# 1 MONTH OF
# FREE
# READING

## at

## www.ForgottenBooks.com

By purchasing this book you are eligible for one month membership to ForgottenBooks.com, giving you unlimited access to our entire collection of over 1,000,000 titles via our web site and mobile apps.

To claim your free month visit:
www.forgottenbooks.com/free882487

ISBN 978-0-266-73876-3
PIBN 10882487

Forgotten Books is a registered trademark of FB &c Ltd.
Copyright © 2018 FB &c Ltd.
FB &c Ltd, Dalton House, 60 Windsor Avenue, London, SW19 2RR.
Company number 08720141. Registered in England and Wales.

For support please visit www.forgottenbooks.com

# COBBETT'S

*Political,*

# W~~EEK~~LY REGISTER.

•••••••••••••••••••••••••••••••••••

## VOLUME LXI. — 62

## FROM JANUARY TO MARCH, 1827.

*and April To June, 1827*

•••••••••••••••••••••••••••••••••

LONDON:

Printed and Published by W. COBBETT, No. 183, Fleet-street.

1827.

V,61-62

DA20
C6
v,61-62

# CONTENTS OF VOLUME LXI.

# COBBETT'S WEEKLY REGISTER.

**Vol. 61.—No. 1.]    LONDON, SATURDAY, DEC. 30, 1826.    [*Price 6d.***

*Published every Saturday Morning, at Seven o'Clock.*

" In like manner did Cicero provoke Anthony, to the great mischief of
" the Empire; and Demosthenes incensed Philip, to the ruin of the
" Athenians; and there is no State or Government but has been highly
" injured by this wicked art: no society of men that ever lent their ears
" to the charms of eloquence, that has not been extremely mischiefed
" thereby: wherefore Socrates thinks rhetoricians worthy of no respect,
" and will not allow them any power in a well ordered commonwealth.
" And Plato excludes them from his commonwealth, with the same con-
" tempt that he rejects PLAYERS and POETS, and not without reason;
" for, there is nothing more dangerous, in civil affairs, than this deluding
" mystery, as from whence all prevaricators, juggling shufflers, back-
" biters, sycophants, and all other lewd and vile tongued persons derive
" their malice and knavery."—CORNELIUS AGRIPPA. *Chapter VI.*

## POSTSCRIPT

### TO

## MR. CANNING.

*Kensington, 27th Dec. 1826.*

SIR,

WHEN I concluded the last Letter which I addressed to you, I did not imagine that it would be necessary for me to address you again upon the subject of this kind of mongrel war: half peace and half hostility, half royalist and half jacobin. But, since that Letter was written, some curious things have occurred. I called upon you, in my first Letter, to

A

Printed and Published by WILLIAM COBBETT, No. 183, Fleet-street.
ENTERED AT STATIONERS' HALL.

disavow the jacobin speech, if it were not yours. You have not disavowed it; you have not published any thing, declaring to us that the speech, which had been published as yours, was not your speech; but, your speech has been published in a pamphlet, which pamphlet is entitled, a "corrected report" of the speech. The title does not say, that you have corrected this report yourself; but this is *said for you*, in various paragraphs, scattered through the newspapers. So that, after all, we have only newspaper authority for supposing (if we do suppose it) that you have retracted your sentiments; or, as the newspapers call it, eaten your words.

However, it is but fair to presume, that you have corrected this speech yourself; that you have edited the pamphlet, in short; and that, of course, you have eaten your words, if we shall find that there has been a devouring of this sort going on in the getting up of this pamphlet. Before I come to a comparison of the pamphlet-speech with the newspaper-speech, it will be necessary to see a little what the newspapers have said upon the subject; and, first, Anna Brodie has this passage in her paper of Saturday, the 23d Dec.: —" A corrected report of the " speeches of Mr. Canning, on " the affairs of Portugal, has just " been published by Mr. RIDG- " WAY. As it is *understood that* " *Mr. Canning has himself su-* " *perintended this publication,* it " is but common fairness to judge " of his opinions rather by the de- " liberate avowal of his *written* " *testimony,* than by the *glowing* " *and impetuous expressions* which " burst from an orator in the hurry " of excited feeling. The speeches " now printed are certainly less " eloquent, but they are decidedly " *more discreet* than those uttered " in the House of Commons. " Whole sentences have been " omitted, and vehement expres- " sions are neutralized by calm " and qualifying adjuncts. This " at least shows that if Mr. Can-

" ning,, from the ardour of his " nature, is liable to err,.he has " sufficient candour and manliness " of mind to avow and correct " his errors."

Thus, this paper, which actually led the way, which actually, as I shall show by-and-by, called for the speech, just as it stood reported; this paper does not pretend to say that the newspaper report was *incorrect*; does not pretend to say, that you were misrepresented even in any.one particular; but seems to admit, and, indeed, does admit, that the speech was *indiscreet*; that it was uttered in the heat of oratory; or, as it pretends, of debate. The *Morning Herald* has, however, made some remarks of a much more sensible character, upon the subject of this correcting pamphlet. It says, after observing on the fact of the publication of the pamphlet, that whole passages of what you uttered are left out, and passages which were not uttered, and which convey a sense different from what you did utter, are added. The

*Herald* is surprised at this, having been firmly convinced, not only that the original report was correct, but that it contained the sentiments of the whole of the ministry: On the subject of the incorrectness of the first report, or, rather, on the subject of the *explanation* now sent about by your friends; namely, that the words were uttered in the " heat of debate;" that there was *no debate;* and, besides, the speech being an opening speech, and coming from the War Minister as an *exposé* resulting from mature deliberation, and stating the principles on which the Government intended to act; that the public had a right to consider this speech as something equal in point of authority to a speech from the King himself. Then the *Herald* observes on what must have stricken every man; namely, the altering, by a written speech, a man's actual speech, and the altering of it by himself, too, and that, moreover, without any pretext of having been misrepresented. It is, as the *Herald* says, a dangerous thing, as a precedent, if a man is to be allowed to do this, *under pretence of having been carried away by his subject!* Very true; but the mischief has been done; and, I shall be much deceived if this speech do not give rise, at a near or more distant date, to consequences which will verify the truth of the words which I have taken for my motto.

Now, before I come to the fact of alteration or no alteration in the speech, let me observe, that I have seen three several gentlemen who were present at the delivery of the speech; and, one of them related to me, even before I saw the newspaper which contained the report, the substance and many of the expressions of the speech, as published in the newspapers, and as inserted by me in the Register. I believe these gentlemen. I cannot disbelieve them: their account of the speech corresponded with what afterwards I saw in print: it is next to impossible that both should be in error. Besides, is it not very singular, that the passages, and precisely the passages which I marked by italic characters when I inserted the speech in the Register, *should have undergone alteration and great alteration in the pamphlet-speech?* This is very singular; and, whatever you may think about the matter, the public both think and say that the pamphlet never would have appeared, had it not been for my commentary on the speech.

Let me, now, take a view of these alterations: let me see how the pamphlet differs from the newspaper, and, then, I shall, perhaps, have time and room to show, that the speech, even as amended, is odious in the extreme, and calculated to produce, like the flippant and insolent speeches and paragraphs with regard to America before the late war, the worst of consequences to this country.

## In the Pamphlet.

I dread war from an apprehension of the tremendous consequences which might arise from any hostilities in which we might now be engaged.

## In the Newspaper.

I dread war from a consciousness of the tremendous power Great Britain possesses, in pushing hostilities, in which she may be engaged, to consequences which I shudder to contemplate.

---

So, so! the tremendous consequences, mentioned in the pamphlet, may be interpreted to apply to *ourselves*, as well as to those with whom we should be at war. It is a vague expression: quite different from the newspaper version; for, there the consequences are to come from *our pushing hostilities* to the extent of *our tremendous power*. There is, in the new version, nothing about *shuddering*; and I can produce three gentlemen that can take their oaths that you uttered the word *shudder*. There is a story about an Irishman, who met a lady in the streets of Dublin, and, going up to her in a begging attitude, asked her for a shilling, saying, at the same time, that, if she refused him, he should be *driven to do that which he shuddered but to think of*. The affrighted lady, having thrust her hand into her pocket, pulled out the shilling and gave it him; and wishing to know the amount of the effects of her charity, asked the supplicant to tell her, now that the peril was over, " *what was that* which he was afraid he should be *driven to do?*" The sturdy vagabond answered, with a soft smile, " Why *to go to work*, by Jases!" Now, when it was related to me, before I saw the newspaper report, that you had made use of this word *shudder*, I immediately observed, to the gentleman who related the substance of the speech to me, why, that is like the fellow in Dublin; only, that was a case of working and not of fighting. And, Canning tells the foreign powers, that if they do not remain at peace, he shall be driven to fight; and that then he shall be a very devil incarnate.

But, there is a monstrous difference in these two passages; a difference so great, that, if the pamphlet be correct, these newspaper reporters are pretty fellows to be suffered to publish exparte examinations taken before magistrates. Either these reporters are a set of persons unfit to make reports; or, they make false reports, and have made a most wickedly false one upon this occasion; or, your amendment of the speech is that which it is unnecessary for me to call by its right name.

| In the Pamphlet. | In the Newspaper. |
|---|---|
| It was by neutrality alone that we could maintain that balance, the preservation of which I believe to be essential to the *welfare of mankind*. | It was in the position of neutrality, alone, we could maintain that balance, the preservation of which I believe to be essential to the *peace and safety of the world*. |

| | |
|---|---|
| You have been very nice in weeding. Your half poetry and half prose has undergone a pretty sharp operation. There is a great deal of difference between the welfare of mankind thus loosely expressed, and the *peace and safety of the world*. Upon reconsideration, | you began to perceive, that this boast of having the peace and safety of the world in your hands, was a little too bold. You, therefore, ate up a little piece of this sentence; or, as the country people say, *drew in your horns*. |

| In the Pamphlet. | In the Newspaper. |
|---|---|
| It is, to be sure, within narrow limits that this war of opinion is at present confined: but, it is a war of opinion, that Spain (whether as a Government or as a nation) is now waging against Portugal; it is a war which has commenced in *the hatred of the new institutions of Portugal*. How long is it reasonable to expect that Portugal will abstain from re- | I fear that the next war to be kindled in Europe, if it spread beyond the narrow limits of Spain and Portugal, will be a war of a most tremendous character; a war, not merely of *conflicting armies*, but of conflicting opinions [*much cheering*]. *I know*, that, if into that war this country enter (and if she do engage, I trust it will be with a most sincere |

*taliation?* If into *that* war this country shall be compelled to enter, we shall enter into it with a sincere and anxious desire to mitigate rather than exasperate, and to mingle only in the conflict of arms, not in the more fatal conflict of opinions. But *I much fear, that* this country (*however earnestly she may endeavour to avoid it*) could not, in such case, avoid seeing ranged under her banners all the restless and dissatisfied of *any nation with which she might come in conflict.*

desire to mitigate rather than exasperate, and to contend with arms rather than with the more fatal artillery of popular excitation), *she will see under her banners, arrayed for the contest,* all the discontented and restless spirits of the age; all those who, *whether justly or unjustly,* are dissatisfied with the present state of their own countries.

Never in this world was there such a palpable eating of words; and never was there act of speechmaker which more fully came up to the description of Cornelius Agrippa. Let us look into this matter a little bit. The newspaper speech told us, that the next war kindled in Europe, was to call forth the furies which we had in our leash; that war was to be a contest of the discontented of all countries against their Governments; but, now behold the opinions, the war of opinions, is become a war commenced in hatred of the new institutions of Portugal! Then comes the question put by you, how long it is reasonable to expect that Portugal is to abstain from retaliation? So that, here, the war of opinions, in which all the restless *spirits of the age* were to be engaged; this war of opinions is now to extend only against Spain, according to the pamphlet - speech, at any rate. Nothing was ever more palpable than this total disagreement. The furies of war, war applied to all nations; dissatisfied spirits, and of several *countries* (in the plural, mind): all this is now made to mean merely that, if Spain cherishes the malcontents of Portugal, Portugal and we at her back shall be compelled to cherish the malcontents of Spain. That is all.

So that Æolus has put forth one of his bags and catched up some of the most dangerous of the winds.

But, this which I have just quoted, is the "BANNER" scene. It resembles, only that it is on the other side of the question, the "DAGGER-scene" of Burke. By the way, Sir, that dagger-scene is worth talking of, just at this time. In one of your half prose, half poetry things in the Anti-jacobin, you called Burke the " lamented sage," he being dead when the poem, as it is called, was published. Now, this "dagger-scene" was as follows: Burke, whose conversion from Foxiteism to Pitt-iteism has already cost this country somewhat approaching to *a hundred thousand pounds*, being inspired by the touch of his new pension, came into the House of Commons, where he described the works and the disposition of the jacobins of that day; where he spoke of the restless and discontented spirits of the age; and, where, after having declaimed for a good while against the then Go-vernment of France as having the seditious, the traitors, and the desolating ruffians of all countries ranged under her banners, he, after having three or four times, in his truly hibernian style, called upon the Parliament, or, rather, upon the Foxites to say, *what the French Government had in reserve for them* : " I will show you what it is!" said he; and, while he said this, he rammed his hand under his coat, by his side, and, drawing forth a long and bloody dagger, flung it upon the floor of the House. Now, Sir, if an orator in France, or in Spain, were to act this part; were disposed to do so ridiculous and despicable a thing as this "lamented sage " did upon this occasion; if even a Spanish monk were disposed to do such a thing as this, has not he just as good ground for doing it; would he not be full as much justified in representing your friendship to consist of a dagger as Burke was in representing the friendship of the Convention of France as being represented by that bloody instrument! Curious enough to observe, that you were amongst the most devoted followers and the loudest eulogists of Burke!

Let us, however, come to the " banner-scene "; and, here the twisting and turning is curious, indeed. But, before we actually come to the " banner," let us see how impossible it is to believe, that your speech really was what it is now in the pamphlet. First, you say in the pamphlet, that this war is at present confined within narrow limits. Then, you say *that it is* founded in the hatred of Spain against the new institutions of Portugal ; then you suggest that Portugal may retaliate, and, then comes the strange assertion that you hope that any part that we shall take in that war, will *not be a conflict of opinions.* So that, away goes entirely the whole pith of your speech. You expect that Portugal will retaliate. You expect that she will carry on a war of opinions ; and here we have you saying, that if we enter into that war with Portugal, we shall,

you trust, not meddle with the conflict in the way of opinions, but in the way of arms!

Now comes the " banner-scene." In the newspaper report, you are made to say, that if the war spread *beyond the narrow limits of Spain and Portugal,* it will be a war of a most tremendous character ; that if this country enter into that war, she will see *under her banners,* arrayed for the contest, all the discontented and restless spirits of the age ; all those who, whether justly or unjustly, are dissatisfied with the present state of their own countries. Here, then, is the " banner-scene ": you will see, under your banners, arrayed for the contest, all these dissatisfied persons. You will see (the reported speech says) not only all the discontented persons in one country, but all the discontented persons in all countries ; and the context says that you would employ them ; and, indeed, that OUR SECURITY CONSISTS in the knowledge which foreign sovereigns have, that you would and could, in such case, employ these mischievous persons in this work of devastation and desolation. But, how all this is frittered away; how the fire is taken out of the component parts of the thunder; how the bullet is taken out of the barrel; aye, and the powder, too, and nothing left but a hissing flash in the pan; how all this is accomplished by the pamphlet version of your speech. Here you much *fear* that this country *could not avoid seeing ranked under her banners;* then she would *earnestly endeavour to avoid seeing it;* then, it is no longer the restless spirits of the age; it is no longer all those who, whether justly or unjustly, are dissatisfied with the present state of their own countries (in the plural, mind, as I said before); but only, " of *any nation* with whom we might come in conflict." If this be not an eating of words; if you be not here flagrantly and shamelessly unsaying that which so many persons heard you say, these reporters and " best public instructors" are amongst the greatest liars and villains that ever walked on the face of the earth. Yet, you do not accuse them. Nobody reproves them. Nobody charges incorrectness upon them: so that, here is the strangest thing that ever was heard of in the world; a minister of state publishing, under the form of a corrected speech, a disavowal and contradiction of that which had been published from the debate actually taken; and, at the same time, he makes a complaint against nobody as having misrepresented him.

### In the Pamphlet.

It is the contemplation of this new power in any future war, which excites my most anxious apprehension. It is one thing to have a giant's strength, but it would be another to use it like a giant. *The consciousness of such strength is, undoubtedly, a source of confidence and*

### In the Newspaper.

The consciousness of such a situation [having the dissatisfied under our banners] excites all my fears; for, it shows that there exists a power, to be wielded by Great Britain, more tremendous than was, perhaps, ever yet brought into action in the history of mankind [hear

security; but, in the situation in which this country stands, our business is not to seek opportunities of displaying it, but to content ourselves with letting the professors of violent and exaggerated doctrines on both sides feel, that it is not their interest to convert an umpire into an adversary.

One thing would rather dispose me to believe that this part of the pamphlet is more your own than the corresponding part of the newspaper speech; and this thing is, that the pamphlet is nonsense, and the speech sense. In the pamphlet, you talk of "this *new power.*" What power? The pamphlet says nothing of any power: it describes no power; but, the newspaper speech speaks of a power, to be wielded by Great Britain, more tremendous than was, perhaps, ever brought into action in the history of mankind; that power is the aid of the restless spirits ranged under our banners; and our security is to arise, according to the newspaper speech, from the knowledge that foreign

hear!]. But, though it may be excellent to have a giant's power, it may be tyrannous to use it like a giant. The knowledge that we possess this strength, IS OUR SECURITY; and our business is, not to seek opportunities of displaying it but, by a partial and half shown exhibition of it, to make it felt that it is the interest of exaggerators on both sides, to shrink from converting their umpire into their competitor.

powers have that we possess this power; that these terrible jacobins are always at our command; and that to touch us is like a powdered beau's coming in contact with a chimney-sweep. Adopt the doctrine of this newspaper speech, and the American skunk is no bad type of our government: men hate it and despise it both: it would be knocked down and killed a hundred times over: but, it has the power of sending its stink out upon its pursuer; and that stink is so dreadful, that it compels people to burn every garment that has been touched by it, and, if it have touched their hair, compels them to shave their heads. The skunk owes its security to the knowledge which the hunters have, that it possesses this pestilent power of flinging out its stink. But, when we come to the pamphlet, what a dull and inconsistent affair do we find! You do not, here, talk of a power arising from people under your banners; for, here you say that you would avoid having them under your banners if you could; and then comes the curious twist, that, instead of "*the knowledge that we possess this strength,*" which means the knowledge that our *foes* have, you have got, in the pamphlet "*the consciousness of such strength:*" and then, when we have seen that this applies to our own knowledge or opinion, and not to the knowledge of the enemy that may be at war with us, comes the curious assertion, that this consciousness is to be a *source of our security!* Stupider stuff than this never was put upon paper, or uttered by lips. The passage from Virgil you could not alter nor suppress: that was down in black and white; and, yet, if you had in contemplation no other power than merely that of assisting Portugal to retaliate the fight of opinions upon Spain, or, at the most, no other power than that to be derived from seeing ranked under your banners, men whom you would see ranked there with *great reluctance,* and whom, of course, you would not think of employing, how does the comparison of England to that of Æolus answer; and, what worse than miserable nonsense is it to talk of deriving security from the mere consciousness of having the opinions and the bodily efforts of jacobins at your command; and how does it answer with your assertion, which you could not expunge from the speech, that you had the furies of war in your hands, and that you had the power of letting them slip at your pleasure?

Having now shown that the speech which obtained you . the shouts of the thoughtless, has been almost wholly frittered away by your pamphlet version, I have to observe, that there is still enough left in it to form a just ground of complaint, at the least, on the part of any and of all the great powers of Europe. That the jacobin threat was foolish is now evident to all the world: every body says it; but, folly is not the worst of its qualities: it has a tendency to produce great mischief. It is despised, as you may learn from reading the French newspapers; but, acts contemptible in themselves have very frequently been the original cause of most enormous national mischiefs. If you have retracted for yourself, however, you have not retracted for Mr. Brougham, who, outstripping his leader, praised the principles which you laid down, in the loftiest strain. He called them sound, enlightened, liberal and truly English principles; he bestowed these praises on your declaration, amongst other things, that our security consisted in the knowledge which our foes had, that all the discontented in the world were ranked under our banners. His praise was not bestowed on the pamphlet speech, but on that speech, the report of which we read in the newspapers. This sound gentle-man admired the jacobin principles so much, the banner and the leash, and all the rest of the incomparable rubbish, that he appears to have thought it a sovereign remedy even for the National Debt. "If," said he, "war should "come upon us, *whatever may* "*be our burthens,* whatever may "be the difficulties with which we "may have to contend, let but "his Majesty's Government act "steadily up to the principles "which they have avowed, and "let the country but remain *true* "*to itself,* and I have *no fear for* "*the rest.*" Oh Lord! no: no fear at all: no fear of adding another five hundred millions to the National Debt: no fear of another Bank Restriction Act: no fear of an issue of assignats: no fear of seeing a pig, worth half-a-crown in money, sell for five pounds in paper. This old hackneyed phrase about the country being "*true to itself,*" has produced, before now, mischiefs enough: it is now played off again by another of CORNELIUS AGRIPPA's men

TO MR. CANNING.

and, in all human probability, with something resembling its former effects. PITT made use of it hundreds, and, perhaps, thousands of times : it was a sort of standing excitation to the spending of the public money, for which spending this beggared nation is now bleeding at every pore. One would think that for a nation to be true to itself was for it to consult, and act according to, its own interests : to save its money from the claws of contractors and commissaries and the mouths of standing armies. One would think, that, being true to one's self meant, the taking care of No. 1 ; but, Mr. Brougham seems to think, that for a nation to be true to itself has no meaning at all connected with that common sense which is, unhappily, but too frequently gone a wandering when this learned gentleman's speeches are composed.

It is impossible to find terms and epithets too severe to apply to this hectoring manner of talking about our power to make war, and, at the same time, saying nothing that has any distinctness in it, as to the means of carrying on that war. This is not the way in which a sensible man ought to talk : such a man ought to estimate the means as justly as he can, and, when he has so done, to state whether, or not, those means be sufficient. Every man in England, who knows any thing of such matters, knows that we cannot enter into war to any extent and for any length of time, without making *enormous loans*. It may be very well for stock-jobbers and loan-mongers, the latter of whom have nothing to do but merely to write their names upon bits of paper, to draw to themselves, and out of the pockets of the people at large, millions of money. It may be very well for such people to praise warlike undertakings ; but, before a sensible man, not having a mercenary object in view, had praised this wild incentive to war, he would have asked himself a question or two : *First*, whether such war would not inevitably produce another Bank Restriction with all its consequences, which consequences, as described by Lord GRENVILLE, at the time when Peel's Bill was passed, were more to be deprecated than revolution itself? *Second*, he would have asked himself what was to be the tenor of the future loan-bills ; whether the interest on those loans was to be paid as the interest of the last loans is, in a gold and silver currency? And, *thirdly*, he would have asked himself what might possibly be the *consequences at home*, of acting upon your "*truly English principles*"?

None of these, however, were, I must confess, to be expected from Mr. BROUGHAM, who has never, as far as I recollect, discovered one grain of sound and sober judgment. It is all flight with him : all hop, skip and jump : all the apparent effect of that sort of caprice, that sort of unsettled mode of acting, which is, in the oldfashioned phrase, described as the *biting of the maggot.* He never has, according to my recollection, proved to be right, in the end, upon any one great subject. But, there appears to be, at this time, a sort of intrigue going on, the expected effect of which probably is, to change the situation of Mr. BROUGHAM. I pretend to understand nothing at all about these intrigues ; but, I will tell you what many people think, and what some people say. They say, then, that Lord LANSDOWN and Mr. BROUGHAM are about *to come into the ministry*, and are to turn out two of that part of the ministry who are supposed not to agree with you. I am very much disposed to laugh at this opinion ; but, certainly, it does receive some countenance from the circumstance of your speech having been, *under your authority*, and with your revision, PUBLISHED AT RIDGWAY'S SHOP.— Mr. RIDGWAY was one of the greatest of all the sufferers in the terrible days of PITT and DUNDAS, and, I might say, of you, too ; for, you were in place and in power at the time of his suffering. Mr. Ridgway was shut up, at two separate times, four years in Newgate, for being the publisher of things not a thousandth part so seditious, so hostile to every establishment, civil and religious, as the newspaper edition of your speech. But, this is far from being all, for, Mr. Ridgway might have changed, like you, from an anti-jacobin to a "liberal"; Mr. Ridgway has, however, never changed at all. He has been what is called the Whig-publisher for a great many years. He sends forth to the world all the profound and learned lucubrations of John Cam Hobhouse and of Lord John Russell. He is, in short, the political bookseller of that portion of the aristocracy who belong to what are ludicrously called the *Whigs*, or, still more ludicrously, "the gentlemen opposite." Now, it is no trifling circumstance, that your speech is published by Ridgway. The speeches of Lord Liverpool, and others of the ministers, have, of late years, been published by Mr. Hatchard; and, it would be curious to discover the reason why you have resorted to the shop of the "Whigs." The truth is, I believe, that there is no political party, no opposition worth speaking of, *except in the cabinet itself!* This is a curious state of things; but, such I believe it is. Now, Sir, what the people, who engage in that very pleasant and profitable amusement, commonly called talking politics; what these people say, is this: that you, Mr. Huskisson, and one or two more, who are of the enlightened, liberal, and free-trade sect, are endeavouring to obtain a greater influence than those of whom the Lord Chancellor is the head; and that, Mr. Brougham, seeing this, and loving the Chancellor as an old dark-faced personage is said to love holy-water, cries you up, not so much for your own sake, as for the purpose of giving a pluck at the robes of the Chancellor. Mr. Brougham has, as I said before, always appeared to me to be deficient in point of judgment, and, if he were not deficient here, he would, if such be his object, take care, above all things, to abstain from praising you. Of this I am quite certain, that, if the expedition to Portugal fail, and bring on us expense for the purpose of purchasing nothing but disgrace, the words of my old author, CORNELIUS AGRIPPA, will be in the mouth of every man in England, and that you are for ever extinguished as a minister, Mr. BROUGHAM sinking, at the same time, into the socket, and *going off in* a smell much more sympathetic than savoury. Like SAUL and JONATHAN, you will have gone along together in your lives, and in your deaths you will not be divided. Something may depend upon flesh and blood ; but, if the Chancellor be sound, wind and limb, and thus continue (as I am told he is likely to do) for several years longer, he will beat you, and every other enterprizing free-trader, whatever may be the quantum of noise that nature has enabled him to make with his tongue. The Lord Chancellor, and his brother still less, is not a great talker ; they are none of CORNELIUS AGRIPPA's men ; they never shone much in the art of haranguing ; but they have had three fourths of the governing of this country in their hands for a great many years ; and, while the Chancellor has the full confidence of a very great majority of the noblemen and gentlemen, he has at his back, sticking to him everlastingly, that body called *the Church*, of which you, great talker as you are, appear to think so little.

Nevertheless, I do verily believe that Mr. Brougham expects that some lucky chance will put it in your power to show that you are not insensible of his support upon this occasion. You have with you, too, the very sapient Member for the Borough, who was, we recollect, a most strenuous advocate for the Cortes of Spain, and who now seems to sigh for a war against the priests of the Peninsula, forgetting (as

B

great wits are apt to have short memories) that, when we obtained victories on that Peninsula, we actually fought under the banners of the priests. Priests are priests, Sir, in all countries, and in all religions; and, as the late Bishop HORSLEY tendered his open arms to receive the Catholic refugee priests from France; so, be you assured, that the present new Constitution of Portugal, and the present armament to support it, will never be popular with the clergy in England; I mean, that clergy whose property consists of tithes and church-lands, and whose families depend on the existence of the Establishment. This Establishment is already enough shaken in the minds of the people of England, without their being called upon to pay taxes to support a war against priests: such a war could not possibly be carried on for any length of time, without adding greatly to this shock, which our clergy have not failed to feel.

As to the state of the struggle in Portugal, it appears, from all the published accounts that have been received, that the great body of the common people are opposed to the new Constitution. I do not know that this is the case, but such is the conclusion fairly to be drawn from all the published accounts that I have seen. Now, if this be the case, what right have we to interfere? As to duty, that is wholly out of the question. You remember, as well as I do, and you ought to remember it better, because you have been well paid for it; you must remember that, in the year 1792, the then French Government, of which the King, observe, was still at the head, complained that we had grossly violated the treaty of amity and commerce that was then existing between us and France; and all the world knows, that the complaint was just. Our answer was, *that the form of Government in France had been changed,* and that we were not strictly bound to adhere to the letter of our treaty in this new state of things. How, then, are we bound by our treaties with the ancient Government of Portugal? If Portugal were to become a sheer democratical republic, should we still be bound to adhere to our treaties, made with the ancient Government of Portugal? Recollect, Sir, that when Louis XVI. was put to death, we withdrew our ambassador, the half brother, I believe, of the present ambassador at Paris. We sent away the French ambassador; or, at least, ceased to give him credit, alleging that the embassy was sent by the King of France, and that our ambassador was sent to Paris to the King of France; and that the Government of France having been totally changed, our compacts with her came all to an end at once. Now, at the time when this took place, or very soon afterwards, you were Under Secretary of State to Lord Grenville, who was the person that gave M. Chauvelin his dismissal. Let me ask, then, upon what principle it is that you contend, that we are

still bound, though at the risk of our own safety, to plunge into a war, in consequence of our treaties with the ancient Government of Portugal. The King of Portugal; or the sovereign of Portugal, whatever he may call himself, who lives in the Brazils, is not dead indeed, but by what right has he ordered a change to be made in the fundamental laws of the kingdom of Portugal? Have not the nobles of Portugal, have not the clergy of Portugal, rights as well as their King? And, unless their consent had been previously obtained, aye, and the consent of the people at large too, was a new Government, was the form of a new mode of governing Portugal to be sent over from a colony of that same Portugal, and left there, good naturedly, by Sir William A'Court, the English ambassador, as he was coming home: just as one neighbour takes a letter from another, and leaves it on his way to his own house! I respect those Portuguese who have not been willing its subjugation to a foreign state; but they never bound us to interfere, except in cases of that sort. So that, after all that you can say, one of two things will take place: a real war with Spain, France, Russia and America; or an expensive armament, kept up by us in Portugal, for the purpose of upholding the new Constitution.

The *Old Times* newspaper has urged you on to this contest. It well knows the popular prejudices contracted against FERDINAND: it seeks its own interest in its bullying balderdash against that king; but, recollect, that it was this identical newspaper, that put forth the prologue to that tragedy in America, which cost us seventy millions of money, and brought on the English arms more disgrace than they had had to sustain for ages and ages. This paper said, "No peace, till we have deposed "James Maddison, till we have "destroyed the American constitution, and have obliterated for "ever that successful example of

" democratical rebellion!" Sir JOSEPH YORKE, then a Lord of the Admiralty, responded from his place in Parliament to the senseless cry, in which he was soon joined by a large part of the Parliament and the nation. We shall have yet to rue the consequences of that cry. We have tasted of some of them, but the much larger part is still behind; for, though you, when bidding for your present office, could talk so prettily at Liverpool, amongst the hungry sycophantic merchants of that place, about "the mother and the daughter," and though Mr. HUGHES, the American envoy to some place or other in the north of Europe, could rival you and, indeed, surpass you in the novel-like stuff about everlasting friendship, that stupid war, first provoked by your flippancy in your despatches during the Presidency of Jefferson; that stupid war, carried on for the purpose of asserting that which England, in former times, had never asserted; that stupid war has actually created a navy;

a great navy; a navy fairly fit to cope with more than two-thirds of our whole force, taking into view the advantageous circumstances of various sorts, which that republic possesses.

You are, Sir, a sprightly, a witty, a voluble man; but, you have said, if the several reports of your speeches speak truth, more foolish things; have given us more instances of ministerial indiscretion; have oftener gratified your greediness for applause as a speaker at the expense of the good and honour of the country; have more frequently excited or aggravated hostility against the State from parties as well at home as abroad, than any man, according to my recollection, that ever made a figure upon the political stage. That the event will, in this case, add another instance to the many that we have formerly beheld, I have no scruple in believing; but, if it do add that other instance, we may console ourselves with the confident belief, that this instance will be the last.

I am, Sir,
Your most obedient and
Most humble Servant,
WM. COBBETT.

---

TO

# DOCTOR BLACK.

---

DOCTOR,

I PERCEIVE, with great grief, that you still keep pecking on upon the Judges with regard to the police-reports. You contend for the monstrous privilege of publishing *just what you please* (for, mind, that is it) under the name of police-reports, containing your own representation of what takes place in examinations before magistrates. If this were law, it would be impossible for the character or, even, the property or life of any man to be safe. It is not law; the judges maintain that it is not, and they act accordingly.

We have, before us, at this very moment, a striking instance of the consequences that may attend reports, taken by reporters and published in newspapers. Such reports have held up our Secretary of State for Foreign Affairs as the first jacobin in Europe; and we have Mr. BROUGHAM held up as the eulogist of his jacobinical principles. To this dilemma we come, then: that Mr. CANNING has deliberately published a falsehood, or, rather, several falsehoods, in a pamphlet edited by himself; or, that, the newspaper reports respecting his speech are falsehoods. But, be this as it may, the mischief was done by the newspapers, whom Mr. BROUGHAM calls the best possible public instructor: so that, here is the " best possible instructor " misrepresenting and disgracing the man whom the eulogist of the " instructor" eulogises to the skies !

Doctor, take my advice : when you write about Judges, let it be about " Dutch Judges," as I used to do, when I was penned up in Newgate. You have been work-ing upon this twelve long enough ; and, be assured, that if the whole of the thing were swept away to-morrow, even by jacobins, those jacobins would be compelled to get the same thing back again. That which has stood and has weathered the storms for a thousand years, is something like the great works of nature herself. You may praise Mr. PEEL for his ameliorations of the police system; and he may, from the red waistcoat, blue coat and blue trowsers, get, as I see he has done, to red collar and red cuffs; then to red facings; then to turning up the laps of the coat, and, at last, to the sabre or the lance, like the *gens d'armes* and *gardes champétres* of France; but, he and you and all of you together, will never root out of the hearts and souls of Englishmen, the Judge, the Jury, the Sheriff, the Justice of the Peace, and the Constable; and, God Almighty forbid that you should !

Doctor, I have heard of a Lord Chancellor stuffed with the twelve Judges ; and, really, you seem to have a relish for a Judge stuffed with Justices of the Peace. Restrain your monstrous appetite, Doctor: content yourself, like me, with a turkey stuffed with sparrows, which I promise myself as soon as any body (you will say this is " throwing a sprat to catch a herring ") will send me a turkey. The sparrows I have got, from a friend in Hampshire, and though these will not keep long, I shall have a supply. Try this dish, Doctor Black ; take after it a pottle of good strong beer, and I'll engage that you shall sleep for eight hours and never dream of Judges or of Justices of the Peace.

Doctor, I wish you a merry Christmas and a happy new year. I have had many a pelting at you during the last, and I trust that God will spare your life, and give you good health for the year that is coming. I am, Doctor,

Your very sincere friend,

And most obedient servant,

Wm. Cobbett.

## AMERICAN SEEDS.

In the first place, I have about forty, or fifty or sixty bushels of Dwarf Kidney Beans, just received, which I shall sell, by the whole lot, or by a large part, several bushels, at any rate, for seventeen shillings a bushel. They are of two sorts, speckled and yellow, and they are, both, as fine in their quality and as good in their condition, as any that I' ever saw in my life. Being grown in a very hot climate, they are a great deal harder than if grown in England ; and, very much to my own surprise, I found, last year, that the American beans, two years old, were just as good as those one year old. Those that are grown here, or that come from Holland, are good for little beyond the first year. I dare say, that a hundred persons have written to me, or told me, verbally, of the excellent quality of these American beans. I am not *mounted,* as the French call it, as a seedsman, and, therefore, I wish rather to sell by wholesale than by retail; but, I shall keep some, at any rate, to sell by retail; and those I shall sell at the rate of, perhaps, about thirty shillings a bushel; for, a man cannot keep a shop and make up small parcels and sell articles of this sort for much less than double what he purchases them at by wholesale.

TREE AND SHRUB SEEDS.—I have received, and shall receive in a few days, American Tree and Shrub Seeds of about *fifty different sorts.* Some of these have been collected by my correspondent at eight hundred miles from his home, which is New York. I intend to make up a packet of each, to put these packets in a box, and to sell the boxes completed. I cannot dispose of the seeds in small parcels and in single sorts, because I have no convenience for this species of retail, which requires numerous drawers, great regularity, and a person well skilled in the whole of the business. I must therefore do as I propose; must see the boxes made up at Kensington myself, and must send them into Fleet-street for sale. Some of the seeds, such as the three sorts of *Magnolia,* for instance, will require little boxes of tin or of wood, to contain them and the matter in which they are packed. It is, if I recollect rightly, the same with the *Cornus Florida,* the *Snow-drop* Tree, and several others; till, therefore, I see what the expense of package will be, and have had time to calculate, accurately, the cost of the several Seeds, I cannot say what the *price* of each collection will be. Some of the Seeds lie in the ground two years; that is to say, they do not come up until the second year, unless great pains be taken and artificial heat be applied. I will, in the list of the Seeds, when it is prepared, note this circumstance against each sort of Seed.

## THE WOODLANDS.

THE *Second Number* of this Week will not be published, as I expected, on the 1st of January. It is all ready but *two engravings,* which this Number must contain, and for which we are obliged to wait for the engraver. I am very sorry for this disappointment; but, the delay will be of a very few days.—When I promised it for the 1st January, I forgot the *Christmas-time.*

---

### WANTED,

Any where within the distance of four or five miles, or thereabouts, of Kensington, A PIECE OF GROUND, WALLED IN. It is wanted to be rented, on a lease of not less than ten years.— Please to make communication by letter (post paid) to 188, Fleet Street, or, personally to me, at Kensington.

In order to save gentlemen the trouble of applying, it is right that I should notice, that I sold my little HORSE, the second day after he was advertized, to a gentleman who wrote for him from the country.

---

A THIRD EDITION OF

## A RIDE IN FRANCE,

BY JAMES PAUL COBBETT.

*Sold at* No. 183, *Fleet-Street.*

2s. 6d. *boards.*

## MARKETS.

Average Prices of CORN through-out ENGLAND, for the week end-ing December 15.

*Per Quarter.*

| | s. | d. | | s. | d. |
|---|---|---|---|---|---|
| Wheat .. | 56 | 4 | Rye .... | 41 | 8 |
| Barley .. | 36 | 11 | Beans ... | 51 | 1 |
| Oats .... | 30 | 5 | Pease ... | 52 | 0 |

Total Quantity of Corn returned as Sold in the Maritime Districts, for the week ended December 15.

| | Qrs. | | Qrs. |
|---|---|---|---|
| Wheat .. | 43,746 | Rye ..... | 196 |
| Barley .. | 48,968 | Beans . .. | 2,518 |
| Oats ... | 9,055 | Pease .... | 931 |

*Corn Exchange, Mark Lane.*

Quantities and Prices of British Corn, &c. sold and delivered in this Market, during the week ended Saturday, December 18.

| | Qrs. | £. | s. d. | | s. | d. |
|---|---|---|---|---|---|---|
| Wheat.. | 5,206 for 15,960 | 19 | 7 Average, 58 | 7 | | |
| Barley.. | 6,953 .. 13,637 | 8 | 10.......... | 36 | 11 | |
| Oats.. | 2,704 .. 4,377 | 6 | 1.......... | 32 | 3 | |
| Rye.... | 10 .. 18 | 8 | 6.......... | 36 | 10 | |
| Beans .. | 1,155 .. 2,861 | 19 | 8........: | 50 | 5 | |
| Pease.. | 517 .. 1,367 | 8 | 3.......... | 52 | 10 | |

Friday, Dec. 22.—The arrivals of all kinds of Grain this week are abundant, and there is a great sup-ply of Flour. The Wheat trade is very heavy, and may be again re-ported 1s. per quarter lower. Bar-ley has met a very dull trade at hardly so good prices as Monday. Beans and Pease may each be re-ported 1s. per quarter lower. The supply of foreign Oats has quite glutted this market for the present, and the trade remains in a very heavy state, at a further decline of 1s. to 2s. per quarter on light ordi-nary descriptions, of which the fo-reign supply chiefly consists. There is very little sale for Flour, but the top price is unaltered.

*Price on board Ship as under.*

Flour, per sack ,......50s. — 53s.

—— Seconds ........42s. — 46s.

—— North Country ..40s. —45s.

Price of Bread.—The price of the 4lb. Loaf is stated at 9½d. by the full-priced Bakers.

COAL MARKET, Dec. 22.

*Ships at Market. Ships sold. Price.*

6    Newcastle  8  ..28s. 0d. to 33s. 3 l.

39¼ Sunderland  6½..30s. 0d.— 36s. 9d.

Account of Wheat, &c. arrived in the Port of London, from Dec. 18 to Dec. 23, both inclusive.

| | Qrs. | | Qrs. |
|---|---|---|---|
| Wheat | 5,658 | Tares | 811 |
| Barley | 8,982 | Linseed | 3,575 |
| Malt | 5,654 | Rapeseed | — |
| Oats | 542 | Brank | 120 |
| Beans | 724 | Mustard | — |
| Flour | 15,311 | Flax | — |
| Rye | 2,015 | Hemp | 12 |
| Pease | 4,994 | Seeds | — |

Foreign. — Wheat, 610; Barley, 1,416; Oats, 69,535; and Beans, 10,061 quarters.

---

## HOPS.

*Maidstone*, Dec. 21.—There is no variation in the Hop trade, which continues exceedingly dull for all sorts, excepting the best, and they sell at a much greater proportion in price than usual.

---

SMITHFIELD, Monday, Dec. 25.

On Friday good Beef sold quite as well as on the preceding market day; but Mutton took a jump of 4d. to 6d. a stone, the weather being highly favourable. Though there is to-day a short supply of every thing, prices have given way, owing partly to the weather having become close and damp, and partly to the heavy state of the dead markets. Even the best Beef does not support the terms of last Monday, 5s. 8d. being quite an outside price. The Mutton trade opened at nearly Friday's prices, but became very flat and lower towards the close: 4s. 4d. is the top price for best polled Sheep, light weights; and 4s. 8d. for choice Downs.

*Per Stone of 8 pounds (alive).*

| | s. | d. | | s. | d. |
|---|---|---|---|---|---|
| Beef | 4 | 0 | to | 5 | 8 |
| Mutton | 3 | 8 | — | 4 | 8 |
| Veal | 5 | 4 | — | 6 | 0 |
| Pork | 5 | 0 | — | 6 | 0 |
| Lamb | 0 | 0 | — | 0 | 0 |

| Beasts | 1,025 | Sheep | 10,850 |
|---|---|---|---|
| Calves | 50 | Pigs | 70 |

NEWGATE, (same day.)

*Per Stone of 8 pounds (dead).*

| | s. | d. | | s. | d. |
|---|---|---|---|---|---|
| Beef | 2 | 8 | to | 4 | 8 |
| Mutton | 2 | 4 | — | 3 | 4 |
| Veal | 3 | 4 | — | 5 | 4 |
| Pork | 3 | 8 | — | 5 | 8 |
| Lamb | 0 | 0 | — | 0 | 0 |

LEADENHALL, (same day.)

*Per Stone of 8 pounds (dead).*

| | s. | d. | | s. | d. |
|---|---|---|---|---|---|
| Beef | 3 | 2 | to | 4 | 4 |
| Mutton | 2 | 8 | — | 3 | 4 |
| Veal | 3 | 4 | — | 5 | 0 |
| Pork | 4 | 0 | — | 5 | 4 |
| Lamb | 0 | 0 | — | 0 | 0 |

## POTATOES.

SPITALFIELDS, per Ton.

|  | l. s. | | l. s. |
|---|---|---|---|
| Ware | 2 10 | to | 4 10 |
| Middlings | 2 0 | — | 0 0 |
| Chats | 1 15 | — | 0 0 |
| Common Red | 0 0 | — | 0 0 |

Onions, 0s. 0d.—0s. 0d. per bush.

BOROUGH, per Ton.

|  | l. s. | | l. s. |
|---|---|---|---|
| Ware | 2 9 | to | 4 6 |
| Middlings | 2 0 | — | 3 0 |
| Chats | 1 9 | — | 2 0 |
| Common Red | 0 0 | — | 0 0 |

## HAY and STRAW, per Load.

Smithfield.—Hay....80s. to 105s.
Straw...30s. to 36s.
Clover. 100s. to 126s.

St. James's.—Hay.... 75s. to 110s.
Straw .. 28s. to 39s.
Clover.. 83s. to 126s.

Whitechapel.—Hay....70s. to 105s.
Straw...32s. to 36s.
Clover..80s. to 126s.

---

AVERAGE PRICE OF CORN, sold in the Maritime Counties of
England and Wales, for the Week ended December 15, 1826.

|  | Wheat. | | Barley. | | Oats. | |
|---|---|---|---|---|---|---|
|  | s. | d. | s. | d. | s. | d. |
| London* | 59 | 0 | 39 | 0 | 33 | 3 |
| Essex | 57 | 5 | 36 | 10 | 31 | 4 |
| Kent | 57 | 5 | 38 | 4 | 29 | 9 |
| Sussex | 52 | 9 | 40 | 8 | 29 | 6 |
| Suffolk | 54 | 11 | 35 | 1 | 30 | 7 |
| Cambridgeshire | 53 | 11 | 35 | 6 | 28 | 10 |
| Norfolk | 54 | 9 | 34 | 10 | 29 | 8 |
| Lincolnshire | 55 | 0 | 40 | 1 | 27 | 6 |
| Yorkshire | 55 | 10 | 40 | 6 | 28 | 4 |
| Durham | 57 | 0 | 41 | 0 | 30 | 6 |
| Northumberland | 57 | 3 | 38 | 6 | 35 | 2 |
| Cumberland | 63 | 10 | 40 | 6 | 35 | 9 |
| Westmoreland | 61 | 10 | 47 | 0 | 34 | 0 |
| Lancashire | 66 | 5 | 44 | 2 | 33 | 1 |
| Cheshire | 59 | 1 | 50 | 10 | 31 | 4 |
| Gloucestershire | 58 | 0 | 43 | 8 | 36 | 11 |
| Somersetshire | 56 | 1 | 40 | 4 | 32 | 6 |
| Monmouthshire | 65 | 9 | 51 | 1 | 0 | 0 |
| Devonshire | 58 | 0 | 38 | 2 | 29 | 0 |
| Cornwall | 57 | 6 | 37 | 11 | 29 | 7 |
| Dorsetshire | 53 | 11 | 37 | 5 | 32 | 9 |
| Hampshire | 55 | 0 | 37 | 7 | 30 | 1 |
| North Wales | 65 | 6 | 46 | 7 | 31 | 5 |
| South Wales | 58 | 11 | 43 | 7 | 28 | 2 |

* The London Average is always that of the Week preceding.

*Liverpool*, Dec. 19.—With a very moderate importation only, the demand was very slack during the past week for each description of Grain, excepting for the finest qualities of Oats, which obtained late prices.—The market of this day was tolerably well attended; sales, however, were effected only to a moderate extent—last Tuesday's prices for fine qualities of Oats were, notwithstanding, supported.—Wheat was at a decline of about 2d. per 70 lbs.—In other articles of the trade the prices of this day se'nnight were barely maintained.

Imported into Liverpool, from the 12th to the 18th December, 1826, inclusive:—Wheat, 4,730; Barley, 565; Oats, 4,689; Malt, 110; Beans, 201; Pease, 681 quarters. Flour, 1,682 sacks, per 280 lbs. Oatmeal, 1,206 packs, per 240 lbs.

*Norwich*, Dec. 23.—The supply of Wheat to this day's market was small. —Red, 53s. to 57s.; White to 59s. Only a moderate supply of Barley, and 1s. lower than last week—30s. to 36s.; Oats, 28s. to 33s.; Beans, 43s. to 45s.; Pease, 44s. to 47s.; Boilers, to 56s. per quarter; and Flour, 42s. to 43s. per sack.

*Bristol*, Dec. 23.—A very great dullness prevails in the Corn trade at this place. Sales are limited, and those few that are effected, may be considered at about the prices below stated :—Wheat, from 5s. 6d. to 7s. 7½d.; Barley, 4s. 3d. to 5s. 6d.; Oats, 3s. 3d. to 4s. 6d.; Beans, 5s. 6d. to 7s. 6d.; and Malt, 5s. 6d. to 3s. 6d. per bushel, Imperial.—Flour, Seconds, 32s. to 43s. per bag.

*Ipswich*, Dec. 23.—We had a short supply of Corn at market to-day, the sale of which was very dull, and prices rather lower, as follow :— Wheat, 50s. to 60s.; Barley, 32s. to 36s.; Beans, 42s. to 44s. ; and Pease, 46s. to 48s. per quarter.

*Wisbech*, Dec. 23.—The business done in Corn to-day was at the terms of last week.—Red Wheat, 50s. to 56s.; White ditto, 56s. to 58s.; Oats, 22s. to 30s.; and Beans, 48s. to 50s. per quarter.

*Wakefield*, Dec. 22.—We have a fair supply of Wheat here to-day, and having a good attendance of buyers, the best dry samples have been taken off at last week's prices, and, in some instances, a trifling advance has been obtained; there has been rather more doing in middling and inferior descriptions. Oats and Shelling are heavy sale, without alteration in prices. The supply of Barley fresh up is moderate; the best heavy samples are dull sale, and hardly support the rates of last week, and there is scarcely any demand for the light qualities. Beans are dull sale, and 1s. to 2s. per quarter lower. Rapeseed is more inquired after, and 1l. per load dearer.

*Newcastle-on-Tyne*, Dec. 23.—We had a large supply of Wheat from the farmers this morning, but there has been very little coastwise during the week, and prices were much the same as on this day se'nnight. Rye is slow sale at last week's prices, although we have had not any arrivals this week. The Barley trade is very much depressed, and only the best heavy Norfolk samples are saleable at 40s. per quarter, the other kinds are offering at all prices down to 36s. per quarter. Malt dull sale, and 2s. per qr. lower. We have had some arrivals of foreign Oats this week, but the holders do not seem disposed to force sales, and the farmers' supply was readily sold at last week's prices.

## COUNTRY CATTLE and MEAT MARKETS, &c.

*Horncastle*, Dec. 23.—Beef, 6s. to 7s. per stone of 14 lbs.; Mutton, 5d. to 6d.; Pork, 6d.; and Veal, 6d. to 7d. per lb.

*Norwich Castle Meadow*, Dec. 23.—We had some lots of good Cattle for slaughter at this day's market selling at 8s. to 8s. 6d. per stone of 14 lbs. sinking offal, and a large supply of store Scots at about 4s. per stone when fat; also a few lots of Short Horns at 3s. to 3s. 6d. Cows and Calves but few to-day, and those and homebreds of all sorts, a flat sale; of Horses a few good ones of the Cart kind offered, but few of them sold. We had more Sheep penned than last week.—Shearlings, 24s. to 28s.; fat ones to 37s.; Lambs, 13s. to 17s. 6d.; Pigs at low prices; fat ones, to 6s. 6d. per stone; Meat, Beef, 7d. to 9½d.; Veal, 7d. to 9d.; Mutton, 5¼d.; and Pork, 5¼d. to 8d. per lb.

At *Morpeth* Market, December 20th, there was a good show of Cattle and Sheep; but there being a great demand, they sold readily at last week's prices.—Beef from 5s. 6d. to 6s.; Mutton, 5s. 3d. to 6s. 3d. per stone, sinking offal.

*Birmingham* Smithfield Market, Dec. 21.—A moderate supply of Beasts and Sheep, and better in quality, and readily sold at a little more money. A fair supply of Pigs, and the trade dull.—Beef 5½d. to 6½d.; Mutton, 5d. to 6½d.; and Veal, 5d. to 7d. per lb. Pork, 8s. 6d. to 9s. per score.—Neat Cattle, 330; Sheep, 502; Pigs, 508.

At *Abingdon* Fair, Dec. 11, there was a considerable show of Stock of all Kinds. Good Horses, both of the Nag and Cart kind, sold pretty well, as well as Colts, which were nearly all cleared off. There appeared but little doing in neat Stock: high prices were asked, but could not be obtained, and many Beasts of the lean sort were left unsold. Sheep and Lambs may be fairly said to be selling at half the price they were at the December Fair last year. Upon the whole, there was little business done, except in good Horses, which sold readily, and at higher prices than have been obtained at some of the preceding Fairs.

# COBBETT'S WEEKLY REGISTER.

Vol. 61.—No. 2.]　　LONDON, SATURDAY, Jan. 6, 1827.　　[Price 6d.

*Published every Saturday Morning, at Seven o'Clock.*

" Notwithstanding all this, however, if the manufacture of straw were
" of a description to require, in order to give it success, the collecting of
" the manufacturers together in great numbers, I should, however great
" the wealth that it might promise, never have done any thing to promote
" its establishment."—COTTAGE ECONOMY, *Letter to the Secretary of the
" Society of Arts.*

TO

# THE LANDOWNERS OF ENGLAND.

*Kensington, 3d Jan. 1827.*

GENTLEMEN,

For a great number of years it has been the fashion to cry up, to extol, in language the most exaggerated, the manufacturing branch of business in this country. This thing, which is generally called *manufactures*, a word used to represent the whole of the interests and property appertaining to this branch of national affairs, has, for a long while past, been so cried up, represented as so great in point of importance, so momentous as a source of national wealth; it has been so everlastingly talked of as being the pride and support of the country, especially during the last war, that, at last, you have, and by your own acquiescence

C

Printed and Published by WILLIAM COBBETT, No 183, Fleet-street.
ENTERED AT STATIONERS' HALL.

and instrumentality, too, been
brought down, not only to a level
with these spinners and weavers;
but to be actually something beneath them, in the eyes even of
your own tenants. At last, however, a state of things is come,
which would enlighten any portion of God's creatures, yourselves
only excepted.

It has been the fashion to speak
of *"our manufactures"* as something new; as something created
by George the Third and by Pitt.
Just as if England were not always
famous for manufactures; just as
if the produce of her own rare
soil and climate had not, even a
thousand years ago, enabled her
(in conjunction with her power
and her valour) to lay under contribution all the nations with whom
she condescended to carry on
trade. Just as if maritime commerce and the business of merchants were things of modern
date? Just as if the race of merchants were created by George
the Third and by Pitt, and just as
if the Royal Exchange were

erected by them! To be satisfied
that England had merchants, in
great numbers, and that those
merchants were of great weight
in the country, and possessed
great riches, what need we more
than this one fact, that a considerable number of the convents, of
the abbeys, priories and other religious foundations, which existed
in England, were *founded by merchants of London*; and that, too,
some of them, more than a thousand years ago. The persons who
were founders of these religious
and charitable establishments,
were Kings, Queens, Noblemen
and Ladies, great knights and
merchants of London, and, these
latter, known as to their rank, as
merchants of London, and nothing more. England was not,
then, erected by George the Third
and by Pitt. Observe, too, that
the merchants of those days were
none of your loan-mongering
crew; for (and pray mark it well),
their religion positively forbade
them to take interest for money in
any shape, even if the money

were lent upon mortgage. This was the sort of merchants that gave England her character for fairness and integrity in her dealings: it was not a crew of base, interest-taking, grasping, monopolizing, discounting, gambling miffs, that are a disgrace to the name of merchant; and that reflect dishonour and even affix infamy on every thing that is mean enough to connect itself with them. In those remote times, there were, indeed, no villanous Jews and Jobbers; no miscreants, who swallow whole batches of widows and orphans at a breakfast. But, again I say, it is another specimen of the vanity and insolence of the present day, to pretend that this commercial greatness, as it is called, is any thing new in England; and equally impudent it is to pretend, that the manufacturing powers are something new.

But, Gentlemen, there is something new in the manner and shape of this manufacturing. Formerly the business was carried on in all parts of the country: now it has been so managed; the taxing and paper-money system has created such a mass of monopolies; has drawn the wealth of the country into such great heaps, as to cause the manufacturing working people to be collected into enormous masses, and that, too, in those parts of the country least productive of food. He must be next to an idiot, who does not perceive, that this is a most unnatural state of things; that it must rob the land of all that which would be earned by the wives and the small children of the agricultural labourers; and that, in case of any fluctuations in the manufacturing business, all the horrors attendant upon ruin and poverty must be witnessed, in the parts of the country in which great numbers of persons are collected together.

For fifteen or sixteen years I have been endeavouring to call the attention of the country to this great evil. I have stood alone; and have, indeed, been opposed by the whole of the press, and by every speaker that I have heard of, that ever uttered a word upon the subject. For several years past, until very lately, the Editor of the *Morning Chronicle*, in observing upon the reports that have been published concerning the low wages and miserable state of the farming labourers, has invariably advised them *to go to the North*, and there to become manufacturers, that being, according to him, the only possible way of obtaining for themselves and their families a sufficiency of food. He has, indeed, suggested another mode of lessening their wants; namely, that of *abstaining from breeding*, which mode, if it had been recommended to people upwards of three score years and ten, might have had some chance of success; but, as the recommendation addressed itself to bouncing girls of eighteen or twenty, with the blood ready to burst through their skins, and to young fellows that valued life itself only because it afforded them the gratification of their tastes and passions, the recommendation dropped dead from the Doctor's press. To quit the plough, the bill-hook and the spade, and to fly to the spinning-jenny and the shuttle was, however, Doctor Black's grand remedy; and urge the adoption of it he did with as much zeal and pertinacity as ever quack did remedies by which he was to get so much for a packet. " Look to the North, dear fellow-subjects," exclaimed the Doctor: " see how " enlightened they are in the " North! Look at Scotland, un- " happy ploughmen and poachers " of Sussex and Hampshire! It " is not from the land and the " woods, that the food and shelter " of man come: these are not to " be found in the South : it is in " the North where you find them : " they are created by mental im- " provement and by perfection in " the art of twisting and platting " together the down which comes " out of the seed-pods of little " plants which grow in Carolina, " Georgia and other distant parts

" of the world." The *Edinburgh Reviewers*, all children of the same family with the Doctor, proved, in manner most elaborate, that it was, not to the land, not to light taxes or no taxes at all; not to these, nor to any thing else of a vulgar nature, that a people owed their happiness; but to a *judicious distribution of labour*; to the farmer not wasting the time of his family, in making the women and girls knit stockings and spin sheets and shirts; but, to his first selling the wool and the flax, at the rate, perhaps, of a shilling a pound, and buying it back again from the manufacturer at the rate of ten shillings a pound. These enlightened political philosophers proved beyond all question, that it was better for a farmer to carry his fat ten miles, sell it to a tallow-chandler for threepence a pound, let him make candles of it, and then buy the fat back again in the shape of candles at a shilling a pound: they proved that this was much better for the farmer than to make the fat into candles him-self, by the hands of his wife or daughters or maid-servants, and by these means have his candles for about *fourpence* a pound, including the wick.

In short, the monstrous fooleries which these Scotchmen have played, in this sort of way, within the last twenty years, is even beyond conception; and, in twenty more years, the thing will not be believed to be possible by the young men of that day. The truth is, however, that these men are *mere writers:* they are writers by trade: they understand that trade pretty well; but, they know nothing of the real situation of the people of this or of any other country. When they are writing about the labouring classes, and about the means of bettering their lot, they utter that which those labouring classes would not at all understand if they were to read it. These men are all of one and the same description and character. They have begun in poverty, accompanied with ambition. They have been compelled to write for their bread, their daily bread. They have not associated with noblemen, clergymen, gentlemen, tradesmen, mechanics, farmers, labourers, soldiers, nor sailors. They have moved no where but within their own little circle: a circle of sameness and of everlasting reaching after something or other, tending to put money into their pockets or victuals into their stomachs. Their very dress has had an influence on their minds. At once as showy and as cheap as possible. The washer-woman's bill has been, with them, a document of no small importance. In a word, a life spent in endeavours to disguise their poverty, and to get, if possible, something to change the poverty into riches. Such men may know a great deal about *words*, but, what the devil can they know of *men* or of *things*; and it requires a *personal acquaintance* with what we write about, to enable us to write about it with sense and with effect. Lords are generally thought to know very little about the affairs of the common people. The most unobservant of Lords, however, know a thousand times as much about them as these men do. They really *know* nothing; they are extremely enlightened; but they have *no knowledge*; and, if upon any subject, they be correct, it is by the merest accident in the world. I mean any subject connected with national or domestic economy; for they have no nation and no family: they come forth to get the means of living out of their facility of publishing great parcels of words.

Hence all this stupid stuff in praise of manufacturing establishments: hence all their exultations at the prosperity of Manchester and Paisley: hence all their everlasting clamour in praise of paper-money. No creature that has ever seen the common people in their natural manners, lives, and habits, would think of recommending to them an abstinence from breeding, any more than of recommending them to cut their throats. But, the greatest error of all, perhaps, of these parts anxious word-mongers has been, their praises on manufacturing establishments. Their devil seems to owe them a grudge, and to be resolved to punish them for their sins even in this world ; for, now we have before us all the natural fruit of these manufacturing establishments, and, never was there bitterer fruit produced in this world. The newspapers, and particularly, I think, that of Doctor Black, tell us, that trade and manufacturing *are reviving*; and are *likely* to be in a more *healthful state* than they have been during the last year. That may easily be, without the state being a bit too healthful. But, what proof *have we of this*? I shall mention a thing or two presently, which clearly demonstrate that there has been and that there is likely to be, no change at all for the better. There needed no one to tell us this, however ; but, the astonishing thing is, that all this body of writers will still shut their eyes against the real and only cause of the depression which now prevails. There are, certainly, many men in England, who now see the real cause of their depression, and who freely declare their opinions upon certain occasions. There are some few, very few, of the country newspapers, which have,

after years of laughing at me and abusing me, adopted my opinions upon this subject; but, the main body of the writers appears to be still as blind and obdurate as ever. To all sorts of causes, except to the true, the one, the all-efficient cause, they ascribe this depression and decline, though the real cause is as apparent to every sensible man that has thought or read upon the subject, as the ground before him is apparent to his eyes. Or, as it was apparent to Mr. Hume, that fifty-four pounds were better in his pocket than to be squandered away in a war against the Turks. This band of Scotch scribblers have seen the paper-money put out in great quantities ; they have seen prices rise, and that which is called prosperity come. They have seen the paper-money drawn in, and they have seen prices fall, and distress and ruin follow. Three several times ; at three distinct periods, within the last twenty years, have they seen these things take place. They saw the paper-money pushed out in 1822; they saw low prices changed into high prices ; they saw the false prosperity immediately follow. They now see the paper drawn in ; they see distress and ruin follow, and, yet, oh yet! the pertinacious, stupid, perverse brutes continue niggling along expressing their expectations of returning prosperity, while the law says that the paper-money shall be further and most prodigiously reduced in quantity. There is not a man of sense in the whole country, who is, at the same time, a reading man, that does not know that a large part of the currency of the country, and a very large part of it, too, still consists of country bank-notes, and, those notes of *one pound*. I travelled, last fall, about six hundred miles. I was in nine counties; in several cities and great market-towns; at the greatest fair that is held in England; and, I know that the far greater part of the currency in all those counties is country bank-notes; and the Scotch themselves tell us that, in their parts, they have nothing else, there being thousands upon thousands of Scotchmen, who have attained the age of thirty years, without ever having once set his eyes upon the King's gold coin. What brutes, then, must these Scotch writers be; what obstinate, what ill-conditioned, what thwart-over devils they must be, still to write on as if they believed that it was not the quantity of the currency that produced alternately the depression and the flashy prosperity;

and as if they still believed that the prosperity, as they have the impudence to call it, would come back again, while the paper-money continued to diminish in quantity!

It being a fact, which no man that has any regard for character will attempt to deny, that a very large part of the currency, especially if you take its efficiency into view, consists of country bank-notes; and, it being certain that, as the law now stands, those country bank-notes must, for the greater part, cease to exist in the month of April, 1829, it is impossible for any man of common sense and with an understanding not wholly perverted, to expect a rise of prices, except in some case where the seasons, or some other accidental cause, has to do with the matter. However, where are the symptoms of this returning prosperity? There has been a public meeting held at Blackburn, in Lancashire, which place is in the very centre of the manufactures of England. This meeting was not held in the fields and liable to be dispersed by the bayonet. It was held in the *ball and concert room* of that town; and, at the meeting, Mr. DEWHURST, who was twice imprisoned, twice dungeoned as a radical, made a speech, which is extremely well worthy of your attention, containing, as it does, more valuable matter than you would hear at St. Stephen's if you were to be present there during the whole of this session. This speech I shall, if I have room, insert in another part of the Register; but, I shall here confine myself to the resolutions passed at this meeting, and which resolutions unquestionably express the sentiments of the great majority of the people in that county. They give us a picture of the people whom the Pitt-system has drawn together in great masses; and, if you can read that picture without feeling, at once, sorrow and shame, you *deserve* something a great deal worse than the loss of your estates.

## TAXATION, CORN LAWS, PARLIAMENTARY REFORM, &c.

At a Meeting of the different Trades of Blackburn and the neighbourhood, held on Monday, the 25th instant, in the Ball and Concert Room, the following Resolutions were unanimously agreed to:—

Moved by Mr. E. Hammond, and seconded by Mr. J. Laycock:

1st. That the distress and misery which pervade the whole of the working classes of this town and neighbourhood are such, that if not speedily changed for the better, a convulsion of some sort or other must at no distant period inevitably take place; that we look forward to the future with much alarm, for that, in addition to our sufferings from hunger, we are at this inclement season of the year destitute of clothing, bedding, and fuel; that his Majesty's Ministers know our real situation, therefore for them to turn a deaf ear to our complaints would be to add insult to injury; that those distresses have not been caused by untoward seasons, or through the agency of Divine Providence, but through the acts of a self-elected House of Commons, who have had no other end in view than their own aggrandizement, to the ruin and degradation of the industrious working classes of the community.

Moved by Mr. Geo. Dewhurst, and seconded by Mr. Thomas Austin:

2d. That this now unhappy country owes all its calamities to an over taxation and a fictitious currency, and that this excessive taxation cannot be wrung from the people; in a healthy state of the currency, without producing misery, if possible, greater than that we now suffer; therefore this Meeting respectfully calls upon the Legislature to reduce the army, all sinecures, pensions, grants, and emoluments not merited by well known public services, and an appropriation of the public estates called Crown Lands, and Church property, to the liquidation of the National Debt, and also an equitable adjustment with regard to all con-tracts between man and man.

Moved by Mr. James Park, se-conded by Mr. Thomas Ellensworth :

3d. That this Meeting views with abhorrence the passing of the Corn Bill in 1815, and its continuance to the present time, in opposition to the repeated and urgent prayers of a starving people; that the passing of this Corn Bill has had the greatest tendency to destroy our home and foreign trade, thereby raising the price of food on the one hand, and decreasing the demand for our la-bour on the other, while at the same time our self-elected Representatives have done this injustice to the peo-ple, for the purpose of supporting in splendour and affluence themselves and adherents, whilst those who labour for the benefit of the nation are totally neglected.

Moved by Mr. John Laycock, and seconded by Mr. Thomas Austin :

4th. Believing that taxation is the cause of all our calamities, and that the Corn Laws are the consequence of such taxation, this Meeting calls upon the two Houses of Parliament to remove such grievous and oppres-sive imposts; and to prevent a re-currence of the evil in future, to cause an efficient Reform in the Commons House of Parliament, upon the principles of Universal Suffrage and Election by Ballot; that such a reform in the Commons' House of Parliament and an Ex-tension of the Elective Franchise,

would give to the Manufacturing In-terest its due weight in the Legis-lature of the Country; and that a repeal of the Corn Laws and a re-duction of taxation ought imme-diately to take place.

Moved by Mr. Edward Hammond, and seconded by Mr. Thomas Austin :

5th. That separate Petitions, found-ed upon the above Resolutions, be forwarded for presentation to both Houses of Parliament, from the dif-ferent Trades of Blackburn and the Neighbourhood:

Moved by Mr. Edward Hammond, and seconded by Mr. Geo. Dew-hurst :

6th. That the Thanks of this Meeting be given to the Chairman, for his able and impartial conduct in the Chair this day.

ANTHONY M'GREGOR,
In the Chair.

*Blackburn, Dec. 25th, 1826.*

———

Here, then, we have Norfolk Petition once more. There will be, very shortly, not a county, either in England or Scotland, that will not have sent up its own edition of the Norfolk Petition; and, whatever else may be omit-ted in any of those editions, a prayer for a new disposition of the *Church property* is never omitted. Other matters apart for the present, how-ever, will any one believe, that these resolutions, moved and passed in the face of the whole town of Blackburn, and by persons allowed to assemble for that purpose, in the *ball and concert room* of that place; will any body believe, that these resolutions, passed in such a place and under such circumstances, *contain a tissue of falsehoods*? Yet, a tissue of falsehoods these resolutions must contain, or the Scotch philosophers are either the greatest liars or the greatest fools that ever put pen to paper. These philosophers, however, are totally ruined for ever; from shabby-genteel coats and shirts with false collars and breasts, they must come to holes at their elbows and no shirt at all, whenever the present infernal system shall be blown to pieces. They now stand with their political souls pledged to the devil of politics for the soundness of the paper system. "MALACHI MALAGROWTHER," who, they say, is that *Walter Scott*, that I have always despised, and that was the first Baronet that the present King made, being followed closely by that other famous Baronet, COUTTS TROTTER, whose very name, the bare sound of whose very name is enough for any man of common stomach; Malagrowther is, they say, a fictitious name taken by the first of these two Scotchmen. He wrote,

last spring, three pamphlets upon the subject of the Scotch paper-money. To notice all the absurdities, all the falsehoods, all the instances of impudence and of insolence contained in these two pamphlets; to bestow a suitable degree of censure upon each, would occupy more than the space of a whole *Register*. But, a duty due to truth is, just to notice the JET of these pamphlets, which may be expressed thus: he asserts, *that, if a Bill be passed to cause the Scotch banks to cease to issue one pound notes, in like manner as the English banks are to cease, all sorts of ruin and misery will fall upon Scotland, and that, if Scotland be left alone in this respect, her flourishing condition will continue.* Now, mind, this is the assertion of WALTER SCOTT, who was the first man that this King made a Baronet, and who, as the newspapers tell us, dined with ÆOLUS CANNING the other day. This is the assertion of Walter Scott. It was made in February last, or, at latest, in March; and the month of October saw Scotland plunged into all sorts of ruin and misery, *notwithstanding the threatened Bill had never been brought into Parliament!* Sir Malagrowther ought to have listened to me, when I told the people in Lincoln's Inn-fields that it was the greatest folly in the world to suppose, that the one pound notes could be abolished in England, without, in effect, their being abolished in Scotland; that whether the intended Act extended to Scotland or not, prices would be affected in Scotland by the Act, in the same degree as in England. Malagrowther could not see this. He thought that if there were no law to put down the one pound notes in Scotland, they would all keep out in as great quantity as ever, and that Scotland would continue to flourish while England would be experiencing distress. The suffering has been great in England, it is great, and it will be greater; but, as yet, it has been nothing (the relative population considered) to the suffering which has been experienced in Scotland, since Malagrowther wrote his pamphlet; or (and mind this *or*), the Scotch lords and Scotch manufacturers and Scotch newspaper writers are the brazenest liars and the meanest knaves under the sun. I do not accuse them of this; but, I must, then, insist on the other proposition of the dilemma.

Is this Malagrowther, then, really the first Baronet that the present King made? Is this a fel-low to turn a government aside from its purpose? From the Report of the Committee on the Scotch banks, it appears that the Ministers were frightened by a threat of the Scotch bankers, that, if the Bill were passed, *they would all stop in one day*, and, thus, of course, throw the country into confusion. This is, doubtless, the real cause why the Ministers did not extend the Bill to Scotland. It is not always wise to take counsel from fear; but, the Ministers acted wisely in this case without suspecting that they did; for, it would not have been wise to tempt these greedy desperadoes, who, like Harpagon, in the "Avare" of Molière, are capable of quarrelling with themselves and even of biting and tearing themselves at the prospect of being thwarted in their schemes of monopoly. It would not have been wise to tempt these horrible rooks to throw things into confusion, and to injure so many thousands of innocent persons as they would have injured; that is to say, it would not have been wise to do this, if the thing which these Harpagons dreaded, could be effected by means not calculated to enrage them to mischief, and yet quite as effectual. Luck, therefore, rather than any thing else, induced the Ministers to desist; but, the ruin and misery have come creeping slowly over Scotland in *just the same manner and in just the same degree as they would have done, if the Bill had extended to Scotland by name*. And this is precisely what stupid Malagrowther could not see. He thought, soft-brained poet as he is, that if there were no *law* to abolish one pound notes in Scotland, they would continue to circulate there in abundance as great as of late years, though the *law* would diminish their quantity in England. Malagrowther, good soul, thought that a man would give a sovereign for a bushel of wheat, on the south side of the Tweed, and that a one pound Scotch note would, at the same time, buy a bushel of wheat on the north side of the Tweed; and he thought, too, good soft-headed bookseller and baronet, that the Scotch notes would not be diminished in number and amount. He thought, now, I dare say, that if a man in England owed a man in Scotland a sovereign, and that, if he could get two Scotch notes for a sovereign, he would choose to pay the sovereign, and not to buy a Scotch note for ten shillings and pay him that! Malagrowther appears not to have perceived, that, if the Scotch paper kept up

to the value of the English paper, the Scotch paper must be diminished in quantity in proportion to the diminution in the quantity of the English paper; and that, then, of little consequence indeed, would it be, whether this effect would be produced *by law* or *without law*, in the first instance. Malagrowther, the great Malagrowther, does not appear to have perceived that, if the Scotch paper did not keep up in value with the English paper, or other money, no matter what, then there would be an exchange against Scotland; and that, for every pound of taxes, collected in Scotland, more than a Scotch pound must be paid in England, when the collector-general sent up his collections. But, the gross absurdity is, to suppose that a difference in the value of the currency could exist, for any length of time, in different parts of the same country, all having constant transactions with each other, without some part or other of the currency coming to an open discount. I always said, "Pass the Bill for "England, or even for Middlesex, "and I will pledge myself that "you drive out all the one pound "notes in every other part of the "kingdom." If the Bill had been passed for Middlesex only, its effects would have extended all over the country in the course of one week. Scotland, therefore, has felt all the ruin and misery which England has felt from this Bill, and from the panic which preceded it; and, if Malagrowther had one single grain of political honesty clinging about his baronetship and his booksellership, he would confess, that he had written three most stupid as well as most insolent and impudent pamphlets upon this subject.

The conclusion from all this is, that the country is like that crazy hulk which I described in a *Register* written during " late panic," which DOCTOR BARING, the loan-monger, asserted to have proceeded from a hot commercial fit. The country is in a state of gradual decline; but, it will not be gradual towards the arrival of the day when no more one pound notes are to be issued in England. It is *sinking* now; but then it will go down *souse*. Ask any man in Norfolk: ask any man in Hampshire: ask any man in any part of the country, what he thinks would be the consequence, *if all the one pound notes were taken out of circulation to-morrow morning?* His answer would be, " *universal ruin.*" If Peel's Bill had gone into full effect at the time appoint-

ed for its going into effect, wheat would have been sold at three and sixpence a bushel at this day; and, in case of an abundant harvest, for three shillings a bushel; and there would not have been one man amongst you, the landlords; not one man amongst ten thousand of you, that would not have been stripped of his estate. Well, why is not the same consequence to follow in the present case? The Act of last year brings us back to Peel's Bill. It is to bring us back to Peel's Bill, in April 1829. I care not a straw about Scotland or Ireland: let that Bill go into effect, and, then, wheat will be at three and sixpence a bushel. There must be a gold currency. Five pound notes of country bankers will be made use of merely as bills of exchange, wherever they are made use of at all. No man will lay one of them by for an hour: we come to a real gold currency: the rag-rooks go to the devil that made them; and your estates go to the Jews and loan-mongers. Let that Bill go into full effect, and I would not give a farthing for the interest that nine-tenths of you will have in your manors and your acres; and, if it do not go into full effect; if you baulk me this time, I will have revenge upon you by actual-

ly hanging up the Gridiron at
Fleet-Street, which I already have
in my yard, made and painted,
(only wanting that gilding, which,
for the honour of gold, it shall
have,) unless this Bill go into full
effect. So that, we come to this,
at last, you cannot keep your estates without seeing me hoist my
Gridiron, which measures *six feet
by seven*, and has handle and legs
that it would do your heart good
to see.

I now come to my, other proof
of the horrible state to which the
country has been reduced; and
this is a proof which, I am sure,
no *loyal* man will call in question: I mean the King's surprising
Letter to the Archbishops, which,
before I proceed further, I shall
here do myself the honour to
insert.

---

*His Majesty's Letter to the Arch-
bishops of Canterbury and York.*

(Copy.)    Whitehall, Dec. 18, 1826.

My Lord,—I have the honour,
in obedience to the commands of his
Majesty, to transmit to your Grace a
letter signed by the King, authorizing your Grace to take proper measures for promoting subscriptions
within your Grace's province, for the
relief of the Manufacturing Classes
in some Districts of the United
Kingdom.

It is proposed that these Subscriptions shall go in aid of those which
have been entered into in the Metropolis for the same benevolent and
charitable purpose. I have accordingly to desire, in compliance with
the terms of his Majesty's letter,
your Grace will take immediate
steps for promoting the objects
therein set forth.—I have the honour
to be, my Lord,

Your Grace's most obedient
humble servant,
ROBERT PEEL.
To the Archbishops of Canterbury
and York, &c. &c. &c.

---

GEORGE R.

Most Reverend Father in God,
Our Right Trusty and Right Entirely Beloved Councillor, We greet you
well! Whereas the Manufacturing
classes, in some districts of the United Kingdom have suffered, and are
still suffering, severe distress; and
whereas many of Our subjects have
entered into voluntary subscriptions
for their relief, and have, at the same
time, most humbly prayed Us to
issue Our Royal Letters, directed to
the Lord Archbishop of Canterbury
and the Lord Archbishop of York,
authorising them to promote contributions within their several provinces
for the same benevolent purpose:
We, taking the premises into Our
Royal consideration, and being always ready to give the best encouragement and countenance to such
humane and charitable undertakings,
are graciously pleased to condescend

to their request. And We do hereby direct, that these Our letters be communicated by you to the several suffragan Bishops within your province, expressly requiring them to take care that publication be made thereof, on such Sunday, and in such places within their respective dioceses, as the said Bishops shall appoint ; and that upon this occasion the Ministers in each parish do effectually excite their parishioners to a liberal contribution, which shall be collected the week following, at their respective dwellings, by the church-wardens or overseers of the poor in each parish, and the Ministers of the several parishes are to cause the sums so collected to be paid immediately into the hands of Messrs. Smith, Payne, and Smith, bankers, of our City of London, to be accounted for by them, and applied to the carrying on and promoting the above-mentioned good designs. And so we bid you very heartily farewell. Given at our Court at Windsor, the 16th day of December, 1826, in the seventh year of our reign.

     By his Majesty's command,
         ROBERT PEEL.

To the Archbishops of Canterbury and York, for a Collection in aid of the Subscriptions entered into for the Relief of the Manufacturing Classes in the United Kingdom.

----

My loyalty restrains me from affixing degrading epithets and appellations to any thing, be it what it may, that comes from under the hand of the King ; otherwise, there present themselves for my selection such a string of them upon this occasion, that they frighten even myself barely to think of. But, in plain and modest terms, let me ask if England ever saw the like of this before the reign of George the Third ? Here we are, living, as our forefathers lived, under a certain law, which has been the law of the land nearly three hundred years, and which provides effectually for the relief of all indigent persons. This law appoints that the means of such relief shall be taken from the land; this relief, or, rather, the amount of it, is a lien upon all the land in the kingdom ; there are officers appointed by this law, to say in what proportion the several portions of the land shall contribute towards this relief; there is a mode of collecting this amount, specified by the law ; all judges, sheriffs, justices of the peace, and all persons in authority of a civil nature are authorized and commanded to aid and assist in the enforcing of this law ; there is, in case of non-payment of the assessment, a power of distraint of goods, of taking possession of chattles and lands, and even of seizure and imprisonment of the person. So that, here this relief is secured; here this effectual relief of all indigent persons is secured by every power with which the King, his magistrates and all his officers of every description are invested. Here are means, which can never fail, because they consist of the land itself and of all that it bears upon it; and here is a mode of coming at those means which can never fail, without a failure of power or of justice on the part of the government itself. Yet, with this law in full force; with this law, unquestioned by any one, whether as to its validity, its meaning, or its efficiency; with this law in existence, here is a King who comes and calls upon the two archbishops to cause their bishops, who are again to call their clergy to call upon his people at large to relieve the indigent by the means of voluntary charity! What must the state of that country be, where such an appeal and under such circumstances can take place!

· But, Landowners, what ought to be your thoughts upon this occasion! Ought you still to applaud that system which has collected together people in such masses, as to cause suffering to such an extent as to form an apology for a measure even like this!

In the first place, this system has robbed your estates of the employment which belonged to the women and the children, of the husbands and fathers necessary to the cultivation of your land. Then, the same system huddles great masses of the people together; throws them, at times, out of all employment; makes them unfit to return to the cultivation of the land; and then it calls upon you to assist in maintaining an army, a standing army in time of peace, to provide against the danger which might arise out of the miseries of these masses of people! Could the devil himself, if he had cogitated for five centuries, have hatched a system more pregnant with misery and destruction?

The Call, however, which is intended to be made, in all parts of the kingdom, for money to relieve the indigence of the manufacturers, will have no effect, I imagine, upon any but tax and tithe eaters and upon very stupid or very timid people. If there be great scarcity of other things in the north, it can hardly be that there is a scarcity of land. Numerous as the swarms of unfortunate creatures are, they are not nearly so numerous as the acres of land; and I believe that, to every human creature in Yorkshire and Lancashire, little babies

D

and all, there are about *six or seven acres of land.* Before, therefore, an application of this sort is made to us, we ought to be informed from what cause it is that the land in those counties cannot relieve the indigent, as well as the lan 's in other counties. Why is Norfolk to subscribe money to relieve the distressed manufacturers in Lancashire and Yorkshire? Or, to put the question rightly, why are the people of Norfolk, first to maintain their own indigent persons, and then subscribe money for relieving the indigent persons in Yorkshire and Lancashire, who have been sacking, for great numbers of years, the high rents which have been caused by the establishment of those very manufactories that have, at last, created a demand upon their land for relief of the poor? Besides, if these counties cannot maintain their poor, there is a power to extend the demand for relief on the lands of the neighbouring counties. Why is Norfolk, why are Sussex and Hampshire and Dorsetshire and Devonshire and Cornwall; why are they, whose lands have been most monstrously injured by being stripped of that in-doors employment which has all been conveyed away to Lancashire and York-

shire; why are those eastern and southern and western counties to be called upon to subscribe money to save the purses of the sharp and greedy landlords in the North?

For my own part, if I were to give a shilling (and I certainly shall not give one farthing) to be conveyed by the means of archbishops and bishops and deacons and God knows what besides, " into the hands of Messrs. Smith, " Payne and Smith, bankers of " our city of London"; if I were to give a farthing to be conveyed into the hands of these people, whose names being introduced in this way makes this Royal Letter smell of those dignified documents, an invoice or a bill of exchange; if I were to give one single farthing into the hands of these people, I should look upon it as a farthing given, not to the poor spinners and weavers of Lancashire and Yorkshire; not to those poor creatures and their wives and children; but *to the landowners of those counties*; and for what *reason* I should do this, neither this document nor any thing else that I have yet seen, gives me any information.

There are a great many persons who will look upon this Royal Letter as containing a royal command. In the several parishes, the parsons will go, attended by the parish officers and by the tax-gatherers. This formidable group every man will have to face, unless he has the good fortune to be absent from his house. Some will take care to be absent; some few will have the spirit to refuse to part with their money for such a purpose; but, the far greater part will submit to the request as to a demand; and will pay as a tax that which will be represented as a voluntary gift. But, what is the sum which can be collected in this way to do; and when are the collections to end? The starvation arises, not from a scarcity of food in the country; not from any want of victuals, drink, or clothing in the country; there is an abundance of all these in the country; but here are hundreds and hundreds of thousands of people, destitute of the means of purchasing these necessaries of life, not because they are unable to work; not because they want strength or want skill; but, because those who used to employ them and to pay them wages wherewith to buy a sufficiency of food and of clothing, are no longer able to do this. The cause of their being unable to do it is, the alteration which has taken place in the value of the money; that value is proceeding on in a course which must necessarily make the difficulty of paying wages to these people greater and greater every day that they live. Where, then, is this work of subscribing to end? The sum will be nothing compared with the sum that is wanted; but, if it were sufficient for the present, another sum must follow it; another sum must follow that; and, at last, a perpetual contribution must be going on all over the kingdom to support these masses of people which a blind and greedy system has gathered together.

It is for you, Landowners, to think of these things. But, very strongly am I persuaded that you will never seriously think of them until it be too late. There are the masses collected together: despise them you cannot; maintain them you must, in one way or another, and, my consolation is, that whatever of evil shall arise to you out of this state of things, will be far short of what a great part of you deserve for your conduct during many years past.

WM. COBBETT.

P.S. I here insert the speech of Mr. DEWHURST, one of the dungeoned-men of 1817 and 1819.

D 2

He has lived to see him, who brought the Dungeon-Bill into the House of Commons, *cut his own throat at North Cray, in Kent*; and, Landowners, I would advise you now to listen attentively to this *radical*, and turn away your ears from the men of *Cornelius Agrippa*. This is the sort of matter that you ought to read about and think about; and not that rubbishing stuff that some of you hear, in places that it is not convenient for me to name. The close of Mr. DEWHURST'S speech, or, rather his second speech, must be *very flattering* to your man, CANNING.

---

*From the Bolton Chronicle.*

MR. GEORGE DEWHURST next addressed the meeting. Mr. Chairman and Gentlemen,—It will not be necessary for me to offer any apology for my attendance here this day. The distress that exists is a sufficient motive; it comes home to every man, to every individual in society, except those who are empowered, by a self-elected House of Commons, to receive the public money, without rendering any services to the nation, as an equivalent. [Here was a spontaneous burst of applause from the meeting.] Mr. Dewhurst then read the 2d Resolution, and afterwards commented upon it in the following terms: — Gentlemen, meetings have been held in different parts of the country, and the object at these meetings, seems to have been a desire to instil into the minds of the people, an idea, that the Corn Laws, and the Corn Laws alone, were the causes of our distress; but I entertain an entirely different opinion; and whoever pays proper attention to the nature of causes and effect, must necessarily arrive at the conclusion, that Taxation is the *real* cause. Eighty millions sterling per annum, are, in one shape, or another, wrung from the hard earnings of the people of this country; and do the idlers, whose individual incomes exceed the income of a German Prince, contribute any thing towards the payment of this immense sum? Some of these hold their estates by hereditary title, and are thereby hereditary legislators. They have consequently had the privilege of augmenting, by their own acts, the value of their hundreds and thousands of acres; and also been enabled to gratify the wants of their hungry dependants, at the expense of the people. If we, who now surround this table, were to collect 10*l.* a week from the remainder of the meeting, and had the disposal of this sum without control, we should undoubtedly enrich our friends and dependants, and neglect the great body of the payers. The poor working man is generally content with a bellyful of beef; and the man who is not satisfied with the gratification of his natural wants, acts in the double capacity of a miser and a robber of the public. He is essentially the same as the highway robber; but of the two, the highway robber is the preferable character; for, if a man is driven, by distress and poverty, to the highway, he does it to satisfy the cravings of his wife and children; whilst the enormous income of the other, derived solely from the produce of the labourer, is expended in luxury and extravagance, and in pampering worthless minions and servants. The Duke, Bishop, Earl, or Commoner, whatever situation he may occupy, if he receives any more than merited wages, is a robber. It is not morality to go to Church, receive the Sacrament, fast, and make long prayers; yet, if your actions are blameless, and you neglect these, the miscreants will denounce you as Deists and Atheists, as beings unworthy the protection of the laws; but I maintain, that the morality of Jesus Christ was, to " Do unto others, as you would they should do unto you." I maintain, that excessive taxation is the cause of all the evil. The Corn Laws were more strictly enforced in 1821, 1822, 1823, than they are at present; for, within the last three months, considerable imports of grain have been made, and yet our sufferings are infinitely greater than they were at those periods. I contend, that the prices of all commodities are regulated by the quantity of money in circulation, and I held in my hand an estimate of the expenses of the year 1813, just previous to the close of the war. In that year they amounted to 112 millions, and some odd money. The price of a calico piece, at that time, was 30s.; the same cloth is now selling at 7s.; and the prices for weaving have been reduced in a similar ratio. There were 40 or 50 millions more, of what is called money, in circulation, in 1813, than there is at present; and as tradesmen are not in the habit of keeping money in their pockets, that must have been the cause of the high prices of 1813, as compared with those of the present day. Shortly after the war was ended, and the blessings of peace and plenty were chaunted from one end of the nation to the other, prices suddenly fell, and the wages of every individual fell at the same time; and the Parsons, the Magistrates, and the tax-eaters of every description, said that it was the sudden transition from a state of war to that of peace, which was the cause, and all would again be right after the first ebullition had subsided. When Bonaparte returned from Elba, an improvement took place; but, at the conclusion of the war of 100 days, as it was called, prices again fell, and have since continued to fall, in the exact proportion as the circulating medium has been contracted. There was a revival a few years since, when the Blackburn Banks, and other Banks of a similar description, issued their paper, and speculation arrived at an amazing height, through the facility with which money could be raised. In the good old times, you might have made calculations on your contracts, to a nicety, for a century to come; but, if a man now makes a contract for any lengthened term, such is the fluctuating nature of a fictitious currency, that he is certain to be deceived. But, I may be asked, how is the medium of exchange to be carried on, if the paper money is withdrawn? I answer, take off taxes in the same proportion as the money is withdrawn, and the real value of the workman's wages will not be reduced. I am certain, that if the money wrung from the people, to support idleness and extravagance, was distributed amongst us, every man, woman, and child, in the kingdom, would have plenty to eat. Some people cry out for a foreign trade, and others for monopoly; but the one makes a German Prince, and the other a Polish beggar. These are plain truths, not mystified with the intricacies of political economy. If we can get the Corn Laws abolished, many other good things must follow: a link of the chain that binds us down will be broken; but we should recollect, that the great landed proprietors are also the legislators, and as self-interest is the stimulant of every human action, they have carried the laws for their own aggrandisement too far. Nor need they flatter themselves, that private benevolence can ever do more than afford mere temporary relief. The 5,000l. they sent down to this town

has done good; but if the money had been circulated in trade, it would have been much better: besides, this charity system is breaking down the spirits of Englishmen—once the admiration of the world. The inventions of genius have sent numbers to the work-house—but who can prevent inventions? Yet, if there were 20 reed makers in Blackburn, and a machine was invented to supersede their labour, it is self-evident that these people would be thrown upon the parish. I now come to the appropriation of the Church property and Crown Lands to the liquidation of the National Debt. This is a delicate subject to treat upon, but the Church property and Crown Lands are the property of the people; and the people want it; for how can it be supposed for a moment, that the interest of 8 or 900 millions of debt can continue to be paid, under the present state of things? There is no prospect for the labouring man but the work-house. He is justly entitled, by his industry, to sufficient meat, drink, and clothing; and when he fails to obtain these, there must be something wrong in the system. The Church property amounts to 9 millions a year, and whilst the Bishop receives 20,000l. per annum, the Curate, who performs all the duty, gets perhaps only 60l. per annum; yet, we call ourselves free-born Englishmen. Many a good man has suffered for speaking the truth, and I myself was confined one hundred and twenty weeks in a gaol, for saying less than I have done this day; but my present observations will pass by, as the idle wind. I next come to the propriety of an equitable adjustment of all contracts between man and man. Suppose I took a farm, on a lease of twenty years, and, during that period, the price of its produce was materially depreciated; still, if I had the same rent to pay, and my poor rates and other taxes were tripled, is it not evident, that if my landlord is inexorable, and will not lower my rent, that I am a ruined man? The Government is in a similar situation; they entered into an agreement with the fundholder, to pay him a certain per centage for the accommodation he afforded them. This contract was made during the existence of a depreciated currency; and, upon what principle of right is the fundholder to receive two-thirds more for his money now, than when he first made the agreement. Whilst our labourers are suffering the extreme of misery, and I own tradesmen are realizing scarcely any profits, the fundholder remains steady. We are in a state of insolvency; and why should the whole of the people be robbed to pay the national creditor? All contracts then being regulated by the value of money, it follows that, to prevent panic after panic, we must have a metallic currency; and, if this were the case, there could not happen any thing more than an occasional fluctuation from the scarcity of bullion. We are but plain unlettered mechanics; yet, I say, these are plain facts, and I cannot but rejoice to learn, that Mr. Canning has almost declared himself to be a Radical. He has avowed, that the next war would be a war of opinions, and that all the discontented and restless spirits of the age would be ranged under the banner of England. I confess I am a character of this description, and may possibly enlist under the banners of the Right Honourable Gentleman. Mr. Canning and Lord Liverpool are certainly loyal men, and, of course, the Radicals will now be considered as loyal subjects;— they were always loyal subjects. Did I ever recommend violence? No. But because I called upon the people to come forward, and demand their rights, I was dragged from my family to a dungeon. It is impossible for me to swallow the infamous doctrine, that our sufferings are the visitations of Providence for our sins, for the poor are not the authors of the calamities that surround us. Then, why punish them? We are told that " it is easier for a " camel to pass through the eye of a " needle, than for a rich man to " enter the kingdom of Heaven;" but when, in spite of this solemn warning, we see the very teachers of these sentiments wallowing in all the luxuries and follies of the age, is it to be wondered at, that Deism and Atheism prevail? Let us, then, make one grand effort to extricate ourselves by petitioning the Legislature for a removal of all our grievances. But I still affirm, that if the Corn Laws were repealed to-morrow, and the rest of our taxes to be continued, our situation would be very little improved. (Loud cheers.)

Mr. DEWHURST again rose. He expressed a wish that the advocates for Catholic Emancipation would join the ranks of the Reformers; for, if a Reform in Parliament was effected, Emancipation would follow as a matter of course. He was aware that no country suffered so much as Ireland; for in no other country were the inhabitants forbid to quit the threshold of their doors before sunrise, or after sunset. He praised the Irish leaders for their exertions, but said, whenever they came in contact with the pestilential breath of an English Parliament, they were immediately contaminated; witness O'Connell—he came fully determined not to barter the liberties of his country, but how soon he fell! He was tempted like Eve, and had no doubt passed many a sleepless night since his fall. He might be said to have mourned in sack-cloth and ashes. But the national curse of Ireland is absenteeism; and whilst provisions of every description are shipped off from thence to other countries, the poor Irish are doomed to feed on hog's meat. We are, my friends, fast approaching to a similar state; and much as we despise the tattered garments and forlorn looks of the impoverished and oppressed Hibernians,

on their first arrival in this country I maintain, that another year will not elapse (unless a change takes place), before we shall cut as sorry a figure as they do. It is true, we have had clothing sent down, and it is all very well, after our keeping the soldiers, to be allowed to wear their cast-off clothes as a favour; but when these miserable substitutes are worn out, we cannot by our industry replace them; so that we must have another supply, or perhaps we may be seen skulking behind the hedges, cleansing ourselves from vermin. I am sorry to be obliged to relate these unwholesome truths; but, could I call forth the brave spirits of our forefathers, they would, on seeing the half-starved appearance of their descendants, skulk back into their graves and say, " *I know you not!* "

## WAR WITH SPAIN.

THERE is no believing one single word that the newspapers say on this subject, Mr. Brougham's " best possible public instructor" being, for one thing, the very greatest liar upon the whole face of the earth. From the contents of the French newspapers, it would appear that France and Spain (for they are closely united in this affair) appear to be disposed to be satisfied with seeing a civil war raging in Portugal, which, as the worst possible termination to them, will saddle us with the charge of maintaining an army to support the new Constitution in Portugal, to make that Constitution most heartily detested by a great majority of the Portuguese, and to expose this Constitution and all its upholders and abettors to all the consequences of such detestation, making the situation of Portugal, in its state of what the fops of Whitehall call *Liberalism*, an object of contempt with the Spaniards. Thus we shall have given Spain the best of security on that side, and neither France nor Spain, nor any other not mad nation, will envy us the expense we shall incur by this senseless intermeddling.

---

## AMERICA.

Mr. CANNING! I speak in a whisper; nobody is listening I hope; but, have you read the message of John Quincy Adams? I have; and, between you and I, though I would not say it publicly for the world, if you do get into a war with Spain, you must fight as they do in the north, with your *feet* and your *teeth*, for the former of which, the gout is by no means favoura-

ble, and for the latter you are not, possibly, too well armed. As to HANDS, you will have none to use in such a contest; for, France and Russia will hold your left hand, and Jonathan will hold the right. I have not time at present to say more upon this American message, than just to add, that it is the sound of the hammer upon another nail, driven into the coffin of that system, of which you have been so long receiving such immense sums of our money for being the clamourous and audacious supporter. All this, mind, is between you and I: I would not say. it to another soul upon any account whatever.—A happy new year to you, and, pray, never forget *the " making a stand " against democratical encroach- " ment,"* when it called out for bringing a seat-seller to the bar of the House; never forget that *" the reformers were a low degraded crew ;"* never forget how the House *laughed* (though I confess that I *know* that some of the Members did not laugh, for I had the fact from my Lord Folkestone) when you uttered the words, *" the revered and ruptured Ogden."* Pray never forget these; preserve these plumes to the last moment of your life, whatever may be the result of your *constitution-making*

and warlike and free-trade projects. Once more begging you to
let all this be between ourselves,
and once more wishing you a
happy new year,

I remain, Sir,
Your most obedient and
Most humble Servant,
Wm. COBBETT.

TO

DOCTOR BLACK.

Ah, Doctor! If you had but
dined with me on New Year's
day! and, upon my word, I should
have been glad of your company.
Some charitable lawyer sent me
a banging turkey, on Saturday evening last, to be stuffed
with the sparrows, which I had
already received from my country cousins. Just as this turkey
arrived, or about a quarter of an
hour before, came in a turkey,
from an excellent friend and
faithful disciple, in Essex; on the
Sunday the sworn brother of this
Essex turkey came along the
Macadamized road from Berkshire. Ah Doctor! say you *feelosophers* what you will, this is the
sort of stuff that produces enjoyment. There was one *Reid*, who
wrote a book on what he called
the "*Human Mind*," when I was

a bookseller, in Philadelphia,
and used to bait and laugh at this
Gallatin, who is now here the
American Ambassador: I used to
sell a great many copies of this book
of Dr. Reid; but never in my life
did I open that book, always having observed that it was the *belly*
and not the *head* which has the
greatest influence on the actions of
mankind in general. But, Doctor,
to return to the sparrows! Plump
and fat little things of themselves;
a little grain of pepper and salt put
into each; and then, undergoing
the operation of baking or stewing,
not in vessels of earth or iron,
or copper, or of that metal of
which a *Scotch feelosopher's*
face is supposed to consist;
but in a cavern, the sides, ends,
top and bottom of which consist
of some of the richest of meat;
then coming out swimming in their
own and the turkey's gravy! Ah,
Doctor! I can go no further; but
again I say, that if you had dined
upon these sparrows as I did,
and had taken after them a pottle,
or even a pot of my beer, you
would not, for the next twelve
hours at any rate, have thought
any more about your favourite
dish, a Judge stuffed with Justices
of the Peace. Your Scotchmen's
dishes are all metaphorical. Mine
are of the contrary nature: all

ualities; and, if I could but get that twist out of your head; if I could but bring you to witness the effects which the three B.'s, Bread, Bacon and Beer, have upon human actions, never should I hear you cant about your *mental improvement* again. I am,

My dear Doctor,
Your most humble and
Most obedient servant,
Wm. COBBETT.

P. S. All my country cousins think that you are a real Doctor; and so you are; and I have made you a Doctor for nothing, when to have got your title from Scotland would, I dare say, have cost you a couple of shillings, or eighteen pence at least. The price generally is, I believe, a cast coat or an old pair of shoes; but, then, *feelosophers* manage so economically, that they can be hardly thought of for so high a dignity.

## ICE HOUSES.

In a new edition of "COTTAGE ECONOMY," there is a plan and explanations upon this subject. The ice is now come; and if any gentleman should think proper to put my plan into execution, he will oblige me very much by letting me know the result.

## AMERICAN
## TREES AND SEEDS.

The far greater part of my trees is sold, except APPLE TREES, of which I have a pretty good store still on hand. The frost has now locked up the ground. Those orders which I have received, and which I have not executed, I most distinctly promise to execute, and to send the trees off, in *four days* after the frost shall be again *out of the ground.* Here I except those trees which are ordered to be kept by me until February.

The tree and shrub seeds, which I, last week, expected to have arrived from America, have arrived, or the ship, at least, has arrived at Deal, or is somewhere thereabouts, I having received the invoice and bill of lading by post from Deal: so that, I shall be ready next week to state the particulars of the collection of which I spoke in the last Register.

## A CLASSICAL
## TEACHER,

Of long experience, and great success for the rapid progress of his Pupils, before and after they enter College, could spare a few hours of the morning or evening, to give private Lectures for any genteel Family, in the west end of the town, or any where in the suburbs, contiguous to his present situation. Terms moderate; references the most satisfactory. A note, directed to Mr. Dean, 182, Fleet-street, shall meet punctual attention.

5th Jan. 1827.

## MARKETS.

Average Prices of CORN through-out ENGLAND, for the week ending December 22.

*Per Quarter.*

| | s. | d. | | s. | d. |
|---|---|---|---|---|---|
| Wheat .. | 55 | 6 | Rye .... | 39 | 4 |
| Barley .. | 36 | 3 | Beans ... | 49 | 7 |
| Oats .... | 29 | 4 | Pease ... | 50 | 9 |

Total Quantity of Corn returned as Sold in the Maritime Districts, for the week ended December 22.

| | Qrs. | | Qrs. |
|---|---|---|---|
| Wheat.. | 44,309 | Rye ..... | 151 |
| Barley .. | 55,392 | Beans ... | 2,563 |
| Oats ... | 10,797 | Pease .... | 951 |

*Corn Exchange, Mark Lane.*

Quantities and Prices of British Corn, &c. sold and delivered in this Market, during the week ended Saturday, December 23.

| | Qrs. | £. | s. d. | | s. d. |
|---|---|---|---|---|---|
| Wheat.. | 5,517 for | 16,067 | 9 2 | Average, 58 | 2 |
| Barley.. | 7,815 .. | 15,197 | 2 9 .......... | 38 | 10 |
| Oats.. | 1,767 .. | 3,037 | 9 4 .......... | 33 | 11 |
| Rye.... | 20 .. | 38 | 15 .6 .......... | 38 | 9 |
| Beans.. | 888 .. | 2,187 | 5 8 .......... | 48 | 9 |
| Pease.. | 607 .. | 1,593 | 2 6 ........ | 52 | 5 |

Friday, Dec. 29. —The arrivals this week are very good of all descriptions of Grain. The Wheat trade continues in a very heavy state, and may be reported 1s. per qr. lower than last Friday. Barley, Beans, and Pease, may each be stated at a reduction of 1s. per quarter. The quantity of Oats for sale is so large, that the prices have further declined 1s. to 2s. per quarter. The Flour trade is extremely heavy.

Monday, January 1, 1827.—There were very good supplies of all descriptions of Grain last week, and this morning we have good quantities of Wheat, Barley, Beans, and Pease, from the surrounding counties, and several more vessels fresh up with Oats. Superfine Wheat is rather scarce, and such has sold at 1s. per qr. reduction, but all other sorts are so cold in hand, that they meet scarcely any demand, even though offered at 2s. per qr. below the terms of last Wednesday.

Barley is so very plentiful that hardly any progress can be made in the sales, at an abatement in value of 1s. to 2s. per quarter. Beans and Grey Pease may each be reported 1s. per quarter cheaper; Boiling Pease very heavy in sale, and rather lower. The market is quite overdone with Oats, and this article continues to decline in value, and may be stated rather lower than on Wednesday last. There is much uncertainty about the top price of Flour, the trade being extremely heavy.

*Price on board Ship as under.*

Flour, per sack ......50s. — 53st

—— Seconds ........42s. — 46s.

—— North Country ..40s. — 45s.

Price of Bread.—The price of the 4lb. Loaf is stated at 9½d. by the full-priced Bakers.

Account of Wheat, &c. arrived in the Port of London, from Dec. 25 to Dec. 30, both inclusive.

| | Qrs. | | Qrs. |
|---|---|---|---|
| Wheat .. | 5.089 | Tares .... | 735 |
| Barley .. | 12,959 | Linseed .. | 910 |
| Malt .... | 5,228 | Rapeseed . | 12 |
| Oats .... | 18,789 | Brank .. | — |
| Beans ... | 614 | Mustard.. | 25 |
| Flour .... | 10,662 | Flax .... | — |
| Rye .... | 2,554 | Hemp ... | 40 |
| Pease.... | 4,212 | Seeds ... | 4 |

Foreign.—Wheat, 3,393; Barley, 2,964; Oats, 22,589; and Beans, 5,356 quarters.

———

Monday, Jan. 1.— The arrivals from Ireland last week were 17,253 firkins of Butter, and 6,235 bales of Bacon; and from Foreign Ports, 1,322 casks of Butter.

## HOPS.

Borough, Jan. 1.—We had more demand for Hops during last week, particularly pockets, than at the early part of last month, with an advance of about 2s. per cwt. Currency as under : — Kent, pockets from 84s. to 112s.; ditto bags, 65s. to 90s.; Sussex, pockets, 74s. to 86s. per cwt.

Maidstone, Dec. 28.—There have been a few sales made this week of middling Bags, at full as good prices, and we consider the Hop Trade has a better appearance.

Worcester, Dec. 27.—On Saturday 157 pockets were weighed ; average prices 93s. to 100s.—The number of pockets of Hops weighed in Worcester Hop Market, from Dec. 25, 1825, to Dec. 25, 1826, was—New, 29,208; Old, 3,640.

SMITHFIELD, Monday, Jan. 1, 1827.

It is our rule to make a report of this market that shall apply to the general trade, neither taking in a few very particular choice Beasts, for which a customer may always be found at prices totally in discordance to the legitimate trade; nor the things that go to the sausage-maker. In our last we stated that 5s. 8d. was a strained price; this was the fact, as but very few realized more than 5s. 6d., which was the fair top price. On Friday both Beef and Mutton were heavy in demand, and a shade lower. To-day is fine and cheerful; but Beef is still receding from the Christmas terms, and though the supply is short, there are quite enough. There is a good market of Mutton, and polled Sheep have recovered the depression of Friday, the best light weights making 4s. 4d.; and best Downs 4s. 8d.

*Per Stone of 8 pounds (alive).*

| | s. | d. | | s. | d. |
|---|---|---|---|---|---|
| Beef . | 4 | 0 | to | 5 | 4 |
| Mutton ... | 3 | 10 | — | 4 | 8 |
| Veal ..... | 5 | 4 | — | 6 | 0 |
| Pork ..... | 5 | 5 | — | 6 | 0 |
| Lamb .... | 0 | 0 | — | 0 | 0 |

| Beasts . . | 2,359 | Sheep . . | 18,000 |
|---|---|---|---|
| Calves ... | 177 | Pigs ... | 130 |

NEWGATE, (same day.)
*Per Stone of 8 pounds (dead).*

| | s. | d. | | s. | d. |
|---|---|---|---|---|---|
| Beef ..... | 3 | 4 | to | 4 | 4 |
| Mutton ... | 2 | 8 | — | 3 | 8 |
| Veal ..... | 3 | 8 | — | 5 | 8 |
| Pork ..... | 4 | 0 | — | 5 | 8 |
| Lamb .... | 0 | 0 | — | 0 | 0 |

LEADENHALL, (same day.)
*Per Stone of 8 pounds (dead).*

| | s. | d. | | s. | d. |
|---|---|---|---|---|---|
| Beef ... . | 3 | 4 | to | 4 | 6 |
| Mutton ... | 2 | 8 | — | 3 | 10 |
| Veal .... | 3 | 8 | — | 5 | 4 |
| Pork ..... | 4 | 4 | — | 6 | 0 |
| Lamb .... | 0 | 0 | — | 0 | 0 |

## POTATOES.

SPITALFIELDS, *per Ton.*

|  | L. s. | | L. s. |
|---|---|---|---|
| Ware | 3 0 | to | 4 10 |
| Middlings | 2 0 | — | 0 0 |
| Chats | 1 15 | — | 0 0 |
| Common Red | 0 0 | — | 0 0 |

Onions, 0s. 0d.—0s. 0d. per bush.

BOROUGH, *per Ton.*

|  | L. s. | | L. s. |
|---|---|---|---|
| Ware | 3 0 | to | 4 5 |
| Middlings | 2 0 | — | 0 0 |
| Chats | 1 15 | — | 0 0 |
| Common Red | 3 0 | — | 4 0 |

## HAY and STRAW, per Load.

Smithfield.—Hay....80s. to 105s.
Straw...30s. to 36s.
Clover. 100s. to 126s.

St. James's.—Hay.... 75s. to 110s.
Straw .. 28s. to 30s.
Clover.. 83s. to 126s.

Whitechapel.—Hay....72s. to 105s.
Straw...32s. to 36s.
Clover..84s. to 126s.

## AVERAGE PRICE OF CORN, sold in the Maritime Counties of England and Wales, for the Week ended December 22, 1826.

|  | Wheat. s. d. | Barley. s. d. | Oats. s. d. |
|---|---|---|---|
| London* | 58 7 | 38 11 | 32 3 |
| Essex | 56 8 | 35 1 | 29 5 |
| Kent | 56 7 | 37 4 | 30 0 |
| Sussex | 53 6 | 38 11 | 30 2 |
| Suffolk | 54 6 | 34 4 | 29 0 |
| Cambridgeshire | 52 1 | 34 6 | 34 1 |
| Norfolk | 54 0 | 34 6 | 30 1 |
| Lincolnshire | 53 5 | 37 6 | 25 6 |
| Yorkshire | 54 4 | 39 6 | 28 1 |
| Durham | 56 1 | 41 0 | 32 0 |
| Northumberland | 55 1 | 38 3 | 33 6 |
| Cumberland | 61 4 | 38 9 | 34 1 |
| Westmoreland | 62 1 | 48 0 | 34 7 |
| Lancashire | 59 10 | 40 9 | 37 0 |
| Cheshire | 57 6 | 53 7 | 30 9 |
| Gloucestershire | 56 11 | 42 8 | 37 5 |
| Somersetshire | 55 2 | 39 7 | 29 1 |
| Monmouthshire | 61 10 | 51 5 | 0 0 |
| Devonshire | 57 6 | 37 2 | 26 11 |
| Cornwall | 57 6 | 36 11 | 29 1 |
| Dorsetshire | 53 5 | 36 9 | 36 3 |
| Hampshire | 54 6 | 37 1 | 29 5 |
| North Wales | 65 7 | 45 6 | 30 8 |
| South Wales | 60 4 | 42 2 | 27 10 |

* The London Average is always that of the Week preceding.

*Liverpool*, Dec. 26.—The arrivals of Grain, particularly of Wheat, Oats, Flour, and Oatmeal, have been considerable since Tuesday last, and, as may be observed, very principally from Ireland : the whole are not reported in the Import note annexed, owing to the intervenience of two holidays, and although the demand was languid in the past week, late prices were tolerably well maintained. At this day's market, which was but thinly attended, but little business was done : fine qualities, however, supported the quotations of this day se'nnight.

Imported into Liverpool, from the 19th to the 25th December, 1826, inclusive :— Wheat, 9,775; Barley, 3,945; Oats, 16,693; Rye, 790; Malt, 1,396; Beans, 963; Pease, 791 quarters. Flour, 1,418 sacks, per 280 lbs. Oatmeal, 1,069 packs, per 240 lbs. American Flour, 818 barrels.

*Guildford*, Dec. 30.—Wheat, new, for mealing, 14*l.* to 16*l.* per load. Rye, 52*s.* to 56*s.*; Barley, 35*s.* to 38*s*; Oats, 33*s.* to 38*s.*; Beans, 56*s.* to 60*s.*; Pease, grey, 58*s.* to 60*s.*; ditto, boilers, 60*s.* to 64*s.* per quarter.

*Norwich*, Dec. 30.—We had only a moderate supply of all Grain to this day's market.—Red Wheat selling at 52*s.* to 56*s.*; White to 57*s.*; Barley, 30*s.* to 36*s.*; Oats, 26*s.* to 31*s.*; Beans, 41*s.* to 43*s.*; Pease, 42*s.* to 45*s.*; Boilers, to 54*s.* per quarter; and Flour, 41*s.* to 42*s.* 6*d.* per sack.

*Bristol*, Dec. 30.—Our Corn markets here are very dull, and although the supplies are moderate, they are quite equal to the demand. Oats have declined in price, in consequence of the very great arrivals of foreign ones, in London, during the last fortnight. Present prices of Corn, &c. are about as follow :—Wheat, from 5*s.* 3*d.* to 7*s.* 6*d.*; Barley, 4*s.* 3*d.* to 5*s.* 6*d.*; Oats, 3*s.* to 4*s.*; Beans, 5*s.* 3*d.* to 7*s.* 7½*d.*; and Malt, 5*s.* 6*d.* to 8*s.* 6*d.* per bushel, Imperial.—Flour, Seconds, 32*s.* to 42*s.* per bag.

*Ipswich*, Dec. 30.—Our market to-day was not largely supplied with Corn, and prices were much the same as last week; as follow :—Wheat, 52*s.* to 60*s.*; Barley, 32*s.* to 36*s.*; Beans, 44*s.* to 46*s.*; and Pease, 46*s.* to 48*s.* per quarter.

*Wisbech*, Dec. 30 —We had a short supply of Wheat to-day, and the little dry offered made full as much as last week. Oats and Beans about the same.—Red Wheat, 50*s.* to 56*s.*; White ditto, 56*s.* to 58*s.*; Oats, 22*s.* to 30*s.*; and Beans, 44*s.* to 48*s.* per quarter.

*Wakefield*, Dec. 29.—The supply of Wheat fresh up here to-day is tolerably good ; the Flour trade in Lancashire being very flat, and having a slender attendance of buyers, the sale has been rather heavy, at the rates of last week.—Oats and Shelling are not plentiful, and fully maintain late prices. Fine heavy Barley is in fair demand, at last Friday's prices, but the light samples are difficult to quit. Beans are very dull to-day. Rapeseed is without alteration.

*Newcastle-on-Tyne*, Dec. 30 —The farmers' supply of Wheat was less this morning than it has been for some weeks past, and there being few arrivals coastwise, the sale was brisk, at last week's prices. Rye is more in demand, at the prices of last week. Barley continues dull sale. The maltsters occasionally buy a little of the best Norfolk, but all other descriptions are neglected. Malt dull sale. We had only the farmers' supply of Oats at market this morning, which was readily sold, at last week's prices.

*Manchester*, Dec. 30.—We continue to have but little doing in sales of Grain, Malt, and Flour: however, this week is generally an exception, being holiday time. We had a moderate attendance of town and country dealers on 'Change to-day, with but a small show of samples : however, the demand has been so slack, that scarcely a sale has been effected in Wheat.

## COUNTRY CATTLE AND MEAT MARKETS, &c.

*Horncastle,* Dec. 30.—Beef, 7s. per stone of 14 lbs.; Mutton, 6d.; Pork, 6d.; and Veal, 6d. to 7d. per lb.

*Malton,* Dec. 30.—Meat in the shambles: Beef, 6d. to 7½d.; Mutton, 5d. to 5½d.; Pork, 6d. to 6½d.; and Veal, 6½d. to 7½d. per lb. Fresh Butter, 16d. to 17d. per lb. of 16 oz. Small Hams, 8s. 6d. per stone.

*Norwich Castle Meadow,* Dec. 30.—The supply of fat Cattle to this day's market was very limited.; prices 8s. to 8s. 6d. per stone of 14 lbs., sinking offal. The supply of store Scots was large, sale quite flat, at about 4s. per stone, when fat; only a few Short Horns here, at 3s. to 3s. 6d. Cows and Calves, and Homebreds, of all sorts, a very flat sale. Horses, of both kinds, but little doing with them. We had only a small supply of Sheep penned: Shearlings, selling at 25s. to 29s.; fat ones to 38s. Lambs, 13s. to 18s. 6d. each. Pigs, a large number, fat ones, to 6s. 6d. per stone.—Meat: Beef, 7d. to 9d. ; Veal, 7d. to 8½d.; Mutton, 5½d. to 7d.; and Pork, 5½d. to 8d. per lb.

*Birmingham* Smithfield Market, Dec. 28.—The supply of fat Beef and Mutton short. Stores plenty, and a little lower. Fat Pigs plentiful, and a dull trade.—Beef, 5d. to 6½d. ; Mutton, 5d. to 6½d.; and Veal, 5d. to 7d. per lb.; Pork, 8s. to 8s. 6d. per score.—Neat Cattle, 265; Sheep, 505 ; Pigs, 254.

*Wakefield* Cattle Market, Dec. 27.—There was a very short supply of Stock to this day's market, (being what might be termed a holiday market,) and a fair attendance of buyers, which, although their purchases were limited, caused nearly the whole to be taken off, at an advance of ½d. per lb,

*Skipton* Cattle Market, Dec. 26.—We had only a thin supply of fat Beasts, but the show of Sheep was good : there was a good demand, at advanced prices.—Beef, 6d. to 7d.; Mutton, 6d. to 6½d. per lb.

# COBBETT'S WEEKLY REGISTER.

Vol. 61.—No. 3.]     LONDON, SATURDAY, Jan. 13, 1827.     [*Price 6d.*

*Published every Saturday Morning, at Seven o' Clock.*

" As, in the disputes between a mother and her daughter, ill-blood may
" exist for a while; but, there the maternal and filial affection is still at
" the bottom of the heart, these causes these to rekindle into mutual love,
" and that, too, more ardent than ever; so, in this case the former dis-
" putes between Great Britain and the United States are now producing
" greater harmony and more sincere attachment than ever animated their
" minds at any former period."—Mr. Canning's *Speech at Liverpool*,
27 *Oct.* 1822.

TO

# THE NOBILITY OF ENGLAND,

## On the Blessings which Messrs. Canning and Huskisson

### HAVE IN STORE FOR THEM.

### LETTER I.

*Kensington,* 10*th Jan.* 1827.

My Lords,

You are great men, for, you have in your hands all the real powers of a great nation, and you have estates, which, if divided equally amongst you, would make each of you a greater man, in respect of dominion, than the average of the Sovereign Princes of Europe. Many of you derive a considerable part of the power and a great part of the domains from your ancestors; and these domains have been held by laws, under which the people were, for numerous ages, the most free and most happy in the world. But, you have, at last, found something to shake you. You are not the men that even your grandfathers were, and nothing at all like the

E

Printed and Published by William Cobbett, No. 183, Fleet-street,
[ENTERED AT STATIONERS' HALL.]

men that your ancestors were four hundred years ago. In your carriage towards the common people, you are loftier than your ancestors. You are not insolent and rude like the upstart jobbers and loanmongers; but, these *halls* in which your forefathers used to sit at the head of their tenantry, are now objects of wonder at what they were made for. The communication between you (even the most gracious and condescending amongst you) and those who till your lands has been growing more and more slender; until, at last, it has been completely cut off by the intervention of attorneys, stewards, land-agents and surveyors. It is, I confess it with pleasure, a compliment to your minds, that the hard things which have to be done to those beneath you, are such that you cannot bring yourselves to do in person. *You know nothing of the matter*, when a hard thing is to be done: you leave it all to your steward or whatever other name he may bear: but, the thing is not less hard for that; and the sufferer fails not to trace the hardship to its source.

This, however, is beginning a Letter with a digression, for I mean to address you upon the subject of the way in which you are likely to be affected by the schemes and contrivances, the novelties and the fooleries of "anti-jacobins" who have all of a sudden turned to be "liberals"; and I particularly mean to address you on the prospects of this country, should a war be commenced, either now or at any future time, and, should the main part of the people be excluded from their due weight in the Government by a continuation of a rejection of the great measure, a reform in the House of Commons.

The present situation of the country is that of pretty nearly disorganization, arising from the sufferings of the people from want of food and clothing. All men now agree; even the hired reviewers and other hired writers agree, that the sufferings of the people are caused by heavy taxation. They all agree also, that a war cannot now be carried on, unless the law respecting the currency be again changed; that is to say, that it cannot be carried on without an issue of assignats; and that is only another word for describing a total dissolution of the Government. There is, then, quite enough to make your Lordships sober. The old saying, "as drunk as a Lord," if it applied to you, which I suppose it does not, in its literal sense, would not be applicable to you any longer, if you could once be brought to contemplate the dangers which menace you. I say you in particular; because, it is you who have every thing to lose. A nation never dies: a nation, unless completely subjugated, can, as a whole, really lose nothing. To the main body of the people, there is very little risk; but, to you, there is every thing to risk; and, as I shall endeavour to show you, you may, if you will, get rid of that risk. Not, however, by listening to the schemes of the schemers of this day; but, by treading back the steps of the last hundred years, and "gaining back the people," as Sir James Graham calls it, not by a bare-faced robbery committed upon three hundred thousand families, as he would recommend, but by means such as I shall do myself the honour of suggesting.

You feel, because you must feel, that you are not the men that your grandfathers were; but you have come into your present state by slow degrees, and therefore you cannot tell, even to yourselves, not only how the change has come about, but you cannot tell what sort of change it really is. You may know what it is, however; or, at least, you may form some little no-

tion of the nature of it when you reflect that your grandfathers would as soon thought, aye, and sooner thought of dining with a chimney-sweep than of dining with a Jew, or with any huckstering reptile, who had amassed money by watching the turn of the market; that those grandfathers would have thought it no dishonour at all to sit at table with farmers, or even with labourers, but that they would have shunned the usurious tribe of loan-jobbers and other notorious changers of money, as they would have shunned the whirlwind or the pestilence. These usurers now take precedence of you in many cases, and many of you really live in awe of them. To this you have brought yourselves, by your jealousy of those who are justly denominated the people, who are your natural friends, and whose friendship you have lost; and thereby made yourselves the dependants, in some degree, at any rate, of this tribe of loan-jobbing vagabonds whom you despise in your hearts, and whom you compliment in your words and by your looks. Never, every reader of this Register will say, were truer words than these put upon paper.

What, then, is to be your attention, if a new series of loans and jobs is to be entered upon? And how are you to weather the storm and preserve your estates, if another war come and find the nation in its present state? This leads me to what it is my principal object to call your attention to; namely, the nature of that next war, let that next war come when it may; and, in speaking of this, the topic most worthy of being considered by you is, the disposition, the means and the employment of the means of that great power, that great maritime power which the impolicy, the folly, the madness of this Government has created, absolutely created, on the *other side of the Atlantic.*

Every man of sense knows, as well as he knows how to distinguish daylight from dark, that England must continue the greatest naval nation in the world, or be reduced to be one of the most contemptible nations in the world. Burke has said, and, though he was a horrible, pensioned old hack, he said it well and truly, that "a nation, *once become great,* "can never sink into a middle "state and there remain; that it "must continue to be great, or, "sink so low as hardly to be worthy "of the name of a nation." There are many men, and those by no means fools, who think that Eng-

land will sink down into the last mentioned state. I am of a different opinion. The whole of the history of my country tells me, that that never will be. Divers have been the times when England seemed to be torn to pieces; seemed to be incapable of ever recovering; but, in every such case, whether from a change of the government; from the destruction of the sovereign; or, from some cause or other, such a change has taken place as to put every thing to rights, and to make the nation as formidable as ever to its neighbours. It has always been, with the people of England, the most monstrous of crimes in their rulers, to do any thing tending to pull down the country; and, if my observation do not deceive me, that spirit is as much alive at this hour as it was in the days of King John or of Edward the Second; but, something must suffer; something must go to wreck; somebody or something must be overturned, when the nation recovers itself by means so convulsive. If, then, my Lords, somebody or something must go to wreck in consequence of such convulsive movement; and if I should be able to show to you that the dreaded depression, degradation, abasement, must come, without suitable means of prevention, who or what, is it, my Lords, that, in such case, would be most likely to go to wreck?

It is now about seventeen years since I began to endeavour to impress upon the minds of the people of this country and upon that of its Government, the great danger to be apprehended from the United States of America becoming a naval power. The calculations of English statesmen have consisted of items relating to the probable duration of the union of those States. They were always ready to concede to you that the danger would be great, if you could ensure the Union to continue; and, while they have had it in their power, completely in their power, to prevent such continuance, they have done every thing that human wit could have suggested, if the object had been to cause the Union to last for ever. *They have kept up with that country an everlasting dispute,* about something or other. From the day of the date of the acknowledgment of the independence of the United States to the day on which I am writing, we have had commissioners or negotiators of some sort or other *in our pay for adjusting disputes with the United States!* Monstrous fact to state: yet notoriously true. Disputes sometimes about something and sometimes about nothing; but always disputes; never-ending disputes. Like the debts of the Nabob of Arcot, subjects of discussion, of the length of which it is no very great exaggeration to say, that it reminds us of the awful word eternity!

Yet, in the midst of all this, and just as if there were no disputes at all, we have, from the lips of the man who was just about to become Secretary of State for Foreign Affairs, the childish caterwauling trash, a part of which I have quoted as my motto to this Letter. I put to your Lordships this question: What a state must that country be in; and what a state must a lord's estate be in, which is situated in that country which has this caterwauling talker for a Secretary of State for its Foreign Affairs? To this Letter I subjoin, or somewhere in this *Register* I shall insert, the Message of Mr. ADAMS, the American President, to the Congress, sent to that body about two months ago. I request your Lordships to read this Message throughout, long-winded as it really is; but, I beg your particular attention to paragraphs 10,

11, 12 and 13; and then to paragraphs 30 and 31. These are
the sort of things that are worthy
of being attended to. Here is
the menace, and there are the
means; and, whatever other faults
Yankees may have, they are not
*jesters*; they deal neither in jokes
nor bombast; and they always
tell you what they mean to be at.
I said in a *Register* some few
weeks back, in addressing myself
to Mr. CANNING, that he had the
*people* of America to combat;
that it was not the government of
America; that Mr. ADAMS was,
in his heart, a good deal of an
Englishman; but that, to obtain
the smallest chance of a re-election, he must vie with his rival in
hostility to England. Luckily for
him, our pretty pair of politicians,
Messrs. HUSKISSON and CAN-
NING, sworn brothers in liberality
though one began his career in
the *Club quatre-vingt neuf*, and
the other at Boodle's or Noodle's,
or some such place of meeting of
the anti-jacobins; luckily for Mr.
ADAMS, this pair of pretty politicians have given him a fine opportunity of showing his decided hostility to us, having, at the same
time, reason on his side; and
your Lordships will perceive how
nicely he is prepared for *making
a move* in case this surprising war

of our renowned ÆOLUS should
happen to assume any thing of a
really warlike character. I dare
say that Mr. ADAMS wishes for
nothing less than for war; but, in
this case, Mr. ADAMS's wishes are
of no more weight than mine: he
has masters to obey; and those
masters are everlastingly hanker-
ing after the means of humiliating
England.

If your Lordships read with attention paragraphs from ten to
thirteen, both inclusive, you will
see that Mr. CANNING and Mr.
HUSKISSON were heirs in the right
line to quite disputes enough with
America before this *new ground
of dispute*, which is of a nature
infinitely more important, especially as connected with the views
of Russia, France and Spain,
than all our other disputes with
all the powers in the world put together.

To describe in detail the *grounds*
of this dispute can hardly be expected, when, if Mr. ADAMS is to
be believed, they consist of certain
provisions in an Act of Parliament, so *difficult to understand*
the meaning of, *so vague*, and *so
unintelligible* as not to be understood by our officers in the West
Indies who are charged to carry
it into effect! This is a pretty
sharpish "*daughter*" to criticise

her good "mother's" words in this manner. It does not discover any strong symptoms in her of that returning affection of which Cornelius Agrippa's man spoke in his caterwauling at Liverpool, to the great delight, no doubt, of all the wives and daughters of the greedy, grasping, huckstering, jobbing crew now denominated merchants, of that most huckstering and jobbing town of Liverpool. But, words are wind: I mean in the mouth of a flash-orator: not so when they come from the pen of Mr. Adams. Yet, even he does not state in detail the grounds of his complaint: I know them, and, with your permission, I will state them, and, I hope, with a little better chance of my words being understood than were the words of that unfortunate Act of Parliament which, though passed by your Lordships, could not be understood even by our own officers in the West Indies.

Be it then known by your Lordships; also to all the faelosophers that Scotland has spewed forth, not excluding Mr. Brougham; be it known to this be-bothered nation, who are caught in a moment at the sound of *liberty* or *liberal* or almost of any word that begins with an L, by no means excluding the word *No*; be it known to all, that here we have the first fruits of that applauded system of "*liberality*," commonly known by the name of *free-trade*, the authors of which discovered (as the two young officers that Swift mentions discovered that there was no God), without the smallest particle of political science; without the smallest degree of knowledge of the relationships between the United States and the West Indies, solely by their own instinctiveness and genius, aided a little by the lucubrations of the Edinburgh Reviewers and my three Doctors, MACCULLOCH and BLACK and BARING: these authors, Messrs. Huskisson and Canning, discovered, that all that our ancestors had ever thought, said or enacted on the subject of trade and commerce, was *radically wrong*; that navigation laws, that prohibitions of every sort, were all mischievous; that all the Acts of Parliament from the reign of Henry the Third down to that of George the Fourth and unto the year one thousand eight hundred and twenty-five, as far as they related to matters of external trade, were heaps of senseless trash; that it was a great mistake to suppose that one nation had an interest different from other nations; that they all belonged to the one great family of mankind; and that it was just as foolish and, indeed, as wicked, for the Government to endeavour to gain advantage over France, as it would be for it to endeavour to cause Wiltshire to gain advantage over Berkshire.

There is a discovery, my Lords! How happy you are to have such lights rise up, one out of an apothecary's shop and the other out of God knows what; such blazing lights to guide you out of the darkness in which you had been left by such a long series of benighting ancestors! They have not said it yet, but, doubtless, they have discovered, that, as one nation ought not to take advantage of another in commerce, so it ought not to take advantage of it in war; that the community of nations ought to love one another, as men ought to love their neighbours; that God made a mistake when he made islands, peninsulas and continents; that all the earth ought to have been in one single patch; that all the people ought to have had the same colour of skin, to have spoken the same language, to have been of the same character, to have had the same tastes and habits. It would have been devilish work if, after assimilating the community of nations to men in a community,

they had applied their national doctrine to the latter; for, then, my Lords, they would have found out, that your interest and the chimney-sweeps' was the same, and that, by only going a little further, they must have called it *monopoly* in you not to let the chimney-sweeps share in your estates.

Of all the stupid things that ever were engendered in the minds of a couple of callow and purblind politicians, this *free-trade* project is the most stupid; yet, it is very likely to saddle your Lordships' estates with the expenses of another war; or, rather, to take from you that part of those estates which the Jews and the loan-jobbers have left you; for, the cause of this new strife with the United States is as follows.

The pair of pretty politicians before-mentioned, and some others, perhaps, of the Ministry, began to put this project in execution last year. The project was to get other nations to admit our manufactures into their countries duty free, and for us to admit their manufactures duty free. If our neighbours were to gain by this change as much as we gain by it; if their power and resources were to be augmented by it in the same proportion as ours were augmented by it, common sense would have told the projectors that the traffic would be as useless as it would be for me to give one of your Lordships half-a-crown and for you to give me thirty of old Lord Liverpool's pennies in exchange; and if we gained an advantage in the traffic, either directly or indirectly; if our power and resources were augmented in a greater degree than those of our rival neighbour; then the very principle upon which the projectors proceeded was violated; for their principle is, that, as Hampshire would be injured by an impairing of the resources of Wiltshire, so England would be injured by any Act which should impair the resources of France. This reasoning, my Lords, is the reasoning of shallow pates: it evinces that it originates in that sort of brain which Swift describes to be like poor cream that will stand but one whipping. I think, or, at least, I hope, for the honour of my country, that there are very few amongst your Lordships, who must not have perceived, at some time or other during your lives, that it is the constant practice of very shallow and narrow-minded men, to reason about the acts and interests *of nations*, just as if they were reasoning about the affairs of men making part of the same *community*. The truth is this: such men are incapable of taking that view of things which the complicated affairs of nations require to be taken. You will hear them begin talking of these affairs, of these great and complicated interests; but, unable to trace them in their ramifications, and to show how commerce, for instance, bears upon or connects itself with public feeling, national power, national honour, and various other things; unable to do this, unable to proceed on to a rational conclusion, they resort to *comparisons* (always the resource of weak minds); they quit their subject entirely, and talk about men in the same nation instead of talking about two nations. Just in the same manner, and in consequence of just the same sort of reasoning that Pitt adopted that prodigious blunder of borrowing money wherewith to pay off the national debt.

It is curious to observe, that the Petition from the merchants of London, got up, doubtless, by the pretty pair of politicians themselves, proceeded *expressly* upon this very vulgar error. It stated, that it was as impolitic to have restraints upon commerce between nation and nation, as it would be to have such restraints upon the commerce between *two counties in the same kingdom*, and as it would be to have restraints upon the commerce between *man and man* in the same community. The great loan-man, Baring (one of my Doctors, my hot and cold-fit Doctor), stood at the head of these petitioners, and was justly enough reproached by the *membre du club de quatre-vingt neuf*, when the former joined in the silk-weavers' cry against the free-trade. But, these pretty politicians and petitioners forgot that their comparison about *counties* and *man and man*; forgot that the comparison was not worth a straw. They forgot that the two counties, for instance, are members of the same community, and that two nations are not: they forgot that the two counties are governed by the same laws, owe allegiance to the same sovereign, that their power and resources are brought into one common stock, and that in all these points, it is precisely the opposite with regard to two nations; they forgot that two nations are, and everlastingly must be, the rivals, and always may be the enemies, of each other, and that two counties never can be either; they forgot, that the objects of

commerce between nations are, to augment the resources and the power of each, in order that it may be more a match for the other, than it would be without such commerce, and that this never can be the case with two counties; they forgot that foreign trade is not worth a straw; that it is a base and worthless thing; unless it be carried on with a view of augmenting your power and resources, *relatively;* that is to say, in *augmenting them more* than it augments the power and the resources of the nation with which you carry on that commerce, while, on the contrary, commerce carried on between two counties may be *greatly and equally advantageous to both,* because, there can be no enmity between them, there can be no hostile rivalship between them, one never can be the enemy of the other, and never can desire to employ its power and resources against the other.

All these dissimilarities in this famous simile, the pair of pretty, prattling politicians and all their babbling devils of loan-mongers and cent. per cent. jobbers, now-a-days called merchants, forgot: forgot! the thought never came into their skulls. If clever men, if really clever men had made use of the comparison, it would have been just to accuse them of sophistry. These turtle-stuffed fellows are not chargeable with that crime. They were incapable of any other sort of reasoning; they put forth their vulgar, stupid stuff: it was swallowed by t' other place, and your Lordships swallowed it too, amidst the uproarious din of the exulting brothers of the broad sheet, stimulated thereunto by my three Doctors, by the scabby reviewers on t' other side of the Tweed, and by the whole tribe of "liberals" from one end of the kingdom to the other. One thing ought to have made your Lordships hesitate before you gave your sanction to this project, which is a thousand times greater "innovation" upon the principles of your ancestors, than any thing which the radicals have ever been accused of proposing; and it is curious enough to observe here, that, while these pretty politicians stigmatize our ancestors as fools as to matters of trade, while they talk of the "spirit of the age," the "enlightened age," as to matters of trade, they will allow of not the smallest alteration in the world in the article of rotten boroughs; though there the hand of time has been visibly at work: has killed or removed the inha-

bitants and even demolished the houses! "I will disfranchise Grampound," said the head man of these two pretty politicians; "but, I will disfranchise it only "because I will preserve Old "Sarum." Ah, my Lords! this is the man and such men as this, to bring your domains into jeopardy. Your really constitutional power, your titles, your honours, your property in your estates, would all be as firmly settled as the hills making part of those estates, were they not all exposed to politicians like this!

One thing, as I was saying, ought to have made your Lordships hesitate before you gave your sanction to this great innovation; and that is, the uniform tenor of these numerous Acts of Parliament, which, from the date of Magna Charta till within these two years; from the days of Bishop LANGTON till the days of WILLIAM HUSKISSON, breathe, in every line, principles directly opposed to this project of free-trade. Precious fools our ancestors must have been, then, for so many ages! The statute-book tells us, however, that they were by no means unmindful of these matters of trade. No reign passed without some, if not many Acts of Parliament on the subject. One would have thought that the wool-sack, on which the Lord Chancellor sits at the head of your Lordships, might have induced you to hesitate long, before you condemned the principles of all antiquity at the mere suggestion of William Huskisson!

I now return to Mr. Adams and his Message, first observing, that, in his Message of last year, he spoke contemptuously of this free-trade project. With as much of ridicule as the dignity of the document would admit of, and as a Yankee permits himself upon almost any occasion, to employ against any body, he spoke of those *new-fangled notions* which had recently been broached *in certain quarters with regard to free-trade.* The truth is, the English consuls, agents and merchant-jobbers in America, and the newspaper fellows that they have there in their pay, had begun to echo the wise sayings of our pretty pair of politicians. Mr. Adams is a man of great experience, has spent half his life in England and in Russia, is partial to England in his heart, as compared with other European nations, as is very natural he should be, for his father was, before him, though he was the first or second man that began the rebellion;

Mr. Adams venerates England; venerates particularly her laws and her courts of justice; but Mr. Adams loves America better; and if he did not, he knows well that he would not dare to show the true feelings of his heart. Therefore, when, last year, the pretty prattle about free-trade began to be echoed in America, he gave it a cut down at once, in his Message to the Congress; and he very pointedly observed, that if they would look at the European nations, they would find that *great resources and great power* had always attended those nations that had always adopted and adhered to the restrictive system: than which a nicer slap in the face was never given to any two of Cornelius Agrippa's men.

It is, then, not at all surprising that, when the free-trade project was offered to America, she should reject it. She did reject it. "No", said the daughter to the mother: "I am close enough to you already, Mamma: we will keep "at this convenient distance, if "you please: I will keep my "restrictions, Mamma, and you "may keep yours. We have "some disputes to settle already, "dear mother, and let us not "have more about this free-trade "that you have recently taken

" into your head in your old " age."

Without figure, the Americans rejected the project; which, to say the truth, *was intended almost exclusively for them.* Our pretty pair of prattlers had heard, that there were *thirty or forty of steam engines making rotten cot--tons at Philadelphia alone,* and they thought that if they could get off the duty upon our rotten cottons by their free-trade project, the rotten cottons would go from that hell-hole, Manchester, to cover the carcasses of the negro-wenches in America; and that the *monish* would come back to the Cotton-Lords and would, through their hands, bring pretty good grist to Treasury Chambers, White-hall. Finding that Jonathan was not to be taken in thus, our pair of pretty prattlers fell into a passion; and then the Act of Parliament, of which Mr. Adams speaks, was passed. This Act *was to shut out American ships from our West India Islands, unless the Americans agreed to adopt the free-trade project before first day of last month.* Mr. Adams says that the devil himself could not understand the Act clearly; but that this was evidently the point that it aimed at, and that it could be levelled at no nation but America.

This is the ground of the present dispute: it is quite within the compass of possibility that it may be the ground of a war: it is *sure* to be a strong inducement to America to be inclined to take part against us in any war that we may have in Europe and especially with Spain. It is sure to be a strong inducement to America to help any body to expel us from the West Indies, if they can, by all the means in their power. So, here we have these pretty, prattling speech-makers, or rather, this speech-maker and his almost dummy: here we have them exerting themselves to their utmost; here we have these " *liberals*" engaged in the consistent undertaking of *forcing* "*free*-trade" down the throats of the silent, sober, long-faced, long-sided, long-headed and brave Americans! *Forcing,* and that, too, by just as mean a trick as ever was attempted to be played in this world!

And how is this to work, if these pretty prattlers should, my Lords, be permitted to persevere! Who are to be the *sufferers,* in this case! In the first place, the West India planters and those who have mortgages on West

India estates, who must purchase their necessaries, of various sorts, at a much dearer rate than before. In the next place, the people, the wretched people of England, Scotland and Ireland, who must pay dearer for the produce of our West India Islands, while the planters and merchants will not gain, but lose, by this additional price to the consumer: In the next place, the whole of us, your Lordships in the foreground, must pay for additional armaments, military and naval, to hold in security these trans-Atlantic dominions; and then comes the risk created hereby, nay, the almost certainty that, in case of war with France or with Spain, the Americans will fight on their side, in order to secure the paring of our nails in that quarter of the world. And all this, observe, my Lords, solely to prop up an innovation upon all the principles and laws of your forefathers. And, what is the *object?* That more manufactured goods may go from England; that the negro-wenches of the United States may have their skins half hidden by the rotten cottons from Manchester, sent out by the spinning-jenny baronet and others, there to dissolve at the sight of a washing-tub. That wise man, Mr. Can-

ning, told a parcel of drinking, bawling creatures, that he got round him at some place, I have forgotten what, that England must in future *rely mainly for her resources on her supplying of foreign nations with her manufactures!* He forgot your Lordships' estates; he forgot the land of England: he forgot the vale of Evesham; he forgot the vale of Taunton; he forgot Kent and Norfolk: in short, he did not forget, for he never knew any thing about the matter; and he knows no more how to estimate the resources of a nation than he knows how to estimate the effects of a change in its currency. He is a talker: he is a Cornelius Agrippa's man; he is a true Æolus, for he deals in nothing but wind; but he is precisely the man to disencumber your Lordships of your estates.

Pray, my Lords, mark the conclusion of Mr. Adams in paragraph 18. After telling the Congress that the British Government *refuses to negotiate upon the subject;* that she will not permit foreign nations *even to talk with her about the matter,* he says, that he leaves it to the Congress to adopt such measures as they may think necessary, in consequence of this measure of the free-trade gentlemen. Now, my Lords, what these measures will be I cannot say exactly, but I imagine that they will give a pretty good blow to the lords of the loom and of the anvil; and I should not much wonder if the rotten cottons were shut out from the United States, altogether. We can do Jonathan but very little harm, unless we were well prepared for resolute war, and that we cannot be, without taking those steps which I shall not have room to point out to your Lordships in the present letter. America is our greatest and best customer for manufactured goods; and, it will be curious enough, if the free-trade project should be the cause of our losing that customer. This will be a curious result of the project of free-trade; and if Mr. William Huskisson do not merit the two thousand pounds a year addition to his salary *after that*, and that, too, expressly for his great labours in perfecting the system of " free-trade," then merit must go without its reward to the end of time. " Merit was ever *modest* known," says some poet or other, but who I have forgotten; and if this be not a modest man, let us hunt for one and find him, if we can, upon the face of the earth. Your Lordships may remember, that this additional salary was

voted him on account of the immense labour which he had had in finding out and preparing for repeal, A HUNDRED OR TWO ACTS OF PARLIA-MENT. Ah! my Lords! here we see the principles of the " *club quatre-vingt neuf*," the seed-bed of the jacobins of France. A hundred or two of the Acts of your ancestors, all hunted out by this single, this industrious, this laborious, this public-spirited, this enlightened, liberal, for which he was cheered, till I think I hear the din in my ears yet, by Doctors BARING, BLACK and M'CULLOCH and by all the scale-covered fellows from the north of the Tweed. Another good joke is, that the " *Whigs* " and the Scotch ones in particular, claim the merit of the invention! And, at a dinner given at Edinburgh to the eulogist of the " best possible instructor," one of the hoot awa' mon fellows said that it was the gentlemen opposite that had *forced the Ministers to* adopt the enlightened principles of Adam Smith and David Ricardo! Just as TIERNEY claimed the invention of Peel's Bill, at the time when it was passed; but, he has had the prudence to refrain from claiming it since 1821. He, good man, now leaves all the merit to poor Mr. Peel, and, be you assured, my Lords, that the Scotch will soon leave all the merit of free-trade to the member of *club quatre-vingt neuf*, who had hunted out a hundred or two of Acts of Parliament passed by your forefathers, in order that he might sweep them out of the statute-book. I wonder he had not (I am sure his brother liberal would if he had thought of it) gone, in the true " spirit of the age," and torn the wool-sack *from beneath the Lord Chancellor ;* and (Lord, have mercy upon us!) he might, in the hurry of his zeal, have tossed sack, Chancellor and all, out of the window into the Thames, where his lordship might have taken the tide and gone on a foreign voyage, huzzaing, as he went, "*free bottoms* make *free goods !*" the meaning of which words (words very old amongst civilians) we shall all soon know if Mr. Canning's jacobinical flippancy, joined to Mr. Huskisson's sweeping away of Acts of Parliament, should happen to get us into a war with ANY BODY.

These, my Lords, are the men you have to fear. We, radicals, are turtle-doves compared to these men. We do not want to burn the statute-book for many years back. We want to *get rid of in-* *novations* made either by the hand of time or by the tongue of man : we want to do nothing that would tarnish the honour of your Lordships, that would lessen your dignity, that would take a hair's weight from your just powers or your ancient prerogatives ; we wish you to enjoy that which your ancestors enjoyed, if you will only let us enjoy that which was enjoyed by ours. Close with us, my Lords : we want to sweep away none of the principles nor of the immortal works of your ancestors. We never belonged to the *club quatre-vingt neuf*, nor to Boodle's nor Noodle's, nor the devil of gambling knows what. We (for I can safely speak for the whole) want no novelties, nor any one thing, but that which is just, that which belongs to us, and the possession of which by us is really more necessary to your safety than it is to our good. With these sentiments, expressed with perfect sincerity,

I am,

Your Lordships'

Most obedient and

Most humble servant,

WM. COBBETT.

# DEATH

# OF THE DUKE OF YORK.

---

" When the fountains of thy eyes are dry,
Mine shall supply the place and weep, for
both."                              ROWE.

---

WHEN I was a great lubberly boy, and had a mind much about like that of Mr. Canning, when he was talking the soft, novel-like nonsense, a part of which forms the motto of the preceding article of this Register; that is to say, when I was about fourteen or fifteen years old, and had just begun to read plays, I was, I remember, delighted with the bombastical stuff of ROWE, the play-writer, and particularly with the passage, part of which I have quoted above, from memory. It is a curiously contented cuckold that utters the words to his intended bride, who is weeping over the corpse of the man that had crckolded him in the shell. The language of the disconsolate brothers of the broad sheet upon the subject of the death of his Royal Highness the Duke of York, brought to my mind this piece of ridiculous bombast. They have dressed their papers in mourning; their words would make any man that did not know them, paint them in his imagination, all drowned in tears, sobbing like a great hog when the vital spark is just leaving him in consequence of the violence of the butcher; tearing their hair; clenching and wringing their hands; looking up to heaven in despair, and with that wild, distracted look which I once saw Mrs. SIDDONS exhibit in the character of *Belvidera*, when she comes, with her hair all dishevelled, claps her hand with violence upon her head and cries, " hot! hot!" In short, every reader that did not know them, would suppose that these fellows, these " best possible public instructors " were all as mad as March hares, and that it would take a regiment of dragoons at the least to prevent them from precipitating their own carcasses into the grave with the body of the Royal Duke.

Now, I, whose taste it is not to play second fiddle, should, if I were to attempt to mourn upon this occasion, appear like a mere ballad-singer, coming after the great, noisy, squalling, quavering devils upon the stage. I should appear like a mere shop-keeping maker-out of bills, who should come after such a man as Mr. HUME. I, therefore, shall not, in spite of the example of the broad-sheeted brotherhood and in spite of the rather *more than expectations* expressed by the Lord Chamberlain, *mourn* either in words or in dress; but, I say, nevertheless, that I am as sorry, and, perhaps, more sorry, for the death of the Duke, than any man in England is. The Royal Brothers must all die, first or last; and, if it were God's good pleasure, I should like that they might be taken to himself, according to their age; that they might go out of the world in the same order in which they came into it; and, in saying this, I wish to be understood as not meaning any thing in levity, but being as serious in my wishes as the subject itself is serious.

F

## LAMENTABLE EVENT.

THE broad sheet does, however, give us an account of another death, which really is not calculated, in my mind, to excite thoughts of a very serious nature; namely, the death of "*Counsellor Brick*." As the Counsellor does, in my intense Comedy, swear by the hod of "his *fadder*," he, most likely, has a *fadder;* and, I will venture to say, that even that *fadder* is not half so much mortified at the Counsellor's fate as I am. The readers of the Register will recollect, that, when I was, in the latter end of September or beginning of October last, riding on the Cotswold hills, I saw, stuck up in a new-sowed wheat-field, to frighten away the rooks, a most bewitching female shoy-hoy. To this lady I intended to marry the Counsellor, being, I am well satisfied, a match far preferable to any of those "*ladies*" who, as the newspaper report told us, clapped their hands and cracked their fans when he, at the meeting at Cork, in 1825, told them that he was "*a stout special pleader.*" I intended to have the wedding celebrated in an old pig-sty at Withington, and I meant that SIR GLORY should stand father upon the occasion, and give the bride away. In all this, and in every thing that would have grown out of it, I have been disappointed, by the unlucky ball proceeding from the pistol of one whose friend had been called a ruffian by this very Counsellor Brick, whom I saw clench his two big fists at a gentleman who had committed no other offence than that of beating him in point of argument. And, speaking now to the sober sense of the Catholics of Ireland, do they think that their cause can be aided by men of this description? Men whose existence in the world is not more necessary nor more useful, or, rather, not less mischievous than the existence of pole-cats and skunks. The death of this man, an account of which has filled whole columns of newspapers, is of no more consequence to the *public*, than the death of a bull-finch or a chaffinch. The Irish Catholics may think just what they please; but, they never will succeed in getting any thing done for them, until they can enlist the great body of the people of England on their side; and, whatever faults we may have, our general fault is not that of being carried away by mere bombast. For a short time we may, and sometimes are; but we think about the matter afterwards; and, in all my experience, I have never yet seen the sounding brass succeed in the end.

Men in England can know nothing of the Irish, and they do know nothing, but what they hear; and, the noisy, rattle-brained, everlastingly bothering speech-makers in Ireland, really make them stare with astonishment. They say, what must that cause be that has such men for its principal advocates? They say, the manner of governing the Irish may be very bad; but, God preserve us from these everlasting botherers. I say, and I say it with a certain knowledge of the fact, that a vast proportion of the good and right feeling in England, with regard to the Catholics, has been worn away by the senseless botheration of the Boards and Associations and other ridiculous exhibitions in Ireland. Men grow tired of it; and, when once they grow tired of any thing, that thing is in a thousand times worse state that if it had their clamorous hostility. While there is life there is hope: hostility implies life and vigour; but wearisomeness is death: it puts an end to all inquiry and discussion: the ears are shut up, and you talk as to a stone. Just thus is it with regard to what has been and still is called the Catholic cause; and this effect has been produced by that series of bombastical speeches which has been published in England from the Irish newspapers. The effect produced here by the news of the death of Brick was, in ninety-nine cases out of every hundred, a laugh: and, as loud a laugh, too, as the Counsellor himself used to record in his reports of the dull witticisms uttered in the House of Commons. Yet, this was one of the champions of the Catholic cause! That cause must have other advocates than it now has, or it never can prevail. It is the Catholics themselves who have the just ground of quarrel with these noisy men. Their " fine " speeches do us Protestants no harm: the harm they do is to the Catholics themselves. They saw a strong feeling rising in their favour; but, these meddlers; these everlasting and impudent and brazen botherers, could not find in their hearts to let that feeling have fair play. Oh, no! that was not their game: the work must be theirs: they must have a finger in the pie, and they must convince us, too, that they meant to have all the pie to themselves. This

very Brick said, distinctly, in his botheration at Cork, that he would gladly accept of " emancipation," by means of a disfranchisement of the forty-shilling freeholders of Ireland; that is to say, that he would sell the rights of half a million of men and their families, for the sake of a chance of getting a silk gown upon his own rough and broad back. Since that, he has been a most clamorous advocate for the maintenance of these forty-shilling freeholders, and has been also one of the managers of a fund, raised by subscription for keeping them in possession of their freeholds.

Having thus fallen in amongst the affairs of the Catholics, I cannot omit noticing, that an Irish newspaper informs us that the precious trustees of the *Catholic rent*, as it was called, have determined to lend five hundred pounds of that rent to the editor, or conductor, or proprietor, of a newspaper, which is well known to be the constant trumpet of the praise of Mr O'Connell. Is it possible for the people on this side of the water, to think well of a cause supported by such means. And, the letting out of this money, and other sums of this money *at interest:* is this the way to revive, in the minds of Protestants, or, to put into those minds, respect for the religion of their fathers? Why, one of the great things that distinguished that religion was, its abhorrence of *usury* in all its forms and shapes. If you tell us that the *times have altered;* our answer is, that if your religion change with the times, it is no longer that religion in which our forefathers lived. The Jews, whom our sensible and just forefathers regarded as little better than dogs, and whom the laws of England made the property of the King, who might, at any time, cause them to be knocked on the head, or flung into the sea; and I believe, that those laws have never yet been directly annulled by statute; those villanous Jews were allowed to receive money for the use of money, if they could get it by other means than those of the law. But, before the Reformation, no Christian ever dreamt of such a thing. Yet, here we see a committee appointed by this association of emancipators, to contrive measures for letting the Catholic Rent out at interest. They will not conform to the Church: they will not abjure the supremacy of the Pope; but, they will carry on the vile traffic in money, in defiance of all those laws of the Church, of which the Pope is the head. If they can do this, why cannot they abjure the supremacy? In short, it proves them to be a mongrel crew, who care not a straw about the religion for which they appear to be contending, and who really have no other object in view than that of getting their paws into the scramble for silk gowns, places and pensions. As long as this is the case; as long as the people of England view the thing in this light, never will the Catholic cause move one inch; it being no matter to any man of sense, whether, if he be to be taxed for idlers, those idlers be Protestants or Catholics; and, as every man of sense must see, that an addition to the number of blood-suckers, would add to the quantity of blood drawn away, men in general must and will desire that there should be no such change.

And thus I close the funeral oration of Counsellor Brick, saying, in the words of the intense comedy, " Not ashes to ashes, but, *brick-bats to brick-bats!* "

----

# PRESIDENT'S MESSAGE.

*Message of the President of the United States, communicated to both Houses, at the commencement of the Second Session of the Nineteenth Congress.*

FELLOW CITIZENS OF THE SENATE, AND OF THE HOUSE OF REPRESENTATIVES:

1. The assemblage of the Representatives of our Union, in both Houses of Congress, at this time, occurs under circumstances calling for the renewed homage of our grateful acknowledgments to the Giver of all Good. With the exceptions incidental to the most felicitous condition of human existence, we continue to be highly favoured in all the elements which contribute to individual comfort and to national prosperity. In the survey of our extensive country, we have generally to observe the abodes of health and regions of plenty. In our civil and political relations, we have peace without, and tranquillity within, our borders. We are, as a people, increasing with unabated rapidity in population, wealth, and national resources; and, whatever differences of opinion exist among us, with regard to the mode and the means by which we shall turn the beneficence of Heaven to the improvement of our own condition, there is yet a spirit, animating us all, which will not suffer the bounties of Providence to be showered upon us in vain, but will receive them with grateful hearts, and apply them with unwearied hands, to the advancement of the general good.

2. Of the subjects recommended to the consideration of Congress, at their last Session, some were then definitively acted upon. Others left unfinished, but partly matured, will recur to your attention, without needing a renewal of notice from me. The purpose of this communication will be, to present to your view the general aspect of our public affairs at this moment, and the measures which have been taken to carry into effect the intentions of the Legislature,

as signified by the laws then and heretofore enacted.

3. In our intercourse with the other nations of the earth, we have still the happiness of enjoying peace and a general good understanding—qualified, however, in several important instances by collisions of interest, and by unsatisfied claims of justice, to the settlement of which, the constitutional interposition of the Legislative Authority may become ultimately indispensable.

4. By the decease of the Emperor Alexander of Russia, which occurred contemporaneously with the commencement of the last Session of Congress, the United States have been deprived of a long tried, steady, and faithful friend. Born to the inheritance of absolute power, and trained in the school of adversity, from which no Power on earth, however absolute, is exempt, that Monarch, from his youth, had been taught to feel the force and value of public opinion, and to be sensible that the interest of his own government would best be promoted by a frank and friendly intercourse with this Republic, as those of his people would be advanced by a liberal commercial intercourse with our country. A candid and confidential interchange of sentiments between him and the Government of the United States, upon the affairs of Southern America, took place at a period not long preceding his demise, and contributed to fix that course of policy which left to the other Governments of Europe no alternative but that of sooner or later recognising the independence of our Southern neighbours, of which the example had, by the United States, already been set. The ordinary diplomatic communications between his successor, the Emperor Nicholas, and the United States, have suffered some interruption by the illness, departure, and subsequent decease of his Minister residing here, who enjoyed, as he merited, the entire confidence of his new Sovereign, as he had eminently responded to that of his predecessor. But we have had the most satisfactory assurances, that the sentiments of the reigning Emperor towards the United States are altogether conformable to those which had so long and constantly animated his Imperial Brother; and we have reason to hope that they will serve to cement that harmony and good understanding between the two nations, which, founded in congenial interests, cannot but result in the advancement of the welfare and prosperity of both.

5. Our relations of commerce and navigation with France are, by the operation of the Convention of 24th June, 1822, with that nation, in a state of gradual and progressive improvement. Convinced by all our experience, no less than by the principles of fair and liberal reciprocity, which the United States have constantly tendered to all the nations of the earth, as the rule of commercial intercourse which they would universally prefer, that fair and equal competition is most conducive to the interests of both parties, the United States, in the negotiation of that Convention, earnestly contended for a mutual renunciation of discriminating duties and charges in the ports of the two countries. Unable to obtain the immediate recognition of this principle in its full extent, after reducing the duties of discrimination so far as was found attainable, it was agreed, that at the expiration of two years from the 1st of October, 1822, when the Convention was to go into effect, unless a notice of six months on either side should be given to the other, that the Convention itself must terminate, those duties should be reduced by one-fourth; and that this reduction should be yearly repeated until all discrimination should cease while the Convention itself should continue in force. By the effect of this stipulation, three-fourths of the discriminating duties which had been levied by each party upon the vessels of the other in its ports, have already been removed; and, on the 1st October next, should the Convention be still in force, the remaining fourth will be discontinued. French vessels, laden with French produce, will be received in our ports on the same terms as our own; and ours, in return, will enjoy the same advantages in the ports of France. By these approximations to an equality of duties and of charges, not only has the commerce between the two countries prospered, but friendly dispositions have been, on both sides, encouraged and promoted. They will continue to be cherished and cultivated on the part of the United States. It would have been gratifying to have had it in my power to add, that the claims upon the justice of the French Government, involving the property and the comfortable subsistence of many of our fellow-citizens, and which have been so long and so earnestly urged, were in a more promising train of adjustment than at your last meeting; but their condition remains unaltered.

6. With the Government of the Netherlands, the mutual abandonment of discriminating duties had been regulated by Legislative Acts on both sides. The

Act of Congress, of the 20th of April, 1818, abolished all discriminating duties of Impost and Tonnage, upon the vessels and produce of the Netherlands in the ports of the United States, upon the assurance given by the Government of the Netherlands, that all such duties operating against the shipping and commerce of the United States, in that Kingdom, had been abolished. These reciprocal regulations had continued in force several years, when the discriminating principle was resumed by the Netherlands in a new and indirect form, by a bounty of ten per cent. in the shape of a return of duties to their national vessels, and in which those of the United States are not permitted to participate. By the Act of Congress, of the 7th of January, 1824, all discriminating duties in the United States were again suspended, so far as related to the vessels and produce of the Netherlands, so long as the reciprocal exemption should be extended to the vessels and produce of the United States in the Netherlands. But the same Act provides that, in the event of a restoration of discriminating duties, to operate against the shipping and commerce of the United States, in any of the foreign countries referred to therein, the suspension of discriminating duties in favour of the navigation of such foreign country should cease, and all the provisions of the Acts imposing discriminating foreign tonnage and impost duties in the United States, should revive, and be in full force with regard to that nation.

7. In the correspondence with the Government of the Netherlands upon this subject, they have contended, that the favour shown to their own shipping by this bounty, upon their tonnage, is not to be considered as a discriminating duty. But it cannot be denied that it produces all the same effects. Had the mutual abolition been stipulated by treaty, such a bounty upon the national vessels could scarcely have been granted, consistently with good faith ; yet, as the Act of Congress of 7th Jan. 1824, has not expressly authorized the Executive Authority to determine what shall be considered as a revival of discriminating duties by a foreign Government to the disadvantage of the United States, and as the retaliatory measures on our part, however just and necessary, may tend rather to that conflict of legislation which we deprecate, than to that concert to which we invite all commercial nations, as most conducive to their interest and our own, I have thought it more consistent with the spirit of our institu-

tions, to refer the subject again to the paramount authority of the Legislature, to decide what measure the emergency may require, than abruptly, by proclamation, to carry into effect the minatory provision of the Act of 1824.

8. During the last Session of Congress, Treaties of Amity, Navigation, and Commerce, were negotiated and signed at this place with the Government of Denmark, in Europe, and with the Federation of Central America, in this hemisphere. These Treaties then received the constitutional sanction of the Senate, by the advice and consent to their ratification. They were accordingly ratified, on the part of the United States, and during the recess of Congress, have been also ratified by the other respective contracting parties. The ratifications have been exchanged, and they have been published by Proclamations, copies of which are herewith communicated to Congress. These Treaties have established between the contracting parties the principles of equality and reciprocity, in their broadest and most liberal extent : Each party admitting the vessels of the other into its ports, laden with cargoes, the produce or manufacture of any quarter of the globe, upon the payment of the same duties of tonnage and impost that are chargeable upon their own. They have further stipulated, that the parties shall hereafter grant no favour of navigation or commerce to any other nation, which shall not, upon the same terms, be granted to each other ; and that neither party will impose, upon articles of merchandise, the produce or manufacture of the other, any other or higher duties than upon the like articles, being the produce or manufacture of any other country. To these principles there is, in the Convention with Denmark, an exception, with regard to the Colonies of that kingdom in the Arctic Seas, but none with regard to her Colonies in the West Indies.

9. In the course of the last summer, the term, to which our last Commercial Treaty with Sweden was limited, has expired. A continuation of it is in the contemplation of the Swedish Government, and is believed to be desirable on the part of the United States. It has been proposed by the King of Sweden, that, pending the negotiation of renewal the expired Treaty should be mutually considered as still in force ; a measure which will require the sanction of Congress to be carried into effect on our part, and which I therefore recommend to your consideration.

10. With Prussia, Spain, Portugal,

and in general all the European Powers, between whom and the United States relations of friendly intercourse have existed, their condition has not materially varied since the last Session of Congress. I regret not to be able to say the same of our commercial intercourse with the Colonial Possessions of Great Britain in America. Negotiations of the highest importance to our common Interests have been, for several years, in discussion between the two Governments; and, on the part of the United States, have been invariably pursued in the spirit of candour and conciliation. Interests of great magnitude and delicacy had been adjusted by the Conventions of 1815 and 1818, while that of 1822, mediated by the late Emperor Alexander, had promised a satisfactory compromise of claims, which the Government of the United States, in justice to the rights of a numerous class of their citizens, was bound to sustain. But with regard to the commercial intercourse between the United States and the British Colonies in America, it has been hitherto found impracticable to bring the parties to an understanding satisfactory to both. The relative geographical position, and the respective products of nature, cultivated by human industry, had constituted the elements of a commercial intercourse between the United States and British America, insular and continental, important to the inhabitants of both countries. But it had been interdicted by Great Britain, upon a principle heretofore practised upon by the colonizing nations of Europe, of holding the trade of their colonies, each in exclusive monopoly to herself. After the termination of the late war, this interdiction had been revived, and the British Government declined including this portion of our intercourse with her possessions in the negotiation of the Convention of 1815. The trade was then carried on exclusively in British vessels, till the Act of Congress concerning Navigation, of 1818, and the Supplemental Act of 1820, met the interdict by a corresponding measure on the part of the United States. These measures, not of retaliation, but of necessary self-defence, were soon succeeded by an Act of Parliament, opening certain colonial ports to the vessels of the United States charging directly from them, and to the importation from them of certain articles of our produce, burthened with heavy duties, and excluding some of the most valuable articles of our exports. The United States opened their ports to British vessels from the Colonies, upon terms as exactly corresponding with those of the Act of Parliament, as, in the relative position of the parties, could be made. And a negotiation was commenced by mutual consent, with the hope, on our part, that a reciprocal spirit of accommodation, and a common sentiment of the importance of the trade to the interest of the inhabitants of the two countries, between whom it must be carried on, would ultimately bring the parties to a compromise, with which both might be satisfied. With this view, the Government of the United States had determined to sacrifice something of that entire reciprocity which in all commercial arrangements with Foreign Powers they are entitled to demand, and to acquiesce in some inequalities disadvantageous to ourselves, rather than to forego the benefit of a final and permanent adjustment of this interest, to the satisfaction of Great Britain herself. The negotiation, repeatedly suspended by accidental circumstances, was, however, by mutual agreement and express assent, considered as pending, and to be speedily resumed. In the mean time, another Act of Parliament, *so doubtful and ambiguous in its import as to have been misunderstood by the officers in the Colonies who were to carry it into execution,* opens again certain Colonial ports, upon new conditions and terms, with *a threat to close them against any Nation which may not accept those terms as prescribed by the British Government.* This Act passed in July, 1825—not communicated to the Government of the United States, not understood by the British Officers of the Customs in the Colonies where it was to be enforced—was nevertheless submitted to the consideration of Congress, at their last Session. With a knowledge that a negotiation upon the subject had long been in progress, and pledges given of its resumption at an early day, it was deemed expedient to await the result of that negotiation, rather than to subscribe implicitly to terms, the import of which was not clear, and which the British authorities themselves, in this hemisphere, were not prepared to explain.

11. Immediately after the close of the last Session of Congress, one of our most distinguished citizens was dispatched as Envoy Extraordinary and Minister Plenipotentiary to Great Britain, furnished with instructions which we could not doubt would lead to a conclusion of this long controverted interest, upon terms acceptable to Great Britain. Upon his arrival, and before he had delivered his letters of credence, he was met by an

Order of the British Council, *excluding, from and after the first of December now current, the vessels of the United States from all the Colonial British ports, excepting those immediately bordering upon our territories.* In answer to his expostulations upon a measure thus unexpected, he is informed that, according to the ancient maxim of policy of European nations having Colonies, their trade is an exclusive possession of the Mother Country; that all participation in it by other nations is a boon or favour, not forming a subject of negotiation, but to be regulated by the Legislative Acts of the Power owning the Colony; that the British Government, therefore, *declines negotiating concerning it;* and that, as the United States did not forthwith accept purely and simply the terms offered by the Act of Parliament of July, 1825, Great Britain would not now admit the vessels of the United States, *even upon the terms on which she has opened them to the navigation of other nations.*

12. We have been accustomed to consider the intercourse with the British Colonies, rather as an interchange of mutual benefits, than as a mere favour received; that, under every circumstance, we have given an ample equivalent. We have seen every other nation, holding colonies, negotiate with other nations, and grant them, freely, admission to the Colonies by Treaty; and, so far are the other colonizing Nations of Europe now from refusing to negotiate for trade with their Colonies, that we ourselves have secured access to the Colonies of more than one of them by Treaty. The refusal, however, of Great Britain to negotiate, leaves to the United States *no other alternative than that of regulating, or interdicting, altogether, the trade on their part, according as either measure may affect the interests of our own country;* and, with that exclusive object, I would recommend the whole subject to your calm and candid deliberations.

13. It is hoped that our unavailing exertions to accomplish a cordial good understanding on this interest will not have an unpropitious effect upon the other great topics of discussion between the two Governments. Our North-eastern and North-western boundaries *are still unadjusted.* The Commissioners under the 7th Article of the Treaty of Ghent have nearly come to the close of their labours; nor can we renounce the expectation, *enfeebled as it is,* that they may agree upon their Report, to the satisfaction or acquiescence of both parties. The Commission for liquidating the claims for indemnity for slaves carried away after the close of the war has been sifting, with doubtful prospects of success. Propositions of compromise have, however, passed between the two Governments, the result of which, we flatter ourselves, may yet prove satisfactory. Our own dispositions and purposes towards Great Britain are all friendly and conciliatory; nor can we abandon, but with strong reluctance, the belief that they will ultimately meet a return, not of favours, which we neither ask nor desire, but of equal reciprocity and good will.

14. With the American Governments of this hemisphere, we continue to maintain an intercourse altogether friendly, and between their nations and ours that commercial interchange, of which mutual benefit is the source, and mutual comfort and harmony the result, is in a continual state of improvement. The war between Spain and them, since the total expulsion of the Spanish military force from their continental territories, has been little more than nominal; and their internal tranquillity, though occasionally menaced by the agitations which civil wars never fail to leave behind them, has not been affected by any serious calamity.

15. The Congress of Ministers from several of those nations which assembled at Panama, after a short Session there, adjourned to meet again, at a more favourable season, in the neighbourhood of Mexico. The decease of one of our Ministers on his way to the Isthmus, and the impediments of the season, which delayed the departure of the other, deprived us of the advantage of being represented at the first meeting of the Congress. There is, however, no reason to believe that any of the transactions of the Congress were of a nature to affect injuriously the interests of the United States, or to require the interposition of our Ministers, had they been present. Their absence has, indeed, deprived us of the opportunity of possessing precise and authentic information of the treaties which were concluded at Panama; and the whole result has confirmed me in the conviction of the expediency to the United States of being represented at the Congress. The surviving member of the Mission, appointed during your last Session, has accordingly proceeded to his destination, and a successor to his distinguished and lamented associate will be nominated to the Senate. A Treaty of Amity, Navigation, and Commerce, has, in the course

of the last summer, been concluded by our Minister Plenipotentiary at Mexico, with the United States of that Confederacy, which will also be laid before the Senate, for their advice with regard to its ratification.

16. In adverting to the present condition of our fiscal concerns, and to the prospects of our revenue, the first remark that calls our attention, is, that they are less exuberantly prosperous than they were at the corresponding period of the last year. The severe shock so extensively sustained by the commercial and manufacturing interests in Great Britain, has not been without a perceptible recoil upon ourselves. A reduced importation from abroad is necessarily succeeded by a reduced return to the Treasury at home. The net revenue of the present year will not equal that of the last. And the receipts of that which is to come will fall short of those in the current year.—The diminution, however, is in part attributable to the flourishing condition of some of our domestic manufactures, and so far is compensated by an equivalent more profitable to the nation. It is also highly gratifying to perceive, that the deficiency in the revenue, while it scarcely exceeds the anticipations of the last year's Estimates from the Treasury, has not interrupted the application of more than eleven millions during the present year, to the discharge of the principal and interest of the Debt itself. The balance in the Treasury on the first of January last, was five millions two hundred and one thousand six hundred and fifty dollars, and forty-three cents. The receipts from that time to the 30th of September last, were nineteen millions five hundred and eighty-five thousand nine hundred and thirty-two dollars, and fifty cents. The receipts of the current quarter, estimated at six millions of dollars, yield, with the sums already received, a Revenue of about twenty-five millions and a half for the year. The expenditures for the three first quarters of the year have amounted to eighteen millions seven hundred and fourteen thousand two hundred and twenty-six dollars, and sixty cents. The expenditures of the current quarter are expected, including the two millions of the principal debt to be paid, to balance the receipts. So that the expenses of the year, amounting to upwards of a million less than its income, will leave a proportionally increased balance in the Treasury of the 1st of January, 1827, over that of the 1st of January last. Instead of five millions two hundred thousand,

there will be six millions four hundred thousand dollars.

17. The amount of duties secured on merchandize imported from the commencement of the year until the 30th of September, is estimated at 21 millions 250 thousand dollars; and the amount that will probably accrue, during the present quarter, is estimated at 4 millions 250 thousand; making for the whole year 25½ millions, from which the drawbacks being deducted, will leave a clear revenue from the Customs, receivable in the year 1827, of about 20 millions 400 thousand dollars; which, with the sums to be received from the proceeds of Public Lands, the Bank Dividends, and other incidental receipts, will form an aggregate of about 23 millions—a sum falling short of the whole expenses of the present year, little more than the portion of those expenditures applied to the discharge of the public debt, beyond the annual appropriation of 10 millions, by the Act of 3d March, 1817. At the passing of that Act, the public debt amounted to one hundred and twenty-three millions and a half. On the 1st of January next it will be short of seventy-four millions. In the lapse of these ten years, fifty millions of public debt, with the annual charge of upwards of three millions of interest upon them, have been extinguished. At the passing of that Act, of the annual appropriation of the ten millions, seven were absorbed in the payment of interest, and not more than three millions went to reduce the capital of the debt. Of the same ten millions, at this time scarcely four are applicable to the interest, and upwards of six are effective in melting down the capital. Yet our experience has proved that a revenue, consisting so largely of imposts and tonnage, ebbs and flows to an extraordinary extent, with all the fluctuations incident to the general commerce of the world. It is within our recollection, that even in the compass of the same last ten years, the receipts of the Treasury were not adequate to the expenditures of the year; and that in two successive years it was found necessary to resort to loans to meet the engagements of the nation. The returning tides of the succeeding years replenished the public coffers, until they have again begun to feel the vicissitude of a decline. To produce these alterations of fulness and exhaustion, the relative operation of abundant or unfruitful seasons, the regulations of foreign Governments, political revolutions, the prosperous or decaying condition of manufactures, commercial speculations, and many other causes not always to be

tracted, variously combine. We have found the alternate swells and diminutions embracing periods of from two to three years. The last period of depression to us was from 1819 to 1822. The corresponding revival was from 1823 to the commencement of the present year. Still we have no cause to apprehend a depression comparable to that of the former period, or even to anticipate a deficiency which will intrench upon the ability to apply the annual ten millions to the reduction of the debt. It is well for us, however, to be admonished of the necessity of abiding by the maxims of the most vigilant economy, and of resorting to all honourable and useful expedients, for pursuing with steady and inflexible perseverance the total discharge of the debt.

18. Besides the seven millions of the loans of 1823, which will have been discharged in the course of the present year, there are nine millions, which, by the terms of the contracts, would have been and are now redeemable. Thirteen millions more of the loan of 1814 will become redeemable from and after the expiration of the present month; and nine other millions from and after the close of the ensuing year. They constitute a mass of thirty-one millions of dollars, all bearing an interest of six per cent.; more than twenty millions of which will be immediately redeemable, and the rest within little more than a year. Leaving of this amount fifteen millions to continue at the interest of six per cent., but to be, as far as shall be found practicable, paid off in the years 1827 and 1828, there is scarcely a doubt that the remaining sixteen millions might, within a few months, be discharged by a loan at not exceeding five per cent., redeemable in the years 1829 and 1830. By this operation, a sum of nearly half a million of dollars may be saved to the nation; and the discharge of the whole thirty-one millions within the four years may be greatly facilitated, if not wholly accomplished.

19. By an Act of Congress of 3d March, 1825, a loan, for the purpose now referred to, or a subscription to stock, was authorised, at an interest not exceeding four and a half per cent. But at that time, so large a portion of the floating capital of the country was absorbed in commercial speculations, and so little was left for investment in the stocks, that the measure was but partially successful. At the last Session of Congress, the condition of the Funds was still unpropitious to the measure; but the change so soon afterwards occurred, that, had the authority existed to redeem the nine millions now redeemable by an exchange of stocks, or a loan at five per cent., it is morally certain that it might have been effected, and with it a yearly saving of ninety thousand dollars.

20. With regard to the collection of Revenue of Impost, certain occurrences have, within the last year, been disclosed in one or two of our principal ports, which engaged the attention of Congress at their last Session, and may hereafter require further consideration. Until within a very few years, the execution of the laws for raising the Revenue, like that of all our other laws, has been ensured more by the moral sense of the Community, than by the rigours of a jealous precaution, or by penal sanctions. Confiding in the exemplary punctuality and unsullied integrity of our importing merchants, a gradual relaxation from the provisions of the Collection Laws, a close adherence to which would have caused inconvenience and expense to them, had long become habitual; and indulgences had been extended universally, because they had never been abused. It may be worthy of your serious consideration, whether some further Legislative provision may not be necessary to come in aid of this state of unguarded security.

21. From the Reports herewith communicated of the Secretaries of War and of the Navy, with the subsidiary documents annexed to them, will be discovered the present condition and administration of our Military Establishment on the land and on the sea. The organization of the Army having undergone no change, since its reduction to the present Peace Establishment in 1821, it remains only to observe, that it is yet found adequate to all the purposes for which a permanent armed force in time of peace can be needed, or useful. It may be proper to add, that, from a difference of opinion between the late President of the United States and the Senate, with regard to the construction of the Act of Congress of 2d March, 1821, to reduce and fix the Military Peace Establishment of the United States, it remains hitherto so far without execution, that no Colonel has been appointed to command one of the Regiments of Artillery. A supplementary or explanatory Act of the Legislature appears to be the only expedient practicable for removing the difficulty of this appointment.

22. In a period of profound peace, the conduct of the mere military establishment forms but a very inconsiderable portion of the duties devolving upon the

administration of the Department of War. It will be seen by the returns from the subordinate Departments of the Army, that every branch of the service is marked with order, regularity, and discipline. That from the Commanding General through all the gradations of superintendence, the officers feel themselves to have been citizens before they were soldiers, and that the glory of a Republican Army must consist in the spirit of freedom by which it is animated, and of patriotism by which it is impelled. It may be confidently stated, that the moral character of the Army is in a state of continual improvement, and that all the arrangements for the disposal of its parts have a constant reference to that end.

23. But to the War Department are attributed other duties, having indeed relation to a future possible condition of war, but being purely defensive, and in their tendency contributing rather to the security and permanency of peace. The erection of the fortifications provided for by Congress, and adapted to secure our shores from hostile invasion : The distribution of the fund of public gratitude and justice to the pensioners of the Revolutionary war : The maintenance of our relations of peace and of protection with the Indian Tribes : And the internal improvements and surveys for the location of roads and canals, which, during the last three Sessions of Congress, have engaged so much of their attention, and may engross so large a share of their future benefactions to our country.

24. By the Act of the 30th April, 1824, suggested and approved by my predecessor, the sum of 30,000 dollars was appropriated for the purpose of causing to be made the necessary surveys, plans, and estimates of the routes of such roads and canals as the President of the United States might deem of national importance in a commercial or military point of view, or necessary for the transportation of the public mail—the surveys, plans, and estimates for each, when completed, to be laid before Congress.

25. In execution of this Act, a Board of Engineers were immediately instituted, and have been since most assiduously and constantly occupied, in carrying it into effect. The first object to which their labours were directed, by order of the late President, was the examination of the country between the tide-waters of the Potomac, the Ohio, and the lake Erie, to ascertain the practicability of a communication between them, to designate the most suitable route for the same, and to form

plans and estimates in detail of the expense of execution.

26. On the 3d of February, 1825, they made their first Report, which was immediately communicated to Congress, and in which they declared that, having maturely considered the circumstances, observed by them personally, and carefully studied the results of such of the preliminary surveys as were then completed, they were decidedly of opinion that the communication was practicable.

27. At the last Session of Congress, before the Board of Engineers were enabled to make up their second Report, containing a general plan, and preparatory estimate for the work, the Committee of the House of Representatives upon Roads and Canals closed the Session with a Report, expressing the hope that the plan and estimate of the Board of Engineers might at this time be prepared, and that the subject be referred to the early and favourable consideration of Congress, at their present Session. That expected Report of the Board of Engineers is prepared, and will forthwith be laid before you.

28. Under the resolution of Congress, authorising the Secretary of War to have prepared a complete system of Cavalry Tactics of the United States, to be reported to Congress at the present Session—a Board of distinguished Officers of the Army, and of the Militia, has been convened, whose Report will be submitted to you, with that of the Secretary of War. The occasion was thought favourable for consulting the same Board, aided by the results of a Correspondence with the Governors of the several States and Territories, and other citizens of intelligence and experience, upon the acknowledged defective condition of our Militia system, and upon the improvements of which it is susceptible. The Report of the Board upon this subject is also submitted for your consideration.

29. In the estimates of appropriations for the ensuing year, upwards of five millions of dollars will be submitted for expenditures to be paid from the Department of War. Less than two-fifths of this will be applicable to the maintenance and support of the Army. A million and a half, in the form of pensions, goes as a scarcely adequate tribute to the services and sacrifices of a former age ; and a more than equal sum, invested in fortifications, or for the preparations of internal improvement, provides for the quiet, the comfort, and the happier existence of the ages to come. The appropriations to indemnify those unfor-

tunate remnants of another race, unable alike to share in the enjoyments, and to exist in the presence of civilization, though swelling in recent years to a magnitude burdensome to the Treasury, are generally not without their equivalents in profitable value; or serve to discharge the Union from engagements more burdensome than debt.

30. In like manner, the estimate of appropriations for the Navy Department will present an aggregate sum of upwards of three millions of dollars. About one half of these, however, cover the current expenditures of the Navy in actual service, and one half constitutes a fund of national property, the pledge of our future glory and defence. It was scarcely one short year after the close of the late war, and when the burden of its expenses and charges was weighing heaviest upon the country, that Congress, by the Act of 29th April, 1816, appropriated one million of dollars annually, for eight years, to the *gradual increase of the Navy*. At a subsequent period, this annual appropriation was reduced to half a million for six years, of which the present year is the last. A yet more recent appropriation, the last two years, for building ten sloops of war, has nearly restored the original appropriation of 1816, of a million for every year. The result is before us all. We have twelve line-of-battle ships, twenty frigates, and sloops of war in proportion; which, with a few months of preparation, may present a line of floating fortifications along the whole range of our coast, ready to meet any invader who might attempt to set foot upon our shores. Combining with a system of fortifications upon the shores themselves, commenced about the same time, under the auspices of my immediate predecessor, and hitherto systematically pursued, it has placed in our possession the most effective sinews of war, and has left us at once an example and a lesson, from which our own duties may be inferred. The gradual increase of the *Navy was the principle of which the Act of 29th April,* 1816, *was the first development.* It was the introduction of a system to act upon the character and history of our country for an indefinite series of ages. It was a declaration of that Congress to their constituents and to posterity, that it was the destiny and the duty of these Confederated States to become, in regular process of time, and by no petty advances, *a great Naval Power.* That which they proposed to accomplish in eight years, is rather to be considered as the measure of their means, than the limitation of their design.

They looked forward for a term of years sufficient for the accomplishment of a definite portion of their purpose; and they left to their successors to fill up the canvas of which they *had traced the large and prophetic outline.* The ships of the line and frigates which they had in contemplation will be shortly completed. The time which they had allotted for the accomplishment of the work has more than elapsed. It remains for your consideration, how their successors may contribute their portion of toil and of treasure for the benefit of the succeeding age, *in the gradual increase of our Navy.* There is, perhaps, no part of the exercise of the Constitutional Powers of the Federal Government, which has given more general satisfaction to the People of the Union than this. The system has not been thus vigourously introduced, and hitherto sustained, to be now departed from, or abandoned. In continuing to provide for the *gradual increase of the Navy,* it may not be necessary or expedient to add for the present any more to the number of our ships; but should you deem it adviseable to continue the yearly appropriation of half a million to the same objects, it may be profitably expended in providing a supply of timber to be seasoned, and other materials for future use, in the *construction of docks,* or in laying the foundations of a School for Naval Education, as to the wisdom of Congress either of these measures may appear to claim the preference.

31. Of the small portions of this Navy engaged in actual service during the peace, squadrons have continued to be maintained in the Pacific Ocean, in the West India Seas, in the Mediterranean; to which has been added a small armament, to cruise on the Eastern coast of South America. In all they have afforded protection to our commerce, have contributed to make our country *advantageously known to foreign nations,* have honourably employed multitudes of our seamen in the service of their country, and have enured numbers of youths of the rising generation to lives of manly hardihood and of nautical experience and skill. The piracies with which the West India Seas were for several years infested, have been totally suppressed. But, in the Mediterranean they have increased in a manner afflictive to other nations, and, but for the continued presence of our squadron, would probably have been distressing to our own. The war which has unfortunately broken out between the Republic of Buenos Ayres and the Brazilian Government has given

rise to very great irregularities among the Naval Officers of the latter, by whom *principles in relation to blockades and to neutral navigation have been brought forward to which we cannot subscribe,* and which our own Commanders have found it necessary to resist. From the friendly disposition towards the United States constantly manifested by the Emperor of Brazil, and the very useful and friendly commercial intercourse between the United States and his dominions, we have reason to believe that the just reparation demanded for the injuries sustained by several of our citizens from some of his officers, will not be withheld. Abstracts from the recent dispatches of the Commanders of our several squadrons are communicated with the Report of the Secretary of the Navy to Congress.

32. A Report from the Postmaster-General is likewise communicated, pre-

Officers have been established within the year; and the increase of revenue with the last three years, as well as the augmentation of the transportation by mail, is more than equal to the whole amount of receipts, and of mail-conveyance, at the commencement of the present century, when the seat of General Government was removed to this place. When we reflect that the objects effected by the transportation of the mail are among the choicest comforts and enjoyments of social life, it is pleasing to observe, that the dissemination of them to every corner of our country has outstripped in their increase even the rapid march of our population.

33. By the Treaties with France and Spain, respectively ceding Louisiana and the Floridas to the United States, pro-

vision was made for the security of land titles derived from the Governments of those nations. Some progress has been made, under the authority of various Acts of Congress, in the ascertainment and establishment of those titles; but claims to a very large extent remain unadjusted. The public faith, no less than the just rights of individuals, and the interest of the community itself, seems to require further provision for the speedy settlement of these claims, which I therefore recommend to the care and attention of the Legislature.

34. In conformity with the provisions of the Act of 20th May last, to provide for erecting a Penitentiary in the District of Colombia, and for other purposes, three Commissioners were appointed to select a site for the erection of a Penitentiary for the District, and also a site in the county of Alexandria for a County Jail; both of which objects have been effected. The building of the Penitentiary has been commenced, and is in such a degree of forwardness as to promise that it will be completed before the meeting of the next Congress. This consideration points to the expediency of maturing, at the present Session, a system for the regulation and government of the Penitentiary, and of defining the class of offences which shall be punishable by confinement in this edifice.

35. In closing this communication, I trust that it will not be deemed inappropriate to the occasion and purposes upon which we are here assembled, to indulge a momentary retrospect, combining, in a single glance, the period of our origin as a National Confederation with that of our present existence, at the precise interval of half a century from each other.—Since your last meeting at this place, the Fiftieth Anniversary of the day when our Independence was declared, has been celebrated throughout our land; and on that day, when every heart was bounding with joy, and every voice was tuned to gratulation, amid the blessings of Freedom and Independence which the sires of a former age had handed down to their children, two of the principal actors in that solemn scene—the hand that penned the ever-memorable Declaration, and the voice that sustained it in debate—were, by one summons, at the distance of seven hundred miles from each other, called before the Judge of All, to account for their deeds done upon earth. They departed cheered by the benedictions of their country, to whom they left the inheritance of their fame, and the memory of their bright example. If we turn our

thoughts to the condition of their country, in the contrast of the first and last
day of that half century, how resplendent
and sublime is the transition from gloom
to glory? Then glancing through the
same lapse of time, in the condition of
the individuals, we see the first day
marked with the fulness and vigor of
youth, in the pledge of their lives, their
fortunes, and their sacred honour, to the
cause of freedom and of mankind. And
on the last, extended on the bed of
death, with but sense and sensibility left
to breathe a last aspiration to Heaven of
blessing upon their country. May we
not humbly hope that to them, too, it
was a pledge of transition from gloom to
glory; and that, while their mortal vest-
ments were sinking into the clod of the
valley, their emancipated spirits were
ascending to the bosom of their God!

     JOHN QUINCY ADAMS.

Washington, Dec. 5, 1826.

---

## MARKETS.

Average Prices of CORN throughout ENGLAND, for the week ending December 29.

### Per Quarter.

| | s. | d. | | s. | d. |
|---|---|---|---|---|---|
| Wheat | 54 | 4 | Rye | 40 | 4 |
| Barley | 35 | 9 | Beans | 48 | 2 |
| Oats | 29 | 1 | Pease | 51 | 0 |

Total Quantity of Corn returned as
Sold in the Maritime Districts, for
the week ended December 29.

| | Qrs. | | Qrs. |
|---|---|---|---|
| Wheat | 39,614 | Rye | 222 |
| Barley | 42,581 | Beans | 2,218 |
| Oats | 8,434 | Pease | 940 |

### Corn Exchange, Mark Lane.

Quantities and Prices of British
Corn, &c. sold and delivered in
this Market, during the week ended
Saturday, December 30.

| | Qrs. | £. | s. | d. | | s. | d. |
|---|---|---|---|---|---|---|---|
| Wheat | 4,709 | for 13,316 | 15 | 0 | Average, | 56 | 1 |
| Barley | 5,405 | 10,092 | 17 | 0 | | 37 | 4 |
| Oats | 1,579 | 2,501 | 11 | 9 | | 31 | 8 |
| Rye | — | — | | | | | — |
| Beans | 723 | 1,693 | 14 | 6 | | 46 | 10 |
| Pease | 567 | 1,437 | 16 | 3 | | 50 | 8 |

Friday, Jan. 5.—The continuance
of the frosty weather, together with
moderate fresh arrivals of Grain in
general, occasions the trade to be
very stiff for every article, at full as
good prices as on Monday last. The
supply of Flour is considerable, but
some sales are making this week with
more freedom.

Monday, Jan. 8.—Last week's
supplies of most kinds of Grain
were again liberal. This morning
the fresh arrivals are moderate, but
the quantities left on hand, from former supplies, constitute a large market for all sorts of Grain. The weather is mild and damp, and most of
the Wheat samples being affected
thereby, they are consequently neglected by the millers; but the few
superfine dry samples that have appeared obtained last week's quotations.

The best samples of Malting Barley have sold at 1s. per qr. advance
on the terms of last Monday, other
qualities are unaltered. Beans meet
a very heavy sale, and hardly support the prices quoted. Boiling
Pease are more in demand, and 1s.
to 2s. per qr. higher. Grey Pease
are unaltered. The quantity of
Foreign Oats for sale here still continues very large, and the frost
being gone, there is a very slack
demand for this article to-day, but
prices cannot be quoted lower than
this day se'nnight. Since the reduction in the top price of Flour the
trade continues heavy.

---

*Price on board Ship as under.*

| Flour, per sack | 50s. — 53s. |
|---|---|
| —— Seconds | 43s. — 46s. |
| —— North Country | 40s. — 45s. |

---

Price of Bread.—The price of the
4lb. Loaf is stated at 9½d. by the
full-priced Bakers.

Account of Wheat, &c. arrived in the Port of London, from Jan. 1 to Jan. 6, both inclusive.

| | Qrs. | | | Qrs. |
|---|---|---|---|---|
| Wheat | 6,311 | Tares | .... | 21 |
| Barley | 8,249 | Linseed | .. | — |
| Malt | 9,937 | Rapeseed | . | — |
| Oats | 7,174 | Brank | .. | — |
| Beans | 935 | Mustard | .. | 21 |
| Flour | 15,485 | Flax | .... | — |
| Rye | 250 | Hemp | ... | — |
| Pease | 1,006 | Seeds | ... | — |

Foreign.—Wheat, 1,473; Barley, 187; Oats, 10,546; and Beans, 1,293 quarters.

———

Monday, Jan. 8. — The arrivals from Ireland last week were 7,661 firkins of Butter, and 3,703 bales of Bacon; and from Foreign Ports, 20 casks of Butter.

———

Price of Hops, per Cwt. in the Borough.

Monday, Jan. 8.—New Kent and Sussex pockets are a ready sale, say Kent, 90s., 98s. to 112s.; Sussex, 80s., 86s. to 88s. Bags, 70s. to 95s. per cwt. Old Hops of every description more in request.

*Another Account.*

Jan. 8.—Our Hop Market, during the last week, has been very firm, and fully maintains last week's prices.

*Maidstone*, Jan. 4.— The Hop Trade continues in the same dull state as last week.

———

COAL MARKET, Jan. 5.

Ships at Market. Ships sold. Price.
121½ Newcastle 26½..26s. 6d. to 36s. 6d.
37 Sunderland 12½..34s. 0d.—37s. 6d.

SMITHFIELD, Monday, Jan. 8, 1827.

Monday, Jan. 8.—The trade for both Beef and Mutton was heavy on Friday, and sales were effected on rather reduced terms. To-day the great change in the weather, with a fair supply of Beasts, and a full one of Sheep, have rendered this market very heavy. The best things are taken off but slowly: here and there a Bullock may have made our top currency of Monday last—but the general trade is decidedly lower. This is also the case with Mutton, though a few choice old Downs have reached 4s. 6d. Top price for polled Sheep, light weights, 4s. 2d.

*Per Stone of 8 pounds (alive).*

| | s. | d. | | s. | d. |
|---|---|---|---|---|---|
| Beef | 3 | 8 | to | 5 | 2 |
| Mutton | 3 | 8 | — | 4 | 4 |
| Veal | 4 | 4 | — | 5 | 2 |
| Pork | 4 | 4 | — | 5 | 2 |
| Lamb | 0 | 0 | — | 0 | 0 |

| Beasts | 2,349 | Sheep | 23,570 |
|---|---|---|---|
| Calves | 166 | Pigs | 220 |

NEWGATE, (same day.)

*Per Stone of 8 pounds (dead).*

| | s. | d. | | s. | d. |
|---|---|---|---|---|---|
| Beef | 3 | 6 | to | 4 | 9 |
| Mutton | 3 | 0 | — | 3 | 10 |
| Veal | 3 | 4 | — | 5 | 4 |
| Pork | 3 | 0 | — | 5 | 0 |
| Lamb | 0 | 0 | — | 0 | 0 |

LEADENHALL, (same day.)

*Per Stone of 8 pounds (dead).*

| | s. | d. | | s. | d. |
|---|---|---|---|---|---|
| Beef | 3 | 8 | to | 4 | 8 |
| Mutton | 2 | 8 | — | 4 | 0 |
| Veal | 3 | 4 | — | 5 | 4 |
| Pork | 4 | 0 | — | 5 | 4 |
| Lamb | 0 | 0 | — | 0 | 0 |

*Liverpool*, January 2, 1827.—The arrivals of Grain appearing considerable, as reported in the Import note annexed, it is here proper to observe, that the most material part thereof were antecedent to those of last Tuesday, and the demand, in consequence, was very languid throughout the week. At this day's market. sales were very limited, even for fine qualities of Wheat, which alone obtained late prices; other descriptions were at a decline of 1*d.* to 2*d.* per 70 lbs., and middling samples of Oats were fully 1*d.* per 45 lbs. lower. Beans, Pease, Malt, and Malting Barley gave way in value 1*s.* to 2*s.* per quarter, as did Flour and Oatmeal 1*s.* to 2*s.* per sack.

Imported into Liverpool, from the 26th December, 1826, to the 1st January, 1827, inclusive:—Wheat, 14,354; Barley, 4,386; Oats, 13,035; Rye, 212; Malt, 1,834; Beans, 3,802; Pease, 125 quarters. Flour, 4,283 sacks, per 280 lbs. Oatmeal, 1,735 packs, per 240 lbs. American Flour, 1,627 barrels.

*Bristol*, Jan. 5.—The prices of Corn, &c. continue nearly the same as last week, and sales are heavy, at the following rates:—Wheat, from 5*s.* 6*d.* to 7*s.* 7½*d.*; Barley, 4*s.* 8*d.* to 5*s.* 6*d.*; Oats, 3*s.* 3*d.* to 4*s.* 6*d.*; Beans, 5*s.* 6*d.* to 7*s.* 8*d.*; and Malt, 5*s.* 3*d.* to 8*s.* 3*d.* per bushel, Imperial.—Flour, Seconds, 32*s.* to 42*s.* per bag.

*Guildford*, Jan. 6.—Wheat, 14*l.* to 16*l.* per load. Rye, 43*s.* to 46*s.*; Barley, 35*s.* to 36*s.*; Oats, 29*s.* to 40*s.*; Beans, 55*s.* to 66*s.*; Pease, grey, 57*s.* to 60*s.* per quarter.

*Ipswich*, Jan. 6.—We had to-day a short supply of all Corn, and prices were somewhat higher; for Barley about 1*s.* per quarter; as follow:—Wheat, 50*s.* to 60*s.*; Barley, 32*s.* to 37*s.*; Beans, 44*s.* to 45*s.*; and Pease, 46*s.* to 48*s.* per quarter.

*Manchester*, Jan. 6.—During the present week we have had a material alteration in the weather, from mild to frosty, which caused the holders of all kinds of Grain, Flour, and Malt, to anticipate higher prices; but this day it began to thaw again, and the consequence is, that the articles before-mentioned have been offered on less terms than this day week. English Wheats, of fine quality, barely support their prices; Irish 1*d.* to 2*d.* per 70 lbs. lower. Grinding Barley more inquired for, and 1*d.* per 60 lbs. dearer. Oats are dull in sale, and ½*d.* to 1*d.* per 45 lbs. lower. Beans steady. Boiling Pease are more inquired after, but, no dearer. There is a better demand for Malt, but prices remain the same. Flour is still a dull article, with very little doing in it.

*Newcastle-on-Tyne*, Jan. 6.—The stormy weather we have had during the week has induced the farmers to thrash freely, and we had to-day rather a large supply of Wheat; which sold slowly at last week's prices. Rye continues in demand at the prices of this day se'nnight. We have not had arrivals of Barley this week, and the market is nearly cleared of good quality. The farmers' supply of Oats was only moderate this morning, and last week's prices were fully supported.

*Wakefield*, Jan. 5.—The supply of Wheat to-day is very moderate; very short of Barley, and quite trifling of all other articles. The canals being closed by the frost, the demand for Wheat has been confined to a few needy millers, the chief of them not being sufficiently bare of stock to employ land carriage: what sales are made are at last week's prices. Oats fully maintain last Friday's prices, and Shelling, being scarce, is rather dearer. Good Barley is not plentiful, and obtains an advance of nearly 1*s.* per quarter. Beans support late prices. The stock of rapeseed is much reduced, and this article is held rather higher.

# COBBETT'S WEEKLY REGISTER.

Vol. 61.—No. 4.]　　LONDON, SATURDAY, JAN. 20, 1827.　　[Price 6d.

Published every Saturday Morning, at Seven o'Clock.

" The Debt says to the King of England, ' You shall never go to war
" again, while I am in existence.'"——REGISTER, TWENTY DIFFERENT
PLACES.

TO

# THE NOBILITY OF ENGLAND,

## ON THE BLESSINGS WHICH MESSRS. CANNING AND HUSKISSON HAVE IN STORE FOR THEM.

### LETTER II.

Kensington, 17th Jan. 1827.

MY LORDS,

IN my last Letter, I had not room to notice some of the most important parts of the President's Message; and, I consider no parts of it as being important unless they relate to matters affecting this country. I shall notice the parts here alluded to in the present Letter; but, before I do that, let me beg your Lordships' attention to a few sober reflections on the inevitable consequences of a war, on whatever grounds and with whatever nation. As a preface to these reflections, let me observe on and quote from the language of one of the London newspapers, which may be taken as a pretty fair sample of the whole of that immense mass of printing which Mr. BROUGHAM, in the fulness of his wisdom, has designated as the " best possible public instructor." And, here, let me beg your Lordships to observe, that the character of the parties who own or who

.G

Printed and Published by WILLIAM COBBETT, No. 183, Fleet-street.
[ENTERED AT STATIONERS' HALL.]

conduct these vehicles, has nothing at all to do with the effect produced by the vehicles. The far greater part of these parties are persons profoundly ignorant on the subject which I am endeavouring to place before your Lordships; and, the whole of them, without a single exception, have no motives in view but such as are merely mercenary. That is no matter: their weight is not the less for that: despicable as their conductors were, you saw them listened to and you saw them ruin hundreds of thousands of bondholders. They are always prepared to do the same, or any act of similar amount of mischief. They write for the profits of the day; and, so that they insure those profits, they care not a straw about the reproaches that will fall upon their writings, after they have eaten, drunk, or worn the fruits of these writings. I have often expressed a wish, and still oftener I have entertained that wish, that the people of England could SEE these instructors all assembled together upon one spot! If they could but once see the wretches, never would they believe in them again. The mass of the people believe them to be gentlemen of learning and talent and fortune. Little do they imagine what a set of reptiles it is; at what rate these reptiles are paid; how they are lodged and fed; what a despicable crew it is, in

short, from head to foot. However, we must take things as we find them: it is impossible to make the people see this: they will believe in these reptiles: they will listen to them, echo their sentiments, set up a foolish cry, dictated by these mercenary wretches: and, in the end, enable creatures made by nature to black shoes or feed swine, to cause the greatest calamities to their country.

Nor, are we to be so much surprised at this, when we see many, even of your Lordships, influenced by these same newspapers. There is a sort of joint effort going on, at this time, between the newspapers and the "*liberals*" amongst the ministers, of which liberals Mr. Canning appears to be at the head. It is monstrous to suppose, that, with the present Debt, this country can go to war without a total blowing-up of the present order of things. This opinion is universal, amongst all men of sense in every country where there exists any knowledge of the real situation of England; while, at home, there is no man of sense and sincerity who does not think and say, that we cannot have war and continue to pay the interest of the Debt in full. I know that we cannot do the latter IN PEACE, if the enactments now existing be carried into full effect. I know that it does not need a war to blow up the present order of things, if the bills passed last year be carried into full effect. I know this : I know that those bills cannot be carried into full effect ; I know that the one-pound notes cannot be banished from circulation in England without producing something very near to a political revolution ; without, at the very least, blowing up the present system of finance ; without a total revolution in property : I know that these Acts cannot be carried into full effect without producing these things, even though there should be no war at all. What then, my Lords, is to be the consequence if a war take place, at this time ; and, especially, if that war demand ships and men to the full extent of the power of the country, such as it was at the close of the last war ?

Yet, with facts before them, such as a rational answer to this question would require, and such as common sense would suggest : with facts like these before their eyes, the stupid, the mercenary, the vile wretches who conduct the newspapers of London, are daily pouring forth empty rubbish, such as your Lordships will behold in the article which I am now about to insert, from that most stupid, most impudent, most vile and corrupt, and, therefore, most read of all the infamous newspapers of London, commonly called the OLD TIMES. It is useless to observe that the thing is unworthy of notice : the same observation may as reasonably be made with regard to a heap of rubbish which is laid upon the road, and that upsets your carriage in the dark. That heap is, in itself, unworthy of notice ; but, the mischief which it does, the wound which it causes, the limbs which it breaks, make it an object worthy of the greatest attention. I give this article, too, as a specimen of the means by which this public is deluded. There is no getting on without the public : the work of mischief moves but slowly, unless there be a loud cry in its favour : it was the national howl ; the big, bullying, hectoring, toasting, feasting, bragging : these it was that saddled the nation with eight hundred millions of *Fundholder-debt*, with pretty nearly two hundred millions of *Dead weight-debt*, and with more than two hundred millions of *Pauper-debt* ; this howl, this hallooing ; this clapping of hands and hectoring it was, that saddled your Lordships' estates with all these Debts ; that fixed all these mortgages upon them ; and I am now going to give you a specimen of that bullying rubbish, which, as sure as you are Lords, would, if it were to be fully acted upon, cause the mortgages to be foreclosed, and take from you even the liberty of seeking shelter for your bodies in the worst room in the worst of your farm-houses. Here it is, my Lords. Pray read it with attention; and say, before you begin, *" Let us now look at that which we have to avoid!"*

Only yesterday we thought it worth while to notice those dreams of the ultra-servile party at Madrid, Paris, and other points of Europe, which fed their imaginations with the hope *that England was now in a condition to be bearded with impunity.* By a curious coincidence, the next mail has brought us an illustration of the folly which we were just exposing, in a passage from the *Allgemeine Zeitung,* where the Editor speaks of the present crisis in Portuguese affairs.

This German *illumine* begins by discovering, in one short sentence, an extreme ignorance of fact, and a gross error in judgment. He tells us, that " by the " armed intervention of Great Britain, " in the present *internal* dissensions in " Portugal, it cannot be denied that the " flames of war may be kindled in the " Peninsula."

Now it is pretty plain, as we conceive, that England has armed for any thing but to intermeddle in the " internal dissensions " of Portugal ; having studiously disavowed all regard whatever to the civil broils of the Portuguese among themselves, and directed her power to the single end of repelling a foreign invasion.

Nor is the *Allgemeine Zeitung,* as it seems to us, more fortunate in his opinions than in his facts. He represents the military interference of this country as likely to " kindle the flames of war in " the Peninsula ;" whereas the flames having been already kindled by the monks of France and Spain, we defy the most

ingenious man living to suggest an expedient better calculated to put out the fire than this same prompt, and vigorous, and well-timed movement on the part of the British nation.

But " it must be remembered," we are told, " that of all the countries of " Europe, Great Britain perhaps more " than any other, NEEDS THE PRESERVA- " TION OF PEACE, as well to heal the " wounds which it has sustained in its " finances by more than 20 years' war, " as to gain time to conjure the storms " of internal discord, especially in Ire- " land."

All states, be it recollected by the *Allgemeine Zeitung,* can be considered as feeble or powerful, only, first, in comparison with themselves at some former period ; or second, when they are compared with other communities. *And is it now a question with any journalist who pretends to speculate on the history of the last 30 years, whether England possesses now, in 1826, more or less capacity for supporting an extensive war than when she was forced into that of the French revolution? Look at the population of the United Kingdom, increased from 14,000,000 to more than 21,000,000 of men.* To those who talk of the discontents of Ireland, we answer that a single vote of Parliament would allay at once all such discontents as can affect the application of our military power ; and the enemies of British glory and greatness may assure themselves, that were a serious war to break out, the party (for it is no more) which resists the claims of our Catholic countrymen, would *soon be deprived of the influence which now enables them to flatter the envy and hatred of foreigners with hopes of our disunion as a people.*

*For those, again, who argue from the debt of England, to the certain exhaustion of the country which sustains it, we say that our funded debt of 800,000,000l. bears no higher interest per cent. than when it amounted to only one-third of the money; this proves that the credit of the Government is quite as good as in 1793, far better than that of any other kingdom in the world; for nowhere has a loan of 5,000,000l. been raised on terms at all comparable to those for which England has procured a credit of more than 800,000,000l. But this is of little signification. Look at the general progress of the empire in the materials of wealth and power, since the beginning of the war in 1793.* Her commerce trebled, her means of productive industry quadrupled, her works of defence, and of communication, by land and water, her concentration of available riches, her immense acquisitions of exterior strength, which give her the keys of three quarters of the world, and more especially the absolute command over all the direct maritime intercourse which can be carried on by the nations of the north, of central and southern Europe, whether through the road of the Mediterranean or of the Atlantic, with Africa or with the eastern hemisphere. The fleets of England were never so predominant as at the hour at which we now describe them, over those of every actual or possible rival. The elements, and frame, and spirit of the army never so well arrayed or constituted. Her arsenals are provided 'for more than ten years of war—but above all, and paramount, stands that strength, which consists in the just and defensive character of British policy, inspiring the great body of nations with confidence, and the members of their several governments with respect.

*With whatever warmth of language* those Englishmen *whose duty* and genius lead them to conduct the discussions of our national interests, may happen to express their feelings of a public wrong, or their solicitude for a remedy, it may bring foreigners into an unlucky predicament if they venture on such grounds to build any hope of profiting by our apparent quarrels with each other. *In free countries,* where opinion is the great mover of the commonwealth, it is unavoidable to paint grievances in strong colours, that they may catch the eye and fix the public attention ; but we repeat, that the power which fancies that because Englishmen remonstrate boldly with their public functionaries, where they feel that some partial defect in the political system might be repalied, they will not, therefore, make common cause with their Government against the intrusions or designs of strangers, will find itself in a very unfortunate mistake, and exposed to perils which it would be wise to avoid by timely abstinence from provocation.

Did you ever see such a beast, my Lords ! He has been reading in German newspapers that England, *more than any other country, stands in need of peace.* What is his answer ! " That the popula-" tion of the kingdom has, since " the beginning of the last French " war, that is to say, during the " last thirty years, increased from " *fourteen* to *twenty-one* millions." Here is an *answer !* Every man of sense knows that this story about an increased population is a sheer, a naked, a monstrous lie. All Englishmen know that I have proved the documents upon which the assertion is founded to be a lie. Besides this positive proof of the falsehood of the assertion taken with such a foundation, there is not a man of sense in the whole world who will believe, that the increase of the population in this kingdom, in the course of 30 years, has amounted to more than the whole of the population of England must have been (according to this) thirty years ago. The lie is too monstrous to be swallowed by the most credulous of mankind; and, the putting of it forward upon this occasion will only tend to prove to foreign nations, that we have, in fact, nothing better than a monstrous lie to put forward.

But, supposing the population to have increased; aye, even in the proportion stated by this monstrous beast; for argument's sake, suppose the fact to be true; what, then, has this increase of population been a source of *strength* to the country? Your Lordships will hardly think that, when you have volumes and volumes of evidence and reports lying upon the tables of your houses, all alleging that the *overstock of population is the cause, the great cause of the miseries of the country!* Nay, more than this, when your Lordships have *voted, for several years past, pretty large sums of money to cause the over-population to emigrate to foreign lands!* These are undeniable facts; and, therefore, if an increase of population have given no increase of strength to combat foreign nations, your Lordships have been pretty wisely set to work, in voting away our money and your own, to export and to get rid of this additional strength. The paper from which this article is taken, is owned by a bouncing dame, one ANNA BRODIE, the wife of one BRODIE, a Church Doctor of Divinity, rector of East Bearne in Sussex, and by her sister, who is the wife of one CARDEN, an Attorney. At least, these are the two principal proprietors. Now, Anna and her sister hardly wrote this themselves: but they cause it to be sent forth; and it is just the same to the public whether they write it or pay for writing it. These are a couple of Mr. BROUGHAM's " best public instructors," who find out that we are more able to go to war than we were thirty years ago, because we have more of those people whose existence your Lordships' proceedings and votes prove to be a source of weakness! What, my Lords, have we become *stronger*, in consequence of an increase of the number of those for whom the *King himself goes round with a begging box!* What, my Lords, have we gained national *strength* by these vast increased real or pretended wretches, for whom the famous law of Queen Elizabeth is insufficient to provide the means of existence! My Lords, read the following article from the best possible public Scotch instructor, Dr. Black's paper, the Morning Chronicle. Read it, my Lords, and if you do not blush as you read, you are unworthy even of the breath of life in your nostrils: you are a disgrace to the form of man. However, I will not believe that your cheeks will not burn with shame as you read this most horrible article. Here it is, and if, after this, there be an Englishman found to talk of the degraded state of the people of other countries, he will deserve to be flogged throughout the world. " SUPREMA " LEX.—A Correspondent sub- " mits, whether, with a view to " the triple purpose of preventing " the future profanation of the " sanctuaries of the dead—*of de-* " *terring, perhaps, in some degree,* " from the *least venial kind of* " *pauperism*—and of ministering, " in an *hour* of extreme need, to " the *vital interests of a science,* " of all others the most important " to human happiness on this side " the grave—a law would be " deemed, by the public, humane " or harsh, which provided that, " in the event (of course with pro- " per exceptions) of any person " dying between the ages of " eighteen and fifty-five, *in a* " *parish workhouse, his or her* " *body should be at the disposal* " *of the Overseers,* the *money* " *arising* from the *sale thereof to* " *a surgeon, for dissection, to be* " *carried to the poors' rate.* The " date of its operation, for the " first time, might be a certain " number of years after its enact- " ment."—Read *that,* my Lords,

and then hear the boasting about " *admiration of the world*"!

But, to return to these women: these noisy, empty-headed women, or the people that they hire to put this stuff upon paper, seem to look upon the affairs of the Catholics as a mere dispute that can be settled without any thing taking place to affect any *institution* of the country. They call *the Church;* the established Church; they call that great branch of the property and power of your Lordships; they call that a mere nothing at all; " a party" *to be deprived of its influence in a moment!* Precious things as rotten boroughs are, my Lords; strong as those rotten things are, though rotten as med-lars when they are ripe, it were much better to be deprived even of them, than to be deprived of the influence given by the established Church. And, yet, here are these women, or their hire-lings, ready to make ducks and drakes of the Church, which they call a mere party, and which they appear to think could be brushed away without the smallest inconvenience, if necessary to secure the means of carrying on another war, and making other loans.

Remark, next, my Lords, what these shocking beasts say about the *debt,* and about the means of borrowing money. Mark the *argument,* above all things, my Lords, and be astounded at the grossness, the brutality, the horrid brute-creation ignorance of these creatures! So, because the Government, by means of immense taxes wrung from your estates and from the labour of the people; because the Government has a fund raised by such means, out of which it can pay an interest for money; because every man's purse is put in a state of requisition by the Government; because the people can have the fruits of their labour wrung from them even to the reducing of them to the last stages of want; and because this immense fund, and the other branches of its system has created a fictitious money, in which loans are made and by the means of which interest is extracted for money really never lent: because these things are, we are to be able to go on and add to the interest of the debt, though every man in the ngdom knows, that there is scarcely a newspaper in the kingdom, not excepting the one from which I am quoting, which has not, within the last six months, expressed a doubt of the ability of the nation to continue to pay the interest of the debt though there should be no war at all.

However, this is the sort of stuff, the hectoring, bragging stuff, which has preceded every ruinous war. I do not pretend to wish that there may not be war: I wish for ANY THING; for any thing, no matter what, that will restore to us *a gold and silver currency and nothing but a gold and silver currency.* I wish for any thing that will effect this; and I care not whether it be effected by war or by peace. War would effect it in a short time; but, the mode must be violent. I wish for a peaceable mode; and, therefore, I am rather inclined in favour of peace. But, my wishes have nothing to do with the question of the policy of this war, or possible war. It is my business to show what will be the consequences of this war, if it really take place. In another part of this *Register*, I shall insert (if I have room) a not badly written paper, signed "A TORY." This paper was sent to the *Morning Herald*, with a request to the Editor, that, if he did not like to insert it in that paper, he would send it to the office of my *Register*. The *Morning Herald* man did not like it. I dislike some parts of it, and particularly those parts where the author seems to praise the throat-cutten CASTLEREAGH, who brought in the Dungeon-Bill of 1817, and also the Six Acts. I dislike some further parts of his paper; and I must particularly express my dissent from what he says about America having *attacked us* in the time of Buonaparte. But, I perfectly agree with this old smoker of a Tory; this old shaffle-breeches, who seems to tremble like a poor little half-starved caitiff before the rod of a pedigogue; who seems frightened out of his senses at the prospect of seeing the radicals uppermost: I perfectly agree with him in his opinion as to the probable consequences of Mr. Canning's war, if he should hatch out one at last. Nothing is clearer, than that we cannot have war with Spain, and with Spain ALONE. FERDINAND, who has been charged with all sorts of vices and of follies, who has been thus charged by the whole tribe of our bullocking newspapers, has, as far as I can judge from what I read and hear, acted as wise a part as man could act in a similar state of things. He has acted against revolutionists in precisely the same manner, and on the same principles that England acted with regard to the revolution going on in France. He has acted purely on the defensive, and his army of observation is only chapter the second of the cordon sanitaire. If we have war with him, his councillors will take special care that we shall be the *aggressors*. He is said to be under the government of monks and friars. If his present measures be the result of the advice of monks and friars, I verily believe that we shall soon think that it would not be amiss if we had a pack of them at White-

hall. Monks and friars are not great talkers, it seems; but, if we may judge from what FERDINAND has hitherto done, they are a good deal of the *thinking* sort, and think it right to look a little forward. The army which Spain has or is about to have on the frontiers of Portugal, and which no nation upon earth can find fault with her for having there, will be pretty nearly as efficient against the pigeon-hole constitution gentry as if that army were drawn up and besieging Lisbon. The "rebels," as Doctor BLACK calls the royalists, will have nothing to fear, so long as the Spanish army is on the confines of Portugal. Mr. CANNING recollects, I suppose, notwithstanding the frenzy of his joy at having the "furies of war" in his "leash;" he recollects, I suppose, that it is no breach of neutrality in one nation to admit deserters, or refugees of any description, into its territory, even if they take their arms along with them. This is no breach of neutrality; but, it is not only a breach of neutrality, but an act of hostility, an act of invasion, in one nation to pursue fugitives from it into the territory of another nation. There can, in fact, be no question of neutrality in this case. There are not two acknowledged independent powers engaged in hostility it is a nation divided within itself: it is two parties of the same nation at war against each other. Either party may take shelter in Spain, without any breach of the peace on the part of Spain; and, the moment they cross the Portuguese frontiers to enter Spain, that moment they are under the protection of the laws and of the Sovereign of Spain. But, that Sovereign may choose between the parties, when once they enter his territory : he is then their Sovereign for the time being ; and he can deal with them according to his laws and his prerogatives. This being the case, and Portugal being bounded by Spain on three sides out of the four, that party in Portugal who has the king of Spain for its enemy, must stand but a poor chance, indeed, even if backed at the expense of millions upon millions from England.

And, yet, all the while, the King of Spain commits no act of hostility against Portugal, does no act of war, breaks the peace in no way whatever, does nothing, and shows a disposition to do nothing, to justify any act of hostility of ours against him. Therefore, my Lords, the monks and friars appear to me to have beaten the newly-enlightened " liberals " of Whitehall. They appear to me to have made it clear to the whole world, or, at least, to have taken measures for making it clear to the whole world, that our inter-ference, that our fuss, that our bullying, that our jacobinical threatening has all been without the smallest provocation on the part of Spain, even if we were bound by treaty, as we clearly are not, to defend Portugal against any attempt levelled at her independence. Our treaties with her were dissolved with the dissolution of her government ; but, supposing them to be still in existence, *the case contemplated by them has no existence*. It is notorious to the whole world, that the conduct of Spain has, in this case, been *purely defensive*; and our treaties with Portugal contemplated, and, contemplated alone, the protection of the whole country of Portugal against the territorial encroachments of Spain.

All these things had in view, there is not a man upon earth, that will attempt to look upon Spain as having been the aggressor *thus far*. We have so good, ground for war with her *as yet* as and King FERDINAND's monks and friars are not such fools as some people are, to get into a war, manifestly against their own interest, and without the smallest necessity. Our newspapers are carrying on the war in Portugal, very much to the advantage of the " liberals." I believe, however, that the monk and friar party will be the strongest at last; and, if it should, if ever there were a pre-

per occasion for employing the
fool's-cap and bells, upon my soul,
my Lords, I shall never forgive
you if you do not get one as high
as the tiara itself, and put it upon
the head of whom you and I know,
but whom, if your Lordships
please, we will not name at this
time. A pretty figure he will cut
with his constitution, the first-born
of his pigeon-holes, flung into the
fire, with twenty or thirty millions
of money for us to pay, and with
an everlasting expulsion, very
likely, of the port-brewers of the
southern peninsula of Europe;
while FERDINAND and his friars
will sit quiet and safe at Madrid,
and laugh at this miserable attempt at making new governments
for other nations. Why, as my
Tory-correspondent very reasonably asks—why could not we let
Portugal remain with her old government? It had served our
ends very well, at any rate. Why
must we needs set to work to hatch
a thing that would make the
priests and the monks of Portugal
call us heretics? They knew,
doubtless, or, at least, they thought,
that we were all to go to the devil
at last; but, in the meanwhile,
we answered their purpose very
well, and, they answered our
purpose, and we had all the
people of Portugal for friends.
Now, the question of right aside;
and, well it may be aside; for, no
more a right had we to be juggling

a new government for Por-
tugal, any more than I have a
right to come and dictate to your
Lordships what you shall have
for dinner: the question of right
aside, was there ever, in this
world, folly equal to that of our
doing, and *gratuitously*, too, that,
which, according to all probability, would enlist against us, and
place in implacable battalions, the
priests, the monks, the whole body
of the clergy of that people whom,
heretics as they say we are, we
have grace enough left to call
the "MOST FAITHFUL"! My
Lords, was there ever madness
like this; for nothing at all, too;
without a possibility of gain, and
with almost a certainty of tremendous loss?

Here, then, we are, with the
fairest chance in the world of
seeing one of two things: our
party put down in Portugal and
our constitution burnt by the
hands of the common hangman,
our troops coming back and glad
to get home and save their bacon,
having been rejected by the nation that they went under the pretext of defending, and, to close the
account, another loan of ten or
fifteen millions to be added to the
National Debt, to pay for this
Æolian exploit; or, of seeing ourselves plunged into a war with
Spain in the first place, we being
the aggressors, and clearly such
to all the world; with France and

Russia in the next place; for, interfere they must and will; with America, to a certainty, if we attempt either of these two things, namely: to take the Spanish West India islands, or to enforce that great right of our maritime dominion, the right of searching neutral ships for enemies' goods. If our hands be tied up as to these two particulars, what war can we carry on? We shall fight like a muffled cock; but we shall spend money as fast as if we were unmuffled. In short, we are destined, if Mr. Canning should get us into this war, to experience humiliation such as would have made Englishmen mad to think of only sixty or seventy years ago.

Did your Lordships do Mr. ADAMS the honour to read the fourth paragraph of his Message, in page 169 of the last *Register*? Mr. ADAMS, though at the head of a, really, very great nation, does not receive so great a salary as Mr. CANNING, to say nothing about the sinecure place of the latter, and about the pensions and places of his relations. But, my Lords, Mr. ADAMS (to describe the proportions of the faculties of the mind by the members of the body); Mr. ADAMS has, I am convinced, as much sound sense in the parings of the nail of his little finger, as Mr. CANNING has in his whole carcass. Read, there-

fore, my Lords, Mr. ADAMS's Message. Do not call him a mean, fellow for taking so small a salary; for, I dare say he would take more if the people were fools enough to give it him; and if you were to ask Mr. GALLATIN's opinion upon this subject, he would say that I am right. Read, then, the fourth paragraph, my Lords, and there you will find, that when Æolus CANNING was flinging about his arms like a true Cornelius Agrippa's man, and bragging that HE (what a shame!) had given independence to South America, had wrested the New World from Spain; there, in that fourth paragraph, you will find that the job was done, as far as it has been done, *by the United States of America, and not by* Æolus CANNING *at all;* for, Mr. ADAMS explicitly says, that, " in " consequence of representations " made by them to the Emperor " ALEXANDER, he took that course " of policy which *left to the other* " *governments of Europe no other* " *alternative* but that of sooner or " later recognizing the independ- " ence of our southern neigh- " bours."

Now, my Lords, what becomes of the bragging, of the blustering Æolus? But, there is much more in this than the mere recognition of the independence of the Spanish colonies. It shows, that what I have always insisted on was true;

namely, that the United States and Russia were inseparably bound together. The cabinet of Washington convinced the Emperor ALEXANDER, that his interest was on the side that they were taking. They convinced him that, first or last, that which they recommended would work injury to England. So here it comes out, at last, that Mr. CANNING's famous "*balance*," which he had found in the New World to compensate the loss of the one in the Old World, was a balance not only desired, but actually *gotten for him*, by a couple of sly, leaguing, sworn foes to the power of England! There is a clever Minister for you, my Lords! And what clever men you are, for finding out so clever a man to carry on your affairs! JOHNNY ADAMS seemed to have had a foreknowledge, a dream or an apparition to tell him of our ÆOLUS being going to boast about his giving independence to South America. It was a spiteful devil to play him this trick, to be sure; and, especially, after the wise House had cheered him, particularly when he made this bragging; and, more especially, the knowing and far-seeing "Whigs," while Mr. BROUGHAM is said to have shouted between a hickup and a blubber. Oh, Lord, it was so moving! it was so melting! And, after all this, for this cool, long-sided Yan-

kee (I beg his pardon, he is a truss little English-looking man); for this cool, placid, never-smiling Yankee, to send us over the news that it was he and the Emperor ALEXANDER that had done the thing! My Lords, it is too bad: it is too much to endure; and I should not wonder if Mr. CANNING were to call upon you to depose Mr. ADAMS, as the *Times newspaper* and Sir JOSEPH YORKE called upon you to depose Mr. MADDISON.

Let us quit this melancholy subject, my Lords, and look at the thirtieth paragraph of Mr. ADAMS's Message. There we see the devil, indeed! There we see that which those great captains, WILLIAM PITT CANNING, FREDERICK SPENCER, SAUNDERS DUNDAS, EDMOND WOODHOUSE and all the swarm of HOPE JOHNSTONES; and all those other famous young heroes who have been put over the heads of so many thousands of men: there we see what these heroes will have to face. Now, I do not pretend that I had any thing to do in causing this American navy to be made; but, in 1815, when all the anti-jacobins were crowing over us; when the insolence of the looks of these scoundrels told us, that they expected to see the day when they would have their feet actually upon our necks; when the French had just had their museum stripped, their frontier towns taken away, and were doomed to pay tribute to those who falsely bragged that they had conquered them; at that time, though I never, for one moment, despaired of the ultimate effects of the good and righteous DEBT that still sticks by us; still, I was afraid for the United States. I knew that there were men in England, who longed for an opportunity of tearing them to pieces; and, if that were once accomplished, we might have become the most villanous slaves that ever disgraced the human shape. You never read such naughty books as *Registers*, my Lords : if you were to do it, you would find, in the *Registers* of 1815, scores of exhortations from me to the Americans, always concluding with these very words : " *again I say, build ships and cast canons !*" Curious enough, that, in April 1816, the Congress, as Mr. Adams now tells us, in paragraph 80, laid the foundation of the navy which now exists. The newspaper fellows think they have discovered great *inaccuracy* in me, because I told Mr. Canning, that if he got into a war, he would have thirty American ships of the line to fight; whereas, Mr. Adams says that he has *only* twelve ships of the line. These cunning fellows think, I suppose, that the Americans cannot augment the number of their ships during the war. I said he would have thirty ships of the line to fight; and thirty he will have to fight and more than thirty, if more be required, before the end of a war of only four years with the United States. And, these *twelve ships of the line*. Our Blue-and-Buff will tell you, that each of them is equal to a hundred gun ship; and they will swear like thunder that an American frigate is as *big* as an English seventy - four. Either, therefore, the feelings of Blue-and-Buff swell the Yankee ships beyond their real size; either their imaginations cause them to see double; or, Mr. Adams has got a goodly collection of ships of the line. However, let us quiet the imaginations of Blue-and-Buff; let us assure them, in the strongest manner possible; let us pray of them to dismiss the persuasion that a frigate is more than a frigate, because she is manned by Yankees; let us convince them if we can that Mr. John Quincy Adams has told us the plain truth; let us prevail upon them, however difficult it may be to do it, not to think that they see a seventy-four coming down upon them when it is only an American frigate ; but, after all is said and done, here are the twelve ships of the line, and a goodly pack of frigates and sloops of war ! Here they are ! And not these " six fr frigates with bits of striped bunting flying at their mast heads," that Mr. CANNING told us of *and made the wise House laugh at* a few years ago! "A loud and general laugh," said the reporter. Ah, ah, my Lords! dear laughs; very costly laughs; very expensive horse laughs, for all of us, but, particularly for your Lordships. Many and many an estate have vanished, and many more will vanish, as the price of that man's jests, and dull jests, too!

In paragraph 31 of his Message, Mr. ADAMS gives us a side-wind hint at some of the uses which the Americans intend to make of this navy of theirs. A part of it is, it seems, employed, at present, on the eastern coast of South America; there is war going on between the Emperor of Brazil and the republic of Buenos Ayres. During this war, the Americans claim to exercise all the *rights of neutrality*. The Emperor of Brazil (always having a good friend from Whitehall at his elbow) has, it seems, put in force our searching and blockading doctrine. But, Mr. Adams says that the United States *will not subscribe to such doctrine*, and that *his naval commanders have resisted it accordingly*. That little sentence is worth a Jew's eye, my Lords. That little sentence tells you what we have to expect, my Lords, if Mr. Canning should

get us into a war with Spain. Then comes down the crest of England: if she submit to this, she comes down, indeed; and, submit she must and will, *unless there be a radical reform in the House of Commons*.

Now, then, let us return to the probabilities of seeing such war. When Mr. ADAMS delivered his Message, he had not heard of our Portuguese affair, and of our threatening the Spaniards with war. The Americans seem to have felt sufficiently hostile without hearing of this Portuguese project of ours. The moment they hear of the probability of a war made upon Spain by us, they will begin to prepare themselves for protecting the Spanish West India Islands against us. I should not wonder if this point had already been settled between Russia and the United States. They are sure to have France with them in such a case. Of this they are quite certain; and we shall have to fight them all, and to pay interest of Debt, dead-weight and poor-rates at the same time. It will not be a war like the last: we shall not have a Dutch and French fleet come over to us and give themselves to us. We shall not have American neutrality. We shall not have Russia with us, and the northern powers either neutral or our allies: we shall have the whole swarm upon us, like all the birds upon the jay to strip him of the plumes which he had stolen from the peacock.

Then shall we call upon ÆOLUS, indeed! Then shall we see how many of the " furies of war" he has in his " leash." We shall see the amount of his " discontented spirits of the age." We shall see, in truth, that he has no resource at all; and that he will be ready to submit to any terms which the enemies may dictate; but, we may also take comfort in reflecting, that, if words will do for us, he will brag just as much after he is beaten as he does at this hour. It is very true, nevertheless, that, if war do not take place now, it will, in all likelihood, take place in a very few years' time; and the strong probability is, that it will be provoked by some flagrant aggression, committed against England by some other power. Therefore, though war be so horrid a thing to contemplate at this moment, *we ought to be prepared for war.* And, my Lords, you, above all other men in this world, ought to think, betimes, of making such preparation. Let Mr. BROUGHAM; let that Cornelius Agrippa's man; let that wild and surprising genius, whom the Irish envy, almost to splitting; let his " *astonishing powers*"; let them, my Lords, be employed to their fullest extent, in amusing those soft pates that can be amused with thundering phrases about the nation appealing to its " *honourable feelings*"; about the nation's " *awakening its mighty soul,*" pronounced with a sort of half hickuping voice, with the mouth three parts open and eyes like the picture of a saint that I have seen holding his hands up towards the crucifix. Yes, yes, my Lords: let this great orator amuse the soft pates with talking about the " re- " sources of war being found in " the *spirit* of the nation"; let

him bleat as long as he pleases about " our burthens *being no- " thing* if the nation be but *true* to " itself." Let him go on with shocking nonsense like this; but, do you, my Lords, put to yourselves this plain, common-sense question: you, my Lords, are no hunters after silk gowns: you have got all the gowns you want; and you have got all the coronets and crests and all the stars and garters amongst you; and, what is a devilish deal better, you have, most of you, got the lands and the villages and the churches and the parks of the spots that your titles are taken from: 'tis not for you, therefore, to talk precious nonsense, nor to listen to precious nonsense, about a nation's " *bear- " ing its burthens, however heavy " they may be, by thinking of its " honour "; by being " true to it- self*"; or by any such ideal means, which are like a Scotch philosopher's dinner, *not tangible:* 'tis for you, my Lords, to put this plain, common-sense question to yourselves: " If it be doubtful " whether our estates can be pre- " served to us even now, without " blowing up the National Debt, " is it possible for us to preserve " those estates, if a war come " upon us before a reduction of " that Debt shall have taken " place? "

That is the question, my Lords, for you to put to yourselves. I think the answer that only a very small portion of common sense would give to that question; and I am not to suppose any of your Lordships destitute of that common sense: I think that the answer which common sense would give to that question, would convince you, in the first place, of the great danger of listening to these loud-talking, vague-talking, loose-talking, wild-talking, bragging men; and, next, that it would convince you, that you ought, with all possible speed, to set about the means of reducing the interest of that Debt; and that, too, upon principles which all the world should say were equitable. The first step, however, is, in my opinion, to regain your natural allies, the great body of the common people, from whom you have alienated yourselves for so many years past, whom you have cast off and taken in their stead the jews, jobbers, loan-mongers, land-screwers, up-start top-boot farmers, and all sorts of reptiles that have crept out of the infernal toad-stool of paper-money. This is the first step; and this is much easier of accomplishment than it would be to get one single farthing out of the Jews, without first having the people with you. Your Lordships will observe that there must be sacrifices somewhere. The system cannot go on as it is in war. The Funds, Dead Weight or the Church: something must give way, or there can be no war any more. Is it not time, then, to consider what it is that shall give way? Spain seems resolved that if she have war we shall be the aggressor upon this occasion. But, do you not see, my Lords; do not you see from the language of the foreign newspapers, that " Late Panic " has proved to the world what our real situation is? Do you not see, that we begin to be looked upon as a party that even a beginner at kicking may try his toe upon? It is impossible, therefore, to avoid war, or, at least, next to impossible to avoid it, for any considerable length of time. I beseech your Lordships to be prepared for it; I beseech you to think of the means of carrying on such war; and, above all things, I beseech you to remember that the affair is yours a great deal more

than it is that of any body else. When I can find time to address another Letter to your Lordships, I may, perhaps, point out in detail that which it is my opinion you ought to do; but, I would have you consider that convulsions do not always give notice of their approach, and again and again I beseech you to observe, that this affair is your own more than it is that of all the rest of the na ion, and that there is, perhaps, no man of that whole nation who would be less, as an individual, affected by it, than would be,

Your Lordships'
Most obedient and
Most humble servant,
WM. COBBETT.

---

## AMERICAN SEEDS.

I HAVE Seeds of FIFTY-TWO sorts of TREES and SHRUBS, which I have received from America, during this last Autumn, and just now. Part of the Trees and Shrubs are *evergreen*, and part *decidnous*. There are, amongst the rest, seeds of the *Magnolia Glauca*, of the *Magnolia Tripetola*, the *Magnolia Grandiflora*, the *Pride of India*, the *Georgia B.rk*, the *Bass Wood*, and, in short, of (I really believe) more rare and fine Trees and Shrubs than is, or is ever likely to be, in the possession of any other man in England, through any other means than mine. My Correspondent has, in person, rummaged the country from Boston to Savannah. If I were to. publish his letters, the readers of them would certainly be tempted to think, that neither he nor I ever had, in our whole lives, thought of any thing else than of getting American Trees and Shrubs into England.——I shall, next week, publish a *List of the Seeds*, and,

H

as far as I am able, on account of the Trees and Shrubs. I shall put up some seeds of each of the 52 sorts, *in a box;* and shall sell the boxes, if any one choose to buy them, at 5*l.*, including box, bags, and every thing. I shall not have *many* to sell : not more, I think, than 20 or 30 ; and I do not offer these for sale with *a view to profit.* The charge will be less than 2*s.* for each sort of seed, and, the portion that there will be of the *Georgia 'Bark,* or the *Pride of India,* is, either of them, worth more than the whole of the *five pounds.* Last year, my Correspondent gave *a dollar* for a single pod of one of these. To gentlemen, who have *hot-beds,* and other such like conveniences, and who have gardeners that *will be doing mischief,* if their masters be so hard-hearted as to give them *nothing new to do,* this collection of seeds is very well worth having. A handful of the seed of either of the *Magnolias* is worth more than the cost of the box.— However, it is my delight to see these things introduced and made common, and therefore, I am repaid in this way. — I have to thank *the Gentlemen at the Custom-House,* for great civility in the landing and other matters connected with these Seeds, which are now come in very nice order.

## AMERICAN BOOKS.

IN 1825 I imported a collection of books, printed in the United States. I wished to have them for my own use, and that of others nearly connected with me, in order, as I then expressed myself, that I might "see what a state brother Jonathan was really in," or, as our poetical Secretary of State for Foreign Affairs would express it, what a state our "*loving daugh-*

*ter*" was in, what she was *aiming at,* and what were really and undoubtedly *her means,* as well in their extent as in their nature. I conceived a project upon the principles of "*free trade*"; that is to say, a project for getting this collection of books *free of cost to myself,* while the books would still come at a reasonable price to any other person in England that might choose to buy them. I imported, therefore, several copies of each work, all of which, or, at least, the far greater part of them, were very soon sold ; and two or three gentlemen, one of whom, a pretty eminent lawyer, has told me, or at least, caused me to be told, that he never had a true view of the state and of the extent of the resources of the United States, until he had an opportunity of examining these books. These, together with other considerations, have induced me to import a fresh parcel of the same works, together with some others, the list and the prices of which are as follows. I give here, with regard to the works imported and advertised in 1825, the same descriptions which I gave in the Register of September 3, in that year. The prices are, now, somewhat lower than they were in 1825, which is chiefly owing to the extinction of a large part of the execrable paper-money on both sides of the water.

I. LAWS OF THE UNITED STATES OF AMERICA. .... Price 10*l.*

I have no copy of this book left. It is a book that every English gentleman ought to have. Treaties are considered as laws in America; accordingly, this collection contains all the treaties that the United States have ever made with any power whatsoever. It also forms, of course, a complete legal history of the country, from the first meeting of delegates to resist the power of the King of England. The book is dear, sovereigns are scarce, and may become scarcer; I am not a bookseller, properly so called; but, if any gentleman, be he who he may, wishes to have a copy of this work, and will write to me to that effect, I will import the work for him, charging him nothing more than the prime cost of the book, the duty which I shall have to pay upon it, and a trifle (nothing more than what is reasonable and real) for freight, insurance and post charges. I have a set myself, and I have no book, the Statutes at large excepted, upon which I set so high a value.

II. OFFICIAL DOCUMENTS, RELATING TO THE LATE WAR, BETWEEN THE UNITED STATES AND GREAT BRITAIN.—One Vol. large 8vo., full bound and lettered, excellent paper, 510 pages . . . . . Price 10s.

Here we have the *real history* of the late war. The book begins with the President (Madison's) Message to the Congress, stating *the complaints* of America against England. Next comes the report of the Committee of Congress, recommending war. Next, the Act of Congress, declaring the war. Next, the *Yeas* and the *Noes* upon the passing of this Act. Next the Proclamation of the President, announcing the war. Then come all the official documents relating to all the transactions and events of the war, by land as well as by sea. And, lastly, the *Treaty of Ghent*, by which the war was, in December 1814, put an end to. This is the real history of that war. Here is no *commentary*; no lying history; garbling and disguising. Here are the facts, as they were, at the time, stated officially, and in the face of all the world.—It is impossible for an Englishman to read this volume without writhing under the disgrace which he feels almost every page perpetuating against his country. I have writhed often enough upon reading these documents. But my anger against JONATHAN has not only been neutralized, but turned into a contrary feeling, when I have reflected on the *consequences* which would have accrued TO US, if Sir JOSEPH YORKE and his compeers, including SIDMOUTH and CASTLEREAGH, could have " deposed James Madison." If they could have done *that*, it would have been better to be a dog than an Englishman. This is a very cruel dilemma to be reduced to; but, reduced to it I am, and so is every Englishman, who is not content to be a slave himself, and to leave his children slaves behind him:—I would, in a more particular manner, recommend this volume to *Blue and Buff*, and to the *Duke of York's* goodly company. They will here see what attends them another time, unless they bestir themselves. The *young* heroes of the Navy, the EDMUND WOODHOUSES, the many HOPE JOHNSONS, the Hon. CHARLES ABBOTTS, the Hon. F. SPENCERS, the WILLIAM PITT CANNINGS, the SAUNDERS DUNDASSES, and the rest of the long list of those *fortunate youths*, who have been *put over the heads of so many thousands*, will here see the sort of stuff that they will have to face; and, if the sight of it should scare any of them into fits, it will be better that this take place now than at a later period. From the moment that the last war began, and even before it began, I, who knew JONATHAN well, most distinctly foretold the general result. I said, that it would be disgraceful to us, and would create a great Navy in America, consisting of the best ships, and ablest and bravest commanders, and the strongest and most active and heroic seamen, that the world had ever seen. When that war began, America had but *six frigates* and some sloops of war. Mr. ' CANNING called them, "half a dozen *fir-* "*frigates*, with bits of striped " bunting flying at their mast- " head." They were not *fir-fri-* gates. They were made of live- oak, locust, black-walnut, cedar and pine, their blocks of occi- dental plane, and their hand-spikes of hickory. There were, how- ever, but *six* of them; but, look, Blue and Buff, without shame, if you can, at what was *done* by those six frigates! There were more than six before that fatal war was over; and, what there is *now* another book will tell.— When, at the close of this vo- lume, I see " GAMBIER, HENRY GOULBURN, and WM. ADAMS," ought I to be surprised at the thing I have read. These famous negotiators gave a " *sine qua* *non,*" and afterwards *abandoned* *every particle of it!* The Ameri- cans answered this "*sine qua* *non,*" by giving that name *to a* *new sloop of war*, just then about to be lanched! This is their laconic and quiet way of doing things. Disgraceful, however, as that peace was, it was *lucky;* for, had the war continued but two years longer, every one of our West India Islands would have been either captured, or in a state of revolt. The Americans were in the full tide of victory in every quarter. PACKENHAM and COCH- RANE were driven in disgrace from before New Orleans, even after the treaty was signed, and JONA- THAN was just getting into fighting order. If any English Minister be still empty enough to think, that that is a people to be insulted with impunity, let him read, in these documents, of the deeds of General Jackson and his *militia-* *army.*

III. CONSTITUTIONS OF THE SE- VERAL STATES OF THE UNITED STATES OF AMERICA. — One Volume duodecimo, full bound and lettered, 410 pages,
Price 6s. 6d.

This is simply a collection of all the *Constitutions of all the* *States* as they *now stand;* and, at the head of these, is the Constitu- tion of the United States.

IV. A GEOGRAPHICAL DESCRIP- TION OF THE UNITED STATES, WITH THE CONTIGUOUS COUN- TRIES, INCLUDING MEXICO AND THE WEST INDIES. WITH THIRTEEN MAPS. — One Oc- tavo Volume, fine paper, very neatly half bound and lettered, 500 pages. — BY JOHN MEL- LISH ............ Price 13s.

This is a work of very great re- search. It arose (as far as it re- lates to the United States) out of an *actual survey* made by Mr. MELLISH, for the purpose of making a great map, many feet square, of that whole dominion. The map was particularly in- tended to mark the exact boun- daries of the several States, and to define, with precision, the limits of lands, located and unlocated. Therefore the map on *that scale* was of no use to me. But this volume (with the present maps) was of great use, containing, as it does, a very well arranged account of the *United States as a whole;* then of every *separate State;* then of the *British American Colonies;* then of the *West India Islands,* English, French, Spanish, Dutch, and Danish. Then of *Mexico and* *Columbia.*—The account of these latter is short; but, as to that of the United States, the several separate States, and the contiguous British possessions of the two Canadas, Nova Scotia, and New Brunswick, the account is most admirable. Limits, extent, soil, climate, timber, other products, waters, population (always distinguishing *free* from *slave*), prices of land and of other things, agriculture, commerce, manufactures, topographical and meteorological tables; in short, every thing that one wants to know about these countries is to be found in this very laborious performance, which I take the liberty to recommend to our Daddies down at Whitehall, in order that they may *see* what, in a short time, they will have to contend with. When the Daddies have read this book *through* (if they ever do such a thing), they will know a little more about our own *colonies* than they now appear *to know*. If the Lord Johns and the Lord Williams and the Lord Charleses could possibly deduct a little time from their *important* pursuits, and apply it to the reading of this book, it would be of great use to us as well as to them. If LORD JOHN RUSSELL, for instance, could, for a while (only for a week) withdraw himself from Mr. Brougham and Peter Doctor Ricardo Macculloch, with whom he is employed in establishing the "*London University*"; if, in short, he were himself to go to school to JOHN MELLISH for a little, previous to his entering on his office of Vice-Chancellor of the London University, I am satisfied, that that seminary would be all the better for it.—At the close of his work, Mr. MELLISH, who died last year, and who was a hard-headed and indefatigable Scotchman, has given us an essay upon Peter Doctor Macculloch's subject, "*polectecal economy*",

and has herein shown us, that *eyes and hands* differ very widely from *brains*. However, even in this part of the work, there are some *tables*, relating to agriculture, commerce and manufactures, which are very interesting.—The Map of the United States, points out the boundaries of all the several States. The other 12 maps, represent the plans of the great cities and towns, their several ports and harbours, and the country round about each.

V. MORSE'S POCKET GAZETTEER OF THE UNITED STATES, WITH A COLOURED MAP; WITH SOME VERY USEFUL TABLES AT THE END, RELATIVE TO THE EXPENSE OF BUILDING SHIPS OF WAR, AND TO OTHER IMPORTANT MATTERS. One Vol. full bound in calf, and lettered, 320 pp. Price 4s. 6d.

This is useful along with the former; for here are all the cities, towns, rivers, counties, and so forth, in *alphabetical order*, with the population, and other things appertaining to each state, county, city, and so forth. It is also called the "*Traveller's Companion*," and must be very useful to persons going to America.

VI. MORSE'S GENERAL GEOGRAPHY. — THE FIRST VOLUME RELATING WHOLLY TO AMERICA; THE OTHER TO THE REST OF THE WORLD. Two large Vols. Octavo, fine paper, full bound in calf and lettered, nearly 900 pages in each volume .. Price 1l. 2s.

This edition is of 1819, which is the last edition. I remembered this Geography of Doctor Morse, which was first published in 1798, while I lived at Philadelphia. I then thought it the best work of the kind that I had ever seen, and, therefore, I have now got a few copies of it.

COMMERCIAL DIGEST. — A Digest REGULATIONS OF ALL THE DIFFERENT FOREIGN NATIONS, WITH WHICH THE UNITED STATES HAVE INTERCOURSE; PREPARED AND PUBLISHED CONFORMABLY TO A RESOLUTION OF THE HOUSE OF REPRESENTATIVES, OF THE 21st JANUARY, 1823. — One large royal Octavo Volume, fine paper, bound in boards, 525 pages ......... Price 17s.

This work proceeded, as its title imports, from a resolution of the House of Representatives. It was prepared under the instructions of the Secretary of State, and was, by him, presented to, and received the sanction of the House, in January, 1824. It contains all the regulations (relating to commerce with America) of Great Britain and Ireland, the kingdom of the Netherlands, France, Sardinia, the Two Sicilies, Russia, Hayti, Chili, Colombia, and Spain. Coming from under such hands, the reader need not be told, that the matter is ably arranged. The detail is full; all the duties, imposed by these several States, on American ships and articles, are particularly stated; so that here the Americans have, in one volume, a view of all the commercial regulations of all the nations that they trade with by treaty. — If our Daddies at Whitehall and Saint Stephens were to treat us to something of this sort, would it not be as well as for them to expend so many tens of thousands a year in the printing of things which never can be of any use to any human being, the paper-maker, printer and trunk-maker excepted?

VIII. DEGRAND'S TARIFF. One Vol. duodecimo, fine paper, neatly half bound, 300 pages. Price 7s. 6d.

account of the commercial regulations of all the foreign countries with which the Americans have commercial intercourse, so this work gives an account of all the commercial regulations of the Americans themselves. First there is a TARIFF OF THE DUTIES, paid in the American ports; then there is a very well arranged digest of all the existing REVENUE LAWS and of the CUSTOM-HOUSE REGULATIONS.—This edition was published only nine months ago; and comes forth sanctioned by the Collector of the Port of Boston. This book seems dear; but, the reader should know, that tables and figures make dear printing.

IX. THE NORTHERN TRAVELLER, CONTAINING THE ROUTES FROM NEW YORK TO NIAGARA, QUEBEC, THE SPRINGS, AND LAKES, WITH DESCRIPTIONS OF THE PRINCIPAL SCENES. WITH PLATES AND MAPS. — One Volume, fine paper, neatly half bound, 213 pages. Price 5s. 6d.

A very pretty travelling book, and very interesting to those who wish to be informed about those stupendous undertakings, the CANALS. Here is one canal 362 miles in length! along two of these canals, produce to the amount of 2,809,432 dollars was carried during the last year. These canals are somewhat different in their uses, from those that our Daddies have made us pay for digging in the Highlands of Scotland! What a scandalous job was this! Here is a canal which unites the Lakes with the North River, into which the canal falls at 145 miles from the City of New York, making, in the whole, a length of 507 English miles. By this canal the Ocean and those fresh-water seas, the Lakes, are joined. This puts Canada, whenever the Americans please, into their hands, and our Daddies are sending out English money and Irish *people*, under Scotch *governors* and *overseers*, in order to make Canada worth *having* to the Americans! Well done, Daddies of Whitehall!

X. THE NATIONAL CALENDAR, AND ANNALS OF THE UNITED STATES, FOR 1824.—One Vol. fine paper, neatly half bound, 280 pages. .... Price 5s. 6d.

This is the American " Red-Book;" but, as they have very few placemen, and no *pensioners*, and no *grantees* and *sinecure* people to cram it full of, they have room for useful matters: for the list of the Congress, for the list of their army and *navy*, specifying the *pay* which the several parties have. Above all things, they have room for their *navy*; and let the reader see what a nutshell this thing, which so cruelly beat big Blue-and-Buff, lies in, with regard to *officers* and to *expense!* We have, I believe, more *Admirals* than they have Commodores (they have no *Admirals*), Captains, Lieutenants and Midshipmen, all put together! The half pay of our navy (or *dead weight* of it) costs us more annually than their whole navy, full pay, half pay, ship-building, dock-yards, and all put together! And (see page 248 and 249 of this CALENDAR) our DEAD-WEIGHT of army and navy, that ALONE costs us about one-third more annually than the whole of their annual expenditure on ALL ACCOUNTS WHATEVER, the ANNUAL INTEREST OF THEIR DEBT INCLUDED! This is the price we pay for our vaunted victories; and no small

part of it for our *beatings*. Let any Englishman read, if he can, without blushing, General Jackson's farewell address (page 469 of the work mentioned 2d in this list); let him there see the brave men, who had quitted their comfortable homes to march three hundred miles in the dead of winter to face invaders of their country; let him see them at the end of four months of constant risk of life, and leaving so many dead behind them, returning home to enjoy, not *half-pay*, to come out of the sweat of a toiling and half-starving people; not to live in luxury, and content with being a " *dead-weight* " upon their country. " Towards you," says the General, " fellow-soldiers, the " most cheering recollections ex- " ist, blended, alas! with regret, " that disease and war should " have ravished from us so many " brave companions. But, the " memory of the cause in which " they perished, and of the virtues " which animated them while " living, must occupy the place " where sorrow would claim to " dwell. Farewell, fellow-soldiers. " The expression of your Ge- " neral's thanks is feeble; but, the " gratitude of a country of free- " men is yours: yours the ap- " plause of an admiring world."— And, away they went, back to their ploughs and hoes and spades! There were no titles, no brevets, no medals, no allowances, no pay, no everlasting " *dead-weight* " of men, women, and children; no taxing of the country, no enslaving it for them: they went back to their homes, again to work, to be free and bold, and did not become *genteel* mumpers, to breed litters of children to be beggars or thieves or forgers, or something or any thing but *workers*. There is an ALMANACK prefixed to this CALENDAR, not crammed up with *birth days* and *prognostics about the weather:* but having its vacant space occupied with things that the people ought to remember. About a quarter part of the days in the year are anniversaries of victory gained by them over " *the British,*" as they call us. Then they do not forget such things as the following :

APRIL 6. American prisoners, confined at Dartmoor, England, fired upon by the British guard. 1815.

JUNE 13. Trinity Sunday. The British, under cover of a flag of truce, entered Wareham, and burnt the stores and shipping. 1814.

—— 25. Outrages of the British at Hampton. 1813.

JULY 25. Great destruction amongst the cattle and poultry, at Portsmouth (Carolina), by about ten thousand of the British. 1813.

Let the reader judge, from this, of the marks and mementos that the people of our Daddies left behind them in this formidable country.—But (page 160 and 161 and forward) look at the NAVY ! Look at the *pay of the sailors;* look at the *distribution of prize-money;* look at *the laws, respecting prize agents;* and then wonder, if you can, at the result of our sea-fights with this people. And, above all things, think of the *manner of promotion;* the *fairness* of it; the skill and zeal and bravery that it is calculated to produce in *all ranks.*

XI. A REPORT TO THE SECRETARY OF WAR OF THE UNITED STATES ON INDIAN AFFAIRS, COMPRISING A NARRATIVE OF A TOUR PERFORMED IN THE SUMMER OF 1820, UNDER A COMMISSION FROM THE PRESIDENT OF THE UNITED STATES, FOR THE PURPOSE OF ASCERTAINING, FOR THE USE OF THE GOVERNMENT, THE ACTUAL STATE OF THE INDIAN TRIBES. Illustrated by a Map of the United States ; ornamented by a correct Portrait of a Pawnee Indian. 1 Vol. 8vo. Bound. Pp. 496.. Price 9s.

The author of this " Report," is the same Dr. MORSE who wrote the above work on Geography. It is an official Report to the Secretary at War. The facts stated are of unquestionable truth ; and when we consider the great learning and diligence and uncommon experience of the author, we must suppose that here is the best account ever yet published of the state, the manners, the propensities, the opinions and the views of the North American Indian tribes. It is a work full of curious and most interesting matter, and the character of the author gives the stamp of truth to every line.

XII. ANNALS OF THE AMERICAN REVOLUTION ; INTERSPERSED WITH NUMEROUS DOCUMENTS AND ANECDOTES ; A SUMMARY ACCOUNT OF THE FIRST SETTLEMENT OF THE COUNTRY AND SOME OF THE PRINCIPAL INDIAN WARS ; TO WHICH IS ADDED AN APPENDIX, CONTAINING A BIOGRAPHY OF THE PRINCIPAL MILITARY OFFICERS WHO WERE INSTRUMENTAL IN ACHIEVING THE INDEPENDENCE. Compiled from authentic Documents. Numerous Plates. 1 Vol. 8vo. bound in leather. Pages 450. By JEDEDIAH MORSE, D. D. ....Price 9s.

Here we have, again, the same Dr. JEDEDIAH MORSE, whom I remember, more than thirty years ago, on his way through Philadelphia to go to Louisiana, for the purpose of collecting materials for making his " Pocket Gazetteer." He was one of the most industrious and indefatigable men that ever lived. He was a Presbyterian parson; but there was no sourness belonging to his character; and he was universally regarded as a man whom nothing upon earth would tempt to put a falsehood upon paper if he knew it. He was, in a great measure, the teacher of America. He explored the whole country in a manner the most minute. He brought the people of one part of the country acquainted with another part of the country. He recorded every thing which he seemed to think would be instructive to posterity; and, though universally respected for so many reasons, the strongest reason of all was his scrupulous adherence to truth, a quality always estimable, always amongst the first; but, the very first of qualities in the author of " *Annals* " of a revolution, in which he himself had acted a part rather conspicuous than otherwise. The Doctor was a republican in grain; but it used to be said of him, that he would rather bend the knee to King GEORGE than tell a lie to please WASHINGTON. I take this opportunity (the only one, probably, that I shall ever have) of paying this tribute to the memory of this most exemplary author.

XIII. HISTORICAL AND TOPOGRAPHICAL SKETCHES OF THE FLORIDAS. — One Vol. 8vo., bound in leather, 226 pages. By JAMES GRANT FORBES... Price 5s. 6d.

This is a very good account of these interesting provinces, which, owing to the folly and the debts of England, the Americans have recently got from Spain. It will be seen how completely these provinces command the *Gulf of Mexico*, and how they render it difficult for us to annoy the American States which lie along the Mississippi and the Ohio. If they, *at Whitehall*, would study this little history of the Floridas, they would be better employed than in grinding new constitutions for Portugal, or in hatching speeches to be blown forth by the breath of ÆOLUS CANNING. What a strange thing, that we should seem to take delight in plucking feeble Spain, and sticking the plumes into the wings of a country, already preparing to spur and to buffet us. But, she is *our daughter*, says wise Mr. Canning!

XIV. FAUNA AMERICANA: BEING A DESCRIPTION OF THE MAMMIFEROUS ANIMALS INHABITING NORTH AMERICA. By RD. HARLAN, M. D. — One Vol., bound in leather, 318 pages ......... Price 11s.

I do not pretend to understand much about this work; but this I can say of it, that if its philosophy be true, that of those great philosophers, Messrs. HUSKISSON and CANNING and Doctors BLACK, BARING and MACCULLOCH, is *directly contrary to the very nature of man.* With this remark, I must leave these our political philosophers and Dr. HARLAN to settle it as they can. Just observing, however, that the Doctor gives this description of the species, *Homo Sapiens:* he says, " They inhabit all parts of the " earth, are omnivorous, disputing " for territory; uniting together " for the express purpose of de- " stroying their own species." There! at him, Æolus! *Fall on* him, *membre du club quatre-vingt neuf!* Tell the philosopher that he lies, and that all men are, by nature, sworn brothers, and want nothing but "*free-trade*" to make them *all winners*.

XV. LETTER FROM THE SECRE-
TARY OF THE TREASURY,
TRANSMITTING STATEMENTS
OF THE COMMERCE AND NA-
VIGATION OF THE UNITED
STATES, DURING THE YEAR
ENDING ON THE 30TH SEPT.
1824.—One Vol. 8vo., bound
in leather, 304 pages.—Price
11s.

Being a public document, and
one put forth by a Government
which stands in no need of lies to
prop itself up, we may rely on the
*truth* of this document; and, at
this time in particular, a very great
importance it is to us. Whitehall
never takes advice but that which
it pays for; and, people in general like to pay for drams or
wines rather than for physic.
Therefore, Whitehall will not, I
dare say, take the trouble to look
at this volume. It will much
rather deal in the speeches of
Æolus, which, perhaps, it has
already paid for with our money.
But, to gentlemen of sense, whatever number there may be of them
left in the country, after the dis-
emboguings of Æolus; to gentlemen who have got *estates*,
above all things, this volume is
most deeply interesting. They
will here discover, pretty quickly,
what a hair-brained membre du
club quatre-vingt neuf it must
have been, to imagine that the
government of the United States;
that that jealous House of Representatives; that that sober and
grave Senate; that that President,
with forty years of experience on
his brow, acquired, too, in all the
courts of Europe; to imagine that
all these were going to be cajoled
out of the great, solid, permanent
interests of their country, by a
prattler about *free-trade*, though

the nobility of England had been
weak enough to give him the
power to begin, at least, to make
ducks and drakes of their fortunes
and their titles: for, what are
those fortunes and those titles, if
the *naval dominion* of England
be lost?

XVI. LAWS OF THE STATE OF
NEW YORK, IN RELATION TO
THE ERIE AND CHAMPLAIN
CANALS, TOGETHER WITH
THE ANNUAL REPORTS OF
THE CANAL COMMISSIONERS,
AND OTHER DOCUMENTS RE-
QUISITE FOR A COMPLETE
HISTORY OF THOSE WORKS.
WITH MAPS, DELINEATING
THE ROUTES OF THE ERIE
AND CHAMPLAIN CANALS, AND
DESIGNATING THE LANDS
THROUGH WHICH THEY PASS.
—Two Vols., Royal Octavo,
in Boards, 1,278 pages. Pub-
lished by the order of an Act
of the Congress. . . . . Price
1l. 18s.

"*Wawst improvements, Ma'am!*"
but, whether really improvements
or not, this is a most prodigious
affair. Here is a canal upwards
of three hundred miles in length,
joining the fresh-water sea to the
salt-water sea. This undertaking
only began to be talked of when
I fled from CASTLEREAGH and
SIDMOUTH in 1817. Observe, it
is the work of the single State of
New York. These volumes contain an account of all the acts,
regulations, proceedings, disburse-
ments and profits, relating to this
great concern. And, here is a
model for all Governments and all
public bodies who may have undertakings of a like nature in view
or in hand.

XVII. TRAVELS IN THE CENTRAL
PORTIONS OF THE MISSISSIPPI
VALLEY; COMPRISING OBSER-

VARIOUS ON ITS MINERAL GEOGRAPHY, INTERNAL RESOURCES AND ABORIGINAL POPULATION. (Performed under the sanction of Government, in the year 1821.)—One Vol., in boards; with Maps and Plates, 459 pages.—By HENRY R. SCHOOLCRAFT, U.S. I.A. . . . . . . . . . Price 10s.

This work relates to a very interesting part of the world. It is the Mississippi Valley of which we here have an account. That Valley will, one day or other, be separated from the sea-board of the United States; that is to say, if ever there should be, again, Ministers in England more fit to manage its great concerns than any dozen washerwomen that I could pick up at Kensington. This work, also, is of great authenticity; the author was employed by the Government of the United States; Dr. MORSE speaks of the book in his Indian Report, and with great approbation. It is a work full of very curious matter, relating to natural philosophy as well as to branches of knowledge, which the statesman ought to desire to possess.

XVIH. TOUR ROUND HAWAII. A JOURNAL OF A TOUR ROUND HAWAII, THE LARGEST OF THE SANDWICH ISLANDS.—One Vol., half-bound, 264 pages. —By a DEPUTATION from the Mission on those Islands.— With Plates . . . Price 5s. 6d.

This is a very curious work of its kind, and the plates represent objects of singular curiosity. It has been published by the Boston-Missionaries; and coming thus, from the " Saint," grafted on the Yankee, it has, doubtless, something false about it, either in matter or in motive; but, if only one-half of it be true, or a tenth part, it is very well worth reading;

as, however, I will not, on any account, vouch for the truth of even a tenth part of it, I leave the public to do as they like, without any recommendation of mine.—How my Correspondent came to send it me, I cannot think. He has, however, sent me several copies; and, as the true and great principle of that "free-trade," which Messrs. Huskisson and Canning are now establishing in my native land, is, if I rightly understand it, "buy the devil, sell the devil," I offer, merely offer, this work for sale.

The amount of a complete set of the above works (exclusive of the last) is 11l. 14s. 3d.; and, I shall sell a whole set for 10l. 10s.

## TO THE
## ROMAN CATHOLIC CLERGY
### of the City of Dublin.

*Dearly Beloved Brethren,*

AMONG the Resolutions of the Aggregate Meeting held on Tuesday 19th December last, in Clarendon - street Chapel, as published in " The Irishman " newspaper, of the 20th, I find the following extraordinary one : " Moved by Francis M'Donnell Esq. : Seconded by D. O'Connell Esq."

" Resolved—That the Trea-" surer of the Old Catholic Rent " be authorized to lend to Michael " Staunton, Esq., the sum of 500l. " at legal interest, upon sufficient " security for the repayment " thereof ; and that it be referred " to the Committee of Thirty-one, " to ascertain and decide on the " sufficiency of such security."

Moreover it is read in the same paper, of the 29th of said month, "That the 13 or " 14000l. (of the Catholic Rent) " has not been let out at usurious " interest to a Noble Lord ;—it is

" vested in Government securi-
" ties." O! what scrutiny, what
searching these thirty-one usurers
had in the borrower's substance!
They certainly are the curse
mentioned in the *Psalm* cviii.,
*May the usurer search all his
substance.* Now we have a clew
to understand their insatiable
thirst these three years for
Catholic Rent. You should no
more trust any man when he
becomes a usurer, than you would
a mad dog. The wretch sells his
God for usury and for gain; he
would readily sell you or even
his country and religion, if he
could only meet a purchaser.

How fortunate would these
thirty-one usurers find themselves,
if the Catholics of Ireland continue to pour into their hands
100,000*l.* a year, of Catholic
Rent! Then we would have in
every paper flowery speeches on
Civil and Religious Liberty; then
should be endowed schools in all
parishes of the Island; Missionaries sent to convert the benighted Indians; Maynooth College
redeemed from the diabolical
oaths required of the students on
entrance, and from the periodical
inquisition of Orange Commissioners. But the usurers must
take care to subtract 16 or 1700*l.*
yearly from the fund to forward
their own missions; that is, 1000*l.*
yearly for advertising their proceedings, 200*l.* for the rent of
their debating-house, 100*l.* for the
porter or door-keeper, and 300*l.*
a year for their London Agent.
That 1000*l.* per annum is a
pretty drawback, at the onset,
from the Rent. Why not apply
the residue to the original purposes—Schools and Missionaries?
why apply it, contrary to the law
of God and of the Catholic
Church, to usurious loans?

We must all die; we are but travellers in this vale of tears; whether
we depart this year, or during the
next, is of little moment either to
ourselves or to society, if we find
a happy death, in friendship with
our Redeemer. But alas! one of
these thirty-one notorious usurers,
these sharp scrutineers of the
borrower's substance, has appeared under his loads of usury,
and unsent for, in the presence of
the all-seeing Judge: six days
after they insulted the Most High,
by passing their heretical usurious
Resolution in his temple, before
the Holy of Holies in the tabernacle, he was killed in a duel—
in the actual commission of mortal sin, giving no sign of com-
punction: he did not say, " Christ
have mercy on my soul;" nor
even cast a contrite look towards
heaven; no, no, he only muttered
*"I am hit, I am afraid mor-
tally;"* and thus, alas! he falls
into eternity! What a melancholy doom: a young man just
fresh from his usurious speeches
in the house of God, after his
sharp and keen searching into
the poor borrower's substance,
thus snatched away, whilst he
was bent on the destruction of the
other unfortunate man, to the
presence of his Judge, for to
undergo the searching and scrutiny of his own accounts!

You are aware, that to charge
interest, or any increase, that is,
any thing more than the capital or
sum lent, is usury; and that usury
is a crime detested in both Testaments, and condemned more than
any other sin against the Creed or
Commandments, by the sacred
canons of the Catholic Church.
Usurers are excluded from the
tabernacle and mountain of God,
in *Psalm* xiv.; and declared, in
*Ezekiel* xviii. 18, to be the future
prey of eternal death; not only the
increase, but even the mere *hope* of
more than the sum lent, is forbid
den by our blessed Redeemer,

*Luke* vi. 35. It would be endless to give all the canons that were passed during every age, down from the time of the apostles to the present, over all Christendom, against usurers and usury; but still the desperate malady seems to be more virulent than ever it was, particularly in these islands, where it threatens nothing less than the total annihilation of the human race.

The general council of Lateran, under Alex. III., *an.* 1179, excommunicates notorious usurers during their life, and deprives them of Christian burial, if they die in that sin; moreover, she suspends, *ipso facto*, any Clergyman who would receive their offering or afford to them (usurers) Christian burial; Lib. 5, Tit. 19, c. 3, *Quia in omnibus.*

The General Council of Lyons, under Gregory X., *an.* 1273, decrees, under pain of heaven's malediction, that the above constitution of the Council of Lateran " be inviolably observed;" decreeing, moreover, *suspension, ipso facto,* against all Archbishops and Bishops, *excommunication* against singular personages of minor dignity, and *interdict, ipso facto,* against all convents and colleges, or assemblages of men and women who should practise or tolerate the practice of usury : Lib. 5, Tit. 5, C. *Usurarum voraginem.* in 6°.

The General Council of Viene, under Clement V. *an.* 1312, decrees an excommunication against the superiors and governesses of monasteries or convents, and against all notaries and clerks, who should write, or make others to write, the bonds or instruments of the usurious loans; and who should not rescind them, if already written, though confirmed by an oath; decreeing, moreover, that *if any person fall into that error that he assert obstinately that usury is not sin, he be punished as a heretic:* Clem. Lib. 5, Tit. 5, C. *Ex gravi.* These canons, and several others, can be seen at length in the little book which I wrote on usury, and which is in the hands of several in Dublin.

Though you are aware, My beloved Brethren, that the lenders for gain sake or for interest, called by whatever name, and their abettors, are *heretics*, under more interdicts, excommunications, suspensions, maledictions, than any other class of heretics, this scandalous Resolution, passed in one of your chapels, under the eyes of your Bishop, passes by unnoticed.

*Banks, debt, usury,* invented in London in the year 1694, by the Prince of Orange, (see Cobbett's valuable Reformation, par. 404,) for the mere purpose of crushing the Church of Christ, is now producing bitter fruits for all classes of society. The unchristian Jewish infection did not penetrate into Ireland until within these forty years : having been always branded, as rapine or theft, with infamy and detestation by your pious predecessors, it sought private shelter in the miser's cursed house, and behind the avaricious trafficker's counter—never, never appearing in open day without mask or palliatives; but, in our miserable days, throwing off the mask, it walks abroad with lofty front, under the garb of virtue : a usurious Meeting must choose the house of God himself—a house that should be the house of prayers, of alms, and of free loans (*Luke* vi. 35), to manage their usurious contracts, to authorise thirty of the most wise sharks and sharpers amongst them to "ascer- " tain and decide on the measure " of security which the poor bor- " rower can give." Are these persons Catholics? are they the descendants of the ancient O'Connels, MacDonnells, O'Loughlans, O'Briens, who covered the fields of Erin with convents for the pious friars and nuns, with hospitals for the orphans, widows, the aged, the sick, and the travellers? They lent at usury to Christ, in the person of the hungry, the naked, the sick, and the captive (*Matt.* xxv. 35), who has not failed to pay them the usury a hundred fold in the land of the living. They never authorised thirty sharpers over the poor borrower's securities, but pious inspectors to ascertain his want and poverty. We read in no history that they were such staunch patriots, such sanguine liberators, or advocates of civil and religious liberty over all the globe as their spurious degenerate descendants. Nor do we read that famine, nakedness, pestilence, then raged in any corner of Ireland, with such ghastly, terrific features, as they do now in the usurious city of Dublin, the theatre of all oratory and patriotism. The multiplicity of paupers occasioned by these usurers and bankrupts forced the inhabitants to erect, five or six years ago, a *poor-house.* It seems that the finances were inadequate for their support, as the "poor-house box" was carried about through the city, from door to door, seeking any offals of the kitchen, whether potatoes, meat, greens, vegetables, or musty broth; the gatherings were altogether thrown into this box or chest, about five feet long, three broad, and four feet high, which was carried in a cart drawn by a mule—not unlike the machine with which the streets are sprinkled with water in the summer season. The collections of this machine was to be the mess of the unfortunate poor: a mess, I am sure, that could hardly be touched by hungry dogs. When I saw this machine, two years ago, on its daily visits through the city, the exhalations from its rotten sides and musty contents would indeed make you vomit. What, then, must be the state of the poor in yonder asylum who were to make it their food! As that was the case then, when there was no noise about want and distress, what was their deplorable misery this last season, when all the Dublin papers were filled with heart-rending accounts of fever and famine.

PROTEUS, in order to shake off the chains, and regain his liberty, assumed various shapes and forms; now became a filthy hog, then a fierce lion, again a gloomy tyger and a scaly dragon; and sometimes a flame of fire (Virgil, Georg. 4, 408); but after all his shifting and changes, he was obliged to resolve himself into his natural form at the hour of sleep. So the usurers, trying to evade the chains of hell fire pronounced against them in both Testaments, assume all the shapes and palliatives in the world: for the scriptural word usury they substitute the novel terms *funds, debentures, omniums, consols, interest, securities.* The Dublin usurers "lent not, they say, the 13 or 14,000*l.* at usurious interest to a noble Lord;—it is vested in Government *securities.*" See what mild term they give to their unchristian, Jewish usury. Securities indeed! no poor or distressed man, none but the man of securities shall partake of their loans; it is not to poverty, but to the securities they lend; where is the charity then, where the Christian religion? Did Christ lend at usury for securities; or the Apostles or the Saints? In the name of common sense, what difference is there between lending to an individual and to the

Government? There is on both sides a loan made *in hope of gain.* Nay, the public lender is on better footing than the private one: for whilst the loan is on the one side exposed to danger from the insolvency and villany of the borrower, there is hardly any risk on the other: until the whole country is corroded by taxes and reduced to national bankruptcy, the public usurer draws his yearly interest, and can regain his capital, whenever he pleases, by taking it from the hands of Government, or by selling it to other usurers. Though usurers palliate their horrid practice under the name Securities, or any other names, it retains the nature and dreadful effects of Debt and yearly interest, on the part of the impoverished Government. If usurers were not so numerous these fifty years, there would not have been such extravagant wars, no taxation, no sinecures, no standing armies, no dead weight. When we reflect that security-men, or usurers, gave rise to all these curses, and then turn our thoughts to the millions of the brave Irish and Britons, who fell by sudden, unprovided death in the field of Mars abroad; on the famine and distress of all classes in both Islands; on all the burnings, murders, robberies and other black outrages already committed in Ireland by a famished population; on the floggings, executions, and banishments that naturally followed; on the same tragical scenes that are now making their appearance in England; and lastly, when we look to the prospects just opening to our view— the scourges, the convulsions, must we not say that no term in any language is sufficiently odious for usurers or security men? are they not murderers of mankind, devourers of society, agents from hell?

My beloved Brethren, Your Catholic Board assumes all the hideous features of usury : they lend at interest or security to an individual 500*l.*, and to the public or Government 13 or 14,000*l.* This they do not deny; they are therefore notorious usurers. Will you admit the 30 sharks to Communion and to Christian burial, if they die in that sin? Remember that the priest, who should afford Christian burial to notorious usurers, dying in their sin, or who should accept their offerings, incurs, *ipso facto,* an excommunication and suspension, and that by attempting to offer up Mass, under any of these two Censures, *a jure,* he incurs, moreover, the horrid guilt of Irregularity. Have you received any new revelation, or discovered any warrant from heaven, or any new decree of the Catholic Church, by which all the existing passages of Scripture, and all the decrees of the Catholic Church may be set aside? If an angel from heaven should preach a gospel contrary to that which you have learned, you ought not to believe him : the law of God abideth for ever; neither one particle nor one iota can be taken from it, until the end of time. Is that miserable time, foretold by the Apostle, 2 *Tim.* iv. 3, arrived, when they will not in Dublin endure *sound doctrine, but will heap together according to their own desires, doctors having itching ears?* If any nation or people advance so far in wickedness, as to set aside the law of God and the Catholic Truth, and to insist on having elastic, temporising teachers, according to their own desires; nothing less than some terrific scourge from heaven cures the wicked race of infidels. Though God is patient and long-suffering, not wishing for the death of the sinner, he comes like a thief in the night; one day with the Lord, is as a thousand years, and a thousand years as one day.

My dearly beloved Brethren, whether these usurers obey you, or not, announce to them the will of God; receive not their impious offerings; let not the notorious sinners pollute with their usurious Resolutions your sacred temples, or insult God in your tabernacle I am certain, from the general character for piety and learning of the Reverend Superior of Clarendon - street Chapel, that he would no more admit the Meetings of usurers in his Chapel, than he would those of robbers, had he foreseen what was to happen. When a desperate infection, such as usury, spreads at every side, it is extremely hard for the Pastor of souls to pass through without partaking, by silence or inadvertence, of the contagion. May Providence grant you grace to do his will upon earth, that you may reap your reward in heaven; may He inspire you to pray for your humble servant,

            J. O'CALLAGHAN,
            R. C. PRIEST.

*Kensington, Jan.* 10, 1827.

TO
JOHN LAWLESS, ESQ.
DUBLIN.

My DEAR SIR,
    YOUR justice and fortitude this time past, have endeared you to every man who is a friend to Ireland, and erected for you a monument of fame more lasting than brass. You have a melancholy warning in the fall of your neighbour: had he persevered in the same career which he ran for 25 years, the future historian would rank him amongst the greatest men that Ireland ever bred. Let those who stand take care that they do not fall; *let them work out their salvation with fear and trembling*, and constantly pray for the uplifting grace of God. You see the rock upon which many great and good men have been wrecked—*avarice*, the rock of perdition and root of all evils; beware of it. Attempts will be now made to shift the care and responsibility of the Catholic Rent to other unblemished shoulders: have nothing to do with it; leave it to the original managers. Neither be a dabbler in usury, nor allow your paper to become the abettor or vehicle of usurious proceedings. When the usurers in every corner of both islands, and of America too, read in your journal of the 20th ult., the *interest* resolution of the Aggregate Meeting of the Roman Catholics of all Ireland, they will imagine that that cursed Jewish practice is the Catholic doctrine, and they will therefore be fastened more and more in the mire. Charity, therefore, and justice to your own and to their souls, and to the souls of future generations, require of you to give insertion also to the above feeble opposition of your most humble and most respectful servant,*

            J. O'CALLAGHAN,
            R. C. PRIEST.

*Kensington, Jan.* 10, 1826.

* Every Paper that published the Resolutions will, I hope, insert the foregoing also.

For want of room, the insertion of the Letter of "A TORY" on "THE THREATENED WAR" is postponed till next week.

# COBBETT'S WEEKLY REGISTER.

**VOL. 61.—No. 5.]   LONDON, SATURDAY, JAN. 27, 1827.   [*Price 6d.*

*Published every Saturday Morning, at Seven o'Clock.*

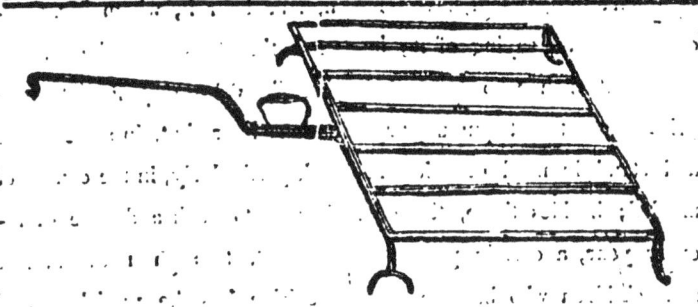

" They will not laugh by-and-by! They will not laugh, when there
" remain neither *rents* nor *tithes*; and, mind, to preserve *either* of these,
" there must be some measures of a *decided assignat* character, unless
" there be a reform of the Parliament, for reduce establishments much,
" and reduce *debt at all*, they cannot without a *reform!* The landlords
" and parsons have, therefore, to choose of these three : *Reform; Assig-
" nats;* or *loss of rents and tithes:* and I would defy the Devil himself,
" if he were Premier, to prevent one of these.' I would recommend the
" first; but, really, it is much more, now, the affair of the landlords and
" parsons than it is that of any body else."—REGISTER, *of May* 1822.

## CORN BILL.

### TO THE DISTRESSED MANUFACTURERS.

*Kensington, 24th Jan. 1827.*

MY FRIENDS,

THE subject of the Corn Bill being one of the first which the Ministers have pledged themselves to bring before the Parliament when it shall assemble next month, it may be useful to you, or, at least, you may like to have my opinions relative to such measure, before the measure be brought forward; and, I hate to anxious a desire to do you good, or, even, to give you any trifling pleasure, that I set about this task with singularly great satisfaction. To be sure, it would seem to be next to impossible for me to lay down any principle, or to use any argument, which has not been laid

Printed and Published by WILLIAM COBBETT, No. 183, Fleet-street.
[ENTERED AT STATIONERS' HALL.]

down or used by me heretofore. But, besides that the circumstances in which a thing is said, have some effect upon the saying of it; besides that men who have their private avocations to pursue, forget and stand in need of being reminded; besides these, there is, every year, a certain portion of mere children who become boys, and of boys who become thinking young men. Therefore, repetition, in such a case, and in a work like mine, is no more to be found fault with than are new editions of spelling-books or catechisms.

Before, however, I enter upon the subject of the Corn Bill itself, let me request your attention to some of the strange things which we now behold. In some parts of the north, particularly, and in several parts of the kingdom, theft and robbery are become so common, that, at last, men seem to begin to doubt whether society will not be dissolved, even in this way. In the meanwhile, severity of punishment has gone on increasing; the gaols enlarging; new sorts of prisons; new sorts of prison-discipline; and, let those nations hear it, whom Mr. CANNING threatens with the " *moral force*," as he calls it; let those nations hear that, in some cases, and, particularly, in the county of Surrey, to such a degree of refinement, to such mathematical precision has the punishment of criminals been reduced, that the prisoners are actually WEIGHED, at certain periods, in order to ascertain the effect which the punishments, of various sorts, have upon their bodies! In my last *Register* I mentioned, that the hellish Scotch writers, those pests of England and disgrace to all honest Scotchmen; those detested wretches, had published a proposition for selling the dead bodies of paupers from the poor-house, to the surgeons for dissection, in order to lighten the burthen of the poor-rates! To be sure, the monstrous wretch who put this upon paper, did not put his name; but, it was published in the London newspapers, and I have not perceived that it has any where met with reprobation. The malefactor who robs on the highway, who breaks a house, who commits any felony short of that of *murder;* short of that of deliberate, wilful murder; any criminal short of this receives from the law no infliction of disgrace upon his dead body: it is only the wilful murderer and the traitor, whose body the law consigns to the hands of the dissector. But, here is a monster, or, rather, a band of monsters, who, in the capital of that country, in which the courts established by ALFRED still exist; here are a band of monsters to propose to sell to the surgeons for dissection, the bodies of those, who, after enduring all the various degrees of anguish which are found on the several steps to the poor-house, die in that poor-house, not only without having committed crime; but, possibly, having been reduced to poverty, having actually been brought into that very poor-house in consequence of their forbear-

ance to enrich themselves at the expense of others, in consequence of their generosity, and, perhaps, in consequence, even, of their tenderness, their compassion and their charity.

Why, my friends, did our ancestors ever dream that England would come to this pass? That lying devil, ANNA BRODIE, is endeavouring to make the public believe, that I am a Roman Catholic, and the woman, drunk or sober, has the audacity to assert, distinctly to assert, that I have had my daughters educated as Roman Catholics, and that they took letters of recommendation to the chief of the Jesuits at Saint Omer's, last year! In the Wife of Bath's words, I say of her: " All this thou sayest, and all thou sayest is lies." ANNA has recently appeared two or three times in the Court of King's Bench, and, in one case, particularly, for her infamous slanders respecting the private affairs of a family. ANNA is surprised, I dare say, that she, " notwithstanding her coverture," is thus handled by judges and juries; but, ANNA should remember the observation of SWIFT, namely, " That when women de-" part from the softness, the mild-" ness, the modesty belonging to " their sex; when they talk loudly, " impudently, and clench their " fists and stamp their feet, they " ought to be considered as bul-" lying men, and ought to be " kicked down stairs accordingly"; and, if I recollect rightly, the Dean goes on very wisely to observe, that to look upon such women in any other light, and to bestow on them any other sort of treatment, would be to do gross injustice to those women who conduct themselves in a manner suitable to their sex. Remember this now, Anna: you have got a Doctor of Divinity for your husband, and he is rector (that is to say, *ruler of* the souls) of the parish of East Bourne, in Sussex. Ask your Doctor of Divinity whether the Doctor of Divinity that I have just quoted is not right. Whether he will be man

enough to tell you what he thinks, is more than I can say; but, I shall be at East Bourne sometime in the month of May, and then I will take the liberty to ask the Doctor how he makes shift to get on with one who has been so very foul-tongued with me, and so monstrous a liar into the bargain.

But, though I am a Protestant, and all whom I have had the educating of are Protestants, it would be not only to discover great ignorance, but great baseness, too, if I were not to recollect, and to remind my readers, also, that, when the Roman Catholic religion was the religion of England, a wretch, or set of wretches, who should have proposed, who should even have talked of, condemning people to be dissected, because they died after having lived some time upon alms, would have been torn to atoms. Oh, no! such thoughts as these never entered men's minds until these *enlightened* days of funding and free-trade! Nor did it ever before occur to the mind of man, that a King of England would issue instructions to the Archbishops and Bishops to cause collections to be made from door to door for such of his labouring subjects as were in distress. The law of the land was, for pretty nearly a thousand years, that the poor were to be maintained out of the tithes and other endowments of the Church. Since that, the law of the land has been, and it is now, that every indigent person shall have a suitable maintenance out of *the land.* The law *is,* also, that men shall *not beg*; that they shall be *punished for begging*; that to beg is a *crime;* and, while there are boards stuck up about almost all the parishes in England, forbidding begging, stating the punishment which begging is to receive; while these notices every where stare us in the face, the parish-officers and others, even in some cases with the beadles to precede them, are actually going a begging from door to door! It may be worth your knowing, that this begging work has met

with but a very cold reception in London and Westminster. The begging agents have been distinctly told, in many, many places, that money would not be grudged to the *poor manufacturers,* but that it was not easy to perceive why the tradesmen of London should give their money to pay poor-rates *due from the land-owners in the North.* .

It is impossible for any man in his senses to believe, that a state of things, that can have engendered the above-mentioned novelties, should be of permanent duration. It must have an end; and that end may be not very distant. We find the distress, as it is called, to extend itself all over the kingdom. At Sheffield, at Paisley and Glasgow: all over Yorkshire and Lancashire, in Nottinghamshire and in Norfolk: everywhere do we hear of distress; and, excepting in the lying columns of newspapers, no man can see the smallest chance of a change for the better. There are some persons, however, who are of such a hoping disposition, that they are always expecting that some change for the better will take place, without ever being able to give the smallest reason for such an expectation. Some poet says that hope sticks to us to the last; and hope is a very good thing; but, hoping and *wishing* are things very different from each other. For there to be hope, there must be some *reason* as a foundation. A man may wish with or without reason, as I may wish that I could fly over the moon; and this sort of wishing it is, that assumes the name of hope in the politicians to whom I have alluded. These hopers rely, amongst other things, upon the effects of a *change in the Corn Laws*; it is worth while, therefore, for us to consider, before this grand expected measure can be adopted, what reason there is for believing that such change, if it take place, will have a tendency to remove the present distress.

First, however, is it certain that any change at all will be made e in the Corn Laws; next, what sort of change is it likely to be, if it take place; and, if a change take place, such as to admit even of a free importation of corn, what effect will that produce with regard to those who are now suffering distress?

Some people think, that, after all the talk about it, no alteration at all in the Corn-Laws will take place. The subject must be brought forward, and there must and will be a great deal of discussion. The result may be, a Bill passed in one house and rejected in the other; but, I do not think that this will be the result; because then all the blame, coming from a very numerous class of persons, would rest distinctly and visibly upon the Lords; for though, as to all practical purposes, the two Houses are one and the same, all the world does not see that: the forms indicate the contrary: and forms, in cases like this, pass for substances. I, therefore, think, that a Bill will pass, and that an alteration will be made.

As to the sort of alteration ; or, rather, the degree, I suppose that it will consist of a little and a very little lowering of the price of English wheat, at which foreign wheat will be admitted. There will be a monstrous deal said about remunerating prices: poor WELLS HALL will seem to have been conjured up from the grave. All his doctrines will be repeated ; and we shall hear, from one end of the country to the other, of the necessity of giving to the land such prices as shall enable it to pay the tithes, the poor-rates, the county-rates; and some other burthens, which, as the land-people are always asserting, "*fall exclusively upon the land*," which phrase is, I verily believe, the foolishest that ever issued from the mouth or dropped from the pen of mortal man. It is curious to observe, that this notion of tithes, county-rates, and poor-rates falling *exclusively* upon the land, is a thing wholly new. Tithes have existed in England about twelve hundred years; and, until since the time of Pitt, and during his time, there never was such an idea in existence as that of the tithes coming out, finally, of the pocket of the farmer ; or, as he is now-a-days called, the "*agriculturist,*" which accursed hard word seems to have been made for the express purpose of rendering this new batch of doctrines even more harsh and disgusting than it otherwise would be. I wonder that it does not come into the head of my neighbour Tucker, the tallow-chandler, that the tax upon his candles falls *exclusively upon him.* Mr. Tucker is not such a fool : he knows very well that those who buy his candles pay the tax and not he; and if he were a landlord or a farmer, would not he say that those who eat his wheat paid the tithe, in the same manner that those who burn his candles pay the tax ? Would not he say, that, as all the candle burners in England pay all the tax upon candles, so all the wheat eaters in England pay the tithes upon all the wheat that is grown in England ! This is what he would say; because this is what would be said by every man of common sense. It is hardly possible to believe that any one would be so foolish or so perverse as to say that there is a difference in the two cases, because the tithe can be taken in kind, while the tax is taken in money; for, in the first place, the tithe is taken in money in nineteen cases out of every twenty; and, in the next place, if the candle-maker were to give one candle out of ten to the tax-gatherer, instead of giving him one penny out of ten on the price of the candles, where would the difference be? Seeing, therefore, that no candle-maker, no maltster, no currier, no tobacco-man, no cotton-printer; seeing that no creature upon earth who has to pay taxes upon the article that he makes for sale; seeing that no one of these has ever been beast enough to pretend, that the tax falls *exclusively upon him*, upon what ground is it, I wish to know, that the land-people believe, or affect to believe, that the tithes fall exclusively upon them?

Precisely the same argument is applicable to the poor-rates, the road-rates, the county-rates, and all those charges, if there be any others, which the land-people pretend fall exclusively upon them. When a pot of beer is put into the hands of the drinker, and he is called upon for six-pence in the way of payment, there is, perhaps, a penny for barley, a halfpenny for hops: all the rest is for tax on malt, tax on beer, tax on the iron of the barrel, tax on the barrel-staves very likely, tax on the house that the beer is sold in, tax on the brew-house, tax on the harness of the horses that draw out the beer, tax on the landlord's house that sells the beer, tax on his permission to sell it, tax on the candles that he burns in serving it out, tax on the fire that he burns to warm the drinkers, tax on the tawdry gown of the dirty wench that brings it up out of the cellar, tax on his windows that give him light when he does not burn candles, tax on the deal-boards that make the benches for the drinkers to sit upon; in short, the whole is tax, all but three half-pence at most, and this, too, you will observe, exclusive of all the farmer's taxes upon the barley and all the tithe which he has paid or yielded on that barley, and also exclusive of both tithe and tax which the hop-grower has paid upon the hops. The truth is, that if there were no tax at all upon the barley after it left the farmer, and through the whole progress of the malt to the lips of the drinker, beer of the present average strength would come to the drinker's lips for even less than three half-pence a pot; and, if it were such good stuff as that, a pottle of which I intend to send to Doctor BLACK one of these days, and which pottle, if he drink it in the course of two hours, I pledge myself shall give him ten hours of the soundest sleep that he ever had in his life; even a pot of such stuff as this would not cost three-pence. Very well, then: if the beer drinker, when he gives a sixpence for a pot of beer, gives fourpence half-penny for tax, and three half-pence for beer, what would he say to the publican who should affect to believe that all the tax upon beer fell exclusively upon the publicans? And, if this would be a gross absurdity; if it would be a piece of ignorance or impudence unparalleled in the publican, what is it, I pray, in the farmer, to pretend that the tithes, the poor-rates, and so forth, fall exclusively upon him? When he comes with his bushel of wheat, and asks six and sixpence a bushel for it, which is much about what he gets at the present time, " what is that for?" says the miller: " why, you get forty of these " bushels to an acre, and you only " scratch the ground about a little " and throw in a few seeds!"— " Aye," says the farmer, " but I have rent to pay."—" Yes," says the other, " what, thirty shillings " an acre, and you ask two hun- " dred and sixty shillings for the " wheat of an acre!"—" Well," says the farmer, " but you do not consider that the parson has taken away a tenth part of my wheat in tithes ; that I have paid poor-rates to the amount of thirty or forty shillings an acre ; that I have paid road-rates, county-rates ; that I have paid tax upon my leather, tax upon my iron, tax upon my windows, tax upon the rotten cotton that my wife and daughters wear; (and, rotten cottons they must have, or they will plague me worse than the couch-grass) ; tax upon my malt; tax upon my own fat after it is turned into candles ; that I have paid all the taxes that all my labourers pay, and a part of all the taxes that my blacksmith and wheelwright have paid ; so that you see, my friend, that my bushel of wheat, though I sell it for six and sixpence, leaves me devilish little for myself."—" I see it clear enough," answers the other, " and, therefore, here is the six and six-pence, which I shall make the baker pay me, and which he will make the weaver, the spinner, the shoemaker, the blacksmith, the hod-man, or the chimney-sweeper, pay him : this is all true ; but, pray, my good honest farmer, never let me hear you again pretend that the tithes, poor-rates, road-rates, and so forth, ' *fall exclusively upon the land !* ' "

After this, I will not insult you, my good friends, by saying another word upon this part of the subject. It must, now, be clear to you, if it were not before, that, out of a certain place, which, for reasons easier to be understood than safe to explain ; out of that certain place, a man ought to be regarded as a born idiot, or possessed of idiotism acquired by infinite pains, to be capable of being persuaded, that the land bears any burthen exclusively ; to be capable of being persuaded that any sum of money or any portion of produce taken from the owner or occupier ; that the amount of these do not distribute themselves throughout the community, and finally fall in exact and due proportions upon all the consumers of all the produce of the land. The pretence, therefore, that the land bears exclusive burthens is wholly groundless; and, the notion is, as I said before, one that never entered into the minds of our forefathers. Poverty and misery have always a tendency to bereave men of their sober senses; and, particularly, of their sense of fair-dealing and of probity. The funding system has, at last, bereft the land people of their senses. They see their estates melting away; and they find out this pretended cause for it; namely, that they do not get a remunerating price for their produce. It is strange that it never entered into their heads to carry this principle of theirs further than the wheat-stack, or, at least, the corn-stack. The corn does not form above a third or a fourth part; nay, not a fourth part, in amount, of the produce of the land. The baker is a poor thing, compared to the butcher, not to mention the clothier and the linen-draper, and divers other persons who sell us the produce of the land. Get upon a hill half a mile high, and look round you: see what the corn land is in extent, compared with the woods and the pastures of various descriptions. It is, comparatively, but a little patch here and a little patch there. How happens it, then, that the wiseacres of remunerating prices never say a word about the price of *wood* or of *meat*? Why do they not call for a wood-bill or a meat-bill? For, observe, they fall in price as the corn falls in price: not caused by the fall of the corn; but falling from the same cause that makes the corn fall. Poor WEBB HALL was strangely puzzled, when, at a time when he was bellowing for a Corn-Bill that would drive the bonded corn back to foreign countries; he was strangely puzzled when he was asked, how the price of *coppice-wood* came to fall, even in a greater degree than that of the corn had fallen, when it was notorious that coppice-wood had never been imported, even to the amount of one hundred of lime-kiln faggots. This puzzled the head of poor WEBB exceedingly. He was, at last, the subject of general laughter : but, those who laugh at others, do not always take care to avoid being laughed at themselves; and, accordingly, we shall now hear as much bleating about remunerating prices as ever; and, some miserable attempt will be made to pacify those who are crying for an alteration in the Corn Laws, and, at the same time, *to keep up the price of corn.*

This, however; this last, namely, to keep up the price of corn, which means, if it have any sense at all in it, keeping up the price of all the produce of the land; this last is impossible to be effected, without driving the gold out of the country; without repealing the Small-note Bill passed last year; without again returning to Bank-restriction, or without producing another " Late Panic "; without one or the other of these, it is as impossible to make corn dear in England, or *to keep it any length of time even at the present price*; this is as impossible as it is for Mr. CANNING to utter one single sentence of common sense upon any of these subjects. There would appear to be a sort of pre-destinated blindness upon this subject. Noblemen, commonly called Lords, in a lump, are, as a sort of fashionable talk, generally represented as men that never think at all. I will not apply the term which is commonly applied to them ; and, as far as my very limited personal knowledge of them has gone, I must confess that I have discovered nothing in them to justify this vulgar opinion. But, at any-rate, they have sense enough to be trusted to walk about without leaders; they do not, when they ride out, plunge into rivers, or go down chalk-pits; they can be trusted to cut their own victuals at dinner without danger of laying open their cheeks with the knife, or running the fork into their eyes. One may suppose all this, to be sure, without implying any great degree of elevation in the scale of intellect. Yet, it implies humanity : what my American philosopher calls the species *homo sapiens*. Let it be on the lowest scale, if the disputant will insist upon it (but which, observe, I myself by no means admit); let it be on a scale but one degree above that class of negroes who do not know what causes the smart when they are cut with a knife : that is quite enough for the present purpose ; quite enough to excite astonishment in me, that any one nobleman in England should not see that it is impossible to keep up the price of corn without producing one or other of the effects which I have enumerated at the beginning of this paragraph.

They have seen the corn continue steadily to fall in price from the year 1819 to the middle of 1822, while they most carefully excluded grain of every description from the country. They have seen a Bill passed that caused an increase of the paper-money, and they have seen the wheat rise gradually with that increase from an average of about four and sixpence to an average of about nine shillings a bushel. They have seen "Late Panic" come, and the paper drawn, in part, in again, accompanied by a law, which is finally to have the effect of Peel's Bill ; and, in the course of twelve months, they have seen the wheat come down from nine shillings a bushel to six and sixpence a bushel. They have seen a crop of corn so short (this last year, taking the crop altogether) that the government thought itself justified in opening the ports for some sorts of grain, merely by an order of the King in council. They must know that when other sorts of grain are scarce or short in crop, wheat is applied in numerous cases so as to supply the place of those other sorts of grain. They must, therefore, know that wheat would have been dearer this year than last year, according to all ordinary rules and calculations : yet, they actually see that it is cheaper by one-fourth, at the least. Between harvest and Christmas is the time when wheat is, generally, and, indeed, always, at a lower price than at any other time of the year. Yet, their Lordships have seen that the wheat was at fifty-seven shillings and seven-pence a quarter on the twelfth of August last; and, that, last Saturday, the price was fifty-three shillings and ten-pence, it being to be borne in mind, too, when we are comparing the prices of this year with the prices of about a year ago, that the new measure makes a difference of about two shillings upon a quarter of wheat, supposing the price to be about fifty-six shillings the quarter; so, at this time, the price of wheat, according to the old measure, is, according to the average return, about fifty-two shillings the quarter; and, it is equally true that, at one time, within the last eighteen months or thereabouts, only just before "Late Panic," it was between seventy and eighty shillings a quarter.

Now, my friends, I ask if it be possible for any of the species of the *homo-sapiens*; any creature rational enough to be set up by the side of a table with an edged instrument in one hand and a pointed one in t'other hand, who has been viewing all these changes, not to perceive, that the Corn Bill, which, with regard to wheat, has been equally in force during the whole of the time; I ask if it be possible that any creature fit to be intrusted with those instruments in its hands, can want the capacity of perceiving, that it is not the Corn Bill that is the great cause affecting prices; and that it can fail to perceive that the *main* cause, and the only cause worth the landlord's thinking about, is the *paper-money*? If you do think that this be possible (and I have a great opinion of your judgment in such cases), then no more of your edge-tools, say I. Great, blunt silver forks for your life, with a bit of bread in the other hand, and let them lick up their dishes like the beastly

French, wiping round their chaps with the remnant of their bread, and then stick that into their mouths as a finish. Oh! by heavens, no more English knives and forks! no more English joints of meat; nothing that wants cutting; nothing that cannot be torn to pieces with the hands or pinched off with the fingers; these latter were made before forks, and, in God's name, let them have them and have nothing. else, who can now stand up and bawl like Stentor for a " *Corn Bill to give them remunerating prices* " !

Well, then, respect for our " pastors and masters," decent reverence for our " betters," must, my friends, make us presume that we shall never, any more, hear such abominable nonsense come from their lips. Nevertheless, it must be allowed, that the introduction of foreign corn would, *at this time*, somewhat lower the price; and, therefore, a strong endeavour will be made to prevent it being introduced. If foreign corn had been introduced in July

1822, it would not have lowered the price one single penny per bushel. In short, it would not have been brought in, for it was selling as cheap here at that time, as it was, on an average, selling upon the continent, taking the quality and the expenses of importation into view. If Peel's Bill had gone into full effect, corn would have been at as low a price here as it would have been in France. That Bill has now been, in effect, RE-ENACTED. The law now stands just as it stood in 1821. At that time, the law was suffered to go on towards coming into full effect, which period of full effect was the month of May 1823; but, in July 1822, nine months before the period for the Bill going into full effect, the Bill was, as to its most material parts, repealed. That repeal, however, though it sent up prices, produced "Late " Panic." The snails at Whitehall, feeling the effects of " Late Pa- " nic," just as snails do the approach of hot lime, drew in their horns: they saw that one-pound notes were the devil, and they enacted that one - pound notes should cease in three years. One year of the time will have passed on the fifth day of April next: we have only had nine months of the three years yet; but, these nine months have brought down the wheat, even in a season of scarcity, one-fourth lower than it was before the re-enactment of Peel's Bill took place. It is notorious: it is a fact, that even the silver-fork gentry must be acquainted with, that the far greater part of the currency, in almost every county in the kingdom, consists of one-pound notes. Go to any farmer in Kent, Sussex, Hampshire, Wiltshire, any where: ask him how he thinks he should get on if the one-pound notes were to cease to circulate. He will tell you directly that he could not go on at all: he will tell you that it is absolute madness to think of it.

- Therefore, my friends, let them do what they please. about the Corn Bill, corn must, if they keep the Paper-Bill in force, come down to the price of the corn in France; and, lower price than that of French corn at *this time*, because, to supply the place of the one-pound notes; gold must be brought from other countries, and amongst the rest, from France; and that will cause a falling in the price of French corn. The difficulty of the landowners, that is to say, of our law-makers, is this: if they repeal the Paper-Bill which they passed last year, without, at the same time, making a Bank restriction, they produce another "Late Panic." Bank restriction is, in other words, an issue of *assignats*, two prices in the market, and a total blowing up that way. Another "Late Panic" I need not describe the effect of: he that does not, as to this, recollect the past, and anticipate the future, is not fit to be trusted, even with a blunt silver fork. There remains, then, nothing for these landholders to do but to let the thing go on as it is going; to let the one-pound notes cease to exist; to reduce the corn in price, so that a bushel of wheat shall sell for about three and six-pence; and then, the landowners may go, take a last kiss of their domains and bid. them adieu for ever! It must be confessed, my friends, that this is a pretty pickle to be in, and might well bring a very rational creature to be unfit for the use of edge and pointed tools; but, you and I, at any rate, have the consolation of re-flecting, that no part of this diffi-culty of these our betters is at all ascribable to us. We have be-sought them, time and often, to make provision against this day of danger. A million and a half of us, in 1817, prayed to them, implored them as if we were beg-ging for an alms, to adopt mea-sures for the prevention of this danger. They turned a deaf ear to our prayers, they scouted our implorings, they called us design-ing and seditious, and they enact-ed that the Secretaries of State should send to dungeons those of us whom they might think proper

to suspect; to dungeons, there to be kept from the sight, if they chose, of relations, friends, or as-sociates, and there to be deprived of the use of pen, ink and paper, and of the use of any book except such as our keepers might choose to allow us to read. While, there-fore, we view the pickle in which they are now placed, if we refrain from exulting at their trouble and their peril, if we, at last, begin to feel compassion for them, and that we shall feel, after all (for some of them, at least), if they enforce the law which they last enacted; if we thus feel (and I have no objection to any one feeling thus), let us always remember that their suffering will not be ascribable to us; and let us always remind them, that, if they had, in 1817, listened to our humble and dutiful prayers, instead of enacting that a dungeon might be our lot, they never would have seen the present day of trouble, of doubt, of fear, of anxiety and of real danger. For my own part, I have no de-sire to add wormwood to the bit-

K

terness of their mess; but, I must remind them that, when we met on Portsdown Hill, to beseech them to provide for our safety and their own, they had provided troops of yeomanry-cavalry, mounted, ready to surround us, with swords by their sides and carabines loaded with bullets. Let the landowners, who were then our bitterest enemies, now read the petition signed on Portsdown Hill, on that day; let them only read that petition, and that is the utmost stretch of that revenge which is sought for by

Your faithful Friend,

WM. COBBETT.

---

### THE CABINET.

—

I TAKE the following paragraph from the *Morning Chronicle*, the Editor of which says that he took it from the *Dublin Evening Post*.

"POLITICAL CHANGES.—Notwith-
"standing the sneer of *The Times*,
"we can, we think, confidently
"state, that the Earl of Liverpool's
"health will not allow him much
"longer to remain in office; and it

"is equally certain, that *Lord West-
"morland* and *Mr. Canning cannot*
"continue to sit together at the same
"Council Board. We may add, and
"we regret to be obliged to do so,
"that *Mr. Robinson continues to*
"*press his resignation.* Upon these
"facts, we think, the reader may
"*implicitly rely.* On the other hand,
"we are sorry, at the same time, to
"be obliged to state, that *Mr. Can-*
"*ning's health has declined so much,*
"that his friends fear he will not be
"able to support the labour of the
"Session."

Now, besides that it is an odd sort of route for news of this kind to take, going from London to Dublin and then back again; besides this, here is rather too much to swallow at once; and I would advise my readers not to swallow even the smallest part of it; for, here goes, at one single smack, a Prime Minister, a Lord Privy Seal, a Secretary of State, and a Chancellor of the Exchequer. This is too much to swallow; but, I must inform my readers that I have heard of stories of this kind, especially as relating to Lord Westmoreland and Mr. Canning; that is to say, I have heard it through the newspapers, who have been talking about this ever since the sort of half-declaration-of-war against Spain. If the news be true, which I neither believe nor disbelieve, however; but, if it be true, I should suppose Lord WESTMORELAND to be a man of very tenacious, or adhering disposition; or, rather, perhaps, I should say, of a very affectionate disposition; that is, I mean, having a strong affection for, an unalterable attachment to, his estate; a parental fondness for the square acres, the trees, underwoods, pastures, corn-fields, parks, orchards, gardens and parterres, by no means forgetting the deer and those precious commodities, the hares, pheasants and partridges, adding thereunto, with singular consistency, the foxes which devour them. In short, if it be impossible, as this Irishman assures us it is, as he bids us "implicitly believe," that my Lord WESTMORELAND can sit any longer at the same council-board with Mr. CANNING, it is a strong argument for my believing that his Lordship

has formed a firm resolution still to have a board to sit at in his own mansion house, which, upon my honour and soul I think it is likely he would not, if the policy, developed, even in the speech printed by RIDGWAY as of Mr. CANNING's editing, were adopted and acted upon by the Government of England. That policy appears to me to be little short of the fruit of insanity or of something very much like it. According to that policy, we are to have all the hazards of war and none of its benefits: we are to risk every thing, and be sure to gain nothing. Above all things, we are to act upon principles which no English jacobin or one that has been called a jacobin, has ever attempted to preach or to justify.—What a pretty figure do we make in the world at this moment! Whole bales of the Minister's corrected speech, shipped to Paris to be distributed in order to remove the impression created by the newspaper speech! One of the French papers observes that the public mind in England had been changed by my first Letter to Mr. CANNING. Nothing was ever more true than this. The truth is in the mouth of every body; but, the pride that I should naturally feel at bearing such power truly ascribed to me, is, in this case, smothered by the shame which it makes me feel for my country. What! an English Minister, one of the King's principal Secretaries of State, edite and publish a pamphlet eating his words, or, at the very least, exposing himself to that imputation! An English Minister sending, or winking at the sending, parcels of that pamphlet in order to quiet foreign nations! This is something new in our history; something upon a perfect level, however, with all the projects of constitution-making and of free trade that we have, of late, been compelled to witness. When I think of these things, I am the more disposed to believe that there is *some* ground, more or less, for the rumour about some of these

changes in the ministry. I do not wholly agree; and, in some things, I wholly disagree, with my correspondent whose letter I shall by-and-by insert, and who signs himself "A TORY"; but, there are parts of his letter very well worthy of great attention; and, I do verily believe, that a great part of the Members of both Houses of Parliament, and, particularly, the Lords, will be found to concur in most of the sentiments of that letter. To get into a war at this time; even to be placed in a state of likelihood to be at war, is what any wise Minister would have avoided. Here are quite difficulties enough at home. Mr. Canning would have found quite enough to do to accomplish his wish of getting " a piece of gold " into every man's pocket," and " *a fowl into every man's pot,*" which latter is absolutely not to be accomplished without a general robbing of hen-roosts. How the devil the fowl got into his head, I cannot imagine. It is precisely the idea of a Sussex poacher; whose motto is "*fleck or feather*," and, into the pot it goes. He never either broils, fries, or roasts. Into the paste and then into the pot. Mr. CANNING would have found quite enough to do in effecting his project for having "a lofty mountain of paper money, the base of which should be irrigated with gold," which, though it discovered, no doubt, a great extent of knowledge in matters of agriculture, was a thing not easily practised in matters of finance. Mr. CANNING would have found quite enough to do in redeeming his pledge of "never again returning "to Bank restriction." Many other things would have required his attention, without getting into a war, at the very best a one-sided war, all out-going and no in-coming, for the sole purpose of enabling a party in Portugal to force a new-fangled constitution down the throats of at least a very large part of the people, including, as is agreed on all hands, the great body of the clergy, who, of whatever description they may be,

have never been found the most docile in swallowing things which they do not like. We have *no news* from Portugal. If there were news at all favourable to us, we should hear it, fast enough. It seems to be agreed on all hands, that there is a large Spanish army on the confines of Portugal. Now, suppose Sussex (look at the map, reader) to be in a state of civil war, one party being called *smugglers*, and t'other party *fair-traders;* suppose Kent, Surrey, and Hampshire, well backed up by six or eight other such counties, to be all for the smugglers, and to have drawn an army round Sussex from Havant to Rye, coming up, in the middle, to Godstone, and along round upon the edge of Sussex through Kent. Suppose this army to be, as I said before, for the smuggling party: suppose it not to *invade* Sussex; not to step a foot over the boundary lines. Oh, by no means! but, to stand there to let the smuggling party take refuge in Kent, Surrey or Hampshire, if necessary, and to prevent, most effectually, the fair-traders from taking such refuge, or, if they sought such refuge, to take them and lay them by the heels. Suppose that to be the case; you then have a pretty correct view of the state of our concern in Portugal; and it seems to me quite improbable that we should succeed in establishing this new constitution in Portugal; and, at the very least, it must cost us immense sums of money to effect that which, as far as we know to the contrary, might be injurious to us after it was effected.—Now, it does seem very likely that some of the Members of the Cabinet may have seen this matter in the light in which I see it; and, if they have, it is possible, and even probable, that some change may take place in that Cabinet; for, it is very clear, that Mr. CANNING is pledged to the project: his reputation for the remainder of his life, and his character as a statesman for ever, depends, in a great degree, upon the result of this, which

I deem one of the wildest projects that ever entered into the head of mortal man. As to my opinion of him, the "*mountain of paper, irrigated with gold at the base*"; the "*fowl in the pot*"; the "*setting the question at rest for ever*"; the "*British mother*" and the "*American daughter*"; the "*half a dozen fir frigates with bits of striped bunting at their mast heads*": these, together with many other sallies of the same description, not forgetting "*the revered and ruptured Ogden,*" the "low, *degraded crew*" of Reformers and the "*making a stand against democratical encroachment,*" when the wicked democrats wanted to produce at the bar proofs of the selling of a seat: these and many other things of the same sort have long ago marked, and fixed in my mind, the character of Mr. CANNING as a statesman: but, I am but one man: I and my readers are many thousands, to be sure, and reflecting thousands too; but, in a comparison of numbers, we are nothing to the mass; but, even with that mass, he is destroyed for ever in point of character as a statesman, if he fail in this undertaking; and fail he will, I verily believe.

---

## AMERICAN SEEDS.

---

SINCE last week, I have received news of the arrival of the ship *Columbia* from New York, which has ten or twelve sorts of seeds, some of them very rare, which I have not, as yet, in my possession. The ship was off Plymouth on Monday last, and is, possibly, now in the river. This will make a great addition to the number of sorts of seeds, a list of the whole of which shall be inserted in my next. I think I can say with truth that I now possess a larger collection of fine trees and shrubs (or, rather the seed of them) than ever was before possessed by any man in England at one time.

## THE MARKETS.

---

IN answer to such Correspondents who have complained of the non-insertion of the accounts of the MARKETS in the last *Register,* I have to observe that I have received from the Commissioners of Stamps, through the Solicitor to that Board, an intimation that there have been certain articles published in the Register, which, being deemed articles of "*public news or intelligence,*" will, if continued to be published in the Register, expose me to the penalties of the Act in that case made and provided. I have not yet ascertained of what description the articles alluded to are; but, until I am able to ascertain that, I must leave out every thing which can possibly, as far as my judgment goes, come within the meaning of the prohibition contained in the Act. An account of the state of the markets may, possibly, be meant : I have, therefore, left them out for the present, being extremely anxious to avoid any transgression of the law.

# THE THREATENED WAR.

———

THE exercise of the duty of every citizen to prevent a war, especially a war threatening dreadful consequences, requires neither apology or explanation.

Mr. Canning has menaced his country with this calamity ever since he last came into power; and now he calculates upon the aid of a " tremendous power," the assistance of all the discontented spirits throughout Europe, that is, that the jacobins of every state will rise in rebellion against the governments they live under, and co-operate with us, a co-operation which now avowedly we will accept and rely upon. If thirty years' experience has been lost upon Mr. Canning, it is necessary to undeceive him: if he will re-enact and republish in the English Parliament, the jacobin Decree of the French Convention on the 19th of November, 1792, granting assistance and fraternity to every people desirous of throwing off their existing government, his memory should be recalled to the consequences which experience have made history.

About the time that celebrated Decree was passed, several deputations from political societies in England and other countries, went to the bar of the French Convention, and presented addresses congratulating the French on their emancipation, and assuring them that millions of the countrymen of these addressers, panted for an opportunity also to break their chains. The alarm spread in England that the population was moving on to a revolution, the Whig party split, and one half of it went over to Mr. Pitt, to support him in resisting the revolutionary mania. The nation was in a state of fever, agitation, and alarm. Already we had recalled our Ambassador from France, and had manifested unequivocal marks of a spirit hostile to the French Revolution. War was apprehended between the two countries; but the French Conversion, then, like Mr. Canning now, boasted that England dared not make an attack, as the English people would revolt, and join the standard of liberty. So fully did they calculate on the aid which " the holy duty of insurrection" would afford them, not only among the English, but the Germans, and the other nations of Europe, that directions were given to enclose the Rights of Man in canisters, translated into suitable languages, that they might be fired into the enemies' lines in the confidence revolt would instantly follow the knowledge of oppression. What was the result ? Not a man deserted the standard of his country! The English royalists trembled for the trial; but not one English bayonet wavered in the face of the enemy. The war had the effect of crushing jacobin principles in England, and Mr. Pitt was accused (it was the ground of the most loud and general of the accusations by the jacobins in Britain) of having made war, for the sole purpose of smo-thering the rising spirit of liberty in England, an object in which it was said he too fatally succeeded. In no part of Europe did French principles assist the French arms during that war. The moment a nation entered upon a foreign war, domestic dissension disappeared, either suppressed, ashamed, or superseded by nationality.

Upon other and more recent occasions this important truth was proved. Rebellious as a great part of the Irish were, they never joined the French. This is the opinion in France. When the French appeared at Bantry Bay, they complained of the want of even a manifestation in their favour. General Humbert marched over a great part of Ireland with a French force, yet none but a very few ragamuffins came to him, rather as he said for what they could pilfer, than to fight under his standard. Read the deplorable accounts of General Moore and his officers, complaining that the Spaniards gave them no sup-

port, but treated the English unkindly, though they came to fight,
not for political principles, on
which there might have been a
difference of opinion, but for the
independence of Spain. The Duke
of Wellington, during some of his
first campaigns, made the same
complaints, till he was advised
to follow the example of the
French in that respect, by publicly
pretending the natives were most
friendly, however annoying in
reality might be their conduct.
Our French subjects in Canada
could not be seduced by republicanism, but fought most gallantly
on our side. Read the history of
the same hopes of domestic assistance from opposite principles.
What was the fate of the French
royalists at Toulon and LaVendee
when assisted by the English?
Many more instances might be
given; but they shall be closed
with the very recent and applicable one. Three years ago, when
the French first entered Spain
under the Duke of Angouleme,
Savory, LaBemande, and others

of Buonaparte's officers, calculated, like Mr. Canning and Dan-
ton and Robespierre, that liberal
principles would seduce the
French troops from their allegiance. They dressed themselves
in the French republican uniform,
with the insignia of the Corsican
Emperor, and exposed their persons almost to the very grasp of
their advancing countrymen, persuaded liberal principles and
glorious recollections would make
them throw down their arms, and
embrace as brothers. Yet, not a
man faltered. The French troops
directed their shot against their
countrymen, the friends of liberty,
with as much sincerity as ever
they had done against Austrians
or Prussians. And has the French
Government, like Mr. Canning,
forgotten the history of these important events!

Suppose a war takes place,
England and Portugal against
Spain and France, for no other
war requiring serious consideration can occur. England will of
course have all the Portuguese

liberals on her side. They are evidently the minority of the people, and the least powerful of the two parties in Portugal, excepting only that they have the Government in their hands, and are supported by England. But the English are disliked by the Portuguese, notwithstanding all favours, and most of all are they disliked by the liberals. We cannot forget with what eagerness the English officers were dismissed from the Portuguese army a dozen years ago, as soon as the Portuguese became their own masters. In relying on the support of the liberals in Portugal, on account of political principles, we should be relying on a rotten staff. In Spain, Mr. Canning admits the majority of the people are in favour of the present most illiberal, unwise, deplorable system; and whether he admits it or not, the fact is so. The English are still more odious to the Spaniards than to the Portuguese. The ruling faction hate them as heretics, and they as well as the liberals, but

more particularly the liberals, hate them for having separated the American Colonies from Spain. Of all the liberals and illiberals in Europe, the English are hated the most by the Spanish liberals, among whom commercial men take a strong lead.

Where, then, are we to find this " tremendous power " which is to shake the Holly Alliance and every throne in Europe? Not certainly in France. There the ascendancy of a military spirit would make any war popular; but a war against England would of all others be the most popular. The last peace left England so proud and powerful, France so humbled and helpless, that shame and envy have engendered in Frenchmen's breasts a deeper hatred of England than ever before existed; a more blind and furious passion of revenge, which some may call a noble zeal to revive their country's glory. Republicans and royalists, bigots and Bonapartists, all Frenchmen, will unite eagerly to humble England

and exalt France. The Abbe Sieyes and some few old dotards of the revolution may indeed turn up their eyes, and sighing, lament that England should be embroiled for enforcing liberal principles in Portugal; but not a pen, much less a musket, will be lifted in France to assist her. Where, then, is this " tremendous power" to be found ? Not in Germany, divided into small states, or into great military monarchies. Not in Italy, where 20,000 Austrians would sit down upon the imbecile revolutionists like a night mare. So much for the " tremendous power," respecting which, it would have been prudent to be silent. While left to remain in the shade, in the back ground, it would have been a mystery to excite doubts and fears in the French Govern- ment; but the moment the light of day is thrown upon it by in- vestigation, its terrors vanish. By no step have the Bourbons strengthened their position more than by the war they have made on the liberals in Spain. Mercy

on us ! That this lesson should have been thrown away upon Mr. Canning!—May he become sen- sible of the truth without attempt- ing another experiment, pregnant as it would be with calamity to his country. If it led to a general war, as it would do if France em- barked in it; if we had all Europe, as we should have, against us, ex- cept Portugal, which neither could nor would give much assist- ance, and which, at any rate, we could not long hold, what could be the consequence but loss and disgrace? The governments of the continent would fight against us with all their heart, which they never did under Buonaparte. France would take the Nether- lands, Spain would take Portugal, Prussia Hanover; and Russia and Austria would find ample equivalents in Germany, Italy, Poland and Turkey. From the proud and powerful eminence on which Lord Castlereagh placed us, Mr. Canning would tumble us down to the condition which Buo- naparte ordered; and England would have nothing to do with the continent.—Aye, but there is the new world! Oh! yes; the new world!! It would be on our side; it must be thrown into the scales in weighing the balance of power in Europe! Indeed! Why all America, the United States excepted, could not render so much assistance in a war in Europe as an English nobleman or gentleman occasionally has done. While the South American States could draw from us loans which were sent out in our manufactured goods, all went on swimmingly. But now that the folly of such loans is felt in England, the South American States and our manufactures, from the same cause, are sinking into poverty and distress. And, for the United States,—they would probably pick a quarrel in the hour of our difficulties, that they might ravish from us the object nearest their heart, the Canadas. On whatever grounds we began the war in 1793, all the world felt that, in 1812, our cause was that of liberty, and of national independence. Yet the United States attacked us, attacked us when our danger was supposed to be so great that her success was certain; attacked us when every friend to the liberties of the world prayed for our success; attacked us for the selfish object of plundering us of the Canadas. And it is on the new world and the liberals of the old world we are to rely for aid in a war against Europe in arms! And this reliance was proclaimed by our leading statesman, nay, it was cheered by an unanimous Parliament! Has Providence confounded men's reason to show the world how highly it can exalt, and suddenly humble a nation?

So much for the " tremendous power " abroad; what is to be done with it at home? Is the Government to rely for support in the war on the disaffected, and to receive coldly the counsels of the loyal, which certainly will be given against such an enterprise? The disaffected already see, in this measure, great financial difficulties, producing revolutions in property, which will produce revolutions in political institutions. The disaffected are as eager for this war, as they were eager in opposing that of 1793, and for the same reason. The one frustrated their views, the other facilitates them. The late reduction of interest in the Funds, produced prodigious agitation and discontent in private circles, among many well disposed persons; yet what would be such trifling occurrences compared with a suspension of the payment of the dividends till the peace!— But this has been better described in the Weekly Register, than it can be here.

So much for "the tremendous power;" so much for the revival of jacobinism, and rehatching of jacobins. We shall soon be without allies, and soon be without money. Then every thing must be sacrificed for the national safety, and all property must be laid open, given up as far as

occasion requires to Government. Discontent will occasion severe laws, the suspension of the Habeas Corpus, and of the constitution. And then it will be found that we were only bound by treaty to protect the integral independence of Portugal, without regard to her laws, constitution, or form of government. If indeed we were bound to these, it was to the ancient institutions of that country, not to the new fangled constitution of modern fashion. And why not have allowed the ancient institutions to remain? That would have been our easiest course. But the sneers of the Whigs had effect, and something different from what Lord Castlereagh did, must be done. Say what they will, it is evident Sir Charles Stewart was sent to Lisbon, thence to Brazil, and back again to Lisbon, to establish a constitution on "liberal principles." It was to be shown that England had a new, a different Government, a Government acting in compliance with "the spirit of the age; " and the new American States, with the liberals all over the world, were to be conciliated. It was with ancient Portugal that England prospered; but, indeed, with the new principles of free trade our ancient alliance could not exist, though so highly praised by Mr. Canning, the champion of free trade. That alliance was founded on prohibition and monopoly. Portugal nearly monopolised the English wine market, and England nearly monopolised the Portuguese market for manufactured goods. As the Corn Laws must be repealed to make way for free trade; so probably Portugal must have free institutions, to make way for free trade also. Free trade will annihilate the advantages of the ancient commercial connexion between England and Portugal. The Portuguese, no doubt, foresee the effects of Mr. Huskisson's efforts to open a free trade with France, by lowering the duties on French silks, wines, &c. At the moment we are going to war to preserve our commercial connexion with Portugal; at the very same moment we are enforcing free trade, which must annihilate the value of that connexion. There is no proof, nay, there is no pretence, that Spain, or any

other power, intends to invade, much less to seize, or conquer, any part of Portugal. We therefore have no right, by treaty, to move. If the Portuguese quarrel among themselves about their constitution, what is that to us? Are we " to interfere in the internal concerns of other nations; " to commit so monstrous a breach of public law as this, against which, with reference to France, the Whigs so loudly exclaimed every night in Parliament, thirty years ago? It was said, Mr. Pitt sent to the Dutch Government, in 1793, begging them to solicit assistance from England, to protect Holland against the French; and that, upon the request being made by the Dutch, the guards, and other troops, were sent with as much expedition and eclat as they are now sending to Lisbon. And there is every appearance that, on the present occasion, the English Government has sent to the Portuguese Ministry, requesting them to require us to send military aid. Military aid to protect Portugal, we trust; only to protect Portugal; not to invade Spain. That will produce a general war in Portugal. Let the English army and the English navy combat the Portuguese who love their ancient institutions.

Let them crush the majority, that a minority may force their countrymen to wear a piece of English manufacture, called a free constitution. This is not exactly consistent with the principles of free trade, to be sure; but it will be a harmless work compared with a war against Spain and France.

Ever since Mr. Canning came last into power, he has betrayed symptoms of warlike designs. Mr. Hume and the Whigs had worried the ministry to reduce the army to the lowest ebb, and yet they cried, Lower, lower still. They were not satisfied. When Mr. Canning came into power, the same ministers increased the army, and then Mr. Hume and the Whigs were satisfied. *Why*, does not appear. Whether there was a secret understanding, that liberal principles were soon to be set up, and fought for, we know not. But, however inconsistent and unaccountable this conduct of the Whigs might appear, it was nothing compared with the conduct of the Tories in power. They sit in the same Cabinet, and, if it be true, that they unanimously agree to call into action all the jacobins of Europe, to effect revolutions in established governments, they apostatize from all the political principles of their lives; they virtually condemn all their political actions during the last thirty years, and constitute themselves a committee of public safety. In nothing does the brilliancy of Mr. Canning's genius shine so brightly, as in effecting this astonishing change; for it can only have been his persuasive powers that could have effected it. It cannot be a sordid love of lucre, an unprincipled love of power, a readiness to sacrifice country, rather than sacrifice place. No! Tories are honourable, disinterested patriots, who would sacrifice their " lives and fortunes," rather than countenance the revolutionary jacobins of the age; but unfortunately, on the present occasion, those in power must be weak, though honest, men, easily deluded by the fascinations of the magician who is placed so high in power. He has avowed himself ready to become the leader of the political incendiaries throughout Europe, thus filling the station from which Buonaparte fell, and standing confessed the successor of that person whom Mr. Pitt called " the Child and Champion of Jacobinism. "

A TORY.

16 *Dec.* 1826.

# COBBETT'S WEEKLY REGISTER.

Vol. 61.—No. 6.]  LONDON, SATURDAY, Feb. 3, 1827.  [*Price 6d.*

*Published every Saturday Morning, at Seven o'Clock.*

" Had I, Sir, been in your place, the Ministers never should have heard
" my voice, the professed object of which is to *protect the farmer*, but
" the real tendency of which must be, if it have any effect at all, to *keep*
" *up the amount of the taxes*.  Law cannot give you price any more
" than it can give you sunshine and showers.  That peace does not and
" cannot make any material difference permanently, in the price of corn,
" has been proved by me, as clearly as daylight.  The only end which
" this Corn Bill will answer you is, after having deceived you for some
" time, to expose you along with the other owners and occupiers of land,
" to be regarded as monopolizers, and to be justly detested, accordingly."
—Letter to the Daddy, in *Register*, *May* 14, 1814.

TO

## MR. HUSKISSON,

### On his Project for Free-Trade in Corn.

*Kensington, 31st Jan. 1827.*

Sir,

I suppose that you begin to feel the comforting and cheering effects of the two thousand pounds a-year, which the last Parliament voted you, in addition to your salary, for having employed your surprising genius in demolishing two or three hundred Acts of Parliament passed by our ancestors. This addition to your already enormous salary must make you outrageously zealous in the cause of that "*free-trade;*" for the promoting of which you got these two thousand pounds a-year of our money; of the money of this miserable people, thousands upon

L

Printed and Published by William Cobbett, No. 183, Fleet-street.
[ENTERED AT STATIONERS' HALL.]

thousands of whom have now, confessedly, neither victuals to eat nor roofs to cover them, while you are wallowing in wealth and luxury, attended by troops of menials and lolling in coaches or on sofas. For you to be thus distinguished from, to be thus raised above, to be thus set over, the crowds of men in the common, or rather, the lower rank of life in which you were born; for you to be thus favoured, there ought to have been *something done by you*, proving to all the world, manifesting to all the world without any inquiry at all, that you possessed capacity superior to that of men in general, at the least, and that you had performed some service or other to your country, which men in general were either unable or unwilling to perform.

Let us see a little, then, what you have done to entitle you to the good things which this Government and Parliament have heaped upon you. Until very lately, you were never heard of but as a mere underling in office,

moving along in the old style, gently upwards to higher and higher emolument, just stopping at one time to secure twelve hundred a-year in a pension to yourself, and six hundred a-year in a pension to your wife, in case you should die before her. Thus you have jogged on, cheek by jowl with John King, Charles Long and others of that stamp; but, within these two years, you have figured in a new line. You have broken through the barricadoes of the paths of the old Whitehall people: you have found out the secret of "*free-trade*," in contradiction to all the principles and maxims which have governed our ancestors from the days of King John to the days of King George. When Selden was writing his " Mare Clausum," in answer to Grotius's " Mare Liber," and, when Needham was writing his eulogium on the work of Selden, little did these famous, learned Englishmen imagine that there would, one day or other, come a spruce clerk from an apothecary's shop, with fingers habituated, perhaps, to the tying on of labels in the neatest of manners, to propose to an English Parliament, the adoption of principles, which, not to be rendered perfectly inconsistent and ridiculous in themselves, must blow at once to the devil all the great principles which these learned men had established by the clearest of proof, and the maintenance of which principles they deemed absolutely necessary to preserve to England the great power and the great fame which she had possessed for more than ten centuries. Adopt your principle of "*free-trade*," and away go, for ever, all the doctrines of Smith and all the glorious circumstances attending an adherence to those doctrines; and England becomes a mere mart for huxterers, a residence for Jews and jobbers, and nothing else; a scene of bustling roguery and cheatery, without one sentiment of honour or of love of country to mingle itself with the mass of corruption.

It is not, however, on this more extended view of the subject that I mean to address you at present. My object, at this time is, to inquire of you how you are likely to make your proposed alteration in the CORN LAWS comport with your principles of "*free-trade*," and, at the same time, comport with the principles (very explicitly expressed) upon which you so strenuously advocated the passing of the Corn Laws in 1814 and 1815. These are the matters to which I am at present desirous of drawing your attention. The day is not far distant, when your projected alteration of the Corn Laws must come before us in a tangible shape; and, when it do come before us, it will be of importance for us to bear in mind the part which you have heretofore taken with regard to these Corn Laws. The present Corn Bill, with some little modifications, was brought in by Mr. Prosperity Robinson and supported by you; and, supported by you, too, upon broad and general principles, applicable now just as much as they were then. At the time when that Bill was in agitation, and all the great landowners were crying aloud for it, I opposed that Bill, the short grounds of my opposition being, those which are expressed by the motto to this Letter, that motto forming a part of an expostulatory, but a very civil and even polite Address to the great Daddy of Norfolk, who has since collected his dependent fools together in barns and holes and corners, in order to calumniate me for endeavours, the tendency of which were to preserve to him his estate. Your project of altering this law must, now, soon see the light. Your liberal Æolian colleague has pledged himself that the project shall be forthcoming. He, poor man, appears to be likely to have quite enough to do in his own department, in order not to give us an instance of the complete fulfilment, or rather, verification, of the opinion of CORNELIUS AGRIPPA. He must take special care how he

now moves; or, he will soon give us woeful experience of the tremendous effects produced by that which St. James so appropriately calls the *unruly member*, vulgarly termed the *red rag*. What Iliads of woes have not been occasioned by the unmeasured movements of that red rag! The world would be astonished, or, rather, would turn away with a smile from any one that should say that the state of ILLINOIS, one of the States of the great American republic, which has, now, a " *constitution*" of its own, observe (and which constitution will last a great deal longer, I believe, than Mr. Canning's Lusitanian constitution); the world would smile and look on it as a jest, if I were to say, that this new member of the grand confederation of States was actually created, actually caused to come into existence, merely because an English husband did not think that the great Atlantic, without three thousand miles distance of land, was sufficient to protect his courage about the sound of a voice which had once charmed those ears? Nothing, however, ever uttered by man is more true or more capable of proof than this fact. The wrath of ACHILLES (about a woman, too, observe) brought on the ten years' war of Troy. This may be a fable; but what I relate is true. Mr. CANNING seems very likely to afford the world another instance to be added to the thousands upon thousands already well known of the mischievous effects proceeding from the movements of this unruly member. What the German papers tell us about the anger of the Emperor NICHOLAS having been excited by that speech which Mr. BROUGHAM praised to the skies may be false: these papers may lie as much as ours, as far as I know; but, there can be no doubt that that speech will have produced great anger in the breasts of all the sovereigns of Europe; and, in the meanwhile, the affairs in Portugal and Spain appear to be proceeding in a way which will leave to your liberal colleague

very little time to assist you in projects of " *free-trade* " and, especially, in projects of free trade in corn.

Returning now to my subject, let me first beg you to read the motto to this Letter. If you do not read it the public will, and they will recollect, that it makes part of a Letter to the Daddy, written thirteen years back. One would think, that the Daddy, when he takes a view (if he can do it) of what has passed between that time and this, would feel a little shame in reflecting on his hole-and-corner calumnies on me. From the time that that motto was written until the present day, the Daddy and all the other land-owners, and all the nation, have been witnessing the soundness of its principles. In a *Register*, published just about the same time, namely, on the 21st May, 1814, I stated, as clearly as it was possible to state, the impossibility of a Corn Bill affording any security whatever to the landlord or the farmer, if the *restoration of the gold currency* were to take place agreeably to the then law. I showed, that it was the currency that would do every thing; that would produce ruin universal to all except tax-eaters, if it were restored to its ancient standard, without a reduction of the taxes, to something like their amount before the war. I will here insert a short passage from the Register just mentioned; and when I have so done, I shall, I think, have a right to call upon this Government, upon this Parliament, and even upon this nation, to blush for their obstinacy, their wilful blindness, their suicidal perverseness; and (with some exceptions, certainly, and those pretty numerous) their injustice and their ingratitude towards me. I, however, may be satisfied; I am not now suffering in purse or in person: a gracious God has given me health to live, to behold and spirits to enjoy and exult in the fulfilment of the doctrines, which I so long ago taught with such an anxious desire to save and to

serve my country without the smallest particle of selfishness of any description. Now read the extract, Sir: you remember my features and the sound of my voice: imagine my looking at you while you read: and, if you do not feel your chin descend towards your breast as you proceed, take my word for it that your mind is not yet prepared for those feelings of humiliation which are to be your lot.

" As very closely connected " with this view of the corn sub- " ject, I will here notice what has " been said about *bringing round* " *our* CURRENCY to the stand- " ard of 1796; that is to say, " when gold was in free and ge- " neral circulation. How such " an idea came into the head of " any one accounted sane I am " at a loss to discover. We were " told, that peace, upon a firm " foundation, would do the thing " of itself. It is notorious that a " *light* guinea will sell now for " 26 or 23 shillings in paper. But " the worst, the most foolish part

" of the conduct of those who en-
" tertain the notion of restoring
" our currency to the standard of
" 1796, is, that they allow, at the
" same time, that the paper-mo-
" ney is depreciated; and (now
" observe) that this depreciation
" has had the effect of *raising*
" *prices.*—Very well. It is *depre-*
" *ciated* and it has *raised prices.*
" —Keep this in mind, and then
" ask these wise men, what would
" be the effect of ' restoring the
" currency to its former *healthy*
" *state.*'—These gentlemen, in
" their anxious desire to restore
" guineas, overlook the *interest of*
" *the debt.* But, is it not mani-
" fest, that they ought to have the
" object continually in their view,
" when they are talking upon the
" subject of restoring guineas and
" lowering prices? And is it not
" also manifest, that in whatever
" degree prices be lowered for a
" permanency, the interest of the
" debt must, invariably, though not
" equally, be augmented!—
" Now, then, what is the annual
" interest of this debt? I will not

" plague the reader with any mi-
" serable detail about funded and
" unfunded, and redeemed and
" unredeemed; but will state, in
" round numbers, that the Debt
" requires taxes to be paid to the
" amount of about forty millions
" a year.—Suppose, then, that
" *wheat* (to take that article as an
" instance) be now, upon *an ave-*
" *rage of years,* 27*l.* a load, of
" five quarters; the paper-money
" has, at the rate of exchange with
" Paris, depreciated *one-third* be-
" low gold; and, of course, has
" *raised prices one-third.* Bring
" the currency back to the stan-
" dard of 1796; and the conse-
" quence is that wheat will be
" upon an average of years 18*l.* a
" load. Well, then, farmer Stiles,
" whose share of payment of inte-
" rest of the Debt is 27*l.* a year,
" and who, of course, used to pay
" a load of wheat a year, must,
" upon the restoration of the gui-
" neas, pay *a load and a half of*
" *wheat a year.* This would make
" the farmer scratch his head, I
" believe! It is as clear as day-

" light, that the restoration of gui-
" neas would, in reality, make the
" Debt cost sixty millions a year
" instead of forty millions a year.
" But, this is not all. The Civil
" List, officers of all kinds, pay,
" pensions, annuities, fixed sti-
" pends of every sort, leases,
" ground - rents, rent - charges,
" must all become more expen-
" sive by one-third to those who
" have to pay them. What a re-
" volution would be here! What
" smashing, what work for lawyers
" and bill-framers ! ".

Ah, indeed! " What SMASH-
" ING ; what work for lawyers
" and bill-framers " ! And, Sir,
remember (and if you do not, the
public will, observe) that this was
written and published by me *thirteen years ago*, come the twenty-
first day of May next. When
those who now are little children ;
when those who now are eight or
ten years of age, shall see themselves steeped in poverty, and remember that their fathers were
gentlemen when they were little
boys ; when they shall behold a

sort of breaking up of society,
property all disturbed, the remnants of it scattered here and
there ; and, possibly behold a
general convulsion sufficient to
shake the most solid and venerable
institutions of this country, which
has been famed throughout the
world for those very institutions ;
when these children become men,
shall behold these things, and shall
contemplate the immediate causes,
will they not, if some one should
state the fact to them, turn to their
beggared and distracted fathers,
and say : " And was there, fathers,
" was there, indeed ; is it true,
" fathers, that there was a man in
" England who not only distinctly
" foretold all these fatal conse-
" quences, but who clearly proved
" the truth of his foretellings ; was
" there, indeed, such a man, and
" were you so obstinate as not to
" listen to him, were you so dull
" as not to understand him, were
" you so blind as not to see the
" light that he held up before your
" eyes, or, understanding him,
" seeing the light, believing in

" the truths which he inculcated,
" were you so base as to abandon
" your country and your families,
" to expose the one to certain
" disgrace and to possible sub-
" jugation, and the other to that
" beggary and that frantic sway
" which we now experience: were
" you so base as this: had you
" the baseness not to demand that
" the wisdom, the zeal, the dis-
" interestedness of this man should
" be brought into play for the
" salvation of your country: is it
" possible that you had the base-
" ness to be content to see power
" in the hands of Canning and of
" Huskisson, while success was
" suffered to attend every artifice
" and every act of violence, to
" keep even a particle of that
" power from, and even to stifle
" the voice and cut off the hand
" of William Cobbett ! "

This, or something very much
like it, is, I verily believe, what
the next generation will have to
say to the present; and, observe,
that next generation will be
amongst us in about five or six

years. You and I and Canning
and Lord Liverpool shall, I hope,
all live to see that generation, face
to face; and, if we do, we shall
*all have our due*, even in this
world; and, I am a great advocate for people having, if convenient, their reward before they die.
At this moment these doctrines of
mine are just as applicable as
they were in 1814 and 1815. One
would think that the passage that
I have just quoted was written but
yesterday. It is the CURRENCY
now which is at work, just as it
was then. Many acknowledge
this, at the present day. Not a
soul, except my readers, acknowledged it thirteen years ago. However, the thing was written: it
was in print: it was then where it
is now, and where it will live for
ages: where it will live long and
long after you and Canning and
Jenkinson, and Brougham, and
Burdett, and the whole band of
you shall have your memories
preserved by no other means than
such as those by which are preserved the memories of the *heroes
of the Dunciad.*

Well, Sir, you, who got two thousand a-year for demolishing at a stroke, at one single chop of your blunt weapon, two or three hundred Acts of Parliament, containing the result of the experience and the wisdom of ages: let us, now, hear what were your doctrines at the time that the Corn Bill was first agitated. The Bill was, as I said before, brought in by Mr. Prosperity Robinson. It was, finally, passed with soldiers drawn up round the Houses of Parliament. It was foolish, on the part of the landlords, to the last degree; but, no matter for that, at the present: let us hear what you said in support of this Bill; and here it is, taken from the debate of the 6th of June, 1814.

"Mr. Huskisson said, every "subject alluded to by the Hon. "Gentleman would, as the motion "was shaped, come before the "Committee; for the first refer- "ence to that Committee was that "of all the petitions on the table "on the subject of the Corn Laws.

"In some of these petitions the "freedom of trade was surely in- "troduced. He hoped, therefore, "that the Honourable Gentleman "would give his vote for the Com- "mittee. He would state the "reason why he supported the "present motion for a Committee, "though he objected to the ap- "pointment of a Committee on a "former occasion. He believed "now, as he did then, that there "was no probability of any im- "portation of Corn into this coun- "try, before the next harvest. "The only circumstances which "raised his view, was that of the "number of petitions which had "been presented to the House. "The views of these petitioners, "even if founded in misrepresen- "tation, although they ought not "to induce any Member to do "that which he was not convinced "was just and proper, were still "entitled to the most respectful "consideration of the House. "Although the petitioners were in "many instances, the result of "malevolent and mistaken ap-

" peals to the feelings of the peo-
" ple, they ought to be met by
" temperate inquiry and the fullest
" investigation. The circumstance
" of such a number of petitions,
" therefore, afforded a ground for
" those who were favorable to the
" measure, to support the present
" inquiry ; for, the object of those
" petitions was not to make any
" alteration in the Corn Laws, or
" to make no alteration in them
" without further inquiry. With
" respect to the encouragement
" which ought to be afforded to
" the farmer, it should be consi-
" dered, that there was now a
" great diminution in the value of
" money; and, that the capital
" necessary for carrying on of
" farming operations, must now
" be double to what it was before
" the war. The Noble Lord (Lord
" A. Hamilton) deceived himself,
" therefore, if he thought, that
" things could return to what
" they were before the war. This
" was one of the most dangerous
" errors which could be enter-
" tained. What was like to be

" the permanent change of this
" country, now that the war was
" at an end ? The whole expenses
" of this country, including *all our*
" *establishments*, before the war,
" only *amounted to 16 millions*.
" Would this produce no altera-
" tion in the money value of arti-
" cles ? When gentlemen talked
" of the increased price of bread,
" was not every thing else raised
" in proportion, and that *not in*
" *consequence of the high price of*
" *bread; but the amount of taxa-*
" *tion ?* It was *impossible for the*
" *country to return to the prices*
" *before the war.* It had been
" said that the obvious remedy was
" to lower the rents. He had
" not the good fortune to be a
" land holder, and he had no in-
" terest but that of the public in
" general in view. The propos-
" ion of the gross proceed of land,
" which now came to the landlord,
" however it might be represented
" in money, *was now much less*
" *than what it was in 1792.* Pre-
" vious to the war, in a farm of
" moderate extent, the farmer

" considered himself requited if he
" made three rents from it. But
" it was necessary in the case of
" such a farm now, that the farmer
" should make at least five rents
" to be enabled to go on. *If even
" the whole rental of the country
" were remitted, it would be im-
" possible to return to the prices
" before the war.* He was not
" afraid to declare that the people
" of this country must not expect,
" be the law on the subject what
" it may, that, *with our burthens,*
" the price of bread can ever be
" LESS THAN DOUBLE TO
" WHAT IT WAS BEFORE
" THE WAR."

Here, then, we have your doctrines. Here we have the grounds
upon which you supported the
Corn Bill. Upon what ground,
then, are you, now, to propose an
alteration in that Corn Bill, which
alteration is to have the effect, or
intended to have the effect of lowering the price of corn? No
matter for the shuffling and the
trickery and the mere rattle of
words to be employed upon this
occasion: the object must be to
cause corn to be *cheaper by the*
alteration which you propose to
make in the Corn Bill. If this be
not your professed object, you are
flagrantly, foolishly, gratuitously
inconsistent. Your folly is so
great, that nothing can possibly
equal it, except your insolence
towards those who petitioned for
the change. You must explicitly
declare your intention *to make
bread cheaper than it now is;* and
to make it permanently cheaper,
too, allowing for the effects of
seasons. Very well, then: what
has taken place to warrant you in
proposing this alteration? You
tell us, in the above speech, that
if the taxes continued to amount
to between fifty and sixty millions
a year; and I beg you to mark
this *if;* if the taxes continued to
amount to between fifty and sixty
millions a year, it would be impossible to return to the same
price of bread as that which existed
before the war, *even if the whole
rental of the country were remitted;* that is to say, if the farmers

had the use of the land, without paying any rent at all ; and, of course, if the landlords were all bundled into the workhouse with their coronets and stars and garters tied about their necks.

Stick a pin there, Mr. Huskisson: bear that in mind, if you please: and, now, do not the taxes still amount to nearer sixty than fifty millions a year? Aye, do they, Sir, and to more than the sixty millions, in the gross amount. There are about fifty-four or five millions paid *into the Exchequer ;* but, observe, there are more than sixty millions collected from the people. Therefore, according to your own speech, *" bread cannot " be less than double to what it " was before the war "* ! When you said *cannot,* you meant, of course, that it could not be without utter ruin to the proprietors and occupiers of land, in the first place, and without a breaking up of society and a total subversion of the State, in the end. Our meaning, in cases like this, has always an understood qualifica-

tion; as, upon one occasion I observed that, when I said that they *could not* carry Peel's Bill into full effect, I meant, of course, that they could not do it without producing general ruin and convulsion; just as I say to a man, " you *cannot* jump down that chalk-pit ;" I know he *can ;* but I know that he cannot do it without breaking his neck or dashing himself to pieces. Thus it was that an understood qualification was conveyed to us in these words : " Be the law on the subject what " it may, *with our present bur-* " *thens,* the price of bread can " never be less than double to " what it was before the war." These were words of sense. I praised them at the time, and I scolded my neighbours of Havant because they burned you in effigy for having uttered them.

But, Sir, Mr. Huskisson, " free-trade " gentleman, demolisher of the laws of the Edwards and the Henrys, and receiver of two thousand a-year for that demolition ; what, Mr. Huskisson, are to be your arguments NOW, when you come forward with a project for making bread cheaper and permanently cheaper, than it is at this time? The taxes are sixty millions a-year: the taxes remain plump up to the mark of your then calculation; and, of course, bread must now be double the price of what it was before the war, or, *the landlords must lose their estates;* an alternative of which I propose to say a little more, by-and-by. Now, then, what was the price of bread before the war? This Register of mine, which contains, in one place or another, almost every thing necessary for a law-giver or a statesman to know, contains, under date of 4th of June, 1814, an account of the price of bread for half a century back. It will there be seen, that the average price of the quartern loaf, for ten years previous to the late war with France, was *seven-pence and five-sixteenths of a penny.* What is the price of that quartern loaf now? It is about *eight-pence,*

*three farthings,* on an average, because the quartern loaf weighed 4lb. 5oz.; the present is a 4lb. loaf, and the average price of that 4lb. loaf is, as near as I can be certain it, about *eight-pence half a farthing.* So that, while the quartern loaf, according to your doctrine of 1814, ought to be at this time *fourteen-pence, and ten-sixteenths of another penny;* while it ought to be, according to that doctrine of yours, *fourteen-pence halfpenny and half another farthing;* it is, as I have just said, *eight-pence three farthings;* and yet, you (without any accompanying proposition to reduce the taxes) propose to reduce it to a lower price still: though, according to your own doctrine, the landlords must, even at the present price, evidently lose their estates!

And, you are a " *minister,*" are you? You are a " *minister of trade,*" are you? You are a Cornelius Agrippa's man, are you? You are a *law-demolisher,* are you? You are a " *statesman,*" are you? You bring us the light

of *club quatre-vingt neuf*, do you?
—Those landlords must be asses
more veritable than those which
carry panniers, if they trust you
with their estates *one hour* after
the making of such a proposition.
They must have very little care
of that which they derive from
their ancestors; the poachers that
kill the game on their estates are
more fit to enjoy the estates themselves, than they are if they suffer
you to have any thing to do with
measures affecting those estates,
if you once venture to make this
proposition; that is to say, unaccompanied (as you intend it to be)
*with any proposition for the re-
duction of the taxes.* I am an
enemy to the Corn Bill: I have
always been an enemy to this Corn
Bill. I would not be a Minister
an hour, unless I were empowered
to demolish this Corn Bill: I have
always reprobated the Corn Bill:
I reprobate the Corn Bill now:
but I have always said, and I still
say, that the taxes ought to be
reduced so as to render a Corn
Bill unnecessary to preserve to
the landlord his estate and to the
farmer his stock. You have just
got a new grant out of the taxes.
You swallow a good slice of them.
You want to augment, rather
than diminish them; and, while
you reprobate us radicals as wishing to overturn the constitution
and the law, as wishing to destroy
all the ranks in society, you have
notoriously a measure in preparation, which, if it could possibly
answer the end which you have in
view, would not leave one single
lord in the land that would not be
an object of scorn in the course
of five years. Your project cannot answer the end which it has in
view: it cannot injure the land-
people *much*, because they will
be totally ruined by the enforce-
ment of the laws passed last winter:
your project will give them a gash
in the cheek while the deadly lead
has done the work for the body. But,
if it could go into full effect, and
if it could produce the ends that
you wish to produce; if it could, at
the fall of a year of scarcity, make
the quartern loaf cheaper than it is

now, *while all the taxes remain the same*, it would strip even the heir of the Duke of Buckingham of every park, mansion, manor, advowson, farm and cottage, which he is destined by heirship and by law to possess, and, this it would do in the course of five or six years at the most. The "George and Garter" might again "dangle "on the curtains of the worst ".rooms' worst bed." If I were the Duke, I would take special care that my George and Garter should not so dangle from such a cause. The curious circumstance is, that out of five or six hundred of these noblemen (peers and heirs apparent to peers) there are, I verily believe from my soul, not one hundred, each of whom has not infinitely more learning, more experience and more sense than you. What the devil can possess them I know not, to suffer you to play at ducks and drakes with their honours and their fortunes. The truth is, however, that they find themselves steeped up to the ears in all the difficulties which an infernal funding and paper-money system has drawn about them by degrees; and, by a bawling press, not less infernal, they are kept in awe of that system. There is no refuge for them but in *regaining the common people*, who were

their natural friends, and of whom they are the natural protectors, but whom they have left to be flayed alive by Jews, Quakers, and every species of money-devil that prowls about over the face of this unhappy land. They will never regain the people without ceding something to the people.; and, what can they cede *less* than what we have so humbly and so often prayed for in vain? With what shame they must look at the punishments which they are compelled to inflict, in order to preserve their game from that very people, whose fathers so reverenced their fathers, and were so sedulously careful not to offend them. We have been accused of a desire to pull them down to a level with ourselves. I defy the accusers to produce a single instance of the fact. Our great accuser, Mr. Canning, who has, in his various harangues, accused us to all the sovereigns and all the countries of Europe, stands, at last, self-accused of that which he has falsely imputed to us; and those sovereigns and those countries have all heard the self-accusation. The people want, and they have always wanted, to take no just constitutional right from the Lords or from any body else. Their dreaded power is a bug-bear; for, God knows, their great fault is, not want of respect, not want of veneration for their superiors; but, if any thing. too large a quantity of it upon all occasions. Nothing was ever uttered with more sincerity than I utter these opinions. The opinions are perfectly correct; and, yet, those who own the land, those who have every thing at stake, those who will finally have no protection but that which is to be found in the hearts of the common people, turn their backs upon that common people, and with both arms embrace the vipers of the funds and paper-money; and they listen to loan-jobbers and almost doff the hat to them, as if they were their actual masters.

To return, now, to you and your small wares, I think I read some speech made during the last session of Parliament, in which the speaker reminded you of this speech which I have quoted above, delivered by you in 1814. He accused you, if I recollect right, of inconsistency; and, if I do not forget, you scratched about and said that an opinion delivered *at one time* might not be applicable to *another time*; that "circum- "stances had changed very great- "ly, since 1814; and that, *there-* "*fore*, the opinion then delivered,

"though correct as applicable to "the circumstances of that day, "might not be correct if applied "to the circumstances of the pre- "sent day."

Now, "*membre du club-quatre-vingt neuf*," though you might plead with some show of reason, that, though you thought the ja-cobins of France good fellows, and very wise reformers, in 1789, you did not think them so after they had cut the King's head off and you were got snugly into Dundas's office, in 1793. "Cir-cumstances" had changed then, I allow; but, what are the circum-stances, pray, that have changed, in this case! The people of Li-verpool, the hang-dog flatterers and tax-hunters of Liverpool, deem you a wonderfully clever man, and so they would Satan, if he could furnish fat posts for their lazy sons. But, clever man as you are, you will find no change of circumstance here. Your opi-nion was this: that bread could not, *as long as our burthens con-tinued to amount to nearer sixty than fifty millions a year*; that, while these burthens continued, bread could not be sold for *less than double the price at which it was sold before the war*, without a total ruin of the owners and occupiers of the land. The cir-

M

cumstances have not changed, then; the circumstances continue the same; bread is not much dearer than it was before the late wars; it is now, after a year of scarcity, *not one-seventh dearer than it was before the late war*; you said that, to bring it down to the price of what it was before the late war, and to continue the taxes to nearer sixty than fifty millions a-year; you said that these would wholly take away the rental of the land; and yet, at a moment when the bread is very nearly as cheap as it was before the late war, you are, without any proposition to diminish the taxes, coming forward with a project to make bread cheaper; that is to say, you are, according to your own principles, coming forward with a project to send the peers and their families to grass. Well for those it will be who live in the fat pasture lands of Hereford-shire and Lincolnshire, and the like; or, perhaps, the nuts and acorns of Hampshire and Sussex, may, in a last extremity, afford them a resource.

You will ask me, then, if I sup-pose that you mean actually to take away their fields and houses and goods and clothes. Take away! Oh no, things are not done in this homely manner. Your project, if it could be executed, would only take away their rents: that is all. Lords, however, must eat, as well as other folks: to eat, they must have eatables: they would soon learn to "stand cook": there is no difficulty in that: but, they must have something to cook: to have something to cook, they must have money to buy it: to have money they must sell their things; and, if they get no rents, how are they to avoid going on pawning, selling and swapping, till they have not even a shirt left to their backs? Pray, clever man, answer me that question. Observe (for I will hold your nose tight to it) you explicitly said (and you said what was very true) that, with taxes amounting to nearer sixty than fifty millions a-year, *the whole of the rental must be remitted* to enable the farmer to raise the corn, unless bread were double the price that it was at before the war. The taxes are nearly or quite sixty millions a-year: the bread is only *a penny farthing* upon a quarters loaf dearer than it was before the war: and you propose to make it cheaper than it is! There, "clever man," get out of that; and then I will join in the praises bestowed upon your cleverness, by the nasty, greedy, huckstering, sham gentlemen, tax-hunting fellows of Liverpool.

In speaking of the consequences to the landholders, of these wild and extravagant measures, even the reflecting part of the public, and of my own constant readers, may think that I exaggerate my expectations. I wish such persons to bear in mind, that revolutions have taken place; that convulsions have shaken property to its foundations; that the greatest Lords have been reduced to beggary; that I had a French Count binding books for me in London; and, in short, that Lords are Lords, 'squires are 'squires, Baronets are Baronets, because they have RENTS; and that, without rents, they are no more than other men. Degradation marches at a much swifter pace than exaltation, even if the exalted happen to have such extraordinarily good luck as you have had. You have been one of the luckiest of those, that have put into the lucky lottery of Whitehall, where people get tickets for nothing, and where all are prizes, and no blanks. Yet, you have been thirty-seven years in reaching your present point, and, I can conceive, if you cannot, a course of events which would bring you back to your starting point, in thirty-seven months or less. I remember that, about three years ago, in a letter which I addressed to one of the three, I reminded you, Mr. CANNING and Lord LIVERPOOL, that we four all started at the same time, or much about the same time, in our political career. I told you, that only about three years before that, all that I could muster in the world, upon a particular evening, every thing that I possessed upon the face of the earth, my clothes excepted, amounted to only *three shillings*. This was perfectly true. I told you, "even now, I would "not exchange situations with "either of you, taking all things "into view; and, said I, mind, I "tell you, that our destiny has "not yet done with us." Our destiny has been at work with us from that day to this. That was just after you had passed the small-note bill: since that we have had " Late Panic ". We are now going to have another " Late Panic ", or a something prodigiously more dreadful to you. Day by day, my doctrines are received with more and more attention: day by day the confidence in my judgment increases: and, just the reverse is, day by day, taking place with regard to you. I have courted nobody; I

have flattered nobody; as connected with my opinions, and
views as to public matters, and
my expression of those opinions,
and delineation of those views, I
have been influenced by, and have
cared for, nobody. I have taken
no pains to get at secret information of any sort; I have been
guided by principles, which I
have believed to be sound, and by
events and transactions obvious to
all the world. There has grown
up a great question, upon which
hinges the property of the rich,
the well-being of the common
people, and eventually, the peace
of the country, and the safety
of the State. Upon this great
question, you (the ministry), with
the Parliament at your back, and
I, have been, and still are, at
issue. Your hostility to me, shown
in so many, and in such deadly
forms, my talents, and, far beyond them, my perseverance,
have, at last, made this question
familiar to every person of any
information in the kingdom. The
question is, by far, the most interesting one ever propounded to
a people: it is of importance,
more or less, to every human being, from the highest to the lowest. The trial between us is
going on. Impartial time is our
judge; and all men are looking

for the decision. You are endeavouring (I mean the Ministry and
the Parliament) to obtain such a
decision as shall not be destructive to your reputation; but, above
all things, *such as shall not be
honourable to me.* This is the
object of your greatest anxiety:
in this anxiety, gentlemen in and
gentlemen opposite unite, joined
by Jews, jobbers, Quakers, and
money-devils of every description. But, there is still a very
great mass of virtuous and impartial men in the middle rank of
life; and it is these, who will, after
all, have to declare and promul-
gate the decision of our judge.
On these we must rely at last;
and these I shall have for me.
As to the length of time that it may
take, a tight-twisted THING
like this does not easily give way;
but, when it does give way, the
consequences are terrible. For
these consequences be you prepared: I am, I assure you; and,
in the meanwhile, the worst that
I wish you, is, that your health
may be as good, and your sleep
as sound, as that of

Your most obedient and

   Most humble servant,

     Wm. COBBETT.

## TO
## DOCTOR BLACK.

————

Dᴏᴄᴛᴏʀ,

You have called my 'History of the Protestant Reformation' pig's meat: you have, during the two last years, seemed to have three principal objects in view: *first* (after taking care of yourself, of course), to ridicule and run down, if possible, my statements relative to the happiness of the people of England in catholic times; *second*, to cause it to be believed, that a vast deal of benefit to every class of people had been occasioned by the putting down of monks, friars and nuns, and by the putting an end to holidays; *third*, to cause it to be believed that new inventions, as you call them; improvements in science, as you call them, have been a great benefit to the people at large. Of all this, your readers must be well assured: mine know it, too, from the quotations that I have made from you. I, therefore, now lay before my readers, an article of yours of the 29th of January, containing, in substance, and, almost, in words, a recantation of all that you have said on this subject in opposition to me. Strange change, Doctor; but, that

which is a vast deal more consequence than this change in you, is, the argument, which may fairly be built upon the premises which you now state; the argument which those premises afford, in opposition to the policy of our Æolian Secretary of State, and in opposition to the doctrines of all his " *liberal* " admirers.

Your article begins with a commentary on a pamphlet of Bᴇɴ- ɴᴇᴛᴛ, the Member for Wiltshire, who, in this pamphlet, exhibits himself as the most stupid ass that ever browzed or brayed. I saw the pamphlet advertized; in the hearing of a friend I said I should like to see it: without more ado he got it: he paid Ridgway two shillings for it, and, though this Bᴇɴɴᴇᴛᴛ is not thought to be much of a liberal in the dealing way, never did he sell such a bargain as this before. I wish Mr Ridgway would give me sixpence for that for which I have given two shillings. There are some natural fools: some fools by acquirement: others are fools in consequence of excessive conceit. These three sorts of folly differ in their outward appearances; but, in this Bennett's book, you have the outward and visible sign and proof of them altogether. Doubtless, a very able law-giver; very fit to make laws for us; but, as an author, it is, assuredly, the most consummate ass that God ever suffered to wear short ears, or to walk about upon two legs instead of four. There are many expressions of opinion contained in this book: now I will be bound, by a wager of ten to one, to point out twenty passages, wherein this man expresses opinions, of which passages, or any one of which passages, he himself shall not be able to tell you the meaning! Mr. Bennett, Lord of the beautiful village of Norton Bovant, in Wiltshire, go home to Norton Bovant, or, if you must to London, dawdle about and *jaser*, as the French call it, so that no one may have your words down in black and white. Write no more books, great knight of the shire of Wilts; or, if you must, down upon all fours at once, and let your ears come out to their natural length: an excellent farmer, a monstrously fine country 'squire, doubtless a most suitable representative of the county; why, then, put all these in peril by assuming the character of the author! Be quiet, Mr. Bennett: keep your tongue still, if you can; except in that place of which you are so worthy and which is so worthy of you; with this exception, keep your tongue still, *if you can*; but, as to the pen and the press, if you cannot keep your fingers still, get a friend, male or female, if you have one upon earth, to chop them off.

Now, Doctor Black, I shall insert the article to which you made the notice to this Bennett's pamphlet a sort of text. I desire your readers and my readers to go through it with great attention. I shall trouble them with no commentary upon it: they will see that the authors whom you have quoted, and that you yourself establish, as far as your authority goes, the correctness of my opinions upon this subject. This is so manifest; here is such direct commendation of the monastic institutions; here is such an almost repetition of my sentiments upon these subjects, that I really have nothing to do but to insert the article in order to fill my readers with surprise. When I have inserted the article, I shall make an observation or two, not on what some would, but which I do not, call your *inconsistency*; but, on *the lesson which this article ought, at this time, to give to Mr. Canning*. Now, for the article, which will certainly be regarded as an atonement for a part, at least, of your sins.

" The manner in which Mr.
" Cobbett speaks of the abun-
" dance enjoyed by our Catholic
" ancestors, and his abuse of the
" Scotch economists for their in-
" difference to human happiness,
" *are no doubt exceedingly extra-*
" *vagant*; but the manner in
" which Englishmen speak of the
" condition of the people of other
" countries, and the scale by which
" they estimate their happiness,
" are seldom less extravagant.

" The first observation, for in-
" stance, which escapes from an
" English traveller in Spain or
" Italy is—Good God! what a
" number of days are lost by fes-
" tivals and holidays! What a
" number of idle people are fed
" *in Convents*! Lisbon has 7,000
" Priests, and Edinburgh has
" only 70, and so forth.

" This would all do very well
" in the mouth of a Noble or other
" Aristocrat; but the lower orders
" themselves repeat the language
" like parrots. There are a few
" distinguished Protestant writers,
" as the celebrated John Mul-
" ler, the Historian of Switzer-
" land, who regret the subtraction
" of so much of the land of a
" country from tenantries for life,
" which the religious houses are,
" to properties in fee. But these
" are only Protestants who are

" intimately acquainted with both
" Catholic and Protestant coun-
" tries.

" And yet the cool selfishness
" with which an English 'Squire
" contemplates the reduction of
" the great body of the labouring
" population to a state of priva-
" tion without example in Catho-
" lic countries, and which enables
" the said 'Squires to extract an
" amount of labour from them
" which could be extracted only
" in England, might have led
" Englishmen (above the vulgar)
" to suspect, that whoever have
" gained by the change, the lower
" classes have not.

" The Italians, though they
" could not read English books,
" used to feel a great reverence
" for the nation that could export
" so many *Mi-Lords*, any one of
" whom could spend as much in
" a month as an Italian Prince
" could spend in a year, and they
" used to devour our political
" writers with great eagerness in
" French translations. Judging
" of the nation from the sample,
" they imagined Englishmen were
" the wealthiest and happiest race
" on the face of the earth, and
" they thought they had only to
" imitate us, to be equally rich
" and happy. Among the English
" tourists of those days, there were,

"perhaps, as many coxcombs as
"there are among the present
"race of tourists; and they used
"to fall foul, on all occasions, of
"the numerous holidays, which
"were such a heavy deduction
"from the industry and wealth of
"the country. BARETTI, a most
"agreeable writer, as well ac-
"quainted with England, from
"long residence here, as with
"Italy, informs us, that the con-
"tinued declamations against
"these abuses at length made an
"impression on the POPE himself,
"and that BENEDICT XIV. 'once
"offered all the Italian Princes
"an utter abolition of all holidays,
"Sundays excepted, which offer
"procured him the appellation of
"the Protestant Pope.' ' Had the
"abolition taken place (he adds)
"it would certainly have demo-
"lished a large portion of those
"superstitious raree-shows so
"nauseated by Protestants in
"general; but after long debates
"and consultations, every one of
"those Princes rejected his Ho-
"LINESS's offer, and chose rather
"to go on in the old way.'

"BARETTI gives us a specimen
"of the debates on the occasion;
"and, what is curious enough,
"the great opponent of the change
"began his speech with the very
"same observation which was

"made by the Wiltshire 'Squire,
"'The plurality must needs be
"ever poor, let their industry be
"ever so great, and their labour
"ever so incessant.' 'Alas, Gen-
"tlemen!' he concludes, 'let us
"saddle an additional weight of
"labour on our poor, and deprive
"them at the same time of their
"rejoicing, festivals and raree-
"shows, what will be the conse-
"quence? The consequence
"will be, that they will work
"their own destruction. It is
"true that our stock in trade will
"certainly grow a little larger for
"a while after the abolition, and
"bring perhaps some few cart-
"loads of money into our country
"from foreign parts. But then
"the cheapness of money will
"cause dearness of provisions,
"and increase much the price of
"all the necessaries of life; and
"then our poor will be very poor
"indeed, as it is certain they have
"as good backs as any poor in
"Christendom to undergo labour;
"but have, on the other hand, no
"more wit than the other poor in
"Christendom to make their pro-
"fit of their labour, and get their
"share of the aforesaid cart-loads
"of money. Skilful computers,
"who are seldom of their class, will
"get all the money to themselves;
"and a few will have palaces and

" large estates, while thousands
" shall be obliged to labour, pine,
" and starve. Then, dearness of
" provisions and other necessaries
" will often make them angry, and
" upon the least ground of com-
" plaint, they will assemble riot-
" ously, and burn and destroy
" granaries and mills, and throw
" corn and cheese into ponds and
" rivers, to make them cheap, and
" seditiously surround the dwell-
" ings of our nobility and chief
" people, whom they shall dream
" to be the authors of their wants,
" and create great confusion in
" all parts of the country; and
" thus we shall bring upon us
" such evils and calamities as we
" are total strangers to. Let us,
" therefore, suffer the good crea-
" tures to live on as they have
" done these many ages; let them
" gaze with wonted superstition
" on their wooden Saints and
" pasteboard Madonas; let them
" enjoy their festivals and raree-
" shows; and a fig for these out-
" landish politics imported in
" French books, that turn the
" heads of all our reading youth,
" and never will do Italy any
" good.'

    " BARETTI, then, in his own
" name, asks one of these poli-
" ticians what he would have said
" to the old MACHIAVELIAN!

" ' Did you not say that the gon-
" doliers of Venice are better fed
" and better dressed than your
" boatmen on the Thames? that
" the low people of Naples look
" as athletic as MILO, in times of
" yore? that the beggars of Tus-
" cany are better clad, and more
" cleanly lodged, than your beg-
" gars through Middlesex and
" Surrey? Heaven knows what
" you would have said if you had
" ever entered the cheerful and
" hospitable habitations of the
" Lombard, the Piedmontese, and
" the Genoese peasantry! Will
" you now, Sir, say, that their
" festivals and raree-shows are
" totally impolitic, as well as su-
" perstitious?'

    " It is curious that nearly all the
" Catholic Governments, which,
" in imitation of JOSEPH, obtained
" from the POPE permission to
" abolish holidays, have been
" gradually restoring them, and
" we believe on a principle of
" *humanity to the lower orders.*
" They say the principle of popu-
" lation will, in all old settled
" countries, always keep the la-
" bourers up to the level of the
" employment for them; and
" though the abolition of holidays
" would add to the wealth of the
" country, it would not add to the
" happiness of the poor them-

" selves, who in the one case " would, as in Protestant coun- " tries, have all work and no " play, and in the other, would " have both work and play, and " the same food and necessaries " in both cases.

" In a delightful article in the " last number of *The Westmin-* " *ster Review*, from the pen of a " writer, long a resident in Italy, " and intimately acquainted with " its rural life, we everywhere " find the contrast between the " lower orders of Italy and Eng- " land in favour of the former. " ' The man of peace and domes- " ticity (says the writer) finds in " its fertile soil, and the happiness " of its peasantry, an ameliorated " likeness of beloved but starving " England.' Some very curious " details of the manners of the " peasantry are given, which seem " to bear out the writer. MARIA " GRAHAM, in her interesting " ' Narrative of a Residence in " the Neighbourhood of Rome,' " gives nearly the same ac- " count :—

" ' Upon the whole (she says) the " peasantry of these mountains may " be considered rich, although they " have seldom much property in " money. Their riches consist in " the yearly produce of their labour, " in which their happy climate per- " mits them to depend with more " certainty than in the northern " parts of Europe. They have not " the habit of laying up a store for " the future, but the price of what " is over and above of the produce " of their ground, after the propor- " tion to the superior proprietor is " paid, is laid out in silver buckles, " and head ornaments, and coral " beads, which are easily converted " into money in times of pressure. " This sort of easy poverty, above " want, but below the state of luxu- " ry, in which ambition begins to " push men on to distinguish them- " selves, or to better their condition, " produces great indifference as to " public interest, and renders them " acquiescent under any Govern- " ment, so long as they remain in " peace, and can sit every man un- " der his own vine, and his own fig " tree.'

" Wisdom comes with lack of " food. If men had been always " able to sit in peace under their " own vine, they would have " made few advances either in " the arts, or in politics.

" But, at all events, the ab- " sence of invention is often also " the absence of crime. We " will answer for it, that there is " more prison room in one county " in England, than there is in all " Italy."

Well done, Doctor ! Your last sentence completely contradicts your first ; but, far be this from being a subject of censure with me. Why live we but to correct our errors? You commence in error, you finish in correctness: you set out a sinner and you finish almost a saint: here you are an advocate for Roman Catholic holidays, for convents and all the rest of the Roman Catholic affair; and you maintain your predilection by argument which is quite unanswerable. However, it is the LESSON; the lesson it is, which this article offers to Mr. Canning; it is this that is the most important circumstance belonging to it; for, Doctor, if the account which you now give of the effect of the Roman Catholic institutions upon the people at large; if this account be true, what hope is there of a CANNING or JERRY BENTHAM constitution being a favourite with any Roman Catholic people upon the face of the earth? I have always contended, that the people in Roman Catholic countries were better off than the people of England: I have always contended that the vagabond Cortes would have beggared the people of Spain: I have always contended that the people of those countries, including South America, must naturally detest and ought to detest, the rogues and ruffians that sought to sell them to Jews and jobbers, and to saddle them with everlasting burthens as the people of England have been saddled: I have always contended that FERDINAND ought to be beloved for over-setting the loan-jobbing Cortes and the loan-mongering bond-holders of London: I have always said that the people of Spain ought to be grateful to him for it; I have always said that they would be grateful to him for it and would stand by him: all this I have said, and all this you have been contradicting for now nearly three years. The varying devil of a press of London, Mr. Brougham's "best public instructor," has constantly been on your side; to cry up liberal principles; to represent the people of Roman Catholic countries as detesting their Governments, and, especially, as detesting the clerical part of their Governments; this has been, in the jacobin jargon, the order of the day. At last, the contagious folly has reached our Secretary of State: the mob of Westminster carry bits of laurel (the instructor tells us) to stick in the caps of the guards who are going to give Ferdinand a drubbing, while the Secretary of State, standing at only a few hundred yards from the spot, is telling his hearers that our

security consists in the knowledge
of the fact, that we have " *all the*
" *discontented spirits of the age*
" *ranged under our banners.*"
From words we come to deeds:
the guards march; the ships sail,
the King sends his message; the
declaration is made; enormous
expense is incurred; and, if we
escape indelible disgrace, we shall
not yet have lost our ancient good
luck.

All this has arisen, Doctor
Black, from opinions respecting
the state of body and mind of the
people of Roman Catholic countries; these consequences have
arisen from the preaching and the
belief in opinions, precisely the
opposite of those inculcated in
this article of yours, which article,
I repeat, ought to be a lesson to
Mr. CANNING for the remainder
of his life, and to this nation for
ever. In conclusion, let me observe that I have talked once or
twice of sending you a pottle of
ale. You shall have it to-morrow,
in proof of my sincere approbation of this article; and, in the
mean time,

I remain

Your most obedient and

Most humble Servant,

WM. COBBETT.

# AMERICAN SEEDS.

I INSERT, below, the article
which I published last week upon
this subject. Since that article
was published, the ship *Colombia*,
with my additional seeds on board,
has arrived in the London docks,
and, surprising to say, the seeds
were put on board in New York
on the 31st day of December.
'Till I *see* them I cannot publish
the *list;* because I do not know
the precise quantity that there is
of each, nor do I know the state
of them. There will be, however,
at least, as I imagine, nearer
seventy than fifty sorts, which
shall not, nevertheless, induce me
to raise my proposed price. As
I said before, one single handful of any one of more than
twenty of these sorts, is, considering their rareness, really worth
more than the money that I charge
for the whole; and this will be
evident to the lovers of planting
and botany, when they see the
list. But, when I was in America,
last, it was one of the pleasing
prospects of my life, that I should
be able to introduce into England,
and to make plenty in England,
many of these valuable Trees
and Shrubs, which were almost
unknown there at that time. I

am, in great part, therefore, repaid by the accomplishment of this my intention.

___

SINCE last week, I have received news of the arrival of the ship *Colombia* from New York, which has ten or twelve sorts of seeds, some of them very rare, which I have not, as yet, in my possession. The ship was off Plymouth on Monday last, and is, possibly, now in the river. This will make a great addition to the number of sorts of seeds, a list of the whole of which shall be inserted in my next. I think I can say with truth that I now possess a larger collection of fine trees and shrubs (or, rather the seed of them) than ever was before possessed by any man in England at one time.

___

## MARKETS.

___

Average Prices of CORN throughout ENGLAND, for the week ending January 19.

### Per Quarter.

| | s. | d. | | | s. | d. |
|---|---|---|---|---|---|---|
| Wheat | 53 | 2 | Rye | | 39 | 9 |
| Barley | 34 | 10 | Beans | | 45 | 8 |
| Oats | 27 | 5 | Pease | | 46 | 11 |

Total Quantity of Corn returned as Sold in the Maritime Districts, for the week ended January 19.

| | Qrs. | | | Qrs. |
|---|---|---|---|---|
| Wheat | 36,963 | Rye | | 271 |
| Barley | 40,073 | Beans | | 1,914 |
| Oats | 11,371 | Pease | | 847 |

*Corn Exchange, Mark Lane.*

Quantities and Prices of British Corn, &c. sold and delivered in this Market, during the week ended Saturday, January 20.

| | Qrs. | £. | s. | d. | | s. | d. |
|---|---|---|---|---|---|---|---|
| Wheat | 4,557 for 12,554 | 2 | 8 | Average, | 55 | 1 |
| Barley | 5,678 | 10,409 | 6 | 5 | | 36 | 7 |
| Oats | 3,138 | 4,915 | 2 | 5 | | 31 | 5 |
| Rye | 24 | 43 | 9 | 9 | | 35 | 4 |
| Beans | 800 | 1,871 | 16 | 5 | | 45 | 7 |
| Pease | 476 | 1,191 | 13 | 5 | | 50 | 0 |

Friday, Jan. 26.—The supplies of this week are moderate, and the frosty weather continuing, for the present, occasions little business to be doing here. Wheat continues dull at Monday's prices. Barley of fine quality looks upwards. Beans fully support Monday's terms. Oats obtain rather higher prices, with a limited trade.

Monday, Jan. 29.—Considering the impediments of last week, the supply of all kinds of Grain may be reported as good, and of Flour the quantity was considerable. This morning's market is furnished with very few fresh arrivals of any description of Corn; the samples, therefore, for sale, are chiefly the remains of former supplies, which appear quite sufficient to meet the present limited demand. The frost having gone, the buyers all appear to be very easy about doing business.

The Wheat trade remains dull at last week's prices, for such damp parcels as were offered; a few picked samples made rather more money. Fine Malting Barley is 1s. per qr. higher, but there is little trade for other kinds. Beans for seed again obtain more money, but not other sorts. Peas continue to meet a very heavy trade. The demand for Oats is so limited, that very little progress can be made in sales, at last quotations. The Flour trade remains as before.

*Liverpool*, January 23.—Owing materially to easterly winds, the importations of Grain to this port were very small during the past week, and the demand limited for Wheat and Oats, excepting for the finest qualities of each, which, of picked samples, (and which were sparingly offered for sale,) obtained a mutual advance of 2*d.* per bushel beyond the value of last Tuesday. The market of this day was but poorly attended by purchasers; the few however of whom bought only of the choicest parcels, for which they paid the above noted advance. Oatmeal was 1*s.* per 240 lbs. dearer.

Imported into Liverpool, from the 16th to the 22d January, 1827, inclusive:—Wheat, 2,334; Barley, 991; Oats, 3,754; Beans, 1150; Pease, 15 quarters. Flour, 2,482 sacks, per 280 lbs. Oatmeal, 751 packs, per 240 lbs. American Flour, 500 barrels.

*Bristol*, Jan. 27.—A little more business is doing here in the Corn Markets than was last week, especially in Barley and Oats, at an advance, in both articles, of 2*s.* per quarter, and in some instances rather more. In Wheat, Flour, and Malt no variation from last week's prices. Supplies very moderate, and present prices may be considered, nearly, as below quoted :—Wheat, from 5*s.* 3*d.* to 7*s.* 6*d.* ; Barley, 4*s.* 6*d.* to 5*s.* 9*d.* ; Beans, 5*s.* 6*d.* to 7*s.* 6*d.* ; Oats, 2*s.* 3*d.* to 4*s.* 1½*d.* ; and Malt, 5*s.* 6*d.* to 3*s.* per bushel, Imperial. Flour, Seconds, 32*s.* to 42*s.* per bag.

*Guildford*, Jan. 27.—Wheat, old, 13*l.* 10*s.* to 16*l.* per load. Rye, 44*s.* to 46*s.*; Barley, 36*s.* to 41*s.* ; Oats, 30*s.* to 40*s.*; Beans, 53*s.* to 56*s.*; Pease, grey, 56*s.* to 60*s.* ; ditto, boilers, 60*s.* to 64*s.* per quarter.

*Ipswich*, Jan. 27.—We had to-day a good supply of Wheat and Barley, which sold freely at full last week's prices, as follow :—Wheat, 50*s.* to 57*s.*; Barley, 34*s.* to 39*s.*; Beans, 40*s.* to 47*s.* ; and Pease; 43*s.* per qr.

*Manchester*, Jan. 27.—Throughout the week we have had a steady demand for most articles in the trade, in consequence of our navigation being impeded by the frost. At our market to-day, all descriptions of Grain (if up) met a free sale, at an advance on Wheat of 2*d.* per Bushel, Barley 1*d.* to 2*d.* per 60 lbs. Oats 1*d.* to 2*d.* per 45 lbs., and Beans 1*s.* per quarter. Pease in better demand, at last week's rates. Malt is free in sale, but the prices are unaltered. The holders of Flour are wanting 1*s.* per sack advance, which was, only in a few instances, reluctantly complied with.

*Newcastle-on-Tyne*, Jan. 27 —We had a good supply of Wheat from the farmers, but very little coastwise, at this morning's market, and the millers being rather bare of stock, sales were readily effected at last week's prices. Rye continues in demand, and prices are unaltered. Barley is 2*s.* per quarter dearer, and as the light Norfolk parcels which were landed a few weeks since have been taken off by the maltsters at about 40*s.* per quarter, the market may be said to be now quite bare of all descriptions. Malt rather more in demand. We have had some arrivals of foreign Oats this week, and the farmers' supply being rather large this morning, the sale was dull at last week's prices.

*Wakefield*, Jan. 26.—The supply of Wheat here this morning, is large, and the navigation of the canals westward, being partially interrupted by the frost, there is a slender attendance of buyers, and the sale of all descriptions has been heavy at last Friday's prices. The supply of Oats and Shelling is not adequate to the demand, and they are both rather dearer. The quantity of Barley offering is only moderate, and it is ready sale at an advance of 1*s.* per quarter. In Beans no alteration.

# COBBETT'S WEEKLY REGISTER.

**Vol. 61.—No. 7.]   LONDON, SATURDAY, Feb. 10, 1827.   [*Price 6d.***

" This Bill (Mr. Peel's) was grounded on *concurrent Reports* of both
" Houses; it was passed by *unanimous votes* of both Houses; it was, at the
" close of the Session, a subject of high eulogium in the Speaker's Speech
" to the Regent, and in the Regent's Speech to the two Houses: now, then,
" I, William Cobbett, assert, that, to carry this Bill into effect is *impos-
" sible;* and I say; that, if this Bill be carried into full effect, I will give
" Castlereagh leave to lay me on a *Gridiron* and broil me alive, while Sid-
" mouth may stir the coals, and Canning stand by and laugh at my groans."
—*Taken from Cobbett's Register, written at North Hempstead, Long
Island, on the 24th of September,* 1819, *and published in England in
November,* 1819.

The Small-Note Bill, passed in 1822, partly repealed Peel's Bill, before
the day for its going into full effect: and, in December 1825, *the one pound
notes of the Bank of England came out again.*—So that here was the above
prophecy completely fulfilled.

## WHAT IS COMING?

## TO THE READERS OF THE REGISTER.

*Kensington, 7th Feb. 1827.*

MY FRIENDS,

WHEN PITT seemed to be ba-
lancing whether he should or
should not be bullied by the Boroughmongers into the war against
the republicans of France; when
it was believed by great numbers
of well-informed persons (and I
believe it still) that he wished not
to go into that war: at that time
Mr. PAINE wrote and published a
pamphlet, entitled "the Prospects
on the Rubicon"; or an *Address*
under some title or other, for, I
really forget precisely what the
title was, desiring the Minister to
pause, to reflect upon the consequences of such war; and, I remember well that, amongst other

N

Printed and Published by WILLIAM COBBETT, No. 183, Fleet-street.
[ENTERED AT STATIONERS' HALL.]

things, he warned the nation, that, let the war end how it might; let what might be its professed object, let it be marked in its progress by whatsoever events it might, it would, in the end, leave consequences behind it, that would be fatal to the aristocratical families in England. We have the terrible consequences of that war now before us. The uncertainty, as to the value of property of every description, the gold coin excepted; the fluctuations in the affairs of men of all ranks in society; the general depression of the whole community; the intolerable, the disgusting workings of misery amongst the labouring classes; the horrible spread of crime and of madness; and, the awful foreboding which every man of reflection has in his mind: these are the natural fruits of the policy prescribed by BURKE and pursued by PITT. I verily believe, that Kings, as well as people, have enormously suffered by that policy. The people of France, if they had been left to themselves; if they had not been menaced in so insolent a tone and treated as a sort of persons entitled to no quarter, never would have touched the life of the King; and, as to ourselves, never should we have seen the begging-box carried round in virtue of a royal rescript, and never should we have heard of such things as horse police and transporting for poaching.

It would have been well, then, if Pitt had stopped, if he had paused, if he had looked at the *prospect* before he crossed the Rubicon of war with France. Of war, too, entered into for the avowed purpose of preventing a revolution of property in England. We, too, ought now to pause; we ought to reflect, while there is time for reflection. We ought to ask ourselves, in the words of my title, **WHAT IS COMING**? The Parliament is to meet again to-morrow; and, I shall have no opportunity of noticing any thing that it may do, until the next *Register*. I know what it can do, and what it cannot do, with regard to those matters which are of the deepest interest to us all; but, I by no means pretend to know what it will *attempt* to do; for, it has attempted so many strange things, and it seems to be so little docile in the school of experience, that I may safely defy any man breathing to foretell what it will, or what it will not, attempt to do.

We are told by the vagabond "best public instructer," that the discussion on the corn-bill is intended to be put off from next Monday to next Monday week; and one branch of the base "best instructer" has told us, that a peer of great power has interfered with the Ministers before-hand, and, as it were, made them give up, to a certain extent, at any rate, their projected alteration of the corn laws. This may, possibly, be true, and, I dare say that the great landowners will, if they think that too much popular discontent will not be excited by it, prevent any real alteration being made in that law. If they do thus expose themselves to the hatred of the great body of the people, they are even weaker than they have ever been represented to be. It is impossible that the present corn-bill, or that any corn-bill, can do them good (except for a few months, perhaps) as long as the Bank of England and other bankers are compelled to pay their notes in gold. It is a clear error; an unmixed error, to suppose that a corn-bill, be it what it may, can prevent prices from falling down to a very low mark, unless a new change were to be made in the laws respecting the currency.

I yesterday saw a gentleman from Norfolk and another from Kent. The report of both was, that the almost only circulating medium in their counties, consisted of one-pound country notes; and both agreed, that it was impossible to take these notes out of circulation without reducing wheat, on an average of years, to three shillings a bushel or less. Their report was, that no man, scarcely, expected that the laws passed last winter would be carried into effect; and, in Norfolk I find that the Gurneys (some branch of the family) have been issuing *new one-pound notes*, ever since the month of September last. This they have, I believe, a right to do, having obtained the stamps previous to the passing of the late Acts; but, they can receive no more stamps, and they can issue no one-pound note, new or old, in twenty-five months and twenty-eight days from this time! What, then, is to take place, when a one-pound note cannot be put forth without exposing the issuer to the risk of a penalty of fifty pounds? Since the panic, there has been a great check upon the country-bankers in the knowledge which people have that every holder of a note has a right to demand it to be exchanged for gold. This has been a great check to the rag-rooks throughout the whole country; but, as long as there are people who want to borrow money;

as long as the numbers of these are very considerable; and very considerable they will be while the value of property is falling and pecuniary distress so very extensive as it must be in such a state of things: as long as this is the case, the rag-rooks will lend their notes, and those who borrow them will circulate them; and hence it is, that though the vile rags are nothing worth in law; though it is manifest folly to keep possession of one of them for an hour, almost the whole of the circulating medium, every where except in London, consists of one-pound notes, either of the country-banks or of the Bank of England. For, the big Borough-Bank herself now issues one-pound notes again, as she has done ever since the time of "Late Panic." She is to lose that power as well as the country-bankers on the 5th of April, 1829. Notwithstanding what we hear about Mr. CANNING's health; notwithstanding the newspapers tell us that his health is nearly restored; notwithstanding that this their assertion is of a most ominous character for him, I hope he will live to see; I hope he will have health to see that 5th day of April; for, that is the day that will tell us who is the fittest to make laws about money, he or I.

Long before that 5th day of April, some great change or other will, in all human probability, take place. If the present law remain in force, a corn-bill that should completely prohibit the importation of corn at any price whatever, would not keep that price up above the price of four shillings for a bushel of wheat; that is to say, on an average of seasons and for any length of time. Such a law, passed at this moment; or, even, a refusal to alter the present law, might, and would, cause wheat, and perhaps all sorts of corn, to take a little rise for a time; because there are great deposits of corn now held in order to ascertain whether such alteration will take place or not. Whatever corn-holder expects to see such alteration, is anxious to sell before the alteration shall come to depress the value of his corn. Many corn-dealers must be in this situation; and, their eagerness to sell has naturally had a tendency to cause corn to fall faster, for some time past, than it otherwise would have fallen. So that, if the Parliament make no alteration in the corn-bill, corn may, and in all likelihood will, rise in price for a few months, perhaps, after the discovery shall be made.

But there will be nothing permanent in this; this will be but for a short time; the price of corn and of every thing else as well as corn, will continue to grow less and less as we approach nearer and nearer to the fifth day of April, 1829. All things will fall in value except the annuities, the salaries, the pensions and the pay of all sorts, proceeding from the Government; and except the income of mortgagees and of those persons who have fixed and permanent charges and demands upon other persons. All this description of persons, including the clergy, will gain by the ruin of the landlord, the farmer, tradesmen of all descriptions, ship-owners, seafaring people, merchants and manufacturers: in short, all that live not upon the taxes or upon incomes which are fixed, will be in a declining and perishing state. It is impossible to prevent this; and, before the fifth day of April shall arrive, and, perhaps, long before, the pressure will, in all likelihood, have become intolerable. But, should we see that fifth day of April; should we see that day arrive, and the present law remain in full force; should we see the one-pound rags swept away out of circulation; should we see Peel's Bill, at last, really

go into full effect: it is not a hundred thousand soldiers, nor ten hundred thousand soldiers, that will prevent scenes in this country, such as hardly any country upon earth ever yet beheld.

Every farmer would be a beggar. His stock would be wholly taken from him; his bed would be taken from under him; he would have no means of paying rent, and hardly a sufficiency to pay his rates. No matter how rich he may be now; a beggar he must be if that law go into full effect. It is this great error; this error; the natural fruit of gross ignorance; of blindness without a parallel; and, above all things, the fruit of *insolent obstinacy*; that insolence which led stupid men to believe, that their power would be more than a match for my penetration, my fore-sight, and my capacity for explaining causes and effects; it is this error, proceeding from this source, and from no other source, which is still at work, tumbling and tossing men's fortunes about, elevating one at the expense of another, shaking all property to its very base, disfiguring the country with crimes and with insanity: it is this monstrous error; this perversion of truth; this criminal adherence to false and foolish notions;

it is this which is still at work, and the final and fatal consequences of which we have yet to witness.

It is for you and I, my friends, constantly to bear in mind the long battle that we have fought against the authors of these false-hoods and these follies. The words of my motto, and the cir-cumstances under which those words were committed to paper, are never to be forgotten. PEEL's BILL arose, in part at least, from a desire, in the breast of both the parties of politicians, the posses-sors of power and the hunters after power; it arose in part from a strenuous desire in them all *to adopt a measure that should give me the lie.* They adopted it: they enacted Peel's Bill; and the mo-ment I heard of it I said that the Bill never could go into full effect; that it never could be acted upon to the full extent; or that, if it were, I would suffer myself to be broiled upon a gridiron. Urged on by their pride; goaded forward by the fear of my falling upon them if they recoiled, they pro-ceeded, in the year 1822, to within nine months of the time when the Bill was to go into full effect. In this attempt they ruined thousands upon thousands and hundreds of thousands of families; they caused a mass of suffering and of crime

such as England, at no period of its history, had ever witnessed be-fore. Frightened at the prospect before them, they suddenly stop-ped; they partly repealed the Bill, and hoped to come back again to something resembling a state of prosperity. A delusive prosperity did return. They boasted that the prosperity was permanent; before six months had expired after they had put that sentiment into the mouth of the King himself, a new species of ruin and desolation was pro-duced by the very means which they had used to effect their pro-sperity, and which ruin and deso-lation I had forewarned them of, from the moment of their attempt to obtain it by such means. Frightened at this new species of ruin; more terrified at that than they had been at the ruin which they had only just escaped in the year 1822; seeing not an inch before their noses, and think-ing about nothing but the present hour, they hastened back to Peel's Bill, and enacted that it should now, in reality, go into effect, in three years from that time; that is to say, on the fifth of April 1829. Here we are, then, again at issue with these bungling, these ignorant, these obstinately blind politicians. They say, that there shall be no one-pound notes in circulation, after the fifth of April 1821. Not only has the Parliament enacted this; but the Ministers have, individually, declared, that they will stand to the enactment.

If they do stand to that enactment, most terrible will be the consequences; and, yet (the debt continuing what it now is), the only method they have of avoiding standing to the enactment, is still more terrible in its prospects than it would be to stand to the enactment itself. If they repeal their Bill of last year, and Mr. Canning treat us with his mountain of paper having a base irrigated with gold; if they do this, it will be impossible to keep the paper-money within those bounds which would prevent the gold from quitting the country. They would, then, be compelled to authorise the Bank to refuse to pay in gold; that, as I have a hundred times said, would be, in fact, to authorise an issue of assignats: half the property in the country would make an instant change of hands; and we should see men, who are now riding in their coaches, sweeping the streets or begging their bread; besides seeing this immense Wen plunged into all the horrors of starvation and its consequent strife.

What, then, is coming? There is a way out of this difficulty. There is a way to avoid both these monstrous evils: and, that way has been clearly pointed out in the Norfolk petition. Do I believe, however, that that petition will be called up and listened to? Indeed I do not. I believe no such thing; and I expect to see the Thing end as it naturally must end, without the application of that remedy, and of that remedy alone. The question at present, however, is, *what will, now, be attempted?* If the Ministers be so blind, or so obstinate, as not to see, or pretend not to see, the real cause of the distresses of the land and of the country in general, all men are not thus blind and thus obstinate. There will be some persons, even in Parliament, to think and even to talk more about the *currency* than about the *corn*. There has, for some time, been an anxious desire, on the part of many of the landowners, to lessen the sum which their estates pay to the fundholders. They have been almost afraid to open their lips upon the subject. They are shockingly under cow to the loan-mongers and other Jews; but, they have now and then ventured to hint that they think that these vile jobbers ought not to have the whole- of their estates, hares, phaesants, and all. Now, though it is impossible for any human being to have a lower opinion of the spirit of other human beings than I have of the wretched creatures to whom I am alluding; though I most sincerely look upon them, in general, as being much lower, in point of spirit, than even the Jews and Genoese, that the old soldiers used to tell me that they used to kick about the streets of Gibraltar; still, I do believe that there will be found amongst them some three or four, at any rate, who will say, in pretty plain language, that they do not mean that the monsters of 'Change Alley, that the loan-jobbers and paper-money makers shall take from them the last acre of their land. Opinions, particularly when they are favourable to the interests of the crowd, by which the opinion-giver is surrounded, are as contagious as a certain cutaneous disease, which, for the honour of our great enlighteners from the north, shall, for the present, be nameless. Such opinions spread about like wildfire; and if there should be found (a thing that I despair of, indeed) only one man of real spirit, to maintain these opinions openly and boldly, the effect would be prodigious.

What I expect, however, is this; that no manly attempt will be made; that there will be a great deal of talk about the currency; that some sort of middle-going measure will be proposed by somebody; and that, after all, nothing will be done, during the present session, to alter the law of last year. But, I also expect, that the language of the Ministers will be such, as to hold out something of a hope that the Bill of last year may, before the day of its awful full execution shall arrive, *receive some degree of mitigation!* That will be enough. The rooks will be all alive, just like the winged inhabitants of a rookery, when they see the farmer's cart coming loaded with corn to be sown in the neighbouring field. There will be such a cawing and such a fluttering, such a riding about in post-chaises, such parcels of new gowns for the wives and daughters of the rag-rooks, such smirking and shaking by the hand amongst the sleek and sly old vagabonds of Quakers: in short, the whole rookery will be in such a state of exultation, that the very din will half scare the nation out of its senses. Thus I think it is possible that the thing may go on for another year, *it* being " *the understood sense* " that the Bill of last year is not to go into full effect. If the rooks get into too high feather, we shall have another " late panic," or, to use the words of Doctor Baring, another *cold fit.* If they keep within moderate bounds, the thing may stagger along till this time twelvemonth; but, then, we shall be coming too close to the terrible fifth of April without something in the law-making way being done. The rooks will begin to require something a little more than the " *understood sense*": they will begin to want a little work in the act-making way. And, now, I hereby give full warning, that, if the Bill of last year be repealed; if it be altered so as to extend the time for the use of the paper-money; or, if there be Bank-restriction; in short, if there be any thing done, in the law-making way, to attempt this revival of Peel's Bill going into full effect, *I shall hoist the gridiron, and fix it on the front of my house in Fleet-Street.* I had a full right to do this, long ago; but, I was resolved to give the pretty gentlemen every possible chance of falsifying my predictions. The gridiron is made; it is of iron, seven feet long and five feet wide: it has been painted, and only wants gilding; and. if any alteration be made in this

law, up it goes upon that house; if I am, that day, in existence. Take the warning, therefore, pretty gentlemen: think of it betimes; for, if that gridiron be hoisted, it never comes down again for many years to come, and as long as it shall remain and as you shall remain, you will be the laughing-stock of this whole nation.

What ought to be the sentiments of this nation with regard to you, if you were now to act in a manner to justify the hoisting of that gridiron? And, it is not only by a repeal of the law that you would justify this: it is by any other measure that would be substantially to the same effect. Another Bank-restriction would, indeed, be to do a great deal more than repeal the last year's Bill. A Bank-restriction must include a repeal of the Bill, and make other provisions in addition to that. But, *lowering the standard* of the currency; or any shuffling trick of this kind, would fully authorize the hoisting of the gridiron. Deducting from the interest of the Debt would also authorize it. In short, unless you carry the last year's Bill into full effect; unless you cleanly sweep away all the one-pound notes, and continue to pay the interest of the Debt in full, in coin of the present weight and fineness, you fully authorize me in hoisting the gridiron; and, as I said in my last year's petition to the Parliament, I know, as well as I know that fire burns, that you cannot do these things.

Well, then, if I be right here; and, time will speedily show whether I be right or wrong; if I be right here, what a scandal it is, what a shameful thing it is, that this mischief should be done; that all this wrong should be thus done, and that there should be no man to say that responsibility ought to rest upon the head of the authors of such mischief! Responsibility, if it be not a mere mockery, means that men should be answerable for the injuries which they do to others; and, what injuries ever done to mortal man equal those which have been done to this country, in the face of all the warnings, all the proofs, which you have received at my hands! Surely we have heard of Ministers being made responsible; actually, in very deed, responsible for the injury they had done to their country. They undertake their offices not only voluntarily, but at their own pressing requests. It is not new in the history of the world, that there have been Ministers to force themselves into power. But, at the very least,

they freely enter their offices; they like them; they contract to receive pay for executing those offices; and, in England, they are paid better than in any other country in the world. In all other businesses of life, the undertaking to do a thing implies a contract, or condition, rather, on the part of the undertaker, that he is capable of doing it; that he knows how to do it: as, for instance, in the case of a cook, he contracts to cook for you; but, if it be found that he does not know how to cook, he has made a false contract, as much as a man would who should undertake to teach French, and who should be discovered to know not a word of that language. In such cases, the parties are punished by having payment refused them. It is not long ago, since I read of an action, brought against a man who had been employed as a surgeon; who had pretended to set a leg or an arm, I forget which; who had spoiled the limb, who was afterwards discovered not to understand surgery, and who was soused in heavy damages for the mischief that he had done.

Now, then, pretty gentlemen, let us try you, according to these principles, the soundness of which, I am sure, nobody will deny. It is notorious to all the world: there are no twelve honest men to be found in England who would, upon their oaths, declare, that the measures, proposed by you, and procured by you to be adopted; that these measures, relative to the currency of this country, have *not done monstrous mischief to his Majesty's subjects, and to his Majesty's kingdom and state*. This is what any twelve honest men in the kingdom would declare upon their oaths; and that, too, without quitting the box for one moment. *What, then, would be your defence, if this notorious fact were* moulded into a charge against you?

Would you plead incapacity to propose better measures? Would you plead innate ignorance? That would be no defence at all; for, you voluntarily undertook to perform the office for so much money; and, you have received the payment. The surgeon was not excused upon a plea of having done his best; because, he ought not to have undertaken to do the thing at all, seeing that he did not understand how to do it. Would you plead, that you advised his Majesty to the best of your wit and cunning; that it was impossible for you to foresee the consequences of the measures which you advised; that no Minister is expect-

ed to be infallible; and that any other man, however wise and diligent, might have recommended the same or similar measures, with the best possible intention? This would be a very good defence; this would be a defence, which the ablest and wisest of men need not be ashamed to set up; but, pretty gentlemen, this defence cannot serve you. For, not only was it possible for you to foresee the consequences of the measures which you advised, but, the consequences were foreseen for you, ready to your hand: they were pointed out to you with the greatest possible accuracy, even before you proposed the measures. Not only was not infallibility required at your hands; but, nothing but mere attention to what was told you was required. You adopted Peel's Bill in the month of July, 1819. In the month of November of the preceding year, I, in a publication, sent forth within a few hundred yards of Whitehall; in a publication of which between twenty and thirty thousand copies were sold in London; in that publication, which you must have seen, or, at any rate, you might have seen, you were duly and fully warned of the fatal consequences of any measure, the tendency of which should be, to re-

store the currency to its ancient
state, without a reduction of the
interest of the Debt. You were
not only warned of the general
tendency of any such measure;
but you were told of the precise
manner in which such measure
would produce its various mischiefs; and, yet, you persevered,
nay, you originated the measure,
even after that warning was given
you. All this admits of regular
*judicial proof.* Hundreds of public
men have had to plead, in *due
form,* in answer to charges founded
on evidence which was vagueness
itself compared to the evidence in
this case. There is The *Register;* there are the witnesses to
prove the publication of it and the
number published; there is *Peel's
Bill* and the date of that Bill, and
witnesses and records to prove the
passing of it, and to prove, also,
your having proposed it. I say,
again, that I know nothing about
the meaning of the word *responsibility,* if it do not mean, *being answerable for the mischief that one
does with one's eyes open.*

But here is " late panic " to
answer for. You proposed, you
procured to be passed the *Small-
note Bill* of 1822. There are the
*Registers,* foretelling the consequences of that Bill before it was
passed; warning you against

those consequences; warning you
afterwards of the consequences of
persevering in it; telling you that
if you persevered you would blow
up the country banks: in short,
warning you, before-hand, of every
one of the evils, which arose out
of these measures of your proposing and procuring. What defence, then, is there? And, if
Ministers are not to be responsible for the mischiefs produced
by measures, which they have
adopted in spite of the plainest
and most impressive warnings,
what a despicable farce is ministerial responsibility!

To say that you never read the
Register, never heard of its contents; to say, that if you did read
it or hear of its contents, you were
not bound' to believe in any part
of those contents, you being such
monstrous great men, while the
author of the *Register* was a mere
nobody, or at best, as Scarlet
said, a contemptible scribbler:
this would not answer your purpose, in the judgment of any sensible and honest man: it would
be at once shuffling and sauci-
ness, either of which would deserve a horse-whip at least. No;
your only defence would be, that
you thought it was better to make
the King's subjects suffer; to expose the peace and tranquillity of

his Majesty; to humble the country to the dust; to do any thing, no matter what, rather than have it be said and let it be notorious to all the world, that you had acted upon the advice of WILLIAM COBBETT; or that you had suffered his predictions to be fulfilled. This is your only defence: you have no other; and you have this comfort, that (I verily believe), a pretty large part of those who will at last be most severely punished by your measures, would say that this defence was perfectly satisfactory.

I have said it, I believe, several times, and I delight in repeating it, that I am convinced that you could have listened to sound advice long ago; that a remedy could have been applied to these evils, years ago; that infinite mischief would have been left undone : had it not been for fear of giving the nation room to say, that now, COBBETT's *predictions were verified.* But, alas, this comes after all, though the mischief has taken place. Those who were so anxious to keep me in a state of depression, that they could even expose themselves to suffering, to accomplish that object; thousands and thousands of these are now actually ruined, thousands of others are upon the point of ruin, and they have, at the same time, the mortification to see, that my doctrines have all been verified to the very letter, and that all the world is satisfied, that, if my advice had been followed, these sufferings would all have been avoided. For my own part, I care not how much the vermin suffer. They are destined to suffer a great deal more yet. Justice has not half done with them; and my real opinion is, that before the 5th of April, 1829, there will be sufferings, compared to which all that we have seen is a trifle.

Now, my friends, readers of the Register, who must feel pretty much as I do, with regard to the stupid, the envious, the perverse, the selfish, the base reptiles that have been calumniating me for so many years past; you, my friends, look forward, I beseech you, to the manner in which you may be affected by the events which are at hand. A rag of the Old Mother Bank, having two dates, one in 1821, and the other in 1826, and signed *C. Tabor,* I think it is: one of these rags, for one pound, is now lying upon the table before me, having printed upon it, in large letters, the word "FORGED," in five different places. I received this

...ing from the country, by letter, for some trees; I gave it to my maltster almost as soon as I had got it, making it a rule never to sleep with one in the house; the maltster took it to the Old Mother, and she disfigured it by printing " FORGED " upon it five times. The maltster brought it back to me; I gave him a sovereign for it; and here it lies upon the table before me, in proof of the soundness of Peter M'Culloch's doctrines relative to " *cheap currency*." Cheap enough this is now, for I shall send it into Fleet Street to-morrow, and order Mr. Dean to stick it up as a Shoy-hoy, or, rather, as *a warning to the readers of the Register*.

Now, my friends, let that bit of " cheap currency," which is No. 62,327, and contains a promise to pay to Henry Hase, or bearer, on demand, the sum of one pound; let this little bit of cheap currency be a specimen quite sufficient for you! This is about the eighth or ninth time that I have had to undergo the pains and penalties of cheap currency. Never through any fault of mine. My order to Mr. Dean is, never to sleep with a bank note of any description in the house, and I adhere to the same rule myself. The thing for you to think of,

however, is this : that, if the act of last year be not repealed, every sovereign that you can put by now, and save for a couple of years, will purchase twice as much of any thing as you can purchase for a sovereign now. This is a capital consideration: It is what every man ought to have constantly in his eye. Forbear a little in your spending now: *keep your money;* but, KEEP IT IN GOLD. If, on the contrary, there should be a repeal of the last year's bill, then there will be a bank-restriction, in a very short time; then a sovereign will sell, perhaps, for four or five pounds in paper: then will be the time for you to congratulate yourselves on your providence, your foresight, and your resolution to keep the gold. It is impossible that any thing should happen, to make you repent of having laid by and kept the king's coin. I conclude in the words in which I have concluded many letters to you, words more necessary to be addressed to you now than at any former period; GET GOLD, AND KEEP IT; and receive an expression of the best wishes of

Your Friend and

    Most obedient Servant,

      WM. COBBETT.

## AMERICAN SEEDS.

————

I do not think any apology (to any of my readers) called for on account of the great length, to which I perceive this article must extend. It is not for my *own advantage*, that I offer the following named seeds to the public; it is not for the purpose of indemnifying myself against loss; but, solely with a view, and in the hope, of introducing into England, and that, too, with as much speed as possible, a widely extended cultivation of some of the finest and most valuable timber-trees, and of the most beautiful shrubs, in the world, several of which are, as yet, almost wholly, and some of them wholly, unknown, in this country.

I have in former Registers stated that it was my intention to put up collections of seeds in boxes; and to sell each collection together with the box, bags, &c., for 5*l.* I have not known till now, precisely what number of sorts of seeds I should have to dispose of; nor could I with any chance of being nearly correct state the probable quantity of each that would be put into the box. I have now arranged the whole matter; have made up some boxes, and therefore now know precisely what I have to dispose of. Each box will contain seeds of TWENTY-TWO sorts of American forest trees; and of FORTY-ONE sorts of lower trees and shrubs, of the whole of which I shall now proceed to give a list, subjoining to the name of each tree and shrub such information, relative to it, as I may deem useful and as I may be able to give. There are two circumstances, which must be attended to: the manner of *naming* the plants, and the manner of *numbering* them. As to the naming, I have sometimes given the botanical name without the vulgar name, and sometimes I have done the reverse. This has arisen from my being unable, in spite of all my ransacking of books, to make the thing more perfect in this respect. With regard to the numbering, the utility of numbering, is manifest enough; because it saves writing the names upon the several parcels; it furnishes a distinctive mark for the beds where the several sorts of seeds are sown. But, I have not, for a reason to be stated presently, been able to begin at *number one*, and to go on to the end, in that ordinary way. It will be seen that I begin with *number nineteen*, then take *number six*, and so on in this promiscuous manner; it will be seen also, that I have a number 124, though the whole of the sorts of seeds amount to but sixty - three in number. The reason of this is, that I have, in the whole of my collection, whether of last year or of this year, whether lying in the ground or now in package, seeds, making altogether 124 sorts, and I believe more. I have been obliged to number these sorts just as I received them, or, in some cases, as I sowed them; and, as Black Walnut, for instance, happened to have originally number nineteen fall to its lot, it still retains in my general list number nineteen. I have got into most troublesome confusion by departing, in certain cases, from this mode of numbering; and therefore I have returned to it, and adhered to it here; it will be productive of no inconvenience whatsoever to persons who purchase the seeds; because, the number which each parcel will have marked upon it will correspond with the numbers contained in this list. There is another reason for this sort of numbering, namely, that having numbered the whole of my collection, I found, upon *examin-*

*ing the seeds*, that there were many, which I could not venture to sell, for fear of exposing the purchaser to disappointment; for, though some part of every sort of seed was good, the part was so small as to make it possible, and even likely, that I should put up some packages containing not one good seed. I was very desirous, for instance, to put in some seeds of the Live Oak, of the Chincapin, of the Yellow-flowering Horse-Chesnut, of other Oaks; but there was no way of distinguishing the good seed from the bad seed without cutting them open, and the proportion of good seeds was so very small, that I could not venture to expose gentlemen to the disappointment, I myself knowing what it is to experience disappointments of this sort. All the seeds I offer for sale I know to contain a very large proportion of good seeds.

I now give the list; merely the list, first, in the order in which they have been put up. I shall afterwards repeat the names and numbers contained in the list, and place against each such information as I think likely to be useful and such as I am able to give. I have read all the books, that I have in my possession, as far as they relate to these trees and shrubs.

With regard to many of them, I find that neither EVELYN nor MILLER knew any thing at all. MICHAUX and Dr. BARTON speak of most of the trees and shrubs; but neither of them give us any information relative to the time that the seeds lie in the ground, and relative to several other circumstances, without some information with regard to which the possession of the seeds must, in many cases, be nearly useless. Many of these seeds, or seeds of these sorts, I have sown myself in former years. I know, experimentally, a great deal about them. I am able to say, as to the greater part of them, whether they come up the first summer or not. I know the precautions necessary to be taken in the sowing and the cultivating of the most delicate sorts. This knowledge I shall endeavour here to communicate in a manner different to the greater part of my brother gardeners who take pen in hand; that is to say, I shall endeavour to do it in a manner that will give the reader a fair chance of understanding my meaning. First, then, I shall, as I said before, insert a mere list of the trees and shrubs, and I shall then take them one by one as subjects of observation addressed to the reader.

## FOREST TREES.

No.
19. Black Walnut. Juglans nigra.
6. Occidental Plane.
107. Ontario White Elm.
7. Red Maple. Acer rubrum.
81. Sugar Maple. Acer Saccharinum.
8. Red Cedar. Juniperus virginiana.
9. White Cedar. Cupressus thioïdes.
22. Black Wild Cherry.
10. Deciduous Cypress. Cupressus disticha.
81. Larch. Larix.
114. Carolinian Ash. Fraxinus platicarpa.
116. Red Ash. Fraxinus tomentosa.
17. White Beech. Fagus Sylvestris.
18. Red Beech. Fagus ferruginea.
74. Bass Wood. Tilia Americana.
14. White Birch. Betula populicolia.
16. Black Birch. Betula leuta.
118. Yellow Birch. Betula lutea.
88. Black Spruce. Abies nigra.
101. Hemlock. Abies canadensis.
92. White Pine. Pinus strobus
119. Hornbeam. Carpinus.

## SHRUBS.

No.
59. Carolina Allspice. Caryophyllus Aromaticus.
62. Sumach. Rhus Carolinianum.
28. Ilex Casine.
80. Ilex Dahoon.
104. Callacarpas Americana.
87. Red bay. Laurus Caroliniensis.

O

97. Black Gum. Nyssa sylvatica.
64. Magnolia Glauca. Small Magnolia or White Bay.
65. Magnolia Tripetala. Umbrella tree.
82. Magnolia Grandiflora. Large Magnolia or Big Laurel.
86. Pride of India. Melia azedarach.
43. Chionanthus.
62. Viburnum.
61. Cornus Florida. Large flowering Dogwood.
77. Cornus Alba.
109. Cornus Sirecea.
111. Cornus Paniculata.
63. June Berry. Mespilus arborea.
89. Crataegus.
105. Pyrus Melancarpus.
106. Choke Cherry.
108. Olive.
110. Viburnum lantana.
112. Prunus depressa.
57. Iron wood. Carpinus ostrya.
55. Arbor vitæ.
75. Box thorn. Lycium.
49. Cercis. Judas tree.
11. Tupelo. Nyssa aquatica.
90. Large Tupelo.
89. Sour Tupelo Nyssa capitata.
45. Nettlewood.
114. Pyrus.
79. Georgia Bark. Pinckneya pubescens.
117. Water Locust. Gleditsia monosperma.
120. Sorrel. Andromeda Arborea.
69. Gordonia Pubescens. Franklinia.
124. Gordonia lasyanthus. Loblolly Bay.
85. Dwarf Rose Bay. Rhododendrum Maximum.
123. Ever-green Anthromeda.
96. Azalia.

No. 19. Black Walnut (Juglans nigra). There are of this sort two gallons in each box. The number of walnuts being between three and four hundred: and I think nearer to four hundred than three hundred. The seed is perfectly good. I have broken many with a hammer, and I do not believe that there is one bad seed out of ten. These seeds are loose in the box. The manner in which I sow them is this. The ground is dug very deeply as for all other seeds; it is laid out in beds three feet wide, with alleys of fifteen inches wide; the walnuts would (if I had room) be deposited about a foot apart upon these beds; when so deposited they are pressed down close into the ground; earth is taken from the alleys and laid upon the bed until the walnuts be covered to the depth of two and a half inches; the ground being made pretty neat and smooth at top. The sooner the walnuts are put into the ground, the better, I am sowing mine now, when I catch an open and dry day; but, I have sown them so late as the month of May, and, in my rich and moist ground they have still done well. The best way, however, is to sow them as soon as you conveniently can; and in the mean while, keep them in a little dry sand.

As to the size and utility of this tree; it is one of the largest trees in the world, and one of very quick growth.

There may be seen at Fleet-Street, a plate recently published at New York, representing the trunk of a Black Walnut tree, scooped out, and furnished as a drawing room. It is exhibited in the Chatham Museum in that City. It measures at its base *thirty-six* feet in circumference, and, as will be seen from the plate, it cannot be much smaller, at the height of fifteen or twenty feet from the ground. The wood is of the colour of the darkest mahogany, but has not the brightness and beauty of the mahogany, though it is very often made use of in the furniture of the best houses. It is a tree that grows to a great height; but is more remarkable for its wide-spreading than for long and straight shaft.

It was under the shade of one of these trees, that I sat, in the month of July, 1818, and wrote that Letter to TENANT; in which I warned this now suffering nation of the fatal effects which would inevitably ensue, if the Government, following the advice of TENANT, should pass a Bill like

that of PEEL.—MICHAUX, in speaking of the uses of the timber of this tree, says, that it is in great use as KNEES in the building of ships, the timber being full, as strong as ordinary oak, though not equal to the Live Oak or the Locust, and the manner of growing in the tree, furnishing such a prodigious quantity of knees.—Like all other North American trees, the leaves continue bright and fresh through the hottest of our summers; and the leaves of this Walnut, hanging in very large lobes, make it altogether a magnificent tree.

No. 6. OCCIDENTAL PLANE, (*Platanus occidentalis.*) This is, I believe, the very largest tree in the world. We have never heard of a cedar of Lebanon approaching to the size of this tree. MICHAUX measured one, which was, at some distance from the ground, (several feet distance I believe), *forty-seven feet round*; that is to say, almost sixteen feet through. There are several in America which have actually served, and many that still serve, as rooms for families of new settlers to live in, and that, too, for a year or two at a time. MICHAUX says, that this tree begins to take its spread about sixty or seventy feet from the ground, where it overlooks the general mass of the forest. The timber of this tree is made use of for all those purposes that white wood is generally employed about; but, it is also made use of for all the purposes where *splitting* is a thing to be avoided; accordingly it is made use of in the making *of blocks for ships*, and in that way, is very useful. In this country we never see this tree in its natural shape. To raise it from seed is an affair, requiring the greatest care and attention. Nothing is so easy as to raise it from *layers*; but (and I beg the reader to remark this well), a *layer* is not a *tree* but the *limb* or *branch* of a tree; and it never can be otherwise than a limb or a branch. Hence it is that we see in England no fine straight and lofty trees, the seed of which it is difficult to make grow, and the cuttings, layers or suckers of which, are pretty nearly as easy to make grow as the root of a dock or dandelion.

I have two or three of these Planes, which I raised from seed three years ago. They were refuse plants, and left by accident in the bed; they are now about eight or nine feet high, and they exhibit a very different shaped thing from those which are raised from layers. Now then for the

seed. It is the most contemptible looking thing upon the face of the earth; it somewhat resembles a most miserable starveling oak, but the pith which it has, is not bigger than the smallest pin, at nearly the point; and it was a long time after I first got the seed, before I could discover any pith at all. There are about four thousand of these seeds in the box in a bag, distinguished by its number; and I now proceed to give instructions for the sowing of this seed, with this prefatory remark, that if it be too troublesome to attend to the instructions, the better way will be to throw the seed into the fire. Time of sowing, about the middle of March, when the ground works well. Make a bed, as in the case of the Walnut; make the earth at the top of the bed very smooth, with the spade; then take a little earth out of the alleys, and sift it evenly over the bed; sow the seed at an inch or two apart upon this sifted earth; then press the seed down hard upon the sifted earth; then sift upon that about a half an inch of earth, and press that down well with the hand; then sift up n the bed another half an inch of earth, and let that remain without pressing down. The seed will come up in about six weeks or two months, and in its seed-leaf, you will find it very much resembling, both in shape and colour, the *bee-root*, when it is in seed-leaf. "Here is a *great deal of trouble*," the reader will say; but recollect that there will be a hundred seeds, or thereabouts, to a square foot of ground, and recollect that the gardener ought to do the whole job, from beginning to end, in *an hour*.

No. 107. ONTARIO WHITE ELM. —Knowing how much more valuable and how much more beautiful the Elms of America are than the Elms of our own country, and knowing that every tree in the world bears its seed, I last year wrote very pressingly to my correspondent, to get me seeds of the Elms, and particularly of the *White Elm* mentioned by MICHAUX. This brought me the seeds of the subject upon which I am now writing. My correspondent, who is a persevering Englishman, went back to the *Genesee country;* that is to say, better than a thousand miles from New York, and very near to the Lake Ontario, to hunt after this Elm seed. It is impossible for me to give a better account of this fine tree than he himself has given of it. I will, therefore, here insert an extract from his letter to me upon the subject, dated New York, 23d June 1826; from which extract, the reader will see the sort of pains that have been taken to get together this collection:——

" I came home last night from " the river Genesee, where I have " been to get *Elm seeds*. The " seeds of the two sorts of elms, " the red and the white, that are " described by Michaux, I have " not been able to obtain. I was " too late. I ought to have gone " off on the first of May, for the " Genesee, instead of going into " New Jersey; but as I did not " know this, and as I went to " Jersey because I would fain " save the expense of so long a " journey as that which I was " obliged to take at last, I acquit " myself of blame, and I hope " you will also acquit me of " blame. If I could have been " 50 or 60 miles west of Utica, " where the land of elms com- " mences as you go west, so early " as the 20th, or 25th of May, I " should most certainly have ob- " tained a barrel of Michaux's " white elm seeds, and perhaps, " also, some red elm seeds; but, " unfortunately, I did not get here " until the 28th, and on the 27th " and 28th there was a most tre- " mendous tempest of wind, rain, " thunder, lightning, which was " cleared off, on the 29th, by

"heavy gales from the north-west.
"The seeds, being quite ripe, were,
"during this tempest, all stripped
"clean from the trees, and I had
"the mortification to see them fly
"off in clouds. I pushed on to
"the west, as far as Rochester,
"in the hope that the storm had
"not reached so far as that, but I
"was disappointed. However,
"three or four miles east of Ro-
"chester, in a township called
"Brighton, I had the good fortune
"to discover, or rather to have
"pointed out to me, an elm, of a
"sort different to any laid down
"by Mr. Michaux, and which
"the pointer-out insisted upon
"calling the true and genuine
"white elm. It was on the 2d of
"June when I first saw this tree.
"I paid great attention to the
"man who pointed it out to me,
"and I immediately looked out
"for a person to chop me down a
"tree of the kind, that I might
"see it all over, leaf, branch,
"seed, everything belonging to it.
"The tree we felled was 70 feet
"high to where it ramified. Seed
"not quite ripe. Stem 20 inches
"through, as straight as a ram-
"rod. Having satisfied myself
"that it is of a sort not spoken of
"by Michaux, and not knowing
"what name to call it by, I set
"about with all possible despatch

"an inquiry as to the real good-
"ness of the wood, in order
"that I might discover whether
"it is better or worse than the
"other sorts of Elm. I took three
"men to see the tree we had cut,
"and the man who helped me
"cut it was a fourth; they all
"called it White Elm. Michaux's
"White Elm, is called by these
"men, Piss Elm, Water Elm,
"Swamp Elm.—I found that this
"New Elm was by all called
"White Elm, and, by all, it is
"regarded as far superior to the
"other sorts. It is used for all
"such purposes as the toughest of
"Hickory is used, namely; for
"whip - stocks, yoke - bows,
"plough-handles, and the like.
"I took care to have ample testi-
"mony as to the common name
"of the tree, and I find that it is
"uniformly called White Elm in
"the Genesee country; at least it
"is so called by numerous persons
"for at least 40 miles east of
"where I gathered the seeds; and
"none of the numerous persons
"that I examined upon this point,
"knew it by any other name. I
"saw a plough maker at Roches-
"ter using this Elm for plough-
"handles, and he tells me that he
"prefers it to every other kind of
"wood for that purpose. However,
"I, as a plough-maker, and having

" an eye to my reputation; as my correspondent tells me, that
" honest plough-wright, think I to avoid the difficulty of picking
" should prefer the White Oak. the seeds up amongst the leaves
" But, in Genesee, White Oak is and rubbish upon the ground, he
" scarce; and, upon this fat land felled the tree in such a way that
" and in the comparatively humid the head of it went *into the river*,
" atmosphere in the vicinage of and that he and his companions
" the great lakes, the White Oak, got into the river and gathered
" and indeed all sorts of timber, is the seeds. He has sent me a
" 'bragger' than that which piece of one of the limbs of the
" grows upon the more arid soil tree. This is too large and too
" and purer atmosphere of the sea long to send whole to Fleet
" board.—I did not see an Elm Street; but I shall have a block
" whip-stock nor an axe elve, but I of it sawed off and sent thither to
" am assured that it is used for be seen by any body who may
" these purposes, and that for such choose to see it. He has also
" uses it has no rival.—RAISE. sent me three of the twigs of this
" The White Elm easily splits, tree; one of which I shall send
" and makes rails that outlast to Fleet Street: and from these it
" the other sorts of Elm; but, like will be seen how widely this tree
" all Elms, it warps a good deal, differs from the elms of England.
" and it is on that account not I have put up, as nearly as I can
" very proper for boards. It guess, about *three hundred of these*
" makes pretty good sills for build- *seeds*, the whole of which are good,
" ing." and every one of which will grow

The English reader will laugh if sown at the time and precisely
at the idea, or perhaps, if a tree in the same manner as directed in
owner or fancier, he will shudder the case of number six. In the ar-
at the thought of cutting down a ticle of elms, our misfortune is, the
tree which had a straight shaft up the great facility of raising them
to seventy feet from the ground, from suckers and layers. If
before it began to branch; he will raised from suckers they are al-
shudder at the thought of cutting ways a sucker, and they fill the
down such a tree, merely to get ground all round about them with
at the seeds, and that, too, without suckers; if raised from layers
asking the permission of the they are always nearly a limb of
owner! In a subsequent letter a tree, and they begin to branch

away before they attain any
height, if you attempt to prevent
which by pruning, you have a
nasty knotty thing, good for very
little as timber, and ornamental
in the eyes of those only who like
to see a sort of broom at the top of
a handle forty or fifty feet long.
We have gone on at this rate till
people in general actually believe
that the common English Elm
never has any seed, than which,
a more false idea never entered
into the head of mortal man.

No. 7. RED MAPLE. (*Acer Rubrum.*)

No. 31. SUGAR MAPLE. (*Acer
Saccharinum.*)—I put these two
together because the time and
manner of sowing them are the
same. Both should go into the
ground as soon as possible,
though the middle of March will do
very well, though, perhaps, a little
later if the seeds be kept in sand.
The manner of sowing, the
same as *number six*, *with the
addition of another inch of mould
at the top*. I am not sure
whether number seven lie a whole
year in the ground before it comes
up; but, I know that number
thirty-one, does; that is to say,
that it does not come up till the
next spring after it is sown.
I know, too, from pretty dear
bought experience, that it

comes up very early in that
next spring; and that a good hard
frost in March (such as we had
last year) will relieve you from
any further care respecting it, as
it did me last year. To avoid
being played a trick like this, one
way is, to keep the seeds in some
safe place, and in sand, rather
moist, until the fall, until November perhaps, then sow them and
you will have them up in April
or May. This will, too, give you
the use of the ground for the
summer. But, I prefer sowing
the seed properly the first year,
and protecting the beds against
the effects of frost, the next spring,
as soon as you begin to see the
plants bend out of the ground.
This is what I shall do, and it is
of course what I recommend to
others, and especially in the case
of the Red Maple, the time of
the coming up of which I do not
yet know. These Maples are all
very beautiful trees, the Red Maple especially. They grow to a
great height, and some of them
furnish most beautiful wood of
great dimensions. My correspondent has sent me a chest made
of Maple, the boards of which are
two feet four inches wide; and the
beauty of the wood surpasses, I
think, that of any wood that I ever
saw. It is a tree easily culti-

vated; will grow very fast and in very poor land. I have sold a few this year that came up the year before last, that were transplanted last spring, and some of which were more than four feet high when I sold them. As an ornamental tree, hardly any lofty tree is equal to the Maple. And only think of the pleasure that friend CROPPER will experience at having an opportunity afforded him of raising *sugar* from the arid fields of England! I have *seen* sugar, and good sugar too; I have seen it with my own eyes made from these trees in that most blackguard and beggarly of all countries " Nova Scotia." I was getting some milk and bread at a tavern; I complained that the milk was rather of the sourest, and my landlady went out very kindly and fetched me some syrup from the Maple tree. Think of that Jemmy Cropper!

No. 8. RED CEDAR (*Juniperus virginiana.*) Every body knows that this is a lofty evergreen, throwing out numerous small branches, having in its timber a red heart (such as the pencils are made of), surrounded with a white wood, which, I suppose, may be called the sap. The seed is contained in a little rough hard pod or shell, a good deal resembling the seed of the red beet or mangel wurzel. There are several seeds in the same pod or shell. They do not come up the first year; and they must be sown in moist ground or kept very carefully watered, to make them come up the second year. I am trying several tricks with these obstinate devils; fire, water, hot dung; all sorts of things, the result of which I will communicate in time. At present I can only say that I know the seed to be good, and I recommend it to be mixed with fine earth, put into a flower-pot, kept in the shade during the summer, being properly watered in dry weather, and sown next spring, in he manner I have directed for No. 7 and 31.

No. 9. WHITE CEDAR. (*Cupressus thioïdes.*) The White Cedar Tree is a lofty and very lofty evergreen, growing as straight as a gun-stick. It is one of the most useful woods in America. It makes the best of *shingles* for the covering of houses: every good house in the whole country has a covering of this wood, and a roof so covered lasts for fifty years. It cleaves so well that no sawing is ever necessary. I have dog-hutches at Kensington, covered with some of these shingles; they have had no paint, though they

have been exposed to the weather
almost ever since I have lived
here, and they will last a lifetime.
The seed of this tree is contained
in a little round cone; or rather a
cone the general shape of which
is round, but which is not smooth
by any means. Each of these
contains three or four seeds, which
are small and flat. They ought
to be sown at the same time, and
in the same manner as I have directed for number 6. They will
come up in a month or six weeks
after they are sown. The little
cones should be broken, or pinched to pieces, and then sown altogether with the seeds.

No. 22. BLACK WILD CHERRY.
A very large and lofty tree; hard,
heavy and beautiful timber. I
have a chest of it at Kensington,
the boards of which are *two feet
three inches wide*. The colour
of the wood is a pale red. It is
made use of in America for the
making of handsome articles of
furniture.

The time of sowing the seed, and
the manner of sowing it, are the
time and manner of No. 19; with
this difference only, that the earth
that goes upon the cherry-stones
ought to be a little finer than that
which goes upon the walnuts, and
not so thick, nor so deep above
the seed by half an inch. A little

more pains may be also taken in
making the ground more smooth
before the seed be deposited upon
it. I suppose that there will be
at least two or three hundred
plants come up from the parcel of
seed which I have put into each
box; for the seeds are all good.
If they be put in the ground late
they will not come up till next
year. They have played me this
trick this last year, though I reserved to have the trick played
me. When they do come up they
are as hardy as that devil of the
vegetable creation, the Scotch
thistle.

No. 10. DECIDUOUS CYPRESS.
(*Cupressus disticha*.) When I called
the Plane the largest tree in the
world, I forgot the Deciduous
Cypress, which, perhaps is,
generally speaking, as large, if not
larger. Michaux says, that the
largest sized trees, and those in
great numbers, are a hundred and
twenty feet in height; and from
twenty to forty feet in circumference above the conical base of the
surface of the earth. He says
that many are standing now in the
city of Mexico which were planted
there in the ancient gardens of
the Emperor of Mexico. He
says that almost all the houses at
New Orleans are built with
the timber of this tree. He

says, that the wood has been proved to be twice as durable as the pine. It certainly is a very fast growing tree; for, I have a few which were sown very late last spring, and, I am ashamed to say it, in a very coarse manner; they did not come up till after Midsummer; and even in their seedling shape they discover all the marks of greatness in point of size and height. The seeds are contained in balls a little bigger than a walnut; each parcel contains a good parcel of seeds, to come at the sight of the kernel of which is a matter of great difficulty. The best way is to take the balls and pinch and squeeze them all to pieces, and to sow the seed, shelly stuff and altogether, in the same manner as I have directed for No. 6, covering with a little more earth than is directed for No. 6.

No. 81. Lᴀʀᴄʜ. (*Larix Americana*.) This tree, Mɪᴄʜᴀᴜx says, is called the Hackmatack. Mɪᴄʜᴀᴜx speaks greatly in praise of this tree. It differs in its foliage, and in the manner of its growth, from the European Larch. I have put the seeds in the cone, so that they must be got out in the usual way. Almost every body knows how to sow Fir Trees; but I should think that to sow them in the man-

ner I have directed for 107, will be the best way. These seeds, it is well known, will come up the first year.

No. 114. Cᴀʀᴏʟɪɴɪᴀɴ Asʜ. (*Fraxinus platicarpa*).—This is a variety of the Ash that I never saw and never heard of before. It is described as a very beautiful ornamental tree, having the usual properties of the Ash as to its timber; but, *Michaux* says that it does not frequently rise to the height of thirty or forty feet. I am not sure that this seed will come up the first year; and if I were compelled to bet upon the point, I would bet that it did not; it might be forced up by artificial heat; and I dare say I shall get some up in this way; but, as to the time and manner of sowing, as to the expectation relating to the seeds coming up; and as to the precautions necessary to be taken in the case of its coming up early in the second year, I beg to be understood as repeating here, all that I said under the head of No. 7 and No. 31.

No. 116. Rᴇᴅ Asʜ (*Fraxinus tomentosa*.)—As to the seed, and every thing relating to the sowing of it, I repeat what has been just said in the last article. This is a large and lofty tree, growing sixty feet high, and covered, as the fall of the year, with a sort of red down, which causes it to be called the Red Ash. The bark upon the trunk is of a deep brown colour, and the wood has something of a bright red in it. Michaux gives a very high character of this tree, and the plate which he gives us of it, shews it to be singularly beautiful. I remember seeing it in America very frequently, and was always struck with its beauty, although it is certainly not so fine a tree as the White Ash, nor so lofty, of the seeds of which latter, I am sorry to say, I have not received any this year.

———

I am compelled to break off here for want of room. I will continue my instructions in the next Number of the Register, and conclude them; and as I said before, without making any apology for the space I am compelled to take up; because this is a matter solely for the benefit of the public, and not at all for the benefit of myself.

———

## MARKETS.

———

Average Prices of CORN throughout ENGLAND. for the week ending January 26.

*Per Quarter.*

| | s. | d. | | s. | d. |
|---|---|---|---|---|---|
| Wheat | 53 | 0 | Rye | 38 | 10 |
| Barley | 35 | 3 | Beans | 45 | 7 |
| Oats | 27 | 6 | Pease | 48 | 6 |

Total Quantity of Corn returned as Sold in the Maritime Districts, for the week ended January 26.

| | Qrs. | | Qrs. |
|---|---|---|---|
| Wheat | 39,520 | Rye | 242 |
| Barley | 40,148 | Beans | 2,462 |
| Oats | 13,129 | Pease | 831 |

*Corn Exchange, Mark Lane.*

Quantities and Prices of British Corn, &c. sold and delivered in this Market, during the week ended Saturday, January 27.

| | Qrs. | | £. | s. | d. | | s. | d. |
|---|---|---|---|---|---|---|---|---|
| Wheat | 6,598 | for 18,496 | 6 | 6 | | Average, | 55 | 10 |
| Barley | 6,734 | 12,863 | 18 | 6 | | | 38 | 5 |
| Oats | 1,941 | 3,002 | 6 | 5 | | | 50 | 11 |
| Rye | 0 | 0 | 0 | 0 | | | 0 | 0 |
| Beans | 608 | 1,386 | 14 | 6 | | | 45 | 7 |
| Pease | 608 | 1,501 | 13 | 1 | | | 49 | 4 |

Friday, Feb. 2.—The supplies of Grain in general this week are rather short. Fine Wheat is very scarce, but other sorts are very dull and almost unsaleable. Barley, of good quality, rather looks upwards. Beans for seed, are rather dearer. Oats are rather dearer, but the trade continues limited. Tares for seed, are again higher.

Monday, Feb. 5.—The arrivals of nearly all sorts of Grain last week were tolerably good. This morning there are moderate supplies of Wheat, Barley, Beans, and Pease, from Essex, Kent, and Suffolk, and a few more foreign vessels with Oats from the near ports. There has been a free demand for superfine Wheat at rather higher prices, but all other descriptions still continue to meet a heavy sale.

Barley finds an increasing demand, and all qualities may be quoted 1s. per qr. higher than this day se'nnight. Beans, of the growth of this country, are 1s. per qr. higher, and such as are fit for seed, obtain a greater advance; but foreign parcels, being mostly ordinary, still meet a very limited demand. Grey Pease are 1s. per qr. dearer. Boiling Pease, except for seed, are very heavy in disposal, especially the foreign parcels. There has been more business done in Oats than for some time past, and this article may be reported rather higher than on this day se'nnight. In the Flour trade there is no alteration. Tares, for seed, are advanced 8s. to 10s. per quarter.

———

Account of Wheat, &c. arrived in the Port of London, from Jan. 29 to Feb. 3, both inclusive.

| | Qrs. | | Qrs. |
|---|---|---|---|
| Wheat .. | 3,785 | Tares .... | 113 |
| Barley .. | 4,240 | Linseed .. | 633 |
| Malt .... | 4,383 | Rapeseed . | — |
| Oats .... | 3,364 | Brank .. | 230 |
| Beans ... | 247 | Mustard.. | — |
| Flour .... | 8,747 | Flax .... | — |
| Rye .... | 488 | Hemp .... | — |
| Pease.... | 844 | Seeds ... | 13 |

Foreign.—Wheat, 170; Barley, 248; Oats, 14,881; and Beans, 3,934 quarters.

———

Monday, Feb. 5.—The arrivals from Ireland last week were 13,706 firkins of Butter, and 11,762 bales of Bacon; and from Foreign Ports, 461 casks of Butter.

———

Price of Hops, per Cwt. in the Borough.

Monday, Feb. 5.—Our market has continued very brisk since our last week's quotation, and at an advance of several shillings per cwt., particularly for Sussex pockets.—Currency as under: East Kent Pockets, 90s. to 126; Kent ditto, 88s. to 112s.; Bags, 76s. to 92s.; Sussex pockets, 78s. to 96.; Ditto, bags, 65s. to 72s.

Maidstone, Feb. 1.—The Hop Trade continues very steady, and prices are about the same as last week.

Worcester, Jan. 31.—On Saturday, fine Hops fetched higher prices; 59 pockets were weighed.

SMITHFIELD, Monday, Feb. 5, 1827.

The Beef trade was heavy on Friday, and somewhat lower, but Mutton was brisk in demand, on better terms than this day se'nnight. To-day we find that the best Beasts sell much about the same as on Monday last; and that there are buyers enough for the supply; but they do not give so willingly the price of last week for meat of second quality. The Mutton trade is brisk, and at a further improvement.

*Per Stone of 8 pounds (alive).*

| | s. | d. | | s. | d. |
|---|---|---|---|---|---|
| Beef . | 3 | 8 | to 5 | 0 |
| Mutton . | 4 | 0 | — 4 | 8 |
| Veal . | 5 | 4 | — 6 | 0 |
| Pork . | 4 | 8 | — 5 | 6 |
| Lamb . | 0 | 0 | — 0 | 0 |

| Beasts . . | 2,433 | Sheep .. | 20,740 |
|---|---|---|---|
| Calves ... | 114 | Pigs ... | 120 |

NEWGATE, (same day.)

*Per Stone of 8 pounds (dead).*

| | s. | d. | | s. | d. |
|---|---|---|---|---|---|
| Beef . | 3 | 4 | to 4 | 8 |
| Mutton . | 3 | 0 | — 3 | 8 |
| Veal . | 3 | 8 | — 5 | 8 |
| Pork . | 3 | 8 | — 5 | 8 |
| Lamb . | 0 | 0 | — 0 | 0 |

LEADENHALL, (same day.)

*Per Stone of 8 pounds (dead).*

| | s. | d. | | s. | d. |
|---|---|---|---|---|---|
| Beef . | 3 | 0 | to 4 | 4 |
| Mutton . | 2 | 10 | — 3 | 8 |
| Veal . | 3 | 8 | — 5 | 8 |
| Pork . | 4 | 4 | — 5 | 8 |
| Lamb . | 0 | 0 | — 0 | 0 |

———

COAL MARKET, Feb. 2.

Ships at Market. Ships sold. Price.
36  Newcastle  9½..29s. 0d. to 35s. 3d.
7  Sunderland  3..32s. 6d. — 36s. 6d.

## POTATOES.

### SPITALFIELDS, per Ton.

| | l. | s. | | l. | s. |
|---|---|---|---|---|---|
| Ware | 3 | 0 | to | 4 | 10 |
| Middlings | 2 | 0 | — | 0 | 0 |
| Chats | 2 | 0 | — | 0 | 0 |
| Common Red | 0 | 0 | — | 0 | 0 |

Onions, 0s. 0d.—0s. 0d. per bush.

### BOROUGH, per Ton.

| | l. | s. | | l. | s. |
|---|---|---|---|---|---|
| Ware | 3 | 0 | to | 4 | 10 |
| Middlings | 2 | 0 | — | 2 | 5 |
| Chats | 2 | 0 | — | 0 | 0 |
| Common Red | 0 | 0 | — | 0 | 0 |

## HAY and STRAW, per Load.

Smithfield.—Hay ... 80s. to 107s.
Straw . 30s. to 36s.
Clover. 100s. to 126s.

St. James's.—Hay ... 80s. to 120s.
Straw .. 27s. to 40s.
Clover. 100s. to 130s.

Whitechapel.—Hay ... 72s. to 105s.
Straw . 32s. to 36s.
Clover . 90s. to 126s.

---

AVERAGE PRICE OF CORN, sold in the Maritime Counties of England and Wales, for the Week ended January 20, 1827.

| | Wheat. | | Barley. | | Oats. | |
|---|---|---|---|---|---|---|
| | s. | d. | s. | d. | s. | d. |
| London* | 55 | 1 | 36 | 7 | 31 | 5 |
| Essex | 54 | 3 | 34 | 5 | 27 | 3 |
| Kent | 52 | 8 | 36 | 8 | 25 | 8 |
| Sussex | 51 | 4 | 38 | 8 | 27 | 9 |
| Suffolk | 52 | 3 | 36 | 4 | 26 | 0 |
| Cambridgeshire | 51 | 6 | 33 | 4 | 24 | 0 |
| Norfolk | 52 | 2 | 32 | 6 | 26 | 6 |
| Lincolnshire | 52 | 2 | 38 | 4 | 24 | 0 |
| Yorkshire | 52 | 0 | 37 | 0 | 25 | 0 |
| Durham | 53 | 0 | 41 | 8 | 30 | 10 |
| Northumberland | 50 | 8 | 36 | 4 | 31 | 8 |
| Cumberland | 58 | 6 | 38 | 2 | 32 | 8 |
| Westmoreland | 59 | 2 | 46 | 0 | 34 | 2 |
| Lancashire | 58 | 0 | 43 | 0 | 33 | 6 |
| Cheshire | 56 | 8 | 45 | 2 | 33 | 6 |
| Gloucestershire | 56 | 2 | 42 | 6 | 38 | 0 |
| Somersetshire | 54 | 3 | 37 | 8 | 25 | 9 |
| Monmouthshire | 60 | 4 | 51 | 0 | 0 | 0 |
| Devonshire | 54 | 7 | 36 | 0 | 23 | 5 |
| Cornwall | 56 | 7 | 35 | 9 | 28 | 4 |
| Dorsetshire | 51 | 10 | 35 | 1 | 33 | 1 |
| Hampshire | 53 | 1 | 35 | 7 | 29 | 6 |
| North Wales | 63 | 2 | 42 | 7 | 28 | 10 |
| South Wales | 57 | 8 | 41 | 3 | 24 | 6 |

* The London Average is always that of the Week preceding.

*Liverpool*, January 30.—The arrivals of Grain since Tuesday last, although light, have exceeded the demand during that period, but such few sales as were effected, were at late prices for each description. The attendance at this day's market was very limited, probably, as regards country buyers, owing to the appearance of canal navigation being shortly closed by the frost, since when, however, a fine thaw has succeeded. But few sales were made, and a small decline in value was generally submitted to, but not in such a proportion as to warrant an alteration in the prices of this day se'nnight.

Imported into Liverpool, from the 23d to the 29th January, 1827, inclusive:—Wheat, 4,640; Barley, 2,100; Oats, 6,806; Rye, 458; Malt, 487; Beans, 1,210; and Pease, 231 quarters. Flour, 2,539 sacks, per 280 lbs. Oatmeal, 592 packs, per 240 lbs. American Flour, 7 barrels.

*Bristol*, Feb. 3.—The Corn Markets at this place are steady at last week's prices. Supplies rather improved. There have been some arrivals of Barley, Beans, and Oats from France during the last fortnight, the qualities of which are not equal to that of English growth. Present prices, about as stated:—Wheat, from 5s. 6d. to 7s. 6d.; Barley, 4s. 6d. to 5s. 9d.; Beans, 3s. 6d. to 7s. 6d.; and Oats, 2s. 3d. to 4s. 3d.; per bushel, Imperial. Flour, Seconds, 32s. to 42s. per bag.

*Guildford*, Feb. 3.—Wheat, new, for mealing, 13l. 10s. to 16l. 10s. per load. Rye, 44s. to 46s.; Barley, 35s. to 41s.; Oats, 30s. to 40s.; Beans, 58s. to 56s.; Pease, grey, 58s. to 60s.; ditto, boilers, 60s. to 64s. per quarter. Tares, 10s. per bushel.

*Ipswich*, Feb. 3.—We had to-day a good supply of Barley and Wheat. Barley sold full 1s. to 2s. per quarter dearer, prices as follow:—Wheat, 52s. to 53s.; Barley, 35s. to 41s.; Beans, 45s. to 47s.; and Pease, 46s. to 48s. per quarter.

*Manchester*, Feb. 3.—During the week the Corn trade has been dull, and to effect sales lower prices have been submitted to. We had a good attendance on 'Change to-day. Wheat, of fine quality, was dull sale at a reduction of 2d. per 70 lbs. Our Millers have purchased freely for the last week or two, which purchases have only arrived this week, the canals, &c. having been frozen up, Barley met free sale at last week's rates. Oats barely maintain the prices of this day se'nnight. Beans stationary. Boiling Pease dull sale. Malt in rather better demand. Flour same as last advised.

*Newcastle-on-Tyne*, Feb. 3.—We had a large supply of Wheat from the farmers, with several arrivals coastwise, at this morning's market, and the flour trade being much depressed, the millers bought Wheat very sparingly at a decline of 1s. per quarter from the prices of last week. Rye not so much in demand, but no alteration in the price. The supply of Norfolk Barley has been more than equal to the demand, and prices continue the same as last week. Malt more in demand. The supply of Oats continues to be equal to the demand, and no alteration can be noted in prices since last week.

*Wakefield*, Feb. 2.—We have again a good supply of Wheat; good dry samples are heavy sale, and scarcely support the prices of last week, and there is very little demand for damp and inferior sorts. Oats and Shelling are in fair demand, and fully maintain their value. The supply of Barley is short, and prices are supported, but the sale has been less lively than on last Friday. Fine Beans are scarce, and rather dearer. Other articles are without variation.

## COUNTRY CATTLE AND MEAT MARKETS, &c.

*Bristol,* Feb. 1.—Beef, from 6*d.* to 7*d.*; Mutton, 5*d.* to 5½*d.*; and Pork, 5*d.* to 5½*d.* per lb. sinking offal.

*Horncastle,* Feb. 3.—Beef, 8*s.* per stone of 14 lbs.; Mutton, 6*d.*; Pork, 7*d.*; and Veal, 6*d.* to 7*d.* per lb.

*Manchester* Smithfield Market, Jan. 31.—We had a good show of Beasts and Sheep at our market to-day as to quantity, but the greater part of the Cattle were of the lean kind, which was difficult of sale at ½*d.* per lb. less, whilst the few prime ones readily met with buyers. Fat Sheep also readily found purchasers at last week's rates, but other sorts were dead to quit.

At *Morpeth* market, Jan. 31, there was a good many Cattle and a very short supply of Sheep, which met with ready sale, at an advance in price.—Beef, 5*s.* 9*d.* to 6*s.* 6*d.*; Mutton, 6*s.* to 7*s.* 3*d.* per stone, sinking offal.

*Norwich Castle Meadow,* Feb. 3.—We had a very large supply of fat Cattle to-day, many of them remained unsold, prices varying a trifle, 8*s.* per stone of 14 lbs. sinking offal; Store Stock was supplied very scantily: a very few Scots sold at 3*s.* 9*d.* to 4*s.* per stone, when fat. Not a single lot of Store Short-Horns, Irish, or Devons; Cows and Calves, and one and two-years old Homebreds, a very flat sale. Sheep, a very few penned; Shearlings, 23*s.* to 28*s.*; fat ones to 35*s.*; Hoggets, 14*s.* to 19*s.* 4*d.*; Pigs in good supply, and cheaper: fat ones to 6*s.* 6*d.* per stone.—Meat, Beef, 7*d.* to 9*d.*; Veal, 6*d.* to 8½*d.*; Mutton, 5½*d.* to 7*d.*, and Pork, 5½*d.* to 8*d*, per lb.

# COBBETT'S WEEKLY REGISTER.

VOL. 61.—No. 8.]   LONDON, SATURDAY, FEB. 17, 1827.   [Price 6d.

*Published every Saturday Morning, at Seven o'Clock.*

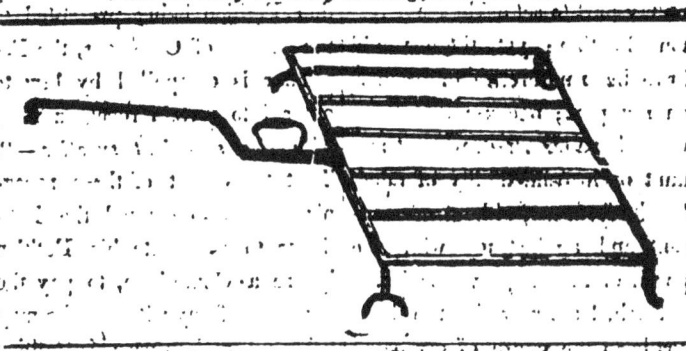

## TO THE ELECTORS OF PRESTON.

*Kensington, 15th Feb. 1827.*

MY EXCELLENT FRIENDS;

I HAVE to announce to you, and to all those numerous political friends and supporters, who have shown so anxious a desire to see me in Parliament, that that object *will not be accomplished at this time,* owing to occurrences of which it is my duty now to give you the true history. When we promise to do a certain thing, it is understood that we mean, that we will do it if we live to the time of performance; for, nobody would charge us with breach of promise for dying before the arrival of the time necessary for doing the thing. We are also understood, in all such cases, to mean that we will perform, what we promise, if nothing intervene, of a nature such as for it to be wholly out of our power to resist. In this way, my promises to you, that I would set aside *Grimshaw's* return, must have been understood. If, for instance, the Government had, since the Election at Preston, passed another Power-of-Imprisonment Bill, such as they passed in the year 1817, I should

P

Printed and Published by WILLIAM COBBETT, No. 183, Fleet-street,
[ENTERED AT STATIONERS' HALL.]

have got out of the country as quickly as possible, if I could have done it; and, of course, there would have been no attempt on my part to set aside the Preston Election; yet, there would have been no breach of promise on my part; because something would have occurred, without any fault or instrumentality of mine, to take from me, without my consent and against my will, the power of fulfilling my promise.

Such, I am now about to show, has been the cause of my being prevented from fulfilling the promise made to you of setting aside the return of Grimshaw, and of giving another sweating at least to the purses of Stanley and Wood. I shall have to give an account of conduct, and that, too, on the part of a man professing the sincerest of personal friendship, the purest of political principles, and the greatest anxiety for our success on this occasion; I shall have to give an account of conduct, on the part of a man thus professing; of conduct that will excite in you feelings, that you yourselves will be unable to describe. In order to enable you clearly to understand the nature of this man's conduct, and more particularly to make you perceive clearly, how it is that our great

purpose has been defeated by that conduct, I must first beg your attention to the following facts:

1. That in case of an Election Petition being presented to the House of Commons, the Petitioner is compelled by law to enter into certain recognizances, with two sufficient sureties.—2. That the object of these recognizances is, to compel the Petitioner to prosecute his Petition before a Committee, to pay the expenses of any witnesses he may bring up, and, in case his Petition be voted frivolous and vexatious, to pay the costs of the persons against whom he petitions.—3. That he shall, within a certain number of days after presenting his Petition, give in to the Speaker the names of the two men who are to be his sureties. —4. That the Speaker shall then appoint a day (within eight days of that time), for examining into the sufficiency of these sureties.— 5. That when the Speaker has appointed the day for such examination, the Petitioner shall give formal personal notice to the parties against whom he petitions, that the examination of the sureties is to take place on such a day, and this notice he is to give them in such time that there may be TWO CLEAR DAYS, between

the time of giving them the notice, and the time of examination.—6. That if the sureties be found to be insufficient, or, if they FAIL TO ATTEND to undergo the examination relative to their sufficiency, then, the Petitioner at once LOSES HIS RIGHT TO PURSUE ANY FURTHER THE PETITION. This is my case: one of my sureties failed me; and it is now my business to inform you, and to inform all our friends, in every part of the country, who this man is, and precisely what he has done to defeat our object.

The man's name is JOSEPH THOMPSON. The thing having been buzzed about, and people always being prone to imagine that they know something of the party that is mentioned: these circumstances have made several people to suppose, and even to ask me, whether the *Thompson* that people were talking about, was not Mr. CHARLES THOMPSON, whose case has been so frequently mentioned in the Register. It should, therefore, be clearly understood, that this man has no relationship and no acquaintanceship, that I know of, with *Mr. Charles Thompson*. This man's name is *Joseph Thompson*; he lived at Hampstead,

of late years, until last fall; he now lives in a new place, on *Lord Holland's* estate, in this parish of Kensington, which place is called Addison Road. He has one son settled in Pennsylvania; he has a daughter married to a law-stationer or something of that sort near Lincoln's-Inn, of the name of Duncombe; is a man of about seventy years of age, and, is possessed of property of various sorts far beyond what would have been necessary to make him a good and sufficient surety in my case.

This man had introduced himself to me originally; the acquaintanceship began on his part; it commenced, when I was in the King's Bench, and by an act on his part, which showed the best of feelings and the best of principles. He gave me some money, with the greatest of apologies for the liberty he was taking, but observing at the same time, that, as he thought that the public in general ought to compensate me for the sufferings I endured for the sake of that public, he, at any rate, was determined to discharge his duty. From that time I have known this man; was always happy to see him; went to see him as often as I could; got him to come to my house as often as I could prevail upon him to do it; was always

very much pleased with his conduct upon all occasions; always
thought him a singularly sound
and sensible man.

When, therefore, I had to nominate sureties, the first name
that occurred to me, was that of
my friend *Mr. Walker* ; and the
next was that of *Mr. Thompson*,
both twenty times more than sufficient in point of property; the
first would have thought himself
neglected and slighted, if I had
not put his name down ; the latter
was chosen in preference to one of
twenty or fifty others that I might
have had, because he lived close
by me; because I knew Mr.
Walker would be staying at my
house ; because we should be thus
all on the same spot and be ready
at any moment, and thus prevent
the POSSIBILITY OF FAIL-
URE, from any of those little accidents which sometimes occur to
prevent the accomplishment of
great objects.

Thus, by over-precaution ; yes,
actually by taking *too* great care,
by having this surety under my
own roof as it were, all your hopes
have been disappointed and all
my labours thrown away. When
the time came to nominate the
sureties, before I gave in the name
of *Joseph Thompson*, I went to
his house, in company, accidentally, with a Gentleman, who was
well acquainted with us both. In
the presence of this Gentleman I
asked *Thompson* if he would be
one of the sureties; I fully explained to him the nature of the
recognizances, and having done
that, I said, " Now, *Thompson*,
" there are plenty of others ready
" to do what I am asking you to
" do : I ask you in preference,
" because you are upon the spot ;
" but, if you have the smallest
" objection in the world, say so
" without the least scruple or hesi-
" tation ; and, be assured, that
" your objection will not be the
" least in the world offensive to
" me." He said he had no objection ; he said he would willingly
and gladly be one of the sureties ;
he authorized me to give in his
name accordingly ; and I did give
in his name. All this took place
in the presence of the Gentleman
who accompanied me to Thompson's house, and who is a Barrister.

When this had been so firmly
settled, all that remained for me
to do was to give my notices to
Grimshaw and his brother returning officers, and to Stanley and
Wood. The Speaker had ap-
pointed Thursday, the 14th of
December, at one of the clock in
the day, for the sureties to come

before the examiners at the House of Commons. I have observed before, that the law required me to give notice to the opposite parties of the time for examining into the sufficiency of the sureties. I gave this notice accordingly; on Wood it was served in London, on Stanley in his bed in Lancashire, and on Grimshaw and his comrades at Preston. My messenger who went for this purpose into Lancashire, returned to London on Sunday the 10th December; so that here we were, every thing prepared; every step carefully taken; my case was already drawn up; my testimony all arranged regularly on paper; a complete MODEL of Grimshaw's traps (such as would have been sworn to, and produced in evidence), had been constructed and was ready at my house: in short, I could, on Monday the 11th day of December, have taken my case before a Committee, and have obtained a decision in my favour, or have made that Committee appear before the public in colours much more facile as a work of the imagination than convenient as a task for the pen, or at any rate for my pen.

I can believe in *great lengths*, on certain occasions: I am not so miserably stupid a dog as to imagine, that, I should have had to experience, in such a case, the benefit of one single expression of friendship, and that I should not have had to experience the full weight, aye, and a little more than the full weight, of all that which "Justice," and Justice not in good humour, too, could have suggested. Nevertheless, with all this duly impressed upon my mind; giving my adversaries double credit for every item on their side of the account, I was, on the 11th December, *in the morning*, firmly convinced that I should not fail, that I could not possibly fail, in setting aside the return of Grimshaw and his comrades. In the evening of that same day, I was as firmly convinced that it came next to impossible, if not quite impossible for me ever to get before a committee at all! Some poet exclaims :—" How *poor a thing* may do a noble office !"—In this case, how poor a thing has defeated the honest and honorable hopes and expectations of hundreds of thousands of sensible Englishmen! About five o'clock in the evening of that day, a sort of blind verbal message reached me that Mr. Thompson wished to speak to me that night or next morning early; I was engaged, and could not go; but I sent my eldest son in my

stead. Thompson lives at about
seven hundred yards from my
house, so that my son was not
long gone. He returned about
eight o'clock, with the following
account, which I state from a paper drawn up by him; which
paper corresponds exactly with
the report he made to me at the
time, and to the truth of the statement contained in which he is
ready to make oath. His statement is this:—That in the evening of the 11th Dec. 1826, he
went to the house of this Joseph
Thompson, whom he found at *tea*
with two ladies; that Thompson
said that he wished to speak with
him privately, on which the two ladies left the room; that Thompson
then began by saying, that he
could not be one of the sureties in
the case of the Preston Election,
for that his brother was just dead,
that he was only a few years older
than himself, that it seemed to
him that he himself was *spoke to,*
that he had got a *shake,* that he
was all of a *tremble,* and that he
was altogether unfit to go out.—
My son states, that, he observed
to Thompson, that he hoped he
would be better by *Thursday*;
that Thompson said he should not
be better by Thursday; that this
was a great shake to him; that
his brother had died suddenly on

the Friday before, and that his
daughter had been into town, and
brought him the news on the Saturday, and it seemed (he repeated) as if he were spoke to. My
son states, that he then observed
to Thompson, that it was very
little for him to do; that a carriage would be brought to take
him down to the House of Commons; that he would have only
to hear his affidavit read, and to
sign it; that he would be detained
a very short space of time; that
the notices were now served in
Lancashire; that nothing was
wanting but his attendance, agreeably to his engagement; that if he
failed, it would be a cruel disappointment to me and to hundreds
of thousands of others. My son
states; that he appeared totally
dead to all this; but, that he then
said that he wanted to advise his
father to do the best thing that he
could in this state of affairs.
" Now you see," said he, " I can-
" not go; that's quite positive,
" and *whether some money can't*
" *be got from them.* They are
" in a *precious fright.* I don't
" know what they don't say of
" me for promising your fa-
" ther. My daughter was at
" my son-in-law, Duncombe's,
" on Saturday, and Mr. Lewis had
" been talking to him and telling

"him that my name was posted
"up in Westminster Hall. She
"says my son-in-law told Lewis
"to come to me, as he could not
"help it."—He went on to say
that this Mr. Lewis was a relation
of Wood.—"Well, sir," said my
son, "but you should have told my
"father before if you were afraid
"of Wood."—"I am not afraid of
"Wood," said he; "but I think
"your father can get some mo-
"ney from them to drop it alto-
"gether, as they are in such
"a way about it. Indeed I
"KNOW, that two or three hun-
"dred pounds could be got from
"them." He pronounced this
"I know" as if he had no manner
of doubt upon the subject.—My
son told him, that he now understood him, but that he had not
understood him when he had mentioned money at the first. My
son expressed his surprise that
such a thought should have come
into a man's head. Thompson
said, that he thought it right to
mention it, because, as he could
not fulfil his promise, he was
ready to do the best he could.
"What," exclaimed my son, "take
money!" "Why," said Thompson, "you know it is better than
"throwing good money after bad."
He added, that he did not think
that the election could be set

aside; "and," said he, "it would
"be better to get a little money,
"than run the risk." My son states
that all this took place under great
expression of impatience on his
part, and he wished Thompson
good night several times, wanting
to get away from him; but that
Thompson still persevered about
getting some money from them,
and said, that "he wished my
"father to consider, whether he
"might not, before they knew my
"father could not give the bail, get
"some money from them;" and,
that, if he would consent to it, he
would send for MR. LEWIS TO
HIS HOUSE AND MAKE A
COMPROMISE WITH HIM.
My son concludes his statement
in these words: "I should not
"omit to state that Mr. Thompson
"*appeared* perfectly well, or, at
"least, as well as I had ever seen
"him. I found him drinking tea,
"eating, looking fresh-coloured,
"and he spoke with a sound
"voice."

After my son came home and
made his report to me I sent for
the Gentleman who was present
when Thompson made the promise
and, indeed, entered into the most
solemn engagement. He went to
Thompson, represented to him
the horrid breach of faith of which
he had been guilty; but he found

him perfectly obdurate. Thus, then, my power of proceeding was completely put an end to. As to the REAL MOTIVES of this man, I shall not trouble you with any conjectures. I know Lewis to be a sort of crony of his. I dined with him once at his house at Hampstead. This Lewis has a brother who is a land-jobber in America. The Lewises come from Maidstone, I believe, or somewhere there, and they are a sort of Whig patriots. In estimating Thompson's conduct, particularly his motives, we must look at TIME.

He made his promise to me on the 24th of November; and, he keeps his peace upon the subject, even after the first petition was, on account of want of form in the proceedings, set aside, and another presented; he keeps silence upon the subject, until the 11th of December; and until it was *absolutely impossible to avoid setting the petition aside if he withdrew his name!* It was not until his daughter went into town, and held as it appears from my son's narrative, a conference with Duncombe, the son-in-law, and others upon the subject, that Thompson changed his mind; but, observe, he took care not to change it, or at least, not to communicate the change to me, until it became quite impossible for me to avoid having the Petition set aside.

You, my good friends of Preston, and my readers in general, will want nothing now to convince you, that I have done every thing in my power in order to fulfil my promise made to you; and that I had no more the power of protecting my Petition, and your and my rights, against this fellow Thompson, than I have to prevent the frost from hardening the ground, or the snow from covering it. No man upon earth can have protection against a fellow like this, in such a case. We cannot search hearts. Who would have believed, that a man, *upwards of seventy years of age,* would, having voluntarily, and with all appearances of zeal, entered into such an engagement; who would have believed that such a man, so pledged, would have barefacedly broken his engagement; and, while he professed to fear that the hand of death was almost upon him; while, to use his own bugaboo slang, he was professing to believe that a supernatural agent had spoken to him to warn him of his death: who, my friends, would have believed, that such a man, thus aged, thus being, thus feeling, thus professing, thus expressing his expectation of appearing shortly before his Maker or his Judge; who would have believed, that, being thus "all in a tremble" of both body and soul, he would propose to become the negotiator, in order to obtain a sum of money from another man which was to be a compensation to me for his breach of promise; and for the sake of which I was basely to betray your interests and those of my country? Oh no! No man is to be expected to be on his guard against the heart that could conceive and entertain, the head that could organise and the tongue that could give utterance to projects like this. I feel myself fully acquitted of all blame. Every man who knows him, would say that Thompson was a proper man to be chosen; to be upon your guard in such a case is utterly impossible.

In another Register I shall have to speak to you upon our *future prospects*; and of the means it will be necessary for us to put in motion, should it please God or the King or both, to give us another chance at working Stanley and Wood. Whatever they may do in Parliament, it shall be my business to take care that they do not get there for nothing. In the meanwhile, look at them, and see what they will do. We shall have rare sport before this day fifteen months, let the Parliament attempt to do what it may; and, my friends, be you well assured, that, before the end of that fifteen months, you will not be the only persons that will regret that I am not in Parliament. It is possible, and indeed it is probable, that it is much better for me, that the "*Thing*" should work on a year or two longer before I have any thing actually to do with it, otherwise than with the pen. Some great change *must* take place in the course of a very few years; and you will see what a figure Stanley and Wood will cut when the hour of change comes. One thing I do believe; and that is, that if I had been in the House, looking him in the face, our old anti-jacobin assailant Canning, never would have made that speech, which is very likely to cost this country the expenses of of a decent war or two. I shall, in the course of a few weeks, resume and finish my little Work, entitled "The Poor Man's Friend;" I shall cause to be distributed gratis among you, three thousand three hundred of the future, as I have done of the past Numbers. I present it to you and your children, as a mark of that gratitude and affection with which I am, and shall always remain,

Your faithful Friend, and

Most obedient Servant,

**Wm. COBBETT.**

---

TO

## DR. FINN,

*Chairman of the O'Connell Association, Dublin.*

---

*Kensington, 15th Feb. 1827.*

Sir,

Having more than nine months ago publicly expressed my anxious wish that the Society would for mercy's sake drop all other matters and amuse themselves with that very entertaining occupation, playing at push-pin; having actually sent over half a pound of pins to the Society for this purpose, and that too by the hands of Mr. O'Dwyer, who has now appeared so conspicuously, and I must say, rather ungratefully, upon the stage: this being the case, you will naturally conclude, that I must have seen, with unmixed satisfaction, the result of your "intense deliberations" and "talented discussions" on the 10th instant;

for, Sir, it is the absence of mischief that I am so anxious to see prevail in that luminous body; and, perhaps, next to the ancient and moral game of push-pin, nothing in this world could be more harmless, than the pushing out of the Register. One more Number, however, I should like you to receive; for, it is destined to contain that which must be most "intensely" admired by the association; namely, a sort of Elegy, which appears to have been written on the borders of the Cotswold Hills, celebrating in one and the same breath, as it were, the *nuptials* and the *death* of that famous heap of brick-bats, the end of which the association so "intensely" lament. Pray, Sir, receive the Register containing this poem, dedicated by me (the editor) to the "intense" association.

With my best wishes, that, by some means or other, no matter what, you may keep your tongues still,

I remain,

Your most obedient, and

Most humble Servant,

**W. COBBETT.**

## SCHEMES AND SCHEMERS.

Almost all the schemers are either in Scotland or come from it. Sir John Sinclair has been a schemer these forty years, and he is a schemer yet. He recommends that the standard of gold should be lowered so as to make an ounce of gold pass for 5l. That is to say, he wishes three pounds seventeen shillings and tenpence halfpenny, to be converted by Act of Parliament into five pounds; or, in other words, if any man owe me 5l. of the present money, if any man owe me five sovereigns, this pretty prattling Privy Councillor; this right honourable adviser of his Majesty wants to compel me by Act of Parliament to receive three sovereigns and 17s. 10½d., instead of the five sovereigns! Oh, much injured Bedlam! much calumniated mad-houses! no wonder that county asylums are wanted for the inland; if projects like these can come from Privy Councillors: I say if such projects can come; for, God forbid that I should think that this coin-clipping, this gold-sweating, this so then swindling project should have actually come from the Right Honourable Baronet in question; whose great love for virtue, innocence, and simplicity, has been known throughout the world, ever since he prepared a straw pen for Lord Malmsbury to sign the treaty he was going to negotiate at Lisle with the Jacobin regicides of France. I find his project published in the Edinburgh Observer of the 9th of this month. But, I have seen my name published and put to things I never wrote. I therefore acquit the privy councillor of having written this letter; but, there it is, and his name at the bottom of it; and it is pretty certain that there are some people, at any rate, in Scotland, who really are mad enough to think of such a project being adopted. What will be done at last, no man can tell. The sensible people of Blackburn have, in their excellent petition, called for the true and only remedy; but, it is to be feared, that this remedy never will be thought of by those who have power, until it be too late.

## MR. CANNING.

In spite of the consolation which the "master mind" of this

gentleman must have received, from the various epistles which I have, of late, done myself the honour to address to him, on the subject of his " intense speech," lately delivered in the House of all Houses; in spite of the still more flattering and more consoli- tary notice which has been taken of that speech in the various Courts upon the Continent; in spite of the puissant " intense- ness of the master mind " itself, we have reason to fear (if reason will ever suffer us to fear any thing that newspapers assert to be true), that in this case, as well as in so many others, though the spirit is willing, the flesh is weak. In short, and in plain words, that Mr. Canning is devilish sick; though the Morning Chronicle tells us, that the " Right Honour- able *Secretary* " was dangerously Ill one day, and the " Right Ho- nourable *Gentleman* " was a great deal better the next. As a man; as a lump of flesh and bones and skin, I cannot care any thing about Mr. Canning; he cannot as such be more to me than any man that I see walk along the streets. As a man to render services to my Country, I know that his death would be no loss to us; but, as an *antagonist*; as a man that I should like to see

to live to see the workings of this system to their result; his life is in my eyes truly valuable; and, though I join not in the canting expressions of the newspapers, I verily believe that I am much more sincere than they in my expression of desire to see him restored to health. The lies that the newspa- pers tell us are so numerous, and so frequently proved to be lies, that we never can believe what they say. If we compare dates we shall find, that they *now* tell us, that he was *dangerously* ill at the time when, as they then told us, he had a slight touch of the gout. Ill he must be, and that in right earnest, or he would be here at this time, where things really seem to be going on as if there were no heads at all; and that, too, at a time when every man of any sense sees and declares that the country is beset by perils.

---

## AMERICAN SEEDS.

---

THE list which I published last week, had some little inaccuracies in it. It contained one repetition, and there was one omission which has now been supplied. The names were not so perfect as they ought to have been. I therefore publish the list anew, and it now corresponds exactly with the numbers on the several bags put into the boxes. I, last week, published my instructions for the sowing, as far down the list as the *Red Ash* inclusive. I shall now insert the list anew, and then I shall continue my instructions or recommendations, relative to the sowing of all the seeds mentioned in the remaining part of the list. The Reader has been apprised, that the price of a box of seeds complete is 5l.; that the boxes may be had at Fleet-street, or be sent to order to any part of the kingdom; that nothing will be charged for box or booking at the coach-office, to which I will now add, that I can supply no Gentleman, who does not make application on or before the last day of March.

### FOREST TREES.

No.
19. Black Walnut. Juglans nigra.
6. Occidental Plane.
107. Ontario White Elm.
7. Red Maple. Acer rubrum.
81. Sugar Maple. Acer Saccharinum.
8. Red Cedar. Juniperus virginiana.
9. White Cedar. Cupressus thioides.
22. Black Wild Cherry. Cerasus Virginiana.
10. Deciduous Cypress. Cupressus disticha.

81. Larch. Larix.
114. Carolinian Ash. Fraxinus platicarpa.
116. Red Ash. Fraxinus tomentosa.
17. White Beech. Fagus Sylvestris.
18. Red Beech. Fagus ferruginea.
74. Bass Wood. Tilia Americana.
14. White Birch. Betula populicolia.
16. Black Birch. Betula lenta.
118. Yellow Birch. Betula lutea.
88. Black Spruce. Abies nigra.
101. Hemlock. Abies canadensis.
92. White Pine. Pinus strobus.
119. Hornbeam. Carpinus.

### SHRUBS.

No.
59. Carolina Allspice. Caryophyllus Aromaticus.
62. Sumach. Rhus Carolinianum.
28. Ilex Casine.
80. Ilex Dahoon.
104. Callicarpa Americana.
87. Red bay. Laurus Cariniensis.
97. Black Gum. Nyssa sylvatica.
64. Magnolia Glauca. Small Magnolia or White Bay.
65. Magnolia Tripetala. Umbrella tree.
82. MagnoliaGrandiflora. Large Magnolia or Big Laurel.
86. Pride of India. Melia azedarach.
43. Chionanthus. Snowdrop tree.
61. Cornus Florida. Large flowering Dogwood.
77. Cornus Alba.
109. Cornus Sirecea.
111. Cornus Paniculata.
63. June Berry. Mespilus arborea.

39. Crataegus.
105. Pyrus Melanocarpa.
106. Choke Cherry. Prunus vir-
    giniana.
110. Viburnum lantana grandi-
    flora.
112. Prunus depressa.
57. Iron wood. Carpinus es-
    trya.
55. Arber vitæ. Thuya Ooci-
    dentalis.
75. Box thorn. Lycium.
49. Cercis. Judas tree.
11. Tupelo. Nyssa aquatica.
90. Large Tupelo. Nyssa grandi-
    dentata.
89. Sour Tupelo. Nyssa capi-
    tata.
45. Nettlewood. Celtis occi-
    dentalis.
115. Pyrus. Pear.
79. Georgia Bark. Pinckneya
    pubescens.
117. Water Locust. Gleditsia
    monosperma.
120. Sorel Tree. Andromeda
    Arborea.
69. Gordonia Pubescens. Frank-
    linia.
124. Gordonia làsyanthus. Lob-
    lolly Bay.
35. Dwarf Rose Bay. Rhodo-
    dendrum Maximum.
123. Ever-green Andromeda.
36. Azalia. American Honey-
    suckle.
121. Milocrium Ligustrium. Old
    man's beard.

## AMERICAN SEEDS.

Continuation of the remarks on
the Trees and Shrubs, the list of
which was published in the last
Register.

No. 17. WHITE BEECH. (Fa-
gus Sylvestris.)

No. 18. RED BEECH. (Fagus
Ferruginea.)

Every body knows the Beech
tree and the Beech nut. These
American Beeches differ from
each other in appearance, and
both differ from our Beech. They
grow to a great height, and attain
to a great size, as our Beech
does. The merits of the timber,
compared with those of our Beech,
I do not know; I have no experience upon the subject, and the
books say nothing at all about the
matter. As to the seed, it is in a
very good state; perfectly sound;
and it is to be sown, with regard
to time, and to every other thing,
in the same manner as directed
for No. 22; always bearing in
mind, that even in this roughish
sort of sowing, the ground ought
not to be in lumps.; for, if it be
*hollow*, and the seed not *touched
in every part* by the mould, the
seed will either not vegetate at all,
or vegetate but feebly.

No. 74. BASS WOOD. (*Tilia
Americana.*) Why the Yankees
call this beautiful tree the Bass
Wood I cannot tell. *Tilia Americana* means *American lime*; and
this is the American lime, growing according to Michaux, and
indeed, according to my own observation, to the height of eighty
or ninety feet, and being in all
respects, whether as to trunk, timber, or leaf, very different from,
and vastly superior to, the European lime. The leaves are larger,
and they continue bright under
the hot sun which turns the European lime quite brown. The
trunk of the American lime is covered with a very thick bark,
which is worked by a certain process into *ropes*, which are in great

use in some parts of the country. The timber of this tree is used in the making of thin things, like the pannels of carriage bodies. Michaux says, that the timber is not so good as that of the Tulip Tree for certain purposes; but, that, it is a very useful timber, and very much in use in and about Boston. The seed of this tree, of which I have put up about three hundred perhaps for each box, consists of a kernel, covered by a hardish shell, and that shell covered by a grey thin pulp or coat, the whole forming a round bulk a little larger than the largest kind of marrow-fat pea. Having no experience to guide me, and the books, with their usual modest reserve, not thinking proper to take upon themselves the office of teaching me, I cannot say positively, whether this seed come up the first year, or lie two years in the ground. I should think, that it would come up the first year. I recommend it to be sown, each seed about six inches from another, as early as the weather will permit; and, as to manner of sowing, preparation of the ground and all the rest, to follow the instructions given with regard to Nos. 7 and 31.

No. 14. WHITE BIRCH. (*Betula populicolia.*)
No. 16. BLACK BIRCH. (*Betula lenta.*)
No. 118. YELLOW BIRCH. (*Betula lutea.*) -

These American Birches, like the Beeches, differ very considerably from our Birch in size and shape of leaf, in colour of leaf and wood, and also in shape of cone, which contains the seed. In all these respects they differ also materially from each other, presenting, in themselves, a very pleasing variety. But they all differ from our Birch in another respect; namely, that they all grow, if left to themselves, up with straight trunks, to lofty and stately trees. In the north of North America, they grow to a very great size, and with the straightest and finest trunk imaginable. Some years ago, there were some ships built of their timber at St. John's in New Brunswick. The scheme did not answer, I believe, but the circumstance shows that it must be common for the Birch to attain to a very great size in that country. After contemplating the height and size of these trees, how one is astonished at beholding *one* of the *seeds* from which such an immense mass springs! The Birch seed is amongst the smallest, amongst the very smallest of the creation. It is a little thing not bigger than the point of a pin, surrounded by a little web-like sort of wing. It is extremely difficult to raise Birch plants from seed. In general our Birches are obtained from the coppices, where sometimes they are found self sown, and sometimes got from suckers. In this way, however, we cannot get the American Birches; and therefore we must endeavour to raise them from seed, which we assuredly can do if we take the necessary pains. As there are many of the shrub seeds which ought to be sown in the same manner as the Birch, I will here give particular directions for the sowing of these very fine seeds; and then, I shall in future, in all cases where the same sort of sowing will be proper, merely have to refer to these instructions for sowing the seeds of the Birch. A small piece of ground will suffice for an immense number of plants. When they come out of the ground they are hardly so big as a seedling lettuce when it comes out of the ground. The Birch plants will get to be about three inches high the first summer. A couple of hundreds of the plants may stand upon a square foot, so that fifty square feet might give you ten thousand plants. Now, a bed seventeen feet long and three feet wide, contains fifty-one square feet; and, according to the foregoing computation, this bed might yield you ten thousand plants of the Birch tree. In order that you may make sure of the seed growing, you must sow that seed well. In the first place, the ground is to be well and deeply dug and finely broken. After the bed is marked out, it is to be made as smooth as you can possibly make it with the spade, picking out all stones and hard lumps. Then you are to sift some mould upon it through a fine wire sieve. Upon this bed of soft and fine mould, you are to sow the seed; and, in order to prevent the seed from falling thick in some and thin in other parts, mix it well with fine sand or fine mould, and thus sow it over the bed. When you have done this, press the seed down upon the mould with the flat of your hand or with some smoother thing made for the purpose. Having pressed the seed close down into the soft mould, cover it with about a quarter of an inch of mould sifted equally fine, press this down also, and thus the seed, though so small, will be touched by the earth in every part of it; and, observe, that it is for the want of this touching the

seeds by the earth, that such millions of small seeds perish. After having pressed down this quarter inch of fine mould upon the seed, put over the bed a quarter of an inch of the same mould. The bed must be protected, if possible, against heavy rains and against a hot sun, until the plants be up. When they have been up one fortnight they set sun and rain and every thing at defiance. The next year they are transplanted. They grow away at a surprising rate; and, without any exception, they are the hardiest of all the trees that I know any thing of, and will flourish upon the poorest ground. The birch is found to flourish in America, where no other tree of any sort will grow; and in New Brunswick it is found growing, where there appears to be not one particle of earth, nothing but rocks, which do not bear even moss. But, in its seed it is the most delicate of all trees that I ever heard of.

No. 88. BLACK SPRUCE. (*Abies Nigra.*)

No. 101. HEMLOCK. (*Abies canadensis.*)

No. 92. WHITE PINE. (*Pinus strobus.*)

These being all of the fir kind, every thing said about the sowing of the Larch (No. 81) applies to these. The seed is in the cone and must be got out in the usual way. The sun, or the heat of a warm fire, is necessary to get the seed out of the cone. The Hemlock is a most superb tree; and, as an ornamental tree, is worth any degree of pains that can be bestowed upon it. The pines are so well known as to their outward figure and the character of their amber, that little need be said respecting these; but, I cannot help observing on the immense height of the White Pine. Its beauty as a tree is very great; but its height is something quite surprising. *Michaux* has measured the stocks a hundred and fifty-four feet long. He says that they attain the height of one hundred and eighty feet, and he quotes from Belknap's History an account of a White Pine, *twenty-five feet round.* So that this may be fairly considered as the loftiest tree of which we have any knowledge; but in *bulk,* taking in limbs, branches and all, it is still greatly inferior to the Occidental plane, No. 6 in the above list; and, let me here notice an error of the press, contained in the last Register, respecting the seed of the Occidental plane. I had written that the seed was a smaller and a more contemptible looking thing than the pith of the most contemptible OAT. The printer, or compositor, or press corrector, thinking, I suppose, that I must have told a lie, and being laudably anxious for the preservation of my character, put a " K " instead of a " T ; " thus making me, in my efforts to describe the smallness and contemptibleness of the seed of the Plane, most emphatically observe, that it was not so big as the smallest of *oaks.* The Black Spruce, I should observe, is called in New Brunswick and the other northern parts of America, Double Spruce. This is on account of the thickness of its leaves. This is the tree that the spruce beer is made out of. When I was in New Brunswick, where I had, along with divers other worthy persons dressed in red coats, the honour to serve his late Majesty of Jubilee memory; when I was thus happily situated, we used to call the branches of this tree " malt;" we had an immense copper put up at the base of a rock, a little way raised above the high water mark of the sea; we used to go into the wood, which began just at the top of the rock, and ran back for hundreds of miles; we used to go into this wood, cut down the trees, chop off the malt, bring it to the top of the rock and toss it down into the copper, with a great quantity of moss leaves and rubbish along with it. Then to assist the malt, we used to put in a certain number of gallons (I forget how many) of that stuff which the Yankees call molasses, and which we in England call treacle. The trunks and limbs of the trees served us for fuel for the brewery. This precious matter we used to carry away in pork tubs with the heads out, and every gang of us had their own tub, standing on the outside of their barrack room door, to go and dip into. From this general store, the beverage was carried away in pots, pans, kettles, canteen bottoms, cows' horns stopped at one end with a cork; famous drinking vessel. I have seen many a fellow dip it out with his shoe and drink it upon the spot. But, after all, strange as the reader may think it, this was the best spruce beer that I ever tasted. It was as clear as wine; and even the rich people used to beg it of us to drink. So that I have rather a particular affection for this Black Spruce; though I must say that I recommend its cultivation only as an ornamental tree. We have, thank God, a better sort of malt

Q

here, and as to its timber, I believe it is worth nothing.

No. 119. HORNBEAM. (*Carpinus Americana*.) This tree has
much smaller leaves and much
finer leaves than our Hornbeam. Its seed is in a little hard
pointed pod, which comes at the
bottom of a small leaf, which
appears to serve it as wings.
—Whether the seed of this tree
come up the first year or not,
I cannot say; but I am inclined
to believe that it does not come up
the first year. It will be prudent,
therefore, to sow the seed just as
if you expected it to come up the
first year; and, in short, to manage it in the manner recommended for the Maples, Nos. 7
and 31. Sow it in the same manner, and at the same depth, as
you sow the Maples; and if you
find the seed coming up very early
the year after, protect the bed
against frosts.

## SHRUBS.

No. 59. CAROLINA ALLSPICE.
(*Caryophillus Aromaticus*.) This
is not the real Allspice called by
this botanical name; but it is an
Allspice, and it is aromatic. The
plant is a shrub which rises sometimes to the height of ten or twelve
feet. It bears a purple flower,
very much like that of a plant of the
climatis kind, which is called the
Virgin's Bower; and this flower,
only one single flower, will communicate its odour to a whole room
of moderate size. The seed is a
kernel, in a not very hard shell,
about the size of a wild cherry-
stone. These seeds should be
sown in the manner directed for
No. 6, with a little more earth as

a covering at the top. They may
be sown at any time in March, or
early in April. This shrub is
very rare in England, though a
thing which one would suppose
every Gentleman would like to
have in his garden. The cause is,
I suppose, that it is raised by
nurserymen, by layers and by
cuttings, a process very tedious,
uncertain, and one that very seldom produces a thriving and free-
growing plant. The seeds that
I have put up in the boxes, will,
if the reader rub one of them a
little in his fingers, convince him,
that, though this is not the Allspice
of Asia, it would serve instead of
it, and that, too, in a way to deceive even the connoisseurs in
spices. The seed will not, however, ripen in England, though
the flowers are as fine here as in
America.

No. 62. SUMACK. (*Rhus Carolinianum*). Most people know
this plant; which is generally pro-
pagated here from suckers. The
seed is contained in a little red
pulpy pod. If you rub the pulp
away, you will find a little flat
brown seed, which, I believe, does
not come up the first year. I am
not sure of this; and therefore the
best way will be to proceed, as to
time and manner of sowing, precisely as in the case of the Nos. 7
and 31.

No. 28. ILEX CASINE.
No. 80. ILEX DAHOON.

These are two different sorts of
American holly. One has smooth
leaves, which leaves are large, too,
and the other small and prickly
leaves. Both differ from our hol-
lies, and both of them grow much
taller. The seed is a little pulpy

thing, pretty much like that of our holly, and, like it, lies in the ground to the second year. I would recommend these seeds to be dealt with in precisely the same manner as that of the red cedar, No. 8. These are famous trees for shelter to houses, gardens or yards; and therefore they are worth a great deal of pains to get them.

No. 104. CALLICARPA AMERICANA.. This is a low flowering shrub, very handsome and very rare. There is a portrait of a limb or branch of this shrub in *Catesbey's* Natural History of Carolina. Leaf, flower and fruit, all is very beautiful, and very curious. Fifty or sixty plants must be as many as any gentleman can ever want. I have put up seeds sufficient I dare say for four times that quantity. This is too small an affair to be committed to the natural ground, in beds. I would recommend to others what I shall do myself; namely, fill some broad top pots to within two inches of the top, with some fine mould; then, suppose that earth a bed, put half an inch of very fine mould upon it, rub the seed out of the pods and put them upon that mould, then press down mould and all together with something very smooth; and proceed to finish the covering or topping up in precisely the same manner which has been recommended for the sowing of the *Birch.* The pots may, if you have such a thing, be plunged into a gentle hot-bed, until the seeds be up, taking great care to give plenty of air the moment you see the plants appear. The pots may afterwards be brought out and partly sunk in the earth, so that they can be shaded in very hot, and sheltered

in very wet weather. They may be then taken care of until the next spring, when they may be planted out perhaps into some rich and sheltered spot, till they become big enough to be put out to where they are to grow and to blow. It will be advisable to screen them a little from the frost during the first winter, and perhaps during the second.

No. 87. RED BAY. (*Laurus Caroliniensis.*) *Michaux* tells us that this Laurel rises sometimes to sixty or seventy feet high, and has a trunk from fifteen to twenty inches in diameter; that is to say, four or five feet round. Nothing more need be said in order to induce every one to wish to possess some of these trees; and the pains which my correspondent has taken to get the seed, surpass every thing except my thanks to him for those pains. The seed is a pretty large berry. It is rather soft, and requires great attention in the preserving of it and in bringing it hither. I beg the reader to look back and pay particular attention to my advice as to the sowing of No. 6, and then to sow the Red Bay in the same manner, with a little more earth upon the top. But, it is so very desirable not to miss getting a few at least of these trees (for tree and not shrub it ought to be called), that I would recommend the putting of a few of the seeds into pots, treated in the same manner as is recommended as to the pots of the *Callicarpa Americana.*

No. 97. BLACK GUM. (*Nyssa Sylvatica.*) This shrub also, *Michaux* says, rises sometimes to the height of sixty or seventy feet, and is four or five feet round the bottom of the stem. The seed is an oblong stone covered by a blue looking pulp. I should think that to a certainty this seed will not come up the first year. It is of the same species as the Tupelos; and I know from experience that they do not come up till the second spring. I would, therefore, recommend this seed to be treated in the same manner that I have pointed out for the Red Cedar; or, in the same manner I have recommended for the Sugar Maple.

No. 64. MAGNOLIA GLAUCA.
No. 65. MAGNOLIA TRIPETALA.
No. 82. MAGNOLIA GRANDIFLORA.

These are well known to be amongst the finest plants in the world. It is very rare that the latter sort is seen in England higher than about twenty or thirty feet, and then against a house. *Michaux* tells us that the grandiflora rises in America to the height of eighty or ninety feet; and I have not the smallest doubt, that if these trees were commonly

here as

re and parts of the United Florida to Canada.

You never see fine trees or plants of any sort unless they become somewhat plentiful in a country, and get into numerous hands. I have but very few seeds of the Magnolia Tripetala, but of the others a sufficient quantity. They are, however, necessarily few in number; because it requires a great space of matter to preserve them in, and they must not be suffered to be exposed to get too dry. Pretty women are sometimes ticklish enough, but the most ticklish of them are not more ticklish than these seeds: too dry, they shrivel: too wet, they rot. I have got them safe here; but not without infinite pains and astonishing good luck into the bargain. As to the sowing of the seed, the time is, as soon as the ground is dry enough to sift: the manner, that recommended for No. 6, with a little more earth on the top; but, the Magnolias are amongst those things which ought to be honored by being sown in pots as above mentioned in the case of the Callicarpa Americana. Above all things the seeds ought to be well pressed into the soft mould.

No. 86. PRIDE of INDIA (*Melia Azedarach*). This is certainly one of the finest flowering shrubs, or rather flowering trees, in the world. *I do not believe that there is one* of them in *England*. The description of this tree, as given by Michaux, is so interesting, that I shall here copy it entire from his AMERICAN SYLVA.—
" This tree is a native of Persia.
" For the beauty of its flowers
" and the elegance of its foliage,
" it has long been in request in
" southern climates for embellish-
" ing towns and adorning the en-
" virons of dwellings. It is pro-
" pagated for this purpose in In-
" dia, in the Isles of France and
" Bourbon, in Syria, Spain, Por-

" tugal, Italy, and the southern
" departments of France. In the
" New World it is found in seve-
" ral towns of the West Indies
" and of South America; and on
" the Northern Continent it is so
" abundant and so easily multi-
" plied in the maritime parts of
" the Southern States, as to be
" ranked among their natural pro-
" ductions. This claim upon our
" attention is enforced by the va-
" luable properties of its bark and
" of its wood. The Pride of In-
" dia rises to the height of thirty
" or forty feet, with a diameter of
" fifteen or twenty inches; but
" when standing alone, it usually
" rests at a smaller elevation, and
" diffuses itself into a spacious
" summit. Its leaves are of a
" dark green colour, large, dou-
" bly pinnate, and composed of
" smooth acuminate, denticulated
" leaflets. The lilac flowers,
" which form axillary clusters at
" the extremity of the branches,
" produce a fine effect, and exhale
" a delicious odour. The ripe
" seeds are large, round, and
" yellowish; they are sought with
" avidity by certain birds, parti-
" cularly by the red-breasts, in
" their annual migration to the
" south, which, after gorging
" themselves immoderately, are
" sometimes found stupified by its
" narcotic power. The venomous
" principle which resides in this
" tree is taken notice of by
" Avicenna, an Arabian Phy-
" sician, who flourished about the
" year 960. In Persia the itch
" is cured with an ointment made
" by pounding its leaves with
" lard.—The Pride of India pros-
" pers in a dry and sandy soil,
" and magnificent stocks are seen
" in the streets of Charleston and

" Savannah. Its foliage, which,
" as well as the flowers, is deve-
" loped early in the spring,
" affords a delightful refreshment
" to the eye, and yields a shelter
" from the fervour of the sun
" during the intemperate season.
" It grows with such rapidity, that
" from the seed it attains the
" height of 12 or 15 feet in four
" years. This surprising vege-
" tation is chiefly remarked in
" stocks less than ten years of
" age, in which the concentrical
" circles are more distant than in
" any other tree. Like the Locust,
" it possesses the valuable pro-
" perty of converting its sap into
" perfect wood in the earliest
" stages of its growth; a stock,
" 6 inches in diameter, has only
" an inch of sap, and consequently
" may be employed almost entire.
" The wood is of a reddish co-
" lour, and is similarly organized
" with that of the Ash; it receives
" a less brilliant polish than the
" Red Bay, the Wild Cherry, the
" Maple, and the Sweet Gum;
" but this defect is unimportant in
" a country which possesses the
" species just mentioned, and can
" easily procure mahogany. The
" Pride of India is sufficiently
" durable and strong to be useful
" in building, and it will probably
" be found adapted to various
" mechanical uses; it has already
" been employed for pullies,
" which, in Europe, are made of
" Elm, and in America of Ash."
" This succinct description de-
" serves attention in the southern
" parts of North America, and in
" those countries of Europe where
" the Pride of India is considered
" as an ornamental rather than as
" an useful tree. Fields exhausted
" by cultivation and abandoned,

"might be profitably covered
"with it."

The seed of this tree agrees of
course with the description of
Michaux. The purchaser will
find it to be about the size, and
very much like the White Sloe.
First there is a spongy pulp; that
taken off, you have a shell about
the size of a very large marrow-
at pea: break the shell, and you
have a kernel, which produces the
tree. Michaux, who is very full
as to his description of what the
thing is after it has become a tree,
seems to have forgotten that those
whom he wished to propagate it,
might want to know something
about the manner of causing this
seed to become a tree. So that
all that I can do is to guess at it,
and to say how I intend to manage
the seed I intend to sow. I shall
sow, as soon as the ground will
work well in March, a little bed
in the same manner as described
for the sowing of No. 6 (Occidental Plane); only putting about
half an inch more of earth upon
the top; but I shall also sow some
in pots, and manage the pots as
directed for the Magnolias and
the Callicarpa.

No. 43. CHIONANTHUS. (*The
Snowdrop, or Fringe Tree.*)—
There are very few of this shrub
in England; but its reputation is
very widely spread. It is a beautiful shrub, and, with care, not
difficult to raise. In this country,
I believe it is raised from layers;
but here we have the seed. Miller, in speaking of this seed, says,
that it will not come up till the
second year. I will give a history
of my experience, and then the
reader will know pretty well what
he ought to do. I sowed a bed of

this sort of seed last April. I did
not expect it to come up until next
April, or thereabouts; but, a few
days ago, (Feb. 1.) after the last frost,
and before the present frost, I went
to the bed with an intention of
moving the earth with my knife,
in order to see what condition the
seeds were in; whether the hard
shell was beginning to dissolve, or
how it was. To my great astonishment, I found that the seeds
were actually coming up very
thickly; that many of them had
come up previous to the former
frost, and had been destroyed by
that frost, and I concluded that
another such a frost would destroy the whole. I immediately took
precautions to prevent this, and I
expect my bed to make a very
decent appearance by the middle
of April. Now, therefore, my
opinion is, that if these seeds be
sown in March, or earlier, they
may possibly come up the first
year; and, if they do not, the sower
ought to take special care to protect them if they should come up
before the month of April in the
second year. The manner of
sowing is that recommended for
the Occidental Plane, with about
an inch more of mould on the top,
and with good hard pressing down.

No. 61. CORNUS FLORIDA,
*Large flowering Dogwood).*
No. 77. CORNUS ALBA.
No. 109. CORNUS SIRICEA.
No. 111. CORNUS PANICULATA.

I have never seen, that I know
of, any of these sorts, except the
first, of the plants of which I have
sold several this year. Michaux
classes this tree amongst the forest
trees of America. In speaking of
it he says, as I said of it in the
*Register;* namely, that its flowers

... in full before there is the appearance of a leaf on any other tree. He says the flowers are collected in "bunches which are "surrounded with a very large "involucre, composed of four "white floral leaves, sometimes "inclining to violet. This fine "involucre constitutes all the "beauty of the flowers, which are "very numerous, and which, in "their season, robe the tree in "white, like a full blown apple "tree, and render it one of the "fairest ornaments of the Ameri- "can forests." The leaves die in the autumn of a deep red colour rather inclining to black; and they hang on pretty nearly throughout the winter; for, the few plants that I have now left, though seedlings, have had their leaves all on until within these ten days, and they have some of their leaves on yet. Of all the plagues of my life of this sort, the seeds of this shrub have been the greatest. I was struck with the beauty of the tree, when I was last in America; I resolved to make them pretty common in England if I could. I began to sow the seed in 1820: I proved that the seed was good by breaking it with a hammer; and I had no idea that the wretches lay sulking two years in the ground; till, by mere accident I took some earth which had been upon a hot bed, where some of these seeds had been sown (for I tried the effect of artificial heat upon them); I took some of this earth to put into pots to plant some tuberoses in. I planted the tuberoses, and up came the Cornus Floridas. I now found that I had been living in the "dark ages!" light broke in upon me as from those lumi- nous pages which issue from the office of the Edinburgh Review. In the April before the last I sowed a bed of these seeds, and last April up they came. So that here I have pretty dear bought experience for my guide. I shall sow, and I recommend others to sow, all these four sorts of seeds in precisely the same man- ner, and with the same atten- tions and precautions that I have pointed out with regard to the Su- gar Maple. There are much finer shrubs than the Cornus Florida; but it blows in that season of the year which would make it one of the fairest ornaments of our plant- ations; and, which is a circum- stance by no means to be over- looked, it is never seen so lofty and in a more thriving state than under the shade of loftier trees. Of the other three sorts, as I said before, I know nothing; but I have put up enough of the seeds of the Cornus Florida to furnish plants enough for any gentleman in England.

No. 63. June Berry. (*Mes-pilus Arborea*.) This flowering tree reaches, *Michaux* says, to the height of thirty or forty feet, and has a trunk two or three feet round. Its wood is of a pure white, and has no difference be- tween the heart and the sap. It sends out large bunches of flowers early in the spring; not a great deal less early than the Cornus Florida. It bears a fruit resembling that of the red currant, and about the same size as our red currants, which fruit is sold in the markets of America early in June: hence the vulgar name of June Berry. This is a very fine and lofty shrub, of which I never saw or heard of one in England. As I never had any of the seed before, I cannot tell whether it come up the first or second year; but I imagine that it comes up the first year, like the wild cherry, if sown early enough. I recommend it to be sown and in all respects treated as the seed of the Sugar Maple.

No. 39. CRATAEGUS. This is one of the American White-Thorns. There are several of them, all differing very considerably from ours, and, in general, having more than one seed in each pod or haw. Our own white-thorn stones do not come up the first year ; neither do these of America. The seeds ought to be preserved to the second year like those of the red cedar mentioned above. The best way is, to put the seeds together with a pretty large proportion of earth into a flower-pot, and sink that flower-pot into the ground to the usual depth, that is to say, just leaving the rim above ground. Let the seed remain thus during this spring and next summer, and sow it in any dry weather that you find about October or November. The plants will come up next spring, and when they come they are very hardy.

No. 105. PYRUS MELANOCARPA. Why they call this a *Pear* I cannot tell. The vulgar name in America is choke berry. It is not a very large flowering shrub. Each berry contains several seeds about the size of the seed of the Cress; and, it ought to be sown at the time and in the manner directed for No. 6.

No. 106. CHOKE CHERRY. (*Prunus Virginiana*). This is a pretty high shrub, with beautiful

and abundant blossoms early in the year; and the seed is to be treated precisely like that of the Black Wild Cherry, No. 22 in this list.

No. 110. VIBURNUM LANTANA GRANDIFLORA. The Americans call this Hobble Bush. There are very few seeds of this sort. The seed is, a kernel in a little shell, to be sown in the same manner as the Wild Black Cherry, No. 22.

No. 112. PRUNUS DEPRESSA, vulgarly called *Sand Cherries*. It blows in May (it would blow in April in England), and bears great quantities of white blossoms. It is to be treated in the same manner as the Black Cherry, No. 22.

No. 57. IRON WOOD (*Carpinus Ostrya*). The seed of the Iron Wood I know by experience lies in the ground until the second year. I know of no means of bringing it up the first year, and would therefore treat it as I just directed with regard to the seed of the Crataegus. The Iron Wood gets to be a largish tree. *Michaux* speaks of it as being sometimes forty feet high and four feet round the trunk. The timber is perfectly white, very compact, fine grain, and heavy. It is used for *levers*. And he says that it is very good for mill-cogs, mallets, and any purposes where great hardness is wanted and where great bulk in the wood is not required.

No. 55. ARBOR VITAE. (*Thuya Occidentalis*). Whether this be the common Arbor Vitae or not, I do not know. *Michaux says that it*

... be forty-five or fifty feet high. Its seed is contained in little cones, some of which will be found in the bag No. 55. The seeds must be got out in the usual way in which seed is got out of cones, and sown at the same time and in the same manner as directed for the Larch, No. 81, with a little more care, if possible; because the seed is smaller and more delicate than that of the larch.

No. 75. Box Thorn. (*Lycium.*) The seed of this beautiful shrub is a large oft kernel in rather a soft shell. Sown in the manner of the Wild Black Cherry it will come up the first year.

No. 49. Cercis. (*Judas tree.*) This shrub is pretty well known; but still it is rare, on account of its being raised generally by layers or cuttings, which prevents it from getting to is natural height. There are two or three hundred of the seeds of this shrub (in the pods) put up in each box. The best way of sowing them is, to lay down the pods flat upon the ground at about a foot or a foot and half apart, press them well down, then proceed as in the case of No. 6, only putting on a little more earth at top. Sow in fine weather in March, and every seed will be a little tree by the month of September.

No. 11. Tupelo. (*Nyssa Aquatica.*)
No. 89. Sour Tupelo. (*Nyssa Capitata.*)
No. 90. Large Tupelo. (*Nyssa grandidentata.*)

These I have called shrubs, though *Michaux* numbers them amongst the forest trees of Ame-rica. The first, he says, attains the height of from forty to forty-five feet, the second does not rise quite so high; but the large Tupelo, he says, sometimes attains the height of seventy or eighty feet. From the colour of the wood, of the leaves and of the fruit, these, especially when they attain a great height, must be all very beautiful trees. The fruit of the Sour Tupelo is red, and that of the others a deep purple. The flowers are not remarkably fine, but in great abundance. The seed very much resembles that of the *Cornus Florida*. It appears to be as hard as a bit of iron; I know from experience, that it does not come up till the second year, and I recommend it to be treated in the same manner that I have recommended with regard to the seeds of the *Cornus Florida*, No. 61. It has been remarked by Michaux, that though these trees flourish best in wet situations in America, they do not require such situations in Europe, where the climate is more humid, and this must be particularly the case then with regard to England.

No. 45. Nettlewood. (*Celtis Occidentalis.*) Michaux calls this the American Nettle tree. He says, that it sometimes rises to the height of 60 or 70 feet, with a trunk *five* feet round. He says, that the wood is hard, compact, supple, and tenacious; that it makes excellent hoops, whip-stocks, and ramrods; and that wheelwrights used it for shafts. This tree is very rare in every part of America. The French called it *Bois inconnu*. It is found only here and there a tree, and my correspondent writes to me to say he obtained the seeds with infinite difficulty. It bears small white flowers early in the spring, which are followed by a little sweet berry of a dull red colour, which berry, if sown at the same time, and in the same manner as directed for No. 6, will produce a tree a foot high by the month of September.

No. 115. PYRUS. That is to say, Pear; and this is a pear, of which I can find no account in any of the books. It is a little red thing, a little larger than the largest of marrowfat peas; but, it is to all intents and purposes a *pear*. It has a tail like a pear; it has a pulp like a pear; it has an eye like a pear; its shape is precisely that of a bergamot pear; it has *pips* exactly like those of a pear. My correspondent tells me, that this sort of shrub is exceedingly rare. The seed ought to be squeezed out of the pulp, and sown in the manner directed for No. 6. The seeds will come up in May, and be little trees in September.

79. GEORGIA BARK. (*Pinckneya pubescens*.) This is one of the most beautiful shrubs in the world. It appears to have been not at all known to Miller, and I have never seen or heard of a plant of it being in England. The younger *Michaux* represents it, and perhaps truly, as having been discovered by his father, long since the "*daughter*" quarrelled with the "*mother*." He named it after Mr. Pinckney of South Carolina, who had in *Michaux's* eyes the merit of being very partial to France. Dr. Barton, in his American Flora, gives us this flower in full bloom; and a most

magnificent flower it is. Before I speak of the seed and the manner of sowing, I must do this fine shrub the justice to copy what *Michaux* has said about it—" This tree, still
" more interesting by the proper-
" ties of its bark, than by the ele-
" gance of its flowers and of its
" foliage, is indigenous to the most
" southern parts of the United
" States: probably it grows also
" in the two Floridas and in Lower
" Louisiana. My father found it
" the first time in 1791, on the
" banks of the St. Mary. He
" carried seeds and plants to
" Charleston, and planted them
" in a garden which he possessed
" near the city. Though en-
" trusted on an ungrateful soil,
" they succeeded so well, that in
" 1807 I found several of them
" 25 feet high and seven or
" eight inches in diameter; which
" proves that the vegetation of
" this tree does not require a very
" warm climate, nor a very sub-
" stantial soil. With a *great*
" affinity to the Cinchona, which
" yields the Peruvian bark, my fa-
" ther discerned in the Georgia bark
" sufficient difference, to distin-
" guish it as a new genus. In testi-
" mony of his gratitude and respect,
" he consecrated it to Chas. Cotes-
" worth Pinckney, an enlightened
" patron of the arts and sciences,
" from whom my father and my-
" self, during our residence in
" South Carolina, received multi-
" plied proofs of benevolence and
" esteem.—The Georgia Bark is
" a low tree, dividing itself into
" numerous branches, and rarely
" exceeding the height of 25 feet,
" and the diameter of five or six
" inches at the base. A cool and
" shady exposure appears the
" most favourable to its growth

" his leaves are opposite, four or
" five inches long, of a light-green
" colour, and downy underneath,
" as are also the shoots to which
" they are attached. The flowers,
" which are white, with longitudi-
" nal rose-coloured stripes, are
" pretty large, and are collected
" in beautiful panicles at the ex-
" tremity of the branches. Each
" flower is accompanied by a
" floral leaf, bordered with rose-
" colour near the upper edge.
" The capsules are round, and
" compressed in the middle, and
" stored with a great number of
" small winged seeds. — The
" wood of the Georgia Bark is
" soft, and unfit for use in the
" arts; but its bark is extremely
" bitter, and appears to partake
" of the febrifuge virtues of the
" Cinchona, for the inhabitants of
" the southern parts of Georgia
" employ it successfully in the in-
" termitting fevers which, during
" the latter part of summer and
" the autumn, prevail in the
" Southern States. A handful of
" the bark is boiled in a quart of
" water till the liquid is reduced
" one-half, and the infusion is
" administered to the sick. From
" the properties of its bark the
" Pinckneya has taken the name
" of Georgia Bark. It is to be
" wished that some intelligent
" physician would examine these
" properties with care, and indi-
" cate with accuracy the manner
" of employing this indigenous
" remedy, and the effects to be
" expected from it; the tree which
" produces it so nearly resembles
" the Peruvian vegetable, that
" some botanists have included
" them in the same genus."—
The seed of this fine shrub
is a very curious thing. It is

contained in a pod, somewhat
resembling that of a poppy
Each pod contains perhaps thirty
or forty seeds, which resemble
very nearly the seed of the birch,
in colour as well as in shape; but,
in size, the Georgia Bark seed is
perhaps six times as large as that
of the white birch. As to the sowing, I have been very particular
in my advice with regard to the
sowing of birch seed, and with
regard to the after-treatment of
the beds or pots. Precisely the
same time and manner of sowing, with a trifling addition of top
mould, I recommend for the
Georgia Bark. But this is so
valuable a shrub, and it must be
so desirable for every lover of
botany to possess it, that I by all
means recommend the sowing of
part of the seeds in pots; and taking care of those pots in the manner recommended in the case of
the Magnolias.

No. 117. WATER LOCUST.
(*Gleditsia monosperma*.) A very
beautiful tree, sometimes rising
to the height of fifty or sixty feet.
The flower is insignificant, but the
leaf is very beautiful. Of the
timber *Michaux* seems to think
very little. The seeds are about
as big as one of Mr. Western's
shillings would be, if he could
carry his little shilling project into execution; that is to say, about
half the superficial dimensions
and half the thickness of one of
the sixpences of our gracious
sovereign, agreeably to that
" *standard*," in which the Ministers have sworn to pay the interest of the debt in full, and
which " standard " the famous
" House," the sensible " House,"
on the motion of Mr. Huskisson,

resolved should not be altered in weight or fineness. This seed is also pretty nearly as hard as his Majesty's coin; and therefore I recommend it to be sown in the time and manner pointed out for the Sugar Maple, and recommend that it should receive a similar measure of patience and precaution on the part of the sower.

No. 120. SOREL TREE. (*Andromeda Arborea.*) This tree mounts, according to *Michaux*, to the height of 40 or 50 feet, with a trunk two or three feet round. Such height, however, is rare, and generally it is rather a low shrub. Its flowers, which it bears in great abundance, are very beautiful, and as *Michaux* observes, render the tree very proper for the embellishment of fine gardens. It stands the winter well, even in the latitude of New York. Its leaves are *sour*; hence its vulgar name. The seeds are contained in little *capsules*, and are exceedingly minute. As small as the point of a pin; but, as to numbers, multitudinous. These seeds must be sown with the greatest care. When you have broken the pod open and let the seeds fall upon white paper, you may discern them with the naked eye, but that is as much as you can do. I have never seen or heard of a tree of this sort in England; and little wonder is this when we consider the great nicety requisite for raising the plants from seed. They are really so small, that I should have little hope of them in the natural ground; but, as several hundreds will come up in a flower pot a foot over at the top, there cannot be much difficulty attending the pro-

cess. The way is, to fill the pot with earth sifted through a cinder sieve, to within about two inches of the top; then put on about half an inch of earth, which has been sifted as fine as flour; shake the pot to make that top earth pretty level; scatter the seeds upon this fine earth; then press them down with some smooth thing upon this earth; then put on some more fine earth to the depth of between a quarter and a half an inch; then press that earth down with the same smooth thing, leaving the top perfectly level and smooth; and when you water, take care to do so with so fine a rose to the watering-pot and so small a watering pot, as not to disturb the surface of the earth. The most effectual protection against heavy rains, would be glazed lights; and, to hasten their coming up, a gentle hot-bed would, in all probability, be efficacious. When the plants are once up, there requires nothing but ordinary care; a little protection, perhaps, during the first winter; but if they be then put out into the natural ground in rich and fine earth, they will soon become trees.

No. 69 GORDONIA PUBESCENS. (*Franklinia.*) This shrub, *Michaux* says, was discovered by John Bartram in 1770; and, I have never seen or heard of its being in England. It rises to the height of 20 or 30 feet; the flowers are more than an inch in diameter; they are white and have an agreeable smell; they open in succession during two or three months; and, the tree begins to bear flowers when it is only three or four feet high: it bears any frosts; *Michaux* says that its growth is luxuriant within a short distance of Philadelphia, and it is on all accounts one of the finest shrubs. The seeds are contained in a hard round pod, which must be broken with a hammer or something like one, to get out the seeds, which are of an angular form, which are not very small, being of about the bulk of a grain of buckwheat, and of which seeds each pod contains about thirty or forty. I have put up ten of these pods in each parcel; and the sower must have bad luck indeed, if he dont get a hundred plants. The shells of the seeds are as hard as the shells of nuts, and the kernel which is within side of these angular shells does not appear to be bigger than the head of a pin. I would sow these in the same manner as is recommended for the Sorel tree; only, in this case, I would not sow above thirty or forty seeds in a pot; and I would cover with *double* the *quantity* of earth recommended for the Sorel tree.

No. 124. GORDONIA LASYAN-THUS. (*Loblolly bay.*) This shrub has been so long the admiration of all who have ever seen it; and it is so long since it was discovered, that there must be doubtless some of these bays in England. It is an evergreen of the most beautiful description; its leaves, their shape, the white flower, the shape of the flower, its straight trunk when raised from seed, its height of fifty or sixty feet, the regularly pyramidical form of the whole tree: all contribute to make this one of the finest, if not the very finest flowering tree in the world. Add to all these, the *easy raising of it.* The seeds are little winged

things, very much resembling a Fir tree seed, contained in a pod, which when broken open give you for each pod ten or a dozen seeds. Doubtless the seeds would grow, if sown in the natural ground, in the manner directed for the Pines, for the Larches and the Spruces; but, these seeds are worthy of the greatest care, and, therefore, I recommend them to be sown in precisely the same manner and to be attended to with the same care that has been suggested for the Franklinia, No. 69.

No. 35. DWARF ROSE BAY. (*Rhododendrum Maximum.*)
No. 123. EVER-GREEN ANDRO-MEDA.
No. 36. AZALIA.

The first of these three is known to every body, as a dwarf shrub producing a large flower, and to be bought in all the nurseries in England, where they are invariably (I believe) raised from layers. In America they cover the surface of the sides of rocky hills for miles at a stretch. I requested my correspondent to gather the seeds promiscuously, that the shrubs may have flowers of all the various colours. — The EVER-GREEN ANDROMEDA is a very fine shrub; but is very little known in England.—The AZALIA (or American Honeysuckle) is known well enough. The first and the last of these shrubs give us their seeds in small pods about half an inch long; the Ever-Green Andromeda gives us its seed in a round pod, about the size of a small pea. One pod of either of the sorts contains two or three hundred of seeds. The pods should be broken to pieces with the fingers; the seeds suffered to fall on white paper; and they should then be sown, in precisely the same manner in all respects, from first to last, as the seed of the Sorel tree, No. 120.

No. 121. MILOCRIUM LIGUSTRUM. (Old Man's Beard.) Whether there be any of this shrub in England, I cannot say; I do not believe that there are; because Doctor Mitchell, the justly celebrated Botanist and Naturalist of New York, is good enough to give my correspondent information upon all these matters; because, therefore, I believe this name to be correct; and because I cannot find this name in Catesby, nor in Miller; and, which is much more conclusive, I cannot find it in Mr. AITON's Epitome of the Hortus Kewensis. My correspondent writes to me on the subject, in these words, under date 31st Dec. 1825:— "This is a most beautiful ever "green shrub, or tree. It is as " big as the generality of Apple " trees. It has large clusters of " White blossoms, that grow in " the manner of tassels. The " tassels are so large, that a man " cannot encircle them with both " hands. I am sorry that I cannot " obtain more of the seed." The seed of this fine tree resembles, in some sort, a beech nut; but is not a twentieth, and perhaps not a fortieth, part, so big as the beech nut. With much pains and patience, you find a little pith in the centre of it; but to make it grow, great pains must be taken. I would recommend it to be sown in pots, in the same manner directed for the Sorel tree, with an inch more of earth upon the top.

I cannot send forth to the English public this account of my collection of seeds, without expressing in the most public manner I am able, my profound gratitude to DR. MITCHELL of New York, without the aid of whose scientific knowledge, my correspondent never would have been able to do a tenth part of that which he has done for me. Dr. Mitchell, who is a native of Long Island, and whose brother gave me one of the Locust posts that are now at Fleet Street, is a striking specimen of that truly noble generosity in the American character, which, as I observed in my " Year's Residence," makes, every American wish to communicate every blessing of his own country to every other country, particularly to England. I am sure, that, if you could poll the whole of the people, natives of America, you would not find one man out of a thousand, who would not, if he could, cause Indian corn, orchards of peaches, and fields of melons, to grow in England. This is the general character of that people, and of this character Dr. Mitchell exhibits a singularly fine specimen, because his wishes are accompanied with zeal and exertion as great as if he were seeking to confer so many benefits upon himself. He has recently done me the honour to send me an engraving of his portrait, as a mark, my correspondent tells me, of his admiration of my exertions to cause the cultivation of the Locust, and other American trees, in England. I beg leave to return him my thanks in this public manner, and to assure him, that there are very few things that I could have received with so much pleasure; that I deem the possession of it of the highest value, and that, thus it will be considered to the last hour of my life.

---

## MARKETS.

Average Prices of CORN throughout ENGLAND, for the week ending February 2.

Per Quarter.

| | s. d. | | s. d. |
|---|---|---|---|
| Wheat | 53 10 | Rye | 39 10 |
| Barley | 36 3 | Beans | 45 9 |
| Oats | 27 9 | Pease | 48 9 |

Total Quantity of Corn returned as Sold in the Maritime Districts, for the week ended February 2.

| | Qrs. | | Qrs. |
|---|---|---|---|
| Wheat | 34,575 | Rye | 186 |
| Barley | 38,491 | Beans | 2,170 |
| Oats | 12,825 | Pease | 1,023 |

Price of Bread.—The price of the 4lb. Loaf is stated at 9d. by the full-priced Bakers.

---

Corn Exchange, Mark Lane.

Quantities and Prices of British Corn, &c, sold and delivered in this Market, during the week ended Saturday, February 3:

| | Qrs. | £ s. d. | s. d. |
|---|---|---|---|
| Wheat | 3,756 (or 10,367 | 9 4 Average, 55 | 1 |
| Barley | 3,540 | 6,834 7 3 | 38 7 |
| Oats | 1,819 | 2,669 8 9 | 32 9 |
| Rye | 0 | 0 0 0 | 0 0 |
| Beans | 664 | 1,488 17 11 | 44 10 |
| Pease | 464 | 1,136 14 9 | 49 11 |

---

Per Stone of 8 pounds (alive).

| | s. d. | s. d. |
|---|---|---|
| Beef | 3 8 to | 5 0 |
| Mutton | 4 2 — | 4 10 |
| Veal | 5 6 — | 6 0 |
| Pork | 4 6 — | 5 4 |
| Lamb | 0 0 — | 0 0 |

Beasts . . 2,502 | Sheep . . 22,960
Calves . . . 151 | Pigs . . . 110

NEWGATE, (same day.)

Per Stone of 8 pounds (dead).

| | s. d. | s. d. |
|---|---|---|
| Beef | 3 4 to | 4 4 |
| Mutton | 3 4 — | 4 0 |
| Veal | 4 0 — | 5 8 |
| Pork | 3 8 — | 5 8 |
| Lamb | 0 0 — | 0 0 |

LEADENHALL, (same day.)

Per Stone of 8 pounds (dead).

| | s. d. | s. d. |
|---|---|---|
| Beef | 3 2 to | 4 6 |
| Mutton | 3 0 — | 4 0 |
| Veal | 3 8 — | 5 4 |
| Pork | 4 0 — | 5 4 |
| Lamb | 0 0 — | 0 0 |

COAL MARKET, Feb. 9.

Ships at Market. Ships sold. Price.
89½ Newcastle 28..29s. 0d. to 36s. 9d.
23 Sunderland 15..31s. 0d.— 37s. 3d.

## POTATOES.

### SPITALFIELDS, per Ton.

|  | l. | s. | l. | s. |
|---|---|---|---|---|
| Ware | 3 | 0 | to 4 | 10 |
| Middlings | 2 | 0 | — 0 | 0 |
| Chats | 2 | 0 | — 0 | 0 |
| Common Red. | 0 | 0 | — 0 | 0 |

Onions, 0s. 0d.—0s. 0d. per bush.

### BOROUGH, per Ton.

|  | l. | s. | l. | s. |
|---|---|---|---|---|
| Ware | 3 | 0 | to 4 | 10 |
| Middlings | 2 | 5 | — 0 | 0 |
| Chats | 2 | 0 | — 0 | 0 |
| Common Red. | 3 | 0 | — 4 | 0 |

## HAY and STRAW, per Load.

*Smithfield.*—Hay....80s. to 105s.

Straw...30s. to 36s.

Clover. 100s. to 126s.

*St. James's.*—Hay.... 80s. to 115s.

Straw .. 30s. to 42s.

Clover. 115s. to 130s.

*Whitechapel.*—Hay....76s. to 105s.

Straw...32s. to 36s.

Clover..90s. to 126s.

---

AVERAGE PRICE OF CORN, sold in the Maritime Counties of England and Wales, for the Week ended February 2, 1827.

|  | Wheat. | | Barley. | | Oats. | |
|---|---|---|---|---|---|---|
|  | s. | d. | s. | d. | s. | d. |
| London* | 55 | 10 | 38 | 2 | 30 | 11 |
| Essex | 54 | 6 | 34 | 5 | 27 | 7 |
| Kent | 54 | 6 | 37 | 5 | 28 | 8 |
| Sussex | 52 | 0 | 36 | 1 | 30 | 9 |
| Suffolk | 52 | 9 | 34 | 8 | 28 | 2 |
| Cambridgeshire | 51 | 4 | 35 | 8 | 23 | 7 |
| Norfolk | 52 | 8 | 33 | 9 | 27 | 4 |
| Lincolnshire | 52 | 3 | 39 | 0 | 28 | 4 |
| Yorkshire | 52 | 3 | 38 | 1 | 27 | 6 |
| Durham | 54 | 0 | 41 | 3 | 30 | 3 |
| Northumberland | 51 | 4 | 36 | 5 | 31 | 8 |
| Cumberland | 58 | 3 | 38 | 0 | 33 | 6 |
| Westmoreland | 58 | 10 | 47 | 0 | 35 | 3 |
| Lancashire | 59 | 0 | 40 | 7 | 33 | 0 |
| Cheshire | 58 | 6 | 46 | 6 | 31 | 3 |
| Gloucestershire | 56 | 11 | 43 | 4 | 35 | 4 |
| Somersetshire | 54 | 5 | 38 | 0 | 27 | 10 |
| Monmouthshire | 59 | 6 | 46 | 6 | 0 | 0 |
| Devonshire | 55 | 1 | 36 | 0 | 24 | 4 |
| Cornwall | 56 | 7 | 36 | 10 | 29 | 9 |
| Dorsetshire | 52 | 3 | 36 | 0 | 31 | 4 |
| Hampshire | 53 | 3 | 36 | 3 | 29 | 6 |
| North Wales | 61 | 2 | 44 | 0 | 29 | 0 |
| South Wales | 58 | 1 | 40 | 4 | 25 | 0 |

* The London Average is always that of the Week preceding.

# COBBETT'S WEEKLY REGISTER.

**Vol. 61.—No. 9.]   LONDON, SATURDAY, Feb. 24, 1827.   [Price 6d.**

" Lord Liverpool said, that he felt the full importance of the
" question : he was prepared to meet it ; and he would suffer no odium
" to frighten him from the STERN PATH OF DUTY."—Lord Liverpool's Speech (as reported in the Courier newspaper), on the Power-
of-Imprisonment Bill, on the 24th day of February, 1817.

## TO THE
## PARLIAMENTARY REFORMERS.

*Kensington, 22d. Feb. 1827.*

MY FRIENDS,

Of all the acts of baseness of which men can be and so frequently are guilty, there is scarcely one which surpasses that hypocritical sorrow and hypocritical humanity which induces them to affect to lament the death, or the illness of those about whom they either care nothing at all, or whom they must, of necessity, dislike, if not hate. In the course of a life some years longer than that of Lord LIVERPOOL, and beset with circumstances, which might almost form an apology for this species of deviation from the paths of sincerity, I have never, in one single instance, given way, even in the smallest degree, if I perceived it, to this at once detestable and despicable species of baseness ; and, my friends, you shall find that I will not give way to it now, though my ears are dinned with the sounds of lamentation from the scores of those who, at any rate, ought to be above self-abasement so horrible as this. That which has now befallen this man may, I shall be told, befal me to-morrow. Surely it may : we are all in the same hand : we

R

Printed and Published by WILLIAM COBBETT, No. 183, Fleet-street.
[ENTERED AT STATIONERS' HALL.]

are all accessible in the same manner: we are all liable to the same afflictions of the body. But, am I to compassionate and even to praise the man who dies on the gallows for murder, because I may die in twenty hours after him? This is not a case exactly in point; because Lord LIVERPOOL does not stand before us as a male-factor; but, am I to act this part with respect to him, whom I have been constantly accusing of pur-suing measures calculated to pro-duce all the manifold miseries and disgraces with which my country is now afflicted; am I, who must be the most factious and hypocri-tical wretch that ever existed if I do not believe that his measures have been the great cause of these intolerable calamities; am I, who have notoriously been engaged, during the whole of his adminis-tration, in warning him against those measures which have, at last, produced difficulty and dis-tress wholly without a parallel; am I, who have thus been warn-ing him against these measures, who have been acridly and with voice (not to be profane) per-fectly prophetic, in a political sense, at any rate; am I, who have seen my forebodings and foretell-ings so amply accomplished, and who now behold, amongst the consequences of that accomplish-ment, the ruin, the total ruin of the middle class of society and the beggary and starvation of the la-bouring classes; am I, who have laboured with as much earnest-ness to induce this man not to pursue his destructive measures as ever man laboured for the sal-vation of his soul: am I, my friends, after all this, seeing an affliction fall upon this man; am I to ex-press sorrow at that, which, in all human probability, will prevent him from adopting any future pub-lic measure; am I, upon hearing that there is no probability of his ever being able again to pursue acts which I have so conscienti-ously condemned: am I to set up a hypocritical howl, making my-self the rival, in the science of blubbering, with one of O'Con-nell's lazaroni of lawyers? Your answer will be, NO.

As I said the other day, respect-ing the illness of CANNING, as a man, merely, I can care nothing about Lord LIVERPOOL. None of us can care much about the death of those, with whom we have no personal acquaintance, unless there be peculiar circumstances of distress or misery arising from their illness or death. In this case, there are none of those cir-cumstances. There are no widow and children left in a state of misery and hunger. His Lordship must have left more money behind him or money's worth, than would amply suffice for a hundred considerable families. To pretend to feel sorrow at every death that we hear of would be to make us habitual hypocrites. Oh, no : I am not to set up a sigh and begin a blubber, every time I hear the tolling of the passing bell of the parish. This is not humanity; nor is it common sense. If I lament, therefore, the death or the illness of any man with whom I am not acquainted, and whose family is left with a sufficiency to keep the wolf from the door, my lamentation must be founded on an opinion, that the death in question or the illness in question is likely to be attended with some injury to my country, or, at least, to some considerable number of those persons, for whose welfare I am anxious. Now, then, can I discover in the severe illness or in the probable death of this man, any injury at all likely to arise to my country, or likely to arise to any considerable number of persons in that country? I frankly say, that, so far from seeing this, I see something which would lead me to hope for the contrary.

Thus, then, I am not one who is disposed to swell the ranks of the boisterous blubberers of the broad sheet. But, besides this, we are not to forget what has been, in divers instances, the conduct of the party thus afflicted. In matters of private life, it may not be necessary to rip up, as it is called, old stories to deprive the sufferer of the compassion of his neighbours. This, however, is not such a case. It is not a case of private life : it is not a powerless individual of whose illness we are speaking : it is the illness of a Minister and of a Prime Minister, too. It will hardly be contended, that the moment a man becomes ill, your mouth is to be locked as to his conduct and measures, or left open only for the purpose of putting forth praise upon that conduct and those measures. This will hardly be contended by any one, who is not ready to contend, that, if a condemned criminal should happen to be seized with the yellow fever, you are not only not to put the sentence in execution, but to praise his character, though he may have committed murder or treason. In short, whether the man be well or ill, alive or dead, the deeds which he has done, the acts which he has committed, or in which he has participated, are still the same.

As such, I should, for the presen , have left the character and acts of this man; but, when I see the base parasites of the press; those most efficient of all instruments in effecting and perpetuating the slavery and misery of a people; when I see these slaves, these corrupt knaves, these prostituted hirelings at work, without, hardly, a single exception, from one end of the country to the other, applauding the character of this man; holding him up as a paragon of public virtue; representing the blow that he has received as the heaviest blow that England could have received; when I thus see that, through the channel of praise bestowed on him, an universal sort of praise is bestowed on that horrible system, which, after having produced misery and degradation such as the world never before saw, has just come to the horrible point of making the people of England silently endure the suggestion, that it is necessary to *transport beyond the seas* hundreds of thousands of unoffending persons, they being in a state not to be enabled to find food and raiment in this once happy England: when I see this, I am not to hold my tongue; I am not to suffer these praises to pass without something, without making an

effort, at least, to steady men's minds and make them look soberly at the matter.

One would imagine, that the state of the country, as described by these eulogists themselves, would be sufficient to restrain even the most shameless of men from affecting to lament that he, who has been at the head of public measures for fifteen years past, is likely to be at the head of them no longer. One of their reasons for lamenting the blow which this man has received, is, that the affairs of this country were never in so difficult and so dangerous a state, as they are at this moment. What the devil, then! do they *lament* that something has happened which is likely to lead to the adoption of a new sort of measures? Do I, when I find my affairs all deranged, my farms all in ruins, my tenants all a set of worthless scoundrels, my debts every day increasing, and my income every day diminishing; when I find, in short, that, with a noble estate, which maintained my ancestors like princes, I am reduced to be only a sort of sturdy beggar with a title; do I, when, such being the state of my affairs, I hear of the sudden illness of my steward, exclaim, " O Lord, I " am ruined! what an unlucky

" accident! just at this time, too,
" when I am reduced to such
" misery! "— If I were, under
these circumstances, thus to exclaim, and to state the circumstances of my ruin and distress
while I was so exclaiming, all my
friends and neighbours would set
me down as mad; for, they would
naturally say, " How can you
" suffer from this accident ?—
" What harm can it possibly do
" you? "

The wretched ruffians of the
broad sheet, who are extolling
this man's gentleness, integrity
and wisdom to the skies, in the
very same breath that they describe the country at the head
of the government of which he
has been for fifteen years as
being in much greater difficulty
and danger, both abroad and
at home, than it ever was at
any former period; and while
they, still in the same breath, represent many parts of the kingdom as being actually in a state
of disorganization approaching to
a dissolution of society: these
wretched ruffians of the broad-
sheet are not mad, my friends.
Fools enough they are, generally
speaking: quite worthy of a cap
and bells; but, not mad! They
all feel; they cannot tell you how
it is, but they all feel that they

are enabled to live without work,
that they are enabled to put lard
upon their own ribs, or round
their own intestines, at the expense of the tradesman, the
farmer, the artisan, and the labourer. They all feel, instinctively,
that any thing that will change
that system, the consequences of
which they affect to lament, will
endanger their ability thus to fatten upon the fruit of the labour of
others. This is the true cause of
their lamentations over this man:
they care not a straw about him,
personally: they have no sort of
regard for him, or for any one
belonging to him: they know the
measure of his puny talents as
well as you or I do; but, they
know that he has been, for a long
while, a sort of key-stone to the
system: they think that his death,
or even his illness, must produce
what the French call a remumenage. It certainly will do that, in
the course of some short time, unless the remumenage is produced
by the workings of the system
itself. Therefore it is that they
howl; therefore it is that they set
up their hypocritical lamentations.

It is for me, my friends, and
for you also, to act a very different
part. It is for us duly to estimate
the character of this man by the

only standard in our power,
namely, his conduct; and, in
speaking of that conduct, it is not
less just than it is natural, for us
first to advert to *his conduct towards ourselves.* Look at the
motto, my friends, Parliamentary
Reformers ; look at the motto, to
the paper which I am now doing
myself the pleasure of addressing
to you. You will see that it is
taken from a report of a speech
made by this man against us,
Reformers, in the memorable
year 1817. I have frequently
reminded him of this expression
of his, about the " stern path
of duty;" and though, properly
speaking, I cannot be said, perhaps, now to remind *him* of it
again; I have no scruple to say,
that I would, *even at this moment,
sound these words in his ears if I
could.* He would pursue the
" stern path of duty," would he ?
And, my friends, shall not we
pursue the stern path of duty ?
He would suffer not even odium
to frighten him from that stern
path; and shall I be frightened
therefrom by the howlings of the
curs of the broad sheet, for whose
censure I ought to care no more
than the farmer cares for the howlings of his curs while he is ring-
ing a pig, than which howling,
perhaps, nothing in all this world

so nearly resembles, in all respects whatsoever : in manner, in
motive, in *matter* even, as the
howlings now set up by these despicable shag-tailed curs of the
press. He was not to be *frightened* from the " stern path of
duty;" he, brave fellow, who had
a hundred thousand regular soldiers at his back, who had, at his
nod, an army costing this miserable nation, at that time, ten millions a year; who had all the justices of the peace, all the police,
all the powers of restraining and
destroying of every description, in
his hands; he, gloriously brave
fellow, was not to be *frightened*
from " sternly " pursuing his march
against a set of poor and helpless
men, who prayed, and who only
prayed to be relieved from a state
of misery, and to be protected
against the recurrence of that misery in future.

But, if no odium was to frighten
him from the stern path of duty,
as he called it; shall we be afraid
to inquire a little, just at this
time, what sort of duty that was,
and how it was called forth ? And,
moreover, let us ask, in what manner that duty was performed; what
this man meant by pursuing the
" stern path of duty " ?

In the year 1817, the working
classes were, in every part of the

country, in great distress. They ascribed their distresses to the heavy and unsparing taxation, which is now done, you will observe, by almost every man, even in the Parliament itself. These 'suffering classes,' whose misery was excessive, thought that the weight of taxes arose from too large establishments; from an improvident expenditure of the public money, generally, and, especially, from the payment of a larger sum to the fundholders than ought to be paid to them. In most humble petitions to the Parliament, they stated these opinions; and, they added that this improvident and unjust application of the public money was manifestly owing to grants and votes of the House of Commons, and arose out of a want of that House being elected by the people at large, agreeably to the principles of the venerable constitution of their country, according to which no Englishman could be taxed without his own consent. They, therefore, prayed THAT AN EFFECTUAL REFORM MIGHT BE MADE IN THE MANNER OF CHOOSING THE MEMBERS OF THAT HOUSE.

They attempted no force, they never spoke of the use of force; they conducted themselves in a legal manner, and in the most peaceable possible manner. They were guilty of no acts of sedition; they instigated nobody to commit such acts. Yet, instead of granting the prayers of their petitions; instead of a patient hearing of their petitions; instead of any attempt to convince them of their error, if it were an error, an Act was passed to authorise the Government to seize any man in Great Britain, whom they chose, merely on saying that *it suspected him of treasonable practices;* to send him to any gaol that they chose, without being first confronted with his accuser, without being informed of the offence that it was alleged he had committed, and without any warrant or other document, stating the nature of the alleged offence. This Act gave the Government the power to put the imprisoned person into any dungeon that it chose; to keep him in that dungeon, in a solitary state, as long as it chose; to deprive him of the use of pen, ink and paper; to deprive him of the sight of his wife, children, parents, brethren, relations and friends. It authorised this same Government to turn the dungeoned man out of prison, when it chose, without bringing him to trial;

and, another Act was after ward passed to indemnify, to bear harmless, any Minister, or any person authorised by any Minister, who had *over-stretched the powers, even of this Act!*

It was when the first of these terrible Acts, which placed every Englishman at the absolute mercy of the Government; it was when the first of these terrible Acts was passing, that this man, Robert Bankes Jenkinson, made the speech, from the report of which, as contained in the *Courier* newspaper, I have taken my motto, containing the declaration of this man, whose illness the vile reptiles of the London press lament in howl so unanimous and so melodious. As to the manner in which the "stern path" was pursued, I shall give no description of my own, but I will here insert (for, God forbid that the thing should ever be forgotten!) a set of queries, addressed to Sidmouth, then Secretary of State for the Home Department, by the acting magistrates for the county of Berks. These magistrates were in the constant habit of visiting the gaol at Reading. When they visited it after the passing of the above Act, they were *refused admittance* to see the poor reformers who were prisoners there.

They, therefore, addressed certain queries to Sidmouth, a copy of which, together with his answers, was published immediately afterwards. There needs very little beyond this document to prove to us the state to which the people of England were at that time reduced, under the Prime Ministership of this man, whom the newspaper vagabonds say is one of the most amiable creatures alive.

" In consequence of the acting
" magistrates for the county of
" Berks having been refused ad-
" mittance to the state prisoners
" in the gaol of Reading (though
" they were in the constant habit
" of visiting that gaol), they ad-
" dressed queries to the Secretary
" of State for the home depart-
" ment on the subject, and re-
" ceived answers. The following
" is a copy of the queries and
" answers.

" (Copy.)—The Visiting Ma-
" gistrates of Reading Gaol wish
" for answers to the undermen-
" tioned questions from the Right
" Hon. Secretary of State :—

" 1. *Q.* May Magistrates gene-
" rally of the county of Berks
" visit the State Prisoners in com-
" mon with the other Prisoners,
" which they are privileged to do,
" and ask questions, and enter
" into conversation with them ?—

" *A. No, except upon special rea-*
" *sons being assigned, which must*
" *be submitted to and be judged*
" *of by the Secretary of State.*

" 2. *Q.* If State Prisoners may
" have a copy of Official Direc-
" tions to Gaolers ?—*A. No.*

" 3. *Q.* If they may have a free
" use of pen, ink, and paper, under
" certain restrictions, as ordered
" by the official directions?—*A.*
" *Vide Official Directions, which*
" *must be strictly observed.*

" 4. *Q.* If they may read the
" public London or provincial
" newspapers under certain re-
" strictions ?—*A. No.*

" 5. *Q.* If they may have books
" to read from circulating libra-
" ries ?—*A. Such books as are ap-*
" *proved of by the Visiting Ma-*
" *gistrate.*

" 6. *Q.* If they may have wine,
" or strong beer, or ale, in limited
" quantities, at their own expense,
" or that of the Government ?—*A.*
" *What quantity is desired ?*

" 7. *Q.* If through the day they
" may be confined in solitary cells,
" and at night in better apart-
" ments, if such can be procured
" by Magistrates for them ?—*A.*
" *To be confined in such manner*
" *as has been usual, and in such*
" *apartments as have been hereto-*
" *fore allotted to State Prisoners.*

" In consequence of new direc-
" tions sent down, the *three pri-*
" *soners were confined in separate*
" *rooms, after having been left all*
" *together in one room for a*
" *fortnight !* "

The man we are now talking of
was not the Secretary of State.
SIDMOUTH was the Secretary of
State; but JENKINSON was the
Prime Minister: he was at the
*head* of this same government.
Let it be recollected, that not one
of these men was *ever brought to*
*trial.* There were Dr. WATSON,
Mr. THISTLEWOOD and another,
I believe, who were brought to
trial. They were duly committed
to trial. Their crime was specified and alleged distinctly. There
were overt acts which were alleged to have been committed by
them. They were brought to
trial; and, though the prisons were
crammed with persons charged
on suspicion; though alarm had
been excited in every quarter;
though they were tried in the
Wen; though Ellenborough pre-
sided, and though the prosecution
was carried on by the Attorney
and Solicitor General; though all
the talent and every thing necessary for such a prosecution was
put in motion, even these men
were acquitted. What reason is
there, therefore, to suppose that
there was any guilt at all attach-

ing to those men, who were thus imprisoned and who were never brought to trial? When a man is brought to trial; when he once gets before a jury, though he may, in certain cases, have great reason to complain of foul play, and of severity: still, in this case, he does not suffer without the consent of twelve of his countrymen; but what is the situation of a man, who can be imprisoned at the pleasure of the government, without being confronted with his accuser, without knowing the crime that he is charged with, without it being possible for him to offer any thing in his defence, without ever being brought to trial or before the face of any magistrate or jury from first to last, and without being permitted to use pen, ink, or paper in his prison, or to see, in that prison, the face, or hear the voice of any relation or any friend! And what must be the impudence, what the shamelessness, what the hardened brass of the fellow, that could call this a measure necessary to the preservation of the liberties of Englishmen?

How individuals were treated; what each man suffered under the execution of this Act, whole volumes could not adequately describe. One man, whose name was RILEY, unable to endure the sufferings which he had to endure in his dungeon, put an end to his existence in that dungeon. No crime had been alleged against RILEY: he had committed nothing that was specifically laid to his charge: he had been committed on *suspicion of high treason*, but, never was he confronted with his accusers; never had he been told when, where, or how that suspicion rose in the mind of any man. The case of poor OGDEN, of Manchester; I mean, the bare *existence* of the case, has become familiar to the ears of the nation by the *jest* which the newspaper reports ascribed to Mr. CANNING, and the loud laugh which those reports have told us was produced in the House by that jest. Whether the jest did actually come from the lips of the now not very hale Right Honourable Gentleman, is more than I can say. It was a jest, an alliterative jest on Ogden, who had complained that he got ruptured by the violence of his treatment after he was seized at Manchester, and in the bringing him off to London. The particulars of Ogden's rupture, therefore; the cause of it, and the nature of it, are worth having, at this time, fully and plainly before us. Mr. Ogden (who is now dead) published his statement at Manchester, in the month of May 1818, in the following words :—

"On Sunday, the 9th March, 1817, I was arrested, early in the morning, by warrant from Lord Sidmouth, charging me to be suspected of high treason; which was in every respect false, as the event has proved. I was immediately conveyed to prison in Manchester, and placed in confinement among felons, till Tuesday, after three o'clock in the afternoon; nor had I any allowance either in meat or drink for the whole time save a threepenny pie, ordered, at my request, by Col. Sylvester, a magistrate, which I eagerly ate, just before I set off for London. I was ironed before the said magistrate, with a trammacle not less than 30 lbs. weight, and treated in the most daunting manner.—On my applying to be confronted with my accuser, I was treated with insult, and posted off to London, as before mentioned, and lodged in Horsemonger-lane gaol. The very ponderous irons I was loaded with, broke my belly, and caused an hernia to ensue, about eight o'clock in the evening, when going to bed; and as it was impossible for me to

alarm the gaoler, I remained in that dreadful state for more than fifteen hours, in the most excruciating pain and torture. On the turnkey appearing next morning, two surgeons were sent for by Mr. Watson, the governor, who, after using such means as seemed proper, found nothing would do but the knife, and they apprehended, from my age (74) that I should die under the operation. The pain was so great that I could endure it no longer, and therefore, at all hazards, I insisted on the operation being resorted to, which continued for one hour and forty minutes. Praised be God and the skill of my surgeons, I survived it, contrary, however, to the surgeon's expectation, and much weakened in my constitution. Mr. Dixon, the surgeon, and his partner, performed the operation in the infirmary of the prison. The wound in my groin was above seven inches in length, and Mr. Dixon had my entrails out of my belly in his fingers like a link of sausages; a circumstance on which, I learn, a Right Honourable Gentleman was afterwards so jocular and entertaining in the House of Commons. Mr. Watson, the governor,

"was present during the opera-
"tion, and he, as well as the
"surgeons, can attest the truth
"of my statement.—Thus have I,
"at the AGE OF SEVENTY-FOUR,
"been torn from my family,
"crushed almost to death with
"irons, suffered near nine *months'*
"*solitary confinement*, and ruined
"in my employ, as a printer;
"and I declare before God, who
"is omnipotent, omniscient and
"omnipresent, that I had done no
"wrong. I may add, that I am
"the father o fseventeen children,
"whom I have supported and
"educated, at my own expense,
"*by my own labour*, and I may
"truly say, that I have always
"been a bringer to the general
"stock, and not like he who made
"a jest of my sufferings, been a
"taker from it during his whole
"life.

"WM. OGDEN.

"*No. 26, Wood-street, Manchester.*"

Now, you mercenary ruffians
of the London press; you shameless parasites; you basest of all
the tools of Corruption and would
be the basest of all the tools of the
tyranny of Nero, if you could
thereby add to the quantity of the
meat and the gin that you swallow; ruffians as you are, can you
look at Ogden in his dungeon,
with his body actually bursted for
*fifteen hours* without being able
to make any soul hear him; with
nothing but treble stone walls to
listen to his groans; can you see
him lying for an hour and forty
minutes under the knives of the
surgeons; can you see his entrails
in the hands of one of those surgeons; can you reflect on his age
of seventy-four years; can you
think of him being the father of
seventeen children, brought up
by the labour of his own hands;
unfeeling ruffians as you are,
unjust and base ruffians as your
acts have proved you, can you
picture this innocent man thus
suffering before you; can you
reflect that the sufferings were
occasioned by an Act introduced
by a government of which this
Lord Liverpool was the head; and
can you pass over all this, and go
on extolling the justice and amia-
bleness of this Lord Liverpool to
the skies! Yes, you can do all
this; for, as CASSIUS says of the
base flatterers of CÆSAR : "Hang
them, reptiles; they would have
said no less if Cæsar had murdered their mothers!"

So much as a specimen; as a
mere specimen of what I shall
have to say of this man and his
measures; but, I cannot quit this
affair of 1817, without observing,
that all the calamities of the pre-

sent day; that every thing which now alarms the rich and that pinches the poor; that the whole of this is to be ascribed to the petitions of the Reformers of 1817 having been rejected. This is a most interesting fact: notoriously true it is; and it is interesting in proportion to its truth. In the Green Bag Reports, on which the Act before-mentioned was founded, it was stated, that the Reformers wanted to see an *extinction of the funded property of the country*; that they deemed the fund-holder a great monster, and that these rapacious wretches took fifteen pence out of every quartern loaf. This was actually stated in the Report, brought into the House of Commons by Cᴀsᴛʟᴇʀᴇᴀɢʜ, who afterwards cut his own throat at North Cray in Kent. There was very little truth in this, to be sure: Reformers were not jackasses enough to think that fund-holders could get fifteen pence out of a quartern loaf that did not cost a shilling in the shops; nor did the Reformers pray for the taking away of the whole of the income of the fundholders. Nor did they pray for any such monstrous robbery as that now-recommended in a pamphlet published under the name of Sir Jᴀᴍᴇs Gʀᴀʜᴀᴍ. However, here they were accused of hostility to the fundholders and their property: here they were accused of a wish to take away the property of the fundholders.

The crime, for which, amongst others, I suppose, of a like nature poor Oɡden had his bowels shook out of his body was, wishing to take away the property of the fundholder; for this was one of the charges against the Reformers upon which the Power-of-Imprisonment Bill was urged to be passed. Now, then, you base revilers of these reformers! do you wish the property of the fundholder to be taken away? Aye, do you; you are waiting to see if the Reformers will join you in the enterprize; and I can tell you for your comfort that they never will, until the army be disbanded, the Church made to contribute largely, and the sinecures, pensions and grants abolished for ever. Just retribution, Good God!

I hardly think it worth while to say any thing about the *changes of men* which this illness of Lɪᴠᴇʀᴘᴏᴏʟ may produce or tend to produce. It does not signify a straw to the mass of the people, who may take his place. Certain it is, that no new man (of sense) will take it, unless with the resolution to act upon the Norfolk Petition, or quit the place immediately. Those who are actually in the mess may do well to keep in it as long as they can; for they would hardly get much by quitting it, unless they quitted it in the same sort of way that Liverpool is like to do. They are in the thing; and it is not very likely that they will choose to run the risks to which they would be exposed by quitting it.

Some people have thought that the King will send for Lord Grey, and make him his Minister. We are, I should suppose, at a great distance from that point, yet; that is to say, at the distance of some months, at any rate: but, even if the King were to send for Lord Grey, and if Lord Grey were to become Minister, with that pretty general high opinion of him which prevails in the country; if this were to be the case, what could Lord Grey do? If Canning can, indeed, find gold to "*irrigate the base*" of his "*mountain of paper*"; if this most wild and absurd idea that ever came in a puff out of the head of Æolus; if this idea could be realised, having first been reduced to common sense; if, in short, Canning could come and find us gold enough to pay the interest of the Debt in full, without ruining the blue coat, yellow button, and ash-stick gentlemen, then I should say, that Canning would be

the man; or, if Lord Grey could do the same, that he would be the man. This is the point: it signifies not a straw about rotten boroughs, about votes, about parliamentary interest; about any of the things which were formerly of so much importance. What is wanted is, a man that will find the means of keeping wheat up to ten shillings a bushel, and keeping the gold in the country at the same time; or, in other words, paying the interest of the Debt in full in gold of standard weight and fineness, without sending the Lords and 'Squires to the poor-house. That is the man that we want; and, if we cannot find such a man, we may, just as well keep the man that we have, or take any washer-woman or cook that happens to be out of place.

What would my Lord Grey do, with a concern such as ours is at present? He would have plenty of people to serve under him, plenty of people full of eulogiums on his lordship's great talents, and everlastingly talking of the exhaustless resources of the country; but, his lordship, all this while, would have the country looking up to him: would have hundreds of thousands of ruined farmers and tradesmen looking up to him for relief, and millions of starving labourers and mechanics and manufacturers looking up to him for bread, not one morsel of which would it be in his power to give them. Things are not come to that mark when Lord Grey would be permitted to do or to talk of doing that which I am very sure he knows must be done, at last. So that, my opinion is, that, if the King were to send for Lord Grey to-morrow, he would send for him in vain.

There has been a talk of Lord LANSDOWN and Mr. BROUGHAM becoming part of the ministry. If this were actually to be the case: or, if only a rumour of it were to reach Scotland, the swarms of place-hunters there would be all, instantly, trimming their toe-nails, plucking their great sandy eyebrows, preparing their kelts and their phillybegs, filling their mulls and getting ready to tramp off upon the first breaking up of the frost. Good lord, what an invasion! I declare to God I would open entrenchments the other side of Highgate: I would send them word, as the Prince of Orange did to Louis the fourteenth, that I would die in this my last ditch, rather than be devoured by them. I am quite serious when I say that if the event were like to take place, I would decamp from Kensington and take my flitches of bacon along with me.

Good Heavens, what a scene there would be, if these two people where to come into power! What a talking! I remember this Lord Lansdown's project for reducing the National Debt. He was Lord Grenville's Chancellor of the Exchequer, and, great progress they made in the good work; but, as in every case of this sort, they began by adding a few tens of millions to the Debt. But to see Mr. Brougham and Lord Lansdown; to see them Ministers; to see them with all their schemes for carrying on this tremendous concern; to hear a repetition of their a thousand times made professions, to adhere inviolably to national faith; to hear of their plans of education and mental improvement; to see Doctor Black strutting in and out of the Treasury Chambers and walking half a foot higher than he now does; to meet the innumerable hordes of Scotch feelosofers, rehearsing a sort of whistle, snapping their fingers and almost jigging along the streets; every where in the purlieus of the palace! Same town, indeed! The same kingdom would be much too confined a place to contain one, such men, so stationed, being in it!

However, all these conjectures are, I dare say, the mere dreams of anxious place-hunters, just as our dreams are almost always about victuals, when we go to bed hungry. Liverpool's illness; his being put *hors de combat* can hardly help disturbing the harmony of the family, of which he has so long been at the head. He was at the head, observe, not because others had not much better pretensions, supposing the system to be what it might; but he was at the head, because others could not agree about which of them should be at the head. He was an exceedingly cunning man; and we have frequently seen the greatest of cunning where there has been the smallest portion of almost any thing else that one is apt greatly to admire. His post is a post that cannot remain vacant any time: there may be some difficulty in fixing upon a substitute, but, for my part, even if he was to die, about which, I care not a straw, I do not expect to see it lead to any thing like what could be called a *change of the ministry*; for, a real change of ministry would inevitably produce, in a short time, a total change of the system that now exists; and, none of the aspirants seem to be pre-

pared for any such thing, as yet. Events soon prepare them, as a sharp frost prepares a fellow for putting on a great coat; but these events may keep off for another year, or thereabouts. So that the conclusion in my mind is, that these ailments, or deaths, or whatever they may be, even the ailment of the great Mr. HUSKIS-SON, will not produce, for some months to come, at any rate, any change that will excite fears in the jews and jobbers and tax-eaters and monopolizers, and hopes in the rest of the nation.

> I am,
> My Friends,
> Your faithful friend and
> Most obedient Servant,
> WM. COBBETT.

---

TO

# DR. BLACK.

*On his Criticism on the Doctrine relative to Speculation, as laid down by the Chief Justice of the Court of Common Pleas.*

---

*Kensington, 23nd Feb. 1827.*

DOCTOR,

WHEN I did myself the pleasure of sending you that pottle of ale, of which you have made such honourable mention in your broadsheet of the 10th instant, I "*fondly* hoped," as my friend Mr.

Tʜᴡᴀɪᴛᴇs, the linen-draper, says;
I "fondly hoped" that it would
have the effect of tranquillizing
your spirit, for, at least, some little
time; and that, their Lordships
the Judges and their Squireships
of the "Great Unpaid," would
be held sacred against your censure until, at the very least, the
taste of the ale should have been
forgotten. But, I am afraid, that
you altogether (from inadvertence
no doubt) omitted, on your part,
to perform a principal condition
on this affair; which condition
was, that you should swallow the
whole pottle between the commencement of a certain hour and
the termination of the next hour
following; for, as in the case of
the ever famous Doctor of Valla-
dolid, *moderation* in the quantity,
defeats altogether the objects of
the specific. " Water," said he,
" my dear Gil Blas; water taken
" in small quantities, so far from
" being useful, is really perni-
·" cious.    It is necessary, my
" friend, to take large draughts;
" for, taken in small quantities, it
" merely *agitates the bile*, and
" adds to the virulence of the
" complaint, rather than tending
" to produce an abatement of it."
To the same tune sings the Poet,
who, you know, enjoins on us to
"*Drink deep* or taste not."

For want of due attention to
these precepts, and, which is
more, to the condition above mentioned, my ale appears merely to
have agitated your bile; and, in
fact, to have tended to increase
rather than diminish your disposition to censure their above-said
Lordships and Squireships. One
instance of your criticism on the
conduct, or rather doctrines of
these distinguished personages, I
cannot help noticing; because, in
the first place, your criticism is,
in my opinion, extremely unjust;
and, in the next place, because
you openly declare that you put
it forth, "NOTWITHSTAND-
ING" the effects of my ale!
That is to say, in *spite of my ale*;
in defiance of my ale, and all
its mollifying effects. Ah, Doctor!
if you had acted up to the condition; if you had swallowed the pottle in the space of one hundred and
twenty consecutive minutes, you
would not thus have set the beverage at defiance: I should have
had the credit of keeping a Scotch
feelosofer's pen from paper for
one twelve hours at any rate.

But, let me now come to the
real object of this letter, which is,
to remonstrate with you on the
censure which you, on the 10th
instant, thought proper to bestow
on the opinions of the Chief Jus-

tice of the Court of Common Pleas. There had been a trial, or rather a nonsuit, on the subject of a *contract for nutmegs*, which contract had been declared by the Judge to be null, because made, contrary to the statute, on the Lord's-day, commonly called Sunday. You say that the *decision* of the Chief Justice was right; but, that, he then proceeded to make some extra-judicial observations, in which he was wrong, and that it was probable that he was indebted *to Mr. Cobbett for his false notions.* In "hauling you over the coals" for this, I shall be accused, perhaps, of saying one word for the Chief Justice and two for myself. No matter for that; no matter at all, if what I say be true. I will now insert the passage from your sheet, to which passage I have here been alluding.

"We wish we could extend our approbation to the doctrine afterwards laid down by the Lord Chief Justice. Indeed (said his Lordship), he was rather pleased than otherwise, that a loss should fall on a man who had broken the Sabbath for the purpose of carrying on *speculation*, which had lately increased to such an abominable extent, that the honourable purposes of commerce had been perverted, and the Royal Exchange had been converted into an arena of gamblers.' So far so good.— The gambling propensities of merchants, which have such a corrupting influence on the national morals, are deserving of all the reprobation

which his Lordship has bestowed on them. But his Lordship could not stop here—he was determined to display not only virtuous indignation (always because in a Judge,) but also great political sagacity and acuteness in economics—a science with which he is evidently very little acquainted. 'Through these *speculations*,' added his Lordship, 'the price of every article of consumption had been factitiously raised; and the result was, that the purchaser was in fact cheated out of the money which he paid over and above what would have been the price of the article, if it had not been for these unwarrantable speculations.'—This is Lord Kenyon all over, though it is possible his Lordship may have been indebted for his views to Mr. Cobbett (whose notions, by the bye, respecting trade, and forestalling, and regrating, notwithstanding his present of a pottle of most excellent ale, which we received from him, we cannot conscientiously approve of); but whatever the source whence his Lordship has derived his views, it would have been prudent in him to have kept them to himself. His Lordship says, 'the price of every article of consumption has been factitiously raised.'—We wish he could point out a mean by which the goods, the produce of our various manufactories, which, for more than a year past, have been a drug in the market, could possibly be raised in price. If he could have pointed out a way of raising the price of these goods half a year ago, he would have done more for the starving workmen than all the Subscription Committees in the metropolis and elsewhere."

Nothing, in my opinion, was ever more just than these observations of the Chief Justice; and, I, of course, think your criticism very foolish at the least. The only fault, if fault it may be called, in the remarks of the Chief Justice, consists in his having given the name of speculation (a word designating an operation of the mind, which is perfectly harmless), to an act, which the law calls *gambling*, or *forestalling or monopolizing*. With this little correction, the Judge's observations were perfectly correct; and, in whatever degree they had a tendency to produce an effect upon the public, that effect must have been good. This people owes a large part of its calamities to the monopolies which have been created by the paper-money. Perhaps the taxes, enormous as they are, do not press upon the people with so much severity, as the all-pervading monopolies, to which the paper-money has given rise.

You, Doctor Black, are so extremely fond of "new light," and have such a hearty contempt for every thing which our ancestors either thought or said, that it may be in vain to tell you, that it has been a settled maxim in all ages, and in every country, and amongst every people on earth, from the days of Moses until the days of William Huskisson, Prosperity Robinson and Co., that one great thing for a Government to keep in view was to prevent the *growth of* the *number of idlers;* to make the number of persons, living upon the labour of the rest, as small as possible, consistently with the sustaining of those ranks in society which are necessary to its good order, its peace and happiness. It always has been, it always will be, because it always must be, that there will be a certain portion of the community, to live without labour of any sort. Call them Noblemen, or call them what you like, there must and will be certain portions of persons of this description; for, without them there can be no civil society. Indeed, this exists even in savage life, as has been shown by Dr. Morse, and by all attentive observers who have visited the savages of North America. There can be *no government*, where there are no distinctions of this sort. But, because it is necessary to the order and happiness and power of a nation, that there should be a certain portion of the men in it, who, by their wealth, either with or without distinctive honours, shall become a sort of natural magistracy; because this is so manifestly true; and because this implies a certain portion of persons, who live not only without bodily labour, but without the fruit of science, either natural or

S 2

acquired; because this certain portion of *idlers* is necessary in the organization of society; because there ought to be, and because there must and will be, great estates going down from father to son; and because it is obvious enough that the general run of these owners of estates will do little or nothing, but pursue the objects of their pleasure: does it follow, because all this is unquestionably true; does it follow that laws should be made, that a system should be pursued, calculated to *convert into idlers*, a very large part of the whole of the community?

This is our case. The laws of England (and I believe of every Christian country upon earth) had constantly in view to prevent such an enormous thing as this. It was easy to see that if men were suffered to forestall a market, for instance, a clear profit would remain in the pocket of the forestaller: it was easy to see that these profits would accumulate in such hands: it was easy to see, that the *consumer* (that is to say *the mass of the community*) must finally pay the amount of these profits; and it was easy to see that as the wealth of the forestaller increased, the number of forestallers would increase, till, at last, the *idlers* would be so numerous, and would take away so large a part of the earnings of those that laboured, that the lot of the latter would become so hard as to be almost insupportable. The lawgivers amongst our ancestors took, therefore, special care that no such race of monopolizers should rise up. It was the duty of the government to protect the people in general against the arts of those whom the Scripture invariably denominates " extortioners," and against whom it denounces vengeance. This was, as I observed before, the law of every Christian land; and it is the LAW of ENGLAND even yet; though that law has been overwhelmed, has been stifled, has, by the vile paper-money and funding systems, been deprived of the far greater part, if not the whole of its force.

Daylight is not clearer to the healthy eye than the wickedness of this work of monopolizing is clear to every man of common sense and impartial mind. If, for instance, I sell a pig which I am taking to market to a forestaller, who meets me upon the road, and the price be ten shillings; if the forestaller take it into the market and sell it to another man for eleven shillings, that forestaller gets a shilling from the man he sells the pig to; and that shilling is so much a loss to the final purchaser of the pig. I remember an instance; or, at least, I was told of it, of a farrow of pigs (three or four months old) that were sold *seven times* before their final departure from Fareham market, on one and the same market day. These pigs were, I dare say, sold to different people, some poor men and some rich men, perhaps; and, whoever the final purchasers were, they had the profits, the " gain of oppressions," as the Scripture calls it, of the seven forestallers to pay. So that, as these seven wretches gain their livelihood in this manner, as they thus provide themselves with the means of living without any labour at all, they were of course maintained by the industrious part of the community. That which was evidently true and just in former times, is true and just now; and we at this moment feel all the horrible effects of departing from these wise provisions and principles of the law of the land.

Infinite indeed were the pains which our forefathers took in providing against this species of robbery of the people. As amongst the most effectual means of preventing this hugger-mugger deal-ing, markets and fairs were established by law in such numbers, with such frequent recurrence and under such wise and strict regulations, that it was very difficult for even the most crafty monopolizer to escape detection. It is curious enough also to observe that our Catholic ancestors, who have been ridiculed everlastingly about their " *superstition*," not only permitted markets and fairs to be held on a *Sunday*; but, established more markets and fairs on that day than on any day of the week. They acted very wisely in this. It was a day of rest; it was a holyday; it was a day of leisure, even in harvest and hay-making time. Almost every person who lives in and near the " *Wen*," knows that Bagshot in Surrey, is a little hamlet, belonging to a parish which is, *I believe*, called Worldham. This hamlet had formerly *three fairs in a year*, one of which was, if I recollect right, held on a Sunday. Amongst the vastly beneficial effects of these *truly paternal laws*, was that the people, even the poorest of the people, treasured up their money for the time of the market or the fair; that all their dealings were for *ready* money; that the fatal system of trust, from which extortion is inseparable, was unknown amongst our happy forefathers, who have been succeeded by a race of trust-takers, of debt contractors, who, according to the express words of the ancient philosophers as well as the fathers of the Christian Church, must always be the real slaves of the trusters and the lenders.

Amongst the consequences of the departure from these just, wise, and paternal laws, we have seen rise up the monstrous, the cruel, the worse than savage code of *debtor* and *creditor*; a code which confounds indiscretion and misfortune with crime; a code which gives the crafty and cheating truster or monopolizer, a power over the estate, goods, and, even, body of the person to whom he has *voluntarily* trusted and lent, which power, if possessed by the King over any portion of his subjects, would be regarded, and justly regarded, as constituting him a tyrant, even the existence of whom ought not to be endured.

If you, Doctor, were any thing short of a Scotch feelosofer, I should flatter myself, that, by this time, you began to perceive, that the views of the Chief Justice were not so astonishingly absurd as you would fain represent them to be. " But," say you, " if his " Lordship be right, when he says

" ' *that the price of every article of* " *consumption has been factitious-* " *ly raised,*' we wish he could point out the means by which " the goods, the produce of our " various manufactories, *could be* " *raised in price.*" Indeed! I do not wish this, nor does his Lordship, I dare say. It is not a rise in the price of the manufactures that is wanted, good Doctor. It is a taking off of the taxes and an abolition of the monopolizing system that is wanted; and, if these were accomplished, the price of the manufactures would be high enough. In fact, this has nothing at all to do with the question; for, though forestalling or monopolizing, has, under certain circumstances, the effect of raising the price of rotten cottons as well as of other things, other circumstances may divert the forestalling from that object, and make it fall with double force on objects of more vital importance; and, this is the case at the present moment. Nor, because monopolizers live in idleness upon the labour of the rest of the community, does it follow that they are *always* to thrive: that would be sad work indeed: they would run the risk of the next world, if they were *sure* always to succeed in this: hence the Quakers (the most renowned monopolizens upon the face of the earth) keep, as they think, two strings to their bow; the "gain of oppressions," in the first instance, and the hope of being enabled to cheat the Devil by their professions of humility, their buttonless coats, and their sanctified looks, which, they have found, by experience, are quite sufficient to over-reach every thing upon the face of the earth.

*Things ought to be left to find their own level: men's own interest will teach them what is best to be done: competition is of itself quite sufficient to keep prices down to their proper standard: all trade ought to be left perfectly free.* If we do not believe all these things most implicitly, it assuredly is not for want of their having been dinned into our ears; verbally; *in* parliament and *out* of parliament; at meetings of all sorts and sizes and through the columns of sheets, the most bread, boisterous, bold, and blackguard that ever came forth blackened by base metal and stinking ink. Yet, these are all so many false or rather senseless assertions. Things can never be suffered to find their own level in a civil community. Man's own interest may teach him what is best to be done for himself; but it requires law to teach him that which he ought to do or leave undone with regard to the interest of his neighbour. Competition (fair competition) would be quite sufficient to keep prices to their proper standard; but, it is competition in open market or fair; it is competition, where the consumer, or the changer of the nature of the article, comes and deals with the *producer*, that is to say with the grower, the manufacturer, or the actually importing merchant. There is no competition that can be useful to the mass of the community, while the competitors are " *speculators,*" as the Chief Justice called them, or, as he should have called them, forestallers or monopolizers. The observation, that trade ought to be left *perfectly free,* is equal to observing that we ought always to have fine sunshine by day, and rain, when necessary, by night. It is a thing that never was, and never can be; and, it would be just as sensible to say, that men ought to be left perfectly free in all their actions; and that theft is no more than a particular species of industry. It ought to be left perfectly free, in so far as the conducting of it does not tend to the injury of the community; but, as there always will be found traders and dealers to be ever ready and willing to overstep these bounds, the bounds must be guarded by law, or, we very soon come to a state even worse than savage life.

After all, Doctor, it is in the CREATING OF IDLERS, that the monopolizing system is most mischievous. These idlers must live upon the labouring part of the community. It was the constant practice of our ancestors not to suffer any body to live in idleness unless he had the visible means of living without labour of any sort. It was in the spirit of their wise laws, that the Vagrant Act compelled every one, if called upon, to *account how he got his living.* And, what justice is there in compelling the poor man or woman to give this account, while it is notorious that whole bodies of buttonless blackguards have skins as soft as those of mice, and ribs with an inside lining like those of a Hampshire hog, without ever having done any thing, but forestall and regrate; that is to say, without having done any thing, since the hour of their birth, but fatten upon the rest of the community, and that, too, by a constant violation of the law of the land!

Now, Doctor, if I had room and time, I would say a word or two upon the remedy necessary to be adopted to rid us of this curse; for, the ancient law is wholly insufficient to grapple with a monster like this, the existence of which it never could have contemplated. If our ancestors had been told that a day would come when the Devil would find advocates in England, they would have believed it as readily as they would have believed that there would be men found in England to eulogize a system, the direct and obvious tendency of which is, to give the cunning knave an advantage over a simple and honest man; to enable the former to enjoy, without any labour at all, fifty times as much as is enjoyed by the most industrious man. In their provisions, therefore, nothing can be found sufficiently energetic for the present emergency. Flinging the monopolizers into the sea would not be a bad way; but, perhaps, treating them as King Richard and King John treated the Jews would be sufficient; however, perhaps no direct measure will be necessary. The vermin have been engendered by the paper system, as botts (like that at Liverpool) are engendered in a diseased horse. The vermin, like the minute animals that come in the buds and blossoms of the fruit trees, are not CAUSE but effect.

It is the diseased state of the tree that brings the insect: when it is come, it adds monstrously to the mischief of the disease; and just so do these base gormandising vermin that have been produced by that horrid state-disease, funding and paper-money.

Horrible situation! When it is notorious that there are hundreds of thousands of these monopolizing idlers, swollen by gluttony and drunkenness, there is before the Parliament a project for *transporting a portion of the labouring classes of the people,* on the ground of their being too numerous in proportion to the means of their sustenance!

This is the state which once happy England has been brought to, by her statesmen acting upon the principles of the impudent Scotch feelosofers. Delivered, however, she must be; and that deliverance will sink for ever the beggarly, upstart, conceited and brazenfaced race, to whose unfeeling suggestions so much attention has, for so many years, been paid. Hoping that you and I shall live to witness this event,

      I remain,

        Doctor,

   Your most obedient and

     Most humble Servant,

       Wᴍ. COBBETT.

TO

## MR. O'DWYER,

*Who originated the Motion for expelling the Register from the Room of the new Catholic Association of Dublin.*

*Kensington, 22nd Feb. 1827.*

Sɪʀ,

Iɴ my last Register, I expressed my sorrow that one more number of that work was not likely to have the honour of being admitted into the room of the Association; and it will not be many moments before you will be convinced, that that expression of sorrow was likely to be sincere; and that it was founded in substantial reason.

At the time when I made this observation, I was not so very anxious for the sale of one more Register, as I was for the Association to see that there were Englishmen, whose breasts sympathize with theirs, whose sighs were responsive to their sighs, drawn forth by the untimely end of their late worthy associate. I am sure, Sir, that you will do me the justice to acknowledge, that, however roughly I may have been handled by that very rough-headed ornament of your body; whatever degree of want of respect, or whatever degree of contempt I may at any time have expressed

for his manners, his motives, his
character, his talents, or his principles, I have uniformly, whether at home or abroad, whether
mewed up in this hellish Wen,
or rambling about amongst the
sweets of the country; I have uniformly, from the date of the
" intense comedy " to the hour of
the Counsellor's lamented demise,
expressed an anxious desire to
see him suitably matched in the
holy state of matrimony.

In the intense theatrical piece,
to which I have just alluded, I expressed my sorrow, at the utter impracticability of uniting him with
my old friend Anna Brodie. Seeing no chance in that way, I next
suggested that a suitable match
might, I thought, be made amongst
the Mawmes of Suffolk, or amongst
the Shoy-Hoys of some of the
Western Counties. These are
families, principally, and, indeed,
exclusively, engaged in that very
healthful and useful and rural
occupation, the scaring of mischievous birds from the corn and
the fruit; and, it is an uniform
and never-failing characteristic of
both families, that the females,
though in some respects not altogether what we could wish, are
never addicted to that loquacity,
which is but too frequently found
to be a great disturber of domestic

bliss; and a symptom of which
was so very apparent in the Counsellor's female admirers, at the
meeting at Cork.

This subject, always alive in
my mind, was mentioned by me
in my Register of the 14th October last. You will, if you have not
voted that number also out of your
room, find the following passage
at page 111. " Mem. To ask,
" when I get to London, what is
" become of the intense ' Coun-
" sellor Bric;' and whether he
" have yet had the justice to put
" the K to the end of his name.
" I saw a lovely female Shoy-
" Hoy, engaged in keeping the
" rooks from a newly sown wheat-
" field on the Cotswold Hills, that
" would be a very suitable match
" for him; and, as his manners
" appear to be mended; as he
" now praises to the skies those
" 40s. freeholders, whom, in my
" hearing, he asserted to be ' be-
" neath brute beasts;' as he does,
" in short, appear to be rather
" less offensive than he was, I
" should have no objection to
" promote the union; and, I am
" sure, the farmer would like it
" of all things, for, if Miss Stuffed
" o' Straw can, when single, keep
" the debouchers at a distance, say,
" you who know him, whether the
" sight of the husband's head

" would have a rook in the coun-
" try !"

It was, doubtless, and, indeed,
there can be scarcely any doubt
on the matter, that it was this intended union, to which Mr. O'Connell, in his usually "intense"
style, so "intensely" alluded,
when he made his motion for eject-
ing the Register from the room.
He said, in accents between a
blubber and a bawl, "that his dear
" departed friend was upon the
" point of an HONOURABLE
" CONNEXION, when so sud-
" denly snatched away from
" them;" that is to say, beyond
all doubt, the connexion suggested
by me in that Register from which
I have just given an extract; and,
the disappointment to which " honourable connexion," has been, in
the following " ELEGY," celebrated by an anonymous poet, residing on the banks of the Colne
river, which winds through the
vales formed by the Cots-Wolds,
where I saw her, whom, from the
moment I set my eyes upon her, I
allotted to Bric, for a "help-meet
unto him." The poet was, it appears, induced to invoke the muse
upon the subject, in consequence
of the above-noticed passage in
the speech of Mr. DANIEL O'Connell; for, until then, he hardly
believed that the projected mar-

riage was any thing more than a
joke of mine; but, when Mr. DA-
NIEL actually came out, and in
the open Association, as good as
declared that the "honourable
connexion" had been all but con-
summated, the poet, anxious to
celebrate the fame of one of the
damsels of his neighbourhood,
called upon the muse to assist
him; and, as the reader is now
about to see, did not call upon her
in vain.

### THE LIVES, LOVES, DEATHS, AND BURIALS OF LAWYER BRIC, AND THE FAIR SHOY-HOY.

Poor Bric is dead ! What Bric ? Why he
That was the husband doom'd to be
Of fam'd Shoy-hoy ! Shoy-hoy was she,
Whom oft-times in the fields you see
Fright'ning the birds ! Was she Bric's
flame,
His earliest love—Shoy-hoy by name.
  But more at length I must relate
How Bric met Shoy—and she her fate.
  One cold raw morning, in the spring,
When crows are early on the wing,
To dig for grubs, or nip the wheat,
Bric was betimes upon his feet;
And, plodding onward, did espy
The rural nymph, the fair Shoy-hoy,
As in a field she took her station,
To guard the corn, her occupation.
  But first, kind Muse, bestow thy aid,
To dress the ever-watchful maid.
  A whisp of straw of curious plat,
Serv'd the dear damsel for a hat ;
Her hair, a most becoming crop,
Was formed of some discarded mop ;
The cloak that on her back was slung,
And at her feet dependent hung,

Some Irish swain relinquish'd keeping,
Last harvest when he left off reaping;
Her body was a besom's tail,
Or staff from some forsaken flail.

But can the Muse e'er hope to trace
The wonders of her matchless face?
Yet what the Muse dares undertake
She shall perform.—Her teeth a rake,
And round the roots as yet there clung
The cold remains of hard cow-dung;
A Swedish turnip was her head,
For cap, a cabbage leaf was spread;
Her eyes potatoes did compose,
And red beet-root was stuck for nose;
And thus array'd, she stood to gain
The heart of Bric, rough-headed swain!

Cupid, transformed into a crow,
Sat perch'd upon a distant bough;
For he it was that set the snare
For Bric, and deck'd the sylvan fair;
He brought about their mutual loves
To avenge the wrongs of Venus' doves;
For Shoy so guarded all the grain,
They scarce had strength to draw her
    train.

As thus she stood with solemn air,
Bric gazed with most astonish'd stare,
Alarm'd with love, and then assay'd
With timid grace to greet the maid;
But first he bade the saints attest
His love was pure; then crossed his
    breast.
Says he, " Chaste nymph, will you com-
ply,
And be my own, my lov'd Shoy-hoy?"
Silence ensued; quoth Bric, " Content;
" For, silence always gives consent:
" Our loves," he cries, " shall ever
    last:"
Then vows, and kisses sweet were past.
To Dublin he;—she lingers yet
About the place where first they met.

'Tis needless here, I'm sure, to tell
The fate which Lawyer Bric befel;
Alas! too well 'tis understood,
That full of hot Hibernian blood,

To which Love added fire and fuel,
He fought, and fell in Dublin duel;
'Tis known, too, that he cried, " I die
" For Love, for Honour, and Shoy-
    hoy!"
    This news soon reaching Shoy-hoy's
    ears,.
Her hopes gave way to instant fears.
" My Bric!—My Bric!" she, screaming,
    said
(Or seem'd to say) : " My Bric is dead."
Then tears distilling drop by drop,
Came gently trickling down the mop;
'Twas then that Cupid watch'd her nose
Begin to rot, and decompose;
'Twas then that he rejoic'd to trace
The falling honours of her face;
'Till Love in league with wind and rain
Laid Shoy-hoy level with the plain,
And there she lies full-length extended,
The sad remains of Bric's intended,
Upon that very self-same place
Where first she met him face to face.

For Epitaph, what shall we say?
A short, and yet a moving lay!
He sought the Bar! She shunn'd the
    city,
The verse should be both wild and witty.
    " Here lies a pair who died in youth,
" Drop dirt and dung upon them both
" Bric was the lad, Shoy-hoy the lass,
" Stop O'Connell ——— and pass!

———

I am not impertinent enough to
attempt to add to the poignancy
of poetry by my miserable prose;
but, as I have taken the liberty to
make a slight alteration at the
close of the Elegy; that is to say,
as I have, in conformity with the
" high state of civilization," " the
" high state of education, mental
" refinement, and mental enjoy-
" ment," of the present happy
age, when the lion, or, rather, the
wolf, lies down by the side of the

lamb, while he is as hungry as the devil; as I have, in conformity with the "intenseness" of the delicacy of this most delicate age and nation, particularly that part of it to which the feelings of my readers may, upon this occasion, be supposed to be most intensely directed; having in conformity with all these, ventured to put a blank after the name of the great DANIEL, in the last line of the Elegy; I beg leave, in the way of mitigation of my temerity, to observe, that the word thus left out, gave us a proof of the profound philosophy, as well as of the humanity of the Poet. He had in his mind the ancient and sage maxim, expressed in the pithy and laconic style of John Bull; namely, that, "the more " you cry, the less you do some- " thing else." Reasoning like Aristotle and all the ancient philosophers, from the known to the unknown, he appears to have concluded, that the more you did *that "something else, the less you would cry."* Taking doubtless into his compassionate consideration, the good people who may be compelled to live within a few hundred yards of your Association room; and, thinking of the infernal annoyance that the vicinage must experience, from the blubberings and bellowings of a whole lazaroni of silk-gown-begging-lawyers, he, like a humane and public-spirited man, took this method of suggesting a mode, how the saline particles might be drawn away from Daniel and his lazaroni, without producing that disturbance of the peace of the neighbourhood, which must have been amongst the consequences of those saline particles being

squeezed from the two outlets under the forehead.

I remain,
Sir,
Your most obedient and
Most humble Servant,
WM. COBBETT.

## AMERICAN SEEDS.

BOXES of these seeds, made up agreeably to the Lists contained in the two preceding Registers, may be had at 183, Fleet-street, or by means of application by letter, directed to Mr. Cobbett, at Fleet-street, as above. I have to repeat here, what I have said before; namely, that I will sell none of these boxes after the 1*st day of April;* because, if I were to do that, I should be pretty certain that the purchaser would not have the seeds in the ground till the middle of April at soonest; and that would be exposing him to disappointment, that I would be, by no means, instrumental in producing. The whole of the lists, and the whole of the instructions for sowing, which were published in the two preceding Registers, have now been reprinted, and formed into a pamphlet; which may be called a Catalogue, if the reader pleases; one of these will be put into and sent with every box of seeds that will be sold in future; and this has been done indeed during the whole of the last week. Nothing will be charged for these pamphlets; and really, they contain matter, which may be useful to almost any English gardener; relating, as they do, to the sowing of Trees and Shrubs, of which, ninety-nine times out of every hundred, English gardeners cannot, as yet, know any thing. If any person want this pamphlet, unaccompanied by the seeds, he must, of course, pay for it, but, at a price a little more reasonable than that which is put upon the "Corn Pamphlets," by their great, rich, hectoring, conceited, stupid jackasses of authors.

## MARKETS.

Average Prices of CORN throughout ENGLAND, for the week ending February 9.

### Per Quarter.

| | s. | d. | | | s. | d. |
|---|---|---|---|---|---|---|
| Wheat | 53 | 5 | Rye | | 39 | 5 |
| Barley | 36 | 2 | Beans | | 46 | 2 |
| Oats | 28 | 4 | Pease | | 47 | 5 |

Aggregate Average of the six weeks preceding Feb. 15, by which importation is regulated.

### Per Quarter.

| | s. | d. |
|---|---|---|
| Wheat | 53 | 6 |
| Rye | 39 | 7 |
| Barley | 35 | 5 |
| Oats | 27 | 10 |
| Beans | 45 | 10 |
| Pease | 48 | 3 |

Total Quantity of Corn returned as Sold in the Maritime Districts, for the week ended February 9.

| | Qrs. | | Qrs. |
|---|---|---|---|
| Wheat | 39,870 | Rye | 224 |
| Barley | 35,690 | Beans | 2,140 |
| Oats | 10,380 | Pease | 1,083 |

### Corn Exchange, Mark Lane.

Quantities and Prices of British Corn, &c. sold and delivered in this Market, during the week ended Saturday, February 10.

| | Qrs. | | £. | s. | d. | | s. | d. |
|---|---|---|---|---|---|---|---|---|
| Wheat | 4,456 | for 12,537 | 2 | 9 | Average, | 56 | 3 |
| Barley | 7,613 | 14,944 | 1 | 6 | | 39 | 3 |
| Oats | 1,815 | 2,981 | 6 | 8 | | 31 | 6 |
| Rye | 12 | 22 | 3 | 7 | | 36 | 10 |
| Beans | 1,708 | 2,593 | 5 | 6 | | 46 | 9 |
| Pease | 895 | 855 | 13 | 4 | | 50 | 0 |

Friday, Feb. 16.—There have been moderate arrivals, this week, of all sorts of Grain, but Barley, which again is considerable. Fine Wheat sells freely, at Monday's prices; other sorts are dull; but not cheaper. Barley sells very heavily, and is rather lower. Beans and Pease are unaltered. Oats meet buyers slowly, at the same terms as at the beginning of this week.

Monday, Feb. 19.—The supplies of Grain in general last week were moderate, except good quantities of Barley and Malt, and a considerable arrival of Flour. This morning's fresh supply is scanty of all descriptions of Corn. Wheat of prime quality being scarce, has advanced 1s. to 2s. per quarter, and there is a better sale than of late for other kinds.

Barley hangs on hand, and is 1s. per quarter lower than this day sennight. Boiling Pease still continue a drug on the market. Beans and Grey Pease are rather dearer. — Those samples of Oats that are stout and good, obtain rather more money; but feed Corn continues to meet a limited demand. In Flour no alteration. All kinds of Spring Corn for seed are considerably higher than the annexed quotations.

Account of Wheat, &c. arrived in the Port of London, from Feb. 12 to Feb. 17, both inclusive.

| | Qrs. | | Qrs. |
|---|---|---|---|
| Wheat .. | 4,005 | Tares .... | — |
| Barley .. | 5,897 | Linseed .. | — |
| Malt .... | 6,174 | Rapeseed . | — |
| Oats .... | 6,515 | Brank .. | — |
| Beans ... | 1,612 | Mustard .. | — |
| Flour .... | 10,007 | Flax .... | — |
| Rye .... | — | Hemp ... | — |
| Pease.... | 1,445 | Seeds ... | — |

Foreign.—Oats, 1,731; and Beans, 1,116 quarters.

---

Monday, Feb. 19.—The arrivals from Ireland last week were 975 bales of Bacon; and from Foreign Ports, 4 casks of Butter.

---

Price of Hops, per Cwt. in the Borough.

Monday, Feb. 19.—The price of Hops continues the same, with the exception of Old, which are 2s. per cwt. dearer. A good demand.

*Another Account.*

Feb. 19. Our market remains firm, although not very brisk.

*Maidstone,* Feb. 15.—The Hop Trade has been rather dull this week. Prices much the same.

*Worcester,* Feb. 15.—The supply on Saturday being larger than the demand, Hops scarcely maintained the last quoted prices : 277 pockets were weighed.

---

COAL MARKET, Feb. 16.

Ships at Market. Ships sold. Price.
39 Newcastle 13½..28s. 6d. to 37s. 0d.
16 Sunderland 12 ..32s. 6d.— 36s. 0d.

SMITHFIELD, Monday, Feb. 19, 1827.

This market, though very short in supply on Friday, was exceedingly heavy, and no disposition on the part of the butchers to buy any thing but on lower terms. A few prime Beasts could hardly obtain a crown a stone. The Mutton trade was equally flat : the large supply of sheep this morning, and the extreme coldness of the weather, have had a material effect on the trade generally. The very best Beef is in slow demand, at 5s. a stone; but things of second quality hang on hand. The Mutton trade is also very dull, and prices lower, by 2s. and 3s. a head. The top quotation for Downs is 4s. 6d., and polled Sheep 4s. 4d.; though a few choice lots have perhaps made a trifle more.

*Per Stone of 8 pounds (alive).*

| | s. | d. | | s. | d. |
|---|---|---|---|---|---|
| Beef ...... | 4 | 6 | to | 5 | 0 |
| Mutton ... | 4 | 2 | — | 4 | 6 |
| Veal ..... | 5 | 0 | — | 5 | 3 |
| Pork ..... | 4 | 6 | — | 5 | 4 |
| Lamb .... | 0 | 0 | — | 0 | 0 |

| | | | |
|---|---|---|---|
| Beasts . . | 2,853 | Sheep .. | 26,600 |
| Calves ... | 112 | Pigs ... | 120 |

NEWGATE, (same day.)

*Per Stone of 8 pounds (dead).*

| | s. | d. | | s. | d. |
|---|---|---|---|---|---|
| Beef ..... | 3 | 4 | to | 4 | 4 |
| Mutton ... | 3 | 0 | — | 3 | 10 |
| Veal ..... | 3 | 8 | — | 5 | 8 |
| Pork ..... | 3 | 8 | — | 5 | 8 |
| Lamb ..... | 0 | 0 | — | 0 | 0 |

LEADENHALL, (same day.)

*Per Stone of 8 pounds (dead).*

| | s. | d. | | s. | d. |
|---|---|---|---|---|---|
| Beef ... . | 2 | 8 | to | 4 | 8 |
| Mutton ... | 3 | 0 | — | 3 | 10 |
| Veal .... | 4 | 0 | — | 5 | 4 |
| Pork..... | 4 | 0 | — | 5 | 4 |
| Lamb .... | 0 | 0 | — | 0 | 0 |

*Liverpool*, Feb. 13.—The arrivals of Grain since Tuesday last, into this port, have been pretty considerable, including the weight of Oats brought in from Ireland, but the demand very limited throughout the week, both in this and the country markets of the district. The market of this day, although tolerably well attended, was not productive of much business, and I must therefore reduce the quotations for Wheat 1d. per 70 lbs.; Oats ½d. to 1d., per 45 lbs.; and Flour, 1s. per 280 lbs.

Imported into Liverpool, from the 6th to the 12th February, 1827, inclusive:—Wheat, 4,867; Barley, 1,983; Oats, 15,199; Rye, 1,985; Malt, 683; and Beans, 343 quarters. Flour, 536 sacks, per 280 lbs. Oatmeal, 542 packs, per 240 lbs.

*Bristol*, Feb. 17.—Very little business is doing here in Corn, &c. except in Barley, which sells freely. Present prices about as follow. Supplies not abundant.—Wheat, from 5s. 6d. to 7s. 6d.; Barley, 4s. 4½d. to 5s. 9d.; Beans, 5s. 6d. to 8s. 3d.; Oats, 2s. 3d. to 4s. 1½d.; and Malt, 5s. 6d. to 8s. per bushel, Imperial. Flour, Seconds, 32s. to 42s. per bag.

*Guildford*, Feb. 17.—Wheat, new, for mealing, 13l. 10s. to 17l. 5s. per load. Rye, 44s. to 46s.; Barley, 36s. to 41s.; Oats, 31s. to 41s.; Beans, 52s. to 56s.; Pease, grey, 58s. to 60s.; ditto boilers, 60s. to 64s. per quarter. Tares, 11s. per bushel.

*Ipswich*, Feb. 17.—We had to-day a small supply of all Grain, and prices were rather dearer, for all except Barley, which was 1s. per quarter cheaper, as follow:—Wheat, 52s. to 60s.; Barley, 33s. to 39s.; Beans, 46s. to 48s.; and Pease, 48s. per quarter.

*Manchester*, Feb. 17.—During the week we have had a steady demand for most articles in the trade. At our market to-day, English Wheat, of fine quality, met tolerable free sale, at 8s. 9d. to 8s. 10d. per 70 lbs.; also, there was more doing in fine Irish and Foreign. Barley, for grinding purposes, was ready sale. The demand for Oats was good, at the quotations above. English Beans are held at higher rates, but not much doing in them; Foreign and Irish more sought after. Boiling Pease, Malt, and Flour, dull in sale.

*Newcastle-on-Tyne*, Feb. 17.—The supply of Wheat from the farmers this morning was not so large as it has been for some weeks past, and the millers being short of stock, sales were readily effected at 1s. per quarter advance. No alteration in the price of Rye. The supply of Norfolk Barley this week has been scarcely equal to the demand, and the market is at present quite bare of malting Barley. Fine Malt rather dearer. The supply of Oats was about equal to the demand, and sales were made readily.

*Reading*, Feb. 17.—We had a better supply of Wheat at our market this day. Old Wheat, 58s. to 68s.; New, 54s. to 66s. per qr. by the Imperial measure. Barley was in fair demand, and 1s. per qr. dearer. In Oats, Beans, or Pease, there was no material alteration. Flour, 45s. per sack.

*Wakefield*, Feb. 16.—We have a fair arrival of Wheat, and a pretty good supply of Oats, to this day's market, but that of Barley is moderate. Good dry Wheat has been tolerably ready sale, at an advance of 1s. per quarter, and there has been more done in middling sorts. Good Mealing Oats are without material variation, but middling samples of Foreign are dull sale, and rather lower. Seed Oats are much inquired after. Shelling is unaltered. Fine heavy Barley obtains the rates of last week, but the middling descriptions are very dull sale. Beans are much the same. Malt is very dull.

# COBBETT'S WEEKLY REGISTER.

**Vol. 61.—No. 10.]** LONDON, SATURDAY, March 3, 1827. [*Price 6d.*

" It is impossible that the present Corn-Bill, or that any Corn-Bill,
" can do the landlords good (except for a few months, perhaps) as long
" as the Bank of England and other bankers are compelled to pay their
" notes in gold. It is a clear error; an unmixed error, to suppose that
" a Corn Bill, be it what it may, can prevent prices from falling down to
" a very low mark, unless a new change were to be made in the laws
" respecting the currency."—REGISTER, 10*th February*, 1827.

## CORN PROJECT.

### TO THE
### WEAVERS IN THE NORTH.

*Kensington, 2d March, 1827.*

MY FRIENDS,

THE Corn Project; that famous measure of "*liberality*" which was to relieve you, is, at last, come out. It has been a long time a hatching, and, now it is hatched, it will, as I shall presently show, have the effect of making bread *dearer instead of cheaper*, as far as it can have any effect at all. We shall see, in the end, that other circumstances will come, and defeat the intentions of the projectors; but, in the meanwhile, we here have their intentions; and, those intentions clearly are, to make bread to be at all times dearer than it is now! This is *the relief*, is it, that these liberal Ministers had in store for you! This is the proof that CANNING is

T

Printed and Published by WILLIAM COBBETT, No. 183, Fleet-street.
[ENTERED AT STATIONERS' HALL.]

to give us, that the House *works well*, and that it needs no reforming. However, let me now proceed to state the substance, at least, of what passed last night relative to this Corn Project.

Various rumours have been afloat with respect to the menaces dealt out by the landowners against the Ministers, if they proposed any thing that would have a tendency to lower the price of corn. Most monstrous threats have, certainly, been uttered on the part of the land people against the poor apothecary, who was bound, solemnly bound, as much as a man could be without parchments and wax, to propose *something like* a free trade in corn. He, accordingly, poor man, was taken ill upon this occasion, and did not even appear in his place. He, poor man, was at a Cabinet Council on Wednesday, but could not attend in the House to look the landlords in the face on Thursday; though he is the Minister of Trade; though he is the advocate of free trade; and though he has just received an addition to his salary, from this very House, of two thousand pounds a year, as a mark of admiration of his surprising genius as a Minister of Trade. The measure is not even owned by Mr. Canning himself,

who brings it forward; but is ascribed to the master mind of the great Liverpool himself! So that, here it came as a sort of begging creature in its shroud, bespeaking indulgence, and deprecating all opposition and all discussion.

However, the main thing is, to ascertain what will be the EFFECT of this measure, as far as the paper-money affairs will let it have any effect. You, my good friends, and all the rest of the half-starving millions of England, Scotland and Ireland, want bread to be cheaper than it is; you want to have your bread at as low a price as the French silk-weavers and cotton-weavers have their bread. Aye, to be sure you do; or, how the devil are you to carry on a competition in the sale of your goods against the silk-weavers and cotton-weavers of France, Germany, and other countries? This is what you want; this is what all of you who have sent up petitions to the Parliament have been earnestly praying for; and this, as far as this measure can accomplish the purpose, you are to be most *effectually prevented from ever having*. The measure now proposed is nothing at all without measures relative to the paper-money; but, that is no matter: we are to speak of this measure as a thing intended to produce certain effects; and we are now going to see what these effects are; and how kindly the Ministers and the landowners, how humanely, they have listened to the voice of a starving people! Lord Milton, the great advocate for the starving weavers; Burke's great Corinthian Pillar; oh, this compassionating Lord, seems satisfied with the course pursued by Canning. He is reported to have said that the Ministers had his thanks for proposing this scheme: nay, Mr. Alderman Wood is, by the *Morning Chronicle*, reported to have expressed himself *favourable to the propositions.* On the other hand, the landowners seem delighted with the propositions; so that, really, if the farm of these propositions, if their wondrous power in producing harmony could be fairly got to the ears of the unfortunate saint, who is asserted to have been the author of them, he might be inclined to carry them and to lay them under his pillow, as the base, rascally, beastly, nauseous parasite of the *Courier* newspaper tells us he did with a PRAYER-BOOK the other day.

But, my friends, though Alderman Wood was one of his hands to help Knatchbull make a clap in favour of these propositions; though both sides and both ends and top and bottom of the big House; though all agree to applaud this measure, pray be not you such despicable fools as to applaud it, until you have ascertained what its EFFECT will be. That effect will be; that effect must be; that effect must be intended to be, to make bread *permanently dearer than it is now.* I do not say that this effect, and that the whole fabric will not be swept away by the operations of the paper-money; but, if the paper-money could be kept steadily in its present state; if the taxes could remain just what they are; if all other things could remain as they are, the inevitable effect of this measure must be, to make bread constantly and permanently *dearer than it is now!* And this I am now going to make as clear to your minds as the sun on the brightest day is, at noon, clear to your eyes.

The average price of wheat, at this time, in England is, according to the government accounts, fifty-three shillings the quarter, of the Winchester bushel, eight bushels being a quarter. There may be some pence on one or the other side of this fifty-three shillings; but, fifty-three shillings is much about the price throughout England; the price being lower in Scotland and in Ireland. As the law now stands, wheat cannot be brought into the country, until English wheat sell for *seventy shillings* a quarter; and then the wheat brought in has to pay a duty of *ten shillings* a quarter. I beg you to mark these sums well; for you will presently see how necessary it is to bear them in mind.

Now, this being the law at present, you wanted such an alteration of the law as would permit wheat to be brought into the country at times when English wheat should be at a great deal *lower price than seventy shillings a quarter*. Indeed, you, and all just men, wanted a great deal more; for you wanted the ports to be as freely open to French corn as they were to French silks. But, at any rate, you wanted wheat to be permitted to be imported, when English wheat should sell in the market *at a lower price than seventy shillings a quarter*. Well, and your wishes are to be gratified now; for, the PORTS ARE TO BE OPENED, and wheat may, at all times, be brought into England, Ireland, or Scotland, from foreign countries! Huzza for Liverpool, Canning and Co.! Now the wiseacres will meet on the " Royal Exchange " of Man-

chester; now they will meet at the " New Bailey," and at the " Police office," and shake one another by the hand and congratulate themselves on the prospect of seeing cargoes of rotten cottons fill the holds of those ships which have brought in cargoes of wheat: " fine times," says 'Squire Cottonfuz, meeting 'Squire Gas, " fine times, brother 'Squire: the ports are open!"—Yes, you great, haughty, insolent, tyrannical, parasitical, half-gentleman looking, smudgy-faced beast; the ports *are open*, and so they have been ever since God made the island; but, when this measure shall have been made a law, go you and try to get a cargo of wheat freely into one of those ports, and you will soon find yourself lying by the heels as snugly as poor JOHN KNIGHT or poor OGDEN ever lay!

Yes, my Friends, the ports will be open enough: wheat may, at all times, be brought in from foreign countries; but, now you are going to see on what conditions it may be brought in. These conditions I beg you to attend to. I beg you to observe that they have been approved of by the whole of the House that works so well; the whole of the House that wants no reforming. These conditions, then, are as follows : when the average of wheat in England, shall be

SIXTY SHILLINGS a quarter, there is to be a DUTY of *twenty shillings paid upon each quarter of foreign wheat brought into the country!* Mark that. Then, if wheat shall, on an average, be at a lower price than sixty shillings a quarter in England, there is to be an additional duty of two shillings a quarter upon the foreign wheat brought in; I say an additional duty of *two shillings a quarter for every one shilling a quarter that the English wheat shall sink below sixty shillings a quarter!* For instance, if English wheat be at 58s. a quarter, then the duty is to be 24s. a quarter; and, to take the present price, English wheat is now at 58s. a quarter: the duty, therefore, on a quarter of foreign wheat is to be THIRTY-FOUR ENGLISH SHILLINGS; that is to say, about four shillings a quarter more than the foreign wheat costs, at this moment, to bring it into this country, and about two shillings a quarter more than the WHOLE OF THE PRICE which the French silk-weaver and cotton-weaver pay for their wheat! This is that "liberality" which Sir FRANCIS BURDETT praises: this the *Morning Chronicle* tells us is viewed favourably by Mr. ALDERMAN WOOD! This is what you are to get in answer to your petitions; this is what

we are to have while the begging-box is going round the country, by royal authority, for your relief. Well did our sensible friends at Stockport decline voting thanks to the Ministers, till they saw what they would finally do for them!

When the average price in England; the average price of English wheat, shall rise above sixty shillings, then the duty on foreign wheat is to be *lowered*, in the same proportion as it is to be raised on the under side of sixty shillings; so that, when the landlords get eighty shillings a quarter for their wheat; that is to say, ten shillings for the Winchester bushel, they are, then, to let wheat in at no duty at all. Kind gentlemen! Only eighty shillings; that is to say, the quartern loaf at about fifteen pence! They will be content to let us have the quartern loaf at fifteen pence: when it comes to that, they, in the excess of their liberality, will impose no duty at all; will have no direct tax upon our bread.

So that, you see, my Friends, here is a famous alteration in your favour. As the thing now stands, foreign wheat cannot be brought in unless English wheat be seventy shillings a quarter in the market; and, then, the foreign wheat is to have a duty of ten shillings fixed upon it. So that, we are not to have wheat from abroad, unless wheat at that time shall cost us eighty shillings a quarter, in one shape or another. The "liberal" Jenkinson has hatched a plan, as Canning tells us, by which we are to be made better off. According to this plan, when English wheat sells for sixty shillings a quarter, there is to be a duty of twenty shillings on the foreign wheat: when English wheat sells at fifty shillings a quarter, there is to be a duty of forty shillings per quarter on foreign wheat; so that, if our English Wheat were to come down to fifty shillings a quarter, we should have to pay ninety shillings a quarter; in reality, we should have to pay this to English landlords, before we could touch a morsel of bread. Suppose English wheat to fall down, as it did some years ago, to forty shillings a quarter; we should, then, to get at a mouthful of foreign wheat, be compelled to pay a duty of *sixty shillings a quarter upon that wheat*; or, in other words, the pretence of there being open ports would be manifest, then, to all the world, the most shocking delusion that ever was attempted to be practised upon a credulous people, habituated to a quiet submission to every species of insult.

Let us, now, see how the thing will work immediately; in what degree it will be likely to relieve your horrible distresses. You want bread to be cheaper than it is now: this measure almost declares it, in so many words, to be already too cheap. The measure declares, in substance, that the proper permanent average price of English wheat is SIXTY SHILLINGS A QUARTER: this is what it declares; and it is to impose duties, restrictions; it is to work effectually for causing this average permanent price of English wheat not to sink below sixty shillings a quarter, Winchester measure. Mind, my friends, this is the only object of the proposed measure: this only object is, to cause English wheat to be constantly sold, if possible, for not less than SIXTY SHILLINGS THE WINCHESTER QUARTER; and, then observe, that the average price of English wheat in the market NOW is FIFTY-THREE SHILLINGS A QUARTER. Thus, then, it is undeniably true: thus, then, all the cant of the liberal school; all the really or pretendedly ailing gentry; all the sophistry and dying backward and forward of the

Scotch foolosophers: nothing that can be said or done by anybody, can amount to a denial of this fact: namely, that this measure will, that it must inevitably tend to make bread dearer than it now is. It must have this effect, unless that effect be destroyed by the workings of the paper-money. Such, at any rate, must be the intention. It can have no other intention than that; and, yet, the *Morning Chronicle* understands Mr. Alderman Wood to have viewed this measure favourably.

However, my Friends, when this measure is adopted (and adopted it will be) we shall know precisely the amount of the tax which we pay to the landowners on our bread. The amount will be exactly that of the duty which is imposed on the foreign wheat. Here am I, for instance, with my little mill, at which I sometimes grind my own wheat. I want a quarter of wheat; and, of course, I want it as cheap as I can get it. There are five hundred thousand quarters of foreign wheat in the King's warehouses. They cost, I believe, about thirty-four shillings a quarter, freight, insurance, and all expenses upon their head. Well, says I, I will go and get me a quarter of this wheat; for, our land-owners will not sell me their's, under fifty-three shillings a quar-

ter; so that I shall, here, save nineteen shillings by buying a quarter of this foreign wheat. Look at me, my friends, marching off as cheerly as possible, my thirty-four shillings in my pocket, and my cart behind me ready to carry home my wheat. Down I go to the warehouse and ask for a quarter of wheat. Say I to the Dantzicker,

Your price, my buck?

DANTZICKER—Only dirty four schellings.

COBBETT—There they are, my boy, and here are my sacks: come, you Sir, bring the bushel here, and let us fill them, for I want sadly to be tasting this cheap bread.

(*Enter Custom-House Officer.*)

OFFICER. Holloa, what the devil's going on here.

DANTZICKER. Why, may it please your honour (bowing very low), I have sold this man, here, a quarter of my wheat for dirty-four schellings.

COBBETT. Yes, 'Squire, and I am going to take it away, if your worship pleases.

OFFICER. Take it away!

COBBETT. Yes, why not take it away: I have bought it and paid for it. Come; John, take this sack upon your shoulder, and carry it to the cart.

OFFICER. Holloa, there! Thames

Police! Here, smuggling; cheating the revenue; robbing the landlords!

COBBETT. What 's the matter? A measure has been adopted for opening the ports: this wheat has been brought in: may I not be permitted, now that I have bought it and paid for it, to carry it away?

OFFICER. (*To the Police.*) Ah, there, you may go away: this fellow is only a fool that does not know what he is about. (Turning to Cobbett.) My good fellow, you have been reading the newspapers, I dare say!

COBBETT. Yes, I have.

OFFICER. Aye, I thought so: and the *debates*, now, I dare say, as they are called?

COBBETT. Yes, I have been reading an account of Mr. SECRETARY CANNING's opening the ports.

OFFICER. I tell you what, my good fellow: those d——d newspapers are the ruin of half the world. Here they have brought you, now, upon a Tom Fool's errand all the way from Kensington down to Rotherhithe, " nine miles to suck a bull and go back a-dry," as my old grandmother used to say.

COBBETT. Well, but, Mr. Officer, must not I have my wheat, now I have bought it and paid for it?

OFFICER (*laughing*). Why, my poor fellow, you may have the wheat, to be sure; but, you have got *another thirty-four shillings to pay me before you take it away.*

COBBETT. The devil I have!

OFFICER. Devil or devil not, I can't let it go, until you give me thirty-four shillings, for that is the duty upon a quarter of foreign wheat when English wheat is at fifty-three shillings a quarter, and that is the price of English wheat now.

COBBETT. Oh, Lord! What a fool I have been! I believed Sir Francis Burdett, when he extolled the "liberality" of Mr. Canning. I could not believe that Mr. Alderman Wood would view favourably any thing that was not for my good.

OFFICER. You would better, I believe, remember the Scripture, that tells you not to put trust in the children of men, whether land-patriots or water-patriots.

COBBETT. Well, but, Mr. Officer, if I give you thirty-four shillings in addition to the thirty-four shillings which I have just given to Mr. VON SNIGGERSNEE, I shall have paid *sixty-eight shillings for my quarter of foreign wheat,* when I could have gone to 'Mark-lane and bought a quarter of English wheat for *fifty-three shillings.* So that this new measure of the Ministers, instead of making bread cheaper, must make it dearer, if it have any effect at all.

OFFICER. Why, as you say, if there be truth in arithmetic, it does seem to be so, indeed.

COBBETT. But, Mr. Officer, don't you think that it is a d——d shame that these landlords should make us pay a tax of thirty-four shillings upon every thirty-four shillings worth of wheat which we eat; and don't you think that a Government that supports them in such proceedings ought to be....

OFFICER. Don't say any thing against Government: I.won't hear any thing said against Government: if you say any thing against Government I'll,...........

COBBETT. But, as I was going to say, don't you think that such a Government ought to be ......

OFFICER. No: I do not; and G——d d——n you, if you dare say such another word, I'll send you before the Police Magistrate for treason against his Majesty.

COBBETT. But is it treason for me to complain of paying thirty-four shillings tax upon thirty-four shillings worth of bread? I said, and I will say it again, that such a Government ought to be....

OFFICER. (*Calling his people.*) Here, lay hold of this rebellious rascal; fling him out into the street, and if he offers to come in again, cram him into the police watch-house.

Aye, and a merciful fellow, too.

This would be much about the end of my economical expedition to Rotherhithe; and, if there be any creature upon two legs and without feathers upon its carcase; if there be any such creature in England who does not, now, see this matter in its true light, it ought to have feathers upon it without delay, or to come down upon four legs and be covered with hair. I am sure, my Friends, that you will see it in its true light; I am sure that you will see that one half of the amount of our bread is now tax, and to continue to be tax. I am sure you will see now, if you never saw it before, that there can be no remedy, except in a reform, a legal and con stitutional reform of the Commons House of Parliament.

Let me not conclude, however, without taking care not to imitate the miserable deluders of the broad-sheet, who will, in general, represent this as a *clear gain to the landlords, at the expense of the rest of the community.* It is so much money which we pay to the landlords, tax upon bread. But, pray mark if they do not get this tax from us, *they lose their estates.* They are compelled to give; they, their tenants, their tenants' work-people, their tenants' tradespeople: all these are com- pelled to give the amount of this enormous tax to the fundholder, the dead-weight people, the army, the navy, the pensioners, the sine-care-people, the grantees, the tax-gatherers themselves; and to all the endless swarms of tax-eaters. The landlords get this enormous tax upon bread from us; but they do not keep it; and, with the present taxes imposed upon them, upon the land and upon every thing, their estates must be taken away from them, even if their wheat be sold at sixty shillings a quarter. What, however, is that to you and I? What is that to you, who are starving? What answer is that to you; especially when these very men who impose this enormous tax upon bread, have the power as completely so to reduce the taxes as to enable them to sell their wheat as cheap as the German farmer: what answer have these men to give you, whom they allow to be in a state of half-starvation, while the begging-box is sent by royal authority round the country for your relief.

Their whole case lies in this short question: *Why do they not take off the taxes, and render a Corn Bill unnecessary?* Their case rather lies in the short answer to this question; namely: BECAUSE THEY AND THEIR RELA-TIONS RECEIVE A VERY LARGE PORTION OF THOSE TAXES!—That is their case, my friends: there is the cause of your suffering; there is the cause of the continual agitations in property; there is the cause of all the difficulties, the embarrassments, the uncertainties, nine-tenths of the bankruptcies, ninety-nine hundredths of the suicides, and more than that proportion of the various crimes which have long disgraced, and which now threaten to produce a dissolution of that society, the "Improved State" of which is the boast of our great minister, Mr. Peel.

Other opportunities will offer for making observations upon this subject; but, I could not refrain from saying a few words upon it at this time, though it will compel me, I fear, to cause some little delay in the dispatching of the Register to the country.

I am, My Friends,
Your most obedient and
Most humble Servant,
W. COBBETT.

N. B. I am of opinion that the schemes of Æolus Canning in Portugal are in such a state as to cause us not to be surprised at the most *wonderful silence* which has been observed upon the subject, ever since the parliament met. One would almost think the members bound by an oath not even to pronounce the word *Portugal*.

TO

## MR. O'GORMAN MAHON,

*On the subject of the expulsion of the Register from the Association Room at Dublin.*

---

Kensington, 26th Feb. 1827.

Sir,

To be indiscriminate is almost always to be unjust; I have often felt great pain in being unable, without the introduction of ever-lasting exceptions, to speak of the "Scotch" in the manner that I do frequently do, knowing as I have through the course of my life, so many excellent men of that nation, and having found amongst them, some of the warmest and most disinterested friends. But I have made exceptions, in this case, which I wish to be regarded as being, at all times, to be understood to be repeated, when I should be bestowing my censure on the conceited, the mean, the greedy and unfeeling, pretended philosophers of Scotland.

In the present case discrimination is more easy; for, there are the names of those who lent themselves to the purposes of Mr. O'Connell; there are the names of his unprincipled Lazaroni; and there are the names also of those who had the spirit openly to scorn to range themselves in the ranks of that despicable lazaroni; and, believe me, Sir, to be perfectly sincere when I say, that the unaffected politeness, the frankness, the sincerity, the great store of good sense and of talent, which, when I had the happiness to see you here, I perceived to mark your character, have given me singular satisfaction when I perceive that you are one of those who opposed this consummately mean and despicable proceeding. With most explicitly declaring, that I, by no means, confound the members of the Association generally with Mr. O'Connell and his tribe; and with expressing my best thanks to all those gentlemen, who, either by their speeches or votes, thus defended

me when I was not present to defend myself: with this declaration
and with this expression I should
stop : but, having seen, in two or
three publications, an expression
of anger against the lazaroni and
their leader, for having done that,
which might, by possibility, tend
to cool my zeal in the just cause
of my Catholic countrymen, I now
proceed to assure you, that, were
I to be stung by a wasp, in an endeavour to drive him from my
fruit, I should no more think of
hacking to pieces and tearing up
those fruit-trees, which I have
reared with so much care, and the
growth of which I have watched
with so much delight, than I
should think of doing any thing
hostile, with regard to my Catholic
countrymen or the people of Ireland, or of leaving any thing undone, that I could possibly do to
serve them, because O'Connell
and his lazaroni have made this
attempt to injure or to mortify me.
You will have seen, in spite of the
vote of the lazaroni, that this
affair has been treated by me, in
a manner which is any thing but
serious. Indeed, my readers in
England, who cannot be expected
to discriminate, in such a case,
with that degree of accuracy
which I can, and which it becomes
me to do, would have been almost
unanimous in their ridicule of me,
if I had treated the thing in any
other manner. I did think, at one
time, of sending over to Dublin,
by way of *answer* to the Catholic
Association, a copy of a French
translation of the Protestant
Reformation, made and published at Paris; a copy of an
Italian translation published at
Rome; a copy of a Spanish translation, published at Philadelphia,
to be sent and circulated throughout South America; a copy of
each of two stereotype editions in
English, published in the United
States of America; and, to these
I did intend to add the original of
a manuscript letter of Mr. Ma-
thew Carey, of Philadelphia,
informing me that the sale of these
English editions, had been, in the
United States, perfectly prodi-

gious, and had produced an effect corresponding to the extent of the circulation.

Why, Sir, supposing that Bric had not been so contemptible a creature as he was; supposing him to have been a person to reflect some credit instead of discredit upon the Association; supposing him never to have been notoriously eager to barter the best rights of the people of Ireland manifestly for the sake of getting his shoulders covered with a silk gown; supposing him never to have called (as I heard him in your presence) the forty shilling freeholders in Ireland "*worse than brute beasts*;" supposing him never, when he found that a continuation in that line did not suit his interest to turn round, and not only eulogise those forty shilling freeholders to the skies, but to dub himself a knight of an order founded to celebrate their fame; supposing him never to have done any of these things, and supposing even that he had died from causes other than those growing out of

that ruffian-like insolence, which marked him for her own when you and I saw him clench and hold up in boxer-like style his two fists at Mr. Lawless, at my table, in answer to an argument of that gentleman in defence of the poor forty shilling freeholders : supposing all this ; supposing him to be a perfectly harmless as well as ignorant creature, and that I, from mere wantonness, had chosen to disport myself over the hyperbolical praises bestowed upon his memory ; supposing me to have discovered less feeling of compassion than I might, or ought to have shown in such a case : let us suppose all this ; and this is supposing a vast deal more than the most slavish of the lazaroni can call upon us to suppose ; supposing all this, was it possible, Sir, for any man, not devoured by ever craving vanity, not rendered insanely vindictive by the mortification that I had given to that vanity ; was it possible for any man except a man like this, or except a man wishing, at bottom, to do injury to the Ro-

main Catholic religion and Roman
Catholic people; was it possible,
Sir, for any man, except one or
the other of these descriptions
suited him, to lay a long train of
dirty intrigues, in order finally to
effect the purpose of causing, as
he hoped, some degree, at any
rate, of disrepute to fix upon my
writings? Put these questions
seriously to yourself, Sir, and I am
sure you will say that the thing
was impossible.

Let the world; but, beyond all
others, let the unreflecting part of
the Irish people, reflect upon this.
They must now see, what they
ought long ago to have seen, that
there is no sincerity in that man.
Is it the habit of our lives to endeavour to destroy things that are
of great value to us because they
occasionally amuse themselves
with destroying things which are
of no value to us? This was not
the case here; but if it had been
the case; would this Leader of
the Lazaroni have evinced, upon
this occasion, sincerity of desire to promote the cause of the

Roman Catholic religion? Do
we endeavour to kill the cat because she is not quite so conside-
rate as we should wish in dealing
with the purloiners of the pantry?
What would you think of the zeal,
fidelity, and, above all things, of
the good sense, of your game-
keeper; if he with his blundering
bludgeon were to endeavour to
cripple your best and perhaps
your only pointer, merely because
the latter had amused himself
with doing something more than
point at one of your tame rabbits,
the place of which the poulterer
would supply you for nine-pence
or ten-pence.

Oh, Sir! miserable is that
country, which groans under oppressions unspeakable; but ten-
fold more miserable is she, if she
look up to such a man for deliverance! She is sure to suffer from
his meddling in her cause—
Thousands upon thousands of men
will say; and hundreds of thousands of Englishmen do say it:
that that cause cannot be good, in
which such a man is the "Leader."

When, or how, unhappy Ireland is to receive relief, no man can tell; but of this, Sir, be assured; on this I would pledge my existence, and every consideration which is dear to me, that she never will receive relief, except through means with which this man shall have no more to do than he now has to do with regulating the movements and preserving the order of the planets. In conclusion, I most solemnly assure you, that the transaction which has given rise to my doing myself the honour of addressing this letter to you, has awakened in my breast no feelings except such as are called forth by reflecting on the hopelessness of the Catholic cause, while such a man is called its Leader; together with a revival of that anxious desire which I entertained, three years ago, to see something done for the relief of that wretched people, who, though reviled and scorned by every haughty, base, and selfish wretch upon the face of the earth, will always, in proportion to his power, find an unshaken friend in,

Sir,

Your most obedient and

Most humble Servant,

Wm. COBBETT.

---

## EMIGRATION PROJECT.

I HAVE always said that the system would, in its last stages, take *monstrous plunges*, cut capers beyond its usual and far beyond its natural strength; just as we see a rat, which, when it is in health, scarcely ever jumps a foot high from the ground, jump a yard or two high when it has got a shot through the heart or through the head. Divers are the plunges which the system has taken: it has cut capers that have made the world laugh : its Corn Bills ; its Paper Bills ; its Small-note Bills ; its Cash Bills ; its surplus produce measures; its Six Acts; its Ogden's Bills ; plunges of all sorts, capers of every description, has this system cut; but, (except perhaps the *Æolian* capers) scarcely any one has equalled this EMIGRATION PROJECT, which will be talked of, in a very few years from this time, as one of the strongest proofs of the damnable consequences of a system of funding and paper money. One *Horton Wilmot* or *Wilmot Horton* (for they shift and change their names backward and forward in such a manner that I know not which it is), who is, it seems, a species of Secretary of State of some sort or other, has, the newspapers tell us, proposed a scheme for diminishing the miseries of the people of this kingdom, by sending a part of them away to Canada; and, the same villanous newspapers tell us that the Parliament is likely to impose taxes upon us for the purpose of sending these people away; or, which must be the fact, to borrow money for the purpose, and thereby add to what is called the national debt, and thereby add to the mortgage upon the landlord's estate and upon the fruit of the labour of the child who is now in the cradle.

We have seen the Prime Minister stand up in his place in Parliament, and ascribe the *sufferings of the country to a surplus produce of food*, while, at that very moment, the begging box was carried round by Royal command to raise the means of preserving part of the people from starving to death; we have heard the distress of agriculture gravely ascribed, by houses as well as by committees, to *over production*, while those same houses at that very same time, voted large sums of money out of the taxes to induce *mouths* to leave the country: these things, and many others equal to these, we have seen: it is not, therefore, with much surprise, that we have to contemplate this project of emigration. The newspapers tell us that this project is the result of the deliberations of a committee of whom *Stanly, Wood, Alexander Baring* (the hot and cold fit man), *F. Baring, Horton Wilmot,* " Col." *Torrens* and some.

others were members. They (the newspapers) lament that the "gallant Colonel," who is, I fancy, a captain on half-pay, *is no longer* a MEMBER. I dare say that the English bundle of empty aristocrats, who call themselves the *English Catholic Association*, lament this circumstance too; seeing that they had just passed a vote of thanks, to the "*honourable and gallant officer*," and were got into as sweet and as silly an interchange of compliments with him, as one would expect to see come from the pens of a *cast*, not more sunk by a long train of oppressions, than their own apparent proneness to self-debasement.

The project of this committee is a *Scotch project*: it is, in fact, avowedly founded on the opinions of *Macculloch*, that celebrated Scotch adventurer, who, only a very few months before late panic broke out, maintained on his own authority as well as that of his brother Scotchman, the sinecure placeman *Adam Smith*, that paper-money was a "cheap currency;" that the use of it was a clear gain to the nation; and that the country was much more liable to suffer from the counterfeiting of the gold coin, than *from the forgery of bank notes and the breaking of bankers!* "Late panic" came, and gave the lie to all the doctrines of this impudent pretender to political knowledge; and yet, this man is the oracle now, and on his opinions we are to be taxed, it would seem, for the purpose of lessening that which is called the superabundant population of the country, by transporting part of the people to Canada.

In remarking upon this project, two observations occur at the outset; first, that when the census was first taken in the year 1801, the result of that census being compared with the random estimates of Chalmers and others relative to the population of former times, showed a *great increase of population*. This showing was perfectly fallacious; it was a great popular political lie, and intended to bolster up that very system

U

which is now shaking the country to its centre. When the abstract of the census was brought up by old GEORGE ROSE and laid before the House of Commons, he spoke of the increase of the population as a *most glorious circumstance*; and PITT and CANNING, and JENKINSON, and that WILLIAM GIFFORD, who has just died covered over with sinecures; aye, and that Mr. IRELAND, who is now Dean of Westminster; the whole of the Pittite tribe, who wagged either tongue or pen, pointed to this " *vast increase of the population,*" as an undoubted proof that the country had prospered; that the people had been, under the administration of Pitt, *happier* than they formerly were; and that his system was therefore thus *proved* to have added to the happiness, the resources, and the power of the kingdom! What! and was this true then, and is this increased population a *curse* now? And is it a curse so great that we must be taxed in order to diminish the population by *physical force?* Oh,

monstrous! but, not a tenth-part so monstrous as the things which we have to bear of, before this system comes to its close.

The other observation that at once occurs to us upon the bare mention of the project, is this; that in no country, under no species of government, in no state, whether called republic, kingly government, monarchy, ecclesiastical government, despotism, wild democracy; or, by whatever name known or designated; in no country upon the face of the whole earth, from the days of Moses to the present day, have we before ever heard of a government entertaining a project of taxing the whole body of the people, in order to raise money to *send part of those very people out of the country,* upon the ground of the people in the country being *too numerous!* It is the first time that the world ever heard of such a thing: the thought never before entered into the mind of man. Powerful despots, tyrants, of irresistible power, have frequently transported whole multitudes, natives of the soil, in order to rid themselves of what they alleged to be a restless and rebellious spirit; in order to ensure the duration of their own sway by exchanging a turbulent for a docile people. The Irish have, partially, been treated in this way, at different times, particularly by the savage tyrant CROMWELL. But, this is the very first time, that the world ever heard of a scheme for transporting to foreign climes the innocent and peaceable natives of the land, and those too of the labouring class, merely upon the ground that there are *too many of them in their native land*; and that, observe, in addition, while every soul of these pretended supernumeraries pays taxes to the amount of one half of the fruit of his labour. This is the very first time that the world ever heard of such a thing; and, that circumstance alone is enough to convince any reasonable man, that the system which could have given rise to such a scheme, must finally produce the most awful of calamities.

After these two observations, the conclusiveness of which must rest upon the mind of every reasonable man, it is really not necessary to say another word upon the subject; but, I cannot resist the temptation to insert here, and to make a remark or two upon, the observations which the Scotch philosopher, DOCTOR BLACK, has published, by way of commentary upon the Parliamentary proceedings in this case. The project is, the reader will please to observe, purely a *Scotch* project: it comes from the other side of the Tweed; it has in it, all the *brain-twist* and all the obduracy of the Scotch philosophy; it considers men, women, and children, merely as it considers beasts of different ages; it considers the mass of the people as it views the cattle, sheep, pigs and poultry upon a farm; and it supposes a legitimate power to dispose of these cattle, sheep, pigs and poultry at the pleasure of the Government, whom it regards as their absolute owner. The whole of this philosophy has entered into entire possession of the heart and mind of Doctor Black. He, therefore, is an advocate for the project; but, the project *does not go far enough* for the Doctor; and, as we shall see, if the project be proper to be adopted in any part, the Doctor has reason on his side.

I request the reader to go particularly through the observations of the Doctor; for though we shall find him afraid openly to avow the horrid lengths to which he and his tribe would go, his observations clearly point to those horrid lengths and enable us to draw the conclusion which he himself has not the courage to draw. I number his paragraphs, in order to save time in referring to the different parts of the article.

1. " The persons more immediately concerned in this matter " may be classed thus—

" 1. Those who desire to emigrate.

" 2. Those who from benevo-" lence, and from want of " information, are willing " to promote emigration.

" 3. Those who are to act as " legislators.

2. " The first class consists of " persons whose situation is so " very deplorable, that it is next " to impossible to make it worse; " they are pretty certain that by " being removed to Canada it " must be bettered. They look " simply to the hope of escaping " from misery, and they cannot " reasonably be expected to look " at it in any other point of view.

3. " The second class are also " operated upon by their feelings; " and without adverting to any " other circumstance than bene-" fitting those who may be re-" moved, are willing to subscribe " their money, their wishes, or " their advice, or, at any rate, to " acquiesce in the request of the " first class.

4. " The third class have a " most important duty to perform; " and yet, strange as it may ap-" pear, not a single Member of " the House of Commons who " spoke on Mr. Horton's motion " for a Committee, took a com-" prehensive view of the subject.

5. " The debate was just such " an one as might have taken place " in any common club or society " of half-informed men who were " disposed to give way to their " feelings, and willing to promote

" a loose project for the advan-
" tage of the petitioners. This is
" doing any thing but what is
" right; and, as it usually hap-
" pens when men in a public
" situation trifle with important
" subjects, it was mischievous. It
" encouraged hopes which can
" never be realised. A legisla-
" tor ought not to allow himself
" to be governed by his feelings,
" however painful it may be to
" him to pronounce sentence on
" the fate of others.

6. " The state of the case is
" this :—*There are in these king-*
" *doms so many more hands than*
" *can be employed, that the wages*
" *of labour have, by their compe-*
" *tition, been reduced to the starv-*
" *ation point, and the misery of a*
" *vast number of them has become*
" *excessive. This is universally*
" *admitted.* What, then, should
" a legislator have done when
" Mr. Horton moved for his Com-
" mittee ? He should have asked
" himself this question, Can I by
" any means remove so large a
" proportion of the people, as will,
" by reducing the demand for la-
" bour, raise the wages of those
" who may remain ? And unless
" he could answer in the affirma-
" tive, he was bound not to hold
" out any hopes by which the peo-
" ple would be deluded.

7. " Great Britain and Ireland
" contain about 23 millions of
" people, and if it were possible
" annually to remove 150,000,
" only one in every 153 would be
" removed. He who knows any
" thing of the state of the people,
" knows that the number is kept
" down to what it is by the impos-
" sibility of increasing it at a more
" rapid rate than that at which it
" does increase, simply by starva-
" tion, and the consequences of
" starvation ; and that if this
" pressure were taken off, more
" people would be immediately
" produced, or more of those who
" die in consequence of privation
" would be preserved. It is of no
" use to blink the matter; we may
" cheat ourselves as much as we
" please, but we cannot prevent
" the consequences here noticed.
" The legislator is bound *not to*
" *blink* the question, not to cheat
" himself—his duty is to meet it
" *openly, manfully, wisely;* and
" *fearlessly* to encounter *any ob-*
" *loquy* which those who either
" cannot or will not look at it in a
" large way, may bestow upon
' him.

8. " Can we remove and settle
" 150,000 persons annually ? The
" answer must be, No. This may
" be shown hereafter—at present
" we will take it for granted we

"said; and then what follows? "What but this—that there would "not be one person less at the "year's end from the respective "days of embarkation.

9. "What is one person in 153 "in such a community as we "have in England?—what in "such a people as inhabit Ire- "land! Can any reasonable "man doubt, for a single instant, "that there is one person for every "153 removed ready to fill up the "void?—and this being the case, "what would be the consequence "of 150,000 persons emigrating "annually? Simply this—that "so many persons would be pro- "vided for at an enormous ex- "pense, which could in no way "lessen the misery of those at "home; and, after many millions "of money had been expended, "bitterly disappoint those who "still remained in misery; bring "upon those who so absurdly at- "tempted to catch water in a "sieve the contempt they would "have merited, for having so "fruitlessly employed themselves "in an absurd attempt to accom- "plish what was not possible, "after having added many mil- "lions to the present enormous "public debt.

10. " Our limits will not allow "us to pursue the subject further "at present."

The Doctor, at the beginning of paragraph 6, states the *evil; name- ly, the existence of more hands than can be employed at wages sufficient to sustain life.* And, having stated this, he says "THAT THIS IS UNIVER- SALLY ADMITTED." When he makes use of the word univer- sal, he certainly is guilty of a very audacious falsehood: the assertion has been repelled by me for more than twenty years consecutively and I have had at my back a very considerable part of the intelligent persons in this kingdom. The fact is notoriously false. All the hands could be employed and constantly employed, and with sufficient wages, if the taxes, the enormous taxes, the bands of paper-money- monopolizers, and all those things were removed, which take from the farmer and other employers, the means of paying those sufficient wages. Stupid or perverse Doc- tor Black, go to any farmer in England, I care not in what coun- ty or of what opinions the man may be: ask him if he have not a great deal of labour left unperformed which he would like to have performed, and the performance of which would be profitable to him, if he could spare the money to pay for it. Ask him *what it is that disables him from sparing the money.* Here he may be a little puzzled; but, if he were to take a pen and piece of paper and put down what he himself pays for the consumption of his own house in tax on tea, tobacco, malt, sugar, soap, candles, leather, hops, wine, spirits, glass, windows, dogs, horse, starch, blue, paper, pepper, mustard, almanack, newspaper, in short, on every thing that he touches, that touches him, or that is at all necessary to the existence of his body and the bodies of his wife and family; if he were to take a pen and put these all down in a string; then add the stamps on his receipts, the enormous deduction from the legacy he got the other day; the tax on the stamp of his lease: in short, he would find himself a thing incrusted over with taxes. Tell him that all the taxes

shall be taken off, or the far greater part of them; and then ask him whether he could not have his land better tilled, and pay his men higher wages. "Oh! yes," he would say, "instead of six men "at eight shillings a week I could "then have eight men at twelve "shillings a week." "Stop, my "good friend," I should say, "You "*need not raise their wages at* "*all:* that's the good of the thing; "for they could work for even less "wages than they have now, and "live well and be well clothed "into the bargain." "Ah! sure "that never can be," he would say. "Yes it could and would "be, for, your labourers now pay "out of their earnings, even out "of their pauper-pay, all the taxes "in proportion to their consump-"tion, which you have to pay, and "which make you so poor as to "make you unable to employ them "upon good wages. And, farmer of "common sense, is it not manifest "to you, that, if your labourer got "as much beer, as much tea, as "much sugar, as much tobacco,

" soap, candles, and leather, for " sixpence as he now is compelled " to purchase for *eighteen-pence* " *or two shillings*; is it not mani- " fest that he would be well off " and live as he ought to live, and " that, too, for a great deal less " wages than what he receives " now from you?" Is not this as clear as day-light? Take article by article, and you will find, that the enormous taxes and the horrid paper-money monopoly, cordially co-operating as they do, take from every labouring man, whether he be ploughman or weaver, a great deal more than one-half of that which he receives under the name of wages or of pauper-pay. For labour, *thus loaded*, there is not a sufficient demand; but for labour, retaining its fruits, the fields of England; the half-cultivated fields of England, and the half-covered backs of the English people, would call aloud for hands.

Thus, unless I greatly deceive myself, the very foundation of this unnatural project is torn up, and blown into air. Men prone to self destruction are never to be taught. Nothing will open their eyes. Like the moth, do what you will, they will rush to the candle. If this were not so, what would this nation have wanted more to open its eyes, than these two undeniable propositions; namely, that the people of the manufacturing districts are plunged into a state of indescribable misery *for want of somebody to purchase the goods they have made*; and that a subscription is on foot, for collecting old cast clothes to *cover the nakedness of the distressed people*. It must be a Scotch feelosopher at the least, to want any thing more than this. It is not then *want of employment*. There would be employment enough, but the means of requiting the labourer, whether ploughman or weaver, are taken from the employer, and carried away, to be given to fundholders, to standing army in time of peace, enormous dead-weight, pensioners, sinecurists, grantees, to tax-eaters

and monopolizers, of all descriptions, not forgetting two or three
hundred thousand persons (including their families) *employed solely*
in the collection of those taxes.

Now, Doctor Black, I do conjure you, not as you have a *soul* to
be saved, for I will say nothing
about that; but, as you have a
*reputation* to be saved, I do conjure you, that you cast aside, for
one day, at any rate, all other matters, and take me up and answer
me upon this question. At the
beginning of your 6th paragraph,
you have clearly asserted a certain thing; you have said that
that thing is universally admitted.
I, denying the admission, have
offered arguments to prove that
your statement, relative to the
supposed evil, *is totally false.*

I have not met assertion by assertion. To have demanded the
proof of you would have been
useless, when you cut me short by
saying that the "*fact was universally admitted.*" You had no
right to go to work in this manner; but no matter; I have taken
hold of your assertion; I say that
I have proved it to be false; and
the public will say so too. Here
we stand, English plain sense opposed to the crotchety Scotch
feelosophy. If thou "beest a
man," answer, Doctor! I am very

much afraid that you will not.
However, here I challenge you;
and, if you do not answer my
challenge, recollect that the bra'
kelted feelosophy will suffer.

For the rest of the Doctor's article, it is of less consequence;
but, still, I must notice it, were it
only for the curiosity of the thing.
The Doctor is right enough in
saying that this scheme must be
*nugatory*, even according to the
principle upon which it is founded,
unless SOMETHING MORE
be done, and which SOME-
THING MORE, the Doctor
does not NAME. It was named,
I believe, in the hand-bills that
were sent from Charing-Cross to
Mrs. MARY FILDES, of Manchester, who, as she has since published, sent that worse than
beastly hand-bill to all the King's
Ministers, to all the Judges, and
to the Attorney and Solicitor General!

The Doctor, at the close of his
seventh paragraph, observes, in
very awful accents, " that the le-
" gialator is bound not to blink
" the question, not to cheat him-
" self; his duty is to meet it
" *openly, manfully, wisely*; and
" *fearlessly* to encounter any OB-
" LOQUY in effecting his pur-
" pose." What the devil can the
Doctor mean ?

He wants a great parcel of the people to be sent away, mind.; but, what he says is this; that *more will be BRED in their STEAD*, if the legislator should blink the question, if he should not be *open, manly,* and *wise*, and if he do not fearlessly encounter obloquy. What the devil then can the Doctor mean?

Mean what he will, however, he takes special care, while he is calling upon others to act a *manly part* and *fearlessly to encounter obloquy*; while he does this, he takes special care to endeavour to avoid the obloquy himself! This is true Scotch all over: making a cat's paw of others; urging fools on to do that, which Sawney himself knows it is prudent not to do. But, what is it, after all, that the Doctor can aim at? He is gratified, or it seems he is to be gratified by a sending of a parcel of the people away; yet, he is not satisfied unless something be done to prevent the REMAINDER from BREEDING so as to fill up the gap made by the transportation.

The short and the long of the matter is, the Doctor must mean, because he can mean nothing else, the use of that sort of means; which, without an absolute destruction of the existing animals,

is made use of to prevent an overstocking of the farm yard! The Doctor means this, because he must mean it, and because he can mean nothing else, when he is talking of a LAW to enforce his wishes.

The project addressed to Mrs. FILDES; the Charing-Cross project; that, though superlatively beastly and nasty; though a pretty good answer to Mr. PEEL about the "improved state of society"; that project contemplated *voluntary conformity*; but here we have the Doctor urging the legislator to go to work with his *irons*. Here we have the constable, the justice of the peace, the gaoler, the hangman, all in the contemplation of the Doctor. FORCE of some sort he must have in view. Mark this, reader: this Scotchman must have *force of some sort in view to prevent us English people from breeding*. This he must have in view. He says that the member of Parliament does not do his duty, who does not openly and manfully and fearlessly encounter obloquy, by meeting this question and adopting this efficient remedy; that is to say, a remedy of a *legislative force* to prevent the breeding; and, yet, the sly Scotchman, after having endeavoured to push forward his cat's-paws this, has not the pluck even to name this *absolutely necessary measure*; but, slides away, slips away out of the subject by abruptly observing: "OUR LIMITS will not allow "us to pursue the subject farther "at present"!

A true Scotchman every inch of him! His "limits" allowed him to fill another column or two of the same broad sheet, with rubbish that would have disgraced the pages of even "ANNA BROOME." A *Scotchman's* "limits" always accommodate themselves most wonderfully to his wants; however, the Doctor has here said enough to show us what stupid, what beastly notions are afloat; and I am satisfied that I have said more than enough to expose those notions to the ridicule, or, rather, to the detestation of every man of common sense.

WM. COBBETT.

---

# SCOTCH IMPUDENCE.

---

I read in the Morning Chronicle an account of what is called the "Theatrical Fund Dinner" lately held in the all-stinking town of Edinburgh. The whole thing was in the true Scotch style. Sir Walter Scott was in the chair and he (who has a son in the army) chose to give the *Duke of Wellington* as a toast. But the toast, most attractive of my attention, and most perfectly characteristic of the arrogance and impudence of this Scotch crew, was the following one:—

"Lord Melville and the Navy, "that fought *till they left nobody to fight with*, like an arch spouter "man, who clears all, and goes "after the game."

The fellows might have coupled the Duke of Clarence's name with the Navy; but, that they left *nobody to fight* with, is a lie, well known to all those who recollect the drubbings which they got from the *American* Navy, who not only fought them to the last hour of the war; but, who actually fought them *after the peace was made*; and, which is singular enough, with a vessel of inferior force, tacked, beat, captured, and carried in as prize, a Scotch-commanded vessel, carrying out from England the dispatches announcing the peace. Sawney cried out to Jonathan, "Hoot a' wa' mon, we are at peace!"—Slap, answered Jonathan with a broadside; and finally, when he came to rummage the papers of his prize and to find that the peace had really been made, he observed that he was sorry for what had happened.— Scotch impudence is, to be sure, beyond all understanding ; but if the " Waverly Poet " had been apprized of this fact, which he will find recorded even by the Scotch historian, JAMES, who was cudgelled by Captain Phillimore, he certainly would not have been jack-ass enough to give this toast !

## MARKETS,

Average Prices of CORN throughout ENGLAND, for the week ending February 16.

*Per Quarter.*

| | s. | d. | | s. | d. |
|---|---|---|---|---|---|
| Wheat .. | 53 | 4 | Rye .... | 40 | 4 |
| Barley .. | 37 | 5 | Beans ... | 47 | 9 |
| Oats .... | 28 | 4 | Pease ... | 48 | 11 |

Total Quantity of Corn returned as Sold in the Maritime Districts, for the week ended February 16.

| | Qrs. | | Qrs. |
|---|---|---|---|
| Wheat.. | 43,137 | Rye ...., | 243 |
| Barley .. | 43,599 | Beans . .. | 3,542 |
| Oats ... | 12,058 | Pease .... | 1,677 |

*Corn Exchange, Mark Lane.*

Quantities and Prices of British Corn, &c. sold and delivered in this Market, during the week ended Saturday, February 17.

| | Qrs. | | £. | s. | d. | | s. | d. |
|---|---|---|---|---|---|---|---|---|
| Wheat.. | 3,926 | for | 11,349 | 14 | 3 | Average, | 57 | 3 |
| Barley.. | 4,949 | .. | 9,868 | 12 | 5 | .......... | 39 | 9 |
| Oats.. | 2,342 | .. | 3,963 | 1 | 9 | .......... | 33 | 10 |
| Rye.... | 10 | .. | 18 | 9 | 0 | .......... | 36 | 10 |
| Beans.. | 1,004 | .. | 2,426 | 9 | 2 | .......... | 48 | 4 |
| Pease,. | 937 | .. | 2,405 | 12 | 3 | .......... | 51 | 4 |

Friday, Feb. 23.—The supplies of Grain are moderate. In consequence of the great accumulation of ice in the river, the lightermen object to work, apprehending danger ; there is, therefore, very little business transacted here to-day, and prices may be considered the same as on Monday last.

Monday, Feb. 26.—The supplies of all descriptions of Corn last week, were rather limited. This morning there are moderate fresh arrivals of Wheat and Barley, but more Beans and Pease than of late; of Oats, the quantities fresh up, both Foreign and English, are trifling. The factors endeavoured to obtain considerably higher prices for Wheat this morning, but in this they did not succeed, our Millers being unwilling to comply in the present state of the Flour trade; the prices of Wheat, therefore, may be quoted the same as last week, except for a few picked samples, which have obtained 1s. per quarter advance.

The Barley trade remains in the same dull state as lately reported, with no alteration in prices. Beans and Pease, being more plentiful, are each 1s. per quarter cheaper, except for seed. There has been rather more trade for Oats to-day, and stout parcels are rather dearer, but cannot quote any alteration in the currency. There is rather more doing in Flour than of late.

Account of Wheat, &c. arrived in the Port of London, from Feb. 19 to Feb. 24, both inclusive.

| | Qrs. | | Qrs. |
|---|---|---|---|
| Wheat .. | 3,207 | Tares .... | — |
| Barley .. | 4,721 | Linseed .. | 2,406 |
| Malt .... | 5,644 | Rapeseed . | — |
| Oats .... | 3,896 | Brank .. | — |
| Beans ... | 1,578 | Mustard .. | — |
| Flour .... | 6,645 | Flax .... | — |
| Rye .... | — | Hemp ... | — |
| Pease.... | 1,893 | Seeds ... | — |

Foreign.—Barley, 584 ; and Oats, 5,448 quarters.

———

Monday, Feb. 26.—The arrivals from Ireland last week were 4,789 firkins of Butter, and 3,300 bales of Bacon; and from Foreign Ports, 360 casks of Butter.

———

Price of Hops, per Cwt. in the Borough.

Monday, Feb. 25.—Our market remains dull, but prices continue much the same as last week. Currency as under :—East Kent pockets, 90s. to 120s. ; Kent pockets, 88s. to 112s. ; bags, 76s. to 90s. Sussex pockets, 78s. to 94s. ; bags, 66s. to 72s.

Maidstone, Feb. 22.—We have had but little business this week in the Hop Trade, and the prices about the same.

———

COAL MARKET, Feb. 23.

*Ships at Market. Ships sold. Price.*
21½ Newcastle 6½ ..29s. 0d. to 37s. 9d.
16½ Sunderland 2½ ..35s.'0d.— 38s. 6d.

SMITHFIELD, Monday, Feb. 26, 1827.

The trade was generally heavy on Friday ; and prices considered lower. To-day the supply is not overdone, but the buyers are very reluctant to give the terms of last Monday ; and the demand is consequently slow. The best Beasts, as well as choice pens of Sheep, nearly support the terms of this day se'nnight ; but middling things are rather cheaper.

*Per Stone of 8 pounds (alive).*

| | s. | d. | | s. | d. |
|---|---|---|---|---|---|
| Beef . . . . . | 3 | 10 | to | 5 | 0 |
| Mutton ... | 3 | 8 | — | 4 | 6 |
| Veal : .... | 5 | 4 | — | 5 | 8 |
| Pork ..... | 4 | 6 | — | 6 | 0 |
| Lamb .... | 0 | 0 | — | 0 | 0 |

| Beasts . . | 2,340 | Sheep .. | 23,210 |
|---|---|---|---|
| Calves ... | 136 | Pigs ... | 130 |

NEWGATE, (same day.)

*Per Stone of 8 pounds (dead).*

| | s. | d. | | s. | d. |
|---|---|---|---|---|---|
| Beef ..... | 3 | 4 | to | 4 | 4 |
| Mutton ... | 3 | 0 | — | 3 | 8 |
| Veal ..... | 3 | 8 | — | 5 | 8 |
| Pork ..... | 3 | 8 | — | 5 | 8 |
| Lamb .... | 0 | 0 | — | 0 | 0 |

LEADENHALL, (same day.)

*Per Stone of 8 pounds (dead).*

| | s. | d. | | s. | d. |
|---|---|---|---|---|---|
| Beef ... . | 3 | 2 | to | 4 | 6 |
| Mutton ... | 3 | 0 | — | 3 | 8 |
| Veal .... | 3 | 8 | — | 5 | 4 |
| Pork ..... | 4 | 0 | — | 5 | 4 |
| Lamb .... | 0 | 0 | — | 0 | 0 |

## POTATOES.

SPITALFIELDS, per Ton.

| | L. | s. | | L. | s. |
|---|---|---|---|---|---|
| Ware | 3 | 5 | to | 4 | 10 |
| Middlings | 2 | 0 | — | 0 | 0 |
| Chats | 2 | 0 | — | 0 | 0 |
| Common Red | 0 | 0 | — | 0 | 0 |
| Onions, 0s. 0d. —0s. 0d. per bush. | | | | | |

BOROUGH, per Ton.

| | L. | s. | | L. | s. |
|---|---|---|---|---|---|
| Ware | 3 | 0 | to | 4 | 10 |
| Middlings | 2 | 0 | — | 2 | 5 |
| Chats | 2 | 0 | — | 0 | 0 |
| Common Red | 8 | 0 | — | 5 | 0 |

## HAY and STRAW, per Load.

*Smithfield.*—Hay....80s. to 110s.

Straw...30s. to 36s.

Clover. 100s. to 126s.

*St. James's.*—Hay.... 70s. to 120s.

Straw .. 31s. to 39s.

Clover. 105s. to 135s.

*Whitechapel.*—Hay....75s. to 105s.

Straw..:32s. to 36s.

Clover..90s. to 126s.

---

**AVERAGE PRICE OF CORN, sold in the Maritime Counties of England and Wales, for the Week ended February 16, 1827.**

| | Wheat. | | Barley. | | Oats. | |
|---|---|---|---|---|---|---|
| | s. | d. | s. | d. | s. | d. |
| London* | 56 | 3 | 39 | 3 | 31 | 6 |
| Essex | 55 | 6 | 37 | 3 | 28 | 7 |
| Kent | 55 | 0 | 38 | 11 | 29 | 0 |
| Sussex | 53 | 1 | 38 | 10 | 29 | 3 |
| Suffolk | 53 | 1 | 36 | 4 | 29 | 3 |
| Cambridgeshire | 44 | 7 | 36 | 0 | 26 | 1 |
| Norfolk | 52 | 1 | 36 | 0 | 29 | 0 |
| Lincolnshire | 52 | 2 | 41 | 0 | 27 | 6 |
| Yorkshire | 51 | 8 | 38 | 11 | 27 | 0 |
| Durham | 53 | 3 | 39 | 8 | 31 | 9 |
| Northumberland | 51 | 2 | 36 | 7 | 31 | 10 |
| Cumberland | 59 | 0 | 38 | 2 | 32 | 6 |
| Westmoreland | 59 | 7 | 43 | 0 | 36 | 2 |
| Lancashire | 58 | 10 | 49 | 4 | 35 | 4 |
| Cheshire | 58 | 0 | 49 | 10 | 0 | 0 |
| Gloucestershire | 57 | 6 | 43 | 7 | 37 | 4 |
| Somersetshire | 54 | 9 | 38 | 1 | 27 | 2 |
| Monmouthshire | 59 | 4 | 49 | 3 | 30 | 0 |
| Devonshire | 54 | 10 | 37 | 4 | 24 | 6 |
| Cornwall | 55 | 11 | 36 | 4 | 29 | 10 |
| Dorsetshire | 52 | 5 | 37 | 3 | 29 | 6 |
| Hampshire | 54 | 0 | 38 | 5 | 29 | 7 |
| North Wales | 60 | 5 | 44 | 5 | 30 | 0 |
| South Wales | 57 | 8 | 40 | 6 | 25 | 5 |

* The London Average is always that of the Week preceding.

*Liverpool*, Feb. 20.—The sales of all kinds of Grain, during the past week, were very limited in this and the country markets of the district, when Wheat, Barley, and Indian Corn, experienced a small decline. Beans, Pease, and Rye, were at a little advance. Oats, Flour, and Oatmeal, supported late prices. The supplies of Wheat, Flour, and Oats, to this day's market, were considerably augmented by the arrivals of yesterday and Sunday, and sales were very limited for each description of Grain, &c.

Imported into Liverpool, from the 13th to the 19th February, 1827, inclusive:—Wheat, 10,274; Barley, 4,130; Oats, 22,490; Rye, 385; Malt, 1,176; Pease, 63 quarters. Flour, 4,347 sacks, per 280 lbs. Oatmeal, 1,543 packs, per 240 lbs.

*Bristol*, Feb. 24.—The Corn Markets here are very dull, and the sales effected are limited. Supplies moderate. Present prices as below quoted:—Wheat, from 5s. 6d. to 7s. 6d.; Barley, 4s. 4½d. to 5s. 9d.; Beans, 5s. 3d. to 8s. 3d.; Oats, 2s. 3d. to 4s. 1½d.; and Malt, 5s. 6d. to 8s. 3d. per bushel, Imperial. Flour, Seconds, 32s. to 42s. per bag.

*Guildford*, Feb. 24.—Wheat, new, for mealing, 13l. 10s. to 17l. per load Rye, 44s. to 46s.; Barley, 36s. to 41s.; Oats, 32s. to 40s.; Beans, 54s. to 56s.; Pease, grey, 58s. to 60s.; ditto, boilers, 60s. to 62s. per quarter. Tares, 11s. per bushel.

*Horncastle*, Feb. 24.—Wheat about 1s. per quarter higher. Oats in good demand at last week's prices. Beans and Rye the same.—Wheat, from 50s. to 54s.; Barley, 36s. to 42s.; Oats, 30s. to 40s.; Pease, 70s. to 75s.; Beans, 56s. to 60s.; and Rye from 42s. to 44s. per quarter.

*Manchester*, Feb. 24.—We have had a steady demand for most articles in the trade: our canals, &c. being closed by the frost, caused the holders of fine Wheats to demand higher rates at this day's market, which was only partially complied with. There has been more doing in the first qualities of Oats to-day, at an advance of ½d. to 1d. per 45lbs. Beans are full 1s. per quarter dearer. Boiling Pease are in better demand, and fully support last week's rates. In Barley, Malt, and Flour, no alteration.

*Newcastle-on-Tyne*, Feb. 24.—We had a large supply of Wheat from the farmers this morning, but not much coastwise, and there being a good many buyers, the sale for fine qualities was brisk at a small advance; but there was not any improvement in the value of other descriptions. Rye is more in demand, and 1s. per quarter dearer. The market continues bare of Norfolk Barley, and prices remain the same as last week. Fine Malt more in demand. The supply of Oats from the farmers was small, and the foreign arrivals this week being of inferior quality, the sale for best descriptions of seed Oats was rather brisk at 1s. per quarter advance.

*Reading*, Feb. 24.—We had a fair supply of Wheat at our market this day, which sold freely for full as much money as last week. Old Wheat, 58s. to 68s.; New, 54s. to 66s. per qr. by the Imperial measure. Of Barley the quantity was very short; it sold readily at an advance of 1s. per quarter. The supply of Oats was very large, and sales in consequence rather heavy. There were more Tartary Oats for seed than we have observed for a long period. The demand for Beans and Pease was dull at last week's prices. Flour, 45s. per sack.

*Wakefield*, Feb. 23.—The canal a few miles below this place being under repair, we have a very trifling fresh supply of all Grain to this day's market. The canal westward being closed by the frost, we have a thin attendance of buyers, and not much business has been done.

## COUNTRY CATTLE AND MEAT MARKETS, &c.

*Horncastle*, Feb. 24.—Beef, 8s. per stone of 14 lbs.; Mutton, 6d. ; Pork, 6d. to 7d.; and Veal, 6d. to 8d. per lb.

*Manchester* Smithfield Market, Feb. 21.—The briskness noticed last week has not been fully supported to-day. We had a larger supply of Sheep, and only a few prime ones reached our highest quotations. The best Cattle were difficult to quit at the top price, and the general runs were from ½d. to 1d. per lb. below that price. Veal fully supports last week's rates, and Pork 1d. to 1½d. per lb. dearer.—Beef, 5d. to 7d. ; Mutton, 6½d. to 7½d.; Veal, 6d. to 7½d.; and Pork, 6d. to 7½d. per lb. sinking offal.

*Norwich Castle Meadow*, Feb. 24.—Our market this day was well supplied with fat Cattle, at 7s. 6d. to 8s. per stone of 14 lbs. sinking offal; also with a considerable number of small store Scots; and some very good ones at 3s. 9d. to full 4s. per stone when fat. Pigs, a great many and cheap; fat ones to 6s. 6d. per stone.

At *Morpeth* market, Feb. 21, there was a good supply of Cattle and Sheep; there being a great demand, fat of both sold readily at an advance in price.—Beef, 5s. 6d. to 6s. 3d; Mutton, 6s. 9d. to 7s. 6d. per stone, sinking offal.

*Birmingham* Smithfield Market, Feb. 22.—The supply of fat Beef and Mutton small, and the trade pretty good. Of Stores dull.—Beef, 5½d. to 6½d.; Mutton, 5½d. to 6½d.; and Veal, 5d. to 7d. per lb. Fat Pigs, 9s. to 9s. 6d. per score.—Neat Cattle, 186; Sheep, 50?; Pigs, 413.

*Skipton* Cattle Market, Feb. 20.—We had a good show of fat Beasts and Sheep, and there was no lack of buyers.—Beef, 6d. to 6½d.; Mutton, 5d. to 6d. per lb.

# COBBETT'S WEEKLY REGISTER.

Vol. 61.—No. 11.] LONDON, SATURDAY, March 10, 1827. [Price 6d.

4 Hear this, O ye that swallow up the needy, even to make the poor of the land to fail,

5 Saying, When will the new moon be gone, that we may sell corn? and the sabbath, that we may set forth wheat, making the ephah small, and the shekel great, and falsifying the balances by deceit?

6 That we may buy the poor for silver, and the needy for a pair of shoes; yea, and sell the refuse of the wheat?

7 The LORD hath sworn by the excellency of Jacob, Surely I will never forget any of their works.

8 Shall not the land tremble for this, and every one mourn that dwelleth therein? and it shall rise up wholly as a flood; and it shall be cast out and drowned, as by the flood of Egypt.—Amos, Chap. viii.

## TO THE

# PEOPLE OF PRESTON;

## ON THE CATHOLIC PROJECT AND ON THE CORN PROJECT.

*Kensington, 8th March, 1827.*

MY EXCELLENT FRIENDS,

In addressing myself to you, I address myself to all the working classes (especially those of them who are manufacturers) in the whole kingdom. As to the *Catholic*-Project, indeed, you may have a little deeper interest than the people of England *in general;* but, as to the *Corn*-Project, all are equally and most deeply interested.

On the first of these subjects I shall not have to detain you long. There are, however, a few things that strike me as being worthy of your attention; and the

X

Printed and Published by WILLIAM COBBETT, No. 183, Fleet-street,
[ENTERED AT STATIONERS' HALL.]

first of these is, that this question was brought forward, the other night, with great ostentation, and, apparently, great assumption of meritorious generosity, by Sir FRANCIS BURDETT, who piques himself upon being the most *consistent* politician in the whole world, and who, more than ten years ago, I believe, rose, when this old, battered question was brought forward, said that he would not sit in the House to give his countenance to such a farce, as he called it; and, thereupon, marched out of the House with back as straight as a curtain-rod. In proof of his boasted *consistency*, this is the second time that he has been at the head of those actors who have exhibited this piece upon the stage.

As further proofs of his consistency, he highly complimented the Government upon its habit of keeping good faith; he praised Pitt a little above the skies; he said that Pitt had promised the Catholics emancipation; that it was evidently his great final object,

to accomplish that purpose, and that he had done every thing that he could to produce such accomplishment. Just towards the close of his speech, he observed, that he was *almost ashamed* to say any more upon this subject. It was pity that this sentiment did not prevail with him at an earlier stage of his speech; but, after the above compliments and many others to the Ministers and to Pitt, he appears to have made a motion in somewhat the following words; namely, "That this House " deeply felt impressed with the " necessity of taking into con- " sideration the present laws in- " flicting penalties and disabilities " upon their Roman Catholic fel- " low-subjects, with a view to re- " moving them."—I copy this from the *Morning Chronicle*, and, it is possible, that it may be incorrect; but, if these were really the words; if this mover upon this "great occasion" did actually put such a sentence together, let the rest of the world judge of the truth of the following words, taken from another part of the report of his speech; namely, that "England stood first of all the "nations that *ever existed* in point "of *intellect, information,* and "general *instruction.*" Not in grammatical instruction, at any rate; for, if such be the grammar of "England's Glory" what the devil must be the grammar, what the intellect, what the information, and what the general instruction of the ordinary man of men?

At the end of two days' or, rather, two nights' debating, the last of which was on Tuesday the 6th instant, the House divided, when, as the newspapers tell us, there were two hundred and seventy-two votes for the motion, and two hundred and seventy-six votes against it; so that, the question of Catholic Emancipation, as it is called, was thus negatived even in the House of Commons, by a *majority of four*; thus sparing the Lords the trouble attending a rejection, which rejection they certainly would have given to the motion or to any measure founded upon it.

Before I make any remarks with regard to the *merits* of the question, I must go on to the close of the second day's debate, where Mr. Canning, in adverting to something that had been said about Pitt having changed his opinion upon this question, positively asserted and declared, that, he was ready to take his oath of his own belief in what he said; positively asserted, that Mr. Pitt never changed his opinion upon the subject, but continued firmly, to entertain it, to the end of his life. But, both "England's Glory" and England's famous "Æolus" forgot to account for the *why* and the *wherefore* in this memorable conduct of Pitt. He went out of office in 1801, *because the old King would not agree to Catholic Emancipation.* This was expressly stated by him at the time; it was asserted by all his partizans; it was believed in by the whole nation. In 1804 he came into office again; he put out Addington, who had been Minister in his place; a motion for Catholic Emancipation was made, after Pitt thus came in in 1804; and Pitt and all his vast majority *voted against that motion for Catholic Emancipation!* And yet we, though we recollect all his suspensions of the Act of Habeas Corpus; though we recollect all his loans and his sinking fund schemes; though we know well that the calamities of the present day all spring from the seed which he and his creatures sowed; though we remember and know these things, and though we see him, in the plenitude of his power, stand, at the head of that immense majority which he had at his command, voting against that Catholic Emancipation to which he was pledged; though we remember and see all this, we are to stand by like soft and silly culls, and applaud those who insist upon the consistency and sincerity of this Pitt.

The apology, or, rather the shuffle, put forward for him is this; that, when he came the second time into office, he still re-tained all his opinions about this emancipation; still remained determined to accomplish the object in the end; but, " came to a de-" termination not to stir it *during* " *the life of the late king.*" Honest and consistent fellow! He would not only remain in office, but he would take office upon this determination, in 1804; but, he wished so much to accomplish the object, that he quitted office because he could not accomplish it in 1801! If tenderness towards the late king;—it was all a lie, mind; it was all false pretence, mind, on the part of these tricky politicians;—but, if it had been tenderness for the scruples of the late king, which induced him to abandon the Catholic Emancipation in 1804 and to *take* office, with a determination thus to abandon it: if tenderness for the scruples of the late king had induced him thus to act in 1804; pray, my good friends, where was that tenderness, in what curious corner of the fellow's breast was that tenderness towards his late Majesty lodged, when he turned his back upon the old king and his scruples in 1801 ? The cause of the Catholics was the same; it was precisely the same in 1804 that it had been in 1801, with this exception, that there were three years of additional injustice to be removed. The scruples of the old king were still the same. *The opinions* of the Minister were still the same. His majority was as great in 1804 as it had been in 1801. The country was at war in both these years: all things and all parties remained the same as nearly as possible; and, yet, we are to be told; there are men to be found impudent enough to tell us, that this was a sincere, and even a wise minister; and, what is still worse, if possible, we are to see no man to stand up to contradict, to expose, to scout, to trample under foot such bare-faced assertions!

So much for what we may call the *extrinsic* matter of this long, and noisy affair. As to the *merits of the question itself*, they lie in a very small compass. Those who are for the question talk about the feelings of the people of Ireland; about the probable dreadful consequences of their discontents; about the wonderful effect which the putting of a dozen lords into the House of Peers, three score Catholic Members into the other House, and silk gowns upon the backs of three or four dozen of O'Connell's lazaroni, the wonderful effect that these would have in making the people of Ireland *happy and peaceable*. They *ought*, indeed, to show what tendency these would have to put meat, bread and beer into the bellies, cloth and linen upon the backs, leather upon the feet, and blankets and sheets upon the beds, of the working classes in Ireland; for, unless the change had a tendency to produce these effects, i some degree, at any rate; unless the change had a tendency to produce these effects, what man worthy of the name of legislator or politician; what man desirous not to be thought a fool or a hypocrite, will affect to believe, that it is a want of a sufficiency of food and of raiment; that it is bodily suffering; that it is *horrid want*, that produces ninety-nine hundredths of the broils, of the crimes of every description, committed in that unhappy country!

Those who take the other side of the question, those who oppose Catholic Emancipation, as, for instance, the MASTER of the ROLLS, during the present debate, rail in good round hand manner against the pope and the devil; they bring up " bloody Queen Mary," as they have the injustice to call her; they call up the massacre of St. Bartholomew, the burnings of the Duke of Alva; the hangings and rippings up of all the Catholic persecutors that they can think of; and this they do with the greater security, because, having nobody but Protestants to face them, they are sure to be told of none of the bloody works, and unexampled cruelties of every description of good Queen Bess, that first *female head of the church*

that ever was heard of in the world. When they have exhibited a pretty full picture of what they call " the atrocities of Popery," they then assert that Popery remains *wholly unchanged*; when they have done that, they proceed to show that, give the Catholics an inch they will take an ell; let in the Pope's toe, slap will come his foot; and that, therefore, unless we have a mind actually to be burned in Smithfield, we must make a stand where we are. Some men may laugh at this; but, this is a mode of proceeding, the best possible for carrying the point which these orators have in view.

For carrying their point with the *mass of Protestants*; but, they have a select body to address themselves to, in this case; namely, those who are interested in the maintenance of *the Protestant Church as by law established*. If they can convince this body, that the granting of the prayers of the Catholics would endanger any part of the established Church, that is to say, if they can con-vince them, or even make them believe it *possible*, that the grant-ing of the prayers of the Catho-lics would tend to lessen the value of the Church lands, of the bishop-rics, of the several livings; if they can convince them of this, their work is completed; and to con-vince them of this (supposing them to have but a very moderate por-tion of common sense) is *by no means difficult*. It was to this great point that the MASTER of the ROLLS (Sir John Copley) directed the main strength of his battery during the late debate. I do not think that his speech had any influence at all, as to the *divi-sion*; for, that which is called the Catholic cause has been blasted, in England, ever since O'Con-NELL wanted to barter away the rights of the forty-shilling free-holders. On the division, there-fore, I do not think that Sir John Copley's speech produced any, or, at most, but very little effect; but, it confirmed men in the opi-nions which they had formed; it

was an able statement of that which was dictated by common sense; and it proceeded upon the basis that men are to be and will be governed by their interests, by their known, settled, solid in-terests, rather than by speculative patriotism; that you in vain en-deavour to terrify them with pos-sible and distant dangers, if, in order to remove those possible and distant dangers, they must make certain and immediate sa-crifices. It was, in short, the great argument; and it unfortu-nately happens for the Catholics, that those who have to plead for them have *no answer to* SIR JOHN COPLEY, *founded in reason*; that they have nothing but assertions; those assertions not admitting of proof, and being, too, such as NO MAN WILL BELIEVE TO BE SINCERE.

The plain statement is this: the opponents of the Catholics say, " We would grant you what you " ask, but it would enable you to " overset the Protestant Establish-" ment and to cause its immense

" property to be applied to public " purposes; and we offer you rea- " sons to show that you would be " naturally desirous of making this " use of the power which we should " give you."—This was, in sub- stance, what Sir John Copley urged home. It was quite admir- able to behold the various shapes and forms in which he presented it to the House. It was sense, and it was sense which appears to have been wonderfully well ex- pressed. PLUNKETT, BROUGHAM and CANNING, the three greatest talkers of our day, all made long speeches in answer to him; but, not one particle of the *effect* of his speech did they remove, or, even, make any thing like a sensible at- tempt to remove, from the mind of any one of his hearers. The utmost that they arrived at was this: to assert that the Catholics HAD NO DESIRE *to overturn* the Protestant Establishment! This was all, and this was to be be- lieved by no man upon earth in his senses.

The great disadvantage which this cause of Catholic Emancipa- tion, as it is called, labours under, is, that its pretended advocates dare not avow that the wishes of the Catholics are what they are. If the Catholics were to petition, in so many words, for a REPEAL of the Established Church, and, of course, for an abolition of all tithes and Church rates and Church dues of every description; if they were to do this, they would have with them ninety-nine hundredths of the Protestants of England; if they were to petition for an appli- cation of the tithes to the mainte- nance of the poor, as was the case in Catholic times, they would have us all with them to a man, except those who give away and those who possess the bishopricks, the livings and all the eight millions' worth a-year which is now kept for the use of this established Pro- testant Church and its clergy; if they were to petition for such an alteration of the law as would pre- vent the tithes and other Church property from being possessed by *married men*, they would have all

the Protestant men with them, at
any rate, except the parties before
mentioned, their relations and immediate friends.   To petitions of
this sort, Sir John Copley would
not find it so easy to give an answer.  He would then have to defend tithes, which Mr. Plunkett is
quite as ready to do as he is; he
would then have to show that it is
*better* to have a religion, the clergy
of which swallow up all the revenues of the Church, than to have
a religion, the clergy of which
kept all the indigent poor out of
these very revenues.  This would
give Sir John Copley something
to do; but, as long as the pretended advocates of the Catholics shall
continue to assert that six millions
of people would be made as happy
as princes and as harmonious and
loving as turtle-doves by merely
putting about six dozen of Catholics into Parliament, putting big
wigs upon the heads of, perhaps,
a quarter of a dozen of lawyers,
and silk gowns upon the backs of
perhaps a couple of dozen of fellows that are now bawling in cam-

let; as long as the pretended advocates of the Catholics shall continue to assert this; as long as they
shall continue to talk for whole
hours without enabling us to perceive that any possible practical
good to us Protestants would be
the effect of that which they plead
for; so long will they plead to us
and to the Parliament with just as
much effect as they would plead
to Gog and Magog, requesting
them to descend from their stations
in Guildhall.

Those who " *support*," as they
call it, the Catholic Petition, talk,
as I observed before, a good deal
about the dangers to the " *Empire*," as they bombastically call
this kingdom; the dangers that
will arise to the " Empire," to
this puffed-up " Empire," from
something or other which, in case
of WAR, might happen, from the
discontents of the Catholics, arising from their not being " *emancipated;* " they talk about this,
however, in so very vague a manner, that one can hardly guess at
their meaning.  They do not men-

tion the manner in which the danger would show itself; but you can perceive that they think, or would seem to think, that France, in case of war, would assist the Catholics of Ireland in obtaining something or another for the Catholic religion; or would at least endeavour to do it, and would thereby foment rebellion and greatly divide the strength of the bladder-blown *empire*. Now, for my part, I, were I an Irish Catholic, should never rest my hope on the disposition of France to do any thing efficient in this way; but there is ANOTHER COUNTRY, to which I, were I an English Minister, should, in case of war of any duration, look with a great deal of apprehension, unless Ireland were in a state of real tranquillity and content: I MEAN THE UNITED STATES OF AMERICA, where there are always 40,000 volunteers, Irishmen by birth, or the sons of Irishmen, ready to embark, finding their own arms, accoutrements, and clothing, in an expedition, for what

they would deem the deliverance of their country. BOSTON HARBOUR, or the Narrows at *New York*, are a great deal farther off in measured miles than the Harbour of Brest; but, if there were on a certain day a convoy with twenty transports in the ports of BREST, consisting of French ships and French men, and, on that same day, a convoy with a similar number of transports at Boston or New York; if both were to be ready to start on the same day, for any given point in Ireland, I would make an even bet to the amount of all I should be worth in the world, shirt and all, that, if there were no impediment in the way of either, JONATHAN *would be first upon the land*. It is a great way to come, to be sure; but I came it once in eighteen days; ships without number have come *from New York to Ireland in fourteen days*; an American ship will, on an average, cross the Atlantic in three-fourths of the time required by English ships, and in half the time required by French ships. JONA-

THAN knows, not only the shortest way, but precisely the time, the manner, all the circumstances, which, in such a case, it is necessary to understand. PAINE said, in one of his pamphlets, it was indeed in a letter to Jefferson, which was not intended to be published, "ten thousand Americans, "landed in Ireland, with 30,000 "stand of arms, would make a "*prodigious change in the affairs* "*of this world.*" I know, almost as well as any man can know, who does not see with his own eyes; at least I most firmly believe, that, if the late war for "deposing JAMES MADISON," had continued another year, there would actually have been an *expedition from the United States for an invasion of Ireland!* I had this information from what I deemed very good authority; and the gentleman who talked to me about it, told me, that he had no doubt at all of something more than a fair chance of success. I heard him at first, in a manner, as one listens to ban-

ter; but, he soon convinced me that it was by no means a matter to laugh at. In the United States there is every requisite at all times ready; the best of ships; the best of sailors; the ablest of ship commanders; men, at once the most sober, the least talkative, and the most resolute; at once the best of heads upon the stoutest and hardiest of bodies. The Irishmen who are in America, are become pretty much like the natives themselves; and, it is not "*Catholic Emancipation*" that would content *them,* if they were once put in motion. They do not amuse themselves about "*Catholic Emancipation.*" They think and talk about quite other things. I hope, I pray, that such a change will be made in Ireland as shall make the people happy and contented, and firmly attached to their Sovereign and to England; but if that should not be the case, and there should arise a war of any considerable duration, between England on one side, and France and America on the other side, I know

of nothing that I should dread so
much as an attack to be expected
from the other side of the Atlantic.
One would imagine, that the
Yankees did enough during the
last war to fill us with most serious thoughts when we contemplate
the probable effects of future hostilities against them; they have
performed the most wonderful feats
of hardihood and of dexterity
mixed that ever were heard of
in the world. A man who was
a prisoner in DARTMOOR prison,
assisted others, though he had all
his life been a sailor, in a manu-
factory of forged bank of England
notes in that prison; he traversed
the country, living upon some of
those notes; got to Liverpool; by
means of his friendly notes, he
got carried out from Liverpool,
and put on board of an American
privateer, that was swaggering up
and down St. George's Channel, making prizes of fishing-boats
and other small craft, and sending them off with printed papers,
declaring the islands of Britain
and Ireland to be in " *a state of*

*rigorous blockade."* Yankees can
stretch as well as other people;
but this man, who had been a captain of a vessel, and whose vessel
had been sold at a port in HOL-
LAND, had come to England in
1817, and went out to NEW YORK
in the same ship with me in the
month of March of that year.
He might *stretch*, as sailors are
very apt to do; but it is certain that he was in DARTMOOR
prison; it is certain that he
traversed the country from DE-
VONSHIRE to LIVERPOOL; and it
is certain he there found the
means of getting out into the
channel, on board of an American privateer, for I had these
facts related to me by a gentleman, at NEW YORK, who
knew them all well. We should,
therefore, know beforehand the
sort of people we should have to
fight with. They coolly undertake
things which nobody else would
dream of; and to observe their
coolness in situations the most
perilous, is perfectly astonishing
to those who are strangers to their

manners and their conduct. In every way they would be enemies most formidable; but in no way so formidable as in that which I have above pointed out. If we had a paper-money afloat, they would stuff us with forgeries: there is no artifice that they would not employ, and no hazard that they would not run. Let us therefore be *prepared*; and let us, above all things, make Ireland happy and contented; and that too by something a great deal more efficient for the purpose than that mockery which is called the "*Catholic Emancipation.*"

Here I should put an end to my remarks upon this annual, or biennial, discussion. But, I cannot help just observing upon the constant practice of the Catholics of duping themselves. How they triumphed upon the *increase of liberal members*! How they exalted in the vast acquisition which they had in the "honourable and gallant Colonel Torrens!" I, for my part, do not believe that their cause has, in reality, either advanced or retrograded. I believe that it is just what it was two years ago, with this trifling exception, that, perhaps, a few men in Parliament may have been influenced by the disgusting conduct of O'Connell and his lazaroni; and, that many thousands, out of doors, have been disgusted by that conduct. The difference between this time, and the month of March, 1825, is this; that, then, many men would hear you with *patience* when you pleaded for Catholic emancipation; and that these same men will not, now, hear you at all, either with patience or without it; and, beyond all doubt, this change has been produced by the attempt of O'Connell and his lazaroni to barter the rights of half a million of their countrymen, for the sake of gaining silk gowns and seats for themselves. I put it to you, Catholics of the borough of Preston: you know what *you felt* at the last election, upon being cut off from your right to vote; upon being compelled to be false to your religion, or to withhold your voice at that election. You know what you felt then. Now, then, let me put it home to you; let me put this question home to every one of your bosoms: if the law, as it stood in May last, had allowed you to vote; and, if one of your Catholic countrymen had proposed to the Parliament to pass a law to take this right from all the poorer part of you, upon condition of his acquiring a privilege to sit upon the bench, or to sit in Parliament, would you not have cried out against him as the most iniquitous of all mankind? And, if you had failed to do this; if you had huzzaed him and carried him upon your shoulders after this attempt, could you have blamed us, your Protestant countrymen, if we had grown cold in your cause; if we had cared nothing about you, or about what became of you, especially when we reflected that the argument of *poverty*, on which you were to be disfranchised, would, with equal reason and justice, be applied to all the poor Protestants of Preston? In your answer to that question, you will find a great deal more than sufficient reason for what is now called the decline of the Catholic cause. That justice will be done to all our Catholic countrymen at last, and that, too, at no

distant day; I not only hope, but believe; but, come the redress how it may, or when it may, certain I am, that it never will come, in consequence of any act or any proceeding of any sort, in which this O'Connell and his crew shall have any hand.

So much for the CATHOLIC PROJECT. I now come to the CORN PROJECT; and, here, I have a great deal to say, though I have hardly left myself time to say it in. In my last Register, which, as my readers must have perceived, was sent to the press in great haste, I made a slight mistake as to one particular point; namely, I said that there never could be a handful of foreign wheat brought into the country to be consumed, under *eighty shillings the quarter*. It should have been *seventy shillings the quarter*. The tax being twenty shillings when our own wheat sells at an average of sixty shillings, I added the twenty to the sixty, which made eighty, not adverting to the circumstance that the tax was to diminish two shillings on every one shilling of our own price above sixty.

I notice this merely to obviate cavil, all my objections to the proposed measure remaining substantially the same as before stated,

My adventure in search of cheap wheat at Rotherhithe, as that adventure is detailed in the last Register, remains precisely what it was; namely, a clear elucidation of the effect of the proposed measure. What you are all praying for; what you all expected; what, at least, you had a right to expect, was, that some measure would be adopted to cause you to get your bread cheaper than you are now getting it. Without troubling your heads about statements of principles; about general definitions, about details of particulars; what you all expected was, that something would be done to make your bread a little cheaper, at any rate. On this ground; relying upon this; you were desired to be patient; to bear your sufferings with patience; to hope for better times; to hope that that same free trade which had let in such large quantities of foreign manufactured goods, would, at last, let in corn in such a way as to enable you to eat bread as cheap or nearly as cheap as the manufacturers of those foreign goods. Your horrible situation was acknowledged; it was proclaimed, throughout the world, by a royal edict; a general begging by authority was on foot; to keep you from dying of hunger and of cold: but, the day was at hand; when an opening, of the ports, on the principle of free-trade, was to bring you, in one and the same wind, *cheap bread* and *customers for your goods.*

Now, it is impossible to deny that this is a true representation of your case and of your expectations; and, with hundreds, nay, with thousands of petitions before the Parliament from you and persons like you, praying for a law to make bread cheaper than it is, a measure is proposed; a measure, in all likelihood, that will be adopted and become the law, to make bread *dearer* than it now is. That is the main point for you to keep in view; that this measure will (unless counteracted by the workings of the paper-money) make bread at all times dearer than it now is. I said this in my last Register. That very day the wheat rose two or three shillings a quarter at Mark Lane; and, even before the propositions be moulded into an Act of Parliament, it is not at all improbable that they may have made wheat, ten shillings a quarter dearer than it was before; and, it is equally probable that they may have added *a penny or three half-pence to the price of every quartern loaf:* and, observe well, the very same measure must inevitably have a tendency to diminish still further than it has been diminished, the price of manufactured goods. On the evening when these propositions were brought forward in Parliament, I, being desirous to ascertain what was intended to be done; being desirous to possess this knowledge at an hour sufficiently early to enable me to communicate it through the pages of the last Register, went down into the lobby of the House of Commons; but, tired, at last, of remaining there, I went to a house called the *King's Arms*, kept by one *Brown*, which is very near to Westminster Hall. In the room adjoining that in which I was, there was a committee of "*agriculturists*," as they call themselves. The partition between the two rooms was so thin, and the agriculturists spoke so loud, that I could hear, very plainly, the greater part of what they said. Amongst other wise sayings, was this, or something to this effect: *Plenty of French claret but no French corn*. And, observe well, that, while the free-trade, as it is called, has made French wines cheaper, has made French silks cheaper, has made every foreign article cheaper which the owners and occupiers of the land consume, a project is brought in even by these boasters about free-trade, for making their corn; the corn which they have to sell, and the bread which you have to eat, **NEARLY DOUBLE** the price that they would be at, if the trade in corn were as free as the trade in foreign silk goods.

I should be, however, a most scandalous deluder; I should be worthy of being put upon a level with ANNA BRODIE, BAINES of Leeds, TAYLOR of Manchester, BACON of Norwich, or even with that beast of all beasts, BOTT SMITH, were I to endeavour to disguise from you my belief that the ministers have been induced to do, upon this occasion, that which, if left to their own choice, they would not have done. The declaration of Mr. Huskisson, made so fully last year; his declaration that the restrictions on the corn trade were more injurious to the country than all the other restrictions put together; the eagerness of ministers to let in the bonded corn in the month of May; their anxiety to be enabled to let in foreign corn during the recess; their actually letting in the foreign corn by Order in Council, to, at least, a very considerable extent; their great backwardness in bringing forward this measure now;

the illness of Mr. Huskisson on the Monday, when the measure was brought forward, though it was stated in the newspapers, he attended a Council on the Saturday: all these circumstances lead me to believe, that the ministers, if left to themselves, would not have proposed such a measure as this. It is, therefore, but justice to them, to say that I believe they have been, upon this occasion, influenced by the remonstrances of the *landowners*. I do not say, that these remonstrances ought not to have had weight with them, any more than that your petitions ought not to have had weight with them: but, I think it right, thus explicitly to state my opinion as to the real source of the proposed measure.

On the other hand, justice to the landowners; justice to my own character; the duty of not deceiving you or of undeceiving you: all these call upon me to say that, in thus exercising their influence, the landowners have merely been acting from motives of *self-defence*; not from motives of unfair gain; not from a desire to profit by your loss; but, merely, from a conviction in their minds, that, if they let foreign corn into the English market, they themselves would be reduced to beg-gary. The pretty paper-kites will reduce them to beggary fast enough, if the present law continue in force until 1829, in spite of every thing that they can do about Corn Bills. They do not see that, however; and, no man in his senses can blame them, they believing, most firmly, that the foreign corn, if let in, would take away their estates; no just man can blame them for endeavouring to prevent a measure and for preventing a measure, which they are firmly persuaded would make them beggars.

They have, too, more than one argument in favour of their assertion, *that dear corn is no harm to you.* They may cite ample experience in support of this assertion. They could remind you that, during the late wars, you had ample employment, your goods were always at high price, your wages were exceedingly great, and that corn was, upon an average, at nearly double the price that it is at now! They could remind you that, when corn became cheap, you fell into misery. They could remind you, that when corn rose again in price during the years of "prosperity," 1823, 1824, and part of 1825, silk-mills and cotton-mills arose by hundreds, your wages became

Y

high, and you were living in abundance. They could remind you, if in so short a period you could stand in need of reminding, that, the moment corn began to fall in price, you began to fall into misery, and that your miseries have increased, as the price of corn has decreased.

Now, these things are undeniably true. They present to the mind a deceptious mass, to be sure; but, landowners are as likely to be deceived as other people; and, when their estates are at stake, is it surprising that they make use of arguments thus apparently conclusive in their favour, though those arguments be wholly founded in error? The truth is this: the price of corn has never had but very little influence in producing your happiness or your misery; never until now; because now it is forcibly kept (though only for a short time, perhaps) at a high price, when the money which is afloat is, comparatively, so small in quantity, as to keep your goods at a low price. It has been the divers variations in the value of money, which have caused your plenty at one time, and your misery at another time. If the paper money were to be poured out in great abundance, you would soon cease to complain of the dearness of bread.

The state of the matter is this: the sum of taxes to be raised is so great; the expenses of the monopolies arising from paper-money are so great, that the produce of the land must be sold at a high price; wheat, for instance, must be sold at seventy shillings a quarter or more, or the present amount of taxes cannot be collected, *or rents cannot be paid.* This is the state of the case, if the money continue at its present value. But, money is daily and hourly rising to a higher value, and it must continue so to rise (if the present law remain in force) until the month of April, 1829. When that month arrive, the present law having been duly enforced up to that time, you will no longer pray for free trade in corn, for, corn will be as cheap in England as it will be in France.

For the present, and, perhaps, until after next harvest, this corn measure will produce effects favourable to the landowners. It will become nugatory, however, or pretty nearly so, before this day twelve months. The landlords do not see this: they think nothing at all about the paper-money. They think that all that they

ment to secure their estates in a high price for their produce; and they are firmly convinced that this measure will always give them that high price. Nobody can expect men who have estates, to stand quietly by while those estates are taken away from them. You do not expect this : you are not such fools : but, if you can suggest a method, by which the owners may preserve their estates, and suffer you to have cheap bread too, you may very justly say, that they ought to listen to your suggestion.

The fact then is, that it is the taxes ; it is what these take from the land, that compels the land to resort to high price in its defence, or, as I should rather say, which induces the land to resort to that high price. You have a right to call upon the landowners to desist from making you eat dear bread, and, if they wish to preserve their estates (to which you can have no objection), *to take off the taxes.* This is what you have a right to call upon them to do; because they have the *power* to take off taxes, as completely as they have the power to pass a Bill to raise the price of corn. Here, too, they would have your hearty concurrence. You want to be relieved from taxes as well as they.

Your week's wages, is loaded, even, in greater proportion, than their land is loaded with taxes. So that, here all ought to be of a mind; and, the question is, the very interesting question, is, why do not the landlords prefer to save their estates by the taking off of taxes rather than by calling for a price of food which tends to ruin your employers and to starve you ? This, my friends, is the vital question. All men of sense now see that the Corn Bill, and that all the efforts of the landlords to maintain and preserve *high price,* proceed from the *taxes;* that is to say, that the present amount of taxes cannot be collected and rents collected at the same time, *unless the produce of the land bear a high price.* This, every man of sense now knows; the landlords, dull as they generally are, cannot but know this too. In short, they do know it; and, you will ask then, WHY do they not take off the taxes, and save their estates in THAT way ; why do they not save their estates in a way that would receive the approbation and even the acclamations of us all, instead of resorting to Corn Bills, and to all those odious means, which are now made use of to impose an enormous tax upon our bread! Ah!

my friends, this WHY is the all important word! When we get an answer to this WHY, we shall want nothing more upon the subject. You may then shut up the Register, the readers of the botheration newspapers may fling them into the fire; we may all draw ourselves into our shells as safely as we can, and patiently wait the END.

An answer to this WHY *you shall have* from me next week. You shall see clearly, that there is no remedy; no means of saving the estates, except that one description of means, which I have long been pointing out. You shall see; you shall be thoroughly convinced; the fact of your own existence shall not be more evident to your senses, than this fact; namely, that the lazy, grunting, conceited, haughty, greedy, and cruel beasts, who would much rather see the devil in authority than see me in authority, will at last be blown pretty nearly to the devil, unless they *swallow my dose*, bitter as that dose may be to their throats. We shall all triumph over them, my friends, but no one can grudge me a little more of triumph than any body else. The nasty conceited wretches are in a pretty puzzle-wit at this moment; but I have no time for further observation at present. Next week you shall have my full answer to the great WHY; and in the meanwhile

I remain

Your faithful Friend, and

Most obedient Servant,

Wm. COBBETT.

P.S.—I understand that the Morning Chronicle, on the report of which I remarked last week, had misunderstood, and, of course, misrepresented what Mr. Alderman Wood said in the House. The report of the Chronicle stated, that Mr. Alderman Wood said that he was "*favourable to the propositions.*" This did not please me, who am a liveryman of London, and, of course, one of the Alderman's constituents. I spoke of it as something that I was very much displeased at; and this has been attended with very good effect, with regard to this my representative; for, it has brought me that which I am sure is a correct report of what the Alderman did say, and which was as follows: he said, " that he should " not have said a word upon the " subject, if he had not heard " such extraordinary sentiments " delivered by the members for " the Scotch counties, who as-

"serted that the duty on barley "and oats was much too low. "Did they consider that barley "was subjected to a duty (in- "cluding that on beer and malt) "which amounted, in the whole, "to the enormous sum of 50s. per "quarter? and that the additional "one of 10s. now proposed, would "increase it to 60? that this heavy "imposition would press chiefly "upon the labourer and artisan, "*whilst the nobility and gentry* "*were enabled to save the duty of* "*30s. per quarter charged upon* "*beer*? That he would ask such "county] members, whether they "could think of imposing a heavier "duty on oats, the general food of "the wretched poor of Scotland. "That after what had fallen from "the Honourable Baronet, the "member for Somersetshire, and "since he appeared to approve of "the proposed measure, he (Mr. "A. Wood) thought it was highly "necessary for the representa- "tives of populous places to be on "their guard; and that he con- "sidered the proposed duties much "too high, and had no doubt that "the price of corn would be up "the next day, since the resolu- "tions were in favour of the corn "growers, and against the inte- "rests of the consumers."

I am glad to have this opportu-

nity of wiping away that which I really deemed a stain upon Mr. Alderman Wood, who would pro- bably have said a great deal more, if he had been in any place where he could have got a quiet hearing. But I do not very well understand what Mr. Alderman means by complaining that the "*nobility* and *gentry*" save the duty on the beer tax; why, I take special good care myself to save that duty; I have exhorted the whole country to save that duty; ninety-nine hundredths of the farmers and of country trades- men save that duty; a great pro- portion of the labourers and jour- neymen, badly as they are off, might save that duty if they would; and, if they be too lazy, their wives too sluttish; if they be such improvident devils as to be re- duced to the necessity of swallow- ing the infernal drugs of the mo- nopolizing brewers; if, to their la- ziness, their improvidence, the stinking sluttishness of their wives, they add a *taste*, a *relish*, for the drugs; or, which is still worse, a desire to enrich the grasping mo- nopolizers that sell the drugged stuff: if this be the case, let them not complain of the Government; let them not complain of the beer tax; and, Mr. A**LDERMAN**, as one of my representatives, let me be-

beseech you not 'to *find* *fault* *with* me, because I wish to keep my purse shut against these enormous monopolizers and to keep my throat closed against their deleterious floods.

---

## MR. COBBETT'S PETITION.

---

YESTERDAY (the 7th March) the following Petition was presented to the House of Lords by Lord King. His Lordship is reported to have said that he wished the Minister for Ecclesiastical Affairs had been present to hear the Petition read. The Petition will speak for itself; and I have only to add, I will not say my *hope*, much less my expectation; but my most earnest wish that the prayer of the Petition may be granted, and especially the latter part of its prayer.

---

*To the Right Honorable Lords Spiritual and Temporal, of the United Kingdom of Great Britain and Ireland, in Parliament assembled.*

The Petition of William Cobbett, of Kensington in the county of Middlesex; dated this 7th day of March, 1827,

Most humbly sheweth,

That, reluctant as your Petitioner is, and as it becomes him to be, to trespass upon the time of your Right Honorable House, he hopes that it is unnecessary for him to inform your Lordships, that, in beseeching your attention to the representations, which he, with all humility, is about to submit to your Lordships on the state of his Roman Catholic fellow-subjects, he can have been actuated by nothing short of that sense of duty to his Sovereign and his Country, which he is sure, your Lordships will readily admit, ought to supersede every other earthly consideration.

Though, after the most mature consideration; though after the most diligent inquiry; after the most patient and most impartial historical researches; though the result of all these has, notwithstanding the early planted and deep-rooted prejudices of his youth, and even of a large part of his riper years; though the result, notwithstanding every obstacle in its way, has been a settled conviction in his mind, that the departure from the religion of our forefathers has produced, and from its outset has been producing, great injury to our country; though he cannot look at the state of England in former times, compared with its state in latter times; though he cannot look into the statutes, passed by our Catholic ancestors, and there behold the indubitable proofs of the ease, the happiness, the plenty of food and raiment, the harmony, the order, the almost total absence of crime; though he cannot, when he compares these with those things of the same nature, now existing in this same country; though, when he makes this comparison, he cannot but feel, that he should be guilty of the basest injustice, were he to withhold an expression of his opinion, *that England has suffered from the change:* still he is too well aware of the violence, the injustice, the numerous and great dangers to his country, which must necessarily arise from any attempt whatever to restore and reestablish that, the abolition of which he regards as so great an evil.

But your humble Petitioner, though he entertains no wish to see the Roman Catholic religion restored and established, in any part of his Majesty's dominions, does, nevertheless, most anxiously desire two things; namely, *first,* that his Roman Catholic countrymen may be, as to political and civil rights, placed upon the same footing with himself, and with all the rest of his Protestant fellow-subjects; and, *second,* that the revenues of that Church, which now enjoys what the Roman Catholic Church enjoyed, may, like the revenues of the Roman Catholic Church, be applied in the like manner as they were in the days of our Catholic ancestors, *to the maintenance of the destitute poor.*

As to the *first* of these, your Lordships' most humble Petitioner beseeches you to reflect, that the Roman Catholic subjects of his Majesty, suffer great privations, great degradation; and, that they suffer these solely because they adhere to the religion of their and our forefathers; because by quitting that religion, by disowning it, by apostatizing from it, they can, at any moment, remove all the privations and all the degradation, of which they so bitterly, and, in your Petitioner's humble opinion, so justly complain: he beseeches your Lordships to reflect, that we owe the colleges, the universities, the cathedrals, and churches, in which we now worship God; that we owe the division of our country into counties, hundreds and parishes;

that we owe our proudly-claimed and long-exercised dominion of the. seas ; that we owe the common law of the land, and those courts of justice, which law and which courts have done more than every thing else done by man to make England happy and great : that we owe, in short, every institution that we really venerate, not only every institution which is worthy of our veneration, but every institution which we really do venerate : your humble Petitioner beseeches your Lordships to reflect that we owe all these ; that we owe all the real renown of our country, to the institutions and deeds of our Roman Catholic forefathers : and, hoping that your Lordships will, in your benignant condescension, be pleased thus to reflect, he cannot but hope, that, thus reflecting, you may be disposed to listen to his humble prayer, that you will, at last, pass such laws as shall cause a cessation of the suffering and degradation of those of our countrymen, who suffer for no other cause than that of adhering with unshaken fidelity to the faith and worship of these our Roman Catholic forefathers.

As to the *second*, your humble Petitioner, though he seeks not to destroy any of the establishments or institutions of the country, cannot behold without feelings of shame, millions of Englishmen become miserable *paupers* ; and, he cannot but recollect, and your Lordships cannot but know, that Pauper was a name unknown in England in the days of our Catholic forefathers ; and, seeing that your Lordships cannot but know, that the indigent poor were wholly maintained out of the tithes and other revenues of the Church ; seeing, that your Lordships cannot but know that provision was made for the indigent poor, even in the Canons which established a Roman Catholic Clergy ; seeing that your Lordships cannot but know, that it was part of the duty of that Clergy to provide effectually for the indigent poor, out of the revenues of the Church ; seeing that your Lordships cannot but know, that laws were made to transfer those revenues to the Clergy of the present Establishment ; seeing that your Lordships cannot but know, that the Clergy of the present Establishment do actually enjoy those revenues : seeing these things, and bearing in mind the representations above humbly made to your Lordships, your Petitioner, with the most profound respect for your Right Honourable House, but with an earnestness and anxiety equal to that respect, and with that confidence in the wisdom, the justice and the mercy of your Honourable House, which it becomes him to entertain and to express, he prays, that your Lordships will be pleased to pass an Act or Acts for the accomplishment of the following purposes:

1. For placing his Majesty's Roman Catholic subjects upon the same footing, with regard to political and civil rights, as the law has placed his Majesty's Protestant subjects.

2. For causing the indigent poor to be, as they were in the days of our Roman Catholic ancestors, maintained by the Clergy, out of the tithes and other revenues of the Church; and for causing thereby, the degrading, the odious name of *pauper*, to be unknown amongst us, as it was unknown amongst our happy Catholic progenitors.

And your humble Petitioner will, as in duty bound, ever pray.

WM. COBBETT.

## CHEAP BREAD,

*The unhappy cause of Poaching and Thieving!*

---

THE above seems at first sight to be a strange proposition; but, if the reader will look into the Morning Chronicle of the 28th Feb., and into the report of the debate of that evening in the House of Lords, on the subject of the Game Laws, he will find the Earl of Malmsbury represented as having said, that the great increase of poaching, and of crime generally, was not owing to the Game Laws, but owing to the LOW PRICE OF AGRICULTURAL PRODUCE! Now, it is clear that a low price of agricultural produce there must be if bread be cheap; therefore, it follows of necessity, that, if the assertion of Lord Malmsbury be true, CHEAP BREAD IS THE CAUSE OF POACHING AND THIEVING.

His Lordship argued thus; owing, said he, to the low price of produce, farmers are unable to employ nearly so many labourers as they otherwise would employ; and, the labourers being from this cause without a sufficient employment, are compelled to become poachers or thieves.

Fair enough, my Lord, supposing your premises be true ; supposing me to admit that *it is the low price of produce* that thus disables the farmer from. giving employment. But, this is not the case, my good LORD of MALMSBURY : it is not the low price of produce, but the double rent, the double tithes, the five-fold taxes, which the farmer has to pay : these it is that prevents him from giving employment ; and, if old HARRIS, the venerable *schoolmaster* (though a very cunning fellow in his day and. way) were to rise from the grave, and swear till he was black in the face, that *cheap bread was an evil to the labouring man,* that labouring man would not believe him.

What I have been noticing here, I give not as the assertion of Lord Malmsbury, who, having a pretty large slice annually out of the taxes, must of necessity understand how it is that those taxes operate. He must feel that they *bring good to him.* Well, then, he that receives and he that pays cannot *both of them have good out of the same money.* . Suppose that the whole of the noble Lord's share were now to be taken away from the farmers of one particular

*parish,* in addition to what the poor devils already pay. Would they not thereby be rendered *less able* to give employment to labourers ?

However, this is all so plain ; it is so evident ; it is so clearly the taxes and the monopolies arising out of paper-money ; it is so plain that these are the causes, and the only causes of the monstrous increase of misery and crime, that it is useless to say more upon the subject.

---

## HORRID SCOTCH LIE.

—

I take the following monstrous Scotch Lie from the Morning Chronicle of this day, 1st. March :

" Many very original opinions
" have, in this country, been pro-
" pounded from the Bench ; it may
" truly be said, that both Divinity
" and Political Economy are high-
" ly indebted to the venerable
" Judges for their volunteer con-
" tributions.—We shall always
" remember the demonstration of
" the infinite *benefit* this country
" *derived from her National Debt,*
" *and the ingenious theory of*
" *Price, sported the other day by*
" *a Lord Chief Justice, who has*

"since been so powerfully backed "by Mr. COBBETT."

Now the plain meaning of this is, that Mr. COBBETT has powerfully backed the Lord Chief Justice in his assertion that the *National Debt was a benefit to this country*; and in sporting the theory of *Price*. DOCTOR BLACK here tells the public, or, he here clearly wishes the public to believe; that I have backed a Lord Chief Justice in these two things; and, all but that bamboozled part of the public who suck down the nostrums of the broad sheet, know that the Doctor here puts forth a horrid Scotch lie. Here is a lie, too, upon the Lord Chief Justice of the Court of Common Pleas; for it was not HE that at any rate cried up the blessings of the National Debt; and in those observations of him, the justice of which I maintained the other day, he, by implication, at any rate, condemns the monopolising system of paper-money.

But what a sneaker this Doctor Black is. He would fain be understood as *sneering* when he talks of my powerful backing of the Lord Chief Justice. Sneering does very well sometimes, but it does not do when there is an argument by which the sneerer is tackled and gets pinned up into a corner; then sneering looks like an angry grin, and is sure to expose the affected sneerer to ridicule and contempt. Let these Scotch feelosophers deal by me as I deal by them: let them first *insert my statement or argument at full length*; and then let them write down their answer on the same paper. This is what they never do. They have neither the industry, nor the talent, necessary to face me; and therefore they slip and slide and shy about; and, when driven from all their skulking places, they come out at last with a brazen lie, as Doctor Black has done upon the present occasion.

## MARKETS.

Average Prices of CORN throughout ENGLAND, for the week ending February 23.

#### Per Quarter.

|          | s. | d. |          | s. | d. |
|----------|----|----|----------|----|----|
| Wheat .. | 53 | 8  | Rye .... | 37 | 6  |
| Barley .. | 38 | 1 | Beans ... | 48 | 7 |
| Oats .... | 29 | 5 | Pease ... | 50 | 3 |

Total Quantity of Corn returned as
Sold in the Maritime Districts, for
the week ended February 23.

|          | Qrs.   |          | Qrs.   |
|----------|--------|----------|--------|
| Wheat .. | 37,542 | Rye ..... | 330   |
| Barley .. | 33,874 | Beans . .. | 3,116 |
| Oats ... | 12,065 | Pease .... | 1,719 |

*Corn Exchange, Mark Lane.*

Quantities and Prices of British
Corn, &c. sold and delivered in
this Market, during the week ended
Saturday, February 24.

| | Qrs. | | £. | s. | d. | | s. | d. |
|---|---|---|---|---|---|---|---|---|
| Wheat.. | 2,033 | for | 5,739 | 4 | 3 | Average, 56 | 5 |
| Barley.. | 3,115 | .. | 5,997 | 13 | 1 | ..........38 | 0 |
| Oats.. | 1,919 | .. | 2,958 | 2 | 1 | ..........30 | 9 |
| Rye..... | — | .. | 0 | 0 | 0 | ..........0 | 0 |
| Beans.. | 857 | .. | 2,073 | 7 | 6 | ..........48 | 4 |
| Pease.. | 478 | .. | 1,241 | 15 | 9 | ..........51 | 11 |

Friday, March 2.—The business
of this market has chiefly consisted
of conversation on the plan of Government relative to the Corn Laws,
and there has, therefore, been very
few sales made. The Factors all
hold Wheat at higher prices, and
demand an advance of 2s. to 3s. per
quarter; but there is no difference
from Monday's currency on the rates
of other articles.

Monday, March 5.—Our supplies
of Corn coastwise are not large; and
land samples of Wheat are likewise
short. The opinion entertained here
of the Propositions of Government,
is, that it will operate as a prevention
to the importation of Foreign Wheat
in any quantities; and prices have,
therefore, risen 3s. to 4s. for fine qualities of Wheat; but inferior samples
are very little, if at all affected. On
the contrary, the duties for other articles not being in proportion to
those on Wheat, the prices of this
day se'nnight for Rye, Barley, Beans,
Pease, and Oats, are barely maintained, with a heavy sale. There
was some intention of advancing the
price of Flour; but it was not finally
settled.

*Price on board Ship as under.*

Flour, per sack ......46s. — 50s.
———— Seconds ........42s. — 44s.
———— North Country ..40s. — 44s.

Price of Bread.—The price of the
4lb. Loaf is stated at 9d. by the
full-priced Bakers.

Account of Wheat, &c. arrived in the Port of London, from Feb. 26 to March 3, both inclusive.

| | Qrs. | | | Qrs. |
|---|---|---|---|---|
| Wheat | 2,904 | Tares | | 8 |
| Barley | 4,125 | Linseed | | — |
| Malt | 3,777 | Rapesced | | — |
| Oats | 828 | Brank | | — |
| Beans | 1,002 | Mustard | | — |
| Flour | 4,918 | Flax | | — |
| Rye | — | Hemp | | — |
| Pease | 608 | Seeds | | 60 |

Foreign.—Oats, 519 ; and Beans, 32 quarters.

———

Monday, March 5.—The arrivals from Ireland last week were 4,055 firkins of Butter, and 2,257 bales of Bacon. No arrivals from Foreign Ports.

———

## HOPS.

Price of Hops, per Cwt. in the Borough.

Monday, March 5.—Since our last our market remains dull, and prices at our last quotations.

*Maidstone,* March 1.—There has been some trade this week, and at much about the same prices. The market appears steady, and the Hops will all soon be out of the planter's hands.

———

### COAL MARKET, March 2.

*Ships at Market. Ships sold. Price.*
8¾ Newcastle 5¼ ..28s. 6d. to 37s. 6d.
1½ Sunderland 1½ ..34s. 0d.— 38s. 0d

---

SMITHFIELD, Monday, March 5.

Though the supply on Friday of Beasts and Sheep was unusually short, yet very little business was done; and the Mutton trade was particularly dull. This morning being fine and cool, and a very short market, have occasioned some briskness. Prime beef sells a shade above our currency, but not so much as 1l. in 20l. For choice sheep an advance has taken place of 2s. to 3s. a head; but the middling and inferior obtain no better terms than last week. A few choice downs have made 4s. 10d.; and the best polled Sheep have realized 4s. 6d.

*Per Stone of 8 pounds (alive).*

| | s. | d. | s. | d. |
|---|---|---|---|---|
| Beef | 3 | 10 to | 5 | 0 |
| Mutton | 3 | 8 — | 4 | 10 |
| Veal | 5 | 4 — | 6 | 0 |
| Pork | 4 | 8 — | 5 | 4 |
| Lamb | 0 | 0 — | 0 | 0 |

| | | | |
|---|---|---|---|
| Beasts | 2,071 | Sheep | 17,560 |
| Calves | 102 | Pigs | 120 |

NEWGATE, (same day.)

*Per Stone of 8 pounds (dead).*

| | s. | d. | s. | d. |
|---|---|---|---|---|
| Beef | 3 | 4 to | 4 | 4 |
| Mutton | 2 | 8 — | 3 | 8 |
| Veal | 3 | 8 — | 5 | 8 |
| Pork | 3 | 8 — | 5 | 8 |
| Lamb | 0 | 0 — | 0 | 0 |

LEADENHALL, (same day.)

*Per Stone of 8 pounds (dead).*

| | s. | d. | s. | d. |
|---|---|---|---|---|
| Beef | 3 | 4 to | 4 | 6 |
| Mutton | 3 | 0 — | 3 | 8 |
| Veal | 3 | 8 — | 5 | 3 |
| Pork | 4 | 0 — | 5 | 4 |
| Lamb | 0 | 0 — | 0 | 0 |

## POTATOES.

**SPITALFIELDS,** *per Ton.*

|  | *l.* | *s.* |  | *l.* | *s.* |
|---|---|---|---|---|---|
| Ox-Nobles | 3 | 5 | to | 3 | 16 |
| Middlings | 2 | 5 | — | 2 | 10 |
| Chats | 2 | 0 | — | 0 | 0 |
| Common Red | 3 | 0 | — | 3 | 10 |

Onions, 0s. 0d. —0s. 0d. per bush.

**BOROUGH,** *per Ton.*

|  | *l.* | *s.* |  | *l.* | *s.* |
|---|---|---|---|---|---|
| Ox-Nobles | 3 | 0 | to | 4 | 0 |
| Middlings | 2 | 10 | — | 0 | 0 |
| Chats | 2 | 0 | — | 0 | 0 |
| Common Red | 3 | 0 | — | 3 | 10 |

## HAY and STRAW, per Load.

*Smithfield.*—Hay....80s. to 110s.

Straw...30s. to 36s.

Clover. 100s. to 135s.

*St. James's.*—Hay....94s. to 115s.

Straw .. 33s. to 40s.

Clover . 126s. to 135s.

*Whitechapel.*—Hay....75s. to 105s.

Straw...32s. to 36s.

Clover..90s. to 126s.

---

**AVERAGE PRICE OF CORN,** sold in the Maritime Counties of England and Wales, for the Week ended February 23, 1827.

|  | Wheat. | | Barley. | | Oats. | |
|---|---|---|---|---|---|---|
|  | *s.* | *d.* | *s.* | *d.* | *s.* | *d.* |
| London* | 57 | 3 | 39 | 10 | 33 | 10 |
| Essex | 56 | 0 | 38 | 0 | 28 | 8 |
| Kent | 55 | 2 | 39 | 5 | 29 | 3 |
| Sussex | 52 | 6 | 39 | 8 | 28 | 3 |
| Suffolk | 53 | 0 | 35 | 8 | 29 | 0 |
| Cambridgeshire | 50 | 0 | 35 | 10 | 25 | 8 |
| Norfolk | 52 | 4 | 36 | 6 | 28 | 2 |
| Lincolnshire | 52 | 6 | 40 | 10 | 27 | 2 |
| Yorkshire | 51 | 8 | 39 | 2 | 27 | 6 |
| Durham | 53 | 6 | 40 | 8 | 30 | 9 |
| Northumberland | 51 | 2 | 37 | 10 | 32 | 6 |
| Cumberland | 57 | 0 | 35 | 4 | 34 | 6 |
| Westmoreland | 60 | 4 | 45 | 0 | 36 | 3 |
| Lancashire | 59 | 0 | 42 | 6 | 33 | 8 |
| Cheshire | 57 | 1 | 52 | 9 | 31 | 0 |
| Gloucestershire | 57 | 4 | 44 | 7 | 35 | 10 |
| Somersetshire | 54 | 1 | 41 | 2 | 26 | 9 |
| Monmouthshire | 58 | 8 | 48 | 0 | 30 | 0 |
| Devonshire | 54 | 1 | 37 | 1 | 26 | 0 |
| Cornwall | 57 | 1 | 36 | 6 | 29 | 11 |
| Dorsetshire | 51 | 11 | 38 | 8 | 36 | 8 |
| Hampshire | 54 | 1 | 38 | 8 | 28 | 6 |
| North Wales | 60 | 8 | 44 | 7 | 30 | 7 |
| South Wales | 57 | 9 | 89 | 8 | 26 | 0 |

\* The London Average is always that of the Week preceding.

*Bristol*, March 3.—Little business is doing here in Corn, &c. Seeds, generally speaking, sell heavily. The supply of Corn, Flour, and Malt, is not abundant, but fully equal to the demand. The following prices are nearly correct at present:—Wheat, from 6s. to 7s. 6d.; Barley, 4s. 4½d. to 5s. 9d.; Beans, 5s. 6d. to 6s. 3d.; Oats, 2s. 3d. to 4s. 1½d.; and Malt, 6s. 6d. to 8s. per bushel, Imperial. Flour, Seconds, 33s. to 48s. per bag. The prices of Wheat and Flour are expected to advance next week.

*Chelmsford*, March 8.—The prices of Grain at our market this day are as under :—White Wheat, 60s. to 64s.; Red ditto, 56s. to 60s.; Barley, 36s. to 40s.; Oats, 28s. to 35s.; Beans, tick, 40s. to 48s.; Pease, Grey, 50s. to 52s. per quarter. Clover Seed, 40s. to 42s. per cwt. Tares, 12s. 6d. to 13s. 6d. per bushel.

*Guildford*, March 3.—Wheat, new, for mealing, 15l. to 17l. 10s. per load. Barley, 38s. to 40s.; Oats, 33s. to 42s.; Beans, 54s. to 58s.; Pease, grey, 60s. to 62s.; ditto, boilers, 62s. to 64s. per quarter. Tares, 12s. per bushel.

*Horncastle*, March 3.—There was a good supply of Wheat and Barley, but not much other Grain. The demand for the best Wheats was something higher; Barley nearly the same; very little doing in Oats; Pease lower; Beans and Rye as our last.—Wheat, from 52s. to 55s.; Barley, 38s. to 42s.; Oats, 35s. to 40s.; Pease, 70s.; Beans, 60s.; and Rye from 40s. to 44s. per quarter.

*Manchester*, March 3.—The demand during the past week has been trivial, the consumers declining to purchase until his Majesty's Ministers' views on the Corn Question were made known. This morning the news brought Mr. Canning's speech in the House of Commons on Thursday evening, when, at our market to-day, the holders of Grain and Flour demanded more money for most articles in the trade. Wheat, of fine quality, was 2d. per 70 lbs., Oats, 1d. to 1¼d. per 45 lbs., Beans, 1s. per qr., Pease 3d. per bushel, and Flour 6d. to 1s. per sack dearer, but slow in sale at the advance. In Barley and Malt no alteration.

*Newcastle-on-Tyne*, March 3.—We had a good supply of Wheat from the farmers, and a large arrival coastwise this morning, for which considerably higher prices were demanded at the early part of the market, under an impression that accounts had been received that the proposition made to Parliament on Thursday night, was to prohibit importation below 60s. per quarter; but when it was ascertained that no account had been received, sales were effected at 1s. to 2s. per quarter above the prices of last week. Rye continues in demand. The ships which have been so long kept back by contrary winds have now arrived, and bring a considerable quantity of Barley, and the maltsters (wishing to see what effect the measures proposed in Parliament will have upon the market) have bought very sparingly of the best samples at 40s. and 42s. per quarter. Fine Malt continues in demand. We had only the farmers' supply of Oats to-day, which sold readily at last week's prices.

*Reading*, March 3.—We had a short supply of Wheat to-day, which met a ready sale, at an advance on the average of 1s. to 2s. per quarter. We note it, Old Wheat, 58s. to 68s.; New, 54s. to 66s. per quarter by the Imperial measure. In Barley, Oats, and Pease, no alteration. Beans, are 1s. per quarter cheaper.

*Wakefield*, March 2.—We had a good supply of Wheat here to-day, with many samples from vessels which are in the river, and will be here in a day or two; good and fine samples sold at an advance of 1s. to 2s. per qr.

## COUNTRY CATTLE AND MEAT MARKETS, &c.

*Horncastle*, March 3.—Beef, 8*s.* per stone of 14 lbs.; Mutton, 6*d.* ; Pork, 6*d.* to 7*d.* and Veal, 6*d.* to 8*d.* per lb.

*Manchester* Smithfield Market, Feb. 28.—Our market was well supplied with Beasts and Sheep; the former were principally of Irish produce, which were not so good to sell only at our lowest quotations. The best Yorkshire were taken off readily at 6½*d* to 7*d.* per lb. Sheep were tolerably well sold; best at 7*d.* to 7½*d.* per lb.; other sorts became heavy sale, particularly at the close of the market, as the weather became very unfavourable for standing. Pigs were very dull and lower.—Beef, 4½*d.* to 7*d.* ; Mutton, 6*d.* to 7½*d.*; Veal, 6*d.* to 7½*d.*; and Pork, 4*d.* to 5½*d.* per lb. sinking offal.

At *Morpeth* market, Feb. 28, there was a very great supply of Cattle ; fat sold readily at last week's prices : inferior stood long, and were not all sold. There being a short supply of Sheep, they met with ready sale at an advance in price.—Beef, 5*s.* 6*d.* to 6*s.* 3*d*; Mutton, 7*s.* to 7*s.* 9*d.* per stone, sinking offal.

*Norwich Castle Meadow*, March 3.—We had a good supply of fat Cattle to this day's market, prices, 7*s.* 6*d.* to 8*s.* per stone of 14 lbs. sinking offal ; and a very small supply of store stock : Scots, 3*s.* 9*d.* to 4*s.* per stone when fat. Pigs, very cheap; fat ones to 6*s.* 6*d.* per stone. Meat, Beef, 6½*d.* to 8½*d.*; Veal, 6*d.* to 8*d.*; Mutton, 5½*d.* to 6½*d.*, and Pork, 5½*d.* to 8*d.* per lb.

# COBBETT'S WEEKLY REGISTER.

Vol. 61.—No. 12.] LONDON, SATURDAY, March 17, 1827. [*Price 6d.*

" I do not know what I may become at last : I may, for aught I know,
" become an oyster before I die ; but, no one can, at any rate, say that
" I am not a CONSISTENT *politician.*—Sir Francis Burdett's Speech
at the Crown and Anchor, in the year 1818.

TO

## SIR FRANCIS BURDETT, Bart.

### ON HIS SPEECH OF THE 9th. INSTANT, RELATIVE TO THE CORN PROJECT.

*Kensington, 15th March, 1827.*

Sir,

In my last Register, I told the good fellows of the North, that I would, in the present Register, clearly explain to them the important WHY : that is to say, WHY the Landlords, the Landowners, the Landsquires, the Pheasant Gentry, the tread-mill inventors ; WHY this *generous class*, to whom you declare it an honour to belong, do not choose to save their estates by a reduction of the taxes, rather than by the means of a tax on the people's bread. Before I have closed this letter, I will fulfil my promise as to the explaining of this important WHY ; but, I address myself to you instead of addressing myself to the Weavers of the North, not by any means, however, because you are more entitled to any one's respect than they are ; but, because, if the newspapers speak truth, you have been poking and blundering *round about and about* the. subjects which are most closely connected with that of the great WHY.

I do not pretend to assert that the thing which I am about to comment on as your speech, really was your speech. But, I find it as I found Canning's Æolian production, published in the newspapers ; and, I may further observe, that, as to the substance, I find the Old Times and the Morning Chronicle per-

Printed and Published by William Cobbett, No. 183, Fleet-street,
[ENTERED AT STATIONERS' HALL.]

fectly agree in their report of this speech. In this publication, I find all manner of wild and foolish matter. Inconsistency and almost self-contradiction in every other sentence. Several true statements, several just observations, several profound suggestions; several of these mixed up with the crude, inconsistent, fallacious rubbish before mentioned; but, if this report be a true report of your speech, the most shameless plagiarist you are that ever lived; for, not one particle of valuable matter does it contain which you have not read a hundred and a hundred times over in the Register; besides having the principles urged upon you from my lips a greater number of times than the number of my fingers and toes, and of all the joints in those fingers and toes.

I need not say this to the readers of the Register, who, when I come to quote this thing called your speech will be astonished at the barefacedness of the plagiarism. The points; that is to say, the principal points, of the speech are as follows :

1. The excellent character of the people called country gentlemen; their great generosity and their remarkable attachment to fair play.

2. The prosperity which reigned throughout the country during the late war with France.

3. The cause of that prosperity being turned into distress.

4. The necessity of an "*equitable adjustment*."

5. The necessity of bringing back the paper system, in order to cause a restoration of the state of prosperity which existed before the war.

As to the first of these, the excellent character of the people called country gentlemen; their great generosity and their remarkable attachment to fair play, it was a pity (seeing how desirable it is that this should be true) that you did not produce some *proof* of it : one little instance or two, would surely have done no harm ! Why not then give us one instance, at any rate, of the justice ; and above all things, of the generosity of these Ash-stick Gentlemen? You asserted, that there was not any set or class of men "more liberal, more virtuous, "more respectable in every point "of view, in this country or in "any country in the world, than "the class to which you have "the *honour to belong ;* that that "class formed, indeed, the *grand* "*distinction* among the nations "of the *civilized world.*" So it does ; and a very grand distinction it is ; for, it distinguishes the country from all other countries, by abetting and supporting a system which is more productive of crime, moral and legal; more productive of baseness of every description; more productive of bribery, corruption, perjury ; more productive of injustice, cruelty, bodily and mental misery, deaths, ignominious by the executioner's hand or by suicide; more productive of all these, than any other system ever invented by mortal man. The whole of the "set or class," including those of them who are in Scotland and in Ireland, contain in their breasts, carry about constantly in their bosoms, a greater quantity of contumely, arrogance, tyranny, and insolence, than, so may God help me, as I sincerely believe to be contained in the breasts of all the rest of mankind. If the fact could be ascertained, I would stake my existence on it; and, having thus endeavoured to describe their vast superiority over the rest of mankind in point of insolence, it is hardly necessary to say that their ignorance is equal to their insolence. Their cruelty and insolence are manifested by the *game affairs*, the *tread-mill affairs*, the anti-population schemes, and by a thousand other things equally horrible. Of their ignorance, we want no other proof, than the bare existence of the *mess, in which they now are!* What more do we want to show, that this is at once the most stupid and most insolent set of men that ever breathed. You did not, I confess, extol very highly, the *wisdom* of this class to which you had the *honour* to belong; and, the only proof, that you attempted to produce of their justice, was merely, that some country gentleman had said that he would *strip the coat off his back*, before he would consent to a reduction of the interest of the debt. The words put into your mouth are these; and, words more silly never dropped from tongue or pen. They cannot have been your real words; or, if they were, Lord have mercy upon the noddles of your constituents! " The Hon. Alderman " had charged the landed gentle- " men with being reckless of all " interests but their own; and he " had intimated that they were " ready, for their own relief, to " apply a sponge to the national " debt. He (Sir F. Burdett) had " heard declarations made in that . " House, which *could leave no*

" *doubt of the groundlessness* " *of that imputation.* When " hints of that kind had been " thrown out, some landed gentle- " men had declared, sooner than " lower the interest of the public " debt, they would strip the *coats* " *off their backs*; and even " stronger expressions had been " uttered, which he would not re- " peat. But he would say, that " on such occasions, none had " expressed themselves *more* " *warmly than the Landed Gen-* " *tlemen.*"

Famous logic! There could be *no doubt* that the landowners did not want to apply a sponge because you had heard some of them declare that they would strip the coats off their backs, before they would apply the sponge! It is curious enough, that the man (for there was but one), who said that he would strip the coat off his back, was the very man, who declared, and in the same place too, that your words, uttered against these very country gentlemen, made *his hair stand on end;* and, therefore, *he moved that you should be sent to the Tower*, whither you were sent, and out of which you came in the manner we all so well recollect! Oh! no, "Mr. Country Gentleman," we are not to be satisfied by reasons like this; there is printed evidence, now on the table of the House itself, to prove, that, while poor starving creatures were and are transported for seven years, for being out by night in pursuit of hares, pheasants and partridges; and while the same code of laws, makes it criminal to *sell* hares, pheasants and partridges; while this is the case, and while the

Z 2

gaols are full of men, whose only crime is that of having killed or sought to kill some of these animals; while this is the case, there is evidence before the House of Commons to prove, that the " Country Gentlemen " are *great sellers of game themselves*; and that, the mean blackguards regularly make a traffic in it, as much as higglers carry on a traffic with the poulterers in pigeons, fowls, ducks, geese, and turkeys. An *honor* is it to belong to a set like this! This honor is a commodity that has one great convenience to it, at any rate; and that is, that nothing above the rank and office of hangman will grudge you the possession of it. 'Tis your acres: 'tis your acres that people grudge you: in all other respects there is no " set " in the country more despised, and, none more worthy of being despised; for this is their real actual situation: they *have lost their estates* (or they are just going, mind!) because they approved of loans, approved of wars, approved of Habeas Corpus suspension acts, of power-of-imprisonment bills, of gagging bills; and all this because they thought that these measures would prevent the *people from having a chance of recovering their just rights.* This is the cause of their losing their estates. Their desire to *prevent the people from being restored to the enjoyment of their rights*: this desire caused them to approve of measures which have at last produced the prospect which now frightens them out of their senses; those of them, I mean, who have any senses; for those of them who appear to have none are by no means few in number. Never was there a set of men, of mean, cruel, cowardly, tyrants more justly punished than the " Country Gentlemen, " as you now call them, have been, and will be. Their great object has been to *prevent the people from regaining their rights*: their reward will be (in many cases it already has been) the *loss of their estates*. Never was justice more perfect than this; and this I have heard you assert as many times as you have individual hairs in your beard. I said it *then*, and the difference between you and I, is, that I say it *now*; while you are rummaging about to see if you cannot find out some scheme or other, for preserving the estates to the Country Gentlemen-fellows, without doing any thing that shall expose the concern to the *danger of letting in the people to the enjoyment of their rights*. This is your present object; an object directly at variance with that which you have been professing to have in view, the whole course of your political life, till within these last two or three years. I have the satisfaction to know, however, that, in this object you *cannot* succeed: the very nature of things is against you: the people must have those rights for which you affected to be so long contending, or, you must lose your estates. The people *may* regain their rights and you lose your estates too. That is amongst the *amiable* chances, secured to themselves by the haunters of Brooke's and Boodle's: that is among the chances that their wisdom has secured for them; but, they have the CERTAINTY of losing their estates or seeing the people restored to their rights; and if you can recommend an equitable adjustment, and not at the same time expect the people to be restored to their rights, you are no longer a person to be reasoned with.

Leaving your amiable " Country Gentlemen :" or, rather, endeavouring to pull you from their beloved company for a little while; though you used to talk wildly about late hours and bad company ; drawing you away a little, from the mild and just and intelligent set of which you are now so much enamoured, let me ask whether it be really true, that you did, on Friday last, the 9th day of March, pronounce an *eulogium on the late war against* France ? The words imputed to you are these :—" It was his opinion, how-" ever, that, *if the currency had* " *not been altered, there would* " *have been no agricultural dis-* " *tress.* What was the evidence " of facts on this subject? *During* " *the twenty years* previous to the " late change in the currency, " there had been *no distress in* " *the country* ; but, on the con-" trary, while there was a large " annual importation of foreign " corn, *every interest,* including " that of agriculture, *flourished* " *in an extraordinary degree.* " The only wonder was, how, after " so prodigal an expenditure, the " country had not only been able " to bear it, but, at the close, to " find *itself more flourishing and* " *prosperous than it was at the* " *commencement of the war.* The " agricultural interest had never " been injured by the importation " of foreign corn till another cause " had operated upon it ; and then, " and not till then, the distress " ensued."

So then, that war was, after all,

a most excellent concern. The country was, you say, more flourishing and prosperous at the end of it, than it was at the beginning of it. If this were true, then, the war was a good thing. All the interests flourished, you tell us. What a pity it was then that the war ever ceased ; and, what a couple of wretched jackasses, or something a great deal worse and more despicable, must *you and I have been,* who were, during so many years, and you, during more years than I, representing that war as unjust, unnecessary, profligate in principle, desolating in practice, *tending,* to a certainty, and fairly presumed to be *intended,* to *crush the spirit of reform for ever ;* to destroy the reformers root and branch, and to stifle for ever the voice of liberty in England ! What a couple of pretty fools, or of most villanous knaves, you and I must have been for putting forth these representations almost every day of our lives, and for pressing them upon the public by every means in our power : nay, for censuring very harshly, all those of our countrymen who did not agree with us in opinion and who did not join us in effort ! What a couple of pretty scoundrels we must have been, or what cell in any mad-house was dark enough for us, if your opinions, if your assertions, now delivered, respecting that war, be correct.

Here, there is no change of circumstances to justify your change of opinion : no new light could have broke in upon you : you cannot have learned any thing now that you did not know at the time when you condemned that war, its authors, its abettors, its principles, its practice, and when you ascribed to it every calamity that the country was suffering; for, you continued to bellow forth this condemnation until the year 1816 inclusive; that is to say, two years after the conclusion of the war! So that, whether you begin to feel the oystershell creep round you or not, in fulfilment of the hypothesis expressed in the motto of this letter; whether you really be getting into that state which may place you in danger of being, at last, actually gobbled up by some Rag-rook, or his fat-sided or sooty-necked wife; whether you be really getting into this state or, perhaps, rather into the state of a crab more than that of an oyster; whether this be the case is more than I can say; but I surely may venture to say, that, if you were to become an oyster the moment you ceased to be a "consistent politician," an oyster you would have been long and long enough ago.

But there is something in this passage, a great deal more astonishing than any inconsistency on your part. You seem to have been in a trance for the last twenty or thirty years. You seem to have been *dreaming*, and to have gotten a set of indistinct and jumbled notions into your head, respecting what has taken place in the country during that time. You have been a *Member of Parliament all the time, too.* That's strange! For a considerable part of the time you have been "Westminster's Pride and England's Glory:" at any rate, you have been making speeches about politics; about the measures of the Government; you have been finding fault of the acts of the Government; you have been censuring kings, royal

families, nobles, bishops and parsons. You have a thousand times been declaring, and in the most authoritative manner, too, that the House in which you sit ought to be reformed. A man that meddles in this sort of way ought to know *something* at least of the things he is talking about. He ought to be able to recollect something about dates and acts. A man that has been sitting at the passing of all the Acts of Parliament, for so many years, ought to know something of the time when the Acts were passed. Let us try you then by this standard. You here tell us, unless the reporter of the Morning Chronicle be a liar, that " during the *twenty years* pre-" vious to the late change in the " currency, there had been *no dis-*" *tress in the country!*" Awake! Cease to dream, good Member for Westminster. The change in the currency took place in 1819, in the month of July; that is to say, that change was enacted at that time, but no change did really take place until the year 1821. Now, the twenty years previous to 1819, would carry us back to the month of July 1799, just about the time, I believe, that General Brune, who had been a printer's boy in Limosin, was pursuing, in the most unmannerly manner, his late lamented Royal Highness the Duke of York, from Valenciennes to the Helder; or (I really forget which it was), when Buonaparte was thumping old Suwarrow in the Tyrol; and, at any rate, not only much about the time, but at the very time, when you were making the whole country ring with the name of Governor Aris !

This, then, was " *twenty years*

" previous to the late change in " the currency." The twenty years were between July 1799 and July 1819; and, if there were " NO DISTRESS IN THE COUNTRY," during that twenty years, those who reported your speeches during those twenty years, were the most infamous liars that ever marked words upon paper; those who heard your speeches during those twenty years, of which hearers I was one, were all stricken with stupidity, so as to be deprived of their comprehension; or, he who made the speeches was —— —— what I will not describe!

As to the facts, however, since you ask, " What are the facts upon this subject?" I will tell you what the facts are ; namely, that great distress has prevailed in the nation for the last thirty years and more; that, during the "twenty years" in which you now tell us there was " no distress in the country," the poor rates *rose from four millions to eight millions a year*; that in the year 1812, and previous to that, but particularly in 1812, singular distress prevailed in the manufacturing districts; that a woman and a little boy were hanged in Lancashire in that year, the woman, at least, for seizing potatoes, at her own price, out of a market-cart in Manchester; that the combination laws were passed in that year for the purpose of keeping down the starving weavers; that in 1814 and 1815, the most horrible distress prevailed in the farming districts ; that, in those two years, several parishes were left without the means of supporting the poor; that MR. BRAND (now Lord Dacres) stated in the House of Commons that the labouring poor had formed themselves *into bands* and were prowling through the country in search of food ; that a report of the Agricultural Society, or *Board of Agriculture*, stated that horrible distress prevailed in all the Agricultural districts ; that report recommended various most desperate remedies, every one of which clearly indicated that the ailment was most dreadful ; that, in 1816, there were meetings in all parts of the country on the subject of means to alleviate the general distress; that there was one held in London, at which Lord Cochrane attended, when he suggested that the weight of the taxes was the cause of the sufferings, and his conduct on that occasion *received your unbounded applause;* that, in the year 1817, the manufacturers in the north were plunged into, then, unexampled distress ; that they, penetrated by the truths which you had assisted to inculcate, and, acting upon the principles which you had taught, and particularly upon the advice which you had so urgently pressed upon them, petitioned for a Reform of the House of Commons ; that forth came the power-of-imprisonment bill, and opened the dungeons to receive the more intelligent and public-spirited part of these distressed and starving petitioners. Yet, with these facts, notorious to all the world, the newspapers tell us that you boldly asserted that there was " no distress in the country " for twenty years previous to " the late change in the cur- " rency," which change, it is notorious to every body, was not enacted until 1819 ! You will, perhaps, be a little more cautious, for the future, how you challenge the evidence of facts in support of what you assert.

In speaking of the alteration in the value of money caused by the acts of the government, you repeat, with true school-boy-like fidelity, that which you had learned from the everlasting dunnings of the Register. You apply, apparently in a very *adroit* manner, an illustration suggested by the late change in the capacity of the English *corn measure*. You are reported to have said, " some- " thing had been said, in the course " of this discussion, respecting the " change that had been made from " the Winchester Measure to that " which was termed the Imperial " Measure. This change would " illustrate his opinion of the cause " from which all the difficulties of " the country had arisen. He was " one of those who thought that " the distress was altogether arti- " ficial, that it resulted *from bad* " *legislation*, and from bad legis- " lation alone. There had been " another very material change, " not only of the bushel that was " applicable simply to corn, but " of that common measure of the " value of all commodities in the " land, which was called cur- " rency ; and this change had " been nearly in the *same propor-* " *tion* as that from the Winchester " measure to the Imperial, namely, " *about one-third*. The Country " Gentlemen found themselves " embarrassed because they were " called upon to pay the same " amount of taxes out of a dimi- " nished income. Suppose, for " example, an Act of Parliament " had been passed, requiring per- " sons who had entered into con-

" tracts in the *Winchester measure* " *to fulfil them in the Imperial* " *measure*, could such a proceed- " ing be justified ? Would it not " be a gross fraud upon those who " had entered into the contracts ? " This was *just the case of the* " *country. Government*, he be- " lieved, was *not aware* of the " effect it would produce when it " changed the currency."

Very pretty, a very pretty il- lustration :—" *fine words ; I wonder* *where you stole 'em*," as Swift said in answer to some fellow, who had taken the motto of " Libertas et natale solum." Very fine words indeed, Sir Francis ; but did you not read this very illustration, in a petition, sent by me from Long Island in the year 1817, and pub- lished in London early in the year 1818. And here we have to ad- mire the wonderful way in which your memory works. You had forgotten all about the horrible distress which prevailed in the country during the twenty years preceding the year 1819 ; but, you remembered well the simile of the " *Winchester bushel* ;" and, your convenient memory shut itself up so as to prevent you recollecting the author of the illustration !

The truth is, that nothing TRUE and NEW can be said upon this subject. I have said it all : I have said it all a hundred times over : I've said it all in every way, and put it in every shape that fact or argument can assume. I wish the whole band of you did hate the devil with the thousandth part of the cordiality that you hate me :" I wish you feared the devil a thousandth part as much ; but hate or fear, or what you will, my principles you must adopt, my ar- guments you must repeat, almost my very words you must resort to the use of; you may swear and rave, and vow that you will perish rather than come to my shop; but, TO MY SHOP YOU MUST COME, AND TO MY SHOP WILL COME! It is always open to you; there is a cordial reception for you; but you shall come by *day-light*, and in at the *front door*. Mind, I tell you that you shall, and you will, come to that shop: and the longer you keep from it, the worse it will be for you, and I beg you to *mind that too*. In the debate of the 8th of March, Lord Clive had said, that before the rates of duty on corn were fixed, "*the question of the currency ought to be settled*." A very wise observation; for, before you settled on *how many shillings* the farmer ought to receive for his quarter of wheat, you ought to have settled what the *value of each shilling should be;* for, if the present law continue in force until it come into complete operation, I am quite sure that a shilling of May 1829, will be equal in value to two shillings of the present day. That I am sure of. I have no idea that the Thing can go on to that point; but, if it could, such would be the result. Mr. Prosperity Robinson, however, always good humoured and with a tongue that seems to run as glibly, and not much more unde the control of thought, than that of a youth just broke loose from school, gave, as the newspapers tell us, the following answer to Lord Clive: "My Honourable " Friend says, that we ought not " to make any alteration in the " Corn Laws at present, because " we have not settled the question " of the currency. *Why I*

" *thought it was settled. Have I* " *been in a dream on that subject?* " Do I merely fancy that my " Right Honourable Friend the " Secretary of State for the Home " Department introduced a Bill " in 1819 for the purpose of bring- " ing back the currency to its for- " mer condition? It is true that " a temporary deviation from that " Bill took place in 1822, a *devi-* " *ation which I for one greatly* " *regret;* but last year we applied " a practical remedy to the evil " of that deviation by accelerating " the period at which country " notes should cease to be issued. " Really, Sir, I know not *what we* " *can do more with respect to the* " *currency.* I shrewdly suspect, " however, that what is meant by " settling the question of the cur- " rency, is making *an alteration* " *in the standard.* That appears " to be the object recommended " in all the pamphlets which have " been written on the subject; " together with something, of " which I confess I can make " neither head nor tail, but which " is called '*equitable adjust-* " *ment.*' If that be the real ob- " ject, if it be proposed as a pre- " liminary to any change in the " Corn Laws to alter the standard, " I hope to God that such a pro- " position will never be listened to " by this House, *and I am quite* " *sure that as long as his Majes-* " *ty's present Government exists,* " *such a proposition will never be* " *successful.*"

Mr. Peel is by the newspapers reported to have said, in the same debate, that, if a great settling of the money out of the country took place under a limited importation of corn, "let honourable Mem- " bers consider how much more

" extensive it would be if, under " the present system, corn rose to " *eighty shillings*, and the ports, " of necessity, kept open for three " months [hear, hear!]? In the " case of such a scarcity, as " opened the ports in this way, " speculations would be indulged " in to the greatest extent, and " must be paid in gold, so that " *such a run would be caused upon* " *the Bank as must disturb the* " *present currency of the country* " [hear, hear!]. An Honourable " gentleman had *complimented* " him (Mr. Peel) upon having " introduced the measure which " established that currency; let " them now adopt a measure, " which would *bring back upon* " *the country a return of those* " *evils* which a different system " had brought upon them, and " *which he now hoped and trusted* " *were nearly overcome.*" This notion about "*danger of disturb-ing our currency,*" is a very ugly notion. If our currency can be *disturbed* by commercial trans-actions, it is not in so very firm a state as Mr. Robinson would have us believe it is. The chief value, however, of the sayings of these two ministers is this, *that they do really believe that all the one pound notes can be done away with, without producing any very great distress in the country.* We gather this from what they said; and we gather further, *that they are resolved to push on their law, which has doomed the one pound notes to destruc-tion.* If they do that; if they destroy the one pound notes; if their law of last year go into full effect: it never will, I should suppose, because horrible convulsion will stare the Ministers

in the face long before they come to that point: but, if this law were to go into full effect, the average price of English wheat would not exceed about *three shillings and three pence a bushel!* I have not the least doubt upon this subject: the price will in some measure depend upon the seasons. In very dear years the wheat might be five shillings a bushel; but I do think that three and three pence will be about the average. There is one happiness here, which does not frequently accompany us in political discussions; namely, that we shall *soon know who is right and who is wrong.* There you are, all together, both Houses, both parties, all the " collective wisdom," all unanimous in your measure; and here am I to assert that you can never carry the mea-sure into full effect, and still pay the interest of the debt in full.

I must not conclude, and, in-deed, I ought not to go any far-ther, without observing that you (though very late in the day) seem to be of my opinion in this respect. You jostle about, and endeavour to avoid, as much as possible, the appearance of coming to my *shop*; but you do come to it; you say that an " *equi-table adjustment* " is wanted; you want an adjustment of contracts, grounded upon the changes of the value of the money: you, in short, though with a devilish wry face, come to my shop and swallow my dose: you hold up the empty glass to the spectators, who appear to have stared most surprisingly; but not a man of whom appears to have had the pluck to utter a single breath against the doctor, the patient, or the dose. The me-morable words, as reported to us by the Morning Chronicle, were as follows:—"The great object " to be gained for the relief of " the country was, that all its "burdens should be reduced in pro- " portion to the increased value of " the currency. The distresses " of the country resulted from the " existing contracts having been " made during high prices, while " the parties were called upon to " fulfil them at the standard of low " prices. *An equitable adjust-* " *ment of contracts was that which* " *alone could fully relieve the* " *country. He admitted that the* " *difficulty of carrying such a* " *measure into effect would be* " *great ;* but it was *nonsense* to " deny *that it was desirable.*"

That was well said : in none of your excellent speeches against the tyrannical boroughmongers, the fraudulent seat-sellers, the feeders on corruption, bribery, and perjury, did you ever say any thing better than that. But there was a great deal more which you ought to have said. While you were swallowing the dose, the healing dose to which you must all come at last, you forgot (a thing ,which you are very apt to forget by-the-bye) that it was your duty to tell your audience where you got the dose from; and, if you really were convinced that it possessed the healing qualities that you asserted it to possess, it was your duty to avenge the Doc- tor on DADDY COKE, on SUF- FIELD, on KNATCHBULL, on CAL- CRAFT, on JOHN SMITH, on JOHN MARTIN, and, generally, on the whole of the tribe by whom his doses have been so decried and abused. It was your duty also, I think, to explain to Mr. PROSPE- RITY ROBINSON, what was meant by an EQUITABLE ADJUSTMENT,

of which he said he could make neither head nor tail. You will all find the dose at full measure and clear as claret, in NOR- FOLK PETITION, which lies on the table of the house, there to be finally taken into considera- tion and acted upon, and that, too, with the concurrence of that very DADDY COKE who presented it and abused it just now about four years ago.

You see, or affect to see, great difficulty of carrying such a mea- sure into effect. Fox-hunting and aristocrat-seeking must have ob- literated a great deal from your memory. Seventeen years ago, or thereabouts, I proved to you, as clearly as any thing was ever proved to mortal man, that one sin- gle year's collection of the income tax was attended with infinitely more difficulty and with ten thou- sand times as much personal in- convenience and vexation, as this adjustment of contracts would be, beginning at the million-holding fundholder and going down to the annuitant of forty shillings a year. Those cursed dogs and their equally noisy and not half so in- telligent two-legged companions in the chase, must have wholly driven out of your head that which I am sure was once fixed there as firmly as it ever was in mine. Come to me, Sir Francis Burdett : I'll set you down in the very same chair in which you sat down before, though *not in the same building.* It will not take above five minutes to convince you that there is now, as there was then, no difficulty, no obstacle, except those, which are raised and interposed by those and those only who live upon the tithes, the taxes, and the paper monopolies.

But, you have, while you appear to have lost your recollection as to these matters, contracted a twist, a sort of Scotch crotchet, which more than overbalances the good sense which you appear to retain upon the subject. You see great difficulty in carrying an equitable adjustment into effect ; and, yet, you see that Corn Bills, and every thing else will be useless in preserving the estates, if the debt is to be paid in gold and in full. Therefore you fly back for refuge to the paper ; and, your opinion clearly is that we ought to go back to the paper system ; that is to say, to bank restriction and legal tender. In the former part of your speech you say, that as long as the former system (meaning the bank restriction system) remained, " all the interests of the country flourished," and that it is your opinion, that, " *if the currency had not been altered, there would have been no agricultural distress.*" You must, therefore, have been sorry at the passing of PEEL's BILL; but be it observed, however, that you never said a word in opposition to that bill. If any doubt as to your meaning could remain, with regard to your meaning, we have another passage, at the close of this speech, which would effectually remove that doubt :—" He " thought it unlikely that corn " would ever rise to such a price " as to give practical effect to the " proposed Resolutions. It was " true, it might do so through a " famine ; but that, instead of " benefit, would only inflict in- " jury on the agriculturist. He " believed that no country ever " had two such distressing mea- " sures imposed upon it at once

" as this, when the Corn Laws " and the Bullion Act were both " put into operation, each of them " deeply affecting the vital in- " terests of the country. An es- " sential object with every Go- " vernment should be, to prevent " the common measure of value " from being exposed to any fluc- " tuations or alterations. If, in- " stead of restoring the gold stand- " ard, the Government of this " country *had adhered to the " system of currency as it existed " at the close of the war*, applying " such remedies as the case of " Scotland proved would have " been sufficient to remove the " evils belonging to it ; this coun- " try, instead of struggling with " difficulty and distress, *might " have been in a state of unri- " valled and unexampled pros- " perity.*" (Cheers.) Here we have you asserting, that if we had adhered to the currency as it was at the close of the war, we should have never known distress ; so that 'if we had adhered to the vile and fraudulent system of legal tender, to a banishment of the king's coin, and to the placing of the chief prerogative of the king in the hands of a set of note makers and discounters of bills, we should have been the happiest people on earth ! And, I hear this, do I, from one of that most liberal, most virtuous and most respectable class to which it is an honour to belong ! God preserve my throat from ratsbane, halters, and pen-knives ; but I declare to God that I would sooner end my days even as CASTLEREAGH did than entertain an opinion like this ; and, the good of it is, that you yourself *really do not entertain it.* You have a parcel of fellows repeating everlastingly in your ears that a " *paper-money is necessary to a great commercial nation;*" that, as the nation prospered so long with a paper-money it would doubtless prosper with a paper-money again. These stupid houni-kins do not reflect; they are incapable, most likely, of reflecting, and you are charmed to be saved the trouble of doing it : you, therefore, do not reflect upon *two things*; namely, that the *prosperity*, as it is called, which the nation enjoyed, or, rather, appeared to enjoy, in the days of *bank-restriction*, was not "*prosperity*," but a *contracting of debt*; that it was like the effect of mortgaging upon a mortgager, enabling him to live gaily and expensively for the present, but laying in for him a store of embarrassment and poverty for the future. Another thing on which you do not reflect is, the *consequence* of returning to bank-restriction, that being clearly what you mean.. The very first consequence would be a falling of the English funds twenty per cent below the French, and perhaps a great deal more. Two prices would follow in a very short time, and, to get *real* money enough to feed the common soldiers and common sailors, would require laws very little short of the sanguinary code of ROBES-PIERRE. No man would give his gold to a taxgatherer if *bank notes were a legal tender;* and, legal tender they must be, or else they would not circulate at all.

It is impossible to escape this rock, except by going boldly on the rock of low prices, as the Government is now doing. There is no passage, no channel, no round-about way to escape one or the other of these rocks. The lowering of the standard, which Mr. WESTERN has recommended, would only add to the evils of either of the other two. For, it would be an open and barefaced violation of all contracts; and even with that, it would not answer the purpose which its inventors think it would answer. The gold would still leave the country, though a sovereign should be reduced to the diameter of a pea.

The truth is, I verily believe, that you must see, that there *is no remedy except mine;* but that your aristocratical and whiskered companions have so be-bothered you, and so terrified you with the idea of the danger of going back to the Radicals again, that you are, at last, afraid or ashamed to say what you think. I believe, most firmly, that a very large part of the landowners see the matter in its true light; but, that they are ready to knaw their own flesh, when they also see, that it is utterly impossible for them to adopt any measure that will save them, without having the mortification of hearing every man in the nation say, " THAT MEASURE IS COB-BETT'S."

There is, however, another obstacle to their acting upon those principles, and indeed upon that plan, suggested to the House of Commons in the NORFOLK PETITION. Norfolk Petition recommends an equitable adjustment of contracts; and, who but such men as DADDY COKE, SUFFIELD, KNATCHBULL, and the like, ever abused a proposal to do that which is *equitable*. But, Norfolk Petition prays for SOMETHING MORE ; and it is this *something* more, that you "liberal, virtuous and respectable" creatures, exceedingly dislike. And, this brings me to the stating of that important WHY, which I mentioned in my Register of last week, and which I mentioned again at the outset of this letter. It is so manifest, that the taxes are the cause of all the distress; it is so manifest, that the landlords must lose their estates, unless they get high prices wherewith to get these taxes; these things are so manifest; it is so clear to every man of sense, that even you who are a sort of *leviathan*, or, at least, a very stout *grampus*, must become a sprat, in a very few years, unless you have higher prices or *lower* taxes, that no one can be surprised that you should wish for one or the other. No man ever yet was stripped of his very garments by his own consent; and therefore, to blame you or any of the landlords for wishing to keep your estates, is censure absolutely against nature.

But, though no one can blame you, for wishing to preserve your estates, and of course for adopting the means necessary to preserve them, every man in the community has a right, when the means of doing this are various; when some of these means are injurious to the country at large, and some of them not injurious if not beneficial: in that case, every man in the community has a right to censure you, if, in the means which you choose to preserve yourselves, you do injury to the people at large. Now, this is precisely the case, in the present instance. There are two ways of preserving the estates: by a CORN BILL or TAX on BREAD;

and, by a LOWERING of ALL THE TAXES. Men ask, therefore, why it is, that the landlords do not choose the latter instead of the former, when, in the latter case, all the people would be applauding their conduct; while, in the former case, in the bread-taxing case, they are sure to have the whole body of the people against them. Landlords, like other men, do not court hatred and contempt. They will, indeed, very frequently set both at defiance; but they do not wish to have them; they are not things that they voluntarily seek after; and, therefore, as a reduction of the taxes to what they used to be before the late wars, would most effectually preserve their estates, and would most wonderfully delight the great body of the people at the same time, we again and again ask, why do they not prefer to take off the taxes? The answer is, THAT THEY THEMSELVES AND THEIR RELATIONS AND THEIR DEPENDANTS, AND ALL BELONGING TO THEM, ARE VERY GREAT SHARERS IN THE RECEIPT OF THOSE TAXES.

Look into the place list, the pension list, the sinecure list, the list of grantees, the late ambassador list, the colonial lists, the law lists, the dead weight list, the live soldier list, the navy list; look into these; see who have all the great prizes; see who it is, that receive the large sums; inquire who they all belong to; and you will find, that nineteen-twentieths of them are landowners or landowners' connexions. But, there is the CHURCH at the back of all this, with its bishoprics, its deaneries, its prebendaries, its canonships, its immensely rich livings, and its enormous fees; the whole of this Church, all its immense property and revenue, you know, Sir, as well as I know, belongs to the landowners. And, if you remind me that the Church revenue, consisting, as it principally does, of rents, is, like other rents, affected by the taxes, and that the receivers of this revenue must, therefore, like the landowners, naturally wish for a reduction of the taxes: if you remind me of this, I answer, that if you will look into the *Norfolk Petition*, you will. there see a short prayer, *for appropriating to the payment of the fundholders a considerable part of this Church property*! Ah! sayest thou so! This, in short, is the whole history and mystery of the important WHY. Reduce the taxes and you must reduce the interest of the Debt; but, mark me well, Sir; pray mark me well, and whisper it with solemn tone in the ears of your aristocratic cronies; that three hundred thousand families of fundholders; that a hundred thousand families, perhaps, of saving-banks-people, are not to be ruined, and that a million of people in and about this *Wen*, are not to be flung out of the means of satisfying their hunger and their thirst while the landowners keep all that they have got, and while they continue to receive all that they are now receiving through the various channels of places, pensions, sinecures, grants, dead weight, army, navy and church. They are . not to keep all this, while millions are plunged into ruin. An *equitable adjustment*, therefore, must necessarily in-

clude a taking away of these things from the landowners; there can be no equity in any other species of adjustment; and therefore it is, Sir, that the landowners dread an equitable adjustment, as a murderer dreads the sight of the murdered man's ghost. Therefore it is that they talk of *stripping the coats off their backs* rather than reduce the interest of the debt. Various circumstances have tended to make them bold, and regardless of public opinion. They are foolish enough, too, in general, as is usual with men born to power and wealth; but they are not foolish enough to believe,. that they can keep all they have got and continue to get as they have hitherto gotten, while a million of creatures shall be actually raving with hunger, in this metropolis alone. The fundholders may be justly called upon for a reduction of their interest; but, not one single farthing can be deducted. from them, till the landowners give up a far greater part of what they receive out of the taxes. This is *"equitable adjustment,"* which Mr. Robinson may now understand, if he did not understand before. Thus is the great and important WHY explained; and thus I close this Letter.

WM. COBBETT.

P. S. I here below insert my Petition, above mentioned, sent from Long Island. I read it, or rather I looked into it, for the purpose of seeing how you had stolen the illustration about the Winchester bushel. I have numbered the paragraphs of the Petition, and the reader will find your illustration, only stated a little better than you have stated yours, in paragraph 28. The Petition was written ten years ago, come next November; and yet, in paragraph 80, you will find a prayer for an "*equitable adjustment of contracts*," and foretelling the fatal consequences of deferring such *adjustment* till it was too late. You, who seemed to have become the most gentle and indulgent creature in the world, say the Ministers *meant well* in their PEEL's-BILL affair. CANNING, in one of his poems, very justly ridicules the candid cant, which ascribes *bad actions* to *good intentions*. But, Sir, read this Petition once more; and, which is of a great deal more importance, let those who were mere boys now read it; and let these boys who have become men say, whether all the true principles are not here laid down, whether all the dangers are not here anticipated, whether all the sufferings of the country at this moment, would not have been avoided if the Parliament had listened to this petition, which I now send forth, to receive those congratulations which are due to it, in consequence of the fulfilment of all its predictions by the melancholy experience of the years since it was written.

## MR. COBBETT'S PETITION.

*To the Honourable the Commons of the United Kingdom of Great Britain and Ireland, in Parliament assembled.*

The Petition of William Cobbett, of Botley, in the County of Hants, now residing at North Hampstead, in the State of New York, this 20th day of November, 1817,

Humbly sheweth,

1. That your Petitioner, always tremblingly alive to those feelings of respect, reverence and awe, which the character and conduct of your Honourable House are so well calculated to excite and perpetuate in the breasts of all mankind, could not, though thereunto urged by a sense of imperious duty, have been induced thus to venture to beseech even one moment's attention from your Honourable House, had he not been sustained by reflecting on the well-known indulgent and benign deportment of your Honourable House towards all his Majesty's subjects, and more especially towards those who approach you with their petitions.

2. Your Petitioner, though living in safety and happiness; though in no danger of arbitrary arrests; though in no danger of changing his house for a dungeon and his own clothes for a criminal's garb; though surrounded by his friends who can lay their heads on their pillows unhaunted by the apprehension of seeing him no more; though there is no fiscal extortioner to wrest from him his money, and no spy to sell his blood: though thus happily situated, under the protection of a Government, founded on the Common Law of England, and carried on by men, amongst whom bribery, corruption, vote-selling and seat-selling, are not only not as notorious as the sun at noon day, but are wholly unknown and almost unintelligible in point of meaning; though, as the natural consequence of this just and wise Government, your humble Petitioner sees around him no starvation, no beggary, and scarcely

bears be of any of those acts which the law regards as crimes; though his eyes are never shocked by those erections, exhibitions and circumstances inseparable from the ignominious exit of malefactors, and though his ears are never annoyed and his heart wounded by the cries of fatherless children and the widows of men, who have sought shelter from the shame of pecuniary ruin in death inflicted by their own hands; though, in short, your Petitioner is in the midst of a state of things, where all is order, content, peace and good will, yet the calamities of his native country are ever present to his mind, and that true and faithful allegiance which he bears to his lawful king, together with the unalterable attachment which he bears to his country, impel him to submit to your Honourable House his opinions as to the causes of those calamities and his prayer as to the remedy to be adopted, all which, however, he does with sentiments of deference the most complete and of humility the most profound.

3. Powerful as are the motives, by which your Petitioner is actuated, the contemplation of the dignified character and of the renewned wisdom of your Honourable House produces in his mind so complete a conviction of his utter insignificance, that it would be altogether impossible for him to support himself under the thought of becoming an object of the displeasure or contempt of your Honourable House, a thought, however, which is, happily for him, wholly removed from his mind by that great indulgence, that kind condescension, that extreme candour, that charitableness of interpretation, that scorn to listen to abuse of persons who have no power to answer, that magnanimous disdain of taking advantage of involuntary error, that fairness in representing, that abhorrence of foul play, and that more-than-maternal tenderness for a petitioning people, which have, as the nation and the world so well know, invariably marked the proceedings of your Honourable House.

4. Emboldened by reflecting on these facts, not less important to him than they are notorious throughout the world, your Petitioner, though still filled with a sense of his insufficiency for the performance of so arduous a duty, will, with all humility, proceed to submit to your Honourable House his opinions as to the principal causes of the calamities, under which his native country is now suffering, calamities which have already swept away whole classes of the community, and which, if not speedily arrested in their course, appear to your Petitioner likely to produce a total dissolution of society,

5. In pursuance of this object your Petitioner humbly begs to be permitted to state to your Honourable House, that he has seen, in documents of high authority, but to which documents, from his profound respect for the sacred privileges of Parliament, he refrains from directly referring; in these documents your humble Petitioner has seen, that the calamities of the nation have, in great part, at least, been traced back to the *Poor-Laws*, operating, as here laid down, so as to create a *redundant population*, a population exceeding a proportionate exertion of labour and production of food.

2 A

6. Your Petitioner most humbly beseeches your Honourable House to permit him to express his surprise, that this doctrine should have ventured to show its face, while the Statute Book of your Honourable House proves, that the Poor-Laws have existed nearly three hundred years, and while the facts are undeniable, that, during those three hundred years the nation has, for a long space of time, enjoyed the highest degree of prosperity, and that, until now, a redundant population has never been regarded as amongst the effects of that now reprobated code; and, if your Petitioner be indulged by your Honourable House in a permission to express his surprise as to this novelty, he fears not that your Honourable House will refuse to permit him to express his astonishment, and, if he may presume, in your presence, to exercise such a feeling, even his indignation, at the doctrine of an augmented and augmenting population being an *evil*, when it is well known, that the records of your Honourable House contain volumes upon volumes of details, collected and arranged at great expense, to establish the fact of a greatly augmented and augmenting population, as an incontestible proof of greatly augmented and augmenting national prosperity, wealth and power.

7. With not less surprise, and with scarcely less indignation, can your Petitioner hear the calamities of the country ascribed to a surplus of mouths exceeding the quantity of the produce of the exertion of labour, when not only is your Petitioner sure that your Honourable House is well aware, that the food produced by the labour of one labourer is, on an average, more than sufficient to sustain a hundred persons, but when the Statute-Book and other Records of your Honourable House, of not more than twenty months' standing, prove to the world, that your Honourable House imputed all the distresses of the country to a superabundant quantity, not of mouths, but of food; and that, upon this very ground, clearly and formally expressed, in several solemn Reports, your Honourable House proceeded to pass, and actually did pass, and now keep in force, a law, the real as well as the avowed object of which was to raise the price, by diminishing the quantity of human food.

8. Impotent as is your Petitioner, feeble as is his voice, insignificant as he knows his means to be, he, nevertheless, humbly begs to be allowed to express his hope, that your Honourable House will not disdain and treat with scorn the jealousy which he feels for the consistency, nay, for the common sense of your Honourable House, at which qualities in your Honourable House these new doctrines appear to your humble Petitioner to be aiming a mortal blow; for, though your Petitioner is too well aware that the wisdom of your Honourable House is invulnerable to all sorts of assault, yet the pride with which, as an Englishman, he must necessarily contemplate the spotless character of your Honourable House, and the zeal which he feels for your renown, urge him to resent, with all the hostile feelings of his heart, the affront offered to your Honourable House, in the formal and authoritative promulgation of doctrines directly at war with the

records and acts of your Honourable House.

9. Were it the misfortune of your humble Petitioner to be addressing himself to an assembly ignorant of such subjects from the nature of its component parts, or rendered such by a disregard of every thing not connected with the gratification of a desire to amass private wealth, by base and corrupt means; were your humble Petitioner addressing himself to an assembly of this low and disgraceful description, he should think it necessary to endeavour to prove the absolute impossibility of the Poor-Laws and of a Surplus of Mouths having produced the calamities under contemplation; but, having the good fortune to be addressing himself to your Honourable House, not less famed for your profound knowledge of all the various branches of political science than for your extreme disinterestedness and matchless purity, he dares not to seem to suppose such proof to be necessary, more especially as all the propositions of the innovators alluded to stand decidedly negatived in the Reports, the Resolutions, and in the venerated Acts, of your Honourable House; and, therefore, your Petitioner will, without longer trespassing on the great indulgence of your Honourable House, proceed, though with inexpressible deference and humility, to submit to your Honourable House a brief exposition of what he deems to have been, and to be, the real immediate causes of the nation's calamities, of which calamities your humble Petitioner and his family bear their full proportionate burthen.

10. Your Petitioner is confident that your Honourable House will not withhold your candid and ready acquiescence from the following undeniable propositions; to wit: that the Poor-Laws continued in operation, from their first enactment, two hundred and seventy years, without producing, and without having imputed to them, any national calamity;—that, in all ages, there have been alternately times of scarcity and times of plenty, times of high price and times of low price, and that never, until now, a *want of employment* accompanied adverse seasons any more than favourable seasons;—that it is manifest, that the want of employment, which is the great symptom of the present national disease, and which is altogether peculiar to the present times, has not arisen from bad seasons, or high prices of food, it being notorious, that it began to be severely experienced in 1814, and has continued to increase, under all circumstances of good seasons as well as of bad seasons, and of low prices as well as of high prices;—that, in 1815, the advocates for the Corn Bill all proceeded upon the principle, taken by them for granted, that the *low price* of farm produce was the cause of the want of employment and of the national distress;—that the Board of Agriculture, and that a Committee of your Honourable House, made reports containing an assertion of this principle;—that the numerous Reports made to the Board of Agriculture to prove, that want of employment, a great increase of pauperism, and wide ruin amongst farmers and traders, had taken place along with a great reduction in the price of food;—that it was a

then held, by all those who sought the enactment of a Corn Bill, that high prices were necessary in order to remove the *prevalent want of employment*, and in order to diminish pauperism and to prevent the total ruin of landlords, farmers, and traders;—and that, it was upon the ground of these principles and of the evidence produced in support of their truth, that your Honourable House passed the Corn Bill, the real as well as the declared object of which was to raise and keep up the price of the produce of the land.

11. To these propositions; which are altogether undeniable, your Petitioner begs leave to add some others, to the truth of which he also believes your Honourable House will not hastily refuse your assent; to wit: that, though it be possible, that the case may in nature occur, that national calamity may arise from a superabundance of population, such calamity can never arise from this cause, while the already enclosed lands of the country are imperfectly cultivated;—that the already enclosed lands of the kingdom admit of a great quantity of additional labour being profitably employed upon them;—that this proposition has been maintained in several Reports sanctioned by your Honourable House;—and that, therefore, it is an obvious conclusion, that it is not the want of materials whereon to employ labour, but the want of means to pay for that labour, from which the now-deeply-felt want of employment has arisen.

12. That this want of employment, together with all the dreadful calamities, of which it is

only one characteristic, should have arisen from *a sudden transition from war to peace*, is in such direct hostility to the experience of the world, as well as to the dictates of reason, that your Petitioner is sure that the wisdom of your Honourable House will treat with scorn the advancing of a doctrine so preposterous;—that the transitions from war to peace, being changes from one state to another, which states are directly opposite in their natures, and can by no possibility co-exist in any degree, *must always be sudden;* —that changes of this sort have taken place in all the civilized nations in the world, a great number of times, and that never, until now, has it happened, that such a change has produced great and general national calamity;—that a transition from war to peace has, in all former cases, if accompanied by success, or by no loss of dominion, in war, invariably been attended by a return, or an increase, of national prosperity and happiness;—that, from the nature of things this must be, seeing that peace naturally restores to productive labour the enjoyment of a large part of that which war requires to be given to unproductive labour, seeing that peace naturally renders certain many things which war keeps in a state of uncertainty, and seeing that a great mass of individual bodily and mental suffering is removed by a change from war to peace, on all which and numerous other grounds, all mankind speak of the *calamities of war* and the *blessings of peace* as they speak of the *torments of hell* and the *enjoyments of heaven.*

13. That, besides what has, in

the above propositions; been; by your Petitioner, most humbly submitted to the wisdom of your Honourable House, he begs permission to add, that even the experience of the present case affords ample ground for asserting, that a transition from war to peace has not been the cause of the nation's distresses and calamities, in proof of which your Petitioner has only to remind your Honourable House, that the want of employment and all the other symptoms of national pressure, began to assume their present character in the autumn of the year 1818, and that the progress of the calamity through war and through peace, through high prices and through low prices, through plenty and through scarcity of food, has been undeviating from that time to this, though, at particular periods, its pace has been rendered quicker or slower, by the adventitious circumstances of seasons or of foreign commerce.

14. In the face of these undeniable propositions, these notorious facts; in the face of the experience of all civilized nations in all ages; in the face of reason and of nature: in the face of these, no one will, your Petitioner would fain hope, have the hardihood to insult your Honourable House, by persevering in imputing the calamities of the nation to causes so perfectly imaginary, and, if they were real, so entirely inadequate to the producing of such tremendous effects.

15. That no effect can proceed from an inadequate cause, is a proposition not necessary to be stated to your Honourable House, and, it is not less obvious, that the cause of great and general na-

tional calamity, bordering on an extermination of the people, must be not only powerful in its nature, but all-searching in the objects of its operation and influence: in short, your Petitioner scruples not to express his conviction, that when your Honourable House shall deign to turn your great contemplative powers to the *amount of the taxes* and the operation of the *paper-money system*, you will seek no farther for a *cause* of the calamities of the country, and that the *remedy* will not long remain hidden from your sight.

16. It is so well known, it must be so obvious to common sense, that the welfare of every community must depend on productive labour receiving just remuneration; that labour is property, and that not to pay for it when received, or to take from it its produce, is to destroy, or set at nought, the vital principles of property; that to take from those who labour and give to those who do not labour, is to put a band round the arms and prevent the blood from flowing into the hands, while the hands, thus benumbed, are called upon to produce food for the body; that in whatever degree a man *pays* without receiving *to his own use* the *worth in return*, he is *the poorer*; that what a man pays in taxes has no channel whereby to return to him other than the channels by which he may expect the return of money lost by him at the gaming-table or on the highway: these things are so well known, they are truths so obvious, that your Petitioner begs your Honourable House to be assured, that he states them merely to show his great

anxiety to keep clear of all conclusions, absurd in themselves, or in anywise offensive to your Honourable House, without whose kind indulgence he is but too conscious that he is less than nothing.

17. Deeply penetrated with this sense of his own weakness, but feeling strong in his reliance on the cherishing countenance of your Honourable House, your humble Petitioner proceeds to express his conviction, that, as in whatever degree a man pays without receiving to his own use the worth in return he must in that degree be poor, it inevitably follows, that, in whatever degree the great mass of the people pay without receiving to their use the worth in return, they must also be the poorer; and he begs leave to think, that from these premises it again inevitably follows, that taxes, in proportion to their amount, produce straightened means in some of the classes of society, poverty in other classes, actual want of a sufficiency of food and raiment in a third, and extreme misery bordering on starvation and accompanied with numerous crimes, and occasional madness, and death, in the lowest and most numerous class of all; whence it has come to pass in our unhappy country, that Taxes, Public Debts, Standing Armies, Military Staffs and Colleges, Lists of Placemen and Placewomen and Pensioners, Police Establishments, Penal Laws, Poor-houses, Jails, and new modes and means of Hanging and Transporting, have all gone on increasing together.

18. The thought of appearing to prefer, in any respect, any country in the world before his own country, would be too painful for your Petitioner to endure, and he trusts that your Honourable House, in your well-known justice, will not suppose him to entertain such a thought, merely because he states to your Honourable House, that, in the country, which now affords him protection against dungeons and dealers in human blood, there are few taxes, and those in amount so insignificant as for their very existence to be unknown to the far greater part of the people; and, that the consequences are, that instances of misery and of crimes are so rare as to be a subject of wonder; that ease, happiness and content every where abound; and that an increase of population is regarded as a blessing and not as a curse.

19. Manifest, however, as your Petitioner humbly presumes your Honourable House will perceive it to be, that taxes, in proportion to their amount, must necessarily occasion poverty and all the evils attendant on poverty, and that the amount of the taxes in the kingdom is calculated to produce such effects in an unprecedented degree, yet he ventures, under the indulgence of your Honourable House, to express his conviction, that this cause of evil has received great additional and most mischievous force from the co-operation of a *paper-money*, forced into circulation and acceptance by divers artful and unjust contrivances, and *changeable in its value* at the pleasure of those by whom it has been made, issued and managed.

20. Your Petitioner fears not to state, that, if your Honourable House will be pleased to refer to the history of the calamities and convulsions, which have taken place in civilized states, during

the last hundred and twenty years, you will find, that one of the most powerful of the causes has been a false, or fictitious money, under the denomination of Bills, Notes, Assignats, and others, and always composed of Paper, bearing on it a promise to pay such or such sums to the bearer or possessor of such paper. In France, many years ago, a scheme of this description spread ruin far and wide, and, of late years, it has actually produced, by its co-operation with heavy and vexatious taxes, two distinct and sanguinary revolutions. In some of those colonies of North America, which are now the United States, a colonial paper-money, introduced more than sixty years ago, spread ruin and beggary amongst a people, who appeared to be so happily situated as to have no want ungratified. In the States of Austria, in Denmark, in Sweden, and in every other country, where such a system of fiction has prevailed, ruin and misery have always, sooner or later, been its fruits, of which fruits the United States themselves have not, as your Petitioner will hereafter beg leave to be permitted to show, wholly escaped the bitter taste.

21. The chief reason of this universally evil effect of such fictions is not less evident than the effect itself is notorious. Money being the universal standard, by comparison with which the value of all things bought and sold is ascertained; or, being the sign, which represents the value of all things which men buy, sell, or with regard to which they enter into contracts of loan, or otherwise, in a pecuniary way; such being the character of, or the office per-

formed by, money, and money being inseparable from the daily concerns of every man from the Prince to the Ploughman, it is obvious, that when money, when this standard of value, is *changeable*, whether at pleasure or from accident, and especially if the changes be sudden as to time and great in degree, a real violation of contracts, a transfer of property unjustly from one to another and ruin, misery and confusion must ensue.

22. It is out of these just notions of the sacredness of money, as a standard of value and as the vital principle of contracts, that the law has arisen which considers to be *treason* the counterfeiting of the coin of the realm, such act of counterfeiting being to strike at the very root of society itself; and, as your Petitioner humbly presumes to believe, *counterfeiting* is neither more nor less than *a changing of the value of money*, an operation, which, when it takes place partially and in a small degree, produces injuries in a similar extent; but, when such changing of the standard of value is *general*, *sudden*, and, with regard to the community, as *secretly performed* as the works of the traitorous coiner, then it becomes a scourge more mortal than the pestilence that walketh by day and the arrow that flieth by night.

23. If your humble Petitioner were addressing himself to a body less enlightened than your Honourable House; if he had the misfortune to have to offer his opinions and prayers to men so profoundly ignorant of all the principles of political economy as to hope to cure the national calamities by voluntary contributions, or by setting

labourers to dig holes one day and to fill them up the next; if he had the mortification to be addressing his prayers to men of this shallow and vulgar-minded description, he might think it necessary to illustrate his representations by supposing the number of cubic inches of the Winchester bushel, or the number of ounces of the pound weight, or the number of longitudinal inches of the foot measure, to be, all of a sudden, changed in a great degree, and without any previous notice to the public; and he is certain that even the most stupid assembly that ever disgraced the forms of legislation would perceive, that such changes would cause a real violation of innumerable contracts, and that distress and ruin to innumerable persons must inevitably follow; but, having the unspeakable felicity to be addressing himself to your Honourable House, whose fame for profundity is surpassed only by your fame for candour and purity, your Petitioner has no need to resort to illustrations of any kind, and, therefore, hastened on by the fear of abusing the well-known indulgence of your Honourable House, he proceeds to trace to your Honourable House the progress of this unrelenting scourge, called Paper-Money.

24. In the early stages of its existence this mortal enemy of human happiness and freedom, was, like the first fibres of the cancer, felt only in occasional twitches; but, as it advanced in bulk, its effects became more and more regularly and severely felt, till, at last, it has produced all the deadly effects now before our eyes. For a long series of years its visible effects

were a regular increase of gambling, of fraud, and of all the vices engendered by a dependence on trick rather than on industry and talent; and its visible effects were a gradual changing of the real property of the country from the hands of the ancient owners into the hands of the dealers in Paper-Money, a gradual undermining of that natural magistracy which is ever the best bond of society, a consequent gradual hardening of the penal laws, and finally a gradually produced dislocation of all the joints and ligaments which held together without grudging and without violence all the orders of that admirable community that formed the people of England. As the powers of Paper-Money increased real property naturally grew into larger parcels, small farms became gradually less numerous, till, at last, they became wholly extinguished, while their industrious and virtuous cultivators sunk down into a state of labourers, and while the labourers, seeing no hope of ever acquiring any share of the profits of their labour, became less and less desirous of abstaining from demands on the parish rates.

25. Such, as your Honourable House must have perceived, were amongst the effects of this baleful system of Paper-Money previous to the year 1797, when it assumed a bolder and more desperate character; for, at that period, the makers and issuers of this fictitious representative of value, who had amassed to themselves, in exchange for their paper, large portions of the real wealth of the nation, under promises to exchange the paper into

gold at the pleasure of the holder, did, all of a sudden, and by an act unparalleled in its extent as well as in its wickedness, fulfil to the very letter the predictions of that Great Political Writer, who had foretold, only a year before, that such would be their conduct. Thence forward these makers and issuers poured forth their fictitious money so as to enhance prices to an astonishing degree, and, when they had given their paper in exchange for men's real property, for their estates in fee, or, more generally, in exchange for mortgages or other securities, they suddenly, and without any previous notice, so diminished the quantity of their paper in circulation as to lower prices one half in nominal amount, to lower the nominal value of real property, of stock in trade and of labour; and they thus, by a changing of the standard of value at their own arbitrary will, acquired a legal demand upon all borrowers to double the real amount of the sums lent.

26. When your Honourable House reflects, that it is in the class of *borrowers* that you see all the greatest motives to exertion, all the most active and most enterprising part of the persons engaged in agriculture, trade, manufactures, and commerce; when your Honourable House reflects on this circumstance, and sees clearly, as your Petitioner humbly presumes you will, the mortal blow that this numerous and active part of the community must have received from this arbitrary change in the standard of value, he is quite sure that your Honourable House will need seek no farther for the cause of a want of employment and great national misery; and yet, in this sweeping violation of all private contracts, in this ruinous oppression of private borrowers, in this stab into the heart of individual industry, enterprize and hope, your Petitioner is convinced that your Honourable House will permit him to say, that there is seen a part only of the cruel effects of this arbitrary changing of the standard of value; for, it must be manifest to your Honourable House, that, if the private borrower must inevitably be ruined by this fraudulent operation, the bare possibility of which never could have entered his mind at the time of receiving the loan, the whole nation, except the lenders to the public and except those persons who derived emolument from the taxes, must also be ruined by the same operation, by which, in fact, the sums required in taxes, great as those sums were, were doubled in real amount.

27. Here then, and, as your Petitioner presumes humbly to express his belief, here only, is the real immediate cause of the present frightful calamities of the nation; for, when your Honourable House reflects on the numerousness of the class of borrowers, on the great portion of the productive labour of the country which this class sets and keeps in motion; when you reflect on the vast proportion of the product of labour which the taxes take away from those who labour and convey to those who do not labour; when you reflect that the total ruin of many borrowers, the straightened means of others, and the discouragement of all, must necessarily cause the money raised in taxes

and paid to the lenders to be retained in a state of comparative inactivity, and, in numerous instances, transferred in loans public and private and in other investments to foreign countries; when your Honourable House reflects on these circumstances, your Petitioner is sure that your Honourable House will here find the real immediate cause of the nation's calamities, and that all the new notions of the injurious effect of the Poor-Laws, of a Surplus-Population, and of a Sudden Transition from War to Peace, will, at once, vanish, leaving behind them nothing but amazement at the monstrousness of their folly.

28. Could it be possible, however, for a doubt still to remain in the mind of your Honourable House, the experience of the United States of America must, as your Petitioner confidently believes, wholly remove that doubt; for, though the whole of the principal of the Public Debt in this country does not exceed in amount the annual interest of the debt with which our country is unhappily burthened; though the taxes here be so light as for their very existence to be absolutely unknown to the great mass of the community; yet, *from a sudden diminution of the quantity of Paper-Money* which had been in circulation previously to 1815, ruin and misery were spread far and wide over all the commercial part of the community, a consequent stagnation of trade ensued, and, for the first time in the history of the country, a want of employment and pauperism and soup-shops began to rear their hideous heads, and to produce what in their very nature they must pro-

duce, idleness, mendicity, and crimes. A wise and economical system of Government, an absence of standing armies, a reliance on the hearty good will of the people for the defence and due execution of the laws, a return, in peace, to all the habits and diminished expenses of peace, will, it is hoped, wholly eradicate the evils produced by the Paper-Money, and which evils had been confined to the commercial towns and their immediate environs; but, if a country, situated as to pecuniary matters, and governed, as the United States are, could feel sensibly a blow from a sudden changing of the standard of value; if a country, in which there is scarcely any such thing as a lease of lands, where mortgages are comparatively unknown, and where borrowing for purposes of agriculture and trade in general is carried to so trifling an extent; if, in such a country, the changing of the standard of value could be felt as a blow at its prosperity, and could produce, even in the smallest degree, *a want of employment*, while the richest of land is calling for cultivators, your Honourable House will not, your petitioner is certain, entertain any doubt that a cause, similar in its nature but a thousand-fold greater in degree, has, as it necessarily must have, produced proportionate calamities in England.

29. Therefore, as your humble Petitioner has the unutterable happiness to be confident that he shall be honoured with the concurrence of your Honourable House as to the great immediate *cause* of the nation's manifold sufferings, so is he not less confident, that, in seeking for a *remedy*, your

Honourable House will reject, as the vision of weak-minded dreamers, any project for altering the Poor-Laws, and that you will treat with ineffable contempt and scorn all the schemes for collecting the savings of a starving people, for preventing the labouring classes from marrying, and for causing holes to be dug one day and filled up the next; but, that, following the dictates of your own instinctive energy and wisdom, you will put an end to the evil by removing the cause; and that, as that cause manifestly is the taxes which drain away from productive labour so large a portion of its fruits to be, as above stated, conveyed, by the hands of the lenders of Paper-Money, into unproductive or foreign depositories, you will largely reduce the proportion of the money so raised and so conveyed away.

30. Therefore, your Petitioner, full of confidence in the well-known justice of your Honourable House, and fearing that he may already have trespassed beyond the bounds even of that great patience and indulgence which are traits so prominent in the now-well-established character of your Honourable House, proceeds, with all humility, distinctly to pray, that your Honourable House will be pleased, by measures, which, to your great wisdom may seem meet, to cause the interest of the Public Debt to be reduced; to cause all salaries, pensions and pay of every description proceeding from the public money to be reduced; to cause a revision of contracts between lenders and borrowers and letters and renters: so that the nation at large and that individuals in their several particular

cases, may receive from the hands of your Honourable House protection from that injustice, which has been done them by an arbitrary change in the standard of value, and which change has produced such dreadful and so notorious calamities.

31. To this his humble and earnest prayer your Petitioner begs leave only to add a representation, that, long foreseeing the calamities, which have now fallen upon his country with such astounding force, your Petitioner has, during eleven years, omitted no means within his humble sphere and capacity to produce the adoption of measures such as those now humbly submitted to the transcendent wisdom of your Honourable House; and that, upon several occasions, he has earnestly besought members of your Honourable House to aid him, by proposing resolutions or otherwise, in the discharge of this important public duty; but, that, whether from indolence, indecision, or some other cause to your Petitioner unknown, he has never been able to obtain any thing beyond repeatedly broken promises of such aid; and, therefore it is that your Petitioner, in whose breast no time, no distance, no calamity, no injuries, can ever extinguish or damp the ardent love which he has always borne his native country, has now ventured, though with great deference and humility, to address directly to your Honourable House the exposition and prayer contained in this his most humble Petition.

And your Petitioner,
As in all duty and humility bound,
Will ever pray.
WM. COBBETT.

## MARKETS.

Average Prices of CORN throughout ENGLAND, for the week ending March 2.

*Per Quarter.*

|  | s. | d. |  | s. | d. |
|---|---|---|---|---|---|
| Wheat .. | 54 | 0 | Rye .... | 38 | 10 |
| Barley .. | 37 | 1 | Beans ... | 46 | 3 |
| Oats .... | 29 | 9 | Pease'... | 49 | 11 |

Total Quantity of Corn returned as
Sold in the Maritime Districts, for
the week ended March 2.

|  | Qrs. |  | Qrs. |
|---|---|---|---|
| Wheat.. | 35,831 | Rye ..... | 266 |
| Barley . | 27,332 | Beans . .. | 3,338 |
| Oats ... | 10,159 | Pease .... | 1,385 |

*Corn Exchange, Mark Lane.*

Quantities and Prices of British
Corn, &o. sold and delivered in
this Market, during the week ended
Saturday, March 3.

|  | Qrs. | £. | s. | d. |  | s. | d. |
|---|---|---|---|---|---|---|---|
| Wheat.. | 3,537 for 10,577 | 1 | 5 | Average,58 | 1 |
| Barley..5,459 | ..10,494 | 18 | 1 | ..........36 | 5 |
| Oats.. | 4,065 | .. 7,679 | 18 | 0 | ..........38 | 11 |
| Rye.... | — | .. | 0 | 0 | 0 | ..........0 | 0 |
| Beans..1,210 | .. 2,889 | 3 | 7 | ..........47 | 9 |
| Pease.. | 851 | .. 2,216 | 2 | 1 | ..........60 | 3 |

Friday, March 9.—The arrivals
of Grain this week are small, owing
to the boisterous weather. As the
top price of Flour has not yet advanced, the Wheat trade has become
dull at the advance of last Monday.
Barley and Beans are heavy in sale,
and hardly maintain the terms last
quoted. There has been little done
in the Oat trade this week, and the
prices of this article are unaltered.

Monday, March 12.—The ex-
tremely boisterous state of the
weather, during the early part of
last week, kept the supplies back,
but, towards the close of the week,
the arrivals increased, and this morning, having a further accession of
samples, the market presents a tolerably full appearance of nearly all
descriptions of Grain. The attempts
to advance the top price of Flour
having entirely failed, the Wheat
trade has become very dull, and
prices may be reported 2s. to 3s. per
qr. lower than on Monday last.

The Barley trade is very heavy,
and as very little, even of Malting
quality, exceeds 40s. the quarter, the
trade may therefore be stated lower.
Beans and Pease are more plentiful
than of late, and each kind of these
articles, are quoted 1s. per quarter
cheaper. There has been so limited
a demand for Oats to-day, that to
effect any sales, 1s. per quarter reduction in price must be submitted
to. Beans, Pease and Oats, fit for
*Seed*, are so scarce, as to sell at prices
considerably above the annexed quotations. Spring Tares are again considerably advanced; some few are
held as high as 14s. per bushel.

*Price on board Ship as under.*

Flour, per sack ......46s. — 50s.
—— Seconds ........42s. — 44s.
—— North Country ..40s. — 44s.

Account of Wheat, &c. arrived in the Port of London, from March 5 to March 10, both inclusive.

| | Qrs. | | Qrs. |
|---|---|---|---|
| Wheat .. | 4,490 | Tares .... | 313 |
| Barley .. | 4,393 | Linseed .. | 1819 |
| Malt .... | 8,561 | Rapeseed . | — |
| Oats .... | 5,923 | Brank .. | — |
| Beans ... | 1,151 | Mustard.. | 8 |
| Flour .... | 9,915 | Flax .... | — |
| Rye .... | 71 | Hemp ... | 69 |
| Pease.... | 1,185 | Seeds ... | 50 |

Foreign.—Oats, 1,865 ; and Beans, 5,256 quarters.

Monday, March 12.—The arrivals from Ireland last week were, 5,363 casks of Butter, and 4,426 bales of Bacon; and from Foreign Ports, 129 casks of Butter. The stock of fine Butter is unusually small, and very high prices are obtained for such. The stock of Bacon is very large, prices nearly as before; demand moderate.

## HOPS.

Price of Hops, per Cwt. in the Borough.

Monday, March 12.—Our trade remains dull, but we cannot quote any alteration in price since last report. Currency as under :—Kent, pockets, from 90s. to 120s.; bags, 76s. to 90s. Sussex pockets, 82s. to 92s.; bags, 66s. to 74s.

Maidstone, March 8.—The Hop Trade has been very dull this week, and what few bags were sold, did not fetch such prices as before.

Price of Bread.—The price of the 4lb. Loaf is stated at 9d. by the full-priced Bakers.

## COAL MARKET, March 9.

Ships at Market. Ships sold. Price.
28 Newcastle 24 ..33s. 0d. to 40s. 3d.
20 Sunderland 17 ..35s. 0d.— 41s. 9d.

SMITHFIELD, Monday, March 12.

Though the number of sheep at this market on Friday would be considered a customary supply, yet an eagerness of demand occasioned an extraordinary rise in price, as compared with that day week, say 7s. or 8s. a-head, and in some instances more. Good Beef was also a ready sale, on the terms fully of last Monday.—The supply to this day's market is moderate. In Beef there is little or no alteration; it sells quite as well as on Monday last; and here and there, for choice things, something more has been given; but Mutton does not sell so high as on Friday. The best polled Sheep reach 4s. 10d., and shorn 4s. 4d., and the highest price for Downs is 5s. Trade pretty good.

Per Stone of 8 pounds (alive).

| | s. | d. | s. | d. |
|---|---|---|---|---|
| Beef . . . . | 3 | 10 | to 5 | 0 |
| Mutton ... | 4 | 0 | — 5 | 0 |
| Veal ..... | 5 | 0 | — 5 | 8 |
| Pork..... | 4 | 8 | — 5 | 6 |
| Lamb .... | 0 | 0 | — 0 | 0 |

| Beasts . . | 2,261 | Sheep .. | 20,120 |
|---|---|---|---|
| Calves ... | 182 | Pigs ... | 185 |

NEWGATE, (same day.)

Per Stone of 8 pounds (dead).

| | s. | d. | s. | d. |
|---|---|---|---|---|
| Beef ..... | 3 | 4 | to 4 | 4 |
| Mutton ... | 3 | 4 | — 4 | 2 |
| Veal ..... | 3 | 8 | — 5 | 8 |
| Pork ..... | 3 | 8 | — 5 | 8 |
| Lamb .... | 0 | 0 | — 0 | 0 |

LEADENHALL, (same day.)

Per Stone of 8 pounds (dead).

| | s. | d. | s. | d. |
|---|---|---|---|---|
| Beef .... | 3 | 2 | to 4 | 6 |
| Mutton ... | 3 | 2 | — 4 | 2 |
| Veal .... | 4 | 0 | — 5 | 8 |
| Pork ..... | 4 | 4 | — 6 | 0 |
| Lamb .... | 0 | 0 | — 0 | 0 |

## POTATOES.

SPITALFIELDS, per Ton.

|  | l. s. | l. s. |
|---|---|---|
| Ox-Nobles | 3 10 to | 3 15 |
| Middlings | 0 0 — | 0 0 |
| Chats | 2 0 — | 0 0 |
| Common Red | 0 0 — | 0 0 |
| Onions, 0s. 0d.—0s. 0d. per bush. |  |  |

BOROUGH, per Ton.

|  | l. s. | l. s. |
|---|---|---|
| Ox-Nobles | 3 10 to | 4 0 |
| Middlings | 3 10 — | 0 0 |
| Chats | 2 0 — | 0 0 |
| Common Red | 3 10 — | 4 0 |

## HAY and STRAW, per Load.

Smithfield.—Hay....90s. to 115s.

Straw...32s. to 38s.

Clover. 110s. to 125s.

St. James's.—Hay.... 84s. to 135s.

Straw .. 34s. to 45s.

Clover. 120s. to 135s.

Whitechapel.--Hay....75s. to 115s.

Straw...32s. to 36s.

Clover..80s. to 135s.

## AVERAGE PRICE OF CORN, sold in the Maritime Counties of England and Wales, for the Week ended March 2, 1827.

|  | Wheat. | | Barley. | | Oats. | |
|---|---|---|---|---|---|---|
|  | s. | d. | s. | d. | s. | d. |
| London* | 56 | 5 | 38 | 6 | 30 | 9 |
| Essex | 56 | 5 | 37 | 6 | 28 | 4 |
| Kent | 55 | 8 | 38 | 10 | 30 | 6 |
| Sussex | 54 | 0 | 42 | 1 | 28 | 9 |
| Suffolk | 54 | 0 | 36 | 3 | 29 | 5 |
| Cambridgeshire | 54 | 4 | 35 | 4 | 26 | 8 |
| Norfolk | 52 | 0 | 35 | 3 | 29 | 0 |
| Lincolnshire | 53 | 7 | 40 | 11 | 29 | 0 |
| Yorkshire | 52 | 3 | 39 | 10 | 29 | 1 |
| Durham | 53 | 9 | 40 | 9 | 32 | 0 |
| Northumberland | 52 | 0 | 37 | 8 | 33 | 6 |
| Cumberland | 59 | 6 | 35 | 6 | 34 | 4 |
| Westmoreland | 59 | 7 | 45 | 0 | 36 | 7 |
| Lancashire | 59 | 3 | 41 | 0 | 33 | 9 |
| Cheshire | 57 | 7 | 48 | 0 | 34 | 5 |
| Gloucestershire | 58 | 0 | 43 | 10 | 38 | 3 |
| Somersetshire | 55 | 4 | 39 | 11 | 31 | 8 |
| Monmouthshire | 58 | 0 | 49 | 4 | 0 | 0 |
| Devonshire | 54 | 9 | 37 | 4 | 24 | 5 |
| Cornwall | 56 | 9 | 37 | 0 | 32 | 1 |
| Dorsetshire | 52 | 0 | 38 | 4 | 35 | 0 |
| Hampshire | 54 | 3 | 38 | 4 | 28 | 4 |
| North Wales | 59 | 8 | 44 | 1 | 29 | 3 |
| South Wales | 57 | 4 | 39 | 4 | 26 | 1 |

* The London Average is always that of the Week preceding.

*Liverpool,* March 6.—The arrivals of Grain from Ireland, and Coastways, have been very considerable, and the sales, up to last Saturday, were very languid, at previous quotations ; but on the arrival here of the Resolutions proposed by his Majesty's Ministers, a re-action immediately took place, when we had an advance of every description of Wheat of 4d. to 6d. per 70 lbs. In other Grain there was no alteration.

Imported into Liverpool, from February 27th to March 5th, 1827, inclusive:—Wheat, 13,364; Barley, 5,277 ; Oats, 32,617 ; Rye, 513 ; Malt, 2,812 ; Beans, 1,300 ; Pease, 147 quarters. Flour, 3,629 sacks, per 280 lbs. Oatmeal, 1,713 packs, per 240 lbs. American Flour, 1,435 barrels.

*Bristol,* March 10.—The Corn Markets at this place are by no means lively. Considerable quantities of foreign Beans, Oats, and Indian Corn, have been imported here within the last ten or twelve days, which, in some degree, accounts for the dullness in our Markets. Supplies good, and present prices about as follow:—Wheat, from 6s. to 7s. 9d. ; Barley, 4s. 4½d. to 5s. 9d.; Beans, 5s. 6d. to 8s. 3d. ; Oats, 2s. 3d. to 4s. 1½d. ; and Malt, 6s. to 8s. per bushel, Imperial. Flour, Seconds, 34s. to 44s. per bag.

*Chelmsford,* March 8.—The prices of Grain at our market this day as under : — White Wheat, 62s. to 68s. ; Red ditto, 56s. to 62s. ; Barley, 36s. to 40s.; Oats, 28s. to 35s. ; Beans, tick, 46s. to 50s. ; Pease, Grey, 48s. to 52s. per quarter.

*Guildford,* March 10.—Wheat, new, for mealing, 15l. to 17l. 15s. per load. Barley, 37s. to 40s.; Oats, 33s. to 40s. ; Beans, 53s. to 58s.; Pease, grey, 60s. to 62s. ; ditto, boilers, 62s. to 64s. per quarter. Tares, 12s. per bushel.

*Horncastle,* March 10.—We had a moderate supply of Wheat. Barley and Oats were plentiful, and something lower. Other articles nearly as last week.—Wheat, from 56s. to 58s. ; Barley, 35s. to 38s. ; Oats, 32s. to 38s. ; Pease, 68s. to 70s. ; Beans, 58s. to 60s. ; and Rye from 42s. to 45s. per quarter.

*Manchester,* March 10.—Since this day week the Corn Trade has been in a very unsettled state. The advance in the London market on Monday, and Liverpool on Tuesday, caused the holders of Wheat and Flour to demand higher rates, which were only complied with by necessitous buyers : the Millers and Bakers who were pretty well stocked, declined purchasing until they were nearer out. Our Market to-day was well attended, and there was a fair demand for fine Wheats, at an advance of 4d. to 6d. per 70 lbs. The arrivals of Oats into Liverpool being large, a small advance of ¼d. per 45 lbs. was with difficulty obtained. Boiling Pease being scarce, an advance of 3d. per bushel was readily obtained. Malt dull sale. Flour has been held at 3s. per sack advance, but only 1s. or 2s. could be obtained. In Barley and Beans no alteration.

*Newcastle-on-Tyne,* March 10.—We had this morning the largest supply of Wheat that we have had this season from the farmers, and we had also some arrivals coastwise. The market commenced by the sellers demanding much higher prices, but the millers succeeded in buying at not more than 2s. and 3s. per quarter above the prices of last Saturday. Rye is rather dull sale.

*Reading,* March 10.—We had a small supply of Wheat at our market this day, the general quality of which was not so good as that of the week before, which caused a dull sale, at much the same prices. Old Wheat, 57s. to 68s.; New, 55s. to 68s. per quarter by the Imperial measure. The quantity of Barley was rather short, but it met a heavy sale, at a reduction of 1s. per quarter.

## COUNTRY CATTLE AND MEAT MARKETS, &c.

*Horncastle*, March 10.—Beef, 8s. per stone of 14 lbs.; Mutton, 7d.; Pork, 6d. to 7d.; and Veal, 7d. to 8d. per lb.

*Manchester* Smithfield Market, March 7.—Our supply of Beasts and Sheep to this day's market was not so large as last week, but fully adequate to the demand, and only the best qualities reached our highest quotations. Veal being scarce and more in demand, an advance of ½d. per lb. was readily complied with. The supply of Pigs was large (principally Irish), and met tolerably free sale, at an advance of ½d. per lb.—Beef, 5d. to 7d.; Mutton, 6½d. to 7½d.; Veal, 6d. to 7½d.; and Pork, 4½d. to 6d. per lb. sinking offal.

At *Morpeth* Market, March 7, there was a good supply of Cattle; and there being a great demand, both sold readily, at a little advance in price. —Beef, 5s. 6d. to 6s. 6d; Mutton, 7s. to 8s. per stone, sinking offal.

*Norwich Castle Meadow*, March 10.—A large supply of fat Cattle to-day caused many of them to go off unsold; those disposed of, were at 7s. 6d. to 8s. per stone of 14 lbs. sinking offal; the supply of Store Stock was also good; Scots sold at 3s. 9d. to 4s. per stone when fat; only a few Shorthorns at 3s. to 3s. 6d.; Only a small number of Sheep penned; Shearlings, 24s. to 29s.; fat ones to 35s.; Hoggets, 16s. to 23s.; Pigs, a flat sale. Meat: Beef, 6½d. to 8½d.; Veal, 6d. to 8d.; Mutton, 5½d. to 6½d., and Pork, 5½d. to 8d. per lb.

# COBBETT'S WEEKLY REGISTER.

**Vol. 61.—No. 13.]** LONDON, SATURDAY, March 24, 1827. [*Price 6d.*

" And they said, the GREAT MEN are surely slain, and they have *smitten one another* : now therefore MOAB to the spoil ! "—2 KINGS.

## THE MINISTRY.

### TO THE READERS OF THE REGISTER.

*Kensington, 23d March, 1827.*

MY FRIENDS,

THERE is, as in the case of my motto, which, fear of being deemed profane, prevents me from calling my text; there is, as in the case referred to by the words of this my motto, a sort of slaying amongst the great men of this our " *imperial nation*." First, the great commander of all makes his last retreat ; retreats not from VALENCIENNES to the HELDER, with that saucy scoundrel the printer's boy at his heels ; but from this troubled state of Old England, to another and a better world, *mourned by*, and followed by the benedictions of ........ those whom I will not attempt to describe, because every thing I could say of them, of their sense, of their public spirit, of their re-, spect for morals, of their gratitude, and of various other qualities belonging to them, and elicited upon this occasion : those, whom I will not attempt to describe, because these their qualities admit not of having justice done to them by a

2 B

Printed and Published by WILLIAM COBBETT, No. 183, Fleet-street.
[ENTERED AT STATIONERS' HALL.]

pen like mine. One ought to exclaim, in the Shaksperian bombast, " Oh, for a muse of fire! " to
describe the various virtues, the
astonishing sublimity of soul, of
these wearers of black silk stockings and bombazeen gowns. But,
not to continue further, at present,
this melancholy subject, no sooner
was the Royal Duke gone, but a
couple of Bishops seemed to have
contended who should have been
the first to go after him. Next
came the Prime Minister; not
dead indeed; not physically dead;
not put under ground; but, so far
" hors de combat " as not to afford
us the smallest hope of his being
able to guide us in future. Next
came the Secretary of State for
Foreign Affairs, with, as the newspapers told us, " a lumbago,"
which was of that severe and peculiar nature, as to induce his
couple of doctors to forbid him to
read the despatches that came
from Portugal. All the world
will allow, that this must have
been a most singular species of
" lumbago;" or, that it was a lie

from the beginning to the end;
that there was no lumbago at all,
but something of a nature very
different to that of lumbago. However, let it be lumbago; let it be
lumbago, that renders it unsafe for
the sufferer to read. Next comes
the Right Honourable the Minister for Free Trade, who seems to
have been smitten in a still more
unaccountable and singular sort
of way. Nobody seems to be
*able to tell us what is the matter
with him!* He attends Councils,
they tell us; and they tell us too
(which is well worth noticing)
*that Councils attend him;* and
those councils consisting, too, of
Dukes, Earls, and other men of
title! This Minister of Free
Trade must have surprising merit
of his own! Must be a creature
endued with wonderful sagacity;
must possess, in a singularly great
degree, the capacity and the will
to do good to the "*Empire.*"

As to the ailments of these
" *Great Men;* " that is to say, as
to the nature of their bodily complaints and sufferings, the news-

papers tell us just what they please, or, perhaps, what the people please who have the management of the houses of the sick men. For my part, I do not believe any thing that we have been told about their illness; except the bare fact of their being ill. I have seen nothing to make me believe, that Lord Liverpool, for instance, has had a *paralytic stroke;* and, I do *not believe that he has had such stroke.* I saw him in the month of May last in his place in the House of Lords; and the remarks I then made, tend to strengthen my total disbelief of the present account. I told several persons what I thought of him at that time, though I do not choose to state here what those thoughts were. Then, again, there were newspaper rumours about his being indisposed during the summer and during the fall of the year. The newspapers remarked, that his Lordship seemed to be *extremely and queerly agitated, during the time that the King was reading his Speech to* the *Parliament.* What, my friends, do you think was the inference which the brethren of the broad-sheet drew from this queer agitation? Why, that his Lordship was in a state of excessive anxiety about the King's reading his speech; and, carrying their inferences one step further, they concluded that his Lordship must have some *extraordinary reason* for this anxiety; and, then they broke off short, as it were with a significant nod, a cocking of the eye, and a pointing of the finger to that forehead of theirs, stored as it is with such a surprising quantity of sagacity. Certainly nothing could be more illogical than the reasoning of these brothers of the broad-sheet. Their facts might all be lies, and ten to one they were all lies; but, at any rate, if the facts were true, the reasoning was the worst that was ever heard of in the world. Now, if we put all these circumstances together; if we observe, that Lord Liverpool was ailing off and on during the summer and fall; if we observe, that he was reported to have been ill, and was recently absent from the House of Lords for a day or two, soon after the beginning of the first session; if we remember that he then went to BATH during the recess, and that a great many blind stories were told us about the state of his health; if we remember, that the newspapers told us, that DR. DREVER had been *in attendance is the house* for some time previous to the apoplectic stroke; if we remember, that all these things took place preliminary to the apoplectic stroke; and if we remember, at the back of all this, that the physicians have never certified under their hands, that there was any apoplectic or paralytic stroke at all: if we remember all these things, what reason have we to believe the notorious liars of the press, when they tell us about an apoplectic or a paralytic stroke?

As to Mr. CANNING, the lumbago lie would be quite sufficient to convince any man of common sense, that his illness, or at least the cause of it; and, indeed, that the whole affair altogether has been totally misrepresented to the public. WHY SAY that it was a lumbago? It comes out the next day that the physicians will not allow him to read the despatches

received from abroad! What then, is it a lumbago in the head? It is a curious sort of lumbago in the loins; a curious sort of ache across the hips, the pains of which can be augmented or prolonged merely by the reading of papers. The girl who became " in a family way " in consequence of a broomstick laid across her shoulders by her sweetheart, was not, unless the brothers of the broad-sheet be liars, of more singular organization and susceptibility than is our wonderful Æolean Secretary of State. This story about the lumbago and the despatches will be remembered after CANNING shall have been forgotten. The whole enterprise, all taken together from first to last, the message of the king, the *Æolean* speech, the choice spirits of the age, the huzzaing of the Parliament, and the now astonishing silence of that collective wisdom: all these things taken together, form a mess to be remembered; but, in the whole mass, there is no ingredient that surpasses that curious lumbago which renders it dangerous for a man to read despatches! One would think that the Parliament also were afflicted with this curious lumbago; for they seem to have an insuperable objection even to hear the despatches read.

In short, we must guess at the real ailments of MR. CANNING. We can *know* nothing at all about the matter. We know very well that something keeps him away from the House of Commons, and that is all we do know or can know. Time will tell us all about the matter. Tell-tale time will let all the secrets out, and then many of us will stare each other in the face, ashamed to reflect on our present, almost beastly credulity.

With regard to Mr. Huskisson, his friends seem to think that there is wisdom in the old maxim, namely, "least said soonest mended." It is a queer sort of way in which the brethren of the broadsheet speak about this gentleman, but, at any rate, nobody seems to be very sanguine, as to his appearing again upon the stage, in any reasonable space of time. Alas then, for free trade! Alas then, for "*liberal principles,*" supported by the supporters of rotten boroughs. Alas then, for the augmented salary of £2000 a year, given for the demolition of two hundred Acts of Parliament! Alas for all these: but, this prudent gentleman has provided *a contingent pension for his life!* That is to say, he is to have, for his life, one thousand two hundred pounds of our money every year, *whenever he do not fill a place that will give him more than* £2000 *a year!* There is a curious way of riding a people! it is neither straddle nor side saddle: it is foot in stirrup with 'tother leg always ready to go over the back; and the poor devil of a public, like the tantalized horse, really knows not what to wish for, whether for the rider to mount and seat himself or to remain where he is. Besides this, Mrs. Emily Huskisson, wife of the minister of "liberal principles," has a pension settled upon her of £600 a year. She is to have this for her life, *after the death of her husband.* This is a singular sort of way of insuring a *dower* for a widow! So that, neither sickness nor death falling upon this *great* man can wholly relieve us from the expense of maintaining him. Of what nature his complaint is, I cannot pretend to say; and the newspapers are pretty nearly silent upon the subject; what they have said has clearly proved their pretences to be false, in that we are in the dark here also, except that we know that the Right Honourable orator does not make his appearance on the stage.

Thus we are in a state of very great uncertainty as to the sort of illness, or the degree of the illness, or the prospect of the duration of the illness which keeps these men out of their places in Parliament. Nay, I should be very loath to take my oath that they *have any illness at all* ; and, at any rate, I would advise you, my friends, and all those who wish to see a change of this system, to keep your tears, at least, to yourselves, till there is a certainty, the only possible certainty, that while you are shedding these tears for the dying men, they may not *give you a stroke* pretty nearly as fatal as that of the palsy and the apoplexy. Pray, my friends, whatever the "*loyal*" may do, expose not yourselves to the laughter of the world on this score. Be taught, my friends, by the story of the Wife of Bath, in the Canterbury Tales of CHAUCER. This virago had sent three husbands to the grave by the bangings of her tongue, and the various tricks she played them. Having amassed a pretty good fortune, by robbing the three first, she then took a fourth for her enjoyment. Here, however, the devil deserted her ; for this fourth was a stout young fellow that seemed to be destined to avenge the wrongs of the former three. He was more than a match for the shrew in all sorts of ways ; not forgetting the

corporal chastisement that she frequently received at his hands. She tried all her old tricks over again ; but all she found unavailing. Even *swooning* and *going into fits* had no effect. At last she resorted to the trick of DYING! This surely would melt the hard heart of the husband. She was dying : she wished just to bid him adieu ; and he, thinking that there was no danger in softening for a minute or two, just as the breath was going out of her body, went to her bed-side, and stooped down, just to imprint a parting-kiss upon her cheek ; a kiss that he gave without much grudging, seeing that it was the last that he was to be called upon to give. Down he stooped then, was just tempering his lips, and beginning to utter " Farewell, my beloved," when she, drawing her right arm slily back under the bedclothes, with a clenched fist at the end of that arm, suddenly gave him a blow behind the ear, laid him sprawling upon the floor, whence he was lifted to be put into the coffin, while she got up to wear her weeds, to look out for a fifth, and to triumph to the end of her days.

Therefore, my friends, be cautious : do not begin to weep too soon over these unfortunate Ministers. I saw Liverpool in his place in the House of Lords last May; and I thought what I thought when I saw him, but I also remembered, that, the last time that I saw him in that place before was, when, in urging the necessity of the Power-of-Imprisonment Bill, he said he was determined to pursue the STERN PATH OF DUTY; words which I have never forgotten whenever I have heard his name mentioned. I, therefore, conjure my readers to restrain their pity, till, at any rate, they be quite SURE, that the objects of their pity will not live to make them measure their length upon the floor. Let them recollect the fate of the melting spouse of the Wife of Bath. Let them, above all things, not begin to forgive too soon; and, indeed, the only safe way is, not to forgive till it is impossible that the forgiven party can ever offend you again; that is to say, unless explicit confession of error or wrong-doing, and ample *atonement*, precede the exercise of your power of pardoning.

But, now, what is to be done? *Who is to be Minister?* This last is the great question; and, at any other time than this; at any former time, until within these ten or fifteen years, it would have been a question not only of uncommon interest, but one which would have kept the whole country in a state of agitation. The MOABITES, or Whigs, would have flown to the spoil. There would have been a running up and down and to and again by the fellows of Brookes's gambling house, as if all their wives and mistresses were in the straw at once. Now very little is said about the matter. A question has been modestly asked in each House, as to when it is likely that a new Prime Minister will be appointed; but, that is all; not a word has been said about the WHO; about the PRINCIPLES; about the MEASURES: not a word has been said about these things. Not that there is any lack of *Moabites;* not that the *Moabites* have ceased to have a relish for good things; but, it is manifest that the Moabites see, that it is not so clear, that there will be any good things for them to get at. They look at the concern as a parcel of sparrows look at food which you have scattered upon the ground, and about and amongst which you have set a parcel of limed twigs! They turn their heads upon one side, turn up their bills, and have faces so full of a mixture of eagerness to get at the food and of doubts relative to the dangers of getting it, that one cannot help admiring at the provident arrangements of nature!

The Moabites would gladly take upon them the immense trouble of imposing, levying, collecting, distributing, fingering, and fumbling the sixty millions sterling a year paid by this wretched and " *imperial* " people of this " *imperial empire.*" They would fain have the fingering of these sixty millions; but all of them, except the exceedingly stupid, see that there is danger, attending the getting possession of this fingering. He who fingers must *account* by-and-by; and, exceedingly stupid as the Moabites generally are, they must see, that to have to settle the account will not be so very pleasant a thing.

The truth is, that there is nobody, of either party, who sees what ought to be done, and who has both the courage and the talent to do it. That is it. There are men enough who want the *places* and the immense power and riches which the places give; but we are now got into a state, which says that those who fill these places shall, at last, be responsible, really responsible for the measures which they adopt.

Egyptian darkness, whatever that might be, could not have been much thicker, could not have been much less contrary to light, than the inside of the heads of these Moabites generally is contrary to what ought to be called enlightened. They are, nine out of every ten, the grossest of fools, as far as relates to great public affairs; but, they have the understanding of brutes, at any rate; and it wants very little more than the understanding of brutes to enable them to see that this *system must go to pieces;* that there must be a great, a terrific change in the whole of the affairs of the Government. They all seem to feel this: they want the courage, they want the skill, they want the every thing necessary to encounter either the consequences of a change like this or the making of the change. That great CORNELIUS AGRIPPA's man, BROUGHAM, for instance: it is very fine to hear him TALK about measures of Government; but put him into office and ask him whether he mean to continue on the law until he has extinguished all the one-pound notes; or whether he mean to return to Bank restriction or legal tender? Let him be in office; let him be responsible for what he says; put these questions to him, and you frighten him out of his senses.

The present men, sick, well, lame, lazy, or anything but dead, must and will carry on the system as long as it will last. If they go, the system goes. Nobody else can carry it on, for a *remedy* would be called for from others; and, *remedy* means a *destruction of the system*. It is nonsense, therefore, to talk of a *change of the Ministry*. If the Moabites were in office, they must do precisely what these men do, or, they must adopt measures which would destroy the system. There has been a talk about MR. CANNING and "*liberal principles*" having triumphed in the Cabinet; and, from the circumstance of *Canning* having been so applauded by BROUGHAM; from the circumstance of his having published his amended speech at the Moabites' shop; from these and various other circumstances, there is reason to suppose that there may have been a silly project of this sort; but, what could the project *effect:* it could do nothing to obviate the convulsion which is coming: it could not have prevented anarchy from low prices or anarchy from two prices. In short, it could have done nothing to save the system; and this is so strongly felt, by both parties, that the one does not care much about remaining in place, and the other has very little desire to get into place.

One of two things must happen in a comparatively short space of time; that is to say, the present law relative to paper money must be repealed, there must be two prices and assignats proceeding from what is called Bank Restriction and legal tender, or, there must be a cessation of all payment of rents. One or the other of these must take place, and that at no distant day. The present Ministers are quite as capable as any others of going back to Bank re-restriction and legal tender. They dare not face the devil of low prices. They dare not cause rents to cease to be paid. What they are to do they themselves do not know; and this is the reason, and the only reason, why there is no bustling and pushing and shoving to get into their places. The places are as valuable as ever for the day; but, then, the *tenure* is hardly worth a pin; while, on the other hand, the danger is great. The House is the same house; there is, for the present, the same table kept; and there is just the same carousing and squandering; but, the *tenure* is not as it used to be; the tenure is from hour to hour; while the very foundations of the house begin to shake, and it may come tumbling at any hour down upon the ears of the occupants. I saw, the other day, a large and good looking house, with a showy garden to it, to be let, on a long lease, or to be sold at a very cheap rate. I was surprised at the cheapness of the thing; but, upon talking about the house to a man who was working hard by, he very significantly pronounced the words " *dry rot* "! That was enough! I needed no more to explain to me why the house was cheap; and, it is precisely from feelings similar to those which would actuate persons going to look at this house; it is from feelings precisely like these, that the present apparent apathy of the Moabites springs. They are as fond of the good things as ever they were: they are as eager to get at them: they see the grain, but they see the limed twigs also: they would fain take the former, but they dread the latter.

To this state, my friends, are the two factions come at last. They have both been our enemies; and that, too, in much about an equal degree. The Whigs have hated us most, but have wanted the power to act according to their hatred. To what state lower than the present can they very well be reduced? There is the Thing, for the preservation of which; for the maintenance of which, with all its abuses, they have so long been at war against us: there is this very concern; this Thing which they deem to be so precious: there it is reduced to such a state, that one party is afraid to keep it, and the other party is afraid to take it, though it continues to pour down riches upon all who have it. This is the state to which we have seen the Thing brought by its own supporters. It does little more at present than merely reel along; and that it may cease even to reel, unless it be radically reformed, is the most anxious wish of

Your Friend, and

Most obedient Servant,

Wm. COBBETT.

---

## DUKE OF YORK.

I CANNOT think what the devil the hangers on of the THING can possibly mean by making all the worry that they are making about the Duke of York. In low matters, they are as cunning as the father of lies himself; but I really cannot discover what they expect to *get*, or what they expect to *keep*; what selfish purpose they expect to answer; how they suppose they shall thereby coax the working part of the community to give them more readily the means of living in laziness; what end, in short, they do propose to answer by this incessant bawling about the *virtues* of the Duke of York, is what I cannot for the life of me dive into.—There is a bookseller, I see, who is now publishing an account of the " *last illness and* " *decease of the* DUKE *of* YORK. " By LIEUTENANT GENERAL SIR " HERBERT TAYLOR, G. C. H. " &c. &c. &c." Now this Taylor really seems to have done no more than what a grateful man ought to do. The Duke of York made him every thing; and, if it was justifiable in him to accept of riches and honours through that channel, he was right in doing what he could to extol the channel. Very different is the case of the man who has been working hard all his life-time, to pay taxes, part of which went to the support of this Duke of York, and this HERBERT TAYLOR, and the Dead Weight; thousands, including the parsons, who are at once military officers and called by the Holy Ghost to teach the Gospel. Very right in this HERBERT TAYLOR with his title of Lieut. General, G. C. H., to cry up DUKE YORK; but NOT SO VERY NATU-RAL, in some of those whom I have seen dressed in blank for the purpose of doing honour to his memory.—But again, to re-turn to the point I am starting from, I cannot imagine *what good these catterwauling* aristocrats think they shall achieve by thus braving every good feeling in the country.

---

## IMPOSSIBLE!

### WHAT! WILBERFORCE DEAD!
———

To my utter astonishment I read the other day, the following words in a speech ascribed to Dr. LUSHINGTON, and said to have been spoken on the 14th instant. The Doctor, after telling a long and tough story about a Church parson in Jamaica, who had, by means of a sermon, set the people to work to mob a Methodist parson; fire several shots into his house, and to do several other acts of great violence: the Doctor, after this account, is said to have proceeded thus:—" It would be " comparatively well if the matter " had stopped even here. Would " the House hardly credit him " when he told them, that on the " ensuing Sunday, but one or two " days having intervened, the " same clergyman mounted the " same pulpit, alluded to the out- " rage which had been committed, " and re-preached the same ser- " mon! (Hear, hear.) The House

" ought to be informed who
" this Rev. Mr. BRIDGES was.
" He was an individual who first
" attained public notoriety by the
" promulgation of a libel upon the
" *memory of a man entitled to the*
" *repectful recollections of all*
" *those endued with creditable*
" *feelings of humanity.* The
" first public proceeding of
" Mr. BRIDGES was a libel
" upon the memory of Mr.
" WILBERFORCE, in which
" were introduced these words:
[Here follow the words.] —
" As a reward for this compo-
" sition the House of Assembly
" in Jamaica voted him £500,
" and as a further encouragement,
" the BISHOP of JAMAICA appointed
" him his Chaplain. He (DR.
" LUSHINGTON) trusted, if the
" facts which he had recited could
" be brought home, some means
" would be devised of punishing
" not only those who had been
" guilty of a violation of the law,
" in firing into the house of MR.
" RADCLIFFE, but also the foun-
" tain and author of that outrage;
" for undoubtedly those who suf-
" fered themselves to be made the
" instruments of such an act of
" violence, however culpable,
" were less guilty than those, at
" whose instigation it was per-
" petrated."

And is it really true that this
chap is dead? Is it really true,
that this representative of " almost
a little kingdom," as I once heard
him call himself; is it really true
that this fellow is gone off, actually
gone off for ever without making
more noise in the country than
would have been made by the
killing of my cat! No, no! it never
can be; the modern saints and
Bible men would certainly set up
a howl: there would certainly have
been some canting printer fellow
found to sell a space of his publication for the putting of black
marks round some part of this
fellow's demise. If he really be
dead, as one would gather from the
words imputed to DOCTOR LUSH-
INGTON, it would almost make me
hope that the sons and daughters
of cant are not incurable. This,
however, is too much to hope.

If the above account of DOCTOR
LUSHINGTON's sayings be correct,
I differ completely from the Doc-
TOR, as to the whole of what he
is here reported to have said. I
commend MR. BRIDGES, not for
urging the commission of breaches
of the peace; not for writing any
LIBEL upon WILBERFORCE, but
for doing every thing which he
lawfully could do in order to counteract the workings of that man.
All that the DOCTOR has given of

the libel, as he calls it, appears to have been in latin, and I shall not quote the latin because I should not like to have a legal contest even with the memory of Wilberforce; but, when the Doctor asserts that all those who have a respect for *humanity* must necessarily dislike the conduct of Mr. Bridges, I deny the fact; for, I have been a strict observer of the conduct of this Wilberforce ever since he began to figure upon the political stage. He began as a Parliamentary Reformer, and he was a supporter of Pitt in every one of his dreadful acts against the Parliamentary Reformers; and there never was an Act passed, from the year 1793 to the passing of the Six Acts in 1819; never an Act hostile to the liberty of the Press; never an Act for suspending the Habeas Corpus; never an Act giving absolute power of imprisonment to the Ministers, never an Act for shutting men up in dungeons without regular commitment, and without being confronted with the accuser; never one single Act of this sort; never a Bank Stoppage Act, and never a Bill of Indemnity, which had not the decided support of this very Wilberforce; and, yet, the above report says, that Doctor Lushington had the boldness to declare, that this "man was entitled to the respectful recollections of all those who were endued with creditable feelings of humanity." My recollections of him are contemptuous in the highest degree; and I think that I herein discover more humanity than the maker of this speech. I feel for Ogden, and for those who suffered with Ogden. Wilberforce's feelings were for Blacks, who were, and who are better fed than the labouring people of England.

---

# AFFAIRS
# OF PORTUGAL.

The following Letters will speak for themselves, and the reader will not fail to draw the proper conclusion, from the fact of the "Times" newspaper having declined to insert that letter which I now insert below. This is an instance of the *foul play* of this abominable press. It hires a wretched creature whom it stations at Lisbon, to send it home what it calls "*intelligence;*" that is to say, materials wherewith to compose doses of misrepresentation, to flatter and cajole and noodle along in error its duped readers, and on whose passions and prejudices it lives and thrives.—Nothing could be more mischievous; or, at least, more detrimental to the English cause at Portugal than the article which appeared in the "Times," and of which my Correspondent has so ably remarked. The conductor of that newspaper felt this truth, and therefore took special care not to expose the follies of his own article, by inserting that of my Correspondent. Infinite has been the mischief done by this press: this "*best possible public instructor*" of the best possible CORNELIUS AGRIPPA's man, of which this country now has to boast. It was this senseless and unprincipled press, with this very "Old Times" newspaper at its head, that drove the country into the last war against the American United States, for the avowed purpose of deposing JAMES MADISON! And, no small part of the public had, by this same stupid and mercenary press, been maddened up to the notion, that the Guards were marching away from LONDON, for the purpose, if not of deposing, of doing something very like deposing, FERDINAND, King of Spain!—What but the everlasting din of these newspapers could have put such a notion into the minds of the common people? When the Guards were marching

away, they were accompanied by crowds of people in the lowest walks of life, carrying LAUREL BOUGHS, and giving the soldiers leaves of that shrub, that symbol of glorious victory, to stick in their caps, crying out, at the same time, "Down with that rascal, Ferdinand!" I heard that there was a crowd assembled at the door of SIR WILLIAM CLINTON, at the moment of his departure for Portsmouth; that they exultingly cheered him when he got into his carriage, and that they cried out, "Pull down that Tyrant FERDINAND!" What, I say, but the base and stupid lies of the Scotch lawyer's "best public instructor," could have produced such effects as these. FERDINAND had done nothing against our Sovereign or ourselves; he had committed no act of hostility against England, either direct or indirect. Whether he had strictly adhered to the principles of the law of nations, even if he had done what had been imputed to him, was matter of great doubt: it was, at any rate, too nice a point to be settled in this sort of way. In short, he had done nothing but endeavour to keep what he deemed anarchy and premeditated sacrilege out of his dominions; and, for this, he was to be execrated by the people of England, and they were to halloo for his destruction. Such an effect never could have been produced by any thing but these horrible newspapers. The poor souls, who were deluded to set up this outcry were not aware, that they, who were already half bankrapts, and others of them nearly half-starved, were to assist *to pay* for this exploit, for this pulling down of FERDINAND, and still less were they aware, that the exploit would not pull him down, and that those soldiers, whose departure they cheered, might have to return without any of the laurel leaves which they had stuck in their caps.—It is very curious, that the Parliament should have separated, *cheering,* nay, *huzzaing* ÆOLUS CANNING on his projected pulling down of FERDINAND; and that the same Parliament should now have been assembled for more than five weeks, without any member of it, in either House, saying one single word about this Portuguese exploit! Not one single word, good, bad or indifferent, has been uttered by one member of either House, any more than if we had not a soldier in Portugal, and than if we were not actually paying, at this moment, for the sending of *hay to Portugal,* to feed the English cavalry horses that are there.—Other occasions will offer, for remarking on the consequences of this enterprise : at present I shall only add a repetition of the opinion which I have always entertained on the subject ; namely, that the "thing," called the "New Constitution," was a scheme hatched in England; that it was wholly unfitted to the Portuguese nation, that it will be blown completely away, leaving behind it no lasting effect other than that of disgrace to its projectors.

To Mr. COBBETT.

*March 16th, 1827.*

SIR,—On Tuesday the 6th inst. the Editor of the Times newspaper published a long letter from his LISBON correspondent. The next day, the 7th, I delivered at the Times Office, Printing House Square, a letter for publication, in which I made manifest the impolicy and indiscretion, and unmasked the character of this Lisbon Correspondent. As the Editor has not published my Letter, I now send it to you ; in order, if you consider the information it contains of general interest, that my letter may appear in that Weekly Register which has so often exposed the injudicious conduct of Government agents, and the humbug and delusions played off upon the public.

I remain; &c.

FAIR PLAY.

*To the Editor of the Times.*

SIR,—As a friend to constitutional liberty, I cannot but express my regret, that you should have thought proper to publish in your widely circulated paper, (this day March 6,) the Letter of two columns without signature, dated the 28th of February, 1827.

I have nothing to do with the subject which gave rise to that letter; the parties accused may, for what I know, be innocent or guilty. I merely address you to expose the injurious effects which such publications may have upon the cause of the Constitutionalists.

One of the things which has most tended to make that cause unpopular, is a report, generally spread in Portugal, that Sir Charles Stuart had obtained Don Pedro's consent, that the estates of monasteries, and other ecclesiastical property, should be sold or mortgaged as a security to those who would advance funds to repay the British Government all expenses incurred, in the establishment and maintenance of the Constitution. Of the truth or falsehood of this report it is not for me

to inquire; but this I must say, that no publication could be better calculated to impress upon the public the truth of this report, than this letter from your Lisbon correspondent.

As almost his whole letter is taken up with the common-place abuse of monks, friars, priests, the processions of the Host, and other religious usages of the Portuguese, I at first thought the writer might be some Biblical itinerant, who, as is usual with those personages, by way of conciliating expends his pious rhetoric in virulent abuse of the doctrines most revered by those he means to bring into his fold. But from the anxiety he expresses for the sale of monastic and other ecclesiastical property, which, as he says, *must follow the restora-*"*tion of social order under the* "*charter*," and the "*astonish-* "*ment felt by some people here*" (in Lisbon) that this "*ecclesiasti-* "*cal property is not immediately* "*made available to the distressing* "*wants of Government*," I am rather inclined to believe that he must be one of those British or Portuguese circumcised or uncircumcised Jews, connected with some joint-stock worthies here, who hold themselves ready to speculate on this ecclesiastical property; of such speculations arising in Portugal they have made sure, particularly since the Minister's *descamisado* Æolian blast, which is once more to let loose the fiends of spoliation and sacrilege, the *liberaux frères et amis*, the vauntingly proclaimed auxiliaries of the present British Ministry.

Now, Sir, there is no one more anxious that the people of Portugal, and indeed of every other country, should enjoy liberty, than I am; but I must own that I have no faith in the zeal of those who hold that liberty is to be founded on robbery, and can only be maintained by the destruction of the Christian religion; for, let us not deceive ourselves, the destruction of the Catholic religion is not the end, but the means by which the end which all *Liberaux* aim at, the "*Ecrasez L'Infame*," is to be attained. This is the great *Liberal*, the *frère et ami*, Cᴏᴜɴᴛ Toʀʀᴇɴo, distinctly expressed in his Preface to his book on the constitution of the Spanish *Cortes*. *Liberaux* seem to be quite fanatics on this subject, but there is something quite other than fanaticism at bottom. They are aware that such is the rooted attachment of the people of Spain, and of course of Portugal, to the Catholic religion, that they cannot uncatholicise without unchristianising

them, and without this total change they know that they cannot be secure in the enjoyment of the plunder of the church, or of their fellow-citizens.

It does appear to me, Mr. Editor, that in the multiplicity of your business, this communication from Lisbon escaped your usual vigilance, otherwise I cannot conceive that you would have suffered the publication of a document so insulting to the feelings of our allies, and indeed so very ill calculated to conciliate the good will of the Portuguese towards our gallant countrymen, who thus are, in the face of Europe, made by your correspondent to figure as the mercenary *alguazils* of a rapacious banditti of Jobbing Jews and *Liberaux*.

If, besides, those Priests and Friars are as really averse to the Constitution as your correspondent represents them to be (which I much doubt), they must be delighted to see such a publication in a respectable English Paper, and they will not fail to produce it as evidence of the hostile intentions of our Government towards their order and their church. Indeed I should not be at all surprised if that very article was translated into Portuguese, and every where circulated by those very same Priests and Friars, as few productions, in my humble opinion, would more effectually tend to injure the Constitutional Cause.

FAIR PLAY.

*London, March 6, 1827.*

PS.—Wednesday, March 7.— I have just heard that a Great Jew has dispatched a detachment of Israelites to establish a house in Lisbon. How sweetly now, if he pleases, may the Jew (aided by the more than Hebrew rapacity of the *Liberaux,* far outdoing the " *alieni appetens*" of Catiline's band of " *frères et amis* ") avenge on the Portuguese nation the wrongs heretofore suffered by his Portuguese brethren.

## INTERMENT OF THE DEAD.

THE same ties and endearments, that link together friends and relatives during life, seem to influence them at the hour of death : nothing is more anxiously sought at that awful hour, than to be interred with the ashes of our fathers. When colonies spread beyond the ocean from the mother hives, they would also, if possible, be buried with their relatives and Christian brethren. There is perhaps no other affection of the human heart stronger, nor more consistent with nature and with religion : it characterized the most holy men under the Old and New Laws. We read in St. Jerome, " That Hbron is called the city of the four great men, because there, in a double sepulchre, were deposited the three Patriarchs and their wives; that is, Abraham and Sarah, Isaac and Rebecca, Jacob and Lia, together with Adam himself and his wife Eve. Tobias (iv. 8.) said to his son, *When God shall have received my soul, bury my body,* and honour thy mother all the days of thy life; but when she will also finish her days, *bury her alongside of me.* Let one grave bring together those whom one wedlock has joined, because they are but one flesh : Matt. xix. 6." Joseph, at the hour of his death in the land of Egypt, requested his brethren to carry his bones and bury them in the tomb of his forefathers; Gen. l. 5. ; and it is said to the prophet who ate contrary to the command of God in Bethel (3 Kings, xiii. 22), Your carcass shall not be interred in the sepulchre of your ancestors. It is also related in the New Testament, that Philip erected a tomb for himself and his daughters.

But the ancient Christians always selected for the interment of the dead the precincts of God's temples, or the spots that were sanctified by the residence or sufferings of the saints and martyrs; their motives for so doing take from ST. AUGUSTINE: " Let us not " imagine that our care for the " dead avails them, unless we offer " on their behalf either the solemn " sacrifice of the altar, or prayers, " or alms-deeds; though they do " not benefit all persons for whom " they are offered, but only those " who, during life, rendered them- " selves worthy of being thus re- " lieved after death. But as we " know not who are worthy, suf- " frages ought to be made for all " the faithful, so that none be omit- " ted for whom these benefits could " and should be performed : for it " is much better that our suffrages " be redundant for those whom " they neither hurt nor serve, than " be wanting to those whom they " could benefit. Let each person " be however more careful to dis- " charge this duty towards his " friends, in hope that he may be " equally dealt with by his own " survivors. But the funeral ob- " sequies is no relief to the soul, " but a display of that human af- " fection which *never allowed man* " *to hate his own flesh: Ephe.* v. " 29. Hence he should take as

" much care as possible of his " neighbour's flesh after the de- " parture of him who ruled it. " And if they, who disbelieve in " the resurrection of the flesh, do " this, how much more are we, " who believe in it, bound to per- " form this duty? Let this sacred " attention paid to the dead body, " that shall rise again and live in " eternity, be a testimony of our " faith in the *resurrection of the* " *flesh.* But it seems to me to be " beneficial also for the dead that " each person be interred in the " places allotted for the comme- " moration of the martyrs, in or- " der that whilst he is recom- " mended to the patronage of the " martyr, the suffrages on his be- " half be multiplied. " 13. Q. 2 C. 19.

GREGORY the GREAT. *Dialog. Lib.* 4, C. 50, *An.* 592, said, " It is useful for those who " are not loaded with grievous " sins, if they be buried in the " church, because their neigh- " bours, as often as they assemble " to those holy places, turn their " thoughts on the persons depo- " sited in the monuments, and " present their prayers for them " before the throne of God. But " with regard to those who are " sunk under mortal sin, they " gain not release, but greater

" damnation by being interred in
" the churches." *Ibidem*, C. 17.

Providence in his own inscru-
table decrees has prepared trials
for all the sons of Eve, and chas-
tises in a greater degree his own
favourites—the Apostles and the
martyrs. The heavier falls his
hand upon any of our fellow-
creatures, the louder he calls for
our sympathy and relief : *When I
was sick, you visited me ; when
in prison*, you came to me ; Come,
ye blessed of my Father, possess
the kingdom prepared for ye
from the beginning of the world.
Matt. xxv. 34. It was in hope
of this future reward that thousands of men and women, during
every century since the birth of
Christ, until the present time, devoted their whole life and property in attending the sick and
burying the dead. Nothing more
edifies the traveller than the
pious heroism of the " Ladies of
Charity" all over the European
Continent : they, pious souls,
abandon in the bloom of youth
the fleeting allurements of society,
to spend their days and nights,
not at the play or dance, not at
the levee or toilet, but consoling
and relieving the sick ; nor plague
nor fever deters them from his
ghastly abode; all thoughts of
personal danger are lost in their

firm hope of the future reward :
Come, ye blessed of my Father,
possess the kingdom prepared for
ye from the beginning of the
world; when I was sick you visited me. They know that God,
who made the promise, is faithful and able to redeem it.

The mode of burying the dead
in Rome is not less edifying, nor
less worthy of the traveller's notice. All the citizens seemed to
have formed themselves into different societies to perform that
work of charity. The shoemakers,
or weavers, for instance, assemble
in a religious costume, generally a
long habit, girded by a cincture.
First they carry the body to the
church, to have the august myste-
ries offered for the departed soul ;
then they move on in solemn procession towards the place of interment outside the city, carrying
on a bier the body, neatly dressed
and decorated with flowers and
religious emblems, with the empty
coffin alongside, to receive the
corpse at the grave. This awful
exposure through the streets, of
that pale image of death—that
face that was full of bloom and
vigour, only two days ago, like
your own, together with the responsive hymn of both clergy and
crowd, generally leaves on your
mind the conviction of the vanity

of this world, and of the uncertainty of your own earthly tenure.

This faith in the merit of good works, and hope in the promise of a God, was no where more visible than in these islands. They founded and amply endowed, in every parish, asylums for the sick, the poor, the aged, and for the traveller, and allotted by the church convenient places for the burial of the dead; little dreading that a race of wolves, in the clerical robe, would ever arise, who would devour the poor flock, demolish their houses, seize on their property, and turn out on the wide world, to famish or to beg, the widows, the orphans, the sick and the lame; and who would moreover make a venal commodity of that sacred, consecrated ground of interment. Behold honest John Ball hard at labour, under the yoke from the beginning of his days, paying annually the tenth part of his labour to feed the parson, and paying perhaps not less than half of the remaining nine-tenths in taxes, both direct and indirect, that were imposed to carry on the " No Popery war," or the war that was carried on since the *funding* reign of *William III.*, for the mere purpose of saving the church property; behold poor John now, after the

very marrow and vital blood was thus squeezed from his heart's core, in tithes and taxes, going heart-broken to take his final repose in the bosom of his mother earth, in hope of a happy resurrection. Will he be met by his own pastor, or his agent, at the church-gate, and told, " John, " you shall not lay down your " bones in this yard, with the " bones of your ancestors, until " you pay us, in addition to all " you ever paid, *thirty shillings!*". What more inhuman, what more terrific! However, this is the practice in and about London, I am told every where. They make a curious distinction: the lodger and man who pays no taxes, is charged thirty, while the householder or payer of taxes, is required to pay but fifteen shillings for his grave.

Some heart-rending cases lately fell under my own observation: I shall mention one. A poor mechanic, of feeble constitution, went, a few weeks ago, to the sexton, to treat about the interment of his baby; he pleaded, as well he might, distress in all her ghastly features, " that his health was " nearly broken down, that he " was hardly able to hold out in " his employment, that he was " already indebted, that his clothes "and furniture were partly sold "and pawned, and that, if now "compelled to pay the burial fees "of his child, he did not know "what to do." But, strange to relate! he was told, that "the "just fees must be paid to his "reverence." And thus the infant was to be waked a few days longer, until the cursed fees were scraped from the humanity of some neighbours. But alas! the same poor man is confined soon after, and continues in the bed of sickness, without friends or hire, to procure him the necessaries of life. Let each parent transport himself in thought to the bedside of that poor man, to see him writhing in the pains of death; the companion of his life in tears at one side, with the surviving little one in her arms, crying for bread; no bread to be given, nothing to buy it; and after his reflections on that house of woe, let him go, on the wings of thought, to see the parson, in his palace, settling with his sexton the interment accounts! with whom he discourses, "As the "lodger or houseless poor have "to pay us double fees, this is the "time to make our fortune; the "'late panic' has unhinged, un- "housed three-fourths of the la- "bouring classes, and thrown "them for lodgings into the ob-

"scure back streets, or upon the "wide world to roam and beg; "what ruined the rest of the com- "munity, yields unto us crops of "gold: good and faithful sexton, "be vigilant." The inventive power of their mind is such, that the monuments erected by the piety or patriotism of Englishmen, in some churches, for their fathers, poets or heroes, could not be look- ed upon by their sons, the stranger, or by the artist, until he pay half- a-crown or three shillings fee to the clergy! Others amongst them are gone so far in the "sin of avarice," in the heresy of simony, that they erect a cemetery, and charge such enormous fees, that no poor man can ever have access to it; and for fear there are not nabobs enough to fill it in the city, they publish, in the yearly Direc- tory, that "There are SPACI- "OUS VAULTS under the "chapel, and a burial ground, "well secured, adjoining it." But the poor, thus hunted, have the consolation of faith, that God, at the other side the grave, *has no respect of persons, nor of bribes.* Deut. x. 17.

Whilst John Ball is fleeced both dead and alive, they amuse him in return from the pulpits, and in pamphlets, with black hideous pictures of the "Scarlet

Whore," of Friars and Nuns, of "superstition," "inquisition,"—Jesuits, "Pope" and "Popery." Surely, John, the compensation which you get is great and valuable; the sacrifice which you have made for your clergy is counterbalanced by your great fortune in being rescued from these terrific monsters. Perhaps you may feel anxious to know the doctrine of the Pope and of the Catholic church, regarding the interment of the dead.

GREGORY the GREAT, *Lib. 7, Regest. An. 599, to the Bishop of Sardinia,* writes, "The "illustrious Lady Nereida has "presented her complaint to us "that your brotherhood wants to "charge her one hundred shil- "lings for the interment of her "daughter. But since our acces- "sion, by the grace of God, to "the Episcopal dignity, we have "both exploded this sin from our "church, and never after allowed "the base practice to revive. "Remembering, that when Abra- "ham demanded for money, from "Ephron, the son of Seor, ground "for the interment of his wife, "(Gen. xxiii. 10; Acts vii. 16,) "he refused to receive the price, "for fear it would appear that he "gained benefit from the dead "body. Therefore, if that Pagan

"had so much consideration, how "far should we Priests be from "being guilty of such things!— "Hence I conjure you not to "allow this sin of avarice to be "repeated even upon the bodies "of strangers. But, if at any "time you allow any body to be "entombed in your church, and "if his parents, friends, or heirs, "voluntarily make any offering "to buy candles, we forbid not "its being accepted, but we en- "tirely forbid that any thing be "demanded or exacted, for fear "either, what is most sinful, the "church become guilty of simony, "which God forbid, (ne aut ve- "nalis fortasse (quod absit) dica- "tur ecclesia,) or that you would "appear to delight in the deaths "of your fellow-creatures, if you "desire to reap profit in any re- "spect from their dead bodies."

CON. TRIBUR, in Germania, *An. 895,* "It is written, (Eccle. "vii. 37,) *prevent not paying re- "spect to the dead, knowing that "we must all die;* again, (xl. 11) "All things that are of the earth "return to the earth again. "Why dost thou, earth, sell the "earth? Remember that thou "art but earth, and that into earth "thou must return, (Gen. iii. 19,) "and that death shall come upon "thee; it approaches, nor is it

" slow in its movements. Recol-
" lect that the earth is not man's
" property, but, as the Psalmist
" (Ps. xxiii. 1) sings, *the earth,*
" *and the inhabitants thereon, are*
" *the Lord's.* If you sell the
" earth, you will be guilty of
" usurping another man's rights :
" you received it gratuitously from
" God, give it gratuitously for his
" sake. Wherefore it is forbid-
" den all Christians to sell the
" ground to the dead, and refuse
" them suitable place of inter-
" ment, unless perhaps the friends
" and relatives of the deceased
" choose to offer any thing, of their
" own accord, in his name, and
" for the salvation of his soul."

INNOCENT III. to the Bishop
of Magalon, *An.* 1208. " An
" abominable custom, that ought
" to be abolished, has grown up,
" it is said, about Mount Pessulan,
" that the grave be not dug for
" the dead, until a certain price
" be paid to the church for the
" ground in which they are to be
" buried. We order that you,
" the Ordinary of that place, do
" compel your clergy not to have
" the presumption of demanding
" any thing whatsoever in that
" respect."

DECRET. GREG. 9. *Lib.* 5.
*Tit.* 3. *C.* 9., de *Simonia :* " As
" all things ought to be done from

" charity in the body of the church,
" and what is gratuitously received
" should be gratuitously imparted,
" it is too horrible that in some
" churches venality is said to gain
" such ground, that for investing
" Bishops, or Abbots, or Ecclesi-
" astics in the see, and also for
" *the interment* and *obsequies of*
" *the dead,* and for the benedic-
" tions of wedlock or for other
" sacraments, *something is re-*
" *quired.* But many persons ima-
" gine that this is lawful ; because
" they think that the penal law
" has lost its force from long, the
" long contrary usage, not minding
" that the more grievous are sins,
" the longer they hold the unhappy
" soul in chains. Therefore that
" these sins be committed in future,
" either that any thing be demand-
" ed for investing in their sees
" Ecclesiastical persons, or for in-
" stituting priests, or for *burying*
" *the dead,* or for imparting nuptial
" benedictions, or for other sacra-
" ments to be ministered, or that
" are already ministered, we most
" strictly forbid. But if any per-
" son presume to contravene this de-
" cree, let him know that he shall
" have his portion with Giezi :"
*Con.Later.* under *Alex. III,Rome.*
*An.* 1179.

Behold that to charge any thing
for the collating of churches, for

the sacraments, or for the interment of the dead, is to sell for price the free gifts of the Holy Ghost, and to fall into simony, that horrible sin committed by Gehazi in the Old Testament: 4 Kings v. 27; by Judas who sold the Redeemer: Matt. xxvii. 5; by Simon Magus: Acts. viii, 20. The law of God against this crying sin stands and will stand until the end of time; nor one iota nor one particle can be taken from it; so the Catholic canons against it are not made for one age or country, but for the whole Church, until time shall be no more. If some persons or nations fall into disbelief, if they throw away the law and faith, *will their incredulity annul the faith of God? God forbid*: Rom. iii. 3. Eye witnesses say that four interments are at least daily made, and very often twelve, in each of the city churches; but let us suppose that six be the average number, and that three be made by tax-payers at 15s. each, comes 2l. 5s.; three by non-payers of taxes, at 1l. 10s. each, 4l. 10s.; making 6l. 15s. daily — 365 days in the year; so that the parson gains yearly, by the [dead alone, about 2468l. 15s.!! together with the tithes and all his other perquisites. However, no people in the world feel more compassion for the " priest ridden" Catholics of Ireland and of other countries than the English. They are for ever sending, at immense expense, missionaries to convert the benighted pagans, and spurious Bibles, that are never received nor read, to emancipate the Irish from " imposition and superstition." Should not their charity begin at home—to redeem the remains of poor John Bull from these greedy vultures; should they not rather purchase Bibles or some good spiritual books that would teach charity or even natural humanity to the parson; or if his heart be hardened by the love of gain, that neither Scriptures nor logical lecture could soften it, would it not be proper to leave his ground of interment to himself, and purchase other spots convenient to each persuasion? If these individuals, who make such fuss, and raise great sums to emancipate the African blacks, to convert the Indians of the forest, and Protestantize the Irish, take no pity upon their own Protestant neighbours, the Government that would, in the tenderness of their soul, relieve the Irish by pensioning the Roman Catholic Clergy, whose entire revenue from the *free donations* of their flocks, is, on an average, from 100l. to 150l. each, should, in consistency, have some compassion for the Englishmen, and free them from this mighty sum, 2463l. 15s., squeezed annually from the fat of the dead by each parson, and make them support the poor, the aged, and the sick, as they were originally supported, out of the tithes. At any rate, his Majesty, who is their spiritual Head, ought to interfere, and bring them to the observance of the law of God, and the S. Canons, and to revere the ashes of the dead.

J. O'CALLAGHAN,
R. Catholic Priest.

Thomas Place,
Hercules Buildings, London.
March 12, 1827.

## TRIP

## TO ROTHERHITHE.

MANY of my numerous and various adventures have had geniuses enough to celebrate them in prose; but, as far as I can recollect, my trip to Rotherhithe, so circumstantially detailed by me in a late Register, when I was giving an account of my vain endeavour to become proprietor of some of ÆOLUS CANNING's cheap wheat:

this trip to Rotherhithe is, as far as I can remember, the only exploit of mine that has ever been celebrated in poetry. I therefore insert the following piece with a degree of satisfaction rather unusual. There are persons who ascribe, to my pen, or to my " muse, " as the rhyming people call it, the verses on BRIO and the SHOY-HOY. Upon my word I did not write a line of them, and I do not know from whom they came. The present piece, which records the sad consequences of my own ignorance, will hardly be ascribed to me. At any rate, it is due to my readers to tell them, that I am totally ignorant as to the name of the author.

## COBBETT'S
## TRIP TO ROTHERHITHE.

THE ruler and the misrul'd alike
Disease's poisonous arrows strike.
This truth Æolus CANNING felt,
As on a sick-bed late he dwelt.
When health anew his nerves had strung,
And servile eloquence his tongue,
Straight to the House he bent his way;
That famous House, whose members
pray,
Each time they meet (and well they
may!),
That virtue may their actions guide,
And wisdom o'er their minds preside:
He there proposed, in solemn strain,
*Admission for the Foreign Grain.*

Which, thanks to Parliament, or fate,
To England comes at cheaper rate
Than grain that springs from British soil,
Than grain produced by British toil.
"*Cheap Corn is come*," was COBBETT's
  cry;
The Weaver Boys "AMEN" reply,
And their dejected eye-balls raise,
As though were dawning better days.
  For Redriff soon did COBBETT start,
With man and horse and bounding heart.
"Holloa! there—Captain Sniggersnee!
"Come here, my buck! a word with
  thee :
"Arriv'd from Kensington am I,
"Some of your foreign wheat to buy;
"Its cheapness makes my mouth to
  water,
"So, Skipper! let me have a quarter;
"But what's the price?"--"O *dirty-four*
"Of yur good schellings:" nothing
  more
Demanded Sniggersnec. To work,
Like hungry ploughman at his pork,
Was COBBETT setting with his sack;
When lo! Exciseman at his back,
Ask'd, with authoritative air,
"What the devil he was doing there?"
"Why, putting up the wheat, my blade!
"For which the Dantzicker I've paid :"
"Stay," said the revenue-harpy, "Stay!"
"You must not bear this wheat away—
"You have a something in your head
"The daily papers just have said ;
"You the *Debates* read o'er, of course,
"And hence your present folly's source;

"This cheap and general education,
"Will ruin bring upon the nation!
"Hark'ye, this wheat you cannot take,
"Unless to me you payment make
"Of shillings *thirty-four*, for that
"The duty now is rated at."
The man-in-office, ceasing, frown'd,
And struck his stick upon the ground.
How COBBETT stared with both his eyes!
Now petrifactions of surprise :
Ere he could speak, some moments past ;
At length he loudly spoke and fast :
"What! pay a duty?—pay for *nought*,
"*A sum, like that the wheat which*
  *bought ?*
"A pretty free-admission this !
"Of Canning's Corn Bill, O the bliss !
"That makes this Dantzic *sixty-eight !*
"Tho' *fifty-four*, the markets state,
"The average price of English wheat !
"Oh ! cheat of cheats—transcendent
  cheat !
"A Government like this, should be—"
"Seditious scoundrel ! come with me—
Roar'd out the officer, "or cease
"With blasphemy to break the peace."
Not soon the war of language ceas'd ;
The Foreign Wheat was unreleased ;
The luckless COBBETT took his sack
And horse and cart, and travell'd back
In such a trim, as when of yore,
He left some damsel's cottage door,
Who late his vows with favour heard,
But now another's love prefer'd.

LEWBO.

# MARKETS.

Average Prices of CORN throughout ENGLAND, for the week ending March 9.

*Per Quarter.*

| | *s.* | *d.* | | *s.* | *d.* |
|---|---|---|---|---|---|
| Wheat .. | 54 | 10 | Rye .... | 36 | 0 |
| Barley .. | 36 | 10 | Beans ... | 48 | 6 |
| Oats .... | 30 | 10 | Pease ... | 49 | 4 |

Total Quantity of Corn returned as Sold in the Maritime Districts, for the week ended March 9.

| | Qrs. | | Qrs. |
|---|---|---|---|
| Wheat.. | 40,104 | Rye ..... | 477 |
| Barley .. | 27,952 | Beans . .. | 3,521 |
| Oats ... | 14,482 | Pease .... | 1,501 |

*Corn Exchange, Mark Lane.*

Quantities and Prices of British Corn, &c. sold and delivered in this Market, during the week ended Saturday, March 10.

| | Qrs. | £. | *s.* | *d.* | | *s.* | *d.* |
|---|---|---|---|---|---|---|---|
| Wheat.. | 4,686 for 14,055 | 8 | 4 Average, | 59 | 11 |
| Barley.. | 4,461 | .. 8,550 | 18 | 11 | ......... | 38 | 4 |
| Oats.. | 3,937 | .. 6,455 | 4 | 0 | ......... | 32 | 9 |
| Rye.... | — | .. 0 | 0 | 0 | ......... | 0 | 0 |
| Beans.. | 1,226 | .. 2,839 | 7 | 6 | ......... | 46 | 3 |
| Pease.. | 843 | .. 2,419 | 5 | 9 | ......... | 59 | 11 |

Friday, March 16.—The arrivals are moderate this week of most kinds of Grain. There is so great a dullness in the Wheat trade, that Monday's prices can hardly be obtained for any samples to-day. Barley and Oats are rather higher, though trade is not lively for either of these articles. Beans and Pease remain in the same dull state as lately reported.

The Flour trade has again become heavy.

Monday, March 19.—There were moderate arrivals of all kinds of Grain last week, and to this morning's market there are again moderate quantities of Wheat, Barley, Beans and Pease, from Essex, Kent, and Suffolk, but not much Corn of any sort fresh in from parts more distant. There has been considerable heaviness experienced in the Wheat trade since this day se'nnight, and only superfine samples maintain last quotations; other descriptions may be reported 1s. to 2s. per quarter cheaper.

There being a good demand for Seed Barley, has occasioned an advance of full 1s. per quarter on the best malting qualities; other sorts are unaltered. Beans still meet a dull sale at last week's terms. Boiling Pease remain in the same heavy state as lately noticed. Grey Pease are unaltered ; fine samples for Seed reach as high as 56s. per quarter. The Oat trade is extremely dull, and notwithstanding the appearance of improvement in the trade last Wednesday, there has been so slack a demand since, that last Monday's prices are hardly supported. In Flour no alteration.

———

*Price on board Ship as under.*

| | | |
|---|---|---|
| Flour, per sack | ...... 46s. — | 50s. |
| —— Seconds | ........ 42s. — | 44s. |
| —— North Country | .. 40s. — | 44s. |

Account of Wheat, &c. arrived in the Port of London, from March 12 to March 17, both inclusive.

| | Qrs. | | Qrs. |
|---|---|---|---|
| Wheat .. | 4,655 | Tares .... | 460 |
| Barley .. | 5,786 | Linseed .. | — |
| Malt .... | 5,620 | Rapeseed . | 7 |
| Oats .... | 5,956 | Brank .. | 24 |
| Beans ... | 1,503 | Mustard .. | 8 |
| Flour .... | 6,635 | Flax .... | — |
| Rye .... | — | Hemp ... | 65 |
| Pease .... | 644 | Seeds ... | — |

Foreign.—Oats, 1,865 ; and Beans, 989 quarters.

Monday, March 19.—The arrivals from Ireland last week were, 1,732 firkins of Butter, and 2,956 bales of Bacon; and from Foreign Ports, 3,261 casks of Butter. The Butter market continues brisk, as the stock is unusually small. Bacon is not so brisk as the preceding week, though the shippers look for advanced prices.

## HOPS.

Price of Hops, per Cwt. in the Borough.

Monday, March 19.—Our Market remains much the same as last week, both in respect to price and demand.

*Maidstone*, March 15.—The Hop trade is particularly dull, and we have not heard of any sales being made during this last week.

Price of Bread.—The price of the 4lb. Loaf is stated at 9d. by the full-priced Bakers.

## COAL MARKET, March 16.

*Ships at Market. Ships sold. Price.*
62½ Newcastle 21½..30s. 0d. to 38s. 0d.
24 Sunderland 12 ..32s. 6d.— 39s. 6d.

SMITHFIELD, Monday, March 19.

The demand for both Beef and Mutton was dull, and the price rather lower than Friday. To-day the Beef trade was sour and heavy, the butchers being reluctant to give last Monday's prices: they were, however, obliged to submit for good things; but middling beasts barely supported the currency of this day se'nnight. There is a jump of 4d. a stone, in choice polled Sheep in the Wool, and they have rather exceeded the terms of the best Downs. The average of the market cannot, however, be quoted higher than 5s. 2d.

*Per Stone of 8 pounds (alive).*

| | s. | d. | | s. | d. |
|---|---|---|---|---|---|
| Beef . .... | 3 | 10 | to | 5 | 0 |
| Mutton ... | 4 | 0 | — | 5 | 2 |
| Veal ..... | 5 | 0 | — | 5 | 8 |
| Pork ..... | 4 | 8 | — | 5 | 6 |
| Lamb .... | 0 | 0 | — | 0 | 0 |

| Beasts . . | 2,409 | Sheep .. | 16,820 |
|---|---|---|---|
| Calves ... | 142 | Pigs ... | 135 |

NEWGATE, (same day.)
*Per Stone of 8 pounds (dead).*

| | s. | d. | | s. | d. |
|---|---|---|---|---|---|
| Beef ..... | 3 | 4 | to | 4 | 4 |
| Mutton ... | 3 | 4 | — | 4 | 4 |
| Veal ..... | 3 | 8 | — | 5 | 8 |
| Pork ..... | 3 | 8 | — | 5 | 8 |
| Lamb .... | 0 | 0 | — | 0 | 0 |

LEADENHALL, (same day.)
*Per Stone of 8 pounds (dead).*

| | s. | d. | | s. | d. |
|---|---|---|---|---|---|
| Beef ... . | 3 | 4 | to | 4 | 6 |
| Mutton ... | 3 | 4 | — | 4 | 4 |
| Veal ..... | 3 | 8 | — | 5 | 6 |
| Pork ..... | 4 | 0 | — | 5 | 6 |
| Lamb .... | 0 | 0 | — | 0 | 0 |

## POTATOES.

### SPITALFIELDS, per Ton.

|  | l. | s. | l. | s. |
|---|---|---|---|---|
| Ox-Nobles | 3 | 10 | to 4 | 0 |
| Middlings | 3 | 0 | — 0 | 0 |
| Chats | 2 | 0 | — 0 | 0 |
| Common Red | 4 | 0 | — 0 | 0 |
| Onions, 0s. 0d.—0s. 0d. per bush. | | | | |

### BOROUGH, per Ton.

|  | l. | s. | l. | s. |
|---|---|---|---|---|
| Ox-Nobles | 3 | 10 | to 4 | 10 |
| Middlings | 3 | 0 | — 0 | 0 |
| Chats | 2 | 0 | — 0 | 0 |
| Common Red | 4 | 0 | — 4 | 5 |

## HAY and STRAW, per Load.

Smithfield.—Hay....90s. to 110s.
Straw...34s. to 40s.
Clover.100s. to 130s.
St. James's.—Hay.... 80s. to 128s.
Straw .. 36s. to 42s.
Clover. 130s. to 140s.
Whitechapel.—Hay.... 80s. to 115s.
Straw...32s. to 38s.
Clover..90s. to 135s.

---

**AVERAGE PRICE OF CORN, sold in the Maritime Counties of England and Wales, for the Week ended March 9, 1827.**

|  | Wheat. | | Barley. | | Oats. | |
|---|---|---|---|---|---|---|
|  | s. | d. | s. | d. | s. | d. |
| London* | 58 | 1 | 38 | 5 | 32 | 11 |
| Essex | 57 | 9 | 37 | 0 | 30 | 3 |
| Kent | 56 | 2 | 38 | 8 | 30 | 8 |
| Sussex | 53 | 8 | 40 | 3 | 29 | 11 |
| Suffolk | 54 | 1 | 34 | 10 | 30 | 7 |
| Cambridgeshire | 53 | 0 | 33 | 1 | 26 | 7 |
| Norfolk | 53 | 0 | 34 | 8 | 29 | 10 |
| Lincolnshire | 54 | 6 | 40 | 1 | 31 | 6 |
| Yorkshire | 52 | 10 | 39 | 2 | 28 | 9 |
| Durham | 54 | 4 | 42 | 9 | 31 | 7 |
| Northumberland | 52 | 0 | 37 | 3 | 34 | 0 |
| Cumberland | 59 | 3 | 39 | 2 | 36 | 2 |
| Westmoreland | 59 | 10 | 44 | 0 | 36 | 8 |
| Lancashire | 59 | 9 | 42 | 4 | 34 | 7 |
| Cheshire | 58 | 3 | 51 | 0 | 30 | 11 |
| Gloucestershire | 58 | 0 | 44 | 7 | 40 | 4 |
| Somersetshire | 55 | 0 | 40 | 0 | 31 | 2 |
| Monmouthshire | 60 | 1 | 45 | 5 | 0 | 0 |
| Devonshire | 54 | 7 | 37 | 9 | 26 | 4 |
| Cornwall | 57 | 4 | 37 | 1 | 34 | 3 |
| Dorsetshire | 54 | 0 | 37 | 11 | 38 | 0 |
| Hampshire | 54 | 8 | 86 | 1 | 0 | 0 |
| North Wales | 61 | 6 | 45 | 9 | 31 | 8 |
| South Wales | 56 | 5 | 40 | 2 | 27 | 0 |

* The London Average is always that of the Week preceding.

*Bristol*, March 17.—The Corn Markets here continue dull, and the supplies quite equal to the demand. Present prices about as quoted below :—Wheat, from 6s. to 7s. 9d.; Barley, 4s. 4d. to 5s. 9d.; Beans, 5s. 6d. to 8s. 8d.; Oats, 2s. 3d. to 4s. 1½d.; and Malt, 6s. to 8s. per bushel, Imperial. Flour, Seconds, 34s. to 44s. per bag.

*Chelmsford*, March 16.—The prices of Grain at our market this day as under :—White Wheat, 62s. to 68s.; Red ditto, 56s. to 60s.; Barley, 36s. to 40s.; Oats, 29s. to 35s.; Beans, tick, 46s. to 48s.; Pease, Grey, 49s. to 51s. per quarter.

*Derby*, March 17.—We had a good show of samples of Grain at this day's market, both from farmers and factors, but the millers not being in immediate want caused the sale of all sorts to be rather heavy, and prices in general rather lower, say from 2s. to 3s. per quarter.

*Guildford*, March 17.—Wheat, new, for mealing, 15l. to 16l. 15s. per load. Barley, 37s. to 41s.; Oats, 32s. to 40s.; Beans, 55s. to 58s.; Pease, grey, 60s. to 62s.; ditto, boilers, 62s. to 64s. per quarter. Tares, 12s. per bushel.

*Horncastle*, March 17.—Our market this day for Barley was rather higher; other articles something lower.—Wheat, from 54s. to 57s.; Barley, 36s. to 42s.; Oats, 30s. to 36s.; Beans, 50s. to 55s.; and Rye from 40s. to 42s. per quarter.

*Ipswich*, March 17.—We had to-day a remarkably short supply of all Spring Corn, and not much Wheat. Prices were as follow:—Wheat, 52s. to 64s.; Barley, 38s. to 39s.; Beans, 44s. to 46s.; and Pease, 48s. per quarter.

*Manchester*, March 17.—There has been very little business transacted in the Corn Trade du ng the week, and prices giving way. At our market to-day, Wheat of fine quality met with purchasers at a decline of 3d. per bushel of 70 lbs. Oats have been dull in sale, at ½d. to 1d. per bushel less than the prices of last week. Flour dull sale, and 6d. to 1s. per sack lower. In Beans, Barley, Pease, and Malt, no alteration can be noted, but each article remains dull.

*Newcastle-on-Tyne*, March 17.—We had again a large supply of Wheat from the farmers, with further arrivals coastwise, at this morning's market, the sale of which was dull at a decline of 2s. per quarter from the prices of last week. Rye continues in demand at fully last week's prices. The market is again bare of malting Barley, and an advance of 1s. per quarter has been obtained, but the demand is very limited. We had a large supply of Oats from the farmers, and the prices were rather lower, excepting fresh samples of seed, which were sold at the same prices as last week.

*Norwich*, March 17.—The supply of all Grain to-day was exceedingly limited, notwithstanding Wheat declined 1s. per quarter.

*Reading*, March 17.—We had a very short supply of Wheat this day, which met a ready sale on much the same terms as last week. Old Wheat, 57s. to 68s.; New, 55s. to 68s. per quarter by the Imperial measure. The quantity of Barley pitched was very small, it was quickly taken off at last week's prices. In Oats, Beans, and Pease, no alteration. Flour 45s. per sack.

*Wakefield*, March 16.—We have a large supply of Wheat here this morning, and the Flour trade being in a heavy state, the trade has been very dull, at a decline of 1s. per quarter, and some quantity remains unsold. The supply of Barley very short, at an advance of 6d. to 1s. per quarter.

### COUNTRY CATTLE AND MEAT MARKETS, &c.

*Horncastle*, March 17.—Beef, 8s. per stone of 14 lbs.; Mutton, 7d. ; Pork 6d. to 7d. ; and Veal, 7d. to 8d. per lb.

At *Morpeth* Market, March 14, there were a good many Cattle ; inferior stood long and were not sold. There being a short supply of Sheep, fat met with a ready sale; prices much the same.—Beef, 5s. 9d. to 6s. 6d ; and Mutton, 7s. to 8s. per stone, sinking offal.

*Manchester* Smithfield Market, March 14.—Our market to-day was well attended, and fat Beef and Mutton were fully ½d. per lb. dearer than last week, with brisk sale, while the lean sorts were neglected. Calves and Pigs were not quite so brisk in sale as last week.—Beef, 5d. to 7½d. ; Mutton, 6½d. to 8d.; Veal, 5½d. to 7d.; and Pork, 5d. to 6d. per lb. sinking offal.

*Norwich Castle Meadow*, March 17.—We had a very large supply of fat Cattle to this day's market, many were bought for Smithfield, and several lots remained unsold, prices 7s. 6d. to 8s. per stone of 14 lbs. sinking offal ; Store Stock was also in good supply ; Scots sold at 3s. 9d. to 4s. per stone of 14 lbs. ; the best here, of about 56 lbs. when fat, selling at 11l. 4s. ; Shorthorns only a few here, and those inferior at 3s.; Cows and Calves, also Homebreds, selling very badly, in consequence of the scarcity of keeping. A very small number of Sheep penned ; Shearlings 24s. to 28s.; fat ones to 37s.; Hoggets, 16s. to 24s. Meat: Beef, 6½d. to 8½d.; Veal, 6d. to 8d.; Mutton, 5½d. to 7d., Lamb, 10d.; and Pork, 5d. to 8d. per lb.

END OF VOL. LXI.

# INDEX TO VOLUME LXI.

# INDEX.

# INDEX.

Printed by W. Cobbett, No. 183, Fleet-street.

# COBBETT'S

# WEEKLY REGISTER.

VOLUME LXII.

FROM APRIL TO JUNE, 1827.

LONDON:

Printed and Published by W. Cobbett, No. 183, Fleet-street.

1827.

# CONTENTS OF VOLUME LXII.

# COBBETT'S WEEKLY REGISTER.

**Vol. 62.—No. 1.]  LONDON, SATURDAY, MARCH 31, 1827.  [Price 6d.**

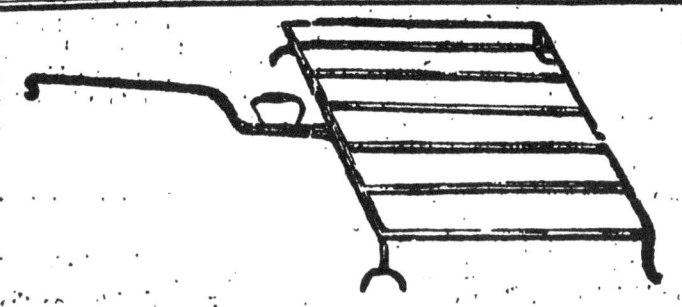

" The question upon which we are at issue involves considerations of
" most tremendous importance; and the decision of it must take place at
" no very distant day. Therefore, though my opinions respecting it stand
" already, over and over again, recorded in terms the most positive as to
" meaning, and the most distinct as to expression, I am anxious, from a
" sense of duty towards my country as well as from a love of honest fame,
" to put them once more into print. If events should prove that *I am in*
" *error*, as to this weighty matter, justice towards those whom I may
" have *misled demands that I put into their hands the power of detection :*
" and, if events should prove that I am correct, *justice towards myself*
" *demands that 'I put beyond all dispute my claim to that public confidence*
" *which may serve as some compensation for all the persecution which I may*
" *have suffered, chiefly for having premulgated these very opinions which*
" *I am now about to re-assert.*"—Letter to Tierney, written the
1st July, 1818, and published in England on the 12th September
of that year.

## TO Mr. TIERNEY.

### ON THE APPROACHING DEATH OF THE SYSTEM.

*Kensington, 26th March, 1827.*

Sir,

Please to look well at the motto which I have inserted above. If you have leisure, please to look at the date as well as at the words of this motto. In the month of May preceding the date of the motto, a bill had been brought in to continue the Bank restriction for another year. You had made a speech, in which you had called upon the House of Commons to adopt effectual measures for returning to cash payments at the Bank. You had given it as your opinion that such return, though it might produce " *some mischief* " for a while, was, nevertheless, perfectly practicable, and that, if the return were " *gentle* and *gradual*," the mischief would not be great; that it would, at any rate, be but of short duration; and that, if such return did not take place, *a dread-*

A

Printed and Published by William Cobbett, No. 183, Fleet-street.
[ENTERED AT STATIONERS' HALL.]

*ful convulsion would be the end of the paper system.* -

The broadsheet, containing the report of your speech, reached me in that retreat, which had happily preserved me from a dungeon such as that of Ogden and John Knight, and of poor Riley, who, never having been confronted with his accuser, never having any thing but bare suspicion alleged against him, unable to bear the torments of his dungeon, to which he had been committed by the warrant of Sidmouth, put an end to his existence. I, more fortunate than these unhappy sufferers, was living happily and jovially, laughing at your troubles, when your speech above-mentioned reached me in the base and infamous Courier newspaper. I had, a thousand times before, exposed the shallowness of the opinions contained in that speech, but, I thought this a pretty fair opportunity of repeating these my exposures. I thought it right to put my opinions once more upon record ; and that, for the purposes mentioned in the motto. I knew well that the time would come when the wisdom of my opinions and the folly of yours would be established by events ; for, I also knew well, that those events were beyond the control of any human power.

After I have closed this letter, I will insert (for the third time) the whole of my letter to you, from which letter the above motto is taken. It was written and published eight years and a half ago. Since that time hundreds and thousands of English boys have become men. It is right that they should know, that there was one man, at any rate, who foresaw the calamities which they and their parents have now to endure, and it is right that they should know also, that that man had been driven into exile, to save himself from the dungeon to which he was destined for having been the foremost, the very foremost, most active and most efficient in endeavouring to bring about that reform of the Parliament, which he had contended would prevent these calamities.

Whenever the Ministry, or the Parliament, or both, shall plead GOOD INTENTION, in having adopted "Peel's Bill," which provided for cash payments which you so strongly recommended ; whenever either or both shall plead GOOD INTENTION in this case ; whenever they shall plead UNFORESEEN EFFECTS, as proceeding from this measure, whenever they shall put forward these pleas, here is the nation's answer to them: " You adopted your fatal measure IN JULY 1819; and, here, in the letter of our countryman, written in America IN JULY 1818, and published in England in *September* 1818 ; here, in this his letter to Tierney, are described, fully described, all the mischiefs which have arisen from this terrible measure ; and, therefore, good intention and unforeseen effects cannot plead you a justification or excuse. It is curious enough, Sir, that, in the letter to you, which I shall re-insert by-and-bye, I exhorted you to read what I had already written upon the subject. " Never mind its *cheapness*," said I, " the blanketeers have all read it. Why " should not you, one of the grave, " reverend, noble, and right ho- " nourable privy council, be as "*wise* as the blanketteers. If you "had read, *you could not have* "*made this speech.*"

I observed then, and I repeat the observation now, that the reformers, even those of them who had not a second shirt upon their backs, understood the whole matter well, while there was not the smallest appearance of its being understood by any member of both Houses of Parliament. Much about the same is the case still, and my opinion is, that thus it will continue, till Noah shall go into the Ark ; that is to say, till it will be much too late to endeavour to prevent that overwhelming desolation which this infernal system of funding and paper-money is naturally destined to produce.

When the bill had been actually passed in England, amidst those universal plaudits, that the ALLWISE-CANNING drew forth, when he congratulated the " collective wisdom" on the question having now been " set at rest for ever ;" when this bill had been passed, and the news of it had reached me, who was still in my retreat from the dungeon; when this news had reached me, I hardly knew how to contain myself for exultation. " Now," said I, " the savage boroughmongers will meet with their match." After about eight and forty hours thinking of the matter ; after riding round to the houses of three or four friends to laugh with them at the trap, which had been set by themselves, and into which our enemies had fallen : after this I began to write upon the subject ; and, in the first article I wrote, I put the passage pledging myself to surrender my carcase to be burned upon a GRIDIRON, if

that bill ever went into full and complete effect. Hence the *gridiron*, now taken as my *crest* ; and hence the fame which will long be attached to the name of that culinary instrument.

On the evening when CANNING brought forward the Corn project, I, who have a greater opinion of his heels than his head, was waiting to see him get out of his carriage at the entrance to the Parliament house, in order that, by seeing how he stood upon his pins, I might be able to judge of him as to other matters. I missed my man, who, it appears, out of pure modesty, I dare say, entered the House through some unostentatious channel. But, I saw you, Sir, and, whether you believe me sincere or not, I was very glad to see you look fresh and stout. You are an old antagonist of mine, and particularly upon this great subject, which is now about to be decided for good and all. I think we are both likely enough to see the system come to its close ; and I do hope, that that close will be as complete ; as much of a *finish*; as radical, and as lasting in its consequences, as it is possible for close to be.

This much, Sir, by way of preface to what I am about to offer you, on what I deem to be the approaching death of the system. There prevails at present, an universal belief, that some great and awful change is approaching. None but the most thoughtless of men, the most contemptible drivellers, or the wretched poltroons who are blinded by their fears, can possibly hope or believe, that the present state of things can long continue. Every where, except amongst the mere tax-eaters, there is most acute suffering, either bodily or mental. Several millions of pounds sterling have actually been taken out of the pockets of the merchants and manufacturers of England, and put into the pockets of the merchants and manufacturers of the continent, by the *new edition* of PEEL's Bill, which came piping hot from the press of the " collective wisdom," in the *month of March last.* No nation ever suffered so much, in one year, from pestilence or from famine, as this nation has suffered during this last year from this *new* and *improved edition* of PEEL's Bill. This I assert most distinctly, and I defy any man to bring me an instance of equal suffering from pestilence or from famine. There have indeed been both pestilence and famine : these rage yet, and in a constantly increasing degree; but, besides these, there has been a mass, and there is still a mass, and a growing mass, too, of moral suffering, of mental agony, such as never was witnessed before in this world.

You will please to observe, that this horrible mischief has all been done in the face of *ample warning* of the consequences. I have nothing to do, but to *open my book.* If the nation were to call upon me for proof that these evils might have been foreseen and prevented; if the nation call upon me, for the grounds upon which I have blamed the measures of mischief ; if thus called upon, I have only to open the Register, which affords me ten thousand proofs, that I foresaw, foretold every consequence, and that I pointed out the means which would have prevented the

evils. Will you say, that this was nothing to any of you ? Will you ask, why you are to believe me ? why you were to think me right and yourselves wrong ? If you ask me for the WHY of this, I refer you to the event for an answer. If you tell me, that it is more by hit than it is by wit, that I am right, I answer, that the proof of the falsehood of this is, that I maintained my opinions by arguments, which not a man of you ever attempted to answer. It was not *assertion* that I called upon you to listen to : it was argument that I called upon you to listen to : it was proof that I called upon you to be convinced by: no attempt to answer has any one of you ever made, while no small portion of you have wantonly calumniated the man, who had tendered you the proof. There has been amongst you, apparently, a tacit, solemn convention to do every thing that you possibly could, to keep my opinions away from the ears of the public, and to prevent even my *name* from being mentioned. The various arts and tricks, that have been used for this purpose, that sort of involuntary and tacit agreement to keep me out of sight; these have been the talk of no small part of the whole nation. The meanness, the baseness, and something worse than baseness, indeed, that has, upon various occasions, been brought into play for this purpose, but especially the MEANNESS, the poor, pitiful, caponlike folly, of supposing that you could make the people not see, if I were the object to be looked at ; this folly has been the subject of ridicule for years ; and, there is not a man of sound sense and of a just way of thinking; there is not one such man in this whole nation, who does not exult with me, when he beholds you embarrassed, bewildered, frightened out of your wits, and your knees knocking together at perceiving the awful workings of the system. "COBBETT IS RIGHT" is the cry of hundreds of thousands of just and sensible men; and, when the system shall finally be destroyed, and shall, by some great and glorious national effort, be hurled down into that hell from whence it sprang, the signal for the onset will be,"COBBETT'S RIGHT." Aye! my worthy representative of the *free and independent borough* of KNARESBORO', these words will live in print; this signal will be repeated by Englishmen, long and long after the present faculty of representative-making by the borough of KNARES-BORO' shall be, if remembered at all, a subject for a ballad or a farce.

As for ME, no compassion whatever is due from me, towards any class of sufferers, except the labouring class and the class of inferior tradesmen and farmers. All the rest have been able to hear *my voice.* They have all had an opportunity of hearing, if they would, and availing themselves of it. Some of them have turned away from the sound of that voice; others have shut their ears against it; others have endeavoured to stifle it by lies and every species of malignity. So that, I should be unjust, as well as foolish and base, if I were to feel any compassion for them: I am not unjust, and I am not foolish and base; and, therefore, I feel no compassion for them. I de-

serve at their hands much greater praises than their tongues and pens are able to bestow. They have heaped their praises on speakers and writers, who have used all the means in their power, not only to counteract my efforts, but literally to destroy me, body as well as mind. I am a singular, and, perhaps, a sole instance of one man having been right all the way through, as to a matter on which the fate of the nation turned, while I have had the whole mass of power belonging to the state, the whole mass of influence proceeding from *sixty* millions annually of taxes, and eight millions annually of tithes, together with the influence of the enormous monopolies arising out of paper-money, all constantly employed in order to counteract, embarrass, distress, and ruin, that one man! This is notoriously true; the whole nation knows it to be true; and, therefore, from me no compassion is due to any class, or to any one person of any class, except those who, from the nature of their situation in life, could not possibly know any thing of me or of my labours. I have said it many times, and I now repeat it, that I verily believe that the present calamities and perils would have been prevented, if they could have been prevented without making the whole nation see, that the measures of prevention were MINE. Let any just man say, then, whether I ought to feel compassion for the sufferers, or to exult at their sufferings! Oh! no, let them have compassion from you, from CANNING, from BROUGHAM, from SCARLETT, from the LOAN JOBBERS, from HUSKISSON, and from all the supporters particularly of the power-of-impri-sonment bill and of the Six-Acts. From me they will have no com-passion : if they bewail their lot, I open my Register and point to the warning. That is my answer to them. My day of triumph is come, and if I do not triumph, and openly triumph, let me suffer even more than any of my enemies. The Gridiron is the distinctive sign of that triumph. It is made : it is painted : it only wants gilding ; and, the colour of gold, and gold in appearance, *up it goes*, on the house whence the Register issues, the moment any . law shall be passed to lower the interest of the debt, to alter the standard of gold, or again to make bank notes a legal tender. I had a full right to hoist it, when Peel's bill was in part repealed in 1822 ; when a further repeal of it took place, by authorizing the Bank of England to issue one pound notes last year ; but, I have reserved the real hoisting of this Gridiron for ano-ther *Bank restriction*, or for a *grand sweep* of the national debt ; and one or the other of those we shall see at no distant day.

Every one *now* says, that *things cannot go on in their present way*. Some change, therefore, *all* men think necessary : some change, *all* men think inevitable : and, the only question seems to be, what is to be the kind and the degree of that change. A conversation in the House of Lords the other night, relative to the corn project, was quite sufficient to convince any reasonable man, that even those who ought best to under-stand the matter, are pretty nearly as much in the dark as ever ; and that they have no notion at all, or, at best, but a very indistinct no-tion, of the cause which is at work, and of the consequences that must follow. The Duke of Richmond criticized the projects of free trade, and seemed to want to prevent the *importation of wool.* He said, in support of this his opinion or wish, that the farmers had two years' wool on hand. He said two or three years' wool ; and that they *could not find a market for it.* Lord Darnley called for further protection for wool, and also said that the farmers had two years' wool on hand. The Marquis of Salisbury said that the farmers had two years' wool on hand, which *was quite unsaleable.* The Duke of Buckingham said, that there was two years' wool on hand, and " that he could not call that " a good market *where nothing was* " *sold for two years.*" This re-port can have hardly been in-correct in all these instances. But, what a strange state of things is this ! Men enabled, farmers ena-bled, to keep their wool two years in hand ; and, yet, complain of *their poverty !*

I agree with the Duke of Buck-ingham, that that cannot be called a *good market* where nothing is sold for two years ; but, why is nothing sold for two years ? Be-cause the makers of paper-money become, in fact, monopolizers of the wool, take the wool, in fact, into *pawn*, and thus keep it out of the market, in the hope, on the part of the farmer, that the market will rise. This is a species of *forestalling* which never entered into the minds of our ancient lawgivers ; and it is a mode of carrying on farming, contrary to every sound principle upon which that calling has ever been heretofore conducted. Dur-ing my " rural ride " of last-fall, I accidentally met, at a friend's house, a big farmer, who made the same complaint about the wool; said that he had two years' wool in hand, and that he could get nothing for it. He was a crusty sort of chap, pretty much inclined to be full as rude, or rather more rude than common prudence would permit him to be, to which general disposition was added, for the time being, what I should suppose was about a *two fifths of a drunk*, being sufficient to leave all the senses in pretty sharp play, and to take away enough of the discretion, to leave to the rudeness of the disposition its full swing. "And so," said I, " you " can get *no market at all for your wool!*"

FARMER. " No."

COBBETT. That's very surprising. I never heard such a thing before in my life.

FARMER. Ah, cunning as you are, you have not heard every thing in the world yet.

COBBETT. I find so, indeed, for I never before heard that a man could not *get any thing at all* for his wool; and, if I had heard it I should not have believed it.

FARMER. What, then, I am a liar, I suppose: eh?

COBBETT. No: I don't say that you are a liar.

FARMER. But you must think me one, for you say that if you had heard what I have said, you would not have believed it.

COBBETT. Why, no, that is not calling you a liar; but, I repeat, that if any one had told me that he could get nothing at all for his wool, I should not have believed him; and I say further, that if you can get nothing at all for yours, you must be a singularly

unfortunate man; for I know that there is a market for wool in every town in England: and I know, that there is even a market in this very village for your wool.

FARMER. I say there is no market at all, and that you had better stay in London and mind your business than to come here and to meddle with ours.

COBBETT. But I have business with you and with your wool; and, to come to the point; to prove to you that you are wrong and I am right, I'll buy all your wool of you, and our friend here, I am sure, will lend me the money to pay for it at once.

FARMER (*Eyes brightening*). You shall ha't. There's my hand.

COBBETT (*Shaking hands*). Well, how much have you got?

FARMER. The wool of about two thousand sheep for two years.

COBBETT. That's right: the more the better: send it here tomorrow morning, and we'll weigh it.

FRIEND. Well, now you two have made a *deal*. The wool is bought and sold. So far so good, and I think I have got money enough in the house to pay for it; but, there is one thing you have not settled; and that is, the price.

FARMER. Oh! ah! what do you mean to give?

COBBETT. I'll give you a *penny a pound*.

FARMER. G—d d—n your blood! *I've been offered seven-pence!*

COBBETT. The devil you have! I thought you told me you could get nothing at all for it; and you were almost ready to knock me down, because I seemed to sup-

pose it possible that your statement was not quite correct.

FARMER (*In a great rage*).
But do you think, then, that seven-
pence a pound is *enough!*

COBBETT. Yes, I do, upon my
word, *if that be the market price.*

FARMER. But how the Devil
then do you think that I am to pay
my rent, rates and taxes?

COBBETT. Ah! that's a matter
for amicable adjustment between
you and your landlord, and the
various sorts of tax-gatherers.
That's a matter quite above my
cut. You said you could get nothing at all for your wool. I
knew that I could get twopence or
threepence a pound for it, and, of
course, I could venture to offer you
a penny.

By the side of every farm house
fire in England, by the side of
every market room fire, talk like
that of this farmer is continually
going on. We talk of the uncul-
tivated state of the minds of savages. There are none of them
so ignorant of their own affairs, of
the causes of their happiness or
their misery, as English farmers
have now been made by the puzzling, by the bothering, by the
cheating, by the shuffling, by the
everlastingly deceiving system of
paper-money. What a hellish
system that must be, that can toss
men's property up and down in
this manner! A thing is worth
*what it will bring in the market.*
If it be kept over-year, it is kept
to the detriment of the public or
the detriment of the farmer; to the
detriment of the consumer or the
detriment of the grower. To the
one or the other it must be injurious. One must buy the cloth
dearer than he ought to have
bought it, or the other must finally

sell the wool for less than he
ought to have sold it. Generally
speaking, the wool, while it is
thus kept, is actually represented
by bank notes. It is a pawn to
the banker, to the wretched Rag-
rook, who now and then visits the
tods, to see that they are safe;
and, finally, when the wool comes
out for use, it comes loaded with
the interest of the money which
has been paid to the Rag-rook.
Upon the *whole*; upon an average
of transactions of this sort, the grower *can gain nothing* by keeping his
wool; for, if all keep, *all must
have to sell at last*; and at last the
price must become lower, in consequence of the keeping, not to
reckon the loss by inevitable waste,
and not to reckon stowage. So
that the farmers, as a whole, can
gain nothing by this species of
forestalling: first or last the whole
of the wool must come out, or be
destroyed by keeping; but, the
Rag-rook *gains to a certainty:* he
gets an interest on the value of the
wool as long as it is kept; that interest is finally paid to the Rag-
rook, partly by the farmer and
partly by the consumer; and thus
it is that the nation is oppressed
by this band of monopolizers, who
could not carry on their monopolies without the assistance of the
paper-money.

As a question between these
noble landlords and their tenants,
the wool affair is settled by the
above dialogue. There is a market; the wool can be sold; and
the MARQUIS of SALISBURY
seemed aware of this, for, when he
said, " *the wool is quite unsaleable*," he slips out at the end of
it, " except at ruinous prices!"
Ah! there's the point! And why
" *ruinous*," my LORD of SALIS-

BURY! Sevenpence a pound, I suppose, for South-Down wool; but why " *ruinous*," my Lord? You can tell me why in a minute if you will: you can tell me that these prices are ruinous because they disable the farmer from paying your rent, calculated on wool at fourteen pence a pound. And, my Lord, why, then, not lower your rents to the sevenpenny scale? You will tell me, that you cannot do that, while the taxes are at the fourteen penny scale. I then ask, with all submission, why you do not reduce you taxes to the sevenpenny scale? Because (you may tell me) there is a thundering army, there is a thundering dead weight, there are thundering places, pensions, sinecures, and grants, and a thundering debt! I dare not venture to ask your Lordship why you do not get rid of these; but I venture to assure you, that free trade, or no free trade, you will not see the price of wool rise much, *as long as the Bank of England shall pay in Gold of full weight and fineness*! The free trade fellows deserve to be laughed at, to be sure; but, it is the small note fellows, the PEEL's Bill fellows, the currency tinkerers, who are aiming to pay off a depreciated paper in gold of full weight and fineness. These are the fellows, that alternately puff up and pull down the price of the South-Down fleece, and that swamp this class to-day and that class to-morrow.

And, Mr. TIERNEY, are not YOU one of, and one of the leaders of, these meddling, tampering, and mischievous tinkerers? The very speech on which my Long-Island letter was a commentary, was an instance of your tinkering;

and, it ought always to be borne in mind, that PEEL's BILL, that the " MERIT " of that fatal bill, was CLAIMED BY YOU! It ought further to be borne in mind, that the wretched faction called " THE WHIGS ;" that that *tail*, or, rather, the be-fouled tip of the tail of that nasty, old, corrupt, riot-act-making, septennial-act-making, bank-note-inventing, loan-jobber-making; that nasty, filthy, corrupt; that rotton-borough-upholding; that tip of the villanous old confiscating and plundering Whig-faction: it ought always to be borne in mind, that it was this despicable *tail* that originated, and that was, in fact, the *real author* of PEEL's Bill, and of all the mischiefs which have proceeded from it. This is *bare justice*: it is hardly full justice; for, the despicable rump of faction was, for a whole year, bragging every day of its life, that it was *it*, which had caused the standard of value to be restored and re-established for ever! In like manner, this despicable rump boasted (and very truly) of being the real authors of the *free trade* project; and the great bleater of all of the dismal rump boasted, at a dinner which the fools at Edinburgh gave him, that it was *he* and his brother rumpites, who had at last *forced* the ministers to adopt the free trade project, than which statement nothing was ever more true, though coming from the lips of a bawler of this despicable faction. Yes, " *cash payments* " and " *free trade* " are presents which the tip of the cow's dirty tail has made the nation a present of.

This faction, then, offers to the miserable nation, a mighty resource in wisdom and in talent. I hear that Brookes's gambling-house is now filled with self-denying feelosophers, who meet each other with looks of perfect resignation; who look up at the places of the government, not as the fox did at the grapes, because they were out of his reach, but as a fox would look at grapes which he could not get at without danger of having his nose chopped off. These *feelosophers*, by way of revenge for the compulsive long fasting which they have been obliged to undergo, do, I understand, pretend that " THEY WILL NOT NOW COME TO THE KING'S ASSISTANCE," but are resolved to leave him to shift for himself! Poor man! they will leave him to shift for himself, because (now mark) " he *deserted* them when he came into his full royal powers." I do not know that he did desert them; but if he did, God knows it was time; and it showed that his Majesty had too much sense, and too much integrity, when he came to man's estate, to stick to these fellows who had surrounded him in his youth. To be sure, there is no telling what is to become of the poor king now, if the septennial-bill-making faction should refuse " to come to his *assistance!*" If he should not have the " *assistance*" of those who invented Peel's Bill and " Free Trade," what the Devil is to become of the King! He would do well to resign his crown at once; for he never can keep it, to be sure, if this *precious* " *assistance*" continue to be refused him! What! none of them;—none of you come to his succour!

Not Mr. Brougham, nor Lord John Russell, nor Lawyer Scarlett, nor Sir Bobby; O Lord, what will the King do! Do! why he will resort to the washerwomen about Windsor and Datchet, to be sure; for, nobody else on the face of this earth can effectually supply the deficiency.

This is a most miserable pretext. I do not know that the hungry cow's tail would not gladly jump at the places, even now, as things are; but, if they would not do it, it is, as I said last week, because they see the grain guarded by limed twigs; because they are afraid, *really afraid*, to dip into the mess of which they themselves have been the principal makers.

Let me be understood here, however; when I say that the tip of the cow's tail was the real cause of Peel's Bill, I do not mean to say, that the system could have lasted, if that Bill had not been passed. But, if the old grubbing dolts of the Pitt and Dundas school had not been worried by the cow's tail tip, they would have *let the* " thing " *go on*; and, by about this time, we should have seen two prices in the market; a paper price, and a gold price. We should have seen the taxes paid in *paper*, and the butcher and baker paid in *gold*, or in paper *at about three for one*. The soldier's shilling or thirteen pence a day, would have been worth about fourpence farthing in real money; and your 1200*l.* a year, my dear old friend, would have been worth about 400*l.* a year in gold. The "THING" would have gone on, like the *Old Whack*, as they call it, in the State of Massachusett's Bay, of which it took, upon one particular occasion, which I have heard talk of, *nine hundred and seventy-two pounds* to pay for a single breakfast. The people, who had one sort of goods to exchange for another, would have been very well by this time; but the army, the dead-weight, the placemen, the pensioners, men, women and children, and all the tax-eaters, and all the fundholders, and all the annuitants of every description, would have been precisely like muscles and cockles; or rather, like the myriads of *gasparaux*, which a spring-tide has gone and left on the beach of the shores of NEW BRUNSWICK, under a burning sun in the month of July! I wish you had ever seen those *gasparaux*, Sir! How they flap and how they gape and how they poison the air, in a few hours afterwards. Such would have been the fate of the innumerable shoals of tax-eaters, if the old Pittite grubbers had continued on in their way. There would, in that case, have been a most dreadful convulsion; and so there will be now; unless the Government and the Parliament come openly to my SHOP, and prevent, by an *equitable and timely* adjustment, the plunder, the confiscation and the bloodshed, which, in all human probability, must take place if such adjustment continue to be obstinately rejected to the last. The TOM TIT, weekly newspaper, which, by-the-bye, ought now to cease its *chee-wee-ing* about my pretended inconsistency, seeing that it, even it has begun to peck at that very man of many acres (BURDETT), whom it so lately praised, and for having attacked whom after having

formerly praised him, this TOM TIT so lately pecked at me! TOMMY TIT will now cease to talk about inconsistency, I hope! The truth is, that TOM TIT must have ceased to *chee-wee* altogether, if he had not shown hostility to this fickle, this crotchety, this inconsistent, this never-to-be-held-to-any-mark man of many acres, who, from being the most thorough-paced democrat that ever made his appearance in England, is now become all of a sudden, and without rhyme or reason, the most unbearable, the most insolent and most disgusting of aristocrats. The readers of the "TOM TIT" do not stand this; and, therefore, if TOMMY were inclined to stand it himself, he must "*chee-wee*" a little to the liking of his readers. This TOM TIT, as I was, above, going to say, affects still to censure my project for an equitable adjustment; and so does the stupid OLD TIMES.; and so does the not much less stupid Chronicle. But, come, Mr. TOM TIT, you who are read by maidens of taste on the upper side of forty; you, who are read by the cuckolds of the 'Change, and by the crowds that fill the cuckold carts that ply between LONDON and BRIGHTON. You affect to believe, that this *Equitable Adjustment* would not be *equitable*, because it would necessarily reduce largely the nominal sum which the fundholder receives in the shape of interest. But, *Tommy*, have you contemplated that which may possibly happen, if no such deduction take place? If no such deduction take place, if no *equitable* arrangement be made, every fundholder will finally lose every farthing of his or her funded property; and every annuitant, in every insurance office, will equally be ruined. Mortgagees may be a little better off, but every species of property coming under the shape of annuity, must, from the nature of things, cease to exist. It is useless to talk about taking vengeance of the aristocracy, or any body else. It is useless to talk of compelling them to make good the loss of the annuitants. There would exist no means of compulsion, nor would there be any tribunal to listen to the complaint of the losers. So that the TOM TIT, if it have any real regard for its maidens and its cuckolds, should take time to consider a little, before it join DADDY COKE and SUFFIELD and KNATCHBULL and JOHN SMITH and CALCRAFT and Lord CLIFTON and other equally wise persons, by no means forgetting Mr. BROUGHAM and LORD JOHN RUSSELL and ANNA BRODIE, in calumniating the author of the proposition for an equitable adjustment.

This adjustment will not, in all human probability, take place. No nation once brought to this pass, was ever yet saved by those who had brought it to this pass; and those who have brought it to such a pass, still have the power to keep their places, and to go on growing richer and richer at the public expense, and to have, at the same time, ninety-nine hundredths of the press speaking in their praise. Such men do not *reform*. They keep on as long as it is possible to keep on; and at last, when they seem to expect it no more than they did ten years back, the whole thing goes to pieces in their hands. There are, however, ge-

nerally, several indications of an approaching end to a system like this. And, what can be a stronger symptom than we now behold in all the various projects for *chopping* and CHANGING the laws?—What is come to the English nation, that English laws will no longer do for it? What is come to us that we cannot live without a foot, and horse, and land, and water *police*, and without a thundering standing army in the time of peace, every soldier of whom now it seems is to swagger along through the country with *ten* rounds of powder and ball in his pouch? What is come to us, when we stand in NEED of all this? What is it all FOR? Answer me that question, thou greatest "Captain of the Age;" a fig for your ten rounds of ball-cartridges, unless they will make *wheat dear and cause the Bank to pay in gold at the same time.* This is what is wanted, and, unless the ball-cartridges tend to produce this effect, they are of no use at all.

I see that *Stanley*, who met with such sweet salutes at Preston, is about to bring in a Bill to regulate the mode of taking the poll at borough elections! He thinks now, I dare say, that this borough work is to go on, and that all the DERBYS, that all the STANLEYS, and all the HORNBYS, and all the EGERTONS, are to go swimming on in the present way with wind and tide! Stanley, a word in your ear: find out a way, my lad, of making the farmers pay rents, and of making the Bank pay the interest of the Debt in gold at the same time: find out that, STANLEY; for, unless you can find that out, I can tell you, as a secret between you and I, that your bill about taking the poll at borough elections will be just as useful to you as one of your own rascally county newspapers, or one of the cards of any one of your once insolent and now broken down Cotton Lords. All these attempts at new projects are like the giving in marriage when Noah was getting ready to go into the ark. The only sensible things which are on foot, are the meetings of the weavers, and other common people, at Oldham, at Bolton, at that hell-hole Manchester, at Huntingdon, and elsewhere. Here the speakers and petitioners strike at the root of the evil; they do not amuse themselves with nonsense like that which comes from the lips and the pens of their pretended superiors: they clearly see the cause of their sufferings, and they manfully strike at it. I was delighted to see, that JOHN KNIGHT, who was the tenant of one of SID-MOUTH's dungeons in 1817 and in 1818, made an excellent speech at Oldham. Never did SIDMOUTH, though once a Speaker of the House of Commons, though once a Secretary of State, and though once a Prime Minister, and once your *patron*, Sir; never did this SIDMOUTH make in his whole life time, a speech half so full of knowledge, half so full of wisdom, a tenth-part so full of talent, as this speech of JOHN KNIGHT, who, by the dungeou-work of 1817 and 1818, was stripped of every thing but his talents and his integrity. JOHN KNIGHT was confined in a dungeon at Reading. When LORD FOLKESTONE described to the House of Commons the horrible treatment of Mr. KNIGHT, CASTLEREAGH answered, that the

man was MAD. Just God! There is KNIGHT making a most able speech at *Oldham*, while CASTLE-REAGH, who cut his own throat at North Cray in Kent, was declared by a coroner's jury to have been *mad* when he cut his throat!

Enough, Sir, for the present. We have to wait to see, now, how this thing will end. Those, who, until this time, have never had any other apparent disposition, than that of a desire to insult the people, now begin to have the feeling of fear. This, however, cannot save them. Such masses of injustice never can be passed over without notice of some sort, or other. For my own part, my complaint is, that the nation has been injured in the most dreadful manner, that it has had to endure sufferings the most terrible; by, or in consequence of, the rejection of *my advice*. That advice cost nothing. The Long Island letter addressed to you was sold for *two-pence*; more than twenty thousand copies of it were sold for two-pence a piece. You had two-pence, or else the devil is in in it. You could afford two-pence out of 1200*l*. a year; and the rest of the whigs, not excepting dead Lawyer HORNER and the Ministers, could surely afford *two-pence*. Their sinecure hack, GIFFORD, whom they have just buried amongst the tombs of that group of despicable slaves, who lie buried in the place called "Poets' Corner:" this vile hack WILLIAM GIFFORD, stuffed with a double commissionership of the lottery, and with a Government sinecure for life: this well-gorged parasite gave the name of "*two-penny trash*" to the Register; and my belief is, that none of you who have the bloated vanity to call yourselves public men, ever used to read the "*two-penny trash*." No wonder then that we are in our present situation; and I always say, that this nation not only *must* suffer, but that it *ought* to suffer, for not resenting the neglect of the Government, to listen to and to follow *my advice*. That it does suffer, and that it will suffer, is certain; but I say it *ought* to suffer. The nation itself has been unjust, with the exception of the working class, and the class of the inferior tradesmen and farmers. *I am able to save the country now;* I would pledge my existence, that I rescued the country from the danger of a convulsion: I am able to do it: I am willing to do it: the nation will not demand that I shall come to do it: the men in power and in Parliament laugh at me for saying I have this ability, while they have before their eyes the clearest of proof, that, hitherto, I have foreseen and foretold *every* thing that has happened, and that never was foretelling so amply fulfilled. You laugh, then, at my tender of services, do you? And, should I *weep* when I see your knees knock together? Shall I weep when I see you bewildered and distracted? Shall I *weep* when Ottiwel Wood and old Nicholas Grimshaw are wringing their hands? Am I to weep when Brougham and Knatchbull and Calcraft and Daddy Coke and Suffield are half frightened out of their wits? You can go on, can you, and make me a liar! Go on, then! Go on, I say! Carry your system on, I will stand and look at you; but the very Devil himself shall not

prevent me from *laughing*, and particularly when I see Stanley with his bill, for improving the manner of taking the poll at elections, and, this too, just at a time, when I am stating, in a rule of three question, how long it will be before an acre of Stanley's grandfather's land will let for a shilling or eighteen pence a year, or, be taken altogether for the use of the poor.

I now leave you, Sir, to the reperusal of my Long Island Letter. As you read it, remember that the author was in exile from his native country, for no other cause than that of having attacked the infernal system of paper-money and rotten boroughs; and that you were in Parliament, and in public pay, for no other cause than that of having been, and of still being, a supporter of that system. You are a lawgiver yet; and I trust that the time is still to come, when I shall hold up the contents of this letter to your face. Whether I do or not, I hold them up in the face of the nation; and again I say, that that whole nation, with the exception of the labouring classes and the lower rank of tradesmen and farmers, OUGHT to suffer, ought to be severely punished, ought to suffer in mind, body and estate, to a very considerable extent, for their baseness, in entertaining enmity towards me, or their not much less criminal conduct, in not calling upon the Government to follow *my advice*.

Wm. COBBETT.

TO THE

RIGHT HONOURABLE

# GEORGE TIERNEY,

*On his opposition to the Bank Protecting Act.*

*North Hempstead, Long Island,*
*1st July, 1818.*

SIR,

I ADDRESS you upon the subject of the debate on the thing called the *Bank Restriction* Act, passed in May last, and in which debate you took a part. I make use of your name upon this occasion for two reasons; *first*, that the Letter, which I am writing, may, without much of circumlocution, have an appellation to distinguish it from other of my Letters on the same subject; and, *second*, that I may directly, and, as it were foot-to-foot, place myself, as to some of your opinions, in opposition to you, whom I regard as being by far the most able man now in what is called the House of Commons. The question, upon which we are at issue, involves considerations of most tremendous importance; and the decision of it must take place at no very distant day. Therefore, though my opinions respecting it stand already, over and over again, recorded in terms the most positive as to meaning and the most distinct as to expression, I am anxious, from a sense of duty towards my country as well as from a love of honest fame, to put them once more into print. If events should prove that *I am in error*, as to this weighty matter, *justice towards those whom I may have misled, demands that I put into* their hands the power of detection; and, if events should prove that I am correct, *justice towards myself demands that I put beyond all dispute my claim to that public confidence, which may serve as some compensation for all the persecution, which I have suffered, chiefly for having promulgated these very opinions, which I am now about to re-assert.*

During the far greater part of my political life I have entertained, and have, with very little intermission, been endeavouring to produce in the minds of others, a hatred and a horror of the funding and paper-money system. In referring to its origin, I found it bottomed in a settled design to sap the foundations of the constitution of England; and, in tracing its progress, I found this design had been but too fully accomplished. But, it is not of the silent, the sapping, the corrupting effects of this system that I am now about to speak: nor is it of the misery, the starvation, the stripes, and the deadly wounds, which it is, at this time, inflicting on the nation. It is of the effects which it has yet in reserve; and with regard to which effects, I perceive, that you hold opinions opposite to mine.

I will not waste my time, as you thought proper to waste yours, in an exposure of the flimsy, the shuffling, the false, the ridiculous pretexts, which the Chancellor of the Exchequer put forward as the grounds of his proposition for continuing the protecting act in force for another year. It can never be worth the ink that one writes with to be listened to by those, who could, for one single moment, listen to those pretexts as something worthy of attention. Your observations on the *future effects* of the system, and your opinions as to the *practicability* and the *means* of preventing those effects: these constitute the only parts of the debate that merit the notice of any rational being.

It has always been an opinion, openly avowed by me, that the funding-system would be marked in its last stage, by a great national change; and, more recently, since it has been upheld as co-partner of the Borough-system, I have been of opinion, as I yet am, that the end of the funding-system will be the end of its associate; that they will die in each others arms amidst the shouting of the people; and this we may, I take it, call a great *convulsion.*

You are, I see, Sir, also of opinion, that the thing will end in a great *convulsion.* "He, there-"fore, exhorted the House to "show its *earnestness* upon this "occasion. If it did not do so, "he feared that the consequences "would be *dreadful;* that a ter-"rible *convulsion* would take "place. This was, probably, the "last struggle to guard against that "*melancholy event,* and let each "man, who felt *for the country,* "have the satisfaction of thinking, "that, whatever be the result, he "had done *his duty.*"—These are the words of the close of your re-ply. Sufficiently impressive: sufficiently awful the warning. But, of *what use* was the warn-ing? . What was it intended to produce? Much able statement in your speech; a great deal of well pointed reasoning. - But for *what?* To what end?

To put the matter into plain propositions, it stood thus: that

the House ought to be in *earnest:* that, if they were not, the paper-money would produce dreadful consequences and a great convul-sion; and that, in order to show their *earnestness,* they ought to appoint a committee to *inquire,* before they passed the Bill.

Thus far I see my way clearly. It is plain, and I cannot err. A great mischief, a dreadful conse-quence, a convulsion, may, in some cases, be prevented by stop-ping to inquire before we proceed to action. But, was this one of these cases? Could any inquiry have tended to prevent that blow-ing up, of which you expressed your dread? Was it *possible;* I will not say *probable;* was it *pos-sible;* was it within the compass of human skill or force, to make provision against that "*melan-choly event,*" which you antici-pated with so much apparent sin-cerity and sorrow? You seem to have been of opinion, that *it was;* I am of opinion that *it was not.*

In order to enter fairly upon the discussion of this question, to wit, whether it was, or was not, *possible* to obtain, by inquiry, any means of preventing a final blow-ing-up of the paper-system, I must look back at what you say, in your own speech, as to the topics and objects of inquiry. These I find stated in the follow-ing words: "There remained little "for him to say, except on the "subject of the *mischiefs which* "*some persons apprehend* from "the resumption of cash pay-"ments by the Bank of England. "To a *certain extent* he was wil-"ling to admit, that these appre-"hensions might, perhaps, be "well founded. He did not be-

" lieve, however, that any *violent* " *shock* could occur. He by no " means supposed that the Bank " would try to secure the continu- " ance of the restriction, by mak- " ing the resumption of cash pay- " ments as difficult and as dan- " gerous as possible; and he was " convinced, that *if the Bank* " *sincerely applied themselves* " *gradually* and *gently to prepare* " *for that resumption, although,* " *undoubtedly, a great diminution* " *must take place in the existing* " *circulation,* yet, that it *would* " *not be productive of any of* " *those fatal consequences which* " *it was the fashion to apprehend* " *from it.* If there were no other " grounds for going into an in- " quiry, the expediency of *trying* " *if a committee of that House* " *could not chalk out some course* " *by which the Bank of England* " *might resume their payments in* " *cash without endangering the* " *tranquillity and welfare of the* " *community, would be one amply* " *sufficient.* (*Hear, hear, hear!*) " Indeed, were we asked how " such a committee as that for the " appointment of which he was " about to move, could best em- " ploy themselves, he would say, " *in endeavouring to devise the* " *means by which the cash pay-* " *ments by the Bank might be* " *gradually brought about, and* " *a limit put to the issue of paper,* " *so as to facilitate those objects* " *without risking any serious* " *shock.* This, he believed, might " be done; but he also believed " that it could be done only by a " committee composed of intel- " ligent individuals, who would " calmly and dispassionately en- " ter into the investigation of the " subject, and collect all possible

" information upon it from those " who were the most competent " to the task of affording such in- " formation."

This, then, was to be the ob- ject of inquiry: the Committee were to " endeavour to devise the " means, by which the cash-pay- " ments by the Bank might be " gradually brought about, and a " limit put to the issue of paper, " so as to facilitate those objects " without risking any serious " shock." Your *opinion* as to the probability of the Committee's *effecting* this object is in the affirmative. You admit, that, to a certain extent, there may be *mischiefs* attending the resuming of cash payments; but, you do not believe that any *violent shock* would occur. You believe, that if the Bank were to apply them- selves sincerely to prepare *gra- dually* and *gently* for the resump- tion, although a great diminution in the circulation would take place, yet that no *fatal consequences* would ensue.

This was your *opinion*, Sir; and no wonder that it was *cheered* by those by whom you were sur- rounded. This opinion came, too, so pat just after my dismal pre- dictions and doctrines, contained in that Petition. This opinion had an effect upon the Borough men like that of æther or laudanum upon a losing gamester; or, like that of Loader's dram upon old Mother Cole. And, so you " went " out of the House *amidst the* " *loudest cheers!*" Thank you kindly, Mr. Loader! Bless you, dear Mr. Loader!

I must be insincere myself, or I must treat you with sincerity; and yet if I do, I am afraid I must offend you; for it is quite impos-

B

sible for me to consider you as
having been sincere upon this occasion without considering you as
extremely shallow with regard to
a matter, which you ought to have
well understood, before you attempted to speak upon it in a
public assembly; and particularly
before you took upon you to be a
leader in the discussion. As being
the least offensive of the two, however, I will suppose you to have
been sincere; and, upon that sup-
position, will proceed to give my
reasons in opposition to this your
consoling and comforting opinion;
which opinion is, that means can
be devised for enabling the Bank
to pay in coin *without* producing
any serious *mischief*, any *fatal
consequences*, any *violent shock*.

As to *mischief* or *fatal consequences*, I may think so too. But,
then, what you may think *mischief*
and *fatal consequences*, I may regard as *most happy events*. To
get rid of all misunderstanding
here, I shall, as I fairly may, suppose you to mean, that the payment may take place *without a
blowing up of the paper, and the
borough systems*; and, that the paper-money and the Debt and the
dividends and army and all can
go on as they now go on.

If, Sir, as a quieter to those
persons, whom you say, *apprehend mischiefs* from the resumption of cash payments; and, if, in
answer to the *fashionable* opinions
about *fatal consequences* to be apprehended from the same cause;
if you, as might have been expected, had, in answer to these
apprehensions, offered some reasons, instead of a naked opinion
in the negative, you would have
saved me a great deal of trouble.
However, your opinion being

wholly unsupported by any reasons does not prevent me from
stating reasons in support of my
opinion; and, if my reasons be
good, your opinion must be erroneous.

Doubtless a Committee of the
House of Commons, as it is called,
would consist of some surprisingly
ingenious gentlemen; but, though
they would have been able to draw
up, in a short time, a Green-Bag
Report, there are certain things
which they could not have done
unless the House could have communicated to them a *real* instead
of an hyperbolical *omnipotence*.
And, amongst the things which a
Committee could not have done,
one would have been, the preventing of the holders of notes
from going to get cash for them,
as soon as the Bank should begin
to pay: yet, unless they could
have done this, it is pretty clear
to me, that the payment would
not have gone on for two days.

That the Bank cannot venture
to pay *now* is certain. That fact
must be taken as *admitted*; because, if it could venture to pay
now, the bill would not have been
passed; no, nor asked for. And,
why cannot it pay now? For the
same reason that many other people cannot pay their bills; namely,
because it has not money enough
to pay with.

There are two ways of enabling
the Bank to pay: one, by *putting
gold into its coffers*, and the other,
by *reducing the quantity of paper now afloat*. As to the first, how
is the Bank to get more gold into
its coffers than it now has in those
coffers, which, I believe contain
very little? I ask *how*, Sir? What
scheme could your committee
have devised to effect this pur-

pence? Suppose I have a parcel of notes out, payable on demand. I wish to take them up; I wish to be able to pay them. I have not money enough to take them up; what am I to do? Borrow some money. But I must give more notes for the money I borrow, or must sell my goods or pawn them. The Bank has nothing to sell or to pawn; and, therefore, it must *buy gold with new issue of notes.* Now, Sir, if a man who had a hundred pounds out in notes, were to buy a hundred pounds in gold with another hundred pounds in notes, and then pay off the first hundred with the gold, and if all his notes were payable on demand to bearer, would he not be sent to a mad-house without any farther proof of his confirmed insanity?

A Member of Parliament, whom I once (in the Bullion Committee time) endeavoured to prevail upon to go to the House and blow all the absurdities into air, asked me, why goods might not be *sent abroad* and sold for gold, and the gold brought home to the Bank? My answer was, that there was no other objection to this scheme, than that the owners of the goods would, in all probability, want to keep for their own use, the gold that the goods would be sold for. His next question was, why the Government could not get gold *from South America.* To be sure, the mines were the places to look towards. But, then, it unluckily happened, that the owners of the gold in South America would demand *payment* for the gold; and, what was more, so little bowels would they have for SAMUEL THOMSON and Company, that they would take care, and have their goods before they would let

the gold go; and, then, if the Bank sent the goods, they must issue paper to pay for the goods. By the help of a fleet and an army, the Bank might, indeed, rob the South American Mine-owners to a trifling extent; or the Bank men might rob the houses and travellers at home, though; perhaps, they would find little except their own paper. This, probably, the Bank men would have some scruple to do, unless assured of an *indemnity* bill before hand.

Their case, then, as far as relates to augmenting the relative proportion of their gold, is desperate; for this last is the only *possible* way, in which they can effect that object. How should there be any other, except, to the asses ears of MIDAS, that Boroughmongers and Bank-men could add his gold-creating touch? They have a parcel of paper, a mass of paper, of *no value*, which they want to convert into pieces of precious metal. A few years ago there was a Norfolk Farmer, who sold five hundred golden guineas to the Guard of the Norwich Coach, for twenty-seven shillings each. The dealer brought down the money the next trip, and asked for the guineas. The farmer had them in London, and up he went with the guard in order to deliver them. He had them *quite safe* in London, for they were in the *Bank*, where he had lodged them three years before, for the sake of *secure keeping!* He went to the Bank, but it was restrained from letting him have them out!

There are very few now-a-days, who are so foolish as this farmer was. When that prime agent, Gibbs, was calling for his fellow labourers to make me a "*blighted example*," he did not, I dare say, imagine, that he was doing that which would produce a *new era*, a totally new era, in political knowledge—"*Paper against Gold*" was amongst the fruits of that deed; and, Sir, whatever those to whom you addressed yourself may think, the *people* of England, the suffering people of England, know all about the paper-money system, and about which, before my foes thought they had murdered me, the people in general knew no more than they knew of the feats of witches and wizards. They did not know what a fundholder, a loan-jobber, or a director was. They knew nothing of the manner of making funds and debts; and, they, if possible, knew less than nothing about the manner in which *they themselves* were affected by this mystery. Little did they, before this period, imagine that this system of funding took from them four pence at least in the price of every pot of beer; and, that it was, in fact, this system, first proposed by BISHOP BURNET, which first by degrees, stripped the artisan and the labourer of all those conveniences and the means of good-living which were enjoyed by their grandfathers. The mass of the people knew, in short, nothing about the matter. But Gibbs and his fellow colleagues had tied me to the stake; and that was destined to be the means of producing a new era in political knowledge. "*Paper against Gold*" will, long and long after the bubble shall have bursted, and overwhelmed all those who now, by various means, work the nation, live to bear testimony to my for-

titude and perseverance, and to the infamy of my persecutors.

But, the good of the thing is, that, while *the people* read this little book, the foes of reform do not read it. So that these latter, to their natural and habit-engendered stupidity, add, in this case, a refusal to use the ordinary means of acquiring knowledge. The *Blanketteers*, who cannot have less than about twenty thousand copies of this little book amongst them, and who have seen all its principles established and its predictions verified, to the very letter, by events; the Blanketteers, Sir, if they happened to read the debate, on which I am commenting, would smile at those *cheers*, with which the House honoured your comforting opinion. The Blanketteers would laugh at the idea of the Bank *adding to its stock of gold*; they would laugh at the idea of the Bank "*sending out gold and re-purchasing it*," as mentioned in another part of your speech; for their little book has, long and long ago, taught them how futile, how childish, how contemptible, all such notions are.

I have said, that it is *impossible*, absolutely impossible, for the Bank to *add to its relative stock of gold*, except by direct *robbery*; that is to say, by a robbery committed in South America (not easy), or a robbery committed on the highway and in the houses at home: a dash at the gold baubles and silver spoons. I can see, I think, what is running in your head upon this subject. You seem to imagine, that, if the Bank were to issue a parcel of notes and to purchase gold with them, though they would thereby *add* to the *positive* quantity of notes, they would *diminish* the *relative* quantity; for that, the new notes would lodge gold equal to themselves in amount, which the old notes have not done. You will say, that if a man has a hundred one pound notes out, and has only one guinea in his coffers, and then put out another hundred notes and buy guineas with them, and put the guineas in his coffers, he will, by this operation, have *added to his relative quantity of gold.*

This is all very true, only you are supposing what it is impossible to effect. But let us see how an attempt in this way would work in practice. Suppose the Bank to have 30 millions of notes in circulation, and to have half a million of gold in their coffers. Well; they want to add to their gold; *why?* Because they want *to be able to pay in gold.* They, therefore, buy ten millions of gold; but, they do it with an *additional issue of notes;* and, mind, this issue must exceed ten millions, because, the paper must be *below par,* else the Bank could now pay in gold, without any purchase of gold. Very well, then; the Bank has now ten and a half millions of gold in its coffers, and much more than forty millions of paper afloat.

You are aware, I suppose, that this new issue of paper would instantly send up prices to an enormous height; you are, I suppose, aware, that it would sink the value of the paper in the same proportion; if you are not aware of these things, the *Blanketteers* are. But, having this gold in its coffers, the Bank *will then begin to pay.* Indeed! If it does, I can assure it, that I, who hold 21 of its depreciated pound-notes, will instantly go and get twenty of its guineas

for them. Thus will every other note holder act, to be sure: so that, in about two days all the gold will be drained out, and the quantity of paper left in circulation will be much greater than before the remedy was applied.

A worthy friend of mine, and one of the most pleasant, hearty, and able men I ever knew, the late Mr. BAVERSTOCK, of Alton, used 'to say of the *Unitarians,* " I want to know what they *would " be at;* they will believe, and " will not believe; they will have " a creed, and yet they will be " infidels." Your financial faith, Sir, appears to me to be of this description. You think this paper-money a very *dangerous* thing; you think it big with fatal consequences, shocks and convulsions; and you think it *very easy,* perfectly *easy,* for the Bank to *pay out its gold* and then *buy it back again,* only by experiencing *some loss.* If this be true, Sir, what ground is there for alarm? If this be true, the borough-men may snore away the whole twenty-four, instead of twenty hours of their time.

That the Bank is quite able to *pay its gold out,* and that it might effect the thing in a very short space of time, nobody, I believe, will dispute; but, as to getting it *back again,* that would be a very different matter: for, as we have clearly seen, it must be effected by the means of new issues of paper; and, therefore, supposing the paying out not to cause a total blow-up at once, the Bank would, when the operation was over, only be just where it was before the operation began.

The " *some loss* " it is, however, that puzzles me the most. I must quote your words here; for, as I can hardly believe my own eyes, my friends, the Blanketteers, may well doubt of their correctness upon this occasion. " Let the " Bank of England send out large " quantities of gold from their " coffers. That would alter the " rate of exchange. The Bank " would have *no difficulty in pur-* " *chasing gold to replenish their* " *coffers,* though certainly at *some* " *loss.* But the question was, " which was best—that Great " Britain should lose the charac- " ter for good faith which she had " hitherto maintained, or that the " Bank *should be obliged to dis-* " *gorge* a part of the enormous " profits which it had made from " the country at large? (*Hear,* " *hear, hear.*) Was it more de- " sirable that the public credit " should be preserved, or that the " Bank, having accumulated mil- " lions upon millions, without con- " tributing in the smallest degree " to the national expenditure, " should be enabled to persevere " in that system!" (*Hear, hear, hear!*)

Yes, yes! they may cry " hear, hear, hear!" But, Sir, the Blanketteers know very well that all this affected reproach on the *Bank* is mere words. Be you assured, that all of the Blanketteer order are quite proof against every attempt to impose on them by affected reproaches against " *the Bank.*"

Aye, Sir, " *Let* the Bank send " out *large quantities* of gold from " their coffers." They must get these quantities in first, to be sure; but, never mind that; let us, for argument's sake, suppose the larger quantities to be there. Well; now the gold is sent out. *How* is the Old Lady to get it back? She is, it seems, to purchase it back. With *what?* With *what?* With *what,* I say! Answer me, or I die! With *what* is she to *purchase* it back? Why, with a *new batch of notes,* to be sure; unless she go and plunder the gold and silversmiths' shops, and rifle the butlers' pantries. In what other way is the old girl to purchase it back? A witch, indeed, she is, as far as tormenting goes; but, as to the turning of paper into gold, she is as harmless as the innocent in the cradle. It is all nonsense; it is all absurdity indescribable; for, what would be done *at home,* while the gold was travelling to and from the continent. But, never mind this: let us swallow this: she would, by the operation, supposing it to be as you say, gain nothing in the way of ability to pay.

But the " *loss;* " the " *some loss,*" that she would experience: what can that mean, I wonder? Pray, Sir, what has the old Lady *to lose?* Do you happen to know the precise, or probable, place of deposit of any of her *valuables?* If you do, it would be but friendly dealing to apprise the Blanketteers of it. Do you allude to *her shop,* or to the *houses and lands and chattels* of the Directors and others of her Company? These she might, indeed, lose; but they would amount to little. Do you allude to the several millions of what is called *Stock,* or *Funds* or *Per Cents.,* of which she is the *owner?* Come, here we have, then, the Great Book before us, and here we find her written down for, suppose, twenty millions. Now, then, what is your notion? That she can get people to come and purchase part of this stock *with gold* at a *loss* to her; that is to say, *below the current paper price!* Why, Sir, the very thought of such an operation would send down her paper fifty to the hundred: and, an attempt to put it in practice would blow up the whole thing.

No: you mean none of these. Your meaning is, that she must give *more* for the gold in paper than the nominal value of the gold, if in coin; and a *higher price* than the real money-price, if in bullion: and this would be neither more nor less than making upon the whole of the operation, an addition, relative as well as positive, to the quantity of her paper.

There remains, then, as I said before, no way, but that of direct robbery and plunder, to add to the relative quantity of her gold by the *bringing in of gold.* I have, indeed, overlooked one way of effecting this grand purpose, and which way I must notice before I proceed to the second part of my subject. It is this; the landowners might give up their estates, equipages, and other moveables. These would bring *gold* quickly. This gold might go to the Bank, and it would, as Mr. CATLEY truly said, enable the Old Lass to face her creditors, pay off her notes, and to pass once more for an honest dame. Whether these conscientious landmen, who cheered you, and who are so anxious to see guineas return, would voluntarily acquiesce in this measure, I must leave for wiser men to decide; but that this (with the exception of the robbery and burglary plan) is the only means by which gold can be brought into the Bank in such a

way as to augment the relative proportion of gold now in the coffers of that prime instrument, must, I think, now be clear as day-light to every one, who is not wilfully and obstinately blind.

We now come, Sir, to the *other* mode of augmenting the relative quantity of the cash of the Bankmen; namely, *the reducing of the quantity of their paper.* It is your opinion that this *can be* done in such a degree as to enable the Bank to resume cash-payments, and that, too, without producing any shock; and that, by this means, the present system of sway in England may be carried on for ages yet to come.

In combating this opinion, I shall hardly be a cool, because I shall be a deeply interested, reasoner; for, if I could believe your opinion to be sound, I should be the most mortified and most miserable of human beings. It is a directly opposite opinion, firmly settled in my mind, that forms the sole foundation of my hope. Were it not for this hope, I should droop down into a state of despondency, and, without another effort, give up my unhappy country.

But, whatever my wishes may be, they cannot impair my reasoning. I know well, that, according to the creed of your hearers, truth is not truth, if it drop from my pen: nor is this of any importance in my eyes: with the rest of mankind the case is different. They will reject, or adopt my opinions, as these are unsupported, or supported, by undoubted fact and conclusive argument. I do not, like you, Sir, hold forth naked opinions to be adopted and acted upon by others: I tender not any thing of *mine* as the grounds of their belief: I ten-der reasoning, which is the com-mon property of all mankind.

You say, Sir, that you think, that "means may be found, by " which cash-payments may be " *gradually* and *gently* brought " about, and a limit put to the " issue of paper, *without risking* " *any serious shock.*" I say, that such means *cannot* be found.

You speak, indeed, with some *diffidence:* and, in a former sen-tence, you "are willing to admit, " that *mischief,* to a *certain ex-* " *tent,* might arise." This is an altered tone. The bullion com-mittee did not talk in this way. They, and especially your wise patron, Lord Grenville, boldly said, that the Bank ought to be compelled to pay on a day to be fixed, as the *only means* of restor-ing the currency of the country to a *healthy* state. A man must be a Lord to utter a foppish phrase like this without being hooted.

But, to get rid of all loop-holes, I admit your qualifications to mean, that the greatest of all pos-sible precautions must be taken, and that, even with all these pre-cautions, some *mischiefs,* as you call them, *something of a shock,* must and will take place. Even this view, which is the most fa-vourable that you, an orator of the Borough-men, can take of the matter, would be quite sufficient to alarm any one but a besotted English fundholder.

I, however, set at nought all your qualifications; and, I say, that the thing must go on as it now is, that the Bank *never* can pay, or, that the whole system, Borough-men and all, must be blown up. This is my opinion; and I now proceed to state the reasons, upon which that opinion is founded.

The use of the words "*gra-dually*" and "*gently*" make a great drawl in the expression of your opinion. They discover great diffidence, great unfixed-ness, and, indeed, great *confusion,* in your mind. You advance like one of us Englishmen here, when, in the burning hot weather, we attempt to imitate the natives in going without shoes. You had been set up by your party, to put to shame the poor stick that had been appointed to bring forward the Bill. You were compelled to oppose him, and yet you had too much regard for your own repu-tation to say point-blank, that the Bank could be enabled to pay. Hence all your qualifications and reservations. But, you do not seem to have perceived, that these, in certain cases, lead to, instead of keeping clear of, embarrass-ment; and, that, instead of saving a general position, they destroy it altogether.

Precisely thus has it happened here; and, if I had a mind to make short work of your opinion, I might stop at showing the com-plete absurdity of this notion of a *gradual* and *gentle* resumption of cash-payments; but from this temptation to laziness I abstain, and will, therefore, reserve the folly of this notion for exposure in a subsequent part of my letter.

To enable the Bank to pay in gold on demand *the Old Lady must reduce the quantity of the floating paper.* Indeed you say, that *a great diminution* must take place in the currency of the country. Now, it is incontestibly true, that such *diminution* must create a great *lowering of prices;* and, it is not less true, that this lowering of prices must be *far greater in proportion* than the diminution in the quantity of paper-money. Because, the first effect of the lessening of the quantity of money afloat, is to straighten and throw into discredit many persons who got along pretty well amidst the abundance of money. The operations of this class, therefore, do not remain in *degree*, but are *put an end to altogether*. When money is plenty, it moves *quicker* than when it is scarce. A horse will be sold and re-sold *ten times* amidst abundance of money, and, perhaps, not *twice* when money is scarce ; and, a shilling which passes twenty-one times a day from hand to hand, is just as efficient in its effect upon prices, on a national scale, as a guinea that changes possessor but once a day.

What, then, are the *unavoidable* consequences of a great diminution in the quantity of currency afloat, and of. this lowering of prices ? The ruin and misery of a great part of the people, and the actual starvation of many. These are the inevitable consequences of a lowering of prices by the means of a *change in the value of money;* and, it is clearly seen, that such change must be effected by a diminution of its quantity.

Suppose me to be a haberdasher. I have my shop full of goods, as many as I shall sell in a year. I lay in my stock to-day. It amounts to three thousand pounds, two of which I have credit for. I deal in gloves, only, and they are laid in by me at 4s. a pair. I begin selling; and 6s. a pair gives me a good profit. But at the end of a month, the Bank goes to work to prepare for cash-payments. It draws in a great deal of its paper. Money becomes scarce. Prices fall. I can sell my gloves at only two shillings a pair, and I am done for at a blow. Thus it must be with the farmer, the manufacturer, and with every person engaged in trade, no matter of what sort.

A man borrows a thousand pounds to-day, upon a house worth two thousand. Next month the Bank draws in its paper, and the house is not worth one thousand. He loses his house for ever.

Another dies to-day, leaves an estate to his son, worth three thousand pounds, with legacies to pay out of it to the amount of fifteen hundred. Before a sale of the estate takes place, the drawings in of the Bank have lowered the worth of the estate to one thousand. The legacies can be paid only in part, and the son is a beggar.

Wheat is 15 shillings a bushel, and a man, calculating upon that price, rents a farm at a hundred a year. The drawings in at the Bank brings wheat down to 5 shillings a bushel. The man cannot pay his rent, his stock is seized and sold. He goes to gaol, and his family to the poor-house.

In the meanwhile, there is no money to pay the journeymen and labourers. Employment cannot be had; and starvation follows. However, men do not, in very great number, starve to death, without an effort to save life. Hence robberies and thefts ; and, to prevent detection, come murders. This is the natural, this is the inevitable progress.

These would be the consequences if there were no taxes at all. What, then, must the conseexpences be, in a country where the taxes amount to double the sum that the rent of all the houses, lands, mines, and canals amount to? And, how is the army and how is the interest of the debt to be paid, if the wheat fall to 5 shillings a bushel? You know very well, Sir, that they are now paid partly by *loans*, in one shape or another. You know, that there is not so much raised as is wanted, by *fifteen millions a year.* You know, that loans to this extent are annually made. You know that these loans go to augment the debt and the dividends, and that this requires an augmentation of the paper-money. How, then, are the dividends and the army to be paid, if prices be lowered to the standard of wheat at 5 shillings a bushel? If money enough cannot be raised now; if the debt keeps on increasing *now*, what is it to do when this lowering of prices shall take place? And you complain of the amount of the debt; blame the poor stick for not making an effort to reduce it; and, yet you would add to it by an attempt to make the Bank pay in coin! You would reduce it by *doubling its real amount!* Yes, by giving the fundholder three bushels of wheat, where you now give him but one! You are sadly pestered! Sadly bemired!

As I am not for arguing upon any *disputed* fact, I do not think it necessary to bind myself down to wheat at *five* shillings a bushel. I am decidedly of opinion, that the resumption of cash payments would bring it down to 3 shillings a bushel. The Bank by its mere *attempt to prepare* for cash-payments brought down the wheat to *seven* or *eight* shillings a bushel.

It brought it down to this price from 15 shillings a bushel; and, why are we to believe, that it would not have come down to 3 if cash payments had really been begun?

The miseries of 1816 and 1817 are hardly forgotten yet; and the acts of those days *never* will be. The thing saved itself then partly by violence; but it could not have done that long; and, therefore, out it tumbled its paper again. Without *this*, dungeons and gags and gallowses and bayonets would have been, in a very short time, of no avail. It is not the return of *prosperity* that you now behold; but the return of *paper*.

When the misery was at its height, the Bank put out their new gold and silver coin. The fools thought they were getting back to *the chink* of coin. But, compelled to slaughter a starving people, or to bring back the paper, they yielded, and brought the paper back; and instantly flew away all their gold and silver; and CASTLEREAGH, during the debate, says, *that the new Sovereigns were all melted down and sent out of the country!* The Bank have, in order to obtain a *respite,* put forth the paper again, and you, their orator, would have them, in order to *avoid a convulsion*, draw it in again!

In " *Paper against Gold,"* Letter XXV., I had said, that, if the Bank attempted to draw in its paper, universal ruin would ensue. Pray, Sir, read that Letter. Never mind its *cheapness.* The Blanketeers have all read it. Why should not you be as wise as they? If you had read it before you had made your speech, you would, I think, not have said what you did.

I there proved, that universal ruin must be the effect of such an attempt. That attempt was made, and the ruin came!

But, you wish the Bank to proceed *gradually* and *gently*. When a man has *means* that are dropping in *gradually*, he may pay gradually; but this is quite another case. The Bank has *now* all the means that it ever will have, or can have. If the paper be drawn in gradually, the approach of the misery and ruin and uproar will be gradual, that is all. The want of employment will come on *gradually* and *gently*, but it will *come*. The convulsion will be the *end* of the scene, but there will be a *convulsion*. The notion of the man, who attempted, by slow, and very slow, very gentle degrees, to teach his horse to live without food, was much about upon a level with this notion of yours. The man succeeded at last; but just at the moment the *horse died*. To draw in the paper-money without reducing the interest of the Debt and all public pay and salaries, is to ruin all persons in trade, and to starve the labouring classes; and what signifies it whether this ruin and starvation come all at once, or by degrees?

But, besides this argument founded on the nature of the case itself, we have before us one of experience. The Bank did proceed *gradually*: it did proceed *gently*. It began drawing in, in 1814; it kept on, until 1816, about October. This was gently enough. The *nonsense* of those years will stand for ever recorded as the tip-top nonsense of the world. The tradespeople called for cheap corn; the farmers and their greedy landlords for dear

corn. The landlords would "*tell the house of it*, that they would!" And away they went to the "*omnipotent house*" to *secure them* a fair price for their corn. The House passed a Corn Bill "to "*protect* the farmer, that useful "member of society." And Corn grew *cheaper* and *cheaper!* I kept telling Mr. COKE and Mr. WESTERN, that they were upon a very wrong scent. I told them, that *the old lady was at work*, and that no Corn Bills would protect them against *her* craft. The distresses kept on increasing; and, in 1816, on came the wise landlords again with long strings of resolutions for *the relief of agriculture*.

The true history of all the miseries of 1815, 1816, and 1817, is this: When *peace* came, the shame, the disgrace, the infamy, and, more than all these, the *danger* of not paying in gold, or, at least, not appearing to pay in gold, stared the administering tools full in the face. An attempt to *appear* to pay could not be made without drawing in a great deal of the paper. These tools were too weak to perceive the full extent of the consequences of even such an attempt. They appear, however, to have been afraid to make it. But, there was I, baiting them weekly with charges of insolvency. Foretelling that they never would pay; foretelling that they would finally be the scorn of all the world; and, in short, galling them in all sorts of ways; not forgetting to remind them, that when their paper money blew up, we should have our *parliamentary reform*. To work they went, therefore, drawing in their paper, and on came the ruin and misery; slowly, gradually, gently enough;

but, still it *came on.* I kept, even on, as the Yorkshire-men say, telling them that their scheme would not succeed; that they would never be able to pay; *that they must put out the paper again.* They, like fools as they were, *persevered.* We, as we had a right to do, pressed them *for reform.* We beset them with arguments and prayers. They threw off their mask.

But while we gained the advantage of seeing them in their naked form, they gained nothing at all. They were, though well set out with dungeons and gibbets, compelled to *bring back the paper again;* and to stand before the whole world, as they now do. The ruin and misery they produced by this vain attempt opened the people's ears to the various causes of their sufferings; they made men listen, who before turned a deaf ear; they were the cause of the spread of knowledge more extensive than any people ever before possessed.

If, Sir, you want *more* proof, than has now been offered, to convince you, that the Bank *never* can pay, without producing a convulsion in the country, I confess my inability to furnish it; and, therefore, I here close my arguments upon the subject.

But, then, there remains the question, *what is to become of the thing at last?* That is quite another matter; and I am as fully convinced as you appear to be, that the consequences will finally be " *fatal;*" in which conviction I am as happy as you seem to be miserable. You say, in one part of your speech, that you are " per-" fectly aware, that there are per-" sons in the country, who are

" *alarmed* at the prospects of cash " payments. These persons ap-" prehend *all sorts of horrors;* " that *nobody will get his rents,* " that *the funds will be at zero,* " and that there will be *a general* " *bankruptcy.*" Oh, oh! They begin to see this, then, do they! Ah, ha! I am glad to find that they are coming to my opinions at last! Very well, then, the thing is, I suppose, to *remain as it is?* Is that what they mean? If it be, they are deceived. It will not remain as it is long. The blowing up will come, whether the Bank draw in its paper, or not. The government must go on *borrowing,* unless they issue such quantities of paper as to make the guineas sell for thirty shillings. This borrowing must regularly add to the quantity of paper. This paper will, in spite of their teeth, come, at last, to an *open* contest with gold: *two prices* will show their faces, and then, good bye Bank-men and all the thing! The taxes will be paid in paper; the law-men and spies and fund-holders and soldiers, will be paid in taxes; and the butcher, baker, and brewer will insist on having real money!

This will be the end, if the thing go on in its present way. Your scheme would, probably, bring the thing to a close sooner; but, be the end when it will, or how it will, the prediction of PAINE will be verified: the Borough-system will last as long as the paper-money-system, and not one moment longer.

Precisely *how* the thing will terminate, whether it will die gradually down into the bottom of the socket, or go out at once by a puff, is a question that I do not pretend to be able to determine:

it is sufficient for me to know, that the total extinguishment will come; and that it will bring with it liberty and happiness; a King and people both enjoying their rights.

I am, Sir,
Your Most obedient
And most humble Servant,
WM. COBBETT.

---

## DUKE OF YORK.

---

EITHER this nation must be openly acknowledged to be the basest in the whole world, or the most duped and insulted. The newspapers, from one end of the country to the other; the whole of this infamous press, without hardly a single exception, is employed in promulgating the most disgusting, the most nauseous, the most corrupt, the most putrid and the most stinking eulogiums on the memory of this man. The eulogiums, to use the words of the late Ellenborough, uttered in the House of Lords, are "*false as hell*"; and, to use the words of Canning, when speaking about that persecuted QUEEN, (with regard to whom the DUKE of YORK's conduct is very well known), to use the words of CANNING, on an occasion connected with that *Queen*, "SO HELP ME GOD," these eulogiums shall not go forth AFTER NEXT WEEK, without having to face SOME TRUTH, at any rate, respecting the object of them. What! has this corrupt press; this mercenary, this vile, this detestable, this nasty scotch-irish; this nasty set of hirelings, half crabbed accents and half blubber; has this base and mercenary crew, this clump of hired pens; has it got such sway over the minds of really enlightened, but *modest* Englishmen, as to cause them to believe, that the DUKE of YORK ought to be held in reverential recollection by Englishmen? *Silence* upon such occasions, is the prudent and becoming course; and, I will pledge my life, the KING would say the same, if the question were put to him; because I have a right to presume, that his MAJESTY is a man of sound understanding. Nobody more than he ought to deprecate the officious babble, the insolent twattle of these pretended friends to the memory of his brother. At any rate, I am resolved, and I say, "so help me God," that this infamous press shall not thus bamboozle the honest and just people of England. It has required a good deal to goad me to this; I have been called upon from all parts of the country, and from the soundest and most sensible of men, that I know of, to stem this torrent of insolent humbug and falsehood. I could see the nasty, greasy wives, the lazy loads upon the backs of the industrious tradesmen, and their tucked up daughters treading in the steps of their insolent and beastly mothers: I could see all these, sitting at or round that piano, which is a mere excuse for not being at work; I could see them drawn off in bombazeen, for which possibly they had run the toiling husband in debt; I could see this, with only a feeling of ineffable contempt for the creatures thus drawn off. When I came to the *husbands* indeed and *fathers*, who had been beggared and perhaps put in gaol, in consequence

of those enormous taxes, arising,
in great part, from that thundering
standing army and that thundering
dead weight, at both of which,
this DUKE was at the head; when
I came to these husbands and
fathers indeed, I felt my contempt
mingled with indignation. Still,
*loathing of the subject, habitual
loathing of the subject,* prevented
me from giving utterance to my
contempt and indignation. But,
goaded on, as I now am, by the
insolent eulogiums before mentioned, and called upon as I have
been, by excellent friends in various parts of the country, I will,
" so help me God," as CANNING
said, endeavour to put forth a little matter of historical truth, respecting this same DUKE of YORK;
and then I shall leave his mourn-
ers to enjoy in uninterrupted tranquillity, those pleasing reflections
which their having mourned for
his Royal grace, are calculated to
inspire in their enlightened and
loyal minds.

## AMERICAN KIDNEY BEANS.

I HAVE two sorts of these, the
finest that ever were in England;
one of them the very earliest that
I ever saw; and the seed, in both
cases, so ripe, sound, and excellent, that a large crop from it is
certain.—One sort is *Yellow*, the
other *Speckled*; both are dwarfs.—
Price—17s. a bushel, and smaller
quantities in proportion, with
something added for paper, string,
and trouble.—They are sold at
the Office of the Register, No. 188
Fleet Street, and may be sent, by
order, to any part of the country,

## MARKETS.

Average Prices of CORN throughout ENGLAND, for the week ending March 16.

Per Quarter.

| | s. | d. | | s. | d. |
|---|---|---|---|---|---|
| Wheat | 56 | 9 | Rye | 38 | 8 |
| Barley | 37 | 3 | Beans | 48 | 2 |
| Oats | 30 | 4 | Pease | 50 | 2 |

Total Quantity of Corn returned as
Sold in the Maritime Districts, for
the week ended March 16.

| | Qrs. | | Qrs. |
|---|---|---|---|
| Wheat | 40,984 | Rye | 331 |
| Barley | 201637 | Beans | 3,335 |
| Oats | 15,943 | Pease | 1,151 |

*Corn Exchange, Mark Lane.*

Quantities and Prices of British
Corn, &c. sold and delivered in
this Market, during the week ended
Saturday, March 17.

| | Qrs. | £. | s. d. | | s. d. |
|---|---|---|---|---|---|
| Wheat | 4,669 | 14,913 | 5 3 | Average 60 | 11 |
| Barley | 5,938 | 11,315 | 18 9 | 38 1 |
| Oats | 4,107 | 6,673 | 0 2 | 32 5 |
| Rye | — | 0 | 0 0 | 0 0 |
| Beans | 1,395 | 3,255 | 8 7 | 46 9 |
| Pease | 862 | 2,033 | 1 8 | 49 5 |

Friday, March 23.—There are moderate arrivals this week of all kinds
of Grain, and a good supply of Flour.
The Wheat trade remains unaltered
from Monday. Barley meets a slow
sale, at last quotations. Beans and
Pease sell heavily at Monday's terms.
There has been little doing in Oats
to-day, and the rates of the beginning
of this week are hardly supported.
Flour meets a very heavy sale.

Monday, March 26.—During the
past week, the arrivals of nearly all
sorts of Grain were tolerably good,
with a considerable quantity of Flour.
This morning there is a limited supply of Wheat, Barley, Beans, and
Pease, from Essex, Kent, and Suffolk;
and scarcely any thing from those

distant ports. Superfine Wheat being scarce, has obtained last Monday's prices, but all other sorts are very heavy in sale, owing to the languid state of the Flour trade.

The best samples of Barley have obtained 1s. per qr. more than this day se'nnight. Beans meet a very heavy trade, and hardly maintain last week's quotations. Pease of both kinds are very dull sale, and rather lower. Good stout samples of Oats meet sale on former terms; while all other descriptions command so little attention, that the sellers are disposed to take rather less money to effect sales.

---

Account of Wheat, &c. arrived in the Port of London, from March 19 to March 24, both inclusive.

| | Qrs. | | Qrs. |
|---|---|---|---|
| Wheat | 5,408 | Tares | 39 |
| Barley | 4,207 | Linseed | — |
| Malt | 5,116 | Rapeseed | 93 |
| Oats | 9,524 | Brank | 23 |
| Beans | 1,763 | Mustard | — |
| Flour | 10,762 | Flax | — |
| Rye | — | Hemp | — |
| Pease | 1,144 | Seeds | — |

Foreign.—Barley, 32; Oats, 3,413; and Beans, 191 quarters.

---

## HOPS.

Price of Hops, per Cwt. in the Borough.

Monday, March 26.—Our Market remains the same as for the last three weeks. There is a report from the Plantations that the stock is very much injured, and cuts very badly.

*Maidstone*, March 23.—The Hop Market continues very dull, and seems for the present quite at a stand.

*Worcester*, March 21.—On Saturday, 95 pockets of Hops were weighed; the sale was brisk at the last quoted prices.

---

### SMITHFIELD.

Monday, March 26.—The market was very heavy on Friday, and the prices of Monday were not supported. To-day, the supply is large for the season; but a very large proportion of Beasts and Sheep came in a very indifferent state. The cutting trade being also bad, there is a great dulness in the demand, and prices have given way. Though a few prime Beasts have made 5s., yet on the whole, the top quotation is 2d. a stone worse than this day se'nnight; and many lean and half-meated things will remain unsold. In Mutton, we can go no higher than a crown for any thing: most of the half-breds come loose and bad; and these, with other ordinary Sheep, are 3s. to 4s. a-head down.

*Per Stone of 8 pounds (alive).*

| | s. | d. | s. | d. |
|---|---|---|---|---|
| Beef | 3 | 10 | to 4 | 10 |
| Mutton | 4 | 0 | — 5 | 0 |
| Veal | 5 | 0 | — 5 | 8 |
| Pork | 4 | 8 | — 5 | 4 |
| Lamb | 0 | 0 | — 0 | 0 |

| | | | |
|---|---|---|---|
| Beasts | 2,561 | Sheep | 19,760 |
| Calves | 131 | Pigs | 131 |

### NEWGATE, (same day.)

*Per Stone of 8 pounds (dead).*

| | s. | d. | s. | d. |
|---|---|---|---|---|
| Beef | 3 | 4 | to 4 | 4 |
| Mutton | 3 | 4 | — 4 | 4 |
| Veal | 3 | 4 | — 5 | 4 |
| Pork | 3 | 8 | — 5 | 8 |
| Lamb | 0 | 0 | — 0 | 0 |

### LEADENHALL, (same day.)

*Per Stone of 8 pounds (dead).*

| | s. | d. | s. | d. |
|---|---|---|---|---|
| Beef | 3 | 2 | to 4 | 6 |
| Mutton | 3 | 2 | — 4 | 4 |
| Veal | 3 | 4 | — 5 | 4 |
| Pork | 4 | 0 | — 5 | 8 |
| Lamb | 0 | 0 | — 0 | 0 |

## COUNTRY CATTLE AND MEAT MARKETS, &c.

*Horncastle*, March 24.—Beef, 8s. per stone of 14 lbs.; Mutton, 8d.; Pork, 7d.; and Veal, 7d. to 8d. per lb.

At *Morpeth* Market, March 21, there was a good supply of Cattle and Sheep, and there being a great demand, both sold readily; the latter at an advance in price.—Beef, 5s. 9d. to 6s. 6d.; and Mutton, 3s. to 9s. per stone, sinking offal.

*Manchester* Smithfield Market, March 21.—Our market to-day was well attended by country butchers, &c., who purchased the best qualities pretty freely at the early part of the day, at last week's prices, while the inferior sorts remained a drug (which is generally the case) at the close of the day. —Beef, 5d. to 7½d.; Mutton, 6d. to 8d.; Veal, 5d. to 7d.; and Pork, 4½d. to 6d. per lb. sinking offal.

*Norwich Castle Meadow,* March 24.—The supply of fat Cattle to this day's market was large, prices 7s. 6d. to 8s. per stone of 14 lbs. sinking offal; we had also a large show of Scots, and the sale slow at 3s. 9d. to 4s. per stone; good Scots that will weigh 50 stone when fat, selling at 10l.; only a few Shorthorns sold at 3s.; Cows and Calves, and Homebreds, a very flat sale. Only a small show of Sheep; Shearlings 25s. to 30s.; fat ones to 48s.; Hoggets, 15s. to 24s. Meat: Beef, 6½d. to 8½d.; Veal, 6d. to 8d.; Mutton, 6d. to 7d., Lamb, 10d.; and Pork, 6d. to 8d. per lb.

# COBBETT'S WEEKLY REGISTER.

VOL. 62.—No. 2.]　　LONDON, SATURDAY, APRIL 7, 1827.　　[*Price 6d·*

*Published every Saturday Morning, at Seven o'Clock.*

" Your merry facetious men seldom penetrate farther than the super-
" ficies of things; which is the very seat of a Jest."—LORD BACON.
*Essay on Rhetoric.*

" This is a business of virtue, not a trial of wit. Who is there that
" would not rather have a Healing, than a Rhetorical Physician? But,
" for esteeming any man purely upon the score of his Rhetorick, I would
" as soon chuse a Pilot for a good Head of Hair."—SENECA, *Epistle II.*

# WHO IS TO BE MINISTER?

*Kensington, 4th April, 1827.*

I HAVE often had to observe, that I thought it likely, that one of the steps leading to a destruction of the funding and paper-money system, would be a sort of *breaking up* of the Ministry. Not a mere change of Ministers; but a sort of new modelling; and that this would arise from the great difficulties that would exist in the carrying on of the affairs of the Government. It was very clear that, when the system arrived at a certain point of danger, all men of real worth and wisdom would

C

Printed and Published by WILLIAM COBBETT, No. 183, Fleet-street.
[ENTERED AT STATIONERS' HALL.]

keep aloof from it. Such men, if they were to be found in the country, could never be expected to take upon them, without compulsion, a responsibility for the effects of the follies or wickedness of others: it was contrary to common sense to suppose that anybody would be desirous of coming into the inheritance of all the embarrassments of *debt*, and of all the obloquy attending the means of meeting that debt. I thought, and I have repeatedly expressed my opinion, that, when the system came to be in a state of obvious peril, the Ministers, who were in place, and who happened to possess any thing approaching to discernment and foresight, would seize some opportunity for retiring; that there would be found, however, enough persons of some sort or other, willing to take their places; that these would, most likely, be for trying some new scheme or other; and that, the machine, once put out of its usual course, would tumble to pieces without one hardly knowing why or how.

The state in which we now are, differs from the one contemplated by me; that is to say, it differs in its *beginning*; but, I think it very likely, that it will not differ from it in its ending. The political demise of Lord Liverpool ought to have produced, in the ordinary course of things, no sensible effect at all. To the whole machine of Government, he was no more than the little bit of leather that the wagoner puts through the eye of of the linch-pin; but, if the wagoner leave out the bit of leather, the linch-pin comes out, the wheel comes off the axle-tree, and, especially if it be heavily laden, crack comes the wagon to the ground. The place of this bit of leather would, in other times, have been supplied in a moment, without the smallest difficulty or delay; but now, the situation of this bit of leather is a situation by no means desirable to men whose ambition is under the control of wisdom; and, therefore, we see weeks and even months elapse without the deficiency being supplied.

We have seen the strangest things happen, as to this matter, that ever were witnessed in the world. But, the strangest of them all is, that there should be even a thought existing in any rational mind, that those who have the power of choosing Prime Ministers, should think of making choice of Mr. Canning. Yet, if we are to believe the brothers of the broad-sheet, the thing is already determined upon, and we are to have the honour, at last, of having the Captain of Eton for the prime adviser of our King. Let me observe, here, that, of all the things in this world, that which I myself most desire, is, *to see the system in the hands of this man!* I want the system to be brought to an end. I am not given to be impatient upon this subject. I have never met with any politician so patient as myself; so willing to wait for the consummation of things; so willing to wait, pa-

tiently, for the overthrowing of that which I abhor. But, the thing cannot come *too soon*, even for me. I want to see the thing accomplished: I am satisfied there is no man on earth who would hasten the accomplishment like this man; who would so soon convince even the wilfully blind, that this system ought to stand no longer; and, therefore, I most anxiously wish that he may be Prime Minister, which, alone, I will bargain to take beforehand, as full compensation made by the system to me for all the evils that I have ever experienced at its hands; and, I hereby declare, that his appointment as Prime Minister, shall be deemed to be, shall be taken to be, and shall be, a receipt in full of all demands given by me to the system.

But, in addressing myself to my readers, I must not suffer my wishes to misguide my pen. At this time those readers will naturally wish to know what is my opinion about *who is to be Minister.* It is impossible for me,

C 2

who never see any of the parties engaged in the intrigues that are going on; who never see any body that ever sees them; it is impossible for me to be able to give any information upon the subject, founded on any positive facts relating to it. I can have no foundation for my opinion but that which is furnished by the reason of the case itself. I know that men very seldom act contrary to their known and obvious interests. I know that nobody can be Minister for more than about a month or six weeks against the will of the owners of the land of this country, and who are owners, also, of some other very valuable things, which, for the present, shall be nameless. I know that a great many of these persons are said, and I believe truly, not to be overburthened with sense; but I have never heard of any one of them who was quite so foolish as to prefer rags and a bit of dry bread and naked feet cut by the flints, to fine clothes, sumptuous living, and a snug carriage to ride

in: and, I know that men must prefer the rags and the crust and the naked feet to the good things before mentioned, if they have those good things, arising out of landed estates, and if they choose Mr. CANNING as the lord of their destiny: he being, in my opinion, of all men living, the man to bring their "noble to ninepence, and their ninepence to nothing."

The brothers of the broad sheet, Mr. Brougham's best public instructor, assure us, upon their honour, for the goodness of which honour each is ready to pledge his pair of shoes without heels: they assure us upon their "*sacred honour*," that the whole nation are calling aloud for Mr. Canning as Prime Minister. This is what is called, I believe, the *puff indirect:* it is telling the readers of the broad sheet what the nation is wanting. That is to say, every individual reader is to believe that *every other person but himself*, at any rate, wishes Mr. Canning to be Minister. This is an old, hackneyed, vulgar, most vulgar mode of puffing; and an ineffectual mode, too; because, as far as it is believed, it deadens the exertion, if he be capable of any, of the reader. This is, however, a most stupid puff: it is wholly false, and it is wholly unlikely to be true. What part of the nation is for Mr. Canning? If you want to know what the Lords think of him, read their speeches and listen to their laughs. As to the people at large, in what way; in what document; in what petition or what address have they uttered a syllable in approbation of this man? He has been the most unmeasured, the most rude, the most merciless, the most insolent assailant of all those, be they of what description they might, who have stood forward, who have dared to open their lips in the cause of public liberty. If we trace him from his very first entrance into the House of Commons about six and thirty years ago, down to the present day, we shall find that there never has been one act tending to abridge the political

and civil liberties of the people, which he has not defended and applauded. In the passing of the Power-of-Imprisonment Bill in 1817, though not, properly speaking, in the Ministry at the time, he was the great advocate for the measure. In 1818, when the Bill was renewed, he was again the advocate, standing foremost of the whole; and, upon this occasion it was, that he cracked his jokes upon the rupture of Ogden. In the affair of SIX ACTS, he was again the most noisy of all the champions of that new code of grinding laws: amongst which was one law (still in force) to compel printers and publishers to give security, *even before they began to print*, for the payment of any fines that might be inflicted upon them *in case they should* print or publish a libel; and, amongst which was another law (still in force) rendering liable to *banishment for life*, any man who might print or publish any thing, having even a *tendency* to bring the House of Commons (of which he himself was a Member) into contempt!

Monstrous, then, is it to suppose, that this man can be a favourite with the people at large; monstrous, indeed, to suppose that this man, who has reviled the people more than any man that I ever knew or ever heard of in my life; monstrous that they should wish to see him at the head of the advisers of the king! And, as to persons who have no kind of public spirit within them; who rather approved than disapproved of his constant and bitter hostility to the friends of freedom and reform: how it is to be believed that such men can wish to see him in an office of great power: to see him the PILOT in this perilous storm! Where is there a man who ever said so many foolish things as this man has said! That part of Rochester's epitaph on CHARLES the Second: that "he never said a foolish thing and never did a wise one," would not suit this witty gentleman; for, though he never yet did a wise thing in his public capacity, no man ever said so many foolish things. A bare string of them, with a short explanation of each; a bare string of those which I myself could recollect, and that I have noticed in print, too, would fill this whole Register. It admits of clear proof that it was his jesting despatches which produced the late most disastrous and disgraceful war with the United States of America. Nothing admits of clearer proof than this; for, though he was not Secretary of State at the time when that war began, his despatches were the real causes of that war; and, is there an Englishman who can now look at the maritime force of those United States of America; and who can think of his contemptuous sneer (in open Parliament) at the half dozen fir frigates with bits of striped bunting at their mast heads; is there an Englishman, who can thus look and thus think, and not blush for his country, when he reflects that this man has been living upon the labour of her people from that day to this, and that there is now a press, infamous enough to be extolling to the skies and wanting to cram down the throat of the King, this very jester on the bits of striped bunting ?

However, that which plodding, selfish men, will be most likely to keep in view is, his conduct with regard to that all-important matter the *paper-money*. He, together with his colleague, Mr. Huskisson, were of the Bullion party, in 1810. In 1819, he called upon the House for an unanimous vote in favour of Peel's Bill, in order to set the question at rest for ever. In the summer of 1825, he gave the most solemn pledge that, let what would happen, he never would consent to return to Bank Restriction again. In 1826, he defended a Bill for the abolition of one-pound-notes at the end of three years; and he made use of arguments, and put forward assertions, and laid down principles, the whole of which, together with the most solemn pledges, he must abandon, in manner the most

barefaced, or really, and in good truth and almost literally, let the furies of war out of his leash.

If he were to be Prime Minister (and this is why I wish he may) he *must persevere with the present law.* He cannot retract ; he cannot move an inch from the stake that he has bound himself to, and there must be an end to the system. I wish to see that end ; but, the far greater part of those who have money and estates, wish for no such thing. Such persons, too, are astounded at the hairbrained enterprise with regard to Portugal, the equal of which, taking all things into view, was certainly never seen before. Men naturally ask themselves what is to become of them, if a head like this is *to preside.* Here are a large part of the expenses of an ordinary war, for no earthly purpose that any man can assign : for a mere whim, it would seem ; and, then the speech, which was corrected and published in a pamphlet, came to crown the whole of a series of such childish proceedings, as are shocking but to think of, and that never could have come into the head of any one not of the character described in the words of that part of my motto, which is taken from Lord Bacon. It is very pretty to hear jesting: nothing is more amusing than to see and hear the player-folks; but, when the affairs of a nation are to be managed, who yet ever thought of intrusting the management to a jester?

I believe, that there are no description of persons in the country, who do not, as I do, wish this paper-system to be destroyed, together with all the misrule and miseries that arise out of it, that can possibly wish this man to be the Minister. The newspaper fellows wish it; but, then, they regard him as *belonging to the corps*, to the regiment of the newspaper press. They can say what they like, in their sheets. They think themselves the nation, and therefore, they say that the nation, with one united voice, call out for him to be the Minister. As I told Mr. Brougham some time ago, *newspaper praise* is very fine, but does not wear well; and I reminded him, that old Sherry discovered that, when it was too late. The newspapers very often make matches, even, almost, in spite of the parties; but, I have never yet heard of one single public man, who was a great favourite with the newspapers, that was confided in by the public. The public read newspapers; often swallow their lies; but, in the long run, they detect the lies; and, in a case like this, they have so many other means of judging of the party that is praised, that the praise thus bestowed, does little more than excite suspicions that make against him. If the newspapers have an advantage in some cases, in keeping hidden the authors of their contents, they have, in the case of praise bestowed by them, this very great disadvantage, that the party praised, is suspected to be the author of it himself, or to have paid for its insertion, every inch of every column being well known to be saleable.

So much, then, for the wishes of the nation upon this point. But that, Mr. Canning's wishes are pretty strong is evident enough. There appears to have been an intrigue, or something very much like an intrigue, going on for a long while, between him and those ridiculous gentry that are still called the *Whigs*. They have been complimenting him for some years; holding him up in the way of contrast with his associates in power; endeavouring to give him a character and a degree of weight with the people, not for the sake of good to him, but for the sake of mischief to his colleagues; endeavouring to make him great in order to diminish the power of his associates in the government. This has been so palpable that every body has seen it. Even BURDETT, who had talked about the " crib," and who had said, upon various occasions, every thing against him that man could well say, has joined in these com-

pliments to him, and for what reason other than the very suspicious one that I have just mentioned, it would, I believe, puzzle the Baronet to tell. At the time when the French were marching into Spain, it was manifest that the parts were arranged before hand, which this Prime Minister and Mr. BROUGHAM were to act. On the recent affair of the Portuguese expedition, when the Æolian speech was made, the latter gentleman over-acted his part; for he applauded to the skies all those " *truly English sentiments* " which the Right Honourable Secretary had, in less than a week afterwards, *to retract,* in a new edition of his speech, with additions and amendments! Nor are there wanting persons to express their belief that it is quite within the compass of possibility that, the other night, Mr. Canning knew, or at least was pretty well able to guess, at what my old correspondent, TIERNEY, was going to say, before either of them entered the House! To be plain, I thought this the moment I saw the report; and several persons have made to me the same observation before hearing my opinion upon the subject.

It is clear that Mr. Canning rests upon the Whigs. His publishing his speech at Ridgway's, his compliments to the Whigs, and theirs bestowed on him; these things can leave no doubt in the mind of any man that he rests upon them as a sort of scarecrows; a sort of body which he can join, if he be not gratified on his own side of the House. But, before he places much reliance upon these gentry he ought to consider a little what these gentry are worth in themselves; and if he were thus to consider, he would find that they were worth not one straw; that they have no reputation with the rich, and that they are detested by the common people. Those of his colleagues, therefore, who are opposed to him, need not fear him on this account; and I sincerely believe that they do not. His chance of being Minister appears to me to consist in this; that it is possible that some of the most powerful of the present Ministers, seeing the state in which things are, and wishing to get away from the approaching responsibility, may, in their new arrangements, insist, even unreasonably, *on his exclusion;* and that they may do this with the view of having an excuse, if refused, for *retiring themselves.* This I think not impossible. It is certainly what I would do, if I were in their situation. It appears evident, that the whole of his schemes; that the whole of his and Huskisson's measures must be abandoned, or that they must have *the whole mess to themselves;* upon the principle mentioned by Swift:

" Thus, when the dirty sloven once has thrown
" His —— into the mess, 'tis all his own."

This I think possible; and, then, stand clear! For, then, on comes the system upon us, back stroke and fore stroke, tooth and nail. I mention this as a possibility, without pretending to say that I believe that it will be so; for, not being jackass enough to pretend even to be able to guess at the thoughts of the King upon the subject, I know how mighty are these interests which are opposed, and must be opposed, to this man being Prime Minister. He cannot be that and continue that, for any length of time, without having the nobility and the gentry with him: he must, in fact, be their man, or he cannot be Minister. I, then, put it to myself, and suppose that I have a title and a thundering estate: it is against nature that I should not wish to preserve these, and I must be the blindest of all mortals if I do not clearly see, that his being Minister would put them in jeopardy. If there were nothing else, there is the *Catholic Question*, as it is called, which he would be compelled to bring forward and *to carry*, or keep his place in a state of disgrace insupportable. He would not have, for a contrary conduct, even the miserable apology of Pitt in 1804, and which apology he repeated the other day; namely, that he could not stir the question *during the life of the old King*. That apology was not worth a straw; but, at any rate, it implied that, if Pitt had remained Minister until the death of his late Majesty, he was bound to carry the question or to retire from his office. It would never do for Mr. Canning to tell us that he could not stir the question during the life of the present King, for that excuse would be as good in the case of the present King's successor; so that here would be a shuffle the most barefaced that ever was practised, even at the Cocoa-tree or at Newmarket. This would never do. He must bring forward and carry the Catholic Question; or, he must retire. And, to carry that question, what is it, short of taking from the aristocracy a very considerable part of the whole of their estates? For, is there a man of sincerity and sense, who does not see and plainly acknowledge, that an immediate consequence of the carrying of that question would

be *a repeal* of the Church of Ireland; that is to say, a taking away
of the whole of the immense property of that Church from that
aristocracy who now, in fact, possess it!

I have always stated this. Look
into the Register of 1811 and 1812.
I there stated that I had no idea
of any change in favour of the
Catholics which did not include a
repeal of the Protestant establishment of Ireland. I have always
been for emancipation, as it is
called, upon this ground. I know
that every thing short of this is
delusive. I know that the con-
cession that is now demanded and
that it is pretended would be satisfactory, would produce no satisfaction at all. It is not the exclusion from silk-gowns, the exclusion from the seats in Parliament,
the exclusion from the Bench and
from high ranks in the army and
the navy, and from seats in the
King's council; it is not these things
that affect the millions of Ireland;
it is the paying to support a Protestant hierarchy; it is the pay-

ing to support churches of the
building of their ancestors to
which they never go; it is, in
short, the Protestant hierarchy,
the dominion of the Protestant
clergy: this is the galling thing,
and without a riddance from which,
no peace will ever be enjoyed in
Ireland.

The opponents of Catholic
Emancipation, as it is called,
maintain that, without going the
length which I would go, nothing
good would be effected; they insist that to go the length that I
would go would be a great evil;
the advocates for the Catholic
claims affect to agree with them
as to the latter; and thus it is
that the advocates for the claims
are always defeated, not only in the
division but in the argument. The
speech of the Master of the Rolls,
in the late debate, was wholly
unanswerable; and, by the bye,
the answer of Mr. Canning to
that speech, if he had never done
any thing else during his whole
life-time worthy of disapprobation,
was a great deal more than suffi-

dient to prove that he was wholly unfit for a Minister; for, piqued by the triumphant speech of the Master of the Rolls, what does he do but divulge, and that, too, in the way of jest, an opinion given at the *request of the cabinet council!* Not an opinion given to himself, by the Attorney and Solicitor-General; not an opinion given to him, merely as Secretary of State; but an opinion given to the King's ministers in Council, or, at least, this is what I gather from his own statement in the debate.

The flabbergaster speech-makers in Ireland, and, particularly, the famous Counsellor Bric, whose nuptials my poetical friend has so lately celebrated, have dealt out abundant reproaches upon me, because I said that nobody attempted to answer the speeches of Mr. WETHERELL and Mr. BANKS, made in 1825. They took precisely the same ground as the Master of the Rolls has recently taken. They said, to express their meaning in few words, this emancipation that you ask is nonsense, unless you mean to overset the Protestant hierarchy. I would overset it, as completely as a brewer's man tumbles down a barrel; I would *repeal* it just as HARRY the Eighth repealed the Catholic Church; I would, to use that old buck's very expression, "betake myself to its temporalities," and apply them to far other uses. Messrs. COPLEY, WETHERELL and BANKS say that this would be a terrible evil and wrong. I say that it would be a good and no wrong: they and I have this preliminary question to discuss: if we agree upon that, we can go on; but, Mr. Canning yields the preliminary point: he concedes to them that the Protestant hierarchy ought to be secured in all its power and all its glory; and then they beat him so shamefully that he flies in a passion, and, like worsted disputants of the other sex, rips up that which ought always to have remained a secret.

However, if he become Prime Minister, things will be wholly changed with him. If pressed (and he will not want pressing), he must bring the question forward; he must carry that question; or he must retire. This is so clear, that there can be no doubt about the matter. He has a vast majority against him, amongst all those that have the power to oppose such a measure. To carry the measure, therefore, he must shift the power into other hands; and I see not how he is to do that without abandoning that dearest object of his most tender affections, *Old Sarum!* " I will," said he, in one of his poetically impudent flights, "*I will* disfranchise Grampound, BECAUSE I will preserve Old Sarum." He would not disfranchise Grampound because Grampound had been proved to be corrupt; but he would disfranchise a borough where there were perhaps, a hundred or two of electors, because he would preserve a thing called a borough, where there were no electors at all! Yet, this object of his tender affections he must give up; and he must, in short, come and join

us radicals (sorry, no doubt, that Ogden is not alive to embrace him), or he must quit his place; for, carry that Catholic question he never can, unless with radical aid.

This, then, is a pretty sort of man to be a Prime Minister in the present state of things. But, besides this, what is he to do as to these matters of *free-trade.* He has here, not only the aristocracy against him, but the most numerous part of the manufacturers, trade-owners and ship-owners, whom these free-trade projects have plunged into a state of ruin hitherto wholly unknown in England. The whole of the projects have completely failed, while the Trade Minister is receiving an additional two thousand pounds a year for having invented the projects. Mr. Tierney, the other night, drew a most dismal picture of the situation of the country, and this he used as an argument for dispatch in the appointing of a Prime Minister, hinting, at the same time, in no very unintelligible terms, that Mr. Canning ought to be that Prime Minister. This was pretty enough as a shot at the disapproving colleagues of Mr. Canning; but, Mr. Tierney seems to have forgotten that the figures pourtrayed in his dismal picture had been, in great part, created by the schemes of that Mr. Canning himself, who has had his full share as well in the remote, as in all the immediate causes of the present sufferings and dangers of the country.

It is plain that the aristocracy do not like Mr. Canning; and, really, when we calmly consider what it is to have a good estate and a life, and how loath men are to put them in jeopardy, one cannot reasonably blame them. Sir Thomas Lethbridge's motion for an address to the King seems to be a most suitable answer or counterpart to the speech of Mr. Tierney. Mr. Tierney had said that there ought to be formed a cabinet in which there should be unity of sentiment and principle; in which the Ministers would pull together; and that he thought that such a Ministry would be able to save the country. Sir Thomas Lethbridge is, therefore, only acting in accordance with this opinion of Mr. Tierney, when he proposes to address his Majesty to select such a Ministry as shall not be divided in principle. The one wishes for a Ministry that shall be *united:* the other wishes for a Ministry that shall *not be divided*. Mr. Tierney ought, therefore, to support Sir Thomas Lethbridge. Both wish for unity; but, I suspect, that the *means* of accomplishing the object are rather different. Mr. Tierney, I imagine, wishes unity to be produced by his and others cordially joining with Mr. Canning, and, I do believe, that Sir Thomas wishes to prevent division in future, by turning Mr. Canning out of the post which he now fills; and, thus, "set the question at rest for ever." And, what is more, I should not be at all surprised if this were the result; for, it must now be clear to every man of common sense, that all the schemes of free-trade, of what are called liberal politics; that all these blandishments bestowed on the settled opponents of his own colleagues; that all these things put together, all the silly compliments bestowed upon Edinburgh Reviewers, clearly indicate that Mr. Canning means to place *his reliance* upon those who are called the *Whigs*, and that, if pushed from his office, he means to endeavour to regain it (or to get something more) by the assistance of his new allies. This must be plain to every man; and, that all his schemes of this sort will fail, I am as certain as that I am now sitting at this table.

The faction, on which he means to lean, is wholly without confidence on the part of the public. They have been laughed at for these ten years last past. They are, indeed, scarcely a faction;

and the whole thing, that used to be called Opposition, is become a mere nothing at all, presenting, in reality, no opposition at all to the Ministry, and being, if possible, still more foolish than the Ministers themselves. Upon the great question of all, the paper-money question, this faction has taken the lead in every thing erroneous and mischievous. In short, the people, almost the whole of the people, despise this faction, this rump of faction, more than they have ever despised any thing of the sort since I have had any knowledge of public affairs. This, therefore, would be a pretty sheet-anchor for a Prime Minister. But, this is a faction, which must eat and drink as well as other factions, and, therefore, to have their assistance, he must give them something for it; and then, we come back to the story of about two months ago, of a Ministry to be composed of MR. CANNING, the MARQUIS of LANSDOWN, Mr. BROUGHAM, and others of the Whigs. When that venerable old veteran patriot and pensioner, Mr. TIERNEY, was talking about an *union* of talents; about a *strong Ministry;* when the venerable old gentleman, who once said, that his constituents of the Borough, had given him a retaining fee for life, to plead against PITT and his principles; when the venerable old gentleman was talking thus, about the country being saved by this sort of *union,* I think it likely that he had running in his head, the very scheme above mentioned, of an union of MR. CANNING and the WHIGS. Besides all the other difficulties, that such a *"strong"* set would have in their way, there would be then, the utter impossibility of returning to Bank restriction and legal tender, without an open and barefaced abandonment of all the principles which these Whigs have been inculcating upon the subject for these last ten years. It would be bad enough if the present set of men were to return to Bank restriction; but, if the Whigs were to do it, they must absolutely be covered with spittle by the people, as completely as poor MR. STANLEY was by the very beautiful girls of *Preston.* The poor Whigs would, too, be destitute of STANLEY's consolation. He was sure of getting his seat, from the very causes that drew forth the spittle upon him; while, on the contrary, the Whigs would see in the cause of the spittle, the cause also of their losing their places. But it is too monstrous to suppose, that these men would go back to Bank restriction. A

**D**

fellow who has stood a half a dozen times in the pillory, would feel horror at the thought of doing such a thing; of doing any thing so flagrantly unprincipled.

Now, though neither Bank restriction, nor any other measure that the wit of man can devise, will save this infernal paper-money system from going to pieces, still there is something, in the *time*, and something also, in the *manner*, of its going to pieces; and, as to both these, the Whigs having to do the thing, or, being in place at the time the thing was done, would certainly have a tendency to add to the mischief. They must keep their present law in force; they must proceed, if they be in power, until the whole of the one-pound notes be annihilated; or, at least, driven out of circulation. If there be force in the Government and in the laws

to push the thing on to this extent; if the progress be not interrupted by a general convulsion and breaking up of society, prices will fall so low, the produce of the land will fetch so small a nominal sum, that *no rents at all can or will be paid.* To this point, if convulsion come not before we arrive at it, the Whig fellows, if they be in power, must push the thing on. But, the same sort of necessity does not exist with regard to the PITTITE fellows, who are not pledged never to return to the paper system. On the contrary, they departed from that system with great reluctance, reluctance which they have expressed over and over again. They are fools for their pains; but, that is no matter. Their returning to the paper, cannot save the thing: the thing must be destroyed, let the Government do what it may;

but, Bank restriction would keep the convulsion away from us for a little while longer than it can be kept away, if the Whig politics be continued to be acted upon. Every man must die at last; but every man thinks that death always comes too soon. It is natural, therefore, for all those who are thriving under the present infernal system, to wish that system to last. Those who have offices that yield them good pay; those whose relations are fastened upon the taxes; those who have fat livings in their gift or in their possession; in short, the aristocracy, including the Church, the Army and Navy, the Civil List, and never forgetting the horrible Dead Weight: all these persons must wish to keep off a total blowing up as long as possible. By a return to the paper, this object might be accomplished for a little while. Gold would be openly at a premium; two prices would soon come into the market; but, they might not come all at once. When they did come, they would be hardly visible, perhaps, for a few months; and, by judiciously employing the *broad-sheet*, the paper system might be made to carry the thing along for a little while; and, as I have just observed, to this system the Pittites might consistently return; and, indeed, I have not the smallest doubt, that, if the free-trade and cash-payments-gentry were pushed out of the Cabinet, there would be a Bank restriction, even during the present session of Parliament.

This is a most weighty consideration with several of the most important classes of the people. Fundholders, as well as landholders; every body who has property and very little public spirit (which generally go together in a state of things like this), dreads the final disappearance of the one pound notes. Farmers, traders of all descriptions, public-house keepers, monopolizing brewers, cormorant quakers, army, navy, dead weight, parsons, parsons' wives and daughters; all of them, including placemen, pensioners and sinecure men, women and children : these all *smell;* they cannot be said to reason about any thing; their faculty of discernment, in a case like this, does not rise higher than merely that of *smelling;* but, they all smell mischief in the disappearance of the one pound notes, and they look forward to the day of their extinction, as sinners do to the day of judgment. Well they may! for the extinguishment of those little dirty bits of paper will do that which one would almost believe was beyond the reach of mortal power, and to be achieved by nothing but Omnipotence ; namely, compel about a hundred thousand tax-eating vagabonds and their families to do that which, as Paddy said, " nature shudders within them but to think of;" that is to say, WORK FOR THEIR BREAD! This is what the vagabonds are afraid of; this is what all their ingenuity is employed to avoid ; this is what, if they think, your efforts tend to reduce them to ; they would spill your blood with as little remorse as they would spill water out of a bowl. What loads of calumny, what loads of malice, have the Reformers had to endure at the hands of these vagabonds! In other respects they are like other people ; but, do any thing that has a tendency to compel them to work for their bread, and they cut your throat, if they have it in their power.

All this numerous tribe are for a return to legal tender. They *smell*, that they must work for their bread, if wheat be sold at three or four shillings a bushel. The vagabond fellows of the press, *smell* to the same effect. They *smell*, that there could be no rents paid, if the wheat were to fall to three or four shillings a bushel; and I have so pummelled their thick skulls, as to make them see that this present system could not go on long, if there were no rents. So that, they fear, that the destruction of the one-pound notes will put a stop to their printing and selling their stuff. This fear of theirs has the same foundation as the blood-inspiring, or rather the blood-shed-inspiring terrors of the tax-eaters; both have the same foundation; namely, an inexpressible horror of *being compelled to work*. This is the cause of these broad-sheeted wretches being so anxious to uphold this system of paper-money, a system productive of mischiefs of all sorts; but, which has for its great characteristic, a constant tendency to enable the insolent, the lazy, the upstarts, the bastardized breed of the country, all the worthless and the children of the worthless to live without labour, upon the fruit of the labour of others. Every wretch that is for this system, no matter in what rank of life; no matter whether male or female; every wretch, that lives, that expects to live, or that wishes to live without labour, out of the fruit of the labour of others, every such wretch smells mischief in the king's coin, and hankers after the paper-money.

A pretty life, therefore, the witty Mr. CANNING and his Whig associates would have to lead, by the time that the one-pound notes would have been gone for about a fortnight or three weeks. Prices would fall so low, as to ruin every farmer and every trader; whose property consisted chiefly in the value of his stock; but, it is useless to waste one's time, in descriptions relative to the state of the country, in case of such a Ministry, and in case of such measures of perseverance. It is useless to talk about this; for, in all human probability, the whole thing would go to pieces, there would be a general convulsion in the country, aye, and a radical reform into the bargain, before the one-pound notes could wholly disappear. It is useless to waste one's time, in further prophecies about the matter; there is, in my yard, the Gridiron, a portrait of which is at the head of this Register. It is to go up at the front of the house, No. 183, Fleet-street, whenever one or the other of the following things shall take place: 1. A repeal of Peel's Bill, in whole or in part: 2. A repeal, in the whole or in part, of the Small-note Bill, passed last year: 3. A reduction of the interest of what is called the National Debt, but which I call the Borough and Church Debt. I say that this Debt is due from those who contracted it, and I say, that those who could have nothing to do in contracting it, who had nothing to do, either directly or indirectly, in choosing the persons who made the loans, cannot, therefore, owe this Debt out of their estates or out of their bodies. However, be this as it may, if there be any reduction of the interest of this Debt, or if either of the other measures be adopted, up goes the Gridiron at the office of the Register, there to remain as long as the Register itself shall continue to be published, a fac-simile of it being prepared, to be nailed upon my coffin, though I may be permitted to hope, I trust, that the fac-simile will not be wanted for some time yet to come. I am · determined to have my revenge, my full measure, if I can get it, upon a system which has done so much mischief to my country in general, and has been the cause of such persecution to myself in particular.

I do not care a straw, with regard to this grand affair, who is the Minister, or what measures he may adopt: I know that nothing but acting upon *Norfolk Petition*, can possibly prevent the result which I contemplate. There is a notion, that the thing may be eked out; it may be pushed along, from hand to mouth, by a succession of bills to *extend the* *time of putting out* the one-pound notes. There is a notion, that by thus keeping an abolition bill constantly hanging over the heads of the paper-money makers, they will be held so much in check as to prevent them from issuing such quantities of paper as would drive the gold out of the country. In other words, that the thing might be thus gently pushed along so as not to produce any great fall from the present prices. This is the notion that I believe the Ministers entertain. Greatly do they deceive themselves; and, if they did not, the very best that they can hope, is, *that things may remain in their present state; a* state as nearly approaching to an. open defiance of the laws of property, as any state well can be. That which used to be called theft or robbery, now scarcely goes by that name. In the neighbourhood of even this well-fed WEN itself, scarcely a family can be said to go to bed in safety. In the country things are infinitely worse; and yet, if the present law continue in force, that which we now behold is a state of peace, plenty and safety, compared with that which we shall behold, *this day two years*, on which day (this being the 5th of April) those truly infernal machines, the one-pound notes, are, as the law now stands, to cease to exist in England, So that, again, I say that, as to this matter, which is of consequence greater than all other matters put together, it signifies not, with regard to the result, who is the Minister, but it signifies something with regard to *time!* and, for the reasons that I have before stated, I look upon Mr. CANNING as a man to hasten the total destruction of the paper-sys-

tem. I am, therefore, for Mr. CANNING: but, for the reasons which I have given, I think that those will be against him who, at present, have the power to let him in or to keep him out.

There is one thing, at any rate, of pleasing novelty; and that is, that we have now a candidate for the Premiership, who would fain make his appeal to the *people;* this is a novelty in the workings of the Thing. To *the people,* I would say, *praise nobody;* keep your praises for your own use; bestow praise upon no pretender to liberal principles, until he distinctly declare his *hostility* to *Gatton and Old Sarum.* The breaking up of the paper-system will, in all likelihood, be so potent in itself, as to prevent even the folly of the people themselves from making them stop short of a real radical reform; but, if the people, having the power to effect such reform, were to neglect this opportunity to effect it, they would deserve, every man of them, and their children after them, to be the most wretched of all the slaves that ever disgraced the face of the earth. As far as the people have recently gone, in their petitions and speeches, they have acted wisely; they have called for reduction of taxes, for disbanding of soldiers, for legal application of Church property to other purposes; for equitable adjustment of contracts; and, as a security against future extravagance, future enormous debts, and future evils of all sorts, they have called for a change in the manner of choosing those who make the laws: in other words, they have called for that reform in the Commons' House of Parliament, of which Mr. CANNING, throughout the whole of his life, has been an implacable enemy. Let the people keep on in this sensible course: let the King, as is his prerogative, choose his Ministers, and let the people never cease to endeavour to recover their right of choosing their representatives in Parliament.

WM. COBBETT.

## DUKE OF YORK.

THE dead can wait, or else the deuce is in it. Several correspondents have begged me to *consider* well before I write upon this subject. I considered very well even before I talked of writing upon it; and that these correspondents will see, whenever I shall find time and room for doing justice to the matter. The living are rather too busy and bustling just at this time to leave me any spare hours wherein to deal with the dead; but, I will deal, and will deal fairly too, with the history of the DUKE OF YORK : I will not, whatever others may choose to do, suffer myself and my readers to be insulted, and to submit in silence to such loads of insults from the miserable parasites of the press.

## AMERICAN KIDNEY BEANS.

---

I HAVE two sorts of these, the finest that ever were in England; one of them the very earliest that I ever saw ; and the seed, in both cases, so ripe, sound, and excellent, that a large crop from it is certain.—One sort is *Yellow*, the other *Speckled*; both are dwarfs.— Price—17s. a bushel, and smaller quantities in proportion, with something added for paper, string, and trouble.—They are sold at the Office of the Register, No. 183, Fleet Street, and may be sent, by order, to any part of the country.

---

## TO CORRESPONDENTS.

---

To the Gentleman who was good enough to remind me of a piece of bad grammar in the Register, I have to say, " between *you* and *me*," Sir, I wish that there might be, one of these days, two Registers running without a grammatical error in either ; for that is, upon my honour, what I never yet saw, though nobody can be more mortified than I am, when I perceive such errors after it is too late.

Just published, price 1s. 6d.
The Second Edition.

A MEMOIR addressed to the SOCIETY OF ARTS, on the PLANTING and REARING of FOREST TREES. By W. WITHERS, Jun. With an Appendix, containing Tables for ascertaining the progressive Annual Increase in the Growth of Trees.

" This excellent little Pamphlet is worthy of the attention of every Landowner in England. Mr. Withers has made divers experiments, and he has given an account of them in a manner, with a degree of public spirit, that do him great honour as well in his character of planter as in that of an Englishman : it being manifest that he can have no motive but that of the good of his country and of his countrymen in general. His account is short, neat, plain, unassuming, and full of interest."— *Weekly Register, Nov. 25, 1826.*

Published by Longman and Co., Paternoster-Row, and to be had at the Office of the Register, 183, Fleet Street; at Ridgway's, Piccadilly, and of all other Booksellers.

# MARKETS.

Average Prices of CORN through-out ENGLAND, for the week end-ing March 23.

*Per Quarter.*

| | s. | d. | | s. | d. |
|---|---|---|---|---|---|
| Wheat .. | 56 | 10 | Rye .... | 38 | 8 |
| Barley .. | 37 | 1 | Beans ... | 48 | 8 |
| Oats.... | 30 | 5 | Pease ... | 49 | 9 |

Total Quantity of Corn returned as Sold in the Maritime Districts, for the week ended March 23.

| | Qrs. | | Qrs. |
|---|---|---|---|
| Wheat.. | 40,335 | Rye ..... | 216 |
| Barley .. | 20,447 | Beans . .. | 8,069 |
| Oats ... | 18,996 | Pease .... | 1,079 |

*Corn Exchange, Mark Lane.*

Quantities and Prices of British Corn, &c. sold and delivered in this Market, during the week ended Saturday, March 24.

| | Qrs. | £. | s. | d. | | s. | d. |
|---|---|---|---|---|---|---|---|
| Wheat.. | 3.936 | for 11,723 | 15 | 9 | Average, | 59 | 6 |
| Barley.. | 3,332 | .. 6,429 | 9 | 9 | ......... | 38 | 7 |
| Oats.. | 4,316 | .. 7,105 | 6 | 4 | ......... | 32 | 11 |
| Rye.... | — | .. 0 | 0 | 0 | ......... | 0 | 0 |
| Beans.. | 842 | .. 1,908 | 11 | 9 | ......... | 45 | 4 |
| Pease.. | 547 | .. 1,122 | 17 | 0 | ......... | 49 | 1 |

Friday, March 30.—There have been fair arrivals this week of every description of Grain, and a consider-able quantity of Flour. Prime Wheat has sold freely at Monday's prices; other kinds are very dull. Barley is unaltered. Beans and Pease meet a heavy trade, at last quotations. Oats are so extremely dull, that 1s. per quarter abatement has been sub-mitted to.

Monday, April 2.—The quantities of all sorts of Grain reported last week were tolerably good, and of Flour considerable. This morning, the fresh supply of Wheat, Barley, Beans, and Pease, from Essex, Kent, and Suffolk, are moderate, and only a few English and Foreign vessels up with Oats and Beans. Superfine samples of Wheat are scarce, and readily command last quotations, but there is a heavy trade for all other descriptions.

The best parcels of Barley have obtained an advance of 1s. per quar-ter on last quotations, with no alter-ation in other kinds. Beans, of good quality, are more in demand than of late, and they are 1s. per quarter higher; but this improvement does not extend to foreign samples. Pease, of both kinds, are unaltered. There is so very limited a demand for Oats, that all sorts may be quoted 1s. per quarter cheaper, with a very slow sale, even at this decline, for Feed parcels. The Flour trade continues very heavy.

*Price on board Ship as under.*

Flour, per sack ......46s. — 50s.
—— Seconds ........42s. — 44s.
—— North Country ..40s. — 44s.

Price of Bread.—The price of the 4lb. Loaf is stated at 9d. by the full-priced Bakers.

Account of Wheat, &c. arrived in the Port of London, from March 26 to March 31, both inclusive.

| | Qrs. | | Qrs. |
|---|---|---|---|
| Wheat .. | 4,873 | Tares .... | 83 |
| Barley .. | 3,355 | Linseed .. | — |
| Malt .... | 7,712 | Rapeseed . | 10 |
| Oats .... | 5,976 | Brank .. | 46 |
| Beans... | 1,477 | Mustard.. | — |
| Flour .... | 10,051 | Flax .... | — |
| Rye .... | 25 | Hemp ... | 10 |
| Pease.... | 548 | Seeds ... | 14 |

Foreign.—Wheat, 539; Oats, 4,156; and Beans, 426 quarters.

———

Monday, April 2.—The arrivals from Ireland last week were, 2,515 firkins of Butter, and 4,000 bales of Bacon; and from Foreign Ports, 3,032 casks of Butter.

———

## HOPS.

Price of Hops, per Cwt. in the Borough.

Monday, April 2.—Nothing doing in the Hop Trade. Prices rather lower.

Maidstone, March 29.—The Hop Market continues in the same dull state, and we do not look for much alteration until the appearance of the bine.

———

### COAL MARKET, March 30.

Ships at Market. Ships sold. Price.
57½ Newcastle 20½..29s. 6d. to 38s. 3d.
12 Sunderland 6¾..38s. 0d.— 39s. 0d.

### SMITHFIELD.

Monday, April 2.—There was no alteration on Friday in the Beef Trade, but Mutton sold at advancing terms. To-day the supply of Beasts is pretty good, and the greater proportion consists of Scots, the best of which make a crown, though not many are in a condition to command so much. Sheep obtain more money than on Friday, and are dearer by 4d a stone than on this day se'nnight, with a free demand. A few very superior Old Downs have obtained 5s. 6d.; and the few choice Leicesters at market 5s. 4d. in their wool. A pen or two of half-breds, as good as any thing here, could not obtain so high a bid as 5s. 4d. Old Ewes, and other ordinary Sheep, have partaken only in a limited degree of the improvement. Lamb is coming tolerably plentiful, and is quoted at 6s. to 7s. per stone.

Per Stone of 8 pounds (alive).

| | s. | d. | | s. | d. |
|---|---|---|---|---|---|
| Beef ..... | 4 | 0 | to | 5 | 0 |
| Mutton ... | 4 | 4 | — | 5 | 4 |
| Veal ..... | 4 | 10 | — | 5 | 8 |
| Pork ..... | 4 | 8 | — | 5 | 4 |
| Lamb .... | 6 | 0 | — | 7 | 0 |

Beasts . . 2,330 | Sheep .. 16,490
Calves ... 128 | Pigs ... 140

NEWGATE, (same day.)
Per Stone of 8 pounds (dead).

| | s. | d. | | s. | d. |
|---|---|---|---|---|---|
| Beef ..... | 3 | 4 | to | 4 | 8 |
| Mutton ... | 4 | 0 | — | 4 | 8 |
| Veal ..... | 3 | 4 | — | 5 | 4 |
| Pork ..... | 3 | 8 | — | 5 | 8 |
| Lamb .... | 0 | 0 | — | 0 | 0 |

LEADENHALL, (same day.)
Per Stone of 8 pounds (dead).

| | s. | d. | | s. | d. |
|---|---|---|---|---|---|
| Beef ... | 3 | 8 | to | 4 | 4 |
| Mutton ... | 3 | 8 | — | 4 | 8 |
| Veal ..... | 4 | 0 | — | 5 | 4 |
| Pork ..... | 4 | 8 | — | 5 | 8 |
| Lamb .... | 0 | 0 | — | 0 | 0 |

## POTATOES.

**SPITALFIELDS,** *per Ton.*

|  | l. | s. |  | l. | s. |
|---|---|---|---|---|---|
| Ox-Nobles | 4 | 0 | to | 0 | 0 |
| Middlings | 2 | 10 | — | 3 | 0 |
| Chats | 2 | 0 | — | 0 | 0 |
| Common Red | 0 | 0 | — | 0 | 0 |

Onions, 0s. 0d.—0s. 0d. per bush.

**BOROUGH,** *per Ton.*

|  | l. | s. |  | l. | s. |
|---|---|---|---|---|---|
| Ox-Nobles | 3 | 10 | to | 4 | 0 |
| Middlings | 2 | 10 | — | 0 | 0 |
| Chats | 2 | 0 | — | 0 | 0 |
| Common Red | 3 | 10 | — | 4 | 0 |

## HAY and STRAW, per Load.

*Smithfield.*—Hay ...80s. to 115s.

Straw...40s. to 45s.

Clover. 100s. to 135s.

*St. James's.*—Hay.... 84s. to 125s.

Straw .. 37s. to 48s.

Clover. 126s. to 135s.

*Whitechapel.*—Hay....75s. to 115s.

Straw...36s. to 42s.

Clover..84s. to 135s.

---

## AVERAGE PRICE OF CORN, sold in the Maritime Counties of England and Wales, for the Week ended March 23, 1827.

|  | Wheat. | | Barley. | | Oats. | |
|---|---|---|---|---|---|---|
|  | s. | d. | s. | d. | s. | d. |
| London* | 60 | 1 | 38 | 1 | 32 | 5 |
| Essex | 60 | 6 | 35 | 11 | 31 | 3 |
| Kent | 55 | 11 | 39 | 2 | 29 | 8 |
| Sussex | 55 | 3 | 40 | 5 | 29 | 0 |
| Suffolk | 56 | 0 | 34 | 8 | 30 | 1 |
| Cambridgeshire | 52 | 7 | 32 | 7 | 26 | 7 |
| Norfolk | 54 | 9 | 34 | 10 | 30 | 6 |
| Lincolnshire | 56 | 5 | 39 | 8 | 27 | 2 |
| Yorkshire | 55 | 9 | 40 | 8 | 31 | 1 |
| Durham | 55 | 1 | 42 | 0 | 33 | 2 |
| Northumberland | 54 | 3 | 37 | 6 | 33 | 10 |
| Cumberland | 63 | 4 | 38 | 1 | 35 | 6 |
| Westmoreland | 63 | 9 | 46 | 0 | 37 | 7 |
| Lancashire | 61 | 6 | 42 | 0 | 36 | 11 |
| Cheshire | 59 | 3 | 49 | 0 | 35 | 5 |
| Gloucestershire | 55 | 1 | 43 | 1 | 37 | 9 |
| Somersetshire | 50 | 5 | 39 | 5 | 29 | 9 |
| Monmouthshire | 59 | 11 | 49 | 1 | 0 | 0 |
| Devonshire | 56 | 7 | 38 | 2 | 37 | 4 |
| Cornwall | 57 | 3 | 37 | 4 | 37 | 4 |
| Dorsetshire | 55 | 6 | 37 | 10 | 35 | 1 |
| Hampshire | 57 | 2 | 38 | 4 | 31 | 9 |
| North Wales | 61 | 10 | 43 | 7 | 32 | 0 |
| South Wales | 58 | 2 | 40 | 10 | 27 | 3 |

* The London Average is always that of the Week preceding.

*Bristol*, March 31.—The Corn markets here continue very dull, except for prime Barley, which is advanced full 1s. per quarter since this day week, the supply of which article is short. Present prices are nearly as follows:—Wheat, from 6s. to 7s. 6d.; Barley, 4s. 4d. to 5s. 10½d.; Beans, 5s. 6d. to 8s. 3d.; Oats, 2s. 1½d. to 4s.; and Malt, 6s. to 8s. per bushel, Imperial. Flour, Seconds, 33s. to 43s. per bag.

*Derby*, March 31.—Grain sold at our market, as below:—Best Wheat, 58s. to 63s.; Barley for Malting, 44s. to 48s.; Grinding ditto, 38s. to 42s.; Oats, 38s. to 44s.; Feed ditto, 30s. to 36s.; and Beans, 56s. to 63s., per eight bushels Imperial.

*Guildford*, March 31.—Wheat, new, for mealing, 14l. to 17l. per load. Barley, 38s. to 42s.; Oats, 33s. to 44s.; Beans, 54s. to 58s.; Pease, grey, 60s. to 64s.; ditto, boilers, 62s. to 64s. per quarter. Tares, 12s. per bushel.

*Horncastle*, March 31.—No alteration in the prices of Wheat, Oats, and Pease; Rye and Barley something better; Beans lower than this day week.—Wheat, from 52s. to 56s.; Barley, 40s. to 42s.; Oats, 30s. to 38s.; Pease, 60s.; Beans, 55s. to 60s.; and Rye from 40s. to 42s. per quarter.

*Ipswich*, March 31.—We had to-day a small supply of all Grain. Barley was 1s. per qr. dearer; other Grain much as last week. Prices as follow:—Wheat, 52s. to 62s.; Barley, 35s. to 40s.; Beans, 45s. to 47s.; and Pease, 48s. per quarter.

*Manchester*, March 31.—There has been nothing material passing in the Corn trade during the week. At our market to-day we had a full attendance of country dealers, &c., and fine Wheats fully support last week's rates, while the inferior (of which there was a considerable quantity offering from Yorkshire) could not be disposed of, at a reduction of 2d. to 3d. per bushel of 70lbs. Barley for grinding in request, at the prices of this day se'nnight. Oats were in better demand, at an advance of ½d. to 1d. per 45lbs. There is a good demand for Boiling Pease, at 3d. to 6d. per bushel advance. The holders of fine Malts are demanding rather more money, which is only complied with by necessitous buyers. Flour continues dull, at last week's rates.

*Newcastle-on-Tyne*, March 31.—We had a good supply of Wheat from the farmers, and having had, through the week, some arrivals coastwise, the market was well supplied this morning, but the millers are short of stock, and they bought freely, at 1s. per qr. advance. Rye continues in demand, at former prices. Malting Barley is very scarce, and the first arrivals will, probably, sell at higher prices than the above quotations. Malt dull sale. A considerable arrival of white Pease, has caused a decline of 3s. per quarter on that article. We had a good supply of Oats, which was sold at fully last week's prices.

*Norwich*, March 31.—The supply of Wheat to-day was but small, and rather dearer.

*Reading*, March 31.—We had a better supply of Wheat at our market this day, the general quality of which was rough; the sale was dull, at much the same prices as last week.—Old Wheat, 58s. to 68s; New ditto, 56s. to 66s. by the Imperial measure. There was a short supply of Barley; the demand was good, and prices advanced 1s. to 2s. per quarter. Oats met a brisk sale, at last week's prices. In Beans and Peas no alteration.

*Wakefield*, March 30.—We have a large supply of Wheat this morning; good dry samples sell very slowly, at last week's prices, and all other descriptions are very dull.

## COUNTRY CATTLE AND MEAT MARKETS, &c.

*Horncastle*, March 31.—Beef, 8*s*. per stone of 14 lbs.; Mutton, 8*d*.; Pork, 8*d*.; and Veal, 8*d*. to 9*d*. per lb.

*Manchester* Smithfield Market, March 28.—The prices of Beef and Mutton have advanced ½*d*. per lb., and the best fat things were soon taken off at the advance, while the lean sorts were dull in sale, there being a considerable quantity sent to market on account of the high price of feed and scarcity of money. Veal and Pork were about ½*d*. per lb. lower than last week.—Beef, 5½*d*. to 8*d*.; Mutton, 7*d*. to 8½*d*.; Veal, 5*d*. to 6½*d*.; and Pork, 4*d*. to 5½*d*. per lb. sinking offal.

At *Morpeth* Market, March 28, there was a good supply of Cattle and Sheep; there being a great demand, fat of the former sold readily, at an advance in price; the latter met with rather dull sale, at a reduction.— Beef, from 6*s*. to 7*s*. 3*d*.; and Mutton, 7*s*. 6*d*. to 8*s*. 6*d*. per stone, sinking offal.

*Norwich Castle Meadow*, March 31.—We had a good supply of fat Cattle to this market, and more money was asked for them, but not complied with; prices 7*s*. 6*d*. to 8*s*. per stone of 14 lbs. sinking offal; the supply of Store Stock was also large; Scots sold for 3*s*. 9*d*. to 4*s*. per stone of 14 lbs., what they will weigh when fat; only a few of inferior Shorthorns at 3*s*.; Cows and Calves, and Homebreds, of one and two years old, almost unsaleable, on account of the great scarcity of keeping. Meat: Beef, 6½*d*. to 8½*d*.; Veal, 6*d*. to 8*d*.; Mutton, 6*d*. to 7½*d*.; Lamb, 10*d*.; and Pork, 6*d*. to 8*d*. per lb.

# COBBETT'S WEEKLY REGISTER.

**VOL. 62.—No. 3.]    LONDON, SATURDAY, APRIL 14, 1827.    [*Price 6d.***

*Published every Saturday Morning, at Seven o'Clock.*

" They flattered him with their mouth, and lied.".
*Psalm lxxviii. v.* 36.

## DUKE OF YORK.

*Kensington, 10th April, 1827.*

SEEING the situation of public affairs of this country at this time; seeing how many subjects there are of great and pressing public interest: seeing, in short, that those of us who are alive, cannot, in a much greater proportion than one out of twenty, say that he has the fair means of decent existence within his reach; seeing that every man of considerable pro-perty, if he be also a man of sense, is, and must be, in a con-tinual state of anxiety with regard to the fate of that property, and with regard to children and other dependants, for whom that pro-perty is intended to provide; seeing these things, I have felt; and I still feel, the greatest reluctance to occupy my pages, and the time of my readers, by observations relative to the dead. But, there

E

Printed and Published by WILLIAM COBBETT, No. 183, Fleet-street,
[ENTERED AT STATIONERS' HALL.]

are occasions, when it is absolutely necessary, for the sake of
the survivors, to speak of those
who are no more.   One of these
occasions now presents itself, and
exterts from me, that which I am
about to write.  If that which is
said of the dead, could do no mischief to the living; if it be not
calculated to give a wrong bias
to men's minds; in such case, as
that which is said of the dead can
do no harm to the living, these
latter may well pass it by without
notice.  But, when the contrary
is manifestly the case; when that
which is said of the dead is clearly calculated to mislead the mass
of the nation; to make it believe
that which is not true; to induce
men to trust to some other means
of obtaining high character, than
the means to be found in their integrity, valour, public spirit, and
other virtues; when that which is
said of the dead, naturally tends
to make men disregard the use of
the only means by which high
character ought to be maintained;
when that which is said of the

dead has a natural and inevitable
tendency to make the mass of
mankind believe, that it signifies
not what you do during your life;
that you are sure of posthumous
fame, if you do but so act, as to
be sure to provide yourself with
eulogists after your death : when
that which is said of the dead has
and must have this tendency, then
the man, who is so situated as to
be able to make a probably successful effort, in counteracting
that which is said of the dead,
may, perhaps, if he hold his peace,
be neither knave nor coward;
but, it would be full as well for
his country if he were both.

Therefore, clear as it is to me,
that that which has been said,
written, and published, relative to
the late Duke of York, has, and
inevitably must have, this mischievous tendency, I should be
ashamed of myself, if I did not,
at any rate, make an effort to
counteract it.

I am not disposed to criticise
any part of the Duke's character
or conduct, in a manner, which—

could possibly merit the epithet severe. But, justice demands, that I expose the baseness of the flatterers of his memory, without, however, insinuating, that he himself, would have approved by anticipation of such immeasurable baseness. The newspapers of England are, unquestionably, the vilest of all human productions; but, in this case, they have been more vile even than usual. They have gone beyond the settled infamy of their character. Their columns are always open for sale, and the reptiles who have filled them in this case have been dealers, to a greater extent, than perhaps was ever before known in the whole of the history of this species of traffic. They have represented the object of their eulogiums as *every thing perfect in man*; particularly as a *saint* and a *hero*. They have represented him as the most humane, the most upright, the most industrious, the most public spirited of mortal men. These base flatterers think, that they know very well what they are

about: they think to imitate the Innkeepers of Oxford; that is to say, "make the *living pay for the dead.*" They ought certainly not to succeed in so villanous an enterprise, but, their success or their failure, is a mere trifle, compared with the mischievous effect, that their base and lying praises are calculated to have upon the nation at large, and particularly upon those young men, who are now coming upon the stage, and whose opinions and principles must eventually have so great an effect on the happiness or misery of the nation. If these praises of the Duke of York be suffered to pass without comment, who shall say that a young man will do wrong if he endeavour, or, permit himself to imitate the life and actions of the Duke of York? If these praises be proper, then the Duke is a model for all men to imitate. Would it, then, be a good thing, if all men were to imitate the Duke of York? All men, literally speaking, cannot; for all men are not *Dukes*; nor, are they in many other situations in which this DUKE was. But all men have dealings and contracts with their fellow-subjects; and, would it be good for *all* men to imitate his ROYAL HIGHNESS in this capacity? I do not pretend to say, what the DUKE's debts are, or are not. I copy the following paragraph from the Morning Chronicle of to-day.

"We are sorry to learn that "the affairs of the DUKE of YORK "are likely to turn out very indif- "ferent as respects the simple "contract creditors—hardly *one* "*shilling in the pound* being likely "*to* fall to their share. This has "not arisen from any failure in the "sales of property that have taken "place, which have realised full "as much as was expected, but "from the immense amount of "liens on that property, and of "*bona fide* bond securities, all of "which must be satisfied before "the other creditors are paid a "farthing. These bonds, it is "said, exceed *two hundred thou-* "*sand pounds*"!

This may be false; and, as I find it in a newspaper, it is but fair to suppose that it is; but, if it be but a nineteen twentieth part of the truth, let me ask whether this is an *example* to hold up to the na- tion, the debtor having had, con- stantly, during his whole lifetime, an income so great, that it is im- possible for common men to con- ceive, by what means it could be expended. Here were no mis- chances, no accidents, no failure in mercantile enterprize, no event to drive the debtor from the regular receipt of his enormous income, the amount of which he always knew, and always was sure regu- larly to receive. What excuse, therefore, for debt at all; and what answer to give to those nu- merous persons who must be suf- ferers from such debt!

All men are not princes and military commanders, but all men are, or are liable to be, *husbands*: and, would it be a good thing if, in that capacity, *all* men were to imitate the DUKE of YORK! I will allude to no *rumours*; I will

proceed upon no scandalous stories ; nothing like cant shall mark
what I have to say of the DUKE of
YORK; but, when I hear these
profligate, these most mercenary
ruffians of the press proclaim him
to the nation as a sort of Saint,
shall I not refer my readers to the
*evidence* taken before the house
of Commons in the year 1809 ?
Shall I not bid them read that
*evidence*? Shall I not bid them
look at the *proof* relative to the
open, the undisguised connexion
with MOTHER CLARKE, while the
DUKE had living, a wife, the
daughter of a king, the sister of a
king, a woman of unimpeachable
character in all respects ; a woman
remarkable for the gentleness of
her manners, and for all those
qualities and characteristics which
made it cruel to the last degree,
to inflict a sting in her bosom.
Had she been otherwise than
strictly virtuous; had she been a
virago; had she been a notorious
squanderer; wasting the substance
of her husband : had she been any
of these, less, and much less would

have been said on the subject.
She was none of them, and her
gentleness, and regard for her
husband's character and feelings
was so great, that she made it a
point of appearing in public with
him, at a moment when all the
world were turning their backs
upon him, though the cause of his
disgrace was that very connexion
which was calculated to inspire
her with the most anxious desire
to obtain revenge.   One cannot
tell any thing about the *mere*
*personal* attachments in such case ;
but the DUCHESS of YORK had to
bear the *pity*, not only of this
nation, but of a great part of the
civilized world ; and *pity* is a thing
which we do not endure very patiently, particularly when we are
in situations, where the very existence of it implies that we are in a
fallen state.   I scorn, as I always
did scorn, cant, upon the subject
of MOTHER CLARKE ; but, let the
eulogists of the DUKE of YORK tell
us plainly, if they dare, that the
man who was the subject of the investigation of 1809, and the sub-

ject of the votes of the House of Commons in that year ; let those eulogists tell us, if they dare, that it would be a good thing, for *all* men to imitate the DUKE of YORK as a *husband :* which, be it observed, is one, at any rate, of the great capacities of human life

Perhaps those eulogists are of opinion, that to pursue that which is generally called, *gaming* has nothing amiss in it. Certainly the thing is common enough, and all that we have heard, relative to this subject, as far as the DUKE was concerned, may possibly be false. If so, however, these eulogists have shown themselves to be very stupid or very insincere friends ; for, they have made no attempt to wipe from his memory, that which was by no means an object of admiration with the wise and virtuous part of the people. They seem to me to have been sensible they were writing a romance, or they would, at any rate, have attempted to palliate the practice so generally imputed to the DUKE. The newspaper ruf-

fians are, generally speaking, addicted to this practice themselves, as far as their means will allow them : it is a practice congenial with the natural turn of their minds : they are penned up amidst swarms of men, and they naturally resort to stimulants of this kind. But, this is not the case with the nation at large : this is not the case with a far greater part of persons in the middle rank of life, nor is it the case with the far greater part of those who move in a higher sphere. These eulogists, then ; these lavishers of indiscriminating praise, must, to be consistent, boldly assert that it would be a good thing, if every one followed the example of the DUKE in this practice, so generally, whether justly or unjustly, imputed to him.

For my part, I can discover nothing " *tangible* " in this praise bestowed upon the DUKE. CHARLES YORKE very indiscreetly called upon WARDLE to bring forward his charges against the DUKE in a

" tangible shape." That worthy ex-Secretary of State and present sinecure placeman, soon found the shape tangible enough. I have endeavoured to find something equally tangible in the praises bestowed upon the Duke; but have been enabled to find nothing of the kind. A monstrous deal about his filial affection, forgetting, I suppose, that he had a grant of 10,000l. a year (in addition to all his other sources of enormous income), merely for the trouble of visiting his aged father once in a week or ten days! How much better it would have been if these injudicious friends had been sensible and honest: if, by way of apology or excuse for the taking of this great sum from the nation, they had said, that the Duke stood in need of the money, and that (which I really suppose to be the truth, because it is against nature to suppose the contrary), if he had no money at all for doing it, he would have watched over his father (who, by-the-bye, had been most particularly kind and good to him), as cheerfully and diligently as if he had been allowed for his trouble a million a year. At any rate, however, he did receive the 10,000l. a year, until the death of his father; and, be it remarked, that the amount so received by him, now makes part of that enormous debt, which is pressing this people to the earth; which makes millions rise every morning not knowing how or where to breakfast; which threatens with beggary even the most wealthy of the community; which renders all men's affairs so uncertain; which, in numerous instances, makes life a burthen; and which, let the military geniuses think what they may, puts every institution in jeopardy.

To talk of the Duke's generosity is, therefore, to suppose that we have all lost our memories, or, that those memories have become so short, that they do not carry us back beyond the space of five or six years. The great burthen of praise, is, however, the surprising kindness of the Duke. He did so many "*keind things*," which word "*keind*" these whiskered, pigeon-cropped and shoulder-padded eulogists pronounce in an accent, partaking of a puke and a lisp. They make me sick, at any rate. He was so " *keind* a soul!" Not so very " *keind*" to poor Queen Caroline, at any rate, though one would have thought, that there were, in the history of his own life, several incidents, that might have induced so singularly a " *keind*" hearted man, to judge her with great lenity, even though he had believed her fully guilty of every thing laid to her charge. Having mentioned the late unfortunate Queen, I will also mention a letter which I have received from a lady, in consequence of the intimation of my resolution, to notice this shameless praise heaped upon the Duke of York. She mentions, amongst other things, the fate which has befallen the most conspicuous enemies of that unfortunate Queen. She notices that the triumph (if triumph it were) arising from her death.

was of short duration in the case of Castlereagh; she notices also, the short-lived honours of Lord Gifford; and she does not forget, that it is not yet seven years since Lord Liverpool ordered her body to be carried round the new road. This is the way in which a lady, writing in a manner as elegant as I ever saw, views the occurrences relating to the men who stood most prominent of all, in the prosecution of the unfortunate QUEEN. The Duke of York did not take a very prominent part upon that occasion. There was nothing peculiarly bitter in his hostility; but, a very large part of the nation will say, let the vile newspapers publish what they will, that that was an occasion, on which for him to shew that tender feeling, that genuine humanity, that gallant generosity which set self at defiance, and of all which these eulogists pretend the DUKE had a store so prodigious.

To return, however, to his excessive " *keindness*," I have, when I was able to overcome the effect of the compound *puke* and *lisp*; when I have been able to overcome the disgust excited by the sound of this word, which is pronounced by a drawing down of the under jaw and by a gape, nearly wide enough to show you the root of an ugly tongue; when I have been able to overcome the disgust excited by this sound and this sight, I have sometimes asked, " Do tell me what are your proofs of this *keindness.*" " Oh! he did so many *keind* things; he gave so many *meritorious* persons good posts; got a regulation to enable old half-pay officers to sell their commissions to young ones; to enable half-pay officers to become parsons; to submit to a ' *call* ' to take upon them the care of souls, and to keep their half-pay at the same time; he was *so good!* made so many families happy: made them so comfortably off!"

In short, I always found, that the Duke was " *keind* " to excess to every body, but to those toiling millions who have to pay the taxes. His " keindness " consisted, in fact, in enabling idlers to live well upon the toil of embarrassed farmers and tradesmen and half-starving journeymen and labourers. Now, mind, I do not accuse the Duke of doing this wilfully. On the contrary, I am quite convinced he was not doing it at all! I am quite convinced, that he never, in the whole course of his life, bestowed a thought on the effect of taxation; that he never reflected, and never thought it his duty to reflect, whence the money came, and that he thought, that if he, as far as related to himself and his office, distributed it pretty fairly, that was all he had to do with the matter. I am ready to acknowledge, that, from what I have heard, it always appeared to be his natural disposition to relieve the distresses of the military people, and to gratify the wishes of any, or all them, who made their application to him. But, what great praise is this, when no part of the millions came out of his own pocket?

It is said, that he greatly improved the *discipline* of the English army. Had the Duke been a friend of mine, I should have preferred to say of him, that he greatly reduced the *numbers* of the English army. England did very well for a *thousand years* without such a thing as a standing army being known, or so much as thought of. It is, said, that, the *state* of the world is altered, and that, if other nations have standing armies, England must have them, too. Those who say this, appear to forget that the other nations of Europe had all of them standing armies; that France, for instance, had a thundering standing army, over which so many victories were gained by the raw levies raised in England by the Norman kings.

It is only since the DUKE of YORK became Commander-in-Chief that there has appeared a settled design to have a great standing army always in England, with all the dresses and manners of a continental army. If you call it an improvement in discipline, to do every thing that can possibly be done to make the hired soldiers a body, *wholly distinct from the people*; to *disunite* the two as much as possible; to create an army, which shall be precisely the reverse of what Judge Blackstone says is congenial to the English constitution; if you call this an improvement of the discipline of the army, then the DUKE of YORK has been as great an improver as ever lived. I must, however, do him the justice to say, that all the items of this system of improvement originated in heads widely different from his. I am far from believing that he was the *inventor* of that *military academy*, which is stuck upon a wild heath, cut off from all communication with towns and villages, and in which you see little boys of *ten* or *twelve* years of age, dressed in military uniform, to *be trained to be officers in the army*, to be kept in a sort of military discipline all the while, to be thus kept *distinct from the mass of the people, to*

have no notion of any sort of obedience, except that due to a military chief, and thus to be made, to all intents and purposes, precisely that description of soldier, which Blackstone describes as wholly incompatible with civil liberty. "In a land of liberty," says he, "it is extremely dan-
" gerous to make a distinct order
" of the profession of arms. In
" absolute monarchies, this is ne-
" cessary for the safety of the
" prince, and arises from the main
" principle of their constitution,
" which is that of *governing by*
" *fear:* but, in free states, the
" profession of a soldier, taken
" singly, and merely as a profes-
" sion, is justly an object of jea-
" lousy. In these, no man should
" take up arms, but with a view
" to defend his country and its
" laws : he puts not off the citizen,
" when he enters the camp ; but
" it is because he is a citizen,
" and would *wish to continue so,*
" that he makes himself for a
" while a soldier. The laws,
" therefore, and constitution of

" *these kingdoms,* know no such
" state as that of a perpetual
" standing soldier, *bred up to no*
" *other profession than that of*
" *war;* and it was not till the
" reign of Henry VII. that the
" Kings of England had so much
" as a guard about their persons."
.................... " Nothing
" ought to be more guarded
" against, in a free state, than
" making the military power,
" when such a one is necessary to
" be kept on foot, *a body too dis-*
" *tinct from the people.* LIKE
" OURS, therefore, it should
" wholly be composed of *natural*
" *subjects;* it ought only to be
" enlisted for a short and limited
" time; *the soldiers also should*
" *live intermixed with the people;*
" *no separate camp,* NO BAR-
" RACKS, *no inland fortresses,*
" *should be allowed.* And per-
" haps it might be still better, if,
" by dismissing a stated number
" and enlisting others at every re-
" newal of their term, a circula-
" tion could be kept up between

" the army and the people, and
" the citizen and the soldier be
" more intimately connected to-
" gether." — *Blackstone's Com-
mentaries, Book I. Chap.* 13.

These are the principles which
were inculcated by a lawyer, not
at all enthusiastic in the cause of
freedom. He was Solicitor-General to the late Queen. Of course
he was a thorough-paced courtier;
yet, only fifty-seven years ago, these
were the principles inculcated by
him. Precisely the contrary of
these principles, have been the
organization, the management,
the discipline, the control over,
the uses made of, and the whole
of the circumstances connected
with the army and its character,
ever since the DUKE OF YORK became Commander-in-Chief of that
army. Here we are told, that it
is dangerous to public liberty to
make the profession of arms a distinct profession, and, that the
making of it a distinct profession,
is grounded on the principle of the
necessity of *governing by fear.*
Here we are told, that the *happy*

constitution of England *knows of
no such state as that of a soldier
bred up to no other station but
that of war.* And, England now
beholds the military profession
made a distinct and a most distinct order; and she beholds a
most expensive and palace like
academy or college, or whatever
else they may call it, stuck up in the
midst of a wild and barren heath,
to hold little boys, who, very soon
after the clouts are taken from
them, are dressed in military uniform, put under a species of military discipline, kept almost as
distinct from the people as if they
were monks of La Trappe; " bred
up to no other profession than that
of war;" and thus hurling contemptuous defiance in the teeth of
what Blackstone tells us to' look
upon as the essential principles
of the constitution. In this book
of our laws we are told, that the
army should *never be a body too
distinct from the people;* that it
should *contain no foreigners;* that
the soldiers should live *intermixed
with the people;* that there ought

to be no BARRACKS, and none of those crafty devices, which are calculated to keep the soldiers and the people in a constant state of jealousy of each other. Since the DUKE OF YORK became Commander-in-Chief, every possible device seems to have been practised to keep the soldiers distinct from the people; and, as to foreigners, the law itself has, in innumerable instances, been wholly disregarded by giving them commissions in our army of natives.

As I said before, I am far from imputing the *invention* of this change to the DUKE of YORK; but, if he be not to have this invention imputed to him, he is to have nothing imputed to him relative to the army. If by *military discipline* be meant a separating of the soldiers from the people; dressing them out in a manner to make them as unlike the people as possible; introducing amongst them every thing in imitation of the armies of the *despots* of the continent; if this be to improve the discipline of the army; then it has been improved, and greatly improved, under the Duke of York; but if improvement of discipline mean an addition made to those qualities of the soldier, which render him more efficient for the purposes of war and more inoffensive and less dangerous to public liberty, when at home and not engaged in war; then I deny that the DUKE of YORK has improved the discipline of the English army. It is pretty impudent to be sure; not more impudent perhaps, not more insulting to the common sense of the nation, than any one of a dozen other things which these base flatterers have said of the DUKE of YORK; not more impudent and insolent perhaps; but, certainly, nothing can well equal in impudence and insolence, the barefaced falsehood, the stupid lie, that the victories obtained by the English army during the late war, are to be ascribed to the discipline taught by the Duke of York! However, these base flatterers seem to forget that the victories; as they are called (and for which we are now paying most dearly), were occasionally interspersed with defeats, or, as they were called about seven and twenty years ago, "negative successes;" an appellation to which the achievements of this same great commander actually gave rise. I shall, by-and-bye, have to speak somewhat at length of these achievements, and then those who were born after the date of the achievements will have a full explanation, a practical and frequently repeated illustration of the phrase "negative success," in the obtaining of successes of which sort, his Royal Highness certainly surpassed any commander from the days of the Moabites to those of the Dutch.

But, as to the merit of these, "victories," gained by our army during the late war; I believe, that there would be a pretty fair balance (leaving out the American ones) between the successes and "negative successes." As to the battle of Waterloo; as to the surrender of Paris; as to the defeat, as it is called, of Bounaparte; as to all these, they were achieved, principally, not by the arms but by the bank notes of England; and, I have no scruple to say, that in the restoration of the Bourbons and of the ancient order of things, the bank directors had a thousand times more influence, than all our armies, all our ships, and all our commanders put together. Nor did the bank directors seem to be blind to their merit in this respect, for they, in a representation to the Ministers, made in 1816, distinctly observed, that, while they joined the rest of the nation in applauding the conduct of our fleets and armies, bare justice to *themselves compelled them to assert their own claim to a large share of the applause due to the successful transactions of the war!* I expressed my approbation of the claim, at the time when it was made. I said then, that the names of the bank directors, the picture of the old lady, ought to be inscribed on the triumphal

columns, which it was then proposed to build; and I do hope
that the "Great Captain" will
suffer the bank directors to be put
upon some part or other of the
triumphal arches, which are now
being built, apparently, for him
and the King.

The victories, as they are called, were generally things purchased with money. It was observed,
by the various parcels of Germans
and Russians which we hired,
that it was *very curious*, that, when
they gained a victory in company
with us, we always claimed it as
*wholly belonging to us*; and that,
when they got beaten along with
us, we always gave them the
greatest share of the "negative
success." Yes, very "curious
perhaps," but, certainly by no
means unjust; for, we *paid* for
the whole of the *victory* when we
got one, and, when the success was
of the negative kind, we might
surely let our hirelings bear their
portion of the honor. The bank
directors were right, to a certainty:
a very large share of the *merits*

of the war, and of all its consequences, assuredly belongs to
them; and, if I could have my will
of every man jack of them, or, if
dead, the heirs or successors of
every man jack of them, should
receive, in the most ample degree,
a *reward suitable to those merits.*
Some people seem to despair of
seeing that day of justice arrive:
for my part I do not, and I trust
that I shall live to record the
event.

Besides, however, this sharing
on the part of the bank directors,
we must set the defeats against
the victories, if we will be base
enough, or, rather, so beastly
stupid, as to ascribe the victories
to the Dᴜᴋᴇ of Yᴏʀᴋ. It would
be the most monstrous absurdity
that ever disgraced the lips of
man, to ascribe the victories to
him without ascribing to him the
defeats also; and, if we do this,
my real opinion is, that, including
his *own famous wars,* of which I
shall presently speak, our army
was present, and took part in, if
we include the war against Ame-

rica, *three* defeats to every *two* victories. So that, the argument, founded on the victories, would be worth very little to his Royal Grace. The victories are taken to be a proof of the excellence of his Commander-in-Chief-ship; but, if the defeats exceed the victories in *number*, which I am sure is the fact; and if the *victories* themselves were purchased, AND REMAIN YET TO BE PAID FOR: if this should turn out to be the case, what then becomes of this proof of the excellence of the discipline taught by the DUKE of YORK; and, who will not be ready to repeat the words of my motto; *" they did flatter him with their mouth, and lied."*

These wondrous parasites either forget, or they never knew any thing about the history of the late wars. Some of them, indeed, may not have been born, at the time when the Duke was in *the field himself*; to such it will be a treat, "especially if they be addicted to rat-hunting," it will be quite a treat, to be introduced into

that field, from which I shall not now, thank God, have much longer to detain them. But, though some of the nauseous parasites may not have been born, at the time of the memorable achievements of Dunkirk and the Helder, they must all have been born (or they have begun the trade of parasite at a very early age) at the time of the battles of CHIPPEWAH, PLATSBURGH, the retreat before BALTIMORE, and the ever memorable battle of NEW ORLEANS, which exhibited to the world, in the bravery and conduct of GENERAL JACKSON and his volunteers, the finest instance of courage, of love of country, of devotion to justice, truth and honour, that ever, as far as I have witnessed, was known since man was man. There may have been, in the history of the world, instances of these virtues equal to these, but it is impossible for human nature to produce any thing to surpass it. There must have been some of the parasites, who were born at the time when that memorable battle took place, yet, perhaps, there is this excuse for them, that that affair was so completely smothered up, in England; so completely shut out of the gazette, as to all its main features, and passed over with such profound silence in Parliament, that this deluded, this wilfully blind and humbugged nation, scarcely ever knew that such a battle had ever taken place, though it decided, for ever, the character of the combatants of both sides, though it read to mankind this useful, this important, this heart - cheering lesson, that all the arts of war; all the perfections of military discipline, all the inventions of military science, all the vaunted rockets of Congreve, all the tactics taught by Prussia, Austria and France, all the stimulants of ribbons, medals, stars and military titles, are as dust in the balance, when weighed against the arms, the simple and rude arms of free men, animated with the resolution to preserve their country against the unhallowed invasions of its enemies. Some of the parasites, however, must have known something of the American war; and, therefore, if they ascribed to the Duke of York's teaching so large a part of what they called the victories of the army, they surely ought to have ascribed to him a share as large of the disgraceful defeats of that war. Leaving out this war, however, why did the parasites stop at the transactions in Spain and France, into neither of which the English army ever entered, until they had *more than one half of the people on their side?* This was the case, observe, or else we were told the most abominable lies. As to Spain, it is notoriously true, that the people were for us almost to a man, and, France was not entered, until, in fact, the tyrant who ruled it, had, so harassed and disgusted the people, as to make them hail us as their *allies.*

Good reason, therefore, as we are now going to see, was there for the parasites to go no further back, than what may be fairly

F

called the fag end of the war, and to leave wholly unnoticed the proceedings of the English army, when in the field against the French, and when the French, whatever might be the fact, were animated by what they deemed the love of freedom. The parasites had, however, more than one good reason for this omission; for, the history of the early campaigns of the war, was a history of little more than the defeats of our army; and another, and a stronger reason was, that, in these early campaigns, the English army was *under the command of this very Duke of York in person.* One would have thought, that no parasite, however barefaced, however profligate, however strongly animated by the desire of making the living pay for the dead, would have wholly overlooked, wholly sunk, this by far the most interesting part of the life of his hero! The office of Commander-in-Chief *at home*, was a thing of trifling importance, compared to the office of Commander-in-Chief *abroad.*

The tactics, practised at the horse guards; the marches and countermarches from PLYMOUTH to HARWICH, and from CHATHAM to LONDON; and then going by sea *on the canal* from BRENTFORD to MANCHESTER and BLACKBURN: these are things easily carried on; they require very little skill; not much more than one could purchase in the shape of a couple of clerks for eight or nine score pounds a year. But, when it comes to commanding an army in the field; when it comes to the facing of brave enemies, and particularly such as are animated by the love of liberty; when it comes to a struggle against such armies as France poured forth during the first ten years of her late wars, then the military merit of the opponent is *put to the test.* The Duke's merit was put to this test; and, let us, then, taking for our guide the page, not of *impartial* history, but of history most partial on his side: taking this history for our guide, advancing no fact as from ourselves, and drawing no conclusion other than the conclusion which evidently proceeds from the premises; taking, in short, for our guide, a statement of those facts, which even parasites could not smother, and that, too, at a time, when it was almost to be guilty of treason to publish any fact contrary to the wishes of those who had the guiding of all things in the nation; when it was dangerous to be even suspected of a desire to make disagreeable truths known to the public: taking for our guide, I say, the cowed down ANNUAL REGISTER of those times, let us try the military merits of the Duke of York even by this test.

In the year 1793, war having been begun against the French, the English army, one of the finest and best appointed that the English ever sent forth, furnished, as our armies always are, even to prodigality, was sent forth under the DUKE of YORK, to join the Imperial, and other German armies, with a view of attacking and putting down the French revolution. It is curious enough, that the Prince of SAXE COBOURG, the father of him, to whom we have now the honour to pay 50,000l. a year, commanded the Austrian army upon this occasion. All these armies united, had taken, in August, 1793, the town of VALENCIENNES, on the confines of France; and all was rejoicing in England, the men got drunk with toasting the DUKE of YORK, while their wives ran them in debt, to vie with their neighbours in sticking up candles to demonstrate their loyalty, and, as was the fashion of that day, their attachment to their "GOD AND THEIR KING," I being by no means certain, that they did not put the king first. The DUKE, though intent enough, perhaps, on putting down "republicanism" and "atheism," did not altogether forget the shop. He knew that DUNKIRK was a famous place for trafficking; and, therefore, in the way of gratitude, I suppose, for the praises which he had received, on account of the conquest of VALEN-

CIÉNNES, which, by-the-bye, was, according to the principle above laid down, ascribed wholly to the Duke; in gratitude, I suppose, for this, his ROYAL HIGHNESS wished to do some signal service to the shop; and, therefore, knowing that the shop would be very much pleased, to possess such a trafficking place as DUNKIRK, he quitted his loving allies (all but the HANOVERIANS, whom he took with him) in order to capture this town. Which capture was deemed to be so certain a result of his undertaking, that handkerchiefs, celebrating the event, and representing the DUKE with a crown of laurel on his head, had been actually printed at that hellhole MANCHESTER, before the news arrived of his having been driven from before the place, with a flea so loudly buzzing in his ear, that the HANOVERIAN GENERAL and our DUKE of CAMBRIDGE " were, for a short time, in possession of the enemy!" In other words, they were prisoners, till a General of the name of WALMO-

DEN came suddenly and unexpectedly to their aid and rescued them. The historian says that the DUKE saved his MILITARY CHEST, took care of the money, but was compelled to abandon his heavy artillery, camp equipage, ammunition, and of course all the rest of the things, to an enormous amount, so necessary to the efficiency of his army. There appears hardly ever to have been a more hasty or helter-skelter retreat; and, which is curious enough, so little were the French Convention satisfied with GENERAL HOUCHARD, and who, they insisted, ought to have *flung the DUKE of YORK and his army into the sea*; that they brought him to trial, condemned him to *die, and put him to death*. Now, though the French Convention consisted of violent men, they would not have put a General to death, unless there had been some ground for the accusation against him. In short, we must believe that HOUCHARD did not do his duty; and, then we must ask, what would have been the fate of the English army if he had done his duty; and that will suggest to us to ask further, what must have been the judgment of him who undertook, and what the conduct of him who had the execution of this enterprize.

After this affair, the Duke rejoined the Austrians; and the first step was to settle a point of *vast importance*, namely, whether the Duke should or should *not be under the command of the Austrian General!* A grand council of war was held to settle this point; but it was of such importance that it could not be settled without a negotiation between the courts of LONDON and VIENNA, by whom it was finally agreed that the DUKE should not be under an Austrian commander unless the emperor came to command in person. While these high blooded gentry were settling this point, the French were preparing for a furious attack upon the whole of them. During the former part of the year 1794, the war was carried on in Flanders, the parties having for them, sometimes victory and sometimes defeat; but the latter generally fell to the lot of the allies, of which the English army formed a part, arising, the historians observe, in some part, at least, from the before mentioned dispute about precedence. At last, VALENCIENNES was abandoned, though fortified anew by the Austrians, and with it such immense quantities of stores and provisions of every sort, that were hardly ever before seen in one fortress. Besides these, an immense military chest fell into the hands of the French, who now pressed the allied army with so much vigour, that they compelled them finally to separate, each army seeking its own safety in retreat, or rather in hasty helter-skelter flight. The DUKE of YORK and his army now hastened away towards Holland, sustaining defeat after defeat, routing after routing, loss after loss, hunted from fortress to fortress, and from some which had never before opened their gates to an enemy, and were, till now, deemed to be impregnable. Winter was coming on apace, the climate was cold, the inhabitants hostile in their hearts, when the English army took shelter in the celebrated fortress of NIMEGEN. Here, however, is a fortress which had always been deemed fit to stand a siege for a year, this unhappy army found no safety. The indefatigable and implacable republicans soon came up, with the view to besiege and take the whole of them. Leaving behind them a large part of the remnant of their heavy stores and implements of war, they traversed the Dutch territories, with the French close at their heels, and, at last, reached the Duchy of Bremin; whence they embarked, or, rather, the remnant of them embarked, and, after being pelted about by the waves, in the bitter cold month of January, landed on the banks of the Humber, and at other places, whither they had been driven, and where, like Job's messengers, they told their dismal tale.

Never have I read of the sufferings of any thing that bore the name of army, to equal the sufferings of this body of men. Without food, without drink, without scarcely a rag to cover them or a shoe to their foot; their backs constantly exposed to the bullets of the French, and suffering every privation that imagination can conceive, frozen to death by thousands, their women and children left dead strewed by the sides of the road, these unhappy creatures came home to England to tell their dismal tale and to put upon record upon the minds of all who heard them, one consequence, at least, of an undertaking, bottomed, as we all well know, in an avowed desire to prevent those which were called French principles from penetrating into England! In other words, to prevent those changes, those very changes, which must even now come, or which must leave their place to be supplied by events beyond all measure more dreadful than those which could possibly have arisen, if even that had taken place for which the reformers are accused of having wished.

But, it may be said by the parasites, and by those who have sold their columns to the parasites, that there might be no *fault* in the Duke of York; that an army may suffer defeat after defeat, and run before an enemy from fortress to fortress, as a rabbit runs from burrow to burrow before a weazel or a ferret that take a grib at her at every resting place, and that still the Commander-in-Chief may be a very *good* Commander-in-Chief. Mark, however, how this works: if there be no *demerit* in such a series of defeat, under every variety of time and place, there can be, under no circumstances whatever, any merit in victory. Say that the Duke of York might be a very *good* *General*, though his army (who were the finest, mind, and best appointed that the world ever saw) got thus hunted about, hacked and trodden to pieces: say that all this might happen, and that the Commander-in-Chief might be *still a very good General*; and then let me ask these "*keind*" parasites, where they will find the evidence to prove, that any man upon earth can by possibility be a *bad General.*

It would be fortunate, however, for the memory of this greatly eulogized *Commander*-in-*Chief*, if the history of this campaign stopped here. It does not stop here: common justice will not let it stop here; but will add, will tell that cajoled public, in whose ears the lofty praises of this Duke have been rung, that HE DID NOT REMAIN TO PARTAKE OF THE DANGERS AND SUFFERINGS OF THIS UNFORTUNATE ARMY! The reader of the present day will hardly believe the fact: the men who have been born within the last thirty years, and who have been stunned by the bawlings of the parasites, will hardly think it possible, but the fact is, that when the cold weather was coming on, and when there could appear a chance of nothing but bare escape, and that, too, by the terrible exertions of hardihood and valour, which this remnant of this army afterwards displayed; when that moment arrived, he who had caused two Governments to negotiate, rather than yield a point of punctilio as to the right of command, quitted that army, of the command of which he had been, and not unjustly, so proud, and left them under a FOREIGN COMMANDER, to be led to the water's edge, and thence to escape, after every species of suffering, mental as well as bodily, of which human beings are capable. Seriously, I say, that, when I think of what he must have felt, while sitting in a double doored, double windowed, carpetted and cushioned room in London; when I think of what his thoughts must have been, what his feelings must have been, while sitting in such room, and reading of the dreadful sufferings of the remnant of his army, of their lacerated bodies, their frozen extremities, their hungry stomachs, and of here a comrade leaving his comrade to perish behind him, here a husband leaving his wife, here a mother leaving her child, which was the case in hundreds of hundreds of instances; when I reflect upon what his feelings must have been, I sincerely say, *that that would have been enough;* but, the parasites provoke an answer, justice to the country demands it, circumstances have given me the power, and duty to my country commands me to exert that power.

If there should be found a parasite so completely destitute of all shame, so wonderfully gifted in the way of impudence and of profligate sycophancy as to say, that the Duke was, at the time here referred to, a young man, and that it was his first essay, I answer, that he was pretty nearly *thirty years of age,* and that he had been studying the art of war all his life time, having lived several years in Prussia, which was looked upon as the school of military commanders. However, the history of the Duke's wars, unfortunately for his parasites, furnish an answer, and a most complete answer, to this miserable excuse; for, in 1799, the Duke had another army put under his command, another English army, appointed and provided in the best possible manner, which was to be joined by a Russian and a Hanoverian army for the purpose of driving the French out of Holland, and for restoring the Stadtholder to his authority. The Duke was Commander-in-Chief of this army. In the month of September, the fighting began. The Duke had under him Generals Abercrombie and Dundas, and many others whom the base newspapers of that day called the *"flower of the English nobility."* There was a maritime expedition accompanied with this, which was intended to *get possession of the Dutch fleet.* This latter object was easily effected, for the Dutch fleet surrendered without striking a blow, and came over as quietly

as possey, and were safely moored, I believe it was, at Torbay! But, to drive the devils of republicans out of Holland was another man's matter, and that matter the Duke had to manage. It is useless to waste time in a detail of the battles that ensued : the *result* being the only thing of any interest, and that result was, that, at the end of about *thirty* days from the commencement of the military operations, in spite of the flower of the *" English nobility,"* the Duke and his army were compelled to retreat to the edge of the land, and that he there signed a capitulation, by which he rescued the bodies of that army from capture, at the least, and, perhaps, from total destruction. The conditions of this capitulation were very simple : the Duke agreed that there should be SURRENDERED TO THE FRENCH EIGHT THOUSAND OF THE SEAMEN, WHETHER FRENCH OR DUTCH, WHO WERE PRISONERS IN ENGLAND, and that, on that condi-

-tion, the Duke's army should be permitted to go out of Holland, safe in body, and as cheerful in mind as circumstances might admit of! Thus ended this celebrated campaign of our late Commander-in-Chief. If any thing could have added; if there had been a possibility of adding to the humiliation of the *Duke* and his "flower of English nobility," that humiliation was at hand in the curious and interesting fact, that the Duke and the "flower," he a prince of the blood royal, and the "flower" having amongst them PRINCE WILLIAM of GLOUCESTER, were defeated by, and the DUKE capitulated with, the French General BRUNE, who had been apprenticed to a PRINTER at *Limoges*, and the Dutch General DANDAELLS, who had been apprenticed to a BAKER at *Amsterdam*. All I shall say more is this, that his MAJESTY, in the order, appointing the DUKE of WELLINGTON Commander-in-Chief to the army, has told us, that

he best merits that post who has led that army to glory. If I approved of standing armies and Commanders-in-Chief, I should agree in this sentiment of his MAJESTY; as the thing is, I leave the parasites up to the chins in that dilemma in which this sentiment of his Majesty has placed them; and thus I take my leave of this subject.

### WM. COBBETT.

P. S.—If the reader should happen to know SIR HERBERT TAYLOR, who has, in his history of the DUKE's last illness, discovered such a profound sense of religion; if the reader should happen to know this gentleman, I should be obliged to him just to ask him, what were the BOOKS, which chiefly composed the library of his late Royal Patron! That the Whole Duty of Man, that BAXTER's Call, and TAYLOR's (perhaps SIR HERBERT's father) Holy Living and Dying; that these works, and other such evidences of the piety of the deceased, made part of the DUKE's library, is to be supposed as a matter of course. But, a Correspondent has informed me that there were

OTHER books, in greater number and variety, than in the collection of any man in England! As to PRINTS, there were, I am told, a VAST VARIETY in all shapes and sizes, and representing, too, other things besides the Crucifixion, the celebration of the Lord's Supper, the Birth of Jesus Christ, the Descent of the Dove, and so forth; these the Royal and pious personage had, of course; but I am told that there was a *great* number of others, which, if SIR HERBERT will be pleased to add a list of them, to that of the books, would form a pretty little *tail-piece* to his history.

## AMERICAN KIDNEY BEANS.

I HAVE two sorts of these, the finest that ever were in England; one of them the very earliest that I ever saw; and the seed, in both cases, so ripe, sound, and excellent, that a large crop from it is certain.—One sort is *Yellow*, the other *Speckled*; both are dwarfs.—Price—17s. a bushel, and smaller quantities in proportion, with something added for paper, string, and trouble.—They are sold at the Office of the Register, No 188, Fleet Street, and may be sent, by order, to any part of the country.

A Young Man, twenty-two years of age, who has resided during the last four years in Paris, and has made himself proficient in the French language, wishes for employment in teaching French, in a Gentleman's family. To his knowledge of French, he begs leave to add that of Latin, and also his capacity to give instruction in the different branches of Philosophy, excepting that of Physic.—Any Gentleman in want of such a person, will please to apply (if by letter, post paid) at the Office of the Register.

### FOR SALE,

AT the Office of the Register, the first 20 Volumes of the REGISTER, half-bound in Russia. Price Seven Pounds.

### ALDERNEY COWS.

JAMES ROBERTS, of Abbotston, near Alresford, in Hampshire, has for sale, Cows and Heifers imported from the Islands. They are of the best breeds, selected with great care, and the Advertizer will warrant them to be what they shall be described to the purchaser. He sends them under the care of his own people, to any part of England; and he has the satisfaction to know, that at nearly three hundred miles from his home, Cows and Heifers sent thither by him have arrived safe and done well. Those Gentlemen and Ladies who live at a distance, and who have no other means of communication, will please to direct their letters as above.    JAMES ROBERTS.

## MARKETS.

Average Prices of CORN through-out ENGLAND, for the week end-ing March 30.

*Per Quarter.*

|          | s. | d. |          | s. | d. |
|----------|----|----|----------|----|----|
| Wheat .. | 56 | 1  | Rye .... | 41 | 3  |
| Barley .. | 37 | 1  | Beans ... | 47 | 6  |
| Oats .... | 30 | 8  | Pease ... | 49 | 5  |

Total Quantity of Corn returned as Sold in the Maritime Districts, for the week ended March 30.

|           | Qrs.   |        | Qrs.  |
|-----------|--------|--------|-------|
| Wheat..   | 36,419 | Rye ..... | 189   |
| Barley .. | 18,277 | Beans . .. | 2,251 |
| Oats ...  | 13,539 | Pease .... | 667   |

*Corn Exchange, Mark Lane.*

Quantities and Prices of British Corn, &c. sold and delivered in this Market, during the week ended Saturday, March 31.

|          | Qrs.  |    | £.    | s. | d. |            | s. | d. |
|----------|-------|----|-------|----|----|------------|----|----|
| Wheat..  | 4,908 | for 14,678 | 10 | 6  | Average, 56 | 9  |
| Barley.. | 4,130 | .. | 8,082 | 6  | 8  | ........ | 39 | 0  |
| Oats..   | 3,988 | .. | 6,396 | 19 | 8  | ........ | 32 | 0  |
| Rye....   | 15    | .. | 29    | 2  | 9  | ........ | 38 | 10 |
| Beans..  | 1,147 | .. | 2,583 | 17 | 11 | ........ | 45 | 2  |
| Pease..  | 641   | .. | 1,300 | 2  | 3  | ........ | 48 | 4  |

Friday, April 6.—The supplies of Grain this week are moderate, and there is again a good quantity of Flour. The Wheat trade is very dull, and hardly supports last Monday's prices. Barley is unaltered. Beans and Pease continue as reported on Monday. There is very little doing in the Oat trade this morning, and prices of last market day are not supported. The Flour trade very dull.

Monday, April 9.—The arrivals of English Grain during the past week were moderate; there was however a good addition made to the quantity of Oats, by the Irish and Foreign supplies, and of Flour the return was again tolerably large. To this morning's market there are few additional arrivals from the adjacent counties, and not much Spring Corn from parts more distant, but Foreign vessels continue to arrive with Oats. Prime samples of Wheat are scarce, and command attention at last week's prices; all other sorts are so very dull, that to effect sales reduced rates must be complied with.

Barley, Beans, and Pease, each find a slow sale at the terms last quoted. The weather being remarkably favourable for Spring opera-tions, occasions our London dealers to purchase very sparingly, and on Friday the trade was reported gene-rally 1s. per quarter lower, but to-day there was an improved demand from country buyers, and the terms of this day se'nnight were nearly ob-tained for such samples as are sweet and good. The Flour trade conti-nues heavy.

———

*Price on board Ship as under.*

Flour, per sack ......46s. — 50s.
—— Seconds ........42s. — 44s.
—— North Country ..40s. — 44s.

———

Price of Bread.—The price of the 4lb. Loaf is stated at 9d. by the full-priced Bakers.

Account of Wheat, &c. arrived in the Port of London, from April 2 to April 7, both inclusive.

| | Qrs. | | Qrs. |
|---|---|---|---|
| Wheat | 4,258 | Tares | 466 |
| Barley | 2,827 | Linseed | 15 |
| Malt | 8,429 | Rapeseed | — |
| Oats | 4,608 | Brank | 8 |
| Beans | 602 | Mustard | 34 |
| Flour | 8,093 | Flax | — |
| Rye | 440 | Hemp | 218 |
| Pease | 942 | Seeds | — |

Foreign.—Wheat, 480; Barley, 570; Oats, 7,231; and Beans, 1,773 qrs.

----

Monday, April 9.—The arrivals from Ireland last week were, 1,800 firkins of Butter, and 1,302 bales of Bacon; and from Foreign Ports, 3,222 casks of Butter.

----

## HOPS.

Price of Hops, per Cwt. in the Borough.

Monday, April 9.—There has been rather more inquiry for Hops during the week, but with no variation in prices.

Maidstone, April 5.—The last week has brought the Hops forward, and they are coming out · of the ground very fast, but the young shoots at present appear rather weakly. Nothing whatever doing in the trade.

Worcester, April 4.—On Saturday, 103 Pockets of Hops were weighed; the demand equalled the supply, and fine samples fully maintained the late prices.—It appears from an Official Return, that in the year ending 5th January, 1827, the quantity of Hops exported to Foreign parts was 3,960 cwt. The imports amounted to 1,874 cwt.

### SMITHFIELD.

Monday, April 9.—On Friday there was a great heaviness in the trade for both Beef and Mutton, and lower terms were of necessity submitted to. For Lamb the demand was brisk, and all that were choice reached the top currency of Monday last. The market to-day is not overdone with anything. The best Beef makes about a crown; but the trade is remarkably flat in other respects; and many middling Beasts, notwithstanding the supply is so moderate, will remain unsold. Sheep being short in number, there was some animation among the buyers in the early part of the day, but towards the close of the market, the demand materially slackened, and the morning's prices could not be obtained. Prime polled Sheep in the wool made 5s. 4d., and best Downs 5s. 6d. The supply of Lamb not being great, the currency of this day se'nnight was fully supported.

Per Stone of 8 pounds (alive).

| | s. | d. | | s. | d. |
|---|---|---|---|---|---|
| Beef | 3 | 8 | to | 5 | 0 |
| Mutton | 4 | 4 | — | 5 | 6 |
| Veal | 5 | 0 | — | 6 | 0 |
| Pork | 4 | 6 | — | 5 | 4 |
| Lamb | 6 | 0 | — | 7 | 0 |

| Beasts | 2,351 | Sheep | 14,720 |
|---|---|---|---|
| Calves | 107 | Pigs | 112 |

NEWGATE, (same day.)

Per Stone of 8 pounds (dead).

| | s. | d. | | s. | d. |
|---|---|---|---|---|---|
| Beef | 3 | 4 | to | 4 | 4 |
| Mutton | 4 | 0 | — | 4 | 8 |
| Veal | 3 | 4 | — | 5 | 4 |
| Pork | 3 | 8 | — | 5 | 8 |

LEADENHALL, (same day.)

Per Stone of 8 pounds (dead).

| | s. | d. | | s. | d. |
|---|---|---|---|---|---|
| Beef | 3 | 0 | to | 4 | 4 |
| Mutton | 3 | 8 | — | 4 | 8 |
| Veal | 3 | 8 | — | 5 | 4 |
| Pork | 4 | 0 | — | 5 | 4 |

## POTATOES.

#### SPITALFIELDS, per Ton.

|  | £. s. | | £. s. |
|---|---|---|---|
| Ox-Nobles | 4 0 | to | 0 0 |
| Middlings | 2 10 | — | 0 0 |
| Chats | 2 0 | — | 0 0 |
| Common Red | 4 0 | — | 0 0 |
| Onions, 0s. 0d.—0s. 0d. per bush. | | | |

#### BOROUGH, per Ton.

|  | £. s. | | £. s. |
|---|---|---|---|
| Ox-Nobles | 3 10 | to | 4 0 |
| Middlings | 2 0 | — | 2 10 |
| Chats | 2 0 | — | 0 0 |
| Common Red | 3 0 | — | 4 0 |

## HAY and STRAW, per Load.

| | |
|---|---|
| *Smithfield.*—Hay | 80s. to 115s. |
| Straw | 40s. to 46s. |
| Clover | 100s. to 140s. |
| *St. James's.*—Hay | 84s. to 128s. |
| Straw | 42s. to 48s. |
| Clover | 120s. to 135s. |
| *Whitechapel.*—Hay | 80s. to 115s. |
| Straw | 36s. to 42s. |
| Clover | 90s. to 135s. |

## AVERAGE PRICE OF CORN, sold in the Maritime Counties of England and Wales, for the Week ended March 30, 1827.

| | Wheat. s. d. | Barley. s. d. | Oats. s. d. |
|---|---|---|---|
| London* | 59 6 | 38 7 | 32 11 |
| Essex | 58 6 | 36 3 | 31 0 |
| Kent | 56 2 | 39 1 | 31 8 |
| Sussex | 55 6 | 41 0 | 30 2 |
| Suffolk | 55 3 | 34 7 | 30 3 |
| Cambridgeshire | 52 2 | 34 9 | 26 1 |
| Norfolk | 55 0 | 34 10 | 32 7 |
| Lincolnshire | 55 8 | 39 1 | 28 1 |
| Yorkshire | 55 5 | 41 6 | 29 8 |
| Durham | 55 3 | 44 0 | 33 3 |
| Northumberland | 53 4 | 36 10 | 33 7 |
| Cumberland | 62 5 | 38 3 | 35 8 |
| Westmoreland | 62 10 | 45 4 | 38 1 |
| Lancashire | 62 1 | 39 6 | 34 4 |
| Cheshire | 60 4 | 49 8 | 30 1 |
| Gloucestershire | 59 7 | 43 8 | 33 2 |
| Somersetshire | 55 9 | 41 3 | 29 10 |
| Monmouthshire | 60 0 | 45 8 | 0 0 |
| Devonshire | 56 0 | 37 5 | 27 4 |
| Cornwall | 57 7 | 38 1 | 37 0 |
| Dorsetshire | 55 7 | 37 9 | 32 5 |
| Hampshire | 56 1 | 38 6 | 34 8 |
| North Wales | 62 4 | 44 10 | 34 0 |
| South Wales | 57 8 | 40 7 | 25 7 |

* The London Average is always that of the Week preceding.

*Liverpool,* April 3.—Since Tuesday se'nnight the imports of Grain have been very light, the demand has been improving throughout the week, and sales have been made of Wheat, Oats, and Barley to a moderate extent, at an increase in value for the former 2d. to 3d. per 70 lbs.; and ½d. to 1d. per bushel on the two latter. We are still without arrivals of White Pease. In prices of Flour and Oatmeal no variation.

Imported into Liverpool, from March 27th to April 3d, 1827, inclusive:—Wheat, 9,202; Barley, 96; Oats, 6,777; Malt, 25; Beans, 600; Pease, 66 quarters. Flour, 130 sacks, per 280 lbs.

*Bristol,* April 7.—We have but little doing in our Corn markets, except for good Barley, which sells freely at a further advance of 1s. per quarter since this day week; the supply of prime Barley continues limited.—Wheat, from 6s. to 7s. 6d.; Barley, 4s. 6d. to 6s.; Beans, 5s. 6d. to 8s.; Oats, 2s. 1½d. to 4s.; and Malt, 6s. to 8s. 3d. per bushel, Imperial, Flour, Seconds, 33s. to 43s. per bag.

*Guildford,* April 7.—Wheat, new, for mealing, 14l. to 16l. 15s. per load. Barley, 38s. to 43s.; Oats, 33s. to 44s.; Beans, 54s. to 58s.; Pease, grey, 60s. to 64s.; ditto, boilers, 62s. to 64s. per quarter.

*Horncastle,* April 7.—The supply of samples of Grain to-day was small, prices nearly the same as last week, except Oats, which were something lower.—Wheat, 50s. to 56s.; Barley, 40s. to 42s.; Oats, 28s. to 35s.; Pease, 60s.; Beans, 55s. to 60s.; and Rye from 40s. to 42s. per quarter.

*Ipswich,* April 7.—We had to-day a remarkably small supply of all Corn for the time of the year. Wheat sold much the same. Barley was 1s. per quarter dearer. Prices as follow:—Wheat, 52s. to 62s.; Barley, 36s. to 41s.; Beans, 44s. to 47s. per quarter; and Pease, none.

*Manchester,* April 7.—The supplies of all kinds of Grain, &c. have been very limited during the week, but fully adequate to the demand, and prices have been on the decline. Our market to-day was but thinly attended, and, from the drooping, dull state of Wakefield market yesterday, the price of the best Wheat declined about 2d., and inferior full 4d. per bushel of 70 lbs. from the prices of last week. Oats dull sale, at a decline of ½d. to 1d. per bushel of 45 lbs. Flour is 1s. per sack lower, and dull sale at the decline. In Barley, Beans, Pease, and Malt, no alteration.

*Newcastle-on-Tyne,* April 7.—There was again a good supply of Wheat from the farmers, but very little coastwise, at this day's market, and prices were nearly the same as last week. Rye continues in demand. We have had some arrivals of Barley from Norfolk, which is selling slowly at prices quoted. Malt rather more in demand. The supply of Oats was not large, but it seemed to be equal to the demand, and prices were the same as last week.

*Reading,* April 7.—We had a fair supply of Wheat, the quality of which was again rough; it met a heavy sale, but the best realized the same prices as last week, while inferior qualities were 1s. lower. Old, 57s. to 67s. New, 52s. to 65s. per quarter by the Imperial measure. There was a very short supply of Barley, which met a very ready sale at an advance of 2s. per quarter. Oats were also a short quantity and 1s. dearer. There were very few Beans and very little demand, prices the same as last week. In Pease no alteration. Samples of Indian Wheat were exhibited in the market, they were stated to weigh from 56 to 58 lbs. per bushel; 5,000 quarters last week arrived at Bristol; 37s. 6d. per quarter was the price asked, to which carriage from Bristol must be added. We did not hear of any sales being effected to-day.

## COUNTRY CATTLE AND MEAT MARKETS, &c.

*Horncastle*, April 7.—Beef, 9s: per stone of 14 lbs.; Mutton, 8d.; Pork, 8d.; and Veal, 9d. to 10d. per lb.

*Manchester* Smithfield Market, April 4.—The supply of Beasts and Sheep to this day's market was small; the dealers demanded and obtained ½d. per lb. advance on fat Mutton, but the lean sorts were heavy in sale, although the quantity was much less than for some time past. Pork has undergone an improvement of ½d. per lb. since this day week, and ready sale at the advance, it being the cheapest meat. Veal the same as last week. As to the few Lambs at market, they were taken away unsold, as being considered not fat enough to kill.—Beef, 5d. to 8d.; Mutton, 7d. to 9d.; Veal, 5d. to 6½d.; and Pork, 5d. to 6d. per lb. sinking offal.

*Norwich Castle Meadow*, April 7.—The supply of fat Cattle to this day's market was large, and the sale for them slow at 7s. 6d. to 8s. per stone of 14 lbs. sinking offal; the show of Scots was large, some few of a good sort, at about 4s. per stone of 14 lbs., of what they will weigh when fat; only a lot or two of poor Shorthorns at 3s. 3d.; Cows and Calves, and Homebreds, continue a flat sale from the difficulty of procuring keep for them.—Meat: Beef, 6½d. to 8½d.; Veal, 6d. to 8d.; Mutton, 6d. to 7½d.; Lamb, 9½d.; and Pork, 6d. to 8d. per lb.

At *Morpeth* Market, April 4th, there were a good many Cattle and Sheep; there being a great demand, the former met with ready sale at an advance in price. Beef, from 7s. to 7s. 9d.; Mutton, 7s. to 8s. 6d. per stone, sinking offal.

# COBBETT'S WEEKLY REGISTER.

VOL. 62.—No. 4.]    LONDON, SATURDAY, APRIL 21, 1827.    [Price 6d.

"Let not, whatever other ills assail,
"A damned Aristocracy prevail."

GOLDSMITH.

## TO THE

# PARLIAMENTARY REFORMERS.

### ON THE CHANGE OF MINISTRY.

*Kensington, 18th April, 1827.*

MY FRIENDS,

We have, at last, seen arise a state of things, which cannot but lead to very important consequences. Consequences of great importance, events which deeply affect nations, come, originally, or distantly, from great causes; but, the *immediate* cause, the act of bringing them forth, is very frequently of a trifling nature. Thus, has the disqualification of Lord Liverpool; that state in which he is, and which, in my opinion, differs in a very slight degree from the state in which he always has been, ever since I have known him, led to such a change, in the persons governing, as must inevitably have a tendency to break up the whole of that system which it seems next to impossible to carry much further without producing sufferings so great and so general, that anarchy and confu-

Printed and Published by WILLIAM COBBETT, No. 183, Fleet-street.
[ENTERED AT STATIONERS' HALL.]

tion must be the final and no distant consequence.

As to the nature of this change, Mr. Canning is, it appears, the First Lord of the Treasury, and Chancellor of the Exchequer, and the King's Prime Minister. In consequence of this appointment, seven of his colleagues, namely, the Lord Chancellor, the Duke of Wellington, Lord Melville, Lord Bathurst, Lord Bexly (Vansittart), Lord Westmorland, and Mr. Peel, have resigned their posts, these being seven out of the twelve Cabinet Ministers. Such is the nature of the change, as far as I have yet heard it represented. Various other noblemen and gentlemen, not being Cabinet Ministers, but persons filling high situations, have also resigned their offices. It is confidently asserted, and many particulars have been stated in proof of the fact, that certain of the nobility, who are pretty well known to have no small influence at *elections*, have had the confidence to remonstrate with the King on this his appointment of Mr. Canning. And, from every thing I see and hear, I cannot help being convinced, that a great body of the persons of this description, not excluding the *clerical aristocracy*, have been by no means backward in expressing their disapprobation of this measure of their sovereign, and their determination to exercise the power they possess, in order to *compel* him to revoke this appointment. Now, my friends, this being pretty nearly, I imagine, a true description of the state of the case, it behoves us to think a little of the part which WE ought to act, during the contest which must inevitably ensue. For my part, had I been one of those, or that person, who advised the King to make this appointment; if I had had the power to obtain the attention of his Majesty upon this occasion, Canning is amongst the last men upon the face of the earth, whom I would have recommended, except as a man, eminently calculated to pull down the whole fabric of the present destructive system. But, if the King had chosen a man still more unfit to be Minister; if he had chosen (I do not suppose it possible) the Right Honourable Gentleman, by whom Eve was seduced, by whom Job was persecuted, by whom our Saviour was tempted, and who is continually roaming up and down seeking whom he may devour, I would have said, " It is " our duty; it is our interest also; " but, it is our bounden duty to " uphold the King against any " combination, or combinations, " that may attempt, that may have " the audacity to attempt, to " thwart his will and compel " him to yield to theirs."

As to the manner in which we, the people of England, can be affected, by any measures that any Ministry may adopt, there are no measures that any Ministers can adopt, worthy of any thing like serious attention, unless these measures have at the head of them regulations and laws relative to the PAPER MONEY.

In this respect there is no difference between CANNING and those who have shunned an association with him. Neither they nor he can do any thing effectual here, without unsaying all that they have said for years past; without breaking pledges a thousand times given; without discovering ignorance almost degrading to human nature; so that, in this all important respect, both parties are upon a footing. The change, therefore, is, in this point of view, of no interest at all. CANNING will go on with the system, till it will hold to pieces no longer; his opponents would do the same if they were to oust him: he would do no more, and no more could they do. It is, therefore, as the groundwork of a great struggle *between the KING and the ARISTO-CRACY*, that we are to view this appointment of Mr. CANNING; and I now address myself to you, in order to induce you, whenever and wherever you may have the means, to support the King against this Aristocracy;

G 2

who, as we have a hundred times over alleged in our petitions, have, in fact, long and long domineered over both King and people. If Canning be the cause of putting an end to this domination, or if it be put an end to merely by the use of his name, he will be entitled, or at least he may expect, from so good-natured a people, forgiveness for all his manifold sins committed against us for the last thirty years; and that is, I think, saying as much for this act of his, as an excess of the generosity of human nature can possibly suggest.

All the miseries of England; its enormous taxes, its irredeemable debts, the abrogation of its best laws, the numerous additions made to the severities of a criminal code, which has at last become terrible but to think of; the horrible code of game laws, the new trespass law, the divers powers of imprisonment bills, the cruel exactions from the industrious part of the community, collected together to be voted away

upon a Church already wallowing in wealth beyond bounds: these things, which are now become so notorious to the nation; all those things, in short, which have embarrassed and ruined the middle class, and which have pauperised or starved the lower class; all these may be fairly traced to the usurped power of that body, who are said now to have pushed their audacity so far as to dictate to the King himself, but whose dictates the King has had the courage to set at defiance.

If, indeed, the body in question had been renowned, if the nation had known them to be wise, disinterested, full of love of country, full of benevolence towards the people, and of proper devotion to the King: if this had been the case, we might have heard with some patience of their pressing their advice, uncalled for, upon his Majesty. When Henry the Eighth was advised to listen to the counsel of Bishop Fisher, it was deemed very harsh in him to say, " Let him take care of "his Bishoprick, and I'll warrant "him I will take care of my "crown." But he was answered, "Recollect that he was deemed "the wisest of your father's coun- "sellors; that his counsels, when "adopted, always led to happy "results; that your mother, on "her death bed, besought you to "listen to him, as you would listen "to your father; that you long "called him 'Father;' that his "counsels always tended to make "you great and your people "happy; and that you have de- "clared this to many, not only "nobles of your own court, but to "foreign princes." If, I say, those who have now attempted to dictate to the King, had had amongst them a man like this; if there had been amongst them a man, whose wisdom, whose disin- terestedness, whose love of coun- try, and whose devotion to his sovereign had been proved by the increased greatness of their mas- ter, and by the happiness of his loyal, most ingenious, and most industrious subjects; if those of the seven seceders who have been the longest in office, had gone to the King, and said, " I, Sir, (the " CHANCELLOR speaking first) " have borne the seals of your " kingdom for something ap- " proaching thirty years, have " received my little reward in " money, it is true; but, what is " that, compared to the diminution " I have seen made in the number " of bankruptcies, especially when " your Majesty considers, how " extremely happy your subjects, " of every description, now are." If, in short, every one had been able to say, and with truth, that under their counsels the nation had prospered, the people had been made happy, the laws had grown milder; that crime and poverty had decreased; that now the nation was in no embarrass- ment, that she was prepared for war at any moment, that the glory of the country, that the renown and safety of the throne, were made as sure as any mortal things could be; if they could, and with truth, have said all this, we might

have been excused for hesitating
a little, before we expressed our
entire approbation of the conduct
of our Sovereign in rejecting this,
the last piece of advice of his and
our benefactors. But, if the
Cabal had gone to him, and said,
as, if they spoke the truth, they
must have said: "Sir, we are come
" to tell your Majesty, that, since
" we have been your Ministers,
" we have seen immense sums of
" money, taken in taxes from your
" labouring subjects, and voted
" away in gifts to a clergy, some
" of the Bishops of whom have
" revenues of forty thousand
" pounds a year; we have pro-
" cured, upon several occasions,
" Acts to be passed to empower
" me to shut your subjects up in
" prison whenever we might SUS-
" PECT THEM of treason;
" these unhappy men have been
" shut up in dungeons, and some
" of them, for years; under our
" sway, the massacre of the 16th
" of August, at Manchester, and
" the letter of thanks to the yeo-
" manry took place; we have

" procured Acts to be passed, to
" occasionally shut your subjects
" up in their houses from sunset
" to sunrise; other Acts, making
" things treason, which were not
" treason before; other Acts, to
" cause men to be transported for
" poaching; other Acts, to make
" the taking of an apple off a
" tree, felony; and to give such
" an extension to the law of tres-
" pass, as to render it almost dan-
" gerous for one of your subjects
" to walk even along the highway.
" From a quarter of a million a
" year, we have seen, during the
" prevalence of our counsels, the
" poor-rates amount to 8,000,000l.
" a year; the annual taxes we
" have seen rise (in time of peace)
" from sixteen to fifty-four mil-
" lions a year; the Debt we have
" augmented more than fourfold,
" in addition to the augmentation
" to the poor-rates; till, at last,
" in every rank and degree, if we
" except those who live upon the
" taxes wrung from the people,
" we every where behold embar-
" rassment, ruin, pauperism, &c.

"starvation; insomuch, and in a
"degree so notorious, that the
"Judges of the Court of King's
"Bench, even when seated on
"that bench, have observed, that
"BREAD and WATER were the
"common food and drink of the
"labouring people of England; as
"a natural consequence, we have
"seen crime increase throughout
"your dominions twenty-fold; we
"have seen every where new
"gaols, of amazing extent, new
"and severer modes of punish-
"ment; we have been obliged to
"assign an additional circuit to
"your Majesty's Judges in the
"winter; to establish a police, a
"thing unknown until now in
"England, and hateful to the ears
"of your predecessors, and their
"happy subjects; in short, may
"it please your Majesty, the
"state of your kingdom, produced,
"in great part, by the choppings
"and changings made in the
"value of money, by our sanc-
"tioning a real invasion of your
"Majesty's greatest and brightest
"prerogative: all these things,

"may it please your Majesty,
"embolden us now to come be-
"fore you, and to beseech you,
"for the love of God, for the
"honour and dignity of your Ma-
"jesty's crown, and for that affec-
"tion and paternal feeling, which
"you have for your people, to
"listen to our advice, and im-
"plicitly to follow it, by giving
"up the exercise of your royal
"prerogative, and to let US ap-
"point your Minister, and not to
"*think* of appointing one your-
"SELF, it being evident, from the
"foregoing statement, which is
"literally true, that your Majes-
"ty must be totally ruined, were
"you to think of ceasing to follow
"our counsels:"

This is what truth would have
bidden them urge in support of
their claim to be attended to by
the King upon this occasion.
Kings have not, very likely, feelings like those of common men;
but, if either of you, my friends,
or I, had been addressed by such
people, in such a way, and for
such a purpose; I do not pretend

TO THE PARLIAMENTARY REFORMERS.

to say what either of you would have done, but I will answer for myself, and I know, that the first thing I could have laid hands on, bottle, glass, candlesticks, ink-stand, hot water: the very first thing I could have laid my hands upon, would have gone, at their heads, wigged or unwigged, and they would have been at the bottom of the stairs and out into the kennel in a twinkling. But, it is surprising to what degree presumption is carried by impunity. Men in power seldom hear the sentiments, the real sentiments of anybody but flatterers. They hear the sound of the voice of nobody else. Formerly Ministers used to have some lessons read to them in Parliament, at least; for the last fifteen or sixteen years, even these lessons have ceased; and, as these men never heard a whisper of disapprobation, even when they ruined whole classes by their dreadful vagaries, played with the King's prerogative of making and issuing money; when they saw that impunity was ready for every

act, be it what it might; when they saw no power on earth to call them to account; when they saw whole descriptions of the people swept, as it were, from the face of the earth; when they heard not a whisper of reproach, even when they proposed to tax the people to obtain the money, to send a part of the people themselves away from their native land, to avoid starvation here; when they heard not a whisper of reproach, even at this, why were they not to suppose, that they were masters of their sovereign, as well as of every body and every thing else! *There*, I, for my part, most gratefully thank the King; they found something to stop their career; and, let them insinuate, and let their blackguards of the quill insinuate in broader language, as long as they please, about that despicable nonsense, " *an influence behind the throne greater than the throne itself*," this act of his Majesty has in it unqualified merit, in my eyes, come the advice from whom, it might. We have no right to presume, that his Majesty wanted any advice at all. He must be deaf and blind, indeed, not to know the situation, not to know the wants, not to know the sufferings and degradations of his people. It is hardly in nature that he should not have wished to change this state of things: his own safety as well as his own honour demanded: the change. Common sense told him (for it required nothing more), that no change of any value could have been effected without a change of counsels. There could have been no change of counsels without a great change of men; and, to begin this salutary change, he was wise in taking a bold and ambitious man, that was not afraid to encounter the formidable opposition, which such a change necessarily implied; a man, wholly ignorant on the subject of the money and of its consequences, and, therefore, wholly insensible of the dangers which he has to encounter; a man, deep enough

in carrying on an affair like that which is now going on, but a man wholly unfitted for the adoption of measures calculated to extricate the country from its difficulties; but, while he is as fit as the resigning sages would have been to put to rights the affair of the paper-money, he is just the man to pull down this aristocracy, of which he has been the eulogist; this *borough* aristocracy, this ruler of King and people, of which he has, all his life-time, until now, been the champion, the daring, the shameless champion. Unless, therefore, the King had seen a probability of obtaining a wise Minister, who well understood the nature of the difficulties of the country, and who would have been likely to find out the means of putting an end to the present miseries of the people by gentle and peaceable means, I do not see how he could have made a better choice than he has made. It was necessary to break up and to rout this band of borough gentlemen: to go on with them any longer was impossible; and again I say, that I do not care a straw about the source of the advice or about the motive to the appointment of Canning.

It is evident to every man of common sense, that we owe all that we suffer to the all-subduing power of the borough aristocracy. There were seven men, at one time, who were so renowned for their wisdom, that they were called the *seven sages* of Christendom. It is said, that they never met but once, and that then they parted for ever, agreeing upon only one maxim, expressed in these two words, " K N O W THYSELF!" Well would it have been for our seven sages, and still better for me, if they had adopted and acted upon this wholesome maxim; for, they would have possessed that very useful branch of knowledge expressed by the maxim, and never would have run their heads against the adamantine rock of royalty, without having one soul amongst the King's subjects at their back,

and it would have been good for me, by saving me the trouble, which I shall now be at, of bringing these arrogant aristocrats into a small degree of acquaintance with themselves: they really do not appear to know who and what they are, whence they sprang, and who it is that has clothed and fed them. It is high time, therefore, when they nose their Sovereign; when they say, "You "shall not choose this man for your "Minister, or we will quit you, "and oppose you:" it is high time that they be made to know themselves; and this they shall before I have done with them, or they will be dull, indeed, of apprehension.

It is impossible, again I say, for any man in his senses not to know, and equally impossible for any honest man to deny, that the present calamities of the country; that the degraded state of the working classes; that the ruin which is sweeping over the farms and the shops and the factories; that, in short, all the cala-

...tions of the country, which exhibit England as just the reverse of what it always used to be; it is notorious that all these have proceeded from the day of the passing of the Septennial Bill to the present hour; that they have all proceeded from the power of the country, all the power of the purse and of every other sort, *being at the disposal of this aristocracy.* It is well known: it is as well known as that this is the month of April, that the present debt, present standing army in time of peace, the present dead-weight, the present poor-rates, are, all, the natural and necessary fruit of wars, waged for the purpose of preventing what the borough-men called and still call, "*anarchy and confusion*"; but which we call, which Sir FRANCIS BURDETT for nearly thirty years called, which the old Duke of Richmond called, which even PITT and WILBERFORCE once called "*a Constitutional Reform* "*in the Commons' House of Par-* "*liament.*" We have heard it

declared in that very House, that the trafficking in its seats was as notorious as the sun at noon-day. We know, as well as we know daylight from dark, what must be the inevitable consequences of those traffickings. The people have long been convinced, that they must continue to suffer every species of public calamity until they have again their legitimate share of power in that House. In 1793, Mr. GREY, now Lord Grey, presented a petition to the House of Commons, stating that he and the other petitioners were ready to prove at the bar of the House, that a majority of the Members were nominated, appointed, and actually put into the House by Peers of the other House and by about twenty or thirty great big thundering commoners, the relations of peers. The petitioners concluded by saying, that the people had, in fact, no efficient share at all in the representation; and that, as far as they were concerned, there might as well be no House of Commons."

There is this petition lying, even to this day, on the table of that House. It has never been taken into consideration, and no act has ever been passed, no measure ever adopted, for the removal of the evils complained of in that petition.

The natural consequence of such a state of things is, such a mode of collecting and expending the public money as to produce the dreadful state of ruin and misery which we now behold. To the seven sages, what we, the people have to say, is this: " You have " rejected the prayers we have " been putting up to you for forty " years; we have prayed to be " admitted to a share in the mak- " ing of laws, in the raising and " expending of our money; you " have rejected all our prayers; " you and the rest of your order " have most severely punished us " for praying. At the end of the " forty years we behold England " the most wretched, instead of " being, as it formerly was, the " most happy country in the world. " We have had no hand in the " producing of this wretchedness; " you have had absolute command " of our persons and our purses; " and, at a moment when we have " this sample of the effect of your " measures before us; when the

" state into which you have " brought the country would fully " justify us in expecting to see " you act an humble part; and, " if not absolutely penitent, at " least modest in your demeanour: " precisely at this moment, we " hear, not only of your retaining " all your usual high tone towards " the people, but of your actually " dictating to the King the manner " in which he shall exercise his " undoubted prerogative."

I should like to have seen these seven sages come in a body before the King, to remonstrate with his Majesty upon the subject of the appointment of Mr. Canning. And, I should like to have been hidden behind a curtain while the work of remonstrating was going on. Suppose me, then, to be thus snugly posted; suppose the King, apprized beforehand of their intention, ready to receive them; suppose the seven sages to enter; and, then, let us imagine, let us not say that such or such a dialogue would have taken place, or ought to have taken place, with regard to his present Majesty; but, let us suppose that there had been a king disposed to be a little jocular, and to handle the seven sages with no great deal of ceremony: let us suppose these things, and then we may imagine that something like the following would have been likely enough to take place.

[Enter the seven sages. His Majesty seated.]

THE KING. I did not send for you, my worthy Counsellors: pray, what may be the cause of the audience which you have solicited.

CHANCELLOR (*Bowing, and bringing his right hand across to his left breast*). May it please your Majesty, we are quite sure that your Majesty will not deem it an intrusion, and will be perfectly convinced that nothing but the most ardent feelings of affection for your Majesty's person and family, could have induced us to come before your Majesty with any thing in the shape of a remonstrance.

KING. Do not be *too sure of that!* I shall know more about it when I have heard the nature of your remonstrance.

CHANCELLOR (*Casting an eye sideways at the rest*). May it please your Majesty, we are come to protest against the appointment of Mr. CANNING, as the head of your cabinet council, as the Minister called your *First Minister*. We beseech your Majesty to reflect on the consequences of such an appointment. These consequences may reach even our Holy Church, and may produce the greatest calamities.

KING. But I have a right to appoint whom I please?

CHANCELLOR. Yes, it is your Majesty's undoubted prerogative to choose your own Ministers; but, it is a right undoubted in us to give you our advice upon the subject.

KING. And if I am bound to *follow* that advice, then my right to choose a Minister is like the *congé d'élire* addressed to the Dean and Chapter of a diocese, when they are about to exercise *their right of choosing a Bishop!* They, in such case, after they have received the *congé d'élire*, invoke the Holy Ghost to assist them in their choice. The ceremony is different in the present case. I have not invoked you to assist me with your advice: the constitution knows nothing about a *congé d'élire* in the choosing of Ministers: if it did, the King would, in fact, be a most contemptible cipher; such as I am not, and as I never will be.

CHANCELLOR. But your Majesty must be perfectly convinced of my loyalty, of my fidelity, of my long and great services.

KING. Very well; but those are not to take from me my prerogative. Besides, as you have been Chancellor for nearly thirty years, and as I have been twice called upon by you and your colleagues during a portion of that time, and once very recently, to issue almost my commands to my people to put money into the begging-box, to save large masses of that people from starving, and as I see that you have measures on foot for making my people pay taxes to raise money, in order to send Englishmen away from their native land, as an escape from their manifold miseries in that land, which was so happy, even at the time when you first became a Minister: this being the case, I must confess that there occurs to me, at this moment, no very obvious proof of the value of those long services which you have been pleased to state as a ground for my yielding implicitly to your advice upon this occasion. I may have made a choice, not the very best. I may be able to accomplish no improvement in the state of my people by this appointment which I have made; but, certain I am, that this appointment, and that nothing arising out of it, can make the situation of my people worse than it is, and can place the state in no greater danger.

CHANCELLOR. What, then, Sir,

are all my sacrifices forgotten! Is all that I have gone through, during so many years, counted for nought! Why, I have clapped your Majesty's great seal to more taxing bills, more power-of-imprisonment bills, to more suspension of habeas corpus bills, more new treason bills, more new game bills, more bills hostile to the press, and more commissions of bankruptcy, than all the Lord Chancellors that ever sat upon the wool-sack from the time of the coming of the House of Brunswick until the time that I began to sit upon that sack! And, after all this, shall not I . . . . . .

KING. Take from me my prerogative?

CHANCELLOR. By no means, may it please your Majesty. We do not want to choose your Prime Minister: that were an encroachment, indeed: we wish your Majesty to choose him: we do not wish to tell you whom you shall choose: we only want to tell you whom you shall not choose.

KING. So, then, you are to have a *veto* upon the exercise of my prerogative! You have, indeed, undergone a great deal, my Lord Chancellor. A man must undergo a great deal in getting from under a coal-merchant's roof to sit thirty years upon the wool-sack. He picks up, generally, some little things on his way; and, I dare say, that these enormous services and sufferings of yours have not been wholly unrewarded, either in your own person or that of your relations, whose names I find opposite the statement of pretty good annual sums. Let them keep what they get; let me keep my prerogative; do what you please with your gains; but, if you have more counsel to spare than you want for other purposes, keep it to yourself, and let me choose whom I please for my Minister. And, now (turning to Wellington), pray what may your pretensions be, for coming to remonstrate with me on the subject of appointing my Minister?

WELLINGTON. What my pretensions! A Wellesley asked for his pretensions!

KING. Yes, I ask for your pretensions, even to *think* about a matter like this.

WELLINGTON. Why, Sir, am not I a Field Marshal; am not I a Knight, a Baron, a Viscount, an Earl, a Marquess, and a Duke; am not I a pensioner for "life (with two succeeding lives after me) for 4000*l.* a year, to come out of the taxes raised on the people; have not I had settled upon me, from the same source, seven hun-dred thousand pounds in money, in public money, to be laid out in lands and houses to be enjoyed by me and to descend to my family; am not I, even at this moment, Master General of the Ordnance, Commander-in-Chief of the army, the Colonel of *two* regiments, Constable of the Tower of London, Governor of Plymouth, the Lord Lieutenant of a county; and do not the people say that they should not wonder if I were to be the next Archbishop of Canterbury?

KING. Well, then, I dare say that you have thought the Constitution very wise in having given me the power to sanction all these numerous and enormous grants and appointments; will you not, then, look upon that Constitution as equally wise when it gives me power to exercise my prerogative in choosing a Minister?

WELLINGTON. I don't know that. My merit was so great, my services so transcendant, the glory I brought upon the country so far beyond all estimate, that........

KING. I have read all about that *in the account of your own Peerage*, where you are represented as something little short of a god; little short of the God of England, and where care has been taken to speak of the " *unsuccessful expedition*", of my late brother.

WELLINGTON. Why, may it please your Majesty, the truth ought to be spoken.

KING. According to this rule, the enormous expense of your campaigns ought not to be overlooked. Your " unsuccessful" campaigns ought to be remembered as well as your successful ones. The great aid which you received from foreign armies, paid for by the nation, ought not to be forgotten; the circumstance of your never having triumphed, except in countries where a large part, and even a majority of the people were on your side, ought to be recollected; and, above all things, the nation had a right to ask, why you were not in those campaigns on the other side of the Atlantic, where there was a brave and united people to combat, and where the armies who had served under you had to experience campaigns not less " unsuccessful " than those which the account of your peerage ascribes to my brother. There it was where the English army had to meet its match; and there you were not. There no subsidies could be of any avail. There money, except to pay soldiers and purchase arms, was useless. Victories were not to be purchased there. That was the close, the winding up of the long war; and, if you take to yourself all the glory of what are called the victories in Portugal, Spain, France, and the Netherlands, take also to yourself the lamentable negative successes of America, or, tell the nation, before you come to remonstrate with me, why, if you had the power, you did not go and prevent the occurrences on the other side of the Atlantic.

WELLINGTON. But, has your Majesty forgotten, then, the ever-memorable, renowned, immortal, and super-human victory at Waterloo!

KING. 'Faith, I am not likely to forget that, as long as there are the means of writing the word, either with brush or chisel; for, it has been stuck up upon every place where it would not be a nuisance indictable at common law for sticking it up. From the Achilles in Hyde Park down to the lowest of sign-posts, the word has been blazoned; and, I am told that a great part of my subjects who see the statue, take Achilles for you, your name being on the pedestal in such very LARGE LETTERS, and all the rest of the letters on the inscription being so very small that they take the image of the colossal warrior to be a veritable image of you. Achilles was invulnerable except in one little point: that point was, at last, found out: take care, my Lord Duke, or you will, in this respect, at any rate, be worthy of having Achilles for your prototype!

WELLINGTON. But, your Majesty will allow that the victory of Waterloo was beyond all praise and all reward!

KING. Your peerage has told me as much: it has told me and my poor, taxed people, that "a "due measure of gratitude for "such services as yours could not "have been rendered; but that "the nation did its best." Your peerage (the grammar of which speaks but too plainly its real author) has told me and my burthened people that your services were the most sublime efforts of human prudence and courage; it has told us that the victory at Waterloo was "unpa- "ralleled in all its features as "well as in the vastness of its "consequences, and raised the "character of this hero to a height "never before attained by any "captain." What! not by Alexander the Great; not by Cæsar; not by Pompey; not by Hannibal; not by Scipio; not by any of the ancients; not by Saint Louis; not by Francis the First; not by Richard the First; not by the Black Prince; not by Henry the Fifth; not by Nelson; not by any one that ever existed upon the face of the earth before: if this be so, and if it were impossible for a due measure of reward to be rendered for your services; if all your appointments, all your pensions, all your grants, all the hundreds of thousands drained out of the sweat of this nation; if the nation did ITS BEST, and yet did not reward you sufficiently, it would be much better for the nation never to have received such services. It had nothing left to give you, but my crown; and, really, the crown is but a poor empty bauble, if you be permitted, either directly or indirectly, to take from me my prerogative. Besides, as to this battle of Waterloo, did you not know that you had the better part of a million of men at your back, and that poor BUONAPARTE had not a single man, and was, besides, beset by traitors and spies, ready to betray and to sell him! And, as to the mere battle itself, it is notorious (else thousands upon thousands are liars) that the battle was won by the extraordinary valour and daring of a man who may probably be your Grace's successor.

H

Wellington (*Raising his hand very high, and looking towards Melville*). Then, may it please your Majesty, I have nothing more to say.

King. Very well. And, now, my Lord of the Admiralty, pray favour me with a statement of your peculiar pretensions. I am aware of the versatility of your talents. I recollect that you are Keeper of the Signet in Scotland, with a salary of 2,069l. a year; that you are Register of Seisins or Chief Baron of Exchequer in Scotland, with a salary of 2,269l. a year; that you are other things besides these, but, these I particularly recollect; that you have had these for about twenty-seven years, and that you have, thus, merely through the means of these sinecures, received, from out of the pockets of my people, 117,122l.; or thereabouts.

Melville. But, will it not please your Majesty to recollect the long services of my venerable father?

King. "Least said is soonest mended", about him, and I do not wish to rip up old grievances. But, if you will press this upon me, I shall cause you to recollect a great many things which the history of his life afforded, to make me resist dictation in a case

like the present. I know that he transacted all India with Scotchmen. I know that he then took to the navy; and that you, his successor, have trodden faithfully in his steps. The Dundases, the Hopes, the Hope Johnstones and the Johnstone Hopes swarm in that service; where, for ages and ages, a Scotch nose never made its appearance.

Melville. But, will it please your Majesty to reflect on the prodigious merit of the Scotch; and, particularly, of the Dundas family in all its branches? Look into the army list, look into the navy list, look into all the lists of place-men, pensioners, grantees. But, particularly, look into that of the navy, which you will find bespangled with their names as the lawn before your Majesty's cottage would be bespangled with daisies, if the scythe were not employed with unremitting vigilance. There your Majesty will see whole strings of the Hope Johnstones, the Johnstone Hopes and the Dundases, lieutenants or captains, while thousands and thousands of Englishmen who were at sea before the former were born, are still midshipmen, though the gray hairs are thickly scattered on their heads.

King. Who has the power of

appointing these people to be lieutenants and captains?

MELVILLE. It is I, may it please your Majesty; and I always appoint and promote men merely for the sake of their merit; merely for the benefit of your Majesty and the country. And, to give your Majesty a proof, an indubitable proof of the surprising talent and merit of our family, I need only mention that there is my own son, a youth of twenty-two or twenty-three years of age, a POST CAPTAIN in your Majesty's navy, while there are nearly five thousand Englishmen, still lieutenants or midshipmen, every dull devil of whom was at sea, and many of them fighting long before that brilliant youth was born.

KING. That is a "proof," indeed, of the great genius and merit of your family; but, you seem to forget that, in that respect, at any rate, the Prime Minister whom I have chosen stands upon a level with yourself; for, he has a son of such surprising genius and merit, that, though, I believe, a year or so younger than your son, he has been, even by yourself, made a post-captain in the navy, over the heads of thousands upon thousands who were sailing and fighting while he was in the cradle. That which is cause for the genius,

my Lord, is cause for the gander; and, if I am to take the appointment of your son as a proof of the merit of the Dundases, let me, I pray you, consider the appointment of WILLIAM PITT CANNING, as a proof of the wonderful talent and merit of the Cannings.— Now (turning to Lord Bathurst) pray, my Lord, on what grounds is it that you come to press your remonstrances upon me in this case?

BATHURST. Need I request your Majesty to look at the quiet, the prosperous, the harmonious, the happy state in which the colonies have been placed under my sway? If your Majesty wants to read speeches, I would beg you to condescend to read mine (Huro, aside, that would be better than hearing them), or those of my secretary, WILMOT HORTON or HORTON WILMOT. There your Majesty would learn how happy we mean to make the Irish, by sending them to Canada, and laying out more money upon each man than would place that man in easy circumstances in Ireland. There your Majesty would learn all the profundity of our political philosophy, all the brilliancy of our schemes of emigration.

KING. But, what has this to do with the exercise of my prerogative, and what right does it give you to interfere in a case of this sort?

BATHURST. If your Majesty will look into the great volume of sinecures, you will find my surprising merit confessed, from my youth. It will hardly be contended, except by some jacobin, some *membre du club quatre-vingt-neuf*, that such rewards are given improperly. There must be, of course, surprising capacity; great fitness to counsel the Sovereign, before such rewards are bestowed. For pretty nearly the whole of my lifetime, I have been receiving the amount of one sinecure of 1,610*l.* a year, which sinecure is to descend to my son, and be by him enjoyed. This son has another sinecure of 472*l.* a year, and this sinecure he has by patent for life. Besides these, I myself was, for a great many years, MASTER and WORKER of your Majesty's Mint, with a salary or income, net receipt, of 3,010*l.* a year. So that, here is a thing, all put together, of, perhaps, the value of a couple of hundreds of thousands of pounds. Now, it would be a libel on that constitution, that fine affair, that wonderful scheme of Government, which is the envy of surrounding nations and admiration of the world; it would be a glaring libel on this glorious constitution, to affect not to believe that nothing short of distinguished merit, profound wisdom, perfect disinterestedness, and ardent zeal for the service of your Majesty and your people, could have obtained for me and my son (not to mention many other of their connexions) these immense sums of the public money. The fact relative to these sinecures, therefore, I put forward as undoubted proof of my fitness to interfere with your Majesty upon the present occasion.

KING. There are, however, my Lord Bathurst, people who would question the conclusiveness of this *proof*, as you call it; but, taking you on your own ground, allowing this proof to be indubitable, the claim of merit is, unfortunately for you, clearly established on the part of the statesman whom I have chosen for my Minister, and against which choice you protest; for, *he has the happiness to be a sinecure placeman, too!* As his son's early promotion in the navy was a conclusive answer to Lord Melville; so his having been, just thirty years, come next November, RECEIVER-GENERAL in the Alienation office, with a salary of 492*l.* 4*s.* 7*d.* a year, amounting now to 14,767*l.*, to say nothing about his famous Ambassadorship to Portugal, where there was at the time no sovereign and no court, ought to be an answer to you.

BATHURST. But, may it please your Majesty, what are fourteen or fifteen thousand pounds compared with the sums which I have received?

KING. You must take the will for the deed: I dare say he got as much as he could: you have been lucky, my lord, heretofore: his time of luck is come now, and, I have not the smallest doubt that if the species of proof of merit for which your lordship contends be to be admitted, he will not long be destitute of proof of that kind in abundance as great as that of the best of you.

WESTMORELAND. Will your Majesty please to hear ME speak, especially as I have but very little to say! I take the doctrine of my noble friend who has just spoken to be a doctrine established by the practice of this glorious constitution, which, as my noble friend has truly observed, is, beyond all doubt, the " envy of surrounding nations and the admiration of the world."

KING. Well, well; get on to the point, my Lord: to the point.

WESTMORELAND. What I ob-ject to, may it please your Majesty, is, not so much the want of a natural and loyal propensity in your newly chosen Minister to obtain a due share of those things which my noble friend has justly characterized as the indubitable roof of merit and wisdom, and particularly of wisdom, as his want of those numerous descendant and collateral branches, vulgarly called family connexions, which are so essential to support the influence of the crown against a constantly encroaching democracy. I, may it please your Majesty, am blessed in this way, almost beyond the extent of man's wishes. Look at the list of my relations and dependents; look at the figure they cut in all the lists where people ought to cut a figure; and then all I have to add is, that when Mr. Canning shall have a tribe equally numerous and equally well provided for, I am ready to sanction his appointment.

KING. All this appears to me to be very unreasonable, my Lords. My Minister is, surely, not to be deemed unfit merely because he has not yet had an opportunity of collecting together and providing for a numerous set of relations and dependants. Still, however, he has not been altogether wanting in this respect. He has provided for Mrs. HUNN and her daughters; there is a Captain HUNN, too, now in the navy. There is a STRATFORD CANNING, who is a pretty well fed ambassador; and, in short, the man seems to have done what he can in this way; he is not to blame because he has not been a great breeder: if he provide for *all*, what can you wish for more? I dare say, that my *people* will not complain against him on this score: they may probably wish that he had less relations than he has; and, for my part, I must confess that I agree with my people in this respect. And now then, (turning to Bexley), let me hear the ground of little Van's objection.

BEXLEY. May it please your Majesty, before I state any objection to the appointment of my friend, Mr. Canning, I beg to be suffered to state my own humble pretensions to advise. About forty years ago, I carried a brief-bag to the quarter sessions of the county of Berks. Of the *contents* of that bag, I will not presume to trouble your Majesty with an account. Feeling myself destined to greatness, and to shine as a financier of this United Empire, I wrote a pamphlet in praise of the money-schemes of Pitt and

Company, proving that the war was just and necessary; that it tended to enrich and not to impoverish the country; that, unlike all former wars, it tended to make your Majesty's subjects easy in their circumstances and to promote prosperity amongst them for ages to come.

KING. What! Did you *prove* all this, do you say?

BEXLEY. Yes, may it please you, as clear as the noon-day sun; and Sir FRANCIS D'IVERNOIS, a Swiss emigrant, pensioned by Pitt, translated my book, and wrote a book of his own to confirm all my doctrines and all my statements; after which I became an Honourable COMMISSIONER of SCOTCH HERRINGS.

KING. But, it was all false then, or else the nation is now in a prosperous state. But, now I think of it, was it not you, who, in the year 1811, moved, in the House of Commons, a resolution, which that house adopted by a very large majority, which resolution expressed *that a one pound note and a shilling were, to all intents and purposes, equal in value to a golden guinea of full weight and fineness;* and did not you vote for propositions, in 1819, in that same house of Commons, founded upon the acknowledged fact, that *a one pound note and a shilling had been worth, in that very 1811, six shillings less than a golden guinea of full weight and fineness?* Were not you the man, the financier, that thus acted upon these two occasions.

BEXLEY. The same, may it please your Majesty: the very same man.

KING (*Turning round towards Peel*). Enough of this honourable Commissioner of Scotch herrings; and now, I have great curiosity to know the ground, Sir, upon which you presume to put on an air of dictation to your sovereign.

PEEL. (*With a sort of smirk on his countenance*). Your Majesty, I presume, is well aware of who I am. There wants nothing, I venture to observe, to prove the identity of my person, or the station which I fill in the state. Your Majesty, the whole nation, the whole world, the universe entire, have heard the name of PEEL.

KING. With the word *garlick* at the end of it, we have, most of us, heard of it; but, really, Sir, the universe, I believe, knows very little of it in its detached state.

PEEL. Has not your Majesty read in the Baronetcy, that my father had a " PRESENTIMENT THAT HE SHOULD BE THE FOUNDER OF A FAMILY"!

KING. Not a family to oust mine, I hope. I have heard or read or something, that you are the son of one ROBERT PEEL, who was a very lucky fellow in the spinning of cotton; that, by the incessant toil of thousands of poor creatures, he gained an immense sum of money; that, when Pitt and Dundas set on foot a voluntary contribution for the carrying on of the war against France, this Robert Peel put his name down for ten thousand pounds; that, not long after this, my father was advised to make him a *baronet*; that he has continued to grow rich; and that, in fact, he is now become one of those who possess that sort of power in this country, of which my people so bitterly complain; that, as to yourself, you, in all human probability, owe your elevation much more to him than to any body else; and that, I cannot recollect any one instance in which you have distinguished yourself in a way that bespeaks capacity, exceeding that of other men, nor which does on any account, whatever, warrant you in pressing your advice against the opinion of any man of experience, much less against the opinion of your sovereign.

PEEL. What! I am surprised! Is it possible that your Majesty never heard of my great states-manlike lawgiving measure, which was productive at last of that miracle of legislation, commonly called " PEEL'S BILL"?

KING. Yes, I have heard of that; a great deal too much of its sorrowful effects; and, if you had been able justly to estimate this act of your life, I should not have been honoured with your presence this day, and especially upon an errand like that on which you are come. My subjects, from one end of the kingdom to the other, have, class by class, suffered, and deeply suffered, from that destructive measure. I remember well, when, in the year 1819, the Speaker of the House of Commons congratulated me on the adoption of that measure. I remember that I was told by him, that, after months of deliberation, the scheme had been happily effected; that it had been brought to maturity by a combination of the greatest of talents, wisdom and zeal; that he assured me that the measure would be productive of most beneficial results, and that it would reflect lasting honour on those who had brought it to perfection. Instead of these anticipated results, the mischievous measure almost instantly began to show that ruin

and misery to class after class, to thousands upon thousands and millions upon millions were to be its final effects. Day by day, from the time of its adoption to the present hour, it has been bringing forth some new calamity. Changed backward and forward it has been, twice; and it must be now changed a third time and be abandoned for ever, with the curses of the whole nation upon its head; or, it will inevitably produce an overthrow of the state of itself. So that, this being the only measure in which you ever bore any conspicuous part, you have, indeed, grounds whereon to be a dictator to your King!

PEEL. May it please your Majesty, the unfortunate consequences of my measure are not to be ascribed to me, any more than the breaking of glass by a hail-storm is to be ascribed to the man who has the care of the house. The man cannot help the hail-storm; nor could I help the fatal consequences of which your Majesty has been speaking. What no one could foresee took place, and, then, the bill, which was good in itself, became fatal in its operation.

KING. What do you say: Was there no one to foresee the consequences?

Cᴏʙʙᴇᴛᴛ. (*In a whisper, peeping out from behind the curtain.*) Push him upon that point. Try his shuttle there.

Pᴇᴇʟ. No, may it please your Majesty. Even Mr. Tierney, that veteran politician, could not see any evil from the Bill. Lord Grenville, Lord Lansdown, the divine Liverpool, Mr. Abercrombie, the great David Ricardo, all congratulated the Houses upon the Bill, and even he whom your Majesty has now chosen for your Minister, called for an unanimous vote in favour of the Bill, and when he had got it, exclaimed, "*now the question is set at rest for ever!*"

Kɪɴɢ. But I have been told; and, indeed, I have read, that there was a man, who, as soon as your Bill was proposed, as soon as its intended contents were known; as soon as any thing like an adequate description of its contents got abroad; that there *was a man*, not only to tell you that such a Bill, if passed, could never be carried into effect, without burying the country in ruin; who not only told you this beforehand, but who proved it to you clearly as day-light; and depicted the consequences of the measure, the embarrassment, the ruin, the breaking up of farmers and tradesmen, the robbing of landlords of their estates, the want of employment, the beggary, the starvation, and every consequence, even to the lowest consequence, not only in substance but in manner, that has been produced by your vain, blundering and fatal Bill, which is, even at this hour, working more mischief than ever, and making it, with many men of great understanding, a serious question, whether a general convulsion be or be not to be avoided!,

Pᴇᴇʟ. But, may it please your Majesty, that one man was an individual of the name of Cobbett; not at all worthy of the attention of your Majesty's Ministers.

Kɪɴɢ. But, if the thing was foreseen and foretold, of what consequence is it by whom it was done? One thing is clear, at any rate, that if I had had that same individual for a *Minister*, all these calamities would have been avoided.

Cᴏʙʙᴇᴛᴛ. (*In a whisper, peeping out.*) You must have me yet, or you have seen only the beginning of the mischief.

Pᴇᴇʟ. A Minister! God preserve your Majesty from suffering such an individual to possess power of any kind or in any degree!

King. Why, Mr. Peel, I really cannot see how it is possible for the individual, as you call him, and as he was called by a spitten upon-fellow in the north; I really cannot see how it is possible for him to do more mischief than you have done; and, indeed, it is preposterous to presume that he who warned you beforehand of the mischief which you would produce, and who must, for his own sake, be, above all things, desirous to repair the mischief, and to make the King and country grateful to him; it is preposterous to believe, that he would not propose to use measures calculated to effect something, at any rate, for bettering the situation of the country.

Peel. But, Sir, the Minister whom you have chosen, has pledged himself to carry through the principles of my Bill.

King. If he have, let him take the consequences to himself. I have given no such pledge: he is, at any rate, as fit as any of you to carry on my affairs: your disliking him, is a proof that he will produce a change of some sort or other; and, as any change must be for the better, I shall persevere in my choice, and you may retire as you came.

This is much about what ought to take place upon such an occasion, and might take place, with very little, if any, departure from the truth. I hope, with all my soul, that the King will persevere: if he do, he will overset every faction that can assail him. As to Canning himself, as Canning, nobody cares anything about him; but, there are millions that care a great deal about maintaining the just and legitimate prerogative of the King. No small part of our sufferings have arisen from this prerogative having, in fact, been taken out of his hands. He has been kept totally cut off from his people. His people have too great a desire to be freed from their present oppressions, not to wish most anxiously for the restoration, the complete restoration and full exercise of the royal authority. Let the King persevere, and we shall soon see that the factions will vanish before him.

What Canning will do with those poor old devils the Whigs, is the most puzzling part of the question. He must give them sops in some way or other, or else they will turn tail upon him, upon pinching occasions. If he take in Brougham and Tierney and Mackintosh, and give no share of the fat things to the others, the others will be jealous; disown the authority of their leaders, and join, upon a pinch, with the powerful foes of the Minister. In the meanwhile, the Paper-money Bill will be going on, reducing, gradually, the price of the bushel of wheat : the landowners, the farmers, the traders and merchants, will not reflect on the true cause of the decline of price and of the consequent ruin. The mischief will be ascribed to this measure, to that measure, but generally to a want of talent and wisdom in the Minister, who will be badgered to death, and, not knowing any thing at all of the true cause himself; being, as to such matters, as ignorant as he was when he was captain at Eton, he will be constantly in a state of uncertainty as to the effect of any steps that he may take, and the whole thing may actually be blown to atoms before he will begin to think seriously of the danger. He is just as fit for the undertaking as the best of his colleagues was : as to this great matter they were all upon a level; but, he is not likely to be content and to let the thing go on as long as it will go; and, therefore, his elevation is favorable to the people. Nobody can save the Thing; that is quite certain; but, by being let alone a good deal; by letting the paper come out in great bales and run itself down, at last, as it

has done in other countries, the final blowing up might be somewhat retarded. At present, all that we have to do is to uphold the authority of the King to the utmost of our power; and, as the reformers have, for years and years, complained that those who filled the seats ruled both King and people, I think it would be proper, and I strongly recommend, that they now address the King for having exercised his royal authority, and expressing a hope that he will persevere in maintaining that authority. I exhort you, my friends, in all parts of the country, if you can form meetings of only one hundred persons, to address the King upon this subject; for, you may be well assured that in this crisis, his cause and our cause are one and the same. Mr. Canning can never stand against the combination with which he is threatened, unless he look to the people. Here, indeed, he may open his *leash* and let out his *spirits* against his arrogant opponents. If he do this, he may be Minister, perhaps, for the remainder of his life; but, if he do not something of this kind, he will either be driven from his post, or will keep it upon terms so degrading as to make life itself a burthen and disgrace.

I am, My friends,
Your Most obedient
And most humble Servant,
Wm. COBBETT.

## AMERICAN KIDNEY BEANS.

I HAVE two sorts of these, the finest that ever were in England.; one of them the very earliest that I ever saw ; and the seed, in both cases, so ripe, sound, and excellent, that a large crop from it is certain.—One sort is *Yellow*, the other *Speckled*; both are dwarfs.—Price — 17s. a bushel, and smaller quantities in proportion, with something added for paper, string, and trouble.—They are sold at the Office of the Register, No 183, Fleet Street, and may be sent, by order, to any part of the country.

---

## MARKETS.

Average Prices of CORN through-out ENGLAND, for the week ending April 6.

### Per Quarter.

|         | s. | d. |          | s. | d. |
|---------|----|----|----------|----|----|
| Wheat .. | 56 | 3 | Rye .... | 39 | 3 |
| Barley .. | 38 | 3 | Beans ... | 47 | 11 |
| Oats .... | 30 | 9 | Pease ... | 48 | 3 |

Total Quantity of Corn returned as Sold in the Maritime Districts, for the week ended April 6.

|         | Qrs. |          | Qrs. |
|---------|------|----------|------|
| Wheat .. | 37,867 | Rye ..... | 247 |
| Barley .. | 15,232 | Beans . .. | 2,651 |
| Oats ... | 11,805 | Pease .... | 715 |

*Corn Exchange, Mark Lane.*

Quantities and Prices of British Corn, &c. sold and delivered in this Market, during the week ended Saturday, April 6.

|        | Qrs. |     | £. | s. d. |          | s. | d. |
|--------|------|-----|----|-------|----------|----|----|
| Wheat.. | 4,909 | for | 14,678 | 0  4 | Average, | 59 | 0 |
| Barley.. | 2,276 | .. | 4,358 | 6  9 | ......... | 38 | 3 |
| Oats.. | 4,164 | .. | 6,640 | 15 11 | ......... | 31 | 10 |
| Rye... | — | .. | 0  0 | ......... | 0 | 0 |
| Beans.. | 574 | .. | 1,272 | 17  0 | ......... | 44 | 4 |
| Pease.. | 277 | .. | 643 | 14  0 | ......... | 46 | 5 |

Wednesday, April 11.—The supplies of all English Grain this week are small, but there is a good quantity of Foreign Oats entered. Wheat remains without alteration from Monday's report. Barley and Beans fully support the terms of last market day. Pease meet a very dull trade. Oats do not find buyers so readily as last Monday, but prices remain the same.

Monday, April 16.—During the past week there were moderate quantities of all sorts of Grain except Oats, the foreign arrivals of which were considerable ; and this morning there are several more vessels from abroad fresh up with this Grain. Of Wheat, Barley, Beans, and Pease, the supply fresh in to-day is moderate. The report of Flour is still considerable, which keeps that trade in a dull state ; and the Wheat trade to-day may be stated very dull at the quotations of last Monday, for all except superfine samples.

Barley does not sell so freely as of late, but prices are unaltered. Beans meet rather more demand, and are advanced 1s. per quarter. Pease are unaltered. The chief part of the large foreign supply of Oats is going to granary in bond, to wait till after the 15th of May, when the average prices are expected to bring the duty to 4d. per quarter under the old Corn Laws, the trade, therefore, fully maintains last quotations, with a fair sale. The recent changes in the Cabinet, render it doubtful whether the New Corn Bill will pass the House of Lords.

Account of Wheat, &c. arrived in the Port of London, from April 9 to April 14, both inclusive.

| | Qrs. | | Qr. |
|---|---|---|---|
| Wheat | 4,058 | Tares | 631 |
| Barley | 1,923 | Linseed | — |
| Malt | 4,841 | Rapeseed | 860 |
| Oats | 904 | Brank | 324 |
| Beans | 546 | Mustard | 15 |
| Flour | 8,903 | Flax | — |
| Rye | 770 | Hemp | 59 |
| Pease | 488 | Seeds | 108 |

Foreign.—Wheat, 900; Barley, 664; Oats, 33,298; and Beans, 443 qrs.

Monday, April 16.—The arrivals from Ireland last week were, 454 firkins of Butter, and 1,200 bales of Bacon; and from Foreign Ports, 11,152 casks of Butter,

## HOPS.

Price of Hops, per Cwt. in the Borough.

Monday, April 16.—Our market is improving, and many sales were effected during last week at an advance of from 2s. to 4s. per cwt. The reports from the plantations are, the plant is weakly, and the flea very prevalent.

Maidstone, April 12.—There has been some little inquiry about the few lots of Hops left in this neighbourhood, but we have not heard of any sales, so that the trade remains much the same.

### COAL MARKET, April 11.

Ships at Market. Ships sold. Price.
27 Newcastle 19½..31s. 3d. to 37s. 9d.
13 Sunderland 9..36s. 0d.— 39s. 0d.

SMITHFIELD.

Monday, April 16.—The Lamb season in this market begins, according to custom, on Good Friday; we were, therefore, well supplied with Lambs, but scantily of Beef and Mutton. There was no variation in the price of Beasts; Mutton sold on higher terms than this day se'nnight; but Lamb remained at the rates last quoted.—To-day our supply is very limited of every thing; so that better terms are obtained for all kinds of Meat. The current top price for Beef is 5s. 2d.; Old Down Mutton, 6s.; and choice Leicester, 5s. 10d. in the wool. Lamb goes off readily at from 6s. 4d. to 7s. The supply of Lincoln Beasts and Sheep unusually short.

Per Stone of 8 pounds (alive).

| | s. | d. | s. | d. |
|---|---|---|---|---|
| Beef | 4 | 0 | to 5 | 2 |
| Mutton | 4 | 8 | — 6 | 0 |
| Veal | 5 | 4 | — 6 | 0 |
| Pork | 4 | 6 | — 5 | 6 |
| Lamb | 6 | 4 | — 7 | 0 |

| Beasts | 1,662 | Sheep | 12,120 |
|---|---|---|---|
| Calves | 120 | Pigs | 80 |

NEWGATE, (same day.)
Per Stone of 8 pounds (dead).

| | s. | d. | s. | d. |
|---|---|---|---|---|
| Beef | 3 | 6 | to 4 | 6 |
| Mutton | 4 | 2 | — 5 | 2 |
| Veal | 3 | 8 | — 5 | 8 |
| Pork | 3 | 8 | — 5 | 8 |
| Lamb | 6 | 0 | — 7 | 0 |

LEADENHALL, (same day.)
Per Stone of 8 pounds (dead).

| | s. | d. | s. | d. |
|---|---|---|---|---|
| Beef | 3 | 0 | to 4 | 4 |
| Mutton | 4 | 0 | — 5 | 0 |
| Veal | 3 | 8 | — 5 | 4 |
| Pork | 4 | 0 | — 5 | 8 |
| Lamb | 5 | 0 | — 7 | 0 |

## POTATOES.

### SPITALFIELDS, per Ton.

| | £ s. | £ s. |
|---|---|---|
| Ox-Nobles | 3 15 to | 4 0 |
| Middlings | 2 10 — | 0 0 |
| Chats | 2 0 — | 0 0 |
| Common Red | 4 0 — | 0 0 |

Onions, 0s. 0d.—0s. 0d. per bush.

### BOROUGH, per Ton.

| | £ s. | £ s. |
|---|---|---|
| Ox-Nobles | 3 10 to | 4 5 |
| Middlings | 2 10 — | 0 0 |
| Chats | 2 0 — | 0 0 |
| Common Red | 4 0 — | 0 0 |

## HAY and STRAW, per Load.

| Smithfield.— | Hay | 90s. to 115s. |
|---|---|---|
| | Straw | 40s. to 45s. |
| | Clover | 100s. to 135s. |
| St. James's.— | Hay | 84s. to 128s. |
| | Straw | 40s. to 48s. |
| | Clover | 120s. to 135s. |
| Whitechapel.— | Hay | 84s. to 115s. |
| | Straw | 38s. to 42s. |
| | Clover | 90s. to 135s. |

---

AVERAGE PRICE OF CORN, sold in the Maritime Counties of England and Wales, for the Week ended April 6, 1827.

| | Wheat. | | Barley. | | Oats. | |
|---|---|---|---|---|---|---|
| | s. | d. | s. | d. | s. | d. |
| London* | 58 | 9 | 39 | 0 | 32 | 0 |
| Essex | 58 | 6 | 36 | 9 | 30 | 10 |
| Kent | 56 | 7 | 37 | 6 | 29 | 8 |
| Sussex | 55 | 2 | 37 | 6 | 29 | 2 |
| Suffolk | 55 | 3 | 35 | 4 | 31 | 2 |
| Cambridgeshire | 53 | 4 | 38 | 4 | 27 | 9 |
| Norfolk | 54 | 6 | 38 | 6 | 28 | 5 |
| Lincolnshire | 55 | 10 | 39 | 2 | 28 | 0 |
| Yorkshire | 55 | 6 | 41 | 4 | 30 | 4 |
| Durham | 56 | 0 | 42 | 7 | 38 | 10 |
| Northumberland | 53 | 9 | 37 | 1 | 33 | 2 |
| Cumberland | 62 | 6 | 39 | 0 | 34 | 0 |
| Westmoreland | 62 | 3 | 46 | 0 | 37 | 0 |
| Lancashire | 62 | 9 | 39 | 7 | 39 | 2 |
| Cheshire | 60 | 2 | 46 | 0 | 34 | 0 |
| Gloucestershire | 58 | 0 | 43 | 11 | 40 | 9 |
| Somersetshire | 55 | 3 | 40 | 9 | 28 | 3 |
| Monmouthshire | 59 | 9 | 47 | 9 | 0 | 0 |
| Devonshire | 56 | 7 | 37 | 8 | 30 | 2 |
| Cornwall | 58 | 4 | 38 | 4 | 35 | 7 |
| Dorsetshire | 55 | 1 | 38 | 0 | 34 | 0 |
| Hampshire | 56 | 1 | 39 | 8 | 31 | 6 |
| North Wales | 63 | 5 | 43 | 4 | 32 | 4 |
| South Wales | 57 | 11 | 41 | 8 | 26 | 8 |

* The London Average is always that of the Week preceding.

*Liverpool*, April 10.—The arrivals in the week have been considerable in Wheat, Flour, and Oats, the great bulk of the latter from Ireland ; the demand has been languid, and prices of last week barely supported; in other articles no alteration, except in Indian Corn, for which there has been a good demand, at an advance of 1s. per quarter of 480 lbs., the weight sold by here; this article is getting into general use in this neighbourhood, as well as in Ireland; heavy shipments have been made from this to the latter place. In Bonded Grain nothing doing. Considerable sales have been made in Bonded Flour, for exportation to Jamaica and Newfoundland, and I have to notice a small improvement in price.

Imported into Liverpool, from April 3, to April 9, 1827, inclusive:—Wheat, 1,134; Barley, 167.; Oats, 17,356 ; Rye, 848; Malt, 2,848 ; Beans, 1,660 ; Pease, 315 quarters. Flour, 3,932 sacks, per 280 lbs. ; and Oatmeal, 219 packs, per 240 lbs.

*Bristol*, April 14.—The Corn markets here are very dull, except for prime Barley, which sells pretty well at last week's prices. Good Oats appear rather more in demand than they have been ; ordinary sorts heavy. Below are about the present prices :—Wheat, from 6s. to 7s. 6d. ; Barley, 4s. 6d. to 6s. ; Beans, 5s. 6d. to 8s. ; Oats, 3s. 11d. to 4s. ; and Malt, 6s. to 8s. 3d. per bushel; Imperial Flour, Seconds, 32s. to 43s. per bag.

*Guildford*, April 14.—Wheat, new, for mealing, 14l. 10s. to 16l. 15s. per load. Barley, 38s. to 42s.; Oats, 32s. to 42s.; Beans, 54s. to 58s.; Pease, grey, 60s. to 62s. ; ditto, boilers, 62s. to 64s. per quarter.

*Horncastle*, April 14.—The prices of Grain remain much the same as last week.—Wheat, 50s. to 56s. ; Barley, 38s. to 42s.; Oats, 28s. to 36s.; Beans, 55s. to 65s.; and Rye from 40s. to 42s. per quarter.

*Ipswich*, April 14.—We had to-day a very small market, and prices remain without alteration from last week, as follow:—Wheat, 52s. to 62s. ; Barley, 35s. to 41s.; Beans, 46s. to 48s. per quarter; and Pease, none.

*Manchester*, April 14.—The Corn trade has undergone little or no alteration during the week. To this day's market we had a good show of samples of Wheat of all descriptions, which were offered on the same terms as on this day se'nnight, without being able to effect sales ; the consumers being well stocked, preferred waiting a week or two longer. In other articles so little doing, as not to be sufficient to warrant any alteration from the prices of this day week.

*Newcastle-on-Tyne*, April 14.—We had a good supply of Wheat from the farmers this morning, which was readily taken off by the millers at 1s. per quarter advance. Rye continues in demand, and is a trifle dearer. The arrivals of Norfolk Barley have been all sold at last week's prices, and as the malting season is drawing to a close, it is not likely that higher prices will be got for the next arrivals. Malt rather more in demand. We had to-day a good supply of Oats from the growers, and some foreign arrivals, but the latter are of very inferior quality, and do not suit the consumption of this district.

*Reading*, April 14.—We had a fair supply of Wheat at our market this day, the quality of which is still rough. The sale was dull, at much the same prices as last week. We note it 54s. to 67s. per quarter, Imperial measure. There was a middling supply of Barley; it was all taken off for seed at high prices. There was a considerable quantity of Oats, and the trade was heavy. In Beans and Pease no alteration.

## COUNTRY CATTLE AND MEAT MARKETS, &c.

*Horncastle,* April 14.—Beef, 9s. per stone of 14 lbs.; Mutton, 8d.; Pork, 8d.; and Veal, 9d. to 10d. per lb.

*Manchester* Smithfield Market, April 11.—The supply of Beef and Mutton to this day's market was rather better than last week, and for fat Cattle and Sheep last week's prices were fully supported, whilst lean inferior qualities were dull sale. What few Calves appeared at market were taken off at last week's rates. There is a better demand for Pigs, but the prices remain the same as last advised.—Beef, 4½d. to 8d.; Mutton, 7d. to 9d.; Veal, 5½d. to 6½d.; and Pork, 5d. to 6d. per lb. sinking offal.

*Norwich Castle Meadow,* April 14.—We had a large supply of fat Cattle to this day's market, which met a ready sale at 7s. 6d. to 8s. 6d. per stone of 14 lbs. sinking offal; the show of Store Stock was also large; Scots sold at 4s. to 4s. 6d. per stone of what they will weigh when fat; Shorthorns, 3s. to 3s. 9d.; Cows and Calves, and Homebreds of one and two years old, selling rather better.—Meat: Beef, 6½d. to 9d.; Veal, 6d. to 8d.; Mutton, 6d. to 7½d.; Lamb, 9d.; and Pork, 6d. to 8d. per lb.

# COBBETT'S WEEKLY REGISTER.

Vol. 62.—No. 5.]  LONDON, SATURDAY, April 28, 1827.  [Price 6d.

" Quand il est question d' estimer la puissance publique, le bel-esprit
" visite les palais du prince, ses ports, ses troupes, ses arsenaux, ses
" villes ; le vrai politique parcourt les terres, et va dans la chaumière du
" laboureur.  Le premier vòit ce qu'on *a fait*, et le second ce qu'on *peut*
" *faire*."—Rousseau.

•When the business is to make a just estimate of the public resources,
the shallow pretender visits the palaces of the Prince, his ports, his
troops, his arsenals, his cities ; the true politician traverses the land, and
goes amongst the country people, and visits the cottage of the labourer.
The first sees what *has been done;* and the second sees that which
*can be done.*

# TO THE KING.

## On the Intrigues now on foot, and on the Measures necessary to restore the Nation to happiness, and to secure the stability of the Throne.

*Kensington, 15th April, 1827.*

MAY IT PLEASE YOUR MAJESTY,

Amongst all your Majesty's
subjects there is not one who has,
in this season of advice-giving,
fairer pretensions to offer you advice than I have.  No one has
addressed himself to you so many
times, and no one has ever been
proved, by time, to have been so
correct and so sound in the ad-

vice which he has offered you.
If your Majesty could now read
the *volume* (and a large one it
would be) of that advice, you
could not but exclaim : " If I had
" listened to *this*, my people
" could not now have exhibited
" to the world that mass of ruin
" and of wretchedness which they
" now exhibit." ;

I might, with no very great im-

I

Printed and Published by William Cobbett, No. 183, Fleet-street.
[ENTERED AT STATIONERS' HALL.]

propriety, beseech your Majesty to look at the motto to this paper, and then to say whether the observation contained in that motto does not give me some pretension beyond that of any man, who has been in your Majesty's councils for many years past. The sort of knowledge which is there pointed out as belonging to the " *true politician*," has been proved to be possessed by me, to a very great extent, at any rate; and the correspondent who has pointed out the motto to me, takes the opportunity of saying that in that motto are described the character and talents, or rather, sort of knowledge, possessed by the man whom your Majesty has chosen for your Prime Minister; and, on the other hand, the sort of knowledge possessed by me. Mr. CANNING can see that which has been done; but, if he could have seen, as I have so frequently seen and so frequently pointed out, that which can be and which ought to be done, your Majesty would not have met with so many hard rubs as you have already had to encounter, and your Minister would not have found himself in that deplorable state to which he has now been reduced by being possessed of ambition without being possessed of reputation for knowledge to justify the gratification of that ambition.

But as I shall, in the latter part of this Letter, take the liberty to offer your Majesty my advice with regard to the measures necessary to restore the nation to happiness and to secure the stability of the throne, it becomes me, out of respect to your Majesty, as well as from a sense of what is due to myself, to state some of the particular instances in which I have offered your Majesty my advice, and in which the nation has experienced the fatal consequences of that advice having been rejected. While your Majesty was Regent, both parties in Parliament concurred, and that, too, by unanimous votes, to enter into a war with the United States of America. Upon that occasion, I, being then shut up in prison, in a felons' gaol, for two years, with a thousand pounds fine upon my head (which thousand pounds were paid to you in behalf of the King), with heavy bail for seven years after the termination of the imprisonment; and all this for having expressed my indignation at the flogging of English local militia-men in the heart of England, under a guard of Hanoverian troops; all this for having expressed my indignation at a thing which would have driven our forefathers to madness but to think of: I being then shut up in such prison for such cause; seeing that both parties in Parliament were bent upon compelling the Americans to yield to our unjust pretensions; I, thus situated, wrote a series of letters addressed to your Majesty, proving to you that the parties in Parliament were wholly ignorant of the nation which they had to contend with; stating to you most respectfully but most urgently, the reasons to prevent an entering into that war; stating to you that the war must be enormously expensive; that it was next to impossible that it should be attended with success; that all the accounts of disaffection in the American people were false; that they would beat your armies by land, and drive them from their shores; that they would beat your fleets by sea, if they met them with equal force; that the war would finally end with having actually created a navy for America and laid the ground of a maritime power equal to our own; and that all this disgrace and this future danger would be purchased by the people of England by an addition to that enormous Debt, which was already so great as to leave not the smallest probability of its suffering the nation to remain many years without a terrible convulsion of some sort or other.

I am not relating, may it please your Majesty, any thing said by me in conversation; I am not referring to a talk of a Cornelius Agrippa's man; I am referring to papers *written and published*, and now making part of volumes which will be read, I trust, long after I shall owe allegiance to any body. I am referring to that which many thousands have in their possession; and, if I had written it at the end of the war, instead of having written it before the war began, the description of the consequences could not have been more correct than it was; that war; that heap of disgrace intolerable, added *seventy millions* to the Debt. The interest of that seventy millions is, probably, equal in amount to all the tax which your poor subjects now pay on their soap, *candles, and leather!* It would have been something, then, to have prevented the necessity of continuing to impose these taxes; and this, to say nothing about the disgrace and the creation, the actual creation of a great navy in America; to have prevented the continuing of these taxes would have been more than your Minister,

Mr. CANNING, is, even if he were well disposed, able to accomplish during the remainder of his life, be that life as long as it may. It is curious enough, too, that this very Mr. CANNING treated with the utmost contempt, sent off with the brightest of his jokes, all the apprehensions of danger from a war with America. His memorable witticism on the half-dozen of fir frigates with bits of striped bunting flying at their mast heads was, perhaps, together with other observations from him and men like him in the same strain, the real source of all the mischief. This bantering; this contemptuous talk with respect to America, blinded the nation; they could see no danger in a war with such a contemptible power; and, hence the war was as popular as it was unwise and unjust. That war has not even yet ceased to *draw new sums from us*; and, it will continue to draw new sums from us for a good long life-time yet to come, if this system can be kept on foot so long.

Many other are the occasions on which I have thought it my duty to address your Majesty; but, I beg to refer, particularly, to three letters addressed to your Majesty from Long Island, in the year 1819. In those letters, I took the liberty to explain to you the nature of the paper-money; to show you how a mere company of merchants had been enabled to take from you in reality the greatest and most important of all your prerogatives, the making and issuing of the measure or standard of value. Your Ministers, and this Mr. CANNING amongst the rest, did, a little more than a twelvemonth ago, put forth this very doctrine of mine as their own. They pretended to have discovered, all at once, that your prerogative had been invaded; but, they took care not to remind you that this had been pointed out to you seven years before. In a subsequent series of letters, published towards the close of 1819, after the Speaker of the Commons had congratulated you on the passing of Peel's Bill, I besought your Majesty to believe that that Bill never could be carried into effect, without endangering your very throne. There are the letters now: every line of them is a, now, *verified prophecy*; and, if your Majesty would now condescend to read them through, you must and you would exclaim: " Had I followed this man's advice: " had I listened to this, none of " the present horrible distresses " and miseries would have afflicted " my people, and I should not

" have been called upon to issue " something approaching to a " command to cause one part of " the people to subscribe their " money to save another part of " them from dying of hunger."

In the course of the Letters here referred to, I described to your Majesty, all those means, and the intention and effect of those means, which had been made use of to *keep your Majesty at a distance from your people!* I described to your Majesty the natural tendency of a regulation which prevented your subjects from approaching your person. I described the object of those regulations. I described the intention of the New-Treason-Bill, made for the avowed purpose of giving your Majesty's person *protection against your subjects*, greater than any king ever had before your father; and I asked you, whether it were *you* that thought that you stood in need of this. I observed, at the same time, that it has been made treason, high treason, to do any thing in order to induce the two Houses, or either House, to act against their will. I expatiated upon all these things, and I showed as clearly as daylight, that they all arose from a desire to play off the king against the people and the people against

the king; and your Majesty may, perhaps, never have heard it, but, it is nevertheless true, that the reformers, in all their petitions, complain of a body of men, who *rule both king and people* at their pleasure, who must continue to do this, who must, finally, totally ruin the people, and bring the crown into jeopardy, unless the king, on his part, were restored to the full and free exercise of all his prerogatives, and the people, on their part, to a free choice, an uncorrupted choice of the Members of the House of Commons. I besought your Majesty to think well of these things while there was yet time to act; I besought your Majesty to recommend by message to the Parliament, a radical reform of the Commons' House; so that, before the paper-money had thrown all things into confusion and had produced general convulsion, the people might be rendered patient and docile by the confidence which they would undoubtedly have in a House of Commons freely and honestly chosen by themselves.

For the want of such a House of Commons; for the want of any real power in the people, in their present unrepresented or partially represented state; for the want of this it is, that we now witness all these intrigues, all that cabalbing, all that conflicting; all that uncertainty, all that chopping backward and forward, both as to men and as to counsels, which must now give your Majesty such exceeding embarrassment. You have not your people at your back; for, though they are with you in their hearts, they have no channel through which to make their approaches toward you, and no organ honestly to declare their will. The thing would be settled in a moment. The choice of your servants, which unquestionably belongs to you, would be the affair of a day, without any intriguing, any paragraph-grinding, any negotiating; all would be over by the declaration of your will, if you had your people at hand to declare their will too. Against king and people, no combination or conspiracy could be successful; but, as things now are, it must be extremely difficult, even for your Majesty yourself to be able to foresee what is to take place as to the appointment of your own servants, who are to bear your seals, to treat with foreign nations, to propose Bills to the Parliament, and to do all other important acts in your name.

The present scene is quite enough to convince any rational man, that this country must fall into something very much like anarchy, unless some very great change take place in the system of governing the country, and, particularly, in managing its pecuniary affairs. We are, now, at the end of a whole month since a Prime Minister was appointed, and, at the end of that month, it is matter of rumour and guess of what persons the Ministry shall

consist. A great body of great men, in point of property and station, oppose themselves to your choice. The people, having no organ through which to make their wishes known, are the same as if they were dumb. The political parties shun Mr. CANNING: all sides seem to say, that they will not be under Mr. CANNING. One of two things, it appears, must take place; he must give way and go out altogether, or must take or keep an office under some other Minister. That he will do this, under one of these queer personages called Whigs, rather than under one of his seceding and satirising former colleagues, is likely enough; but, even this would only show that he can be spiteful though he cannot be powerful. It is impossible to conceive a situation of greater embarrassment, greater peril, as to character, than the situation in which he now is; and, he has not the consolation of reflecting, that this situation was *unavoidable.* Not only might he have avoided it; but, it is clear that he sought it, not reflecting that he had not the people at his back; and, above all things, not reflecting that he had a Debt, a dead-weight, a poor-rate debt, and an enormous military establishment to provide for; not reflecting (when he looked back to the days of Pitt's triumph) that the nation was, then, in a state of prosperity; that it was then really recovering from the injuries of war; that PITT was a *maiden* politician; that Pitt stood upon the reputation of his *father*; that Pitt was able to propose to save millions to pay off the then trifling Debt; that the whole of the taxes then amounted to only sixteen millions a year, and that the present expenditure cannot be faced with much less than sixty-four millions a year, including the expense of collection.

He did not perceive that which I told him, a few weeks ago, he would perceive, that, though place-hunters were still as fond of salaries as the sparrows are of wheat, though they have changed nothing of their nature, they would see that the wheat was now beset with twigs covered with bird-lime; and that they would be as shy as sparrows are, when they see those twigs surrounding the food which they are so anxious to get at. We are told of negotiations with the Marquess of Lansdown and Mr. Abercrombie. Grand accession to a minister! Mighty rock of strength; but, even these *negotiate*; they do not fly down upon the grain without hesitation; and, as to Lord GREY, the news-papers tell us that he will have nothing to do with the matter. Thus, that very state of things has arisen, which I in my letters from Long Island told your Majesty would arise. The concern is become such, that men will not like to have any thing to do with it; and, if the seven ministers retired for the mere purpose of getting out of the concern, they acted a part pointed out by worldly wisdom, however disrespectful their conduct might be towards your Majesty.

If Mr. Canning should, at last, form a junction with the Whigs, as they are called, and it is evident that he can carry nothing without such junction, then, heterogeneous, indeed, will be the mass of principles which will here be brought together. Those Whigs must be consigned to everlasting infamy, unless they immediately adopt measures of *retrenchment*. This word has been constantly on their lips for the last twenty years. As great enemies of Parliamentary reform as their opponents; as great enemies of reformers as those were whom they called Tories; but, always calling for " *economical reform*;" always calling for retrenchment in the public expenditure. Mr. CANNING just the contrary; defending every item of expenditure, and carrying the extravagance of his language to that extent, that he asserted, at the opening of the present Session of Parliament, that times of national embarrassment and distress were suitable times for expending large sums of money on palaces and other public works of ornament. He is a man who has invariably defended, with every argument at his command, every species and every degree of expenditure; and who has, with the most biting jests within his reach, with all the sarcasm that he could muster up, ridiculed those who called for a husbanding of the public resources. Will the Whigs, then, join with a man who will make no reforms in point of expenditure? Will they keep in place and keep up the present enormous establishments in time of peace? Will they suffer such immense sums to be expended in the department of ambassadors, envoys and consuls, sums exceeding those expended, I verily believe, by all the other nations in the world put together? Will they not overhaul this enormous dead weight, and condescend to let us know the reason for a man who is a parson receiving pay, at the same time, as a military officer? Will they not call upon the enormously rich Church of England, to pay back those many hundreds of thousands of pounds which were voted to that Church out of the taxes? Will they not institute an inquiry into the cause of old half-pay officers being permitted to sell their commissions to young men, and of the people being called upon to pay taxes to maintain the widows and children of those young men. Will they not institute an inquiry into any of these things? Will they not *reduce the taxes?* Will they not make good any one of the expectations which they endeavoured to convince people that they might entertain, provided that they came into power?

If they do not; if they take no step of this sort; if they merely come to pocket the money that others pocketted before them, your Majesty will have a Ministry more odious, more detested by the people, than any Ministry that ever existed since your family came to this throne; and the worst of it is, it will be called a Ministry of your choosing. They will endeavour in vain to amuse us with that very pretty, very indefinite, very unmeaning word, *liberality*. I have heard a great deal about this liberality; about liberal principles, and about the liberal principles of Mr. Canning in particular. This is a very fine word; but we must look to the *acts* to which this word is applied, before we look upon it as characteristic of any thing that is very good to us. In common conversation, to be liberal means to be generous, to be free in letting others share in any good that you possess. Now, the way for Mr. Canning and the Whigs to

show their liberality towards the people of England; the way to convince us that this liberality is a good thing, would be for them to begin by *reducing their own salaries* nine-tenths, or thereabouts, and thereby leaving more of our money in our own pockets, to be spent by ourselves. They have two ways of showing their liberality: one by cutting short the expenditure, by giving less of our money to other people than they now give; the other, by continuing to raise as much in taxes as ever, and to give as largely as they can, to all manner of persons out of those taxes; or, in other words, being excessively liberal at our expense. This latter is a species of liberality most detestable in itself, loudly calling for our reprobation, and this is precisely that species of liberality which, I verily believe, the Whigs most admire, and which I also believe, they would resolutely put in practice, and with all the brass not only of conscious innocence, but of acknowledged merit.

If we were to be guided in our judgment by what we hear and read every day, we should imagine that the *Catholic question,* as it has been called for the last seven and twenty years, is the great obstacle to Mr. Canning's obtaining suitable colleagues. Those who have any sense know that this is no obstacle at all; that to abandon the question would be popular, rather than otherwise; that it has been abandoned over and over again by those who had pledged themselves to it; that, after Pitt's famous shuffle of 1804, no one can ever be at a loss to abandon that question, and that, too, without the smallest scruple or the smallest danger of loss of place. That, therefore, may pass for nothing. That keeps no man aloof from place, patronage and emolument. But, there is *another matter*, a matter that is never mentioned by any of the political expounders of these intrigues; a matter that seems to be as carefully kept out of sight, the mention of which seems to be as sedulously avoided, as the mention of halters are said to be in a house where one of the family has been hanged; or, which, perhaps, is a still more complete case, the mention of which is avoided as carefully, with as much anxiety as the pronouncing the word *Portugal* has been, during the last four months, avoided in the House of Commons, though we have an army in that same Portugal, and though several millions of our money, screwed out of a really starving people, have followed and must follow, that army, and for a purpose, which any fellow in Bedlam can explain as clearly as I have, yet, heard it explained.

This other matter, the very naming of which is avoided with such tender concern, is, Mr. Canning's *one pound note affair!* Many of the Whigs are very foolish men; very shallow coxcombs; but, there are some amongst them cunning enough to see that the devil himself is safer to face than wheat at four shillings the Winchester bushel. To face that, your Majesty's new Minister is firmly pledged; for, if he persevere in the Bill which he is pledged to persevere in, to four shillings a bushel the wheat must come. The Whigs are also pledged to this bill: they gave it their support; they urged the Minister on to adopt the measure. They can-

not retract without being hooted through the world, and they cannot go on without blowing the whole system into air, without demolishing the whole fabric of the paper-money; without spreading ruin and real *desolation* over the whole country. They cannot push on this bill without ousting every man from his estate. They will finally see half a million of human beings in this metropolis without bread to put in their mouths; and, after having produced every evil with which a nation can be afflicted, they will only have to contrive and determine what they shall do with themselves.

There are men amongst the Whigs, though I do not believe Lord Lansdown to be one of them, who would not like to be in place when some landlord should move for the *repeal of the malt-tax:* not for a preventing of the supplies from going out of the exchequer, but merely for preventing the taxes from going into it. The repeal of the malt-tax would, in a very short time, operate as a repeal of the beer-tax, the spirit-tax, the tea-tax, a cutting off of the licences for selling these, and, in short, would lop off *twenty millions* of taxes in a year. There goes the system! There goes off Mr. Canning and his new allies in a spare beer-barrel, sailing down the Thames, chanting the blessings of free trade out of the bung-hole! The landowners will not stop the supplies. They will not vote against issuing money to pay the army and the navy and the fund-holders. There they would have the people against them, for, the money being in the exchequer, the people would say, "pay it out, to those whom you owe it to." But, for a repeal of the malt-tax, all the people would be clamorous. Every man who brews a bushel of malt, and every man, indeed, who drinks beer, and, bad or good, it is drunk by every body, would be for this measure; and, to this measure the landlords will resort, to this measure the landlords must resort, if Mr. CANNING push on his Bill, or every landlord must lose his estate.

Now, may it please your Majesty, this is the great matter of all. Your Majesty wonders, I dare say, what can make any body, and, especially, a Whig, backward to come into office. Your Majesty knows, from long experience, that these are gentry who have no doubt of their talents; that they all look upon themselves as CECILS and WALSINGHAMS; that they think they are, every man of them, the greatest statesmen of the age; and, that they have great affection for the *public money*, it were blindness worse than Egyptian to doubt. In plain words, your Majesty knows that it is just as conceited and greedy a set as ever scrambled for place or pelf. You must, therefore, have been very much surprised at their wonderful abstemiousness upon this occasion; but, when you come to perceive that Mr. CANNING and the colleagues whom he retains stand pledged to the extirpation of the one-pound notes, or, in other words, to make wheat sell for four shillings a bushel, you will feel less surprise at this great disinterestedness on the part of your own friends. If he were to break his pledge and they to break theirs along with him, their situation would be very little mended. The short statement of the case is this, may it please your Majesty: the wheat must come to four shillings a bushel, or the gold will go out of this country, if gold payments continue at the Bank. To avoid either, the Ministry may return to paper-money and legal tender. That would be a breaking of the pledges of Mr. CANNING and his Whig associates; but even that would not prevent a blowing up of the paper-system. Those who are wise, who have, indeed, but a very small share of wisdom, avoid touching any thing so ticklish as this. Hence it is that there is a difficulty in filling up the offices: hence it is that Lord GREY and others stand aloof, and wish to have nothing to do with the matter.

As far as I am able to judge, Lord GREY is the most likely man to be able to form a Ministry fit to effect any thing for the good of the country; but, even Lord GREY can effect nothing without a total blowing up of the paper system. He must take the petition of the county of Norfolk in his hand, he must resolve to adopt measures consonant with the prayer of that petition; or, he is unable to do any thing to rescue this country from its distresses and its dangers. I dare say, that your Majesty would think that I, now, for instance, would think it a great prize to be made your Minister, and that I should be by no means scrupulous about the means and the terms; but, if your Majesty would make me every thing that WELLINGTON was the other day, and make me as rich as the CHANCELLOR is, I would not be your Minister, without your solemn assurance, without your word as a king, to stand by me while I carried into effect every proposition, all and singular the propositions, contained in the Norfolk Petition. The truth is, self preservation would be my teacher: if I, knowing what I know, and the nation knowing what I know, or, at least, what I have inculcated with so much industry and earnestness; if I were to attempt to carry on the present system, I must be, notoriously, a perjured counseller of your Majesty, and if I were not to be hanged, I should deserve it. This is the real state of the case. There are men enough, who would accept of offices upon the present occasion; but, they think as I think upon this all important question; they are my disciples, though they have not had the courage to avow it: still less have they the courage to do or to propose to your Majesty to do that which they know ought to be done. They are like proselytes in secret; they want the courage to avow their conviction; but they see the danger, and they wish to keep out of it.

There is, therefore, in my firm opinion, no remedy for the evils that oppress the country; no safe path for your Majesty to pursue; no mode of putting an end to these disgraceful intrigues, so embarrassing to the country and so little honourable to the throne: there is nothing, in my firm conviction, short of an adoption of the prayers of the Norfolk Petition, which, it ought to be remarked, has been imitated by several other counties, and by numerous bodies of men not assembled in county meetings. One of the prayers of that Petition is, however, that there may be a *constitutional* reform of the Commons' House of Parliament. This must be, too, a *previous* measure; it must be a first great step; for, until that step be taken, no other, efficiently, can be taken. Nothing but a reformed House of Commons would be able to effect the objects contemplated by the petition. In such a House of Commons the people would have perfect confidence: all men would submit to its decisions without grumbling and without cavil. Great arrangements are to take place, and must take place. An adjustment of hundreds, nay, thousands of millions, can never be effected without the hearty concurrence of the people at large; and that hearty concurrence never can be had unless the House of Commons be chosen by the people themselves. With such a House of Commons nothing would be more easy than a perfectly equitable and peaceable adjustment: this terrible load would be shaken from the shoulders of your suffering people: the saucy, insolent drones would no longer devour the fruit of the labour of the bees. The prayer of the prophet would be realized, happiness would reign throughout the land; crime would be reduced to its ancient standard of quantity, the idle would be punished with hunger, the industrious rewarded with plenty, public virtue would have its reward, and your Majesty's throne would be established in righteousness.

And, as I took the liberty to ask you, in one of my Letters from Long Island, why, *why* cannot this be done, and that, too, immediately. Mr. CANNING has, it seems, a "*budget*" to bring forward. That vulgar word, applied to so important a concern, is truly characteristic of the whole system. He has a budget to bring forward. Instead of a budget, if he were to bring a message from your Majesty, recommending to the House to make a reform of itself, seeing that in its unreformed state it appeared to be unequal to the task of rescuing the country from its dangers. If he were to do this, and bring forward his budget afterwards, the nation would have a much higher opinion of his judgment than it now has. It has been a favourite assertion of his, that, be the House constituted as it may, it is a House that "*works well.*" He will not, perhaps, find it to work so well, in future, as he has found it work in past times. If he get before this House as a Prime Minister, and there really appears to be an *if* in the case, he will not find it work quite so smoothly as it used to do. For his own sake, therefore, he ought to endeavour to change it. However, this is too much to expect: he must still contend for Gatton and Old Sarum ; for, were he to do otherwise, he would be abandoned, even by the Whigs.

After all, then, there is no ground to hope for a just and peaceable result, except your Majesty be the chief mover ; and, I will now, in very plain language, tell your Majesty how I would act, the advice which I would give, if I were in your Ministry, and, being resolved to give that advice, really giving it, and standing by it, I should not be afraid of all the boroughmongers, both the factions, every thing that could be mustered up against me, I would answer for success with my life, and I should have the inexpressible pleasure of seeing your Majesty the most justly popular sovereign that ever reigned upon the face of the earth. My first step would be, humbly but most urgently, to press upon your Majesty the necessity of issuing your Royal Proclamation, fully and frankly stating to your subjects, the situation of the nation's affairs ; describing the several evils that oppress them, and tracing those evils to their immediate causes ; then tracing them to their more distant causes and stating the great cause of all to be a want of sufficient sympathy and community of feeling between those who make the laws and those who pay the taxes; calling upon them for mutual forbearance towards each other in their pecuniary affairs ; calling upon the rich to be kind and benevolent towards the poor ; enjoining most strictly on magistrates to see the laws well and duly enforced, for preserving the lives and health of the people of the poorer sort; promising to all, every thing in your power for their relief and for their speedy restoration to happiness, concluding with telling them that you would immediately suggest to your Parliament to make such a change in the representation as would be likely to repair the injuries inflicted upon the country.

The next step would be to advise your Majesty to send a message to both Houses of Parliament, recommending them to pass laws for making a constitutional reform of the Commons' House; observing to them that you had examined into the source of the evils which now afflict your people ; telling them that history informed you that, of all the people in the world, the English people had been, for numerous ages, the happiest, the best fed, the best clad, the freest, the most virtuous; that a long list of melancholy but undeniable facts now convinces you that they are, with the sole exception of your still more miserable subjects in Ireland, the most unhappy, the worst fed and worst clad people upon the face of the earth. Telling them that you had diligently inquired into the several causes which had produced this disgraceful, this deplorable change; that, when you looked round the kingdom and saw, every where, new gaols, new modes of punishing criminals: that when you saw that a greater quantity of food was allowed to the convicted felon than to the honest labouring man, you could not but inquire into the causes of all this misery and degradation; that, after long and diligent inquiry, you had traced this mass of evil, this fearful change, this change which seemed to have destroyed every thing of England but its bare name; that, in every instance, you had traced back the original cause to *some act or other of the Parliament.* That, to confine yourself to recent instances, the miseries of the year 1822, the agricultural distress of that year; the panic of 1825; that these, you found, came immediately as the effects of two acts of Parliament; that, therefore, it could not be doubted that there must be something wrong in the manner of electing those who imposed the taxes; that this had been told you by your people a thousand times over; that Earl GREY, then Mr. GREY, presented a petition to the House of Commons in 1793, in which the peti-

tioners declared that they were ready to prove at the bar of the House that a decided *majority of the House were returned by only one hundred and fifty-four persons*; that you find, upon inquiry, that the petition was received, that it now lies upon the table of the House, and that it has never, from that day to this, been taken into consideration; and that, therefore, you recommended to the House of Commons to *take that petition into their consideration, without loss of time.*

There is no man in his senses who must not be well assured that, if your Majesty were to take these steps, an effectual reform of the House of Commons would be the certain and speedy consequence. With such a House of Commons, and with the hearty concurrence of your Majesty, every thing would be speedily done which your dignity and our happiness demanded. This load would be taken from our shoulders, the uncertainty as to the value of property would cease; your corn, like that of your ancestors, would be the only money known to your people; wealth, wherever it existed, would be solid; men would seek to live by industry and not by trick; no fortunes of half a million would be made by watching the turn of the market; the cursed Jews must flee the land, or would be flung into the sea, and England would be once more a really Christian, a free and happy country.

There are people, so wrapped up in this Jewish system as to believe it not to be possible for us to live without it. The monster has worked in such a way as to debilitate men's minds, as to make them think corruptly from their very infancy; but, Sir, every thing portends a great change. If not gentle, it must be violent; and gentle it cannot be unless you be graciously pleased to take the lead in the effecting of it. In such a state of things, a leader is always wanted; a leader in effecting the change. If the leader be an inferior person, he is very likely to be crushed: if a man of high rank, he creates envy and division; but, if the King take the lead, nine hundred and ninety-nine thousandths of the people are with him; and for this very good reason: that, if rightly advised, if he act wisely, he must do that which is for the good of the main body of this people; because, without them he is nothing, any more than a common man. This is, indeed, the great advantage of hereditary, kingly government: the King, and all his family, and all that are to come after him, have no fortune, no possession, not bound up with the fortunes and possessions of the people. Common sense, therefore, instinct, almost, leads the people to think that the King must mean for the best. In the present supposed case, there would not be a soul to gainsay; the discontented would be so few in number and so insignificant, that they would neither be seen nor heard of: the whole would be set to rights without a single breach of the peace proceeding from the change. No rank, no class, no description of persons would be called upon for any sacrifices but such as would be barely necessary; and, for my part, I can see no reason why every thing might not be adjusted and the nation starting in a new career of prosperity and happiness in the course of six months from this very day.

I do not like to describe the opposite picture: that of a reform brought on by dire necessity and originating in another quarter very different from that of the King. If this paper-money system be suffered to work on, till it can work on no longer; if it produce, at last, so menacing an attitude on the part of the people; if it plunge things into confusion; if something very nearly resembling a dissolution of society take place and if reform then come as a last resort, how different will be the situation of us all, and, especially, how different the situation of your Majesty! It signifies not what may have been the secret wishes of your Majesty; it signifies not that you may have been friendly to reform in your heart all the while. It signifies not what gratitude your people may owe you for the desires which you may have entertained in their favour: the fact will not be notorious; your conduct will not have been open and your acts visible; you will not have been the leader in the great work; and, to say nothing about dangers; to say nothing about losses from such a cause, why not act now, and secure the gain!

I beg your Majesty to be assured, that nothing which man can do can preserve this paper system for any great length of time, in any form or in any degree; that it must come to an end, and that its progress towards that end must be marked by shock after shock, ruin after ruin, great misery here to-day and great misery there to-morrow, with a steady and constant general increase of poverty, degradation, and crime. There is no way that man has it in his power to proceed which can prevent this, if the paper-system be suffered to proceed to its natural termination. It never can end in that way, without producing a reform of the Parliament, or something of a nature which every good man would wish to see avoided. To the great, to the monopolizers of power, to the meat-sellers, the very smallest evil that can happen, in such a case, is, a radical reform of the Parliament. For them, therefore, it would be better to consent to such reform now. To every body else, and particularly, to your Majesty and your family, beyond all measure, would it be better. However, I simply say what I would do. Mr. CANNING, the Whigs (as they are called), the seven sages or whoever else may have the power, must do what they please. Difficulty upon difficulty will they have to encounter. They will merit the compassion of nobody, and more especially of

Your Majesty's
Most faithful and obedient
Subject and Servant,
WM. COBBETT.

## THE NEW MINISTRY.

IF one were to believe the rumours which are afloat, one ought not to think it wonderful if CANNING were to cut and run, even before Tuesday next. I saw him riding in the park this morning, at about ten o'clock, looking pretty well; boots rather large, cantering, pretty stoutly, upon an easy pad, looking devilish hard towards the statue of Achilles and the triumphal arches; not melancholy in his countenance, but having in it more of the gravity of a Premier than the smirk of a Jester. However, I did not stop to look at the Premier, for I must confess I was afraid lest he should see me, and, if he had, he certainly would have been for pressing me into the service. If it be true, as the newspapers tell us, that he has been negotiating with Lord Lansdown through Abercrombie, and that he has been sending down to Bow Wood the same ambassador that he sent to St. Petersburgh; if it be also true, as the newspapers tell us it is, that Lord Lansdown came to town, and rejected the propositions that had been made to him; then the affairs of the Premier are in a ticklish state indeed. The gossiping world, especially the admirers of the Cornelius Agrippa's men, are quite astonished at what they hear respecting Mr. BROUGHAM, who, it is said, has "lent his powerful aid" in the forming of Mr. CANNING's Ministry; but who, for a reason which he will state hereafter, is to take no place himself! The reader will remember, that when the Vicar of Wakefield's wife asked Colonel Thornhill to make a declaration relative to marrying her daughter Olivia, the Colonel said that he had his reasons for not doing it. "Oh," said the good lady, "if you have your reasons, that is another thing;" and so the Colonel took the girl off without marrying her. Now, is it not the King, and not Mr. Brougham, who has had "his reasons" upon this occasion? This is a pretty humbug story. Just as if any

Scotchman, and particularly a Scotch lawyer, ever refused to receive public money in any shape or any size. For my own part, I regret that there are reasons to shut out Mr. BROUGHAM. He and CANNING together would have actually talked the House to death; and then there would have been such a haggis of wild schemes, such a trickery with the paper-money, such projects for cramming the skull and leaving the belly empty as would have given us a twelvemonth's laughter, at any rate. It was clear to me, from the beginning, that if Mr. CANNING was to be Prime Minister, he must rest upon the Whigs. He appears to have endeavoured to do without them: they perceived this, and, now, it is likely that they will have nothing to do with him, unless they be allowed to be his master. His endeavours to get the Duke of DEVONSHIRE with him, and to conciliate TIERNEY, BROUGHAM, and all the talkers on that side; the compliments that they have been bandying backward and forward, all prove that he has meditated this stroke of policy for a long time. He knew the state of Liverpool better than any body else, except those who were in the house with him. He appears to have thought that an outward display of the friendship of the Whigs for him would *intimidate his colleagues.* He appears to have thought that his colleagues, perceiving that the Whigs would be for him, would be afraid to oppose him, lest he should call in the Whigs and shut them out for ever. This really does appear to have been his view of the matter; but he does not seem to have contemplated the consequence of

*resistance* on the part of his colleagues, which must inevitably drive him for protection to the rump of the Whigs. His colleagues knew very well, that the sensible part of the Whigs could not be so very eager for place in this state of things; and they were pretty certain that he could not resort to the Whigs, except with an offer of the premiership to them. So that, either he would be reduced to the necessity of being an underling to the Whigs, of returning to be an underling to his former colleagues, or to cut and run altogether. There have been some ugly hints thrown out about his *having no desire to be Premier!* Strange story this; but, it seems to indicate that he begins to feel that he must either decamp, or be something less than the master. He has vacated his seat; but he has not, yet, appeared in the Gazette, which is a very strange thing, seeing that he ought to have appeared there first of all. So that, if he should, finally, be compelled to desist and to yield the Premiership to somebody else, it will not have to be said that he was turned out of it. In short, his affairs are in a very ticklish state; and, I cannot say that I can possibly think of wetting a handkerchief upon the subject, when I recollect that, in 1809, he called us reformers " *a low degraded crew,*" and, when proof was offered at the bar, of the selling of seats in the House, he called upon the House not to hear the proof, and thereby to " make a stand against democratical encroachment." Let Mr. CANNING, in the difficulties in which he finds himself, reflect a little on his long career of cruel, insulting, and licentious abuse of the people; and let him read, in those difficulties, the consequences, or some of the consequences, of such a career : consequences as natural and as just, in such a case, as crippled toes and numbed joints are of the swallowing of gin, grogs, and whiskey.

The appointment of the Duke of CLARENCE has given universal satisfaction. It has cheered the hearts of all the Englishmen in the Navy; and it has given me hopes that our Navy will be fit to cope with that of America, whenever a war shall break out. I know nothing of the Duke personally, of course; but I have always heard that he was a blunt, open, fair-dealing man; and, it is reasonable to suppose that he will have great zeal and great impartiality in the conducting of the affairs of his office. Except as to this point, I care not one straw about Mr. CANNING or his Ministry; but, if this appointment depends upon the stability of Canning's Ministry, I hope it will stand; for, this Navy is a capital consideration, and, when the day of fighting comes, we shall have to feel the effects of what is done at that Admiralty in time of peace. MEL-VILLE, I am told, adopted, when he came to the Admiralty, a regulation to keep him from the sight, from the approach, of *every thing under the rank of Captain*; that is to say, that he laid it down as a rule that he would see no Lieutenant or Midshipman and, of course, no person of inferior rank or station. My God! And this regulation by a Scotchman, placed at the head of that glorious service, which gained all its glory under Englishmen exclusively! I do hope that the Duke of Cla-

rence will keep his station. I hope it was the King's own appointment; and I would rather that almost any thing should happen than that that appointment should be overset. Yet, I fear it will be if our Cornelius Agrippa's man should be driven from the field; and this I think very likely to happen.—The worst sign for Mr. CANNING is the retirement of WALLIE WALLACE, that old veteran placeman, from the mastership of the Mint, with an income of 3,000*l.* a year. One almost hears him coming down the stairs from the Mint, cry aloud, "Scots wha hae wi' Wallace bled!" His going out seems to be a certain sign that the whole will come back again. There are others, too, who never would have quitted, unless torn out by flesh-hooks, if they had not been pretty sure to come back again. If CANNING was deep, and laid his plans long before-hand, the others seem to have been aware of his plans, and to have been perfectly ready to meet him. Take the thing altogether, it is, perhaps, as fine an intrigue, or rather, nest of intrigues, as ever was seen in the world. We have long been in a state of gradual mental improvement; our refinement has been excessive for a long time; this intrigue seems to be the climax. It is one end of it, at any rate, and now, something else must come.

---

## PARLIAMENTARY REFORM.

I am certain that there will be no safety for the country, that it cannot recover itself in any de-

K

gree, without a reform of the House of Commons; that it must go on to he worse and worse off, and that it will finally become the lowest and most degraded country in the whole world, unless such reform be adopted. The young men of the present day have heard of the memorable petition of Mr. GREY and other gentlemen in 1793. They have heard of it, but very few of them have read it. They have heard every body calumniated who have talked of reform of any sort. To petition for reform has been deemed a crime. We have now come to the crisis: we must have that reform, or we must have something a great deal more dangerous to those who have been its most bitter enemies. Mr. TIERNEY, the present Duke of BEDFORD, Lord JOHN TOWNSEND, and several other persons now alive, signed the petition of Lord GREY. I have said that I would recommend it to the King to suggest to the Parliament to have this petition taken into consideration. I have said that such a message from the King would produce a reform. I will here, therefore, insert this petition, long as it is; and, if the Whigs go into office without bringing forward a reform of Parliament as a Cabinet measure, they will not, indeed, deceive me, but they will undeceive the small remnant of their supporters throughout the country.

_Authentic Copy of a Petition praying for a Reform in Parliament, presented to the House of Commons by_ CHARLES GREY, _Esq. on Monday, 6th May,_ 1793; _and signed only by the Members of the Society of the Friends of the People, associated for the Purpose of obtaining a Parliamentary Reform._

To the Honourable the Commons of Great Britain in Parliament assembled.

Sheweth

THAT by the form and spirit of the British constitution, the king is vested with the sole executive power.

That the house of lords consists of lords spiritual and temporal, deriving their titles and consequence either from the crown, or from hereditary privileges.

That these two powers, if they acted without control, would form either a despotic monarchy, or a dangerous oligarchy.

That the wisdom of our ancestors hath contrived, that these authorities may be rendered not only harmless, but beneficial, and be exercised for the security and happiness of the people.

That this security and happiness are to be looked for in the introduction of a third estate, distinct from, and a check upon the other two branches of the legislature; created by, representing, and responsible to the people themselves.

That so much depending upon the preservation of this third estate, in such its constitutional purity and strength, your petitioners are reasonably jealous of whatever may appear to vitiate the one, or to impair the other.

That at the present day the house of commons does not fully and fairly represent the people of England, which, consistently with what your petitioners conceive to be the principles of the constitution, they consider as a grievance, and therefore, with all becoming respect, lay their complaints before your honourable house.

That though the terms in which your petitioners state their grievance may be looked upon as strong, yet your honourable house is entreated to believe that no expression is made use of for the purpose of offence.

Your petitioners in affirming that your honourable house is not an adequate representation of the people of England, do but state a fact, which, if the word "Representation" be accepted in its fair and obvious sense, they are ready to prove, and which they think detrimental to their interests, and contrary to the spirit of the constitution.

How far this inadequate representation is prejudicial to their interests, your petitioners apprehend they may be allowed to decide for themselves; but how far it is contrary to the spirit of the constitution, they refer to the consideration of your honourable house.

If your honourable house shall be pleased to determine that the people of England ought not to be fully represented, your petitioners pray that such your determination may be made known, to the end that the people may be apprized of their real situation; but if your honourable house shall conceive that the people are already fully represented, then your petitioners beg leave to call your attention to the following facts:

Your petitioners complain, that the number of representatives assigned to the different counties is grossly disproportioned to their comparative extent, population, and trade.

Your petitioners complain, that the elective franchise is so partially and unequally distributed, and is in so many instances committed to bodies of men of such very limited numbers, that the majority of your honourable house is elected by less than fifteen thousand electors, which, even if the male adults in the kingdom be estimated at so low a number as three millions, is not more than the two hundredth part of the people to be represented.

Your petitioners complain, that the right of voting is regulated by no uniform or rational principle.

Your petitioners complain, that the exercise of the elective franchise is only renewed once in seven years.

Your petitioners thus distinctly state the subject matter of their complaints, that your honourable house may be convinced that they are acting from no spirit of general discontent, and that you may with the more ease be enabled to inquire into the facts, and to apply the remedy.

For the evidence in support of the first complaint, your petitioners refer to the return book of your honourable house.—Is it fitting, that Rutland and Yorkshire should bear an equal rank in the scale of county representation; or can it be right, that Cornwall alone should, by its extravagant proportion of Borough members, outnumber not only the representatives of Yorkshire and Rutland together, but of Middlesex added to them? Or, if a distinction be taken between the landed and the trading interests, must it not appear monstrous that Cornwall and Wiltshire should send more borough members to parliament, than Yorkshire, Lancashire, Warwickshire, Middlesex, Worcestershire, and Somersetshire united? and that the total representation of all Scotland should but exceed by one member, the number returned for a single county in England?

The second complaint of your petitioners is founded on the unequal proportions in which the elective franchise is distributed, and in support of it,

They affirm, that seventy of your honourable members are returned by thirty-five places, where the right of voting is vested in burgage and other tenures of a similar description, and in which it would be to trifle with the patience of your honourable house, to mention any number of voters whatever, the elections at the places alluded to being notoriously a mere matter of form. And this your petitioners are ready to prove.

K 2

They affirm, that in addition to the seventy honourable members so chosen, ninety more of your honourable members are elected by forty-six places, in none of which the number of voters exceeds fifty. And this your petitioners are ready to prove.

They affirm, that in addition to the hundred and sixty so elected, thirty-seven more of your honourable members are elected by nineteen places, in none of which the number of voters exceeds one hundred. And this your petitioners are ready to prove.

They affirm, that in addition to the hundred and ninety-seven honourable members so chosen, fifty-two more are returned to serve in parliament, by twenty-six places, in none of which the number of voters exceeds two hundred. And this your petitioners are ready to prove.

They affirm, that in addition to the two hundred and forty-nine so elected, twenty more are returned to serve in parliament for counties in Scotland, by less than one hundred electors each, and ten for counties in Scotland by less than two hundred and fifty each. And this your petitioners are ready to prove, even admitting the validity of fictitious votes.

They affirm, that in addition to the two hundred and seventy-nine so elected, thirteen districts of burghs in Scotland, not containing one hundred voters each, and two districts of burghs, not containing one hundred and twenty-five each, return fifteen more honourable members. And this your petitioners are ready to prove.

And in this manner, according to the present state of the representation, two hundred and ninety-four of your honourable members are chosen, and, being a majority of the entire house of commons, are enabled to decide all questions in the name of the whole people of England and Scotland.

The third complaint of your petitioners is founded on the present complicated rights of voting. From the caprice with which they have been varied, and the obscurity in which they have become involved by time and contradictory decisions, they are become a source of infinite confusion, litigation, and expense.

Your petitioners need not tender any evidence of the inconveniences which arise from this defect in the representation, because the proof is to be found in your journals, and the minutes of the different committees who have been appointed under the 10th and 11th of the king. Your honourable house is but too well acquainted with the tedious, intricate, and expensive scenes of litigation which have been brought before you, in attempting to settle the legal import of those numerous distinctions which perplex and confound the present rights of voting. How many months of your valuable time have been wasted in listening to the wrangling of lawyers upon the various species of burgagehold, leasehold, and freehold! How many committees have been occupied in investigating the nature of scot and lot, pot wallers, commonalty, populacy, resiant inhabitants, and inhabitants at large! What labour and research have been employed in endeavouring to ascertain the legal claims of borough-men, aldermen, port men, select men, burgesses, and councilmen! And what confusion has arisen from the complicated operation of clashing charters, from freemen resident and non-resident, and from the different modes of obtaining the freedom of corporations by birth, by servitude, by marriage, by redemption, by election, and by purchase! On all these points it is, however, needless for your petitioners to enlarge, when your honourable house recollects the following facts; namely, that since the twenty-second of December, 1790, no less than twenty-one committees have been employed in deciding upon litigated rights of voting. Of these, eight were occupied with the disputes, of three boroughs, and there are petitions from four places yet remaining before your honourable house, waiting for a final decision to inform the electors what their rights really are.

But the complaint of your petitioners on the subject of the want of an uniform, and equitable principle in regulating the right of voting, extends as well to the arbitrary manner in which some are excluded, as to the intricate qualifications by which others are admitted to the exercise of that privilege.

Religious opinions create an incapacity to vote. All Papists are excluded generally, and, by the operation of the test laws, Protestant dissenters are deprived of a voice in the election of representatives in about thirty boroughs, where the right of voting is confined to corporate officers alone; a deprivation the more unjustifiable, because, though considered as unworthy to vote, they are deemed capable of being elected, and may be the representatives of the very places for which they are disqualified from being the electors.

A man possessed of one thousand pounds per annum, or any other sum, arising from copyhold, leasehold for ninety-nine years, trade, property in the public funds, or even freehold in the city of London, and many other cities and towns having peculiar jurisdictions, is not thereby intitled to vote. Here again a strange distinction is taken between electing and representing, as a copyhold is a sufficient qualification to sit in your honourable house.

A man paying taxes to any amount, how great soever, for his domestic establishment, does not thereby obtain a right to vote, unless his residence be in some borough where that right is vested in the inhabitants. This exception operates in sixty places, of which twenty-eight do not contain three hundred voters each, and the number of house-holders in England and Wales (exclusive of Scotland), who pay all taxes, is 714,911, and of householders who pay all taxes, but the house and window taxes, is 284,459, as appears by a return made to your honourable house in 1785 ; so that, even supposing the sixty places above-mentioned to contain, one with another, one thousand voters in each, there will remain 939,370 householders who have no v ·e in the representation, unless they have obtained it by accident or by purchase. Neither their contributions to the public burdens, their peaceable demeanor as good subjects, nor their general respectability and merits as useful citizens, afford them, as the law now stands, the smallest pretensions to participate in the choice of those, who, under the name of their representatives, may dispose of their fortunes and liberties.

In Scotland, the grievance arising from the nature of the rights of voting, has a different and still more intolerable operation. In that great and populous division of the kingdom, not only the great mass of the householders, but of the landholders also, are excluded from all participation in the choice of representatives. By the remains of the feudal system in the counties, the vote is severed from the land, and attached to what is called the superiority. In other words, it is taken from the substance, and transferred to the shadow, because, though each of these superiorities, must, with very few exceptions, arise from lands of the present annual value of four hundred pounds sterling, yet it is not necessary, that the lands should do more than give a name to the superiority, the possessor of which may retain the right of voting notwithstanding he be divested of the property. And, on the other hand, great landholders have the means afforded them by the same system, of adding to their influence, without expense to themselves, by communicating to their confidential friends the privilege of electing members to serve in parliament. The process by which this operation is performed is simple. He who wishes to increase the number of his dependent votes, surrenders his charter to the crown, and, parceling out his estate into as many lots of four hundred pounds per annum, as may be convenient, conveys them to such as he can confide in. To these, new charters are, upon application, granted by the crown, so as to erect each of them into a superiority, which privilege once obtained, the land itself is reconveyed to the original granter; and thus the representatives of the landed interest in Scotland may be chosen by those who have no real or beneficial interest in the land.

Such is the situation in which the counties of Scotland are placed. With respect to the burghs, every thing that bears even the semblance of popular choice, has long been done away. The election of members to serve in parliament is vested in the magistrates and town councils, who, having by various innovations, constituted themselves into self-elected bodies, instead of officers freely chosen by the inhabitants at large, have deprived the people of all participation in that privilege, the free exercise of which affords the only security they can possess for the protection of their liberties and property.

The fourth and last complaint of your petitioners is the length of the duration of parliament. Your honourable house knows, that by the ancient laws and statutes of this kingdom frequent parliaments ought to be held; and that the sixth of William and Mary, c. 2. (since repealed) speaking while the spirit of the revolution was yet warm, declared, that " frequent and new parliaments tend very much to the happy union and good agreement between king and people;" and enacted, that no parliament should last longer than three years. Your

petitioners, without presuming to add to such an authority by any observations of their own, humbly pray that parliaments may not be continued for seven years.

Your petitioners have thus laid before you the specific grounds of complaint, from which they conceive every evil in the representation to spring, and on which they think every abuse and inconvenience is founded.

What those abuses are, and how great that inconvenience is, it becomes your petitioners to state, as the best means of justifying their present application to your honourable house.

Your petitioners then affirm, that from the combined operation of the defects they have pointed out, arise those scenes of confusion, litigation, and expense, which so disgrace the name, and that extensive system of private patronage which is so repugnant to the spirit of free representation.

Your petitioners entreat of your honourable house to consider the manner in which elections are conducted, and to reflect upon the extreme inconvenience to which electors are exposed, and the intolerable expense to which candidates are subjected.

Your honourable house knows that tumults, disorders, outrages, and perjury, are too often the dreadful attendants on contested elections as at this time carried on.

Your honourable house knows that polls are only taken in one fixed place for each county, city, and borough, whether the number of voters be ten or ten thousand, and whether they be resident or dispersed over England.

Your honourable house knows that polls, however few the electors, may by law be continued for fifteen days, and even then be subjected to a scrutiny.

Your honourable house knows that the management and conduct of polls is committed to returning officers, who, from the very nature of the proceedings, must be invested with extensive and discretionary power, and who, it appears by every volume of your journals, have but too often exercised those powers with the most gross partiality and the most scandalous corruption.

Of elections arranged with such little regard to the accommodation of the parties, acknowledged to require such a length of time to complete, and trusted to the superintendence of such suspicious agents, your petitioners might easily draw out a detail of the expense. But it is unnecessary. The fact is too notorious to require proof, that scarce an instance can be produced where a member has obtained a disputed seat in parliament at a less cost than from two to five thousand pounds; particular cases are not wanting where ten times these sums have been paid, but it is sufficient for your petitioners to affirm, and to be able to prove it if denied, that such is the expense of a contested return, that he who should become a candidate with even greater funds than the laws require him to swear to as his qualification to sit in your honourable house, must either relinquish his pretensions on the appearance of opposition, or so reduce his fortune in the contest, that he could not take his seat without perjury.

The revision of the original polls before the committees of your honourable house, upon appeals from the decisions of the returning officers, affords a fresh source of vexation and expense to all parties. Your honourable house knows, that the complicated rights of voting, and the shameful practices which disgrace election proceedings, have so loaded your table with petitions for judgment and redress, that one half of the usual duration of a parliament has scarcely been sufficient to settle who is entitled to sit for the other half; and it was not till within the the last two months that your honourable house had an opportunity of

discovering, that the two gentlemen who sat and voted near three years as the representatives of the borough of Stockbridge, had procured themselves to be elected by the most scandalous bribery; and that the two gentlemen, who sat and voted during as long a period for the borough of Great Grimsby, had not been elected at all.

In truth, all the mischief of the present system of representation is ascertained by the difficulties which even the zeal and-wisdom of your honourable house experiences in attending to the variety of complaints brought before you. Though your committee sit five hours every day from the time of their appointment, they generally are unable to come to a decision in less than a fortnight, and very frequently are detained from thirty to forty days. The Westminster case in 1789, will even furnish your honourable house with an instance, where, after deliberating forty-five days, a committee gravely resolved, that, "From an attentive consideration of the circumstances relating to the cause, a final decision of the business before them could not take place in the course or the session, and that not improbably the whole of the parliament" (having at that time near two years longer to sit) " might be consumed in a tedious and expensive litigation;" and they recommended it to the petitioners to withdraw their petition, which, after a fruitless perseverance of about three months, they were actually obliged to submit to.

Your petitioners will only upon this subject further add, that the ex-

m only lasted two days
point of fact only six hours, amounted to very near twelve hundred

pounds. And this your petitioners are ready to prove.

Your petitioners must now beg leave to call the attention of your honourable house to the greatest evil produced by these defects in the representation of which they complain, namely, the extent of PRIVATE PARLIAMENTARY PATRONAGE; an abuse which obviously tends to exclude the great mass of the people from any substantial influence in the election of the house of commons, and which, in its progress, threatens to usurp the sovereignty of the country, to the equal danger of the king, of the lords, and of the commons.

The patronage of which your petitioners complain, is of *two* kinds: That which arises from the unequal distribution of the elective franchise, and the peculiar rights of voting by which certain places return members to serve in parliaments; and that which arises from the expense attending contested elections, and the consequent degree of power acquired by wealth.

By these two means, a weight of parliamentary influence has been obtained by certain individuals, forbidden by the spirit of the laws, and in its consequences most dangerous to the liberties of the people of Great Britain.

The operation of the *first* species of patronage is direct, and subject to positive proof. Eighty-four individuals do by their own immediate authority send one hundred and fifty-seven of your honourable members to parliament. And this your petitioners are ready, if the fact be disputed, to prove, and to name the members and the patrons.

The *second* species of patronage cannot be shown with equal accuracy, though it is felt with equal force.

Your petitioners are convinced, that in addition to the one hundred and fifty-seven honourable members above-mentioned, one hundred and fifty more, making in the whole three hundred and seven, are returned to your honourable house, not by the collective voice of those whom they appear to represent, but by the recommendation of seventy powerful individuals, added to the eighty-four before-mentioned, and making the total number of patrons altogether only one hundred and fifty-four, who return a decided majority of your honourable house.

If your honourable house will accept as evidence the common report and general belief of the counties, cities, and boroughs, which return the members alluded to, your petitioners are ready to name them, and to prove the fact; or if the members in question can be made parties to the inquiry, your petitioners will name them, and be governed by the testimony which they themselves shall publicly give. But if neither of these proofs be thought consistent with the proceedings of your honourable house, then your petitioners can only assert their belief of the fact, which they hereby do in the most solemn manner, and on the most deliberate conviction.

Your petitioners entreat your honourable house to believe that, in complaining of this species influence, it is not their intention or desire to decry or to condemn that just and natural attachment which they, who are enabled by their fortune, and inclined by their disposition, to apply great means to honourable and benevolent ends, will always ensure to themselves. What your petitioners complain of is, that property, whether well or ill employed, has equal power; that the present system of representation gives to it a degree of weight which renders it independent of character; which enables it to excite fear as well as to procure respect, and which confines the choice of electors within the ranks of opulence, because, though it cannot make riches the sole object of their affection and confidence, it can and does throw obstacles, almost insurmountable, in the way of every man who is not rich, and thereby secures to a select few the capability of becoming candidates themselves, or supporting the pretensions of others. Of this your petitioners complain loudly, because they conceive it to be highly unjust, that, while the language of the law requires from a candidate no greater estate, as a qualification, than a few hundred pounds per annum, the operation of the law should disqualify every man whose rental is not extended to thousands; and that, at the same time that the legislature appears to give the electors a choice from amongst those who possess a moderate and independent competence, it should virtually compel them to choose from amongst those who themselves abound in wealth, or are supported by the wealth of others.

Your petitioners are the more alarmed at the progress of private patronage, because it is rapidly leading to consequences which menace the very existence of the constitution.

At the commencement of every session of parliament, your honourable house, acting up to the laudable jealousy of your predecessors, and speaking the pure, constitutional language of a British house of commons, resolve, as appears by your journals, "That no peer of this realm hath any right to give his vote in the election of any member to serve in parliament;" and also, "That it is a high infringement upon the liberties and privileges of the commons of Great Britain, for any lord of parliament, or any lord-lieutenant of any county, to concern themselves in the elections of members to serve for the commons in parliament."

Your petitioners inform your honourable house, and are ready to prove it at your bar, that they have the most reasonable grounds to suspect that no less than one hundred and fifty of your honourable members owe their elections entirely to the interference of peers; and your petitioners are prepared to show by legal evidence, that forty peers, in defiance of your resolutions, have possessed themselves of so many burgage tenures, and obtained such an absolute and uncontrolled command in very many small boroughs in the kingdom, as to be enabled by their own positive authority to return eighty-one of your honourable members.

Your petitioners will, however, urge this grievance of the interference of peers in elections no farther, because they are satisfied that it is unnecessary. Numbers of your honourable members must individually have known the fact, but collectively your honourable house has undoubtedly been a stranger to it. It is now brought before you by those who tender evidence of the truth of what they assert, and they conceive it would be improper in them to ask that by petition, wich must be looked for as the certain result of your own honourable attachment to your own liberties and privileges.

Your petitioners have thus laid before your honourable house, what the mischiefs are which arise from the present state of the representation, and what they conceive to be the grounds of those mischiefs, and therefore pray to have them removed.

They now humbly beg leave to offer their reasons, why they are anxious that some remedy should be immediately applied.

Your petitioners trust, they may be allowed to state, because they are ready to prove, that seats in your honourable house are sought for at a most extravagant and increasing rate of expense.

What can have so much augmented the ambition to sit in your honourable house, your petitioners do not presume accurately to have discovered, but the means taken by candidates to obtain, and by electors to bestow that honour, evidently appear to have been increasing in a progressive degree of fraud and corruption. Your petitioners are induced to make this assertion by the legislature having found it necessary, during the last and present reigns, so much to swell the statute book with laws for the prevention of those offences.

As far as conjecture can lead your petitioners, they must suppose, that the increasing national debt, and the consequent increase of influence, are the causes of the increased eagerness of individuals to become members of the house of commons, and of their indifference as to the means used to gratify their speculations. To prove that they do not state this wantonly, or without substantial grounds, they humbly beg to call your attention to the following table, all the vouchers for which are to be found in the journals of your honourable house, or in different acts of parliament.

It is upon this evidence of the increase of taxes, establishments, and influence, and the increase of laws found necessary to repel the increasing attacks upon the purity and freedom of elections, that your petitioners conceive it high time to inquire into the premises.

Your petitioners are confident that in what they have stated, they are supported by the evidence of facts, and they trust that, in conveying those facts to your honourable house, they have not been betrayed into the language of reproach or disrespect. Anxious to preserve in its purity a constitution they love and admire, they have thought it their duty to lay before you, not general speculations deduced from theoretical opinions, but positive truths, susceptible of direct proof, and if in the performance of this task, they have been obliged to call your attention to assertions which you have not been accustomed to hear, and which they lament they are compelled to make, they intreat the indulgence of your honourable house.

Your petitioners will only further trespass upon your time while they recapitulate the objects of their prayer, which are,

That your honourable house will be pleased to take such measures, as to your wisdom may seem meet, to remove the evils arising from the unequal manner in which the different parts of the kingdom are admitted to participate in the representation.

To correct the partial distribution of the elective franchise, which commits the choice of representation to select bodies of men of such limited numbers as renders them an easy prey to the artful, or, a ready purchase to the wealthy.

To regulate the right of voting upon an uniform and equitable principle,

And finally, to shorten the duration of parliaments, and by removing the causes of that confusion, litigation, and expense, with which they are at this day conducted, to render frequent and new elections, what our ancestors at the revolution asserted them to be, the means of a happy union and good agreement between the king and people.

And your petitioners shall ever pray.

---

## AMERICAN KIDNEY BEANS.

I HAVE two sorts of these, the finest that ever were in England; one of them the very earliest that I ever saw; and the seed, in both cases, so ripe, sound, and excellent, that a large crop from it is certain.—One sort is *Yellow*, the other *Speckled*; both are dwarfs.—Price—17s. a bushel, and smaller quantities in proportion, with something added for paper, string, and trouble.—They are sold at the Office of the Register, No 183, Fleet Street, and may be sent, by order, to any part of the country.

# BELL'S
# LIFE IN LONDON,

## AND SPORTING CHRONICLE,

*Price Sevenpence,*

Of SUNDAY, April 29th, will give the best Account of the FIGHT between BURN and BALDWIN, at No Man's Land.

---

**BELL'S LIFE IN LONDON**

Will give (as it has done for the two preceding Sundays) the most authentic and fullest particulars of the New Administration.

**BELL'S LIFE IN LONDON,**

AND SPORTING CHRONICLE,

Combining, with the News of the Week, a rich Repository of Fashion, Wit, and Humour, and the interesting Incidents of Real Life, is regularly published every Saturday Afternoon at Four, and on Sunday Morning at Four o'Clock. It contains Twenty Folio Columns, printed upon the best Paper, with a large Type—is the same size as *The Observer*, and the price only Sevenpence.

Small 8vo., with an Engraving, by Humphreys, Vol. I., price 7s. 6d., in boards, of

## ILLUSTRATIONS
### OF THE
## PASSION OF LOVE.

"Omnia vincit Amor." - - OVID.

CONTENTS:—Abbassa—Agnes Sorel—Abelard and Heloise—Abraham and Sarah—Abou Joseph—Alfieri—Angels—Anne of Austria—Antony and Cleopatra—The Lady Arabella—Sophia Arnoud—Count d'Artois—Aspasia—Athenais—Chevalier de la Barre—Bassompierre--Benyowski Biron—Anne Boleyn—Constable de Bourbon—Madame Bourignon, &c. &c. &c.

Printed for Hunt and Clarke, York street.

---

## MARKETS.
----

Average Prices of CORN throughout ENGLAND, for the week ending April 13.

Per Quarter.

|  | s. | d. |  | s. | d. |
|---|---|---|---|---|---|
| Wheat .. | 56 | 4 | Rye .... | 39 | 5 |
| Barley .. | 38 | 3 | Beans ... | 47 | 2 |
| Oats .... | 30 | 4 | Pease ... | 47 | 4 |

Total Quantity of Corn returned as Sold in the Maritime Districts, for the week ended April 13.

|  | Qrs. |  | Qrs. |
|---|---|---|---|
| Wheat.. | 35,713 | Rye ..... | 209 |
| Barley .. | 13,543 | Beans . .. | 1,597 |
| Oats.... | 11,945 | Pease .... | 366 |

*Corn Exchange, Mark Lane.*

Quantities and Prices of British Corn, &c. sold and delivered in this Market, during the week ended Saturday, April 13.

| Qrs. | £. | s. | d. |  | s. | d. |
|---|---|---|---|---|---|---|
| Wheat..5,242 for 15,463 | 7 | 0 | Average, 58 | 11 |
| Barley..2,143 .. 4,353 | 10 | 9 | ..........40 | 7 |
| Oats.. 1,653 .. 2,763 | 19 | 1 | ..........33 | 5 |
| Rye.... 32 .. 58 | 17 | 0 | ..........36 | 9 |
| Beans.. 545 .. 1,205 | 10 | 9 | ..,.......44 | 2 |
| Pease.. 271 .. 617 | 0 | 7 | ..........45 | 6 |

Friday, April 20.—The supplies of Grain, during the present week, are tolerably good. Wheat meets a slack demand, at Monday's prices. Barley and Pease also find a heavy trade. Beans fully maintain the advance of Monday last. Oats are not so free in sale as on Monday last, and Feed descriptions are rather lower. Flour unaltered.

Monday, April 23.—The report of arrivals for last week was tolerably good, but the fresh samples of Grain this morning form no material addition to the quantities left over from last week, so that there is no great show of samples of any kind of Grain, except Foreign Oats, which continue to come in plentifully. The Wheat trade may be stated precisely the same as on this day se'nnight, with very little fine left unsold.

Barley has met more freedom in sale to-day, but the prices cannot be quoted any higher. Dry Beans are more in demand, and 1s. per quarter dearer. Pease remain as last quoted. Oats find a fair trade, for good parcels, at the terms of last Monday, but inferior sorts still meet a dull sale. Tares are again considerably cheaper.

----

Price of Bread.—The price of the 4lb. Loaf is stated at 9d. by the full-priced Bakers.

## COAL MARKET, April 20.

*Ships at Market. Ships sold. Price.*

42¾ Newcastle 22½..30s. 6d. to 37s. 6d.
15 Sunderland 7. ..35s. 6d.— 38s. 6d.

Account of Wheat, &c. arrived in the Port of London, from April 16 to April 21, both inclusive.

| | Qrs. | | Qrs. |
|---|---|---|---|
| Wheat .. | 4,640 | Tares .... | 1,740 |
| Barley .. | 1,681 | Linseed .. | 3,664 |
| Malt .... | 4,642 | Rapeseed . | 2,671 |
| Oats .... | 6,254 | Brank .. | 560 |
| Beans ... | 400 | Mustard.. | — |
| Flour .... | 9,150 | Flax .... | — |
| Rye .... | — | Hemp ... | 115 |
| Pease.... | 757 | Seeds ... | — |

Foreign.—Wheat, 3,367; Barley, 4,163; Oats, 31,217; Beans, 1,656 qrs.; and Flour 12 barrels.

———

Monday, April 23.—The arrivals from Ireland last week were, 1077 firkins of Butter, and 3,513 bales of Bacon; and from Foreign Ports, 6,461 casks of Butter.

———

## HOPS.

Price of Hops, per Cwt. in the Borough.

Monday, April 23.—We have had considerably more business doing since our last report, at an advance in price; and it is anticipated it will continue, as the reports from the plantations come very unfavourable. New duty called 120,000*l.*

*Maidstone,* April 19. —We have nothing doing this week of any conseqfience in the Hop Trade. The late unkindly weather has kept the bines rather backward, and there is flea in many of the grounds.

*Worcester,* April 18.—On Saturday 155 pockets of Hops were weighed; prices, 90*s.* to 96*s.*—The plants are reported to be springing very favourably.

Monday, April 23.—On Friday, both Beef and Mutton sold at rather higher prices than on the previous market day. This morning there is a brisk trade in the former article, and it fully commands Friday's terms, the best Scots readily obtaining 5*s.* 4*d.*, and prime Lincolns 5*s.* The Mutton trade is not so lively as last week; the best polled light weights, in their wool, go no higher than 5*s.* 8*d.*; but choice Downs make our top currency.— Sheep of secondary quality are certainly lower. In Lamb there is no alteration.

*Per Stone of* 8 *pounds (alive).*

| | s. | d. | | s. | d. |
|---|---|---|---|---|---|
| Beef . | 4 | 2 | to 5 | 4 |
| Mutton ... | 4 | 8 | — 6 | 0 |
| Veal ..... | 5 | 4 | — 6 | 0 |
| Pork..... | 4 | 4 | — 5 | 4 |
| Lamb .... | 6 | 4 | — 7 | 0 |

| Beasts . . | 2,039 | Sheep .. | 12,120 |
|---|---|---|---|
| Calves ... | 134 | Pigs ... | 140 |

NEWGATE, (same day.)
*Per Stone of* 8 *pounds (dead).*

| | s. | d. | | s. | d. |
|---|---|---|---|---|---|
| Beef ..... | 3 | 8 | to 4 | 8 |
| Mutton ... | 4 | 0 | — 5 | 6 |
| Veal ..... | 3 | 8 | — 5 | 8 |
| Pork..... | 4 | 0 | — 6 | 0 |
| Lamb .... | 4 | 8 | — 6 | 8 |

LEADENHALL, (same day.)
*Per Stone of* 8 *pounds (dead)*

| | s. | d. | | s. | d. |
|---|---|---|---|---|---|
| Beef ... . | 3 | 4 | to 4 | 10 |
| Mutton ... | 4 | 0 | — 5 | 4 |
| Veal ..... | 3 | 8 | — 5 | 8 |
| Pork..... | 4 | 4 | — 5 | 8 |
| Lamb .... | 5 | 4 | — 7 | 4 |

## POTATOES.

SPITALFIELDS, per Ton.

|  | L | s. |  | L | s. |
|---|---|---|---|---|---|
| Ox-Nobles | 3 | 10 | to | 4 | 10 |
| Middlings | 2 | 0 | — | 0 | 0 |
| Chats | 2 | 15 | — | 0 | 0 |
| Common Red | 3 | 10 | — | 4 | 0 |

Onions, 0s. 0d.—0s. 0d. per bush.

BOROUGH, per Ton.

|  | L. | s. |  | L. | s. |
|---|---|---|---|---|---|
| Ox-Nobles | 3 | 10 | to | 4 | 10 |
| Middlings | 2 | 0 | — | 2 | 10 |
| Chats | 1 | 15 | — | 0 | 0 |
| Common Red | 3 | 10 | — | 4 | 10 |

## HAY and STRAW, per Load.

| Smithfield.— | Hay | 80s. | to | 115s. |
|---|---|---|---|---|
|  | Straw | 40s. | to | 45s. |
|  | Clover | 100s. | to | 140s. |
| St. James's.— | Hay | 72s. | to | 132s. |
|  | Straw | 40s. | to | 48s. |
|  | Clover | 132s. | to | 140s. |
| Whitechapel.— | Hay | 80s. | to | 115s. |
|  | Straw | 38s. | to | 42s. |
|  | Clover | 90s. | to | 135s. |

AVERAGE PRICE OF CORN, sold in the Maritime Counties of England and Wales, for the Week ended April 13, 1827.

|  | Wheat. | | Barley. | | Oats. | |
|---|---|---|---|---|---|---|
|  | s. | d. | s. | d. | s. | d. |
| London* | 59 | 0 | 38 | 3 | 31 | 10 |
| Essex | 58 | 8 | 38 | 3 | 31 | 9 |
| Kent | 56 | 8 | 39 | 10 | 31 | 0 |
| Sussex | 54 | 11 | 41 | 6 | 29 | 6 |
| Suffolk | 55 | 5 | 37 | 2 | 31 | 9 |
| Cambridgeshire | 53 | 8 | 35 | 4 | 27 | 10 |
| Norfolk | 55 | 1 | 36 | 6 | 28 | 4 |
| Lincolnshire | 55 | 10 | 40 | 9 | 28 | 8 |
| Yorkshire | 55 | 5 | 41 | 10 | 29 | 0 |
| Durham | 56 | 1 | 42 | 4 | 35 | 6 |
| Northumberland | 53 | 9 | 37 | 6 | 32 | 4 |
| Cumberland | 61 | 8 | 39 | 8 | 35 | 5 |
| Westmoreland | 61 | 0 | 45 | 0 | 37 | 3 |
| Lancashire | 61 | 5 | 44 | 10 | 34 | 5 |
| Cheshire | 60 | 2 | 0 | 0 | 30 | 3 |
| Gloucestershire | 58 | 0 | 43 | 6 | 39 | 1 |
| Somersetshire | 54 | 10 | 39 | 10 | 29 | 2 |
| Monmouthshire | 59 | 4 | 47 | 9 | 0 | 0 |
| Devonshire | 55 | 10 | 38 | 2 | 27 | 1 |
| Cornwall | 59 | 8 | 38 | 9 | 36 | 11 |
| Dorsetshire | 54 | 4 | 39 | 3 | 34 | 6 |
| Hampshire | 56 | 4 | 39 | 8 | 30 | 0 |
| North Wales | 63 | 5 | 46 | 10 | 35 | 4 |
| South Wales | 57 | 9 | 43 | 5 | 26 | 1 |

* The London Average is always that of the Week preceding.

*Liverpool,* April 17.—The arrivals of Grain since Tuesday last have been more moderate, but the Corn Trade has been languid throughout the past week here, and in all our country markets,—in some degree owing to the fine seasonable weather we have for Seed-time;—for the few sales effected of Wheat and Indian Corn, the prices last quoted have been obtained, but all other kinds of Grain, Flour, and Meal, might have been bought at a trifling reduction. In Bonded Grain there has been nothing done, but of Flour in Bond, sales are daily making for export, at fully the prices quoted. At this day's market there was a very good demand for fine Mealing Oats, and sales to a fair extent were effected; for other descriptions, and for Wheat and every other article in the trade, sales were very limited,—and although, upon the whole, the prices of this day week were barely obtained, for any description of Grain, (excepting Indian Corn, which was fully 1s. per quarter higher,) we can make no decided alteration in the general prices last quoted. About 300 quarters of inferior Indian Corn, free, and about 200 quarters of Egyptian Beans, in bond, were offered by auction after the market, but withdrawn for want of bidders.

Imported into Liverpool, from April 9, to April 17, 1327, inclusive:—Wheat, 5,652; Barley, 514; Oats, 12,713; Rye, 74; Malt, 1,227; Beans, 909; Pease, 379 quarters. Flour, 3,097 sacks, per 280 lbs.; American Flour, 3,000 barrels; and Oatmeal, 616 packs, per 240 lbs.

*Bristol,* April 21.—The Corn markets here continue nearly the same as last week. The sales of good Oats are increased, and prices rather improved. Other kinds of Grain, &c. dull.—Wheat, from 6s. to 7s. 6d.; Barley, 4s. 3d. to 6s.; Beans, 6s. 3d. to 8s.; Oats, 3s. 1½d. to 4s. 1½d.; and Malt, 6s. to 8s. 3d. per bushel, Imperial. Flour, Seconds, 32s. to 43s. per bag.

*Guildford,* April 21.—Wheat, new, for mealing, 15l. to 17l. per load. Barley, 39s. to 44s.; Oats, 32s. to 42s.; Beans, 54s. to 58s.; Pease, grey, 60s. to 64s.; ditto, boilers, 62s. to 64s. per quarter.

*Horncastle,* April 21.—Wheat and Oats about 1s. per qr. lower; Barley 2s. higher; in other descriptions of Grain little or no alteration.—Wheat, 52s. to 55s.; Barley, 40s. to 44s.; Oats, 28s. to 35s.; Beans, 60s. to 65s.; and Rye from 40s. to 42s. per quarter.

*Ipswich,* April 21.—We had to-day again a remarkably short supply of all Corn, and prices were much as last week, as follow:—Wheat, 52s. to 62s.; Barley, 36s. to 41s.; and Beans, 46s. to 48s. per quarter.

*Manchester,* April 21.—The Corn trade continues in the same dull state as the last two or three weeks. At our market to-day, which was but thinly attended, Wheat of the best quality barely maintains last week's rates; a few sales were made, at an abatement of 1d. per bushel, and for inferior there was no demand. Oats may be quoted ½d. to 1d. per 45 lbs. lower. Beans being scarce, are advanced 1s. per quarter. The season for Boiling Pease being nearly over, what few remain are bought for provender. Malt is very dull, and to make sales to respectable houses, 1s. per load reduction has been submitted to. Flour continues very heavy in sale.

*Newcastle-on-Tyne,* April 21.—We had again a good supply of Wheat from the farmers this morning, but no arrivals coastwise during the week, and the millers being short of stock, the whole was readily sold at 2s. per quarter advance. Rye is 1s. per quarter dearer, and in demand. We have had no arrivals of Barley this week.

## COUNTRY CATTLE AND MEAT MARKETS, &c.

*Horncastle,* April 21.—Beef, 9s. per stone of 14 lbs.; Mutton, 8d.; Pork, 8d.; and Veal, 8d. to 10d. per lb.

*Manchester* Smithfield Market, April 18.—The supply of Beef and Mutton to this day's market was but small, but in general of good quality. The prices having advanced so much of late, of course causes a less consumption, and the butchers buy very sparingly. The supply of Calves is in general small, as our butchers get supplied by the dealers off market day. Pigs were in good supply, which readily found buyers, at last week's rates, and nearly the whole cleared off.—Beef, 4½d. to 8d.; Mutton, 7d. to 9½d.; Veal, 5d. to 6½d.; and Pork, 4½d. to 6d. per lb., sinking offal.

*Norwich Castle Meadow,* April 21.—The supply of fat Cattle to this day's market, was the largest we have had this year, and the prices nearly as last week, 7s. 6d. to 8s. 6d. per stone of 14 lbs., sinking offal; that of Store Stock was also very large; Scots sold at 4s. to 4s. 6d. per stone of what they will weigh when fat; Shorthorns, 3s. to 3s. 9d.; Cows and Calves, a more ready sale.—Meat: Beef, 7d. to 9d.; Veal, 6d. to 8d.; Mutton, 6d. to 8d.; Lamb, 9½d.; and Pork, 6d. to 8d. per lb.

At *Morpeth* Market, April 18, there was a great supply of Cattle; there being few buyers, they met with dull sale, at a reduction in price, and part were not sold. There was a short supply of Sheep, which sold readily at an advance in price. Beef, from 6s. 6d. to 7s. 6d.; Mutton, 9s. 6d. to 10s. 6d. per stone, sinking offal.

# COBBETT'S WEEKLY REGISTER.

Vol. 62.—No. 6.]     LONDON, SATURDAY, MAY 5, 1827.     [Price 6d.

" Gentlemen, that Mr. CANNING (I mention him as the CHAMPION
" of the party, a part for the whole) should defend, to the utmost, a
" system, by the HOCUS-POCUS TRICKS of which *he and his family*
" *get so much public money*, can cause neither in me nor any man suspi-
" cion or anger.;

> " For 'tis their duty, all the learned think,
> " To espouse the cause by which *they eat and drink.*"

" The ox knoweth his owner and the ass his MASTER'S CRIB; and
" these gentry, at least, equal the ox and the ass in knowledge and virtue;
" and are, moreover, superior to the Jews; for they do know their *Maker.*
" I will, however, boldly adduce their example as proof undeniable of the
" benefits the people would derive *from appointing their own Representa-*
" *tives; seeing that these gentlemen are ever true to their and their*
" *patrons' interests.* This identity of interest keeps all smooth, and the
" people may rest assured, that the same cause will ever produce the
" same effect; and that, whenever the people shall have *the appointment*
" *of their own House of Commons*, the public expenditure will be con-
" trolled, the public burdens diminished, the public money applied, in
" words, *liberty and property*, secured, and NOT TILL THEN."—Sir
FRANCIS BURDETT'S LETTER TO THE REFORM-MEETING AT THE CROWN
AND ANCHOR, 4TH APRIL, 1821.

## "THE CRIB."

## TO THE REFORMERS.

*Kensington, 3d May, 1827.*

MY FRIENDS.

When you have read the above motto, and are then told, that on Tuesday night last, Burdett sat perched side by side with Tierney, close at the back of Canning, ON THE TREASURY BENCHES, you will with difficulty be persuaded to believe,

L

Printed and Published by WILLIAM COBBETT, No. 183, Fleet-street.
[ENTERED AT STATIONERS' HALL.]

that the two *backers* have not, a last the CRIB fully in their eye! More of this, however, when I have spoken of what the newspapers tell us took place in the House of Commons on Tuesday last, the 1st of May, and in the House of Lords on Wednesday, the 2nd of May, on which two days the Houses appear to have been wholly engaged in hearing explanations of the motives of the INS and of the OUTS. The retiring Ministers chose to assume that they had been accused of conspiring and caballing against the exercise of the King's prerogative, and on that assumption they grounded the necessity of coming forward to clear themselves from the charge, though nobody cared one straw about the matter. Every one of them, in both houses, alleged that they quitted the Ministry because it had at the head of it a man notoriously an advocate for that which has been so long, so deceptiously and yet so ludicrously called *Catholic emancipation,* that old subject of amusement to the vulgar, that grand store of powder to throw in the eyes of fools, that " *annual farce,* " as Sir FRANCIS BURDETT called it about ten or twelve years ago, and to the acting of which, as he alleged, no honest man would give his

countenance by being present at the exhibition, *whereupon he walked out of the house!*

It is, perhaps, the greatest error, not to call it the most flagrant cheat, that ever was practised upon mankind, to suppose, or, to affect to suppose, that the putting of silk gowns upon the backs of a couple of score of lawyers ; that the hoisting of three or four lawyers up upon the bench; that the putting of thirty or forty Catholic aristocrats or relatives of Boroughmongers into Parliament; that the giving the Catholic aristocracy a chance of getting their noses occasionally into the King's council, privy or cabinet; that the putting of a dozen or fifteen Catholic peers into the House of Lords to enjoy their right of legislation, and which they did enjoy, and in both Houses of Parliament, too, until the foul combinations of the fanatics, combined with the Church clergy, shut them out of those seats in the reign of CHARLES II.: it being curious, indeed, to observe, that the Protestant Reformation was made; was begun, continued and completed through the reigns of good Queen Bess, the famous racking and military-law lady; and through that of JAMES I. and CHARLES I. without any one ever appearing to here thought of any thing so damnably unjust and odious as that of taking from these peers and gentlemen the possibility of sitting in the two Houses of Parliament, and that, too, merely because they and their fathers had never been apostates: however, the above are the things, which "*Catholic emancipation*" would effect, and nothing more; and, again I say, that there never was an error, not to call it a piece of cheatery, so gross as the hope that the accomplishment of that measure (*if accompanied with no other measures*) would produce, not *relief*, not deliverance from misery, not restoration to happiness and freedom, but, the smallest portion of good, that it would add one single miserable potatoe, one single mouthful of hog-meat, and bad hog-meat, or one single rag two inches square to the food or the dress of the average of the great body of Roman Catholic subjects of the King. What a farce, then, what monstrous insincerity, or what more than monstrous folly, to pretend, as Mr. Canning's adherents pretend, that this measure is necessary to the *tranquillity of Ireland*, and to the safety of the "*British empire*," as the foppish style of the day calls this ancient and once

happy kingdom! Yet, the old story; all this intriguing, all this squabbling and quarrelling; all this contest for power and emolument, all these coalitions, these splittings-up, these re-meltings and new castings, are, as it were, by common consent of all the parties, made to turn solely upon this question of emancipation; and, if one may judge from present appearances, on that question the opponents of the lucky Minister mean to found their first grand attack upon him. In the House of Commons, Mr. PEEL has rested his secession solely upon this ground. In the House of Lords, four of the seceders have done the same, while Lord MELVILLE tells us that he was *for Catholic Emancipation*, but that he would not sit in the Cabinet, unless the others, *who were against it*, continued to sit there also. He was very explicit in stating this; and, if, after this, any man can have a doubt as to the real motives of the parties, the head of that man must be of a very peculiar construction.

I may stop here to observe that, from the bottom of my heart I do think that, let Lord MELVILLE's motive be what it might, the act which it produced is likely to be of the greatest possible benefit to the country; because I cannot

L 2

help being convinced that the Duke of Clarence being at the head of the navy, being the source of promotion and of honour in that branch of service, on which the safety, the greatness, the glory of the country must, finally, depend in a great degree; I am firmly convinced, that his Royal Highness, being in this post, having no partialities to gratify, having, not even by possibility, any interest disconnected with that of us all, must be of the greatest importance, and may, perhaps, be the cause of our being finally defended against those growing powers, which are now silently towering up, each and every of them having, as its ultimate view, the pulling down of the maritime power of England. It is not likely, let the fate of Mr. CANNING be what it may, that *this appointment* will be overset. Here is the heir presumptive to the throne; here is a man that nobody will be disposed to displease. I look upon this appointment as permanent, as long as the Duke and his Majesty shall live; and, of such great importance do I deem it, that, were the permanence of the appointment to depend on the permanence of Mr. CANNING's power, I could almost wish that power to be permanent too, and I do wish it most

sincerely, unless it be destroyed by a reformed Parliament. A reformed Parliament would not, if it were to assemble to-morrow, wish to displace the Duke of Clarence. No appointment could have been so proper; and, though this change; this conflict of factions; this general *remu-menage*, this breaking up of all combinations, this putting an end to all the packing, by which the people were both deceived and injured; though this unexpected, and, as it were, providential stir, which is exposing and will finally put in the full blaze of light, so many things hitherto closely hidden from the people; though I am satisfied that this breaking up, this throwing of all the elements of faction into confusion, will finally lead to events more important than any one seems to anticipate, I should hail it as the great blessing to the country, were it, in the end, to have been found to produce nothing but this appointment of the Duke of CLARENCE.

To return from this digression: the Catholic question is to be considered by sensible people as nothing more than a *mere plea*, first, for the secession on the part of the Ex-Ministers, and, next, for the coalition on the part of the stragglers from the Whigs, who have gone over and placed themselves in the stern of the new Ministers, with the avowed object of giving their support to a man who deprecates even a discussion of this Catholic question, and who professes his resolution *not to make it a Cabinet measure.* Read the long, the laboured, the far-fetched, the strange compound of all that is unsatisfactory; read the speech of Mr. PEEL; then read the speeches in the Lords; and then common sense will tell you to believe that the Catholic question has, at bottom, nothing to do with the matter; that, as to Mr. PEEL, he wanted to be Minister himself, or, to secure the reversion of the office; and that, as to the other Ministers, they dislike Mr. CANNING on many accounts, which will clearly be seen to be the case, if we attend to the speech of Lord LONDONDERRY. He frankly, and I say, very sensibly, (though Doctor BLACK laughs at the idea,) stated solid objections, fair objections, and such as I, if I had been one of his order, and had not been desirous of seeing an end to the borough-system, should have stated for myself. The real state of the case is this: the owners of the land; the owners of the titles and the estates do not like Mr. CANNING; *they never liked*

him, and this has been visible upon scores of occasions. He is particularly disliked by *the whole body of the Church,* a body which smells danger where it is sensible to the olfactory nerves of nobody else. As far as he was the champion of that system, which has, at last, seen the country covered with crimes and with misery; as far as he was the champion of that system (as Burdett called him in his Letter to the Reformers, written six years ago), the possessors of borough power, and of all the good things flowing from that source, liked him very well, they cherished him, they applauded his alliterative jests; they patted him on the back; and, if he were detested by a considerable part of the people for his bold attacks upon them, and his vehement sallies against all their efforts to recover their rights, those who profitted from his efforts left him to the enjoyment of that detestation. But, the moment they discovered in him *designs to work up to the head*: the moment they perceived him assume the tone of " *liberality*," as the means of gaining support from the people or any portion of the people, that moment they began to suspect him; suspicion is, with them, quite enough; and, though they did not find it prudent to break with him, they appear to have formed a firm determination never to suffer him to have any great store of power. He, by no means less cunning than they, perceived the workings of their minds, and, that man must have been a very inattentive observer of the conduct of men in power, not to have perceived, that he, on his part, lost no opportunity of making the people, and the trading part of the people, particularly, believe that he was desirous of following, as BURDETT calls it, " the march of mind ;" as PEEL calls it, " the mental improvements of the age ;" and, as BROUGHAM calls it, " the astonishing growth of intellect." All this must have been the devil to the staunch adherents of the old system. It was, in fact, by implication, though not in words, beginning to turn his back upon that Old Sarum by which he had sworn to live and die. Then came all his projects about free-trade ; about emancipation of the New World ; about the right of people to choose their own governments. Meantime, his coquetry with the Whigs, his compliments on the Edinburgh Review ; his publishing his pamphlet speech at Ridgway's ; these would have marked out the staunch adherents of the borough-system for stark fools if they had failed to perceive what was his ultimate object. Both the parties knew the opinion entertained by each other of each other. They knew his designs, and he their determination to thwart them. By what *short cut* he turned their flank at last ; by what manœuvre ; by the assistance of what *angel* or whatever else, it would be hard to say ; but, turn their flank he did ; he got in their rear, secured possession of his post, and they had nothing left for it, but to turn round, abandon their designs of opposing him, place themselves under him in his " march of mind "; and subject themselves to every measure which he might deem necessary to the security of his own power and to the chipping of theirs away, until he had reduced them to a state of perfect insignificance : there was no alternative now left them but to do this or *to bolt.* They chose the latter ; and there the parties are. They resolve apparently, to drive him from his post if they can, and he, not less firmly, resolved to hold that post. Catholic emancipation, as it is called, is the mere pretence, and, if they try him upon that, I think it very probable, that they may be beate     Not beaten in their houses, perhaps, but, I think it very unlikely that they should

succeed in that which is their manifest design, namely, to raise a
stupid, a senseless, a beastly cry
of "NO POPERY" throughout
the country.

"Things are very much altered;
men's minds have undergone a
great change, with regard to this
No-Popery affair, since the day
that little PERCIVAL played his
pranks and that the corrupt and
stupid beasts of Liverpool pelted
with stones and dirt the accomplished and virtuous Mr. ROSCOE.
Men, the people of England,
particularly, have now had time
to consider that this cry, like the
howlings of the worst of the rabble
at the burning of GUY FAWKES,
is a trick played off upon them,
and of deluding them to their own
manifest injury. Of late years the
people have perceived what this
Church of England really is;
how much they pay for its maintenance; what immense sums it
takes out of the pockets of tradesmen, farmers and labourers; they
now know, that the tithes and the
rest of the Church property, which
were taken from a Catholic clergy
and given to a Protestant clergy,
USED TO MAINTAIN ALL
THE POOR, before the pro-
perty was so transferred. They
can clearly see, now, or else they
must be blinder than moles, that

there never would have been poor-
rates nor the necessity of poor-
rates, had it not been for the transfer of the Church property. It
is, therefore, impossible to make
them believe, that a change, that
even a change back again to
Popery would be ruinous to them.
They are not, then, to be frightened in this way any longer. They
now know well, that the cry of
the *Church being in danger* means,
that the *tithes* are in danger; that
the Church property is looked
upon as being in danger; that
there is danger that by restoring
the Roman Catholics to the enjoyment of their civil rights, the
Parliament may be induced to
bethink it of the necessity of going
a little further and restoring the
poor to their right of being maintained out of the property of the
Church instead of being maintained out of the poor-rates. In a
sort of rustic harangue which I
made to a company of farmers and
hop-planters at Andover, last fall,
and which harangue I prefaced
by the toast of "OLD ENG-
LAND", I explained to them
the origin of that toast, or, rather,
of that phrase, I observed, that
the phrase seemed, upon the face
of it, to have very little sense in
it; but that, when its origin was
known, it would appear to be very

expressive, very full of sense. We never heard people talk of or toast *Old* America, *Old* Holland, *Old* France, *Old* Germany, *Old* Scotland, *Old* Italy, or *Old* any thing but Old *England*; that the cause was this: after the Protestant Reformation had taken place; after the tithes and other Church property had been taken away from the poor, and had been given to Church of England parsons to be eaten and drunk by them and their wives and their children; after this had been done, and the Protestant Scotch King JAMES I. had come in and set his hungry northern vultures to tear to pieces, to mulct, to fine, to extort from, to tear away the very beds from under the remnant of the English Catholic gentlemen; these latter, not daring to give vent openly to their just indignation and hatred of the new order of things, used to give as a toast, "OLD England"; that is to say, England as *she formerly was*; the England of our forefathers; the happy England that knew nothing of poor-rates, and the duty and the practice of whose clergy it was to maintain the poor and comfort the widow, the orphan and the stranger; that England (continued I, as I was addressing myself principally to farmers and planters, from Farn-

ham, in *Surrey*), that England which saw WILLIAM of WICKHAM in the palace of Farnham; and who had never seen a bishop that sold small beer out of that palace as the late bishop of Winchester did! Such an explanation could not take place without producing great effect upon the minds of the persons present. That effect showed itself by all those visible signs demonstrative of strong feelings awakened in the breasts of the audience. Now, all the intelligent part of the community are become acquainted with facts like this. They are not therefore to be duped by a hypocritical cry of " no Popery." If Mr. CANNING were to answer that cry (as I would to a certainty), by a proposition made from his seat in Parliament, to make the Church property liable to the maintenance of the poor, that fine young maiden statesman, Mr. PEEL, might, I take it, pack up his budget of mental improvements, and get off to Oxford and take commons with his tutor, Dr. COPPLESTONE, and, between them, they might hatch another cashbill, or amuse themselves in any way that they liked, except that of bellowing about "no Popery," which might afford them a chance of getting broken heads. It was the Catholic Church, or, if you will, it was "Popery;" it was real Popery that caused the poor to be fed out of the revenues of the Church, and it was Protestantism; it was this Church of England, that took away the Church property from the poor, and that laid all the burthen of poor-rates, all the burthen of church-rates, that made overseers and paupers. Therefore, if I were Mr. Canning, I would answer the cry of "no Popery" with the cry of "no parsons that eat up the tithes "from the poor." And I would not confine myself to a *cry*; it is not a hullabaloo that would satisfy me; I would bring in a bill to give the nation all the benefits of Popery; to restore the nation to the blessings of Popery; that is to say, to cause horrid pauperism to cease, and to compel the clergy to maintain the poor, and pay the Church rates out of the revenues of the Church, as the Popish Clergy did. I would teach my Lord Eldon the good of Popery; the certain advantage of it. He talks about civil and religious liberty, and particularly about "religious liberty"; and he tells us that we can have no liberty if we do not have that. What the devil, my good lord, do you mean to say that we have been made more free

by letting the parsons swallow up all the tithes and other revenues of the Church, instead of being permitted to keep only just enough to exist upon while they distributed all the rest among the poor? Strange sort of doctrine this must be. Aye, the *Church is really in danger*, my lord; for, never will it keep all those tithes and other revenues to be devoured by itself for another ten years. Mr Canning must know, well, that the whole body of the Church of England clergy are his enemies. I think he is too cunning to believe that he will wheedle them round to his side. That he will never accomplish. The prudent course therefore is, to attack them; to be the assailing party, and *openly*, too: their tender place is their temporalities: iron bound like Achilles every where else, there they are as sensitive as the galled back of a horse. At their temporalities, therefore, say I; answer "no Popery" with that, my good Æolus, and you may dispense with the backings of Burdett and Brougham and all the shilly-shallies that are now looking on between hawk and buzzard to discover which will be most profitable,—to keep you in your seat or to help shove you out of it. You would have ninety-nine hundredths of the people with you. The people would make the aristocrats pull their hats off as they pass by your door; you would put your enemies under your feet, and would be Minister for life if you chose it. And, now, a word *in your ear*: if if you do not do this, somebody else will. You will, in all probability, be ousted, by endeavouring to play the aristocrat against aristocrats; by pretending your attachment to the Church, and to the inviolability of its possessions. You will, at last, be beaten by your present enemies: they will be beaten, too, by some man who will propose the measures here suggested; a new race of Ministers will surround the King, and you and your present opponents will, supposing you to have great good luck, all sink into one common grave of oblivion, and will hardly be remembered, except the memory of you be kept alive by your being the subject of a jest.

So much for the " no Popery" part of the affair; and, now, my friends, Reformers, you cannot refrain, I think, from viewing with delight this strange, yet total and complete breaking up and confounding of all the factions. I have said, in the Register, four or five times within the last seven years, that the system would be hastened towards its winding up by changes in the Ministry; that some men would become frightened, and would avail themselves of pretexts for quitting their posts; that new and more needy adventurers would come in; that these would resort to schemes of all sorts; that they would listen to every thing new, and would act off-hand at a dash; that men of different principles would get mixed up together; that thus there would be a constant vacillating and a constantly increasing weakness in the government. Now, look at the mixty-maxty mess that the thing presents at this moment: see the obstacles which the several parties themselves have created, each in the way of its own success. As to the Ministry, one does not know whether it be formed or not formed, even to this moment. No one seems to know whether those who are in the places are to stay in them or to go out to make room for somebody else. The Whigs, as they are called, have sent off a sort of detachment to join the Minister. It is really an affair of the lime-twigs. BROUGHAM and BURDETT and TIERNEY have flown across, and settled down near the food, just as you see two or three sparrows from a flock, or two or three rooks, or two or three magpies dispatched from the flock to reconnoitre; to ascertain by actual survey, whether there be likely to be safety in the concern. The main flock stay behind, remain perched upon their old branches. This is just the state of the thing at this moment. The Whigs have not *joined* the Minister: they are waiting to see whether it be *safe* to join. They have sent him a detachment of backers, in order to ascertain what strength he has. Mr. BROUGHAM appears to be very little more than the bearer of a flag of truce, coming over, under "safe conduct;" but he is ready to go back, of course; and BURDETT's errand seems to be of much about the same sort.

The most powerful body is, unquestionably, that which is in opposition to MR CANNING; that is to say, his former invaluable colleagues. But, even they, if they were to muster the utmost of their force, are not what they were before. They might, perhaps, be able to muster a majority in Parliament; but this would not carry them through, if the Minister had the pluck to make even a trifling advance towards the people. His former colleagues would very soon find an immense majority of the people against them: they would meet with execrations from every quarter and corner. He will find, if he take up the muster-roll, that the Lord Charleses form the most formidable body against him. Let him propose to take away their salaries and pensions; let him propose to pinch their purses; or, rather, to pull their hand out of the public purse; let him do this, and he is safe, for the present, at least. But, if he will assail nobody; if he think to triumph and to persevere in his eulogiums on Old Sarum, he will not die a Minister, unless his glass be very nearly run. Still, the old bitter Pittites will never be again what they have been for the last thirty years: their strength is divided; and, though Mr. CANNING may be unable to stand as a Prime Minister, he would, in an opposition to them, be, in this talking and printing age, a most formidable foe.

At any rate, my friends, good to the people must come out of this thing. It is impossible to see what this chopping and changing will finally produce; impossible to see, precisely, how the thing will work; but it must produce good to the people. Each faction, and each limb of a faction, carefully avoids all allusion to the

state of the country. All the
ruin and misery and crime and
dreadful starvation in some parts;
all allusion to the cause or causes
of these; but each faction have
these things in their mind. They
talk about nothing but Catholic
emancipation; but, Mr. CAN-
NING's ranks would have been
full; he would have had crowds
of supernumerary statesmen if it
had not been for the serious, the
alarming, the increasing distresses
and misery of the country. I, for
my part, am thoroughly convinced, that there must be, at no
distant day, a general convulsion
or a *peaceable reform.* Lord
WESTMORELAND is reported to
have asked whether a Minister
was bound to continue to serve
the King as a Minister, in case
his Majesty were to place *a reformer* at the head of the Ministry.
I answer, by no means; and, I
verily believe, that his Lordship
will not be called upon to serve
under such a Minister; but I also
verily believe, that there will be
such a Minister, at no very distant day; and, I wish I could believe, that Sir FRANCIS BURDETT
had now gone over to sit at the
back of Mr. CANNING, in order
to have an opportunity of suggesting to him the absolute necessity of becoming such Minister.

Why should not Mr. CANNING do
this? Why should he not turn his
back upon Old Sarum? Why
should he be afraid of a charge of
inconsistency, after the noble example just now set him by Westminster's pride and England's
glory? Look at the motto to this
paper, my friends. Read the article which will follow this; observe that the Baronet accused
this Mr. Canning of extolling the
system for the sake of the public
money that he and his family got
by the system: observe that the
Baronet, writing to a meeting of
reformers, told them that the nation never could have justice, until there should be a reform of the
Parliament: observe, that he solemnly assured that meeting, that
his abilities, be they what they
might, should always be exerted
for the destruction of this system, and for the producing of a
constitutional reform. Then behold him actually placing himself, placing his corporeal substance at the back of him,
close at his back, so as for his
knees to touch his shoulders, professing his intention to give his
support to that very man whom
he had distinctly accused of supporting the system, merely for the
sake of what he and his family
got by it, out of the public money;

accusing him of being the champion of the system by which liberty and property were taken
from the people, and charging
him with' being as full' of knowledge and virtue as the ass, because with equal accuracy he
knew the CRIB at which he fed;
that is to say, the crib of the public provender. When I saw the
Baronet seated there, what was I
to expect short of a declaration,
that the champion of the system
had become the champion of reform? Not a word about the matter,
from the Baronet, who has, all at
once, become enamoured of that
question of Catholic Emancipation, which, ten years ago, he
called a despicable farce! And,
he was not decided about this
question either; for his words, as
explained by Mr. BROUGHAM,
meant that *he by no means wished
that question to be agitated.* He
did say, once, at the Crown and
Anchor Tavern, that he might,
for ought he knew, be turned to
an *oyster,* at last; and, really, it
is for you to guess whether the
shell be not now actually creeping
over him. If this should be the
case, and if the Minister, who is
said to be a man of great taste,
should be particularly fond of
shell-fish, down goes " Purity
of Election " at a single gulp!

In the mean while, the celebrated 23d of May is approaching,
and that is the Baronet's and the
Rump's anniversary dinner, to
chaunt forth the praises of " Purity of Election." I do hope that
we shall, then, have some explanation, relative to the pledges
which the Baronet has; doubtless,
obtained from Mr. CANNING, of
his intention to favour the great
cause of Parliamentary Reform.
Some one will, to be sure, ask for
such explanation, in spite of the
howlings, the *wands* and the nails
of the Rump. This daring humbug will, assuredly, not be played
off now, without some inquiry
into the motives of the Baronet in
giving his support to this calum-
niator of reformers, this jester
upon OGDEN, this champion of
the " crib." If some one do not
demand this explanation, if some
one do not ask what can be the
meaning of this change, Westminster is sunk for ever, and is
baser than any rotten borough in
the kingdom.

We hear nothing of Lord GREY
in this affair. The press has not
been able; has not dared to publish one single word, expressive
of Lord Grey's approbation of
Mr. Canning and his crew.' I
should suppose that his Lordship
can have very little inclination to

embark on board a vessel ,so crazy. He may dislike, and he must dislike, the late Ministry; but, he must know that, unless we have some declarations relative to acting upon new principles, it is monstrous to pretend that the new set is better than the last; and, my opinion of Lord GREY must always have been very erroneous, if he would, for the sake of any emoluments, or any pitiful political triumph, undertake that which he did not look upon as being for the good of the country at large. Besides this, I gather from several of his speeches, that he understands the nature of the real dangers of the country. He must know that those dangers are not to be obviated without a reform of the Parliament; he must know that nothing short of that is capable of grappling with these dangers. He is almost the only public man, if not the only one, who has never been wrong upon the subject of the paper-money. PITT put him upon the committee to report on the affairs of the Bank, at the time of the stoppage in 1797. He disdained all participation in the report; he stated that he disagreed with those who made it; he said that he washed his hands of it; and, even at that time he declared that

the evils which would result from the proceedings of that day, must, in the end, be terrible to the nation. When Peel's bill was passed, he found the cry in its favour so general, that he did not actually oppose it; but, he expressed his fears that the Marquis of LANSDOWN, who had stated that, it could be carried into effect without inconvenience, would find himself disappointed in his calculations. Here we have these two men before us now; Mr. CANNING has the Marquis at his back; but, greatly deceived am I if he ever receive a word of support from Lord GREY. Why this nobleman do not come boldly forward and explicitly state all his views as to the situation of the country and the remedies necessary to be applied, it is not for me to say: I cannot even guess why he does not do it; but this I know, that, whatever he may think of the matter, he is able, at this moment, to render his country greater services than any other man and than all other men put together. He has every thing for him. Good character, stands high in the opinion of every body, as to his integrity; great talents, long experience.; and a conviction in the mind of every man, that if he were to commit error it would be from accident and never from intention. For my part, I can never account for such men remaining silent and inactive at such a time; and, as far as I have known any thing of mankind, I have never been able to discover that backwardness of this sort was ascribed to the best of motives.

However, every man must do as he likes. The thing has been put into a stir by this little incident of Lord Liverpool; and, I am satisfied, that it will work along in some shape or other, without ceasing to operate, until the end of the paper-system shall arrive. That system will have made great progress before this day twelvemonth, and when Mr. CANNING's remedies shall come to be agitated, if he should remain in office so long, he will find the Catholic question of no more importance than the question relative to the treatment of sheep and of jack-asses, so interesting to poor Mr. MARTIN, who is now, it appears, gone upon his travels, leaving the poor donkeys without a protector.

WM. COBBETT.

P. S. Oh! I had almost forgot, but, pray do not let us forget, that, among the other novelties which present themselves, and that not the least ominous, the PRESS: aye, that the " respectable press" has misbehaved at last. In both Houses it is stated *is in the pay of the* It is now found out
"
"
m
m

secession of the seven sages without previous concert or communication. However, no matter about their purity, whether they be actually at the " crib " or by what herd-like faculty they may all agree together, no doubt we shall see them one and all for the " march" of mind," the " improved state of society;", and, it would be hard, indeed, if the " best possible instructor " was not for the " astonishing growth of intellect." In short, they are all fairly upon this scent, and, now the parties who have so long found them so convenient and manageable, must consider them as fairly let slip from the leash!

## " ENGLAND'S GLORY "
### AND
## MR. CANNING.

#### TO

*The Electors of Westminster.*

Kensington, 20 June, 1827.
GENTLEMEN,

It was not my desire to trouble you with any remarks on " GLORY's " conduct. His adventures since the month of February last were quite sufficient to render all further notice of him wholly unnecessary; but, this recent affair between Mr. CANNING and him really does call so loudly for something, from some quarter or other, that I cannot remain silent. As a mere *duelling* affair, I should, probably, only have joined others in laughing at "*Glory's*" conduct in it; but, the correspondence, is this case, involves matter of political *principle* and *consistency* (that precious quality in "Glory's" eyes); and, therefore, the thing becomes matter of importance, more especially as he is a member for your populous city, and as he still occasionally talks about a *Reform in the Parliament*.

The short history of the quarrel between "*Glory*" and Mr. Canning is this:—The former being at the time passing his *three months* " in the *custody* of the Marshal of the King's Bench," wrote and sent to the Chairman of what was called " *a Reform Dinner*," on the 4th of April last, a letter to be read to the persons then and there assembled. In this letter he spoke *evil* of Mr. Canning, as you will presently see. The latter, who was then in England, took no notice of this letter at the time; and soon afterwards went to France. But, as soon as "*Glory's*" three months "*custody*" were expired, Mr. Canning came home, and wrote to "*Glory*," by the hands of Lord William Bentinck, demanding (and; as you will see, in a most peremptory style) a *disavowal*, or, the "*other alternative*." The *disavowal was made;* and that,

too, in the most *prompt* manner! There was no want of *industry* on this occasion! There was no *shilly-shally*. Prompt enough, saith, in this affair.

Now, gentlemen, if this matter had been a mere *duelling* affair, if it had embraced nothing of politics, it would have passed wholly unnoticed by me. But, you will find, that the *disavowal* strikes at the very root of political justice; and that, if it be to pass uncensured, all that *responsibility* in public functionaries, for which we have always been contending, and for which "Glory" has always been contending, is completely swept away.

We will now take the documents, beginning with " *Glory's*" letter aforementioned. And, here, before I proceed further, let me observe, that I give no *nick-name*. This is the name, or title, given to him by his own band of creatures; his own RUMP; his own friends and partizans. Does he merit it? *Is* he the "*Glory of England?*" Then it is a title *due* to him; and it can be no *nick-name*, no mockery. Is he unworthy of it? Does the application of it to him excite laughter? Then let him no longer surround himself with the band of base flatterers, who have bestowed it on him; and who, by the various arts, of which I shall by and by speak, extort from you that support of him, which your own good sense and honesty, if left to themselves, would never suffer you to give. Gentlemen, we hear enough of flattering *courtiers;* we despise the parasites of *kings;* we think ourselves fully warranted, in this case, to express our contempt of the receiver as well as of the utterer of the flattery; we are moreover, in the habit of commending blunt sincerity, and I hope, this commendation is not unjustly given to us as a nation. But, Gentlemen, Electors of Westminster, was ever flattery so fulsome; was ever flattery so nauseous; did ever subject of the Grand Monarque of France or slave of Turkish Sultan, utter flattery so base and disgusting as that which has been poured on this man by those creatures who have the audacity to put forth their slavish eulogiums in *your name?* We have heard of numerous instances of hyperbolical flattery, but never of one equal to " *England's Glory,*" applied to a fickle, an irresolute, an inert, and inefficient being, who himself acknowledges that *he can do no good,* though placed in a situation, where even the poorest of talents might, and must, if honestly exerted, do *great good.* To apply an appellation like this to such a man, is not only shameful in itself, but it would seem to indicate a widely prevalent want of public principle; and it must have a tendency to disgust men of real worth, and to make them despise, and, of course, to be careless about the fate of, a people who can be at once so base and so unjust. If this man, who can, or, at least, who really does, *do nothing,* be " *England's Glory;* " if he be " *Westminster's Pride;* " if this be the way in which *the people* estimate, what man can think it a duty to make real and efficient exertions for such a people? However, let me dismiss this topic, for the present, by expressing my conviction, that this preposterous and ridiculous appellation has been given without *your* sanction. But, let me add, that it is your *bounden duty* to interfere, and that, too, in an efficient manner, whenever the occasion again may arise. I know, that *you* do not sanction those contemptible annual festivals, where " *purity of election* " is chaunted by impudent men, who have, in effect, made your great city no better than a *rotten borough,* and where the hero of the Rump has the modesty to sit and hear 'himself styled the "Glory of England;" but, those festivals are held in *your name;* and it becomes you to vindicate your character.

To return from this digression, I shall, as I before said, insert the *documents,* beginning with " *Glory's* " letter to the Lord Mayor, who was Chairman of the

M

" *Reform Dinner.*" Then will come Mr. Canning's demand of a disavowal, or ———! Then GLORY's *prompt* and ample disavowal; and then the curious letter of Mr. KINNAIRD (one of "GLORY's" chickens!) accusing the editor of the COURIER of *forgery* and complaining of *breach of confidence.* Lord WILLIAM BENTINCK's exposure of the nonsense of this complaint will close the collection, which collection, unless you separate yourselves from the *Rump* and their hero, will long remain a deep stigma on yourselves ; for, the question naturally arises : if such be " Westminster's *Pride*," what must *the people* of Westminster be.

*King's Bench Prison, April* 4, 1821.

MY LORD,

You will not, I am sure, doubt the sincerity with which I express my regret at being unavoidably detained from the Meeting of this day. My heart is however amongst you, and my mind altogether in the great cause which you are met to promote. That cause has been supported by so much ability, acute reasoning and profound learning, that it baffles ingenuity to offer any thing importantly new upon the subject. Nor do I now take up my pen with the vain hope of doing any thing more than expressing my respect for the gentlemen assembled. Indeed, the question is itself so plain, and has been so elaborately set forth and illustrated, that to use the slang of the Honourable House, the people out of doors, the profane vulgar, perfectly understand it. For in this enlightened age and country, no one is, I take it, so ignorant as not to know, that *to have is to have*, which is *the whole*

of the subject; that if what I acquire, either by good fortune or the sweat of my brow, another can take from me without my own consent, it is not my property, but his; that in that case I am tenant at will; and that if any man, or set of men, can make laws to imprison my person, to which I have never consented, my person is as insecure as my property ; in other words, that " Liberty and Property," the watchword of our forefathers, are sounds as senseless and empty as the beating of a drum—as

"Sounding brass or a tinkling cymbal."

* * * * *

Gentlemen, that *Mr. Canning,* I mention him as the champion of the party, *a part for the whole,* should defend to the utmost a system by the hocus pocus tricks by which *he and his family get so much public money,* can cause neither me nor any man suspicion or anger.

" For 'tis their duty, all the learned think,

" To espouse the cause *by which they eat and drink.*"

Do I therefore say the House of Commons is corrupt ? Not I indeed, even though I should run no risk of being transported—no such thing ; they are true to the interest of those who send them. " *The ox knoweth his owner,* and the *ass his master's crib,*" and they at least equal the ox and the ass in knowledge and virtue, and are, moreover, superior to the Jews, for they do know their Maker. I will, however, boldly adduce their example, as proof undeniable, of benefits the people would derive from appointing their own representatives, seeing that these gentlemen are ever true to their own and their patrons' interest. This identity of interest keeps all smooth, and the public may rest assured that the same cause will ever produce the same effect, and that whenever the public shall have the appointment of their own House of Commons, the public expenditure will be controlled, the public burthens diminished, the public money applied to public purposes, and the public happiness and prosperity, in other words, " Liberty and Property" secured, and not till then. In the mean time I take this opportunity of expressing my satisfaction at the cause being in such good hands, and to add, that the Reformers may always command, such as they are, my services in any way or situation which they can think useful.

I remain, Gentlemen,
Your most obedient,
PRANCIS BURDETT.

---

TO SIR FRANÇIS BURDETT.

*Gloucester Lodge, June 7, 1821.*

Sir—In a letter bearing your signature, and purporting to have been addressed by you to the Chairman of a dinner of Parliamentary Reformers, on the 4th of April, which was published in several of the newspapers of the following day, a liberty is taken with my name, as little justifiable (in my judgment) by differences of public opinion, as it is reconcileable with the ordinary courtesies of private life.— The obvious meaning of that passage in your letter of which I complain, is, to impute to me, that in upholding the present system of Representation in the House of Commons, *I am actuated by the corrupt and dishonourable motive of a personal pecuniary interest.* —It cannot be matter of surprise to you, that I should feel myself under the necessity of *requiring at your hands a disavowal of the imputation* which that passage appears to convey. Should you be unable, or unwilling, to afford me a satisfactory explanation upon this point, *I have then to demand of you the only other reparation which an injury of such a nature admits.* It can hardly be necessary to state to you, Sir, the reason why this demand has not been sooner made: but I owe it to myself to preclude the possibility of any doubt or misrepresentation, as to the causes of that delay. The first and natural impulse of my own feelings, was to address myself to you the instant that I had read your letter in the newspapers. But it was represented to me by the friend whom I requested to take charge of my letter, that your then situation rendered it impossible for you to accept the second of the alternatives proposed to you (a circumstance which, I must be permitted to observe, considerably aggravated the offence offered to me); that the utmost which I could obtain

from you was an engagement to afford me satisfaction, so soon as the term of your confinement should have expired; that the interval must be full of hazard as to secrecy; that without in any degree impeaching either your honour, or that of any gentleman whom you might select, the mere fact (which could hardly be concealed) of a communication between me or any friend of mine, and the King's Bench, could not fail to excite suspicion; and that such suspicion would necessarily be strengthened by my prolonging my stay in England till the middle of May, after having repeatedly and publicly announced my intention of waiting only for Mr. Lambton's motion of the 17th of April. Yielding for the time (and I know not how I could have done otherwise), to the force of these representations, it remained for me only to keep my own counsel, and to quicken, as much as possible, my return from the Continent. I arrived here yesterday evening. My first business on my arrival has been to communicate with Lord William Bentinck, who has the goodness to undertake to deliver this letter to you, *and to settle, on my behalf, all necessary arrangements on the matter to which it relates.* I assure you, upon my honour, that Lord William Bentinck is the only person who has any knowledge of this letter, or of my purpose to write it.

I have the honour to be,
Sir,
Your most obedient Servant,
GEO. CANNING.

---

TO THE RIGHT HON. GEORGE CANNING.

*St. James's-place, June 8, 1821.*

Sir—I am not aware of having made any unjustifiable allusion to you, or of having said of you in my letter to the Chairman of the Reform Meeting, more than *all political men, who benefit from the system which they advocate, are fairly and necessarily subject to.* The letter in question is now before me; and I am at a loss for a form of words in which I could have more guardedly marked the disqualification under which I conceive yourself and others to be from giving authority to your opinions on Parliamentary Reform, and at the same time have

M 2

avoided making any allusion whatever to personal character. Not having intended, and not having made (as I read the letter), any such allusion at the time, I cannot now hesitate in a more particular manner; *to disclaim having ever had such an intention.*

I have the honour to be,
Sir,
Your most obedient humble Servant,

(Signed) FRANCIS BURDETT.

---

## TO SIR FRANCIS BURDETT.

*Gloucester Lodge, June 9, 1821.*

Sir—Lord William Bentinck has just delivered to me the answer, which you have transmitted to his Lordship, through Mr. Kinnaird, to the letter which I addressed to you on Thursday. Lord William Bentinck's opinion (with which my own feelings entirely coincide) satisfies me that I can have no other reply to make to your Letter, than to express my acknowledgment for the frankness and promptitude, with which you have disclaimed any intention of personal offence.

I have the honour to be,
Sir,
Your most obedient Servant,

(Signed) GEORGE CANNING.

---

## TO THE EDITOR OF THE MORNING CHRONICLE.

*St. James's Square, June 12, 1821.*

Sir—Some one has *forged* my name to a letter to the Editor of the *Courier,* authorizing the publication of a correspondence between Mr. Canning and Sir Francis Burdett. Lord William Bentinck has assured me he knows nothing about the matter. I did authenticate copies of the letters that had passed between the two gentlemen in question. But in so doing, *at the special request of Lord William Bentinck,* I stated that, although Sir Francis Burdett could have *no possible objection to their publication,* I should think it *unbecoming on his part to be a party to it.* As far as my own opinion went, of course, I could have opposed no obstacle to that which I thought *would do so much credit to Sir Francis*

Burdett. But his Lordship will recollect I stated *my surprise* if Mr. Canning *should wish to give notoriety to such a transaction.*

I am, Sir,
Your obedient Servant,
DOUGLAS KINNAIRD.

---

We have been requested by Lord William Bentinck to give insertion to the following Letter:—

## TO THE EDITOR OF THE MORNING CHRONICLE.

*Park-lane, June 13, 1821.*

Sir—A letter from Mr. D. Kinnaird, which appeared in your Paper of this day, in reference to the publication of the Correspondence between Mr. Canning and Sir Francis Burdett, requires from me the following explanation:— Certainly, the paragraph to which both our names are signed, though written by us, was not written as *a letter to the Editor of the Courier,* or to any other person. It was intended simply to authenticate the correspondence which it accompanied. The mistake, by which the Editor of the *Courier* considered it as addressed to himself, is explained by him in his Paper of this evening. With respect to the question of publishing, it is perfectly true that Mr. D. Kinnaird, though publication had his perfect assent, and though his authentication of the correspondence was given with *that view,* declined to be *a party to it.* But it is equally true, that publication, in some form or other, was always required by Mr. Canning, and *was uniformly so stated by me to Mr. Kinnaird,* from the moment that there appeared a prospect of the affair being brought to an amicable termination. I regret the mistake into which the Editor of *The Courier* has fallen, more especially as it has given rise to Mr. Kinnaird's letter, which although (as I am convinced, from all that has passed between us upon this occasion) without the intention of the writer, seems *to detract something from that complete satisfaction* to the feelings as well as to the honour of both the parties principally concerned, with which I can truly say Mr. Kinnaird and I mutually flattered ourselves, that this transaction had happily terminated.

I am, Sir,
Your obedient Servant,
W. BENTINCK.

· The same letter *mutatis mutandis* appeared in *The Courier* of last night, with the following note addressed by the Editor of *The Courier* to Lord W. Bentinck, which, says the Editor, his Lordship wishes to be annexed to his own letter :

The Editor of *The Courier* presents his compliments to Lord William Bentinck, and has the honour to inform him, with reference to that part of Mr. Douglas Kinnaird's letter which relates to the alleged "*forgery*" of *his name*, that the mistake originated in a practice ordinarily adopted in giving publication to the communications of Correspondents, viz. that of causing them to be addressed to the Editor of the Journal in which they appear. It is surely superfluous to add, that there could have existed no motive of any other kind for thus introducing the Correspondence.

The following is the *forgery* complained of by Mr. DOUGLAS KINNAIRD.

TO THE EDITOR.

· SIR—The following Correspondence (Nos. 1, 2, 3,) having passed between Mr. Canning and Sir Francis Burdett, we declare it to be authentic.

W. BENTINCK,
DOUGLAS KINNAIRD

June 11, 1821.   ‗

Thus we have all these curious documents before us ; and, let us now see, whether you, Gentlemen, are ready to acknowledge, that *they* too are " *Westminster's Pride.*"

As to the practice of duelling, though I by no means pretend that it includes any *moral offence*, it is any thing rather than a trial of *courage ;* for, nine times out of ten, the parties are urged on to it by *fear ;* and we accordingly see the most perfect cowards fighting duels. Shakespeare has admirably illustrated the real character of the duellist in the play, called " *What you will.*" Sir Andrew, a stupid drunken Knight, has *fallen into disgrace* with his Mistress, he is told ; and he is also told, that he must regain his lost ground by " some " notable expedient of wit or of " *valour.*" Whereupon, after pretty nearly *ascertaining* that his rival *will not fight*, he sends him a challenge, written in a " curst and brief." style and manner. But, despicable as the thing is ; many as are the poltroons which it palms on the world for men of valour and of honour ; monstrous as it is to suppose, that the fighting of a duel can make a rogue an honest man, and still more monstrous as it is to appeal to a pistol for the decision of an argument : still, if a man acknowledges the *legitimacy* of this mode of settling differences ; if he will have the advantage attending the reputation of duel-fighting ; if he will pretend to merit on account of a supposed readiness in him to fight duels ; then, he subjects him‑

self to the *laws of duelling*, and his conduct must be judged of by those laws.

Now, it is clear, that, when the complaining party comes, at once, to the point, and makes *disavowal* the condition, and the express and *only* condition, of *not fighting*, to disavow is to acknowledge *fear to fight*. This is so plain a thing that it cannot be questioned by any one. If, indeed, the injured, or pretended injured, party, call for an *explanation*, and in civil terms, *without accompanying the call with a statement of the fighting alternative*; then, even a high dueller, or, as they call it, " *man of honour*," may *explain*, and may, if truth will bear him out, disavow. But, to say to a fighter, " you shall *disavow or fight*," is to cut off the possibility of honourable *parley*. Upon this principle all men act. If the honest labourer be told to retract *on pain of a slap in the face*, nothing but *fear of the slap* will make him retract.

Here I leave this matter, it being, in my eyes, of far less importance than the political consequences of this, as Mr. Canning calls it, " *prompt* disavowal." Let us see what " *Glory's*" assertion was. It was this: that Mr. Canning defended to the utmost

a system, by the hocus-pocus tricks of which *he* and his *family* got much *public money*; that he espoused a cause by which *he* and his *family eat and drink*; that he was true to those who put it in his power to get this money, and to eat and drink, in like manner as the ox knoweth his *owner*, and the ass his *master's crib*.

This is the clear, the fair, the *only* meaning of the words; and, now, what says " Glory" of those words in his disavowal, or disclaimer? Why, that he had *no intention to make any allusion whatever to PERSONAL character!* The deuce he did not! Well! Let him then keep a glossary-monger to be the bearer of his despatches; for, it will henceforward be extremely dangerous to place the smallest degree of reliance on his *words* as they appear on the paper. Nothing *personal! No allusion* even to *personal character!* Good God! Then this may not be paper, on which I am writing, nor is this a pen that I hold in my hand. My name may not be William; and even " Glory" himself, as he once curiously enough observed, in one of his Crown-and-Anchor harangues, " may be an *oyster*." Plain as " *Glory*," in his Bardolph-like fustian, seems to represent the proposition, "that to have is to have," why are we too enlightened not to doubt of that, if we are to be made to believe, that here was no intention to allude to personal character?

*Personal character!* What! Tell a man that he defends a fraudulent (*hocus-pocus*) system for the sake of the money that *he* and his *family* get by it; tell him that he defends this false and wicked thing for the purpose of getting *eatables* and *drinkables;* tell him that he is, as to his employers, what the ox and ass are to their owner, and not to omit even the *crib:* and, after all this to say, that you mean *no* allusion to *personal character!* It must be confessed, that here is no *shuffle,* no *equivocation:* it is a plain, undisguised *swallowing of words;* and never did hungry ploughman more heartily open his shoulders to bolt down his master's bacon. If, to tell a man these things be not to allude to his *personal character,* neither is it to allude to his personal character to say, that he is a *charlatan,* a *thief,* a *mean dependent toad-eater,* a fellow that supports villany for the sake of getting *enough to eat and drink.*

But, Gentlemen, there is a great deal more than this *swallowing of* words (which is certainly not the least disgraceful sort of *eating*) which hangs to the new doctrine here sent forth by "Glory." It amounts to this: that a man may support a hocus-pocus system for the purpose of getting money; for the purpose of getting eatables and drinkables; that he may be to the chiefs of such a system what the ox is to his owner and the ass to his master's crib: and that, *notwithstanding all this,* he may be a man of *good character,* an *honourable man!* Mind the poison of this doctrine; mark the mischievous tendency of it; and find out, if you can, from "Glory," what *he* would deem *bad character;* what *he* would deem a *dishonourable man.* Mark, I pray you, the sweeping effect of this doctrine! A man may be a peculator, that is to say, a *public robber;* he may *give or take bribes;* he may be a *partial judge;* he may be a *traitor* or *rebel;* and yet bring no stain upon his *personal character!* He is still to be deemed an *honourable man!* He may, with all these atrocious crimes on his head, be the "*Pride* of Westminster:" and may possibly arrive at that pinnacle where the Rump will hail him as "England's Glory."

In order to shift off the charge

of direct individual imputation "Glory" generalizes his assault, and says, that his letter (as *he* read it! Oh, God!) said "no "more than all *political* men, "who *benefit* from a system "*which they advocate*, are *fairly* "and *necessarily* subject to." What "Glory!" are *all* political men who benefit from a system which they advocate *fairly* and even *necessarily* subject to be accused of acting, in such cases, merely from motives of getting money, and getting food and drink! If this be the case no government can ever be carried on by *paid* functionaries; for all such must be mean and base wretches. Now *Mr. Monro and the Congress* are all *paid.* They all *benefit* from the system that they *advocate;* and are *they also, fairly* and NECESSARILY, subject to have imputed to them the corrupt and base motive that your letter (whether justly or not I, *for my part*, do not pretend to say) imputes to Mr. Canning! Go and try your bombast a little upon some Virginian, and see how quickly he will teach you the meaning of words!

Gentlemen, talk not of aristocratical pride and insolence, if you acknowledge this to be sound doctrine. No man, according to this doctrine, is to be *paid* for any *public services;* for, as to the qualification, contained in the word "*political,*" what does it amount to? What is *political!* Why, connected with, or having relation to, *public affairs;* belonging to the *management of a nation's concerns.* Every Minister, every person employed in the affairs of government, every governor of a colony and all those employed under him; every *judge, justice of the peace,* and even the *King himself:* they are all *political men:* and, according to "*Glory,*" if they be *paid;* or, if they *benefit* from that mode of governing which they *advocate* (and which it is their *duty* to advocate, mind); if they *benefit* from it, that is to say, if they be *paid* for their services, they are all "*fairly* and *necessarily*" subject to the charge of advocating it for the sake of the money that it brings them; for the sake of getting eatables and drinkables; and, they are to be compared to the ox and the ass. So that, it comes to this, that all *political* men are to serve the public *for nothing;* and, of course, are to consist of those who have great wealth of their own! The folly of this is manifest enough; but the aristocratical insolence of it exceeds its folly. Why has "*Glory*" wealth? Not because nature has given him any particular claim to it; but, because there have been, and are "*political* men who benefit "from the system they advocate" to prevent people from taking it from him. The fact is, that, in order to fritter away the imputation on Mr. Canning, "Glory" makes a general sweep at all functionaries, in all times, under all circumstances, and in all countries.

But, Gentlemen, electors of Westminster, are you to forget, then, the *colleague* of " *Glory*!" That colleague is, indeed, no *placeman himself*; but Mr. Canning's *family* was introduced. And, is Mr. *Hobhouse's* family to be forgotten? Mr. Hobhouse's father has, for years and years, been a *Commissioner of the Nabob of Arcot's Debts*, with a salary of 1,200 *l.* a year. Mr. Hobhouse's uncle is Secretary to the famous *Sidmouth*, and has, of course, been an adviser and assister of that renowned man during the whole of his renowned works. The family of Mr. Hobhouse has received more public money than the family of Mr. Canning, the latter himself included. Oh! but it is *uncandid* to make Mr. Hobhouse answer-able for this, though, in all human probability his fortune will consist, in part at least, of what his father receives in this way, and though he lives under the roof of that father, studying, day and night, the doctrines hostile to "po-"litical men *benefitting* from the " system *they advocate!*" But, then, where is the *justice* of the imputations on Mr. Canning? If one of the Hobhouses; if a son of the *Commissioner of Carnatic Debts* (an office that I dare not properly characterize), if such a person be to be palmed upon *you* by " Glory," what reason; what sense; what consistency; what *decency* is there in "Glory's" imputing base and corrupt motives to *all* men engaged in the management of public affairs? What decency was there in *his* dragging forth the pension to the mother and sisters of Mr. Canning? It is very true, that " *to have is to have ;*" and, Gentlemen, be you assured, that for Mr. Canning's family to *have* public money is just as well for you as for Mr. Hobhouse's family *to have* it.

So much for " Glory's" doctrines of *disinterestedness*, of which, probably, I shall say more by and by. I now come to the part that Mr. KINNAIRD has acted in this Westminster drama. He writes to the Morning Chronicle complaining that the Courier (or some one in it) has *forged his name*! Forged his name! Now, mind, here is a certificate of authenticity. It is *signed by Mr. Kinnaird*. He is requested to sign it by Lord W. Bentinck who receives it from him. The latter states to him, *at the time of signing, that Mr. Canning requires that it shall be published*. It is published; and, because there is, at the top of it, " *To the Editor of the Courier*," Mr. Kinnaird says that this is a *forgery* of his *name* to the certificate !

What a miserable effusion of mortification ! What folly too! What incomparable and incomprehensible folly! The brains as well as the heart must have been gone. What could be more fair, more open, more honourable, than the conduct, in this case, of Lord William and his principal ! If Mr. Canning will always treat us real Reformers in this way, we will never complain of him. His Ambassador declared before hand, that *publication must take place*. Indeed, publication was absolutely necessary. Without that *nothing was accomplished*. What! for a public insult was there to be a private and secret apology ? Nonsense! And nonsense, too, that no one other than a chicken of " Glory" would ever have suffered to enter into its head, much less drop from its pen.

This querulous letter of Mr. Kinnaird is full of follies. Why make the gratuitous confession, that he *signed* the certificate " at " the *special request* of Lord Wil- " liam Bentinck ?" And, then, to say, that he himself, " could,

" *of course, wish* to oppose no " *obstacle* to the publication of " that which he thought *would do* " *so much honour to Sir Francis* " *Burdett* ;" to say this, at the very moment when he is discovering that he endeavoured to prevail on Lord William to *prevent publication*, and when he is discovering senseless rage at the publication having taken place ; really, to put all this before the public eye, and that, too, without broomstick at back or pistol at breast ; to do this thing voluntarily, and even eagerly, and to seem to think that it would tend to relieve the desperate case of his client, is something wholly unparalleled in the annals of folly ; but it is no more than was to be expected from one of those unfledged politicians that " Glory" chose to take under his wing when he abandoned the cause of the people in 1817. He has supped sorrow for that on many occasions since ; and the dose is not yet half down his throat.

But, Gentlemen, let us have a little more about this *forgery*. For thereby hangs an illustrative tale. This was *forgery*, was it ! This was forging *a name*. Come, then. The *Rump*, the supporters of this very " *Glory*," finding him *hard pushed* in 1818, got from *John Wright* a private letter of mine, written ten years before, in perfect confidence, and they deputed Cleary to read *a part* of this letter on the hustings of Covent Garden. It was then published, the *top and the bottom cut off*, and my *name clapped at the bottom of the middle*. I called *this a forgery*. I was sued for so-calling it ; and, what you will be so just, I hope, as to bear in mind, " Glory" rode, afterwards, in a procession got up and conducted by these very persons : that very Cleary rode the milk-white charger (emblem of purity !) before him, who was seated in the cerulean car, surmounted with the banners of " *Westminster's Pride and England's Glory* !" And yet it is *forgery* in the Editor of the Courier to put at the top of authentic and literally correct papers, *sent to him for publication*, which publication had been expressly stipulated for by Lord William Bentinck ; it is *forgery*, it is to *forge a name*, to put at the head of these documents the words, " *to the Editor of the Courier* ! Bah ! as the French say, when they turn up their noses.

I could go on a little, here, about publishing even *private letters* ; but, I reserve that matter for another occasion, and will now, in discussing this part of my subject, just request you to join me in admiration of the sweet simplicity with which Mr. Kinnaird tells us, that he stated to Lord William his " *surprise* if Mr. " Canning should *wish to give* " *notoriety to the transaction!* " This is a specimen of *naïveté* far surpassing that of the Shepherdess of Frith-street. How Lord William Bentinck must have laughed. If he has any children of his own, the remark must have sent his mind back to the nursery, and set it to wandering amongst the whistles and rattles of the rising generation. And this, oh humbugged Electors of Westminster ! *this* too ; yea, even *this*, was, if " Glory" and the Rump could have had their way, to have been one of the persons that " purity of election" was to send into parliament, there to espouse and to maintain the cause of the people, in times of great difficulty and peril !

# MARKETS.

---

Average Prices of CORN through-out ENGLAND, for the week ending April 20.

### Per Quarter.

| | s. | d. | | s. | d. |
|---|---|---|---|---|---|
| Wheat .. | 56 | 0 | Rye .... | 39 | 9 |
| Barley .. | 39 | 6 | Beans ... | 46 | 9 |
| Oats.... | 30 | 2 | Pease ... | 45 | 8 |

Total Quantity of Corn returned as Sold in the Maritime Districts, for the week ended April 20.

| | Qrs. | | Qrs. |
|---|---|---|---|
| Wheat.. | 32,636 | Rye ..... | 185 |
| Barley .. | 13,407 | Beans . .. | 1,416 |
| Oats ... | 9,528 | Pease .... | 323 |

*Corn Exchange, Mark Lane.*

Quantities and Prices of British Corn, &c. sold and delivered in this Market, during the week ended Saturday, April 21.

| | Qrs. | £. | s. | d. | | s. | d. |
|---|---|---|---|---|---|---|---|
| Wheat.. | 4,730 for | 13,980 | 13 | 6 | Average, | 58 | 10 |
| Barley.. | 2,730 | .. 5,457 | 6 | 10 | .......... | 40 | 10 |
| Oats.. | 3,255 | .. 5,372 | 15 | 1 | .......... | 33 | 0 |
| Rye.... | — | .. | — | | .......... | — | |
| Beans.. | 563 | .. 1,227 | 6 | 2 | .......... | 43 | 8 |
| Pease.. | 242 | .. 544 | 17 | 3 | .......... | 45 | 0 |

Friday, April 27.—There have been very short supplies this week of English Grain and Flour, and a moderate arrival of foreign Oats. Wheat, of fine quality, is so scarce that it looks upward in price, and is expected to be dearer. Barley, Beans, and Pease fully maintain the terms of Monday last. Oats have met a limited sale at last quotations.

Monday, April 30.—During the past week the supplies of all descriptions of English Grain were small; but of foreign Oats there was a good arrival. There is another small fresh supply this morning, of Wheat, Barley, Beans and Pease, from Essex, Kent, and Suffolk, and very little Corn from more distant ports. The supply of Flour now comes short, and most of the country markets near the metropolis being rather higher for Wheat, this article has sold freely here to-day, and the prices may be quoted full 1s. per quarter higher than on this day se'nnight.

Barley well maintains the terms last quoted. Beans find buyers readily at 1s. to 2s. per quarter advance. Pease are without variation, except fine Greys, which are rather dearer. There has been a good demand for Oats, chiefly by country buyers, and the prices of last week have been well supported for this article. No alteration in the price of Flour.

---

Price of Bread.—The price of the 4lb. Loaf is stated at 9d. by the full-priced Bakers.

---

COAL MARKET, April 27.

*Ships at Market. Ships sold. Price.*
24¼ Newcastle 20¼..29s. 0d. to 38s. 0d.
2⅝ Sunderland 1⅝..36s. 0d.— 38s. 3d.

Account of Wheat, &c. arrived in the Port of London, from April 23 to April 28, both inclusive.

| | Qrs. | | Qrs. |
|---|---|---|---|
| Wheat .. | 4,492 | Tares .... | 566 |
| Barley .. | 1,080 | Linseed .. | 2,134 |
| Malt .... | 3,355 | Rapeseed. | 498 |
| Oats .... | 4,459 | Brank .. | — |
| Beans ... | 360 | Mustard.. | — |
| Flour.... | 4,247 | Flax .... | — |
| Rye .... | — | Hemp ... | — |
| Pease.... | 1,241 | Seeds ... | 8 |

Foreign.—Wheat, 2,507; Barley, 3,837; Oats, 18,231; Beans, 1,412 quarters.

———

Monday, April 30.—The arrivals from Ireland last week were, 131 firkins of Butter, and 3,108 bales of Bacon; and from Foreign Ports, 3,830 casks of Butter.

———

Price of Hops, per Cwt. in the Borough.

Monday, April 30.—During last week there was a great deal of business done in new Hops, at an advance of from 2s. to 4s. per cwt. upon our last currency. The reports continue to come very unfavourable from the plantations, which has reduced the duty to 110,000l.

*Maidstone*, April 26.—There is nothing doing with us this week in the Hop Trade. The few growths left are almost at a stand, as both buyers and sellers seem to wait the appearance of the bine.

*Worcester*, April 25.—On Saturday 132 pockets of Hops were weighed. The accounts from the plantation state, that in throwing down the hills the plants in many yards look healthy and strong; but in other places they are either dead or weak.

SMITHFIELD.

Monday, April 30.—Beef being rather short on Friday, the trade was good at about last Monday's terms. Mutton was a heavy sale, though but little alteration in price. Lamb sold at former rates. To-day, Beef and Mutton are both lower; and a dragging trade. The best Beasts do not fetch so much as this day se'nnight, by 20s. a head; and middling things have sustained a still greater reduction. A few prime things have made 2d. a stone above our top currency. The best polled shorn Sheep are quoted at 5s. 2d. a stone; and Downs, in the Wool, 5s. 8d.; but both those prices may be considered rather strained. Lamb continues at 6s. to 7s. a stone.

*Per Stone of 8 pounds (alive).*

| | s. | d. | | s. | d. |
|---|---|---|---|---|---|
| Beef . | 4 | 0 | to | 5 | 0 |
| Mutton ... | 4 | 6 | — | 5 | 8 |
| Veal ..... | 4 | 6 | — | 5 | 4 |
| Pork ..... | 4 | 6 | — | 5 | 4 |
| Lamb .... | 6 | 0 | — | 7 | 0 |

| | | | |
|---|---|---|---|
| Beasts . | 1,967 | Sheep .. | 16,300 |
| Calves ... | 150 | Pigs ... | 193 |

NEWGATE, (same day.)

*Per Stone of 8 pounds (dead).*

| | s. | d. | | s. | d. |
|---|---|---|---|---|---|
| Beef ..... | 3 | 8 | to | 4 | 6 |
| Mutton ... | 4 | 0 | — | 5 | 4 |
| Veal ..... | 3 | 8 | — | 5 | 8 |
| Pork ..... | 4 | 0 | — | 6 | 0 |
| Lamb .... | 4 | 0 | — | 6 | 0 |

LEADENHALL, (same day.)

*Per Stone of 8 pounds (dead).*

| | s. | d. | | s. | d. |
|---|---|---|---|---|---|
| Beef ... . | 3 | 6 | to | 4 | 6 |
| Mutton ... | 4 | 4 | — | 5 | 4 |
| Veal ..... | 3 | 8 | — | 5 | 4 |
| Pork ..... | 4 | 4 | — | 5 | 8 |
| Lamb .... | 4 | 0 | — | 7 | 0 |

## POTATOES.

SPITALFIELDS, *per Ton.*

|  | l. s. | l. s. |
|---|---|---|
| Ox-Nobles | 3 15 to | 0 0 |
| Middlings | 2 10 — | 0 0 |
| Chats | 2 0 | 0 0 |
| Common Red | 4 0 — | 0 0 |
| Onions, 0s. 0d. —0s. 0d. per bush. |  |  |

BOROUGH, *per Ton.*

|  | l. s. | l. s. |
|---|---|---|
| Ox-Nobles | 3 10 to | 4 10 |
| Middlings | 2 0 — | 0 0 |
| Chats | 1 0 — | 0 0 |
| Common Red | 4 0 — | 0 0 |

## HAY and STRAW, per Load.

*Smithfield.*—Hay....90s. to 115s.
Straw...40s. to 42s.
Clover. 100s. to 140s.
*St. James's.*—Hay.... 80s. to 130s.
Straw .. 39s. to 48s.
Clover. 132s. to 140s.
*Whitechapel.*—Hay....80s. to 115s.
Straw...38s. to 42s.
Clover..90s. to 135s.

---

AVERAGE PRICE OF CORN, sold in the Maritime Counties of England and Wales, for the Week ended April 20, 1827.

|  | Wheat. | | Barley. | | Oats. | |
|---|---|---|---|---|---|---|
|  | s. | d. | s. | d. | s. | d. |
| London* | 58 | 11 | 40 | 7 | 33 | 5 |
| Essex | 58 | 5 | 37 | 8 | 30 | 10 |
| Kent | 55 | 10 | 40 | 3 | 30 | 0 |
| Sussex | 55 | 7 | 40 | 9 | 30 | 0 |
| Suffolk | 55 | 7 | 37 | 5 | 31 | 0 |
| Cambridgeshire | 61 | 3 | 35 | 4 | 28 | 5 |
| Norfolk | 54 | 9 | 37 | 1 | 28 | 4 |
| Lincolnshire | 55 | 4 | 40 | 9 | 26 | 0 |
| Yorkshire | 55 | 0 | 42 | 8 | 28 | 0 |
| Durham | 56 | 3 | 41 | 8 | 35 | 2 |
| Northumberland | 54 | 1 | 38 | 6 | 33 | 0 |
| Cumberland | 61 | 2 | 39 | 10 | 35 | 9 |
| Westmoreland | 62 | 10 | 46 | 8 | 37 | 8 |
| Lancashire | 62 | 0 | 42 | 5 | 36 | 4 |
| Cheshire | 61 | 2 | 0 | 0 | 30 | 8 |
| Gloucestershire | 57 | 4 | 43 | 8 | 39 | 0 |
| Somersetshire | 54 | 8 | 42 | 10 | 35 | 4 |
| Monmouthshire | 61 | 3 | 46 | 8 | 0 | 0 |
| Devonshire | 56 | 4 | 38 | 8 | 29 | 3 |
| Cornwall | 60 | 0 | 39 | 9 | 38 | 0 |
| Dorsetshire | 53 | 2 | 39 | 5 | 34 | 0 |
| Hampshire | 55 | 4 | 41 | 7 | 30 | 11 |
| North Wales | 62 | 3 | 44 | 9 | 34 | 8 |
| South Wales | 58 | 11 | 43 | 10 | 26 | 9 |

* The London Average is always that of the Week preceding.

*Liverpool*, April 24.—Although the arrivals of Grain have again been moderate since this day week, the Corn trade has continued very languid here, and in all the Corn markets around us; the dealers and Millers have purchased very sparingly of Wheat and Oats for their immediate wants; prices last noted have been barely supported for the finest qualities, and a small decline has been submitted to on inferior descriptions. For Indian Corn (chiefly of the white) there has been a fair demand for shipment to Ireland, and this article has fully supported last quotations. In all other articles there has been little done, and no alteration in prices. In bonded Grain and Flour we can note no particular transactions, nor any change in prices. At this day's market we have had a moderate demand for Wheat at a small decline, though not sufficient to alter the general quotations in our last. For Oats the sales were very limited, and a reduction of ½d. to 1d. per 45 lbs. was submitted to. Of other articles very few sales were effected, and prices remain without alteration.

Imported into Liverpool, from April 17, to April 23, 1827, inclusive:— Wheat, 6,212; Barley, 71; Oats, 3,547; Beans, 130; Pease, 150 quarters. Oatmeal, 151 packs, per 240 lbs. Flour, 1,105 sacks, per 280 lbs.

*Bristol*, April 28.—There is so little alteration in our Corn markets here since our last statement, that it is not worth notice. The following are about the present prices.—Wheat, from 5s. 6d. to 7s. 6d.; Barley, 4s. 4½d. to 6s. 3d.; Beans, 5s. 6d. to 8s.; Oats, 3s. 3d. to 4s. 3d.; and Malt, 5s. 6d. to 8s. 3d. per bushel, Imperial. Flour, Seconds, 33s. to 42s. per bag.

*Guildford*, April 28.—Wheat, new, for mealing, 15l. 10s. to 17l. 10s. per load. Barley, 39s. to 44s.; Oats, 33s. to 42s.; Beans, 53s. to 56s.; Pease, grey, 60s. to 62s.; ditto, boilers, 62s. to 64s. per quarter.

*Horncastle*, April 28.—Our Corn market continues nearly the same as our last.—Wheat, 54s. to 56s.; Barley, 40s. to 43s.; Oats, 30s. to 35s.; Beans, 60s. to 64s.; and Rye from 40s. to 45s. per quarter.

*Ipswich*, April 28.—Our market was very shortly supplied. Wheat was 1s. per quarter dearer; in other grain no alteration: prices as follow:— Wheat, 54s. to 63s.; Barley, 36s. to 41s.; and Beans, 47s. to 49s. per quarter.

*Manchester*, April 28.—Since this day week the arrivals of nearly all descriptions of Grain have been inconsiderable, but of Flour large, from Yorkshire, &c., and the transactions have been on a limited scale. At our market to-day we had a slender attendance of country dealers, and what few sales were made were on similar terms to this day se'nnight, with the exception of Flour, which is 1s. per sack lower.

*Newcastle-on-Tyne*, April 28.—We had a large supply of Wheat from the farmers, most of it from the northern part of the county, this morning, but having no coasting supply, the sale was tolerably brisk at last week's prices. Rye continues in demand at last week's prices. The arrivals of Barley have been sold at 44s. per quarter, and there is yet a demand at that price. Malt is rather dearer. The supply of Oats from the farmers was large for the season, and we had more foreign arrivals this week. English and foreign free Oats sold slowly at rather lower prices, but Oats in bond are 1s. per quarter dearer.

*Reading*, April 28.—We had a short supply of Wheat this day, but the quality was superior to any brought to market for some time past; it met a tolerably ready sale at an advance of 1s. per quarter; we note it by the Imperial measure, 55s. to 68s. per quarter. There was a short supply of Barley, which sold at 1s. to 2s. per quarter higher.

## COUNTRY CATTLE AND MEAT MARKETS, &c.

*Horncastle*, April 28.—Beef, 9s. per stone of 14 lbs.; Mutton, 8d.; Pork, 7d. to 8d.; and Veal, 8d. to 9d. per lb.

*Manchester* Smithfield Market, April 25.—At this day's market the supply of Sheep was better than on this day week, and the weather being very unfavourable, from the fall of snow, which is rather unusual at this season of the year, the dealers were inclined to take rather less money for fat Mutton, and, at a reduction of ½d. per lb., there was a tolerable good clearance made. Fat Beasts sold on full as good terms as this day week, while lean sorts were totally disregarded. Pigs barely support last week's rates.—Beef, 4½d. to 8d.; Mutton, 7d. to 9d.; Veal, 5d. to 6½d.; and Pork, 4½d. to 5½d. per lb., sinking offal.

*Norwich Castle Meadow*, April 28.—We had a good supply of fat Cattle to this day's market, and the demand was brisk at 7s. 6d. to 8s. 6d. per stone of 14 lbs., sinking offal; that of Store was very large; Scots sold at 4s. to 4s. 6d. per stone of what they will weigh when fat; Shorthorns, 3s. 6d. Pigs cheap; fat ones to 7s. 6d. per stone.—Meat: Beef, 7d. to 9d.; Veal, 6d. to 8d.; Mutton, 6d. to 7½d.; Lamb, 9d.; and Pork, 6d. to 8d. per lb.

At *Morpeth* Market, April 25th, there was a good supply of Cattle and Sheep. From the high prices, and there not being a great demand, both stood long, and the latter met with very dull sale; and part were not sold. Beef, from 7s. 3d. to 8s.; Mutton, 9s. 9d. to 11s. per stone, sinking offal.

# COBBETT'S WEEKLY REGISTER.

VOL. 62.—No. 7.]    LONDON, SATURDAY, MAY 12, 1827.    [*Price 6d.*

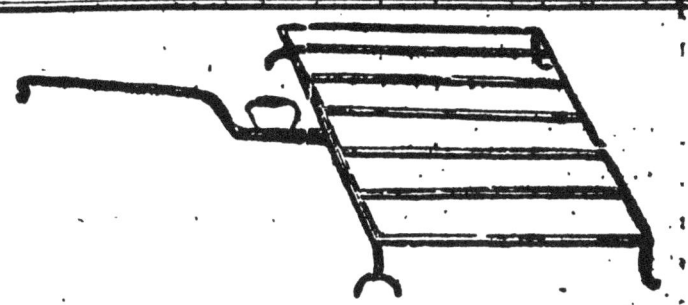

"I would fain hope, that the example given by the people of West-
"minster, might encourage other places still to contend for that small
"portion of Independence which yet remains in the country; and thereby
"keep alive, at least in the remembrance of their countrymen, their
"ancient constitutional right to a *full, fair, and free representation of the*
"*people in Parliament,* their *only quiet and peaceable security,* at all times,.
"for their *rights and property,* against the *despotism and plunder of the*
"*few.* For these purposes you shall *always* find me, either *in* or *out* of
"*Parliament,* READY TO LAY DOWN MY LIFE."—SIR FRANCIS
BURDETT'S LETTER TO THE ELECTORS OF WESTMINSTER, 16TH OCTO-
BER, 1812.

TO THE

# ELECTORS OF WESTMINSTER.

ON THE MONSTROUS INTRIGUES AND THE MONSTROUS COALITION,
AND ESPECIALLY ON THE CONDUCT OF THEIR MEMBER, SIR
FRANCIS BURDETT.

*Kensington, 10th May, 1827.*

GENTLEMEN,

AGAIN I say, "Look at the Motto," and then view the conduct of the author of the Letter (a Letter addressed to yourselves), from which that Motto is extracted. But, before I proceed to comment upon that conduct, before I proceed to show the extent of the insolence, the ingratitude, the perfidiousness of that author towards the people of Westminster; towards that people who have done so much for him, and who have been so unvaryingly faithful

N

Printed and Published by WILLIAM COBBETT, No. 183, Fleet-street,
[ENTERED AT STATIONERS' HALL.]

and indulgent to him; before I proceed to do this, and to show how the people at large are now intended to be sacrificed by both and by all the factions, let me first request your attention to the monstrous intrigues and the monstrous coalition that have taken place. -

At the time when Canning was complimenting Brougham, and receiving the compliments of the latter; at the time when these two wordy politicians were reciprocating compliments upon the subject of the mad project of forcing what they call liberty, but what I call plunder under the name of liberty, upon Portugal; at that time, it was easy to see, that Canning foresaw something that would make it necessary for him to form a coalition with that old, battered part of the "regiment" (as Sir Francis Burdett used to call it) which had for so many years been so heartily despised under the name of Whigs. Indeed, long before that, he seems to have had a pretty clear understanding with some of them that they should join together for the purpose of putting him at the head of affairs, and of obtaining snug things for them under him. It was understood, and, indeed, it was manifest enough to all the world, that Canning and the late Lord Chancellor pretty cordially detested one another; and that, if Liverpool should happen to drop out of the socket, a contest would arise, that would bring the strength of these parties to a trial. That some part of the creatures called Tories would stick to Canning was certain: he had his little band; and that band must stick to him or become mere underlings. For three or four years, the people called Whigs have been playing into his hands, in order to give him weight and power against his colleagues of the other part of the Ministry. Liverpool balanced between the two, and thus kept his place and power. When he dropped out, the contest came. Now, it was manifest to me, that, a long time ago, he was very likely to drop out. In the month of May last, I saw him in the House of Lords; and I could call upon twenty gentlemen to prove that, between that month and the month of September, I gave a description of him, and gave an opinion founded on that description, which opinion was, that he could remain to act in office but a very short time. If I, who could see him only by just getting a squeezing peep at him in the House of Lords; if I could come to this conclusion; and that, too, with perfect impartiality, because I cared no more about his health or capacity than I cared about the health or capacity of any snail or slug that is an inhabitant of my neighbour's garden; if I could, under such circumstances, come to this conclusion, is it not fairly to be presumed, that Canning, who saw him so frequently, who had so many opportunities of ascertaining his state, must have come to something very much like the same conclusion! In short, when I was in the House of Lords, on the day of the debate on Lord MALMSBURY's motion relative to the corn laws, I heard Lord BATHURST make his speech in opposition to Lord Malmsbury's proposed motion, and I heard Lord Liverpool, who sat on the same bench, on the right hand of Lord Bathurst, repeating, loud enough for me to hear the words at the bar (which is a distance nearly half the length of the House between the throne and the bar) the *closing nine or ten words of every sentence uttered by Lord Bathurst;* and this work of repeating he continued in my hearing and to the astonishment of myself and all about me, during the whole of Lord Bathurst's speech, which lasted for more than half an hour. It was impossible to believe, that, to whatever this might be ascribeable, it indicated any thing short of an ailment of some sort or other, that would naturally produce the retirement, in some way, of Lord Liverpool. This would not escape Canning and the Whigs; and, accordingly, we find that their complimenting of each other increased, day by day, till at last it was manifest to every body that there was an intention to form a junction which should enable Canning to oust his colleagues. They are now ousted; and the Whigs are sitting, intermingled with the small Tories, with this same Canning at their head. Whether it be true or not, that Canning received the proposition for a coalition from the Whigs or they from him, is of very little consequence to us; whether it be true, as it has been suggested in the House of Lords, that he received this proposition, kept it ten days in his pocket, then laid it before the King, and never, during the ten days, communicated it to his colleagues; whether this be true or false, signifies not a farthing to us; nor would it signify a farthing to us, whether the coalition were formed or not; whether Whigs or Tories, or partly one and partly the other, composed the new Ministry; but, it signifies greatly to us, when the cause of Parliamentary Reform is to be sacrificed, when that cause is to become the victim of this intrigue; when those who have pretended that they wished for Parliamentary Reform, come and place themselves on the side of Canning, who has always been its bitterest enemy ; come and sit at his back and give him all the support in their power; come and do this, without saying one single word about any thing to be obtained in favour of the people. Nay, when they come and disclaim the cause of Reform ; when they say that the people no longer wish for it; when, in short, they clearly show us that they mean not only to abandon the cause of the people; not only never to do any thing any more with a view of obtaining the people justice; not only to withdraw even all their pretended support of the people's cause; but when they almost openly declare that they will make a sacrifice of the people's rights for the sake of securing power and emolument for themselves. This is a matter that *does concern us:* the miserable renegado reptiles will be deceived: even if you were indifferent to your own security and to the honour of your country, and even if all the people followed your example in that respect; even then the renegadoes would not succeed in their intentions; for, events will speedily arise that will cripple all their projects, that will disconcert all their deep-laid schemes, that will throw them into utter confusion, and make even those whom they have ousted, congratulate themselves upon having lost their power and their places: the renegadoes will find that they have over-reached themselves, and that they have gained nothing but danger and disgrace, greater than they have ever known before; but, this forms no apology for their conduct: they mean well; they mean well for themselves: they mean to get possession of power and emolument, and to keep them for the whole length of their lives; this is what they mean, and we will do them the justice to take the will for the deed.

They will be defeated; but, it is no reason for our keeping silence. Though time, and a short time, will see all their schemes blasted, it is our duty to defend ourselves against those schemes. It is our duty to assert the rights which they have so flagrantly abandoned; and if we do not assert those rights at this time, we shall deserve, and we shall be and our children after us will be to he bandied about, from faction to faction, to be kicked backward and forward, to be tossed up and down, to have our purses emptied at the end of every month, and to be, in short, the most despicable slaves that ever toiled for a set of greedy masters.

But, some one may say, is it not a good thing to see ousted that set of men, who have, during so many years, been doing, every year, so many things which *I* and which you and which the people

at large have so loudly complained of: is it not a good thing to see
this band broken up, divested of
power, and tasting, at last, of
something like humiliation? A
very good thing! A very good
thing in itself, a very good thing
in its natural consequences; for,
my conviction is, that it must lead
to good, and that it will be one
means of accelerating the total
destruction of that system of which
we have been so justly complaining for so many years. But, even
this great good is worth nothing;
it is even an evil, if it be to be
purchased by *an abandonment of
the cause of Parliamentary Reform*. It is not the *men:* it is the
horrible *system*, the Borough-
system which has caused us to
suffer, and which causes us still
to suffer. Why do we pay five-
pence halfpenny a pot for porter,
instead of that three halfpence
which we should pay, if there
were none of those taxes, of which
the remainder of the price is composed? Why do we pay, at this
moment, seven shillings a bushel

for the wheat which we ought to
have for little more than three
shillings and sixpence the bushel?
What is the cause of this? Is not
the cause as plain as the nose
upon one's face? Do we wish to
pay thus for our bread and our
beer? Do we wish to have our
earnings thus taken away from
us? Certainly we do not: we
wish not to have them thus taken
away: what is it that takes them
away? The *law*: and who makes
the law? Not men of our choosing.
The law is made by a set of men,
who are not chosen by the people
at large. According to the petition
presented by Lord GREY, and now
lying upon the table of the House
of Commons, a majority of the
Members of that House are put
into it by less than two hundred
great men; by the will and pleasure of less than two hundred
great men. Therefore it is, that
we pay the taxes we pay; therefore it is that the great mass of us
are poor and miserable; therefore
it is that we are deprived of our
suitable enjoyments. If the laws

were made by men chosen by the people at large, those men would not and could not consent that taxes so enormous should be raised upon the food and drink of the people. Let me put this question to any rational being. Does he believe that, if the people had the choosing of the makers of the laws, those law-makers would ever have given their consent to the giving of half-pay as *military officers*, to men who were now parsons, having livings and receiving tithes, surplus fees, and Easter-offerings as clergymen of the church? It is impossible: no man in his senses and who has any love of truth about him, will say that he believes that men, chosen by the people, would have thus disposed of money arising from taxes on the food and drink of that people, on their soap, their candles, their tea, their tobacco, their sugar, their pepper, their, in short, almost every article forming a necessary of life. No rational man will say that he believes such a thing: how, then, are we to be-

come better off without a change in the mode of electing the law-makers? Is not this the greatest thing of all? Is not this the only thing worth seeking after with earnestness? and if this be abandoned; if those who are to come and succeed the late Ministers are to begin their career by saying that no reform is necessary, or by acting as if they said so, what does this wretched people get by this change? They are made worse off than they were before. They have fast enemies, avowed enemies in the set that are gone out; and they have lost even the pretended friendship of the set that are come in. There is nobody, now, even to speak for them; but, I trust that they are not so base or so foolish as to abstain from speaking for themselves; and that, too, upon every occasion and in every way that presents itself to them.

Nobody can doubt that, before the overture was made to Canning by the Whigs; that long before that, a part of this old rump of politicians, who had been accustomed to speak or to vote for reform of Parliament, clearly saw the difficulty in which they would be placed, if they joined Canning. That they would join him if they could thereby obtain a chance of getting any thing by it, was certain. They knew, well enough, that he could not stand a day if he did not distinctly declare that *he would never consent to a Reform of the Parliament.* They knew that he must make this declaration, or that he would be ousted in a twinkling. They knew that there was that majority in the House of Commons so well described and so positively asserted in Lord Grey's petition: they knew well that that majority would turn him out in a trice if he did not give them an assurance that he would always continue hostile to Reform. They knew that he would declare perpetual hostility to it, and therefore they began to prepare themselves for accounting for going over to his side and supporting him in spite of this declaration of his, of eternal hostility to Reform! This was a pretty tough job to manage: one would wonder how *any* man, however impudently profligate, could, at the end of twenty years of repeated solemn declarations, that the nation never could be freed from oppression without a Reform of the Parliament; one would wonder how even the most barefacedly profligate of all mankind could, after all this, go over, sit at the back of a man, call a man their right honourable friend, pledge themselves to support a man as prime minister, who should solemnly declare to their faces, at the very time that they were supporting {him and pledging themselves to support him, that he would *oppose Parliamentary Reform to the last hour of his having a seat in that House!* Yet, this is what the coalescing Whigs have done; and have thus made good all our charges against them; have thus proved themselves to be the false friends of Reform; have thus proved to actual demonstration that they have made use of Reform as a means of deceiving the people, and of thereby gaining some strength wherewith to annoy the Ministers in order to get possession of power and emolument themselves.

. But, let us hear a little of the *reasons* given by these coalescing Whigs, for having joined the great and mortal enemy of Reform, and for persevering in supporting him, after hearing his declaration that his hostility to it shall cease only with his parliamentary life. The reasons given by Mr. Brougham are these: that, for some years past, particularly since the death of Castlereagh, who cut his own throat at North Cray in Kent, the people have become *indifferent* with respect to the cause of Reform; that there has been much coolness amongst the people with regard to it; that the Government has been conducted in a manner to give general satisfaction; that the nation has felt itself so well off under this new mode of carrying on the Government, since Canning came into office in 1822, that the people have not any longer been anxious about a Reform of the Parliament; and that, therefore, NOW that question may be passed over and these Whigs may agree to support Mr. Canning, though he solemnly declares that he never will consent to Reform. Much about the same thing was said by Lord JOHN RUSSELL, who is now member for a borough in Ireland, while your member BURDETT, the author of the motto to this paper; the author, as I shall show, one of these days, of more than *two hundred solemn declarations*, that every thing was false; that every thing was an infamous pretence which professed to have in view to better the lot of the people, until there should be a Reform of the Commons' House of Parliament, which he, seventeen different times, has pledged himself to defend, to support by all manner of means, and to obtain if possible, and at the risk of his life, if necessary. While the others

give the above *reasons* for supporting the bitter and everlasting
enemy of Reform, this hero says,
this "Westminster's Pride and
England's Glory" says, that "as
" to Reform, he will VOTE for it
" and vote for *any Reforms,*
" *whenever they shall be brought*
" *forward"!* This is what he
says; and, thus, they all abandon the cause of Reform, most
expressly, and they tell us as
plainly as they can tell us, that
they will support the man, he
being Prime Minister, too, who
plainly tells them that he will oppose it to the last hour of his parliamentary life.

Now, as to these *reasons* given
by the coalescing Whigs, and
coming from the mouth of Mr.
Brougham. First, they tell us
that, for five years past, the people
have appeared indifferent with
respect to the cause of Reform.
They choose to forget that, for a
considerable part of that time,
there has been a law actually in
force *to prevent the people from
meeting* to talk about Reform,
unless at the manifest peril of
their lives; and that law, after
having remained in full force so
long, the people regarded as being
the law for ever, and a vast majority of them still look upon it as
law to this day. They choose to
forget, too, the dungeons and bills
of indemnity of 1817 and 1818.
They choose to forget the long
imprisonments; the terrible sufferings, the horrible ruin and lacera-
tion of hundreds of men, for no
other crime than that of being
known to be serious in the cause
of Reform; they forget the fate
of poor Riley; they choose to
forget the choppings and shootings
and tramplings at Manchester;
they choose to forget the Oldham
Inquest; they choose to forget
that the shaking of the bowels
out of the body of poor Ogden,
became the subject of an illitera-
tive jest, which set the House in
a roar of laughter; and they
choose to forget or to appear to
forget, that it is with the jester
that they have now coalesced, for
the sake of coming into the scram-

ble, and getting at a share of what the Reformers wished. to heap from them all.

These things were pretty well calculated to cool the Reformers. If halters, axes, guns, bayonets, the trampling of horses' feet, years in a solitary cell and bowels shaken out of the body; if these be not sufficient to cool men, they must be of a nature like Etna. Still they have not been indifferent: wherever the people have met, they have not shown a coolness on the subject. In the counties of Kent, Surrey, Norfolk, Huntingdonshire, Cambridgeshire, county meetings have all sent up petitions for Reform of the Parliament, and that, too, since the man cut his throat at North Cray in Kent. During this very winter, there has been a petition from Renfrewshire, for Parliamentary Reform. The people, properly so called, the promiscuous multitude, have met nowhere in public meeting, to petition upon any subject, without including Parliamentary Reform.

In stating their complaints against the Corn Bill; in framing prayers against that cruel tax, they have never failed to ascribe it to a want of Parliamentary Reform.; so that, the assertion is false; not sophistical, but really a blunt falsehood; an impudent, barefaced falsehood: the people are satisfied that as long as they have nothing to say in the making of laws, their food, their drink, their raiment,' all the fruits of their earnings will be taxed, as expressed in the words of my Motto, for the benefit of the few. The author of the Motto called it the *plunder* of the few. I make use of milder terms; but the people are still satisfied, are still convinced, that their only security against being half starved, and being clothed in rags, is that Reform in the Parliament, to obtain which your Member BURDETT declared that he was ready *to lay down his life!*

But, if we are to believe BROUGHAM, the Government has been conducted in a manner, during the last five years, to give such general satisfaction, and the nation has felt itself so well off during that time, that the people have not, any longer, been anxious about a Reform of the Parliament. Mark, Gentlemen, how false pretences sometimes trip themselves up. If the Government have been so well conducted, and so much for the good of the nation *during the last five years*, how unjust is it in Mr. Brougham *to find fault of the late Ministers!* It is notorious that *Canning* was not the ruler. Seven out of twelve, or, rather, seven out of eleven of his colleagues, and those filling all the great offices, quit the Ministry rather than serve under him. It is notorious that he was in a minority in the cabinet: it is notorious that the measures were not his: it is notorious that the measures for the last five years, be they what they might, were measures, in which he had only a share, and that, too, a small share. This being the case: this being undeniable, what ground can Mr. Brougham have for wishing at all for a change of the Ministry: and, if the system which the Minister pursued gave such general satisfaction as to make the people cease to wish for a change of the system, and for a Reform of the Parliament, for what could he desire to see a change, except for the obtaining of an opening for himself?

The fact is, however, that the Government has, during the last five years, been conducted in just the same way that it always has been conducted since I or since any of you can remember. It could not have any Six Acts to pass; for they were already passed and they have all been kept in force to their utmost. It could not pass Power-of-Imprisonment Bills, unless in mere sport, for, it had laws already passed to prevent the people from meeting and to muzzle the press, and make the main mass of it completely subservient to those who had the governing power in their hands. It has, however, passed *some* laws;

it has done some things during that five years; and these things ought, by no means, to be forgotten. It has hardened the laws with respect to the game. It has passed a *new trespass law*, which makes it dangerous for a man to set his foot off the turnpike road. It has empowered the magistrate to send the poor man to gaol and to hard labour upon a charge of trespass of even one penny damage; and, it has protected the rich man from being thus dealt with, though he commit damage to the amount of scores of pounds. Nay, it has done this: it has enabled the magistrate, one single magistrate, to send a poor man to prison and to hard labour, under certain circumstances of non-payment of damages, if he walk but ten feet in a corn-field; and, it has protected the rich man, in going through the same corn-field and beating down half the corn, with horses, dogs and followers, and subjected him to nothing but the ancient and usual slow process at law. During the last five years, while the *softener of the criminal code*, who is now, it is said, to be in place; during the last five years, while this softener has been at work to put an end to the laws against witchcraft, this excellent Government of ours; this mild and well-behaved Government, which has given such " general satisfaction;" or that has acted so satisfactorily, at least, to Mr. Brougham, Lord John Russell and Sir Francis Burdett, has brought in and passed a bill, *making it felony to take an apple off a tree!* and, thus, even though the felon may be pardoned, causing him to forfeit all his right to real property to the end of his life! A mightily well-behaved Government, to be sure; a singularly mild and tender-hearted Government; a Government the conduct of which was, to be sure, famously calculated to make the people cease to wish for Reform.

Not to go into other particulars, at present; not to dwell upon a great variety of acts, every one of which proves the necessity of a Reform of the Parliament, and every one of which have been passed at the instigation of the Ministers within the last five years, what will these converted coalescers say to the tricks which have been played with the paper-money? Mr. Robinson, Mr. Huskisson, all were in place, when the Small-note Bill of 1822 was passed, except Canning himself, and he constantly supported and voted with the Government. All the late Ministry, including Canning himself, then, put forth the bales of paper in 1822; that produced the horrible ruin of 1825; that produced the Act of last year; proposed by Canning himself and accompanied with a vow that he would never recede from it; the Act of last year has produced the present steadily increasing ruin; and which ruin will finally produce the overthrow of Canning and of all his newly converted tribe, unless they be overthrown by some other thing, before that great cause comes into full operation. Look at the ruin of the manufacturers; look at the ruin of the merchants. See the thousands and thousands of tradesmen breaking up in spite of all their incessant industry; think of the wide-spreading starvation of the people by thousands and hundreds of thousands, and look at the begging-box carried round by Royal authority; look at all these things, and see new royal and ministerial palaces rising up at the same time at most enormous expense; look at a sham bridge, costing from thirty to sixty thousand pounds; look at the whole thing, even as it is; look at the farmers, and hear their tales; behold the paupers swarming like the lice of Egypt, and thousands actually rotting upon rushes or straw reduced to smaller than chaff by the rub of their miserable carcases; behold these things in England and all over England; hear it observed from the Court of King's Bench, that bread and water are the common food and drink of the labouring people in England,

See the wretched resorts of the "*houseless*;" read the description of them, even in this luxurious metropolis, packed so closely upon the floor that there is not room for the turning of the body: look at all these things, things which no man can deny; things notorious to the whole nation, and then think of the immeasurable, the ten-fold brazen audacity of the man who can assert, in the face of this same suffering and degraded people, this starving, this tread-mill country; who can assert, that, for the last four or five years, the conduct of Government has given such general satisfaction, and the nation has been so *well off*, that the people have not, any longer, been anxious about a Reform of the Parliament, and that, therefore, now he may support Mr. Canning, though he solemnly declares that he will oppose Reform to the last hour of his parliamentary life! Think of the brass of this man, and your rage will be so great, that you will seek for consolation in something that shall give you ground for a hope that the triumph of his audacity will not be of great duration. Such consolation I have; and I wish that each of you should have it too; I shall, therefore, state it to you by and by; but, first of all, we must dispose of our own hero, our twenty years old reformer; that is to say, our champion pretended, for twenty years; our champion pretended, indeed, for thirty years; but our champion receiving reward, ample for even faithful services, if they had been such, during twenty years.

The reports of the debates in Parliament, exhibit BROUGHAM, Lord JOHN RUSSELL, BURDETT and CANNING, making their declarations relative to Reform of Parliament. Mr. DAWSON had asked this strange coalition what they now meant to do relative to several subjects, and, amongst others, relative to the subject of Parliamentary Reform. It was difficult, indeed, to imagine how any of the coalescing Whigs, and particularly how Burdett could shuffle out of this question. It was, with him, the all-in-all; the one thing needful; the *sine qua non*, and the evil, the want of Reform, he had called, over and over again, the *accursed thing* of the country; the sole cause of all its calamities, and the cause which, if not removed, must, in the end, and ought speedily, to produce the overthrow of every thing. How often (good God!) has he called to the people; how often has he invoked them to come forward in a mass, and to demand their rights in a manner not to be resisted: how often has he, and in terms the most vehement and most bitter, reproached the people, accused them of cowardice, accused them of degeneracy, accused them of being unworthy of his exertions in their favour, because they did not come forward simultaneously as one man, and imitate the example of those who had sent him into Parliament; and, now, we see him seated at the back of a man, who has not only always been the bitterest enemy of Reform; who

has not only been the very forwardest in support of every measure for keeping down Reform, by every means that could be suggested; who has not only vilified, calumniated and heaped the most infamous accusations and imputed the most infamous of motives to all Reformers, but who still declares, in the very teeth of this Sir Francis Burdett, that he, who is now Prime Minister, will oppose Reform, *under whatever shape it may appear*, to the last hour of his parliamentary life!

The sayings of these men, their declarations to which I have alluded, agreeably to the report in the *Morning Chronicle*, took place in the House of Commons on Friday, the 4th day of this month of May. These are memorable words. They will have to be repeated many times hereafter; and, as in the case of Prosperity Robinson's speech of the month of February, 1824, I, foreseeing the many times that I shall have to refer to these words, insert them as I find them reported in the above mentioned paper, under the above mentioned date. A time may come, and I am sure that a time will come, and that that time is not distant, when we shall have to call upon the three former of these men, at any rate, to answer to us, the people, for having uttered these words, or to deny (which, however, they must do without loss of time) that they ever did utter such words. They are neither of them the wisest of mankind; but, weak indeed must they be, if they expect that these memorable words will be suffered to sink into oblivion.

---

## MR. BROUGHAM.

" Now we come to the question of Parliamentary Reform, and it is quite unnecessary for me to remind the House that we, who formed the late Opposition, were as a body divided upon that question, many being at one time against Reform altogether, who had so far yielded, however, as to be for moderate Reform, which Major Cartwright and others called *mock* Reform, but which I certainly call by no such appellation; and several still objecting to any Parliamentary Reform. It is impossible to say, with any appearance of reason or sound argument, that we as a body stood pledged in favour of that question, against which the Right Honourable Gentleman at the head of the Treasury, I am apprehensive, does stand pledged. That we, therefore, who have been so long divided among ourselves on that question, should on that ground, as a body, refuse to join an Administration whose principles and conduct we approved of in so many other particulars, would be perfect folly, and injurious to the favourable side of that very question: it would be injustice to ourselves, and dishonesty to our country. The great features of the late Administration, after the loss of the late Lord Londonderry, were marked by large views, and by a liberal and truly English feeling, more particularly in its foreign policy, and its conduct with regard to the rising States of South America [hear, hear!]; and on the most urgent questions respecting trade and manufactures under the conduct chiefly of the Right Honourable President of the Board of Controul, the proceedings of that Administration were founded on liberal and enlightened views, and such as were fully approved in the main by the great body of the Opposition. These have been the three cardinal points of the Administration—the large features upon which they have acted ever since the Right Honourable Gentleman now at the head of the Treasury came into the Foreign Office."

O

LORD JOHN RUSSELL

" Said, that as the subject of Parliamentary Reform had been introduced, and as that was a subject which he had taken considerable interest in, and to which he had on more than one occasion called the attention of Parliament, he wished to remind the House, that that was never a Parliamentary question of the Whigs as a party. It was a question on which there was a great diversity of opinion among those who advocated it, and to which the leaders of the Whigs were always unwilling to be pledged as to a party question. He (Lord John Russell) did not expect that it would be carried as a party question. He had often declared so, and had done so when last he brought the question forward, which, he stated, was brought forward for the last time. The reason which induced him to state that he had brought it forward then for the last time, was, because he observed a great lukewarmness throughout the country and in the House on the question, which lukewarmness was greatly owing to the conciliatory and satisfactory manner in which Government was latterly conducted, and which made him and his Honourable Friends suppose that, by supporting that portion of it which remained, they might contribute to the public service—if it had remained indeed, in the possession of the seceders—if the Government was under the controul of the Honourable Member for Derry (Mr. Dawson), and the discontent and dissatisfaction that would prevail, he might expect the inevitable success of this measure; but, anxious as he was for its successful result, yet he owned he was not desirous to purchase it at such a cost as the return to office of himself and his associates in secession."

- SIR FRANCIS BURDETT.

" One principal ground on which I give my support to the present Administration is, because it does practically and in effect uphold the King in the just exercise of his prerogative. That is my justification on that point. But I will tell the Right Honourable Gentleman further, that. *putting. aside all the great questions* which he *is so singularly anxious* to bring under discussion, *including among the rest that of Parliamentary Reform* [a laugh], I see sufficient reason to support this Administration. [Cheers.] The Right Honourable Gentleman seems never to have known that there was *a schism on the subject of . Reform*. It is news to him that there *were ever shades of opinion upon it*. He was not aware, it appears, that there were as. *many different views* of the general measure as there have always been of comprehensive political questions. Some are for confining it within narrow limits ; others for extending it to the widest. I am ready to vote for *any measure* of Reform. By supporting the present. Government, *I do not abandon or sa-*

crifice one iota of my principles as a friend of *Parliamentary Reform*, or any other question on which I may deem it fitting and prudent to deliver my sentiments. [Cheers.] As a man of common sense, I must wish to *achieve some practical good in my time*. If I cannot *do all I would*, I am bound, without waiting till, perhaps, more extensive views may be adopted, to promote *all the good which the opportunity of the passing moment offers me*. [Hear, hear !]—

\* \* \* \* \* \* \* \* \* \* \* \* \*
\* \* \* \* \* \* \* \* \* \* \* \* \*

" *My Right Hon. Friend (Mr. Canning)* has been accused, among other things of an overweening ambition," &c. &c.

### Mr. CANNING.

" I am asked what I mean to do on the subject of *Parliamentary Reform?* Why, I say—*to oppose it—to oppose it to the end of my life in this House, under whatever shape it may appear*."

———

Here are their declarations; and these declarations are to remain upon record, until the time come, when I do hope we shall have an opportunity of calling upon them for an answer to what may be fairly urged against these declarations. But, we are not going to wait, I hope, before we, by our conduct, give the lie to those, who assert that we are lukewarm, who assert that we feel no interest any longer in the cause of Reform.

Of the silly shuffle contained in the two former of these reports of speeches, I shall say nothing, except that they prove the truth of what we have so often asserted, that the Whig reform was a miserable sham, and that even that sham would be abandoned, the moment the parties found that they could get into place. What does the veteran placeman TIERNEY, who is, they say, to have a snug birth in the new concern; what does he say to this question of Reform; he who signed the petition of Lord GREY, just thirty years ago, in this very month of May, and he who has seen added to the national debt (including dead-weight and peer-rates) a thousand millions of money since that time; he who has seen the number of paupers augmented tenfold; he who has seen large parts of the people of Ireland shut up in their houses from sunset to sunrise; he who has seen, since the time he signed that petition, more bankruptcies take place and more insolvencies than had taken place in three centuries before. He who has seen the labouring people of England reduced to an allowance of food and drink and raiment, smaller in quantity and worse in quality than that which is allowed to convicted felons in the gaols: what does the veteran Tierney say, in the way of reason for giving his support to a man who declares to his face that he will persevere in the present unreformed system to the last hour of his parliamentary life? Does the veteran Tierney think that the right sort of system, think that the best sort of Parliament, which every year or two raises or lowers the value of money, and every year or two crushes one class or other of the community, and which has, even at this moment, no plan of restoration, no plan for producing a settled state of things, while things are going on from bad to worse, and while a convulsion, if not prevented by a Reform, is as sure to be the result as the end of the year is sure to arrive? The veteran Tierney did, in 1793, look upon a Reform of the House of Commons as absolutely necessary to the salvation of the country; but, a thousand millions having been added to the Debt by an unreformed Parliament, an enormous standing army in time of peace having been kept up by that unreformed Parliament, parsons having received military half-pay and being upheld in the receipt of it by that famously unreformed Parliament, that unreformed Parliament having passed *corn bills, transportation-for-poaching bills, new-trespass* laws, and having ordained *banishment for life* as the punishment of a man who shall, a second time, utter that which has a tendency to bring the unreformed Parliament into contempt; the unreformed Parliament having swelled up the taxes from sixteen millions a-year to sixty millions a-year, and the people having been, in consequence, plunged into crimes that have caused new gaols to rise up all over the country; yes, the unreformed Parliament having been found adequate to all these things, it would appear from the newspaper reports that the Right Honourable veteran has gone and placed himself at the back of a Prime Minister, who positively declares, that he will oppose, to the end of his parliamentary life, any Reform of the Parliament, *in whatever shape that Reform may appear!*

BURDETT, who has, doubtless, the same cogent reasons with the veteran Tierney, has, however, a rather tougher task to perform, in order to make people believe that he has not, by pledging himself to support Canning, abandoned one iota of his principles as a friend of Parliamentary Reform. He sets out by saying, that he will put aside that question, and that he then finds sufficient reasons for supporting Canning; but Canning will not *let him put it aside*; for, he gets up immediately and says he will oppose Reform to the end of his political life, and, still Burdett sits at his back, and still he says he will support him. With these facts so plainly before our eyes, are we to be cheated by an observation that there was a *schism* on the subject of Reform; aye, a schism, sure enough, made by the Whigs, whom he denounced, a thousand times over, for hypocrisy and roguery in the making of that schism. He talks about shades of opinion, and Canning himself talked about this difference of opinion amongst Reformers, and the vile Whigs talked about this difference of opinion, and the base hypocrites made it an excuse for not supporting Reform! Burdett says, there were many different views as to the nature of the Reform; I can tell him that there will be not many different views as to his conduct upon the present occasion; and, when the people of Westminster shall have a fair meeting, as I trust they will have NEXT MONDAY

IN COVENT-GARDEN, AT TWELVE O'CLOCK, he will find them perfectly unanimous; he will find no differences of opinion as to his junction with, or, rather, his truckling to, the jester, Canning, who set the House in a roar upon the subject of the bowels of poor Ogden.

But, Gentlemen, do, I pray you, look at the impudence of this assertion. The words form the greatest insult that ever was offered to any people upon the face of the earth. The people of England in general, and the people of Westminster in particular, have now received from this vain and haughty aristocrat, a greater insult than I recollect ever having seen offered to any body before. Here stands up a Prime Minister and says, I will oppose Parliamentary Reform to the end of my political life! *there shall be no Parliamentary Reform, as long as I shall be Minister:* and, Burdett, standing close at this man's back, says, within a few minutes of the same time, I will support this Minister: that is to say, I will support an opposition to Reform as long as this man remains Minister; and, yet, *I do not sacrifice one iota of my principles as a friend of Reform!* Upon my soul, Gentlemen, I believe him, if he mean his real principles; for, from the bottom of my heart, I believe he was always the secret enemy of Reform. If he had said, I do not sacrifice one iota of my *pretended* principles, I should have said, that the declaration argued a sense of past hypocrisy and a determination to be open and fair with us for the future. As the words now stand, they are a piece of base, ungratuitous insolence. If he had said, I must wish to achieve some practical good in my time; that is to say, *good to myself*; to pick up a peerage, or so, "as a man of common sense, when the opportunity is offered by the passing moment;" but, to declare that he will support the man, the Prime Minister, who, at the same moment, tells him to his teeth that he will oppose Reform to the end of his life, in that House, and still to call himself a friend of Reform, is a piece of insolence that could have proceeded from no man who had not been flattered for twenty years by a set of corrupt wretches who made a trade of crying him up for their own emolument. His new master has left him no excuse; he has left him no hole to creep out of, no pretences about shades of opinion and difference in views; for, he has told him that he will oppose Reform *under whatever shape it may appear,* and Burdett has pledged himself to support this man, and, of course, to support this opposition to the end of this man's life, if he himself live so long.

Nothing more need be said upon the subject, with a view of exposing the conduct of the man, who pledged himself to support the cause of Reform to the end of his life; who pledged himself to lay down his life if necessary, to ensure the success of that cause. It is curious enough, that Mr. Brougham says, that, if Dawson and his friends had remained in power, the Reformers might have been encouraged to proceed; but that, now, they will have no encouragement to do so. A pretty assertion, this, and clearly showing that that intriguing lawyer and all his brother coalescers reckon without their host. However, what we have now to consider, is, *what is our duty in this crisis of affairs.* Our duty clearly is, to meet when and where we legally can: there is no obstacle to our meeting now. Seven house-holders are to call a Meeting, when and where they like, upon giving the neighbouring Magistrate notice of their intention. It is very true, that all this stuff will be blown into air, at no very distant day, by troubles, by turmoils, that will shake these jobbers out of their senses; but, we ought to be ready; we ought to be perfectly ready to avail ourselves of the advantages that events will offer us, for the purpose of securing that Reform of the House of Commons, without which we must become a herd of the most beggarly slaves that ever crept about under the sun. I am happy to perceive that a meeting is to be held at Covent-Garden at 12 o'clock on Monday next. At that meeting I shall be; and I understand that *it is the intention of Mr.* HUNT *to be there also.* The precise object of the meeting I do not at present know. Whatever it may be, the meeting affords an opportunity for an appeal to the insulted and ill-treated people upon the subject of their ill-treatment and of the conduct of those who have insulted them. I here insert a notification which appeared in the *Morning Herald* of Tuesday last; and, as I detest roundabout ways, I will state precisely how that notification was produced. I spoke to a gentleman on Sunday last, to request Mr. Hunt, if he had the same views upon the subject that I had, to meet me the next day to deliberate on the means of co-operation in defence of the cause of Reform. The gentleman went suddenly out of town on Monday morning. Finding him gone, I wrote to Mr. Hunt much about what I had expressed to the gentleman verbally, and requested him to meet me that day, if he chose to co-operate with me for such purpose. The consequence of my letter was that a meeting took place, and that, in about ten minutes afterwards, the following notification was sent to be published in the *Morning Herald* Newspaper.

### Purity of Election — Parliamentary Reform.

The Anniversary Dinner-Meeting will, of course, be held, at the Crown and Anchor, in the Strand, on the 23d of this month of May, to celebrate the event, to which the above title alludes; and we think it right, think it a duty that we owe to our country, to notify, that we intend to be present at that Dinner, in the hope of obtaining an explanation of circumstances, which, in our opinion, indicate, in certain quarters, not only a disposition, but a settled design, to betray the cause of the people, and to barter the remnant of their liberties for the gratification of the vanity, or pecuniary interest, of those, who have heretofore professed themselves to be the most zealous defenders of those rights.

WM. COBBETT.
H. HUNT.

London, 7th May, 1827.

Since this notification was written, I have seen advertised in the newspapers, a meeting to take place, in the open air, in Covent-garden, on Monday next, the 14th instant. To that meeting, as I said before, I shall go, and I understand that Mr. Hunt will be there also. The people of Westminster may, by possibility, have become so abominably base as to like to be bartered, like bullocks in Smithfield; but, at any rate, they shall not be bartered without my doing my utmost to make them understand the nature of the transaction. I have, however, supposed this merely for argument's sake. I know they have been deceived, I know they have been cheated, I know they have been muzzled, I know they have been made miserable tools of by a selfish and rascally Rump-committee; but I know that they are not corrupted; I know that,

when they perceive the treason that has been committed against them, they will repel the traitors with indignation; and, I do really believe that this treachery, intended to ruin their liberties for ever; intended to make them slaves, infinitely more base than those of Maryland or Virginia; I do believe that this treachery, which aimed at the utter extirpation of all hope of Reform, will be the cause of the triumph of Reform and of the destruction of the traitors.

As to the dinner, the "twentieth anniversary of the purity of election dinner; if the stewards, as they call themselves; if the promoters of the dinner, suffer it to pass without calling to account the great hero of the feast, they must and will be stigmatized as the basest wretches upon earth. Twenty successive years has this dinner been held to celebrate the triumph of Westminster in having secured the election of a member in spite of the aristocracy. For twenty successive years that member has, in that same dinner room, solemnly declared his immoveable attachment to the cause of Reform, and has, with equal solemnity, assured the parties present, that no good whatever could ever be effected for the country without such Reform; that every thing else was idle and farcical; that the Whig pretence about economy and retrenchment was a hypocritical shuffle; for twenty successive years has he thus been vowing and declaring upon this identical spot; and he now comes to the same spot under the title of " Triumph of Westminster, Purity of Election," having just declared, in that seat into which the " Triumph of Westminster" put him; after having just declared from that very seat, that he who was, that he who continues to be, the bitter and abusive enemy of Reform, is now " his right honourable friend," and after having declared that he will give his support to that enemy of Reform, though that enemy says he will continue to be its enemy to the end of his life! If, therefore, this man can go into that dinner-room, and come out of it without the censure that he merits, the company assembled there will be so base, so entirely worthless and infamous; so rotten, so corrupt and so degraded, that

they will deserve, not to be treated like fallen men, but to be trodden into dirt and dung, like the spawn of those filthy reptiles from which the eye is turned and the touch recoils.

But, this event will not happen. Englishmen are not so degraded, yet. Fellows with age and skill in the art of packing, and well supplied with money, may do much; but I do not believe that they have the power; I do not believe that they could bribe enough of even poor starving creatures in Westminster to bear down the indignant and independent men who will be present at the Crown-and-Anchor on that day. I beg leave to press it upon the real and earnest friends of Reform, and, particularly, upon those who have some *leisure*, to consider, that they have a very sacred duty to perform upon this occasion. Nothing is so clear, as that the people are intended to be sacrificed by both the factions; that the liberties and all the interests of the people are to be the price of the several splittings and jostlings and shufflings and choppings and changings that have been and that are, now, going on. If the people gain no relief now; if the present scheme of sacrificing them succeed, almost every man in the middle rank of life must and will become something very near to that of a pauper. The system is now stripping the laborious tradesmen, who always hitherto escaped. There is no remedy short of a Reform of the Parliament. We have no defence but in such Reform; and this is now become so evident; it is become so evident that we must be beggared by the tax-eaters of various descriptions; by these eternal half-pay parsons and others who feed upon our vitals; this is so evident, that now it is seen by the dullest of eyes. All men see it; and, I trust, that many will now have the courage to come forward and do their best to save themselves and their children from that degradation which, without a Reform, is, assuredly, their lot.

I think that, upon this occasion, many gentlemen in the country ought to come to London; ought to be at the first of the meetings which will now take place. If they will not stir hand or foot, it is in vain to use their eyes in reading and their tongues in chatting by their own fire-sides. It is out in public meeting that they are wanted. I trust that they will not be wanted, but will come forth; that they will show Mr. Brougham that they have not cooled upon the subject of Reform; and, they may be assured, that, as far as I am concerned; as far as my capacity goes; as far as my limbs will carry me, and my voice can be heard, nothing shall be neglected to counteract the schemes and defeat the projects of the treacherous, base, malignant and cowardly enemies of the cause of Reform.

WM. COBBETT.

P. S. I perceive that Mr. Hume has given notice that he intends to bring in a Bill to repeal one of the Six Acts; and nothing has given me more pleasure for a long time. This is one of those famous Acts, passed in Canning's so loudly extolled " short month of legislation," which followed close upon the 16*th of August,* thanks to the *Manchester Magistrates,* and the *Oldham Inquest;* and the particular Act which Mr. Hume's notice relates to, is that which had been conjured up by Canning, Mackintosh and others; who are coalesced, to make it law to *transport a man on the second conviction of writings having a tendency to bring either House into contempt.*—I repeat, that I rejoice to see this notice of Mr. Hume, and I am sure that he can do nothing for which he will better deserve the thanks of the country.

# MARKETS.

Average Prices of CORN throughout ENGLAND, for the week ending April 27.

### Per Quarter.

| | s. | d. | | s. | d. |
|---|---|---|---|---|---|
| Wheat .. | 56 | 2 | Rye .... | 40 | 9 |
| Barley .. | 39 | 5 | Beans ... | 47 | 0 |
| Oats .... | 30 | 6 | Pease ... | 45 | 0 |

Total Quantity of Corn returned as
Sold in the Maritime Districts, for
the week ended April 27.

| | Qrs. | | Qrs. |
|---|---|---|---|
| Wheat .. | 35,634 | Rye ..... | 252 |
| Barley .. | 11,686 | Beans . .. | 1,588 |
| Oats ... | 11,650 | Pease .... | 292 |

*Corn Exchange, Mark Lane.*

Quantities and Prices of British
Corn, &c. sold and delivered in
this Market, during the week ended
Saturday, April 28.

| | Qrs. | £. | s. | d. | | s. | d. |
|---|---|---|---|---|---|---|---|
| Wheat.. | 4,489 | for 13,304 | 18 | 7 | Average, | 59 | 3 |
| Barley.. | 2,222 | .. 4,561 | 10 | 5 | .......... | 41 | 0 |
| Oats.. | 3,800 | .. 6,448 | 4 | 6 | .......... | 33 | 11 |
| Rye.... | 2 | .. 3 | 13 | 8 | .......... | 36 | 10 |
| Beans.. | 419 | .. 933 | 10 | 7 | .......... | 44 | 6 |
| Pease.. | 90 | .. 205 | 3 | 0 | .......... | 45 | 7 |

Friday, May 4.—The supplies of
Grain and Flour this week are moderate. The Wheat trade remains
the same as stated on Monday last.
Barley, Beans, and Pease fully maintain their late quotations. There is
not much doing in the Oat trade to-
day, and prices remain as last reported. There is a fair demand for
fresh made Flour.

Monday, May 7.—The arrivals of
the past week were moderate of most
kinds of Grain, and this morning the
fresh supplies are small. Wheat of
prime quality continues scarce, and
has obtained a further advance of 1s.
per qr. on the terms of this day se'n-
night, and other descriptions meet a
more ready sale than of late.

The Maltsters having nearly done
working, the best parcels of Barley
sell heavy at last quotations; Grinding samples sell freely, and are rather dearer. Beans of good quality
are again 1s. per quarter higher, as
there are so few at market. Pease
of both kinds remain the same as
last quoted, with little doing. In
good sweet Oats there has been a
fair demand to-day, at full as good
prices as last Monday, but other
kinds have not met with buyers
readily. There is a good trade for
fresh made Flour, but the prices are
unaltered.

———

Price of Bread.—The price of the
4lb. Loaf is stated at 9d. by the
full-priced Bakers.

———

## COAL MARKET, May 4.

*Ships at Market. Ships sold. Price.*
32½ Newcastle 15¼..31s. 0d. to 37s. 9d.
10¼ Sunderland 8¾..33s. 9d.— 38s. 9d.

Account of Wheat, &c. arrived in the Port of London, from April 30 to May 5, both inclusive.

| | Qrs. | | Qrs. |
|---|---|---|---|
| Wheat .. | 5,557 | Tares .... | 302 |
| Barley .. | 2,404 | Linseed .. | 92 |
| Malt .... | 6,989 | Rapeseed . | — |
| Oats .... | 3,171 | Brank .. | 18 |
| Beans ... | 433 | Mustard.. | — |
| Flour.... | 6,419 | Flax .... | — |
| Rye.... | — | Hemp ... | 35 |
| Pease.... | 257 | Seeds ... | — |

Foreign.—Wheat, 1,175; Barley, 4,290; Oats, 11,868; Beans, 5,860 quarters.

———

Monday, May 7.—The arrivals from Ireland last week were, 620 firkins of Butter, and 1,792 bales of Bacon; and from Foreign Ports, 4,062 casks of Butter.

———

## HOPS.

Price of Hops, per Cwt. in the Borough.

Monday, May 7.—The accounts from Kent and Sussex state flea as general, and have done some damage to the bines, which at present come up weak and nettley; prices, however, are not improved. Currency: Sussex, 80s. to 95s.; Kent, 84s. to 112s. Duty 115,000l.

*Maidstone*, May 3.—The warm weather and showers this last week, have much improved the Hops, and the Bines, which from the flea and frost were looking very unkindly, are resuming their colour and doing well. In the trade nothing doing.

*Worcester*, May 2.—On Saturday, 166 pockets of Hops were weighed: there was more demand, and an advance in price; the average being 96s. to 100s., and fine 105s. Neither the Merchants nor Planters are large holders. The accounts from the Plantation state that the flea increases.

## SMITHFIELD.

Monday, May 7.—The Beef Trade was heavy on Friday, but the best Beasts made about as much as this day se'nnight. Mutton was in fair demand, and looking upwards. Lamb sold freely at steady prices.—To-day there is a brisk trade, and higher prices given for every thing but lamb, which remains at 6s. to 7s. per stone. We quote Beef no higher than 5s. 2d. for the general trade; but some choice things have made more money. The best polled Sheep, shorn, have freely obtained 5s. 4d.; and Downs in the Wool, 6s. per stone. In the dead market, on Saturday, fore quarters of Mutton were sold at 5s., and whole carcases at 5s. 4d.

Per Stone of 8 pounds (alive).

| | s. | d. | s. | d. |
|---|---|---|---|---|
| Beef | 4 | 4 | to 5 | 2 |
| Mutton | 5 | 0 | — 6 | 0 |
| Veal | 5 | 0 | — 6 | 0 |
| Pork | 4 | 4 | — 5 | 6 |
| Lamb | 6 | 0 | — 7 | 0 |

| | | | |
|---|---|---|---|
| Beasts .. | 2,035 | Sheep .. | 15,600 |
| Calves ... | 130 | Pigs ... | 160 |

NEWGATE, (same day.)

Per Stone of 8 pounds (dead).

| | s. | d. | s. | d. |
|---|---|---|---|---|
| Beef | 3 | 8 | to 4 | 8 |
| Mutton | 4 | 0 | — 5 | 4 |
| Veal | 3 | 8 | — 5 | 8 |
| Pork | 3 | 8 | — 5 | 8 |
| Lamb | 4 | 8 | — 6 | 8 |

LEADENHALL, (same day.)

Per Stone of 8 pounds (dead).

| | s. | d. | s. | d. |
|---|---|---|---|---|
| Beef | 3 | 10 | to 4 | 6 |
| Mutton | 3 | 8 | — 5 | 2 |
| Veal | 3 | 10 | — 5 | 4 |
| Pork | 4 | 0 | — 5 | 4 |
| Lamb | 3 | 8 | — 6 | 8 |

## POTATOES.

**SPITALFIELDS,** *per Ton.*

|                    | l. | s. |    | l. | s. |
|--------------------|----|----|----|----|----|
| Ox-Nobles          | 3  | 15 | to | 0  | 0  |
| Middlings          | 2  | 10 | —  | 0  | 0  |
| Chats              | 2  | 0  | —  | 0. | 0  |
| Common Red         | 4  | 0  | —  | 0  | 0  |

Onions, 0s. 0d.—0s. 0d. per bush.

**BOROUGH,** *per Ton.*

|             | l. | s. |    | l. | s. |
|-------------|----|----|----|----|----|
| Ox-Nobles   | 3  | 10 | to | 4  | 0  |
| Middlings   | 2  | 10 | —  | 0  | 0  |
| Chats       | 1  | 15 | —  | 2  | 0  |
| Common Red  | 3  | 10 | —  | 0  | 0  |

## HAY and STRAW, per Load.

*Smithfield.*—Hay....90s. to 120s.
Straw...38s. to 42s.
Clover. 100s. to 140s.
*St. James's.*—Hay.... 80s. to 132s.
Straw .. 36s. to 49s.
Clover. 120s. to 140s.
*Whitechapel.*—Hay....84s. to 115s.
Straw...38s. to 42s.
Clover..90s. to 135s.

AVERAGE PRICE OF CORN, sold in the Maritime Counties of England and Wales, for the Week ended April 27, 1827.

|                   | Wheat. | | Barley. | | Oats. | |
|-------------------|----|----|----|----|----|----|
|                   | s. | d. | s. | d. | s. | d. |
| London*           | 58 | 10 | 40 | 10 | 33 | 0  |
| Essex             | 58 | 2  | 38 | 3  | 31 | 0  |
| Kent              | 55 | 6  | 39 | 10 | 30 | 6  |
| Sussex            | 54 | 9  | 0  | 0  | 30 | 8  |
| Suffolk           | 55 | 2  | 37 | 6  | 32 | 1  |
| Cambridgeshire    | 53 | 9  | 37 | 0  | 27 | 7  |
| Norfolk           | 55 | 0  | 36 | 6  | 30 | 6  |
| Lincolnshire      | 55 | 0  | 40 | 9  | 27 | 0  |
| Yorkshire         | 54 | 10 | 41 | 8  | 27 | 6  |
| Durham            | 55 | 8  | 42 | 3  | 38 | 8  |
| Northumberland    | 54 | 0  | 39 | 0  | 32 | 5  |
| Cumberland        | 61 | 3  | 40 | 4  | 34 | 2  |
| Westmoreland      | 61 | 10 | 43 | 8  | 38 | 3  |
| Lancashire        | 61 | 8  | 43 | 6  | 35 | 1  |
| Cheshire          | 60 | 10 | 0  | 0  | 0  | 0  |
| Gloucestershire   | 56 | 8  | 43 | 1  | 37 | 1  |
| Somersetshire     | 54 | 1  | 42 | 1  | 31 | 8  |
| Monmouthshire     | 59 | 8  | 45 | 0  | 0  | 0  |
| Devonshire        | 56 | 4  | 38 | 10 | 29 | 2  |
| Cornwall          | 61 | 2  | 40 | 0  | 37 | 3  |
| Dorsetshire       | 53 | 8  | 39 | 8  | 37 | 9  |
| Hampshire         | 55 | 7  | 40 | 8  | 30 | 1  |
| North Wales       | 64 | 10 | 45 | 2  | 35 | 0  |
| South Wales       | 59 | 5  | 45 | 4  | 28 | 1  |

* The London Average is always that of the Week preceding.

*Bristol*, May 5.—The sales of Corn, &c. in our Corn markets, appear more brisk than they have been, and more business is doing. The prices at present are about as below quoted.—Wheat, from 6s. to 7s. 6d.; Barley, 4s. 3d. to 6s. 3d.; Beans, 6s. 3d. to 8s.; Oats, 3s. 2d. to 4s. 3d.; and Malt, 5s. 6d. to 8s. 3d. per bushel, Imperial. Flour, Seconds, 32s. to 43s. per bag.

*Horncastle*, May 5.—There has been so little alteration in our Corn markets for the last two or three weeks, that it is not worth notice—Wheat, 54s. to 56s.; Barley, 40s. to 43s.; Oats, 30s. to 35s.; Beans, 60s. to 64s.; and Rye from 40s. to 45s. per quarter.

*Ipswich*, May 5.—We had to-day a small supply of Corn at market. The sale was dull at about last week's prices, as follow:—Wheat, 54s. to 62s.; Barley, 36s. to 41s.; and Beans, 47s. to 49s. per quarter.

*Malton*, May 5.—Our market for Grain continues in the same dull state it has been for some weeks past. Prices rather lower. Wheat, 58s. to 62s. per quarter for 40 stone; Barley, 44s. to 43s. per quarter. Oats 15d. to 17d. per stone.

*Manchester*, May 5.—During the week, and at our market to-day, there has been a better demand for most articles in the trade. The holders of fine wheat demanded an advance of 2d. per bushel of 70 lbs., which was, in a few instances, complied with. Oats may be quoted ½d. to 1d. per 45 lbs. lower, with very little doing in them. Beans were in request at last week's rates. Flour is rather improved in value as well as demand. In Barley, Pease, and Malt, no alteration.

*Newcastle-on-Tyne*, May 5.—The supply of Wheat from the farmers was again large this morning, and having some small arrivals coastwise, the millers were enabled to supply themselves at a trifle above the prices of last week. Rye continues in demand. Barley sells at the same prices as last week, but the demand is very limited. The farmers' supply of Oats sold very slowly at a decline of 1s. per quarter, but foreign Oats in bond are dearer.

*Norwich*, May 5.—We had only a small supply of all Grain to-day, and the demand being brisk, Red Wheat sold at 52s. to 59s.; White, to 61s.; Barley, 30s. to 40s.; Oats, 28s. to 32s.; Beans, 43s. to 48s.; Pease, 44s. to 48s.; Boilers, to 52s. per quarter; and Flour, 41s. to 42s. per sack.

*Reading*, May 5.—We had a short supply of Wheat, which met a ready sale on much the same terms as last week, viz. 55s. to 68s. per quarter, by the Imperial measure. The quantity of Barley was less than for the last twelve months; it sold at the same prices as this day se'nnight. Oats were also a short supply, and maintained their value. So little was done in Beans or Pease, that prices of both articles must be stated nominally as last week.

*Wakefield*, May 4.—There is a good supply of Wheat fresh up to-day; the factors generally, at the commencement of the market, asked higher prices, but the buyers were unwilling to comply, and the business done has been at last Friday's prices. Oats and Shelling are dull sale, and rather lower. Although the supply of Barley is very small, the sale has been dull to-day, at the rates of last week for the best samples; and the middling sorts are rather lower. Beans are in better demand, and 1s. per quarter dearer. Rapeseed is as dull as possible.

*Wisbeach*, May 5.—Wheat and Beans sold to-day for full as much money as last week. Oats were about 1s. lower.

## COUNTRY CATTLE AND MEAT MARKETS, &c.

*Horncastle*, May 5.—Beef, 9s: per stone of 14 lbs.; Mutton, 8d.; Lamb, 10d.; Pork, 7d. ; and Veal, from 8d. to 9d. per lb.

*Manchester* Smithfield Market, May 2.—We had a short supply of Beef and Mutton to this day's market. Last week's prices were barely maintained.—Beef, 5d. to 8d.; Mutton, 7d. to 8½d.; Lamb, 9½d. to 11d.; Veal, 5½d. to 7d.; and Pork, 4½d. to 6d. per lb., sinking offal.

*Norwich Castle Meadow*, May 5.—The supply of fat Cattle to this day's market, was exceedingly large, and the demand not corresponding with it, prices were a little lower than last week; 7s. 6d. to 8s. 3d. per stone of 14 lbs., sinking offal; Store Stock was supplied also in great abundance; Scots sold at 4s. to 4s. 6d. per stone of what they will weigh when fat; Shorthorns, 3s. to 3s. 9d. Pigs fewer in number ; fat ones to 7s. 6d. per stone.—Meat: Beef, 7d. to 9d.; Veal, 6d. to 8d.; Mutton, 6d. to 7½d.; Lamb, 9d.; and Pork, 6d. to 8d. per lb.

At *Morpeth* Market, May 2d, there were a good many Cattle; being a great demand, fat sold readily at last week's prices. There was a full market of Sheep, which met with dull sale; prices rather lower, and part not sold.—Beef, from 7s. 3d. to 8s.; Mutton, 9s. 6d. to 10s, 6d. per stone, sinking offal.

# COBBETT'S WEEKLY REGISTER.

Vol. 62.—No. 8.]    LONDON, SATURDAY, May 19, 1827.    [Price 6d.

" Gentlemen,—After what has lately passed in review before us, it is
" impossible to shut our eyes to the actual situation of our country.
" Lord Melville, with his associates and abettors, under the pre-
" tence of *loyalty;* and *the leaders of the Whigs under the pretence of*
" *the Constitution;* and the LEADERS OF THE CATHOLICS, UN-
" DER THE PRETENCE OF RELIGION, are ALL evidently strug-
" gling for one and the same object;—A SHARE OF THE COMMON
" SPOIL. Whilst the wholesome power of the Crown, the fair liberty
" of the subject, and the real interest of any religion are all sacrificed to
" the *common object—Plunder.* Of the rights of the people at large and
" of their welfare and independence, not a syllable is even whispered by
" any of these factions : and any attempt by others to bring the people
" or their interests into consideration, is stigmatised as treason."—
SIR FRANCIS BURDETT'S ADDRESS TO THE FREEHOLDERS OF MIDDLESEX,
APRIL 28, 1807.

" Gentlemen, that MR. CANNING (I mention him as the CHAMPION
" of the party, a part for the whole) should defend, to the utmost, a
" system, by the HOCUS-POCUS TRICKS of which *he and his family*
" *get so much public money,* can cause neither in me nor any man suspi-
" cion or anger ;

　　" For 'tis their duty, all the learned think,
　　" T' espouse the cause by which *they eat and drink.*"

" The ox knoweth his owner and the ass his MASTER'S CRIB; and
" these gentry, at least, equal the ox and the ass in knowledge and virtue ;
" and are, moreover, superior to the Jews ; for they do know their *Maker.*
" I will, however, boldly adduce their example as proof undeniable of the
" benefits the people would derive *from appointing their own Representa-*
" *tives; seeing* that these gentlemen are *ever true to their and their*
" *patrons' interests.* This identity of interest ' keeps all smooth, and the
" people may rest assured, that the same cause will ever produce the
" same effect; and that, whenever the people shall have *the appointment*
" *of their own House of Commons,* the public expenditure will be con-
" trolled, the public burdens diminished, the public money applied to
" public purposes, and the public happiness and prosperity, in other

Printed and Published by WILLIAM COBBETT, No. 183, Fleet-street.
[ENTERED AT STATIONERS' HALL.]　　　P

" words, *liberty and property*, secured, and NOT TILL THEN."—Sir
Francis Burdett's Letter to the Reform-Meeting at the Crown
and Anchor, 4th April, 1821.

" I would fain hope, that the example given by the people of West-
" minster, might encourage other places still to contend for that small
" portion of Independence which yet remains in the country ; and thereby
" keep alive, at least in the remembrance of their countrymen, their
" ancient constitutional right to a *full, fair, and free representation of the*
" *people in Parliament*, their *only quiet and peaceable security*, at all times,
" for their *rights and property*, against the *despotism and plunder of the*
" *few*.  For these purposes you shall *always* find me, either *in* or *out* of
" *Parliament*, READY TO LAY DOWN MY LIFE."—Sir Francis
Burdett's Letter to the Electors of Westminster, 16th October, 1812.

" I am asked what I mean to do on the subject of Parliamentary Re-
" form.  Why, I say,—to oppose it—TO OPPOSE IT TO THE END
" OF MY LIFE IN THIS HOUSE, UNDER WHATEVER SHAPE
" IT MAY APPEAR."—Mr. Canning's Speech in the House of Commons, 4th May, 1827.

" Putting aside all the great questions, *including that of Parliamentary*
" *Reform*, I see sufficient reason to support the Administration of my
" Right Honourable Friend [Mr. Canning.]"—Sir Francis Burdett's
Speech in the House of Commons, 4th May, 1827.

" I am accused by some persons as a man who am changing my prin-
" ciples.  None of us knows what we may be changed to at last, and, I
" may become an *oyster* for any thing that I know to the contrary ; but
" this I will say, that no one can truly assert that I am not a CON-
" SISTENT POLITICIAN"!—Sir Francis Burdett's Speech, at
the "Purity of Election" Dinner, at the Crown and Anchor, on
the 23d May, 1818.

TO THE

# ELECTORS OF WESTMINSTER.

*Fleet Street*, 17th May, 1827.

Gentlemen,

Now is the time for you to prove, in every way that you have the power, that you are no longer to be silenced, to be muzzled, to be moulded into things like the inhabitants of a rotten borough, by a despicable Rump Committee, who are the notorious tools of a man of immense wealth, who knows very well how to husband that wealth, how to take care of the pounds and shillings, and how to bestow the odd pence and farthings in a judicious and profitable manner; how to grease the chins and fill with swill the teals of his ambition.

The Meeting which took place in your City, on last Monday, and which brought forth an Address from you to the King, unanimously passed, and which Address I shall presently insert, was attended with circumstances such as can leave no doubt in the mind of any rational man, that it was intended to prevent you from having any Meeting at all; and, as little doubt can remain in the mind of any such man, that the object of this interruption was to save BURDETT and HOBHOUSE, and particularly the former, to shelter him from the consequences of meeting you face to face, and there having his conduct fairly tried.

Pray, Gentlemen, attend to these circumstances; a hundred and ten house-holders of Westminster, each putting his name at full length and his place of abode

at full length, apply to the High Bailiff in writing, and send him a requisition, thus signed, requesting him to call a Meeting in the city, for the purpose of taking into consideration the propriety of *addressing the King*. This was the sole object stated in the requisition. The intention of the parties sending the requisition was to express approbation of the conduct of his Majesty in having exercised his prerogative, *in spite of what the parties believed to have been an attempt unduly to interfere with the exercise of that prerogative*. This was the intention of the parties; but, in their requisition to the High Bailiff, they simply stated their wish that he would afford the electors of Westminster an opportunity of *addressing the King*.

Was there ever any thing, Gentlemen, less calculated to excite the suspicions of a public officer of any improper motive in the parties requesting? Was there ever any thing less calculated to produce objection in such officer to call a public Meeting? Was there ever any thing better calculated to produce in any such officer alacrity in accommodating the requesting parties? Yet, the High Bailiff of Westminster (Morris, I think his name is), in a very laconic answer, and without assigning any reason whatever, *refused to call the Meeting;* though, he had *never, upon any occasion, refused to accede to a requisition presented to him by Burdett's rump committee.*

Another circumstance is, that the gentlemen who sent the requisition, wrote, at the same time, to Burdett and Hobhouse, requesting them to attend the Meeting of their Constituents; and, it had been their uniform practice to attend all such Meetings in Westminster. From these two worthies, however, the gentlemen obtained NO ANSWER AT ALL, and, thus situated, some gentlemen who had taken a lead in the business, called a meeting themselves, as they had a right to do, appointing, as the place of the Meeting, the pavement (not the causeway) in Covent-garden, opposite the east front of St. Paul's church. When the hour of meeting arrived, Mr. Hunt, myself and several others, who had had no previous communication whatsoever with the parties calling the Meeting, went to the spot, where a hustings had been erected under the superintendence, and at the expense of a Committee of the Requisitionists. When we arrived, there were persons at work, under the direction of Mr. Lee, the High Constable of Westminster, who was assisted by a great number of his constables, demolishing these hustings, and that, too, in a manner the most violent.

In this object they, at last, succeeded, to the great peril of one of the gentlemen of the Committee. The hustings having been demolished, Mr. Hunt sent for a van, into which some gentlemen of the Committee, Mr. Hunt himself, I and others, got, and drove to the spot where the hustings had stood, and where there was an immense concourse of persons assembled. A like interruption was now given to the van, by a person calling himself a *surveyor or commissioner of pavements*; who insisted that he had a right, under the Paving Act, to prevent the van from standing on that spot or on any other spot in the parish of St. Paul, asserting that its standing there was an *obstruction to travellers on the king's highway.* You will observe, that it was *not a market-day;* you will observe, also, that it was *not a street*, along which carriages of any sort pass frequently, except on a market-day; you will observe, in short, that it was a spot where no nuisance could possibly be committed by the standing of either the van or the hustings; and, therefore, taking into view the refusal on the part of the High-Bailiff; bearing in mind that he never refused to call a meeting at the suggestion of Burdett's rump Committee; and, adding to all these circumstances, the further circumstance that BURDETT and HOBHOUSE *gave no answer of any sort* to the application of so large a number of their constituents; taking all these circumstances into view, it is quite unnecessary for me to point out to you what persons were the real source of this attempt totally to prevent a meeting of the people of Westminster upon this occasion.

It could not, you may say, or some persons, at least, might say; it could not possibly be BURDETT who was the cause of preventing a meeting of his constituents to *congratulate the king* on a transaction of which he had expressed his approbation in Parliament; it surely could not be Burdett that wished to prevent his constituents from applauding the king for having shown his firmness in a way to get rid of his late ministers? Why, I will tell you, now, Gentlemen: Burdett would have had no objection in the world to come and join his constituents in congratulating the king on his firm-

ness in getting rid of his late ministers; but, Burdett was by no
means sure that his constituents
would *stop there*; he was by no
means sure that his constituents
would approve of the *new Minister*, who was the notorious, the
persevering, the insulting, the
implacable enemy of that reform
of Parliament, which this Burdett
had a thousand times over declared
to those constituents was the only
measure from which they could
possibly derive either security to
their property, peace to their
homes, or safety to their lives.
He was by no means sure that
his constituents would not see
somebody come face to face before
him, accuse him of abandonment
of all his principles and all his
pledges; prove to his teeth that
he had, now, put aside the cause
of Reform; that he had now pledged himself to support an opposition to Reform, during the political life of Mr. Canning; that he
had called this bitterest of all the
enemies of Reform his *Right
Honourable Friend*, though the

other, while Burdett was sitting
with his knees in his back, declared that "*he would oppose Reform
to the end of his political life,
in whatever shape it might appear*"! This would have been
a pretty good dose for him to swallow; he must have had a face of
brass and a throat of iron to get
down even *this* dose.   But, he
would have further had proved to
his teeth that his present miserable
pretence about Catholic Emancipation was upon a level with the
rest of his conduct; and of that
you may now well satisfy yourselves, if you will read the mottos
to this paper and also the extracts from the several speeches
and letters which I shall insert at
the end of this letter to you.  Burdett was aware of all this: Burdett knew that he had represented the leaders of the Catholics
as being, like the leaders of the
Whigs, *in search of a share of the
spoil*; he was well aware that he
had distinctly stated in the House
of Commons, over and over again,
that *the Catholic Question was a*

force; and that he would be reminded that he had, in the most
serious and elaborate manner, declared, and that, too, in the House
itself, that it was monstrous, that
it was contemptible beyond description to believe, or affect to
believe, that any part of his Majesty's dominions, and PARTI-
CULARLY IRELAND, could
have a chance of being made
better off without the adoption of
that great measure, Parliamentary
Reform.

Well was Burdett aware of all
these things; and, though I have
no evidence to prove that it was he
who wished to prevent the meeting from taking place; though,
perhaps, hardly a man of you
have any such evidence to produce; yet, I am fully persuaded
that there is hardly a man of you
who will not be convinced, as I am,
that he was the real source, the
real cause of all those obstructions
which were intended to prevent a
Public Meeting in Westminster
from taking place.

That Meeting did, however,
take place. We, in the van,
moved off round by the north side
of Covent-garden, and went down
through Catherine-street to a
pretty wide and rather quiet place
between the street of the Strand
and the northern commencement
of the Strand-bridge. There the
proceedings were commenced by
a Mr. PITTS, who proposed and
read to the Meeting an Address
to his Majesty, expressing approbation of his Majesty's conduct in
having exercised his authority in
choosing a Prime Minister, and
also expressing approbation of
the known principles of that Minister. This would have suited
Daddy Burdett excellently well!
If he could have been present,
when an Address like this were
carried, he would have been worth
a great deal more to Canning
than he would be worth without it.
But, alas! he was too cunning to
venture upon an attempt like this
to add to his value. He knew his
honest constituents too well to believe that such an Address would
be tolerated by them: he knew

that no Meeting of the Electors of Westminister, in *open air*, would ever agree to an approbation of the principles of a man, who had just declared that he would oppose Parliamentary Reform to the end of his political life. In a *packed assembly* of persons, called the Electors of Westminster; in a room, lined by the rump; at a dinner where the price would operate as an exclusion, even to the middle rank of life; in a room guarded by a set of fellows called stewards, appointed by his rump or himself; in such a place, he might be able to get such an Address carried; but, then, an Address so carried, would rather *lessen than add to his value* in the eyes of CANNING. When Mr. PITTS had concluded, and his Address had been seconded by Mr. HUNT, who, you will please to observe, seconded it merely because there appeared no body else to do it: merely because the Meeting should have an opportunity of expressing their opinion upon it; Mr. Hunt, at the end of a speech of considerable length, proposed and read to the Meeting the following Address.

" TO HIS MAJESTY, GEORGE " THE FOURTH.

" The dutiful and humble Address of a large number of his " Majesty's subjects, assembled " first in the parish of St. Paul, " Covent Garden, and next in " the parish of St. Clement " Danes, in the city of Westminster, on Monday, the 14th " day of May, 1827.

" May it please your Majesty, " —We, your Majesty's dutiful " subjects, think ourselves called " upon, by the sentiments of " loyalty and attachment which " we bear to your Majesty, to " congratulate your Majesty on " your firmness in having exercised your undoubted prerogative, in choosing your Prime " Minister, in defiance of what " did appear, and what still appears, to us, to have been an " attempt, on the part of certain " persons, to dictate to your Majesty in the making of that " choice.

" But, may it please your Majesty, while we thus congratulate your Majesty, while we are " thus mindful of the royal rights " of your Majesty, we, not un-

" mindful of our own undoubted
" rights, and of that which is
" necessary to preserve or to re-
" store them, should be wanting
" in justice to ourselves, and in
" fidelity to your Majesty, were
" we to refrain from expressing
" our deep regret, that the per-
" son on whom the choice of your
" Majesty has fallen, should have
" already declared his decided
" and never-ceasing hostility to
" that great measure, Parliamen-
" tary Reform, which we deem
" absolutely necessary to our
" restoration to real freedom and
" happiness; and, not more ne-
" cessary to these, than to the
" permanent greatness of the
" nation, and to the dignity
" and security of your Majesty's
" Throne."

I seconded this Address, after
having stated my reasons for so
doing. The Address speaks for
itself; and the country will by
no means be surprised to learn
that it was carried, without one
single dissenting voice; and that
not one single hand was held up,
or one single yea pronounced, for
the Address in which approbation
had been expressed of the principles of Canning. Oh, Burdett!
oh, great Daddy of Westminster!
oh, " Westminster's Pride and
England's Glory ! " if you could
but have found leisure to be present upon that occasion, how your
ears would have tingled at the
feelings of indignation which were
expressed by your honest constituents; at their looks of disdain,
at their ejaculations of contempt,
every time that your recent conduct was either mentioned or alluded to ! Thousands of the persons present seized opportunities
of expressing their abhorrence at
that conduct, and the common jest
of the day was, how clever you
had shown yourself, how sound
and excellent your judgment, in
taking care not to be present at
this Meeting.

The extracts, which I have
prepared for insertion in the latter part of this Register, make
it necessary for me to postpone
further remarks, with regard to
this Meeting, to another occasion;
though, I must add, while I think
of it, that I, having a fortnight
ago republished part of a Long

the present; and, as to his "right honourable friend," he may judge of his popularity and of the real influence, at bottom, of the vile and corrupt press of London, by what passed at the Mechanics' Institute last night. It was a Meeting in-doors. Mr. Hume, who "keeps his eye THUS;" who looks hard across the way; who neither lets out nor keeps in; who seems to be friendly; who seems to tender the olive-branch; who stretches it out, and, not being taken, draws it back again; who, doubtless, meant to show that he had a little band that he could play off upon occasion; this gentleman, this nice calculator of interest, *was in the Chair*! Yet, the Address to the King which was carried, dared not even whisper a word in praise of Canning. On the contrary, his principles were manfully attacked, and, it was evidently owing to the diffidence, the personal modesty of the sensible men who attacked those principles, that a clause was not added to the Address, expressive of detestation of those principles. The Prime Minister's popularity does not shine much, then, even in London; even amongst those who are most under the influence of this deluding, base and corrupt press. Mr. Alderman Wood has said that he will support Canning; that his constituents approve of Canning: let Mr. Alderman Wood *call a Common Hall of London*, and he shall smother me in a hop-bag, or distil me into finings for porter, if the decision be not completely and ten to one against this daring, this insolent enemy of Parliamentary Reform. Again, I say, let Mr. Alderman Wood call the Common Hall: he will find that the corrupt press has not corrupted his honest constituents: he will find that that vile instrument has not debauched the minds of the people; and, if he do not call that Common Hall, I trust that somebody else will have the spirit to do it, and, then we shall see whether the people have abandoned the cause for which they have so long been contending.

I conclude this article with observing that I am about to insert a series of extracts from letters and speeches and addresses and resolutions, written, spoken, presented or proposed by Burdett. I beg the young men who read the Register; particularly the *young* men, to attend to these. The mottos are pretty nearly enough, to be sure; but, here, there is a thousand times more than enough. Here is every thing ten times over repeated, to prove him to be destitute of every particle of political principle. Agreeably to the notification made in my last Register, it is the resolution of Mr. Hunt and of myself, to attend at the "*Purity*" dinner, at the Crown and Anchor in the Strand, on Wednesday next, the 23d of this month of May. I am yet to believe, and I am yet to *see* it, before I believe it possible, that one single man who has not been actually hired for the purpose, or who is not constantly retained in pay, will stand up to propose or to second, a motion for drinking the health of this man. At any rate, I will put the party to the test, except some trick he played in order to prevent it: some trick like that of Monday last to prevent the Meeting; a trick more easy to play with success, because the getting up of the thing is in the hands of the cronies of the landlord of the house. But, I warn the old Daddy, that no trick of this sort shall answer his purpose in the end. I warn him, that if there be not a clear stage and fair play, he shall suffer for the obstruction in the end.

Thus, Gentleman, I take my leave of you for the present: I was one of those who put this man into the seat for Westminster; I was one of the principal actors in that affair: I was one of his principal props for many years. Just about ten years ago, I denounced him as being prepared to abandon the cause, for the sake of which, and for the sake of which only, we had put him up and upheld him. He has now proved that that denunciation was just;

" selves to share the booty in such
" different proportions as the
" leader of the gang shall appoint
" to each. From time to time it
" will happen that some thief or
" other amongst them will pur-
" loin a part of the booty, and
" clandestinely appropriate to
" himself more than his appointed
" share. The purloiner is de-
" tected: and the gang, with open
" mouths exclaim against the atro-
" city of cheating the regiment;
" the only crime of the kind which
" they acknowledge to be so.

* * * * * * * * * *

" And unless the public, with an
" united voice, shall loudly pro-
" nounce the abolition of the
" WHOLE of the present SYSTEM
" OF CORRUPTION, I must
" still continue to despair of my
" country. In the mean time, though
" an individual is almost as nothing
" in the scale, I will carry with me
" your sentiments into the House
" of Commons. And I assure you
" that no rational endeavours of
" mine shall be omitted to restore
" to my countrymen the undis-
" turbed enjoyment of the fair
" fruits of their industry ; *to tear*
" *out the accursed leaves of the*
" *scandalous* RED BOOK: and
" to bring back men's minds to the
" almost forgotten notions of the
" sacredness of private property ;

" which ought no longer to be
" transferred from the legitimate
" possessors *by the corrupt votes*
" *of venal and mercenary combi-*
" *nations.*"—Address to the
Electors of Westminster, 23d
*May*, 1807.

———

(4.) *Speech at the first "Purity of*
*Election" Dinner, held on the*
*29th June,* 1807. (*Register* 4th
*July,* 1807. *Vol.* xii. *page* 6.)

" Gentlemen, it is quite impos-
" sible for me to express in ade-
" quate terms the sense I feel of
" the affectionate manner in which
" you have been so good as to
" compliment me.—Your confi-
" dence in my public principles,
" and in the sincerity of my pro-
" fessions, has called me, when I
" least expected it, from the re-
" tirement I had chosen. I have
" but small hope, that any weak
" endeavours of mine will be able
" to benefit my country; because
" the choice of a new House of
" Commons is not what it ought
" to be, and what it is hypocriti-
" cally pretended to be—an ap-
" peal to the sense of the people.
" —In November last, the then
" Ministry, by an unusual disso-
" lution of Parliament, affected to
" appeal to the sense of the peo-
" ple. And this sense of the peo-

" ple, immediately consented to
" drive themselves from the first
" floor to the garret, and to beg-
" gar their posterity by confirm-
" ing to the Ministry a yearly
" tenth of all the income and pro-
" fits of the property and industry
" of the whole nation, together with
" an additional ten per cent. upon
" the already enormous assessed
" taxes.—Only six months after-
" wards, another set of men, the
" present Ministry, follow the ex-
" ample of the last set, and affect
" in their turn, by another disso-
" lution of Parliament, to appeal
" likewise again to the sense of
" the people. What this last-
" taken sense of the people will
" produce it is easy to foresee;
" and we shall soon experience.
" —Gentlemen, they both of them
" laugh at the people—they de-
" spise the people—and those
" who have robbed us most, have
" justly the most contempt for us.
" It is the common cant of both
" parties to deny that there is any
" such thing as the people—and
" they insultingly ask us, where
" such a thing as the people is to
" be found in England?—I can
" now answer their question—in
" Westminster—in the metropo-
" lis of England. And if the cor-
" rupt and mercenary factions
" shall see the other inhabitants of

" England act firmly and perse-
" veringly like a people, they
" will quickly acknowledge them
" to be such—and those who now
" tread oppressively upon their
" necks will be found humble at
" their feet.—I cannot, Gentle-
" men, go back to my place at
" the table, without returning my
" sincere thanks to the electors of
" Westminster, for the honour
" they have conferred upon me ;
" *assuring them that my whole*
" *life shall be devoted to their*
" *service.*"

------

(5.) " Thus, plans are proposed,
" decided on and rejected! The
" indecision of this Government
" contrasted by the blind obsti-
" nacy of the next, and both
" outdone by the nick-name vigour
" of the following! Distraction
" in our councils and impotence
" in our Ministers, while military
" executioners are daring to fix
" the badge of servitude on the
" people. Alas! how deplorably
" do I feel at the sight of the jour-
" neymen politicians opposite;
" feeble is the hope of England if
" such is her dependence! Sir,
" such are my sentiments on this
" bill and on our present situation ;
" they are the result of observa-
" tion, and of the instruction which

" I have gleaned from those pure
" and venerable authors which
" even the new morality has not
" taught me to despise."—DEBATE
ON LOCAL MILITIA. *May*, 1808.

---

(6.) " The Gentlemen who have
" preceded me, have told you very
" truly, that these abuses arise
" from the imperfect state of our
" Parliamentary representation.
" I am fully convinced, that there
" is not, at the present moment,
" any subject worthy of engaging
" the serious attention of the Eng-
" lish nation, except the necessity
" of a REFORM in PARLIA-
" MENT. This sentiment has
" been always entertained, and
" always avowed by me, and I
" do flatter myself that it was this
" sentiment which first recom-
" mended me to your notice.

* * * * * * * * *

" *So far from the House of*
" *Commons representing the sense*
" *of the people of England, I*
" *have ever found, since I have*
" *been a member of the House*
" *of Commons, that the most po-*
" *pular sentiment, which can be*
" *expressed in that place, is a*
" sentiment of CONTEMPT
" FOR THE PEOPLE OF
" ENGLAND, whose represen-
" tatives they still profess to be.

" I do believe that the House of
" Commons is the only spot in all
" *the world, where the people of*
" *England are spoken of with*
" *contempt. There they are ca-*
" lumniated, there the character
" of Englishmen are lightly spoken
" of, and their opinions and feel-
" ings set at nought. If this cir-
" cumstance does not shew you
" *the necessity of Parliamentary*
" *Reform*, there is nothing that I
" can say (were I to speak till
" night), which could convince
" you.

" The abuses of which we com-
" plain, proceed directly from the
" corruption which has taken root
" in the whole system of govern-
" ment. Where the source is
" corrupt, the streams cannot be
" pure. Where corruption has
" fastened in the root, it will be
" discovered in the fruit of the
" tree. Those abuses have ar-
" rived to so flagrant a pitch, that
" even the friends of that system
" thought it necessary to have
" commissions and inquiries in-
" stituted for the purpose of prun-
" ing and dressing the tree which
" now produces such bitter fruit.
" This, however, is not enough:
" ness; WE must LAY THE
" AXE TO THE ROOT OF
" THE TREE. Unless we de-
" stroy this *hydra of corruption*,

" it will destroy the country. The
" monster now stands with harpy
" claws, seizing on all our sub-
" stance, to supply the means of
" its boundless prodigality.

* * * * * * * * * *

" I am free to confess, that it
" is my opinion, that a Parlia-
" mentary Reform is now abso-
" lutely necessary. If it can be
" obtained by quiet means, it will
" be a most fortunate circum-
" stance, not only for the country,
" but for the government, for they
" are the most foolish and wicked
" advisers of the crown, who ad-
" vise the sovereign to treat with
" scorn the wishes and opinions of
" the people.

* * * * * * * * * *

" I HOPE THE NATION
" HAS CEASED TO LOOK
" FOR ANY ADVANTAGE
" FROM ANY CHANGE OF
" ADMINISTRATIONS. We
" must look no more to parties,
" and be assured that we never
" can expect any measures really
" useful, until the people of Eng-
" land have their proper share
" in the constitution of their
" country."—SPEECH AT A MEET-
ING AT WESTMINSTER, 30th March,
1809.

----

(†) " At a meeting of the
" FRIENDS of such a Reform

" as would secure to the People
" the reality and uses of RE-
" PRESENTATION in PARLIA-
" MENT, held at the Crown and
" Anchor Tavern, May 1809,
" Sir FRANCIS BURDETT, Bart.,
" M.P., in the Chair,

" Resolved,

" 1. That it is the grand
" principle of the Constitution,
" that the People should have a
" share in the Government, by a
" just representation in Par-
" liament.

" 2. That the long duration of
" Parliaments greatly facilitates
" the corruption of the members,
" and removes that wholesome
" check or control on their con-
" duct, a frequent recurrence to
" the opinions of their constituents.

" 3. That in a petition pre-
" sented to the House of Com-
" mons on the 6th May 1793, it
" was offered to be proved at the
" Bar, that 154 individuals did,
" by their own authority, appoint
" or procure the return of 307
" Members of that House (exclu-
" sive of those from Scotland)
" who were thus enabled to decide
" all questions in the name of the
" whole people of Great Britain.

" 4. That this meeting believes
" individual patronage in Bo-
" roughs has increased since
" 1793; that in those in which

" the voters are few, and which " are called open, the returns are " for the most part obtained for " money ; that the representation " for Scotland is extremely in- " fluenced ; and that there are " great defects in that of Ireland: " and it is the opinion of this " meeting that a great majority of " the members of the Commons' " House are so returned that the " nation is not constitutionally " represented ; though it is taxed " to support an expenditure of " 70,000,000 sterling a year.

" 5. That in the Act (commonly " called the Act of Settlement) " which placed the House of " Brunswick on the Throne of " these Realms, it was asserted " and recognised as the constitu- " tional principle, That no person " who has an office or place of " profit under the King, or receives " a pension from the Crown, shall " be capable of serving as a " Member of the House of " Commons.

" 6. That it appears by a report " laid on the table of the House of " Commons in June last, about 78 " of its Members are in the regular " receipt under the Crown of " £178,994 a year.

" 7. That in 1782, it was de- " clared by Mr. Pitt in the House " of Commons, that seven or

" eight Members of that House " were sent there by the *Nabob of* " *Arcot*, and that a foreign state " in enmity to this country might " procure a party to act for it " under the mask and character " of Members of that House.

" 8. That such a state of repre- " sentation is a national grievance.

" 9. That in every department " of the state into which inquiry " has been made, scandalous cor- " ruptions and abuses have been " detected.

" 10. That the exclusion of " the public voice from all influ- " ence in, and the consequent " corruption of, the Governments " of the Continental States, have " been the causes of their subju- " gation.

" 11. That so long as the people " shall not be fairly represented, " *corruption will increase*; our " *debts and taxes will accumulate;* " *our resources will be dissipated;* " the native energy of the people " will be depressed; and the " country deprived of its best de- " fence against foreign foes.

" 12. That to remedy the great " and glaring evils of which we " complain, it is not necessary to " have recourse to theoretical " speculations, or dangerous ex- " periments in government, but " to recur to the principles handed

" down to us by the wisdom and " virtue of our forefathers.

" 13. That the remedy is to be " found, and to be found ONLY, " in *a full and fair representation* " *of the people in the Commons'* " *House of Parliament; a reme-* " *dy equally necessary to the safety* " *of the Throne, and the happi-* " *ness and independence of the* " *country.*

" 14. That we therefore re- " commend to every town, city, " and county, to take the state of " the representation into consi- " deration, and urgently, but tem- " perately, to apply to Parliament " to adopt such measures as shall " secure to the nation the reality " and uses of representation."

————

(8.) Speech of Sir Francis Burdett in the House of Commons, on the 15th June, 1809. (*Register*, vol. 15. page 974.)—

" Every part of the Empire " will feel the benefit of the Re- " form; but *no where* will the " great advantages of the mea- " sure be likely to prove more " salutary than in that most inte- " resting part of the empire—*Ire-* " *land!* From the deep interest " I take in the concerns of that " country, from my idea of its " mighty importance, have I re-

" served the mention of it till last; " though the consideration of the " manner in which I could devote " my best service to it has never " been out of my mind, never till " now did it mature any practi- " cable plan, calculated to give " universal satisfaction to that " generous, that insulted people, " with perfect security to the state. " *If Reform is necessary here, it* " *applies much more forcibly* " *there;* indeed, the peculiar situ- " ation of that country makes it a " measure of imperious necessity. " —On the subject of Ireland I " can hardly speak, from the fear " of trespassing on the rule I had " laid down for my conduct upon " this occasion. I dare not ven- " ture to trust myself with the " grievances of Ireland. It is a " subject I cannot discuss without " a more considerable degree of " warmth, than is consistent with " that dispassionate line of con- " duct I am upon this occasion " particularly anxious to main- " tain. My desire is to have Ire- " land united with this country " upon terms, however, very dif- " ferent from those which at pre- " sent exist. I should wish to see " there a perfect equality of ad- " vantage, and no exclusions. Of " the present Union, so called, I " shall speak but little at this

" time : suffice it to say, that it
" was a measure contrary to the
" wishes, repugnant to the interest,
" revolting to the feelings of that
" nation; and effected by means
" the most flagitious, if the most
" unblushing corruption on the
" part of the agents, and the
" breach of every solemn assur-
" ance to the great body of that
" people, not only implied but
" expressed by the government of
" that country, deserve the appel-
" lation. Instead of that parch-
" ment Union, I shall propose a
" real Union of heart and affec-
" tion, founded on the broad basis
" of the Constitution, of equal
" rights, and reciprocal interests.
" ——Away with that crooked
" policy, that narrow-minded bi-
" gotry of legislation, that intole-
" rable intolerance, which keeps
" alive perpetual heart-burnings,
" hatred, and revenge. I wish
" not to dwell upon this system;
" it is high time to put an end to it.
" —Is it to be any longer endur-
" ed, that four millions of Irish-
" men should be aliens and out-
" laws in their native land? Is it
" safe to have four millions of the
" people thrust out of the pale of
" the Constitution? Is it consis-
" tent with reason, with common
" sense, putting justice out of the
" question, any longer to tolerate

" such a system? By the adop-
" tion of Reform, the government
" will have the fairest opportu-
" nity of removing the principal
" grounds of dissatisfaction in Ire-
" land : now will be the time to
" do every thing without yielding
" any thing, to legislate upon en-
" larged principles, knowing no-
" thing of particular parties, sects,
" or factions; keeping alive no
" distinctions of Catholic, Protes-
" tant, and Presbyterian, Tory,
" Whig, or Jacobin ; alarming no
" prejudice, insulting no party,
" they may now include the whole
" within one bond of union of the
" Constitution, embracing and en-
" suring the safety and tranquil-
" lity of the empire at large.——
" We shall then, and not till then,
" have an United Kingdom—one
" King — one People. —— We
" shall by this recurrence to the
" Constitution, not only seat the
" Chief Magistrate upon his
" throne, and fix the Crown upon
" his head, but we shall place
" within his hand the sceptre and
" legitimate power of the King, in
" despite of those 157 Borough-
" mongers, who have TREASO-
" ROUSLY usurped all but the pa-
" geantry and outward show and
" forms of Royalty."

(9.) *Extract from an Address to the Prince Regent, from the House-holders of the City and Liberties of Westminster.*

Presented on the 23d April 1811, by Sir Francis Burdett, Bart. and by the High Bailiff (the present High Bailiff) of the City of Westminster. This Address was delivered to the Prince Regent at the Levee, and was, by royal authority, afterwards published in the London Gazette.— *Register, 8th May,* 1811, *vol.* 19, *p.* 1125.

" Thirty years ago it was de-" clared by Sir George Savile, " in his place in Parliament, that " the Commons' House was no " more a representation of the " people of this kingdom than it " was of the people of France.

" The seats in that House, both " for close and for open boroughs, " are notoriously marketable. One " of them, as we are credibly in-" formed, was once bought by a " French king's mistress for her " English correspondent in time " of war; and it stands on record " that, at another time, those " seats were purchased wholesale " by the Nabob of Arcot for his " intriguing agents. None, then, " Sir, can assure us, that at this " day a whole troop in the pay of

" a Napoleon may not sit and " vote in that House.

" The inveteracy of this disease " was made manifest to the whole " world, when, in the cases of " Mr. Henry Wellesley, Lord " Castlereagh, and the present " Minister, Mr. Perceval, all ac-" cused of trafficking in those " seats, not only no punishment " ensued, but the traffic was vin-" dicated—and for this extraordi-" nary reason, that it was become " as notorious as the sun at noon-" day.

" Here, Sir, is the cancer of " the State. With a House of " Commons rapidly becoming, by " the virulence of this pest, a mere " mass of corruption, death must " ensue, unless the cancer to its " last fibre be eradicated, and " free parliaments restored.

" For such a restoration your " Royal Highness must perceive " that no talent, no wisdom, no " virtue in Ministers can become " a substitute."

———

(10.) Extract from the speech of Sir Francis Burdett, in the House of Commons, on moving an Address in answer to the Message of the Prince Regent, on the 20th July, 1812. —(*Register Vol. xxii. p. 172.*)

" The greatest grievance of
" which the country had to com-
" plain was, the assumption by
" the House of Commons of the
" whole of the powers of the State.
" He (Sir F. Burdett) had been
" constantly held up as the ene-
" my to the constituted authorities
" —to the authorities legally con-
" stituted he was a sincere friend,
" and he would at all times sup-
" port the just power and dignity
" of the Throne. The House of
" Commons, a boroughmonger
" faction, erected itself into an
" odious oligarchy, and usurped
" all the powers of the three
" branches of the Constitution.
" In this cause most of our evils
" originated. The annual sum of
" nearly 23 millions was paid as
" the army expenditure, but on
" calculating the pay of the whole
" military force at the highest
" rate, it did not exceed six mil-
" lions. To what purpose, then,
" was the remainder applied?
" It was divided among the offi-
" cers, and was swallowed by jobs
" in the barrack and other de-
" partments. The same remarks
" applied to the navy, and Lord
" St. Vincent (no light authority
" on this subject) had declared,
" that the marine affairs of the
" nation might be conducted at
" one-third of their present ex-

" pense. What then, it would be
" inquired, was the remedy? But
" he was sure that those who put
" the question could themselves
" answer it without prompting—
" *Parliamentary Reform.* On the
" many occasions when this ques-
" tion had been discussed, some
" gentlemen had professed them-
" selves friendly to reform, but
" they did not see the benefit that
" would result from it. If, as it
" could be proved, the present
" corrupt state of the representa-
" tion was the real cause of all
" the corruption in the various
" branches of Government, the
" benefit that would result from
" reform, must be obvious to all.
" The Ministers themselves, al-
" though, in the present state of
" things, they were supported by
" corruption, were compelled to
" be responsible for many acts
" which originated in the defects
" of the House of Commons.
" Whether war or peace would be
" the issue of our differences with
" America was a question, com-
" pared with Parliamentary re-
" form, of little consequence, and
" without it, the Regent might,
" with any Ministers, in vain
" attempt to satisfy his sub-
" jects."

Extract from the Address moved

as above stated.—(*Register, Vol.*
xxii. *p.* 183.)

" We, however, deeply lament
" that any Privy Councellors of
" this realm could accept of com-
" missions to that end, without
" explicitly laying before your
" Royal Highness the necessary
" means of accomplishing the
" object in view, which could only
" have been effected by restoring
" the people to their rights, and
" so placing your Royal High-
" ness's Government on the vir-
" tues and affections of the nation.
" We lament that your Royal
" Highness's beneficent intentions
" and ready endeavours produced
" no effect advantageous to the
" country, and only gave occa-
" sion to intrigues and cabals, not
" less odious in their too obvious
" motives, than injurious to the
" character of the Government;
" it being made manifest to all
" men, that the persons who pos-
" sess, and those who aspire to
" the offices of state, no longer
" regard themselves as chosen by
" the Sovereign, but as the nomi-
" nees of the borough oligarchy,
" who equally invade the province
" of the Crown, and the rights of
" the people, interposing with the
" one in the choice of its Ministers,
" and depriving the other of the
" election of its representatives.

" If it were, at this day, necessary
" to point out the mischievous and
" disgraceful effects of this uncon-
" stitutional and disloyal invasion
" of the rights of both King and
" people; if, after all the votes
" by which the worst sort of ty-
" ranny and corruption have been
" sanctioned; by which Ministers
" have been screened against a
" charge of trafficking in seats in
" this House, and an Attorney
" General against a charge of
" oppression and partiality; if
" after all that we have witnessed
" in the course of the last twenty
" years, of outrage upon the rights
" and liberties of Englishmen,
" there still wanted proof of the
" pernicious and degrading in-
" fluence of the borough faction,
" that proof we must now regard
" as complete, when we recollect
" that at the end of several weeks,
" during which the business in
" Parliament was suspended, for
" the professed purpose of af-
" fording time to your Royal
" Highness to form a new Mi-
" nistry, that same House of Com-
" mons who had, by one vote, de-
" clared the Ministers to be in-
" competent, recognized by ano-
" ther vote the competence of
" these same Ministers, leaving
" scarcely a possible doubt as to
" the means by which the conver- .

" sion had been effected. While
" we are convinced, that posterity
" will never believe that a King
" and people of England were
" thus made the sport and prey of
" a borough faction, sustained
" solely by a fraudulent pretence
" of being the representatives of
" the people, we of the present
" day feel too sorely the reality of
" the fact, which has been mani-
" fested in a long train of useless
" wars and expeditions; which,
" while attended with a dreadful
" waste of treasure and of life,
" have almost uniformly failed in
" their professed object, and have
" only answered the purpose of
" enriching the borough faction
" and their dependants, as a re-
" ward for political corruption."

(11.) Sir Francis Burdett's fall of
snow letter to his Constituents,
on being invited to attend a Meeting in Westminster to petition
against the property-tax.—(*Register, vol. 26, p. 862.*)

" Malmsbury Manor, Dec. 28, 1814.
" GENTLEMEN,

" I am much disappointed at
" being prevented by a *heavy fall*
" *of snow*, attending the Meeting
" of the Electors of Westminster,

" advertised for the 29th De-
" cember.

" I regret this the more, be-
" cause, I perceive, by the word-
" ing of the advertisement, that a
" large and enlightened view of
" the subject is intended to be
" taken; one worthy the city in
" which this Meeting is to be held;
" not narrowed to the considera-
" tion only of an oppressive tax,
" but enlarged to a general view
" of that whole system of taxation;
" every stroke of which, like the
" cat-o'-nine-tails from the backs
" of our soldiers, brings blood;
" and which is not more galling
" in the mode and severity of its
" correction, than in its profligate;
" corrupt, and wasteful expendi-
" ture. In fact, the Income or
" Property Tax has no title to
" that pre-eminence in infamy, it
" appears in public detestation to
" possess, nor is it a whit more
" arbitrary in its execution, cruel
" in its operation, or ruinous in
" its consequences, or unconsti-
" tutional in its principles, than
" the Excise, or many other sum-
" mary, arbitrary, and unconsti-
" tutional jurisdictions, established
" by Act of Parliament, and root-
" ing out the common law of the
" land; that law which my Lord
" Coke truly says is the best in-
" heritance of the subject : besides

" the torture of our-soldiers, I
" might add the brutal horrors of
" the impress, the inhospitable
" and tyrannical act against fo-
" reigners, with a long string of
" et cæteras, too numerous to in-
" sert here, and too palpable to
" be denied.

" The enlightened and patriotic
" Electors of Westminster know
" full well, that these are only a
" few of the *bitter fruits of that*
" *baleful tree, which nourisheth*
" *its roots in that hot-bed of cor-*
" *ruption from whence it sprung,*
" *Saint Stephen's Chapel;* and
" though it has struck deep in that
" consecrated soil, we are in-
" structed by the highest *autho-*
" *rity how to judge* it, *and by the*

" *same authority how to deal with*
" *it.*

" That we may be *able to deal*
" *with it accordingly,* before the
" whole property of the country
" is absorbed by Government,
" before the nation is plunged
" into fresh wars against human
" liberty, and before the system
" of dragooning introduced during
" the last, is irremoveably esta-
" blished, is the fervent prayer
" of, Gentlemen, your ever grate-
" ful, sincere, and attached Ser-
" vant,

" F. BURDETT."

[The extracts will be concluded
in the next Register.]

## MARKETS.

Average Prices of CORN through-out ENGLAND, for the week ending May 4.

*Per Quarter.*

|          | s. | d. |          | s. | d. |
|----------|----|----|----------|----|----|
| Wheat .. | 56 | 1  | Rye .... | 39 | 5  |
| Barley .. | 39 | 7  | Beans ... | 47 | 2  |
| Oats .... | 31 | 3  | Pease ... | 52 | 0  |

Total Quantity of Corn returned as Sold in the Maritime Districts, for the week ended May 4.

|          | Qrs. |          | Qrs. |
|----------|------|----------|------|
| Wheat.. | 40,045 | Rye ..... | 413 |
| Barley .. | 10,239 | Beans . .. | 1,283 |
| Oats ... | 11,619 | Pease .... | 225 |

*Corn Exchange, Mark Lane.*

Quantities and Prices of British Corn, &c. sold and delivered in this Market, during the week ended Saturday, May 4.

|          | Qrs. | £. | s. | d. |          | s. | d. |
|----------|------|----|----|----|----------|----|----|
| Wheat.. | 5,397 | for 16,963 | 10 | 3 | Average, 69 | | 2 |
| Barley.. | 2,005 | .. 4,053 | 1 | 4 | ..........45 | | 0 |
| Oats.. | 1,367 | .. 2,336 | 4 | 6 | ..........34 | | 2 |
| Rye.... | 0 | .. 0 | 0 | 0 | ..........— | | — |
| Beans.. | 530 | .. 1,251 | 15 | 3 | ..........47 | | 2 |
| Pease.. | 426 | .. 968 | 17 | 1 | ..........45 | | 6 |

Friday, May 11.—The supplies of Grain this week are moderate, with a fair quantity of Flour. The Wheat trade is not quite so lively as on Monday last, at no alteration in prices. Barley, Beans, and Pease have no variation. There is no alteration in the top price of Flour.

Monday, May 14.—The arrivals of all kinds of Corn during the preceding week were moderate, but this morning the fresh supply of Grain in general, consists of limited quantities of Wheat, Barley, Beans, and Pease, from Essex, Kent, and Suffolk. There are a good many vessels now coming in with Foreign Oats. The best samples of Wheat found sale readily at 1s. per quarter advance on the terms of this day se'nnight, but there are several parcels of middling quality left on hand unsold, such being very dull in sale.

Barley is scarce, and Grinding parcels are rather dearer. Beans and Pease firmly maintain last quotations. There have been a few country buyers of Oats here to-day, but the demand for this article is limited, and prices remain as last quoted. There has been some attempt to raise the price of Flour, but up to the present hour it has been unsuccessful.

*Price on board Ship as under.*

Flour, per sack ......46s. — 50s.

—— Seconds ........42s. — 44s.

—— North Country ..40s. — 43s.

Price of Bread.—The price of the 4lb. Loaf is stated at 9d. by the full-priced Bakers.

COAL MARKET, May 11. )

| Ships at Market. | Ships sold. | Price. |
|------------------|-------------|--------|
| 78 Newcastle | 32 ..30s. 0d. to 35s. 0d. | |
| 41⅝ Sunderland 30⅜ ..31s. 6d.— 36s. 6d. | | |

Account of Wheat, &c. arrived in the Port of London, from May 7 to May 12, both inclusive.

| | Qrs. | | Qrs. |
|---|---|---|---|
| Wheat .. | 5,434 | Tares .... | 147 |
| Barley .. | 1,246 | Linseed .. | 29 |
| Malt .... | 5,158 | Rapeseed . | 7 |
| Oats .... | 2,506 | Brank .. | 5 |
| Beans ... | 586 | Mustard.. | — |
| Flour.... | 6,790 | Flax .... | — |
| Rye .... | 38 | Hemp ... | — |
| Pease.... | 322 | Seeds ... | 6 |

Foreign.—Wheat, 5,908; Barley, 3,808; Oats, 18,924; Beans, 2,607 quarters.

---

Monday, May 14.—The arrivals from Ireland last week were, 837 bales of Bacon; and from Foreign Ports, 7,163 casks of Butter.

---

## HOPS.

Price of Hops, per Cwt. in the Borough.

Monday, May 14.—Our market this morning has assumed a very brisk appearance, in consequence of the bad appearance of the Bine in all parts of the Plantations, and the uncongenial state of the weather, and more money has been asked and obtained, particularly for Pockets.

*Maidstone,* May 10.—The accounts this week are not so favourable, as the Flea has much increased in many grounds, where there is but little Bine to be seen, and the cold nights have rather checked those that were forwarder.

*Worcester,* May 9.—In our market on Saturday, 49 pockets of Hops were weighed; price 90s. to 100s. Business was rather flat. The plants were growing rapidly before the late cold winds, which have checked them.

## SMITHFIELD.

Monday, May 14.—On Friday, Beef sold for something more than on Monday, but Mutton was 2s. to 3s. a-head lower. Lamb went off readily on full as good terms as before. To-day the supply of Beasts is moderate, and they will be all sold at a small advance in prime things on the price of this day se'nnight; but Mutton is rather cheaper, with a dull trade:—say 5s. 2d. as the top for short polled Sheep, and 5s. 10d. for the best Downs in the Wool. Choice Lamb is worth 7s., but middling does not sell readily, and is certainly cheaper.

*Per Stone of 8 pounds (alive).*

| | s. | d. | | s. | d. |
|---|---|---|---|---|---|
| Beef .|... | 4 | 4 | to 5 | 4 |
| Mutton ... | 4 | 8 | — 5 | 10 |
| Veal ..... | 5 | 0 | — 5 | 8 |
| Pork..... | 4 | 8 | — 6 | 0 |
| Lamb .... | 6 | 0 | — 7 | 0 |

| Beasts . . | 2,095 | Sheep .. | 17,390 |
|---|---|---|---|
| Calves ... | 170 | Pigs ... | 153 |

NEWGATE, (same day.)
*Per Stone of 8 pounds(dead).*

| | s. | d. | | s. | d. |
|---|---|---|---|---|---|
| Beef ..... | 3 | 8 | to 4 | 8 |
| Mutton ... | 3 | 8 | — 5 | 8 |
| Veal ..... | 3 | 8 | — 5 | 8 |
| Pork ..... | 4 | 0 | — 6 | 0 |
| Lamb .... | 4 | 8 | — 6 | 8 |

LEADENHALL, (same day.)
*Per Stone of 8 pounds (dead).*

| | s. | d. | | s. | d. |
|---|---|---|---|---|---|
| Beef ... . | 3 | 8 | to 4 | 6 |
| Mutton ... | 3 | 8 | — 5 | 4 |
| Veal ..... | 3 | 8 | — 5 | 4 |
| Pork ..... | 4 | 0 | — 5 | 8 |
| Lamb .... | 4 | 4 | — 7 | 0 |

## POTATOES.

### SPITALFIELDS, per Ton.

| | £. s. | | £. s. |
|---|---|---|---|
| Ox-Nobles | 3 10 | to | 0 0 |
| Middlings | 2 5 | — | 0 0 |
| Chats | 2 0 | — | 0 0 |
| Common Red | 3 10 | — | 3 15 |

Onions, 0s. 0d.—0s. 0d. per bush.

### BOROUGH, per Ton.

| | £. s. | | £. s. |
|---|---|---|---|
| Ox-Nobles | 3 10 | to | 4 10 |
| Middlings | 2 5 | — | 0 0 |
| Chats | 2 0 | — | 0 0 |
| Common Red | 3 10 | — | 0 0 |

## HAY and STRAW, per Load.

Smithfield.—Hay ... 60s. to 120s.
Straw ... 36s. to 42s.
Clover ... 90s. to 168s.

St. James's.—Hay ... 60s. to 120s.
Straw .. 40s. to 48s. 6d.
Clover.. 120s. to 140s.

Whitechapel.—Hay ... 84s. to 120s.
Straw ... 36s. to 42s.
Clover .. 90s. to 168s.

---

## AVERAGE PRICE OF CORN, sold in the Maritime Counties of England and Wales, for the Week ended May 4, 1837.

| | Wheat. | | Barley. | | Oats. | |
|---|---|---|---|---|---|---|
| | s. | d. | s. | d. | s. | d. |
| London* | 59 | 3 | 41 | 0 | 33 | 11 |
| Essex | 58 | 2 | 37 | 6 | 31 | 7 |
| Kent | 57 | 0 | 40 | 7 | 30 | 10 |
| Sussex | 55 | 4 | 36 | 9 | 31 | 0 |
| Suffolk | 55 | 10 | 37 | 6 | 31 | 0 |
| Cambridgeshire | 56 | 1 | 36 | 11 | 29 | 10 |
| Norfolk | 55 | 0 | 37 | 4 | 29 | 10 |
| Lincolnshire | 55 | 5 | 41 | 0 | 28 | 2 |
| Yorkshire | 54 | 10 | 41 | 10 | 29 | 1 |
| Durham | 55 | 5 | 42 | 0 | 36 | 9 |
| Northumberland | 54 | 2 | 39 | 4 | 32 | 0 |
| Cumberland | 62 | 9 | 41 | 1 | 35 | 1 |
| Westmoreland | 61 | 2 | 42 | 1 | 38 | 1 |
| Lancashire | 62 | 6 | 48 | 8 | 63 | 10 |
| Cheshire | 60 | 10 | 48 | d | 29 | 10 |
| Gloucestershire | 57 | 5 | 48 | 6 | 40 | 1 |
| Somersetshire | 54 | 3 | 42 | 4 | 32 | 6 |
| Monmouthshire | 62 | 4 | 46 | 8 | 0 | 0 |
| Devonshire | 56 | 7 | 40 | 3 | 32 | 1 |
| Cornwall | 62 | 9 | 39 | 11 | 37 | 5 |
| Dorsetshire | 54 | 11 | 40 | 1 | 35 | 0 |
| Hampshire | 55 | 2 | 40 | 4 | 0 | 0 |
| North Wales | 63 | 11 | 45 | 5 | 29 | 9 |
| South Wales | 59 | 7 | 46 | 8 | 27 | 0 |

* The London Average is always that of the Week preced.

*Liverpool, May 8.*—There was a very thin attendance at this market, and little business doing in Wheat and Flour. Oats and Oatmeal were particularly dull, and a decline may be quoted of 1d. in 45lb. on good, and 2d. on ordinary qualities. Indian Corn, white, advanced 1s. per quarter.

Imported into Liverpool, from April 24, to April 30, 1827, inclusive:—Wheat, 8,308; Barley, 4,443; Oats, 15,666; Rye, 140; Malt, 7; Beans, 4,196; Pease, 795 quarters. Flour, 2,880 sacks, per 280 lbs..; Oatmeal, 58 packs, per 240 lbs..; American Flour, 564 barrels; and Indian Corn, 4,681 quarters.

*Derby, May 12.*—Our Corn market this day was well attended by the farmers and factors; we had also a good supply of Grain, except fine Wheat, which article found some customers at about 1s. per quarter advance. The sales in other kinds of Grain were small, although at some reduction in price.

*Horncastle, May 12.*—Our market for Wheat was something higher. Barley nearly the same as last week; other articles of Grain rather lower. Wheat, 56s. to 59s.; Barley, 40s. to 43s.; Oats, 28s. to 32s.; Beans, 55s. to 60s.; and Rye from 40s. to 44s. per quarter.

*Ipswich, May 12.*—We had a very short supply of Wheat, and a remarkably small one of Barley again to-day. More money was asked for Wheat and Beans, but little disposition was evinced to comply. Prices as follow:—Wheat, 54s. to 63s.; Barley, 36s. to 41s.; and Beans, 48s. to 50s. per quarter.

*Manchester, May 12.*—Our market to-day has been well attended, and most articles fully support the prices of this day week. Wheat of the finest quality obtained an advance of 2d. per 70lbs.; other sorts in proportion. Barley not so much inquired for. The demand for Oats has been good, and last week's rates maintained. Beans are scarce, and 1s. per quarter dearer. In Pease nothing doing. Malt is dull in sale, but no lower. Fresh-made Flour obtained a further advance on last week's rates, with a good demand.

*Newcastle-upon-Tyne, May 12.*—We had a small supply of Wheat from the farmers this morning, and not having any arrival coastwise, the millers were obliged to give an advance of 2s. per quarter upon the prices of last week. Barley continues to be taken off at former prices, but the malting season is nearly over, and the demand for Barley is very limited. The farmers' supply of Oats was small, but we have had several cargoes from the Baltic during the week, and as there seems to be now no doubt that they will next week be imported at 4d. per quarter duty, the price in bond is very nearly the same as for those which are free. English Oats are 2s. per quarter dearer.

*Norwich, May 5.*—The supply of all Grain this day was small, and the demand for Wheat brisk, Red 52s. to 60s.; White, to 61s.; Barley, 32s. to 41s.; Oats, 28s. to 32s.; Beans, 43s. to 48s.; Pease, 44s. to 48s.; Boilers, to 52s. per quarter; and Flour, 42s. to 43s. per sack.

*Reading, May 12.*—We had a better supply of Wheat at our market this day, which met a ready sale at an advance of 1s. per quarter. We note it 55s. to 70s. There was a short supply of Barley, which was taken off at last week's prices. Oats met a heavy sale, in consequence of the ports being about to open for the admission of that article. Beans and Pease were in better demand and 1s. dearer.

*Wakefield, May 11.*—The supply of Wheat to this day's market is good; fine fresh samples sell slowly at rather better prices than were obtained last week, but all other descriptions are without alteration in value.

## COUNTRY CATTLE AND MEAT MARKETS, &c.

*Horncastle*, May 12.—Beef, 9s. per stone of 14 lbs.; Mutton, 8d.; Lamb, 10d.; Pork, 7d.; and Veal, from 8d. to 9d. per lb.

*Manchester* Smithfield Market, May 9.—Our market to-day was better supplied with Beef, Mutton and Lamb. Such Beasts as were fat fully supported last week's rates, but lean sorts were not so good to sell. Fat clipt Sheep met tolerable free sale, at about ½d. per lb. below last week's price, and those that were not clipt barely supported their price. There was a good demand for fat Lambs, at the quotations below. Veal and Pork each maintained the price of this day se'nnight.—Beef, 5d. to 8d.; Mutton, 7d. to 8½d.; Lamb, 9½d. to 10½d.; Veal, 5½d. to 7d.; and Pork, 5d. to 6d. per lb., sinking offal.

At *Morpeth* Market, May 9th, there was a good supply of Cattle and Sheep; inferior met with dull sales; prices rather lower.—Beef, from 7s. to 7s. 9d.; Mutton, 9s. to 9s. 6d. per stone, sinking offal.

*Norwich Castle Meadow,* May 12.—We had a good supply of fat Cattle to this day's market, prices 7s. 6d. to 8s. 6d. per stone of 14 lbs., sinking offal; the supply of Store Stock was also large; Scots sold at 4s. to 4s. 6d. per stone of what they will weigh when fat; Shorthorns, 3s. to 3s. 9d. Cows and Calves and Homebreds, a very flat sale. Horses for riding inquired after; few good ones here: in Cart Horses there is little doing. The Sheep pens were again this day well filled with many excellent Hoggets, but few sold, and those considerably lower than even the prices of last week, 18s. to 26s.; fat ones to 35s.; Ewes and Lambs 20s. to 25s. the couple. Pigs, a flat sale, fat ones to 7s. 6d. per stone.—Meat: Beef, 7d. to 9d.; Veal, 6d. to 8d.; Mutton, 6d. to 7½d.; Lamb, 9d.; and Pork, 6d. to 8d. per lb.

# COBBETT'S WEEKLY REGISTER.

VOL. 62 —No. 9.]     LONDON, SATURDAY, MAY 26, 1827.     [*Price 6d.*

" Whenever the *leaders of contending parties and factions, in a state,*
" *unite*, the history of the world bears evidence, that it never is in favour,
" but always at the expense, of the people; whose *renewed and augmented*
" *pillage* pays the scandalous price of the recociliation."—SIR FRANCIS
BURDETT'S ADDRESS TO THE FREEHOLDERS OF MIDDLESEX, 1806.

TO THE

# ELECTORS OF WESTMINSTER.

REMARKS ON THE WESTMINSTER " PURITY" DINNER.

*Fleet Street, 24th May, 1827.*

GENTLEMEN,

If you had all been present, yesterday, at the Crown and Anchor Tavern, in the Strand; or, if a fair report of what took place, had, or could have been published in the newspapers of to-day, I should have been spared the trouble of writing, and you the trouble of reading, any thing, on the subject, in my Register. But, seeing that, by the high price of admission, by the comparative smallness of the place, and by the want of means, or want of will, in the newspaper people, to give any thing like a full and fair report, there are some essential facts and remarks that I deem it my duty to lay before you, as far as I am able

R

Printed and Published by WILLIAM COBBETT, No 183, Fleet-street.
[ENTERED AT STATIONERS' HALL.]

by my very limited means, to effect that object.

You are aware that I had, by public advertisement, signified my intention to be present at that dinner, and that Mr. Hunt had signified a similar intention. You are aware that these sort of dinners are got up by men, if not actually employed, acting in perfect concert with Sir Francis Burdett, and with others who expect to derive profit in some way or other from the use which is made of such dinners. These persons first call themselves *a Committee.* They bespeak the dinner; they get the cards ready to sell; they dispose of these to a great part of the persons that are to come to that dinner; and, if they or their employers choose to go to the expense, they can give cards away to any extent, and thus fill the room with their own creatures, which, to a certain extent, they invariably do when they have reason to expect opposition of any sort. The Committee then turns itself into a body of " *Stewards,*" and arm themselves with good stout sticks, which they politely call *wands,* about seven feet long, with which wands they are enabled to give a good thrust in the stomach, to put out an eye, or, by an application of the butt end, to knock a man down. They station themselves in different parts of the room, listen to the conversation of the company, communicate frequently with a select Committee of them, stationed in an adjoining room, and, upon an emergency, rush all to one spot, in order to prevent any one from speaking any words or doing any act, at all inconvenient to the great Jupiter, to protect whom against the effect of any speech, is their principal business and object.

It was manifest that there were great expectations with regard to the proceedings at this dinner. There is a cross-table at one end of this immense room, and there are five tables length-wise the room. In the middle of the cross-table is seated the Chairman;

and, then these stewards take upon themselves, not only to invite whom they please at the expense of the company in general, but to seat these invited parties along the sides of this cross-table, which is considered the post of honour. Mr. Hunt made application two days before-hand to have seats for himself and me at this cross-table, it being most convenient to address the whole room from that station. This request was refused, and, therefore, we went and took our station at the upper end of one of the long tables (it was that table which was next to the right hand wall), on the left of the Chairman, and, of course, our station was very near to one of the ends of the cross-table. The stewards had promised Mr. Hunt that he and I should have a fair hearing. I well knew, that, if the miracle existed that they desired this, they had no power of enforcing their desire. It was not to be expected that there would be a fair hearing, and it was easy to perceive, that every possible previous step had been taken to prevent it. If BURDETT came to the dinner, of which there were very great doubts, it was clear to every one that the intention was to smother our voices by some means or other, if possible; and, never, by any means, *to put any question to the vote.*

The room was very full. There were nearly twice as many people as had ever been seen at one of these dinners before. At five o'clock, in marched Sir Glory, accompanied by Daddy Coke, Lord John Russell and others, whose names will be found in the newspaper report, which I shall insert by-and-by, and the reader will find them to be a whole band of place-men, pensioners, sinecure-people, notorious expectants, accompanied by a downright fool or two, who had been wheedled to swell the cortége. As soon as the dinner had been cleared away, in marched a couple of these pretty fellows called *stewards*, at the

R 2

head of a band of about twenty Lord Charleses and fellows of that description, who were conducted round to the back of the cross-table, and there seated down in chairs; and they had manifestly been brought in, contrary to every principle of justice towards the company in general, to give their votes, or to make a noise for Sir Glory.

Every thing being thus prepared, the work of toasting began. By turning to the Morning Chronicle's report, which you will find at the end of my letter to you, you will see the order of the toasts. Sir Glory had been received in a very cold manner. He had come up on the side of the room opposite to that in which we were stationed. Gentlemen sitting there, have assured me, that, comparatively, very few persons rose from their seats as he passed, though accompanied by such a long train of lords and members of Parliament. A few men in a room make a great noise: but I, who sat at the head of a long table, and could see all down that table, saw that not one third part of the people at that table took any notice at all of his entering. The demonstrations were those of curiosity, of expectation of sport; and not at all of that respect which used formerly to be shown upon these occasions. I was determined to put him upon his trial; to have a fair defence from him; to have a fair decision on the part of the people present; to have his conduct fairly put to the vote, and to cause all the world to be convinced that he dared not to meet a VOTE, even in an assembly in which it would not be very difficult to prove that there were more than three score men who had had cards given to them, and who had, in fact, been hired; been fed and hired to prevent any thing being fairly put to the VOTE.

I went prepared to put his conduct to the vote, by moving a resolution, consisting of twenty clauses, and which resolution I intended to move at the time when the Baronet's health should be proposed, concluding the resolution with the proposition that the health of the Baronet ought not to be drunk. This resolution, containing an epitome of the whole of his political life, from the time that he proposed *to tear the leaves out of the accursed red book*, until the time when he went and tickled the shoulders of Canning with his knees, I shall insert, after inserting the Newspaper report of this dinner; and, then, Gentlemen, you will see what wretches those must have been, what despicable slaves, or what detestable hirelings, who would have drunk or would attempt to drink the health of this man as a friend of Parliamentary Reform, and as a consistent politician.

: I soon discovered that it would be utterly impossible to obtain silence sufficient for the reading of this paper; I soon discovered that the object of the Baronet and his crew would be, from one end of the meeting to the other, to prevent a hearing of any body but himself. I had discovered, indeed; I saw it clearly, from the commencement, that there was a great *majority of members* in the room, hostile to the Baronet. We had three to his one; but, his were either stewards, who were persons in authority apparently; or, they were desperate hirelings, in clothes not much worthy of protection; they were distributed in all parts of the room; they had their instructions regularly given what to do, and you might see the principal person who had the superintendence of them, going from group to group, to see that they did their duty. Twenty men, in a room like this, supported in their annoying acts by stewards, will prevent a hearing, in spite of all the rest put together. This was the plan, and on this plan the partizans of the Baronet acted throughout the meeting.

It was not a place for *making speeches*; it was not a place for entering into debates and discussions; it was a place for *drinking toasts*; I, therefore, adopted the resolution to propose *amendments-to-toasts*, as the method, as the channel, of bringing the Baronet's conduct to a VOTE. When, therefore, the old toast about Parliamentary Reform was given, I proposed, before the toast was drunk, to make an addition, by way of amendment to the motion. Nothing could be more fair, nothing more regular than this; and, I will now, Gentlemen, lay before you the toast as amended by me; and here it is:

" A full, fair, and free representation
" of the people in the Commons' House
" of Parliament, the only effectual re
" medy for all our national grievances ;
" — *and a hearty prayer on our part,*
" *that his Majesty will be graciously*
" *pleased to chase from his councils,*
" *instantly and for ever, the minister*
" *who has had the audacity to declare,*
" *that he will oppose, to the last hour of*
" *his parliamentary life, a reform of*
" *the Commons' House of Parliament,*
" *in whatever shape it may appear.*"

You will please to observe, Gentlemen, that the part which is in italic characters was added by me. What could be more just, what more reasonable than this ? Here was nothing offensive to any person present, except that per-son was an enemy of Parliamentary Reform ; an enemy of that which the original toast professed to wish for so anxiously. Yet, the moment the amendment was proposed, the hired crew set up a yell; and, after pretty nearly an hour spent, this part of the affair ended without any motion ever having been put to the meeting, and without the toast ever having been drunk at all.

Next came the health of Sir FRANCIS BURDETT, moved, as usual, by Daddy Sturch; but, the Daddy did not, upon this occasion, venture to call him either *Westminster's Pride* or *England's Hope or Glory.* The Daddy having made his motion, I, in regular order, rose and proposed an addition in the way of amendment. Here follows the whole toast, as amended by me; the part in *italics* being my part, and the part not in italics being the part of Daddy Sturch:

" The health of our Representative,'
" Sir Francis Burdett, the great, con-
" sistent advocate of the rights and
" freedom of the people, whose long,

" disinterested, and zealous exertions in
" their service entitle him to the gra-
" titude and esteem of the country;—
" *yea, that very Sir Francis Burdett,*
" *who, for years past, has represented*
" *Mr. Canning as the great champion of*
" *corruption: that very Sir Francis*
" *Burdett, who recently declared this*
" *Mr. Canning to support the system of*
" *corruption for the sake of the public*
" *money, which he and his family got by*
" *it; that very Sir Francis Burdett, who*
" *now sits at the back of this same Mr.*
" *Canning, and promises to support him,*
" *while this Mr. Canning has the auda-*
" *city to declare, to this Sir Francis*
" *Burdett's face, that he will oppose Par-*
" *liamentary Reform to the end of his*
" *Parliamentary life.*"

Now arose a row, a yelling, a
noise, a hurly-burly, a confusion
and uproar, enough to stun any man
but, far sweeter to the ears of Burdett than a hearing of my speech
would have been. He seemed to
feel, however, that he must be
branded with the basest of partiality, if he did not come forward
as Chairman and demand silence.
He did this; he said that it was
the proper time for me to make
the motion, if I made it at all; and
he requested the yellers to hear.
They knew too well his meaning
to listen to the request. At last,
I said, "put my motion to the
VOTE: it is the VOTE that I
want: it is the SHOW OF
HANDS that the company wants:
refuse that, and sentence of guilty
is passed upon you." Urged in
this manner, manifestly wishing
for a shuffle to get out of putting
the queston to the vote, he asked
to have my amendment communicated to him IN WRITING. A
gentleman carried it to him in
pencil. He wanted it in ink.
Where were ink and pen to be
gotten, and who was to write in a
noise, a pushing, a knocking about,
a confusion like that into which
his fears had plunged us. Having
got it, however, at last, he and
his sagacious colleague discovered
that it was *nonsense*, and that he
would not put nonsense to the
meeting; so that, he never put the
question to the meeting at all;
I called to him and told him that
he dared not put the question to the
meeting; that he dared not venture
upon a show of hands, even in his
own packed assembly; that he dared, not meet a vote, even upon his
own dunghill. I reproached him

with partiality, with political cowardice, with an intention to sneak away from the present test, and I made shift, in spite of the noise, to make his supple band of place-hunters hear me say that he would never dare to look the people of Westminster in the face again, out in the open air. After this, *pretending to believe* that his health had been drunk, he affected to return *thanks for the high* honour ; and I suffered him, without interruption, and my friends were all always ready to hear every body, to proceed upon his *defence.* A most miserable defence it was, a wriggling, a twisting, a shuffling, a winding and working about, in voice so faultering, and with a look so miserable, lips so pale and so quivering, that I turned round to a band of the Lord Charleses who were in a corner to my right hand, and asked them " which " would you rather be, in that man's " situation, or double-ironed in " Newgate!" His speech was received with occasional shouts by the dirty-shirted hirelings, and by the place-hunting tribe that surrounded him ; but, not one minute of it passed, without groans, hisses, or without " No, no, it won't do, it won't do; " ha ha, that will never do," from a considerable part of the assembly. After this exhibition, the most dismal that ever struck my eyes, the most deplorable, when I recollect him in former times, he sat down with a swaggering sort of period that excited a species of *laugh* enough to sting a man to his very soul.

Mr. Hunt replied to him at considerable length, and obtained, in some parts of his speech, a tolerable hearing ; but, whenever he touched on matter that pinched the Baronet, thy myrmidons began to yell, and not a word was to be heard. And, thus ended this second part of the trial, without the Chairman ever having dared to put the question to the VOTE. He now found the benefit, the want of which his neighbour Cobb had had to deplore in St.

Andrew's Hall at Norwich; he now found the benefit of being Chairman, or judge, where he himself was upon his trial; which is, I take it, what is meant by the old saying of "going to law with "the Devil, when the court is held "in hell." Daddy Coke had seen me carry a petition in the county of Norfolk, though myrmidons had been hired to prevent both speech and petition from being heard; but, there was an *upright chairman* in St. Andrew's Hall. There was an honourable man, the Sheriff of the county; he saw me hold up a paper, he saw the meeting agree to that paper; having had that paper handed to him, and finding it to be a petition of the county of Norfolk, which had been fairly put to the vote, he signed it as the petition of the county of Norfolk. If Burdett had acted as fair a part here, he would have been voted out of the chair before the end of the evening, and he would have been requested, by another vote, to resign his seat for the city of Westminster; and this he knew very well.

Next came a motion from Lord WILLIAM RUSSELL, to drink the health of poor little HOBHOUSE, who had, for two hours, or thereabouts, been looking more dead than alive. They said that I was a very devil for mending things; for, now came another amendment. I found no fault of Lord William's motion. I only begged leave to add to it a little; and, I observed, to be sure I should meet with no opposition this time, as the whole of my proposition consisted of additional thanks to Mr. Hobhouse. The toast, as amended by me, stood as follows:—

(Lord William Russell's part.)

"The health of John Cam Hobhouse, "Esq. our Representative, who is not "more distinguished for the diligent "assiduity and ability of his services, "than for the unremitting integrity "which he displays in the discharge of "his duty to his constituents."

(My part.)

"*And our best thanks to him, for the* "*character which he once drew of the* "*enemy of Reform, and especially for* "*his declaration, made during an an-* "*niversary dinner in this room in 1818,* "*that the same enemy was* UNWOR-

" THY THE NOTICE OF ANY RA-
" TIONAL MAN, *and could only be*
" *respectable in the eyes of the Meeting*
" *as having been an object of the animad-*
" *version of* Sir Francis Burdett;
" *and that he could assure the worthy*
" *Electors of Westminster, that, on no*
" *other account, would he,* Mr. Hob-
" house, *have presumed, even for a*
" *moment, to mention that* ABAN-
" DONED NAME."

Now began a row in reality.
Burdett would not put my
amendment; Hobhouse could get
no hearing; I begged of him to
let my amendment be put; "for,
said I, " my dear little Sancho,
I propose nothing but to give you
*additional thanks."* The word
Sancho seemed to fill the little
creature with astonishing rage.
He snatched a " wand" out of the
hands of one of his stewards, dart-
ed at me a furious look, and, as
he ran along towards the end of
the cross-table to get at me, upon
my soul he put me in mind of
Gulliver's swaggering about with
his broad sword upon the table of
the Brobynagians. He said, " If
you say that again, I'll knock you
down!" A tremendous shout of
laughter, in which stewards, Lord

Charleses, and all seemed to join,
sent him back again without his
wand, which some of them had
got out of his hand.

It now became manifest that
there was no such thing as recovering the interest of the humbug;
that the parties must disperse in
disgrace, unless I could be *forced*
*out of the room.* " Out with
" him! Turn him out! Down with
" him! All, all, all, say turn him
" out!" And, on they came,
headed by a dozen or two of
" stewards" with their wands:
one gave a poke at my stomach:
another took an extraordinary
good aim at my eye with the
point of his wand; but a friend,
seeing it coming, snatched hold
of it and broke it, and thrust
the big end of it back against
his throat. Friends seeing
me in danger, rushed from all
parts: in a minute the whole
banditti were knocked back; the
Lord Charleses in our quarter
had, by this time, scampered off
out of their chairs: Mr. Hunt
made a *chevaux de frieze* with

the chairs turned upside down on that side; and, though, at the beginning of the battle, I had been (not being upon my guard) torn off the table with the loss of part of my waistcoat, I was soon surrounded by a body of men, who, if I had pressed it, I verily believe, would have gone and plucked the Baronet from his chair, and tossed him out into the street. I discouraged every thing of the sort. I said, " they are " covered with everlasting dis- " grace : we have beaten them to " nothing ; and it is not for us to " commit acts of brutal violence." Some little time after this, I got upon the table again, out of mere curiosity, to see what the humbugs were at, all, now, being confusion, and the toasting and speech-mak- ing being going on in dumb show. Two fellows got upon the table, with the apparent intention to annoy me. Some of my friends jumped on to drive these fellows off. A battle being apparently approaching, others jumped on in like manner, and down came the table with us all, the crash keeping time with another crash that was going on in the vicinage of the Baronet, just by whose head a butt end of one of his steward's wands had passed, and smashed a pane of glass in the window be- hind his back. By this time, Daddy Coke and several others who had come for the purpose of shining as speech-makers, but who had no taste, it seems, for the harmony produced by these mis- siles, had decamped, leaving the honours of the forum to Mr. Thompson, the Member for Dover (to whom, while he was speaking, the people cried out " Spare the tallow!") to Lord John Russell, and to Lord Nugent and his bottle companion, upon this occa- sion, the renowned Mr. Wooler, who was called forth and who actually made a speech, not de- fending the conduct, but apo- logizing for the conduct of the Honourable Baronet in the Chair, as he called him, while I exclaimed to the Baronet, " Mi- " sery brings a man acquainted " with strange bed-fellows!"

This does appear to have been too much even for the fallen Baronet to bear; and up he got, marched off with the remnant of his retinue, amidst the clapping of the well-stuffed birelings, the rappings of the stewards upon the floor, and the hissings and hootings of all the rest of the assembly.

The close was perfectly worthy of all the rest; for, Mr. JEREMIAH HARMER, Sir Francis Burdett's *London Attorney*, in whose service Mr. Wooler now is, *made a motion, calling Mr. Wooler to the Chair*, in which Mr. Harmer's client had just been sitting. Many of the remaining part of the company pressed Mr. Hunt to take the Chair; but Mr. Hunt apologised by saying that, though he should be very happy to comply with the wishes of the company, he would never disgrace himself so much as by sitting in a chair that had been sitten in by Sir Francis Burdett.

This was a proper finish. There was no staying any longer:

here ended the career of Sir "Glory;" and, now let us wait for the next title that he is to receive.

I conclude with requesting you, Gentlemen, to observe, that, both in the report of the proceedings of this meeting which I have given from the Morning Chronicle, and in the extracts which I have given in the resolution which was to have been moved at this Meeting, I speak not my own words, I give you not my own opinions of men or of things; but I give you matter which is upon record, which is in print, and which has been said, not by me, but by Sir Francis Burdett. When you have read all these, judge not of other men by what he has asserted at various times; but judge of him by what he has asserted; for, if he spoke falsely or truly, he stands, now, convicted of the greatest political inconsistency, of the most flagrant destitution of political principle, that ever was beheld in mortal man.     I am, Gentlemen,

Your faithful friend, and

Most obedient Servant,

WM. COBBETT.

# WESTMINSTER

## ELECTION ANNIVERSARY.

[FROM THE MORNING CHRONICLE, MAY 24th.]

The Twentieth Anniversary of the Triumph of Purity of Election in Westminster was held yesterday, at the Crown and Anchor Tavern ; Sir Francis Burdett in the Chair.

The Meeting was very numerous, and we observed among those who sat at the cross table with the Hon. Baronet, the following gentlemen :—

— — Guest, M. P., Montague Burgoyne, Esq., Lytton Bulwer, Esq., J. T. Clarke, Esq., W. Smith, M. P., Otway Cave, Esq. M. P., Mousieur Renuset, Monsieur Guigorel, J. Blackburne, Esq., J. Smith, Esq., of Liverpool, S. W. Scott, Jones Burdett, Esq., Lord Viscount Ebrington, T. W. Coke, M. P., —— Sykes, M.P. Hon. H. Howard,M.P., Lord J. Russell, M.P., Lord W. Russell, M.P., Sir J. Graham, M.P.,.John Wood, M. P., Sir R. Heron, Bart., T. S. Rice, M.P., J. Paulett Thompson,M.P., Henry Warburton, M. P., S. C. Whitbread, M. P., Lord Nugent, Alexander Dawson, M. P., Sir R. Wilson, Sir J. Barham, —— Dealtry, Esq., Mr. Buckingham, &c. &c. Mr. Cobbett and Mr. Hunt sat near the head of one of the side tables. When Sir Francis Burdett and his friends entered the room, the great body of the Gentlemen assembled stood up till he passed ; but we could not observe that either Mr. Cobbett or Mr. Hunt rose from their places.

After the cloth had been removed, the Chairman proposed, as the first toast—" The people, the only source of legitimate power" — (drunk with acclamations.)

Tune—Britons, strike home.

The next toast proposed was—" The King, and may he confirm his own declaration, that the Crown is held in trust for the benefit of the people"—(drunk with great applause.)

Tune—Rule, Britannia.

The third toast proposed by the Chairman was—" A full, fair, and free Representation of the People in the Commons' House of Parliament—the only effectual remedy for all our national grievances."

Tune—Keep the rogues out.

Mr. Cobbett here rose to address the Meeting ; but the hootings of one portion of the Meeting and the applauses of another part, prevented his being heard.

Mr. Galloway then came forward, and solicited the attention of the Electors for a moment. He stated that he addressed them in the name of the Stewards, to request that they would not refuse to hear Mr. Cobbett, or any Gentleman who was desirous of calling their attention, in a regular way, to any thing that he might think material, if the subject matter introduced was such as was consistent with the nature and object of the Meeting. It was illiberal to prevent any gentleman from addressing them, as long as he confined himself to such matters as were proper to be brought under their attention ; and if any man should abuse their indulgence, and endeavour to introduce extraneous or improper matter, then the good sense of the Company would call him to order. In the mean time, no irregularity had been committed, and they ought to hear any gentleman who chose to address them.

Mr. Cobbett then rose again, but the tumult increased, and for a long time he could not be heard at all ; and owing to the continued uproar, he could not be heard perfectly at any time. If the Meeting chose to hear him, he would not occupy their attention for any length of time, as all he wanted was to make a slight addition to the toast. [Cries of " Down with him !" and " Turn him out !"] The Meeting might accept or reject what he had to propose to them, as they pleased ; but he was resolved that, if he possibly could accomplish it, the acceptance or rejection should be decided by a fair show of hands [uproar]. What he had to say at present was not so much directed against Sir Francis Burdett, as against the implacable and everlasting enemy of Parliamentary Reform — the man who openly and constantly declared, that he would resist Parliamentary Reform, at whatever time, in whatever manner, or in whatever shape it might be brought forward [uproar]. His proposal ought, certainly, to have a fair hearing [The uproar continued, but Mr. Cobbett appeared by no means disposed to sit down. *His toast at length was drunk with tumultuous applause.*]

This toast, as amended by me, stood thus : you will observe that the original toast, is in the common type, and my amendment in the italic type.

" A full, fair and free Representation
" of the People in the Commons' House
" of Parliament,—the only effectual
" remedy for all our national grievances ;
" —and a hearty prayer on our part,
" that his Majesty will be graciously
" pleased to chase from his Councils in-
" stantly and for ever, the Minister, who
" has had the audacity to declare, that
" he will oppose to the last hour of his
" Parliamentary life, a Reform of the
" Commons' House of Parliament, in
" whatever shape it may appear."

Mr. Sturch came forward to propose the next toast, which, he said, was certainly not a new one, but one that had been received in that very room for twenty successive years, with every expression of cordial approbation and applause. He himself had had the honour, and, he would add, the pleasure of proposing the toast now put in his hand, as many who had been in the habit of attending the anniversary of the glorious triumph of Westminster would know. But before he proposed the toast—[Here there was a pause, and a cry of " You must deliberate." Great laughter.]— He certainly did not intend to trouble the Meeting with any thing like an attempt at a speech; yet they would allow him to state, that when he had the honour of proposing this toast at the last Anniversary, he had no expectation then that it ever would be his lot to propose it again. Being advanced in years, no doubt many persons would think he ought to resign the office to abler hands, especially as it was the fashion at the present day for great men to resign, thinking they had held their offices long enough, and, as others had thought, much too long. [Great cheering.] If any were of this opinion, they exactly coincided with himself. At first he had intended to resign his office, with all its emoluments and toils [laughter]; and should have done so, had it not been that he was afraid that many who had usually heard the toast given from his lips would have been led to conclude that he had deserted the men who had never deserted the cause of public liberty [great cheers], and he was sure who never would, as long as they lived. [Continued applause.] Twenty

years had rolled away, marking the steady conduct, principle, spirit, and high talents of that Honourable Baronet, since he had called on the inhabitants of Westminster to elect him, and since he had been elected by an overwhelming majority. He looked back with pleasure on those days, because he was enabled still to see the same man in the Chair [Hear, hear, hear! and great confusion]—to declare his acknowledged principles, and appear as a standard for all the world. He, therefore, rejoiced in once more proposing the health of that Honourable Baronet: he hoped it would be proposed for many years to come, and that when all present would be removed in the course of nature, that the inhabitants of Westminster would ever afterwards maintain that independent spirit—that ardent and zealous love of liberty for which the Honourable Baronet had been so highly distinguished; [Hear!] and that they would be able to spread that love throughout the country, till England, Scotland, and Ireland, were convinced that it was the only effectual security for having a good Government. [Hear, hear!] He then proposed " The " health of their Representative, Sir " Francis Burdett, the great consistent " advocate of the rights and freedom of " the people, whose long and disinte- " rested zealous exertions in their ser- " vice entitled him to the gratitude and " esteem of the country." [Loud cheers, waving of handkerchiefs, and great confusion for upwards of five minutes.]

Mr. Cobbett here mounted the table amidst great uproar, and often attempted to speak, but could not be heard.

Sir Francis Burdett then rose, with a view to restore order, which only increased the confusion for upwards of a quarter of an hour. At last, on being permitted to speak, he said—If the Gentlemen present would only favour him for a short time, he hoped to be able to restore tranquillity. When a toast was proposed, every man present had a right either to drink that toast, or to object to it; the present was the only time at which an objection could be made to the toast that had been proposed; and it appeared to him (the Honourable Chairman) that it would be for the convenience of the Meeting, and better, in every point of view, with respect to Public Meetings, and to the characters of such Meetings in the eyes of the public, that any objections to be made should good-naturedly be heard. He knew that, as Chairman, he had no power except what the Meeting invested him with; that power was to preserve regularity. If there was any irregularity, he trusted he should have power enough to subdue it; but so far nothing appeared to him irregular, and therefore he trusted the Gentleman who attempted to oppose the drinking of the toast, would be heard at this his only opportunity. [Applause.]

Mr. COBBETT then said, if the Meeting would observe the same silence while he addressed it that had been paid to Sir Francis Burdett, he would pledge himself to take up as little time as the Hon. Baronet had done. He was bold to say, that there were persons, and especially when he looked at his left hand (alluding to the great body of the Meeting), that there were persons present, and he believed the majority of the Meeting, who were anxious to object to the toast, as well as himself, unless they got an explanation of some very extraordinary circumstances which had made their appearance in public, within the last three weeks. The Electors of Westminster had expressed as much to him, and he would put it to the vote of the Meeting by and by, if the Honourable Chairman would allow him, who were for, and who against his proposition [great applause and confusion]. Every man had a right to be at this Meeting who had paid for his card—every man who was an Elector of Westminster especially; and surely he had some right to be here above children not born then, he having taken an active part in the very first election [very great confusion]. The Meeting would get nothing by their clamour. He would pledge himself that they did not go off without punishment one way or other for their clamour [much laughter, and continued applause]. The Gentlemen present might drink the health of a fellow with a pot of beer in his hand, and care not a farthing whether the Devil had that fellow or not in three minutes afterwards; but when a toast like the present was given, it was to go forth to the public as the solemn opinion, and the decided declaration of those who constituted the Meeting, and, in short, to stamp their characters, and the characters of the Electors of Westminster. By the toast Mr. Sturch had proposed, the Meeting approved of the principles of the present Government, as far as they could learn those principles, and the too apparent principles of Sir Francis Burdett [hear, hear! and great uproar]. For his own part, he totally disapproved of the conduct of their Representative; and if Mr. Sturch would

only permit him to make a slight addition to the toast, he would not trouble the Meeting a moment longer. The toast, in plain English, expressed approbation of the long-tried conduct of Sir Francis Burdett, as a friend of Parliamentary Reform—nay, and as a consistent man [much confusion]. He called upon the Meeting to be manly in their conduct, and to dare the world with the just and true addition which he should propose to the toast respecting their Representative, who now sat behind a man who, all his life long, as well as his family, according to his own declaration, had been sapping the public [great applause and confusion]. It was true that that individual had had a sinecure for the last thirty years. Sir Francis, he avowed, sat at the back of that man, —countenanced that man—had pledged himself to support that man [hear!]. He maintained that that was the English of the toast. The family of that man had received 17,000l. or 18,000l. of the public money in pensions. He himself had received, in sinecures, about 18,000l. of the public money, and he was the implacable —the abusive—the scurrilous—the villanous—the calumnious, and the eternal enemy of Reform. [Confusion and applause, which lasted several minutes.] Add this to the toast, and he (Mr. Cobbett) would have no objection to its passing [much laughter]. Sir Francis Burdett, whose conduct had been applauded, namely, down to the present day, had now gone across the House and placed himself at the back of Canning the abuser—the mortal enemy of Parliamentary Reform; and yet Mr. Sturch applauded him for being consistent! At the very last Anniversary Sir Francis Burdett called the House of Commons a political Sodom [cheers and confusion]. Sir Francis now sat and said nothing; but he (Mr. C.) would repeat, that on this very day twelvemonth their Representative declared, in the very room in which they were now assembled, that the House of Commons was overwhelmed by a scum such as was never before found on the face of the earth [hissing and clapping]. The reason, he added, of this scum was, because so little of the public voice of the people was that House, and because so few good men were found there—the House of Commons was a political Sodom. He (Mr. C.) said, therefore, that the Meeting could not, according to the cherished principles of Westminster, drink the present toast, unless they compromised those principles. Sir Francis Burdett had said, in allusion to Catholic Emancipation, that all the Catholics were a parcel of rogues, and that they wished for Emancipation merely because they wanted to get into office; but he now slipped out from those declarations in the hope that he might get a Peerage, and walk up to the other House [uproar]. He begged the Meeting would not make a noise, or they would certainly frighten their Representative away [laughter]. In spite of the Meeting—in spite of their high obstreperous voices—before the face of the said Sir Francis Burdett—he would put his Amendment to the Meeting. Sir Francis Burdett had frequently declared himself to be the enemy of that House, which he considered to be a House of corruption, and the Meeting might swallow that for their comfort.

During the uproar, and when it was impossible for Mr. Cobbett to be heard, he turned towards the cross table and said: "I think I see Mr. Wood, the Member for Preston, here. By way of interlude—Mr. Wood promised to *take Mr. Canning by the beard*, in the House of Commons; he must have meant to do so *as a barber*, for that is the only way he can or dare to do it." [Here it was intimated that Mr. Cobbett's Amendment was to be put* from the Chair; *but, after some delay, Sir F. Burdett's friends rose in a body, and drank the toast, with loud acclamations, mixed with the hisses and yells of the Cobbettites.*] While the uproar continued, Mr. Cobbett turned towards his friends, and said, "*He is afraid to put my Amendment, by G—d.*" Here the Gentleman who took the Amendment to the cross-table, returned, and said that the Chairman refused to put the Amendment, *as it was literally nonsense.*

Mr. Cobbett: "Nonsense, indeed! he is a pretty fellow to judge of nonsense; he *is afraid to put it, by G—d.*"

The toast, *as amended by me*, stood thus, my amendment being in Italics;

"The health of our Representative, Sir
" Francis Burdett, the great consistent
" advocate of the rights and freedom of
" the people, whose long, disinterested,
" and zealous exertions in their service
" entitle him to the gratitude and esteem
" of the country;—*yea, that very* Sir
" Francis Burdett, *who, for years
" past, has represented* Mr. Canning *as
" the great champion of corruption;
" that very* Sir Francis Burdett, *who

" recently declared this* Mr. Canning *to
" support the system of corruption for
" the sake of the public money, which
" he and his family got by it; that very
" Sir Francis Burdett, who now sits
" at the back of this same* Mr. Canning,
" and promises to support him, while
" this* Mr. Canning *has the audacity to
" declare, to this* Sir Francis Bur-
" dett's *face, that he will oppose Par-
" liamentary Reform to the end of his
" Parliamentary life.*"

Sir Francis Burdett came forward, and attempted to address the Meeting, and stated that he had not altered a single *iota* of the opinions which he had formerly entertained on the question of Parliamentary Reform, and the other great political principles by which the freedom and happiness of this country might be promoted [some of Mr. Cobbett's party "*We are not to be caught with chaff, Sir Francis*"].

Mr. Cobbett still insisted that his Amendment to the toast should be put, and Sir Francis retired for a short time; but the tumult having somewhat subsided,

Sir Francis Burdett was anxious that every gentleman should, under the present circumstances, have the fullest opportunity for explanation; and it was, no doubt, on that account, that so much indulgence was shown to a few who appeared to have attended in that place, for the purpose of interrupting the proceedings of the evening; an indulgence such as he had seldom seen bestowed upon those who might be supposed to be more friendly to the general object of the Meeting. As Chairman of the Assembly, perhaps, he had been too slow in coming forward to correct the irregularity which had been introduced; but his apology was, that he was very anxious to remove all pretence for the false imputations, and gross misrepresentations in other places, of the nature, temper, and conduct of those who were now assembled to celebrate the Anniversary of the Triumph of Purity of Election in Westminster. But indulgence might be carried too far when they found their proceedings interrupted, and the most persevering attempts made to create confusion by a wretched inconsiderable Rump of a Junto [Loud applause, and some cries of "no, no!"], who had proposed and supported this Amendment. Amendments of this kind, if accepted and put from the Chair, would always put an end to all public proceedings, and to all harmony and social intercourse among Meetings of this description; and the reason that he had not put it from the Chair, when it was handed to him, was, that upon looking at it, he found that there was nothing at all in it, and that it was literally nonsense [Applause and laughter]. He had been reproached with having now set himself down at the back of Mr. Canning, who had so often declared himself to be the enemy of Parliamentary Reform. But in doing so, he had conferred a most important benefit on the public, and that was the only reason why he had done it. The immediate benefit conferred on the public was, that he had by that means done all in his power to exclude, and had assisted others in excluding from power, those Ministers who for so long a time, he might say ever since the year 1760—the period of the commencement of the reign of the late King—sat like an incubus on the breast of the country, and constantly threw the most serious, and even insurmountable obstacles in the way of improvement. When they could find a man of more enlightened mind, and power, and principles, than the present Minister, who might be able to bring his views and principles into operation in the conduct of public business, that man, no doubt, ought to be preferred; but, in the mean time, it was of the last importance that those who had been so long such a dead weight on the country, or worse, should, by all means, be prevented from returning to fix their talons again in the vitals of the nation [Loud applause and cheers]. If, after the experience which they had of him, of his principles, and his conduct, during the whole thirty years of his public life, they thought it necessary for him to make a formal defence against such accusations as were in this way preferred against him—if their confidence in him could be so easily shaken, then he must say that their confidence would not be worth having. But if any person, much more an elector of Westminster, wished to have an explanation from him, and came like an honest man and an Englishman, and a man of practical common sense, to ask it, he would most willingly give any explanation that might be required by such a person. During his whole public life, which began as soon as he could by law be permitted to sit in the House—during a period of thirty years, he had been the constant and earnest advocate of Parliamentary Re-

form, and the liberties of the people, and he trusted that he ever would continue to be the firm supporter of the liberties of his country to the latest hour of his life. Ever since he had been their Representative, he had acted upon the same principles, although he certainly seldom, if ever, alluded particularly to his own conduct. But at the same time, if any thing had occurred which might have rendered it necessary to call their attention to a subject that might be displeasing to them, he never would have hesitated to do his duty, whatever might be the consequence. What he now did, was merely to do the utmost in his power to prevent the unclean birds who had so long sat perched on the top of fortune, and maintained themselves there by means of a system of well-compacted corruption, from returning again to prey on the vitals of the country. Since their overweening confidence in their own strength and importance, or some other motive, whatever it might be, had induced them at last to take a flight, he certainly was willing to take advantage of so favourable a circumstance, and turn it to the highest account in promoting the best interests of the country. The course of policy, both foreign and domestic, which the present Ministers had pursued, was exactly opposed to that of their predecessors, and was calculated for the benefit of the

themselves to see all the links in the chain of causes and events, sometimes misled their masters, but he trusted they would not be permitted to deceive others [applause]. Every principle of freedom which the many had long supported against the few, whether relating to commercial, civil, or religious liberty, was now better understood throughout the country, and he believed more justly appreciated by the Government; for they were now, in a great measure, linked together; and he had no doubt that the time would come when they would be able to say to any Minister (and that would happen when the public at large were as truly enlightened as were the citizens of Westminster) [cries of "That will be one thousand years hence!"] "you shall" or "shall not adopt such a measure," accordingly as that measure

S

was calculated to effect public benefit or public injury. What he had often before asserted he would now repeat—that while the Government was upheld, as it long had been under former Ministers, by the Borough interest, it was impossible for any honest man to be a Minister. To him it was indifferent what Minister was in authority, if a certain set of measures, obnoxious to the interests of the people, were to be pursued; but he trusted, and believed, that such would not be the case with the present Administration, since the Right Honourable Gentleman could not hope to be supported, unless by the strength and influence of public opinion [applause]—a support which he could never expect to obtain, if he did not maintain those principles that in their operation would be beneficial to the public interests. He should apply the same rule both to a Representative of an enlightened city, and to a Minister placed in such circumstances as those which now existed, and he should say, avowing that grand and main principle of public conduct (not knowing whether he should slip into a Peerage or not, for the declaration) [a laugh], that both must exist on the good will, the affection, and the confidence, of their country [loud cheering]. That grand principle—that sound doctrine—such as the Electors of Westminster and himself had long done all in their power to promote, and which alone could give the hope of maintaining the liberties of all countries—namely, a fair representation of the people—he never should abandon ["aye, aye, stick to that and we'll stick to you"]. In what he had done, he had neither manifested an intention of abandoning nor even of retarding it, and he said for himself, exercising his own unbiassed judgment upon the subject, that there was no act or step which he had or should take, that should ever divert him from the view of accomplishing that great end ["Then you only think you were right."] That's a matter of opinion. Well, if he was wrong, he is only wrong in opinion [cheers and laughter]. There were many great public men who had been in the habit of making the strongest and the warmest professions, and who had yet not kept them better than others; from these persons he should take a lesson, and feeling as he did, that he should not entitle himself more to their confidence by vaunting of his own powers, than by confessing the weakness of human nature, he should deal fairly by them, and say, that he did not mean to desert them, and he thought that when they disco-

vered he had broken his promise in that respect, and had deserted the cause of the People, it would be time enough for them to think of deserting him [loud cheers]; as he did not feel that he had ever shrunk from his duty, he knew that he should be excused among them if he had not exercised a perfectly correct judgment, when they saw that it had been his intention to have done so; and he could assure them, that it was upon that feeling that now, without the slightest misgivings of conscience, he appeared before them claiming their suffrages to his conduct with the most perfect confidence [applause]. He would recal recent circumstances to the memory of the Meeting, and he would ask whether there had not been a strong necessity, not for demanding whether, under the New Ministry, Reform should be carried (for at such a time it would have been silly to ask such a question;) but for deciding, and that at once, whether the enlightened part of the Administration, pressed as they had been by their less liberal colleagues, could support themselves without the union of those who had lately gone over to their assistance; or whether, with the conviction that they could not support themselves without assistance, that assistance should have been refused, and by its refusal have tended to restore to place and power, those Ministers, whose principles, if not themselves, had, since the beginning of the reign of George III.—since the year 1760, been the severest affliction to the people [cheers]? So true it was, that they had been so long the domineering principles of the Government, that the men who professed them seemed to consider office as their hereditary right, and the people, whose fathers had witnessed their uninterrupted possession of power, who had themselves never seen that power shaken, and whose children seemed likely still to groan under its influence, had almost begun to imagine that they were immovable—that having obtained power, the King must support them in the possession of it, That charm, that spell, was now broken: the old possessors of office had been driven out—their former colleagues, but their present rivals, had succeeded them; and the new Ministers being supported from quarters where the King had not expected assistance, and where they had not calculated on aid, they were by that unexpected support enabled to maintain themselves in their situations—and as they were indebted for it to public opinion, it was to be expected that they would act for the benefit of the public. It was impossible to doubt, that what he had stated was the fact; it was impossible to deny that the late seceders from office had been so long in possession of it, that not only they, but the people, almost considered them as born to it, and had nearly lost the hope, though not the desire, of ever seeing a better system established [applause]. One great practical good had been effected in getting rid of that deep-rooted opinion, and of affording the people a better prospect. He had been accused of sacrificing every thing for the hope of obtaining Catholic Emancipation; he begged leave to deny the charge, and he would take that opportunity of saying that he was not particularly the advocate for the Catholics, but the friend of the great principle of religious liberty, the acknowledgment of which would secure to all men what he thought they ought to possess—the enjoyment of their civil rights, without any limitation on account of their religious opinions [cheers] He thought it an unjust, an impolitic, and an indefensible act for any Government to say that any well conducted man within its dominions, who possessed talents that qualified him for office, should be excluded from it on account of his religious opinions [applause]. If the question of Catholic Emancipation should be carried, it would be an utter impossibility that any civil disability should continue to exist with respect to any other class of persons whose religious opinions did not coincide with those of the Church. In doing all he could to support that question, he was, therefore, advocating the extension of the principle of religious feeling in the fullest manner; and though the present head of the Administration was not actually pledged to carry the question, yet there could be no doubt that he would give it his utmost support. Of that question the Right Hon. Gent. had long been the able and powerful advocate; and though he (Sir F. Burdett) had, in other times and under other circumstances, been opposed to that Right Hon. Gent. in many great questions, yet, when he saw that, by supporting him, a more liberal policy than had heretofore been pursued might be expected to be followed, it was not easily to be seen how such support could dishonour the man who gave it, as he did, with no other view than that of advancing the great cause of public freedom, and liberating this country from the shackles of a faction that had long been the most determined enemies of liberty [applause]. In the field of political warfare he had often manifested feelings of considerable hostility to that Right Hon. Gent.; but surely there was no dishonour

in merging these feelings in others of a more kindly nature for the public good; indeed, in his opinion, it was the more meritorious to do in proportion as the feelings of hostility had been strong and bitter; and if the wish for the public service had not rode over the feelings of political hostility or personal enmity, he should have feared that his conduct would have required much apology, even if it had not been entirely indefensible. On these grounds, he had no doubt that the Electors of Westminster would feel perfectly satisfied with his conduct, and would thoroughly understand the principles on which he had acted. At the same time he would say, that he did believe they would never find him other than what he had been for the last twenty years; that he should never refuse to do all in his power to advance the interests of the people; that he should never be deterred from performing his trust in an upright and straightforward manner; and that, upon the whole, he hoped they would find his conduct to be such as they, of all men, were most capable of estimating; and in estimating, be trusted they would see good grounds of approval. But for the particular circumstances of that Meeting, he should not have said so much. He should, however, now abstain from going further; and having explained his own conduct, he should avoid discussing some of those great topics in which not only this country, but Europe and the world at large were interested. He had satisfied his own mind that he had done his duty as their representative; and as far as he could collect the feeling of those whom he was then addressing, he saw no reason to doubt that they gave him their unreserved confidence—a confidence which, he trusted, he should always be found to deserve, since he believed he should always act in such a manner as to be able to say, with the same boldness as at present, that he was perfectly ready to explain any part of his public conduct. The Hon. Baronet resumed his seat, amidst the loudest cheering, not unmixed, however, with cries of "It won't do;" "Very poor;" and similar expressions.

Mr. Hobhouse then appeared upon the Table, and was loudly greeted. Some opposition was at first manifested, but comparative silence having at length been obtained, he proceeded to say that he should not have offered himself to their notice but for some of the observations which had fallen from the Hon. Baronet who had just addressed them,

He had heard that Hon. Baronet's speech with as much delight as any man there, and he went far, very far with him in the observations he had made. He went a great way with that Hon. Baronet, and all those who supported him. He agreed fully as to the feeling of execration with which that Hon. Baronet had spoken of those Ministers who were now, thank God, out of office, and whom nineteen-twentieths of the people rejoiced to see out [loud cheers]. The company whom he then saw assembled, had been called on in a most extraordinary way, for their opinion on the conduct of their Representative [Here Mr. Hunt was interrupted by cries of a very discordant kind]. They were Englishmen—they were Westminster Electors; at least, he was one: and they were assembled there on a great occasion; he, for one, had taken part in the first election of Sir F. Burdett, and had been an invited guest to that dinner for eleven successive years, when, although he resided some distance in the country, he had never failed to attend; he was, therefore, one among them—one of themselves; and he hoped and trusted that all who conducted themselves as men and as gentlemen might be allowed freely to express their sentiments, whether in favour of, or against the conduct of their Representative, Sir Francis Burdett [cheers]. Towards that Honourable Baronet, he did not wish to use one harsh expression; but it was both necessary and proper to discuss his conduct freely and fully. They had not met there merely for the purpose of drinking the health of Sir Francis Burdett; but to support and advance those principles in which one and all agreed; and to advocate those opinions of which Sir Francis Burdett himself had been the forcible, the eloquent, the distinguished advocate for so many years. He agreed with the Honourable Baronet in the sentiment of the toast which had been proposed, that " a full, fair, and free Representation of the People in the Commons' House of Parliament," was " the only efficient remedy for all our national grievances;" and he would, add, ought to be the *sine qua non* of any support afforded by the popular Representatives of the present Administration [applause]. Yet he was sorry to say, that although the Hon. Baronet was a supporter of Reform, he had joined the present First Lord of the Treasury, who was notoriously one of the most inveterate enemies of Reform; an union by which they—some of them, at least—himself, for instance, thought the Honourable Baronet had compromised the principles he ought to have supported [applause and disapprobation].

It was perfectly right for such an assembly of Englishmen as the present, particularly for such a body of Electors as he saw before him, to differ from him upon that subject. They differed from him at that moment; but he thought, that when they came to reflect on what had passed, and when they had heard him a little further, they would feel—as, indeed, the best friends of Sir Francis Burdett must feel—to rejoice that an opportunity had been afforded that Honourable Baronet of saying that which, if he had said before, and in Mr. Canning's teeth, perhaps the proceedings of this day never would have happened [applause]. They had been told by the public press, and had learned from other sources, that the Honourable Baronet had felt it his duty, and, no doubt, had felt it his conscientious duty, to support the present Administration, whom he thought more likely to carry into effect measures for the public benefit, being directed by a gentleman whom he believed to be a more enlightened, a more liberal, and a better man than any of those who had gone out of office. Now he confessed he was not fully satisfied with this explanation, although he entertained no unkindly feeling towards the Honourable Baronet [cheers and hisses]. He trusted they would hear what he had to say, and not let it go out to the world, that when the people of Westminster had been assailed, one of their number had been put down by clamour; for the greatest enemies of Sir F. Burdett, of themselves, and of the cause of Reform, would be more rejoiced at such a circumstance than at any other, since it would enable them to make a scorn of those supporters of freedom, who would put down a man without a hearing [cheers]. They had a right to ask why their Representative, the great agent of Reform, the great mover of that important question in this large city, should have joined a man who had always been opposed to it? What had that Right Honourable Gentleman (Mr. Canning) done to justify this confidence? Had he ever been the friend of the rights and liberties of the people? Had he for the last thirty years, on any one occasion, supported their privileges? On the contrary, had he not, on every occasion, been the first to oppose, with all his power, the success of those questions in which their great interests were involved [cheers, mixed with violent clamour]? He appealed to those around him, whether he had in the course of the evening interrupted any gentleman in expressing his opinions? [No, no.] Then he requested that they would afford him equal justice, and listen to those sentiments which he felt it his right and duty to declare. They had been called on to say (and Sir F. Burdett had himself, as Chairman, put that question), whether they approved of his (Sir F. Burdett's) conduct up to that time? [Mixed cries of " Yes," and " No."] In what situation were they placed? [Cries of " not we but you."] They were told that the Right Hon. Gentleman now at the head of the Government was such an enlightened and liberal Minister, that he would bring about all those good things which the people had hitherto been accustomed to look for in any quarter but that of the administration. Had he (Mr. Canning) in any one part of his life, given any ground for such an opinion? Had he, during his recent possession of office, made one move towards it? [A voice, " No, because he has not had time."— Another, " He has in his foreign policy."] Oh! by all manner of means give him time. But before they were called on to support that Minister who had always been opposed to them, they ought to have better guarantees than mere anticipations. He was of opinion that the Hon. Baronet had acted most imprudently in joining the present Administration at this moment. The King had tried to make an Administration without the assistance of Mr. Canning; but, as might have been expected, he had failed in the attempt. He had desired Mr. Peel to form an Anti-Catholic Administration. Mr. Peel declared his inability to do so. He next applied to Mr. Canning to form a similar Administration. Mr. Canning also declared his inability to do so. Then what was the situation of Mr. Canning, when ultimately desired to form an Administration? Did any man believe that he would have been able to form an Administration which would stand a single week? [Yes, with the Ministers who have gone out.] But without them, could he have formed it, unless he had been joined by the Hon. Baronet and the other Members of the Opposition? [No.] Then could these Gentlemen have formed an Administration which would have lasted one week without the assistance of Mr. Canning? [Mixed cries of " No," and " Yes."] He thought they could; and then he said, that if they had not precipitately thrown themselves into the arms of Mr. Canning, he must have gone out, and they must have carried on an Administration formed by their own party, and governed by their own principles. At present he would ask, had they proposed

any guarantee by which they secured the carrying into effect the principles they had so long advocated? He would answer that they had not; but on the contrary, they had thrown themselves into the hands of their opponents, and surrendered at discretion. They had had the power of obtaining that guarantee— they could have made any terms they pleased; and if their terms had not been accepted, they themselves might have formed an Administration, and have come into the House, assured of the applause of that Meeting, and of the people of England [cheers]. If they had properly exercised the power they possessed, they might have compelled the Right Honourable Gentleman at the head of the Government to a declaration in favour of Reform as strong as any of those which he had previously made against it. And what he accused the Honourable Baronet of was, that he had not made those terms with the new Administration which he might have made when he promised to afford them his support—that he had changed his seat without even obtaining from the Right Honourable Gentleman an undertaking that he would cease to be the uncompromising enemy of Reform ; and that, not having done this, he had not stayed in his place, and said something like that which he had addressed to the Meeting that evening [applause]. Those who supported the Hon. Baronet, he meant Mr. Brougham and Lord John Russell, the last of whom he believed to be present, had said in the House of Commons, that the country had been so well governed for the last few years, that the people now cared nothing about Parliamentary Reform. [cries of 'No, no!'] Yet it was strange, if that were the fact, that between three or, four thousand people should have said, at a meeting in Westminster, a few days since, that, without it they could expect to do nothing whatever ; and he trusted that the company whom he was then addressing, felt, and would express the same opinion, and would say, that without Reform any other measures were a mere farce—a mere delusion. Mr. Cobbett had merely proposed an Amendment to the terms of a toast to the health of Sir Francis Burdett ; they were not assembled there to drink that Hon. Baronet's health merely as the Chairman of that Meeting; for if his health had been proposed only as the head of a convivial assembly, any man would have drank it. [" Yes, all."] The proposal of that health, however, involved a great question [applause and hisses]. They gave him some signs, that whatever he might say upon that question would not alter their opinions. ["Certainly not."] He thought they would always agree with him in cherishing those principles of public freedom which had always been nearest his heart. What had been done that day had been merely done for the advancement of those principles, in support of which he had thought it his duty to address them, and he was sure they would approve of his conduct, whether they agreed with him in opinion or not [loud applause].

Lord Wm. Russell wished to call their attention to the object of the Meeting, which was to celebrate, with honour and conviviality, that great cause which was, equally in his own heart as theirs, important beyond all other considerations—he meant the cause of Public Liberty [applause]. They met for that purpose, and not for discussion and debate. [hisses]. Having said that, he did not mean to deny that a Representative ought not to be always open to the scrutinizing severity of the public at large. But there were times and seasons for all things; and it was not at the festive board that such discussions ought to be carried on. If it were thought right to express any opinion on the conduct of their Representative, they had still, thank God, as a remnant of the great public liberty of the country, the means of doing so, by convening a public Meeting, where they could canvass the conduct and character of any public man. And sure he was that there were none near him such a meeting, in whatever way that decision might affect themselves, since they fully acknowledged that toast which they had already drunk—that the will of the people was the only legitimate source of Government [cheers]. He had only now to propose the " health " of John Cam Hobhouse, Esq., their " Representative, who was not more " distinguished for the diligent assiduity " and ability of his services, than for the " unremitting integrity which he display- " ed in the discharge of his duty to his " constituents [applause]."

The toast having been drunk with three times three,

[This is a sheer falsehood. I rose instantly, and prevented the health from being drunk. Hobby rose; but it was not to return *thanks*, but to obtain quiet in order that there might be an appearance of having had his health drunk.— W. C.]

The toast, as proposed by Lord William Russell, and as amended by me, stood thus :

### Lord William Russell's Part.

" The health of John Cam Hobhouse,
" Esq., our Representative, who is not
" more distinguished for the diligent as-
" siduity and ability of his services,
" than for the unremitting integrity
" which he displays in the discharge of
" his duty to his constituents ;

### My Part.

" and our best thanks to him, for the
" just character, which he once drew of
" the enemy of Reform ; and especially
" for his declaration, made during an
" Anniversary Dinner in this room, in
" 1818, that the same enemy was *un-*
" *worthy the notice of any rational*
" *man*, and could only be respectable in
" the eyes of the meeting, as having been
" an object of the animadversion of Sir
" Francis Burdett ; and that he
" could assure the worthy Electors of
" Westminster, that, on no other ac-
" count, would he, Mr. Hobhouse, have
" presumed, even for a moment, to
" mention that ABANDONED NAME."

Mr. Hobhouse rose *to return thanks*; but Mr. Cobbett, at the same moment, presented himself upon the table on the left ; and the cries of " Hobhouse, Hobhouse ! " and " Cobbett, Cobbett ! " were re-echoed through the room. Mr. Hobhouse stood as if patiently determined to obtain a hearing ; Mr. Cobbett appeared equally resolved to do so, at all events ; for, when cried down by the crowd, he kept addressing the persons immediately about him, and, at intervals, expressing to the " upper table," by sawing his arms, gnashing his teeth, and other significant motions, that he was not at all pleased with the opposition which he experienced.

The scene which now took place beggars all description. Mr. Hobhouse appeared still endeavouring to obtain a hearing ; but the screaming, howling, and hissing on the one hand, and the cheers and clapping of hands on the other, were almost deafening. The

Mr. HOBHOUSE renewed his attempt to obtain a hearing, and was for a few moments successful. He observed that

was renewed, and after some little time,

Mr. HOBHOUSE: I know you are, Sir; but I am not speaking of you.

Sir F. Burdett and Mr. Bruce here approached Mr. Hobhouse, and induced him to resume his seat.

During this very disgraceful scene, the Chairman, and the Noble and Honourable Gentlemen around him had taken their hats, and were about to depart, but again resumed their seats.

midst of this confusion, Mr. Hobhouse repeatedly presented himself, and uttered a few sentences with a view to obtain a hearing, but they were completely drowned in the uproar which prevailed.

No health of the Honourable Baronet, even if he were

considered only as a veteran pensioner of the public service; this opposition to such a toast, without affording him an opportunity of explanation, *would be cowardly.* The Honourable Baronet had very properly told them, that if he had not his own esteem, he would not care a farthing for theirs. After some further observations, he concluded by declaring, that those who would not hear Mr. Hobhouse, were not candid to their own cause.

Mr. Hobhouse denied that he was conscious of having done any thing to deserve the disapproval of his fellow-citizens—nor did he know of any charge which the Electors of Westminster could fairly bring against him. It was clearly the intention of the individual who had first introduced this dissension, to disturb and destroy the Meeting. If it was their pleasure that the Meeting should be immediately dissolved, in God's name let it be so; but if it was not, as they had never been put down by power, he trusted they would not suffer themselves to be put down by impudence. If after so many professions of public service and so many acts performed, public men were to be deprived of public confidence by attacks of this kind, there were no men of honour who would consent to become public servants. If any individual had any charge against him, let him come forward and make it, but no insults or interruptions of this kind should deter him from expressing his opinions. The voice of his conscience told him that he had never given a single vote differing from the opinions of a vast majority of his Constituents [applause, mixed with some disapprobation]. [At this part of Mr. Hobhouse's speech, the tables and benches, upon which he and his friends had stationed themselves, to the left of the Chair, gave way, and the whole party—bottles, decanters, glasses and all—went to the ground, with a sudden crash, to the no small delight of their opponents who laughed heartily at their *fall.*]

Mr. Hobhouse made some additional observations; but the clamour which prevailed rendered them totally inaudible, even to those immediately around him.

The Chairman having proposed the health of " Lord Nugent, and the Electors of Aylesbury," which was drunk with three times three.

Lord Nugent said that he most sincerely and gratefully thanked them for that honour—an honour which he felt perhaps the more, after the disgraceful scene they had lately witnessed. He trusted that he entertained a fair estimate of the value of public character; but if his character had been impeached from such a quarter, he would not have condescended to answer it. He would at once name the person to whom he alluded, for he should be ashamed to use a word vaguely that might leave it open to be supposed that he meant any person but Mr. Cobbett. He owed it to his own feelings as an Englishman and a gentleman to say, that Mr. Hunt had behaved both manfully and honourably, but Mr. Cobbett had conducted himself in such a manner, as, if he had any feeling at all, would make him feel the effects of that conduct the longest day of his life. The Noble Lord justified the conduct of Sir F. Burdett in supporting the present Administration, as it had enabled Mr. Canning to break the head of a faction, which, if admitted again into power, would only destroy the glory and interests of the country. So long as he (Lord Nugent) could carry a musket in the cause, he would enlist under the banners of any commander that would destroy such a faction. In the present instance he had done so, and his constituents had approved of his conduct. His Lordship here stated, that he had been returned by those constituents at their own expense. He was so situated that he could not bribe them if he would, and he would not if he could [cheers]. This, he had fairly stated to them, and upon those principles it was that he held his present seat. His constituents had presented to him, upon his entering Parliament, the receipts of the expense of that Election, which expense amounted to 32l. some odd shillings [applause]. He returned his sincere thanks, on the part of himself and his constituents, and he trusted that he should always be found at the side of the Hon. Baronet [applause]. i α

Mr. Wells, of Huntingdon, made some observations, preparatory to a motion of thanks to Earl Grey. The motion was objected to by the Chairman, solely upon the ground that the Noble Earl was not present.

Sir F. Burdett next proposed the " health of a Noble Lord, who had uniformly and zealously advocated the cause of the People — he meant his Noble Friend Lord Ebrington." The toast was drunk with three times three [applause].

Lord Ebrington said, he rose with feelings of the utmost gratitude, to re-

turn thanks for the distinguished honour which the Meeting had done him.
But at that late hour, and considering
the disgraceful interruptions which had
taken place in the course of the evening
—considering, too, that there were
many gentlemen around him more capable of addressing the Meeting than he
could pretend to be, his address should
not detain them more than a few moments. He could not, however, do justice to his own feelings—he could not do
justice to those Honourable Friends with
whom he had so long and so invariably
acted, if he did not avail himself of the
occasion, when the Honourable Chairman's conduct was assailed, to render to
him the humble tribute of his respect
and gratitude for the whole of his Parliamentary conduct [cheers]; and he
must be allowed to say, for no part of it
more than that which was at present
called in question [loud applause, mixed
with disapprobation]. Further, he would
say, that whatever meed of praise or of
blame was dealt out to the Hon. Baronet,
he (Lord Ebrington) must, in a small
degree, take his share. If he had been
asked whether the present Administration was precisely such a one as he
should wish to see formed, his answer
would be—certainly not. But that was
not the question brought under his consideration. What, he asked, was the
choice left to him? What was the
option left to the party with which
he had the honour of acting? Why,
that they must support the new, and
in many instances liberal, Administration, recently established — or else
they must, by turning them out, reinstate
the Ex-Administration, and thereby give
effect to that which had been well described by an Hon. Friend of his in the
House of Commons—to be Toryism in
its most hideous form [cheers]. He and
his friends had been asked if they still
adhered to the great questions of Civil
and Religious Liberty—if they still adhered to the question of Reform? He
said that they did? and for himself he
would also say, that if his retaining his
former seat could have advanced both or
either of these questions, he would have
sat there to the end of his days [cheers].
But was he, because he could not obtain
all he wished, precluded from getting all
he could? [Cries of " No, no!"] He
never did, and he never would, vote
against any question which had for its
object the extension of civil and religious
liberty; but while he said this, he felt that
it was but fair to give a trial to a liberal
Administration. In that trial the Administration might succeed, or they

might fail; but in either event, something must be gained. If it succeeded,
then, to use the words of his Hon. Friend
(the Chairman) in another place, the
High Tory faction, who had so long
fattened over us, would be made to
feel that their power was not omnipotent either in the possession or in public domination [cheers]. But, should
the Administration fail, or should he
and his friends find that in the course
of the next Session nothing had been
gained in support of civil or religious
liberty, then he would say that he
should retire disappointed, but still with
a clear conscience—with a decided feeling that he, and those who acted with
him, had used their utmost efforts to
advance those great public principles
which they had through life supported
[cheers]. He had always had the happiness to agree with their Honourable
Chairman, upon all public occasions;
but upon none was he more proud of
agreeing with him than upon the present
occasion [applause]. He thanked the
meeting for the kind and patient attention with which they had heard him,
and requested pardon for having so long
detained them. He begged to conclude
with a repetition of the kind sense he
entertained of the honour paid to him
[applause].

Sir F. Burdett next proposed " the
health of Lord John Russell;" but the
noise in the room (which we must here,
once for all, observe was more worthy of
Hockley-in-the-Hole, or the *Westminster Pit*, than any place we have ever
yet described,) was so great that not a
single word could be heard beyond the
Noble Lord's name.

Lord John Russell rose to return
thanks, but his Lordship was, from the
causes already assigned, for a short time
inaudible. He had come, he said, solely for the purpose of testifying his regard
and admiration of the character of their
Representative and Chairman [cheers].
It appeared to him, that the question to
be tried there that day was, whether the
Honourable Baronet's conduct was
such as to merit the approval of his Constituents—the Electors of Westminster.
He (Lord J. Russell), judging from the
feeling which he had seen expressed in
that room, must say, that the principles
of the Honourable Baronet had been
fully approved of by the Meeting [cheers,
mixed with some disapprobation from
the left corner of the room]. The Noble Lord, adverting to the two great
questions brought under discussion—
namely, Parliamentary Reform and a

Reform of the Administration—observed that the question was, whether they were to have certain liberal measures brought forward and supported without any pledge upon the question of Reform, or, whether they were to have the domination of a Ministry who would oppose every liberal and enlightened measure, but Reform most of all [cheers]? For his own part, he thought is would be better to preserve the present Administration without any pledge, than to recur to the whole of the old one without any hope [cheers]. He had always supported Reform, but he had always maintained, that an Opposition to Reform did not necessarily imply the existence of a good Minister; the evil was the other way, because a bad Minister necessarily implied an opposition to all Reform. The Noble Lord concluded by the most cordial approval of the Honourable Chairman's conduct [applause].

The CHAIRMAN proposed "the health of Mr. W. Paulett Thompson, and the Reformers of Dover," with three times three [applause].

Mr. W. P. THOMPSON returned his most grateful thanks for the honour done him, and begged to say a few words, and few he assured the Meeting they should be, because he felt, first, that if he were to give expression to his sentiments, he should only repeat that which had been more ably said by those who had preceded him; and, secondly, because he could not presume to expect a hearing, when the Meeting had refused to attend to their Honourable Representative, Mr. Hobhouse. In alluding to the interruption which took place, he acquitted the Meeting collectively of any such intention, but he charged it upon one individual, upon whose head it must and ought to rest. The Honourable Gentleman, after professing himself to be a decided friend to freedom and liberal opinions in their most extended terms, concluded by again thanking the Meeting for the honour they had done him.

Sir F. BURDETT, in rising to propose the only toast which remained, wished, before he retired to give an explanation of something which had been said in the course of the evening. If Mr. Hunt had been in the House of Commons, when he (Sir F. Burdett) stated the grounds upon which he had determined to support the present Administration, he would have heard him utter precisely the same sentiments which he had uttered that evening [cheers]. He said this,

merely to prevent its going abroad that he had held different opinions in different places [loud applause]. The Toast was —"The Liberty of the Press," with three times three [applause].

Mr. WOOLER rose to return thanks, and, in the course of his speech observed, that he considered Mr. Canning to be like an overgrown eel, that, having got out of the reservoir into the current, was obliged to go along with that current, because, if he would, he could not rejoin his companions in the reservoir.

Sir F. Burdett, and those immediately around him, retired at eleven o'clock. They had scarcely left the room, when a discussion took place as to who was to take the Chair. After a great deal of noise and clamour,

Mr. WOOLER was ultimately voted Chairman for the remainder of the evening, during which there was as much noise, to say the least of it, as had prevailed at any earlier period. Mr. Cobbett, in retiring, was not treated with all the kindness he could wish, but he and his friends bore the pushes and elbows which they received, with comparative meekness. The noise (we cannot say the hilarity) of the evening was kept up to a late hour.

---

# TULIP-TREE WOOD.

I HAVE just received from America about *sixteen hundred feet* of tulip-tree plank, two inches and a half thick; and I believe, and all carpenters that have seen it agree with me, that this is the finest lot of plank that ever was seen in England since England was England. Some of the planks are fourteen feet long, each, and *between three and four feet wide*; and there is not, in the whole lot, one single curl or one single knot. The planks are just as wide at one end as at the other. I shall advertize them for sale next week. I have a great desire to introduce this tree into extensive use in England. If properly raised and cultivated, it will grow as fast and get to as great a height and be as straight here as in America; and it has appeared to me that the most likely way of inducing gentlemen to plant the tree is to let them see with their own eyes a specimen of the timber. The tree will grow more than a hundred feet high: I have seen it more than a hundred feet high, many times; and, if raised from seed, it will attain that height here as well as in America; but from *layers*, as it is raised in the nurseries, in general, it is always merely a *branch of a tree*, and will never attain to any thing of a height or size.—Bᴜʀᴅᴇᴛᴛ says, that as a man of common sense, he would achieve something during his life-time; now, I think, that if I succeed in introducing this noble tree into England, as I hope to do, I shall be doing something much more worthy of common sense than he will, though he should get somebody to give him a title, and so creep off on his hands and knees away from us.

---

N. B. For want of room, I am obliged to postpone the insertion of the Resolution, spoken of in the foregoing Letter, until next week.

# MARKETS.

Average Prices of CORN through-out ENGLAND, for the week ending May 11.

### Per Quarter.

|        | s. | d. |        | s. | d. |
|--------|----|----|--------|----|----|
| Wheat  | 56 | 8  | Rye    | 39 | 2  |
| Barley | 39 | 4  | Beans  | 49 | 2  |
| Oats   | 30 | 3  | Pease  | 47 | 0  |

Total Quantity of Corn returned as Sold in the Maritime Districts, for the week ended May 11.

|        | Qrs.   |       | Qrs.  |
|--------|--------|-------|-------|
| Wheat  | 41,824 | Rye   | 263   |
| Barley | 7,247  | Beans | 1,304 |
| Oats   | 8,863  | Pease | 626   |

Aggregate Average of the six weeks preceding May 18, by which importation is regulated.

### Per Quarter.

|        | s. | d. |
|--------|----|----|
| Wheat  | 56 | 3  |
| Rye    | 39 | 7  |
| Barley | 39 | 0  |
| Oats   | 30 | 7  |
| Beans  | 47 | 6  |
| Pease  | 47 | 6  |

*Corn Exchange, Mark Lane.*

Quantities and Prices of British Corn, &c. sold and delivered in this Market, during the week ended Saturday, May 11.

|        | Qrs.  | £. s. d.    |          | s. | d. |
|--------|-------|-------------|----------|----|----|
| Wheat  | 4,847 | for 14,916 13 10 | Average | 61 | 6  |
| Barley | 1,104 | .. 2,230 18 9 |         | 40 | 6  |
| Oats   | 2,433 | .. 4,019 7 1 |         | 33 | 0  |
| Rye    | 14    | .. 25 7 3    |          | 36 | 2  |
| Beans  | 479   | .. 1,140 0 3 |          | 47 | 7  |
| Pease  | 96    | .. 226 13 1  |          | 46 | 7  |

Friday, May 18—There are fair arrivals of most kinds of Grain this week, and a good quantity of English Flour and Foreign Oats. Wheat meets a dull sale, at Monday's prices. In Barley, Beans, and Pease, there is no variation. Most of our buyers are waiting till Monday before they purchase Oats, as the Foreign are then expected to be liberated, at the low duty. There is no alteration in Flour.

Monday, May 21.—During the preceding week the supplies of most kinds of English Grain were moderate, and of Foreign Oats very large. The quantity of Flour was also considerable. To this day's market, the fresh arrival of Wheat, from Essex and Kent, is better than for several weeks past, but there is very little Spring Corn of our own growth fresh in to-day. The attempt to raise the top price of Flour having entirely failed, the Wheat trade has, in consequence, become very dull, and the prices are declined 1s. to 2s. per qr. from the terms of this day se'nnight.

Barley is scarce, and the prices remain as last quoted. Beans and Pease continue without alteration. The Foreign Oats being permitted to enter at 4d. per qr. duty, there is now abundance of Horse Corn for sale; and although there has been a good attendance of country buyers, yet they have not bought freely, and the prices are declined 1s. to 2s. per quarter, from the terms of this day se'nnight. All kinds of Seed meet a very heavy sale.

*Price on board Ship as under.*

| Flour, per sack | 46s. — 50. |
|---|---|
| —— Seconds | 42s. — 44s. |
| —— North Country | 40s. — 43s. |

Price of Bread.—The price of the 4lb. Loaf is stated at 9d. by the full-priced Bakers.

## COAL MARKET, May 18.

| Ships at Market. | Ships sold. | Price. |
|---|---|---|
| 133. | 24¾. | 28s.—42s. |

Account of Wheat, &c. arrived in the Port of London, from May 14 to May 19; both inclusive.

| | Qrs. | | Qrs. |
|---|---|---|---|
| Wheat .. | 4,576 | Tares .... | 150 |
| Barley .. | 498 | Linseed .. | 2,012 |
| Malt .... | 5,849 | Rapeseed . | 1,592 |
| Oats .... | 1,538 | Brank .. | 164 |
| Beans.... | 544 | Mustard .. | 27 |
| Flour .... | 9,583 | Flax .... | — |
| Rye .... | 88 | Hemp .... | 4 |
| Pease.... | 912 | Seeds ... | 16 |

Foreign. — Wheat, 789; Barley, 10,396; Oats, 46,478; Beans, 790 quarters.

Monday, May 21.—The arrivals from Ireland last week were, 108 firkins of Butter, and 5035 bales of Bacon; and from Foreign Ports, 6,651 casks of Butter. The demand continues to take all the Foreign Butter on arrival. Bacon continues without any material alteration.

## HOPS.

Price of Hops, per Cwt. in the Borough.

Monday, May 21.—The bad prospects in the Hop plantations have been increased by the arrival of considerable quantities of fly, which has caused this morning a rapid rise in both bags and pockets. Many people anticipate a similar result, from this early attack, to what we experienced in 1825. Duty called, 95,000l.

Maidstone, May 17.—Our accounts are better every day from the change of weather, and the Bines are generally much improving, with less flea. We have had a few sales this last week, though at not much better prices.

Worcester, May 16.—The easterly winds and frosty nights having given the plants an unkindly appearance, prices rose in our market on Saturday 3s. to 4s. per cwt. The duty is down to 105,000l.

### SMITHFIELD.

Monday, May 21.—On Friday Beef obtained the prices of the preceding market; but Mutton fell 1s. to 2s. a-head; in Lamb no alteration. The supply of Beasts to-day is short, but there will, notwithstanding, be many unsold. In Sheep there is a considerable decline, from last Monday, say 3s. and 4s. a head, with a heavy trade. The best polled Sheep, in few instances, reach a crown, and old Downs do not exceed 5s. 2d., both out of the wool. Lamb also lower; and very few obtain our top figure: 6s. to 6s. 8d. is about the thing for good Lamb; but middling is very heavy in sale.

Per Stone of 8 pounds (alive).

| | s. | d. | s. | d. |
|---|---|---|---|---|
| Beef .... | 4 | 0 | 5 | 2 |
| Mutton .. | 4 | 0 — | 5 | 2 |
| Veal .... | 4 | 8 — | 5 | 4 |
| Pork .... | 4 | 6 — | 5 | 2 |
| Lamb .... | 6 | 0 — | 7 | 0 |

| Beasts .. | 2,014 | Sheep .. | 19,780 |
|---|---|---|---|
| Calves ... | 158 | Pigs .... | 110 |

NEWGATE, (same day.)
Per Stone of 8 pounds (dead).

| | s. | d. | s. | d. |
|---|---|---|---|---|
| Beef .... | 3 | 8 to | 4 | 6 |
| Mutton ... | 4 | 4 — | | 4 |
| Veal .... | 3 | 4 — | | 4 |
| Pork .... | 3 | 8 — | | 8 |
| Lamb .... | 4 | 8 — | 5 | 8 |

LEADENHALL, (same day.)
Per Stone of 8 pounds (dead).

| | s. | d. | s. | d. |
|---|---|---|---|---|
| Beef ... | 3 | 8 to | 4 | 6 |
| Mutton ... | 3 | 4 — | 5 | 0 |
| Veal .... | 3 | 8 — | 5 | 4 |
| Pork .... | 4 | 4 — | 5 | 4 |
| Lamb .... | 4 | 0 — | 6 | 10 |

## POTATOES.

**SPITALFIELDS, per Ton.**

|                     | £. | s. | | £. | s. |
|---------------------|----|----|---|----|----|
| Ox-Nobles.....      | 3  | 10 | to | 0 | 0 |
| Middlings......     | 2  | 5  | — | 0 | 0 |
| Chats .........     | 2  | 0  | — | 0 | 0 |
| Common Red..        | 6  | 10 | — | 0 | 0 |

Onions, 6s. 0d. —0s. 0d. per bush.

**BORROUGH, per Ton.**

|                     | £. | s. | | £. | s. |
|---------------------|----|----|---|----|----|
| Ox-Nobles ....      | 3  | 10 | to | 4 | 5 |
| Middlings...        | 2  | 0  | — | 2 | 10 |
| Chats.........      | 2  | 0  | — | 0 | 0 |
| Common Red..        | 3  | 0  | — | 4 | 0 |

## HAY and STRAW, per Load.

Smithfield.—Hay....90s. to 115s.

Straw....36s. to 46s.

Clover.100s. to 135s.

St. James's.—Hay.... 70s. to 105s.

Straw .. 30s. to 40s. 6d.

Clover. 115s. to 140s.

Whitechapel.—Hay.... 80s. to 120s.

Straw...36s. to 42s.

Clover..99s. to 135s.

---

## AVERAGE PRICE OF CORN, sold in the Maritime Counties of England and Wales, for the Week ended May 11, 1827.

|                  | Wheat. | | Barley. | | Oats. | |
|------------------|--------|----|---------|----|-------|----|
|                  | s. | d. | s. | d. | s. | d. |
| London*          | 60 | 2 | 40 | 5 | 34 | 2 |
| Essex            | 56 | 9 | 39 | 10 | 31 | 3 |
| Kent             | 57 | 9 | 41 | 0 | 31 | 0 |
| Sussex           | 53 | 9 | 0 | 0 | 30 | 7 |
| Suffolk          | 56 | 0 | 37 | 2 | 31 | 10 |
| Cambridgeshire   | 52 | 11 | 36 | 4 | 27 | 6 |
| Norfolk          | 54 | 10 | 37 | 0 | 27 | 0 |
| Lincolnshire     | 55 | 9 | 40 | 1 | 26 | 9 |
| Yorkshire        | 55 | 1 | 41 | 6 | 28 | 0 |
| Durham           | 55 | 7 | 43 | 5 | 29 | 4 |
| Northumberland   | 54 | 4 | 38 | 5 | 31 | 10 |
| Cumberland       | 64 | 2 | 39 | 6 | 36 | 2 |
| Westmoreland     | 68 | 4 | 46 | 0 | 41 | 6 |
| Lancashire       | 61 | 0 | 46 | 5 | 44 | 0 |
| Cheshire         | 65 | 5 | 0 | 0 | 28 | 0 |
| Gloucestershire  | 56 | 9 | 43 | 5 | 41 | 10 |
| Somersetshire    | 54 | 2 | 0 | 0 | 29 | 1 |
| Monmouthshire    | 56 | 11 | 44 | 6 | 0 | 0 |
| Devonshire       | 55 | 6 | 39 | 7 | 33 | 0 |
| Cornwall         | 62 | 7 | 41 | 0 | 27 | 11 |
| Dorsetshire      | 55 | 1 | 39 | 9 | 0 | 0 |
| Hampshire        | 55 | 10 | 41 | 5 | 31 | |
| North Wales      | 65 | 6 | 45 | 5 | 30 | |
| South Wales      | 62 | 4 | 49 | 8 | 27 | |

* The London Average is always that of the Week preceding.

*Derby*, May 19.—Our market this week was but thinly attended, and but little business done; prices for all sorts of Grain nearly as before:—Best Wheat, 60s. to 65s.; Barley for malting, 44s. to 47s.; Grinding ditto, 38s. to 42s.; Oats, 32s. to 49s.; and Beans, 58s. to 62s. per eight bushels Imperial measure.

*Horncastle*, May 19.—Wheat, Barley, and Rye fully obtained last week's prices, and Oats nearly the same. Wheat, 56s. to 60s.; Barley, 40s. to 48s.; Oats, 26s. to 30s.; Beans, 60s. to 63s.; and Rye from 40s. to 44s. per quarter.

*Ipswich*, May 19.—Our supply to-day was small, but equal to the demand. The sale was dull, at rather less prices.—Wheat, 54s. to 63s.; Barley, 36s. to 41s.; and Beans, 49s. to 51s. per quarter.

*Manchester*, May 19.—The Corn trade has been in an inanimate state during the week, owing partly to the result of the Bill now in the House of Lords, whether there will be any alteration in the existing laws. At our market to-day, fine Wheat was difficult of sale, at last week's rates; inferior unsaleable. Barley, for grinding purposes, 3d. per bushel lower. Oats of fine quality barely support the prices of last Saturday. Beans are in limited supply, but no alteration in value can be noted. Malt in fair demand; and, if our manufacturing trade continues to improve, the result will be a proportionate demand for Malt. The dealers in Flour have not experienced such a lively demand as was anticipated, but last week's prices have been fully supported, and, in a few instances, a small advance has been obtained.

*Newcastle-upon-Tyne*, May 19.—The Wheat at this morning's market was confined to the farmers' supply, with some samples from granary, and the millers being short of stock, the sale was brisk, at 1s. per quarter advance upon the prices of last week. The malting season being over, Barley is dull sale, at last week's prices. The farmers' supply of Oats was small, and not having any foreign arrivals of consequence this week, the sale has been tolerably free, at last week's prices.

*Norwich*, May 19.—We had only a moderate supply of Wheat to-day, prices nearly the same as last week.—Red, 52s. to 59s.; White to 61s.; Barley, only a few small parcels, 34s. to 40s.; Oats, 28s. to 31s.; Beans, 43s. to 48s.; Pease, 44s. to 48s.; Boilers, to 52s. per quarter; and Flour, 42s. to 43s. per sack.

*Reading*, May 19.—We had a moderate supply of Wheat this day, which was heavy in disposal, on the same terms as last week. There was a short supply of Barley, but no alteration in the price. Beans were 1s. dearer. In Oats and Pease no alteration, and very little doing.

*Bristol*, May 19.—The Corn markets at this place are not lively for any description of Grain. Supplies by no means great, yet equal to the demand.

*Horncastle*, May 19.—Wheat, Barley, and Rye fully obtained last week's prices, and Oats nearly the same. Wheat, 56s. to 60s.; Barley, 40s. to 42s.; Oats, 26s. to 30s.; Beans, 60s. to 63s.; and Rye, from 40s. to 44s. per qr.

*Wisbech*, May 19.—We had a good supply of Wheat here to-day, which went off slowly, at a decline of 1s. per quarter; Oats are also 1s. lower; but fine Beans exceed the late quotations 2s. per quarter.

## COUNTRY CATTLE AND MEAT MARKETS, &c.

*Horncastle*, May 19.—Beef, 9s. per stone of 14 lbs.; Mutton, 6d. to 7d.; Lamb 8d.; Pork, 7d.; and Veal, from 8d. to 9d. per lb.

*Manchester* Smithfield Market, May 16.—Although the supply of Beef and Mutton was not so large as last week, yet it was fully equal to the demand, and the best quality of the former declined full ½d. per lb.; the latter with difficulty support last week's rates. The few Calves at market were very fine, and ½d. per lb. advance was paid for the best. The supply of Pigs was principally Irish, and bought at rather less price for store. We had a plentiful supply of Lambs, the principal part of which were sold at ½d. per lb below the price of this day se'nnight.—Beef, 4½d. to 7½d.; Mutton, 7d. to 8½d; Lamb, 9d. to 10d.; Veal, 5½d. to 7½d.; and Pork, 4d. to 5½d. per lb., sinking offal.

At *Morpeth* Market, May 16th, there were a good many Cattle and Sheep; being few buyers, both met with dull sale, at a reduction in price, and part of both were not sold.—Beef, from 7s. to 7s. 6d.; Mutton, 8s. to 9s. 4d. per stone, sinking offal.

*Norwich Castle Meadow*, May 19.—The supply of fat Cattle to this day's market was good, prices 7s. 9d. to 8s. 6d. per stone of 14 lbs., sinking offal; the supply of Store Stock, of all descriptions, was very large, and the sale of them very dull; Scots sold at 4s. to 4s. 6d. per stone of what they will weigh when fat; Shorthorns, 3s. to 3s. 9d.; Cows and Calves selling rather better; Homebreds, of one and two years old, hardly saleable. Pigs, a flat sale, fat ones to 7s. 6d. per stone.—Meat: Beef, 7d. to 9d.; Veal, 6d. to 8d.; Mutton, 6d. to 7½d.; Lamb, 8½d.; and Pork, 6d. to 8d. per lb.

# COBBETT'S WEEKLY REGISTER.

Vol. 62.—No. 10.]    LONDON, SATURDAY, June 2, 1827.    [Price 6d.

" Lord Castlereagh found that he was wrong, and he died of a broken
" heart. But it was not unprosperous external affairs of his country which
" destroyed him. It was the unmeasured and unmitigated *ruin which he*
" *saw at home.* I KNOW that he saw it; and I may ALMOST say, I
" KNOW THAT IT KILLED HIM."—Thomas Attwood's Letter to
Sir John Sinclair, December, 1825.

> BARONET.—Cleary, thy faith and love full well I know ;
> But, so low my fortunes, that Atlas self
> Unable were to keep me 'bove contempt.
> Farewell, a long farewell to all my pride !
> Farewell huzzas, farewell big sounding speech !
> Farewell the toasts, the flattery of Rumps,
> And all the pomp and circumstance of Dining !
> Crown and Anchor, scene of all my triumphs,
> Oh ! farewell !
>               COBBETT's WESTMINSTER TRAGI-COMI-FARCE, WRITTEN
>                    IN LONG ISLAND, 11TH SEPT. 1818.

# OLD LADY

### AND

# SIR   GLORY.

### TO THE READERS OF THE REGISTER.

*Fleet Street, 30th May, 1827.*

MY FRIENDS,

Two great personages are now
before us: the Old Lady of
Threadneedle-street, and the old
badgered and battered Sir Glory,
whom some of us had standing
before us, on the 23d of this
month, in the character of a political culprit, wriggling, twisting,
shuffling, whimpering and canting,
till even his own hired and stuffed

T

Printed and Published by WILLIAM COBBETT, No 183, Fleet-street.
[ENTERED AT STATIONERS' HALL.]

ruffians seemed to be ashamed of the exhibition. I did not, in my last Register, do half justice to this dismal old wreck of a pretended patriot; and I intended to make up, in the present Register, for the omission. Something more about the old battered hack and his myrmidons and hangers-on I must say in the present Register; but, just as I was setting to work this morning; or, rather, thinking about setting to work upon him, in came the *Morning Chronicle*, containing the Bank of England CIRCULAR (as it is stated to be), which I shall presently insert, and which, if Burdett had two grains of sense in that noisy head of his, would make him see how slippery is the ground on which he stands; how uncertain the tenure of whatever he may expect to get from Canning; how far from being as solid as the foundations of the hills, is even the title of that estate which he values, apparently, beyond his soul itself. This great, gawky personage, speaking last year to a gentleman that I know, said, " Cobbett may say what he will, " but it is all d—d nonsense to " suppose that, with all the in- " creased wealth of this country, " there can be gold and silver " enough found to carry on its

" affairs : there must be plenty of " paper-money."

The great oaf did not perceive, apparently, that it was not the quantity of money, but the price of things that he ought to have kept in his eye. Only think what a fool a fellow must be; only think what a pretty law-giver, to imagine that money ought to be increased as the quantity of goods is increased. At that rate, there must be an additional parcel of money issued in consequence of a great harvest or a great crop of apples. But, it is waste of time and an insult to you, my friends, to give any serious answer to such a staring fool, who is just as fit as that fish-woman that I see now, going along the street with a basket of mackerel; who is just as fit as she is to suggest means for the putting of this troubled state of things to rights. He seems to understand not one single sound principle connected with the subject; he is notoriously too lazy to go into the detail, even if he understood the principles ; and, if he had all the other requisite qualities, he wants the courage, the steadiness, the political pluck, to make even a slight attempt to carry any necessary measure into execution.

But, before I proceed any further on this part of my subject, let me beg of you, my friends, to look at this new project of the Old Dame of Threadneedle-street. The newspapers tell us, that she has sent it round in the way of a friendly proposal to the principal country-bankers in England. However, here it is: read it with attention, if you please, and, then, I beg you to listen, for a moment, to a remark or two that I have to make upon the subject.

(CIRCULAR.)

" Assuming it to be desirable to retain a paper money currency convertible on demand, the great question for consideration is, how that paper money can be so regulated as to afford the greatest security for receivers, both as regards the solidity of the issuer, and the power of obtaining coin for the same on demand.

" In order to obtain those objects, it is necessary, in the first instance, to free the paper money, as far as may be possible, from the effects of what has been termed panic. In a great commercial country like this, periods of speculation and overtrading may frequently arise; still, no event of that nature ought, under proper regulation of the currency, to affect the credit of the paper money, the discredit of which has hitherto tended very greatly to aggravate the evils which we have in such times sustained. Now, under the present system of issues by the Bank of England, and the country bankers, there is the greatest difficulty, amounting almost to an impracticability, of so regulating the paper money currency as to attain the objects immediately referred to. The confliction of action and interest between these two description of issues is the main difficulty; the fact being that, as prices expand, and even where the notes are returning upon the Bank for gold to be exported, the issues of the country bankers are extending, and are never attempted to be withdrawn, until the Bank makes an evident demonstration to the country of contracting from a continuance of the drain upon that establishment for gold. That action, though of the most trifling amount, immediately lays the foundation of alarm, and the paper money issued by the country bankers becomes discredited, before they can be provided to meet the run upon their establishments. Stoppage is the consequence with many; and although they may eventually realize sufficient assets to meet their engagements to the actual holders of the notes, yet the country has to sustain all the evils attendant on the first discredit, and which no final payment can ever alleviate. It is in this state of discredit, attending the *private* paper money currency, that the Bank of England is looked to, not only for gold in exchange for its own notes, but also to supply an almost instan-

**T 2**

taneous demand to a very great extent on the part of those country bankers who have the command of funded or other tangible property to offer as security, the magnitude of which internal demand for gold actually places the Bank in the greatest possible danger, and with that danger the credit of the country is placed at hazard.

" It may, perhaps, be deserving of consideration, whether the hazard and difficulties of our present system might not be obviated by confining fhe issue of the paper money currency to one body of undoubted solidity ; and believing that such a measure, if practicable, could not be so satisfactorily carried into effect as by the Bank of England, *under proper and efficient parliamentary regulations*, it is proposed that the paper of that corporation should be that alone permitted to circulate. There could, however, be no objection to the substitution of any other body of equal credit, which might be deemed more advantageous for the country. In thus limiting the issue to one body, the accommodation and advantage derived by the public from the country banks ought to be preserved as far as may be practicable ; and which, it is presumed, might be effected by continuing in that channel the issue of the paper money proposed to be adopted, in such manner and at such rate of interest as may afford a fair proportion of the advantage which the country bankers

have for so many years been permitted to enjoy in their own circulation. It remains, therefore, to be shown, in what mode a plan of that nature could be adopted.

" The advantage hitherto derived by the country bankers upon their issues may be estimated at 5 per cent. per annum ; from which, however, should be deducted :—

" 1. The expense of printing, issuing, &c.

" 2. The stamp duty.

" 3. The interest on the amount of Bank of England paper, or bullion, which they *ought* to keep to meet returns.

"*4. The risk of loss in times of general discredit of private paper money, upon realizing funded or other property, which under the present system has generally occurred once in four or five years; and there appears no reason to suppose that it will occur less frequently hereafter.*

" These deductions may be fairly estimated at from 2 to 3 per cent. per annum, the residue forming the amount of net profit. It might therefore be proposed that every country banker, withdrawing his own paper circulation, should receive that of the Bank of England *to the same amount at a reduced rate of interest,* giving to that corporation security for such issue ; one-third of which should be in bills of exchange, or other convertible securities, which, in the event of a contraction becoming necessary to correct the exchanges, might be withdrawn by the Bank upon three months' notice, in sums not exceeding 5,000l. in succession; and any sums so withdrawn should, if required, be again re-issuable in the same manner, and upon the same terms. The remaining two-thirds to be a permanent advance upon funded or landed property, during the term of the Bank charter, at the option of the borrowers.

" The country bankers would thus derive the full benefit between the rate of interest paid to the Bank, and that which they would obtain from their borrowers, free from all anxiety arising from panics, and from other causes discrediting private paper money. There might, perhaps, be some little difficulty in laying down regulations for keeping up this system upon the dissolution of existing country establishments : that difficulty might, in all probability, be got over when the details of the plan came to be considered.

" The Bank paper thus proposed for circulation might be issued from the branch banks established in central parts of the country, affording the facilities of exchange, and payment in coin when demanded; and from which branch banks any further issue might be made upon discount at the current rate of interest, which might be required *by the expansion of prices, so long as the exchanges were in favour of the country;* thus affording at all times a full and efficient currency. In order to give the desired effect to a plan of this description, it would be essential to obtain the concurrence of the majority of the country banking interest, and which, from a *limited inquiry that has been made, it is thought would be given, provided no material difficulty arose in arranging of details.* And, finally, to give stability to the system, the Bank of England should be required to publish in the Gazette every quarter, the amount of notes in circulation, with the bullion, and securities in deposit, that the public might be apprised of any fluctuation in either paper or bullion which might occur, and which publication would, it is conceived, be a sufficient security against any undue use of the power thus placed in the hands of the bank.

" It is presumed, that by the foregoing plan all the advantages and convenience of the country bank establishments might be retained, and permanent solidity be given to our paper money currency, no contraction ever being likely to occur, except in the event of a continuance of an unfavourable exchange, and the consequent return of paper upon the Bank and its branches for gold to be exported, which return of paper, if not improvidently re-issued by the Bank, would in all probability be sufficient to correct the exchanges, and bring back the gold which might have passed abroad. If the demand, however, for gold should at any time be very rapid and extensive, it might, possibly, in such case, require some trifling check, either by contraction of the paper circulating throughout the country, or by a limitation of the mercantile discounts at the Bank, the effect of which would be to contract at an early period that part of the currency which may be termed collateral—viz. bills of exchange and credits; thus lowering the prices of commodities, so as to render them cheaper articles of payment to the foreigner than the bullion previously required.

" If, upon giving this subject the fullest consideration, it *should be deemed objectionable,* to confine the issue of paper money to one body, *it appears to be doubtful whether any real and effectual security can be given against the recurrence of the evils we have so lately sustained.* So long as the Bank and the *many* exist together, so long will the latter always rest upon the former in the day of distress and discredit; and from what has hitherto so frequently occurred, it may be confidently asserted, that under the great existing state of our paper money, the Bank, continuing to act as heretofore, must *necessarily incur the greatest risk of stoppage, and thereby place at hazard the very credit of the country.*

" In considering the preceding statement, the following principle should be admitted :—that all supposed vested interests either in the Bank of England or other establishments issuing paper money, should be deemed subservient to the national interests ; consequently the security of general property should form the

only object of consideration in any plan for *substituting paper money for coin."*

The first thing to observe on is this ; that this circular must have been put forth *with the concurrence of the Ministers;* because, that which it proposes, cannot be carried into effect, without the concurrence of the Ministers and the Parliament. For instance, it proposes that the old mother-bank should supply all her young devil-banks with paper-money. This she cannot do, *without a new Act of Parliament,* because she herself cannot, now, according to law, make small paper-money ; so that, it is clear as day-light, that she must have had the sanction of the Government before she sent forth this circular. Judge, then, my friends, what a pretty state we are in ; judge you of this " solid system of finance," as flabbergaster Pitt used to call it ; judge you of the "*mountain of paper,*" the base of which, according to " the great" Mr. Canning, the " liberal" Mr. Canning, the " *enlightened* " Mr. Canning, whose shoulders are tickled alternately by the knees of Burdett, Brougham and Tierney ; judge you, my friends, of this mountain of paper, the base of which the flashy Canning tells us, is so nicely " irrigated with gold "! Things must be in a pretty state, when a sort of jugglery like this is going on; when the Government makes use of an organ like this to feel its way about; and, when this organ itself is, in fact, neither more nor less than a dependent branch of the Government.

The next thing to observe is, that this Old Lady declares to the country-bankers; declares to the country itself, *that another panic must come;* that there is no way of obviating another panic : another panic is a blowing-up of the system, Burdett's " march of mind " and altogether ; another panic means a blowing of Tierney away from the Mint, of Brougham away from the bait that he has in his eye; another panic means the scattering of the whole thing and all those appertaining to it into the air or under the ground or somewhere or other, as completely as the timbers and tiles and other things belonging to a powder-mill are blown away by one of those explosions that now and then take place : another panic means all this, and it means, probably, a reducing of shifty and shuffling Burdett to a state of life such as he ought to be reduced to : but, mean what it will; if it mean only

what it meant last time, its meaning is pretty satisfactory; mean what it will, here we have it openly declared by the Old Lady herself, that *come it must, unless the present system be changed;* unless the power of making banknotes be taken from the country-bankers; unless all the notes be made at one bank; and then, may it please your old devilish Ladyship, what is there for the paper to rest upon but the Government stock, the Government promises to pay ? What is that but a Government paper-money, such as they have in Austria and Russia; and what is that but the beginning of a sponge, which, if it could possibly be carried into execution, must leave *a million of people, in and about London,* without bread to put in their mouths ! This is what will pinch you, old Daddy Burdett : here is a body that the bread-taxers and the parsons will be unable to cope with. Here are half a million of men, able-bodied men, assembled in and about this Wen. Destroy the value of the paper, or greatly lessen it ; pay the interest of the debt in that depreciated paper, though you find the means of paying the soldiers and sailors in gold ; pay the interest of that debt in depreciated paper, and you have this half million of able-bodied men to persuade to lie down and die quietly, without an effort to get food and drink. Faith, Daddy Burdett, that will put your eloquence to the test! I am afraid, that the hungry half million will not wait for the " march of mind," and will feel little consolation in reflecting that if they could but get victuals and drink, they would, in this " enlightened age," be weighed and measured by the beating of a pendulum in sixty-two degrees of Farenheit's thermometer.

Last year, Canning, Huskisson, Robinson, Peel, all declared that they never would return to Bank-restriction. They passed an Act to put a total end to one-pound notes in the course of three years. I petitioned them, begged them to reduce the taxes more than one-half; for, that, if they did not, and if they adhered to the Bill that they had just passed about the small notes, they would produce sufferings absolutely intolerable. They persevered: the base and stupid reptiles of the press have been asserting and are asserting now, that things are coming about; Mr. Canning says the same thing; but, in the midst of all this, out comes the old she badger from Threadneedle-street, and tells her offspring, that the present system must be totally changed or that another panic must come.

Now, my friends, before we go further, pray look at the first of the two mottos of this letter. It is taken from Mr. Thomas Attwood's letter to Sir John Sinclair, written in December, 1825, written in the midst of the " panic." Sinclair is a Privy Counsellor, and, really, it is a pity that Attwood is not, too, instead of being merely a Birmingham iron man. The doctrine of these two worthies is this, that all we want is plenty of paper-money: that all the distress has arisen from the want of a sufficient quantity of paper-money. When the " late panic" took place, they found their doctrine rather upset, seeing that they were compelled to acknowledge that it was the great quantity of paper-money that had produced the panic. This was undeniable; no blackguard jew, even, had the audacity to deny this; and, therefore, these two worthies were a good deal puzzled. They soon, however, found out a remedy for all the distresses of the country. They proceeded thus: " What caused the panic? Peo- " ple running to the bankers for " gold.—What caused people to " run to the bankers for gold? " Because gold was wanted to " send out of the country.—Why

" was gold wanted to be sent out of " the country ? Because you could " send a sovereign to Paris and " get a Bank of England note and " a sixpence for it.—What, then, " is the remedy ? *Compel people* " *to take paper instead of gold.* " Have another Bank restriction " and legal tender: that is the " only security for the country."

Thus, these two worthies, two great philosophers, great politicians and statesmen concluded. But, Peel and Canning, and Robinson and Huskisson were bound to the contrary, and there was the gridiron everlastingly staring them in the face. Mr. Attwood says, that Castlereagh " *found that he was wrong,*" and that he " *died of a broken heart.*" What soft expressions your ironmonger politicians can find out when they like to use them. If this Mr. Attwood had been speaking of a radical, of which class, by the bye, he speaks in a most beastly manner, in his stupid pamphlet; if he had been speaking of a radical, he would not have said " died of a broken heart ; " he would have said that he *cut his throat at North Cray in Kent*; but, at any rate, I challenge him (Attwood, I mean) to make out, if he can, what the devil this fellow should cut his throat for, on ac-

count of the ruin that he saw in the country, when he had coolly called the people of England the basest populace ; when he had as coolly brought in a Bill to shut them up at his own discretion and that of Sidmouth ; when he, a fellow from Ireland, had had the audacity coolly to recommend that Englishmen should be set to work to dig holes one day and fill them up the next; I challenge him to make out, if he can, why this fellow should have cut his throat, merely on account of the ruin which he saw in the country, when it is notorious that it was Peel and Canning more than it was Castlereagh, that effected the passing of Peel's Bill. Castlereagh assented to the Bill, but was by no means a great advocate of it ; and the good of it is, that he had just brought in and caused to be passed a Bill, which partly repealed Peel's Bill, at the time when he cut his throat. The Small-note Bill was passed in the month of July, and Castlereagh cut his throat on the 12th of August following. So that this is a pure invention of this delicate and tender-hearted man of iron, who chooses to represent radicals as the enemies of their country. This man of iron says, that he KNOWS that Castlereagh saw the ruin which pervaded England at that time. This is not very wonderful: he must have been stark staring mad, indeed, if he had not seen that, for many years before; but, when the man of iron says that he can *almost* say that HE KNOWS, that the seeing of the country's ruin killed Castlereagh, I say that I do not believe the man of iron; that I believe he is as regardless of truth in his account of Castlereagh's feelings as he is in his description of the characters and motives of the radicals. In short, this Attwood is a fellow with a great parcel of money, and most likely he wants to be a Lord. He thinks that the abuse of the radicals will help to pave the way for him; and he has not sense enough to see; his thinking faculties are insufficient to enable him to perceive, that even if his own paper-schemes could be adopted, there would be an end of the whole of the system in which he wishes to thrive and hopes to shine.

Castlereagh knew nothing of the subject: he was an empty fellow, as far as related to such matters. His speeches in 1816, when he began the talk about the effects of a " *sudden transition from war to peace,*" and when I began to laugh at him for the stu-

pid idea. These speeches showed that he understood no more about the matter than a baby. The coroner and the Kentish jury, or the witnesses, were perjured, basely perjured, if he had not been mad for several weeks before he cut his throat, though he was, at the same time, *leader of the House of Commons*, and, during the King's absence in Scotland, had the charge of the offices of all the three Secretaries of State. There is nothing very interesting in this bold assertion of the man of iron. The Duke of Wellington wrote a letter at the time of Castlereagh's death, saying something about his having been over-worked. It seemed to be a pretty hard point to make out; and, therefore, why did not the man of iron hasten up to London to state the cause of his cutting his throat, if he was " almost sure of it"! This man of iron has a great deal to answer for, observe, if he is now almost sure that Castlereagh cut his throat because he saw the distress of the country: the man of iron must have seen some symptoms of a disposition to perform this exploit with the pen-knife. It is impossible that anybody can believe him, when he says that he is almost sure that Castlereagh cut his throat on this score; it is impossible to believe Attwood when he says this, without believing that Attwood had *seen some symptoms* of a design on the part of Castlereagh to kill himself: I repeat, that it is impossible to believe that Attwood can now *almost say that he knows* that Castlereagh cut his throat from this cause, without believing that Attwood perceived some symptoms of an intention to cause self-destruction. Attwood, therefore, now asserts a falsehood, or he was guilty of a scandalous neglect of duty, a most base as well as a most scandalous neglect of duty, in not communicating his almost knowledge to some Minister of the King, or, at least, to the relations of Castlereagh himself: it comes to this, Mr. Thomas Attwood, according to his own showing, has a heart as hard as the metal that he deals in, or he is a most insufferable coxcomb, wanting to pass himself off as familiar with and in the secrets of statesmen and men of high rank. He may choose which he likes: the two, however, are very nearly allied, for, the last, though contemptible in itself, becomes perfectly detestable, when it induces the party, as it has done this Attwood, to impute to the suffering masses of his countrymen, those designs, of

their entertaining which he produces not a shadow of proof. Ah, Mr. Attwood, you and the whole of the insolent crew of calumniators and oppressors of the people will finally be brought to your senses by those events of the approach of which the present Circular of the Venerable Dame of Threadneedle Street is an incipient, but a very strong indication. Those events, though flasby Canning and the balderdash Baronet can see nothing of them, will teach those who now have estates and titles, that, after all, their best ally and their only security is that mass of common people, of injured, insulted, longsuffering, but still loyal and docile common people, whom upstarts like you wish to see rendered more abject than negro-slaves, whom you designate by what you deem the odious name of radical, and to whom you, as Castlereah did before you, falsely impute the worst of motives.

This Circular of the Old Lady; this document coming from no one can tell whom; this paper of equivocal generation, is, however, of most ominous import: it says, and, as it appears, pretty nearly says it on the part of the Government itself, that the *present law cannot stand*; that

the law for which Canning, Robinson,, Huskisson and Brougham
and Burdett, and all the motley crew
now stand directly or indirectly
pledged, cannot last; that something or other must be adopted in
its stead; that the returning prosperity, of which they have,
again, recently been boasting, is
a delusion; and that, in fact,
a total change of system must
be adopted, or that another panic
is at hand. Before this Register
comes from the press, one of those
pretty things called *budgets* will
have made its appearance. I care
not what it shall contain : it must
and will be a thing of no real interest to the country : it has evidently been put off merely because the Ministers *know not what
to do;* and, for my part, I care
not one straw what measure they
adopt : I know that the end must
be a destruction of the paper system, and a return to the ancient
money of the country, together
with a return to something approaching, at any rate, to the ancient liberties and happiness of
Englishmen. To men in common
life, therefore, the measures that
shall be adopted, the way in which
the thing will work is, as to the result, a matter of little consequence;
but, to those who have estates and,
particularly, to those who have

titles as well as estates, these measures and this way of working are
matters of fearful importance. I
defy all earthly powers to do any
thing by which the interest of the
debt shall be reduced, without
the other measures suggested in
Norfolk Petition ; I defy all earthly powers to effect this, without
leaving half a million and I might
say *a million* of men, women, and
children, in and about London,
destitute of bread. This consideration alone is quite enough,
without taking any other into view.
The Lords, who have so much to
preserve, should consider how wide
the difference will be, between a
state of half-barter without a Parliamentary Reform, and a state of
half-barter with such Reform.
However, the affair is much more
theirs than it is mine: let them
look to it if they please: if they
do not please, let them join Thos.
Attwood in abusing radicals and
imputing to them all those designs
which they have never entertained
and which they know that they
have never entertained.

If this document of equivocal
generation, and of which the base
and stupid press seems to be half
afraid to speak, should lead to any
practical consequences, we shall
witness such scenes, such a series
of follies, such preliminary con-

fusion, as never were before witnessed in the world. Men will not know what to think. They will not know what to expect. They are a good deal in that state now; but, their uncertainty will increase daily and hourly. Some attempt must and will be made to lessen the burthen of the debt; and, what the mass of the people have to do is, to make a stand against any project for stripping three hundred thousand families of fundholders, without, at the same time, calling for a participation of sacrifices on the part of the landowners and the Church. If those who have titles and estates were wise; or, which is a better way to put it, perhaps, when they shall see their interest, and have a clear sight of the events that are coming, they will listen patiently to the people's petitions for Reform; they will act graciously towards them; they will not set them at defiance and treat them with disdain; and then they will show their sincerity by some overt act; by doing something for the people; by repealing the septennial Bill; by lopping off some of the rotten boroughs; by doing something that shall prove that they mean that the people shall have fair play. How vast (good God!) would be the difference in their own situation, were they but to give indications like these of a disposition to conciliate the people; but, on the contrary, we have now a Minister, who declares that he never will hear of Reform in any shape, and that he will always oppose it as long as he has power to oppose it, however moderate its tone, however humble the attitude in which it may approach. Here we are, then, as long as this man has power (and Burdett says he is *right in making the declaration*): here we are, then, directly opposed to each other; and the fate of the paper-money, and that alone, is to decide between us. The decision cannot be far distant; and it will be complete and radical, as sure as Burdett has a head upon his shoulders. There are no *tricks* whereby the decision can be avoided. No small coin scheme will answer the purpose: no little shilling project will stifle this great question: wheat at four shillings a bushel, or assignats is the only alternative. Either will do: either gives us Reform of Parliament; and that, too, in a way the most advantageous to the people at large. The document of equivocal generation is, therefore, a thing of very great importance: as such I submit it to my readers: as such I leave it for their serious consideration and their solid consolation.

At the end of this Letter, towards the close of which I am now, for want of more room, speedily approaching, I shall insert the RESOLUTION, consisting of twenty clauses or paragraphs, which I had in my hand, and which I intended to move at the "Purity" Dinner, on the 23d instant. When my readers have gone through it, let each say to himself, " Was there ever any " thing more true, more just, " more moderate than this! and, " what would I not endure rather " than be the man, whose words, " whose five-and-twenty years' " professions and pledges are " here recorded!" I was, in the manner described in the last Register, prevented from putting this Resolution. I found, that it would be impossible to obtain silence sufficient for the reading of such a paper; and, therefore, I adopted the course of moving amendments to the toasts. The result was just as effectual as a reading of the Resolution could have been. Two things marked the character of the whole proceeding. Burdett, who was the chairman of the meeting and the accused party, objected to put, and never did put,

never dared to put, one of my motions, two of which contained, by implication, a censure on himself. The other thing is, that his partisans made an attack, a regular attack, with the avowed, not only with the evident, but with the avowed intention of putting me out of the room; and that his partisans were not only wholly unable to effect their avowed purpose, but were driven in disgrace from the spot where they made the attempt. There he stood, then, upon his own dunghill; the newspapers say, that his stewards came in a body, with their "wands" in their hands (being forty or fifty in number), and cried, "One and all, " one and all, put him out of the " room!" The same newspapers record, that my friends rushed from all parts of the room, drove the assailants back, broke their wands all to pieces, drove the lords and members of Parliament, scampering from that part of the room; placed me in a state of as great security, as if I had been sitting in my own house at Fleet-street. The same newspapers record, that Sir Glory's head narrowly escaped the butt end of one of his stewards' staves, which perforated a pane of glass just behind him. They record that I kept the room after he had quitted it, and that, following the "march of mind," he went off his own dung-hill amidst the confusion of clappings and hootings, the far greater part of the lords and members of Parliament that had come to do him honour and to shine as speech-makers, having scampered off long before, and left all the honours of the forum behind them.

These few facts are quite sufficient; and I am sure that you will all say that Sir Glory may now go and repeat the tragi-comi speech which I wrote for him in Long Island, and which I have placed as the second motto to this Register. It was ten years ago, nearly, when I wrote that speech for him. He had then abandoned the people, though the people were not so sensible of the abandonment as they are now; I then told him what he would come to at last; and I pledged myself, that I would stick to him to the end of his career. This I will do, if it please God to give me life, and to continue to bless me with health. In default of these, man can do nothing; but, this I say, that it shall be in default of these, and in default of these ALONE; that there is nothing else in this world that shall prevent me from sticking to him to the end of his career.

Before I insert the Resolution, it is right for me to observe, that I disavow many of the sentiments and more of the expressions, contained in the extracts which I have made from his speeches and addresses. I never approved of his violent and outrageous expressions. Never did he use such expressions by my advice. I always endeavoured to prevent that course which was so well calculated to excite apprehensions in the breasts of moderate people. It was he, and he alone, that was the cause of furnishing the grounds, or, rather, the pretences, for the horrid Bills of 1817. In the fall of 1816, he being at Brighton and I being at Botley, he enclosed me a letter from Major Cartwright to himself, which he was to forward to me to read. This letter proposed the making of a grand effort for the forming of little Hampden Clubs all over the manufacturing districts, and for drawing forth the people, in great bodies, to petition for Reform. I wrote to him immediately a letter which I requested him to show to the Major, in which I expressed my opinion against any very strenuous and general efforts being made at that time, and particularly against the formation of clubs. I told them that my opinion was that, as long as the paper-money continued to circulate uninterruptedly; as long as no weakness was felt in that quarter, we should carry on a struggle for our rights in vain; and, that all that we should accomplish would be, to point out great numbers of excellent and public-spirited men as objects of vengeance; but, I added, if, after having thus given my opinion, you two think it right to persevere, I will not flinch: I will act with as much zeal as if the undertaking had had my hearty concurrence. He received my letter, forwarded it to the Major, sent me the Major's answer, which was in contradiction to my opinion, and he himself observed, in communicating the Major's second letter to me, that the Major argued his case well, and he added that he agreed with him in opinion. On, therefore, we went. When the hour of trial came, he deserted his post. He went into Leicestershire, instead of being in London to meet the deputies of his own clubs, clubs formed in consequence of recommendations *signed with the facsimile of his own name,* and sent round the country, not by post, but by special deputy. He pledged himself to be in town by a certain day. He shuffled that off and wrote to the Major that he would call upon him as he went down to the House at the opening of the Parliament. He came from Leicestershire on the day of the meeting of Parliament; went down to the House without calling upon the Major; went by the end of Palace-yard when Lord Cochrane was going, carried by the people, loaded with their petitions. There he sat in the House like an unconcerned spectator; and, during the whole of the proceedings by which the Reformers were crushed, and many of them totally destroyed, he never once opened his lips in their defence; and he ostentatiously took to the exercise of fox-hunting, whilst scores of the Reformers were pining in dungeons, and some perishing on the scaffold. I give his tirades, his bombastical professions, his unmeasured abuse of persons in power, his monstrous and outrageous calumnies on individuals as well as on bodies of men; I give them not as things that I approve of, but as things that I censure, and particularly as specimens of the means by which he deluded the people, by which he made them believe that it was impossible that he should not hate their enemies. I remember well when he harnessed men in chains, or, at any rate, when men were harnessed in chains and rode down to Brentford on coaches, decorated with his colours, rattling those chains enough to stun the inhabitants of the streets through which they passed, the exhibition being intended to represent the state of the people, and to hold him forth as the man to set them free. A constant burthen of his abuse was, those whom he called the *great families*; the great families were what he appeared to wish to pull down. In short, he was a *demagogue*, in the true and full sense of that word; and, not being able to succeed in his projects of demagogue, he at last turned about, and is now sticking his knees in the back of that Minister, who says that he will never agree to Reform in any shape or degree. Ten years ago, I, my friends, told you that it would end thus; but, this is not the end with him: there is, yet, the paper-money account to settle, and his share of that account to be inquired into.

With these observations in your minds, I request you to read the whole of the Resolution with attention, and I particularly request this attention from those readers who were, at most, but mere boys, at the beginning of this man's career. I am,

Your faithful friend, and
Most obedient Servant,
Wm. COBBETT.

*Postscript.—31st May*, 1827. The papers of to-day, give a report of what passed in Parliament last night, relative to the CIRCULAR above remarked on by me. I said that this document was of equivocal generation, and I hardly believed it to have emanated from the Bank *officially*. Last night it appears, that Sir JOHN WROTTESLEY gave notice that he should move on the 7th of June for a copy of the Circular Letter which had been " published as " addressed by the Bank Direc- " tors to the leading country " bankers." It appears that Mr. MANNING, a Bank Director, stated, that the Directors knew nothing at all of the document, and that he gave the most complete denial, as far as the Directors were concerned, to the statements it contained. Sir John Wrottesley is stated to have observed, that Mr. Manning's answer was not, to him, satisfactory, and that " the Cir- " cular might have come from ' some individual nearly connect- " ed with the Bank of England, " although it did not emanate " from the Bank Directors."

It is remarkable, that none of the Ministers said a word upon this subject. I truly characterized the thing as of *equivocal genera- tion*: it appeared to me like a

U

feeler: in that light it appears to me yet ; and I imagine that we shall soon see something to convince us, that the ideas contained in this document have not been put forth without a good deal of reflection. Whether the document proceed from any official source or not, it would be hard to conjecture ; but I shall be very much deceived, if there be not on foot some project, somewhat of the nature described in this document. At any rate, something must be done; for the present law cannot go into full effect without producing a real, an actual devastation of the country; or, if it can, I will acknowledge myself to have been the most deceived man alive.

---

### RESOLUTION

*Drawn up by Mr. COBBETT, and intended by him to be proposed at the "Purity of Election" Dinner, at the Crown and Anchor, on the 23d May, 1827.*

---

1. That this is the twentieth anniversary of a meeting intended to keep alive the recollection of the *triumph of the city of Westminster*, obtained on the 23d May, 1807 ; and that that triumph consisted in the Electors of Westminster having succeeded in returning SIR FRANCIS BURDETT

as a member for this city, he having, during several years previous to that time, and especially in the years 1802, 1804, and 1806, professed himself, solemnly declared himself, the uncompromising enemy of the system of corruption ; having, in every form of words that the subject would admit of, declared his hatred of the present mode of returning Members to Parliament, most solemnly vowed his readiness to *lay down his life* for the purpose of obtaining a Parliamentary Reform, which he had repeatedly declared to be the *only possible means* of putting a stop to the plunder which he had as frequently asserted to be continually committed upon the people, by *both* the political factions ; and that, in the last-mentioned year, he expressly declared to the freeholders of the county of Middlesex, that, " whenever the leaders " of contending parties and fac- " tions in a state unite, the history " of the world bears evidence, " that it is never in favour, but " always at the expense, of the " people; whose renewed and " augmented pillage pays the " scandalous price of the recon- " ciliation."

2. That, in an address to the Electors of Westminster, dated

the 23d May 1807, Sir Francis Burdett pledged himself to them, " that no rational endeavours of " his should be omitted, to *tear* " *out the accursed leaves of the* " *scandalous Red Book,* and to " bring back men's minds to the " almost forgotten notions of the " sacredness of private property, " which ought no longer' to be " transferred from the legitimate " possessors by the corrupt votes " of venal and mercenary combi- " nations;" that, in his speech at the first meeting, of which this is the anniversary, he declared to the persons assembled, " that the " two factions in parliament, that " both sides of the House of Com- " mons laughed at the people, " despised the people, and those " who had robbed the people " most had the greatest contempt " for them;" and he concluded that speech by assuring the Elec- tors " *that his whole life should be spent in their service.*"

3. That, from this period until the year 1817 the language of his addresses to the Electors, whether written or verbal, the language of his speeches in Parliament, every act of his public life, were mani- festly calculated to impress the minds of that public with a belief, that he looked upon a reform of Parliament as being absolutely

necessary to give the people even a chance of enjoying either their property or their liberty ; that, in short, he declared them to be slaves, and the worst of slaves, too, *unless they could obtain a reform of the Parliament.*

4. That in 1809, he declared, that "there was nothing worthy " the serious attention of the Eng- " lish nation, except the *necessity* " *of a reform of Parliament*"; that, " so far from the House of " Commons representing the peo- " ple of England, the most popu- " lar sentiment in that House " was, contempt for the people of " England"; and that, " he be- " lieved the House of Commons " to be the only place in all the " world where the people of Eng- " land were spoken of with con- " tempt"; that, " the tree of cor- " ruption, which was now pro- " ducing such bitter fruits, it was " our business to lay the axe to " the root of;" adding, " unless " we destroy this hydra of cor- " ruption, it will destroy the coun- " try ; for, the monster now stands " with harpy claws, seizing on all " our substance to supply the " means of its boundless prodi- " gality": and he concluded his speech with observing (it was a speech at a meeting at Westmin- ster) that " *reform of Parliament*

" *was the only remedy,*" adding,
" I hope the nation has ceased to
" look for any advantage *from*
" *any change of administration;*
" parties are no more to be looked
" to, and be assured, that we can
" never expect any measures
" really useful until the people of
" England have their proper
" share in the constitution."

5. That, in the same year 1809,
he, at a meeting of the friends of
Parliamentary Reform, held in
this place, agreed to, and sent
forth, under his name, fourteen
resolutions, in which it was declared, that, " so long as the
" people shall not be fairly re-
" presented, corruption will in-
" crease, our debts and taxes will
" accumulate, our resources will
" be dissipated, the native energy
" of the people will be depressed,
" and the country deprived of its
" best defence against foreign
" foes; that the remedy was to
" be found, and to *be found only,*
" *in a full and fair representa-*
" *tion of the people in Parliament,*
" a remedy equally necessary to
" the safety of the throne, and to
" the happiness of the people."

6. That, in the year 1811, he,
accompanied by the High Bailiff
of Westminster, presented an address to the Prince Regent at the
levee, beseeching his Royal
Highness to give his countenance
*to a reform of the Commons' House
of Parliament,* which the address
represented to be eaten up by
corruption, observing to the Regent, " here, Sir, is the cancer of
" the state. With a House of
" Commons rapidly becoming,
" by the virulence of this pest, a
" mere mass of corruption, death
" must ensue, unless the cancer to
" its last fibre be eradicated,

" and free Parliament restored.
" For such a restoration, your
" Royal Highness must perceive,
" that *no talent, no wisdom, no*
" *virtue,* in Ministers, can become
" a substitute."

7. That, in 1812, he, in the
House of Commons, proposed an
address to the Prince Regent, in
answer to His Royal Highness's
speech to the Parliament; that,
in that address, he declared, and
there stands the declaration in the
votes of the House, that, " it had
" been made manifest to all men,
" that the persons who possessed,
" and those who aspired to the
" offices of state, no longer re-
" garded themselves as chosen by
" the sovereign, but as the nomi-
" nees of the borough oligarchy,
" who equally invaded the pro-
" vince of the crown and the rights
" of the people, interposing with the
" one in the choice of its Ministers,
" and depriving the other of the
" election of its representatives; and
" that, amongst the consequences,
" were a long train of useless wars
" and expeditions, which, attended
" with a dreadful waste of treasure
" and of life, have only answered
" the purpose of enriching the bo-
" rough faction and its depend-
" ants, as a reward of political
" corruption."

8. That, in the year 1814, he,
in an address to his constituents of
Westminster, asserted, that one of
the fruits of the tree of corruption
was a " system of taxation, every
" stroke of which, like the cat o'
" nine tails from the backs of the
" soldiers, brought blood, and
" which was not more galling in
" the mode and severity of its
" collection, than in its profligate,
" corrupt and wasteful expendi-
" ture." He added, that the pa-

triotic and enlightened electors of Westminster knew full well, that these were a few of the bitter fruits of that baleful tree, " which " nourished its roots in that hot-" bed of corruption from whence " it sprang, St. Stephen's Chapel; " that we were instructed by the " highest authority *how to judge* " *it, and by the same authority* " *how to deal with it ;* and that he " *trusted that we should deal with* " *it accordingly.''*

9. That, in 1819, he, in a letter addressed to the Electors of Westminster, traced the horrible deeds committed at Manchester, in that year, to the want of a reform in the Commons' House of Parliament; asserted the principle of the absolute necessity of obtaining such a reform, and declared that he *held his estate as a retaining fee, for the exertions which it was his duty constantly to make in support of the rights of the people*, always putting the faculty of voting for Members of Parliament at the head of those rights.

10. That, at the close of his re-election, in the year 1818, a dinner was held in this same room, in the month of July, to celebrate his return to Parliament; that at that dinner, he renewed all his protestations upon the subject of reform, and expressed his confident expectation, that the people of England, and especially the people of Westminster, would never abandon the sacred cause of reform; that there were certain banners carried by the several parishes on that occasion; that upon two of those banners were inscribed the words, " BURDETT and RE-FORM"; that, in one part of the procession, came SIR FRANCIS BURDETT himself, seated in a

TRIUMPHAL CAR (on one of the steps of which was inscribed the word "REFORM"), drawn by six horses, preceded by six trumpeters with silver trumpets, and followed by a long dark blue banner carried on horseback, and waving over his head, having on it the motto " RADICAL REFORM"; that, at the dinner aforesaid, the first toast given was : " May a " S P E E D Y and an E F F E C-" T U A L R E F O R M enable " the people of the United King-" dom to choose their own repre-" sentatives "; and that SIR FRAN-CIS BURDETT, in addressing the Electors, again solemnly repeated, that there " could be no security " for the people of England, with-" out a Radical Reform in Parlia-" ment"; that, upon this same occasion, SIR FRANCIS BURDETT, in a written address to the Electors of Westminster, said, " that the " question was, whether those " principles and professions, upon " which they had so long acted, " should be upheld, or whether " they should strive to uphold a " cheat; that the great question " now at issue, in Westminster, " was, whether reform or no re-" form shall take place, or whether " corruption and despotism should " be countenanced. As to my-" self," said he, " I shall at *all* " times be ready to co-operate " with my countrymen, for the " purpose of checking that system " of fiscal spoliation and political " corruption, which takes his due " reward from the poor, his in-" heritance from the rich, and " liberty from all, and must finally " terminate in the establishment " of despotic power. It is against " this formidable enemy we have " buckled on our armour ; and I

" trust *we shall keep our harness*
" *on our backs* until we have ob-
" tained the people's unalienable
" rights, recovered their fair and
" reasonable share of the Govern-
" ment, the appointment of their
" own guardians in a House of
" Commons, freely and constitu-
" tionally chosen by themselves."

11. That, with regard to what
has been called the CATHOLIC
QUESTION, he always (up to
the year 1824) treated it with
scorn; treated it as a *mere pretence*, kept up for the purposes of
deception and plunder; that, in
a letter to the Freeholders of
Middlesex, in the year 1807, he
thus addressed himself to them
with regard to the *Catholics* and
their cause :—" Gentlemen, after
" what has lately passed in re-
" view before us, it is impossible
" to shut our eyes to the actual
" situation of our country. Lord
" Melville, with his associates
" and abettors, under the pretence
" of *loyalty*, and the *leaders of
" the Whigs under the pretence
" of the Constitution*; AND
" THE LEADERS OF THE
" CATHOLICS, UNDER
" THE PRETENCE OF RE-
" LIGION, are ALL evidently
" struggling for one and the same
" object : A SHARE OF THE
" COMMON SPOIL ; whilst
" the wholesome power of the
" crown, the fair liberty of the
" subject, and the real interest
" of any religion, are all sacri-
" ficed to the COMMON object—
" PLUNDER," that in a speech
made in the House of Com-
mons, on the 15th June 1809,
he asserted, that *nothing but a
Reform in Parliament could
cure the evils of Ireland*; that, if
reform was necessary HERE, it

was THERE a measure of im-
*perious necessity*; that no *other
measure could effect any change
for the better*; but that, by the
adoption of reform, " the chief
" magistrate would be seated up-
" on his throne, the sceptre of
" legitimate power would be
" placed in the hands of the King,
" in despite of those 157 Borough-
" mongers, who have traitorously
" usurped all but the pageantry,
" outward show and forms of
" royalty."

12. That such are the doctrines, such the teachings, such
the pledges, such the invocations
to the people, such the promises
of fidelity to the cause of reform,
which the people of Middlesex
and the people of Westminster in
particular, and the nation in general through them, have heard
and received from SIR FRANCIS
BURDETT ; that, for several years
past, there have been great inactivity, a marked silence and shy-
ness in SIR FRANCIS BURDETT,
on the subject of Reform in Parliament ; and, certain parts of
his conduct with regard to the
Corn Bill, showed but too clearly
what we had to expect in the
future.

13. That, in 1824, he supported a proposition, directly in
the teeth of all his former declarations relative to the *Catholic
question*; that he then began to
represent that which is called
*Catholic Emancipation as suffi-
cient of itself* to restore Ireland to
happiness ; that instead of continually insisting, as formerly,
that no good to Ireland could ensue without a Reform of Parliament, he now supported a proposition for stripping the forty
shilling freeholders of Ireland of

their right of voting; to strip half a million of men of their right of voting for Members of Parliament; and that, too, as the price of a measure, which would have subjected all the people of England to be taxed for the *payment of salaries to the Catholic Priests* of Ireland; while all Ireland was, at the same time, to be subjected to the payment of tithes and church rates to the Protestant Clergy, some of whom have from three to seven livings each, and whose followers or flocks, do not, in many cases, form more than a fiftieth part of the people, and, on an average, not more than a seventh part."

14. That, there has recently been a change in the King's Ministry; that Mr. Canning has become the Prime Minister; that from the hour, and even years before the hour, that Sir Francis Burdett became the open advocate of reform, Mr. Canning became its open enemy; that he has continued to be its open, its bitter, its implacable, its most deadly enemy from that day to the day of his recent appointment to be Prime Minister; that he has constantly been the loud, the determined, the inveterate advocate of every measure, whether against the press, or against the pockets or the persons of the people, if such measure were intended to crush, or do injury to, those who advocated the cause of Parliamentary Reform; that the motives and the characters of the reformers have been, with this man, subjects of constant abuse, and their ruin, their sufferings, both mental and bodily, constantly subjects of his cruel and scurrilous jests.

15. That, so flagrant has invariably been his conduct in these respects, that Sir Francis Burdett has been, for years, in the habit of regarding him and representing him as the *champion of the boroughmongering system;* that, in a letter addressed to a company of Reformers assembled in this very room, in 1821, he says, " Gentlemen, that Mr. " Canning (I mention him as the " CHAMPION of the party, a " part for the whole) should de- " fend to the utmost a system, " by the HOCUS POCUS, " TRICKS, *of which he and his " family get so much public mo- " ney,* can cause, neither in me " nor any man, suspicion or anger;

" For 'tis their duty, all the learned think, " T' espouse the cause by which they eat and " drink."

That, at the dinner before mentioned, held in 1818, Sir Francis Burdett said, that, " if Mr. Can- " ning had found himself obnox- " ious to the people, it was be- " cause they had always found " him the interested supporter of " every species of abuse and " tyrannical power;" that, at the same dinner, Mr. Hobhouse, being engaged in imitating Sir Francis Burdett, with regard to his attack upon Mr. Canning, and being interrupted by an elector, said, that he " agreed with the worthy " elector, who had just done him " the honour of interrupting him, " that Mr. Canning was UN- " WORTHY THE NOTICE " OF A RATIONAL MAN, " and could only be respectable " in their eyes, as having been " animadverted upon by the Chair- " man; and that he could assure " them, that, on no other account, " would he have presumed to in-

" troduce, even for a moment, the " mention of that *abandoned name*" (LOUD APPLAUSE!)

16. That, in the House of Commons, on the 4th day of this present month of May, 1827, SIR FRANCIS BURDETT, having first crossed the House and placed himself close at the back of Mr. CANNING, said, that "*putting* " *aside* all the great questions " mentioned by an honourable " Member, *including that of* " *Parliamentary Reform, he saw* " *sufficient reason* to support the " administration of Mr. CANNING," whom, (hear it, Electors of Westminster!) he called " his right honourable FRIEND "; and that, to conclude this series of undeniable and astounding facts, Mr. CANNING rose and said, " I " am asked what I mean to do " on the subject of *Parliamentary* " *Reform*; why, I say,—to OP- " POSE IT,—TO OPPOSE " IT TO THE END OF MY " LIFE IN THIS HOUSE, " UNDER WHATEVER " SHAPE IT MAY AP- " PEAR !"

17. That, thus, SIR FRANCIS BURDETT has abandoned all those principles, for his presumed and believed attachment to which, he was chosen by the people of Westminster; that, twenty-five years ago, he asserted, that, " when the " leaders of contending factions " united, *the pillage of the people* " *formed the scandalous price of* " *the reconciliation*"; that, since the commencement of his assertions respecting the, *deadly effects of a want of reform*, he has seen his assertions proved by fatal experience; that, since he first publicly asserted that a want of reform, if continued to exist, would

increase the debt, the taxes, the poverty, the misery, the hard treatment of the people, he has seen THREE HUNDRED MILLIONS added to the capital of the national debt, and THREE MILLIONS a year added to the poor-rates; he has seen the number and size of the gaols tripled, and the number of the criminals augmented five-fold; he has seen that system of imprisonment, which he so bitterly and loudly complained of at *Cold Bath Fields*, extended to all parts of the kingdom; he has seen new game laws, extending the punishment for poaching to that of *transportation even by the Justices of the Peace*; he has seen ELLENBOROUGH's ACT, which, combined with the new game laws, has been the ground of condemning many men to the gallows; he has seen the new trespass law, which authorizes a man to be sent to prison and to hard labour, for a damage amounting to a *shilling or less*, and which gives no new protection to property of any sort against the damage-doer, who, by horses, dogs, or by any other means, shall commit damage *exceeding in amount five pounds*; he has seen a law passed making it felony to take an apple from a tree; he has seen the invention of a new mode of punishment, called a Tread Mill, the very thought of the existence of which, in England, would have made our forefathers hide their heads for shame; he has heard it observed by the Judges, in the Court of King's Bench, that *bread and water had now become the common diet of the labouring people of England*; he knows that, in one of the counties in which he has great estates, the allowance of food, made by the Magistrates, to the convicted felon in the gaol, *is more than that which the same Magistrates* allow to the honest *labouring man;* he has seen the begging box three times sent round, by Royal authority, in order to collect from one part of the people the means of preventing another part of them from dying from starvation; he has now before his eyes, in printed reports, laid before himself and others of the House of Commons, proofs, that the labouring men in England now have potatoes for almost their only diet; that in Ireland, the poor have been *detected* in *stealing* (for food) sea-weed, which had been laid out upon the land for manure; and he has before him, in these reports, evidence of the anxious desire of thousands upon thousands to be *transported for life* from their native land, in order to free themselves from the dreadful miseries of all sorts, which they have to endure in that land.

18. That, during the last twenty-five years, he has, until very lately, been constantly asserting *that such things must be the effect of the want of a Reform in Parliament;* that there could be no cure, no mitigation of suffering, and no hope of redress, without a Reform of the Parliament; and that, even at the anniversary dinner of last year only; even on this day twelvemonth, in this very room, Sir Francis Burdett, in the course of his speech, said that " the House " of Commons was overwhelmed " by a SCUM, such as was never " before found upon the face of " the earth, because so little of " the public voice of the people " could, by any exertions of *public*

" *virtue,* be got in at all; and this " was because there were so few " men of that description in the " House of Commons : as few as " there were in SODOM, which " a few would have saved from " destruction;" and, that *now*, only at the end of 365 days, after seeing a further augmentation of all these terrible evils, every one of which can, even according to his own doctrines, be clearly traced to a want of Reform, he goes, seats himself at the Minister's back, *puts aside the cause of Reform,* says he sees reasons to support that Minister, while that Minister, at the same time, declares that he *will oppose Reform to the last hour of his political life :* so that, here we have Sir Francis Burdett, at last, declaring that he will support the opposer of Parliamentary Reform, that he will support the upholder of this political Sodom, to the end of that opposer's Parliamentary life, that opposer being, too, the Prime Minister of the country !

19. That at the Westminster dinner before mentioned, in 1818, Mr. Sturch, who proposed the toast " WESTMINSTER'S " PRIDE AND ENGLAND'S " HOPE," in his preface to this toast, uttered the following words : " It was not the private virtues, " the great fortune, nor the splen- " did abilities of Sir Francis " Burdett that induced him to " give a single vote in support of " his election. But, if any man " should ask him why he felt " interested in the return of Sir " Francis Burdett, he should " say, it was because he felt, in " his *heart and soul,* that their " favourite representative was the " *unalterable friend of freedom.*

" If, however, that MELAN-
" CHOLY DAY ever should
" arrive, when their representa-
" tive NO LONGER *possessed*
" *the principles which had recom-*
" *mended him to their choice,* he
" would then SHRINK WITH
" AVERSION FROM THAT
" TOAST which he now gave
" with delight."

20. That all men here present
must feel " *in their heart and
soul,*" that this " *melancholy day*"
has arrived; " that this represen-
" tative no longer possesses the
" principles which recommended
" him to the Electors of Westmin-
" ster," and that, therefore, all
men now here present, ought to
" *shrink with aversion*" from a
repetition of that, or any such,
toast; or that we ought to be prepared to see every sensible and
sound-hearted Englishman " shrink
with aversion" from us.

## TULIP-TREE WOOD.

I have for sale *fifty-four* planks
of this wood, averaging about
*thirty feet* in each plank. They
are *two and a half inches* thick.
Some are about fourteen feet long;
others not, probably, more than
ten feet. Some are between *three
and four feet wide;* others not,
perhaps, more than two feet. The
planks are just *as wide at one end
as at the other;* and there is not a
*single knot,* or *curl,* in the whole

parcel of *one thousand, five hundred and eighty-one feet.* ...

Michaux, in his North American Sylva, says of the *tree,* that
he saw one *twenty-two feet, six
inches* in circumference, at five
feet from the ground; and that he
judged the tree to be *a hundred
and forty feet high.* Of the
WOOD Michaux says what
every body in America knows;
namely, that it is in colour of a
pale yellow; that its grain is very
fine; that the wood is both *light*
and *strong;* that it is used in
rafters, shingles, door - panels,
bedsteads, wainscoting, chair-
bottoms, large bowls, and particularly, in all parts of America,
in making the *panels of coaches*
and other pleasure carriages; and,
so much is this the case, that it is
carried hundreds of miles to be
used in those places, near to
which it does not grow.

The wood admits of a *beautiful
polish,* and is used for various
purposes by cabinet-makers. Of
these planks that I have, a single
plank would make a kitchen-
dresser, or table; a servants'-hall
table; a slab for a dairy or a
larder; fine things, I should think,
for cutting-boards, shop-boards,
counters, show-boards, or almost
any thing, which requires a very
large breadth of wood in one

single, smooth piece. Being 2½ inches thick, these planks are strong enough for any thing.

The price *for the whole parcel,* ONE SHILLING and THREE-PENCE A FOOT; for any quantity less than the whole, and exceeding a hundred feet, ONE SHILLING AND SIXPENCE A FOOT; and for a *single plank,* ONE SHILLING AND NINE-PENCE A FOOT. So that a plank, 14 feet long, and 3½ feet wide, which, with a couple of trestles, would make a table to dine *twenty people,* would cost only *four pounds five shillings*; it might be kept as clean as a marble slab, and with nearly as little trouble, and would last for many a life-time.

The planks are at my *house at Kensington,* where they may be seen, by *application to the gardener,* at any hour between four in the morning and five in the afternoon. There is the *mark* on each plank, expressing the *number of feet* which it contains. The marks were put on in America, and, therefore, are according to our old-fashioned English *kingly* measure, and not according to the grand and sublime "IMPERIAL MEA-SURE," which, being an "*improvement of the age,*" produced by "*liberal principles,*" the off-spring of the "*march of mind,*" gauges (in defiance of Bedlam) ale, metes oysters, and ascertains the length and width of shirting, by the "beat of a *pendulum* in a "heat of sixty-two degrees of "Farenheit's Thermometer"!

# MARKETS.

Average Prices of CORN throughout ENGLAND, for the week ending May 18.

*Per Quarter.*

| | s. | d. | | s. | d. |
|---|---|---|---|---|---|
| Wheat .. | 57 | 6 | Rye .... | 40 | 11 |
| Barley .. | 39 | 5 | Beans ... | 49 | 10 |
| Oats .... | 29 | 5 | Pease ... | 46 | 10 |

Total Quantity of Corn returned as Sold in the Maritime Districts, for the week ended May 18.

| | Qrs. | | | Qrs. |
|---|---|---|---|---|
| Wheat.. | 38,226 | Rye ..... | | 287 |
| Barley .. | 4,631 | Beans . .. | | 1,301 |
| Oats ... | 9,630 | Pease.... | | 130 |

*Corn Exchange, Mark Lane.*

Quantities and Prices of British Corn, &c. sold and delivered in this Market, during the week ended Saturday, May 19.

| | Qrs. | | £. | s. d. | | s. d. |
|---|---|---|---|---|---|---|
| Wheat.. | 4,874 | for 14,491 | 19 | 8 | Average, 62 | 0 |
| Barley.. | 3,153 | .. 4,401 | 4 | 11 | ..........40 | 10 |
| Oats.. | 1,791 | .. 2,971 | 3 | 4 | ..........33 | 2 |
| Rye.... | 52 | .. 96 | 12 | 6 | ..........37 | 1 |
| Beans.. | 523 | .. 1,311 | 4 | 11 | ..........50 | 2 |
| Pease .. | 29 | .. 72 | 10 | 1 | ..........50 | 0 |

Friday, May 25.—This week our market has been moderately supplied with English Corn; but there is another large arrival of Foreign Oats. Wheat continues dull at Monday's prices. Barley and Beans are very scarce. Oats, of feeding descriptions, are very heavy in sale, and rather decline in value, as the quantity for sale is so considerable.

Monday, May 28.—The preceding week furnished a fair supply of Wheat and Flour, and very scanty quantities of Barley, Beans, and Oats of English growth; but another large arrival of Foreign Oats. This morning the fresh supply of all descriptions of Grain is small. Superfine samples of Wheat are very scarce, and such, though taken off slowly, obtained last week's prices, but all other sorts are very dull, and must be reported 1s. per quarter lower.

Scarcely a sample of Barley is to be seen, and the prices of this article may be considered nominal. Beans and Pease are unaltered in value. Nearly all the Foreign Oats are of a feed description, and such being very abundant, may be reported 1s. to 2s. per quarter lower than on Monday last, but stout parcels of Oats nearly maintain the terms last quoted. There is a fair sale for Flour, at no variation in value.

*Price on board Ship as under.*

Flour, per sack ......46s. — 56s.
—— Seconds ........42s. — 44s.
—— North Country ..40s. — 43s.

Price of Bread.—The price of the 4lb. Loaf is stated at 9d. by the full-priced Bakers.

COAL MARKET, May 25.

| Ships at Market. | Ships sold. | Price. |
|---|---|---|
| 44¾. | 24¾. | 28s.—35s. 9d. |

Account of Wheat, &c. arrived in the Port of London, from May 21 to May 26, both inclusive.

| | Qrs. | | Qrs. |
|---|---|---|---|
| Wheat .. | 6,490 | Tares .... | 88 |
| Barley. .. | 515 | Linseed .. | 2,442 |
| Malt .... | 5,620 | Rapeseed . | 550 |
| Oats .... | 3,515 | Brank .. | 103 |
| Beans ... | 600 | Mustard .. | — |
| Flour .... | 6,848 | Flax .... | — |
| Rye .... | — | Hemp ... | — |
| Pease.... | 214 | Seeds ... | 21 |

Foreign.—Wheat, 4,927; Barley, 2,351; Oats, 37,200; Beans, 429 quarters.

Monday, May 28.—The arrivals from Ireland last week were, 36 firkins of Butter, and 2,877 bales of Bacon; and from Foreign Ports, 6,039 casks of Butter. The market is now abundantly supplied with English Butter, and the prices generally are much lower. Bacon was very dull last week: prices may be quoted full 1s. per cwt. lower.

### Price of Hops, per Cwt. in the Borough.

Monday, May 28.—The fly having increased beyond what was expected even by the most sanguine, the Hop market has been very brisk, at a great advance in price since our last report. To-day's letters from the Plantations speak of very great increase of fly since Saturday, which it is expected will prove fatal to the crop.—Kent pockets, from 8l. to 10l.; bags, 6l. 10s. to 8l. 8s. Sussex pockets, 7l. to 8l. 8s.

*Maidstone, May* 24.—About two days after our last Report, we had the first appearance of fly in this neighbourhood, which has ever since generally much increased; in consequence, the market has within the space of the last week advanced full 40s. per cwt.; bags offered last Thursday at 4l. 10s., now selling at 6l. 10s. to 7l.; Pockets in proportion.

### SMITHFIELD.

Monday, May 28.—There was some improvement in the price of Beef, Mutton, and Lamb on Friday, which is fully supported to-day. Good Beasts are from 30s. to 2l. a head higher than this day se'nnight; and a few choice things have exceeded our top currency. Down Mutton is very short in supply, and 4d. a stone dearer than last Monday, 5s. 6d. being readily given for the best; and Polled Sheep have advanced about 1s. per head. The best Lamb obtains 7s. a stone, and has a free sale. The market opened with a brisk trade, but towards the close the demand slackened, and it was thought some things would remain over, both of Beef and Mutton.

*Per Stone of 8 pounds (alive).*

| | s. | d. | s. | d. |
|---|---|---|---|---|
| Beef ...... | 4 | 0 | to 5 | 2 |
| Mutton ... | 4 | 0 | — 5 | 2 |
| Veal ..... | 4 | 8 | — 5 | 4 |
| Pork ..... | 4 | 6 | — 5 | 2 |
| Lamb ... | 6 | 0 | — 7 | 0 |

| | | | |
|---|---|---|---|
| Beasts .. | 1,933 | Sheep .. | 21,020 |
| Calves ... | 210 | Pigs ... | 160 |

### NEWGATE, (same day.)

*Per Stone of 8 pounds (dead).*

| | s. | d. | s. | d. |
|---|---|---|---|---|
| Beef ...... | 3 | 8 | to 4 | 8 |
| Mutton ... | 4 | 4 | — 6 | 4 |
| Veal ..... | 5 | 4 | — 6 | 0 |
| Pork ..... | 4 | 0 | — 6 | 0 |
| Lamb .... | 5 | 4 | — 6 | 8 |

### LEADENHALL, (same day.)

*Per Stone of 8 pounds (dead).*

| | s. | d. | s. | d. |
|---|---|---|---|---|
| Beef ... | 3 | 4 | to 4 | 6 |
| Mutton ... | 3 | 4 | — 5 | 0 |
| Veal ..... | 3 | 8 | — 6 | 0 |
| Pork ..... | 4 | 4 | — 5 | 8 |
| Lamb .... | 4 | 0 | — 6 | 8 |

## POTATOES.

### SPITALFIELDS, per Ton.

|  | l. s. | | l. s. |
|---|---|---|---|
| Ox-Nobles | 3 10 | to | 0 0 |
| Middlings | 2 5 | — | 0 0 |
| Chats | 0 0 | — | 0 0 |
| Common Red | 3 10 | — | 0 0 |

Onions, 0s. 0d.—0s. 0d. per bush.

### BOROUGH, per Ton.

|  | l. s. | | l. s. |
|---|---|---|---|
| Ox-Nobles | 3 10 | to | 4 0 |
| Middlings | 2 5 | — | 0 0 |
| Chats | 2 0 | — | 0 0 |
| Common Red | 3 0 | — | 2 10 |

## HAY and STRAW, per Load.

*Smithfield.*—Hay....90s. to 115s.

Straw...36s. to 42s.

Clover. 100s. to 140s.

*St. James's.*—Hay.... 75s. to 122s.

Straw .. 33s. to 48s. 6d.

Clover. 120s. to 140s.

*Whitechapel.*—Hay.... 84s. to 120s.

Straw.. 38s. to 42s.

Clover.. 90s. to 135s.

## AVERAGE PRICE OF CORN, sold in the Maritime Counties of England and Wales, for the Week ended May 18, 1827.

|  | Wheat. | | Barley. | | Oats. | |
|---|---|---|---|---|---|---|
|  | s. | d. | s. | d. | s. | d. |
| London* | 61 | 6 | 40 | 6 | 33 | 0 |
| Essex | 59 | 5 | 39 | 0 | 32 | 1 |
| Kent | 58 | 8 | 40 | 3 | 30 | 7 |
| Sussex | 56 | 10 | 42 | 8 | 29 | 0 |
| Suffolk | 56 | 3 | 37 | 5 | 31 | 7 |
| Cambridgeshire | 55 | 4 | 38 | 6 | 27 | 7 |
| Norfolk | 56 | 3 | 37 | 10 | 31 | 3 |
| Lincolnshire | 56 | 0 | 39 | 3 | 24 | 9 |
| Yorkshire | 56 | 1 | 41 | 5 | 28 | 8 |
| Durham | 56 | 2 | 42 | 4 | 39 | 8 |
| Northumberland | 56 | 7 | 37 | 5 | 31 | 5 |
| Cumberland | 65 | 8 | 42 | 0 | 35 | 10 |
| Westmoreland | 64 | 4 | 47 | 0 | 41 | 1 |
| Lancashire | 62 | 4 | 0 | 0 | 32 | 5 |
| Cheshire | 62 | 4 | 0 | 0 | 0 | 0 |
| Gloucestershire | 57 | 0 | 42 | 3 | 36 | 0 |
| Somersetshire | 55 | 1 | 42 | 0 | 37 | 6 |
| Monmouthshire | 59 | 9 | 45 | 2 | 0 | 0 |
| Devonshire | 56 | 9 | 39 | 1 | 34 | 7 |
| Cornwall | 64 | 1 | 41 | 2 | 28 | 0 |
| Dorsetshire | 54 | 5 | 39 | 9 | 32 | 0 |
| Hampshire | 57 | 1 | 41 | 9 | 0 | 0 |
| North Wales | 66 | 7 | 45 | 7 | 29 | 11 |
| South Wales | 61 | 0 | 49 | 0 | 27 | 4 |

* The London Average is always that of the Week preceding.

*Liverpool*, May 22.—At this day's market there was a moderate business doing in Wheat and Oats, at about the prices of this day week for the former, and at about 1*d.* per 45 lbs. decline in the latter. In Indian Corn there has been a good demand, and a small advance has been obtained. In other articles little doing.

Imported into Liverpool, from May 15 to May 21, 1827, inclusive:— Wheat, 6,207; Barley, 1,366; Oats, 4,738; Malt, 1,382; Beans, 453; Pease, 214 quarters; Flour, 1,502 sacks, per 280 lbs.; Oatmeal, 204 packs, per 240 lbs.; American Flour, 5,101 barrels.

*Derby*, May 26.—Our Corn market this day was but thinly attended, and very little business done. Prices of all sorts of Grain rather on the decline.—Best Wheat, 60*s.* to 64*s.*; Barley, 38*s.* to 46*s.*; Oats, 34*s.* to 40*s.*; and Beans, 54*s.* to 62*s.* per eight bushels Imperial measure.

*Horncastle*, May 26.—We had only a moderate supply of all sorts of Grain. Wheat and Barley rather lower. Oats, Beans, and Rye, nearly the same as our last.—Wheat, 56*s.* to 58*s.*; Barley, 38*s.* to 40*s.*; Oats, 26*s.* to 30*s.*; Beans, 60*s.* to 64*s.*; and Rye from 38*s.* to 42*s.* per quarter.

*Ipswich*, May 26.—Our supply was very small again to-day of Wheat and all other Grain. The same price was asked as last week, and but little business was therefore done. Prices as follow:—Wheat, 52*s.* to 65*s.*; Barley, 38*s.* to 41*s.*; and Beans, 49*s.* to 50*s.* per quarter,

*Manchester*, May 27.—The Corn trade continues in the same dull state as noted last week. At our market to-day we had a good attendance of country dealers, &c., and a large supply of Wheat and Oats: the finest qualities of the former were offered at a reduction of 2*d.* per bushel of 70 lbs.; inferior unsaleable: the latter were 2*d.* to 3*d.* per 45 lbs. lower, at which reduction sales to a considerable extent were made. The Flour trade was dull at a decline of 1*s.* per sack on last week's rates. In Barley, Beans, Pease, and Malt, no alteration since this day se'nnight.

*Newcastle-upon-Tyne*, May 26.—We had a moderate supply of Wheat from the farmers this morning, which was readily sold at last week's prices, and granary samples were more in demand. Rye sells freely at last week's prices. Barley dull sale at 2*s.* per quarter cheaper. The farmers' supply of Oats was small, but there were a great many samples from granary, and prices were 1*s.* per quarter lower. We had some inquiry for Barley and Wheat in bond, and sales were made of fine Barley at 30*s.*, and Dantzic Wheat at 40*s.* per quarter.

*Norwich*, May 26.—The supply of Wheat to-day was only moderate, notwithstanding prices were 1*s.* per quarter lower than last week.—Red, 52*s.* to 58*s.*; White to 60*s.*; Barley, only a few parcels, at 40*s.*; Oats, 28*s.* to 31*s.*; Beans, 43*s.* to 48*s.*; Pease, 44*s.* to 48*s.*; Boilers, to 50*s.* per quarter; and Flour, 41*s.* to 42*s.* per sack.

*Reading*, May 26.—A general dullness pervaded the sale of Corn of all descriptions this day. We had a fair supply of Wheat. Barley was a shade dearer, but so little is doing in this article, or in Oats, Pease, or Beans, that the prices were little more than nominal.

*Wakefield*, May 25.—The supply of Wheat for this day's market is very large; the sale has been very heavy, at a decline of full 1*s.* per quarter from the prices obtained last Friday, and to quit any quantity a still greater reduction must be submitted to. Oats and Shelling are very dull sale, and something lower. Malt is in limited demand, without alteration in value. Beans are in request, and rather better prices are obtained for them,

## COUNTRY CATTLE AND MEAT MARKETS, &c.

*Horncastle*, May 26.—Beef, 9s. per stone of 14 lbs.; Mutton, 6d. to 7d.; Lamb 7d. to 8d.; and Veal, from 7d. to 9d. per lb.

*Manchester* Smithfield Market, May 23.—The supply of Sheep to this day's market was good, and of Lambs abundant, the greater part of which were sold. The supply of Cattle was short, and such as were fit for slaughtering were sold readily at an advance of full ½d. per lb. on last week's rates. In Calves and Pigs little or no alteration.—Beef, 4½d. to 8d.; Mutton, 7d. to 8½d.; Lamb, 8d. to 9½d.; Veal, 5d. to 7½d.; and Pork, 4d. to 5d. per lb., sinking offal.

At *Morpeth* Fair, May 23, there was a short supply of Cattle, Sheep, and Lambs; and there being a good many buyers, both the latter sold readily, at a little advance in price.—Beef, from 7s. to 7s. 9d.; Mutton, 8s. 9d. to 9s. 9d.; Lamb, 9s. to 10s. per stone, sinking offal.

*Norwich Castle Meadow*, May 26.—We had only a moderate supply of fat Cattle to this day's market, prices nearly the same as last week, 7s. 9d. to 8s. 6d. per stone of 14 lbs., sinking offal: the supply of Store Stock was also large; Scots few, sold at 4s. to 4s. 6d. per stone of what they will weigh when fat; Shorthorns, 3s. to 3s. 9d.; Cows and Calves but few here, sale rather brisker; Homebreds, of one and two years old, a flat sale. Pigs, rather brisk sale.—Meat: Beef, 7d. to 9d.; Veal, 6d. to 8d.; Mutton, 6d. to 7½d.; Lamb, 8d.; and Pork, 6d. to 8d. per lb.

# COBBETT'S WEEKLY REGISTER.

Vol. 62.—No. 11.]   LONDON, SATURDAY, June 9, 1827.   [*Price 6d.*

The Reformers have yet many and powerful foes: we have to contend against a host, such as never existed before in the world. Nine-tenths of the press; all the channels of speedy communication of thought and of fact; all the pulpits; all the associations of rich people; all the taxing people; all the immense military and naval establishments, costing us nearly twenty millions a year; all the yeomanry cavalry tribes; all the Jews and jobbers, who suck up thirty millions a year · Your allies, Mr. Canning, are endless in number and mighty in influence. But, we have ONE ALLY, worth the whole of them put together; namely, THE DEBT! This is an ally, whom no honours, no rewards, can seduce from us She is a steady, an unrelaxing, an ever-persevering and incorruptible ally: an ally who is proof against all blandishments, all intrigues, all temptations and all acts of open violence. She sets at defiance all "*military*," all "*yeomanry cavalry*": they may as well fire at a ghost. This ally cares not a straw about *spies* and *informers*. She laughs at the expenditure of *secret-service money*. She is always erect, night as well as day, and is always firmly moving on in our cause, in spite of all the terrors of gaols, dungeons, halters, and axes. Therefore, Mr. Canning, be not so pert. The combat is not so unequal as you seem to imagine; and confident and insolent as you now are, the day of your humiliation may be not so very far distant. Already do many of your friends, seeing the strength and fidelity of our ally and the tendency of her march, begin to propose measures *for weakening* her; *for diminishing her power* by degrees; for drawing off detachments from her, under the name of *reductions!* Oh, no! She is not to be taken from our cause in this way! She is one and indivisible. She is as staunch as she is strong. She is to be got at only by sap and mine: she is to be beaten only by BLOWING UP; and the explosion is SURE TO BURY HER ASSAILANTS AND OUR ENEMIES IN HER RUINS.—Register, 9 Nov. 1816.

# CANNING'S BUDGET.

## TO THE READERS OF THE REGISTER.

Fleet Street, 6th June, 1827.

My Friends,

There are many parts of my twenty-five years' Register, to which parts I turn back with great delight, and I am sure that many of you are in the habit of doing the same thing. Amongst all the parts, to which I thus turn, I do not know of one, to which I have so often turned, with feelings of self-gratulation, as the passage, which I have selected as a *Motto to this Register*, and which I beg

X

Printed and Published by William Cobbett, No. 183, Fleet-street.
[ENTERED AT STATIONERS' HALL.]

you to read, this once more, at any rate; for, during my present address to you, I shall have to apply it in a most striking manner.

The dirty intrigues that have been going on for some months, seem to have caused a sort of *suspension of thought* with regard to all really important public affairs. At last, however, in CANNING'S BUDGET, together with the real state of the paper-money, we have something that forces itself upon the serious attention of all men, who are capable (as you, my friends, all are) of justly judging as to such matters. We must now, therefore (for one week at least), cast aside "Westminster's Pride and England's Glory," together with his "CRIB" and his "REGIMENT"; or, rather, we must leave him in the "Regiment," fighting hard to get at the "Crib," and preserve our blows for him and his Sancho and their now notoriously battered Rump, until we have leisure to bestow these blows. We must also pass over the curious exhibition of Thursday, the 31st of May, when Mr. HUME made a motion for a repeal of that Act of SIX-ACTS, which compels every printer, or publisher, of *any newspaper*, or of a periodical publication of *not more*

*than two sheets* and of *a price less than sixpence;* which compels every such printer, or publisher, to GIVE BAIL, BEFORE HE BEGIN TO PRINT OR PUB-LISH; to give bail in THREE HUNDRED POUNDS, with two SURETIES in 150*l.* each, for the payment of any fines *that may be imposed on him for libel, after he begin to publish!* This is, however, a mere trifle, when compared with another part of this Act, and with that part of another of the SIX-ACTS, which makes a man liable to be BA-NISHED FOR LIFE, for uttering, in print, any thing which has even "a TENDENCY to bring *either House of Parliament into* CONTEMPT"!!! So that, THOMAS ATTWOOD, and several others, who, if people believe them, MUST have brought both Houses of Parliament *into contempt,* may, even now, be BA-NISHED FOR LIFE! Well, on the day above-mentioned, Mr. HUME made a motion for a repeal of the first of these Acts; and he got TEN *to vote for him!* The whole band of formerly noisy Whigs, who made such a merit of their long and strenuous opposition to these very Acts, now either voted against the repeal, or *they kept away!* and Sir BOBBY, particularly, even *spoke against* the repeal! Burdett and his Little Man were *silent*, at any rate, owing, perhaps, to their *fatigue at the purity dinner* on the 23d! These are such scenes as even this nation never beheld before. There was LAWYER SCARLETT speaking against the repeal of an Act which he had strenuously opposed; there was CANNING defending the Whigs for this conduct, upon the principle that *a barrister is defensible* for speaking for and against the same thing; and there was PEEL insisting that the present conduct 'of the Whigs, in opposing the repeal of this Act, PROVED that it was a MERIT in his lamented friend, Castlereagh, to have been the author and proposer of the Act! After which, if any unsatisfied greedy Whig, if any apostate Reformer disappointed in getting a peerage, were *to happen to cut his throat*, who need wonder, if our SOLON from the Spinning Jenny were to hold it up as a PROOF, that Castlereagh acted a very wise, statesman-like, loyal, patriotic, decorous, and valiant part, in cutting his own throat at North Cray in Kent, at the very time when he had charge of the nation's affairs in the offices of the three Secre-

taries of State! If, indeed, SOLON PEEL had insisted that his "lamented, noble friend" was not proved to have been *just as great a friend to the liberties of the people as the Whigs were*, nobody would, or could, with reason, have disputed the truth of his conclusion; and, all that I should have said about the matter would have been, that SOLON's remark was, as far as related to me, wholly *unnecessary*, seeing that, at the very time, *when the Whigs were voting against the Bills*, I said, that the far greater part of them *wished the Bills to pass*, and that they would have voted for the Bills, if they had not been SURE THAT THEY WOULD PASS IN SPITE OF THEIR VOTES. This opinion of mine is now fully established. It is now settled beyond all dispute, that the Whigs were and are just as *good* as Castlereagh, and *no better*; just as *humane*, and not more so; precisely as great *friends of public liberty*, and not *one jot* greater; and that, as the people of Kent told the leaders of the two factions, in 1815, *all were tarred with the same brush.*

However, though here is matter for copious commentary, we must quit it, in order to get at " CANNING's BUDGET;" for this,

*this* is the subject that is truly interesting; here we have the point on which every thing turns; the intrigues, their expected results, the hopes and fears of the factious, Solon's new laws, " the march of mind," Burdett's monstrous support of Canning; every thing sinks out of sight when we are in the presence of the DEBT and its inevitable consequences.

This annual romance, called the " *Budget*," I have, of late years, taken very little notice of; but, upon this occasion, I shall go fully into the matter; because the Budget has come forth, accompanied *with indications of what we may expect to see take place within a few months*; and because, some of the present supporters of the ministry have been very positive in expressing their *opinions* and their *intentions* on the money-subject. These their declarations it will be convenient to have on record, and to remember. I shall, therefore, notice certain parts of the speeches reported (in the Morning Chronicle) to have been made upon this occasion, beginning with that of Canning himself, who, be it observed, has put off this Budget-affair to the distance of *three months* from the usual time of bringing it forth. Of all the *poor sticks* that I have ever seen making budget-speeches, this is the very poorest; but, as I said from the moment I heard of his elevation, this is the man of all men to bring the thing to a close, to wind it up, to *see the last of it !* According to the report, he began his speech as follows:

- - - - - " The task which " I am this day called upon to per-" form, difficult as it must be at any " moment for a person who is called " upon to undertake it for the first " time, is not in my case lessened by " the consideration that the picture of " the financial state of the country, " which it is become my duty to pre-" sent to this Committee, is not one " of *unqualified prosperity*. Undoubt-" edly a complexion has been thrown " over the whole of it by dark spots " upon particular parts, which have " made a deeper impression, both " upon this House and upon the " country, than I think was war-" ranted by any consideration of the " state of our finances; and I have " the *consolation* to reflect, that the " nearer we approach the subject, " and the more accurately we ex-" amine its details, the more ground " we have to hope that the com-" plexion of our condition has been " much exaggerated; and that if " there are some topics upon which " we may find *much to lament*, and " others in which there may be *much* " *to repair;* yet that there are to be " found *means* which, united with

" *determination*, may repair them.
" The financial situation of this
" country is indisputably one which
" requires to be looked at with a
" *steady and scrutinizing eye* ; but in
" proportion as it is minutely and
" accurately examined, *I see signs*
" which form a justification of the
" sanguine hopes I have ventured to
" express, that the *reparation* of our
" situation is *neither difficult* nor
" even *questionable*."

Oh! you " *see signs*," do you,
to make you believe, that the
" *reparation of our situation* [a
queer phrase !] is neither " *difficult* nor even *questionable*." What
are these " *signs*"! You do not
point them out to us; and, the
truth is, you see no such signs,
and a baby just born understands
as much of the matter as you do.
After this, the jester goes on to
state, that the revenue now falls
short of the expenditure by *three
millions a year*, and that he means
to *borrow* that three millions. Then
he comes to the *Sinking Fund*,
which his *new allies* have, for
years, contended to be a " *gross
deception*," and which he, *with
their approbation*, means still to
keep up! You will observe, my
friends, that, all the while that this
" Sinking Fund," that is, a fund for
sinking, or lowering, the amount
of the Debt; all the while that

this fund is at work, the amount
of the Debt keeps RISING!
And, well it may, when more is,
in one way or another, borrowed
and added to the Debt, than the
" Sinking Fund" takes away from
the Debt. The notions of this
man, relative to this fund, are truly
curious : if we had nothing more
from him than these notions, that
would be quite enough to convince
us, that he is totally ignorant of
the whole subject, and that, if he
keep the thing in his hands for
only a year, it must fall to pieces
without his knowing any thing at
all of the cause.

" The Committee cannot fail to
" perceive, from what I have endea-
" voured to enforce, that I have en-
" tertained the expediency of a Sink-
" ing Fund (whether it be called by
" that name or Surplus Expenditure)
" to assist us in maintaining the na-
" tional faith and national credit. I
" may ask the Committee, what
" would they suppose of a country
" that was not in a condition to pro-
" vide for a sudden defalcation of re-
" venue, or an unforeseen emergency?
" The past year has brought both
" these necessities upon us—a sud-
" den falling off of revenue, and an
" emergency coming upon us sud-
" denly and unawares [hear, hear].
" What would they think of the
" situation of a *private gentleman who
" would squander his ascertained income*,

" and not lay by a part of it to meet
" any sudden call that may be made
" upon him, or demand that may not
" be foreseen [hear, hear!]? What
" should be the amount of such a
" surplus fund, it is not our business
" now to discuss; but I own that it
" does appear to my mind that there
" ought to be a Sinking Fund of not
" less than five millions on a revenue
" of fifty millions—less than this we
" should not have, judging from our
" own experience and acting con-
" sistently with private analogies. I
" abstain now from expressing how
" large that fund should be, but ex-
" press frankly my opinion that it
" should exist; reserving the deter-
" mination of its amount, and the re-
" flections which the intervening
" time may afford, *until the whole*
" *question of our finances shall be con-*
" *sidered.* On such an occasion
" *Government should look to the ad-*
" *vice of Parliament.* The question
" for the Committee now is, whether
" the deficiency, which I have stated
" in round numbers to be three mil-
" lions or something less, shall be
" provided for by *any extraordinary*
" *course,* or by taking credit on the
" Consolidated Fund: and also to
" wait until *next year for the adoption*
" *of any measure of a stronger charac-*
" *ter,* should such a measure be
" deemed necessary."

Only think of the illustration
of the " *private gentleman*"!
This is the way in which these
people have always deceived
themselves. Why, you foolish
man, we " *lay by* " nothing in this
" Sinking Fund." We *borrow* the
amount of it, and *more,* every
year. Where, then, is your illustration? We want the amount of
the " Sinking Fund" to pay back
the sums which we annually borrow; and, the payment is *greater*
than the receipt by the amount of
the profits which the Jews and
jobbers make out of the transaction.—Now, let us hear his
notions of the present state and
of the prospects of the country,
and of those *remedies* which he
has in his eye. He seems to be
*afraid to speak,* and yet he must
say *something* to keep his adherents in countenance. He manifestly *does not know what to do.*
This is so clear that no one can
dispute it. He has found out, at
last, that there is one matter, at
least, on which jesting has no
effect; and that it is necessary,
as to this matter, to have something more than alliterations to
play off. To be convinced, that
he is wholly ignorant upon this
great subject, we have only to
look at his bare words: in every
line we discover, that, if he continue to be the Doctor for only a
little time, the THING must die
in his hands.

" The present condition of the " country is that of *hopeful*, not con- " firmed *convalescence*. I trust and " believe that it is *proceeding to a re-* " *turn of its former power and security* " (of course I mean *financial secu-* " *rity*), provided it is not, at *this cri-* " *tical period, tampered with by any* " *injurious remedy*, or by *any sudden* " *shock*, which may divert it from " *the course of prosperity* in which it " is gradually but directly advancing " [cheers]. *I see improvement in our* " *resources*, which induces me to trust " much to the old natural means for " relief, and not to allow ourselves " to be prematurely tempted from " that system, on a perseverance in " which I think we may rely for a " realization of our hopes, and which " we ought not prematurely to aban- " don *without a due consideration of* " *what course to pursue.* If I were to " decide for myself in taking a course " like this, *without first stating it to* " *Parliament*, I feel that the *respon-* " *sibility would be too great* for me to " assume. But it is because I have " frankly and openly stated it to " Parliament—because I have no- " thing to keep back or to colour— " because there is no concealment— " because I have no object other " than to represent things as they " are, that I have the *courage to wait* " *and expect*, and that I do hope that " more benefit will be derived from " *leaving things for the present as they* " *are*, than from any premature " measure that could be adopted " [hear!]."

Oh! "*hopeful* but not *confirm-ed* convalescence"! *Convalescence* at *best*, then! And that, too, at the end of *twelve years of profound peace*, preceded by a war of such "*success*" and so much "*glory*," that they were almost too great for us to bear! *Convalescence!* Hopeful conva-lescence! Thou art, indeed, a hopeful Minister of Finance. This, in your own words, will tell all foreign nations that they have nothing to fear from us. So that we have been *ill*, while the French and the Americans have been *building fleets!* How those na-tions must laugh at the thought of our being "*proceeding* to a *return* " of our *former* power and finan-" cial security"! Not actually *returning* yet! Oh, no: but, *going on towards a return* to our former power and financial secu-rity! And, even this is, observe, only matter of *belief* with this Budget-man. But, after all, this *belief* that we are thus "*proceed-ing*" to a return to our former power and financial security; even this belief, which is as slen-der as the shadow of a mouse's hair, is, in the mind of this grand financier, dependent on two cir-cumstances; namely, that the country be not tampered with by any injurious remedy, or by any

SUDDEN SHOCK, which might divert it from the course of prosperity in which it is advancing. So that, here we have him already in a course of actual prosperity! But, the "*sudden shock*"! What does he mean by a sudden shock? And, what a pretty state he has got us into, if we are liable, every hour, to some sudden shock! If he had read Mr. Paine's writings, instead of abusing the author, as he so frequently has done, he would have known, that "It is in the last "stages of the system that *all the* "*great shocks come*"; and, as sure as his name is Canning, he will have a great shock of some sort to encounter, before another twelve months have gone over his head, unless he be turned out of his office long before the end of that time.—The whole of this part of the speech, and, indeed, of every part of it, shows ignorance and fear both in the greatest degree. He has no settled opinion upon any part of the subject; and, like all men, who fear that which is to come, he is for putting off the evil which he does not know how to meet. He says, that he has the "*courage to wait and expect*": a new sort of courage, I presume! A courage which may, with much propriety, be called the rankest of cowardice. It is that sort of courage which makes the woodcock poke his long bill and his eyes under the fern, and, being in the dark himself, hopes and believes that the hawk does not see him. This brave, this courageous, this waiting and expecting financier, is for leaving things as they are, though he acknowledges, though every line of his speech makes you see that he is convinced that they cannot continue as they are, and that they cannot mend, unless some great measure of change be adopted. He confesses, in this very paragraph, that he dares not propose any measure of change at all, without first having the approbation of Parliament. He says that the responsibility would be too great for him, and, yet he has the emptiness to talk about his having the courage to wait and expect. After this miserable mess; this mess of nondescribable nonsense, he proceeds to state the several items of the receipt and expenditure of the country, which can be of no interest to my readers, when the result is, that, to get along at all, it is necessary to have a loan, this year, of three millions sterling, to be added to the amount of the enormous debt, which is already greater, and far greater, than ten such nations would be able to pay.—After this, he proceeds, in the same vague and undefined manner as before, to speak of his *intentions with regard to the future.* He describes no intentions, nevertheless: and, you can only still continue to gather from his words, that he knows not what to do; that he cannot even guess at what is likely to happen to the finances; that he does not even hint at any remedy that has occurred to his mind; and, my friends, when you have read the following paragraph, I am satisfied that you will agree with me; that there is no child in the cradle not as fit to face the difficulties of the country as this man is.

"From what I have stated, it is "for the Committee to decide, un- "der the circumstances of the coun- "try, whether we shall go on through "the present year, not in ignorance, "but with a *full knowledge of our si- "tuation*, and abstain from *a change* "until we await the *growing effects* "of our present prospects of prospe- "rity*, rather than hastily press for- "ward to that question of financial "consideration *which stands for next "year*, with a risk before us of de- "ranging our present accounts with- "out knowing the possible effects of "that derangement. In the Supplies "of last year, there is an increase,

"beyond the estimated charge, of "800,000*l*. This increase arose from "certain charges on account of Army "Extraordinaries, and on account of "the Vote of Credit for Portugal. "I know it will be urged that it is "desirable to bring us back to a "fixed and certain expenditure. As "to this, *or any precise limit*, or any "future measure, I *forbear from "making any promises;* and for this "reason, that I have always observed "that promises of this kind are al- "ways exaggerated by those to whom "they are made, and because, as "more is expected than is held out, "they generally end in disappoint- "ment. All I can say on the part "of Government is, that Ministers "*are disposed and determined to apply "their best efforts;* and that they "have resolved *to take the House into "council on the subject.* This is all "that, in the circumstances of the "country, the House can expect, or "that Government can do [cheers]. "In its present state we should not "even aid the country, but leave it "to its natural course, and before "the adoption of any new measure, "wait *until the prosperity of the na- "tion was more unequivocal* [hear, "hear!]. I have a confident hope "that that prosperity *which has com- "menced* will continue to increase; "that hope I found on a knowledge "and reliance of *its intrinsic ener- "gies*—of its ascertained, though "not *now put-forth power*, rather "than on any particular circum- "stances which might, in the state-

" ment, lead into minute and de-
" tailed explanation [*cheers*]."

Yes, "*cheer*" away; these cheers
never yet failed to come forth upon
such occasions. *What* was it that
the good folks cheered? They
cheered this, that he had a confident hope that our *present prosperity* would continue to increase;
that that hope was founded on a
knowledge and reliance of the
"*intrinsic energies*" of the country, and of its "*ascertained though
not put forth power*"! It really
makes one sick to hear and much
more to repeat, such abominable
nonsense. It is worse than the
most beastly balderdash of a novel.
He talks of a CHANGE; but,
this change he puts off until he
sees the effects of our present-
prospect-of prosperity! What reason is this for putting off the
change? He talks of a question
of finance; some great question
of finance, which, he says,
"STANDS FOR NEXT
YEAR." Why, this is the very
first that we have heard of such
standing! He did, indeed, say,
one night, that he meant to have a
Finance-Committee in the next
session of Parliament; but, he
said nothing to convince any man
alive that his whole system would
not be blown up before the next
session of Parliament should commence. I shall have more to say,
by-and-bye, about this Finance-
Committee project; and shall only
now, observe, further, upon these
poor, miserable, unintelligible
remarks; this poor stuff; this
wretched balderdash, that the
"*taking of the House into council
on the subject*" must naturally
give us, who have experienced
such blessed effects of the councils
of the House, a monstrous deal of
consolation. The Ministers are
resolved to take the House into
council with them on the subject!
It is easy to see that this is a mere
pretence for getting over the
present session without proposing
any measure at all for the relief
of the country; it is easy to perceive that the Minister and his
new allies are wholly unable to
suggest any remedy themselves;
and that, if they finally resort to
such Committee, it will be merely
with the hope of obtaining a screen
for themselves. But, a Committee, though it may do excellently
well for discovering reasons for
passing Power-of-Imprisonment
Bills, Banishment Bills, Gagging
Bills, and Bills for various other
such amiable purposes: though a
Parliamentary Committee may be
wonderfully efficient for these purposes, for crushing Reformers,

for shutting them up in dungeons, for making political pamphlets too dear to be purchased, and too big to be sold, without loss to the vendor; though a Parliamentary Committee may be quite sufficient for all purposes of this sort, this grand financier; this SECOND PITT in finance, and this SHERIDAN No. 2 in party-fidelity ; this grand financier, Portuguese warrior, and Cornelius Agrippa man will find that, when he has to cope with the great, the brave, the magnanimous, the incorruptible ALLY, whose qualities are so fully described in the motto to this Register ;. the man of romance will find that, in a combat against her, Parliamentary Committee has no more power than he himself, single-handed, would have ; that is to say, unless the said Parliamentary Committee BLOW HER UP, and, then, let him observe, that the explosion is sure to bury the enemies of Reform in her ruins !

The conclusion of this most dismal Budget-speech consisted of AN OLD SPEECH OF PITT. The man seemed really to be like a newspaper-article writer, who, for want of time or for want of something to say for himself, resorts *to the making of extracts*, in order to fill those columns, which must otherwise go forth blank. This is a man, who, as I have often described him, is totally destitute of the power of *consecutive thinking.* The subjects of money and accounts, and, especially, when the resources are to be taken into consideration, demand, even in the vulgar details of them, something like connexion of thought. You can see, from the whole of this speech, that Sheridan No. 2, had never been able to understand, much less to speak, upon, any such matter ; you can see that, like all men similarly situated, he had avoided looking at the subject, until the last moment ; and that, it must have been with the utmost difficulty that he got worked into his head matter sufficient to make any thing of a speech at all. Now, the other finance fellows, such as Robinson, Vansittart, Perceval, Old Rose, Huskisson, and even Castlereagh, had a devilish deal of *working* in them; got together a multitude of facts; pored over them and talked about them, till they got together a mass of stuff, more or less confused, to be sure, but more than enough to make a good long speech out of; blunderheaded enough, generally wholly destitute of all sound principle ; but, making, when all put together, and put forth with tolerable volubility, a great mass of fallacies and intricacies, rounded here and there by bold and swaggering assertions, which, all-put together, made a mess for the greedy feeders to satisfy their maws with. But, this poor man really seems to have been turned down, as a merciless nurse turns down her baby without the leading-strings upon a hard floor. " *All aloney!*" she cries; and away comes the poor thing, holding out its helpless hands, catching at the first thing it comes near, and at last tumbling upon the floor with a squall. Whether it were conceit and obstinacy, on the part of the Premier, or cruelty on the part of those who sent him forth thus helpless before the public, I know not; but, never, since Budget-making was in fashion, was there beheld a Budget-man so completely contemptible as this.

After having made the senseless speech, almost the whole of which I have given in the above extracts, he, as I observed before, actually concluded with a long extract from AN OLD SPEECH OF PITT; and, this old speech, which, he said, contained the principles on which he himself meaned to proceed; this old speech of Pitt was the very speech

in which that shallow and showy fellow introduced his project for *paying off the Debt by the means of a Sinking Fund:* that very speech, I say, in which the flashy Pitt introduced this sublime project for paying of a Debt, and which very project has caused the Debt to swell up from two hundred millions to eight hundred millions, exclusive of four hundred millions more, which is not less Debt than the Funded Debt, now known under the names of Dead-weight and Poor-rates. Pretty principles, then, this financier of ours means to act upon. But, if these be his principles, what need have we of a Finance-Committee, with one of which he is, it seems, to treat us next year. If these be his principles, we know them: they are principles which sanction incessant borrowing and everlasting Debt: they are principles which sanction paper-money down to one pound notes or under; the acting upon which principles must inevitably lead to shocks, to panics, to the breaking-up of merchants, manufacturers, tradesmen, farmers, and gentlemen; to the unjust transfer of property from hand to hand; to the ruin of innumerable industrious and excellent families; to the degradation of the common people in general, and to the actual starvation of great multitudes of them. Let us, then, once more see this old speech : let us have it before us : let the young men of the present day behold the flashy words by which their grandfathers were induced to consent to that series of measures, to the adoption of that horrible system, which now scourges them, and which, if they had not the sense and courage to abate it, will scourge their children worse than any set of slaves in this world were ever before scourged. But, above all things, let those who have estates, and large estates too, look once more at these delusive words : let them, as they see their parks departing into the hands of the Jews, look back at these words, and see in them the beginning of that train of causes which has led to this departure.

" Before I sit down I will, with " the permission of the House, read " an extract from an eminent autho- " rity in support of the propriety and " efficacy of the principles on which " I have professed and avowed my " reliance. . " But there is still an- " " other cause, even more satis- " " factory than these, because it is " " of a still more extensive and per- " " manent nature—that constant ac- " " cumulation of capital, that con- " " tinual tendency to increase the

" " operation is universally seen in a " " greater or less proportion, when- " " ever it is not obstructed by some " " public calamity, or by some mis- " " taken and mischievous policy, " " but which must be conspicuous " " and rapid indeed in any country " " which has at once arrived at an " " advanced state of commercial " " prosperity. Simple and obvious " " as this principle is, and felt and " " observed as it must have been, " " in a greater or less degree, even " " from the earliest periods, I doubt " " whether it has ever been fully de- " " veloped and sufficiently explained, " " but in the writings of an author " " of our times, now unfortunately " " no more (I mean the author of a " " a celebrated Treatise on the " " Wealth of Nations), whose ex- " " tensive knowledge of detail, and " " depth of philosophical research, " " will, I believe, furnish the best " " solution to every question con- " " nected with the history of com- " " merce, or with the systems of " " political economy. This accu- " " mulation of capital arises from " " the continual application of a " " part, at least, of the profit ob- " " tained in each year, to increase " " the total amount of capital to be " " employed in a similar manner, " " and with continued profit, in the " " year following. The great mass " " of the property of the nation is " " thus constantly increasing at " " compound interest, the progress " " of which in any considerable " " period, is what at first view would -

" " appear incredible. Great as have
" " been the effects of this cause
" " already, they must be greater in
" " future ; for its powers are aug-
" " mented in proportion as they
" " are exerted. It acts with a velo-
" " city continually accelerated, with
" " a force continually increased. It
" " may indeed, as we have ourselves
" " experienced, be checked or re-
" " tarded by particular circum-
" " stances—it may for a time be
" " interrupted, or even overpower-
" " ed ; but where there is a fund of
" " productive labour and active in-
" " dustry, it can never be totally
" " extinguished. In the season of
" " the severest calamity and distress,
" " its operations will still counter-
" " act and diminish their effects;
" " in the first returning interval of
" " prosperity, it will be active to re-
" " pair them. If we look to a pe-
" " riod, like the present, of con-
" " tinued tranquillity, the difficulty
" " will be to imagine limits to its
" " operation. None can be found
" " while there exists at home any
" " one object of skill or industry
" " short of its utmost possible per-
" " fection—one spot of ground in
" " the country capable of higher
" " cultivation and improvement ;
" " or while there remains abroad
" " any new market that can be ex-
" " plored, or any existing market
" " that can be extended. From the
" " intercourse of commerce, it will
" " in some measure participate in
" " the growth of other nations—in
" " all the possible varieties of their

" " situations. The rude wants of
" " countries emerging from barbar-
" " ism, and the artificial and in-
" " creasing demands of luxury and
" " refinement, will equally open
" " new sources of treasure and new
" " fields of exertion, in every state
" " of society, and in the remotest
" " quarters of the globe. It is this
" " principle which, I believe, ac-
" " cording to the uniform result of
" " history and experience, main-
" " tains, on the whole—in spite of
" " the vicissitudes of fortune, and
" " the disasters of empires—a con-
" " tinued course of successive im-
" " provement in the general order
" " of the world." These are the
" words of Mr. Pitt. Adam Smith
" is the authority cited. Let those
" who regard the application of phi-
" losophy to politics as innovation,
" go back with me to the principles
" avowed in this House by Mr. Pitt
" in 1792 [cheers]. I now speak
" them from my mouth—I adopt
" them as my principles—I proclaim
" them to Parliament as the guide
" and polar-star of my political
" course." [The Right Honourable
Gentleman *sat down amid loud and
continued cheers.*]

Oh, yes, " *loud and continued
cheers* "; just such cheers as were
bestowed upon Pitt, when he uttered this old speech, as a preface
to his grand project of a Sinking
Fund ; that project, which has,

even in this House itself, been a thousand times denominated a delusion and a humbug; that project which the feelosophers tell us their own Dr. Hamilton has discovered to be a cheat; that project which I, in "Paper against Gold," written ten years before Dr. Hamilton ever wrote upon the subject, *proved* as clearly as daylight to have proceeded from one of the silliest heads that ever was placed upon a pair of human shoulders. The principles upon which this project was founded, this Second Pitt tells us he has adopted as his principles, and that he proclaims them to Parliament as the guide and polar star of his political course; whereupon he receives " loud and continued cheers"!

Cheers! Aye, to be sure, and so did Prosperity Robinson, when he proclaimed the glad tidings that this prosperous nation was covered with blessings, " *dispensed from the portals of an ancient constitutional monarchy.*" Cheers! loud and continued cheers! And did not Vansittart receive the same, when he, in 1811, proclaimed to Parliament that a one-pound note and a shilling were equal in value to a golden guinea of full weight and fineness? And did not Solon Peel receive equally loud and continued cheers; when he, in 1819, proclaimed to Parliament that a one pound note and a shilling had been, in 1811, worth only about sixteen shillings in gold? Cheers, indeed! When were these cheers wanting, to a man who had the public money to dispense! Loud and continued cheers followed the speech of Castlereagh, when he ascribed the public distress to a sudden transition from war to peace. Lord Liverpool was cheered when he ascribed the distresses of the country to *Over-production*, at the very moment when money was voted by the Parliament to save from starvation a considerable portion of the people. Loud and continued cheers regaled the ears of this same Canning; this very same second Pitt, when he said, upon the passing of Peel's Bill, that now the *question was set at rest for ever*; and cheers not less loud, attended his worthy colleague, Castlereagh, when he, in 1822, proposed the measure that partly repealed that Bill. Loud and continued cheers regaled the ears of this same Canning, when he decried that famous Bill of 1822; cheered again he was, when, last year, he proposed the Act which is, next April twelvemonth, to put an end to the Bill of 1822; but, and here is an end of the cheering, cheers *will not salute his ears* when he shall have to propose a something (God knows what it will be) *to prevent his Bill of last year from going into effect*; for, that is what he must do, or, he will absolutely be lost in the scramble, and will never be heard of or read of again, except in the pages of this Register.

So much for the Budget-speech of this our grand financier, of this our Pitt the second; for, like him he is, in every thing, except that he has a little more of indiscretion, a little more shallowness and a little less of what the other might have had a great deal more of without having a bit too much. So much for his part in this financial debate. Mr. HUME, who followed him, and who appears to have been almost the only person who uttered opinions opposite to his, said many things showing the fallacy of the prospects held out by Pitt the second; pressing for an immediate reduction of expenses; but, containing one fallacy as great, as complete, of tendency as mischievous, and even, more mischievous, than any thing said by the financier himself, whose speech, indeed, was perfectly harmless, calculated to

deceive nobody of any sense, and to excite nothing in the public mind, except that universal contempt which has been bestowed upon it. The chief burthen of Mr. Hume's speech was, that the financial affairs of the country might be retrieved by what he called *economy*. He said, and very truly, that those who used to sit on the same side of the House with himself, but who were now gone he knew not whither, used to say the same thing; but that, now, they either held their tongues upon the subject, or held opinions wholly different from those which they then held. This is very true; but, those opinions were always just as false as those of Mr. Hume are now. Mr. Hume is reported to have said, upon this occasion, that the course to be pursued was *to reduce our expenditure*; and, then, we find these words: " In two short months he would " pledge himself to reduce our " expenditure by from five to " seven millions; and that he " would do this without inflicting " injury upon any department of " the public service."

Now, the army, the navy, the ordnance, the odds and ends belonging to both, the places and pensions and so forth: all these amount to about twenty millions a year. After that, there are upwards of forty millions left of expenditure. Mr. Hume looks merely at the little *deficiency in the revenue*. He seems to think that it would be enough if the present expenditure could be brought down to the present revenue. He seems to forget that it is the present revenue, whether it falls short of the expenditure or not, which is pressing the people to the earth. Besides, though he bids pretty fairly for the office of Chancellor of the Exchequer; though he tells us that he would take off seven millions without inflicting injury upon any department of the public service; he is not condescending enough to tell us in what department he would make his reductions. Fund-holders, tax-gatherers, and all the whole body, except the army, the navy, and their contingencies, including places and pensions: all these would require taxation to the amount of more than forty millions a year; and, does Mr. Hume imagine that that forty millions a year, IN GOLD, observe, as it must be, very shortly; does he imagine, that that forty millions a year could be collected by the use of any means whatever? But, he proposes to take off but *seven* millions. If he were to take off the whole of the twenty mil-

lions, does he imagine that the forty could be collected IN REAL GOLD? If he do, March hare never was madder than he!

Mr. Hume seems to forget that the taxes are now, in effect, paid in paper-money, for the greater part. He seems to forget that this paper-money is to cease in about twenty-one months from this day. The man is mad, stark staring mad, who believes that fifty-three millions of taxes could be collected after the cessation of that paper-money; for, and Pitt the Second will make the discovery, *without one pound notes*, there is, in fact, very little aid to be derived from paper-money; and, Sheridan No. 2, if he ask Hudson Gurney, who never issues any thing but five-pound notes, will find, that five-pound notes without one-pound notes, are like greyhounds without legs and pigeons without wings.

Nevertheless, this notion about "retrenchment and economy;" this economical reform, as the canting old Whigs have called it for so many years, seems to have still stuck in the heads of Lords Althorp and Milton. Mr. Brougham, indeed, contented himself with cutting some sarcasms on Mr. Hume. He contented himself with saying that he thought

Y

that the loan proposed by Canning was the best plan. In short, he made a speech approving of this financial statement and picture of Canning, and uttered words which, as we may have to refer to them hereafter, as we have had to refer so often to those of Prosperity Robinson, I shall put on record, as follows :—

"He was one of those who felt " perfect satisfaction at the state- " ment made by the Chancellor of " the Exchequer on a former occa- " sion, and renewed that night. He " was perfectly satisfied with the " promise of a Finance Committee " in the ensuing year; he looked to " the Report of that Committee for " the greatest and most *important* " *information with respect to the Debt,* " the *Taxes,* and the *Public Expen-* " *diture.* If he looked with confi- " dence to the Report of a Commit- " tee appointed in Mr. Pitt's day—if " he looked with confidence to the " Finance Committee appointed in " 1817—he trusted that he should " not be considered sanguine, if he " entertained strong expectations " from the *Committee to be appointed* " *next year;* and the more so, when " he saw a *better light,* both with re- " spect to trade and to finance, *break-* " *ing in through the walls of that* " *House,* since the appointment of " the last Committee; when he re- " flected that great errors had been " swept away from our commercial

" policy—when he looked back upon " what had been truly remarked " by Dean Swift, in his Financial " Arithmetic—who, speaking of ex- " cise and customs, observed, that " two and two did not always make " four, that sometimes they did not " make three, and often not even " two—when he perceived that the " increase of taxes, instead of adding " to the Revenue, generally caused " a defalcation—when he considered " that taking off taxes had added to " the Revenue in almost every in- " stance in which it had been tried " —when he knew that lightening " the burthens of the people added " to, instead of decreasing the weight " of the public purse—when he found " that the light was slowly, late, but " surely and steadily breaking in, as " well upon the country as upon the " minds of Members of that House, " and enlightening the darkness in " which they had hitherto sat there " —he had great and ardent hopes " in the Report of that Committee " [hear, hear!]. In his opinion the " Chancellor of the Exchequer had " acted right, well, and wisely, in " not giving to the House an exag- " gerated picture of the prosperity of " the country; he had done well, too, " not to draw a too florid, & too pic- " turesque representation of the " financial resources of the country. " He (Mr. Brougham) had had too " much of Budgets brought forward " by different Ministers; to trust im- " plicitly to any statement of that " kind, which it had been his fortune

" to hear. He must say—and he " was sure the Right Honourable " Gentleman (Mr. Canning) would " forgive him, when he made the " observation—that he always felt " the suspicious character in which " a Chancellor of the Exchequer " came forward. It might be, that " a man's feeling or his prejudice " led him to imagine his statements " true; but still they must be received " with doubt; therefore it was that " he gave the Right Honourable " Gentleman credit for not having " overcharged his statement either " of the finances or resources of the " country. There was *no doubt that* " *the country was recovering from that* " *great and pressing distress, under* " *which it had laboured,* and which " every man *must deplore.* The most " extensive sources of information " from various quarters—informa- " tion upon which he could place " the greatest reliance—information " coming, too, from men the least in " the world likely to give an exag- " gerated account] of the country's " prosperity, and they confirmed " him in the conviction—a conviction " for the first time, within the last " eighteen months, was now im- " pressed upon him, *that the country* " *was in a gradual, a slow, but there-* " *fore a more trust-worthy and perma-* " *nent state of improvement* [hear, " hear, hear!]. It seemed to him " that the plan now submitted to the " Committee was a plan *for gradual,* " and, therefore, in all probability, " *for permanent reduction.*"

When Brougham uttered these words, he was not aware, nor is he aware, now, that they would have to be quoted against him. They are subject fit for a good long commentary; but, this is not the time to make that commentary. When his expected *Finance-Com- mittee shall have made their re- port;* when they shall have told us the means by which we are to be saved; then will be the time to remind Mr. Brougham of this his approbation of Canning and his measures. We will now no- tice what was said by Lord Al- thorp and by Lord Milton; what reasons they gave for not oppos- ing the Minister upon this occa- sion.

" Lord *Althorp* said, that although " he was afraid that the statements " of the Right Honourable Gentle- " man were too sanguine, and that " the country was in great difficulties, " and required immediate attention " to retrenchment, he did not there- " fore agree with the Honourable " Member for Aberdeen, that the " House ought, *at the present time, to* " *press upon the Chancellor of the Ex- " chequer.* It was not fair, upon the " Right Honourable Gentleman's " *coming into office,* to compel him to " go into *questions of detail.* It would " be *bad policy* to do so with respect " to the future reduction of the ex- " penditure. He was perfectly well

" satisfied, that if the Chancellor of
" the Exchequer examined into the
" financial state of the country, the
" more deeply he investigated, the
" *more power he would find himself*
" *possessed of to reduce the expendi-*
" *ture.* But if the Right Hon. Gen-
" tleman were *to be forced into such*
" *an inquiry at the present moment*, he
" would have great difficulty and
" less hope of effecting any reduction
" in future. The Right Honourable
" Gentleman had expressed his in-
" tention of proposing the formation
" of *a Finance Committee* in the next
" Session of Parliament, and he
" (Lord Althorp) had no doubt that
" it *would be a Committee entitled to*
" *the confidence of the country.* The
" Chancellor of the Exchequer well
" knew that it was impossible, *at the*
" *present day*, for any Committee to
" give satisfaction to the House or
" to the public, unless *it was fairly*
" *composed of gentlemen able and deter-*
" *mined to do their duty.* He (Lord
" Althorp) looked forward to the
" appointment of that Committee as
" an object of *great importance*, for if
" he did not expect, and if he should
" not hereafter find, that it recom-
" mended the *most strict economy* in
" every branch of the public expen-
" diture, it would be *impossible for*
" *him to give his support to the Ad-*
" *ministration.* Whatever other ad-
" vantages the country might gain
" by possessing the present Ministers,
" he thought it right to state, dis-
" tinctly and positively, that *if great*

" *economy were not introduced into all*
" *the Estimates* of the next year, he
" should feel himself *obliged to with-*
" *draw his support from the Govern-*
" *ment.* If the Committee were fairly
" constituted, he felt no doubt *that*
" *very great reductions would be brought*
" *forward.* He thought the increase
" of the Unfunded Debt extremely
" disadvantageous, and, *under other*
" *circumstances*, no man would be
" more ready than himself to oppose
" it; but under all the present cir-
" cumstances, *he thought it best for*
" *the country that it should be agreed*
" *to.*"

Here, then, his Lordship expressly says, that he shall insist
upon a *reduction of expenditure*,
as the *condition* upon which he
shall continue to support the Minister! Alas, poor Minister! If
he reduce the expenditure, he
may as well at once march out of
his office, for, the devil of any
body will he have to support him
if once he seriously begin any
such reduction. Colonel DAVIES
seems to have had the strangest
idea in his head, that ever came
into the head of mortal man. " He
" thought that the Right Honour-
" able Gentleman was too sound
" a politician, as well as too good
" a tactician, not to know that he
" would *best strengthen his power*
" and add to his popularity by re-
" ducing the expenditure of the

" country, and not to go on as " the *late* administration did."— " Late," Colonel! Why Canning was one of the late administration : he was the *champion* of it, as Burdett called him in the Crib letter : he was the champion of expenditure and of heavy taxes. " Strengthen his popularity," you say. That is possible; but his *power* consists of votes : and do you think, Colonel, that he is likely to get votes by lopping off pensions, places, pay, jobs, and putting an end to loans ? Do you think that, Colonel ? If you do, say so at once. Mr. Canning, however he may be deficient in other branches of knowledge, is too good a " tactician" not to know just the contrary of what you say he must know: Lord Milton seems to be duly impressed with the difficulties that Canning would have to encounter, if he were to attempt to act upon your advice. He seems to see the applications which the Ministers would have to resist. Those applications are so numerous, so various in their nature, coming from so many quarters, that, to think of resisting them and to keep his place too, is what Canning is much too cunning for. Let us, however, before we proceed any further, hear the opinions of Lord Milton.

" Lord *Milton* said, he could not " entirely agree with his Honourable " Friend's (Mr. Hume's) opinions " upon that occasion. His Honour- " able Friend had arraigned his Ma- " jesty's Government for not having " at once come forward with some " specific financial plan. Now he " (Lord Milton) thought, that if ever " there was a period when it would " be improper to introduce a specific " and permanent financial plan, it " was the present [hear, hear!]. " For although the distress and suf- " fering under which the country " had been unhappily labouring for " the last two years were, in a great " degree, decreasing ; still no man " could pretend to say, *that the* " *country was restored to that state* " *of calmness and tranquillity which* " *would enable Government to take a* " *full review of the financial state of* " *the country,* and of the difficulties " which they had to meet, in such a " manner as would justify them in " calling for the confidence and co- " operation of that House. [Hear, " hear !] If former Governments had " exerted themselves, and had, in " fact, exhausted the means of mak- " ing the expenditure meet the in- " come of the country, then, indeed, " *he should despair.* But when he " looked back to what had taken " place within the last few years, " he felt that it was greatly to " be deplored that the public ex- " penditure had not only not been " greatly decreased but had been "considerably augmented. [Hear, "heard]. For this, however, that "House was quite as much to blame "as the Government. As to the "Right Honourable Gentleman (Mr. "Canning), he felt that he should "do him injustice if he thought he "would shrink from proposing to "the Committee to be appointed "next year, the reductions which "were called for by the state of the "country. But if the Right Ho- "nourable Gentleman meant to do "this, he must brace himself up "against all applications; he must "put on the whole armour of denial "to the claims made upon him; he "must stand in a different situation "from his predecessors in office; but, "above all things, he would im- "press upon the Right Honourable "Gentleman the necessity of resist- "ing the importunities of those who "possessed a great share of Parlia- "mentary influence in that House "[loud cries of hear, hear, hear!] "He (Lord Milton) was aware "that there was nothing more "difficult, in the situation in which "the Right Honourable Mem- "ber was placed, than to resist the "applications to which he was exposed. "It would not be proper, or rather "it would not be parliamentary, in "him to make any more direct allu- "sion to those applications [hear, "hear!]. He trusted, however, that "under the auspices of the Right "Honourable Gentleman the claims "would be resisted, and that reduc-

"tions would be made in the public "expenditure."

I cannot say that I am satisfied with what was said by these two noblemen, with regard to *putting off economy to the next year.* One of them says that the House ought not, at the present time, to press upon the Chancellor, just at his coming into office; that it would be *bad policy* to do so. The other lord says, that this is the *most improper period* for going into the subject of finance. But, unfortunately, neither of these lords gives us any *reasons* for this their opinion; except, indeed, the cir- cumstance of Canning having just come into office; a very poor reason, truly; for, if it is a better order of things which he is to in- troduce; why postpone the com- mencement of it, why not let us have the benefit of his improve- ments at once? If these lords be sincere, their conduct seems to me the strangest in the world.

However, we have, in this de- bate, two things stated to us; namely, that Lords Althorp and Milton will not continue to sup- port Canning, *unless he, in the ensuing Session of Parliament, set in earnest about a reduction of the public expenditure.* Let that be borne in mind; and let it be borne in mind, too, that I tell

Canning, that, if he do set in earnest about a reduction of the public expenditure, and if he continue to oppose Parliamentary Reform at the same time, he will be turned out of his office, at the end of a month, or thereabouts, from the beginning of his reductions.

Another thing which we have stated to us in this debate, is, that there is to be a *Parliamentary Committee of Finance* in the next session; that Lord Althorp, Lord Milton, Mr. Brougham, Sir Henry Parnell, and several others, have expressed the great hopes that they entertain of the great benefits to be derived from the labours of this Committee. All is referred, it seems, to this wonder-working Committee. The Catholic world seems never to have been in greater expectation on the prospect of seeing a general council held. Canning says, that the Ministers have resolved to TAKE THE HOUSE INTO COUNCIL WITH THEM; Aye, aye, Canning, "take the House into council with

you," as long as you please; lay your plans of war, sketch your campaign before-hand; but, never, never will you succeed against that gallant ally of the Reformers which I have described in the motto to this Register. It is not the driblets of revenue; it is not the cheese-parings and candle-ends of Downing Street that you have to deal with or concern yourselves about. The angry barkings of *Joseph Hume* are to be effectually enough met by the answers of *Joe Miller*; but our gallant ally is not to be faced by jibes and conundrums; alliterations and antitheses are no weapons to bring into this field. It must be *reduction indeed* that will satisfy our ally. You must put on the whole armour of *radicalism*; you must tear corruption up to the very fibres, or our ally will bury you and all your adherents in the ruins of your own system.

In conclusion, my friends, readers of the Register, either this Finance-Committee is a mere pretence for putting off the work of reducing expenditure, or, it is intended as a sort of assistant to the ministry in proposing some change of system; some mode of getting rid of the Debt, or of a part of the Debt. Sir HENRY PARNELL observed, in this debate, that he thought it incumbent on the Chancellor of the Exchequer to devise some means of reducing the National Debt. If Sir Henry Parnell should go across the House, and get a place, and a look, of course, into the nation's affairs, he would see that this reduction was no child's play, and would, of course, cease, like Mr. Tierney and Mr. Brougham, to talk about the matter. In the mean while, until he shall actually cross the House, I dare say Canning would be very much obliged to him, if he could tell him *how to go to work to reduce the Debt!* Look at her, Sir Henry! Look at our ally, as described in my motto: look well at her. No: you turn away your head, just as the dogs are said to turn away their head at the sight of a lion: instinct bids you to turn away your eyes the moment she appears. .

But, my friends, if this Committee should actually meet, it will meet within about a twelvemonth of the day when one-pound notes are to cease. This will trouble the brains of the Committee. They will have to find out the means of collecting more than *sixty millions of taxes in gold*; and this, I take it, the bare thought of it, if they be sober, will frighten the Committee out of their wits. The revenue, and all the schemes about long and short annuities, and all the brilliant schemes and hopes of Canning, will all vanish from the heads of the Committee, when once they put to themselves the serious question, " How are we to collect sixty millions a year in gold?" Therefore, if there really be to be such a Committee, and if the scheme have originated with any man of sense, this Committee must be intended to be an organ for the introducing of some scheme or other, of ASSIGNATS, or of LITTLE SHILLINGS, or of EQUITA-

. BLE ADJUSTMENT. From Brougham and the Marquis of Lansdown I should expect a something or other not, perhaps, altogether unlike the scheme propounded the other day in the document of equivocal generation. However, this is all mere conjecture: no one can even guess at what is intended. To use the fantastical words of Canning, we must *have the " courage to wait and expect;"* and, in the full assurance that the result, in spite of every contrivance that can be resorted to, will be a shaking of the false money system to pieces, a restoration of the use of the King's solid Coin, and a restoration of the rights of the people; having the " courage to wait and to expect " these things, '

I remain

Your faithful friend and

Most obedient Servant,

WM. COBBETT.

POSTSCRIPT. — Since writing the above. I have seen a manuscript copy of the " *Bank Circular*," relative to which SIR JOHN WROTTESLEY was to : make a motion this night in the House of Commons. This paper was declared by MR. MANNING not to have been authorised *by the Directors*; but, that it came from the Bank, or somebody closely connected with it, there can be no doubt, and there is no doubt in my mind; and I think the concluding part of it, namely, that part which lays it down as a principle, " That all vested interests " of the parties issuing paper- " money, should be deemed sub- " servient to the national interests," must have been dictated by somebody closely connected with the Government. This document, therefore, ought to be considered, , in my opinion, as a certain proof, that fears of the approach of ' another *panic* are very prevalent.

## THE NEXT REGISTER

WILL be addressed to LORD WESTMORELAND. People will wonder WHAT the devil I can have to say to him! They will *see*; but, I will now say, that I intend to show the Lords how to shove out Canning, Burdett, and that motley crew, and how to *secure their own estates*; two things, I take it, that they must want very much to know.

---

## TULIP-TREE WOOD.

---

I HAVE for sale *fifty-four* planks of this wood, averaging about *thirty feet* in each plank. They are *two and a half inches thick*. Some are about fourteen feet long; others not, probably, more than ten feet. Some are between *three and four feet wide*; others not, perhaps, more than two feet. The planks are just *as wide at one end as at the other*; and there is not a *single knot*, or *curl*, in the whole parcel of *one thousand, five hundred and eighty-one feet*.

MICHAUX, in his North American Sylva, says of the *tree*, that he saw one *twenty-two feet six inches* in circumference, at five feet from the ground; and that he judged the tree to be *a hundred* and forty feet high. Of the WOOD Michaux says what every body in America knows; namely, that it is in colour of a pale yellow; that its grain is very fine; that the wood is both *light* and *strong*; that it is used in rafters, shingles, door panels, bedsteads, wainscoting, chair-bottoms, large bowls, and particularly, in all parts of America, in making the *panels of coaches* and other pleasure carriages; and, so much is this the case, that it is carried hundreds of miles to be used in those places, near to which it does not grow.

The wood admits of a *beautiful polish*, and is used for various purposes by cabinet-makers. Of these planks that I have, a single plank would make a kitchen-dresser, or table; a servants'-hall table; a slab for a dairy or a larder; fine things, I should think, for *cutting-boards*, *shop-boards*, counters, show-boards, or almost any thing, which requires a very large breadth of wood in one single, smooth piece. Being $2\frac{1}{2}$ inches thick, these planks are strong enough for any thing.

The price *for the whole parcel*, ONE SHILLING and THREE-PENCE A FOOT; for any quantity less than the whole, and exceeding a hundred feet, ONE

SHILLING AND SIXPENCE A FOOT; and for a single plank, ONE SHILLING AND NINEPENCE A FOOT. So that a plank, 14 feet long, and 3½ feet wide, which, with a couple of trestles, would make a table to dine *twenty people*, would cost only *four pounds five shillings*; it might be kept as clean as a marble slab, and with nearly as little trouble, and would last for many a life-time.

The planks are at *my house at Kensington*, where they may be seen, by *application to the gardener*, at any hour between four in the morning and five in the afternoon. There is the *mark* on each plank, expressing the *number of feet* which it contains. The marks were put on in America, and, therefore, are according to our old-fashioned English *kingly* measure, and not according to the grand and sublime "IMPERIAL MEASURE," which, being an "*improvement of the age*," produced by "*liberal principles*," the off-spring of the "*march of mind*," gauges (in defiance of Bedlam) ale, metes oysters, and ascertains the length and width of shirting, by the "beat of a *pendulum* in a "heat of sixty-two degrees of "Farenheit's Thermometer"!

## MARKETS.

Average Prices of CORN throughout ENGLAND, for the week ending May 25. ·

Per Quarter.

|  | s. | d. |  | s. | d. |
|---|---|---|---|---|---|
| Wheat .. | 58 | 0 | Rye .... | 40 | 9 |
| Barley .. | 40 | 2 | Beans ... | 49 | 11 |
| Oats .... | 29 | 0 | Pease ... | 48 | 11 |

Total Quantity of Corn returned as
Sold in the Maritime Districts, for
the week ended May 25.

|  | Qrs. |  | Qrs. |
|---|---|---|---|
| Wheat.. | 40,941 | Rye ..... | 257 |
| Barley .. | 5,117 | Beans ... | 1,216 |
| Oats ... | 9,025 | Pease .... | 47 |

*Corn Exchange, Mark Lane.*

Quantities and Prices of British
Corn, &c. sold and delivered in
this Market, during the week ended
Saturday, May 26.

|  | Qrs. | £. | s. | d. |  | s. | d. |
|---|---|---|---|---|---|---|---|
| Wheat.. | 5,534 | for 16,985 | 14 | 3 | Average, | 61 | 4 |
| Barley.. | 139 | .. | 286 | 5 | 6 .......... | 41 | 2 |
| Oats.. | 1,318 | .. | 2,129 | 19 | 3 .......... | 32 | 3 |
| Rye.... | 6 | .. | 10 | 15 | 4 ......... | 36 | 10 |
| Beans.. | 444 | .. | 1,115 | 0 | 3 .......... | 50 | 2 |
| Pease .. | 432 | .. | 1,031 | 3 | 8 ......... | 47 | 8 |

Friday, June 1.—There are this
week more moderate arrivals of all
kinds of Corn than for several weeks
past. Wheat remains in a dull state
at the terms last quoted. Barley
continues so scarce as to render the
prices nearly nominal. Beans and
Pease meet very few buyers at present. Oats of good quality fully
maintain the terms of Monday, but
there is not an extensive demand to-
day.

Monday, June 4.—The current
opinion in this market is, that the
additional clause introduced into the
Corn Bill will prove fatal to that
measure, unless it should be expunged in another stage of the proceedings; and as the supply of Wheat
is scanty, higher prices are asked for
that article, and all the Kentish samples were quickly cleared off at 2s. to
3s. per quarter, and most of the
Essex samples at 3s. per qr. advance
on the terms of this day se'nnight.

Barley and Beans are both so very
scarce as to render the prices almost
nominal. There are still several
samples of Pease (particularly White)
left, and they sell slowly at last quotations. There has been a good attendance of country buyers here to-
day, and they have purchased Oats,
but not with much freedom, the
prices, therefore, of this article remain as last quoted, with plenty of
Feed left unsold. There has been a
strong attempt again to advance the
top price of Flour, which, after some
opposition from the Flour Factors,
may be considered as established at
55s. per sack.

---

*Price on board Ship as under.*

Flour, per sack ......50s. — 55s.
—— Seconds ........44s. — 48s.
—— North Country ..42s. — 46s.

---

Price of Bread.—The price of the
4lb. Loaf is stated at 9d. by the
full-priced Bakers.

Account of Wheat, &c. arrived in the Port of London, from May 23 to June 2, both inclusive.

| | Qrs. | | Qrs. |
|---|---|---|---|
| Wheat .. | 3,413 | Tares .... | — |
| Barley .. | 135 | Linseed .. | 1,689 |
| Malt .... | 4,378 | Rapeseed. | — |
| Oats .... | 1,441 | Brank .. | 22 |
| Beans ... | 247 | Mustard.. | — |
| Flour .... | 5,572 | Flax .... | — |
| Rye.... | 8 | Hemp.... | 44 |
| Pease.... | 101 | Seeds ... | — |

Foreign.—Wheat, 290; Barley, 2,216; Oats, 7,838; Beans, 1,820 quarters.

Price of .Hops, per Cwt. in the Borough.

Monday, June 4.—The accounts from the plantations state, generally, a great increase of fly upon the lower grounds, while some of the higher and more exposed situations, the last two days, have rather decreased, owing to the high and cold winds; but the deposit already made is of that extent, that a few warm muggy days, with showers, will bring into life as great a quantity of lice as in 1823 and 1825, and probably may prove as destructive. Prices, owing to many holders being determined to realize for New, gave way 20s. to 30s.; but to-day a greater firmness is general.—Currency: Sussex pockets, 6l. 10s. to 7l. 15s.; Kent, 7l. 7s. to 8l. 10s. The sale to-morrow of about 1000 bags and pockets of Old, will show the confidence of. the trade; duty estimated at 55,000l. to 58,000l. Letters from Essex and Farnham, which ten days ago were clear, are now as much affected with fly as others; and from Worcester accounts are as bad, their duty doing at 6,000l.

*Maidstone,* May 31.—Our accounts are rather more favourable to-day, as the fly does not appear at present to have made that increase which many of the Planters expected, and in consequence the trade has been particularly dull, and several lots of both bags and pockets, although offered at low prices, have not been sold.

SMITHFIELD.

Monday, June 4.—The trade of this Market was very heavy on Friday, and prices fell; though not so much in Beef as in Mutton, which had an extraordinary drop. The former was lower by about 2d. a stone, and the latter 6d. to 8d. a stone. Lamb also experienced a considerable reduction. The fineness of the weather, and the supply, have this day combined to keep the market in a state of depression. Scot beasts are about 10s. a head worse than this day se'nnight; and large Beasts near £1. Polled Sheep are no higher than 4s. 8d.; nor are Downs above 5s., all out of the Wool. Lamb from 5s. to 6s., and the trade dull for every thing.

*Per Stone of 8 pounds (alive).*

| | s. | d. | s. | d. |
|---|---|---|---|---|
| Beef .... | 4 | 4 to | 5 | 4 |
| Mutton ... | 4 | 0 — | 5 | 0 |
| Veal .... | 5 | 0 — | 6 | 0 |
| Pork..... | 4 | 2 — | 4 | 8 |
| Lamb .... | 5 | 0 — | 6 | 0 |

| Beasts . . | 1,719 | Sheep .. | 20,030 |
|---|---|---|---|
| Calves... | 210 | Pigs ... | 161 |

NEWGATE, (same day.)

*Per Stone of 8 pounds (dead).*

| | s. | d. | s. | d. |
|---|---|---|---|---|
| Beef ..... | 3 | 8 to | 4 | 8 |
| Mutton ... | 3 | 8 — | 4 | 8 |
| Veal ..... | 3 | 8 — | 5 | 8 |
| Pork ..... | 4 | 0 — | 6 | 0 |
| Lamb .... | 4 | 8 — | 6 | 8 |

LEADENHALL, (same day.)

*Per Stone of 8 pounds (dead).*

| | s. | d. | s. | d. |
|---|---|---|---|---|
| Beef ... | 3 | 8 to | 4 | 8 |
| Mutton ... | 3 | 4 — | 4 | 6 |
| Veal .... | 3 | 4 — | 5 | 8 |
| Pork..... | 4 | 0 — | 5 | 8 |
| Lamb .... | 5 | 8 — | 6 | 8 |

## POTATOES.

### SPITALFIELDS, *per Ton.*

|  | L. s. | L. s. |
|---|---|---|
| Ox-Nobles | 3 10 to | 0 0 |
| Middlings | 2 5 — | 0 0 |
| Chats | 0 0 — | 0 0 |
| Common Red | 3 10 — | 0 0 |
| Onions, 0s. 0d.—0s. 0d. per bush. | | |

### BOROUGH, *per Ton.*

|  | L. s. | L. s. |
|---|---|---|
| Ox-Nobles | 3 10 to | 4 0 |
| Middlings | 2 0 — | 0 0 |
| Chats | 0 0 — | 0 0 |
| Common Red | 3 0 — | 0 0 |

## HAY and STRAW, per Load.

| Smithfield.— | Hay | 80s. to 115s. |
|---|---|---|
|  | Straw | 36s. to 42s. |
|  | Clover | 95s. to 140s. |
| St. James's.— | Hay | 80s. to 120s. |
|  | Straw | 36s. to 46s. |
|  | Clover | 105s. to 140s. |
| Whitechapel.— | Hay | 84s. to 115s. |
|  | Straw | 36s. to 42s. |
|  | Clover | 90s. to 135s. |

---

## AVERAGE PRICE OF CORN, sold in the Maritime Counties of England and Wales, for the Week ended May 25, 1827.

|  | Wheat. s. d. | Barley. s. d. | Oats. s. d. |
|---|---|---|---|
| London* | 62 0 | 40 10 | 33 2 |
| Essex | 59 10 | 38 10 | 29 10 |
| Kent | 58 4 | 40 1 | 31 8 |
| Sussex | 56 11 | 0 0 | 32 11 |
| Suffolk | 57 2 | 37 5 | 31 3 |
| Cambridgeshire | 56 10 | 36 5 | 26 8 |
| Norfolk | 56 4 | 37 1 | 26 6 |
| Lincolnshire | 57 3 | 40 2 | 26 0 |
| Yorkshire | 57 0 | 41 1 | 26 1 |
| Durham | 57 6 | 41 8 | 35 10 |
| Northumberland | 56 7 | 39 1 | 32 9 |
| Cumberland | 62 0 | 42 4 | 35 4 |
| Westmoreland | 65 0 | 43 8 | 41 0 |
| Lancashire | 64 0 | 0 0 | 33 0 |
| Cheshire | 63 2 | 0 0 | 35 1 |
| Gloucestershire | 57 3 | 42 0 | 40 1 |
| Somersetshire | 56 0 | 37 4 | 33 1 |
| Monmouthshire | 60 3 | 44 0 | 0 0 |
| Devonshire | 58 2 | 39 10 | 33 9 |
| Cornwall | 64 8 | 41 2 | 38 5 |
| Dorsetshire | 56 0 | 40 9 | 34 0 |
| Hampshire | 57 3 | 42 2 | 30 4 |
| North Wales | 67 9 | 46 6 | 36 6 |
| South Wales | 63 0 | 45 0 | 27 1 |

* The London Average is always that of the Week preceding.

*Liverpool*, May 29.—The demand for all sorts of Grain has been very limited during the week, and at our Corn Exchange this day the transactions were trifling. Wheat and Flour in bond, dull.

Imported into Liverpool, from May 22 to May 28, 1827, inclusive:—Wheat, 7,465; Barley, 998; Oats, 14,138; Rye, 400; Beans, 1,313; Pease, 84 quarters. Flour, 1,230 sacks, per 280 lbs.; Oatmeal, 301 packs, per 240 lbs.; American Flour, 300 barrels.

*Derby*, June 2.—Our Market this day was well attended by farmers and millers, and all sorts of Grain rather lower—Best Wheat, 58s. to 63s.; Barley, 38s. to 46s.; Oats, 30s. to 38s.; and Beans, 54s. to 62s. per eight bushels Imperial measure.

*Horncastle*, June 2.—Our Market this day was thinly attended. Prices nearly the same as last week.—Wheat, from 54s. to 57s.; Barley, 40s. to 44s.; Oats, 26s. to 34s.; Beans, 60s. to 61s.; and Rye from 38s. to 40s. per quarter.

*Ipswich*, June 2.—Our market to-day was very shortly supplied with all Grain. Prices were much the same as last week. Spring Corn in general seems almost entirely exhausted; scarcely any Beans; no Pease are to be seen, and only a sample or two of Barley, and 48s. was generally asked for them. Wheat sold at from 54s. to 63s. per quarter.

*Manchester*, June 2.—Our market to-day was well supplied with Corn of most descriptions, the finest qualities of which reached the prices of this day se'nnight; inferior descriptions nearly unsaleable. The transactions have been on a limited scale, not being such as to alter the currency of this day week. In Malt and Flour no alteration.

*Newcastle-upon-Tyne*, June 2.—We had a short supply of Wheat from the farmers this morning, and not having much from any other source, the millers gave readily last week's prices. Rye sells slowly at former prices. Nothing doing in Barley. We had a small supply of Oats from the farmers, but a good many samples from granary this morning, and the demand from the consumers being slack, very few sales were effected, although lower prices would have been taken by the sellers.

*Norwich*, June 2.—We had a tolerable good supply of Wheat to-day, and prices a little lower than last week.—Red, 52s. to 57s.; White to 60s.; Barley, only a few small parcels, at 36s. to 38s.; Oats, 28s. to 32s.; Beans, 43s. to 48s.; Pease, 44s. to 48s.; Boilers, to 50s. per quarter; and Flour, 41s. to 42s. per sack.

*Reading*, June 2.—We had a good supply of Wheat this day, which at the opening of the market met a heavy sale, and prices on the average were 1s. lower.—Towards the close, intelligence arriving that the Warehousing system had been materially altered, last night in the House of Lords, the market became more firm, and the growers held over for higher prices. There were only four parcels of Barley pitched, and these sold on rather better terms than last week. In Oats, Beans, and Pease, very little was done.

*Wakefield*, June 1.—We have again a large supply of Wheat to this day's market, and buyers not being disposed to purchase more than for their immediate wants, the trade has been very dull, and up to the close of the market not much business has been done: the rates obtained generally are the same as last week; in some instances rather lower prices have been taken. Oats are dull, and lower. Shelling is very heavy at 2s. per load cheaper.

## COUNTRY CATTLE AND MEAT MARKETS, &c.

*Horncastle*, June 2.—Beef, 9s. per stone of 14 lbs. ; Mutton, 6d. to 7d. ; Lamb 7d. to 8d.; and Veal, from 7d. to 8d. per lb.

*Manchester* Smithfield Market, May 30.—The 'supply of Sheep, Pigs, and Lambs, to this day's market continues to be large, but of Cattle and Calves it was small. Mutton fully supports the price of this day week, but the quantity sold was not equal to that day's sale. Grass being now plentiful, the drovers preferred waiting another week, rather than submit to less terms. The fat Beasts were taken off readily at an advance of ½d. per lb. on last week's rates. The price of Lamb being nearly that of Mutton, the demand was good at ½d. per lb. reduction from the price of this day se'nnight. In Veal and Pork no alteration.—Beef, 5d. to 8½d.; Mutton, 7d. to 8½d.; Lamb, 8d. to 9d.; Veal, 6d. to 7½d.; and Pork, 4d. to 5d. per lb., sinking offal.

At *Morpeth* Fair, May 30, there was a very short supply of Cattle, which sold readily, at an advance in price.—Beef, from 7s. 6d. to 8s. 6d.; Mutton, 7s. 3d. to 9s. 4d.; Lamb, 8s. 3d. to 9s. 6d. per stone, sinking offal.

*Norwich Castle Meadow*, June 2.—The supply of fat Cattle to-day was small, prices 8s. to 8s. 6d. per stone of 14 lbs., sinking offal : that of all the Store Stock was large; Scots, 4s. to 4s. 6d. per stone of what they will weigh when fat; Shorthorns, 3s. to 3s. 9d.; Cows and Calves and Home-breds, quite a flat sale. Pigs, hardly saleable, unless forward.—Meat: Beef, 7d. to 9d.; Veal, 6d. to 8d.; Mutton, 6d. to 7d.; Lamb, 7d.; and Pork, 6d. to 7½d. per lb.

# COBBETT'S WEEKLY REGISTER.

Vol. 62.—No. 12.]    LONDON, SATURDAY, June 16, 1827.    [Price 6d.

" But, if some event were to happen which would shake the Bo-
" roughmongers by *their own means;* some event which would make them
" stagger under *their own weight;* some event which would bring them
" *to a stand,* not knowing which way to turn themselves; then, indeed,
" they must give way. I could suppose many events, that would have
" operated thus; but, the event, which I was *sure* would be effectual, and
" which I was *sure* would, sooner or later, take place, was the blowing
" up, or, at least, the total discredit of the Funding system by *a failure
" in the means of paying the interest of the Debt* in FULL AND IN
" GOLD. It was, therefore, my opinion, that it was not prudent to urge
" on the cause of Reform to what might be called a *pitched battle* with its
" enemies, until those enemies were at war amongst themselves."——
REGISTER (No. 17, Vol. 32), JULY 26, 1817.

## BANK CIRCULAR.
### A MOST IMPORTANT SUBJECT!

*Fleet Street, 12th June, 1827.*

IT was, as notified in my last Register, my intention to address this present Register to LORD WESTMORELAND, and therein to tell him how the Lords ought to go to work to *shove out* Canning and his Crib-man (Burdett), and all that most motley crew, and how, also, to *preserve their own estates.* But, I must beg his Lordship to wait a bit; for, after the last Register went out of my hands, SIR JOHN WROTTESLEY, who is, observe, a *country-banker,* a dealer in that sort of manu_ facture, to which PROSPERITY RO_ BINSON gave so degrading a name; since the last Register went out of

Z

Printed and Published by WILLIAM COBBETT, No. 183, Fleet-street,
[ENTERED AT STATIONERS' HALL.]

my hands, this WROTTESLEY, this paper-money maker, has made a motion, in the House of Commons, relative to this BANK CIRCULAR, which, from the very first sight of it, I regarded, and pointed out, as a thing of great importance, it being manifestly a *feeler*, put forth by some person, or persons, with the approbation, if not at the suggestion, of more or less of the members both of the *Bank and the Government.* I called it a thing of "equivocal generation": one could not clearly trace it to any seed: but, I was satisfied, that it sprang from the above-mentioned ancient and most amiable partnership: so amiable and so full of affection, indeed, as to almost merit the epithet of *conjugal*; and, I am disposed to believe, that never were there man and wife more truly bone of bone and flesh of flesh, or, rather, so near to being these, as this most loving pair, *the Government and the Bank of England.*

I am, at the end of ten years from the time of writing and pub-lishing it, more firmly than ever fixed in the opinion, expressed in my Motto, that the workings of the DEBT, and that those workings alone, will bring the people into the enjoyment of their rights, and will restore them to something like a sufficiency of food and raiment: and, as I deem no public matter of any importance at all, when compared to the means of accomplishing such restoration, I always make a point of calling upon my readers to bestow special attention on every thing connected with the "*march*" of the DEBT and the PAPER-MONEY, leaving the "*march of mind*" and the "*improvements of the age*," to sublime geniuses like Sir Glory and the son of the Spinning Jenny.

Amongst the things of the sort here alluded to; amongst the symptoms of the system's approach towards dissolution, and, of course, of our advance towards a restoration to full bellies and good clothes; amongst these things, I have seen few of a more cheering aspect than this BANK CIRCULAR, of which I shall speak in detail by-and-by, when I have given an account of Wrottesley's *motion* as to this affair, and of the *confessions* and *opinions*, the promulgation of which it produced.

WROTTESLEY (who is a country-paper-money issuer, mind) was the man that first assailed Mr. JONES's gold-petition in July, 1825, and which petition most assuredly *hastened late panic* by several months. " Late panic" would have *come* without that petition, as apples will, at last, fall from a tree; but, a *shake* will bring them down before their time; and thus it was that Mr. JONES of Bristol worked on the paper-tree. In a case like this, a great part of the import of the words uttered depends upon the person who utters them. This Wrottesley is deeply interested in the perpetuating of the circulation of country bank paper. I am going to notice several parts of his speech, and to offer remarks

on them as I proceed; but, throughout the whole, the reader will be so good as to bear in mind that the individual on the report of whose speech we are going to remark, is a paper-money man; a paper-money-monger, or dealer, the word *monger*, meaning *dealer;* a monger in currency; a rival in office with the King, who has a great many of these money-makers and mongers for his rivals; upon which circumstance, both Canning and Huskisson, in about six weeks after I had pointed it out to them in the Register, most ostentatiously remarked in the House of Commons. Upon the present occasion, this Wrottesley, who is a Member of Parliament for some place in the midland counties, this individual, who, in the debate upon Jones's petition, suggested to Mr. Hume that it might be the work of some " malignant individual," enemy of the prosperity of the country; this individual, Wrottesley, did, according to the report in the Morning Chronicle, con-

clude his speech upon this occasion, with a motion for " The ap-
" pointment of a Select Committee
" to inquire whether the Gover-
" nors and Directors of the Bank
" of England, or any of that
" Body, had circulated through
" the country a Letter tending to
" *cast doubts on the solidity of*
" *Private Bank Paper, and*
" *thereby to injure the commer-*
" *cial, manufacturing, and agri-*
" *cultural interests of the*
" *country."*

I shall have to remark, by-
and-bye, upon the curious doctrine contained in this motion ; I
shall have to ask of this Wrottesley, how the devil it can be, that
the manufacturing classes must of
necessity " *depend for their*
*wages,"* upon a parcel of little
bits of extremely thin and often
not less dirty paper, which are,
a whole cart-load of them, intrinsically worth not one single
straw, except as manure ; they
being too flimsy, even to light a
pipe with, and, in the capacity
of manure, the cart-load would

certainly not be equal to one single shovelful of the meanest of
horse-dung. The report informs
us that this profound maker of paper-money began his speech in
the following manner.

" Sir *J. Wrottesley* rose, in pur-
" suance of the notice he had given,
" to move for the production of the
" Letter relative to advances from
" the Bank of England to country
" bankers. Perhaps the House would
" think he ought to be satisfied with
" the unequivocal denial of one of
" the Directors of the Bank, that the
" Letter in question had *originated*
" *with their body.* He (Sir J. Wrot-
" tesley) would have abandoned his
" motion, but it appeared to him
" that the Letter was intimately con-
" nected with many other circum-
" stances, which induced him to be-
" lieve, that, although it had ap-
" peared without the *positive sanction*
" of the Bank Directors, it had pro-
" ceeded from, and was the result of,
" *many consultations which those Di-*
" *rectors had had upon the subject.*
" He was inclined to believe that the
" Letter was written and circulated
" *by the direction of the Bank.* He
" was not prepared to state any posi-
" tive facts conclusive of the point ;
" but from many circumstances
" communicated to him from vari-
" ous parts of the country, he had
" every reason to suppose *that some*
" *one gentleman who was a Director*

" *of the Bank,* had shown the Letter
" to a variety of persons, asking their
" opinion; and it had thus gone fur-
" ther than it was intended, until it
" had at length been communicated
" to the public, through the medium
" of the newspapers. He trusted the
" House would be prevailed upon to
" look into the subject. At a mo-
" ment when it had been stated in
" that House that there was a gra-
" dual increase of employment of
" the capital and industry of all
" classes, he could not conceive a
" more mischievous contrivance than
" a Letter, which should. be pub-
" lished with the effect of *bringing*
" *into discredit those establishments*
" *upon which the manufacturing classes*
" *must necessarily depend for wages,*
" and all their current advances."

I shall notice, when I come
to the speech of the Director,
PEARSE, what is here said about
the authenticity of the document;
about the origin of it, and about
the manner in which it became
public. In this place, I wish to
direct the reader's attention to
what this paper-money man is
pleased to assert, respecting the
*tendency* of the Circular Letter in
question. He says, that its effect must be, " to bring into
" discredit those establishments,

" upon which the manufacturing
" classes *must necessarily depend*
" *for wages, and all their current*
" *advances."* What a monstrous
idea is this! Or, what a monstrous
state of things is that in which we
are! Here are a parcel of people
at work, making goods for sale;
and is it absolutely necessary that
there should be somebody to make
paper-money for the purpose of
paying them wages for their work?
Surely, the cloth that is made by
the clothier; the goods that are
shipped by the merchant; surely
these will bring the parties something in return, without their going to a man that makes paper-
money! Neither does he except
the farmer, whom he includes
amongst those who are to be injured by doubts being cast on the
solidity of private bank-paper!
What! is the bushel of wheat,
then, good for nothing; is the fat
hog, the milch-cow, the rich ox
and the team of horses; are the
quarters of wheat and of barley
possessed of no intrinsic value;
and, are they to fetch nothing to

the producer; is the worth of them by no means to be obtained by him, except with the assistance and through the instrumentality, solely, of bits of paper, a whole bushel of which is not equal in value to a single barley-corn! Really, these people seem to pore over columns of calculations and to read or listen to gibberish about what they call finance; they seem to get enveloped in fallacies and a sort of mystical political romancing, introduced and taught by the Scotch at the instigation of the devil; they seem to get enveloped and entangled in this sort of way, till they have completely lost sight of common sense, and have been divested of all the perceptions and faculties given by God for the guidance of man. As in the case of poor Job, the devil of "political economy," as the philosophers call it, seems to have been let loose upon this race of paper-money men. How long he is to be allowed to torment them, and through them this afflicted country, it would be pre-

sumption to attempt even to guess; but every man of common sense will agree that some such tortuous devil as this must have been allowed to have his swing over a community, where it can be believed, where the idea can be maintained by overt speech, that little bits of paper intrinsically worthless, are indispensably necessary to procure due compensation for his labour to the maker of a coat or to the rearer of a pig. The truth is, that men who talk in this sort of way have been so long accustomed to this species of fiction, that their minds seem incapable of returning to those dictates of common sense, which, generally speaking, come naturally to all men. I should like to put it to this Wrottesley, whether he believe, whether he really and seriously believe that, if the whole of the paper-money were to be destroyed by fire to-night, and if there were never to be any more; whether, in this case, we should cease to wear coats and cease to eat! His statement would go

this length; for, if the manufacturing classes must necessarily
depend upon the country bankers
for food, in return for the goods
that they make; if they must of
necessity be in this state of dependence, a total destruction of
the paper must be a total destruction of the people. Wrottesley
will say, that he does not mean to
go this length. Will he be so
good, then, as to tell us where he
means to stop? If he stop short
of this, he must talk with us a
little about the quantity of the
paper; and then he must point
out to us, if he can, what power
there is, anywhere at present, to
*regulate this quantity*, which, as
things now stand, may be puffed
up to the size of a mountain, or
reduced to that of a mole-hill, at
the sole will and pleasure of those
whose profit or whose security,
whose self-interest, at any rate,
whose mere private interests, are
to be consulted in a matter, which,
according to his own showing, is
of such immense importance to
the people at large.

This paper-money maker did
not, it appears, confine himself,
upon this occasion, to the subject
of the motion which he appears
to have made. He took occasion,
as the report tells us, to complain
of the general desire of the Bank
of England to profit by the ruin
of the country-bankers; to complain of the Bill of last year, for
putting an end to the issue of one-
pound notes; and to give a sort
of history of this one-pound note
affair, going back so far as the
period of the first Bank restriction.
What he said upon these topics,
which are all of importance, in
themselves, is very well worthy
of the attention of my readers;
for, we may be perfectly assured,
that he has here spoken the sentiments of the whole body of the
paper-money makers, from one
end of the kingdom to the other.
Before I conclude this article, I
shall have to introduce a famous
recent Circular Letter of that indefatigable Privy Councillor and
Scotch feelosofer, Sir JOHN SIN-
CLAIR; but, at present, I will

confine myself to the speech of our worthy Warwickshire (I believe it is) maker of paper-money; and, again I request my readers to pay attention to the words; not for the sake of the man, but for the sake of the subject.

"He was induced, moreover, to "bring forward this measure, because "the objectionable conduct of the "Bank of England was not confined "to this one circumstance. There "had been a rooted determination "upon the part of that body to keep "up their circulation to what it had "been previously to the peace. They "had found it difficult to accomplish "that object. It was, in fact, impos- "sible; and because they had not "been able to keep up the same cir- "culation, and could not realise the "profits they had previously made, "they endeavoured to bring the "country banks into discredit, wish- "ing to build their *own profits upon the* "*foundation of the ruin of others.* "This was a most material part of "the transactions of the Bank of "England. In the last Session of "the recent Parliament, he had taken "an opportunity of addressing the "House upon this subject; but it "was then considered that the coun- "try establishments were not to "have the support that all other in- "terests uniformly enjoyed. *An* "*attack* was made upon them last "year, the object of which was to "withdraw from them the power of

"issuing *one-pound notes.* As he "alluded to this subject, it was only "fair to state upon what grounds "these notes had been first intro- "duced. Originally, the Country "Bankers had no right to expect "that such an indulgence would be "granted to them. Previously to "1797, they had issued nothing less "than five pound notes, and they "had not expected to be called upon "to issue any of a smaller amount. "They had made these issues by *no* "*solicitation* of their own; they pro- "ceeded entirely from the *miscon-* "*duct of the Bank of England.* That "misconduct had brought upon the "Bank the necessity of restraining "their issues, and the Country Bank- "ers had, therefore, been obliged to "issue their small notes. At that "period, they had not conceived that "they had any claim or right to con- "tinue such issues; but the Act of "Parliament was passed to allow "them to proceed in issuing small "notes, upon the ground that the "Bank of England continued their "restrictions. At the expiration of "the war, the Country Bankers na- "turally expected to be called upon "for payment of their one-pound "notes in cash; but the restrictions "still continued, and were not re- "moved until after the peace. At "the commencement of the Session "of 1822, the late Lord Londonderry "induced the House to agree to many "very extraordinary changes. Agri- "cultural distress then prevailed to

"a great extent, and in many coun-
" ties the agriculturists met and re-
" presented their grievances to the
" House in Petitions. To so great
" an extent had that distress pro-
" ceeded, that it was found necessary
" to lend to these Petitioners the
" redress they sought, and to extend
" to the agricultural 'interests every
" protection for which they asked.
" The issue of the one-pound notes
" by the Country Bankers did not
" originate from their own sugges-
" tions. Let the House look at the
" speech of Londonderry. They
" would find that amongst the dif-
" ferent measures which he proposed
" for the relief of Agricultural dis-
" tress, that on which he laid the
" greatest stress, was the Country
" Bankers continuing for ten years
" to 'issue one-pound notes. If the
" Country Bankers were *prepared to
" give up these notes,* and were *called
" upon not to do so,* in order to concur
" with the measures proposed by the
" Administration for the relief of
" agricultural distress, he would ask
" if it was fair or just to call upon
" them to withdraw their notes at a
" moment when there existed a hos-
" tile spirit against them, as well as
" a degree of doubt as to their soli-
" dity and credit, which had never
" existed at any former period ?"

To that which our manufacturer
of paper-money here says about
the greediness of the Bank of
England, I pay little attention.

That "two of a trade can never
agree" is an old proverb; and, I
have often compared the mother-
bank and her litter to an old sow
and her numerous farrow of pigs;
and all agricultural people know
very well how bitter the old devil
is as soon as the young ones begin
to lug her too hard: first she
knocks them about with her snout,
and, if they be not pretty soon
taken away, she sticks her tusks
into them with very little ceremony; if they do not know when
to cease sucking, she knows when
it is high time to cease letting
down her milk; and, really, this
does seem to be pretty much the
state in which the mother-bank
and her young ones are at this
moment.

Sir John, our paper-money-
making Baronet, appears to have
sticking in his stomach, the Bill
that was passed last year, which,
if Mr. Canning, or his successor,
should have the pluck to stick to
it, will totally extinguish the one-
pound notes on the fifth of April
after the next. The paper-money-
making Baronet here enters into
the history of the one-pound country bank-notes, the origin of which
he traces to the " misconduct of
the Bank of England." That is
to say, he gives us to understand,
that there never would have been

any country one-pound notes, if
Pitt had not been pushed to
sanction the making of one-pound
Bank of England notes; therefore, says Sir John, we did not
make country one-pound notes in
consequence of any *solicitations*
of our own. No, 'Squire, there
were, certainly, no solicitations
on the part of the country manufacturers of paper-money; but,
at the same time, I beg you to
remark, that the "misconduct,"
as you call it, of the Bank of
England, arose, in great part,
from the monstrous issues of the
country-bankers, upon which she
had no check; and, as to "*solicitations*" on your part, to be permitted to issue one-pound notes,
there was no occasion for solicitations, any more than there is
for a cow to solicit to go into a
clover-field when she is loose in a
barren lane and sees the gate of
the clover-field open before her.
The law, in consequence of which
you began to make the one-pound
notes, held out no *solicitation to
you to do so;* it did not mention
you at all; it made a gap in the
hedge of the clover-field; it
flung the gate open; but it neither
drove you nor invited you to get
over the one or to enter at the
other. The making of the one-
pound notes was your own act

and deed; it was your own
choice; and now hear something
which you appear to have forgotten, and that is this: that no
country bank-note was protected
by law, until, *at the solicitation*
*of country bankers*, the country
bank - notes became protected
against demand of payment in
gold; and, when you are reproach-
ing the Bank of England; when
you are talking thus slightingly
and haughtily of the Bank of England; when the ungrateful pro-
geny thus turns round upon the
poor old mother, let them recollect, and let them have the justice
to acknowledge, that, in order to
protect themselves against demands in the King's coin; in
order to protect their own notes
against such demands, they *obtained an Act of Parliament to
enable them to tender Bank of
England notes in payment of their
own notes;* thus, returning to the
homestead and taking shelter under the old belly from which they
had drawn their nourishment in
their infant state. Nay, still more
flagrant the ingratitude becomes,
when we recollect that only just
fifteen months have passed over
our heads since these young ones
made a whining and a squeaking
enough to set the teeth of a
ploughman on edge, in order to

obtain from the Parliament the power of paying, even at that time, their own notes in notes of the Bank of England! That virtuous and enlightened body, thanks to them from me from the bottom of my heart, rejected the application. But, after all this, the country bankers continued, in many instances, as petitions presented to the Parliament will show, to refuse to pay their own notes, *except in notes of the Bank of England*.

Pretty decent is it, then, in this paper-money-making 'Squire, to speak of the Bank of England as he is here reported to have spoken of her. She has a deal to answer for, to be sure, as towards the nation; but, as a mother, she has been a good one, and one does not like to see her treated in this sort of way; if we give to Satan his due, surely we may give her due to an old creature like this, who, whatever she may be, certainly is not quite so bad as Satan.

It is curious enough to observe the turn which our Warwickshire 'Squire gives to the affair of the Small-note Bill of 1822. He says, that the Small - note Bill was passed in order to relieve the agricultural distress of that day; that is to say, it was passed with a view of raising prices, putting money into the pockets of the landlords, keeping it out of the pockets of the fund-lords and other tax-eaters, and these by the means of a vast increase of a quantity of paper-money. The country-bankers were, as the law then stood, to cease making one-pound notes on the first day of the next month of June; but, in order to prevent prices from falling down to the money mark, the Small-note Bill was passed in the month of July previous to that month of May. Sir John says, in alluding to this transaction: " If the country-bankers were prepared to give up these notes, and were " CALLED UPON NOT TO " DO SO, in order to concur with " the measures proposed by the " administration for the relief of the " agricultural distress, he would " ask if it was FAIR or JUST " to call upon them to withdraw " their notes, as by the Act of " last year !" I should say, that, taking the paper-'Squire at his word, it was *perfectly fair and just*; at a time when the breaking of the country-bankers had left so many thousands of families with, as the French call it, nothing but their eyes to cry with, unless, indeed, we count for something, the ample possession of what Prosperity Robinson justly denominated "worthless rags." I should say, that, upon his own showing, this Act was perfectly fair and just; and, if the measure were not a measure of the Parliament, I should call it a measure criminally indulgent towards the country-bankers, whose good was by this Act made paramount to the good of the nation. But, if I should say this, *taking the paper-money man at his word*, what shall I say when I revert to the real facts of the case? These facts are, that, during the winter of 1802, there were repeated meetings, in London, of the country bankers coming from all parts of the kingdom, and, that the object of these meetings was to prevail upon the Ministers to give a great *extension to the period for the issuing of one-pound notes by those bankers*. This extension was at last agreed to at the time that we have just seen; and, to the shame of those country bankers, who reproached the Bank of England with greediness of gain, be it remembered that, by the same Act, she obtained a right to continue, for ten years, to issue one-pound notes; that she laudably abstained from resorting to this source of profit; that she never issued a single one-pound note, until, in January 1826, she

was absolutely compelled to do it, to put a stop to the devastation which had been set sweeping over the country by the one-pound notes of these very country bankers; that is to say, by their having eagerly taken advantage of a permission, of which she had never attempted to avail herself. She has now stopped her issues or re-issues of one-pound notes again; and it does appear to be quite monstrous to abuse her on account of a project (visionary enough, I allow) but the object of which evidently is, to prevent a return of that sweeping devastation which she was called upon, only sixteen months ago, to prevent; aye, and that, too, pretty much at her own loss.

The remainder of the speech is of less importance; but there are some parts of it which will be worth remembering, and particularly the part with which the paragraph that I am about to quote concludes.

" If the object of the proposal were
" to regulate the Paper Currency, it
" must be considered as the transac-
" tion of the Bank itself. The mass
" of paper originated from the Bank
" itself. If the Circular related to
" any panic, the first intimation of
" such panic proceeded from the
" President of the Board of Trade.

" In 1821, the President of the
" Board of Trade had given a caution
" to the Bank as to the way in which
" they were going on with respect
" to their issues. The Bank were
" obliged to bring their Exchequer
" Bills into the market, and the con-
" sequence was a general panic and
" dismay in the public mind ; every
" person who held paper, of whatever
" description, became anxious to
" turn it into specie. The Bank
" Directors now alluded to the de-
" mands made upon them by the
" Country Banks, at that period of
" public alarm and distrust, as the
" ground of their conduct. He (Sir
" John Wrottesley) remembered tell-
" ing the late Chancellor of the Ex-
" chequer (now Lord Goderich) at
" that period, to take care how he
" issued Exchequer Bills, as in the
" event of any panic which might be
" caused by a variety of unforeseen
" circumstances, the Unfunded Debt
" would be materially affected, and
" ought therefore to be kept down.
" The Honourable Baronet here read
" an extract from the Budget speech
" made by the Chancellor of the Ex-
" chequer last year, relative to the
" prospective intention (as we under-
" stood him) of applying the Sinking
" Fund to the reduction of the Un-
" funded as well as of the Funded
" Debt. So long as the Bank con-
" tinued to be the holder of Exche-
" quer Bills—so long as it continued
" to make advances to Government
" upon such securities—so long

" would the Country Bankers and the
" money market generally be subject
" to panic and alarm. It was not
" his intention to suggest any plan
" in opposition to the temporary
" measure about to be resorted to by
" the present Chancellor of the Ex-
" chequer in aid of the public reve-
" nue. On the contrary, he thought
" that the best mode of making up the
" deficiency, under existing circum-
" stances, was by an issue of Ex-
" chequer Bills [hear, hear !]. But
" he maintained, that the present
" state of the Unfunded Debt was
" one which ought not to continue
" for any length of time. The Bank
" of England ought to be in such a
" situation as to be able at once to
" meet all demands upon them. They
" ought to be able to do that which
" they were pledged to on the face
" of an instrument which he hoped
" every gentleman who heard him,
" had in his pocket;—they ought
" to be ready to fulfil the simple
" promise on the face of their own
" note, namely, " I promise to pay
" on demand, so and so." If the
" Bank adhered to a few practical
" facts—if they took care to know
" at all times the amount of their
" notes in circulation, and also to
" keep in their possession a suffi-
" cient quantity of specie to meet
" any sudden and extensive demand
" upon them, he would venture to
" say that that establishment would
" stand upon a much more respect-
" able footing than it did at present.

" But the fact was, that the Bank
" was so extensively connected with
" the Government, that it felt an
" itching to have the management
" of the affairs of every body else.
" He admitted, that no men were
" more fit than the Bank Directors
" to conduct their own affairs ; but
" when they undertook to conduct
" the business of the country in ge-
" neral, he must take leave to ob-
" serve, that they did not display
" that general enlightenment which
" would qualify them for such a task.
" He was ready to admit that the
" Bank of England was the most
" respectable Corporation in the
" world ; but still he should object
" to their possessing such extensive
" powers as were contemplated by
" that letter which had caused such
" alarm in the minds of Country
" Bankers, and of the country in
" general. No other country in the
" world had ever attempted to anti-
" cipate its resources to the extent
" that England had done; and
" therefore sudden fluctuations, and
" alarms caused by other circum-
" stances, might, if proper care was
" not taken, be productive of the
" most disastrous and ruinous con-
" sequences. The property of the
" country consisting of land, manu-
" factures, and commerce, would it
" not be better that the paper-cur-
" rency of the country should de-
" pend upon many Corporations, ra-
" ther than upon one ? He should
" like to hear the sentiments of the
" Country Gentlemen upon this

" point, publicly declared. It was
" generally known that the Bank, by
" its power over the paper-currency
" of the country, had the means of
" increasing or decreasing property,
" to the amount of from 25 to 30
" per cent. There were many in-
" stances of persons who had bought
" estates, having been suddenly
" ruined by such sudden fluctuations.
" Looking to the serious events
" which had recently taken place—
" looking to the general panic which
" pervaded the kingdom—he would
" ask the House, whether they were
" prepared to throw the whole cur-
" rency into the hands of the Bank,
" and thereby give a power of alter-
" ing the value of property, and of
" checking and impeding the pro-
" gress of the commerce and manu-
" factures of the country, to be ex-
" ercised by these twenty-four Di-
" rectors at their pleasure ? "

These concluding words contain very good reasons for putting
an end to the paper-money altogether. I defy this paper-money
merchant to show that the Bank
of England possesses any power
over prices, which is not possessed
in a more dangerous degree by
the country banks. They can do
just as much in this way as the
Bank of England itself can ; and,
while, as to every evil effect, their
paper is equal to hers, there is
one good belonging to hers which
theirs has not ; namely, that it is

not, at any hour, liable to become worth not a straw. After this speech of Sir John Wrottesley, Mr. Pearse, who is, I believe, the Deputy Governor of the Bank, is reported to have stated, but in so *low a tone* as to be hardly audible in the gallery, " that the " Letter in question had been " drawn up by a Bank Director, " as a plan for regulating the " paper circulation of the coun- " try; that it had been submitted " by him to some friends whose " opinions he was anxious to ob- " tain; that the Director, not " wishing to part with the origi- " nal, had got about a dozen co- " pies of it struck off at his own ex- " pense for the use of his friends; " and that in this 'manner the let- " ter found its way into the public " newspapers; but that the letter " had never been submitted to the " Governor or Directors as a body, " in any shape; and that they " were in no way whatever privy " or consenting to its being drawn " up or put into circulation. The " Hon. Member added, that no " such plan had ever been dis- " cussed or contemplated by the " Bank Directors [hear, hear!]." —After this, the report says, that Mr. Canning, in a *low tone*, " observed, that, after the clear " and satisfactory explanation gi-

" ven by the Honourable Direc- " tor, there only remained one " observation for him to make— " namely, that his Majesty's Mi- " nisters had never, in any man- " ner, been consulted, or had in " any way given advice, upon the " letter in question."—After this, Mr. Maberly complained of the Bank Directors for not having publicly disclaimed the letter in question, and said that the Direc- tor who had drawn up the letter had acted very ill. After this, the report of the debate proceeds as follows; and every word of it is worthy of the best attention of my readers. Mr. Baring, two Mem- bers whose names are not men- tioned, Lord Milton and Mr. Hume are the speakers; for Sir Henry Parnell is much too profound on these matters for a man like me ever to be able to make top or tail of what he says. What was said by the others is worthy of great attention; and, my readers may be well assured, that this is by no means the last that will be heard of this matter.

" Mr. *Baring* defended the gen- " tleman who had written the Let- " ter, and thought he had been " *hardly dealt with* by his Honour- " able Friend near him. He (Mr. " Baring) thought the *Letter a most* " *ingenious one*, and well *worthy the*

" attention of every gentleman who
" thought proper·to turn his mind
" to the subject.

" An Hon. Member, whose name
" we could not learn, said, that be-
" ing connected with a country bank,
" he was anxious that some such
" plan as that recommended in the
" Letter in question should be adopt-
" ed—namely, that Bank of Eng-
" land paper should be substituted
" throughout the country for local
" notes.

" Sir H. Parnell objected to the
" plan proposed in this Letter, as it
" would be the effect of giving the
" Bank of England the power of
" committing greater errors than it
" had already done, by giving it more
" extensive command over the cir-
" culation of the country. Means
" of a different description might be
" taken to get rid of private banks,
" or the greater number of them.
" For instance, the establishment of
" Joint Stock Companies (giving
" proper security) would have this
" effect, and would prevent fluctua-
" tions in the currency.

" Lord Milton observed, that the
" difficulties under which the coun-
" try laboured last year had not yet
" been got rid of, and he hoped that
" no more tampering with the cur-
" rency would take place until the
" affairs of the country were placed
" upon a more steady footing.

" A Member from under the Gal-
" lery, whose name we could not
" learn, said, that the monetary sys-

" tem of the country was full of
" danger and difficulty, and ought to
" occupy the prompt and serious
" attention of the Legislature.

" Mr. Hume said that the assertion
" of the Honourable Director (Mr.
" Pearse), that the Bank Directors
" always conducted their operations
" with a view to the public benefit,
" and not to their own interests,
" ought to be taken with some small
" share of allowance. For himself,
" he thought that they attended
" pretty well to their own interests:
" He protested against giving to the
" Bank of England any further con-
" trol over the interests of the
" country. If benefit was to be
" derived by the currency, let it
" be derived by a National Bank, in
" the establishment of which, the
" Chancellor of the Exchequer could
" find no difficulty. What confidence
" could be placed in the management
" or resources of the Bank of Eng-
" land? They were pledged to pro-
" vide specie for their paper issues;
" yet, what was the fact? *They lent*
" *the whole of their capital to Govern-*
" *ment, and raised money,—how?* By
" the issue of from 19,000,000l. to
" 23,000,000l. of paper, of which
" sum, no less than 13,000,000l. *in*
" *addition to the whole of their capital,*
" *was also lent to Government.* [Hear,
" hear, hear!] What confidence, he
" asked, could be placed in an esta-
" blishment which acted in this
" manner? By a National Bank,
" established upon sound principles,

" the country would be benefitted in
" the instance of Exchequer Bills to
" the amount of many millions a
" year, while, from the taxes being
" regularly paid in, the extent of any
" over-issue could be always ascer-
" tained with the greatest certainty.
" Whenever Exchequer Bills at the
" present moment came to a dis-
" count, they were always paid in in-
" stantly to the Exchequer on account
" of taxes. This was a method by which
" the over-issues could be ascer-
" tained, and in the same manner the
" payment of the taxes in the issues
" of a National Bank, would regulate
" the amount of paper which ought
" to be afloat in the country. Go-
" vernment would, at the same time,
" by a Bank under its own manage-
" ment, save all the profits which
" now went to fill the coffers of the
" Bank of England. The Honourable
" Member, after some other obser-
" vations to the same effect, con-
" cluded by recommending the Right
" Hon. Gentleman (the Chancellor
" of the Exchequer) to get rid of the
" Bank and its Directors altogether,
" and save the Government from the
" expense of enormous sums paid for
" managing its affairs, as well as the
" country from all the ruinous fluc-
" tuations in the value of property,
" produced by over-issues of paper."

If I had been proprietor of this
newspaper, the reporter of this
debate never should have reported
another for me. Here is " a Mem-

" ber from under the gallery"
stating that *the money system of
the country is full of danger and
difficulty.* Here is another Member who is connected with a country bank, who is anxious that *some
such plan as that recommended in
the letter in question, should be
adopted !* It would have been of
the greatest importance to ascertain the *names* of those Members ;
but, alas ! the reporter *could not
learn their names.* If, for instance,
one of them had been Mr. Hudson
Gurney, as it very likely was, how
different would have been the
effect upon the minds of readers
in general, from the effect which
is now produced on their minds!
These are words of infinite importance ; and they appear to be
thought nothing of by these reporters, who are generally so careful to note down with correctness
every effusion of folly and of
emptiness which comes forth in
the shape of a joke or a sarcasm.
However, the reporter has given
us the name of Mr. BARING, and
has told us that Mr. Baring said
that the gentleman who had written this famous letter had been
hardly dealt with by his Honourable Friend (Mr. Maberly) ; that
he, Mr. Baring, thought the letter
*a most ingenious one,* and well
*worthy the attention* of every gen-

2 A

tleman who turned his mind to the subject. This is quite enough to convince every intelligent reader, or, at least, quite enough to induce him to believe, pretty confidently, that Mr. Baring not only knew the author of the letter; but, had seen the letter before it was published; had approved of its contents, and also approved of its being promulgated. This, I think, is not at all a straining of suspicion. In short, every one must be convinced of the facts. Let us, then, see a little, what are the contents of this letter. The letter contains a project for the putting an end to the making of paper-money (in England and Wales); to the putting an end to the making of any paper-money whatever, *except by the Bank of England herself.* The letter has been inserted in the Register of the second day of this present month of June. It will be useful for the reader to refer to the whole of it; but, it may be sufficient here just to state its substance. It proposes, then, that no body, no person or body of persons, shall issue paper-money, except the Bank of England; it proposes to make the present country-bankers a sort of *agents* for circulating the Bank paper-money. It proposes to give them a certain per centage upon the paper-money issued by them; they *giving security* to the mother-bank for responsibility; or, to use another word, for repayment to her, and for due payment in gold, if called upon, to the holders of the notes which they circulate. This is the substance of the project; and the Circular Letter represents such project as absolutely necessary to prevent the recurrence of panics; that is to say, to prevent a blowing-up of the paper-money and of the whole system.

I have now to notice the very remarkable counter-project of Mr. HUME. This gentlemen, when once he gets on the scent of *profits*, pushes right on through bush and through briars, without being diverted by collateral scents or sounds. The Bank, or at least, the Director who wrote this letter, had spoken to the country bankers of *profits, of sharing in profits.* "Ah ha!" says Mr. Hume; "'gad! I'll get these *profits for the nation!*" And, to work he sets, recommending to our new and most profound Minister, to set up a national bank; *to get rid of the Bank and its Directors altogether;* "to save the Government "the expense of the enormous "sum paid for managing its "affairs"; and to make the currency of the country permanent and of solid value ; to free it from all liability to fluctuations ; and to make property once more fixed and for ever secure!

How various, oh, Folly! is the taste of thy votaries! Yet, among all this variety, strange to relate, no one ever seems to approach towards an idea of the solidity of coin. Gold, which, in every language in the world, is a word illustrative of weight, security, value, solidity, and of every thing else that has permanency and safety in view ; this word gold seems to be shunned by thy votaries, as the light of the sun is shunned by the toad and the slug. When Mr. Hume had got back so far as the nation's issuing its own money ; when he had got so far as to want Mr. Canning to have a national press to make the nation's money at, was not it strange that he could not lift up his eyes only about eighteen inches, and see the venerable TIERNEY, that veteran politician, that new man of the Mint, sitting cheek by jowl with the reformer, Burdett, filling an office, the object of which is, to supply the nation with the King's golden coin! And was it not strange that this venerable veteran, did not call out across the House, to the place where he so lately sat himself, and remind his late honourable friend, that it was at his shop that the true money was to be had? However, this project of Mr. Hume is only one more proof, that nothing is so hideous to the sight of all men of all parties in that place; nothing so hideous as the thought of returning to gold. Gold is the touch-stone of the system. Without gold there is not a moment of safety ; and, the presence of gold drives the system into everlasting oblivion. None of them dare face the gold. You always hear them talking about different sorts of paper-money ; how to manage the paper-money ; how to make our situation safe with paper-money.; how to have nothing but paper-money; and, yet, to have no panics, late or present. The devil of all the rest of the world is black : yellow is the colour of the devil of these politicians.

It is impossible not to perceive that the Bank of England paper is, in fact, the paper of the Government, though it is not so in mere appearance. Mr. Hume himself says, that the Bank has *lent the whole of its capital to the Government; and that it has issued thirteen millions of paper in addition to that whole!* Let me now, before I conclude, go to the debate of Friday last, the 8th

June, and take from that debate the reported speech of Mr. MA-BERLY. These are words deeply interesting to us. We never can have reform, Englishmen never can be well off; they always must be miserable, as long as this system of funding and paper-money shall continue. Our two descriptions of enemies must come to an open contest before either will listen to our propositions for a just and constitutional reform. This Mr. Maberly is a great "*financier*." Be he what he may, however, in reality, he is THERE, and, in all human probability, he will have a great hand in the famous "*Finance Committee*," which all accounts tell us is to sit next year. Let us, therefore, hear what Mr. Maberly said in this last-mentioned debate, and, particularly, what he said on the subject of a *national bank*, or some such establishment as that pointed out by Mr. Hume. We shall find, that he spoke twice upon this occasion, and that Mr. Hume also spoke. The whole is short and pithy, and I shall insert it as it stands in the report, begging my readers to pay great attention to the words which I have put in *italic* characters.

"Mr. *Maberly* wished to take this "opportunity of making a few re-

"marks on the subject of Finance, "and commenced by referring to the "promised *appointment of a Commit-*"*tee early in the next Session*. On *this* "*account* he had *abandoned various* "*motions* of which he had given "notice, and he thought that he "could not have shown greater "courtesy to the Right Hon. Gen-"tleman at the head of his Majesty's "councils. To the Sinking Fund he "was desirous of calling the atten-"tion of the Right Hon. Gentle-"man, because he had himself, re-"cently referred to it in his annual "statement, which was distinguish-"ed by its fairness, and which ra-"ther afforded an unfavourable than "a too favourable view of the "finances of the kingdom. The "Right Hon. Gentleman had not, "indeed, distinctly pledged himself "to any given amount for a Sinking "Fund, but he had thrown out a "suggestion, that with an expendi-"ture of fifty millions, a Sinking "Fund of five millions did not seem "too much. He (Mr. Maberly) "contended, from the practice of "late years, when there had, in "fact, been little or no Sinking "Fund, that it was not necessary in "order to maintain public credit. "At all events, it ought not to re-"quire taxation to support it; and, "as a general argument, it seemed "to him much more expedient to "have a moderate balance of the "public revenue—say two millions "—in hand, and if it appeared "likely to be permanent, to reduce

" taxation to that amount. If, on
" the other hand, a Minister pledged
" himself to any given sum for a
" Sinking Fund, it might be very in-
" convenient to produce it at one
" period, although there might be no
" difficulty in doing so at another.
" He objected to the manner in
" which the vote of credit was to be
" raised, as it was highly desirable,
" under existing circumstances, that
" Government should keep as clear
" as possible of the Bank of Eng-
" land. *The state of the Bank was*
" *this: it had advanced nearly all its*
" *available capital to Government*
" *upon an annuity, and it had in con-*
" *sequence obtained a valuable mono-*
" *poly, which he hoped never would be*
" *renewed, and from which a con-*
" *siderable revenue might be derived*
" *by proper arrangements.* He ad-
" mitted, that by means of Exche-
" quer Bills, the Right Hon. Gen-
" tleman obtained a loan at a cheaper
" rate than he could otherwise raise
" it, but he could find no remedy for
" the calamity that would arise if
" the Foreign Exchanges should be
" against the country, and the Bank
" of England, for its own security,
" contract its issues by the sale of
" Exchequer Bills. He did not look
" for any reply, but he felt assured,
" that what he had offered would
" receive due consideration from the
" Right Hon. Gentleman.

" Mr. *Herries,* in pursuance of the
" Resolution of the Committee of
" Supply, moved a vote for raising
" the sum of 500,000*l.* by Exchequer
" Bills.

" Mr. *Hume* objected to this mode
" of going on adding to the Unfunded
" Debt of the country. He hoped
" that the Right Honourable Gen-
" tleman would be able to assign
" some reasons for pursuing such a
" course.

" Mr. *Herries* observed, that on
" the night when the Budget was
" brought forward, the House had
" universally concurred in the sug-
" gestion that the constitution of the
" Sinking Fund should not be altered.
" If new Exchequer Bills were re-
" quired, the mode of issuing them
" must depend upon the circum-
" stances of the time.

" Mr. *Hume* added, that this was
" the first occasion on which a Chan-
" cellor of the Exchequer *had avowed*
" *that he had not money for the Sink-*
" *ing Fund,* and that he must bor-
" row, in order to obtain it for that
" purpose. At all events, it seemed
" fit only to apply to the Sinking
" Fund the money which the Trea-
" sury actually possessed. The plan
" now persevered in complicated and
" stultified the whole of the accounts.
" He called upon the Right Honour-
" able Gentleman (Mr. Canning) to
" state why he reverted to the absurd
" doctrines of 1822; it was keeping
" up *a humbug,* inconsistent with the
" acknowledged fairness and candour
" of the Right Honourable Gentle-
" man.

" The *Chancellor of the Exchequer:*

" The Hon. Member asks me why I " do not make a new arrangement " of finance upon his sole recom- " mendation, and in opposition to " the expressed opinion of all the " rest of the House [cheers].

" Mr. *Maberly* said, that as *the* " *whole subject would be reviewed by a* " *Finance Committee early next Ses-* " *sion*, it was hardly worth while " to persevere in recommending a " change of system which would " *probably only continue for a few* " *months longer.*"

Well, then, first we see that Mr. Maberly (who is a great financier, as I said before) appears to have entire confidence in the works of this expected Finance Committee. Mr. Hume calls the sinking-fund a shocking humbug. He calls upon Mr. Canning to state " why he keeps up this humbug." Mr. Canning answers, that the " honourable " gentleman asks him why he " does not make a new ar- " rangement of finance upon his " sole recommendation, *and in* " *opposition to the expressed opi-* " *nion of all the rest of the House.* (*Cheers*)." Aye, aye, " cheer " away; but this is a very poor answer, Mr. Canning; and you will find that you will have all the House against you upon this very point, if you continue in your place but another six months. There is no joking with an empty purse, or a purse that is growing empty; and, on this subject Mr. Hume will beat you, with your learned friend Mackintosh pinned on to your back. But, it is Mr. Maberly that I wish the reader to look at; he wishes Mr. Hume to let the " *humbug* " alone for the present; because it, as well as all the other things, " will be review- " ed by the Finance Committee " early next session "! Gad, there will be a pretty review! Never was there such an one upon Hounslow-heath nor Wormwood-scrubs. But (and here is the great point of all), WILL THE BANK PROJECT COME BEFORE THAT FINANCE COMMITTEE! Will the question of reduction of the interest of the Debt come before that Committee? Will the question whether the last year's law about one-pound notes be to be enforced or not, come before that Committee? Leaving these questions for Mr. Canning to consider in his closet, I give it to my readers as my opinion, that the present project of the Bank, of which we have seen so much, would, if put in execution, directly lead to the issuing of a GOVERNMENT PAPER-

MONEY; and, thus, we should, at last, come to the situation of the National Convention of France, and the old Congress of America. This is my decided opinion. I do not say that I believe that the Bank project will be attempted to be enforced; because I can form no opinion as to what is likely to be done by men who manifestly have no settled opinions of their own; but, I know that, before twelve months are over our heads, or thereabouts, there must take place a change which will produce a sensation seldom experienced in any country in the world. The system now exhibits all the symptoms of approaching agony and dissolution. God send it a happy turn; and we have this consolation, at any rate, that no turn that it can take can possibly make the situation of the people of this kingdom much worse than it now is: while it is not only possible, but in the highest degree probable, that the change that will take place, will directly tend to the happiness of the people and the safety, power and honour of the country.

             WM. COBBETT.

P. S. I have not room for the Circular of Sir JOHN SINCLAIR, and shall content myself with observing, that he, also, has his project for making a *"permanent"* and *"safe"* paper-money!

POSTSCRIPT.——Since writing the above (it is now Wednesday noon) I perceive that the Corn Bill appears to have become an abortion. The poor thing appears to have been choked by some queer sort of proceeding of the midwives; and, really, its friends seem not to have been a great deal *fonder of it, at last, than its foes!* I suspect that it was seen, that at a moment *when gold and silver are rising in price*, it would not have been very convenient, either to Whigs or Tories, or by whatever other ridiculous devil's name they are called, to suffer the very moderate quantity of gold which is now in the Bank to be *sent out of the country to pay for corn!* Which must have been the case, observe, if the more than a million sterling's worth of wheat, *now in bond*, had been, by passing the Corn Bill as it stood, suffered to be sold in this country. This I suspect to be the true cause of what has the outward appearance of having been the effect of party contest; and, I cannot give much credit to the report that Mr. Canning, irritable as the shallow man is, has so very grossly characterized the Lords of the Household who voted in favour of the Duke of Wellington's amendment.

Another thing which has taken place, since my writing of the above article, and which is also most closely connected with this great subject of the paper-money, is a renewal of the notice of a Mr. E. DAVENPORT to make a motion for a Select Committee to inquire into the causes of the distresses of the country. He gave this notice last night (Tuesday); and, it appears, that the motion is to come on to-morrow. He had given notice of the motion once before, but, when the time for discussing it came, behold there was NO HOUSE! I shall be mistaken if he gets A HOUSE next time. Mr. Davenport tells the House beforehand, that " HE MEANS TO SHOW " that the one-pound note Act will throw every thing into confusion if it be persevered in ! " A potatoe in your *news-box*, Mr. Davenport!" will say all the Paddies ; a potatoe in your news-box! and, JOHN BULL will exclaim, " *Queen Anne is dead*, Mr. Davenport !" Just as if the House would not think, that this Mr. E. Davenport, who talks about the writings and principles of *Locke*, and who seems as if he had never heard of the POLITICAL REGISTER, were like a country girl who has just been to the fair and has got a new red petticoat; just as if the House would not guess, that he

had been reading the Political Register; that he had got his head full of its matter, that his tongue was running upon it, as the tongue of a country fellow runs upon a new song; that he meant to come forth with that matter as a discovery of his own; just as if the House would not, at least, imagine all this; just as if they could fail to perceive that the author, the real father of these doctrines, would claim them as his own; and that, thereby, the House, by suffering Mr. Davenport to put forth these notions, would only be adding to the fame of that man whom they hate infinitely more than they hate the real eternal Devil himself. Oh, no: they know too well, what would be the effect of Mr. Davenport's motion, to permit it to produce any thing like a debate ; to permit it to stand before the public as a matter worthy of a great degree of public attention. I suppose, therefore, that, either there will be NO HOUSE, or that, by some curious means or other, poor Mr. Davenport will find his motion end in nothing, and that it will hardly be noticed by those profound and faithful gentlemen, the reporters to the newspapers : who, observe, are all sent to sweeping the streets, to dung-cart, or to mending the highways, the moment the paper-money shall receive its final blow. These are amongst the filthy vermin engendered by the paper-money system : they are like the nasty poisonous flies that are engendered under the lights of the pits, where my exotic seedlings are now coming up, and which filthy reptiles I destroy by scalding water, by hot lime, but, above all, by lifting up the lights, and letting in the sweet air upon them. Thus will it be when the covering of corruption shall be drawn away, and when the sweet air of justice and liberty shall be let in upon the accursed vermin that are now nipping in the bud every thing tending to the real peace and happiness of the nation. I conclude by inserting the reported speech of this Mr. E. Davenport, this scholar, as he would have us believe, of "the great *Locke*," as he calls him, who was, indeed, great, as a swallower of the public money; but, who was not more worthy of being quoted upon this subject than Hudibras would have been. I cannot help observing, that Peel talked about nothing but *Locke* and *Queen Elizabeth*, when he introduced that Bill, which has already brought the country three times to the verge of actual convulsion; that

Bill which the profound Canning said " *had set the question at rest for ever*"; and, which Mr. E. Davenport, after having seen it altered three times, backward and forward and backward again, now declares to be calculated to produce inevitable ruin to the country, unless it undergo another alteration; unless (to use his own words) it be *neutralized* by some measure of a counteracting tendency.

" Mr. *E. Davenport* presented a
" Petition from a class of poor, but
" industrious inhabitants of the Me-
" tropolis, the operative Silk-weavers
" of Spitalfields, praying for relief
" from the greatest grievance under
" which any portion of the commu-
" nity could labour ; namely, inade-
" quate remuneration for their la-
" bour. They prayed that an inquiry
" might be instituted into the cause
" of their distress. It might be that
" it was not in the power of that
" House to relieve them ; but as per-
" sons who were drowning, caught
" at the slightest things to save
" themselves, so the Petitioners
" were anxious to seize every pos-
" sible means of remedying the evils
" under which they laboured. They
" admitted that there was an im-
" provement in the trade generally ;
" but expressed their doubts of its
" continuance, and their conviction of
" the little benefit which that improve-
" ment would occasion to the working

" classes, while the masters, by com-
" bination, had the power of diminish-
" ing the rate of wages. They solicited
" Parliament to enact a law, making
" agreements with respect to wages
" between the masters and the jour-
" neymen duly convened, imperative
" on both parties. For his own part,
" he thought that any measure of
" that kind would be merely a pallia-
" tive and not a corrective of the evil,
" which, in his opinion (as we under-
" stood the Hon. Gent.), principally
" resided in the state of the currency.
" *He could never understand how it*
" *was possible to withdraw a consider-*
" *able portion of the currency in the*
" *manner in which it had been with-*
" *drawn, without paralysing all the*
" *industry of the country. The Act*
" *providing for the abolition of one-*
" *pound notes had already produced*
" *the greatest distress, and eighteen*
" *months were still to elapse, before he*
" *whole of the evil which it was calcu-*
" *lated to create would be rendered ma-*
" *nifest. If that evil were not neu-*
" *tralized by some measure of a coun-*
" *teracting tendency, he was persuaded*
" *that it would arrive at a most alarm-*
" *ing height. It was extraordinary to*
" *hear the contradictory opinions on*
" *this important subject. While in*
" *the memorable debate which three*
" *years ago took place respecting it,*
" *one of the Ministers of the Crown*
" *asserted, that the question of the*
" *currency was settled, a Bank Direc-*
" *tor, a man of great ability and ex-*
" *perience, declared, that so far was*
" *the question from being settled, that*

" *the manner in which it was left was*
" *fraught with the utmost danger, and*
" *would spedily require some altera-*
" *ation in the law. Was it not incum-*
" *bent on the House to sift to the bot-*
" *tom such opposite opinions on a sub-*
" *ject of such vital importance? By*
" *what strange fatality was it that so*
" *few persons were disposed to listen to*
" *the discussion of a topic so generally*
" *interesting? It appeared as if some*
" *apprehension existed lest the real*
" *facts of the case should be made ma-*
" *nifest. Various reasons had been*
" *pressed upon him, but in vain, to in-*
" *duce him to withdraw his notice of a*
" *motion on Thursday next, for the*
" *appointment of a Select Committee*
" *to inquire into the causes of the*
" *severe distress which had afflicted the*
" *commercial and industrious classes of*
" *the community, during the last and*
" *present years. However unwillingly*
" *in some respects, he was determined*
" *to do his duty by persevering in that*
" *motion; leaving to Parliament all*
" *the honour or all the shame that*
" *would result from adopting it on the*
" *one hand, or letting it die on the*
" *other.*"

---

## TULIP-TREE WOOD.

I HAVE for sale *fifty-four* planks
of this wood, averaging about
*thirty feet* in each plank. They
are *two and a half inches thick.*
Some are about fourteen feet long;
others not, probably, more than
ten feet. Some are between *three
and four feet wide;* others not,
perhaps, more than two feet. The
planks are just *as wide at one end*

*as at the other;* and there is not a *single knot,* or curl, in the whole parcel of *one thousand, five hundred and eighty-one feet.*

MICHAUX, in his North American Sylva, says of the *tree,* that he saw one *twenty-two feet six inches* in circumference, at five feet from the ground; and that he judged the tree to be *a hundred and forty feet high.* Of the WOOD Michaux says what every body in America knows; namely, that it is in colour of a pale yellow; that its grain is very fine; that the wood is both *light* and *strong;* that it is used in rafters, shingles, door-panels, bedsteads, wainscoting, chair-bottoms, large bowls, and particularly, in all parts of America, in making the *panels of coaches* and other pleasure carriages; and, so much is this the case, that it is carried hundreds of miles to be used in those places, near to which it does not grow.

The wood admits of a *beautiful polish,* and is used for various purposes by cabinet-makers. Of these planks that I have, a single plank would make a kitchen-dresser, or table; a servants'-hall table; a slab for a dairy or a larder; fine things, I should think, for cutting-boards, shop-boards, counters, show-boards, or almost any thing, which requires a very large breadth of wood in one single, smooth piece. Being 2½ inches thick, these planks are strong enough for any thing.

The price *for the whole parcel,* ONE SHILLING and THREE-PENCE A FOOT; for any quantity less than the whole, and

exceeding a hundred feet, ONE SHILLING AND SIXPENCE A FOOT; and for a *single plank,* ONE SHILLING AND NINE-PENCE A FOOT. So that a plank, 14 feet long, and 8½ feet wide, which, with a couple of trestles, would make a table to dine *twenty people,* would cost only *four pounds five shillings;* it might be kept as clean as a marble slab, and with nearly as little trouble, and would last for many a life-time.

The planks are at *my house at Kensington,* where they may be seen, by *application to the gardener,* at any hour between four in the morning and five in the afternoon. There is the *mark* on each plank, expressing the *number of feet* which it contains. The marks were put on in America, and, therefore, are according to our old-fashioned English *kingly* measure, and not according to the grand and sublime "IMPERIAL MEA-SURE," which, being an "*improvement of the age,*" produced by "*liberal principles,*" the offspring of the "*march of mind,*" gauges (in defiance of Bedlam) ale, metes oysters, and ascertains the length and width of shirting, by the " beat of a *pendulum* in a " heat of sixty-two degrees of " Farenheit's Thermometer"!

N.B. I have now but little more than half the above quantity left; Gentlemen, who may wish either to see it or purchase it, must therefore be speedy in their applications.

# MARKETS.

Average Prices of CORN throughout ENGLAND, for the week ending June 1.

*Per Quarter.*

| | s. | d. | | s. | d. |
|---|---|---|---|---|---|
| Wheat .. | 58 | 4 | Rye .... | 42 | 2 |
| Barley .. | 40 | 3 | Beans ... | 51 | 4 |
| Oats .... | 28 | 8 | Pease ... | 47 | 11 |

Total Quantity of Corn returned as
Sold in the Maritime Districts, for
the week ended June 1.

| | Qrs. | | Qrs. |
|---|---|---|---|
| Wheat .. | 35,856 | Rye ..... | 139 |
| Barley .. | 1,878 | Beans . .. | 956 |
| Oats ... | 7,196 | Pease .... | 452 |

*Corn Exchange, Mark Lane.*

Quantities and Prices of British
Corn, &c. sold and delivered in
this Market, during the week ended
Saturday, June 2.

| | Qrs. | £. | s. | d. | | s. | d. |
|---|---|---|---|---|---|---|---|
| Wheat.. | 4,054 | for 12,147 | 15 | 6 | Average, | 59 | 11 |
| Barley.. | 1,571 | .. 3,164 | 7 | 9 | .......... | 40 | 3 |
| Oats.. | 2,302 | .. 3,391 | 19 | 0 | .......... | 29 | 5 |
| Rye.... | 8 | .. 13 | 19 | 4 | .......... | 34 | 1 |
| Beans.. | 385 | .. 950 | 10 | 3 | .......... | 49 | 4 |
| Pease .. | 54 | .. 134 | 8 | 0 | .......... | 49 | 9 |

Friday, June 8.—The supplies of
Grain this week are moderate, but of
Flour the quantity is good. Wheat
has received a check to-day, and the
trade has become so heavy that Monday's prices cannot be obtained.
Barley continues very scarce. Beans
and Pease are unaltered. The trade
for Oats remains unvaried from the
report of Monday. The Flour trade
is very dull at the advance.

Monday, June 11.—There was
last week a small supply of most
kinds of English Grain, with a large
arrival of Flour, and a good quantity
of foreign Oats. The fresh supplies
to this morning's market are inconsiderable. The anticipation that the
Duke of Wellington's clause will be
expunged from the Corn Bill, has
caused great dullness to be experienced in the Wheat trade to-day:
there is scarcely any superfine Wheat
at market, and the general quality
may be reported 2s. per quarter
lower than this day sen'night, with
the chief part of the supply left unsold.

Barley continues so very scarce
that the prices may yet be reported as
nominal. Beans come also very
scantily to market, and the rates are
unaltered. Pease have no variation.
There have been fewer country buyers of Oats here to-day than for some
weeks past, and the trade for this
article being slack, the prices are reported 1s. per quarter lower for thin
feed samples, and even other kinds
can hardly obtain the terms of this
day sen'night. The Flour trade is
so extremely heavy, that most of the
Factors consider the top price as
having fallen to 50s. per sack.

———

*Price on board Ship as under.*

Flour, per sack ......46s. — 50s.
—— Seconds ........ 0s. — 0s.
—— North Country ..40s. — 44s.

———

Price of Bread.—The price of the
4lb. Loaf is stated at 9d. by the
full-priced Bakers.

Account of Wheat, &c. arrived in the Port of London, from June to June 9, both inclusive.

| | Qrs. | | Qrs. |
|---|---|---|---|
| Wheat | 5,026 | Tares | — |
| Barley | 1,443 | Linseed | 1,168 |
| Malt | 8,913 | Rapeseed | — |
| Oats | 2,310 | Brank | 60 |
| Beans | 520 | Mustard | — |
| Flour | 10,863 | Flax | — |
| Rye | — | Hemp | — |
| Pease | 546 | Seeds | 9 |

Foreign.—Wheat, 3,840; Barley, 4,291; Oats, 18,890; Beans, 753 quarters.

### Price of Hops, per Cwt. in the Borough.

Monday, June 11.—The general reports, this day, from the plantations about Maidstone are, that there is rather less fly, and the bines are growing fast; while from other quarters, they state an increase of fly. The market is very dull, and last week's prices can scarcely be realized for either new or old.

*Another Account.*

June 11.—Our market remains dull, and where sales have been forced, lower prices have been submitted to; but such is the confidence generally felt by the trade, that when Hops have been offered at less than the market price of the day, they have readily found purchasers. The accounts from the plantations continue very favourable, and districts where the attack had not been so general, have now been visited by the fly in great numbers. Duty called 55,000 l.

*Maidstone*, June 7.—The accounts from the Weald of Kent, say that there is a very great increase of fly, and, that the plantations are getting in the same bad state as in the year 1825, but here and round this neighbourhood they are more favourable, as it is considered the fly has generally decreased, and the bines are growing and look much better. The trade seems quite at a stand—nothing doing whatever.

Monday, June 11.—On Friday there was but little variation from the preceding market; if any difference, it was that Mutton and Lamb sold on rather better terms. The supply to-day may be considered large, and the weather being extremely warm, there is a great heaviness in the trade. Choice Beasts, not exceeding 100 stones, nearly maintain the terms of last Monday; but large and coarse things are 1l. to 2l. a head lower; and it is very doubtful whether all will be sold. A few prime pens of Sheep, from 7 to 8 stone, have exceeded our top currency; but the general trade is no higher than this day sen'night; and Lamb also remains the same.

*Per Stone of 8 pounds (alive).*

| | s. | d. | | s. | d. |
|---|---|---|---|---|---|
| Beef | 4 | 4 | to 5 | 4 |
| Mutton | 4 | 0 | — 5 | 0 |
| Veal | 5 | 0 | — 5 | 8 |
| Pork | 5 | 0 | — 5 | 8 |
| Lamb | 5 | 0 | — 6 | 0 |

| | | | |
|---|---|---|---|
| Beasts | 1,970 | Sheep | 20,550 |
| Calves | 232 | Pigs | 140 |

NEWGATE, (same day.)

*Per Stone of 8 pounds (dead).*

| | s. | d. | | s. | d. |
|---|---|---|---|---|---|
| Beef | 4 | 0 | to 5 | 0 |
| Mutton | 3 | 8 | — 4 | 8 |
| Veal | 4 | 0 | — 6 | 0 |
| Pork | 4 | 0 | — 6 | 0 |
| Lamb | 4 | 8 | — 6 | 8 |

LEADENHALL, (same day.)

*Per Stone of 8 pounds (dead).*

| | s. | d. | | s. | d. |
|---|---|---|---|---|---|
| Beef | 3 | 6 | to 5 | 4 |
| Mutton | 3 | 4 | — 4 | 8 |
| Veal | 3 | 8 | — 5 | 8 |
| Pork | 4 | 4 | — 5 | 8 |
| Lamb | 3 | 8 | — 6 | 8 |

Monday, June 11.—The arrivals from Ireland last week were, 1,708 firkins of Butter, and 2,466 bales of Bacon; and from Foreign Ports, 7,388 casks of Butter.

## POTATOES.

### SPITALFIELDS, per Ton.

| | £. s. | £. s. |
|---|---|---|
| Ox-Nobles | 3 10 to | 0 0 |
| Middlings | 0 0 — | 0 0 |
| Chats | 0 0 — | 0 0 |
| Common Red | 0 0 — | 0 0 |

Onions, 0s. 0d.—0s. 0d. per bush.

### BOROUGH, per Ton.

| | £. s. | £. s. |
|---|---|---|
| Ox-Nobles | 3 0 to | 3 10 |
| Middlings | 2 0 — | 0 0 |
| Chats | 0 0 — | 0 0 |
| Common Red | 3 0 — | 3 10 |

## HAY and STRAW, per Load.

———

*Smithfield.*—Hay....90s. to 120s.

Straw...36s. to 42s.

Clover. 100s. to 147s.

*St. James's.*—Hay... 84s. to 130s.

Straw .. 36s. to 46s.

Clover. 105s. to 136s.

*Whitechapel.*—Hay... 84s. to 120s.

Straw,..36s. to 48s.

Clover 100s. to 140s.

———

## AVERAGE PRICE OF CORN, sold in the Maritime Counties of England and Wales, for the Week ended June 1, 1827.

| | Wheat. s. d. | Barley. s. d. | Oats. s. d. |
|---|---|---|---|
| London* | 61 4 | 41 2 | 32 3 |
| Essex | 60 5 | 40 8 | 30 4 |
| Kent | 57 8 | 41 7 | 32 11 |
| Sussex | 56 11 | 41 4 | 28 0 |
| Suffolk | 57 4 | 37 11 | 31 8 |
| Cambridgeshire | 54 6 | 34 1 | 26 2 |
| Norfolk | 57 0 | 37 8 | 28 3 |
| Lincolnshire | 58 7 | 39 8 | 28 0 |
| Yorkshire | 56 3 | 40 0 | 28 1 |
| Durham | 59 1 | 42 8 | 36 1 |
| Northumberland | 57 6 | 40 0 | 33 7 |
| Cumberland | 64 6 | 42 10 | 37 0 |
| Westmoreland | 63 11 | 47 9 | 29 10 |
| Lancashire | 63 4 | 0 0 | 31 10 |
| Cheshire | 63 4 | 0 0 | 30 8 |
| Gloucestershire | 67 1 | 42 7 | 42 0 |
| Somersetshire | 55 6 | 38 5 | 29 7 |
| Monmouthshire | 59 7 | 44 4 | 0 0 |
| Devonshire | 58 0 | 39 6 | 34 2 |
| Cornwall | 64 5 | 42 1 | 36 7 |
| Dorsetshire | 55 9 | 38 10 | 34 7 |
| Hampshire | 56 5 | 42 0 | 28 0 |
| North Wales | 70 8 | 50 2 | 29 8 |
| South Wales | 62 6 | 47 8 | 27 7 |

* The London Average is always that of the Week preceding.

*Liverpool*, June 5.—At this day's market higher prices were demanded for Wheat, say from 4*d.* to 5*d.* per 70lbs., and in some few instances obtained. Sales of all sorts of Grain, in bond, at a complete stand. Of Oats, sales to a moderate extent were made at the prices of this day week. In other Grain no alteration.

Imported into Liverpool, from May 29 to June 5, 1827, inclusive :—Wheat, 10,418; Barley, 1,535; Oats, 5,112; Beans, 345; Pease, 81 quarters. Flour, 140 sacks, per 280 lbs.; Oatmeal, 242 packs, per 240 lbs.; American Flour, 2,621 barrels.

*Derby*, June 9.—On account of this day being our Whitsun Fair, our Market was rather neglected. Prices for fine Wheat were rather higher, and with very little demand ; all sorts of Grain nearly nominal.—Wheat, 60*s.* to 65*s.*; Barley, 38*s.* to 46*s.*; Oats, 30*s.* to 36*s.*; and Beans, 54*s.* to 62*s.* per eight bushels Imperial measure.

*Horncastle*, June 9.—We had a very short supply of all kinds of Grain. Wheat something higher ; Barley the same as out last ; Oats dull, and little business doing.—Wheat, from 55*s.* to 60*s.*; Barley, 40*s.* to 44*s.*; Oats, 25*s.* to 30*s.*; Beans, 60*s.* to 64*s.*; and Rye from 38*s.* to 40*s.* per qr.

*Ipswich*, June 9.—We had a fair supply of Wheat at market to-day, but a very short one of other Grain, and prices remain nearly as last week, viz. —Wheat, 54*s.* to 63*s.*; Barley, 36*s.* to 42*s.*; and Beans, 48*s.* to 52*s.* per quarter.

*Manchester*, June 9.—This being almost a holiday week here, very little business has been transacted in the Corn trade. The advance in London, on Monday last, has not had a corresponding effect here to-day, although the holders of fine Wheat were demanding an advance of 2*d.* to 4*d.* per bushel of 70 lbs. ; the Millers were not disposed to comply, and what few sales were made were only at an advance of 2*d.* per bushel ; nor do we expect much life in the trade until the Corn Bill is finally settled. Flour has advanced full 1*s.* per sack. In Barley, Oats, Beans, Pease, and Malt, no alteration.

*Newcastle-upon-Tyne*, June 9.—We had a short supply of Wheat from the farmers, and very little coastwise at this day's market, and the obstruction the Corn Bill has met with in the House of Lords having caused some alarm amongst the millers who are out of stock, they gave readily an advance of 2*s.* per quarter upon the prices of last week ; but the feeling amongst the principal buyers was in favour of the Bill passing, and they bought very sparingly at the advance. Rye rather more in demand. The farmers' supply of Oats was very small this morning, and we have had few foreign arrivals during the week, but the buyers did very little business today, and prices remain nominally the same as last week.

*Norwich*, June 9.—The supply of Wheat to-day was quite equal to the demand, prices of Red, 53*s.* to 59*s.*; White to 62*s.*; Barley, may be considered nominal ; Oats, 28*s.* to 31*s.*; Beans, 43*s.* to 48*s.*; Pease, 44*s.* to 48*s.* Boilers, to 50*s.* per quarter ; and Flour, 42*s.* to 44*s.* per sack.

*Reading*, June 9. – From the remarks made by Lord Goderich, in the House on Thursday night, a pretty general expectation existed in our market this day, that it is his Lordship's intention on the bringing up of the Report of the Corn Bill from the Committee, to move that the Duke of Wellington's Resolution raising the average be expunged—and as proxies can be used in the House, which is not the case when their Lordships go into a Committee, a majority, it is supposed, will be in favour of the Corn Bill, as it stood before amended by the Noble Duke ; under this uncertainty, very little business was transacted in our market, and prices of all Grain must be called nominally as on this day se'nnight.

## COUNTRY CATTLE AND MEAT MARKETS, &c.

*Horncastle*, June 9.—Beef, 9s. per stone of 14 lbs.; Mutton, 6d. to 7d.; Lamb 7d. to 8d.; and Veal, from 7d. to 8d. per lb.

*Manchester* Smithfield Market, June 6.—To this day's market we had an abundant supply of Sheep and Lambs, but of Beasts, Calves, and Pigs, the quantity was short. Mutton and Lamb have declined full ¼d per lb. since this day week. In Beef, Veal, and Pork, no alteration.—Beef, 5d. to 8¼d.; Mutton, 7d. to 8d.; Lamb, 7d. to 8½d.; Veal, 6d. to 7½d.; and Pork, 4d. to 5d. per lb., sinking offal.

At *Morpeth* Market, June 6, there was a short supply of Cattle, which met with dull sale, at a reduction in price; there were a good many Sheep, and a very full market of Lambs; good Lambs sold readily, prices rather lower; inferior of the latter not sold.—Beef, from 7s. 3d. to 8s.; Mutton, 7s. 3d. to 9s.; Lamb, 8s. to 9s. per stone, sinking offal.

*Norwich Castle Meadow*, June 9.—We had only a very small supply of fat Cattle to this day's market, prices 8s. to 9s. per stone of 14 lbs., sinking offal: the supply of Store Stock was very large; Scots, 4s. to 4s. 6d. per stone of what they will weigh when fat; Shorthorns, 3s. to 3s. 6d.; Cows and Calves selling rather better; Homebreds, of one and two-years old, a flat sale; the supply of Sheep was exceedingly large.—Meat: Beef, 7d. to 9d.; Veal, 6d. to 8d.; Mutton, 6d. to 7½d.; Lamb, 6½d. 7½d.; and Pork, 6d. to 7½d. per lb.

# COBBETT'S WEEKLY REGISTER.

VOL. 62.—No. 13.]  LONDON, SATURDAY, JUNE 23, 1827.  [Price 6d.

" Here, then, in THE TAXES is the real cause of the necessity of high prices. It is the
" Government, and not the farmer, who stands in need of high-priced corn. Oh ! ye COKES
" and WESTERNS, be not; be not I pray and supplicate you, made the tools of the taxing
" system. You talk of protection to agriculture ; but, the real tendency of your exertions
" is, to protect and promote the taxing system. Reduce the taxes of the English farmer
" and those of his miserable labourers, and then he will grow corn enough without the aid
" of foreign supply; and, the manufacturers, eating cheap food, will be able to sell cheaper
" than the manufacturers of foreign nations; and, thus, all will thrive together : make
" corn dear, and all will decline together, except the military and naval and tax eating
" part of the community, who will, in the end, obtain a predominance such as they possess
" in the Austrian, Prussian, Russian, and German dominions, and English freedom and
" English manners and English tastes will take their flight for ever to the other side of the
" Atlantic. A Corn Bill would be no protection to the farmer, and, in the end, none to
" the land-owner : what it gave in prohibition, it would take away in tax, and give it to
" the tax-eating tribe. For these reasons I, who am a farmer by taste as well as in fact,
" detest and abhor, from the very bottom of my soul, the idea of any measure tending to
" raise or keep up the price of corn ; and, if there be but one man in all England found to
" petition against such a measure, I, William Cobbett, will be that man."—POLITICAL
REGISTER, 28th January, 1815.

# ·CORN BILL.

### TO THE

## REFORMERS OF BOLTON.

*Fleet Street, 20th June, 1827.*

MY FRIENDS,

IN the way of thanks or acknowledgment for the excellent petition and proceedings at Bolton, a
few days ago, and which do you
all such great honour, and show

you to be so much superior in
point of mind to the far greater
part of those who affect to look
down on you with contempt, but
who hate you because they fear
the final effects of that real superiority which they perceive you

2 B

Printed and Published by WILLIAM COBBETT, No. 183, Fleet-street.
[ENTERED AT STATIONERS' HALL.]

to possess; in the way of acknowledgment for that petition and
those proceedings, which entitle
you to the thanks of the whole nation, I address to you this present
set of remarks on the corn projects
and disputes recently carried on
and still carrying on in the two
Houses of Parliament.

Before I proceed to these remarks, let me beg you, first of all,
to look at the motto which I have
prefixed to this paper. You will
perceive that it was written a little
while before the first Corn Bill
was passed. The truths which it
contains, need not be particularly
pointed out to you; but, it may
not be amiss that I now remind
you, who were men at that time,
and that I inform those of you who
were then but boys, of certain
transactions which took place
during the progress of that Bill.
From the time that the Bill was
first brought into the House of
Commons, every exertion that I
was able to make was made against
it. In these exertions, I was joined
by Mr. Hunt; and, after the

Bill had passed the House of Commons, a meeting, in consequence
of a requisition put forth by Mr.
Hunt, was presented to the High
Sheriff of Wiltshire, to call a
meeting of the county to petition
the House of Lords not to agree
to the Bill.

The High Sheriff, Mr. GEORGE
EYRE, called the meeting to be
held at the city of Salisbury, on
the 8th of March, 1815. At this
meeting, a petition, moved by Mr.
Hunt, and seconded by me, was
agreed to in the following words;
and it was presented to the House
of Lords by the late Lord STAN-
HOPE.

———

" To the Right Honourable the Lords
" Spiritual and Temporal of the
" United Kingdom of Great Britain
" and Ireland, in Parliament as-
" sembled.

" The Petition of the Freeholders,
" Landholders, Tradesmen, Ma-
" nufacturers, and Inhabitants

" of the County of Wilts, in
" County Meeting assembled.

" Humbly sheweth,

" That your Petitioners, at the
" moment when they were justified
" in expecting to enter on the en-
" joyments of the blessings, usually
" attendant on Peace, to which they
" had so long been strangers, per-
" ceive, with the deepest sorrow,
" that attempts are making to pro-
" long and perpetuate the sufferings
" of War, by enhancing and uphold-
" ing the price of Corn.

" That your Petitioners, seeing, in
" other quarters, political corruption
" and private rapacity so firmly and
" resolutely leagued against them,
" fly with confidence for protection
" to your Lordships, and appeal to
" your noble-mindedness, your jus-
" tice, your humanity, against the
" machinations and violence of this
" unfeeling, this merciless league.

" Your Petitioners, therefore,
" humbly pray, that your Lordships
" will reject any proposition that may
" be made to you to entertain any
" Bill, or other measure, tending to

" diminish, or restrain the importa-
" tion of Corn.

" And your Petitioners shall
" ever pray, &c:

(Signed)    " HENRY HUNT,
            " WILLIAM COBBETT,

" And by upwards of three thousand
            " other persons."

You will, my friends, be disposed to laugh when you read the
*second paragraph* of this petition,
especially when you duly reflect
upon transactions of a very recent
date. The truth is, the people
laughed at it at the time, and we
laughed at it, too; but it was well
calculated to arrest the progress
of the measure, if feelings of any
sort could have produced such an
effect. It is a truly curious historical document: it is one amongst
a thousand other proofs that he
who would know the true history
of this country for the last twenty-
five years, must look into this
Register of mine.

To the meeting, who agreed to

this petition without one dissenting voice, it was explained, that the landowners who had promoted the Bill wished still to be able to pay the high taxes. It was explained to the meeting, that the land-owners of this very county of Wilts had petitioned for a Corn Bill; and had told the Parliament, in that petition, that they were still willing to bear heavy taxes, provided the Government and Parliament would pass a law, the effect of which should be to raise and keep up the price of their corn! That is to say, that, so long as they could have a price which would be a protection *to them* against ruin, they did not care how heavily the loaf was taxed, how cruelly the mass of the people suffered, how much money was squandered away, how large a standing army was kept up in time of peace, how the rights and liberties of the people were dealt with. It was fully explained to this meeting, that the Petitioners for a Corn Bill were foolish, even as to their own interests; and, it

was predicted, in terms most explicit, that the farmer, especially, was not at all interested in a rise in the price of corn; that it was his place-holding, his pension-receiving, his sinecure-swallowing landlord, together with his relations and dependants; that it was these who wanted a high price of corn; because, without that high price, rents and taxes could not be paid to a high amount, and without taxes to a high amount their places, pensions, half-pay, and all the receipts of the tax-eaters, could not be met.

The House of Lords received our petition with a little grumbling; but, I recollect, that Lord Stanhope told them that, though it contained some pretty stinging matter, it was, nevertheless, proper for their Lordships to receive it.

After this, before the Bill was passed, I endeavoured to get a county meeting in Hampshire; but, one BOSANQUET, the same fellow, I believe, who was a Bank director, and who carried the message to Pitt, which message pro-

duced the Order in Council for a
Bank-restriction or stoppage in
1797 : this Bosanquet refused to
call the county meeting; and I,
as one man in Hampshire, at any
rate, resolved to petition myself.
On the 17th March, 1815, I drew
up a petition in the following
words, and sent it to Lord Stanhope to present. The Bill had
passed, on the day he got the
petition, and before he got down
to the House. I insert this petition here, in order that you, my
friends, may see, how clear a
view I had of the matter from the
very beginning. It is not to gratify vanity that I thus insert this
petition; for, it is already well
known enough, that I have foreseen every thing relating to the
effects of this dreadful system of
sway. I insert it, in order to show
you how culpable those men must
be, who despised the statements
and advice contained in this petition. They pretend, that no human foresight could have reached
so far as to anticipate consequences at a distance of twelve
years. Read, my friends, the
fourth paragraph of this petition ;
and, then, you will see that those
consequences could be anticipated
by plain common sense ; and, of
course, you will judge accordingly, of those who turn their backs
upon this advice. Soon after this
petition was presented to the
Lords, the foolish and fatal Bill
was passed ; and, there stands, in
the Register of 25th March, 1818,
this everlasting record against the
deadly principle of all such Bills.
I will just add, before I insert this
petition, that the county of Wilts
is the only county that ever met,
in regular county meeting, to petition against this species of infliction upon the people ; that the city
of Salisbury is the only city that
ever saw such meeting; and that
Mr. HUNT had the honour to call
that meeting, or, at least, to origi
nate the requisition in consequence
of which it was called by the Sheriff, who behaved upon the occasion with as much impartiality and
justice, as the High Sheriff of
Norfolk did upon the occasion of

the Equitable Adjustment meeting
of 1828. Greater impartiality and
justice he could not show; and,
when we consider the general conduct of sheriffs, high bailiffs and
other such officers, these two gentlemen must be deemed persons
worthy of our particular commendation. The following was my petition, as a Hampshire freeholder.
I beg you to read the whole of it
with attention; but, particularly,
the fourth paragraph of it. It is
a petition which might be repeated at this moment, with as much
propriety as it was put forth in
1815.

----

" To the Lords Spiritual and Tempo-
" ral of the United Kingdom of
" Great Britain and Ireland in
" Parliament assembled.

" The Petition of WILLIAM COB-
" BETT, of Botley, in Hampshire,
" dated on the 17th day of
" March, 1815.

" Humbly Showeth.

" 1. That your Petitioner, on the
" 10th instant, delivered to the High

" Sheriff of Hampshire, signed by
" your Petitioner himself, and by
" five hundred and eighty-one other
" Inhabitants of the County, many
" of whom are freeholders, land-
" owners, and land-cultivators, a Re-
" quisition in the following words;
" to wit:—

" ' 2. Sir,—We, the undersigned
" ' Freeholders, and other Landhold-
" ' ers, Tradesmen and Manufactur-
" ' ers of the County of Southampton,
" ' perceiving, that, in various parts
" ' of the Kingdom, evil-disposed, or
" ' misguided, persons are endeavour-
" ' ing to prevail on the Legislature to
" ' impose duties on the Importation
" ' of Corn, and being convinced
" ' that such a measure would griev-
" ' ously oppress the labouring classes,
" ' would be ruinous to Tradesmen
" ' and Manufacturers, would, in
" ' the end, be injurious to the
" ' Growers of Corn and the Owners
" ' of Land themselves, and might
" ' possibly disturb the peace of
" ' his Majesty's Dominions, request
" ' that you will be pleased to con-
" ' vene a Meeting of the County on
" ' a day as little distant as may be
" ' convenient, in order to take into
" ' consideration and to discuss the

" ' propriety of presenting a Petition
" ' to the two Houses of Parliament,
" ' earnestly praying, That no such
" ' measure may be adopted, and
" ' also praying for a repeal of laws,
" ' hostile to our rights and liberties,
" ' passed during the late wars, and
" ' for a constitutional Reform in the
" ' Commons' House of Parliament.'

" 3. That the said High Sheriff
" has refused to call such Meeting
" of the County, and that, therefore,
" your Petitioner, deeply impressed
" with the injurious tendency of any
" law to prohibit, or restrain, the im-
" portation of Corn, has thus humbly
" presumed to make his individual
" appeal to the Wisdom, the Justice,
" the Humanity of your Lordships.

" 4. That your Petitioner does not
" presume to be competent to judge
" of the precise degree in which the
" Merchants, Traders, and Manu-
" facturers of this kingdom may be
" affected by the proposed law ; but
" while common sense tells him, that
" it must seriously injure these
" classes of the community, that it
" must so enhance and uphold the
" price of shipping, freight, and manu-
" factured goods, as to transfer the
" building of ships, the employment

" of ships, the making of goods, to-
" gether with vast numbers of our
" best artisans to countries, where
" the necessaries of life are at a much
" lower price : while common sense
" tells him, that to uphold the price
" of food is to drive from their na-
" tive country great numbers of per-
" sons in search of better living on
" their incomes, leaving their share
" of the taxes to be paid by those
" who remain, and that, too, out of
" diminished means arising from a
" diminished demand for their pro-
" duce, their manufactures, and their
" professional labours; while com-
" mon sense says this to your Peti-
" tioner, his own experience, as an
" owner and cultivator of land, en-
" ables him to state, with more pre-
" cision, to your Lordships, the
" grounds of his conviction, that any
" law tending to raise, or keep up,
" the price of Corn, will prove, in
" the end, to be no benefit, but an
" injury to the owner and cultivator
" of the land.

" 5. Your Petitioner is well aware
" that, unless prices be raised and
" upheld, it will be impossible for
" the owners and the cultivators of
" the land to pay the taxes that will

" exist after the Property Tax shall
" have ceased ; he is well aware,
" that to ensure them a high price
" for their Corn is the only means of
" enabling them to pay these taxes ;
" but, then, he is clearly convinced,
" that a very large part of those
" taxes might be dispensed with ;
" that the army and navy, which
" swallows up so considerable a por-
" tion of them, might be reduced to
" the state in which they were pre-
" vious to the late war, and that the
" whole of the public expenses (ex-
" clusive of those attendant on the
" National Debt) might be reduced
" to what they then were, namely,
" to six millions a year; and thus,
" without raising the price of Corn,
" the credit, the safety, the honour
" of the nation, might all be amply
" provided for and secured.

" 6. For these reasons your Peti-
" tioner humbly prays, that your
" Lordships *will not pass any law to*
" *prohibit, or restrain, the importation*
" *of Corn;* and, as the nation, once
" more, happily, sees the days of
" peace, he also prays for the repeal
" of all the laws, *laying new restric-*
" *tions on the Press,* passed during
" the late wars; and, further, he

" most humbly but most earnestly
" prays and implores your Lordships
" to take into your early considera-
" tion that subject, which, in point
" of real importance, swallows up all
" others : namely, the state of the
" Representation of the People in the
" Commons' House of Parliament.

" And your Petitioner shall
" ever pray.

" W. COBBETT."

———

The above petition was, as I
said before, sent to Lord Stanhope on the 17th of March, 1915.
The Bill to which it related received the royal assent very
shortly afterwards; and, under
this system, with a modification or
two at different times, we have
been living from that day to
this ; sometimes in tolerable
abundance; sometimes, suffering,
as the Ministers have told us, from
a surplus of food in one part of
the kingdom, while actual starvation has been spreading its ra-
vages over other parts of the
kingdom; constantly increasing
in general poverty and misery;

and, at this very moment, precisely in that state, in that state of
depression, embarrassment, tur-
moil and misery, which is so fully
described and so correctly anticipated in the fourth paragraph of
the above petition, which was
sent, you will observe, to this very
House of Lords, before the first
Corn-Bill was passed.

There is one thing more, and that
thing of great importance, to remind young men of upon this occasion; namely, that almost the
whole of the cities and towns in
the whole kingdom of England
and Wales sent most urgent petitions against this Corn Bill;
that, the Bill was brought in by
that Mr. Robinson who was lately so gay in his descriptions of
our *prosperity;* that Castlereagh
(who has since cut his own throat
at North Cray in Kent) was, at
that time, what is called the leader
of the Ministerial side of the
House; that he said, upon the
third reading of the Bill, that he
did not care so much about the
Bill in itself, but, that, *now that*
*there were clamours against it,*
he should urge its immediate
adoption; and, lastly, let it be
known to those who do not know
it, and let it be remembered by
us all, old and young, that this
Bill was passed with a great body
of troops, with bayonets upon the
points of their muskets, drawn up
round the Parliament-House; or,
at least, round all that part of it
which is accessible to the people.

So much for the origin and
progress of this law or code of
laws and regulations, relative to
the importation of corn. I now
come to what has recently taken
place upon the subject. There
has been so much talk; so many
stupid statements; such masses of
words with such little meaning;
such a blundering and such a
saying and unsaying; there has
been, in short, such a confusion
of ideas produced by the debatings
and the writings about this matter,
that it seems necessary to say
something in the way of explanation as to the very nature of the
thing. We all know that, some

time ago, a new Corn Bill was passed by the House of Commons and sent to the Lords. We all know that this new Bill has been knocked in the head by an amendment of Wellington (whose titular name is quite long enough, without any thing more), which was made in the House of Lords about ten days ago. I shall speak by-and-bye of the third Bill, which, it appears, is now coming on in the House of Commons; but, at present, let me speak of the new Corn Bill and the old Corn Bill.

According to the old Corn Bill, wheat (we will speak of wheat alone, in order to render the explanation more simple) might, at any time, be brought into our ports from abroad, and *warehoused*; but, not brought into the market to be sold, unless the average price of English wheat in the market *were below a certain price.* According to the new Corn Bill, foreign wheat might not only be brought into her ports and warehoused at any time, but might also *be brought into the market*

and sold at any time; but, then, observe, it was, according to the new Corn Bill, to *pay a duty*, which duty was to be in an inverse proportion to the price of English wheat in the market. The old Corn Bill was a system of *prohibition;* the new Corn Bill was a system of *heavy duties.* The latter, so very high were the duties, was pretty nearly as effectual as the former, for the purpose of keeping out foreign wheat; but, still, it was not a positive prohibition; wheat might be constantly coming in at some rate or other; and, in certain cases, the new Bill would have lowered the price of the produce of the English farms, and have lessened the capacity of the farmers to pay high rents.

Now, I beg you to pay attention to the amendment proposed by Wellington, by which amendment this new Bill was defeated. I have spoken above about warehousing; and, it is right that you understand clearly the nature of this curious affair. There are ever-

mous warehouses in the ports for the holding of goods, until the importers of them choose to take them out and pay the duty upon them. All is TICK, in this our ticking, trusting, accommodating, discounting, speculating and the devil-knows-what-besides system. Formerly, the merchant, when his cargo came into port, went and received it, put it into his own storehouse, and paid the duty upon it, whatever it might be. This was the way of going on, when London acquired, throughout the world, such a reputation for the riches and integrity of her merchants. Pitt, who appears to have been the father of postponement in payments, hatched a system of giving credit, or, rather, opened a sort of national pawn-shop for merchants' goods. He built immense warehouses, into which merchants might put their cargoes, which remained thus locked up by the Government, till the merchants were able and willing to pay the duties upon the cargoes, so that the importer, having first, perhaps, given bills, as they are called; that is to say, gone on TICK for the cargo, next put the cargo in pawn for the duty; then, when he found a customer or could get his price, went on tick again to raise money to pay the duties; then took the cargo out of pawn; then sold the cargo, and, perhaps, got something by it, after paying the bills that he had drawn for the purchase of the cargo and after paying the duties; and thus, had a gain, upon the whole, without ever having possessed, of his own, one farthing of money from the beginning.

Such is the warehousing or pawning system of commerce. Now, wheat, as we have seen, might be pawned to the Government in this way, under the new Bill as well as under the old Bill; but there was this difference, that, under the old Bill, it could never be taken out of pawn to be brought into the English market, until the average price of English wheat in the market was at a certain high amount; while, under the new Bill, wheat might be taken out of pawn *at any time, upon paying the duty* fixed by the Bill.

The amendment of WELLING- TON was this, (hat wheat *should not be taken out of pawn under the new Bill,* until the average price. of wheat in the English market should be sixty-six shil- lings the quarter! This, as you will clearly see, quite destroyed the principle and object of the new Bill. This Bill was to put an end to *prohibition,* and to substitute duties instead thereof. The Lords persevered in this amendment, and the Bill was, of course, put an end to. It must have been put an end to if they persevered in the amendment, because it has long been an inva- riable rule for t'other place to suffer no alterations to be made by the Lords in a money-bill; and this was a money-bill, because it treated of duties; and, in fact, it did treat of a tax upon our bread. There has been a queer sort of *understanding* going on between the Ministers and the opposing Lords upon this occasion. The

opposing Lords were in difficulty; for, the leading men amongst them are those who were in the ministry before the late change; and they had all approved of the bringing in of the new Bill. How were they to contrive, then, to defeat this same Bill! WELLING- TON has been represented by Mr. CANNING as having been in- duced by others to move and per- severe in the amendment. I see no reason for asserting this. He was one of the Ministers that ap- proved of the new Bill being brought in; and, when the new Bill had passed the Commons, without any alteration in the warehousing or pawning part of it, without the introduction of any clause to take away the power of pawning or the taking out of pawn, how was Wellington to find an excuse for this amendment, which totally changed the nature of the Bill; which made it a Bill of prohibitions as well as a Bill of duties?

This great captain, who ap- pears to be as skilful in corn tactics as he is held to be in those of a military cast, got, some how or other, into a correspondence with our free-trade Minister, Mr. Huskisson, whom Lord Lauderdale has asserted to be the real papa of this new Bill, though Mr. Canning did positively assert that it was a sort of legacy of Lord Liverpool, a sort of orphan, which had dropped, as it were, from his Lordship, into the hands of this our new First Lord of the Treasury. Into a correspondence with this our free-trade Minister, the Duke of Wellington, some how or other, did get; and, there, in the columns of the broad sheet, we behold, " My dear Huskisson " and " My dear Duke," to a whole string of letters, making, all together, perhaps, a foot or eighteen inches in length of the said columns. From this correspondence it appears that Mr. Huskisson expressed his opinion that any alteration in the Bill at all; at least, that any amendment at all resembling that of the Duke, would cause the total loss of the Bill.

But, at the same time, it is very clear that Mr. Huskisson did furnish the Duke with a pretext, and, perhaps, it may be called a pretty fair ground for proposing some such amendment as that which he did propose. The passage in Mr. Huskisson's letter to which I allude is this :—" Had your propo- " sal been that no corn bonded " after the passing of the present " Bill should be allowed to be en- " tered for home consumption till " the average price had reached " 66s., and that thenceforward all " corn so bonded, or thereafter " imported, should come under the " regulations of the Bill, individu- " ally I should not object to such " a proviso. It would ensure that " no quantity beyond that now in " bond should be thrown upon the " market, unless, in spite of that " quantity, the price reached a " level which might fairly be taken " as an indication of our being in " want of a further supply from " abroad."

Here Huskisson clearly gives his assent to the Duke's amendment, as far as related to all corn that should be brought into the country and warehoused after the passing of the Bill. He gives his assent to the prohibition system, to the extent of sixty-six shillings a quarter, as far as relates to all corn, not in warehouse before the Bill should be passed. So that, if the Duke had modelled his amendment upon Huskisson's plan, all the wheat *now in warehouse,* now in pawn, might have been taken out of pawn, upon paying the duty; but all wheat taken into pawn after the passing of the Bill, must, just as in the case of the old Bill, have been kept in pawn, or, at least, not suffered to be brought out of pawn into the English market until English wheat rose to the average of 66s. The Duke's amendment differed from Huskisson's assent in this; that, Huskisson wished to let the corn now in pawn out into the market upon paying a duty, but wished to subject all corn brought into pawn in future to the prohibitory regulations of the old Bill, as far, at least, as the price of 66s.; while the Duke's amendment subjected the corn now in pawn, as well as the corn to come into pawn, to the same prohibitory regulation. Huskisson assented to the destruction of the principle of the Bill as far as related to the corn now in pawn: the Duke's amendment destroyed the principle altogether, for time present as well as for time to come.

Thus stood the matter, when the Bill was abandoned in the House of Lords. Next comes Mr. CANNING again to the House of Commons, with a project for patching up the matter for the present. But, before we speak of that project, we must see a little of Mr. BARING's description of the effect which the amendment of Wellington would have had if the Bill had been passed with that amendment in it. These observations of Baring are very well worthy of attention. They show to what extent ignorance has operated upon this occasion. I beg the reader to pay attention to the parts which I have marked in italics. It will be observed, that Mr. Baring here shows very clearly, that the amendment would have caused the corn to be warehoused in countries on the other side of the channel; so that, as the learned Duke's amendment shut out no corn, and was to have effect upon no corn, except that which was in warehouse here in England, the amendment would have had no effect at all upon corn warehoused on the other side of the channel, and would, in fact, have kept out of the market, no corn, except that which is now in pawn in England! I beg the reader, now, to pay attention to Baring's words; for, as we shall presently see, they give a precious cut, either at the sense or the sincerity, of our Minister of trade.

———

: " If the Right Honourable Member for Oxford could think that
" such an Amendment was intro-
" duced from a sincere desire to pro-
" mote the object without injuring
" the principle of the Bill, he could
" only say, that his credulity was
" equal to his candour; for he (Mr.
" Baring) could hardly conceive how
" any persons with common sense,
" who were really friendly to the
" principle and object of the Bill,
" could have proposed such an
" Amendment, especially if they
" knew what would be the fate of
" the Bill, which they must have
" done, as it was to be presumed
" that they were acquainted with
" the privileges of the House of
" Commons, and with their own
" privileges. The effect of the
" Amendment was to *throw the whole*
" *of the Corn Trade of the country*
" *into a state of total uncertainty and*
" *confusion.* He thought the Right
" Honourable Gentleman himself
" ought to have said a few words
" on the nature, object, and effects
" of the Amendment. Could any
" one show that the Amendment
" was good for any thing except to
" throw the Corn Trade *into the*
" *hands of foreigners?* If the object
" was to give a preference to the corn
" directly imported, over the corn
" in bond, that plan would *not have*
" *the slightest effect in protecting the*

" *agriculture of this country;* and if
" it had not that object, it had no
" object whatever, unless that of
" destroying the Bill. It could not
" surely have been intended to *injure*
" *our own shipping,* and to throw the
" whole of the Corn Trade into the
" hands of foreigners; and if that
" was not the purpose, what could it
" be, except to get rid of the Bill?
" He repeated, that as a protection
" to agriculture, the Amendment
" *was the most absurd and inoperative*
" *that could possibly be conceived;* for
" Corn would be *warehoused at the*
" *Hans Towns and Flemish ports, and*
" *would come into competition with*
" *the home growers to the full as much*
" *as if it were warehoused at home.*
" He ought to apologize to the Com-
" mittee for taking up their time
" with such an Amendment as this;
" but every one must be perfectly
" aware, that foreign Corn might be
" easily warehoused at Flushing and
" other parts of the opposite Conti-
" nent, and readily poured into this
" country. Some gentlemen seemed
" to be of opinion, that these foreign
" ports were at an extraordinary
" distance, while some of them were
" not much further from Mark-lane

" than Bolton or Lynn. Parliament
" could have given no greater boon
" to foreigners than by passing this
" Bill in the shape in which it stood
" after the Amendment. Foreign
" Corn would still have flowed in
" abundantly, when the averages
" would have permitted; but *all the*
" *benefits of the warehousing system*
" *would have been transferred abroad.*
" There would have been one differ-
" ence, which he believed had not
" suggested itself to the sagacious
" inventors of this beautiful Amend-
" ment; namely, that while foreign
" Corn would have come in at low
" prices with as much facility as
" ever, if unfortunately the home
" price had risen to 99s. or 100s. in
" consequence of the scarcity result-
" ing from a deficient harvest, this
" country would then have found
" itself entirely at the mercy of those
" foreign countries, where the ports
" were situated in which the Corn
" had been warehoused [hear, hear!],
" and from which the supply neces-
' sary to our subsistence might in a
" moment be cut off [cheers]."

————

This is a very good cutting at
the Lords; but, Baring does not

appear to have perceived that he was, at the same time, cutting as hardly upon his Right Honourable Friend, the free-trade Minister; for, he, good man, he, wise Trade-Minister, would have had no objection to imposing the 'Duke's prohibition upon 'corn taken into pawn after the passing of the Bill, which, as Baring tells us, would have caused the corn to be bonded on the other side of the channel, would have afforded no protection whatever to English agriculture, and would have thrown the profits of the foreign corn-trade wholly into the hands of foreigners, and taken it away from English merchants. And, this really does appear to be the case; for, as Baring observed, the ports on the other side of the channel are as near to us as those of Boston or Lynn, requiring a very few hours to order shipments thence into the Thames, into which the wheat might have been brought, and thrown into the English market at any time; and, thus, the Duke's amendment, while it would have kept the corn now in pawn from coming into the English market, would have kept all future corn out of pawn, and have kept the market constantly open to receive it; because, as you will perceive, my friends, when the merchant brings in corn, he is not, under the new Bill, *compelled to put it in pawn*: he may, upon paying the duty, sell it, at once, out of the ship. According to the old law, no wheat could be brought into the market at all, until English wheat rose to a certain price; according to the new Bill, foreign wheat may be brought into the English market at any time, upon paying a certain duty: if not put into pawn it would not have been affected by the Duke's amendment; so that, if the Bill had passed with that amendment in it, it would have produced all the absurd and mischievous effects which Baring describes; and, if it had been passed, with the amendment suggested by Huskisson, it would have b■■.

2 C

but a very little better : it would not, indeed, have kept the corn at present in pawn still in pawn, while other corn was brought from warehouses abroad to be sold here; but, even our Trade-Minister's own project would have caused the corn to be warehoused on the other side of the channel, and would have produced all the mischiefs which Baring has enumerated.

So much for the past: now let us see what appears to be at present intended. Mr. Canning is about to bring in another Bill, for the mere temporary purpose of suffering the corn, NOW IN PAWN, to be brought into the market and sold upon payment of the duties specified in the new Bill. There are, they say, about half a million of quarters of wheat, besides other grain and meal and flour. This is to come into the market, if the owners choose to bring it into the market before the first day of May next.

This is the new, the last, or, rather, the present, piece of patch-work. This will hardly have much effect upon the price of corn ; but, it will do something ; and it is not very likely that the Lords will make much of a stand against this Bill. What they dislike is, *open ports*, let the duty be what it may. There is a deep-rooted prejudice with the land-owners in favour of *prohibition*. They dread the idea of a competition with countries who are untaxed, comparatively, and untithed. Instinct, almost without the smallest assistance from reason, teaches them that the Jews and jobbers must have their last acre, unless they can get a high price for the produce of the land. They are the real sellers of the corn and the cattle. The farmer has no interest in having a high price; seeing that his rent, his tithes, and all his outgoings, are in proportion to the price of his produce. But, the landlord has a direct and great interest in getting high rent, which he cannot do unless there be a high price of produce. He, therefore, it is, that wants the high price; and high price he must have, unless he give up his estate to the Jews and jobbers, or unless he obtain the taking off of more than one half of the taxes. He is frightened at the idea of either of these: he is shocked at the thought of sweeping the streets or cracking stones on the high-way. He would take off the taxes, with all his heart; but, when he comes to call the roll of his relations and dependents, he finds that if the taxes were reduced, these would all fall back upon him like so many paupers. Besides, there is, perhaps, his own place, his own pension, his wife's sinecure, his own half-pay or something else, or his half-dozen sons quartered upon the taxes in some way or other. There must be money to pay the interest of the Debt. Sweep away the taxes, and the interest is unpaid. He cannot continue to eat taxes while the fund-holder is torn from the crib. Turn him which way he will, he finds himself beset with difficulties. So I have seen, after a shower, a mischievous, greedy, reptile of a slug, surrounded, for one's amusement, by a circle of warm lime, two or three inches in diameter. The reptile advances towards the circumference, pokes out his horns and his nose; just touches the lime; round he turns; pokes away towards another part of the circumference; finds the lime again there; back he twists, making a similar effort in another quarter; and, thus he goes on, till the gardener, having had enough of his torments, and remembering his character and the extent of his devastations, takes a crumb of the lime, puts it upon his back, and the nasty, slothful reptile, made, apparently, to devour the labour of others, made, sometimes black and sometimes white, sometimes yellow and sometimes grey, but always the same devouring monster; till the gardener, remembering his devastations, thus puts the consuming material upon his worthless carcass, and sees him curl up and expire.

Beset with difficulties as completely as a slug so surrounded;

are the landowners, not many years since so insolent, so cruel, so savage towards the common people of England. They are not so insolent as they were. Poverty, and fear for the future, have taught them humility to a certain degree; but, that they may be taught to do complete justice to the people; that the rest of us, like you, my friends, may never cease our efforts, till we have obtained from them every particle of that which they unjustly withhold, is the prayer and the hope of

Your faithful friend and

Most obedient Servant,

WM. COBBETT.

## PAPER - MONEY.

I AM compelled to postpone some remarks that I intended to make on what took place on Thursday last, 15th June, on the motion of MR. DAVENPORT. Some very curious things were said by Sir FRANCIS BURDETT, on this paper-matter. This is the rock, on which the THING will split. Corn Bills are trifles, compared with this affair.

## BANKS BREAKING!

### OR

## ANOTHER "LATE PANIC."

WE shall certainly have famous sport in a short time. I have been told, that even the stopping of the pitiful paper shop at HUNTINGDON, which was a drop of water, compared to the Thames, almost frightened an OLD FEMALE FRIEND of mine out of her senses. I am told that she was actually beset

for two or three days; I mean
haunted by a sort of craving
Devils that seem to threaten to
tear out her very bowels. If this
be true, and I believe it is strictly
true, she will begin to look about
her pretty sharply, and DADDY
CANNING (for he is now upon the
list of my *Daddies*, along with
COKE and BURDETT) may begin
to look sharply about him. I
always thought him just the man
to bring this thing to a close. The
*Bank Circular* was, to me, clear
indication of what was coming.
Some means or other will be resorted to, with the intention and
anxious desire of preventing the
Country Banks from blowing up the
Mother Bank, and from producing
*Parliamentary Reform*; for this
is the way, my boys, in which reform will come, and in no other
way, as God has given it to man
to produce that reform. This

being the case, I rejoice exceedingly at the breaking up of any
bank, however small it may be.
The newspapers give an account
of another recent bank-breaking
in Staffordshire. Thus the thing
began last time; and, the same
sort of panic must come again,
before it be long, with a great addition of force and of mischief,
*unless the Winchester bushel of
wheat come down to five shillings
at most.* I desire my readers to
bear this in mind; and, especially
if they have children, or any other
persons, particularly helpless persons, to provide for, let them act
as reason dictates to them, or let
them, I say, suffer half starvation
at least, with bundles of " WORTH-
LESS RAGS" in their pockets.

## TO THE

## EARL OF WESTMORELAND.

———

*Fleet-Street, 21st June, 1827.*

Mr Loss.

I INTENDED to do myself the honour of addressing a Letter to your Lordship, pointing out a mode of shoving out Mr. CAN-NING and his motley tribe; and also a mode of preserving the estates of the landowners, or at least a part of those estates. I have been induced to defer the execution of my purpose, by the *events,* which have come pressing upon us for the last two weeks; and now other *events* seem to be pushing on, and they appear to be of a nature calculated to decide the whole thing at a single blow. Corn, that is to say wheat (not measured by the beating of a pendulum), must come to 5*s.* a bushel at least; or, another

" late panic " is approaching. I hear from all parts of the country, that which convinces me of this; and that which I see going forward in London convinces me, that every effort will be made to protect the general paper concern against the natural panic-produc-ing progress of the country banks. These efforts, my Lord, though of various descriptions, and, appa-rently, working in ways very *different* from each other, or in-tended so to work, have all, evi-dently *one and the same tendency;* namely, to make the whole of the currency of the country consist of what will, in reality, be a GO-VERNMENT PAPER-MONEY! That is the last stroke, my Lord; and under that stroke the system will linger but a very short space of time; and during that time, short as it will be, the great question must be settled; namely, whether things shall be righted by a Radical Reform of the People's House of Parliament, or the whole fabric go to pieces, amidst a general convulsion; if the latter take place, I am not bold enough to attempt to describe, what I think will be the consequences: if the former take place, it will immediately produce that " Equitable Adjustment" prayed for in the NORFOLK PETITION, which will once more give safety to property, and liberty and happiness to the people; and therefore, that it may take place, is, notwithstanding all the treatment that I have received from the landowners, the parsons and their subalterns, the sincere prayer of,

My Lord,

Your Lordship's

Most obedient and

Most humble Servant,

WM. COBBETT.

P. S. My Lord,—So many things have happened of late, to make me rather out of conceit with a certain august assembly, that I really feel happy at having an opportunity to notice a circumstance which has had a contrary effect upon my mind. I allude to the throwing out of the DROXFORD INCLOSURE BILL, by your Lordships' House, after the said Bill had been passed by the House of Commons. This Bill would have destroyed the very best nursery for OAK TIMBER, that I ever saw in my life. The nature of the soil, is that of the *Wealds* of Surrey, Sussex, and Kent, so famous in the annals of the navy of England: it would have robbed the Crown of a part of its rights by alienating for ever a part of the revenue of the See of Winchester; and, a thing to be deprecated by every man with a heart in his bosom; it would have chased, pretty nearly, if not quite, *a thousand* persons from the happiest cottages, that yet remain in England, and have driven them to slink and starve in the beggarly skirts of towns and villages; and all this, my Lord, solely to gratify the stupid greediness of a dozen or two of that description of persons, on whom GOD himself has denounced vengeance for their desire to " lay house to " house, and field to field, until " the poor and needy be driven " from the land." It is curious enough, my Lord, that, in the close of the First Number of my Work, called the Woodlands, and in the beginning of the Second Number (not yet published), I noticed this very spot as one of the finest in England, for the growth of Oak Timber; and,

during my Rural Ride of last fall, I noticed the surprising growth of two of the spots of this Forest, or *Chase*, as it is called; which spots had been inclosed twenty-five years ago, by the late Bishop, and which had been, agreeably to the old law, thrown out as grazing land again at the end of *twenty years*. I saw these inclosures about three years after they were made. There were then no signs of timber growing within these inclosures. When I saw them last fall, there were thousands upon thousands of *Oak* trees, as big round in the butt as my thigh is big round in the middle (and nature has not made it very small); and thousands upon thousands not much less than *thirty* feet high. Would it not have been a murderous act to have broken up this ancient *Chase*, to have destroyed this nur-

CHASE

sery of Oak trees, so near to a naval arsenal? It has not been done. The greedy applicants have not been gratified; the good of the nation, the rights of his Majesty, and the happiness of the poor have been consulted on this occasion; and it is with great pleasure that I acknowledge, for myself, and that I proclaim to others as far as my voice will reach, that we owe this act of protection to the House of Lords.

## TULIP-TREE WOOD.

---

I HAVE for sale *fifty-four* planks of this wood, averaging about *thirty feet* in each plank. They are *two and a half inches thick.* Some are about fourteen feet long; others not, probably, more than ten feet. Some are between *three* and *four feet wide;* others not, perhaps, more than two feet. The planks are just *as wide at one end as at the other;* and there is not a *single knot,* or *curl,* in the whole parcel of *one thousand, five hundred and eighty-one feet.*

MICHAUX, in his North American Sylva, says of the *tree,* that he saw one *twenty-two feet six inches* in circumference, at five feet from the ground; and that he judged the tree to be *a hundred and forty feet high.* Of the WOOD Michaux says what every body in America knows; namely, that it is in colour of a pale yellow; that its grain is very fine; that the wood is both *light* and *strong;* that it is used in rafters, shingles, door-panels, bedsteads, wainscoting, chair-bottoms, large bowls, and particularly, in all parts of America, in making the *panels of coaches* and other pleasure carriages; and, so much is this the case, that it is carried hundreds of miles to be used in those places, near to which it does not grow.

The wood admits of a *beautiful polish*, and is used for various purposes by cabinet-makers. Of these planks that I have, a single plank would make a kitchen-dresser, or table; a servants'-hall table; a slab for a dairy or a larder; fine things, I should think, for cutting-boards, shop-boards, counters, show-boards, or almost any thing, which requires a very large breadth of wood in one single, smooth piece. Being $2\frac{1}{2}$ inches thick, these planks are strong enough for any thing.

The price *for the whole parcel*, ONE SHILLING and THREE-PENCE A FOOT; for any quantity less than the whole, and exceeding a hundred feet, ONE SHILLING AND SIXPENCE A FOOT; and for a *single plank*, ONE SHILLING AND NINE PENCE A FOOT. So that a plank, 14 feet long, and 3½ feet wide, which, with a couple of trestles, would make a table to dine *twenty people*, would cost only *four pounds five shillings*; it might be kept as clean as a marble slab, and with nearly as little trouble, and would last for many a life-time.

The planks are at *my house at Kensington*, where they may be seen, by *application to the gardener*, at any hour between four in the morning and five in the afternoon. There is the *mark* on each plank, expressing the *number of feet* which it contains. The marks were put on in America, and, therefore, are according to our old-fashioned English *kingly* measure, and not according to the grand and

sublime " IMPERIAL MEA-
SURE," which, being an "improvement of the eye," produced
by " liberal principles," the off-
spring of the " march of mind,"
gauges (in defiance of Bedlam)
ale, makes oysters, and ascertains
the length and width of shirting,
by the heat of a pendulum in a

" heat of sixty-two degrees of
" Farenheit's Thermometer."

N.B. I have now but little more
than half the above quantity left;
Gentlemen, who may wish either
to see it or purchase it, must therefore be speedy in their applications.

## MARKETS.

Average Prices of CORN throughout ENGLAND, for the week ending June 8.

**Per Quarter.**

| | s. | d. | | s. | d. |
|---|---|---|---|---|---|
| Wheat | 57 | 11 | Rye | 41 | 11 |
| Barley | 40 | 0 | Beans | 49 | 6 |
| Oats | 28 | 8 | Pease | 50 | 0 |

Total Quantity of Corn returned as Sold in the Maritime Districts, for the week ended June 8.

| | Qrs. | | Qrs. |
|---|---|---|---|
| Wheat | 30,412 | Rye | 161 |
| Barley | 3,151 | Beans | 772 |
| Oats | 6,904 | Pease | 66 |

*Corn Exchange, Mark Lane.*

Quantities and Prices of British Corn, &c. sold and delivered in this Market, during the week ended Saturday, June 9.

| | Qrs. | | £. | s. | d. | | s. | d. |
|---|---|---|---|---|---|---|---|---|
| Wheat | 5,364 for | 16,208 | 6 | 10 | Average, | 60 | 5 |
| Barley | 617 | 1,315 | 14 | 10 | | 42 | 7 |
| Oats | 1,287 | 2,141 | 3 | 5 | | 33 | 3 |
| Rye | 0 | 0 | 0 | 0 | | 0 | 0 |
| Beans | 488 | 1,213 | 19 | 10 | | 49 | 9 |
| Pease | 83 | 193 | 13 | 5 | | 46 | 8 |

Friday, June 15.—The arrivals of Grain this week are small, except of Foreign Oats, the quantity of which, reported this week, is excessive. The abandonment of the Corn Bill has occasioned an advance in the price of Wheat since Monday last of 5s. to 6s. per qr. Barley and Beans remain nominally as last reported. There is no alteration in the value of Oats since last report. The top price of Flour is considered as established at 55s. per sack.

Monday, June 18.—The supplies of English Grain in general last week were moderate, and of Foreign Oats the quantity was excessive. Of Flour, meantime, the arrivals were likewise considerable. To this morning's market the fresh supplies of Corn are small. The loss of the new Corn Bill had a considerable effect on the Wheat trade last Friday, but to-day there is less eagerness in the millers, and although the prices are quoted 4s. to 5s. per quarter higher than last Monday, yet the sales have been very dull to-day, at this advance.

Barley, Beans, and Pease, are each 2s. to 3s. per qr. dearer than this day se'nnight, but the quantities of each are so very small, that the quotations may be considered almost nominal. There are now so many Oats for sale, that only such as are stout and sweet maintain last quotations; Foreign Feed parcels are 1s. to 2s. per quarter lower than this day se'nnight. The top price of Flour is established at 55s. per sack. Nothing now doing in Bonded Corn of any description.

*Price on board Ship as under.*

Flour, per sack ......50s. — 55s.
—— Seconds ........45s. — 48s.
—— North Country ..44s. — 47s.

Price of Bread.—The price of the 4lb. Loaf is stated at 9d. by the full-priced Bakers.

Account of Wheat, &c. arrived in the Port of London, from June 11 to June 16, both inclusive.

|  | Qrs. |  | Qr. |
|---|---|---|---|
| Wheat .. | 4,239 | Tares .... | — |
| Barley .. | 1,362 | Linseed .. | 2,397 |
| Malt .... | 4,626 | Rapeseed . | 13 |
| Oats .... | 8,015 | Brank .. | 49 |
| Beans ... | 301 | Mustard .. | — |
| Flour .... | 8,204 | Flax .... | — |
| Rye .... | 147 | Hemp ... | — |
| Pease .... | 669 | Seeds ... | 28 |

Foreign.—Wheat, 6,373; Barley, 5,498; Oats, 63,424; Beans, 2,721 quarters; and Flour 503 barrels.

---

### Price of Hops, per Cwt. in the Borough.

Monday, June 18.—This last week has experienced an advance of duty from 55,000*l.* to 90,000*l.*, owing to the partial improvement round Maidstone; this only lasted two days, as on Saturday and this day the duty is again down to 55,000*l.*, and a further decline likely. The accounts generally state an increase of fly; but the blight must have time to go through its stages, and the probable result will be as decisive as at any period since 1802. It is impossible to state prices in such a market: an advance from Friday last is stated of 20*s.* to 30*s.*

#### Another Account.

June 18.—In consequence of reports from the Plantations (particularly Essex) of a disappearance of the fly from many grounds, the duty advanced from 55,000*l.* (our last Report) to 90,000*l.*, on Friday last, and with the rise of that, the prices of all sorts of Hops decreased in proportion. On Saturday, accounts arrived, that with the still warm weather which succeeded the cold and northeasterly winds of this day week, and following days, the fly had again made its appearance in increased numbers in all quarters. This morning has confirmed Saturday's report,

as our accounts speak of the blight increasing rapidly in all parts of the Plantations. There is considerable inquiry this morning for Hops, at higher prices. Duty called 50,000*l.*

*Maidstone,* June 14.—The accounts we receive from the Hop Plantations are this week rather more favourable, particularly round about this neighbourhood; the fly is considered to be much decreased, and the bines are growing, and look more kindly.— Duty advanced to 70,000*l.*

---

### SMITHFIELD.

Monday, June 18.—This market was lower on Friday for both Beef and Mutton; particularly the former. To-day the trade is by no means lively, the weather and the supply combining against it.

*Per Stone of 8 pounds (alive).*

|  | s. | d. | s. | d. |
|---|---|---|---|---|
| Beef ..... | 4 | 0 | to 5 | 0 |
| Mutton .., | 4 | 0 | — 5 | 0 |
| Veal ..... | 5 | 0 | — 5 | 8 |
| Pork ..... | 5 | 0 | — 5 | 4 |
| Lamb .... | 5 | 0 | — 6 | 0 |

| Beasts . . 2,080 | Sheep .. 21,210 |
|---|---|
| Calves ... 227 | Pigs ... 162 |

NEWGATE, (same day.)

*Per Stone of 8 pounds (dead).*

|  | s. | d. | s. | d. |
|---|---|---|---|---|
| Beef ..... | 3 | 8 | to 4 | 8 |
| Mutton ... | 3 | 4 | — 4 | 4 |
| Veal ..... | 3 | 8 | — 5 | 8 |
| Pork ..... | 4 | 0 | — 6 | 0 |
| Lamb .... | 4 | 4 | — 6 | 4 |

LEADENHALL, (same day.)

*Per Stone of 8 pounds (dead).*

|  | s. | d. | s. | d. |
|---|---|---|---|---|
| Beef ... . | 3 | 8 | to 4 | 10 |
| Mutton ... | 3 | 4 | — 4 | 6 |
| Veal ..... | 3 | 8 | — 5 | 4 |
| Pork ..... | 4 | 4 | — 6 | 6 |
| Lamb .... | 4 | 0 | — 5 | 8 |

## POTATOES.

**SPITALFIELDS,** *per Cwt.*

|  | s. | s. | s. | s. |
|---|---|---|---|---|
| Ox-Nobles.....| 0 | 0 | to 0 | 0 |
| Middlings......| 8 | 0 | — 10 | 0 |
| Chats .........| 3 | 0 | — 6 | 0 |
| Common Red..| 0 | 0 | — 0 | 0 |

Onions, 0s. 0d.—0s. 0d. per bush.

**BOROUGH,** *per Ton.*

|  | L. | s. | L. | s. |
|---|---|---|---|---|
| Ox-Nobles ....| 3 | 0 | to 3 | 10 |
| Middlings......| 2 | 0 | — 0 | 0 |
| Chats .........| 0 | 0 | — 0. | 0 |
| Common Red..| 3 | 0 | — 0 | 0 |

## HAY and STRAW, per Load.

*Smithfield.*—Hay....90s. to 126s.

Straw...38s. to 42s.

Clover. 110s. to 150s.

*St. James's.*—Hay... 70s. to 140s.

Straw .. 39s. to 48s.

Clover. 120s. to 145s.

*Whitechapel.*—Hay....84s. to 120s.

Straw...36s. to 42s.

Clover 100s. to 150s.

---

## AVERAGE PRICE OF CORN, sold in the Maritime Counties of England and Wales, for the Week ended June 8, 1827.

|  | Wheat. | | Barley. | | Oats. | |
|---|---|---|---|---|---|---|
|  | s. | d. | s. | d. | s. | d. |
| London* | 59 | 11 | 40 | 3 | 29 | 5 |
| Essex | 59 | 3 | 38 | 6 | 28 | 8 |
| Kent | 57 | 3 | 39 | 7 | 32 | 8 |
| Sussex | 56 | 8 | 34 | 5 | 29 | 10 |
| Suffolk | 56 | 10 | 39 | 6 | 26 | 8 |
| Cambridgeshire | 54 | 6 | 36 | 4 | 24 | 8 |
| Norfolk | 56 | 6 | 37 | 3 | 29 | 0 |
| Lincolnshire | 56 | 1 | 39 | 8 | 24 | 2 |
| Yorkshire | 55 | 11 | 35 | 2 | 28 | 10 |
| Durham | 58 | 10 | 42 | 8 | 38 | 4 |
| Northumberland | 57 | 8 | 38 | 3 | 34 | 6 |
| Cumberland | 64 | 3 | 43 | 4 | 36 | 6 |
| Westmoreland | 64 | 5 | 46 | 0 | 39 | 4 |
| Lancashire | 63 | 1 | 0 | 0 | 32 | 2 |
| Cheshire | 63 | 10 | 45 | 2 | 28 | 0 |
| Gloucestershire | 56 | 3 | 43 | 4 | 43 | 1 |
| Somersetshire | 55 | 10 | 0 | 0 | 28 | 8 |
| Monmouthshire | 61 | 2 | 44 | 4 | 0 | 0 |
| Devonshire | 59 | 7 | 39 | 3 | 32 | 7 |
| Cornwall | 64 | 5 | 42 | 1 | 37 | 0 |
| Dorsetshire | 55 | 8 | 40 | 11 | 0 | 0 |
| Hampshire | 57 | 1 | 39 | 6 | 0 | 0 |
| North Wales | 71 | 5 | 46 | 4 | 29 | 4 |
| South Wales | 62 | 1 | 45 | 8 | 28 | 0 |

* The London Average is always that of the Week preceding.

*Liverpool*, June 12.—Since our last there has been a very limited demand for Wheat, at a reduction of 3d. per 70lbs. For Oats, demand likewise limited, and prices nominal. Indian Corn has become very scarce, and sales have been made at an advance of 3s. per qr. on Yellow, and 2s. on White. In other articles little doing.

Imported into Liverpool, from June 5 to June 11, 1827, inclusive:— Wheat, 10,566; Oats, 8,239; Barley, 4,092; Malt, 50; Beans, 3; Pease, 35 quarters. Oatmeal, 75 packs, per 240 lbs.; Flour, 41 sacks, per 280 lbs.

*Derby*, June 16.—We had but little business done in the Corn trade this day, owing to the sudden rise which had taken place in London on Wednesday, and the price demanded for Wheat could only be complied with by a few needy customers, and that about 1s. to 2s. per qr. advance.

*Horncastle*, June 16.—There is very little business doing here in the Corn Trade; the prices something higher.—Wheat, from 57s. to 63s.; Oats, 28s. to 33s.; Beans, 63s. to 66s.; and Rye, from 38s. to 40s. per qr.

*Ipswich*, June 16.—We had to-day a good supply of Wheat, but no Spring Corn. Considerably higher prices were demanded, and little business was done. Currency as follows:—Wheat, 56s. to 66s. per qr.

*Manchester*, June 16.—From Monday to Thursday morning the Corn and Flour trade was as dull as possible; scarcely a sale could be effected, particularly after the report of the London market on Monday last had been received here; but, on the receipt of the news that the Duke of Wellington's amendment on the Corn Bill was carried, in the second reading, by a majority of 11, and of Lord Goderich's intention of withdrawing the Bill, it caused the holders of Wheat and Flour to demand higher prices; on the former, of 6d. to 8d. per bushel of 70 lbs.; and on the latter, of 2s. to 3s. per sack of 280 lbs., which advance has been fully supported at our market to-day, with brisk sale at the close. Oats have also improved in value 1d. to 2d. per bushel of 45 lbs., with a good demand. Beans are in short supply, and 1s. per qr. dearer. Boiling Pease, little or no demand. There is more inquiry for fine Malt, but at present it has not undergone any improvement in value, but it is expected it soon will. The sales in Flour have been more extensive since Thursday, at the beforementioned advance, with a prospect of going still higher, the supply being short, as well as all kinds of Grain. In Barley no alteration.

*Newcastle-upon-Tyne*, June 16.—The overthrow of the Corn Bill in the House of Lords, and a small supply of Wheat from the farmers, caused a rapid sale for fine new threshed samples this morning, at an advance of 3s. per qr. since last week, and granary samples sold proportionally dearer. Rye is 2s. per quarter dearer. Barley is so scarce that it is difficult to quote prices with precision, but it is considerably dearer. Beans and Pease are each 3s. per quarter higher. We had a small supply of Oats from the farmers, which sold readily for mealing at 2s. per quarter advance; but having had some foreign arrivals during the week, and the principal consumers not buying to-day, prices of feed Oats remain the same as last week.

*Norwich*, June 16.—We had only a small supply of Wheat to this day's market, with a brisk demand, and an advance in price of 3s. per quarter; Red, 56s. to 62s.; White to 64s.; Barley nominal; Oats, 28s. to 31s.; Beans, 43s. to 48s.; Pease, 44s. to 48s.; Boilers, to 50s. per quarter; and Flour, 43s. to 41s. per sack.

## COUNTRY CATTLE AND MEAT MARKETS, &c.

*Horncastle*, June 16.—Beef, 9s. per stone of 14 lbs.; Mutton, 6d. to 7d.; Lamb 7d. to 8d.; and Veal, from 7d. to 8d. per lb.

*Manchester* Smithfield Market, June 13.—The supply of Sheep to this day's market was not so large as for the last two or three weeks, but fully equal to the demand, and the prices may be considered ½d. per lb. lower than last week. There was a better show of Beasts, but the weather being so warm caused a dullness in the trade, and the price gave way about ½d. per lb. Lamb in abundant supply; the price declined ½d. per lb., at which nearly the whole was cleared off. In Veal and Pork no alteration.—Beef, 4½d. to 8d.; Mutton, 6½d. to 8d.; Lamb, 7d. to 8d.; Veal, 6d. to 7½d.; and Pork, 4d. to 5d. per lb., sinking offal.

At *Morpeth* Market, June 13, there were a good many Cattle, and a great supply of Sheep and Lambs; although there was a good demand, they met with rather dull sale, at a reduction in price, and part were left unsold.— Beef, 7s. to to 7s. 9d.; Mutton, 7s. to 8s.; and Lamb, 7s. to 8s. 3d. per stone, sinking offal.

*Norwich Castle Meadow*, June 16.—The supply of fat Cattle to this day's market was small, prices 8s. to 9s. per stone of 14 lbs., sinking offal: Store Stock of all sorts was in large supply; Scots sold at 4s. to 4s. 6d. per stone of what they will weigh when fat; Shorthorns, 3s. to 3s. 6d.; Cows and Calves, but few good ones here; Homebreds, a flat sale; the show of Sheep was large.—Meat: Beef, 7d. to 9d.; Veal, 6d. to 7½d.; Mutton, 6d. to 7½d.; Lamb, 7d.; and Pork, 6d. to 7½d. per lb.

CPSIA information can be obtained
at www.ICGtesting.com
Printed in the USA
BVHW04*1137011018
528939BV00008B/272/P